PHASE EQUILIBRIA IN MATERIALS

PHASE EQUILIBRIA IN MATERIALS

SHANT P. GUPTA
Department of Metallurgical Engineering
Indian Institute of Technology,
Kanpur

ALLIED PUBLISHERS PVT. LIMITED

New Delhi • Mumbai • Kolkata • Lucknow • Chennai
Nagpur • Bangalore • Hyderabad • Ahmedabad

ALLIED PUBLISHERS PVT. LIMITED

Regd. Off.: 15. J.N. Heredia Marg, Ballard Estate, Mumbai — 400038
Prarthna Flats (2nd Floor), Navrangpura, Ahmedabad — 380009
3-2-844/6&7, Kachiguda Station Road, Hyderabad — 500027
16A Ashok Marg, Patiala House, Lucknow — 226001
5th Main Road, Gandhinagar, Bangalore — 560009
17 Chittaranjan Avenue, Kolkata — 700072
81 Hill Road, Ramnagar, Nagpur — 440010
1/13-14, Asaf Ali Road, New Delhi — 110002
751 Anna Salai, Chennai — 600002

ISBN 81-7764-422-X

Senior Editor: Jyoti Mehrotra

Published by Sunil Sachdev and printed by Ravi Sachdev at Allied Publishers Pvt. Limited (Printing Division), A-104 Mayapuri, Phase II, New Delhi — 110 064.

ACKNOWLEDGEMENTS

The financial support for writing this book was provided by the QIP Cell, Indian Institute of Technology, Kanpur.

PREFACE

The experience gained in teaching an undergraduate course on phase equilibria in materials (binary and ternary phase diagrams and quantitative microscopy) has resulted in a textbook, which covers the above subject matter. Although a large number of textbooks have been written on thermodynamics, there is a relative lack of textbooks on alloy phase equilibria. A proper knowledge of phase diagram and interpretation of microstructure is important in analyzing problems in physical and process metallurgy and materials sciences.

Alloy phase equilibria in material systems provides an in-depth treatment of the binary and ternary phase diagrams and quantitative evaluation of microstructural features, resulting due to both solidification of the liquid and solid to solid transformation reaction.

Phase equilibria in materials is an introductory textbook intended primarily for use in an undergraduate course on the subject. In addition to the treatment being general, it includes chapters on phase diagram calculations and quantitative microscopy. These and the chapters on ternary phase diagrams will be immensely useful to graduate students working in the area of physical metallurgy/materials sciences and also to working metallurgists/materials scientists involved in research and development of materials.

The book presents an introductory chapter on basic thermodynamics, as being useful in part of the treatment in Chapters 2 and 7 of phase diagram calculations. The formation of metastable and stable phases from the liquid or solid parent phase is explained through the use of free energy-composition diagrams involving applications of basic thermodynamics. Along with the development of microstructure is given the procedure to calculate stepwise, the relative amounts of various phases in equilibrium with each other. Development of microstructure during non-equilibrium solidification is also described. In order to give students a feel of the subject, selected problems are provided at the end of each chapter. Some of the problems have emerged out of classroom discussions. The calculation of phase diagrams presented in Chapter 7 is based on published data on excess enthalpy and entropy of various phases. The free energy of solutions data was programmed on "C" and plots obtained at a number of temperatures in the whole range of compositions for binary systems. Some of the free energy-composition diagrams are shown in the book and procedures outlined for obtaining the phase diagram.

A brief description of quantitative microscopy is presented in Chapter 8 where the evaluation of parameters such as volume fraction, surface area per unit volume, length per unit volume, number of particles and average particle size, grain size etc., are described. A simple procedure of evaluation is also provided with the help of illustrated examples in each case. This topic is very useful in research and development and for working metallurgists/materials scientists.

The treatment on the ternary phase diagram is sufficiently detailed to enable those learning for the first time to grasp the subject easily, develop variants of the ternary diagrams and apply the knowledge to real systems. The ideas developed in Chapters 9 to 14 have been applied to real systems, some of which are presented in Chapter 15. Only a few selected ternary diagrams are described, the list of real ternary phase diagrams being very vast.

It is my pleasure to acknowledge the help of a few undergraduate students who not only encouraged me to write this book but also read the manuscript and carried out programming for the preparation of Chapter 7. I am very grateful to my wife, Manju, who had to spend a lot of time alone while I was busy working on this project.

Shant P. Gupta

CONTENTS

Acknowledgements *v*

Preface *vii*

1. Basic Thermodynamics and Its Applications **1**

1.1 Introduction
1.2 First Law of Thermodynamics
1.3 Heat Capacity
1.4 Second Law of Thermodynamics
1.5 Enthalpy,Helmholtz and Gibbs Free Energy Functions
1.6 Entropy and Disorder - Statistical Interpretation
1.7 Gibbs Free Energy, Equilibrium and Chemical Reaction
1.8 Heterogeneous Equilibrium and the Phase Rule
1.9 Free Energy of Phase Mixtures
1.10 The Free Energy of Solutions - Quasi Chemical Model
1.11 Single Component System : Pressure - Temperature Diagram
1.12 Effect of Curvature on the Melting Temperature

2. Binary Phase Diagram - Isomorphous Systems **104**

2.1 Introduction
2.2 Application of the Phase Rule
2.3 The Lever Rule
2.4 Equilibrium Solidification and Microstructure
2.5 Non-Equilibrium Solidification - Coring
2.6 Conditions for Phase Equilibrium in Isomorphous Systems
2.7 Free Energy Curves for Solid and Liquid Solutions
2.8 Solute Redistribution During Solidification
2.9 Zone Refining
2.10 Constitutional Supercooling - Formation of Cells and Dendrite
2.11 Formation of Dendrites

3. Binary Eutectic, Peritectic and Metatectic Systems **156**

3.1 Binary Eutectic System

3.2 Application of the Phase Rule

3.3 The Eutectic Reaction

3.4 The Microstructure of Eutectic Alloys

3.5 Hypoeutectic and Hypereutectic Alloys - Equilibrium Solidification

3.6 Hypoeutectic Alloys - Non Equilibrium Solidification

3.7 Terminal Solid Solutions

3.8 Free Energy - Composition Diagrams

3.9 Modification of Eutectic Alloys

3.10 Isothermal Diffusion

3.11 The Growth of Eutectics

3.12 Binary Peritectic Systems

3.13 Equilibrium Solidification of a Peritectic Alloy

3.14 Equilibrium Solidification of Hypoperitectic and Hyperperitectic Alloys

3.15 Natural Cooling of Peritectic, Hypoperitectic and Hyperperitectic Alloys

3.16 Free Energy - Composition Diagrams

3.17 Isothermal Diffusion

3.18 Binary Metatectic Systems

3.19 Free Energy - Composition Diagrams

4. Binary Monotectic and Syntectic systems **240**

4.1 Introduction

4.2 The Monotectic Reaction

4.3 Equilibrium Solidification of Monotectic Alloys

4.4 Equilibrium Solidification of Hypomonotectic and Hypermonotectic Alloys

4.5 Free Energy - Composition Diagrams

4.6 Binary Syntectic Systems

4.7 Equilibrium Solidification of Syntectic Alloys

4.8 The Effect of Gravity Segregation on Microstructural Evolution During Natural Cooling of a Syntectic Alloy

4.9 Free Energy - Composition Diagrams

5. **Intermediate Phases** 272

5.1 Introduction

5.2 Classification of Intermediate Phases - Origin of Formation

5.3 Structure of Intermediate Phases - Principles

5.4 Classification of Intermediate Phases - Structural

5.5 Non-Stoichiometric Compounds

5.6 Congruent Transformations in Solids

6. **Binary Phase Diagrams - Equilibrium of Phases in the Solid State** 294

6.1 Binary Eutectoid System

6.1.1 Eutectoid Transformation in Fe-C Alloys

6.1.2 Transformation of Austenite to Pearlite

6.1.3 Transformation of Austenite to Ferrite

6.1.4 Transformation of Austenite to Bainite

6.1.5 Transformation of Austenite to Martensite

6.1.6 Tempering of Martensite

6.1.7 Transformation at Fixed Subcritical Temperature - The Time - Temperature - Transformation Diagram

6.2 Binary Eutectic and Eutectoid Reactions - Cast Irons

6.2.1 White Cast Iron

6.2.2 Grey Cast Iron

6.2.3 Ductile Iron

6.2.4 Malleable Cast Iron

6.2.5 Alloy Cast Irons

6.3 Binary Peritectoid Systems

6.4 Binary Monotectoid Systems

7. **Binary Phase Diagram Calculations** 360

7.1 Binary Isomorphous Systems

7.2 Maximum and Minimum in the Solidus and Liquidus Curves

7.3 Binary Eutectic Systems

7.4 Binary Peritectic Systems

7.5 Binary Monotectic Systems

7.6 Binary Syntectic Systems

7.7 Numerical Methods of Phase Diagrams Calculations

7.8 Calculation of Slopes of Phase Boundaries

8. Quantitative Microscopy **453**

8.1 Introduction

8.2 Theory of Probability

8.2.1 Sample Space and Elementary Events

8.2.2 Probability of an Event

8.2.3 Probability Distribution

8.2.4 Frequency and Cumulative Frequency

8.2.5 Sample Mean and Sample Variance

8.2.6 Random Variable and Mean and Variance of a Distribution

8.2.7 Normal Distribution

8.3 Geometrical Probability of Intersection of Microstructures with Test Lines and Test Planes

8.4 Volume Fraction Analysis

8.4.1 Area Fraction

8.4.2 Lineal Fraction

8.4.3 Point Fraction

8.4.4 To Show that $\overline{A}_f = \overline{L}_f$

8.5 Specific Surface Area and Specific Length

8.6 Number of Particles and Average Size of Particles

8.6.1 Introduction

8.6.2. Evaluation of Number of Particles Per Unit Volume - Constant Shape and Arbitrary Size Distribution

8.6.3 Evaluation of N_v and $\overline{R}$ for Disc-Shaped Particles

8 .6.4 Evaluation of N_v and $\overline{R}$ for Constant Shape and Constant Size Particles

8.6.5 Separation Between Particles of a Dispersed Phase

8.7 Grain Size Measurements

9. Ternary System - General **537**

9.1 Introduction - Application of the Phase Rule

9.2 Representation of the Ternary System

9.3 Application of the Lever Rule - Tie Lines and Tie Triangles

10. Ternary Alloy System - Two Phase Equilibria **555**

10.1 The Space Model

10.2 Isothermal Sections

10.3 Vertical Sections

10.4 Equilibrium Solidification of Alloys

10.5 Rules Governing Construction of Ternary Tie Lines

10.6 Variants of the Ternary Isomorphous System

10.7 Two Phase Equilibria Involving Immiscibility Gap

10.7.1 Ternary System with Maximum Critical Point at a Binary Composition

10.7.2 Ternary System with Maximum Critical Point at a Ternary Composition

11. Ternary Alloy Systems - Three Phase Equilibria **586**

11.1 Ternary System Showing an Eutectic Reaction, L $\rightleftarrows \alpha + \beta$

11.1.1 The Space Model

11.1.2 Isothermal Sections

11.2.3 Vertical Sections

11.2.4 Solidification

11.2 Ternary System Showing an Eutectic Reaction in One Binary System with a Minimum in the Liquidus Temperature

11.3 Ternary System Showing an Eutectic Reaction in One Binary System with a Maximum in the Liquidus Temperature

11.4 Ternary System with a Maximum or Minimum in Liquidus Temperature and Eutectic Reaction in Two of the Binaries

11.5 Ternary System Showing a Peritectic Reaction in Two Binaries

11.5.1 The Space Model

11.5.2 Isothermal Sections

11.5.3 Vertical Sections

11.5.4 Solidification of Alloys

11.6 Ternary Peritectic System with One Binary System Showing the Peritectic Reaction and a Minimum in the Liquidus Temperature

11.7 Ternary Peritectic System with One Binary Showing Peritectic Reaction and a Maximum in the Liquidus Temperature

11.8 Ternary System Showing a Peritectic Reaction in One Binary and an Eutectic Reaction in the Second Binary. The Third Binary System is Isomorphous

11.9 Ternary System Showing a Monotectic Reaction $L_1 \rightleftarrows \alpha + L_2$ in One of the Binaries and a Minimum in the Liquidus Temperature

11.10 Ternary Alloy System with a Syntectic Reaction in One of the Binaries and a Minimum in the Liquidus Temperature

11.11 Ternary Alloy System with a Syntectic Reaction in One Binary and a Monotectic Reaction in a Second Binary

11.12 General Rules Governing Construction of Three Phase Regions

12. Ternary Alloy Systems - Four Phase Equilibria 664

12.1 The Ternary Eutectic Reaction- Class I

12.1.1 The Space Model

12.1.2 Isothermal Sections

12.1.3 Vertical Sections

12.1.4 Solidification of Alloys

12.1.5 Variants of the Eutectic - Class I Reaction

12.2 The Ternary Quasi-Peritectic, Class II, Reaction

12.2.1 The Space Model

12.2.2 Isothermal Sections

12.2.3 Vertical Sections

12.2.4 Solidification of Alloys

12.2.5 Variants of the Ternary Quasi-Perite Class II Reaction

12.3 The Ternary Peritectic, Class III Reaction

12.3.1 The Space Model

12.3.2 Isothermal Sections

12.3.3 Vertical Sections

12.3.4 Solidification of Alloys

12.3.5 Variants of the Ternary Peritectic Reaction

13. Ternary Four Phase Equilibrium With Congruently Melting Intermediate Phases 723

13.1.1 The Space Model

13.1.2 Isothermal Sections

13.1.3 Vertical Sections

13.2 Ternary System with an Intermediate Phase in One of the Binary Systems Without a Quasi-Binary Reaction

13.3 Ternary System with an Intermediate Phase in One of the Binaries Without a Quasi-Binary Reaction

13.4 Phase Diagram Showing a Ternary Intermediate Phase

13.5 Ternary System with Congruently Melting Intermediate Phase Associated with Each Binary

14. Ternary Four Phase Equilibrium - Liquid Immiscibility 746

14.1 Liquid Immiscibility in the Ternary Phase Diagram with Two Binary Systems Showing Monotectic Reactions and the Third Showing an Eutectic

14.2 Liquid Immiscibility in the Ternary Phase Diagram with One Binary System Showing a Monotectic Reaction at Higher Temperatures and an Eutectic at Low Temperatures. The Other Two Binaries Show Eutectic Reactions

14.3 Ternary Phase Diagram Showing Liquid Immiscibility with One Binary System Showing a Monotectic Reaction

14.4 Liquid Immiscibility in Ternary Systems with Two Binary Syntectic Reactions

15. Selected Examples of Ternary Systems 762

15.1 Ternary Isomorphous System, Ag-Au-Pd

15.2 Ternary Three Phase Equilibrium, $L \rightleftarrows \alpha_1 + \alpha_2$, Ag-Au-Cu

15.3 Ternary Three Phase Equilibrium, $L \rightleftarrows \alpha + \beta$ (Ag-Au-Ge System)

15.4 Ternary Three Phase Equilibrium, $L + \alpha_1 \rightleftarrows \alpha_2$ (Ag-Au-Pt System)

15.5 Ternary Three Phase Equilibrium, $L \rightleftarrows \alpha + \beta$ (Ag-Ge-Si System)

15.6 Ternary Monovariant Reaction Involving Immiscibility in the Liquid (Ag-Cu-Ni System)

15.7 Ternary Eutectic Reaction, L $\rightleftarrows$ $\alpha + \beta + \gamma$ (Ag-Cu-Pb System)

15.8 Ternary Eutectic Reaction, L $\rightleftarrows$ $\alpha + \beta + \gamma$ (Ag-Cu-Cu_3P System)

15.9 Ternary Eutectic Reaction, Al-Si-Sb System

15.10 Ternary Peritectic Reaction, L + $\beta + \gamma$ $\rightleftarrows$ δ (Ag-Cu-Mg System)

15.11 Ternary Phase Diagram of the System Fe-Cr-Ni

15.12 The SiO_2 - MgO - Al_2O_3 System

Index **813**

Chapter 1

BASIC THERMODYNAMICS AND ITS APPLICATIONS

1.1 INTRODUCTION

In materials science, the properties of materials are characterized in terms of the qualitative nature of the phases present. An understanding of the thermodynamics of material for a systems is essential for a study of the stability of phases present in metals and alloys, ceramics, glasses, polymers, etc. The state of a system can be described in terms of the mass, pressure, temperature, position and motion of all constituent particles. It may appear that in order to describe the macroscopic state of the system, a large number of properties need to be known. It turns out that this is not so, and from a knowledge of a few of them the rest can be deduced. Thermodynamics basically deals in establishing relationships between system parameters on which a number of system properties are dependent. As an illustration, temperature and pressure are two independent system variables (which define the state of a system) on which a number of properties depend. Consider the volume of a system to be dependent on the temperature and pressure,

$$V = f(P, T). \tag{1.1.1}$$

The total differential can be written as,

$$dV = \left(\frac{\partial V}{\partial P}\right)_T dP + \left(\frac{\partial V}{\partial T}\right)_P dT. \tag{1.1.2}$$

The change in volume is dependent on the value of two different variables related to the changes in pressure or temperature or both. It is independent of the path taken. This is a consequence of the fact that volume is a state function.

1.2 FIRST LAW OF THERMODYNAMICS

Consider a rigid body being displaced under the action of a force. The magnitude of the work done is equal to the product of the force and the component of displacement in the direction of the force. Work may be done either by the system or on it, when the system exerts a force on its surroundings and the displacement takes place. Work that involves interaction between the system and its surroundings is significant in thermodynamics and is known as external work. However, when a part of the system interacts with another part and work is done, it is termed as internal work. The interaction between molecules and electrons or ions and electrons constitute internal work.

The magnitude of the work done can be calculated for a hydrostatic system. Consider a gas contained in a cylinder fitted with a movable piston on which the system and the surroundings may act. If the pressure acting on the piston face is P, then the force acting on the surroundings will be $P \cdot A$, where A is the cross-sectional area of the piston. The surroundings in this situation will exert an opposing force on the external face of the piston. If the force exerted by the surroundings is also $P \cdot A$ and is in direction opposite to the force exerted by the system, then there will be no displacements. No work will be done in this case. However, if the force exerted by the surroundings differs from $P \cdot A$, even by a small amount, then there will be a net displacement of the piston say, by dx and the system will perform work. An infinitesimal amount of work dW is then said to be done. The magnitude of the work is,

$$dW = P \cdot A \cdot dx. \tag{1.2.1}$$

and since $A\,dx = dV$.

$$dW = PdV. \tag{1.2.2}$$

The work done can be calculated when the volume change from the initial value V_i to the final value V_f is known. However, the change in volume must occur quasi-statically[1] so that the system at each of the infinite number of stages between V_i and V_f is near thermodynamic equilibrium. The pressure can be expressed as a function of temperature and volume by means of the equation of state. The work done during the quasi-static process is,

$$\int_{V_i}^{V_f} PdV. \tag{1.2.3}$$

In the above, the state of the system has been made to change from an initial state to the final state by the performance of work. The state of the system can also be made to change by means other than the performance of work. For example, consider a cylindrical vessel filled with liquid. The vessel is kept in an inverted position and the liquid allowed to heat up from below. The liquid vaporizes with an increase in the temperature and pressure. Since the volume of the vapor phase does not change and there is no displacement of any kind, no work is done. The state of the system, however, has changed.

A similar change in the state of the system is brought about by heating water contained in a vessel by means of the resistor. The resistor being at a higher temperature transfers heat to the surrounding water and its temperature rises. A change in the state of the system is brought about by the temperature difference only. Similarly, in the previous example, the hot combustion products of the Bunsen burner vaporize the liquid contained in the vessel affecting an increase in the temperature and pressure. Thus, the state of the system is made to change due to a difference in temperature only and heat is transferred between the system and the surroundings in the process.

If the system is caused to change from an initial state to a final state by the introduction of an amount of heat dQ and the work done is dW, then a change in the inter-

---

[1] During a quasi-static process the system is under mechanical, thermal and chemical equilibrium. There are no unbalanced forces, no difference in temperature between different parts of the system and no net transport of any of the species from one part of the system to the other.

nal energy dE of the system occurs. This is the first law of thermodynamics and is expressed as,

$$dE = dQ - dW. \tag{1.2.4}$$

The change in work dW, as well as change in heat dQ, is not a function of the co-ordinates of the system but depends upon the path by which the change in the system is brought about. The internal energy, however, is a state function and depends upon the initial and final states. This means that although dQ and dW are not state functions, the difference $(dQ-dW)$ is. For an infinitesimal change in the co-ordinates of the system involving pressure and volume, the first law of thermodynamics is written as,

$$dE = dQ - PdV. \tag{1.2.5}$$

The internal energy of the system is the sum of the kinetic and potential energies of all its constituent parts.

1.3 HEAT CAPACITY

Consider a system at an initial temperature T_i. If Q units of heat are transferred, the temperature of the system changes from T_i to T_f. The average heat capacity is defined as,

$$\overline{C} = \frac{\Delta Q}{T_f - T_i}. \tag{1.3.1}$$

If the amount of heat introduced into the system is made smaller, the final temperature T_f will approach T_i. In the limit $T_f \rightarrow T_i$, when the ratio of the heat, ΔQ, over the difference in temperature $(T_f - T_i)$ approaches heat capacity, then

$$C = \lim_{T_f \rightarrow T_i} \frac{\Delta Q}{T_f - T_i} = \frac{dQ}{dT}. \tag{1.3.2}$$

There are a number of ways the temperature of a system may be made to change by the introduction of heat. One way is to maintain constant pressure while other thermodynamic parameters of the system are allowed to change. Under this condition, the heat capacity is known as the specific heat at constant pressure, defined as,

$$C_P = \left(\frac{dQ}{dT}\right)_P . \tag{1.3.3}$$

The heat capacity of the system may also be measured while the volume remains constant. This heat capacity is known as specific heat at constant volume,

$$C_v = \left(\frac{dQ}{dT}\right)_v . \tag{1.3.4}$$

Similarly, the heat capacity of a substance in different states may be measured at constant surface tension C_F constant length of the wire C_L, etc.
Next, we will establish a few simple relationships between specific heat and the internal energy functions from the first law of thermodynamics for a hydrostatic system,

$$dQ = dE + PdV, \tag{1.3.5}$$

where E, the internal energy of the system, is a function of pressure, volumc and temperature. Selecting any two of the three variables, suppose, V and T, we can write,

$$E = f(V, T),$$

and $dE = \left(\frac{\partial E}{\partial V}\right)_T dV + \left(\frac{\partial E}{\partial T}\right)_V dT.$

Substituting for dE in equation (1.3.5), we get

$$dQ = \left(\frac{\partial E}{\partial T}\right)_V dT + \left[P + \left(\frac{\partial E}{\partial V}\right)_T\right] dV. \tag{1.3.6}$$

Dividing by dT and keeping volume constant yields,

$$\left(\frac{dQ}{dT}\right)_V = \left(\frac{\partial E}{\partial T}\right)_V = C_v. \quad (1.3.7)$$

Also dividing by dT and keeping pressure constant yields,

$$\left(\frac{dQ}{dT}\right)_P = \left(\frac{\partial E}{\partial T}\right)_V + \left[P + \left(\frac{\partial E}{\partial V}\right)_T\right]\left(\frac{dV}{dT}\right)_P. \quad (1.3.8)$$

since $\left(\frac{dV}{dT}\right)_p = \beta V$, where β is the volume expansion coefficient,

$$C_p = C_v + \left[P + \left(\frac{\partial E}{\partial V}\right)_T\right] \cdot \beta V. \quad (1.3.9)$$

or

$$\left(\frac{\partial E}{\partial V}\right)_T = \frac{C_p - C_v}{V\beta} - P. \quad (1.3.10)$$

1.4 SECOND LAW OF THERMODYNAMICS

In order to understand the statement(s) of the second law of thermodynamics it is pertinent to understand the concept of heat and work and how work can be converted into heat and vice versa. The concept of heat and work was introduced in the earlier section. To understand how work can be converted into heat, let us consider an electric wire through which a current I is passed. If the wire is immersed in water it will start heating the water due to the resistance present in it. The process will continue as long as the current in the wire is maintained. In this process, the work (electrical) is completely converted into heat without bringing any change in the system (wire). This is expected because if there is no change in the state ($\Delta E = 0$) of the system, all electrical work must get converted into heat. The work W is done upon the system in contact with a reservoir, giving rise to a flow of heat Q without changing the state of the system. The function of the reservoir is to absorb heat. In this process, the work is converted into heat with 100% efficiency.

Now let us understand the conversion of heat into work by means of a series of processes, which can carry out the conversion without affecting any change in the state of the system; i.e., the thermodynamic coordinates of the system will remain the same after the completion of the process. Consider the isothermal expansion of the gas. The internal energy of the system remains the same ($\Delta E = 0$) because the process is carried out at constant temperature. The heat is completely converted into work. However, the thermodynamic coordinates of the system have changed. For example, in this case the volume of the gas increases and the pressure decreases till atmospheric pressure is reached. In order that the initial thermodynamic state of the system be restored, the process can be carried out in a series of steps and then we can measure the fraction of heat which has been converted into work. The series of steps involved in this case constitute a cycle involving the flow of heat to or from the system and performance of work by or on the system. We represent these quantities as,

Q_H = the amount of heat absorbed by the system at a higher temperature.

Q_C = the amount of heat rejected by the system at a lower temperature.

and W = amount of work done by the system.

If in the process, the system is brought back to the original state, there will be no change in the internal energy of the system and the net amount of work done by the system must equal the amount of heat absorbed in the process ($Q_H - Q_C$). The process can be performed by an engine, whose efficiency can be stated as the ratio of the amount of work W carried out by the system and the amount of heat absorbed by the system. The work done by the system constitute the output and the heat absorbed the input.

The efficiency of an engine, $\eta = \dfrac{W}{Q_H} \times 100,$

and since $W = Q_H - Q_C,$ $\eta = \dfrac{Q_H - Q_C}{Q_H} \times 100,$

$$= \left(1 - \frac{Q_C}{Q_H}\right) \times 100. \tag{1.4.1}$$

There are a number of devices available now which can convert heat into work. These are the sterling engine, steam engine, internal combustion engine etc., each of which can absorb heat at a higher temperature, perform some amount of work and in the process some amount of heat is rejected at a lower temperature.

Depending upon the setup involved, the efficiency of the engine can be calculated by an idealized process which assumes,

(i) the gas to be ideal

(ii) no friction between moving parts, and

(iii) no turbulence of the fluid medium.

In an ideal case, we can construct a system to consist of a hot reservoir and a cold reservoir. An amount of heat Q_H is absorbed by the system through the hot reservoir (at a higher temperature). This is followed by the performance of work by the system. Thereafter the system is brought back to its initial state by passing it through a cold reservoir, rejecting an amount of heat Q_C in the process. The original statement of the second law of thermodynamics after Kelvin is,

> 'It is impossible to construct an engine which, working in a complete cycle, will produce no effect other than raising of a weight and cooling of a heat reservoir'.

A statement having conceptually the same meaning has been given by Planck and the second law can be written as a combined Kelvin-Planck statement as,

> 'No process is possible whose sole result is the absorption of heat from a hot reservoir and conversion of this heat into work'.

It is a consequence of the second law of thermodynamic that, although an infinitesimal change in heat dQ is not a state function (i.e., it depends upon the path followed in reaching the final state f from an initial state i), the quantity dQ/T is a state function. Consider an electric wire immersed in water. When the current is switched on, an amount of work dW is performed in a small time interval. The work gets converted into heat during the irreversible process and a quantity of heat dQ is transferred to the reservoir kept at the temperature T_2. If the heat reservoir is placed in contact (through a diathermal wall) with another heat reservoir at a lower temperature T_1, then there will be transfer of heat from the hot reservoir to the cold reservoir. If the same quantity of heat is allowed to flow through an adiabatic process then the quantity dQ/T_2 is less than dQ/T_1. The quantity dQ/T is termed as the change in entropy dS, which in this case is $(dQ/T_1 - dQ/T_2)$, where S is the entropy function. The magnitude of ΔS indicates the degree of irreversibility of the system. For a reversible process $\Delta S = 0$ and for an irreversible process $\Delta S > 0$.

Let us examine the function dQ/T for its integrability. While discussing the first law of thermodynamics it has been pointed out in sufficient detail that the functions dQ and dW are inexact differentials, i.e., the heat absorbed or evolved by the system or work done on or by the system depends upon the path through which the system is carried. Let us consider a system which can be defined in terms of two independent thermodynamic variables. Consider one of the variables to be the temperature of the system being acted upon by a force F such as to have a change in the positional coordinate x. From the first law of thermodynamic, we can write,

$$dQ = dE + F\,dx. \tag{1.4.2}$$

The internal energy of the system can be written as a function of T and x to give,

$$E = f(T, x).$$

The total differential of E with respect to T and x yields,

$$dE = \left(\frac{\partial E}{\partial T}\right)_x dT + \left(\frac{\partial E}{\partial x}\right)_T dx.$$

Substitution of dE into equation (1.4.2) gives the following results:

$$dQ = \left(\frac{\partial E}{\partial T}\right)_x dT + \left(F + \left(\frac{\partial E}{\partial x}\right)_T\right) dx. \tag{1.4.3}$$

It is assumed that $F, \left(\frac{\partial E}{\partial T}\right)_x$ and $\left(\frac{\partial E}{\partial x}\right)_T$ are known functions of T and x.

If the process has been carried out adiabatically and reversibly, equation (1.4.3) can be written as,

$$\left(\frac{\partial E}{\partial T}\right)_x dT + \left(F + \left(\frac{\partial E}{\partial x}\right)_T\right) \quad dx = 0.$$

or

$$\left(\frac{dT}{dx}\right) = -\frac{F + \left(\frac{\partial E}{\partial x}\right)_T}{\left(\frac{\partial E}{\partial T}\right)_x} \tag{1.4.4}$$

Since F, $(\partial E/\partial T)_x$ and $(\partial E/\partial x)_T$ are known functions of T and x, their values are known and (dT/dx), which is the slope of the T–x diagram, is known at every point of the (T, x) coordinate. Equation (1.4.4) has a solution which consists of a family of curved lines and the solution may be written as,

$$\sigma(T, x) = \text{constant}, \tag{1.4.5}$$

such that for every value of σ there exists a curve. By combining these curves a surface is generated which represented a general solution to equation (1.4.5). The meaning of equation (1.4.5) is that $dQ = 0$ for an adiabatic process and the change in σ is zero, i.e., σ = constant. In the present consideration the internal energy function E can now be treated as a function of σ and x,

$$E = f(\sigma, x),$$

with the total differential,

$$dE = \left(\frac{\partial E}{\partial \sigma}\right)_x d\sigma + \left(\frac{\partial E}{\partial x}\right)_\sigma dx. \tag{1.4.6}$$

Equation (1.2.4) when combined with $dQ = dE + F\,dx$ gives,

$$dQ = \left(\frac{\partial E}{\partial \sigma}\right)_x d\sigma + \left[F + \left(\frac{\sigma E}{\sigma x}\right)_\sigma\right] dx. \tag{1.4.7}$$

For $d\sigma = 0$ (for σ = constant), $dQ = 0$ as obtained earlier, and the coefficient of dx must vanish. Equation (1.4.7) reduces to the forms,

$$dQ = \left(\frac{\partial E}{\partial \sigma}\right)_x d\sigma.$$

If we define $\left(\frac{\partial E}{\partial \sigma}\right)_x = \lambda,$ then

$$dQ = \lambda \, d\sigma, \qquad .(1.4.8)$$

where λ has the same functional relation as the internal energy function has with *T*, *x* and σ. Equation (1.4.8) suggests that 1/λ is the integrating factor such that when *dQ* is multiplied by 1/λ, the result is an exact differential. λ Can be treated as a function of *T* and σ as,

$$\lambda = \varphi\,(T)\,\phi\,(\sigma),$$

which upon substitution in equation (1.4.8) yields,

$$dQ = \varphi\,(T) \quad \phi\,(\sigma)\,d\sigma, \qquad (1.4.9)$$

Writing φ(T) as kT, when k is a constant, equation (1.4.9) can be expressed as,

$$\frac{dQ}{[T]} = k \quad \phi(\sigma) d\sigma, \qquad (1.4.10)$$

$$= dS_R.$$

The right hand side of equation (1.4.10) is an exact differential and therefore *dQ/T* become an exact differential and therefore *dQ/T* becomes an exact differential. The right hand side is equated to dS_R which is the change in entropy of a system carried through a reversible path. For the change in entropy S_i from an initial state *i* to a final state value of S_f, we can write:

$$S_f - S_i = {}_R\int_i^f \frac{dQ}{[T]}, \qquad (1.4.11)$$

where R stands for a reversible process. When the process is carried through a completely reversible cycle, the system is brought back to the original state. The initial and final entropies will be the same because entropy is a state function as first proved and the change in entropy is zero, i.e.,

$$\int \frac{dQ}{[T]} = 0 \tag{1.4.12}$$

In order to illustrate that dQ/T is a state property, we can consider an ideal gas whose equation of state can be written as $PV = nRT$. From the first law of thermodynamics,

$$dQ = dE + P\,dV. \tag{1.4.13}$$

Now, the internal energy can be written as a function of temperature and volume, which yields,

$$dE = \left(\frac{\partial E}{\partial T}\right)_V dT + \left(\frac{\partial E}{\partial V}\right)_T dV.$$

For an ideal gas $(\partial E/\partial V)_T = 0$ as shown earlier, therefore,

$$dE = C_v dT, \quad \text{(equation(1.3.7))}$$

Substitution for dE and P in equation (1.4.13) yields,

$$dQ = C_v dT + nRT\frac{dV}{[V]} \tag{1.4.14}$$

The right-hand side of equation (1.4.14) is an inexact differential but can be made exact by dividing through by T. The result is,

$$\frac{dQ}{[T]} = C_v\frac{dT}{[T]} + nR\frac{dV}{[V]} \tag{1.4.15}$$

From the preceding paragraphs which led to the description of the entropy function, it is to be understood that there is nothing called 'absolute entropy'. We can only define the entropy change of a system, by taking the initial state as the reference state for simplification. Thus, only with reference to a given state can the change in entropy be calculated.

In order to illustrate the concept of reference state and the value of entropy in the selected reference state, let us consider the change in entropy of an ideal gas. Further, let the gas absorb and infinitesimal amount of heat dQ during a reversible process. The change in entropy of the system can be written as, $dS = dQ/[T]$. The amount of heat dQ is not an exact differential and can not be written in terms of the state variables alone; however, when divided by the temperature it becomes an exact differential and thus can be represented in terms of the thermodynamics coordinates P, V and T etc., and subsequently integrated. The infinitesimal change in heat at constant pressure is written as,

$$dQ = C_p dT - V\,dP. \tag{1.4.16}$$

Dividing through by T yields,

$$\frac{dQ}{[T]} = \frac{C_p dT}{T} - \frac{V\,dP}{T} \tag{1.4.17}$$

For an ideal gas, the equation of state is $PV = nRT$. Substituting for V in equation (1.4.17) gives the following result,

$$dS = \frac{C_p dT}{T} - nR\frac{dP}{P}. \tag{1.4.18}$$

Equation (1.4.18) can be integrated between an arbitrarily selected reference state with coordinates T_r and P_r and the final state P and T:

$$\Delta S = \int_{T_r}^{T} C_p \frac{dT}{[T]} - nR\int_{P_r}^{P} \frac{dP}{[P]} \tag{1.4.19}$$

The specific heat at constant pressure can be represented by the polynomial,

$$C_p = a + bT + CT^{-2},$$

where a, b and C are constants whose values for different materials can be obtained from handbooks on thermodynamics. Substitution for C_p in equation (1.4.19) and integration yields,

$$S = a \ln T - a \ln T_r + bT - bT_r - \frac{C}{2T^2} + \frac{C}{2T_r^2} - nR \ln P + nR \ln P_r$$

$$= \left(a \ln T + bT - \frac{C}{2T^2} - nR \ln P \right) - \left(a \ln T_r + bT_r - \frac{C}{2T_r^2} - nR \ln P_r \right)$$

$$= a \ln T + bT - \frac{C}{2T^2} - nR \ln P + S_0, \tag{1.4.20}$$

where $S_0 = -\left(a \ln T_r + bT_r - \frac{C}{2T_r^2} - nR \ln P_r \right)$,

the entropy of the reference state with the pressure and temperature being P_r and T_r, respectively. Thus, with reference to the value of entropy in the reference state, S_0, the entropy of the system can be calculated. A similar expression can be written when an infinitesimal amount of heat dQ is absorbed by the system at constant volume,

$$S = C_v \ln T + nR \ln V + S_0 \tag{1.4.21}$$

Some Useful Relations:

(i) For a reversible process, we can write,

$$dS = \frac{dQ}{[T]}. \tag{1.4.22}$$

If the process is allowed to change from an initial state i to a final state f adiabatically, then $dQ = 0$ or $dS = 0$. Thus for a reversible adiabatic process there is no change in entropy.

(ii) Equation (1.4.22) can be written as,

$$\frac{dS}{dT} = \frac{dQ}{TdT}.$$

At constant volume, $\left(\frac{dQ}{dT}\right)_V = C_v$, thus

$$\left(\frac{dQ}{dT}\right)_V = C_v = T\left(\frac{dS}{dT}\right)_V. \tag{1.4.23}$$

Similarly, $\left(\frac{dQ}{dT}\right)_p = C_p = T\left(\frac{dS}{dT}\right)_p$ (1.4.24)

(iii) From equation (1.4.24) , $dS = \frac{C_p dT}{[T]}$. Substituting for C_p yields,

$$dS = a\ d\ \ln T + b dT - \frac{c dT}{T^2}$$

The integration can be carried out to determine the entropy of a system at some temperature T if the value at some reference temperature T_r is known. The reference temperature is generally taken as room temperature, 298 K.

(iv) Entropy changes of the system and surroundings for a reversible process can be calculated by considering the system to be in contact with a heat reservoir with which it can exchange heat. Consider an infinitesimal amount of heat dQ which is transferred from the system to the heat reservoir (surroundings) reversibly at temperature T. Since the amount of heat transferred is infinitesimal, there will be no change in the temperature of the system or the surroundings. The change in entropy of the system is,

$$dS = -\frac{dQ}{[T]}.$$

and the change in the entropy of the surroundings is,

$$dS = +\frac{dQ}{[T]}.$$

The change in entropy of the universe $= -\frac{dQ}{[T]} + \frac{dQ}{[T]} = 0.$

Thus, if we add the entropy change of the system to the entropy change of the immediate surroundings, we obtain a quantity which is the entropy change of the entire process. The entropy change is found to correspond to that of the universe.

(v) Entropy change during an irreversible process:

Consider a cylinder fitted with a frictionless movable piston containing an ideal gas at a pressure above 1 atmosphere. The gas is allowed to expand isothermally from an initial volume V_i to the final volume V_f. The change in entropy of the system is written as,

$$dS = \frac{dQ}{[T]} = \frac{P\,dV}{T}, \quad (\text{since } dE = 0 \text{ at constant } T) \tag{1.4.25}$$

For an ideal gas, $PV = nRT$ and substituting for P in equation (1.4.25) yields,

$dS = nR\frac{dV}{[V]}$, which upon integration gives the following result:

$$\Delta S(\text{system}) = nR \ln\left(\frac{V_f}{V_i}\right).$$

The change in entropy of the surroundings is zero during free expansion of the gas. The change in entropy of the universe is,

$$\Delta S \text{ (universe)} = \Delta S \text{ (system)} + \Delta S \text{ (surroundings)} = nR \ln\left(\frac{V_f}{V_i}\right)$$

Since $V_f > V_i$ during the expansion of the gas, ΔS (universe) is positive.

(vi) Heat transfer due to a temperature difference during an irreversible process:

Consider a system in contact with a heat reservoir at a temperature T_1, which in turn is in contact with a cold reservoir at a temperature $T_2 < T_1$. If the system transfers an amount of heat Q to the hot reservoir at T_1, there is no change in the entropy of the system. The hot reservoir transfers heat to the cold reservoir. The entropy changes for the irreversible process are written as,

$$\Delta S \text{ (system)} = 0$$

$$\Delta S \text{ (hot reservoir)} = -\frac{[Q]}{[T_1]}$$

$$\Delta S \text{ (cold reservoir)} = +\frac{[Q]}{[T_2]}$$

and
$$\Delta S \text{ (surroundings)} = +\frac{[Q]}{[T_2]} - \frac{[Q]}{[T_1]},$$

which is a positive quantity. The change in entropy of the universe which is the sum of the changes in the entropies of the system and surroundings is positive; i.e., the entropy of the universe increases during an irreversible process.

(vii) From the second law of thermodynamics, $dQ = dE + P\,dV$. From $dQ = T\,dS$, $T\,dS = dE + P\,dV$ or the change in internal energy of the system is expressed by the following relationship,

$$dE = T\,dS - P\,dV \tag{1.4.26}$$

1.5 ENTHALPY, HELMHOLTZ AND GIBBS FREE ENERGY FUNCTIONS

According to the first law of thermodynamics, the quantity of heat either absorbed or given by the system is related to the internal energy, pressure and volume. At this point it is useful to define a new function enthalpy H of the system by the relation,

$$H = E + PV. \tag{1.5.1}$$

Consider the change in enthalpy due to small changes in the internal energy, pressure and volume of the system. This can be written as,

$$dH = dE + P\,dV + V\,dP. \tag{1.5.2}$$

However, since $dE + P\,dV = dQ$, we can write equation (1.5.2) as,

$$\begin{aligned} dH &= dQ + V\,dP \\ &= T\,dS + V\,dP. \end{aligned} \tag{1.5.3}$$

At constant pressure,

$$\left(\frac{\partial H}{\partial T}\right)_P = \left(\frac{\partial Q}{\partial T}\right)_P = T\left(\frac{\partial S}{\partial T}\right)_P = C_P \tag{1.5.4}$$

The Helmholtz free energy is defined as,

$$F = E - TS. \tag{1.5.5}$$

For infinitesimal changes in the internal energy, temperature and entropy of the system, we can write the new function in differential form as,

$$dF = dE - T\,dS - S\,dT. \tag{1.5.6}$$

From $T\,dS = dE + P\,dV$, equation (1.5.6) is written as,

$$dF = -S\,dT - P\,dV, \tag{1.5.7}$$

which for an isothermal process yields,

$$\int_i^f dF = -\int_i^f P\, dV \tag{1.5.8}$$

Equation (1.5.8) suggests that if a system is brought from some initial state i to a final state *f* reversibly and at constant temperature and volume, then there is no change in the Helmholtz free energy.

The Gibbs free energy function is defined by the following:

$$G = H - TS \tag{1.5.9}$$

or

$$dG = dH - T\, dS - S\, dT \tag{1.5.10}$$

Substituting for *dH* from equation (1.5.3) in equation (1.5.10) yields,

$$dG = V\, dP - S\, dT \tag{1.5.11}$$

If a system is made to change reversibly and at constant temperature and pressure, the corresponding change in the Gibbs free energy is zero.

The differential form of the four functions, internal energy, enthalpy, and Helmholtz and Gibbs free energies constitute the set of Maxwell's relations. These are:

$$dE = T\, dS - P\, dV$$

$$dH = T\, dS + V\, dP$$

$$dF = -S\, dT - P\, dV$$

$$dG = -S\, dT + V\, dP.$$

A number of useful relations can be derived from the above,

$$\left(\frac{\partial T}{\partial V}\right)_S = -\left(\frac{\partial P}{\partial S}\right)_V$$

$$\left(\frac{\partial T}{\partial P}\right)_S = +\left(\frac{\partial V}{\partial S}\right)_P$$

$$\left(\frac{\partial S}{\partial V}\right)_T = \left(\frac{\partial P}{\partial T}\right)_V \qquad (1.5.12)$$

$$\left(\frac{\partial S}{\partial P}\right)_T = -\left(\frac{\partial V}{\partial T}\right)_P$$

In order to show the above relations, let us take z to be a function of x and y, $z = f(x, y)$. The differential of z is written as:

$$dz = \left(\frac{\partial z}{\partial x}\right)_y dx + \left(\frac{\partial z}{\partial y}\right)_x dy$$

$$= K\,dx + L\,dy,$$

where $K = \left(\frac{\partial z}{\partial x}\right)_y$ and $L = \left(\frac{\partial z}{\partial y}\right)_x$ and z are all functions of x and y. We can write,

$$\left(\frac{\partial K}{\partial y}\right)_x = \frac{\partial}{\partial y}\left[\left(\frac{\partial z}{\partial x}\right)_y\right]_x = \frac{\partial^2 z}{\partial y \partial x}$$

$$\left(\frac{\partial L}{\partial x}\right)_y = \frac{\partial}{\partial x}\left[\left(\frac{\partial z}{\partial y}\right)_x\right]_y = \frac{\partial^2 z}{\partial x \partial y}. \qquad (1.5.13)$$

This gives

$$\left(\frac{\partial K}{\partial y}\right)_x = \left(\frac{\partial L}{\partial x}\right)_y$$

Using properties of differential calculus, it can also be shown that,

$$\left(\frac{\partial x}{\partial y}\right)_z\left(\frac{\partial y}{\partial z}\right)_x\left(\frac{\partial z}{\partial x}\right)_y = -1 \qquad 1.5.14)$$

and
$$\left(\frac{\partial x}{\partial y}\right)_f\left(\frac{\partial y}{\partial z}\right)_f\left(\frac{\partial z}{\partial x}\right)_f = 1 \qquad (1.5.15)$$

where f is a function of x, y and z.

Maxwell's relations are very useful as they provide means of determining other properties if some are known. For example, $\frac{1}{V}\left(\frac{\partial V}{\partial T}\right)_p$ is the temperature coefficient of volume expansion, which can be written from equation (1.5.12) as,

$$\beta = \frac{1}{V}\left(\frac{\partial V}{\partial T}\right)_p = -\frac{1}{V}\left(\frac{\partial S}{\partial P}\right)_T \qquad (1.5.16)$$

Thus if a material is compressed isothermally, the volume will decrease and the atoms or molecules will occupy a smaller volume. If no other interaction occurs, the arrangement of atoms or molecules will become more orderly. The entropy will decrease because of increased ordering. The term $\left(\frac{\partial S}{\partial P}\right)_T = \frac{\Delta S}{\Delta P}$ (for small changes) therefore becomes negative and the temperature coefficient of volume expansion, for the material will be positive.

Some useful relations:

(i) Show that
$$T\,dS = C_v\frac{\kappa}{\beta}dP + \frac{C_p dV}{\beta V}.$$

Let us consider entropy S to be a function of pressure and volume, which upon differentiating partially yields,

$$dS = \left(\frac{\partial S}{\partial P}\right)_V dP + \left(\frac{\partial S}{\partial V}\right)_p dV.$$

Multiplying both sides by T gives the following,

$$T\,dS = T\left(\frac{\partial S}{\partial P}\right)_V dP + T\left(\frac{\partial S}{\partial V}\right)_p dV.$$

$$= -T\left(\frac{\partial V}{\partial T}\right)_S dP + T\left(\frac{\partial P}{\partial T}\right)_S dV \text{ (from Maxwell's relation)} \qquad (1.5.17)$$

We can write,

$$\left(\frac{\partial V}{\partial T}\right)_S = -\left(\frac{\partial S}{\partial T}\right)_V \left(\frac{\partial V}{\partial S}\right)_T \quad \text{and} \quad \left(\frac{\partial P}{\partial T}\right)_S = -\left(\frac{\partial P}{\partial S}\right)_T \left(\frac{\partial S}{\partial T}\right)_p$$

Substituting for $\left(\frac{\partial V}{\partial T}\right)_S$ and $\left(\frac{\partial P}{\partial T}\right)_S$ in equation (1.5.17) yields,

$$T\,dS = T\left(\frac{\partial S}{\partial T}\right)_V \left(\frac{\partial V}{\partial S}\right)_T dP - T\left(\frac{\partial P}{\partial S}\right)_T \left(\frac{\partial S}{\partial T}\right)_P dV.$$

Upon substitution $T\left(\frac{\partial S}{\partial T}\right)_V = C_v$ and $T\left(\frac{\partial S}{\partial T}\right)_p = C_P$ in the above, we get,

$$T\,dS = C_v\left(\frac{\partial V}{\partial S}\right)_T dP - C_P\left(\frac{\partial P}{\partial S}\right)_T dV.$$

$$= C_v\left(\frac{\partial T}{\partial P}\right)_V dP + \frac{C_p dV}{\left(\frac{\partial V}{\partial T}\right)_P} \qquad (1.5.18)$$

Now from $\left(\frac{\partial T}{\partial P}\right)_V \left(\frac{\partial P}{\partial V}\right)_T \left(\frac{\partial V}{\partial T}\right)_P = -1$, we get,

$$\left(\frac{\partial T}{\partial P}\right)_V = -\frac{\left(\frac{\partial V}{\partial P}\right)_T}{\left(\frac{\partial V}{\partial T}\right)_P} = +\frac{\kappa}{\beta},$$

which upon substitution in equation (1.5.18) yields,

$$T\,dS = C_v \frac{\kappa}{\beta} dP + \frac{C_p dV}{\beta V} \tag{1.5.19}$$

(ii) Show that $C_p - C_v = \frac{VT\beta^2}{\kappa}$

From equation (1.3.9), we can write,

$$C_p - C_v = \left[P + \left(\frac{\partial E}{\partial V}\right)_T\right]\beta V. \tag{1.3.9}$$

The first law of thermodynamics gives a relationship between the differentials of internal energy, entropy and volume,

$$dE = T\,dS - P\,dV$$

or

$$\left(\frac{\partial E}{\partial V}\right)_T = T\left(\frac{\partial S}{\partial V}\right)_T - P. \tag{1.5.20}$$

Substituting the value of $\left(\frac{\partial E}{\partial V}\right)_T$ in equation (1.3.9) gives the following,

$$C_p - C_v = \beta VT\left(\frac{\partial S}{\partial V}\right)_T \quad (1.5.21)$$

From Maxwell's relations, $\left(\frac{\partial S}{\partial V}\right)_T = \left(\frac{\partial P}{\partial T}\right)_V$, which simplifies to,

$$\left(\frac{\partial P}{\partial T}\right)_V = \left(\frac{\partial V}{\partial T}\right)_P\left(\frac{\partial P}{\partial V}\right)_T \quad \left\{\text{from} \left(\frac{\partial P}{\partial T}\right)_V\left(\frac{\partial T}{\partial V}\right)_P\left(\frac{\partial V}{\partial P}\right)_T = -1\right\}$$

Equation (1.5.21) can be written as,

$$C_p - C_v = -\beta VT \cdot \left(\frac{\partial V}{\partial T}\right)_P\left(\frac{\partial P}{\partial V}\right)_T$$

$$= +\frac{VT\beta^2}{\kappa} \quad (1.5.22)$$

(iii) Show that $\left(\frac{\partial P}{\partial V}\right)_S = -\frac{C_p}{C_v \cdot V\kappa}$

From the relation $\left(\frac{\partial P}{\partial V}\right)_S\left(\frac{\partial V}{\partial S}\right)_P\left(\frac{\partial S}{\partial P}\right)_V = -1$, we can write $\left(\frac{\partial P}{\partial V}\right)_S$ as,

$$\left(\frac{\partial P}{\partial V}\right)_S = -\left(\frac{\partial S}{\partial V}\right)_P\left(\frac{\partial P}{\partial S}\right)_V .$$

Now, since S is a function of P, V and T,

$$\left(\frac{\partial P}{\partial S}\right)_V\left(\frac{\partial S}{\partial T}\right)_V\left(\frac{\partial T}{\partial P}\right)_V = +1 \quad \text{and} \quad \left(\frac{\partial S}{\partial V}\right)_P\left(\frac{\partial V}{\partial T}\right)_P\left(\frac{\partial T}{\partial S}\right)_P = +1$$

Hence,

$$\left(\frac{\partial P}{\partial V}\right)_S = -\left(\frac{\partial P}{\partial T}\right)_V \left(\frac{\partial S}{\partial T}\right)_P \left(\frac{\partial T}{\partial V}\right)_P / \left(\frac{\partial S}{\partial T}\right)_V$$

From $T\left(\frac{\partial S}{\partial T}\right)_P = C_p$ and $T\left(\frac{\partial S}{\partial T}\right)_V = C_v$, we can write,

$$\left(\frac{\partial P}{\partial V}\right)_S = -\frac{C_p}{C_v}\left(\frac{\partial P}{\partial T}\right)_V \left(\frac{\partial T}{\partial V}\right)_P = +\frac{C_p}{C_v}\left(\frac{\partial P}{\partial V}\right)_T = -\frac{C_P}{C_V V \kappa} \qquad (1.5.23)$$

(iv) Show that $T\,dS = C_v\,dT + T\left(\frac{\partial P}{\partial T}\right)_V dV$

Consider the entropy of a substance to be a function of temperature and volume, $S = f(T, V)$, which allows us to write,

$$dS = \left(\frac{\partial S}{\partial T}\right)_V dT + \left(\frac{\partial S}{\partial V}\right)_T dV$$

or

$$T\,dS = T\left(\frac{\partial S}{\partial T}\right)_V dT + T\left(\frac{\partial S}{\partial V}\right)_T dV.$$

$T\left(\frac{\partial S}{\partial T}\right)_V = C_v$ and $\left(\frac{\partial S}{\partial V}\right)_T = \left(\frac{\partial P}{\partial T}\right)_V$ from Maxwell's equation.

Thus,

$$T\,dS = C_v dT + T\left(\frac{\partial P}{\partial T}\right)_V dV \qquad (1.5.24)$$

$$= C_v dT - \frac{T\beta}{\kappa} dV. \tag{1.5.25}$$

Similarly it can be shown that

$$T\,dS = C_p dT - T\beta V\,dP. \tag{1.5.26}$$

(v) Show that $dE = (C_p - PV\beta)dT + V(\kappa P - \beta T)dP,$

$$dH = C_p dT + V(1 - \beta T)\,dP,$$

$$dF = -(PV\beta + S)dT + P\kappa V\,dP.$$

From the relation,

$$dE = T\,dS - P\,dV$$

and $T\,dS = C_p dT - TV\beta\,dP$, equation (1.5.26) and

$$dV = \left(\frac{\partial V}{\partial T}\right)_P dT + \left(\frac{\partial V}{\partial P}\right)_T dP = C_p dT - TV\beta\,dP$$

or $dV = \beta V\,dT - \kappa V\,dP$, we can write,

$$dE = (C_p - PV\beta)dT + V(\kappa P - \beta T)dP \tag{1.5.27}$$

From the relation,

$$dH = T\,dS + V\,dP,$$

and, $T\,dS = C_p dT - TV\beta\,dP$, we can write,

$$dH = C_p dT - TV\beta\, dP + V\, dP$$

$$= C_p dT + V(1 - \beta T)dP. \tag{1.5.28}$$

From the relation,

$$dF = -S\, dT - P\, dV,$$

and, $dV = \beta V\, dT - \kappa V\, dP$, we can write,

$$dF = -S\, dT - P\beta V\, dT + P\kappa V\, dP$$

$$= -(P\beta V + S)dT + P\kappa V\, dP. \tag{1.5.29}$$

Example: The pressure on one mole of Cu is increased reversibly and isothermally from 1 atmosphere to 10,000 atmosphere at 300K.

Given: $\beta = 50.6 \times 10^{-6}\ K^{-1}$, $\overline{V} = 7.06\ cm^3\ mole^{-1}$, $\kappa = 0.788 \times 10^{-6}\ atm^{-1}$ and $C_p = 24.5\ J\ mol^{-1}\ K^{-1}$, calculate

(a) the amount of heat transferred during compression.
(b) the amount of work done during compression.
(c) the change in internal energy of copper.

(a) From Equation (1.5.26), $T\, dS = C_P\, dT - T\, \beta\, V\, dP$

T = Constant for an isothermal process hence $dT = 0$.

$$T\, dS = dQ.$$

$$\therefore \quad dQ = -T\, \beta\, \overline{V}\, dP \quad (V = \overline{V})$$

$$Q = -T\, \beta\, \overline{V}(P_f - P_i)$$

$$= -300 \times 50.6 \times 10^{-6} \frac{7.06}{1000}(10000 - 1)\left(\frac{\text{Lit.atm}}{\text{mol}}\right) \times 101\ \text{J mol}^{-1}$$

$$Q = -108.23\ \text{J mol}^{-1}$$

(b) The amount of work done during compression is

$$W = \int P\,dV. \quad \text{from} \quad dv = \left(\frac{\partial V}{\partial P}\right)_T dP + \left(\frac{\partial V}{\partial T}\right)_P dT$$

$$\text{at constant } T,\ W = \int P\left(\frac{\partial V}{\partial P}\right)_T dP$$

$$= -\int_{P_i}^{P_f} \kappa\, V\, P\, dP$$

$$= -\kappa\frac{\overline{V}}{2}(P_f^2 - P_i^2)$$

$$W = -0.788\times 10^{-6}\times\frac{7.06}{1000}\times\frac{(10^8-1)}{2}\times \text{J mol}^{-1}$$

$$= -28.09\ \text{J mol}^{-1}$$

(c) The change in internal energy E is

$$E = Q - W = -28.09 + 108.23$$

$$= 80.14\ \text{J mol}^{-1}.$$

Example: In the previous example, what would be the change in temperature if one mole of copper is compressed adiabatically.

For adiabatic compression, $T\,dS$ in equation (1.5.26) is zero.

$$\therefore \quad C_P dT = T\,\beta\,\overline{V}\,dP$$

$$\Delta T = \frac{T\beta\overline{V}(P_f - P_i)}{C_P} \quad \text{for small change in temperature)}$$

$$= 300 \times \frac{50.6 \times 10^{-6}}{24.5} \times \frac{7.06}{1000} (10^4 - 1) \times 101$$

$$= 4.4 \text{ K}.$$

Example: Calculate the molar heat capacity at constant volume of NaCl at 300K and 1 atm. pressure.

Given: $C_P = 49.4$ J mol^{-1}K^{-1}, $V = 0.027$ Liter mol^{-1},
$\beta = 119 \times 10^{-6}$K^{-1} and $\kappa = 4.38 \times 10^{-6}$ atm^{-1}.

From equation (1.5.22), $C_P - C_V = \dfrac{T\overline{V}\beta^2}{\kappa}$

$$C_V = C_P - \frac{T\overline{V}\beta^2}{\kappa}$$

$$= 49.4 - \frac{300 \times 0.027 \times 119^2 \times 10^{-12}}{4.38 \times 10^{-6}} \times 101$$

$$= 46.755 \text{ J mol}^{-1} \text{ k}^{-1}$$

Example: One mole of silver at 1 atmosphere and 300 K is subjected to the following two processes,

(i) an isothermal compression to 10,000 atmosphere
(ii) an isobaric change to 1000 K.

Calculate the change in enthalpy.

Given: $C_P = 21.3 + 8.53 \times 10^{-3}T + 1.5 \times 10^5 T^{-2}$ J mol^{-1}K^{-1},

$$V = 10.27 \text{ cm}^3 \text{ mol}^{-1}, \quad \beta = 57 \times 10^{-6} \text{ K}^{-1}$$

From equation (1.5.28), $dH = C_P dT + V(1 - \beta T)\, dP$

(i) at constant temperature,

$$dH = V(1-\beta T)\,dP$$

$$\Delta H = \int V(1-\beta T)dP = V(1-\beta T)(P_f - P_i)$$

$$= \frac{10.27}{1000}(1-57\times10^{-6}\times300)(10000-1)\times101 \text{ J mol}^{-1}$$

$$= 10195.3 \text{ J mol}^{-1}$$

(ii) $\Delta H = \int C_P\,dT$

$$= \int_{T_i}^{T_f} (21.3 + 8.53\times10^{-3}T + 1.5\times10^5T^{-2})dT.$$

$$= 21.3(1000-300) + \frac{8.53\times10^{-3}}{2}(1000^2-300^2) - 1.5\times10^5\left[\frac{1}{1000}-\frac{1}{300}\right]$$

$$= 14910 + 3881.15 + 350$$

$$= 19141.15 \text{ J mol}^{-1}$$

The above example illustrates that enthalpy of a system is influenced more by temperature than pressure changes.

1.6 Entropy and Disorder–Statistical Interpretation

The entropy of a system is a measure of the degree of disorder, when applied at the atomic level. For example, in the case of crystalline solids atoms vibrate about their mean position while sitting on the regular lattice sites. There is not much movement of atoms except occasionally when one of the atoms makes a jump to the neighbouring lattice site. The atoms are therefore considered to be in a state of well maintained order. In contrast, atoms in a liquid are free to move from one position to another. This creates a degree of disorder in liquids relative to solids. The atoms or molecules are in continuous motion when they are in the gaseous state. The degree of disorder of the atoms in the gas or vapor state is considerably higher than of those in the solid and liquid states. The entropy of a system in the gaseous or vapor state is, therefore, much higher when compared to that of the same system in the condensed state.

The entropy of a system in the liquid state as compared to that of a system in the solid state can be understood from the enthalpy of fusion when a pure solid melts at its melting temperature. In order to melt a pure solid, an amount of heat ΔH_f is added and the entropy increases by an amount $\Delta H_f/T_f$ in the process. Thus, the liquid state of a substance is associated with an increase in disorder and hence has a higher entropy than the solid state. Similarly, the vapor state of a substance has a higher entropy from the contribution made by the enthalpy of vaporization ΔH_v required to vaporize a condensed phase.

A quantitative relationship between the degree of disorder and entropy can be obtained from statistical thermodynamics, which is developed from the consideration that the equilibrium state of a system is the most probable state, because every system vies to attain this state. The problem reduces to the determination of the probability of occurrence of a given state of a system.

In quantum mechanics each particle is considered to occupy a given microstate and the number of microstates corresponding to a given macrostate is termed as thermodynamic probability. Consider a gas filled in a box of volume *V*. The particles in the gas are in continuous motion and each particle occupies a discrete energy level and a quantum state. However, due to collisions between particles, they either emit or absorb photons. At any given moment each particle occupies a distinct quantum state but due to frequent changes the microstate changes from one quantum state to another. The thermodynamic probability of occurrence of a given microstate is designated by *W*, where *W* is a large number.

In order to determine the number of microstates and hence the thermodynamic probability, let us consider four indistinguishable particles which can be placed in four distinguishable cells, *A*, *B*, *C* and *D*. Let the total energy of the four particles be $4e$, distributed between energy levels e_0, e_1, e_2, e_3 and e_4 where these energy levels have energies, $e_0 = 0$, $e_1 = e$, $e_2 = 2e$, $e_3 = 3e$ and $e_4 = 4e$. The system of four particles can be distributed in the four cells in the following ways:

a. All four particles are in the energy level e_1 with total energy $4e$. Since the particles are indistinguishable there is only one way to make this arrangement, Fig. 1.1a.

b. One particle is in the energy level e_4 and the rest are in e_0 with total energy $E = 1 \times 4e + 3 \times 0 = 4e$. The number of possible microstates are four in this case because one particle with energy $4e$ can occupy only one of the cells A, B, C or D at a time. The remaining three particles will occupy the remaining three cells and have energy zero, Fig. 1.1b.

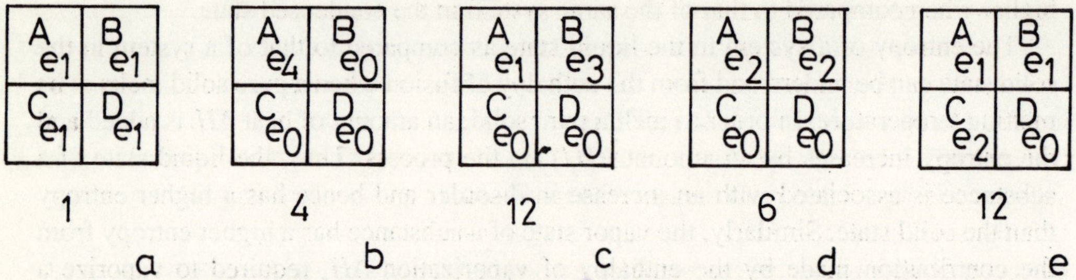

Fig. 1.1 Different arrangements of particles in the four cells A, B, C and D.

c. One particle each occupies energy levels e_3 and e_1 and two particles occupy zero energy levels. The number of such arrangements or microstates is 12 as shown in Fig. 1.1c.

d. Two particles occupy energy level e_2 and the remaining two particles occupy zero energy level with total energy $E = 2 \times 2e + 2 \times 0 = 4e$. The number of arrangements is six, Fig. 1.1d.

e. One particle each occupies energy levels e_2 and e_0 and the remaining two particles are in the energy level e_1 with total energy, $E = 1 \times 2e + 2 \times e + 1 \times 0 = 4e$. The number of microstates for this arrangement is 12, Fig. 1.1e.

The number of molecules in a gram mole of a gas is an enormous number equal to 6.023×10^{23}. Thus the number of microstates for each arrangement is a large number. Let us consider the number of ways of permuting/arranging N indistinguishable particles. The first particle can be arranged in N different ways, the second in $(N-1)$ different ways, the third in $(N-2)$ different ways and so on up to 1. The number of ways of arranging N particles is $N\,(N-1)\,(N-2)\,(N-3)\ldots 1 = N!$. However, since the particles are indistinguishable, the number of arrangements is much less. In general, for a system of N particles, the number of microstates is determined by dividing $N!$ by the number of particles occupied by each state. Thus, if N_0 is the number of particles occupying the energy level e_0, N_1 the number of particles occupying the energy level e_1 and N_i the number of particles occupying the energy level e_i, we can write the thermodynamic probability as,

$$W = \frac{N!}{N_0!N_1!N_2!\ldots} = \frac{N!}{\prod_{i=0}^{r} N_i!} \tag{1.6.1}$$

In the above example, when the four particles are placed in four cells, *A*, *B*, *C* and *D*, the thermodynamic probability of the five microstates can be written according to equation (1.6.1) as,

$$W = \frac{4!}{4!0!0!0!} = 1 \text{ for the arrangement in (a)}$$

$$W = \frac{4!}{3!1!0!0!} = 4 \text{ for (b)}$$

$$W = \frac{4!}{2!1!1!0!} = 12 \text{ for (c)}$$

$$W = \frac{4!}{2!2!0!0!} = 6 \text{ for (d)}$$

$$W = \frac{4!}{1!2!1!0!0!} = 12 \text{ for (e)}$$

In all there are 35 possible ways of arranging the four particles in the four cells. If the particles are in continuous motion and each microstate is equally likely to be occupied, then the first microstate (a) will be occupied 1/35 of the time, the second (b) 4/35 of the time, third and fifth 12/35 of the time and the fourth (d) 6/35 of the time.

The most probable distribution of particles in a system is also the equilibrium distribution and is obtained by maximizing *W*. For a large number of particles (which is close to the real situation, there being 6.023×10^{23} particles (molecules) in a mole of gas), the factorial in the expression for ln *W* can be simplified by using Stirling's approximation,

$$\ln X! = X \ln X - X,$$

or

$$\ln W! = N \ln N - N - \sum_{i=0}^{r} (N_i \ln N_i - N_i) \qquad (1.6.2)$$

$$\delta \ln W = 0 - \sum_{i=0}^{r} \left(N_i \frac{\delta N_i}{N_i} + \ln N_i \delta N_i - \delta N_i \right)$$

$$= -\sum \ln N_i \, \delta N_i .$$

or
$$\sum_{i=0}^{r} \ln N_i \, \delta N_i = 0 \tag{1.6.3}$$

The most probable distribution is to be attained under conditions of constant volume, total internal energy E and number of particles N.

For
$$N = N_0 + N_1 + N_2 + \ldots + N_r = \text{constant}$$

$$\delta N = \sum_{i=0}^{r} \delta N_i = 0 \tag{1.6.4}$$

For
$$E = N_0 e_0 + N_1 e_1 + N_2 e_2 + \ldots + N_r e_r = \text{constant},$$

$$\delta E = \sum_{i=0}^{r} e_i \, \delta N_i = 0 \tag{1.6.5}$$

In order to arrive at the number of energy levels N_i we can make use of the Lagrange's method of undetermined multipliers. Let us multiply equations (1.6.4) and (1.6.5) by $\ln \alpha$ and β, respectively. Combining these with equation (1.6.3) yields,

$$\sum_{i=0}^{r} (\ln N_i - \ln \alpha + \beta e_i) \, \delta N_i = 0 \tag{1.6.6}$$

Since $\delta N_i'^s$ are independent of each other, the coefficient of each term must vanish in the expansion of equation (1.6.6).

Thus,
$$\ln N_i - \ln \alpha + \beta \, e_i = 0 \tag{1.6.7}$$

or
$$N_i = \alpha \, e^{-\beta e_i} \tag{1.6.8}$$

An expression for α can be obtained from the condition that the sum of all N_i must equal the total number of particles N (equation (1.6.4)). Writing each term from equation (1.6.8),
we get,

$$\sum_{i=0}^{r} \alpha e^{-\beta e_i} = \alpha e^{-\beta e_1} + \alpha e^{-\beta e_2} + \ldots + \alpha e^{-\beta e_r}$$

$$= \alpha \sum_{i=0}^{r} e^{-\beta e_i}$$

The term under the summation is known as the 'Partition function' or sum of all states, and plays an important role in the theory of Statistical mechanics. Thus designating the partition function as Z, we get,

$$N = \alpha Z \quad \text{or} \quad \alpha = \frac{N}{Z} \tag{1.6.9}$$

Substituting for α in equation (1.6.8), gives an expression for the number of occupied states with energy e_i

$$N_i = \frac{N}{Z} \exp^{-\beta e_i} \tag{1.6.10}$$

The expression for N_i indicates that the number of levels which maximize W decreases exponentially with increasing energy of the level, shown schematically in Fig. 1.2a and b. The actual shape of the curve is dependent on the value of β which is a positive quantity and is proportional to the reciprocal of temperature. The constant of proportionality is $1/k$, where k is the Boltzmann's constant. This gives $\beta = 1/kT$ and equation (1.6.11) is written as,

$$N_i = \frac{N}{Z} \exp^{-e_i/kT} \tag{1.6.11}$$

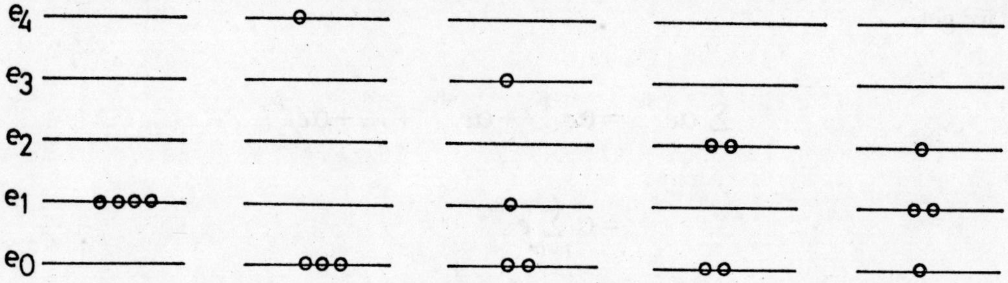

Fig. 1.2a Schematic representation of the distribution of particles in different energy levels.

The value of W can be obtained by substituting for N_i in equation (1.6.2). Accordingly,

$$\ln W = N \ln N - \Sigma N_i \ln N_i$$

$$= N \ln N - \Sigma \frac{N}{Z} \exp^{-e_i/kT} \ln\left(\frac{N}{Z} \exp^{-e_i/kT}\right) \qquad (1.6.12)$$

$$= N \ln N - \frac{N}{Z} \Sigma \exp^{-(e_i/kT)} \left[\ln N - \ln Z - \frac{e_i}{kT}\right].$$

$$= N \ln N - \frac{N}{Z} (\ln N - \ln Z) \Sigma \exp^{-e_i/kT} + \frac{N}{ZkT} \Sigma e_i \exp^{-e_i/kT}$$

$$= N \ln N - \frac{N}{Z} (\ln N - \ln Z) Z + \frac{N}{ZkT} \Sigma e_i \exp^{-e_i/kT}$$

$$= N \ln N - N \ln N + N \ln Z + \frac{N}{ZkT} \Sigma e_i \exp^{-e_i/kT}$$

$$= N \ln Z + \frac{N}{ZkT} \Sigma e_i \exp^{-e_i/kT} \qquad (1.6.13)$$

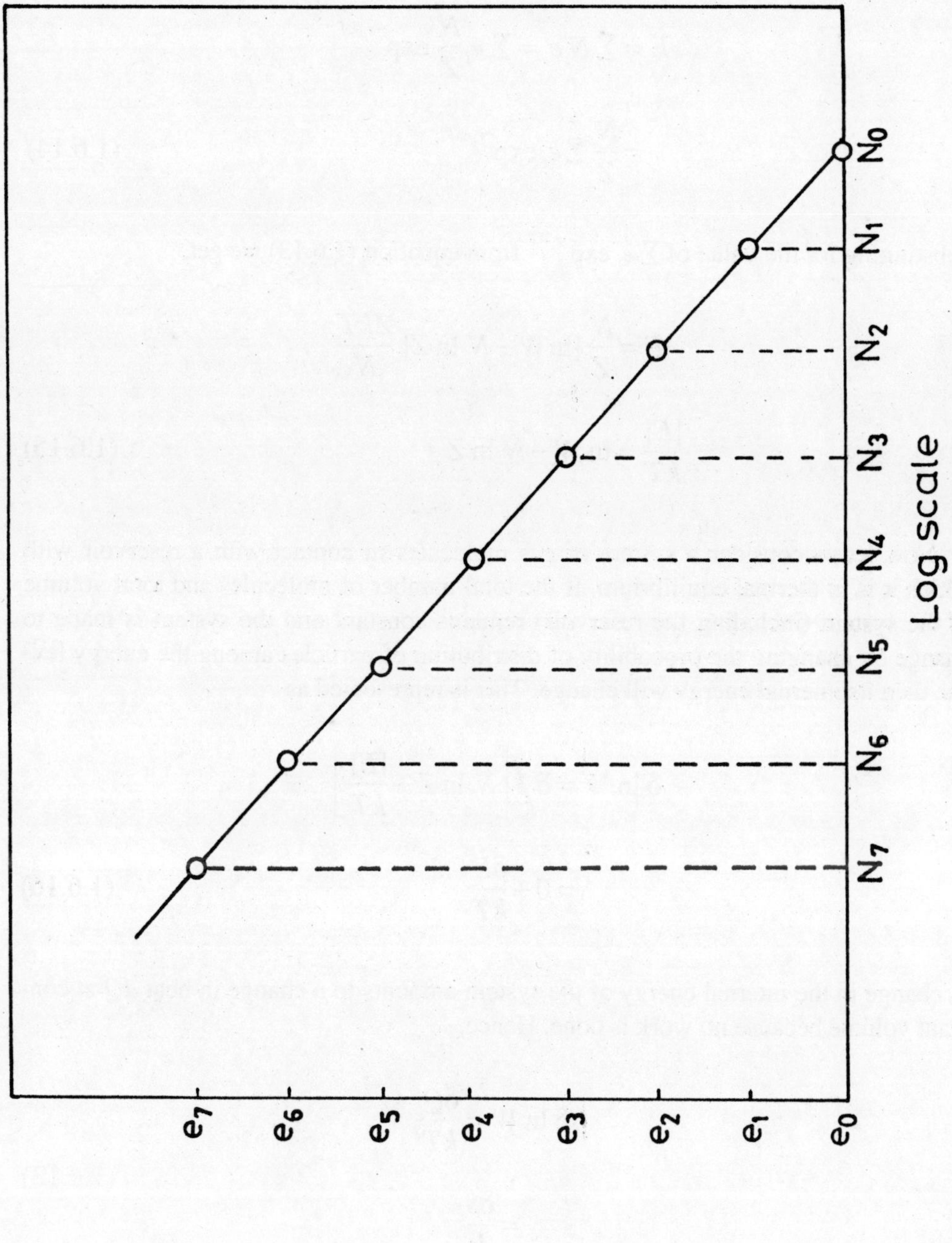

Fig 1.2b Schematic representation of the distribution of particles in different energy levels.

The internal energy of the system consisting of gas molecules can be obtained from

$$E = \Sigma N_i e_i = \Sigma e_i \frac{N}{Z} \exp^{-e_i/kT}$$

$$= \frac{N}{Z} \Sigma e_i \exp^{-e_i/kT} \qquad (1.6.14)$$

Substituting for the value of $\Sigma\, e_i \exp^{-e_i/kT}$ from equation (1.6.13) we get,

$$E = \frac{N}{Z} [\ln W - N \ln Z] \frac{ZkT}{N}$$

or

$$\frac{[E]}{kT} = \ln W - N \ln Z \qquad (1.6.15)$$

Now let us consider a system of gas molecules in contact with a reservoir with which it is in thermal equilibrium. If the total number of molecules and total volume of the system (including the reservoir) remains constant and the system is made to change by changing the probability of distribution of particles among the energy levels, then its internal energy will change. This is represented as

$$\delta \ln W = \delta \not{\beta} \left[N \ln Z + \frac{[E]}{kT} \right]$$

$$= 0 + \frac{\delta E}{kT} \qquad (1.6.16)$$

A change in the internal energy of the system amounts to a change in heat dQ at constant volume because no work is done. Hence,

$$\delta \ln W = \frac{\delta Q}{kT}$$

$$= \frac{\delta S}{k}$$

or $$S = k \ln W \tag{1.6.17}$$

1.7 GIBBS FREE ENERGY, EQUILIBRIUM AND CHEMICAL REACTION

1.7.1 Change in the free energy for a reaction

When a chemical reaction between reactants and products proceeds reversibly at constant temperature and pressure, a stage will be reached when the system appears stationary. The reaction does not stop. The state of the system is under dynamic equilibrium whereby the rate of forward reaction equals the rate at which the product phases dissociate to give the reactants. The system is known to be under equilibrium and a certain number of moles of each component reactant phase will give certain number of moles of each component of the product phase. In order to characterize chemical equilibrium, the free energy concept can be of immense significance in the thermodynamics of a chemical reaction. The conditions under which a particular state of the system is realized under equilibrium and how it is affected by changes in temperature and pressure of the system can now be stated.

It is of interest to determine the free energy change for a chemical reaction using the standard state of the reactants and products. The change in the standard free energy will dictate the spontaneity of the reaction and help to evaluate the equilibrium constant. Let us consider n_A moles of component A combining with n_B moles of component B to give n_L moles of L and n_M moles of M as products (all in their standard states). This reaction is written as,

$$n_A A(S) + n_B B(S) \longrightarrow n_L L(S) + n_M M(S) \tag{1.7.1}$$

The free energy change for the reaction is ΔG_1^0. The reactants and products can be considered to be in equilibrium with each other in the vapor state with their respectively vapor pressure p_A^0, p_B^0, p_L^0 and p_M^0. These reactions can be written such that one can obtain products from the reactants.

$$n_A A(g, p_A^0) == n_A A(s), \qquad \Delta G = 0, \tag{1.7.2}$$

$$n_B B(g, p_B^0) == n_B B(s), \qquad \Delta G = 0, \tag{1.7.3}$$

$$n_L L(s) = n_L L(g, p_L^0), \qquad \Delta G = 0, \tag{1.7.4}$$

$$n_M M(s) = n_M M(g, p_M^0), \qquad \Delta G = 0, \tag{1.7.5}$$

All the above reactions are at equilibrium and hence the change in free energy for each reaction is zero. The free energy change corresponds to the components in the standard state. Addition of equations (1.7.1) to (1.7.5) yields the change in free energy for the conversion of reactants and products in their gaseous state,

$$n_A A(g, p_A^0) + n_B B(g, p_B^0) = n_L L(g, p_L^0) + n_M M(g, p_M^0), \tag{1.7.6}$$

$$\Delta G = \Delta G_1^0.$$

We can now obtain the gaseous state of each component at a pressure p_i^e such that the reaction will be under equilibrium. Thus for each component, the change in the free energy in bringing it from p_i^0 to p_i^e at constant temperature is written as,

$$n_A A(g, p_A^e) = n_A A(g, p_A^0), \qquad \Delta G = n_A RT \ln (p_A^0/p_A^e) \tag{1.7.7}$$

$$n_B B(g, p_B^e) = n_B B(g, p_B^0), \qquad \Delta G = n_B RT \ln (p_B^0/p_B^e)$$

$$n_L L(g, p_L^0) = n_L L(g, p_L^e), \qquad \Delta G = n_L RT \ln (p_L^e/p_L^0)$$

$$n_M M(g, p_M^0) = n_M M(g, p_M^e), \qquad \Delta G = n_M RT \ln (p_M^e/p_M^0)$$

Combining equations (1.7.6) and (1.7.7) yields,

$$n_A A(g, p_A^e) + n_B B(g, p_B^e) = n_L L(g, p_L^e) + n_M M(g, p_M^e),$$

$$\Delta G = \Delta G_1^0 + RT \ln \left[\frac{(p_A^0)^{n_A} (p_B^0)^{n_B} (p_L^e)^{n_L} (p_M^e)^{n_M}}{(p_A^e)^{n_A} (p_B^e)^{n_B} (p_L^0)^{n_L} (p_M^0)^{n_M}} \right]$$

Since the reaction is under equilibrium, $\Delta G = 0$, and hence,

$$\Delta G_1^0 = -RT \ln K, \tag{1.7.8}$$

where the equilibrium constant K is,

$$K = \frac{(p_A^0)^{n_A} (p_B^0)^{n_B} (p_L^e)^{n_L} (p_M^e)^{n_M}}{(p_A^e)^{n_A} (p_B^e)^{n_B} (p_L^0)^{n_L} (p_M^e)^{n_M}}$$

The free energy change for the reactions of equations (1.7.7) can be written from $dG = V\,dP - S\,dT = V\,dP$ (at const. T). Considering the vapor phase of the components of the reactants and products to behave as ideal gases at low pressure, we can write,

$$dG = V\,dP = \frac{nRT}{P}\,dP = nRT \cdot d\ln P$$

or

$$\Delta G = nRT \ln \frac{p_i^e}{p_i^0}. \tag{1.7.9}$$

The ratio of the vapor pressure of the components at equilibrium p_i^e to the partial pressure of the solid p_i^0, which is p_i^e/p_i^0 is termed as the activity of the component i, a_i. The equilibrium constant can be written as,

$$K = \frac{a_L^{n_L} a_M^{n_M}}{a_A^{n_A} a_B^{n_B}} \quad \text{and} \quad \Delta G_1^0 = -RT \ln\left[\frac{a_L^{n_L} a_M^{n_M}}{a_A^{n_A} \cdot a_B^{n_B}}\right] \tag{1.7.10}$$

Equation (1.7.10) gives an expression for the free energy change for the reaction when the reactants and products are in their standard states. The activities of the components can be considered to be equal to 1 for reactants and products in their standard states. Let us now determine the free energy change for components which are not in their standard states but have arbitrary activities. The change can be carried out by writing the reactions:

$$n_A A(a_A) \rightleftharpoons n_A A(a_A = 1), \qquad \Delta G = n_A RT \ln (1/a_A)$$

$$n_B B(a_B) \rightleftharpoons n_B B(a_B = 1), \qquad \Delta G = n_B RT \ln (1/a_B)$$

$$n_L L(a_L = 1) \rightleftharpoons n_L L(a_L), \qquad \Delta G = n_L RT \ln a_L$$

$$n_M M(a_M = 1) \rightleftharpoons n_M M(a_M), \qquad \Delta G = n_M RT \ln a_M$$

and $\quad n_A A(a_A = 1) + n_B B(a_B = 1) \rightleftharpoons n_L L(a_L = 1) + n_M M(a_M = 1), \quad \Delta G = \Delta G_1^0.$

The change in the free energy for the reaction when the components are in arbitrary states is,

$$\Delta G = RT \ln \left[\frac{a_L^{n_L} \cdot a_M^{n_M}}{a_A^{n_A} \cdot a_B^{n_B}} \right] + \Delta G_1^0. \qquad (1.7.11)$$

1.7.2 Variation of Equilibrium Constant with Temperature and Pressure

The extent to which the equilibrium constant is affected by pressure can be determined by writing the free energy change ΔG_1^0 and differentiating it with respect to the pressure. Thus,

$$\Delta G_1^0 = -RT \ln K,$$

or

$$\left(\frac{\partial \Delta G_1^0}{\partial P} \right)_T = -RT \left(\frac{\partial \ln K}{\partial P} \right)_T = 0. \qquad (1.7.12)$$

Since the standard state for the reactants and products is defined such that it is independent of pressure, the derivative of the free energy change w.r.t. pressure will be zero. The equilibrium constant is therefore independent of pressure. A similar procedure can be followed in determining the effect of temperature on the equilibrium constant.

$$\left[\frac{\partial(\Delta G_1^0/T)}{[\partial T]}\right]_P = -R\left(\frac{\partial \ln K}{\partial T}\right)_P \tag{1.7.13}$$

The Gibbs free energy function is written as, $G = H - TS$. From Maxwell's relations, $dG = V\,dP - S\,dT$, or $S = -(\partial G/\partial T)_P$. Substituting for S in the expression for G yields,

$$G = H + T\left(\frac{\partial G}{\partial T}\right)_P. \tag{1.7.14}$$

Dividing both sides by T^2 yields,

$$\frac{G}{T^2} = \frac{H}{T^2} + \frac{1}{T}\left(\frac{\partial G}{\partial T}\right)_P$$

or

$$\frac{1}{T}\left(\frac{\partial G}{\partial T}\right)_P - \frac{G}{T^2} = -\frac{H}{T^2}$$

or

$$\left[\frac{\partial(G/T)}{\partial T}\right]_P = -\frac{H}{T^2} \tag{1.7.15}$$

Equation (1.7.15) is one of the forms of the Gibbs-Helmholtz relation. There is another and more useful form of this relation where the difference in free energy between two states 1 and 2 of a system can be written using the above proceedure.

$$G_1 = H_1 - TS_1 \quad \text{and} \quad G_2 = H_2 - TS_2$$

or

$$G_1 = H_1 + T\left(\frac{\partial G_1}{\partial T}\right)_P \quad \text{and} \quad G_2 = H_2 + T\left(\frac{\partial G_2}{\partial T}\right)_P,$$

or $$G_2 - G_1 = H_2 - H_1 + T\left\{\frac{\partial G_2}{\partial T} - \frac{\partial G_1}{\partial T}\right\}_p,$$

$$\Delta G = \Delta H + T\left(\frac{\partial \Delta G}{\partial T}\right)_p. \quad (1.7.16)$$

Dividing both sides of the equation (1.7.16) by T^2 and rearranging, we get,

$$\left[\frac{\partial(\Delta G/T)}{\partial T}\right]_p = -\frac{\Delta H}{T^2}. \quad (1.7.17)$$

Equation (1.7.17) has the differential of ($\Delta G/T$) with respect to T which upon substitution in equation (1.7.13) yields.

$$R\left(\frac{\partial \ln K}{\partial T}\right)_p = \frac{\Delta H^0}{T^2}, \quad (1.7.18)$$

where ΔH^0 is the change in enthalpy of the reaction for both reactants and products in their standard states, i.e., the same state used in the calculation of the equilibrium constant. Equation (1.7.18) is known as Vant Hoff's equation.

1.7.3 Partial Molar Properties

In the preceding sections we have discussed the molar properties of materials consisting of pure components. In connection with phase diagrams, we are concerned with the thermodynamic properties, for example, Gibbs free energy, enthalpy, entropy etc., of a given component in binary, ternary or multicomponent solutions. The thermodynamic properties of a given component in a solution are known as its partial molar properties. For example, the partial molar Gibbs free energy of the component A in a solution is termed as G_A. It refers to the Gibbs free energy of one mole of A in a solution containing n_A moles of A, n_B moles of B, n_C moles of C etc. In order to make these definitions easily understandable we can consider a definite volume of, say, a binary solution A–B. The binary solution consists of a certain number of moles of A and B types atoms which occupy a definite volume, to make up the total volume of the solution. The total volume of the solution therefore consists of the volumes of n_A number of moles of A and n_B number of moles of B. The volume occupied by one mole of A is known as the partial molar volume of A, V_A and that occupied by a mole of B is known as partial molar volume of B, V_B.

If G_i is the molar free energy of the component i in the solution then the total free energy of the system consisting of n components is the sum of the products of n_iG_i or $G = \sum_{i=1}^{n} n_iG_i$. Let the mean value of any extensive thermodynamic property be denoted by ϕ per mole of the solution. The observed value of the property ϕ_T for a binary solution consisting of n_A and n_B number of moles of A and B, respectively, is given by,

$$\phi_T = (n_A + n_B)\phi \tag{1.7.19}$$

Differentiating equation (1.7.19) with respect to n_B keeping n_A constant yields,

$$\phi_B = \frac{\partial \phi_T}{\partial n_B} = (n_A + n_B)\left(\frac{\partial \phi}{\partial n_B}\right)_{n_A} + \phi \tag{1.7.20}$$

Writing the number of moles of A and B in terms of the mole fractions, X_A and X_B, respectively, gives the following:

$$X_A = \frac{n_A}{n_A + n_B}, \quad X_B = \frac{n_B}{n_A + n_B},$$

which upon differentiation yields,

$$dX_A = -\frac{n_A\, dn_B}{(n_A + n_B)^2}, \quad dX_B = \frac{n_A dn_B}{(n_A + n_B)^2}$$

$$dX_A = -\frac{X_A dn_B}{(n_A + n_B)}, \quad dX_B = \frac{X_A dn_B}{(n_A + n_B)}.$$

Upon substitution of the above result in equation (1.7.20), we obtain the following,

$$\phi_B = -X_A \frac{dn_B}{dX_A}\left(\frac{\partial\phi}{dn_B}\right)_{n_A} + \phi,$$

$\phi_B = \phi - X_A\left(\dfrac{\partial\phi}{\partial X_A}\right) = \phi + X_A\left(\dfrac{\partial\phi}{\partial X_B}\right)$, (since $dX_A = -dX_B$ for a binary solution). The partial molar property of a component in a solution can also be derived graphically. Consider the property ϕ of the solution to be represented by the curve shown in Fig. 1.3. Draw a tangent to the curve at coordinate positions (X_A, X_B) which meets the pure component axes A and B at M and N, respectively. The slope of the line at the point O (X_A, X_B) is $d\phi/dX_B$, which from the triangle PNO may be written as,

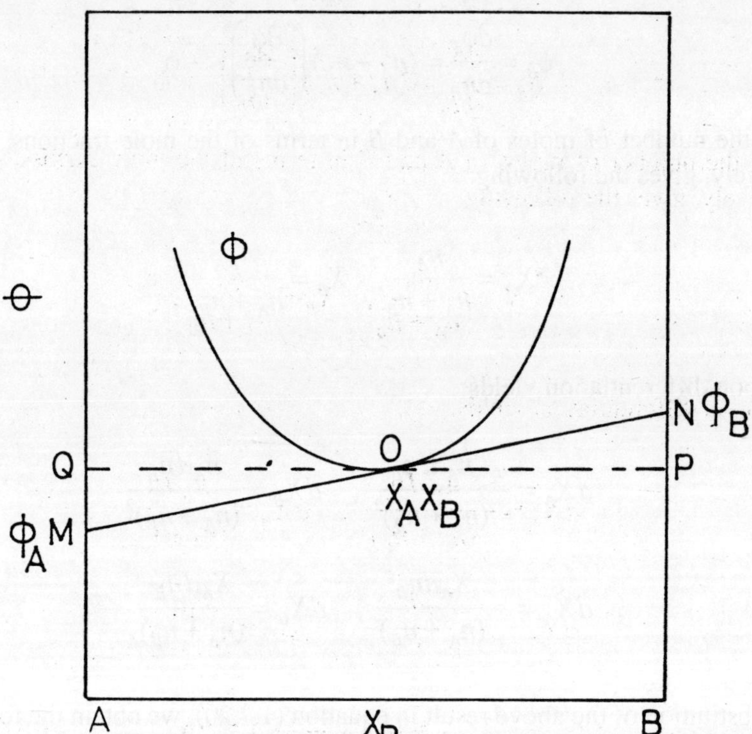

Fig 1.3 Graphical representation of thermodynamic properties. The partial molar property of A, ϕ_A, is the intercept that the tangent at the composition point (X_A, X_B) makes with the y-axis.

$$\frac{d\phi}{dX_B} = \frac{\phi_B - \phi}{X_A} \quad \text{or} \quad \phi_B = \phi + X_A\left(\frac{\partial \phi}{\partial X_B}\right).$$

Similarly from the triangle MOQ, $\dfrac{d\phi}{dX_B} = \dfrac{\phi - \phi_A}{X_B}$

or
$$\phi_A = \phi - X_B\left(\frac{\partial \phi}{\partial X_B}\right).$$

For $\phi = G$, V, S and H, we can write the following,

$$G_A = G - X_B \frac{\partial G}{\partial X_B}, \quad G_B = G + X_A \frac{\partial G}{\partial X_B}.$$

$$V_A = V - X_B \frac{\partial V}{\partial X_B}, \quad V_B = V + X_A \frac{\partial V}{\partial X_B}$$

$$S_A = S - X_B \frac{\partial S}{\partial X_B}, \quad S_B = S + X_A \frac{\partial S}{\partial X_B}$$

$$H_A = H - X_B \frac{\partial H}{\partial X_B}, \quad H_B = H + X_A \frac{\partial H}{\partial X_B}.$$

Treating ϕ_T as a function of X_A, X_B, . . . at constant temperature and pressure, we can write,

$$d\phi_T = \left(\frac{\partial \phi_T}{\partial X_A}\right)_{T,P,X_B} dX_A + \left(\frac{\partial \phi_T}{\partial X_B}\right)_{T,P,X_A} dX_B + \ldots$$

or
$$d\phi_T = \phi_A dX_A + \phi_B dX_B + \phi_C dX_C + \ldots$$

Integration yields,

$$\phi_T = \phi_A X_A + \phi_B X_B + \phi_C X_C + \ldots \tag{1.7.23}$$

Differentiating with respect to ϕ as well as w.r.t. composition variables yields the following,

$$d\phi_T = \phi_A dX_A + \phi_B dX_B + \phi_C dX_C + ... + X_A d\phi_A + X_B d\phi_B + X_C d\phi_C + ...$$

However, since $\phi_A dX_A + \phi_B X_A + \phi_C dX_C + \ldots = d\phi_T$, we obtain,

$$X_A d\phi_A + X_B d\phi_B + X_C d\phi_C + ... = 0.$$

For the Gibbs free energy function, $\phi = G$,

$$X_A dG_A + X_B dG_B + X_C dG_C + ... = 0. \quad (1.7.24)$$

Equation (1.7.24) is known as the Gibbs-Duhem equation which for a binary system can be written as,

$$X_A dG_A + X_B dG_B = 0. \quad (1.7.25)$$

In order to obtain the partial molar property of one of the components when that of the other is known, we can use Gibbs-Duhem integration, which gives,

$$\int dG_B = -\int \frac{X_A}{X_B} dG_A = -\int \frac{1 - X_B}{X_B} dG_A. \quad (1.7.26)$$

The integration can be carried out from $X_B = 1$ to X_B

$$\int_{G_B \mathrm{at} X_B = 1}^{G_B \mathrm{at} X_B} dG_B = -\int_{G_B \mathrm{at} X_B = 1}^{G_B \mathrm{at} X_B} \frac{1 - X_B}{X_B} dG$$

Now, at $X_B = 1$, $G_B = G_B^0$, with the result

$$G_B - G_B^0 = -\int_{G_A \text{at} X_B = 1}^{G_A \text{at} X_B} \frac{1 - X_B}{X_B} dG_A.$$

At $X_B = 1, \dfrac{1 - X_B}{X_B} = 0$. Thus the area under the curve for a G_A vs. $\dfrac{1 - X_B}{X_B}$ plot will give the value of $G_B - G_B^0$ shown as the shaded area under the curve, Fig. 1.4.

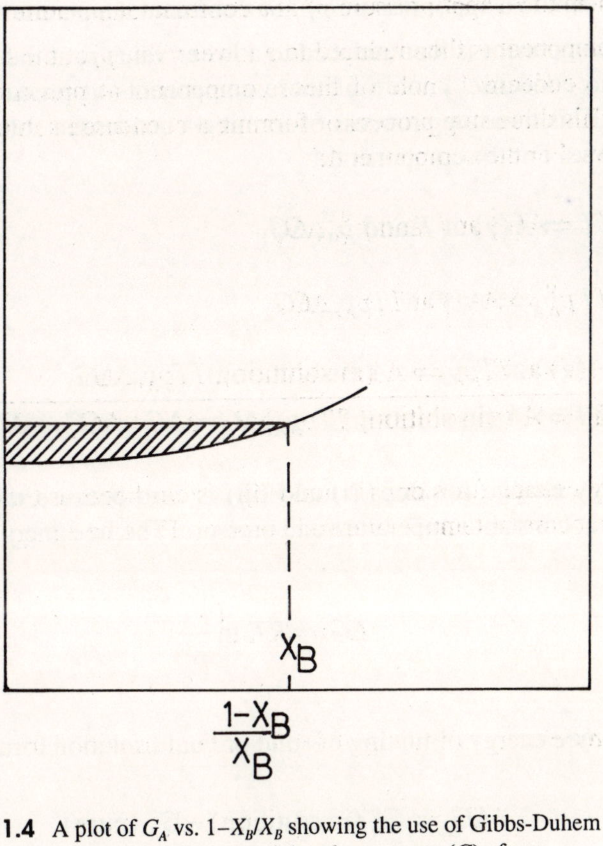

Fig. 1.4 A plot of G_A vs. $1-X_B/X_B$ showing the use of Gibbs-Duhem integration to obtain the partial molar property (G) of one component when that of the other is known.

1.7.4 The Change in Free Energy of Mixing (Formation of a Solution)

Consider a binary system with components A and B both in the condensed state. The components A and B exert a vapor pressure p_A^0 and p_B^0, respectively, when in the pure state. Upon mixing of the two components to form a solution, the vapor pressures exerted by each component will be p_A and p_B, which are less than p_A^0 and p_B^0 respectively. The change in the vapor pressure of the two components from p_i^0 to p_i ($i = A$, B), can be brought about by first evaporating 1 mole of each of these components and bringing them to a vapor pressure p_i^0 at a constant temperature T. The vapor pressure of each component is then reduced to a lower value p_i at the temperature T. The next step is to condense 1 mole of these components at pressure p_i into a binary solution at T. This three step process of forming a condensed solution can be written below as follows. For the component A:

(i) $A(s)$ at $T \Rightarrow A(v)$ at T and $p_A^0, \Delta G_1$

(ii) $A(v)$ at $T, p_A^0 \Rightarrow A(v)$ at $T, p_A, \Delta G_2$

(iii) $$\frac{A(v) \text{ at } T, p_A \Rightarrow A \text{ (in solution)}, T, p_A, \Delta G_3}{A(s) \text{ at } T \Rightarrow A \text{ (in solution) } T, p_A, \Delta G = \Delta G_1 + \Delta G_2 + \Delta G_3}$$

The free energy change for steps (i) and (iii) is zero because the change has been brought about at constant temperature and pressure. The free energy for step (ii) is,

$$\Delta G_2 = RT \ln \frac{p_A}{p_A^0} \tag{1.7.27}$$

The change in free energy of mixing of solid or liquid solution formation is,

$$\Delta G_A = G_A \text{ (in solution)} - G_A \text{ (pure)}$$

The value of G_A in solution is the partial molar free energy and that for the pure component A is G_A^0. Thus,

$$\Delta G_A = G_A - G_A^0 = RT \ln a_A \tag{1.7.28}$$

The free energy of pure components before formation of the solution is,

$$\Delta G'_m \text{ (pure)} = n_A G_A^0 + n_B G_B^0$$

The free energy after mixing is,

$$\Delta G'\text{(in solution)} = n_A G_A + n_B G_B.$$

The change in free energy due to mixing is,

$$\Delta G'_m = n_A(G_A - G_A^0) + n_B(G_B - G_B^0)$$
$$= RT\, n_A \ln a_A + RT\, n_B \ln a_B \tag{1.7.29}$$

For one mole of the solution,

$$\Delta G_m = RT\, [X_A \ln a_A + X_B \ln a_B] \tag{1.7.30}$$

1.7.5 Raoult's Law and Henry's Law

Consider a pure component B in the liquid state kept in a closed evacuated vessel at temperature T. The component B will start forming vapor till a saturated vapor pressure p_A^0 is reached. The liquid still continues to evaporate but the molecules start condensing when they strike the liquid surface. An equilibrium stage is reached at which the rate of evaporation of the liquid B becomes equal to the rate of condensation of the vapor. The rate of evaporation R_B^e is dependent upon the bond energy (attractive interaction) between atoms and in turn the thermal energy sufficient to overcome the activation energy E^*. The rate of condensation R_B^c is proportional to the number of atoms that strike the liquid surface, which is proportional to the vapor pressure of the liquid at the temperature T,

$$R_B^c = K p_B^0 \tag{1.7.31}$$

when K is the constant of proportionality. Since the rates of condensation and evaporation are equal at equilibrium,

$$R_B^e = R_B^c = Kp_B^0 \tag{1.7.32}$$

A similar expression can be written for the component A with constant of proportionality K',

$$R_A^e = K'p_A^0 \tag{1.7.33}$$

Now let us consider a liquid solution consisting of A and B components. In this case, the B atoms are surrounded by A atoms at the liquid surface. Considering that the rate of evaporation from the liquid surface is independent of the presence of A atoms at the surface, the rate of evaporation of B will decrease to a new value p_B. Considering uniform distribution of B atoms in the bulk of the liquid and surface, the rate of evaporation of B should be equal to the rate of evaporation of pure B times the mole fraction of B in solution, i.e.,

$$R_B^e X_B = Kp_B = R_B^c \tag{1.7.34}$$

Substituting for R_B^e from equation (1.7.32) in equation (1.7.34) yields,

$$Kp_B^0 \cdot X_B = Kp_B$$

or

$$p_B = X_B \cdot p_B^0$$

and

$$p_A = X_A \cdot p_A^0. \tag{1.7.35}$$

The pair of equations (1.7.35) are the expressions for Raoult's Law. The above expressions are applicable when the A–A, A–B and B–B bond energies are approximately equal and there is no preferential bond formation of either type.

Let us focus our attention on a very dilute solution of B in A with the condition that the A–B bonds are significantly stronger than the A–A and B–B bonds. Since the solution is very dilute, each B atom will be surrounded by A atoms with preferential

A–B bonds. The activation energy required to overcome the force of attraction between atoms will be higher and the rate of evaporation will decrease from the old value R_B^e to R'^e_B. Equilibrium will be established when the rate of condensation equals the rate of evaporation, which gives,

$$R'^e_B \cdot X_B = Kp_B. \tag{1.7.36}$$

Combining equation (1.7.32) and (1.7.36) yields,

$$p_B = \frac{R'^e_B}{R_B^c} \cdot X_B \cdot p_B^0 = K_B \cdot X_B \cdot p_B^0 \tag{1.7.37}$$

Equation (1.7.37) will be strictly followed for very dilute solutions of B in A. However, as the mole fraction of B in the solution is increased, a stage will be reached when B atoms will not be surrounded only by A atoms. B atoms may also make B–B bonds which are relatively weaker than the A–B bonds. The activation energy required to overcome the force of attraction between B–B bonds will be lower. The rate of evaporation will increase. It thus appears that the rate of evaporation and hence the vapor pressure is composition dependent (after some initial concentration of B in A). The extent of the concentration range over which equation (1.7.37) is obeyed is dependent on the relative bond energies of the A–B, B–B and A–A bonds and on temperature. A similar behavior is expected for the A atoms in solution. Equation (1.7.37) is referred to as Henry's law and the solution is said to show Henrian behavior. In the case when the bond energy of the A–B bonds is higher than those of the A–A and B–B bonds, the rate of evaporation and hence that in the vapor pressure vs. composition plot, p_B will be less than $X_B p_B^0$ as shown, schematically in Fig. 1.5a.

Let us consider the second case when the bond energy of the A–B bonds is less than the bond energy of either A–A or B–B bonds. For a dilute solution of B in A, most of the B atoms will be surrounded by A atoms and it will be easier for the B atoms to evaporate because the activation energy required to overcome the force of attraction between A and B atoms is lower. The rate of evaporation will increase to a new value R'^e_B from R_B^e. In this situation,

$$p_B = \frac{R'^e_B}{R_B^e} \cdot X_B \cdot p_B^0 = K_B X_B p_B^0, \quad (K_B > 1).$$

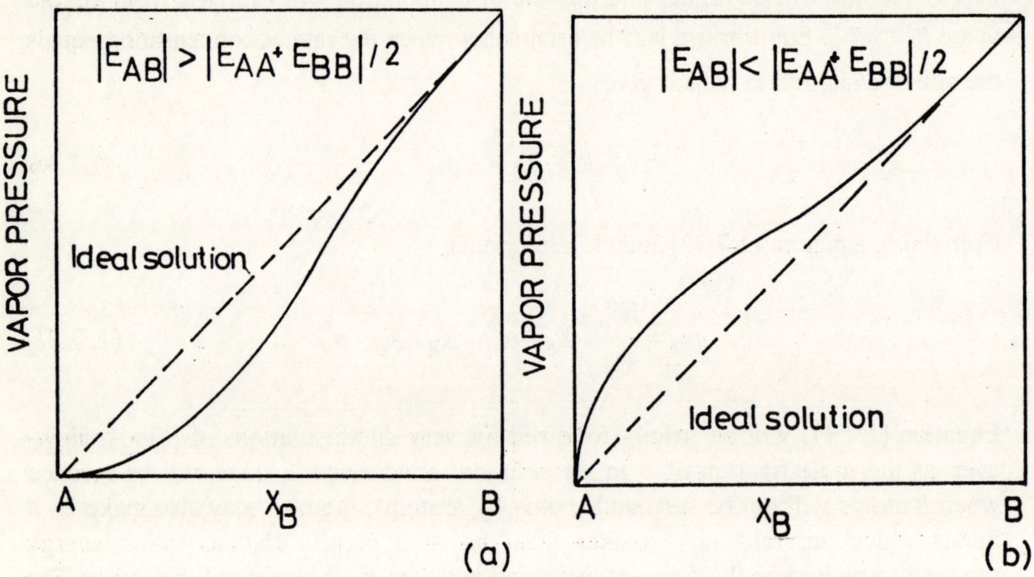

Fig. 1.5 Vapor pressure vs. composition plot (a) when the magnitude of the bond energy of the *A–B* bonds is higher than those of the *A–A* and *B–B* bonds. (b) When the magnitude of the bond energy of the bonds between like atoms is more than that between unlike atoms.

Since $R'^e_B > R^e_B$, the ratio of the two is represented by $K_B > 1$ and hence the vapor pressure of *B* in the solution is greater than $X_B p_B^0$ in the range of compositions where *B* atoms are preferentially surrounded by only *A* atoms. The vapor pressure vs. composition curve lies above the Raoult's law line as shown in Fig. 1.5b.

The activity of a component in a solution is defined as the ratio of the vapor pressure of the component in solution to the vapor pressure of pure component. Thus for component *B*,

$$a_B = \frac{p_B}{p_B^0}, \tag{1.7.38}$$

which for an ideal solution (no preferential *A–A*, *A–B* or *B–B* bonds) gives,

$$a_B = X_B. \quad [\text{from } R'^e_B = R^e_B,\ K_B = 1] \tag{1.7.39}$$

The Raoult's law line is shown in Fig. 1.5. Henry's law can also be written in the alternate form by writing $a_B = p_B/p_B^0$,

$$a_B = K_B X_B = \gamma_B X_B.$$

For an ideal solution, $a_i = X_i$ and equation (1.7.30) can be written as,

$$\Delta G_m^{ideal} = RT\,[X_A \ln X_A + X_B \ln X_B] \qquad (1.7.40)$$

1.7.6 Activity Coefficient and Excess Properties

As shown in the previous section, the activity of a component in an ideal solution equals its mole fraction. An additional thermodynamic parameter, activity coefficient γ, is a convenient way to describe a non-ideal solution and is defined as the ratio of the activity of the component to its mole fraction. Thus for a binary solution,

$$\gamma_A = \frac{a_A}{X_A} \quad \text{and} \quad \gamma_B = \frac{a_B}{X_B}. \qquad (1.7.41)$$

Substituting for the activities of the components in equation (1.7.30), we get the free energy of the formation of real solutions:

$$\Delta G_m = RT\,[X_A \ln X_A + X_B \ln X_B] + RT\,[X_A \ln \gamma_A + X_B \ln \gamma_B] \qquad (1.7.42)$$

The activity coefficient of a given component in a solution may be greater than unity ($\gamma_i > 1$), less than unity ($\gamma_i < 1$) or equal to unity ($\gamma_i = 1$). When the activity coefficient is greater than unity we say that the addition of a given component to a solution results in positive deviation from Raoult's law. Similarly for $\gamma_i < 1$, the solution is said to exhibit negative deviation from Raoult's law. For $\gamma_i = 1$, the solution is ideal. The magnitude of γ_i is important in the theory of solutions as it can be used to predict the behavior of solutions.

The activity coefficient is a function of both temperature and composition and is determined experimentally. From the Gibbs-Helmholtz equation, we can write for the component B,

$$\left[\frac{\partial(G_B/T)}{\partial T}\right]_{P,A} = -\frac{H_B}{T^2}, \tag{1.7.43}$$

and for pure component B,

$$\left[\frac{\partial(G_B^0/T)}{\partial T}\right]_{P} = -\frac{H_B^0}{T^2}, \tag{1.7.44}$$

where H_B and H_B^0 are the molar enthalpies of the component B in the solution and pure state, respectively. Combining equations (1.7.43) and (1.7.44) yields,

$$\frac{\partial}{\partial T}\left[\frac{G_B - G_B^0}{T}\right] = \frac{H_B - H_B^0}{T^2}$$

or,

$$\frac{\partial}{\partial T}\left[\frac{\Delta G_B^m}{T}\right]_{P,X_A} = -\frac{\Delta H_B^m}{T^2}. \tag{1.7.45}$$

For an ideal solution, $\Delta G_B^m = RT \ln X_B$ and hence,

$$\frac{\partial\left(\frac{RT \ln X_B}{T}\right)}{\partial T} = -\frac{\Delta H_B^m}{T^2},$$

or

$$\Delta H_B^m = 0.$$

For non-ideal solutions, $\Delta G_B^m = RT \ln X_B + RT \ln \gamma_B$.

$$\frac{\partial\left(\frac{RT}{T} \ln X_B\right)}{\partial T} + \frac{\partial\left(\frac{RT}{T} \ln \gamma_B\right)}{\partial T} = -\frac{\Delta H_B^m}{T^2}$$

$$\frac{(\partial R \ln \gamma_B)}{\partial T} = -\frac{\Delta H_B^m}{T^2}$$

or
$$\frac{\partial (R \ln \gamma_B)}{\partial (1/T)} = \Delta H_B^m$$

Similarly,
$$\frac{\partial (R \ln \gamma_A)}{\partial (1/T)} = \Delta H_A^m . \tag{1.7.46}$$

In general, there is a tendency for the activity coefficient to approach the ideal value of unity when the temperature is increased. That is, if the activity coefficient is greater than one, its value decreases with increasing temperature and approaches one. In such a case, the partial molar enthalpy of mixing of the components *A* and *B* will be positive, equation (1.7.46) i.e., heat will be absorbed in the formation of a solution. In a non-ideal solution showing negative deviation from ideal behavior ($\gamma_i < 1$), the partial molar heat of mixing of the components will be negative and hence the formation of a solution will lead to heat being released. This occurs during the formation of a compound or intermediate phase.

The Excess thermodynamic property of a solution is defined as the difference between the value of that property in the solution and its value for an ideal solution. For example, the excess free energy is the free energy of mixing of a solution minus the free energy of an ideal solution. Thus for a binary system,

$$\Delta G^E = \Delta G_m - \Delta G_m^{ideal}$$

$$= RT\,[X_A \ln a_A + X_B \ln a_B] - RT\,[X_A \ln X_a + X_B \ln X_B]$$

$$= RT\,[X_A \ln \gamma_A + X_B \ln \gamma_B] \tag{1.7.47}$$

The excess partial properties are defined as

$$G_A^E = \Delta G_A - \Delta G_A^{ideal}$$

$$= RT \ln a_A - RT \ln X_A$$

$$= RT \ln \gamma_A$$

$$G_B^E = RT \ln \gamma_B$$

Also

$$\Delta G^E = X_A G_A^E + X_B G_B^E$$

$$= RT\,[X_A \ln \gamma_A + X_B \ln \gamma_B].$$

1.8 Heterogeneous Equilibrium and the Phase Rule

When a system consists of a single phase, be it a liquid, solid or gas, it is considered to be homogeneous. The liquid, solid or the gaseous phase may be a pure metal or a homogeneous mixture of two or more metals or non-metals. In phase equilibria of materials, we are concerned with system consisting of two or more phases in equilibrium with each other. These may consist of two or more liquids, liquids and solids or two or more solids. A heterogeneous system consists of two or more phases and the equilibrium between these phases is termed as heterogeneous equilibrium.

Phase equilibria in material systems can be described in terms of the number of phases, components and the number of degrees of freedom. A precise definition of these quantities is required. A phase is that part of the system which is chemically and physically uniform throughout. A phase may consist of any amount, large or small, of material being in one unit or subdivided into a number of smaller ones; for example, ice represents a phase whether it be in a single block or subdivided into smaller blocks. This subdivision, however, should not be carried to the molecular level. A number of phases may coexist in equilibrium with each other in a given system. The phases may differ in both composition and crystal structure.

In order to provide information about the chemical composition of a phase, it is useful to describe it in terms of the number of components. The number of components C is the least number of independently variable chemical species necessary to describe the chemical composition of each phase of the system. For example, the α phase of the Cu–Ni binary system may consist of 70% Cu and 30% Ni. It consists of two components Cu and Ni. Similarly, plain carbon steel consists of iron and carbon and ice consists of hydrogen and oxygen as components.

Some properties of each phase of a system are independent of the amount of phases present. The temperature, pressure, molar heat capacity, density etc. of a material are independent of the amount of that material. The properties of a material which are independent of the mass are termed as "intensive properties". Properties which depend on the mass of a material are known as "extensive properties". For example, volume, free energy, enthalpy, entropy etc. are extensive properties. It turns out that in order to characterize a system it is not essential to specify all its properties. If some of the properties (such as temperature and pressure) are specified, other properties of the system may also be said to be specified. Any other set of intensive properties instead of the temperature and pressure might have been specified and the system characterization would still be complete.

The number of degrees of freedom f is defined as the smallest number of intensive variables that must be specified to fix the values of the remaining intensive variables.

Condition for Equilibrium

Let us consider a large quantity of a single phase α consisting of n_A moles of the component A and n_B moles of the component B. The phase is in a state of stable equilibrium at temperature T and P. The Gibbs free energy of the α phase is a function of the T, P and number of moles of A and B, n_A and n_B, respectively. This is expressed as,

$$G' = f(T, P, n_A, n_B) \tag{1.8.1}$$

Now, by making small changes in the temperature, pressure and the number of moles of A and B during a reversible process, the change in the Gibbs free energy for the α phase is,

$$dG' = \left(\frac{\partial G'}{\partial T}\right)_{P,n_A,n_B} dT + \left(\frac{\partial G'}{\partial P}\right)_{T,n_A,n_B} dP + \left(\frac{\partial G'}{\partial n_A}\right)_{T,P,n_B} dn_A + \left(\frac{\partial G'}{\partial n_B}\right)_{T,P,n_A} dn_B \tag{1.8.2}$$

Equation (1.8.2) can be written by substituting

$$\left(\frac{\partial G'}{\partial T}\right)_{P,n_A,n_B} = S', \left(\frac{\partial G'}{dP}\right)_{T,n_A,n_B} = V'$$

$$\left(\frac{\partial G'}{dn_A}\right)_{T,P,n_B} = \mu_A \quad \text{and} \quad \left(\frac{\partial G'}{\partial n_B}\right)_{T,P,n_A} = \mu_B.$$

where μ_i are the chemical potential, S' is the entropy and V' the volume of the α phase

$$dG' = V'\,dP - S'dT + \mu_A dn_A + \mu_B dn_B \tag{1.8.3}$$

The chemical potential is a measure of the change in the free energy of a component in a solution when a component of the phase is introduced.

Let us consider a heterogeneous system consisting of the α and β phases in a binary system. The free energy change of the α and β phases by virtue of small changes in the variables, T, P, n_A and n_B, can be written as,

$$dG'^{\alpha} = V'^{\alpha}dP - S'^{\alpha}dT + \mu_A^{\alpha}dn_A^{\alpha} + \mu_B^{\alpha}dn_B^{\alpha}$$

$$dG'^{\beta} = V'^{\beta}dP - S'^{\beta}dT + \mu_A^{\beta}dn_A^{\beta} + \mu_B^{\beta}dn_B^{\beta} \tag{1.8.4}$$

At constant temperature and pressure,

$$dG'^{\alpha} = \mu_A^{\alpha}dn_A^{\alpha} + \mu_B^{\alpha}dn_B^{\alpha}$$

$$dG'^{\beta} = \mu_A^{\beta}dn_A^{\beta} + \mu_B^{\beta}dn_B^{\beta}$$

Let us assume that a small amount dn_B moles of the component B are transferred from the α to the β phase. The change in the free energy of the α and β phases is as follows;

$$dG'^{\alpha} = \mu_B^{\alpha}dn_B^{\alpha}, \quad dG'^{\beta} = \mu_B^{\beta}dn_B^{\beta} \tag{1.8.6}$$

Since the number of moles of the component A are not changed in either of the two phases, α or β, changes in the number of moles of A are zero, i.e.,

$$dn_A^{\alpha} = dn_A^{\beta} = 0$$

The free energy of the system being an extensive property, the total change in its value equals its change in the component parts, i.e., in the α and β phases. Thus,

$$dG' = dG'^{\alpha} + dG'^{\beta}$$

or

$$dG' = \mu_B^{\alpha} dn_B^{\alpha} + \mu_B^{\beta} dn_B^{\beta} \tag{1.8.7}$$

In the process of transfer of dn_B moles of the component B, the β phase gains whereas the α phase loses B type atoms,

$$dn_B^{\alpha} + dn_B^{\beta} = 0 \quad \text{or} \quad dn_B^{\beta} = -dn_B^{\alpha}$$

Substituting for dn_B^{α} in equation (1.8.7) yields,

$$dG' = -\mu_B^{\alpha} dn_B^{\beta} + \mu_B^{\beta} dn_B^{\beta}$$

$$= (\mu_B^{\beta} - \mu_B^{\alpha})\, dn_B^{\beta} \tag{1.8.8}$$

The change in the free energy of the system is zero at equilibrium which makes us write,

$$(\mu_B^{\beta} - \mu_B^{\alpha}) dn_B^{\beta} = 0 \quad \text{or} \quad \mu_B^{\beta} = \mu_B^{\alpha} \quad (\text{Since } dn_B^{\beta} \neq 0) \tag{1.8.9}$$

Similarly it can be shown that $\mu_A^{\alpha} = \mu_A^{\beta}$. The general criterion for equilibrium in a system consisting of p phases is that the chemical potential of each component is the same in all the phases. Thus for the *ith* component,

$$\mu_i^{\alpha} = \mu_i^{\beta} = \mu_i^{\gamma} = \ldots = \mu_i^{p} \tag{1.8.10}$$

The compositions of the phases in equilibrium can be determined by drawing a common tangent on to the free energy curves. This can be demonstrates by considering two phases α and β in equilibrium with each other. The free energy curves for the two phases as a function of composition are shown in Fig. 1.6a. The tangent to the curve at any composition point is the partial molar Gibbs free energy, G_A or the chemical potential, μ_A as shown at composition X_B^1 on the free energy curve for the α phase. The chemical potential is designated as μ_A^α (X_B^1). We can draw a large number of tangents on both the free energy curves (for the α and β phases) at a number of composition points. The condition for equilibrium between the two phases requires that the chemical potential of each component be same in both the phases, i.e., $\mu_A^\alpha = \mu_A^\beta$ and $\mu_B^\alpha = \mu_B^\beta$. Among a large number of tangents drawn on the two curves, only the common tangent on the two free energy curves can satisfy the equality of chemical potential, as shown in Fig. 1.6b.

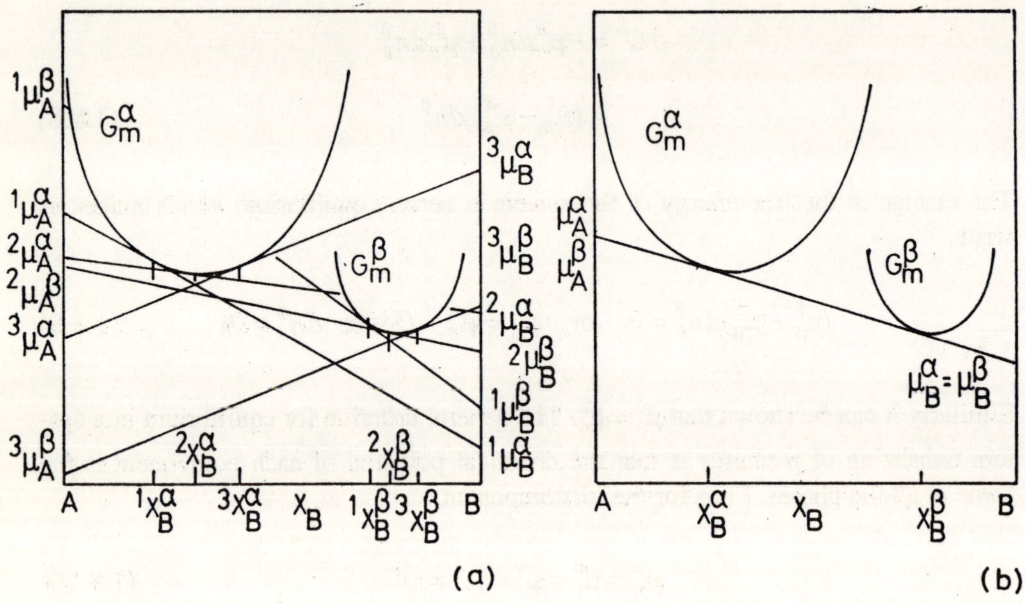

Fig. 1.6 (a) Free energy composition diagram, (b) Free energy composition diagram and construction of common tangent to establish equilibrium.

If the system is not in equilibrium, then for the reaction to proceed in the forward direction, the free energy of the heterogeneous system has to be negative, i.e., $dG' < 0$. This would require $(\mu_B^\beta - \mu_B^\alpha)\, dn_B^\beta < 0$. In this inequality, dn_B^β is positive and thus $(\mu_B^\beta - \mu_B^\alpha) < 0$. In other words $\mu_B^\alpha > \mu_B^\beta$ for the B types atoms to transfer from the α to the β phase. A similar inequality holds for the reaction to proceed in the opposite direction, $\beta \Rightarrow \alpha$ when dn_B^β is negative and $\mu_B^\beta - \mu_B^\alpha > 0$. This would be possible if $\mu_B^\beta > \mu_B^\alpha$.

We come to the conclusion that a net transport of atoms of a particular component occurs from a state where it has a higher chemical potential to state of lower chemical potential. The transfer of atoms from one phase to the other continues till the chemical potentials of the component become equal in the two phases and in general in all the phases. At equilibrium, the chemical potential of each component of the system is the same in all the phases.

The Phase Rule:

Let us consider a system of c components and p phases. At first glance it would appear that $c \times p$ number of variables are required to completely define the system. However, it is known that for each phase the number of variables is described by $(c-1)$ concentration terms and one variable per phase is fixed automatically. From the sum of the mole fractions of each component of a phase, we can write,

$$X_1^\alpha + X_2^\alpha + \ldots + X_c^\alpha = 1$$

$$X_1^\beta + X_2^\beta + \ldots + X_c^\beta = 1$$

$$\ldots\ldots\ldots\ldots\ldots\ldots \qquad (1.8.11)$$

$$\ldots\ldots\ldots\ldots\ldots\ldots$$

$$X_1^p + X_2^p + \ldots + X_c^p = 1$$

In order to describe p phases, $p\,(c-1)$ composition variables are required. In addition to the composition variables, one can also vary temperature and pressure independently. The total number of independent variables of system is $p\,(c-1) + 2$. Since the composition of the *ith* component in a phase is fixed by the equality of chemical potentials at equilibrium, all the above variables are not independent. At equilibrium, we can write for each component,

$$\mu_1^\alpha = \mu_1^\beta = \mu_1^\gamma = \ldots = \mu_1^p$$

$$\mu_2^\alpha = \mu_2^\beta = \mu_2^\gamma = \ldots = \mu_2^p$$

$$\ldots\ldots\ldots\ldots\ldots\ldots \tag{1.8.12}$$

$$\ldots\ldots\ldots\ldots\ldots\ldots$$

$$\mu_c^\alpha = \mu_c^\beta = \gamma_c^\gamma = \ldots = \mu_c^p.$$

Thus, for each component, there are (p–1) independent equations at equilibrium. For example, for a three component system with three phases, we have,

$$\mu_1^\alpha = \mu_1^\beta = \mu_1^\gamma$$

$$\mu_2^\alpha = \mu_2^\beta = \mu_2^\gamma$$

$$\mu_3^\alpha = \mu_3^\beta = \mu_3^\gamma.$$

For component "2", we have

$$\mu_2^\alpha = \mu_2^\beta \quad \text{and} \quad \mu_2^\alpha = \mu_2^\gamma$$

The third equality does not give an independent equation as it can be obtained from the other two. The equality of chemical potentials at equilibrium fixes (p–1) variables for each component and therefore for a system of c components there are c (p–1) variables which are fixed. The total number of independent variables required to define a system is also known as the degree of freedom f:

$$f = p(c-1) + 2 - c(p-1) \tag{1.8.13}$$

$$= c + 2 - p$$

or
$$f + p = c + 2 \tag{1.8.14}$$

The Gibbs phase rule described by equation (1.8.14) relates the number of independent variables that can be exercised in a system of c components and p phases. Application of the phase rule will be demonstrated while describing unary and binary phase diagrams.

1.9 FREE ENERGY OF PHASE MIXTURES

Let us consider a binary alloy of the original alloy composition X_B^0, represented by the point P, Fig. 1.7. The molar Gibbs free energy of the alloy is G_m. Let the solid solution represented by the point P dissociates into two phases α and β at temperature

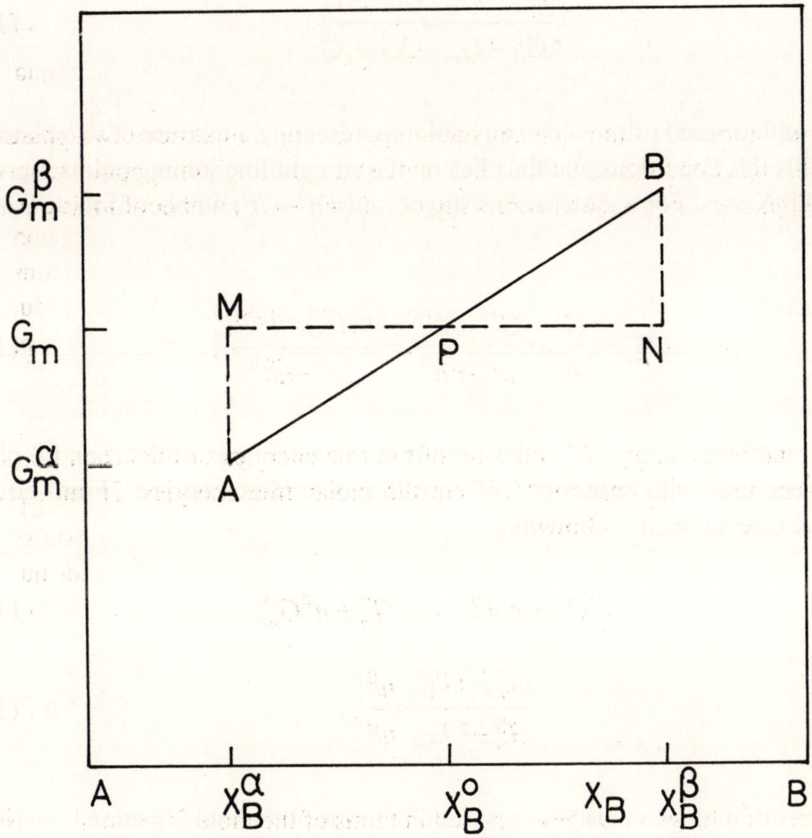

Fig. 1.7 Molar Gibbs Free energy vs. composition for an ideal solution.

T. The compositions of the phases α and β are represented by points A and B, respectively. If the point P lies on the straight line connecting points A and B, then from triangles MAP and NBP, we can write the following

$$\frac{MA}{MP} = \frac{NB}{NP}$$

or,

$$\frac{G_m - G_m^{\alpha}}{X_B^0 - X_B^{\alpha}} = \frac{G_m^{\beta} - G_m}{X_B^{\beta} - X_B^0}$$

or,

$$\frac{G_m - G_m^{\alpha}}{G_m^{\beta} - G_m} = \frac{X_B^0 - X_B^{\alpha}}{X_B^{\beta} - X_B^0}. \tag{1.9.1}$$

Now, we will proceed to show that any point representing a mixture of two phases, (α + β), fulfills this conditions and thus lies on the straight line joining points representing α and β phases. For a system consisting of n (= $n^{\alpha} + n^{\beta}$) number of moles, we can write,

$$G_m = \frac{G'}{n} = \frac{G'^{\alpha} + G'^{\beta}}{n^{\alpha} + n^{\beta}} = \frac{n^{\alpha} G_m^{\alpha} + n^{\beta} G_m^{\beta}}{n^{\alpha} + n^{\beta}}, \tag{1.9.2}$$

where the total free energy G' is the sum of the free energies of the α and β phases. The free energies with subscript "m" are the molar free energies. From equation (1.9.2), we can express the following,

$$n^{\alpha} G_m + n^{\beta} G_m = n^{\alpha} G_m^{\alpha} + n^{\beta} G_m^{\beta} \tag{1.9.3}$$

or,

$$\frac{G_m - G_m^{\alpha}}{G_m^{\beta} - G_m} = \frac{n^{\beta}}{n^{\alpha}}. \tag{1.9.4}$$

The number of moles can also be expressed in terms of the mole fraction by writing,

$$n = n^{\alpha} + n^{\beta},\ n_B^{\alpha} = n^{\alpha} \cdot X_B^{\alpha},\ n_B^{\beta} = n^{\beta} \cdot X_B^{\beta}, \tag{1.9.5}$$

where X_B^α and X_B^β are mole fractions of the component B in the α and β phases, respectively. The original alloy composition can be written as,

$$X_B^0 = \frac{n_B}{n} = \frac{n_B^\alpha + n_B^\beta}{n^\alpha + n^\beta} = \frac{n^\alpha \cdot X_B^\alpha + n^\beta \cdot X_B^\beta}{n^\alpha + n^\beta}. \tag{1.9.6}$$

or
$$n^\alpha \cdot X_B^0 + n^\beta \cdot X_B^0 = n^\alpha X_B^\alpha + n^\beta X_B^\beta, \tag{1.9.7}$$

which gives,

$$\frac{X_B^0 - X_B^\alpha}{X_B^\beta - X_B^0} = \frac{n^\beta}{n^\alpha}. \tag{1.9.8}$$

Comparing equations (1.9.4) and (1.9.8) yields,

$$\frac{G_m - G_m^\alpha}{G_m^\beta - G_m} = \frac{X_B^0 - X_B^\alpha}{X_B^\beta - X_B^0},$$

which is identical to equation (1.9.1). Thus, it is seen that the free energy of phase mixtures lies on a line connecting the same two phases.

1.10 THE FREE ENERGY OF SOLUTION—QUASI CHEMICAL MODEL

The quasi-chemical model of solutions is applied to solutions which have equal molar volumes in their pure state and which have no change in volume ΔV_m during mixing. The interatomic forces are significant and only the nearest neighbour interactions are considered.

Let us consider one mole of a solution consisting of components A and B. If there are n_A number of A atoms and n_B number of B atoms then the mole fraction of A and B type atoms is,

$$X_A = \frac{n_A}{n_A + n_B} = \frac{n_A}{N_0}$$

$$X_B = \frac{n_B}{n_B + n_B} = \frac{n_B}{N_0}, \tag{1.10.1}$$

where N_0 is the Avogadro's number. The *A* and *B* type atoms are situated on regular lattice sites in the solution and one can assume an *A* atom to be situated next to an *A* atom as its first nearest neighbour. An A atom can also be situated next to a B atom as its neighbour. Similarly, a *B* atom can be situated next to a *B* atom or an *A* atom as its nearest neighbour. The solution, therefore, has three types of bonds, i.e.,

$A - A$ bonds, the energy of which is E_{AA}
$A - B$ bonds, the energy of which is E_{AB}
and $B - B$ bonds, the energy of which is E_{BB}.

If there are P_{AA}, P_{AB} and P_{BB} bonds of *A–A*, *A–B* and *B–B* bond types, respectively, then the energy of the solution in the mixed state is,

$$E \text{ (mixed)} = P_{AA} E_{AA} + P_{AB} E_{AB} + P_{BB} E_{BB} \tag{1.10.2}$$

Taking *Z* as the coordination number of the lattice, *A* type atoms will make $n_A Z$ number of bonds. This consists of *A–A* and *A–B* bonds. (The number of *A* atoms) × (the number of bonds per atom) = (the number of *A–B* bonds) + (2) × (the number of *A–A* bonds). Thus,

$$n_A Z = P_{AB} + 2 P_{AA}. \tag{1.10.3}$$

The factor 2 on the second term on the right-hand side of equation (1.10.3) arises from the fact that each *A–A* bond requires two atoms. Similarly,

$$n_B Z = P_{AB} + 2 P_{BB} \tag{1.10.4}$$

From equation (1.10.3) and (1.10.4), we obtain,

$$P_{AA} = \frac{n_A Z - P_{AB}}{2} \quad \text{and} \quad P_{BB} = \frac{n_B Z - P_{AB}}{2},$$

which upon substitution in equation (1.10.2) yields,

$$\begin{aligned} E\ (\text{mixed}) &= \left(\frac{n_A Z}{2} - \frac{P_{AB}}{2}\right) E_{AA} + \left(\frac{n_B Z}{2} - \frac{P_{AB}}{2}\right) E_{BB} + E_{AB}\, P_{AB} \\ &= \left(\frac{n_A Z}{2} E_{AA} + \frac{n_B Z}{2} E_{BB}\right) + \left[E_{AB} - \frac{E_{AA} + E_{BB}}{2}\right] P_{AB} \qquad (1.10.5) \end{aligned}$$

The energy of unmixed pure A and pure B consisting of n_A and n_B number of atoms, respectively, is

$$\begin{aligned} E\ (\text{unmixed}) &= P_{AA}\, E_{AA} + P_{BB}\, E_{BB} \\ &= \frac{n_A Z}{2} E_{AA} + \frac{n_B Z}{2} E_{BB} \qquad (1.10.6) \end{aligned}$$

The change in the energy of the system after mixing is,

$$\Delta E_m = \left(E_{AB} - \frac{E_{AA} + E_{BB}}{2}\right) P_{AB}\,. \qquad (1.10.7)$$

The enthalpy of mixing ΔH_m is

$$\begin{aligned} \Delta H_m &= \Delta E_m + P \Delta V_m \\ &= \Delta E_m, \text{ for } \Delta V_m = 0 \text{ for this model.} \end{aligned}$$

Therefore, $$\Delta H_m = \left(E_{AB} - \frac{E_{AA} + E_{BB}}{2}\right) P_{AB}\,. \qquad (1.10.8)$$

The problem now is to determine the number of bonds in terms of the atom fractions or mole fractions. The probability that a particular lattice site is occupied by A is X_A. The probability that an A atom is situated next to an A atom (to make an A–A bond) is $X_A \cdot X_A = X_A^2$. Similarly, the probability that a B atom is situated next to a B atom in one mole of the solution is X_B^2. The probability that site "one" is occupied by an A atom is X_A and the probability that the nearest neighbour site "two" is occupied by a B atom is $X_A \cdot X_B$. Furthermore, the probability that site "one" is occupied by a B atom is X_B and "two" is occupied by an A atom is $X_B \cdot X_A$. The probability of A–B bond formation is $2X_AX_B$.

The number of bonds $P_{AA} = \frac{1}{2} Z N_0 \cdot X_A^2$,

$$P_{BB} = \frac{1}{2} Z N_0 \cdot X_B^2 \tag{1.10.9}$$

$$P_{AB} = \frac{1}{2} Z N_0 \cdot 2 X_A X_B$$

Substituting for P_{AB} in equation (1.10.8) yields,

$$\Delta H_m = Z N_0 X_A X_B \left(E_{AB} - \frac{E_{AA} + E_{BB}}{2} \right) \tag{1.10.10}$$

$$= \Omega X_A X_B , \tag{1.10.11}$$

where $\Omega = Z N_0 \left(E_{AB} - \frac{E_{AA} + E_{BB}}{2} \right)$. Equaton (1.10.11) shows that the enthalpy of mixing depends upon the bond energy of A–B bonds and the average bond energy of the pure components.

Consider now the entropy of the system consisting of A and B atoms in solution. The mixing of two miscible components into a single homogeneous solution is in all cases an irreversible process. Once A and B atoms are mixed completely into each other, unmixing is impossible. Consequently, mixing always increases the entropy of the system. This is known as the entropy of mixing ΔS_m defined as the difference in the entropies of mixed and unmixed components of a solution. The entropy of a system is given by the Boltzmann expression from statistical thermodynamics, equation (1.6.17), as

$$S = k \ln W,$$

where k is the Boltzmann constant and W is the number of distinguishable ways of placing A and B atoms on possible sites available to them. The entropy therefore is a measure of the state of ordering or randomness of a solution. The entropy of the system consisting of the pure components is

$$S_1 = k \ln W_1.$$

The entropy of the system after A and B atoms are allowed to mix together is given as,

$$S_2 = k \ln W_2.$$

The entropy of mixing is,

$$\Delta S_m = k\,(\ln W_2 - \ln W_1) \tag{1.10.12}$$

As before, let there be n_A and n_B numbers of A and B atoms, respectively, in a mole of the solution. In the unmixed pure state of A, the number of distinguishable ways of placing A atoms on n_A sites is 1 because in the pure state all arrangements of A atoms are identical. Similarly, there is only one distinguishable way of placing B atoms on n_B sites. The value of W_1 in equation (1.10.12) is 1.

If A and B atoms are now allowed to mix together, they would be occupying $(n_A + n_B)$ number of sites. The number of ways of placing A and B atoms is $(n_A + n_B)!$. However, placing different A atoms on a site previously occupied by an A atom does not change the arrangement. The number of distinguishable ways of placing A and B atoms is

$$W_2 = \frac{(n_A + n_B)!}{n_A!\,n_B!},$$

which gives,

$$\Delta S_m = k\left[\ln\frac{(n_A+n_B)!}{n_A!-n_B!} - \ln 1\right] \qquad (1.10.13)$$

Using Stirling's approximation for large number N,

$$\ln N! = N\ln N - N,$$

$$\Delta S_m = k\,[(n_A+n_B)\ln(n_A+n_B) - (n_A+n_B) - n_A\ln n_A + n_A - n_B\ln n_B + n_B]$$

$$\Delta S_m = -k\left[n_A\ln\left(\frac{n_A}{n_A+n_B}\right) + n_B\ln\left(\frac{n_B}{n_A+n_B}\right)\right]$$

$$= -k\,[n_A\ln X_A + n_B\ln X_B]$$

$$= -kN_0\left[\frac{n_A}{n_A+n_B}\ln X_A + \frac{n_A}{n_A+n_B}\ln X_B\right].$$

For one mole of the solution, $(n_A+n_B) = N_0$ and

$$\Delta S_m = -R\,[X_A\ln X_A + X_B\ln X_B]. \qquad (1.10.14)$$

The change in entropy due to mixing is brought about by the different arrangements of A and B atoms, i.e., by placing some A atoms as neighbours of B and some B atoms as neighbours of A. The entropy change, therefore, is configurational is nature. Moreover, there is an increase in the entropy due to mixing (see equation (1.10.14)). The change in the free energy is

$$\Delta G_m = \Delta H_m - T\,\Delta S_m$$

$$= \Omega X_A X_B + RT\,[X_A\ln X_A + X_B\ln X_B] \qquad (1.10.15)$$

The first term on the right-hand side of equation (1.10.15) is dependent upon the bond energies of the three bond types. The second term is temperature dependent.

Depending upon the nature of bonds between atoms of the solution, we can identify three distinct cases.

Case I: Ideal solution. Ideal solution behavior is realized when the bond energy of the *A–B* bonds equals the average bond energy of the like components, i.e.,

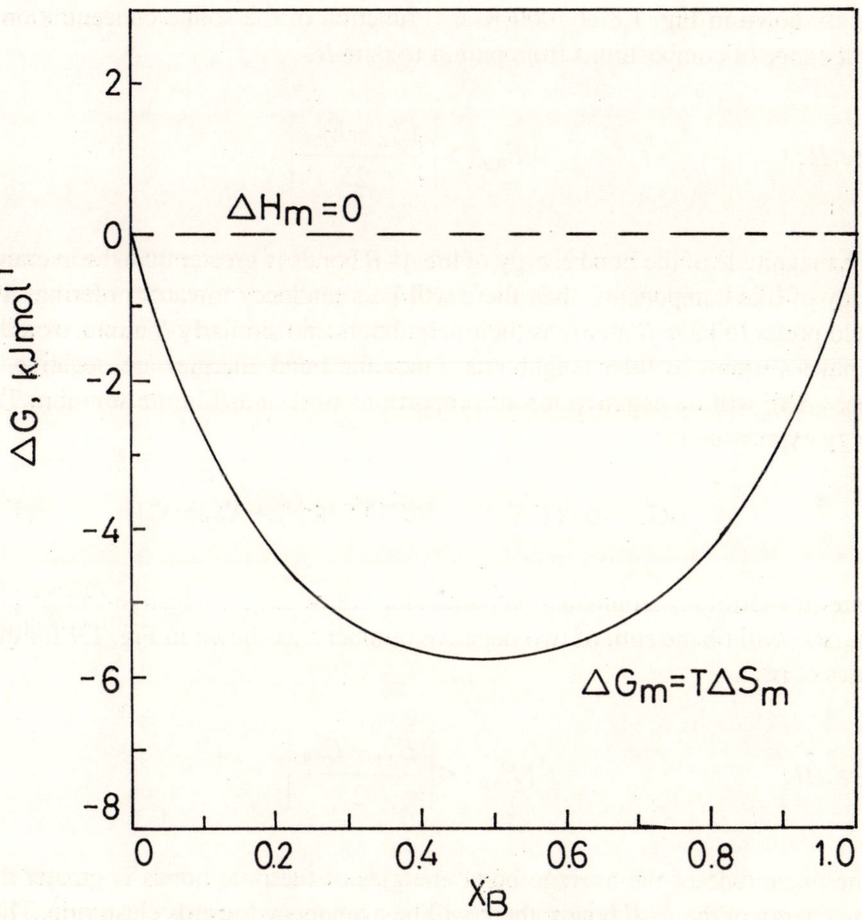

Fig. 1.8 ΔG_m vs. composition for an ideal solution.

$$|E_{AB}| = \left|\frac{E_{AA}+E_{BB}}{2}\right|.$$

The value of Ω in equation (1.10.15) is zero and the enthalpy of mixing of an ideal solution, $\Delta H_m = 0$. The free energy of mixing is represented by

$$\Delta G_m = RT\,[X_A \ln X_A + X_B \ln X_B]. \tag{1.10.16}$$

This is shown in Fig. 1.8 at 1000 K as a function of the solute concentration in the whole range of compositions from pure *A* to pure *B*.

Case II: $$|E_{AB}| > \left|\frac{E_{AA}+E_{BB}}{2}\right|$$

If the magnitude of the bond energy of the *A–B* bonds is greater than the average bond energy of like components, then there will be a tendency towards ordering. *A* atoms would prefer to have *B* atoms as their neighbours and similarly *B* atoms would prefer to have *A* atoms as their neighbours. Since the bond energies are negative, Ω and hence ΔH_m will be negative for all proportions of *A* and *B* in the solution. The free energy expression is

$$\Delta G_m = \alpha\, RT\, X_A X_B + RT\,[X_A \ln X_A + X_B \ln X_B] \tag{1.10.17}$$

where $\alpha(= \Omega/RT)$ is an interaction parameter. Since ΔH_m is negative and ΔS_m is positive, ΔG_m will be the sum of two negative numbers, as shown in Fig. 1.9 for different values of α.

Case III: $$|E_{AB}| < \left|\frac{E_{AA}+E_{BB}}{2}\right|$$

if the magnitude of the average bond energies of the pure bonds is greater than the bond energy of the *A–B* bonds, there will be a tendency towards clustering. The value of Ω and hence ΔH_m will be positive in the whole range of compositions. The ΔH_m and

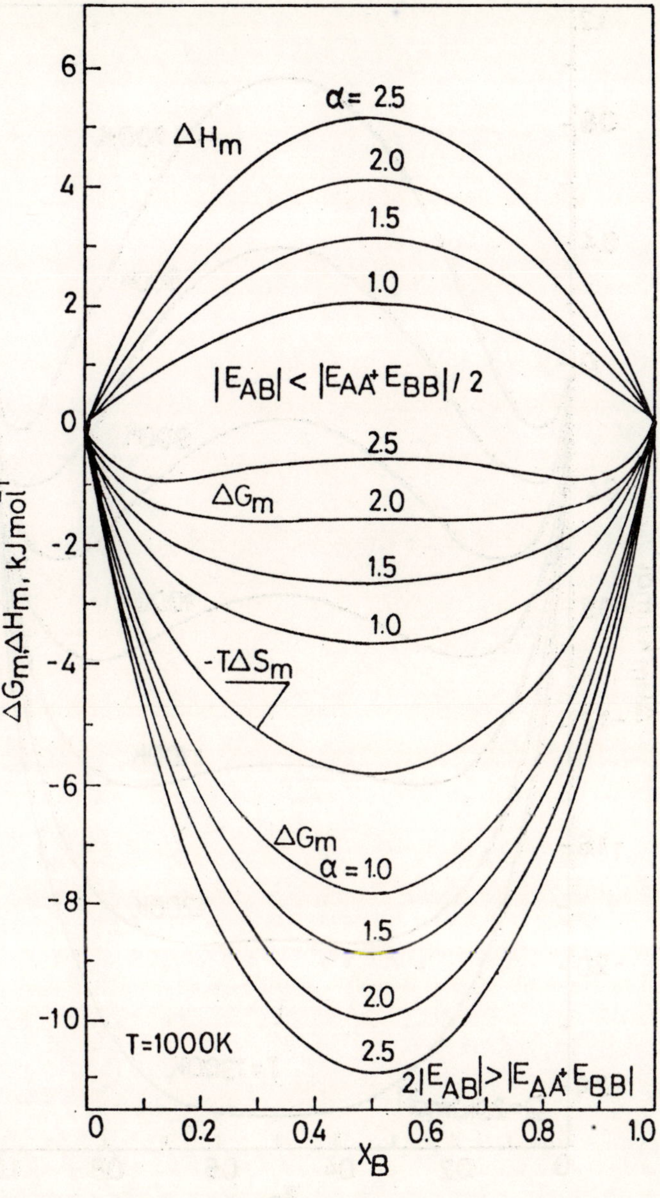

Fig. 1.9 ΔG_m and ΔH_m vs. composition for different values of α at 1000 K.

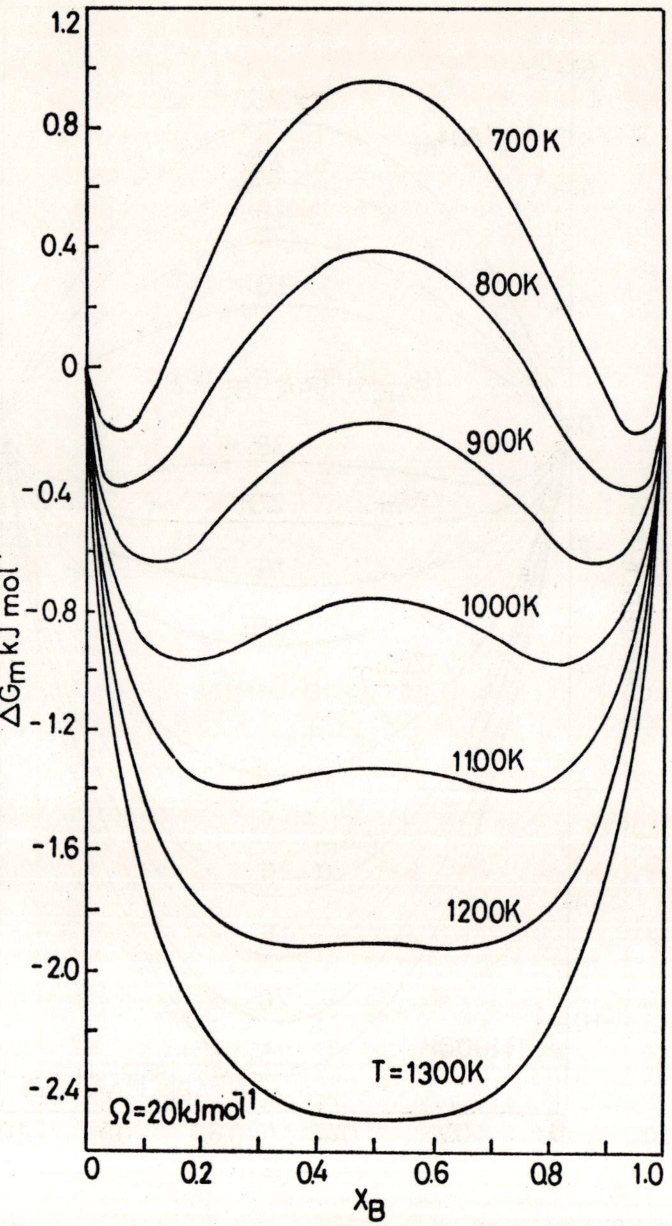

Fig. 1.10 ΔG_m vs. composition and temperature.

ΔG_m curves are shown in Fig. 1.9 at 1000 K for different values of α. At higher temperatures the $T\Delta S_m$ term will dominate which results in the formation of a solution. The free energy composition diagram will be concave downwards in the whole range of compositions as shown in Fig. 1.10 at 1300 K. As the temperature is lowered, the ΔH_m term will begin to dominate and the free energy curve will become concave upwards in some range of compositions. We can define a critical temperature T_c below which the solution will decompose into A-rich and B-rich clusters. The free energy-composition diagram will show two minima and there will be two inflection points which satisfy the condition,

$$\frac{\partial^2 \Delta G_m}{\partial X_B^2} = 0 \tag{1.10.18}$$

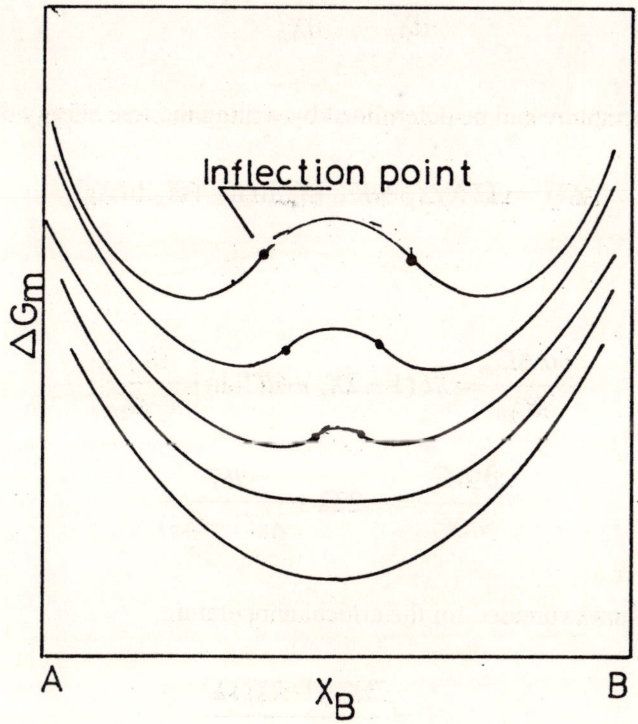

Fig. 1.11 ΔG_m vs. composition showing inflection points.

The free energy curves of Fig. 1.10 show two minima at all temperatures below 1200 K. The inflection points are shown in Fig. 1.11. The free energy-composition diagram of Fig. 1.11 illustrates that the compositions at which the two minima occur approach each other as the temperature is raised. The inflection points will also approach each other as the temperature is raised and at the critical temperature the inflection points and the minima will coincide. Since the condition for the minimum in the free energy-composition diagram is:

$$\frac{\partial \Delta G_m}{\partial X_B} = 0,$$

at the critical temperature we can write,

$$\frac{\partial \Delta G_m}{\partial X_B} = \frac{\partial^2 \Delta G_m}{\partial X_B^2} = 0 \qquad (1.10.19)$$

The critical temperature can be determined by writing the free energy of mixing,

$$\Delta G_m = \Omega\, X_A X_B + RT\, [X_A \ln X_A + X_B \ln X_B],$$

from which,

$$\frac{\partial\, \Delta G_m}{\partial X_B} = \Omega\, (1 - 2X_B) + RT \ln\left(\frac{X_B}{1 - X_B}\right) \qquad (1.10.20)$$

and

$$\frac{\partial^2 \Delta G_m}{\partial\, X_B^2} = -\,2\,\Omega + \frac{RT}{X_B(1 - X_B)}\,. \qquad (1.10.21)$$

From the condition expressed for the critical temperature,

$$T_c = \frac{2X_B\,(1 - X_B)\,\Omega}{R} \qquad (1.10.22)$$

Equation (1.10.20) may be used to determine the two minima composition (of phases in equilibrium with each other due to splitting of the parent solid solution) in the free energy-composition diagram, yielding

$$\ln\left(\frac{X_B}{(1-X_B)}\right) = -\frac{[\Omega]}{RT}(X_A - X_B) \tag{1.10.23}$$

The temperature at which a homogeneous solution of A and B begins to split into clusters of A and clusters of B in neighbouring regions corresponds to the critical temperature. The critical value of α, α_c, also corresponds to the same behavior of the solution. The free energy curves and the corresponding first, second and third derivatives of the free energy are plotted against composition in Fig. 1.12 for values of α less than the critical value of α ($\alpha < \alpha_c$), α equal to α_c and α more than α_c. It is seen that for $\alpha = \alpha_c$, the second and third derivatives of the free energy with respect to composition are equal at the value of $X_B = 0.5$. Applying the condition for the critical value of α,

$$\frac{\partial^2 \Delta G_m}{\partial X_B^2} = \frac{\partial^3 \Delta G_m}{\partial X_B^3} = 0, \tag{1.10.24}$$

we get

$$-2\Omega + \frac{RT}{X_A X_B} = RT\left[\frac{1}{X_A^2} - \frac{1}{X_B^2}\right]. \tag{1.10.25}$$

For $\Omega = \alpha RT$,

$$-2\alpha_c RT + \frac{RT}{X_A X_B} = RT\left[\frac{1}{X_A^2} - \frac{1}{X_B^2}\right].$$

$$\alpha_c = -\frac{1}{2X_A X_B}\left[\frac{X_B - X_A}{X_A X_B} - 1\right]. \tag{1.10.26}$$

at $X_B = 0.5$, $\alpha_c = 2$.

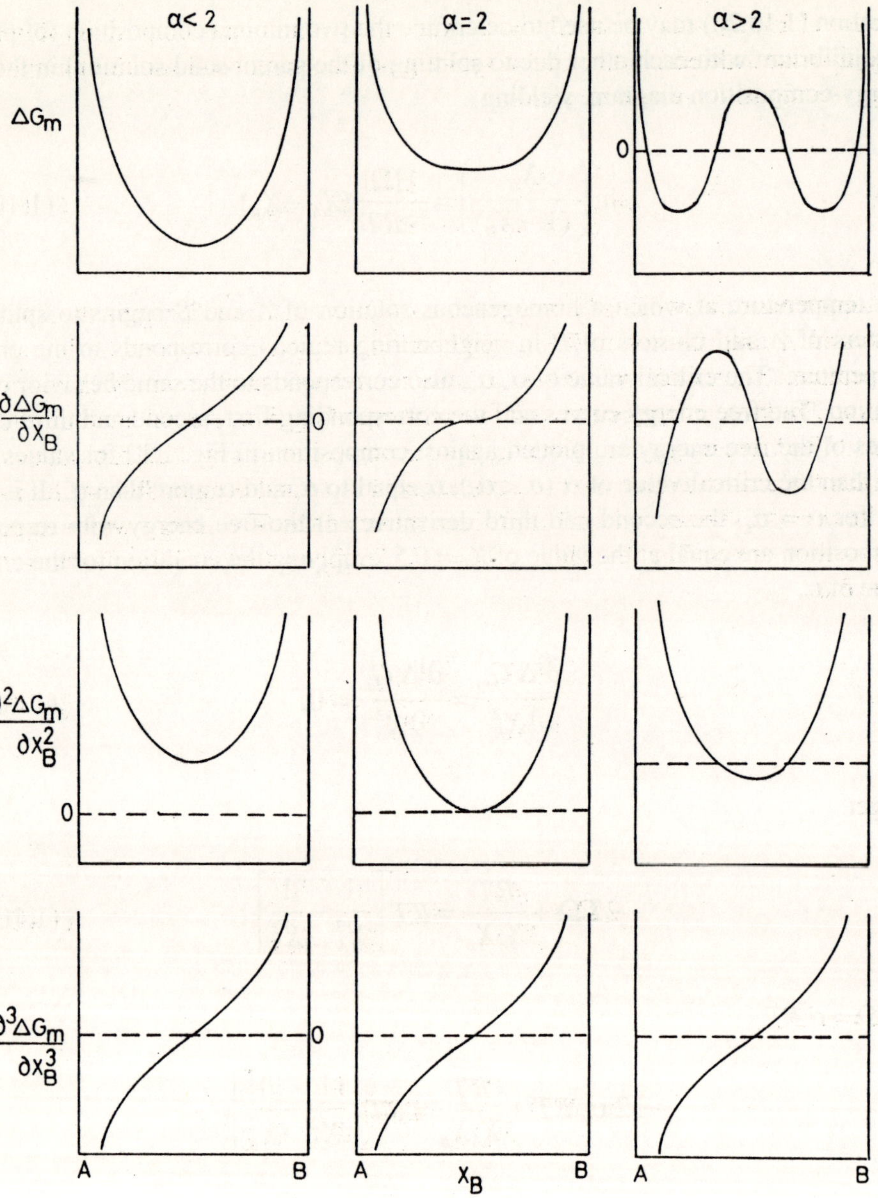

Fig. 1.12 ΔG_m vs. composition diagrams for different values of α. The first, second and third derivatives of the free energy are also shown.

There will be a changeover in the behavior of the solution at the value of $\alpha = 2$ from a homogeneous solution to partitioning into clusters.

A multicomponent system forms a regular solution when $\Delta H_m = 0$ and $\Delta S_m^E = 0$, where ΔS_m^E is the excess entropy change. The relation for the partial molar enthalpy of a solution can be obtained from the partial quantities:

$$\Delta H_A = \Delta H_m - X_B \frac{\partial \Delta H_m}{\partial X_B}$$

and

$$\Delta H_B = \Delta H_m + (1 - X_B) \frac{\partial \Delta H_m}{\partial X_B} \tag{1.10.27}$$

For $\Delta H_m = \Omega\, X_A\, X_B$,

and

$$\left.\begin{aligned} \Delta H_A &= \Omega(1 - X_A)^2 \\ \Delta H_B &= \Omega(1 - X_B)^2 \end{aligned}\right\} \tag{1.10.28}$$

and

$$\left.\begin{aligned} \Delta S_A &= -R \ln X_A \\ \Delta S_B &= -R \ln X_B \end{aligned}\right\} \quad \text{for} \quad \Delta S_m^E = 0, \tag{1.10.29}$$

combination of equations (1.10.28) and (1.10.29) for each component yields,

$$\Delta G_A = \Omega(1 - X_A)^2 + RT \ln X_A = RT \ln a_A,$$

and

$$\Delta G_B = \Omega(1 - X_B)^2 + RT \ln X_B = RT \ln a_B \tag{1.10.30}$$

Since $a_A = \gamma_A\, X_A$ and $a_B = \gamma_B\, X_B$, we obtain,

$$\Omega\,(1 - X_A)^2 = RT \ln \gamma_A,$$

and

$$\Omega(1 - X_B)^2 = RT \ln \gamma_B$$

or
$$\ln \gamma_A = \frac{\Omega(1-X_A)^2}{RT},$$

and
$$\ln \gamma_B = \frac{\Omega\,(1-X_B)^2}{RT}. \qquad (1.10.31)$$

For negative values of Ω (which leads to the formation of intermediate phases) the activity coefficients of the components A and B are less than one ($\gamma_i < 1$). The activity vs. composition graph shows the activity values lying below the ideal solution. For positive values of Ω (which leads to clustering of A and B components) the activity coefficients of the components A and B are greater than one.

1.11 SINGLE COMPONENT SYSTEM: PRESSURE-TEMPERATURE DIAGRAM

In a single component system, e.g., pure metals, compounds etc., the phase diagram is represented by the pressure-temperature relationship as shown in Fig. 1.13. The phases under consideration are, solid, liquid and vapor. The phase equilibrium between any of the two phases is represented by the lines *Ob*, *Oa* and *Oc*, meeting at the triple point *O*. Sublimation of the pure substance is represented by the line *Ob* along which solid and vapor phases coexist in equilibrium with each other. Fusion of the pure substance is represented by the line *Oa* along which solid and liquid phases are in equilibrium with each other. The line *Oc* represents vaporization of the liquid or liquefaction of the vapor phase.

Application of the phase rule reveals that there are two degrees of freedom ($f = c + 2 - p$) in the single phase region of the phase diagram. The two independent variables are temperature and pressure. Selecting pressure P_1 as the independent variable, one degree of freedom is utilized. The other independent variable in the form of temperature can be selected along a horizontal line at P_1. The set of coordinates (P_1, T_1), (P_1, T_2), etc., keep the pure substance in the single phase region, in this case a solid. A similar set of coordinates exist for the pure substance in the liquid as well as in the vapor state. These represent bivariant equilibria in a single component system.

Monovariant equilibrium is represented along the lines *Oa*, *Ob* or *Oc* in the P–T diagram. According to the phase rule there is one degree of freedom in the two phase region of a single component system. Thus one of the variables, temperature or pressure, can be independently selected. Consider the equilibrium between solid and liquid phases represented by the line *Oa* and select P_3 as an independent variable. The solid and liquid phases can coexist in equilibrium with each other only at the temperature T_3. Thus by selecting pressure as the independent variable (one degree of freedom), the temperature is fixed. One degree of freedom can be exercised in the form of temperature, say T_4, and then the pressure (P_4) will be fixed for the solid $\Rightarrow$ liquid equilibrium. A similar selection can be made to represent solid-vapor and liquid-vapor equilibria.

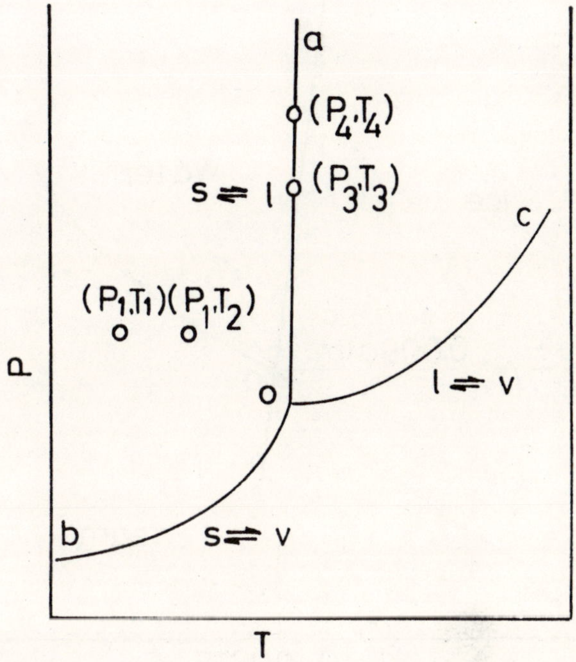

Fig. 1.13 Pressure-Temperature diagram for a pure component.

Application of the phase rule gives zero degrees of freedom at the point *O* of the phase diagram where all the three phases, solid, liquid and vapor coexist in equilibrium with each other. The system is invariant. The invariant point for the ice-water-steam system is an shown in Fig. 1.14.

On The Shape of the Curves *Oa*, *Ob* and *Oc*.

Consider two phases α and β in equilibrium with each other. This can be represented as occurring along one of the curves *Oa*, *Ob* or *Oc* or any such curve along which any such transformation or variant of the transformation in solid, liquid or vapor may occur. At equilibrium, the change in free energy ΔG for the transformation $\alpha \longrightarrow \beta$ is zero. This is represented as,

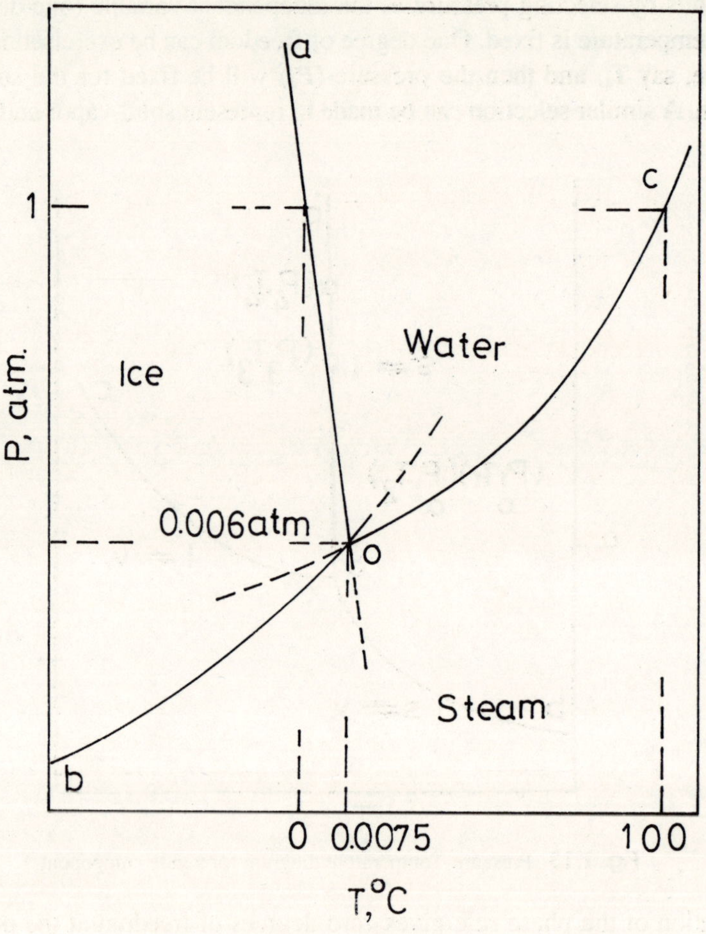

Fig 1.14 *P–T* diagram for ice-water-steam system.

$$G^{\alpha} = G^{\beta} \text{ or equivalently, } dG^{\alpha} = dG^{\beta}.$$

The free energy of the α and β phases can be made to change by making small changes in the pressure and temperature. This is written as,

$$dG^{\alpha} = V^{\alpha} dP - S^{\alpha} dT$$

and
$$dG^{\beta} = V^{\beta}dP - S^{\beta}dT \qquad (1.11.1)$$

From
$$dG^{\alpha} = dG^{\beta} \text{ at equilibrium,}$$

$$V^{\alpha}dP - S^{\alpha}dT = V^{\beta}dP - S^{\beta}\,dT$$

or
$$(V^{\beta} - V^{\alpha})\,dP = (S^{\beta} - S^{\alpha})\,dT.$$

For the $\alpha \Rightarrow \beta$ transformation,

$$\frac{dP}{dT} = \frac{\Delta S}{\Delta V}. \qquad (1.11.2)$$

For a reversible process, $\Delta S = \int_{\alpha}^{\beta} \frac{dQ}{[T]} = \frac{\Delta H}{[T]}$ · Substituting in equation (1.11.2) yields,

$$\frac{dP}{dT} = \frac{\Delta H}{T\Delta V} \qquad (1.11.3)$$

where ΔH is the heat of fusion, vaporization, sublimation or transformation of one phase into another. Consider the solid to liquid transformation (fusion) of a pure metal. In order to melt a pure metal, an amount of heat equal to the enthalpy of fusion ΔH_f is to be supplied to the system. Hence, $\Delta H = \Delta H_f$ in equation (1.11.3) is a positive quantity. There is an increase in volume in general when a solid melts making ΔV positive. The slope of the P vs. T curve during solid to liquid transformation of a pure metal, in general, should be positive. The line Oa should show a positive slope. The melting point of a pure metal will be raised when hydrostatic pressure is applied. This can be understood from the fact that the phase with lower volume per mole will be more stable as compared to the phase with higher volume per mole when pressure is applied. And since, the solid, in general, has a lower molar volume per mole (higher density) than the liquid, the solid phase will be stable above the normal melting point under pressure. The effect of pressure on the melting temperature, however, is very small as illustrated by the following example.

Example: Pure Ni melts at 1726 K at 1 atm. pressure. Determine the melting point of pure Ni when acted upon by a pressure of 10^8Pa. For Ni, ΔV (solid-liquid) = 0.26×10^{-6}m^3 mol^{-1} and $\Delta H_f = 18079.2$ Jmol^{-1}.

For small changes in temperature, equation (1.11.3) can be written as,

$$\frac{\Delta P}{\Delta T} = \frac{\Delta H_f}{T_e \Delta V}, \quad (T_e = \text{ mp at 1 atm pressure})$$

$$(10^8 - 10^5) = \frac{18079.2}{1726 \times 0.26 \times 10^{-6}} \Delta T.$$

$$\Delta T = 0.0248 \times 10^2 = 2.48 \text{ K}.$$

Line *Oa* in Fig. 1.13 is almost vertical and has a positive slope. There is a contraction in volume during melting of the metals Bi and Ga as well as during melting of ice. Thus ice can be made to melt below 0°C under hydrostatic pressure.

Liquid-Vapor and Solid-Vapor Equilibria

Let us consider the liquid $\Rightarrow$ vapor equilibrium (vaporization) of a pure substance. Here the α and β phases can be considered to be the liquid and vapor phases, respectively. The effect of temperature on vapor pressure is given by the equation (1.11.3) where $\Delta H = \Delta H_v$ is the enthalpy of vaporization and ΔV is the change in volume.

$$\Delta V = V\text{ (vapor)} - V\text{ (liquid)}$$

$$= V_v - V_l$$

However, the volume of the vapor phase V_v is very large compared to the volume of the liquid V_l, $\Delta V \cong V_v$. Furthermore, the vapor phase may be treated as an ideal gas, $V = RT/[P]$, which upon substitution in equation (1.11.3) yields,

$$\frac{dP}{dT} = \frac{\Delta H_v}{T \cdot RT} \cdot P,.$$

or

$$\frac{d \ln P}{dT} = \frac{\Delta H_v}{RT^2},$$

or

$$\frac{d \ln P}{d\left(\frac{1}{T}\right)} = -\frac{\Delta H_V}{R}. \tag{1.11.4}$$

Assuming the enthalpy of vaporization ΔH_v to remain constant in the range of temperatures and pressure considered, the integrated form of the equation (1.11.4) is

$$\ln P = -\frac{\Delta H_v}{RT} + \text{constant}, \tag{1.11.5}$$

$$\text{(For sublimation, } \ln P = -\frac{\Delta H_s}{RT} + \text{constant)} \tag{1.11.6}$$

or

$$\ln P = -\frac{a}{T} + b,$$

where a and b are material constants.

Equation (1.11.5) can also be written as

$$P = A \exp^{-(\Delta H_v/RT)}, \tag{1.11.7}$$

where A is an integration constant. A similar relation between pressure and temperature can be arrived at for the solid-vapor equilibrium (sublimation). Equation (1.11.7) shows that there is an exponential increase of pressure with increase in temperature. Lines Ob and Oc show such a behavior, Fig. 1.13.

The relationship between pressure and temperature expressed by equation (1.11.7) indicates that a plot of ln P vs. $1/T$ should be a straight line and that the slope of the line is to be identified with the term $-\Delta H_v/R$. This is illustrated in Fig. 1.15 for the transformation of water to steam. A deviation from the linear behavior of such a plot in some systems is due to the following,

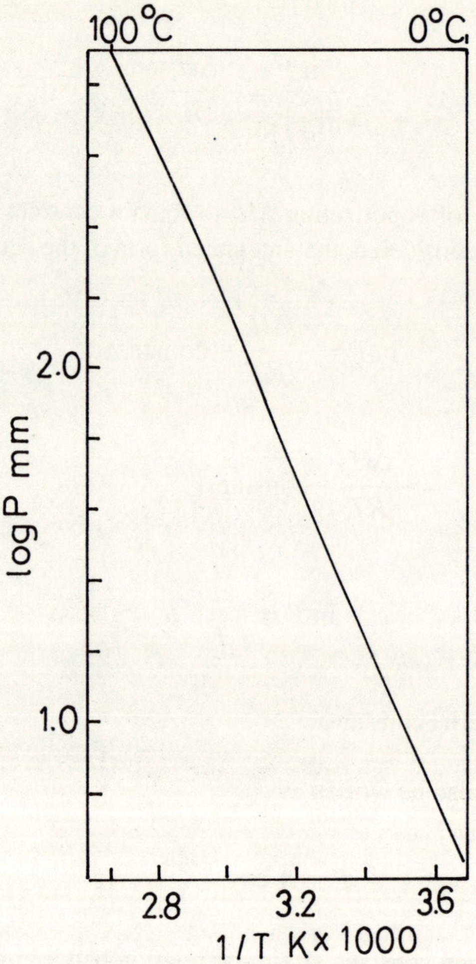

Fig. 1.15 A plot of log P vs. $1/T$ for the vaporization of water.

(i) The vapor phase has been treated as an ideal gas which may not be realistic for the system under consideration.

(ii) The enthalpy of vaporization has been assumed to be constant in the range of temperatures considered.

(iii) The specific heats of the condensed and vapor phases are assumed to be independent of temperature.

A list of triple points for some of the common metals is given in Table 1.1. For a majority of metals, the triple point lies below 1 atm. pressure and the critical point (corresponding to boiling) above 1 atm. pressure. The vapor pressure of the metals is very small at ambient temperature. The heat of sublimation can be determined from vapor pressure data as the following example illustrates.

Table 1.1 List of Triple points for some of the common metals and non-metals

Name of the Element	Temperature (T_t) K	Pressure (P_t) atm.
Ag	1236	1×10^{-4}
As	1087	36
Ba	977	10^{-3}
Cu	1356	7.8×10^{-7}
Fe ($\alpha\gamma G$)	1180	1.65×10^{-10}
Fe ($\gamma\delta G$)	1767	1.14×10^{-5}
Fe (δLG)	1808	8.29×10^{-5}
Ge	1231	8.4×10^{-4}
Hg	234.2	1.3×10^{-9}
Ni	1726	1×10^{-4}
Pb	600	1×10^{-7}
Si	1683	2.65×10^{-4}
Pt	2046	1×10^{-6}
Zn	708	0.05

Example: The vapor pressure of Mg in the temperature range 700 to 739 K satisfies with reasonable accuracy the equation $\ln P = -17320/T + 19.78$.

Similarly for Zn in the temperature range 575 to 630 K, the vapor pressure is given by,

$$\ln P = -\frac{15636}{T} + 20.66.$$

Determine the heats of sublimation of Mg and Zn. Comparison of equations (1.11.5) and (1.11.6) expresses that,

$$a = \frac{\Delta H_s}{R}, \text{ where } \Delta H_s \text{ is the heat of sublimation}$$

$$\therefore \qquad \Delta H_s = a \times R.$$

From the given data, a for Mg = 17320 and for Zn, a = 156336.

$$\therefore \qquad \Delta H_s(Mg) = 144 \text{ kJ mol}^{-1} \quad \text{and} \quad \Delta H_s(Zn) = 130 \text{ kJ mol}^{-1}.$$

The behavior of metals with a triple point below 1 atm. pressure and the critical point above 1 atm. pressure can be understood by heating at constant pressure such as P_1 (= 1 atm.). The vapor pressure of the metal at the lowest temperature of Fig. 1.13 is given by point "b". The remaining pressure P_1b is that due to the partial pressure of air. The solid phase is in equilibrium with its own vapor with vapor pressure "b" and the partial pressure P_1b of air. The vapor pressure of the metal vapor increases along the curve bO, the solid phase remaining unchanged. The partial pressure of air gradually decreases with increasing temperature. Continuous heating leads to melting at the equilibrium melting temperature T_{mp}. Above the melting point, the liquid phase will be in equilibrium with its own vapor with the vapor pressure increasing along the line Oc with increasing temperature. Continuous heating of the liquid leads to boiling of the metal at the temperature T_{bp}.

For a metal or a pure substance whose triple point lies above 1 atm. pressure, the material will sublimate directly to vapor if heated slowly. The metal will melt, however, if heated rapidly. The above behavior occurs, owing to the vaporization process being a surface phenomenon i.e., the vaporization occurs when bonds of the surface atoms are broken. In the mean time the melting temperature of the material will be realized as illustrated at pressure P_2 (which is below the triple point), Fig. 1.16. The extension of the solid/liquid line aO meets the isobar at P_2 at the point d, which corresponds to the melting point at P_2.

Allotropy

Some metals (as well as non-metals) are found to exist in more than one crystalline form. There is a range of temperatures in which a given crystalline form is stable. Such materials are called allotropic. The individual form is known as allotrope or allotropic modification. For example, iron exists in three different allotropic forms, α, γ and δ. The crystal structures of the different allotropes are:

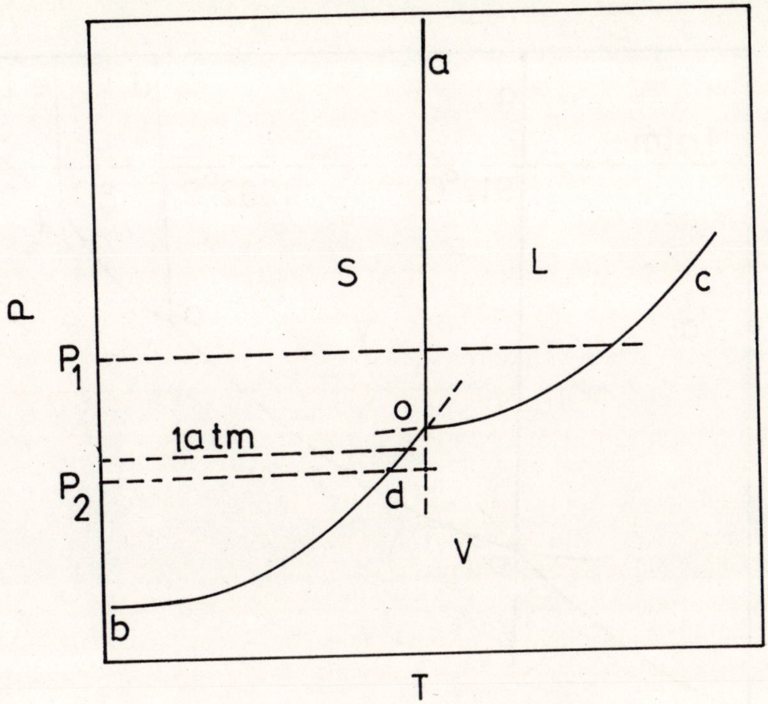

Fig. 1.16 *P–T* diagram for a pure component.

$$\alpha, bcc, a = 2.864\ \text{A}°\ 20°\text{C}$$

$$\gamma, fcc, a = 3.571\ \text{A}° \quad \text{(extrapolated to 20°C)}$$

$$\delta, bcc, a = 2.94\ \text{A}°\ 1425°\text{C}$$

The *P–T* diagram of iron showing its allotropic modification is shown in Fig. 1.17. The diagram shows more than one triple point and two additional monovariant lines corresponding to $\alpha \longrightarrow \gamma$ and $\gamma \longrightarrow \delta$ transformations. When pure iron is gradually heated from ambient temperature, it remains in the α form in equillbrium with its own vapor. The α phase transforms to the γ phase at 912°C, the γ phase is in equilibrium with its own vapor till 1392°C at which it transforms to the δ phase. The δ phase is stable upto the melting point of pure iron.

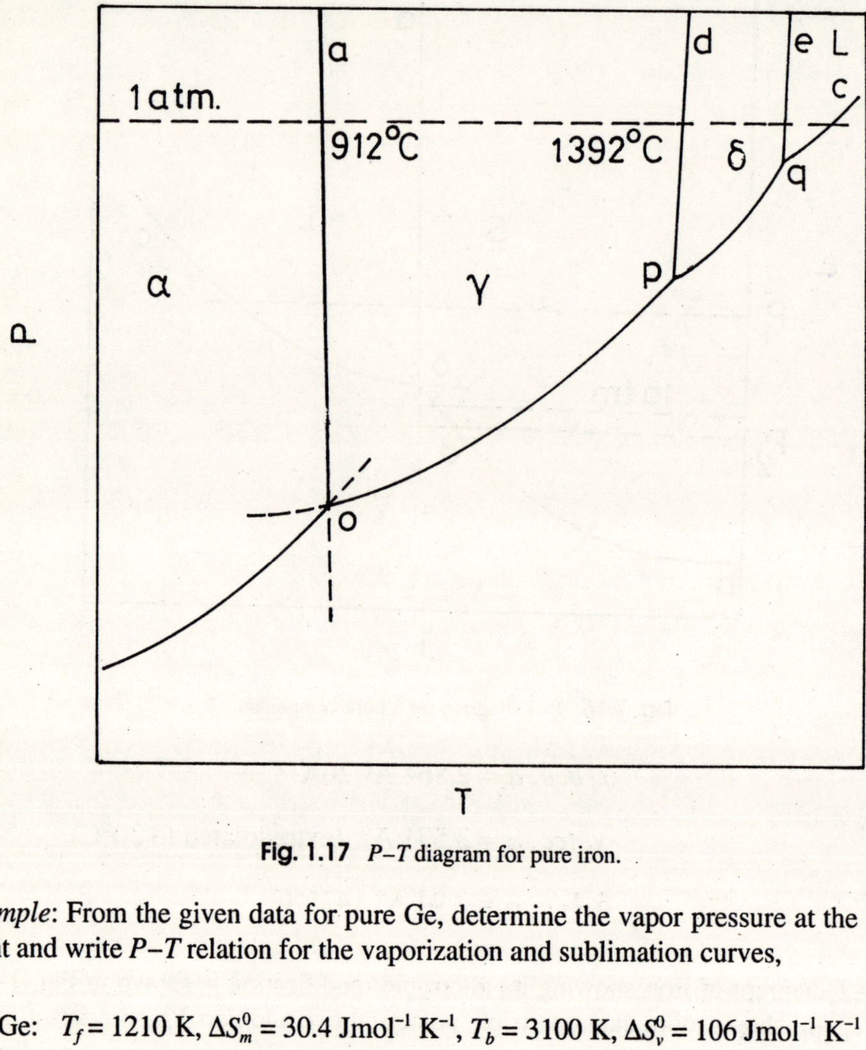

Fig. 1.17 *P–T* diagram for pure iron.

Example: From the given data for pure Ge, determine the vapor pressure at the triple point and write *P–T* relation for the vaporization and sublimation curves,

For Ge: $T_f = 1210$ K, $\Delta S_m^0 = 30.4$ Jmol^{-1} K^{-1}, $T_b = 3100$ K, $\Delta S_v^0 = 106$ Jmol^{-1} K^{-1}

$$\Delta H_f^0 = 30.4 \times 1210 = 36784 \text{ Jmol}^{-1}$$

$$\Delta H_v^0 = 106 \times 3100 = 328600 \text{ Jmol}^{-1}$$

For sublimation and vaporization, we can write from equation (1.11.7);

$$P_v = A_v \exp^{-\left(\Delta H_v^0/RT\right)}$$

and
$$P_s = A_s \exp^{-\left(\Delta H_s^0/RT\right)}$$

Since the curves for vaporization and sublimation meet at the triple point pressure P_t, we can equate the above two equations to yield,

$$P_t = A_v \exp^{-\Delta H_v^0/RT} = A_s \exp^{-\Delta H_s^0/RT}$$

which upon solving gives the following result:

$$T = \frac{\Delta H_s^0 - \Delta H_v^0}{R \ln (A_s/A_v)}$$

and
$$P_t = A_v \exp\left(\frac{\Delta H_s^0}{\Delta H_v^0 - \Delta H_s^0}\right)$$

The metal will boil at 1 atm. pressure. Thus

$$A_v = 1 \times \exp^{+\Delta H_v^0/RT} = \exp^{+328600/8.314\times 3100} = 3.44 \times 10^5 \text{ atm.}$$

The vaporization curve in the P–T diagram is represented by

$$P_v = 3.44 \times 10^5 \exp^{-328600/RT}.$$

At the triple point, $P_v = P_t$ and since the triple point temperature is close to the melting point of the metal,

$$P_t = 3.44 \times 10^5 \exp^{-328600/8.314\times 1210} = 2.245 \times 10^{-9} \text{ atm.}$$

Now
$$A_s = P_t \exp^{\Delta H_s^0/RT_f} = 2.24479 \times 10^{-9} \exp^{365384/R\times 1210}.$$

from $\Delta H_s^0 = \Delta H_f^0 + \Delta H_v^0$ for $S \longrightarrow V = S \longrightarrow L + L \longrightarrow V$.

$$A_s = 1.33 \times 10^7.$$

The sublimation curve in the P–T diagram is represented by

$$P_s = 1.33 \times 10^7 \exp^{-365384/RT}$$

Example: Calculate the heat of vaporization of pure Ge from the following data:

$$T_f = 1210 \text{ K}, \quad T_b = 3100 \text{ K}, \quad P_t = 2.244 \times 10^{-9} \text{ atm}.$$

We can write from equation (1.11.7),

$$2.244 \times 10^{-9} = A_v \exp^{-\Delta H_v/R \times 1210} \quad \text{at} \quad T_f.$$

$$= A_v \exp^{-\Delta H_v/R \times 3100} \quad \text{at} \quad T_b.$$

Solving for ΔH_v, yields,

$$\Delta H_v = 327 \text{ kJmol}^{-1}$$

1.12 EFFECT OF CURVATURE ON THE MELTING TEMPERATURE

In the previous section on the single component systems it has been shown that increasing the pressure on pure solid raises its melting point as given by the Classius Clapeyron equation (1.11.3). It has been assumed in the derivation that the liquid-solid interface is flat with curvature $K = 0$ ($r = \infty$) and pressures in both phases α and β are the same. If the α and β phases are separated by a curved interface, the pressures in the two phases will be the different. Let us assume that the α and β phases are separated by a curved interface with curvature K. The pressure in the β phase is given by:

$$P^\beta = P^\alpha + \gamma K, \tag{1.12.1}$$

where P^α and P^β are the pressure in the α and β phases, respectively, and γ is the interfacial energy. The free energies of the α and β phases due to changes in pressure and temperature are given by,

and
$$\left.\begin{aligned} dG^\alpha = V^\alpha dP^\alpha - S^\alpha dT^\alpha \\ dG^\beta = V^\beta dP^\beta - S^\beta dT^\beta. \end{aligned}\right\} \tag{1.12.2}$$

At equilibrium between α and β phases, $G^\alpha = G^\beta$ or, $dG^\alpha = dG^\beta$, which gives from equations (1.12.2),

$$V^\alpha dP^\alpha - S^\alpha dT^\alpha = V^\beta dP^\beta - S^\beta dT^\beta \tag{1.12.3}$$

Substituting for dP^β from equation (1.12.1) in equation (1.12.3) after differentiating yields,

$$V^\alpha dP^\alpha - V^\beta dP^\alpha - \gamma V^\beta dK = S^\alpha dT^\alpha - S^\beta dT^\beta. \tag{1.12.4}$$

At constant temperature $T^\alpha = T^\beta$, and $dT^\alpha = dT$. At constant pressure in $P^\alpha = 1$ atmosphere. We can write, $dP = 0$ and hence from equation (1.12.4),

$$-\gamma V^\beta dK = (S^\alpha - S^\beta)dT. \tag{1.12.5}$$

Upon integration of the two sides of equation (1.12.5) assuming γ to be independent of curvature, we get the following result.

$$-\gamma V^\beta \int_{K=0}^{K} dK = (S^\alpha - S^\beta) \int_{T=T_e}^{T} dT. \tag{1.12.6}$$

The lower limit is taken at the equilibrium transformation temperature, $T = T_e$ and $K = 0$ ($r = \infty$) for large size particles. Equation (1.12.6) yields,

$$-\gamma V^{\beta} K = (S^{\alpha} - S^{\beta})(T - T_e) \tag{1.12.7}$$

Let us consider solidification of a pure substance, $L\ (\alpha) \rightleftharpoons S\ (\beta)$. The entropy change ΔS, $(S^S - S^L)$, is negative and can be approximated for small changes in temperature as

$$\Delta S = (S^S - S^L) = -\frac{\Delta H_f}{T_e}.$$

Equation (1.12.7) can now be written as,

$$T = T_e\left(1 - \frac{\gamma V^{\beta} K}{\Delta H_f}\right) \tag{1.12.8}$$

The curvature of an interface is represented in terms of two principal radii as,

$$K = \frac{1}{r_1} + \frac{1}{r_2}$$

For a dendrite (with flat ends), $r_1 = \infty,\ r_2 = r$

For a sphere, $r_1 = r,\ r_2 = r.$

Thus equation (1.12.8) for

dendrite is, $T = T_e\left(1 - \dfrac{\gamma V^{\beta}}{r \Delta H_f}\right)$,

and for sphere it is, $T = T_e\left(1 - \dfrac{2\gamma V^{\beta}}{r \Delta H_f}\right)$ (1.12.9)

Example: Calculate the temperature at the tip of Ni dendrites growing in the liquid with tip radius (a) 1 μm (b) 0.1 μm (c) if Ni grows as spheres of radius 0.1 μm. Given $V_{\text{Ni}}^s = 7 \times 10^{-6} \text{m}^3 \text{ mol}^{-1}$, $\gamma = 255 \text{ mJ m}^{-2}$, $\Delta H_f = 18079 \text{ Jmol}^{-1}$ and $T_e = 1726$ K.

From equation (1.12.9),

(a) for dendrites with tip radius $r = 1$ μm,

$$T = 1726\left(1 - \frac{0.255 \times 7 \times 10^{-6}}{10^{-6} \times 18079}\right) = 1725.8 \text{ K}, \Delta T = 0.2 \text{ K}.$$

(b) for dendrites with tip radius $r = 0.1$ μm,

$$T = 1726\left(1 - \frac{0.255 \times 7 \times 10^{-6}}{10^{-7} \times 18079}\right) = 1724.3 \text{ K}, \quad \Delta T = 1.7 \text{ K}.$$

(c) for spheres with radius $r = 0.1$ μm.

$$T = 1726\left(1 - \frac{2 \times 0.255 \times 7 \times 10^{-6}}{10^{-7} \times 18079}\right) = 1722.6 \text{ K}, \quad \Delta T = 3.4 \text{ K}.$$

Example: Calculate the radius of the tip of tin dendrites forming in the liquid if the temperature at the tip is 2°C below the bulk melting point of pure tin at atmospheric pressure. Given $V_{Sn}^S = 16.446 \times 10^{-6} \text{ m}^3 \text{ mol}^{-1}$, $\gamma = 0.055 \text{ Jm}^{-2}$, $\Delta H_f = 7071.4 \text{ Jmol}^{-1}$ and $T_e = 505.1$K.

From equation (1.12.29)

$$T = T_e\left(1 - \frac{\gamma V^S}{r \Delta H_f}\right)$$

$$503.1 = 505.1\left(1 - \frac{0.055 \times 16.446}{r \times 7071.4}\right).$$

Solving for r gives the tip radius as

$$r = 0.032\mu\text{m}.$$

The calculation shows that if the liquid next to the tip of the dendrite is supercooled more than that at the tip, there will be heat flow from the solidification front and the dendrite can grow. However, if the temperature of the liquid near the tip is more than that at the tip, the tip of the dendrite will get blunted and will gradually disappear. In a system consisting of an array of dendrites of distributed tip radii, only these dendrites whose temperature at the tip is more than those of the neighboring liquid will grow. The rest of the dendrites will dissolve. If the surrounding liquid has the same temperature as the tip, the dendrite will remain stationary.

Next, let us consider the effect of curvature on the vapor pressure of a condensed phase in equilibrium with its own vapor at constant temperature. Consider two liquid-vapor systems. In one, the bulk liquid is in equilibrium with its own vapor with the vapor pressure represented by P ($K = 0$). In the second, very fine droplets of the liquid are in equilibrium with their own vapor with vapor pressure P (K). Both systems are at the same temperature.

From equation (1.12.2) at constant temperature

$$V^{\alpha} dP^{\alpha} = V^{\beta} dP^{\beta}. \tag{1.12.10}$$

Where two phases are separated by a curved interface,

$$P^{\beta} = P^{\alpha} + \gamma K \quad \text{and} \quad dP^{\beta} = dP^{\alpha} + \gamma dK.$$

Substituting for dP^{β} in equation (1.12.10), we get,

$$V^{\alpha} dP^{\alpha} = V^{\beta} dP^{\alpha} + \gamma V^{\beta} dK. \quad \text{or} \quad (V^{\alpha} - V^{\beta}) dP^{\alpha} = \gamma V^{\beta} dK. \tag{1.12.11}$$

For the liquid (β)$\rightarrow$vapor (α),

$$\Delta V = V^{\alpha} - V^{\beta}, \text{ and since } V^{\alpha} \gg V^{\beta},$$

$$\Delta V \cong V^{\alpha}$$

$$\cong \frac{RT}{[P]} \text{ for an ideal gas behavior of one mole of the vapor phase.}$$

Substituting for ΔV in equation (1.12.11) and integrating yields

$$\int_{P(K=0)}^{P(K)} \frac{dP}{P} = \int_{K=0}^{K=K} \frac{\gamma V^{\beta} dK}{RT}.$$

or $$\ln\frac{P(K)}{P(0)} = \frac{\gamma V^{\beta} K}{RT} \quad \text{or} \quad P(K) = P(0)\exp^{\gamma V^{\beta} K/RT},$$

where $P(0)$ is the pressure of the vapor phase when in equilibrium with the bulk condensed phase, and $P(K)$ is the vapor pressure in a system of liquid droplets of mean curvature K. For spherical liquid droplets of radius r,

$$P(r) = P(\infty)\exp^{2\gamma V^{\beta}/rRT}. \tag{1.12.12}$$

Example: Calculate the vapor pressure in a system of Mg droplets suspended in its own vapor at 1000 K.

Given: $\gamma^{LV} = 525\ \text{mJm}^{-2}$, $V^{L} = 15.29\ \text{cm}^3\ \text{mol}^{-1}$ and vapor pressure of Mg, $\log_{10}$ P (mm Hg) $= -7550\ T^{-1} - 1.41 \log T + 12.79$.

The vapor pressure over bulk liquid Mg at 1000 K is $P =$ 0.01346 atm.

For, $r =$ 10 μm, $P(K) = P(0)\exp^{2\times 0.525\times 15.29\times 10^{-6}/1000\times 8.314\times 10^{-5}}$
$=$ 0.0134625 atm.
$r =$ 1 μm, $P(K) =$ 0.01372 atm.
$r =$ 0.1 μm, $P(K) =$ 0.01372 atm.
$r =$ 0.01 μm, $P(K) =$ 0.016327 atm.
$r =$ 0.001 μm, $P(K) =$ 0.092827 atm.

The vapor pressure as a function of the radius of liquid droplet is shown in Fig. 1.18.

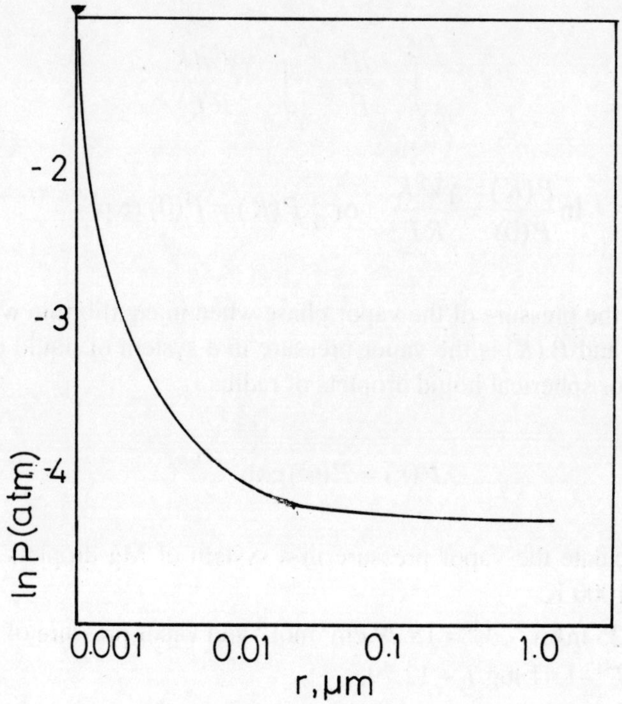

Fig. 1.18 Vapor pressure vs. radius of liquid Mg droplets.

PROBLEMS

1. The pressure on 1 mole of water is increased reversibly and isothermally from 1 atm. to 5000 atm. at 0°C. Assuming the volume, density, volume expansion coefficient and compressibility to remain constant, calculate:
   (a) the amount of heat transferred during compression.
   (b) the amount of work done.
   (c) the change in internal energy of the system.

   Given: $V = 1.0\ \text{cm}^3\text{g}^{-1}$, $\beta = -67 \times 10^{-6}\text{K}^{-1}$, $\kappa = 51.5 \times 10^{-6}\ \text{atm}^{-1}$,
   $C_p = 4.2177\ \text{Jg}^{-1}\text{K}^{-1}$.

2. In problem 1 if the compression is carried out adiabatically, calculate the change in temperature.

3. Calculate the molar specific heat at constant volume of copper at 500K and 1 atm. pressure.

   Given: $C_p = 25.8$ Jmol^{-1} K^{-1}, $\beta = 54.9 \times 10^{-6}$K^{-1}, $\kappa = 0.85 \times 10^{-6}$ atm. and molar volume = 7.21 cm^{3}mol^{-1}.

4. Derive the following relations:

   (i) $$\left(\frac{\partial P}{\partial T}\right)_S = \frac{C_p}{V\beta T}$$

   (ii) $$\left(\frac{\partial V}{\partial T}\right)_S = -\frac{C_v \kappa}{V\beta T}$$

   (iii) $$\left(\frac{\partial H}{\partial T}\right)_V = C_p - \frac{\beta^2 VT}{\kappa} + \frac{\beta V}{\kappa}$$

   (iv) $$\left(\frac{\partial F}{\partial T}\right)_S = \frac{\kappa P C_p}{\beta T} - \beta P V - S$$

   (v) $$\left(\frac{\partial P}{\partial T}\right)_S = \frac{C_p}{\beta V T}$$

   (vi) $$\left(\frac{\partial P}{\partial T}\right)_S = \frac{C_p}{\beta T} - S$$

5. From the given data for pure Zn and Cu, determine the vapor pressure at the triple point and write the *P–T* relation for sublimation and vaporization.

	Zn	Cu
T_f, K	692.7	1356.6
ΔH_f^0, kJmol^{-1}	7.28	13.02
ΔH_v^0, kJmol^{-1}	114.342	305.64
T_b, K	1180	2830

6. Calculate the heat of vaporization of Mg from the following data:

$$T_f = 922 \text{ K} \quad T_b = 1360 \text{ K}, \quad P_t(\text{triple point}) = 4.73 \times 10^{-3} \text{atm}.$$

7. (a) The density of diamond is 3.52 g per cc and that of graphite is 2.25 g per cc. Assuming that the pressure is kept constant at 1 atmosphere, what temperature would bring graphite to diamond?
   (b) Assuming the constant temperature of 25°C, what pressure would produce equilibrium between graphite and diamond. Assume the densities to remain constant over the temperature range. The following values are given:

	ΔH_f^0, kJmol^{-1}	ΔG_f^0, kJmol^{-1}	S^0, Jmol^{-1}K^{-1}
graphite (298K)	0	0	5.74
diamond (298K)	1.89	2.9	2.38

8. Pure water solidifies at 273 k at 1 atmosphere pressure. Calculate the freezing point of water under a hydrostatic pressure of 10^4 atm. Consult thermodynamic tables for relevant values.

9. The free energy of a binary solution obeys the relation,

$$\Delta G = 1000 X_A X_B + RT\,[X_A \ln X_A + X_B \ln X_B].$$

Determine the partial molal free energies of components A and B (μ_A and μ_B) at $X_B = 0.4$.

10. Calculate the partial molal enthalpies of the components A and B for a regular solution given by

$$\Delta H_m = \Omega\, X_A\, X_B.$$

11. Calculate and plot as a function of radius the vapor pressure in a system of water droplets suspended in its own vapor at 300K.

Given: $\gamma = 200$ mJm^{-2}, $V_L = 18 \times 10^{-6}$m^{3}mol^{-1}

$$\log P = -\frac{2900}{T} - 4.65 \log T + 22.613 \text{ (mm Hg)}.$$

12. Calculate the radius of the tip of Cu dendrites forming in the liquid if the temperature at the tip is 2°C below the bulk melting point of pure copper at 1 atm. pressure.

    Given: $V_{Cu}^{S} = 7.48 \times 10^{-6} m^3 mol^{-1}$, $\gamma_{SL} = 177$ mJm^{-2}, $\Delta H_f = 13 kJmol^{-1}$ and T_e = 1356.6 K.

Chapter 2

BINARY PHASE DIAGRAM–ISOMORPHOUS SYSTEMS

2.1 INTRODUCTION

The two components A and B, that make the binary isomorphous system, are completely soluble in each other in the liquid and solid states in all proportions. The product is known as a liquid solution (L) or solid solution (α)

A typical phase diagram of the binary system is represented by a P–T–X diagram. Introduction of the composition variable in the P–T diagram of the unary system (Chapter-1) makes it a three dimensional figure with pressure, temperature and composition as variables represented by an orthogonal axes system; as shown in Fig. 2.1 for the isomorphous system. The two components are always miscible in each other in the gaseous state.

The left-hand face is the pressure-temperature unary diagram for the component A with the invariant point O_A. The right-hand face is the pressure-temperature unary diagram for the component B with invariant point O_B. The equilibrium between solid

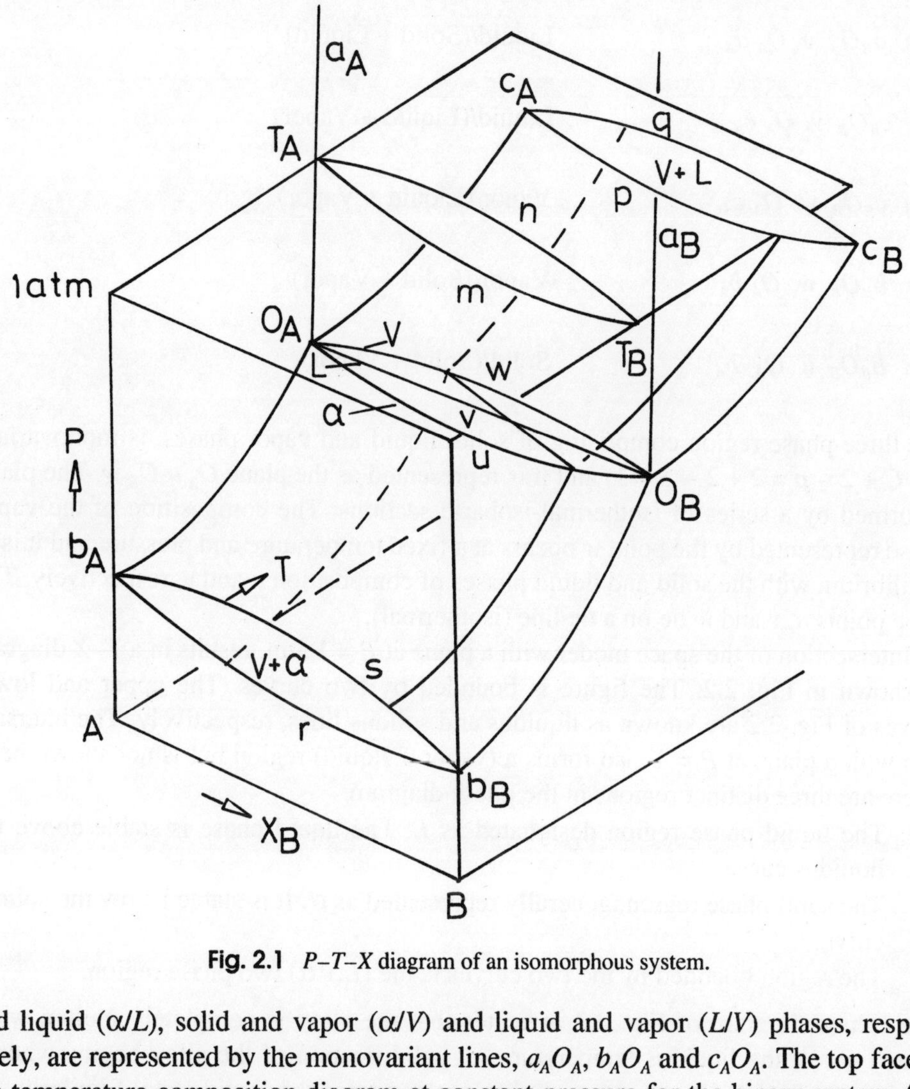

Fig. 2.1 *P–T–X* diagram of an isomorphous system.

and liquid (α/*L*), solid and vapor (α/*V*) and liquid and vapor (*L*/*V*) phases, respectively, are represented by the monovariant lines, $a_A O_A$, $b_A O_A$ and $c_A O_A$. The top face is the temperature-composition diagram at constant pressure for the binary system *A-B* which intersects the melting temperature of pure components *A* and *B* at T_A and T_B, respectively when P = 1 atmosphere. The three two-phase regions are bounded by surfaces which form lenticular shapes upon intersection with a plane (at constant pressure). The six surfaces are as follows:

$a_A\ m\ a_BO_B\ u\ O_A\ a_A$	Solid/(Solid + Liquid)
$a_A\ n\ a_BO_B\ v\ O_A\ a_A$	Liquid/(Solid + Liquid)
$c_A\ p\ c_BO_B\ v\ O_A\ c_A$	Liquid/(Liquid + Vapor)
$c_A\ q\ c_BO_B\ w\ O_A\ c_A$	Vapor/(Liquid + Vapor)
$b_A\ r\ b_BO_B\ w\ O_A\ b_A$	Vapor/(Solid + Vapor)
$b_A\ s\ b_BO_B\ u\ O_A\ b_A$	Solid/(Solid + Vapor)

The three phase region comprising of solid, liquid and vapor phases, is monovariant ($f = C + 2 - p = 2 + 2 - 3 = 1$) and it is represented as the plane $O_A\ u\ O_B\ w$. The plane is formed by a series of isothermal-isobaric sections. The composition of the vapor phase represented by the point w occurs at a fixed temperature and pressure and it is in equilibrium with the solid and liquid phases of composition u and v, respectively. The three points u, v and w lie on a tie line (isothermal).

Intersection of the space model with a plane at $P = 1$ atm. results in a T–X diagram as shown in Fig. 2.2. The figure is bounded by two curves. The upper and lower curves of Fig. 2.2 are known as liquidus and solidus lines, respectively. The intersection with a plane at $P = 1$ also forms a (vapor + liquid) region but is not shown here. There are three distinct regions in the phase diagram.

a. The liquid phase region designated as L. The liquid phase is stable above the liquidus curve.
b. The solid phase region, generally represented as α. It is stable below the solidus curve.
c. The region bounded by the two curves is the $(L + \alpha)$ two phase region.

The phase diagram of Fig. 2.2 indicates that the alloy is completely molten when heated above the liquidus temperature, or solidification of the alloy begins when it reaches the liquidus temperature during cooling from the liquid state. Similarly, the solidification of the alloy is complete when the solidus temperature is reached during cooling, or melting of the alloy begins at the solidus temperature when the alloy is heated from the completely solid state. The solidification of the alloy occurs over a range of temperatures.

Alloy compositions are generally represented in weight percent of component B,

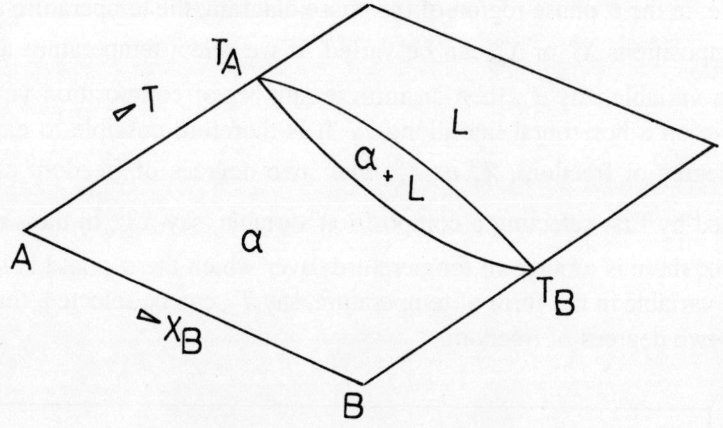

Fig. 2.2 *T–X* diagram at *P* = 1 atm.

especially for engineering applications. However, when quantitative evaluation of structural properties is desired, it is appropriate to use atom percent of component *B*. The relation between atom and weight percent can be represented by the following:

$$\text{at.pct. } B = \frac{(\text{wt.pct.}B)\,/\,(\text{at.wt.}B)}{(\text{wt.pct.}A)\,/\,(\text{at.wt.}A) + (\text{wt.pct.}B)/(\text{at.wt.}B)} \times 100$$

$$\text{wt.pct.}B = \frac{(\text{at.pct.}B) \times (\text{at.wt.}B)}{(\text{at.pct.}A) \times (\text{at.wt.}A) + (\text{at.pct.}B) \times (\text{at.wt.}B)} \times 100$$

Example: A Cu-Zn alloy contains 40 at.pct.Zn. Calculate the wt.pct.Zn in the alloy. The atomic wt. of Cu = 63.54. The atomic wt. of Zn = 65.38

$$\text{wt.pct.Zn} = \frac{40 \times 65.38}{60 \times 63.54 + 40 \times 65.38} \times 100 = 40.68$$

2.2 APPLICATION OF THE PHASE RULE

The phase rule as applied to the condensed system is $P + F = C + 1$, when pressure is kept constant (1 atm.):

(i) Single Phase Region: Application of the phase rule in a single phase region of the phase diagram, Fig. 2.3a, reveals that there are two degrees of freedom. For example, in the α phase region of the phase diagram, the temperature and one of the compositions X_A^α or X_B^α can be varied. If we select temperature as an independent variable, say T_1, then an infinite number of composition variables are available on a horizontal line along T_1. It is therefore possible to exercise one more degree of freedom, X_A^α or X_B^α. The two degrees of freedom can also be exercised by first selecting a composition variable, say $X_B^{\alpha 1}$. In the single phase region α, there is a range of temperatures over which the α phase is stable. The second variable in the form of temperature, say T_2, can be selected, thus exercising the two degrees of freedom.

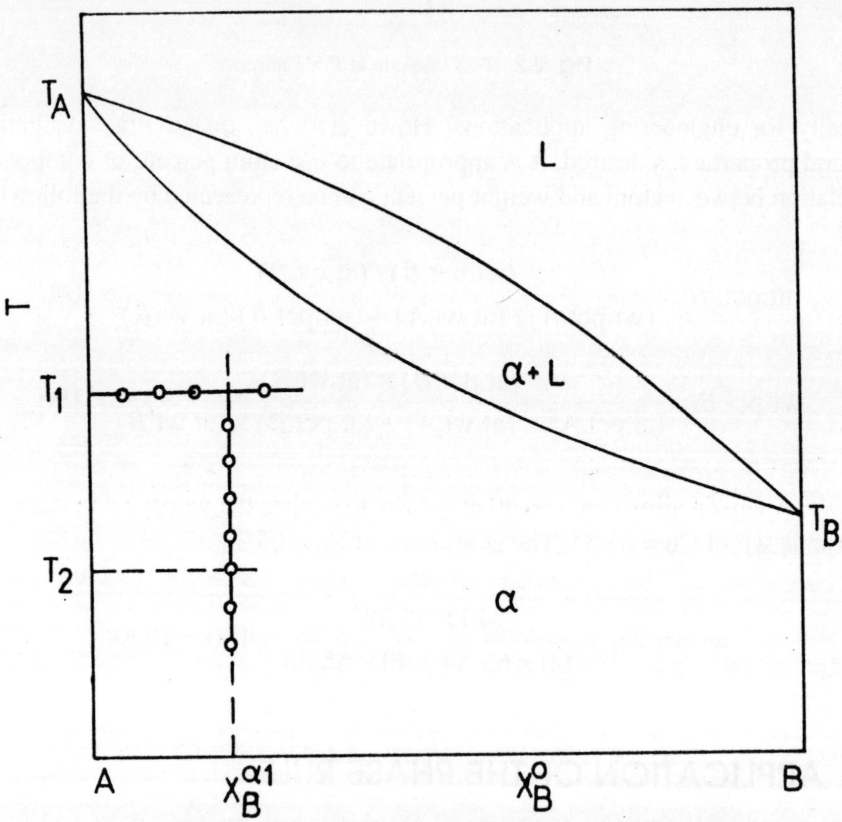

Fig. 2.3a The application of the phase rule to single phase region.

(ii) Two Phase Region: There is one degree of freedom in the two phase field of a binary alloy system. One degree of freedom can be selected out of the four composition variables, X_A^α, X_B^α, X_A^L, X_B^L and the temperature, Fig. 2.3b. The four composition variables are not all independent, from the relation for a binary system, $X_A^\alpha + X_B^\alpha = 1$ and $X_A^L + X_B^L = 1$. Suppose we exercise one degree of freedom by selecting temperature as one of the variables, say T_3. The compositions of the liquid and solid phases that can be in equilibrium with each other at T_3 are determined by drawing a horizontal line at T_3. These compositions are X_B^{L3} and $X_B^{\alpha 3}$, respectively, for the liquid and solid solutions. Similarly, selecting the composition of one of the phases, say $X_B^{\alpha 4}$ for the α phase fixes the composition of the liquid phase, X_B^{L4} in equilibrium with it. The two phases can coexist at the temperature T_4.

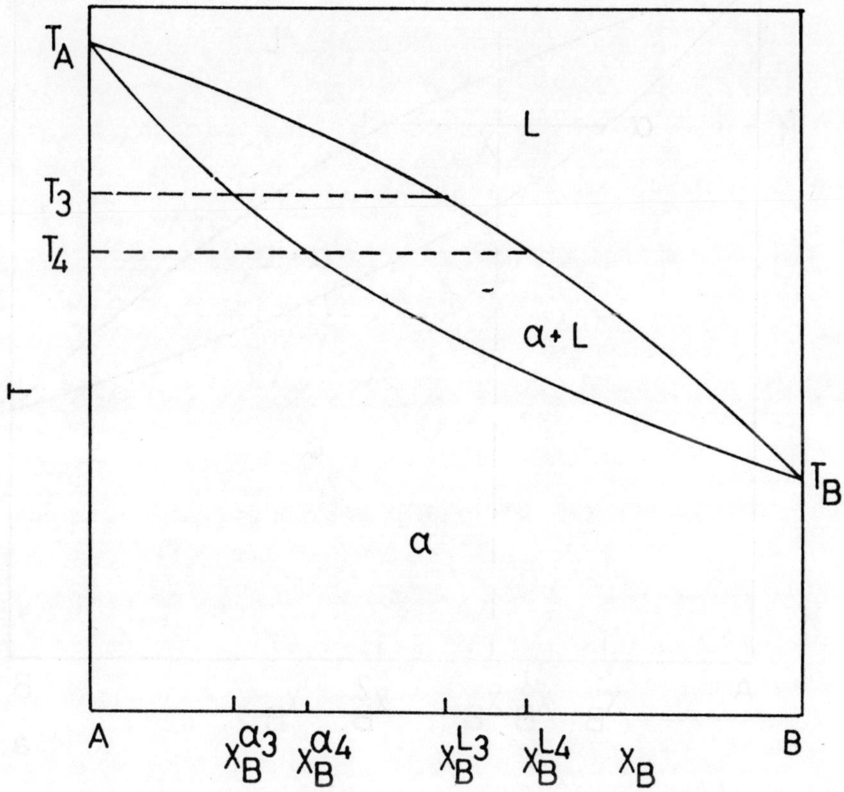

Fig. 2.3b The application of the phase rule to two phase region.

2.3 THE LEVER RULE

In order to determine the relative amounts of phases in a phase mixture, the lever rule is used. Consider an isomorphous system between components *A* and *B*, Fig. 2.4a. If an alloy of composition X_B^1 is selected, it would be 100% α at temperature T_1. Similarly, the alloy composition X_B^2 would be 100% liquid at T_1. For an alloy X_B^3, the two phases α and liquid will coexist in equilibrium with each other at the temperature T_1 in a certain proportion. This is the situation for all alloy compositions selected between compositions X_B^1 and X_B^2. It is clear that the tie-line α*L* represents 100% of the alloy for equilibrium between the two phase at T_1. If the tie-line α*L* is therefore treated

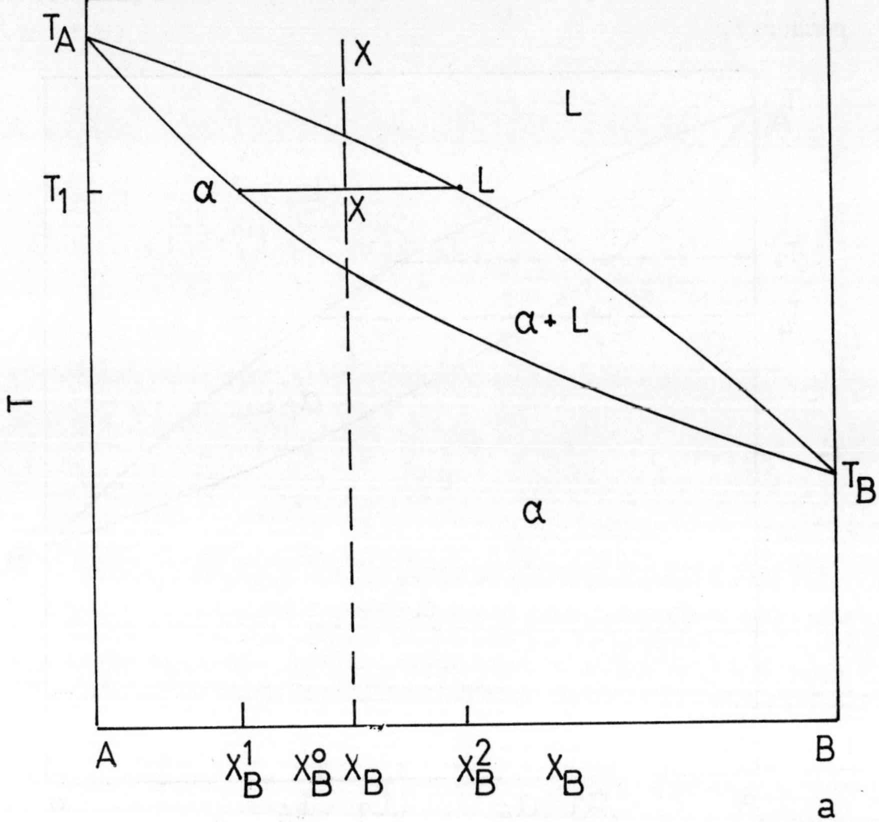

Fig. 2.4a Demonstration of the lever rule with the help of binary phase diagram.

as the arm of a lever, the original alloy composition X_B^0 as fulcrum and the weight of each phase is placed at its respective end, then the lengths of the line XL and αX will be proportional to the relative amounts of the α and liquid phases, respectively. This is the lever rule.

The above idea can be translated into a mathematical derivation of the lever rule. When two metals are alloyed together they either form a homogeneous solution or separate into phases α and β at the temperature T. Let there be N moles of the alloy of composition X_B^0, which separates into N^α and N^β moles of the α and β phases, respectively. Conservation of the component B in the alloy yields,

$$X_B^\alpha N^\alpha + X_B^\beta N^\beta = X_B^0 \cdot N, \tag{2.1}$$

where X_B^α and X_B^β are the mole fractions of the α and β phases respectively. Substituting for $N^\alpha = N - N^\beta$ in equation (2.1) yields,

$$X_B^\alpha \cdot (N - N^\beta) + X_B^\beta \cdot N^\beta = X_B^0 \cdot N. \tag{2.2}$$

Rearrangement of terms yields,

$$N^\beta (X_B^\beta - X_B^\alpha) = (X_B^0 - X_B^\alpha)\, N$$

Similarly,

$$\left.\begin{aligned} \%\beta &= \frac{N^\beta}{N} \times 100 = \frac{(X_B^0 - X_B^\alpha)}{(X_B^\beta - X_B^\alpha)} \times 100 \\ \%\alpha &= \frac{N^\alpha}{N} \times 100 = \frac{(X_B^\beta - X_B^0)}{(X_B^\beta - X_B^\alpha)} \times 100 \end{aligned}\right\} \tag{2.3}$$

Thus if we place N^α moles of the α phase at the point α, N^β moles of the β phase at point β and the fulcrum represents the original alloy composition, X_B^0, then,

$$\text{the relative amount of } \alpha = \frac{q}{p+q},$$

the relative amount of $\beta = \dfrac{p}{p+q}$,

and the ratio of the amounts of α and β, $\dfrac{\alpha}{\beta} = \dfrac{q}{p}$,

where p and q represent the length of the arm of the lever from the fulcrum, Fig. 2.4b. Equation (2.3) represents the lever rule in mathematical form.

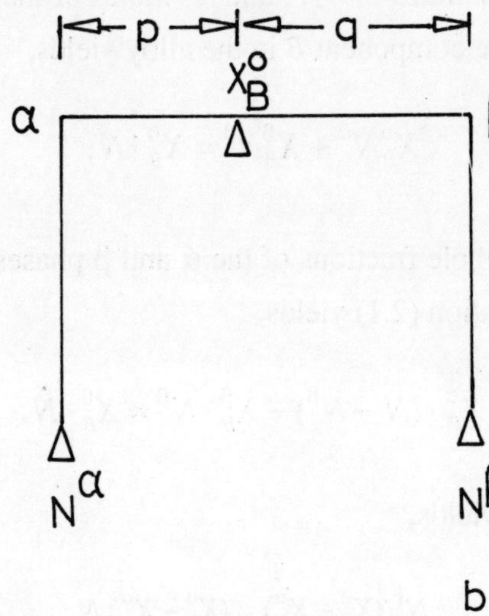

Fig. 2.4b Demonstration of the lever rule (balance of lever with weights of α and β and the fulcrum at X).

2.4 EQUILIBRIUM SOLIDIFICATION AND MICROSTRUCTURE

Let us consider a binary alloy system between components A and B forming liquid and solid solutions in the whole range of compositions, defined as an isomorphous system, Fig. 2.5. An alloy of composition X_B^0 will form a homogeneous liquid solution when kept at T_0 for sufficient lengths of time. No phase changes occur during cooling the alloy until temperature T_1 corresponding to the liquidus is reached. At the temperature T_1, nuclei of the α phase begin to form and the solid phase α, of composition $X_B^{\alpha 1}$, is in equilibrium with the liquid phase of composition X_B^{L1}.

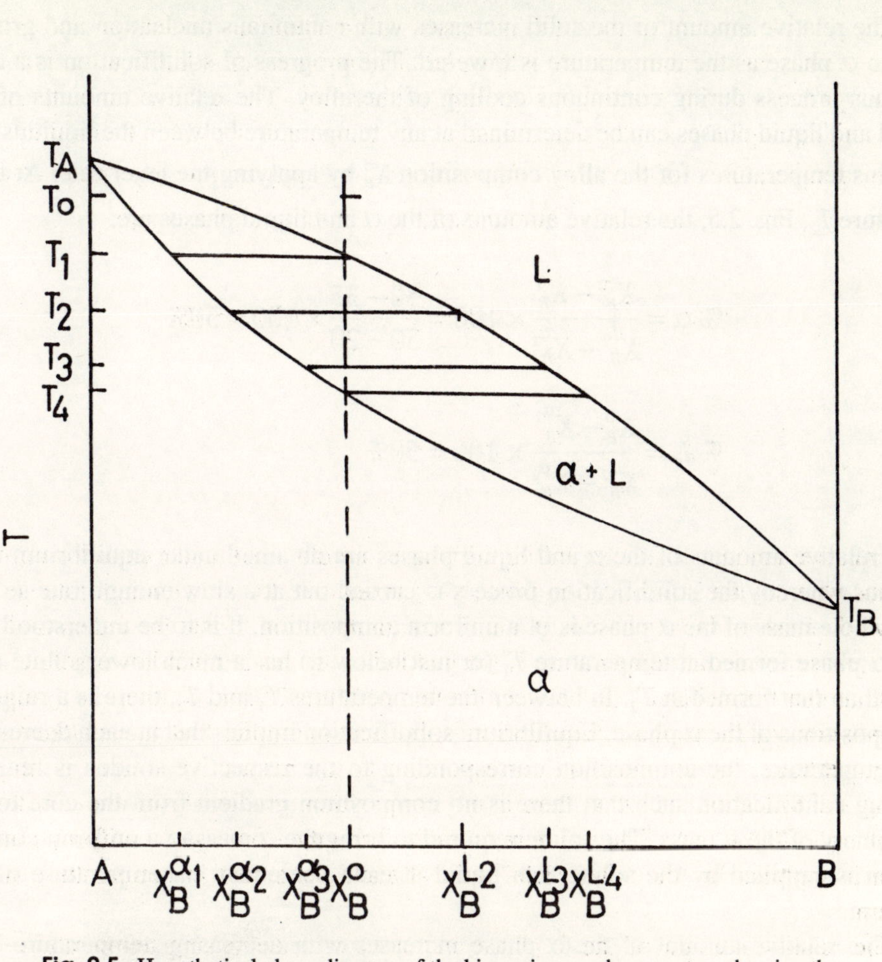

Fig. 2.5 Hypothetical phase diagram of the binary isomorphous system showing the progress of solidification.

In general, solidification does not begin at T_1 since a certain degree of undercooling is required before stable nuclei of the α phase can form and grow. This is essential because a part of the volume free energy change available for liquid to solid transformation below T_1 is used up in forming the solid/liquid interface. At or near temperature T_1, embryos of the α phase form but dissolve quickly. Stable nuclei of the α phase form in the liquid with an increase in undercooling, ΔT. The degree of undercooling varies from a few degrees in some systems to as large as 0.2 T_e in other systems. T_e is defined as the equilibrium melting temperature of the solid. The α phase being rich in component A makes the liquid phase richer in component B.

The relative amount of the solid increases with continuous nucleation and growth of the α phase as the temperature is lowered. The progress of solidification is a continuous process during continuous cooling of the alloy. The relative amounts of the solid and liquid phases can be determined at any temperature between the liquidus and solidus temperatures for the alloy composition X_B^0 by applying the lever rule. At temperature T_2, Fig. 2.5, the relative amounts of the α and liquid phases are:

$$\% \alpha = \frac{X_B^{L_2} - X_B^0}{X_B^{L_2} - X_B^{\alpha_2}} \times 100 = \frac{50-35}{50-20} \times 100 = 50\%$$

$$\% L = \frac{X_B^0 - X_B^{\alpha_2}}{X_B^{L_2} - X_B^{\alpha_2}} \times 100 = 50\%$$

The relative amounts of the α and liquid phases are obtained under equilibrium conditions whereby the solidification process is carried out at a slow enough rate so that the whole mass of the α phase is of a uniform composition. It is to be understood that the α phase formed at temperature T_1 (or just below it) has a much lower solute content than that formed at T_2. In between the temperatures T_1 and T_2, there is a range of compositions of the α phase. Equilibrium solidification implies that at each decrement of temperature, the composition corresponding to the respective solidus is realized during solidification such that there is no composition gradient from the core to the periphery of the α mass. The solute required to bring the α mass to a uniform composition is supplied by the solute rich liquid at each decrement in temperature of the system.

The relative amount of the α phase increases with decreasing temperature. The relative amounts of the α and liquid phases at the temperature T_3 are,

$$\% \alpha = \frac{X_B^{L_3} - X_B^0}{X_B^{L_3} - X_B^{\alpha_3}} \times 100 = \frac{0.6-0.35}{0.6-0.30} \times 100 = 83.33$$

and %L = 16.66.

At T_3, homogeneous α phase of composition $X_B^{\alpha_3}$ is in equilibrium with liquid of composition $X_B^{L_3}$. The solidification process is completed when the composition of the α phase coincides with the original alloy composition X_B^0. This occurs at T_4. The progress of solidification can be understood from the development of microstructure resulting in an equiaxed structure, Fig. 2.6. This is compared with an actual photomicrograph, Fig. 2.6e.

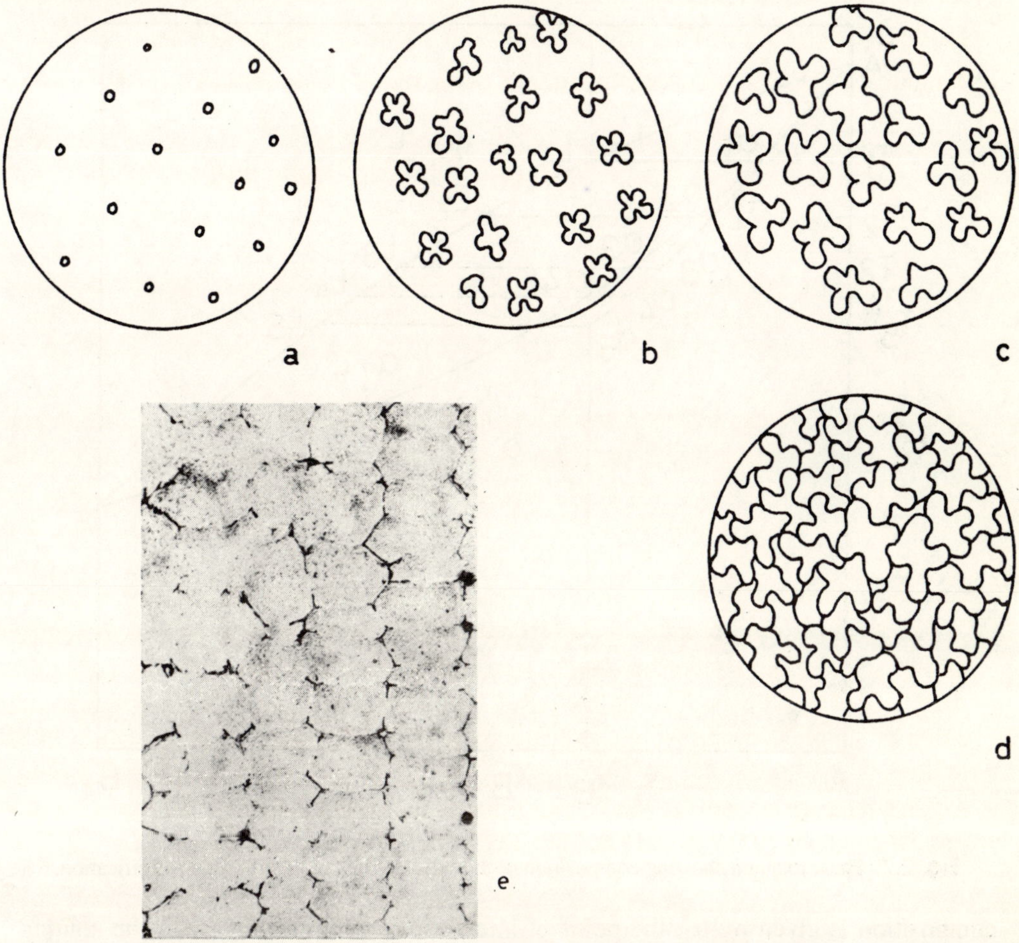

Fig. 2.6 The development of microstructure sketched at T_1 to T_4 (a to d) and compared with the microstructure obtained in an Ag-Cu alloy during solidification (e), optical photomicrograph.

2.5 NON-EQUILIBRIUM SOLIDIFICATION-CORING

The composition of the α phase remains uniform from the core to the periphery of its mass during equilibrium solidification. Equilibrium conditions are difficult to realize in practice because of the very long time required at each decrement of temperature to readjust the composition of the two phases. Consider solidification of the same alloy under natural cooling, Fig. 2.7. The α phase forms at the temperature T_1 and its

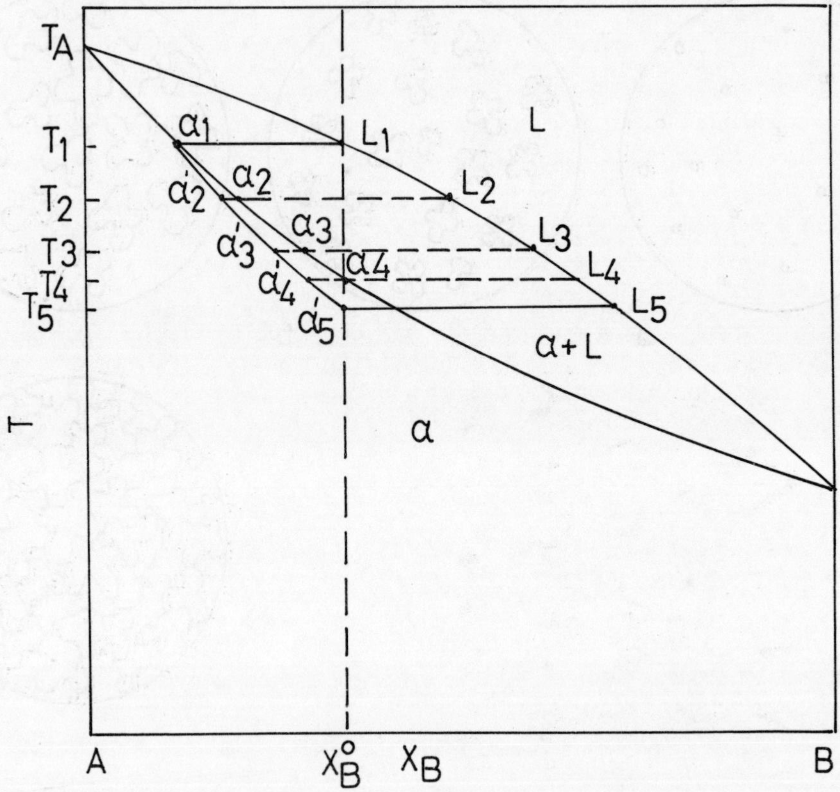

Fig. 2.7 Phase diagram showing composition of the solid during non-equilibrium solidification.

composition is given by α_1; the point of intersection of the tie-line with the solidus curve. This composition of the α phase forms the core of the solid. At each decrement of temperature a new layer of α forms over the existing α and the subsequent layers are richer in solute. The composition of the α phase that forms at each temperature corresponds to the composition of the solidus at that temperature and thus is dictated by the phase boundary. For example, composition of the outermost layer of α which forms at temperature T_2 will be α_2, Fig. 2.7. There will thus be a composition gradient in the α phase from the core to the periphery. The rates of diffusion of *A* and *B* are so slow in the solid that no significant homogenization of α occurs in the time available for solidification under natural cooling conditions. The liquid phase generally becomes homogeneous because of higher rates of diffusion of A and B atoms in the liquid. The composition of the liquid phase is given by the liquidus curve at any temperature in the two phase region.

The average composition of the α phase at temperature T_2 lies between α_1 and α_2, say α'_2. With further cooling a solute rich layer forms on the existing α at each decrement in temperature. The average composition of the α phase at temperature T_3 will be α'_3 although the outermost layer of α has a composition α_3. Similarly, at temperature T_4, the α'_4 is the average composition of the α phase which is less than the original alloy composition. The relative amounts of the α phase at temperatures T_2, T_3 and T_4 are calculated using the lever rule.

$$\text{at } T_2, \qquad \% \alpha = \frac{50-35}{50-18} \times 100 = 46.87\%$$

$$\% L = 53.12\%$$

$$\text{at } T_3, \qquad \% \alpha = \frac{60-35}{60-25} \times 100 = 71.43\%$$

$$\% L = 28.57\%$$

$$\text{and} \qquad \text{at } T_4 \qquad \% \alpha = \frac{66-35}{66-30} \times 100 = 86.11\%$$

$$\% L = 13.88\%$$

The amount of total α formed up to temperature T_4 is 86.11%; 13.88% liquid of composition $X_B^{L_4}$ still remains to be solidified. During continuous cooling, the solidification of the alloy is extended to temperatures below the solidus for the alloy composition under consideration. The alloy will solidify completely at temperature T_5 when the average composition of the solid coincides with the original alloy composition X_B^0. The liquid solidifying last will have composition $X_B^{L_5}$ as shown in the diagram. Non-equilibrium solidification therefore occurs over a larger temperature interval and there

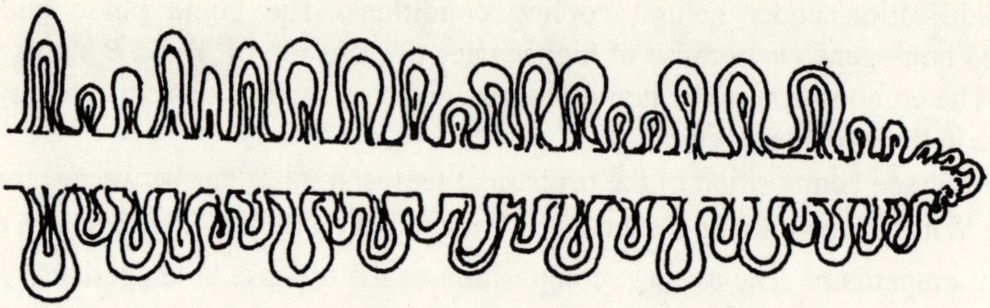

Fig. 2.8a Schematic showing coring in dendrites.

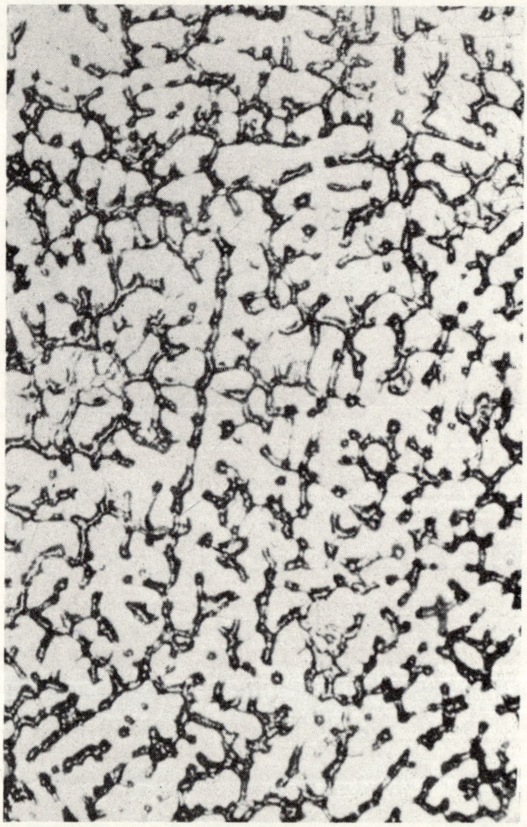

Fig. 2.8b Optical photomicrograph showing cored microstructure in a Cu-Ni alloy.

is large composition difference between the first and the last solid that forms. The microstructure that develops during non-equilibrium solidification is known as a "cored structure", as shown in Fig. 2.8a. The optical photomicrograph of Fig. 2.8b shows the dendritic microstructure of a Cu-Ni alloy cooled naturally. The central region (core) of each dendrite is light coloured which gradually changes to light gray and finally to dark gray at the periphery. The Cu-Ni phase diagram, Fig. 2.9, show complete solubility in the liquid and the solid states for the components Cu and Ni in

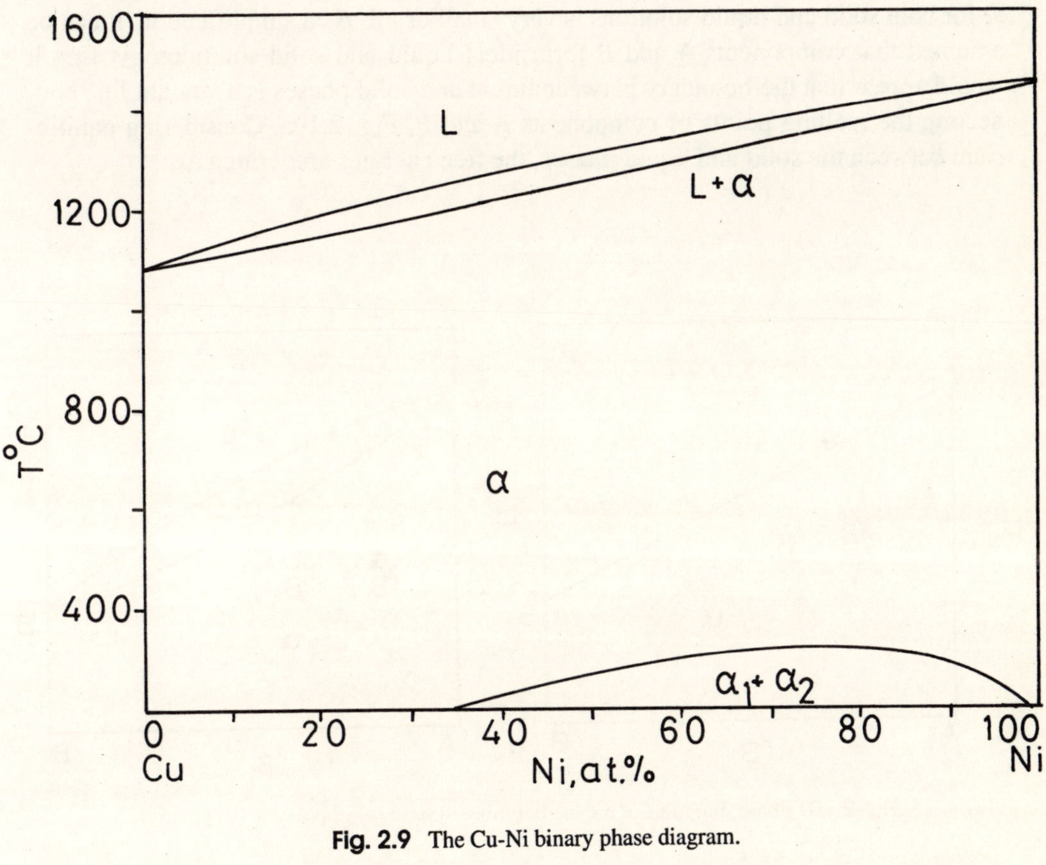

Fig. 2.9 The Cu-Ni binary phase diagram.

each other. The first solid layer (core of the structure) that forms is rich in Ni.[1] Subsequent layers of the solid (that form during cooling through the two phase region) will progressively have more Cu. The etching characteristic of the alloy is, therefore, due to this difference in composition of the α phase.

2.6 CONDITIONS FOR PHASE EQUILIBRIUM IN ISOMORPHOUS SYSTEMS

Consider an isomorphous system in which metals *A* and *B* are completely soluble in each other in all proportions in both the liquid and solid state. This would be possible if both components have the same crystal structure and the interaction parameter Ω for both solid and liquid solutions is very small or nil. As a simplification, it can be assumed that components *A* and *B* form ideal liquid and solid solutions. At first it would appear that the boundary between liquid and solid phases is a straight line connecting the melting points of components *A* and *B*, Fig. 2.10a. Considering equilibrium between the solid and liquid phases, the free energies are written as

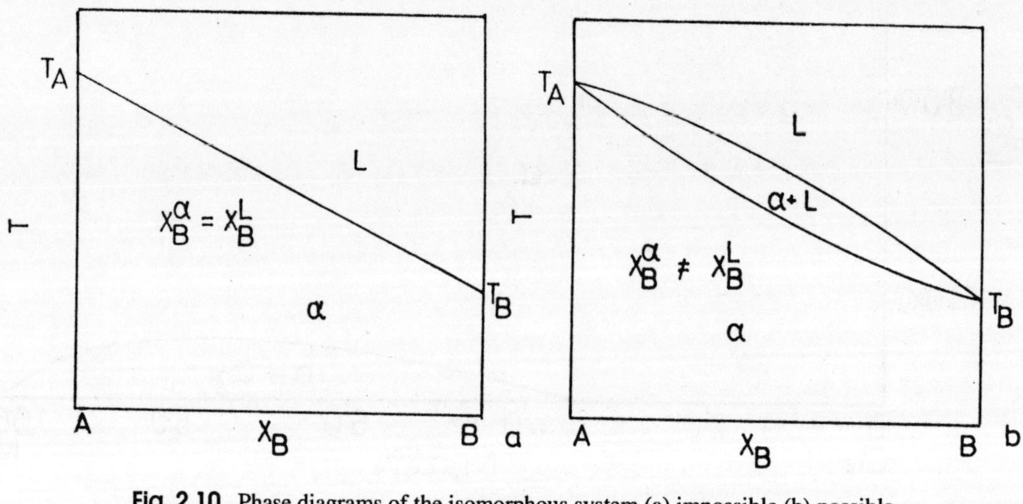

Fig. 2.10 Phase diagrams of the isomorphous system (a) impossible (b) possible.

[1]This follows the general rule that the first solid is always rich in that component which raises the melting point of the alloy.

and
$$\left.\begin{aligned} dG^{\alpha} &= V^{\alpha}dP - S^{\alpha}dT + \mu_A^{\alpha}dX_A^{\alpha} + \mu_B^{\alpha}dX_B^{\alpha}, \\ dG^{L} &= V^{L}dP - S^{L}dT + \mu_A^{L}dX_A^{L} + \mu_B^{L}dX_B^{L} \end{aligned}\right\} \tag{2.4}$$

At equilibrium, $dG^{\alpha} = dG^{L}$, and at constant pressure,

$$-S^{L}dT + \mu_A^{L}dX_A^{L} + \mu_B^{L}dX_B^{L} = -S^{\alpha}dT + \mu_A^{\alpha}dX_A^{\alpha} + \mu_B^{\alpha}dX_B^{\alpha}.$$

Transferring terms between LHS & RHS yields,

$$(S^{\alpha} - S^{L})dT = \mu_A^{\alpha}dX_A^{\alpha} + \mu_B^{\alpha}dX_B^{\alpha} - \mu_A^{L}dX_A^{L} - \mu_B^{L}dX_B^{L}. \tag{2.5}$$

From the equality of chemical potential for components A and B in the two phases, i.e., $\mu_A^{\alpha} = \mu_A^{L} = \mu_A$ and $\mu_B^{\alpha} = \mu_B^{L} = \mu_B$,

$$(S^{\alpha} - S^{L})\, dT = \mu_A\, (dX_A^{\alpha} - dX_A^{L}) + \mu_B\, (dX_B^{\alpha} - dX_B^{L}). \tag{2.6}$$

Relations $X_A^{\alpha} + X_B^{\alpha} = 1$ and $X_A^{L} + X_B^{L} = 1$, can be differentiated to yield, $dX_A^{\alpha} = -dX_B^{\alpha}$ and $dX_A^{L} = -dX_B^{L}$, which upon substitution in equation (2.6) yield,

$$(S^{\alpha} - S^{L})dT = (\mu_A - \mu_B)\,(dX_B^{L} - dX_B^{\alpha}).$$

Dividing by dX_B gives the following:

$$(S^{\alpha} - S^{L})\frac{dT}{dX_B} = (\mu_A - \mu_B)\left(\frac{dX_B^{L}}{dX_B} - \frac{dX_B^{\alpha}}{dX_B}\right) \tag{2.7}$$

The differentials on the right-hand side of equation (2.7), dX_B^{α}/dX_B and dX_B^{L}/dX_B, are equal if the phase diagram of the isomorphous system is represented by a straight line as shown in Fig. 2.10a, because $X_B^{\alpha} = X_B^{L}$. Substituting $dX_B^{\alpha}/dX_B = dX_B^{L}/dX_B$ in equation (2.7) yields,

$$(S^{\alpha}-S^{L})\left(\frac{[dT]}{[dX_B]}\right)=0. \tag{2.8}$$

In equation (2.8) $S^{\alpha} \neq S^{L}$, as heat is always evolved when a metal or an alloy solidifies thus, $[dT]/[dX_B]=0$. This is impossible because the slope of the temperature vs. composition diagram cannot be zero, except when the melting points of the two component metals are the same. Thus, the original assumption that $X_A^{\alpha} = X_A^{L}$ leading to $[dT]/[dX_B]=0$ is not applicable. Instead, there has to be a gap between the liquid and solid phase regions, as shown in the phase diagram of Fig. 2.10b.

The assumption $X_B^{\alpha}=X_B^{L}$ is associated with a minimum or a maximum in the phase diagram, Figs. 2.11, a and b, provided that equation (2.8) is satisfied, i.e., $dT/dX_B=0$ or a tangent drawn at the common composition point between the liquid and solid phases is parallel to the composition axis. Figs. 2.11, c and d, show phase diagrams with $X_B^{\alpha}=X_B^{L}$. However, these are impossible constructions of phase diagrams because $[dT]/[dX_B]\neq 0$. The phase diagram of Fig. 2.11e is also impossible as two solid phases α_1 and α_2 are in equilibrium with liquid L and it violates the phase rule (three phases in equilibrium with each other in a binary system are invariant).

Binary phase diagrams with a minimum or maximum in the liquidus and solidus curves are observed in real systems. The Au-Ni system is an example of minimum in the isomorphous system, Fig. 2.12. Compositions of thc solid and liquid phases are the same at 955°C. An alloy containing 42.5 at. pct. Ni will behave like a pure metal. It will melt and solidify at one temperature without undergoing any change in composition. These congruently melting alloys, as they are known, do not show any coring effect.

2.7 FREE ENERGY CURVES FOR THE SOLID AND LIQUID SOLUTIONS

Consider the free energies for the liquid and solid solutions below the melting point of pure A and above the melting point of pure B. As a simplification of the problem it is assumed that the two components A and B form ideal solutions and have the same crystal structure. The standard state of component A is taken as pure solid A and for component B it is taken as pure liquid B. Thus, for the liquid solution formed from components A and B, we can write,

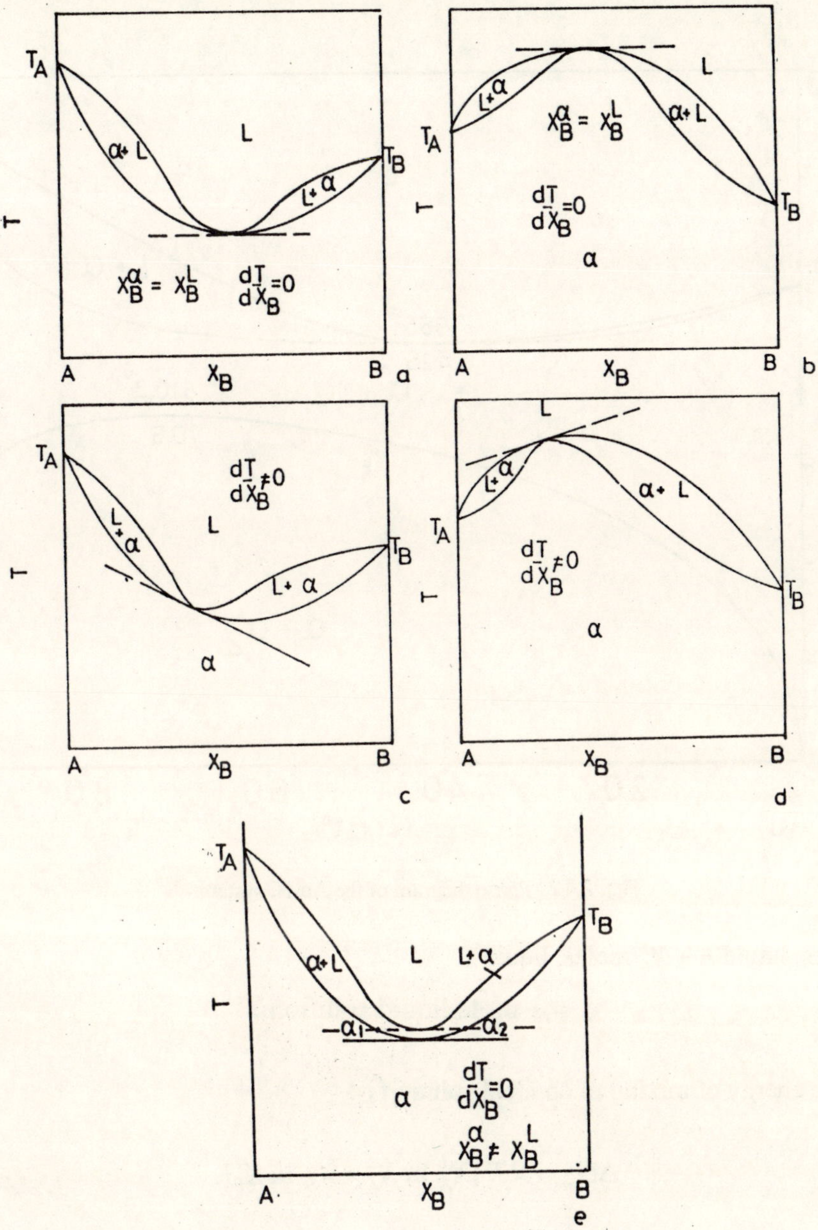

Fig. 2.11 Phase diagrams showing variation of the isomorphous system (a) minimum (b) maximum (c) impossible diagram, $dT/dX_B \neq 0$ (d) impossible diagram $dT/dX_B \neq 0$ (e) impossible diagram $X_A^\alpha = X_B^L$ but violation of the phase rule.

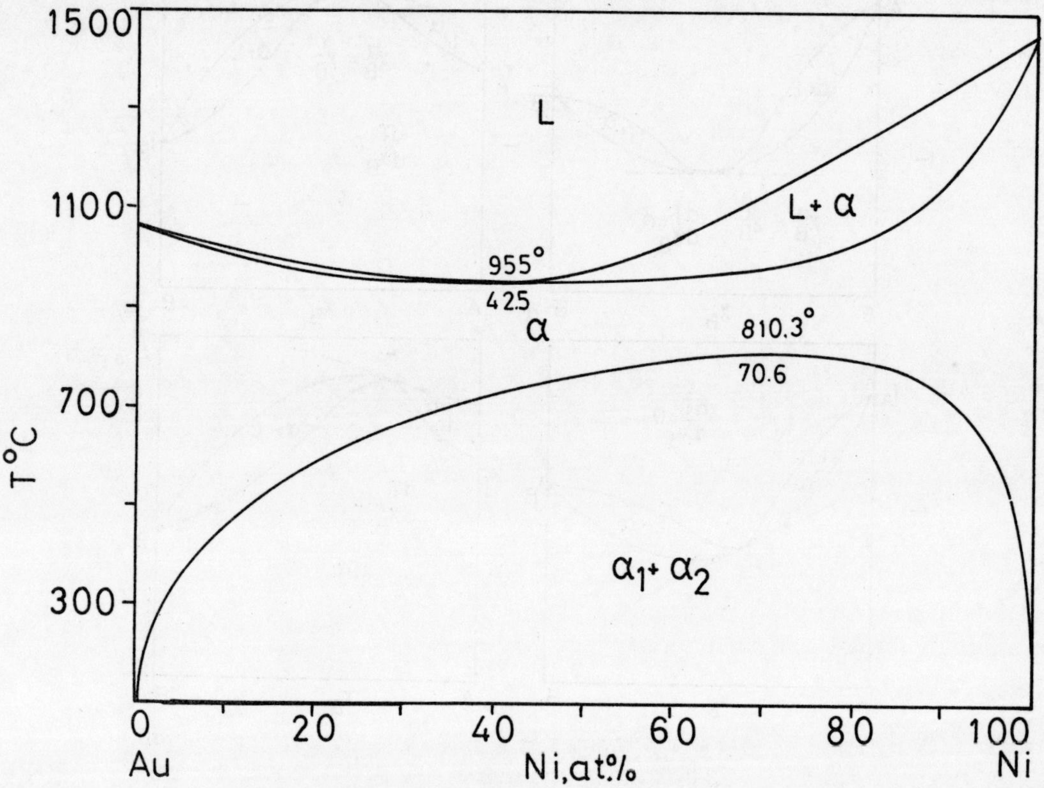

Fig. 2.12 Phase diagram of the Au-Ni system.

X_A^L moles, liquid A + X_B^L moles, liquid B

$$= 1 \text{ mole liquid solution} \tag{2.9}$$

The free energy of mixing of an ideal solution is:

$$\Delta G_m = RT\ [X_A^L \ln X_A^L + X_B^L \ln X_B^L]$$

However, since the standard state for component A is pure solid A instead of liquid A, we must allow the change of state of pure A from X_A^S moles of solid A into X_A^L moles of liquid A, i.e.,

$$X_A^S \text{ moles of solid } A \longrightarrow X_A^L \text{ moles of liquid } A. \tag{2.10}$$

The free energy change associated with the above change of state is

$$\Delta G = X_A^L \, \Delta G_{fA}^0, \tag{2.11}$$

where ΔG_{fA}^0 is the free energy of fusion of pure A. Combining equation (2.9) and (2.10) yields,

X_A^S moles of solid A + X_B^L moles of liquid B

= 1 mole of liquid solution.

The free energy of formation of the liquid solution is

$$\Delta G_m^L = X_A^L \, \Delta G_{fA}^0 + RT \, [X_A^L \ln X_A^L + X_B^L \ln X_B^L] \tag{2.12}$$

Similarly for the solid solution,

X_A^S moles of solid A + X_B^S moles of solid B

= 1 mole of solid solution.

The free energy of formation of the solid solution is

$$\Delta G_m = RT \, [X_A^S \ln X_A^S + X_B^S \ln X_B^S] \tag{2.13}$$

Since the standard state for component B is pure liquid B, X_B^L moles of liquid B must be converted into X_B^S moles of solid B.

Thus,

$$X_B^L \text{ moles of liquid } B \longrightarrow X_B^S \text{ moles of solid } B,$$

$$\Delta G = -X_B^S \,\Delta G_{fB}^0 ,$$

where ΔG_{fB}^0 is the free energy of fusion of component B at the temperature T.

For the reaction,

X_A^S moles of solid $A + X_B^L$ moles of liquid B

$$= 1\text{mole of solid solution,}$$

$$\Delta G_m^S = -X_B^B \,\Delta G_{fB}^0 + RT\,[X_A^S \ln X_A^S + X_B^S \ln X_B^S] \tag{2.14}$$

Equations (2.12) and (2.14) represent the free energies of formation of the liquid and solid solutions, respectively. The free energy curves for the liquid and solid solutions drawn at temperature T_1, above the melting points of both components, are separated from each other and do not intersect in the whole range of compositions, Fig. 2.13a. The magnitude of separation of the two free energy curves at $X_A = 1$ and $X_B = 1$ defines the free energy of fusion at the temperature, written as,

and
$$\left.\begin{aligned} \Delta G_{fA}^0 &= \Delta H_{fA}^0 - T\Delta S_{fA}^0, \\ \Delta G_{fB}^0 &= \Delta H_{fB}^0 - T\Delta S_{fB}^0. \end{aligned}\right] \tag{2.15}$$

In equation (2.15) ΔH_f^0 and ΔS_f^0 are the enthalpy and entropy of fusion, respectively. Considering the standard enthalpy and entropy of fusion to be independent of temperature, the entropy of fusion at the melting temperature can be determined from,

$$\Delta S_f^0 = \frac{\Delta H_f^0}{T_m}.$$

Substituting for ΔS_f^0 for the components A and B in equation (2.15) yields,

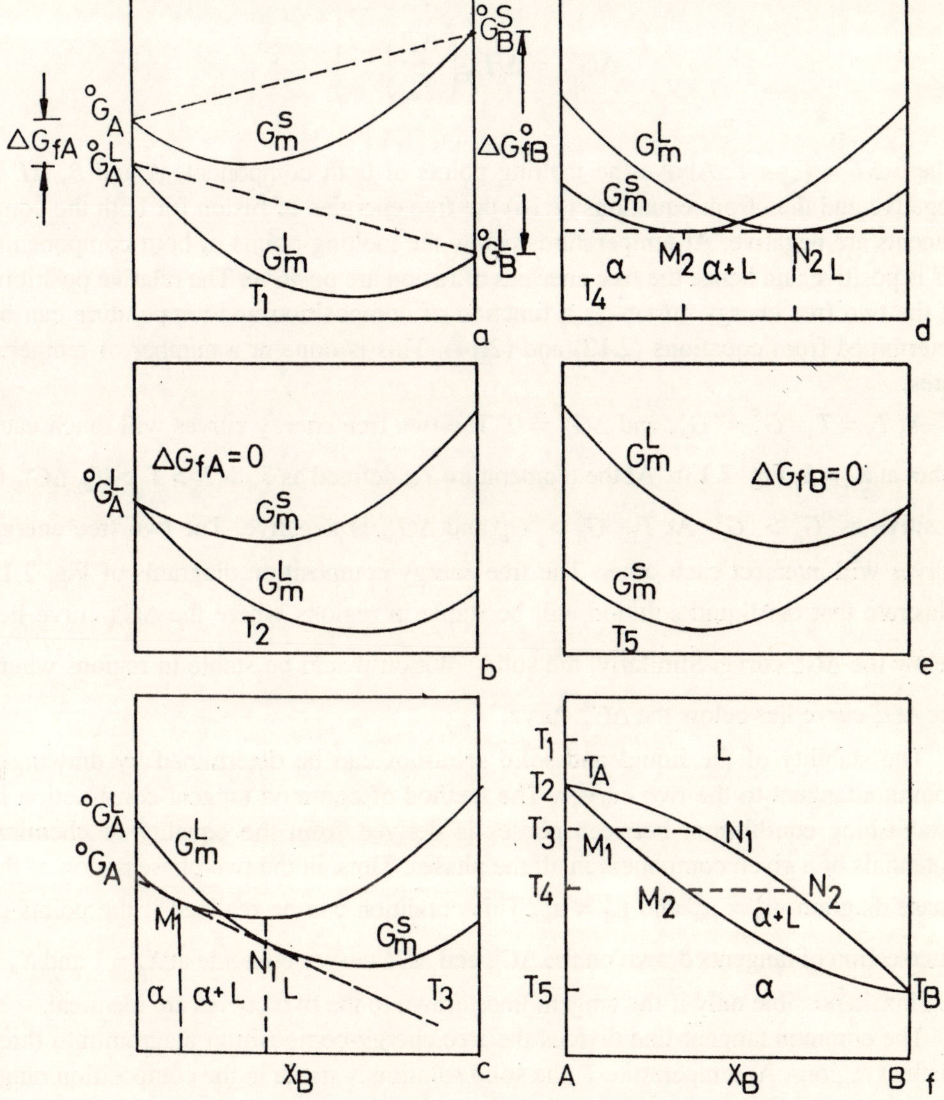

Fig. 2.13 Free energy-composition diagrams (a-e) and phase diagram (f)

$$\left.\begin{aligned}\Delta G_{fA}^{0} &= \Delta H_{fA}^{0}\left(\frac{\Delta T}{T_m}\right)\\ \Delta G_{fB}^{0} &= \Delta H_{fB}^{0}\left(\frac{\Delta T}{T_m}\right),\end{aligned}\right] \tag{2.16}$$

where $\Delta T = T_m - T$. Above the melting points of both components A and B, ΔT is negative and thus from equations (2.16) the free energies of fusion for both the components are negative. At temperatures below the melting points of both components, ΔT is positive and hence the free energies of fusion are positive. The relative positions of the two free energy curves as a function of composition and temperature can be determined from equations (2.12) and (2.14). This is done at a number of temperatures.

At $T_2 = T_A$, ${}^0G_A^S = {}^0G_A^L$, and $\Delta G_{fA}^0 = 0$. The two free energy curves will touch each other at $X_A = 1$, Fig. 2.13b. At the temperature T_3, defined as $T_A > T_3 > T_4 > T_B$, ΔG_{fA}^0 is positive as ${}^0G_A^L > {}^0G_A^S$. At T_3, ${}^0G_B^S > {}^0G_B^L$ and ΔG_{fB}^0 is negative. The two free energy curves will intersect each other. The free energy composition diagrams of Fig. 2.13 illustrate that the liquid solution will be stable in regions where the ΔG_m^L curve lies below the ΔG_m^S curve. Similarly, the solid solution would be stable in regions where the ΔG_m^S curve lies below the ΔG_m^L curve.

The stability of the liquid and solid solutions can be determined by drawing a common tangent to the two curves. The method of common tangent construction in establishing equilibrium between phases is derived from the equality of chemical potentials of a given component in all the phases. Thus, in the two phase region of the phase diagram, $\mu_A^S = \mu_A^L$ and $\mu_B^S = \mu_B^L$. This condition can be realized if the points of intersection of tangents drawn on the ΔG_m^L and ΔG_m^S curves coincide at $X_A = 1$ and $X_B = 1$. This is possible only if the tangent lines drawn to the two curves are identical.

The common tangent line divides the free energy-composition diagram into three distinct regions. At temperature T_3 the solid solution is stable in the composition range from pure A to the composition point M_1 on the tangent line. The liquid solution is stable in the composition range between point N_1 and pure component B. In the composition range between point M_1 and N_1, the free energy of phase mixtures, represented by any point lying on the line M_1N_1, is lower than the free energy of either solid or liquid solutions. Thus, solid solution (α) of composition represented by the point

M_1 will be in equilibrium with liquid solution, point N_1, Fig. 2.13c.

Similarly, at temperature T_4, defined as $T_3 > T_4 > T_B$, the same above conditions apply. The free energy of fusion of the component A will be more positive at T_4 as compared to the value at T_3, i.e., the two free energy curves will be much more separate at $X_A = 1$. The free energy of fusion of component B will become less negative at T_4. The two free energy curves will move closer to each other at $X_B = 1$ as the temperature approaches the melting point of B, T_B.

The common .angent construction indicates that points M_1 and N_1 are shifted to new positions M_2 and N_2, respectively, as the temperature is lowered from T_3 to T_4. The composition range over which the solid solution is stable is enhanced, Fig. 2.13d. At temperature $T_5 = T_B$ the free energy of fusion for component B is zero, and free energy curves for the solid and liquid solutions will touch each other at $X_B = 1$, Fig. 2.13e. The phase diagram is constructed by translating compositions corresponding to the points of tangency on a temperature vs. composition diagram, Fig. 2.13f.

Compositions of the α and liquid phases can be determined by applying equality of chemical potential between two phases in equilibrium, i.e.,

$$\frac{\partial \Delta G_m^S}{\partial X_B} = \frac{\partial \Delta G_m^L}{\partial X_B}. \tag{2.17}$$

Differentiation of ΔG_m^S and ΔG_B^L with respect to X_B and substituting into (2.17) yields,

$$-\Delta G_{fB}^0 + RT \ln (X_B^S/X_A^S) = -\Delta G_{fA}^0 + RT \ln (X_B^L/X_A^L)$$

or

$$\Delta G_{fA}^0 - \Delta G_{fB}^0 = RT\,[\ln (X_B^L/X_A^L) - \ln (X_B^S/X_A^S)]. \tag{2.18}$$

Substituting for ΔG_{fA}^0 and ΔG_{fB}^0 from equation (2.16) into (2.18) yields,

$$\Delta H_{fA}^0\left(1-\frac{T}{T_A}\right) - \Delta H_{fB}^0\left(1-\frac{T}{T_B}\right) = RT\,[\ln (X_B^L/X_A^L) - \ln (X_B^S/X_A^S)] \tag{2.19}$$

Equation (2.19) has two unknown composition variables which can be solved with the following approximation.

As the temperature, $T \to T_A$, $X_A^S \to 1$ and $X_A^L \to 1$. Hence near T_A,

$$-\frac{\Delta H^0_{fB}}{R}\left(\frac{1}{T}-\frac{1}{T_B}\right) = \ln\,(X^L_B/X^S_B) \qquad (2.20a)$$

Similarly, as $T \to T_B$, $X^L_B \to 1$, and $X^S_B \to 1$.

Hence near T_B,

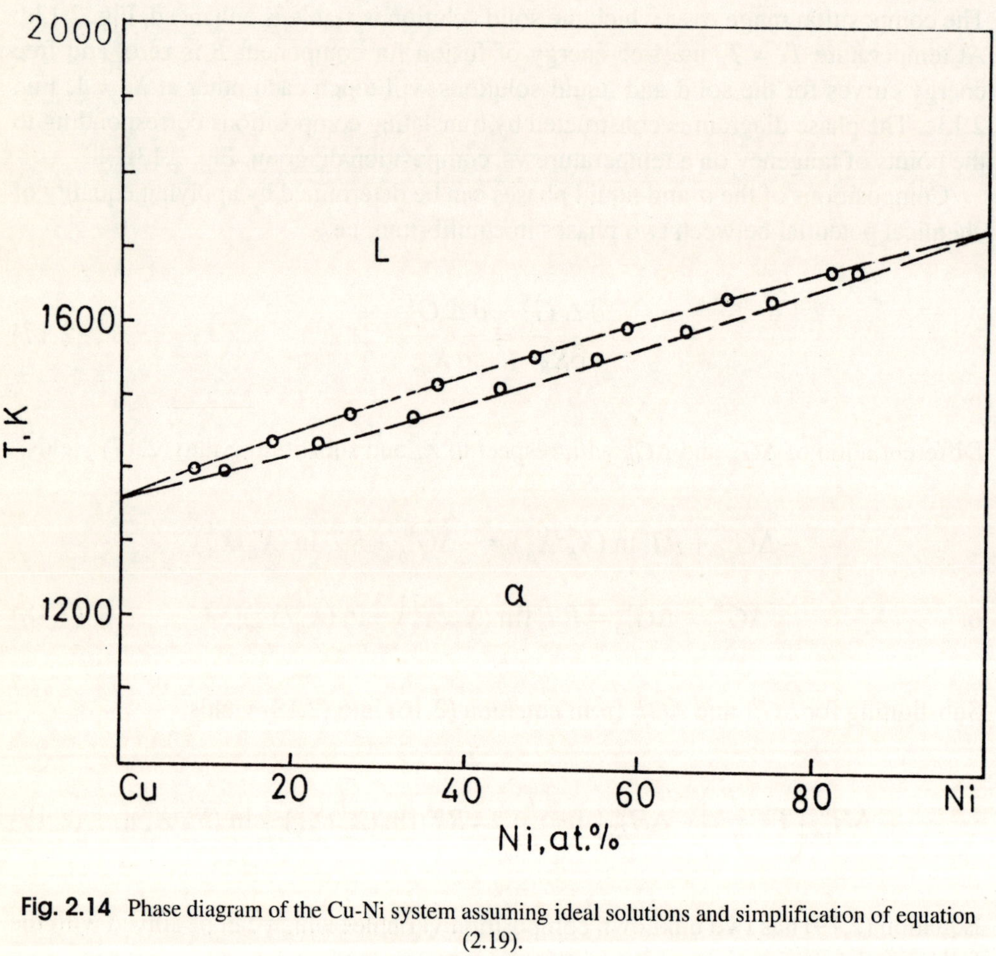

Fig. 2.14 Phase diagram of the Cu-Ni system assuming ideal solutions and simplification of equation (2.19).

$$-\frac{\Delta H^0_{fA}}{R}\left(\frac{1}{T}-\frac{1}{T_A}\right) = \ln\,(X^L_A/X^S_A) \tag{2.20b}$$

From enthalpies of fusion and melting temperatures of the components A and B, equations (2.20) can be solved and the phase boundary compositions X^S_B and X^L_B can be determined. The above calculation has been carried out for the binary system Cu-Ni. The following data are used:

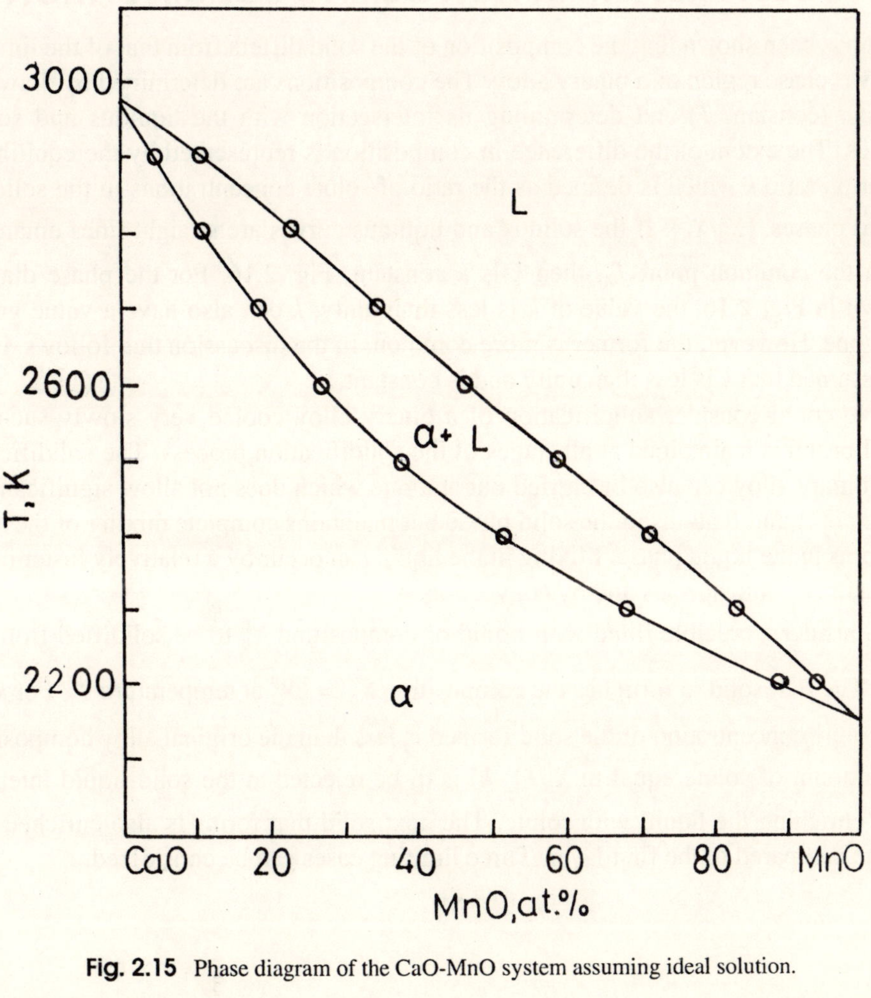

Fig. 2.15 Phase diagram of the CaO-MnO system assuming ideal solution.

$$\Delta H^0_{f\text{Cu}} = 13 \text{ kJmol}^{-1}, \quad T_{\text{Cu}} = 1356.5 \text{ K}$$

$$\Delta H^0_{f\text{Ni}} = 17.5 \text{ kJmol}^{-1}, T_{\text{Ni}} = 1726 \text{ K}$$

The data are plotted in Fig. 2.14 and compared with the actual phase diagram (open circles).

A similar calculation has been carried out for the binary system CaO–MnO. The results are shown in Fig. 2.15.

2.8 SOLUTE REDISTRIBUTION DURING SOLIDIFICATION

It has been shown that the composition of the solid differs from that of the liquid in the two phase region of a binary alloy. The compositions are determined by drawing a tie-line (constant T) and determining its intersection with the liquidus and solidus curves. The extent of the difference in composition is represented by the equilibrium partition ratio k which is defined as the ratio of solute concentrations in the solid and liquid phases, (X_B^S/X_B^L). If the solidus and liquidus curves are straight lines emanating from the common point T_A, then k is a constant, Fig. 2.16. For the phase diagram shown in Fig. 2.16, the value of k is less than unity; k can also have a value greater than one. However, the former is more common. In the discussion that follows, it will be assumed that k is less than unity and is constant.

We could consider solidification of a binary alloy cooled very slowly such that equilibrium is maintained at all stages of the solidification process. The solidification of a binary alloy can also be carried out at a rate which does not allow significant diffusion of A and B atoms in the solid phase but maintains complete mixing of the A and B atoms in the liquid phase. Mixing in the liquid can occur by a relatively faster rate of diffusion of both species and by convection.

Consider a crucible filled with liquid of composition X_B^0 to be solidified from one end. The first solid to form has the composition $X_B^{\alpha_1} = kX_B^0$ at temperature T_1. For $k < 1$, the solute concentration of the solid formed is less than the original alloy composition. An amount of solute equal to X_B^0 $(1-k)$ is to be rejected at the solid-liquid interface, thus enriching the liquid with solute. The next solid that forms is also enriched with solute compared to the first layer. Three limiting cases can be considered.

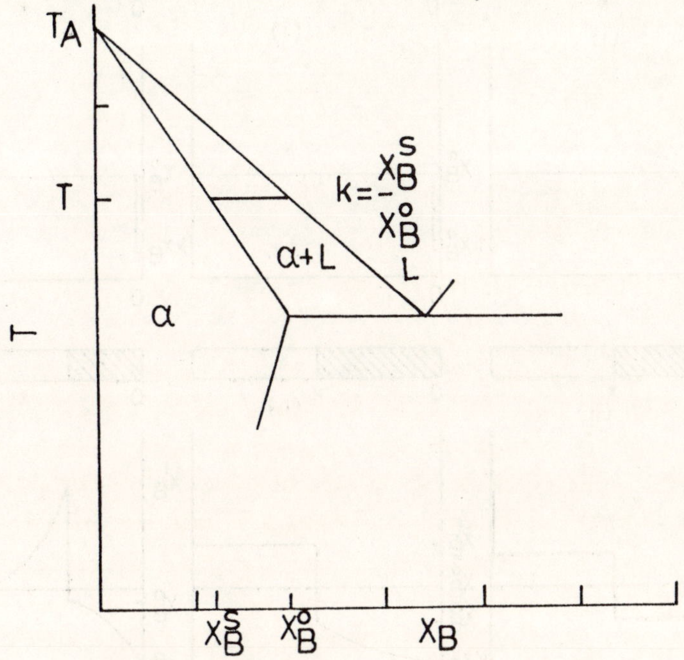

Fig. 2.16 Phase diagram showing the two phase ($\alpha + L$).

(a) Equilibrium Solidification

The first solid to form has composition kX_B^0 as mentioned earlier, Fig. 2.17a. The compositions defined by the phase diagram are maintained at all stages of the solidification process during equilibrium solidification. The excess solute must move away into the liquid which in turn gets enriched with solute. The next solid to form will have the composition $k\,(X_B^0 + \Delta X_B)$. The slow rate of cooling allows sufficient time for the diffusion of solute all the way to the first layer of solid formed. At any given temperature the solid phase is of a uniform composition characteristic of the solidus. The solidification front moves forward with a continuous increase in composition of the solid phase. The solidification process continues till the solidification front moves to the other end of the crucible. The last liquid to solidify has the composition (X_B^0/k). The solid has the uniform composition X_B^0.

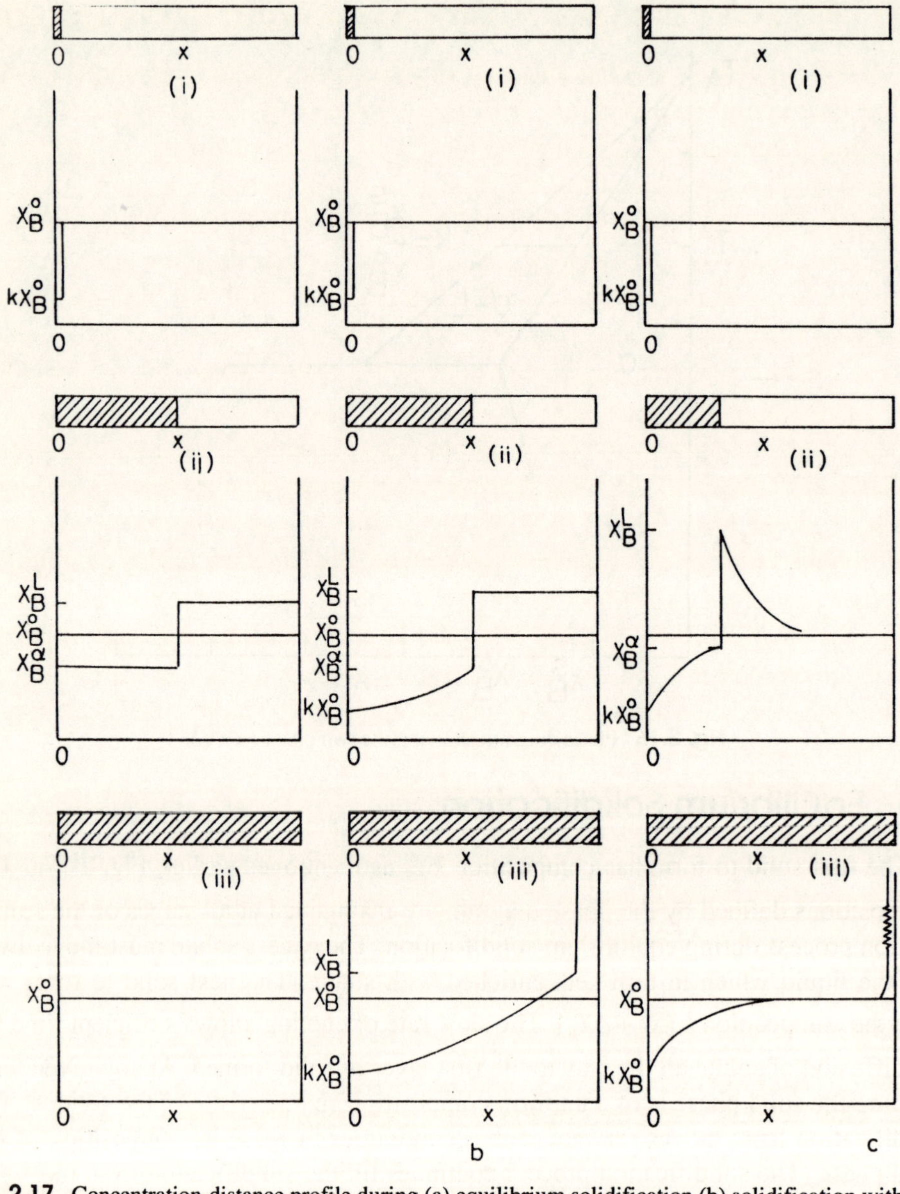

Fig. 2.17 Concentration-distance profile during (a) equilibrium solidification (b) solidification with no diffusion in the solid but complete mixing in the liquid (c) solidification with the conditions of (b) but without convection.

(b) No Solid Diffusion, Complete Mixing in the Liquid

At a faster rate of cooling than that employed for equilibrium solidification, the solute does not get sufficient time to diffuse to the core of the solid phase. The rate of diffusion in the liquid which is three to five orders of magnitude higher than that in the solid, combined with the convection mixing of solute and solvent atoms, may allow uniformity of composition in the liquid phase. The solidification of an alloy under these conditions is of much more practical importance than the one considered in (a).

Consider again the same liquid alloy in a crucible solidifying from one end. The first solid to form has composition $X_B^{\alpha 1} = kX_B^0$. The excess solute rejected at the interface moves away into the liquid thus enriching its solute content. The solid that forms next, therefore, must have a higher solute concentration $k\,(X_B^0 + \Delta X_B)$ where ΔX_B is the small change in composition of the liquid due to a small drop in temperature. The solute concentration of the solid increases continuously along the bar as the solidification front migrates, Fig. 2.17b.The composition of the solid formed at any stage of the solidification process remains unchanged due to slow diffusion rates. The concentration-distance profile of Fig. 2.17b shows increasing solute concentration along the solidified bar. Since the first solid layer has a composition below the original alloy composition, the last layers of solid to form must have a composition well above X_B^0 from mass balance. The solidification front reaches the other end with average composition X_B^0 for the solid phase.

A quantitative expression relating the concentration of solute in the solid to the original alloy composition and fraction of the solid α formed, can be obtained by using mass balance. When a small fraction of the α phase df^α forms from the liquid, the amount of solute rejected is $(X_B^L - X_B^\alpha)df^\alpha$. The solute concentration of the liquid is raised by dX_B^L. Mass balance yields,

$$(X_B^L - X_B^\alpha)\,df^\alpha = f^L\,dX_B^L = (1 - f^\alpha)\,dX_B^L \tag{2.21}$$

Substituting for $X_B^\alpha = kX_B^L$ in equation (2.21) and integrating yields,

$$-\ln(1 - f^\alpha) = \frac{1}{1-k}\ln X_B^L + A, \tag{2.22}$$

where A is the constant of integration. From the initial condition,

$$f^{\alpha} = 0, X_B^{\alpha} = kX_B^0, \quad \text{and} \quad X_B^L = X_B^0, \quad \text{we get,}$$

$$X_B^{\alpha} = kX_B^0 (1 - f^{\alpha})^{k-1}, \tag{2.23}$$

or in terms of the liquid composition,

$$X_B^L = X_B^0 (1 - f^{\alpha})^{k-1} \tag{2.24}$$

These equations are known as the non-equilibrium lever rule or Scheil (1) equation. A comparison with the equilibrium solidification reveals that the average composition of the solid at any given instant will be less when solidification occurs with no diffusion in the solid. The relative amount of the liquid remaining unsolidified will, therefore, be more. The last liquid to solidify will have a composition more than X_B^{α}/k.

(c) No Convection in the Liquid and No Solid Diffusion

In the solidification process (b), it is assumed that the liquid becomes homogeneous by virtue of both diffusion and convection. A third practical case will now be considered where the concentration of solute in the liquid is limited only by diffusion. The mixing of solute in the liquid docs not occur by convection. The solidification process starts with the formation of the α phase of composition kX_B^0 at the left-hand end of the crucible. The rejected solute piles up at the α/L interface. Due to limited mixing by diffusion in the liquid a steep concentration gradient will be built up at the interface. The solute concentration at the interface increases as the interface migrates during solidification. The concentration of solute in the solid that forms also increases, Fig. 2.17c. A situation is reached when the concentration of solute in the liquid reaches a value X_B^0/k at the interface and thus the solid that forms will be of composition $X_B^0 \left(\frac{X_B^0}{k} \cdot k \right)$, which is the original alloy composition.

If the composition of the solid is $X_B^{\alpha} < X_B^0$, then there will be a build up of solute at the solid-liquid interface, modifying the exponential distribution of solute in the liquid such that $X_B^{\alpha} = X_B^0$. In the case where $X_B^{\alpha} > X_B^0$, the growing solid phase will require more solute from the liquid than it can supply from the interface region. The solute is drawn from the far away regions of the liquid. This lowers the exponential distribution of the solute in part of the interface in the liquid. The concentration gradient of solute in the liquid decreases and X_B^α again approaches X_B^0. The solid-liquid interface can only move at a steady state rate and composition of the α phase corresponds to the original alloy composition X_B^0, Fig. 2.17c. Solidification occurs at the temperature T (shown in Fig. 2.17c) corresponding to the solidus at X_B^0.

Under steady state conditions, the flux of solute rejected at the interface is just balanced by the solute moving away from it under the concentration gradient built up at the interface. It is assumed that the diffusion coefficient of solute in the liquid D_L is independent of solute concentration. The solute distribution in the interface region is given by the following differential equation

$$\frac{dX_B^L}{dt} = D_L \frac{d^2 X_B^L}{dx^2} + v \frac{dX_B^L}{dx}. \tag{2.25}$$

Under steady state conditions, $\dfrac{dX_B^L}{dt} = 0$, thus

$$D_L \frac{d^2 X_B^L}{dx^2} + v \frac{dX_B^L}{dx} = 0 \tag{2.26}$$

where x is the distance from the interface and v is the steady state rate of migration of the interface. The solution to the differential equation (2.26) is,

$$X_B^L = A \exp\left(-\frac{v}{D_L} x\right) + B, \tag{2.27}$$

where A and B are constants of integration which can be evaluated from the initial and boundary conditions,

$$X_B^L = \frac{X_B^0}{k} \text{ at the interface, } x = 0 \text{ and } X_B^L = X_B^0 \text{ at } x = \infty$$

The values of A and B are,

$$A = X_B^0\left(\frac{1-k}{k}\right), \text{ and } B = X_B^0,$$

which upon substitution in equation (2.27) relates the growth rate to the distance from the interface and composition as obtained by Tiller et al (2).

$$X_B^L = X_B^0\left[1 + \frac{1-k}{k}\exp\left(-\frac{v}{D_L}x\right)\right]. \tag{2.28}$$

This relationship shows that the liquid composition varies exponentially with distance and (D_L/v) is the characteristic distance at which the composition of the liquid differs from the original alloy composition by $1/e$ of the value $X_B^0\,(1-k)/k$, which is the maximum difference in composition for the steady state growth of the solid.

The concentration-distance profile of the solid α can also be calculated. In order to achieve steady state growth, the solute concentration of the solid must increase continuously (for $k < 1$) from an initial value kX_B^0 to X_B^0 and become asymptotic at X_B^0. This is shown for the two intermediate stages and the final steady state, Fig. 2.18. The shaded areas in Figs. 2.18, b and c, must be equal in order for the solute to be conserved. The initial transient therefore is to the extent that the solidification process reaches a steady state. Solidification proceeds under steady state and it will be maintained if there is sufficient liquid ahead of the interface and v is constant. The presence of liquid ahead of the interface is required for the diffusion of solute which is built up at the interface. This condition is not fulfilled when the growing solid nears the other end. The composition of the solid formed rises above X_B^0 as required by the conservation of solute. The final transient is a narrow region of steep concentration gradient in the solid, Fig. 2.18e.

A solution to the time dependent solute concentration in the solid in the initial transient has been given by Smith et al (3) for $k << 1$ and by Pohl (4) as,

$$X_B^\alpha = X_B^0\,[1 - (1-k)\exp(-kvx/D_L)] \tag{2.29}$$

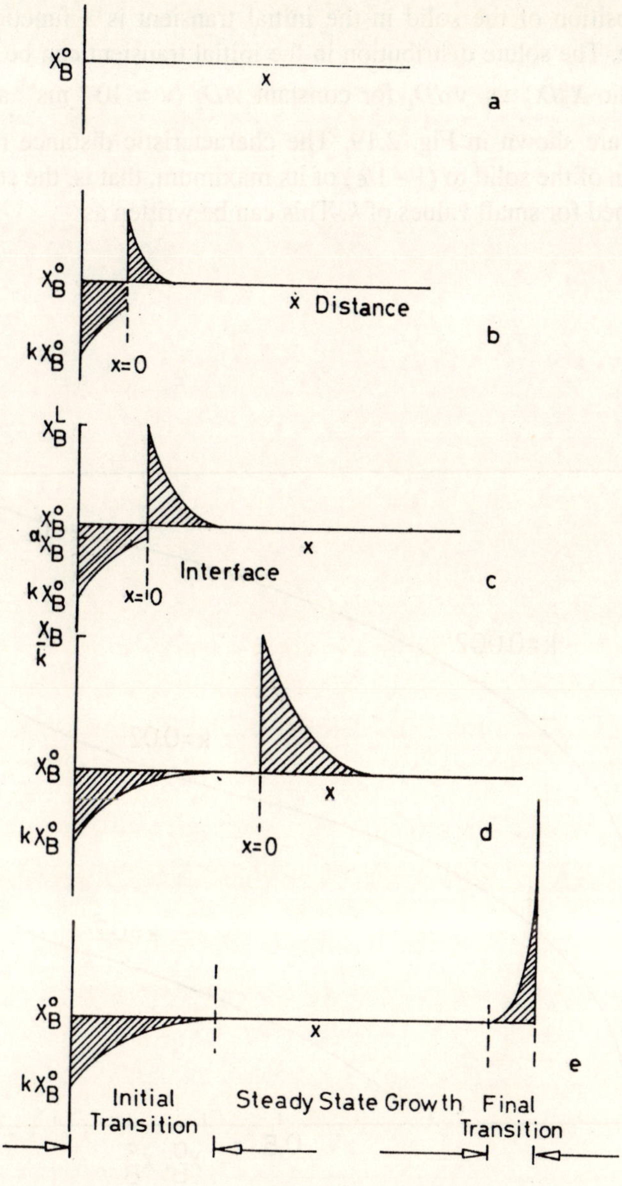

Fig. 2.18 The concentration-distance profile, during initial stages (a), early stages (b-c), steady state (d), and final stages (e) of the solidification process.

The composition of the solid in the initial transient is a function of k, D_L and the growth rate. The solute distribution in the initial transient can be determined by plotting the ratio X_B^α/X_B^0 vs. vx/D_L for constant v/D_L ($v = 10^{-4}$ ms^{-1} and $D_L = 10^{-8}$m^{2}s^{-1}). The result are shown in Fig. 2.19. The characteristic distance required to raise the composition of the solid to $(1 - 1/e)$ of its maximum, that is, the steady state value can be determined for small values of k. This can be written as

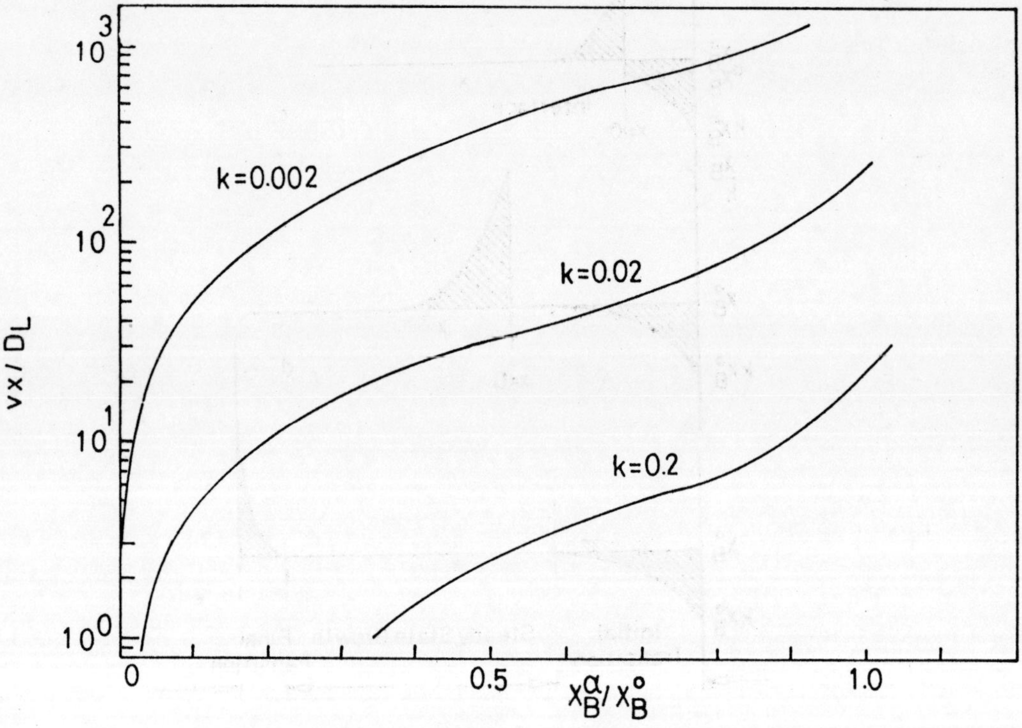

Fig. 2.19 (X_B^α/X_B^0) vs. (vx/D_L) for $k = 0.2$, $k = 0.02$ and $k = 0.002$.

$$X_B^\alpha / X_B^0 = 1 - \frac{1}{e} = 1 - (1-k)\exp(-kvx/D_L) \tag{2.29}$$

or $\quad e^{-1} = (1-k)\exp(-kvx/D_L)$

for small k, $\qquad \dfrac{kvs}{D_L} = 1 \quad \text{or} \quad x = \dfrac{D_L}{kv}$

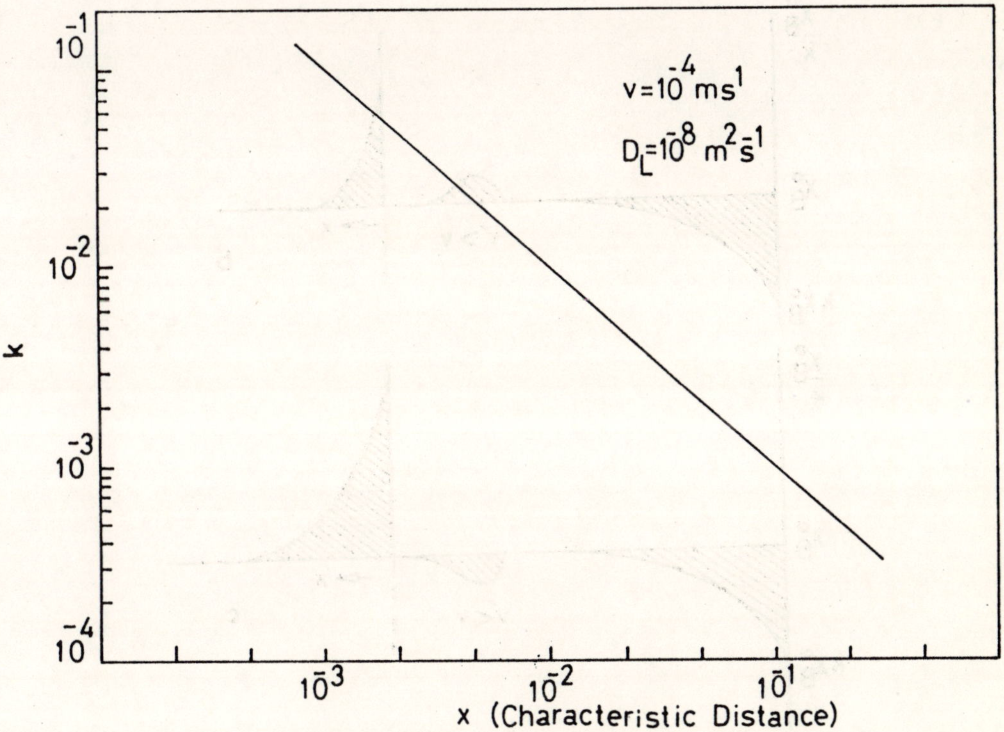

Fig. 2.20 Characteristic distance x vs. k.

For values of k from 10^{-3} to 10^{-1}, the characteristic distance, x, is calculated for v = 10^{-4} ms^{-1} and $D_L = 10^{-8}$ m^{2}s^{-1}, as shown in Fig. 2.20.

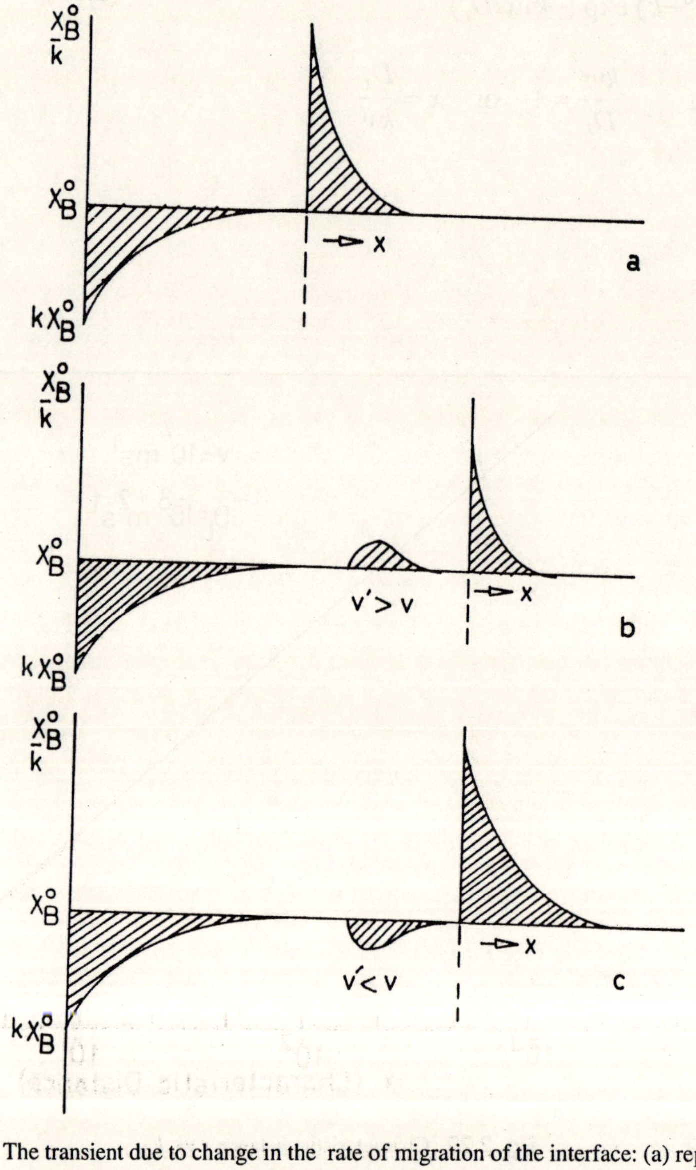

Fig. 2.21 The transient due to change in the rate of migration of the interface: (a) represents the concentration-distance profile at steady state rate v (b) $v' > v$ (c) $v' < v$.

A similar but small transient occurs at the end of the solidification process when liquid very rich in solute solidifies at the other end of the crucible. The length of the final transient is of the order of D_L/v which is the characteristic distance of the solute boundary layer.

Under steady state conditions (v = constant), the amount of solute carried forward is equal to the area under the curve in Fig. 2.21a (cross-hatched). This is proportional to the characteristic distance D_L/v and is therefore inversely proportional to the rate of migration of the solid/liquid interface. If the rate of migration is increased from v to v', the characteristic distance D_L/v' decreases and hence the amount of solute carried forward into the liquid decreases. The excess solute that was present in the liquid next to the interface appears in the solid during the changeover from v to v'. The transient due to change in the rate of migration of the interface is shown in Fig. 2.21.

2.9 ZONE REFINING

In the preceding sections we have observed that a solid growing from either impure liquid or liquid solution rejects solute ($k < 1$) or solvent ($k > 1$). The final transient of the last liquid layer to solidify has very high concentration of solute (for $k < 1$). This property of unidirectional solidification of solutions has been used in refining metals to a high degree of purity. In the zone refining process developed by Pfann (5), a molten small zone is allowed to traverse along the bar from one end to the other.

The concentration-distance profile after the first pass of the zone refining process is shown in Fig. 2.22. The impurity element(s) present in the metal to be purified accumulates at one end of the bar which can be rejected. If the distribution coefficient is very small (of the order of 10^{-5} to 10^{-6}) a high degree of purity is obtained in just one pass. However, for values of k close to unity a large number of zone refining passes would be required to achieve acceptable levels of purity. A substantial part of the bar would be rejected in the process.

The solute distribution along the bar can be determined until the final transient is reached by a simple mass balance of solute entering and leaving the zone. For a bar of an initially uniform composition X_B^0 the solute distribution is given by

$$X_B^{\alpha} = X_B^0\,(1 - (1 - k)\exp(-kx/l)) \tag{2.30}$$

which is obtained by substituting $l = D_L/v$ in equation (2.29), where l is the zone length. If a second zone is traversed along the bar in the same direction as the first,

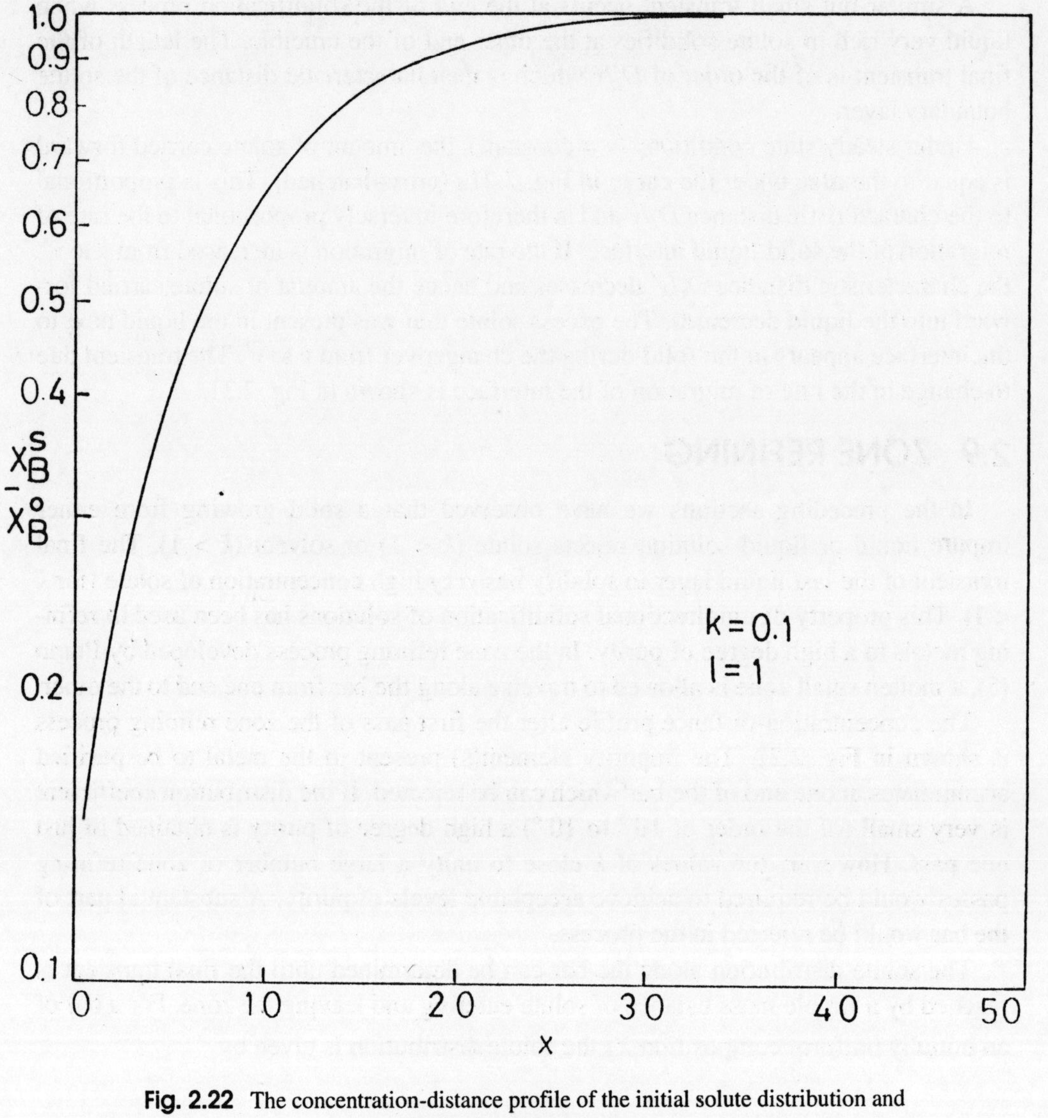

Fig. 2.22 The concentration-distance profile of the initial solute distribution and distribution after one pass.

further depletion of solute ($k < 1$) will occur. This will continue with successive passes till a satisfactory level of purity is obtained. The solute distribution along a bar after 10 passes is shown in Fig. 2.23 for an alloy system with $k = 0.1$ and $l = 1$ unit.

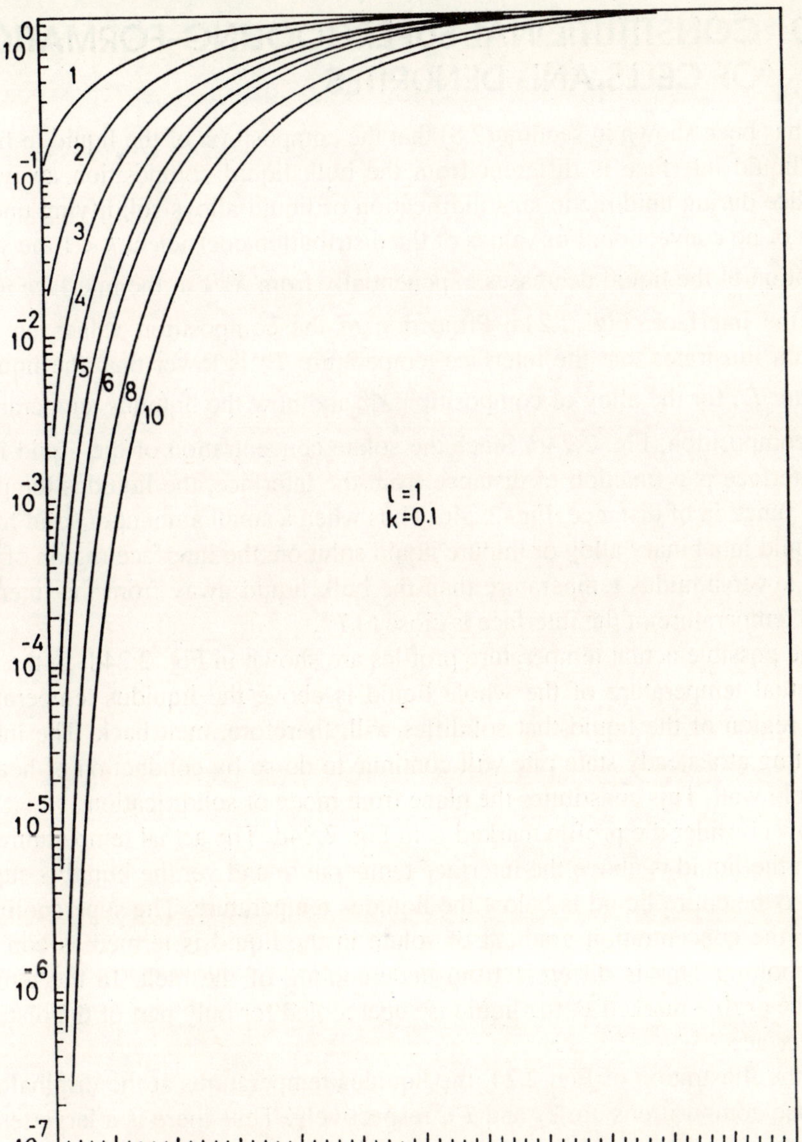

Fig. 2.23 The concentration distance profile after passes of $n = 1, 2, 3, 4, 5, 6, 8$ and 10 zones. $k = 0.1$ and zone length $l = 1$ unit. The distance is in multiples of zone length.

2.10 CONSTITUTIONAL SUPERCOOLING-FORMATION OF CELLS AND DENDRITES

It has been shown in section (2.8) that the composition of the liquid in front of the solid/liquid interface is different from the bulk liquid composition away from the interface during unidirectional solidification of liquid alloys solidifying under a condition of no convection. For values of the distribution coefficient $k < 1$ the solute concentration of the liquid decreases exponentially from X_B^0/k at the interface to X_B^0 away from the interface, Fig. 2.24a. Projection of the composition values on the phase diagram illustrates that the interface temperature T^* is lower than the liquidus temperature T_L, for the alloy of composition X_B^0, and how the liquidus temperature varies with composition, Fig. 2.24b. Since the solute concentration of the liquid in front of the interface is a function of distance from the interface, the liquidus temperature is also a function of distance, Fig. 2.24c. Thus when a small amount of solid forms from the liquid in a binary alloy or impure liquid solution, the interface region of the liquid has a lower liquidus temperature than the bulk liquid away from the interface. The actual temperature of the interface is close to T^*.

The possible actual temperature profiles are shown in Fig. 2.24d. In the profile *A*, the actual temperature of the whole liquid is above the liquidus temperature. Any small region of the liquid that solidifies will, therefore, melt back. The interface, if migrating at a steady state rate will continue to do so by conduction of heat through the mold wall. This constitutes the plane front mode of solidification.

Now consider the profile marked *C* in Fig. 2.24d. The actual temperature distribution in the liquid is above the interface temperature and yet the liquid is supercooled because the entire liquid is below the liquidus temperature. The supercooling arising due to the concentration gradient of solute in the liquid is termed as constitutional supercooling. This is different from undercooling of the melt. In the temperature-distance profile marked *B*, the liquid is supercooled for only part of the distance from the interface.

In the illustration of Fig. 2.24, the liquidus temperatures at the original alloy and interface compositions are T_L and T^*, respectively. Thus there is a large temperature interval over which solidification can occur due to constitutional supercooling. The temperature range can vary from a few tens of degrees to a few hundreds of degrees Celsius. Such large temperature intervals are not necessary because instability of the planar interface is set up by a small fraction of the available constitutional supercooling as observed in a large number of alloy systems.

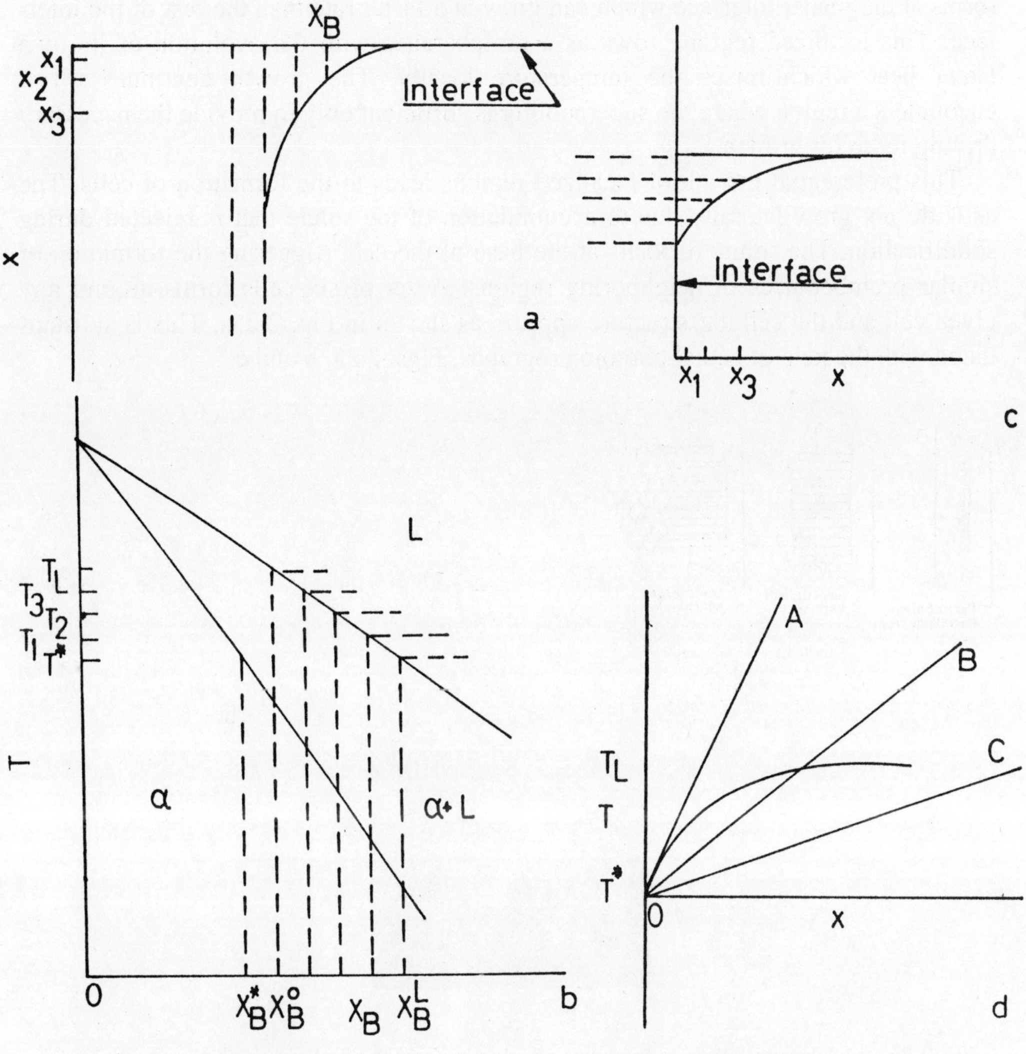

Fig. 2.24 (a) Concentration of solute in the liquid vs. distance (b) temperature vs. concentration (c) liquidus temperature vs. distance (d) temperature vs. distance profiles: *A*-growth of planar interface, *B* and *C* growth of cellular structure due to instability of the planar interface.

Consider a planar interface that has formed when a small amount of liquid has solidified. If a localized region of the planar interface advances ahead of the interface, it finds itself in a supercooled environment and does not disappear. A protuberance forms at the planar interface which can grow at a faster rate than the rest of the interface. This localized region grows as a protuberance with the evolution of its own latent heat which raises the temperature locally. The growth continues till it encounters a region where the supercooling is sufficient only to provide the necessary driving force for growth.

This preferential growth of localized regions leads to the formation of cells. The cells do not grow laterally due to accumulation of the solute that is rejected during solidification. The solute deposits at the base of the cell, triggering the formation of similar protuberances in neighboring regions. A set of six cells forms around any given cell and the cellular structure appears as shown in Fig. 2.25a. This is substantiated with the help of actual photomicrographs, Figs. 2.25, b and c.

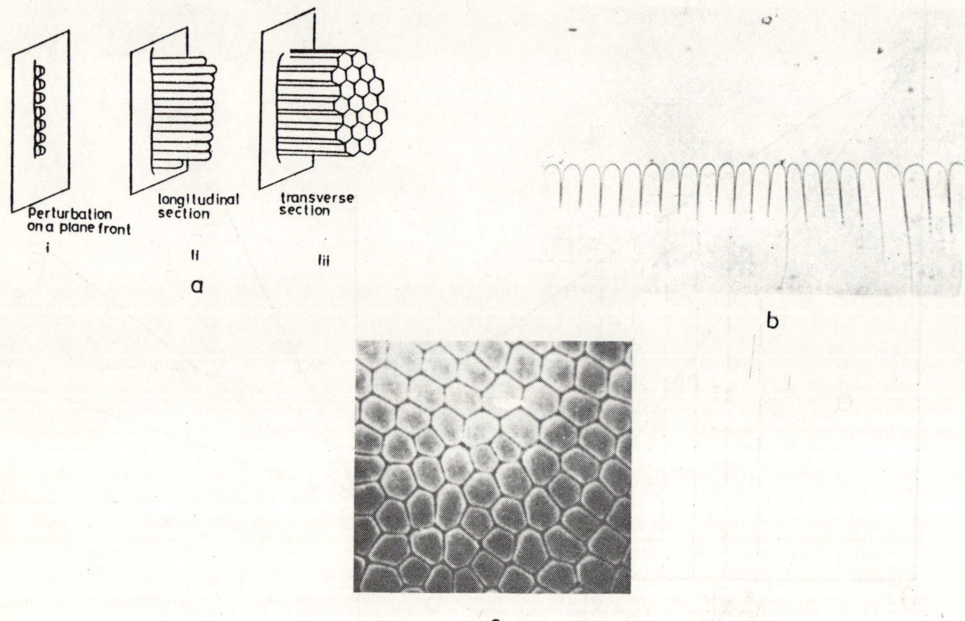

Fig. 2.25 (a) Schematic showing formation of cells, (b) Growth of cells in a transparent organic liquid, carbon tetrabromide (after Jackson, K.A. & J.D. Hunt, Acta Metall, 13 (1965), 212), (c) Optical photomicrograph showing cellularly solidified Pb-Sb alloy (after Morris, L.R. & W.C. Winegard, *J. Crystal Growth*, 5 (1969), 361).

The first quantitative description of the constitutional supercooling criterion was developed by Tiller, Jackson, Rutter and Chalmers (2). This was based on the cell-formation theory of Rutter and Chalmers (6). The theory is based on the heat and mass balance at the interface. The flux of solute in the liquid can be determined from the concentration gradient of solute that is built up when a small amount of the α phase forms. From Fick's law, we can write

$$J_1 = -\frac{D_L}{V_m}\left(\frac{dX_B^L}{dx}\right)_{x=0} \tag{2.31}$$

where D_L is the diffusion coefficient of solute in the liquid, V_m is the molar volume of the liquid, and (dX_B^L/dx) is the concentration gradient at the interface. This must be balanced by the flux of solute rejected.

$$J_2 = \frac{v}{V_m}(X_B^L - X_B^\alpha) \tag{2.32}$$

where v is the rate of growth of the interface. The balance of J_1 and J_2 yields

$$v\,(X_B^L - X_B^\alpha) = -D_L\left(\frac{dX_B^L}{dx}\right)_{x=0} \tag{2.33}$$

The equilibrium liquidus temperature is a function of solute concentration; thus, we can write at the interface,

$$T_L^{\cdot} = \left(\frac{dT_L}{dx}\right)_{x=0} = \left(\frac{dT_L}{dX_B^L}\right)\left(\frac{dX_B^L}{dx}\right)_{x=0} \tag{2.34}$$

where (dT_L/dx) is the slope of the liquidus temperature vs. distance curve and (dX_B^L/dx) is the slope of the solute concentration vs. distance curve, both evaluated at the interface, i.e., $x = 0$. (dT_L/dX_B^L) is the slope of the liquidus line. Constitutional supercooling is absent when the actual temperature gradient in the liquid G_L is equal to or greater than $(dT_L/dx)_{x=0}$. The plane front is stable when

$$G_L \geq \frac{dT_L}{dx},$$

or

$$\geq \left(\frac{dT_L}{dX_B}\right)\left(\frac{dX_B}{dx}\right)_{x=0},$$

or

$$\geq -\left(\frac{dT_L}{dX_B}\right)\frac{v}{D_L}(X_B^L - X_B^\alpha), \quad \text{from} \quad (2.33)$$

or

$$\frac{G_L}{v} \geq -\left(\frac{dT_L}{dX_B}\right)\frac{X_B^L - X_B^\alpha}{D_L} \tag{2.36}$$

Substituting for $X_B^L = X_B^\alpha/k$ in equation (2.36) gives the following result:

$$\frac{G_L}{v} \geq -\left(\frac{dT_L}{dX_B}\right)\frac{X_B^0}{D_L}\frac{(1-k)}{k} \tag{2.37}$$

At steady state growth under conditions of no convection in the liquid, the composition of the α phase equals the original alloy composition X_B^0. The general condition for constitutional supercooling is that the plane front is stable when

$$\frac{G_L}{v} \geq -\left(\frac{dT_L}{dX_B}\right)\cdot\frac{X_B^0}{D_L}\left(\frac{1-k}{k}\right) \tag{2.38}$$

2.11 FORMATION OF DENDRITES

A planar solid-liquid interface is observed during solidification of a pure metal under normal cooling conditions. The solid-liquid interface can be planar, cellular or dendritic depending upon the conditions of solidification and the alloy system under consideration. Direct observation of the solid-liquid interface has been made during solidification of organic liquids which solidify like metals and a comparison made with the resulting microstructure of solidified alloys. Accordingly, four distinct types of solidification microstructures have been observed, as shown in Fig. 2.26. These are:

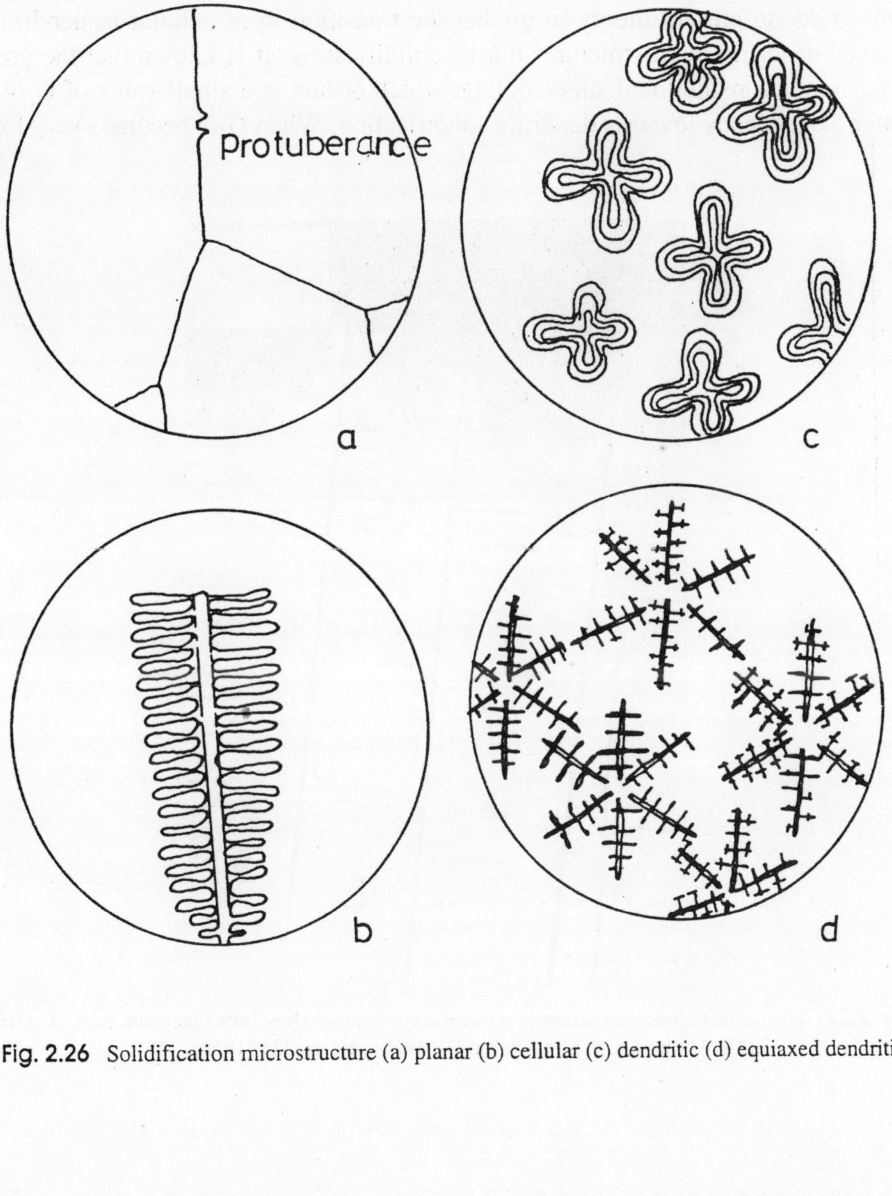

Fig. 2.26 Solidification microstructure (a) planar (b) cellular (c) dendritic (d) equiaxed dendritic.

(i) Planar
(ii) Cellular
(iii) Columnar dendritic
(iv) Equiaxed dendritic

The condition for the breakdown of the planar front is quantitatively given by equation (2.38) and experimentally verified by a number of investigators. The theory predicts closely the transition from plane front to cellular mode of solidification. There exists no present theory to predict the transition from cellular to dendritic to equiaxed dendritic microstructures during solidification. It is known that the greater the degree of constitutional supercooling, which occurs at a small value of G_L/v, the greater the tendency towards dendritic solidification. When G_L/v becomes very low at

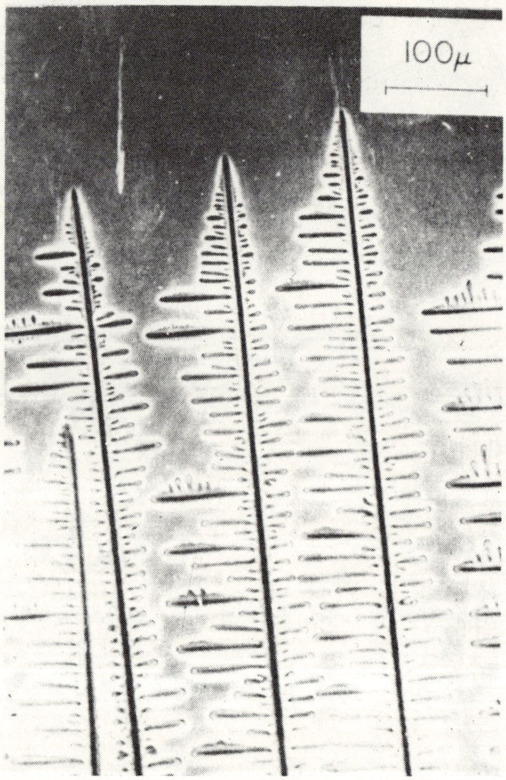

Fig. 2.27 The dendritic microstructure of a transparent organic alloy (after Jackson, K.A., J.D. Hunt, D.R. Uhlmann, & T.P. Seward III, *Trans. AIME*, 236 (1966), 149).

high rates of solidification, the nuclei of the solid form in front of the solid-liquid interface and grow into an equiaxed morphology. The exact reason for such an occurrence is far from clear. It is reasoned, however, that secondary arms form on the cellular or columnar grains for the same reason that lead to the formation of primary arms of the dendrite (cell formation due to constitutional supercooling). If the growth rates are high and the constitutional supercooling large, then protuberances formed on the primary arms become stable and grow as secondary arms of the dendrite. The effect of growth rate on solidification microstructure has also been described in relation to the crystallographic effects that exert an influence on the microstructure. The dendritic structure is shown in Fig. 2.27.

REFERENCES

1. E. Scheil, *Z. Metallk*, 34 (1942), 70.
2. W.A. Tiller, K.A. Jackson, J.W. Rutter and B. Chalmers, *Acta Metall*, 1 (1953), 428.
3. V.G. Smith, W.A. Tiller and J.W. Rutter, *Can. J. Phys.*, 333 (1955), 723.
4. R.G. Pohl, *J. Appl. Phys.*, 25:668 (1954), 1170.
5. W.G. Pfann, *Zone Melting*, 2nd ed. John Wiley and Sons Inc., New York, 1966.
6. J.W. Rutter and B. Chalmers, *Can. J. Phys.*, 31 (1953), 15.

SELECTED PROBLEMS

1. (i) An alloy *A–B* contains 40 at. % B. Calculate wt. % *B* in this alloy.
   (ii) An alloy *A–B* contains 40 wt. % *B*. Calculate at. % *B* in the alloy.
   Given: atomic weights of $A = 30$, $B = 63$.
2. Metals *A* and *B* when mixed together form a binary isomorphous system. An alloy containing 40 at. % *B* when equilibrated at temperature *T* in the two phase region shows 66.66% solid and balance liquid. Another alloy containing 45 at. % *B* shows 33.33% solid when equilibrated at the same temperature *T*. Determine the equilibrium compositions of the liquid and solid phases at the temperature *T*.
3. Metals *A* and *B* when mixed together form a binary isomorphous system. An alloy containing 50 at. % *B* when equilibrated at temperature T shows 50% solid rest liquid. The same alloy when cooled naturally shows 40% cored solid at *T* with average composition of the solid, $X_B^S = 0.35$. Calculate the equilibrium liquidus and solidus compositions at *T*.

4. Draw a series of free energy-composition diagrams to illustrate (a) temperature minimum and (b) temperature maximum in the phase diagram of an isomorphous system.
5. Pure Si and Ge when mixed together form an isomorphous system in the whole range of compositions. Calculate compositions of the α and liquid phases in equilibrium with each other at (a) 1300 K (b) 1400 K and (c) 1500 K. Draw the phase diagram. Assume $C_p(\alpha) = C_p(L)$.

   Given: $\Delta H^0_{f\text{Ge}} = 31.8\ \text{kJmol}^{-1}$, $T_{\text{Ge}} = 1210.4$ K

   $\Delta H^0_{f\text{Si}} = 50.61\ \text{kJmol}^{-1}$, $T_{\text{Si}} = 1685$ K.
6. The oxides of Ni and Mg form an isomorphous system. The entropies of fusion are 23.4 and 25 $\text{Jmol}^{-1}\text{k}^{-1}$ and melting points are 2233 K and 3070 K, respectively, for NiO and MgO. Determine compositions of the solid and liquid phases in equilibrium with each other at 2300 K, 2500 K, 2700 K and 2900 K. Draw the phase diagram. Assume $C_p(\alpha) = C_p(L)$.
7. An Sn-Pb alloy forms a eutectic. However, the Sn–1.1 at. % Pb alloy solidifies as a single phase. In a composition interval of 16.7 at. % Pb, the liquidus temperature drops from 231.9 to 183°C. The composition of the liquidus and solidus are $X^L_{\text{Pb}} = 0.105$ and $X^\alpha_{\text{Pb}} = 0.01$, respectively, at 200°C. Using constitutional supercooling criterion, determine whether the solid will grow as plane front or cells, if the actual temperature gradient in the liquid is (a) $3 \times 10^6\text{Km}^{-1}$ (b) 10^3Km^{-1}. Given: growth rate = 10^{-5} ms^{-1} and $D_L = 10^{-8}\text{m}^2\ \text{s}^{-1}$.
8. an *A–B* alloy containing 0.1% B is zone refined with a zone length of 2 mm. The distribution coefficient is $k = 0.2$ and it is independent of composition. Determine solute concentration in the solid after (a) 2 passes (b) 4 passes at positions 1, 10 and 50 zone lengths along the bar. What fraction of the bar is within 10% of the average composition?
9. A bar of a Ge-Ga alloy containing 0.002 at. % Ga is solidified at a steady state rate of $5 \times 10^{-5}\text{ms}^{-1}$ under conditions of no diffusion in the solid and negligible convection. Calculate and plot the composition of Ga along the length of the bar. What are the critical and final transient lengths? The diffusion coefficient of Ga in the Ge-Ga liquid alloy is $5 \times 10^{-9}\text{m}^2\text{s}^{-1}$ and it is independent of composition. Takè $k = 0.15$.

10. Draw the concentration-distance profile during zone refining of an alloy A–B with distribution coefficient of solute $k = 2$. Use the rest of the data from problem 8.

Chapter 3

BINARY EUTECTIC, PERITECTIC AND METATECTIC SYSTEMS

3.1 BINARY EUTECTIC SYSTEMS

In a binary eutectic system, there is complete solubility of component A in B in the liquid state and vice versa however, the solubility of the two component metals in each other in the solid state is very limited, as indicated by the hypothetical phase diagram, Fig. 3.1. There is a general lowering of the melting point of the two components with a minimum in the liquidus temperature known as the eutectic temperature. The composition at which minimum in the liquidus occurs is known as the eutectic composition.

In the eutectic phase diagram shown in Fig. 3.1, there are three two-phase regions, i.e., $(\alpha + L)$, $(\beta + L)$ and $(\alpha + \beta)$, three single-phase regions, α, β and L, and a three-phase region, $(\alpha + \beta + L)$, occurring at the eutectic reaction isotherm. The α and β

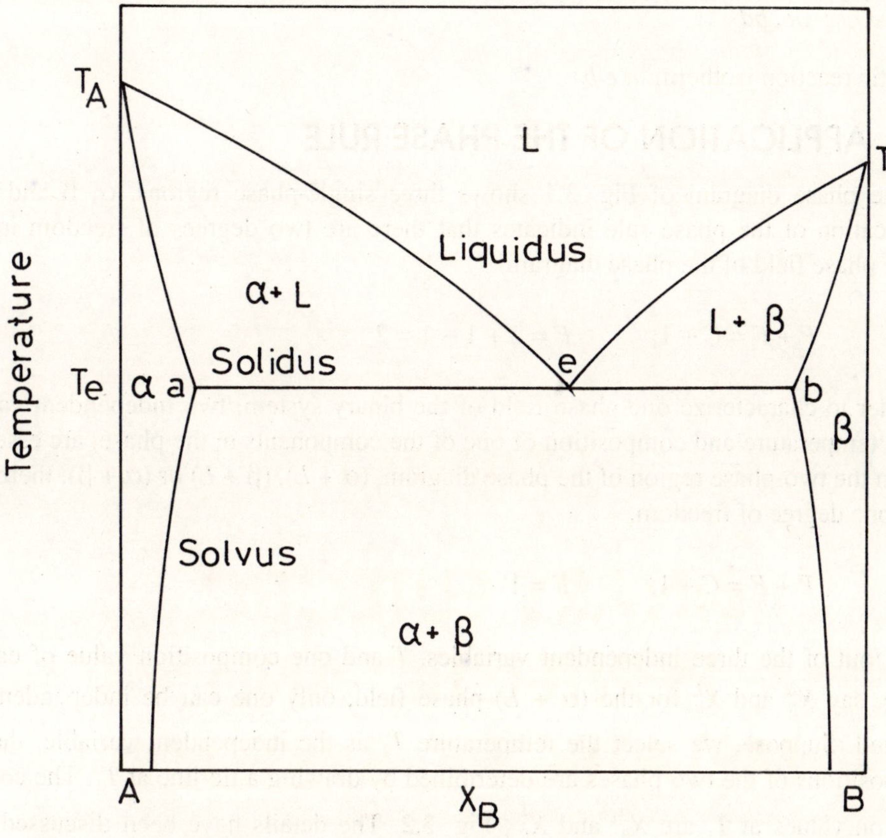

Fig. 3.1 Binary phase diagram showing the eutectic reaction between components *A* and *B*. T_A and T_B are melting points of pure *A* and *B*, respectively.

phases are solid solutions of *B* in *A* and *A* in *B*, respectively. The α phase has the crystal structure of pure *A* and the β phase that of pure *B*.

The (α + *L*) phase region is made up of tie-lines joining the conjugate liquid and solid phases, *L* and α, respectively. Similarly, the (β+*L*) phase region is made up of tie-lines joining the conjugate phases, liquid and β, represented by composition points on the liquidus and solidus, respectively. These two phase regions are analogous to the two phase region, (solid + liquid), of the isomorphous system. There is an additional two phase region comprising of two solid phases α and β. The phase diagram is represented by the following boundaries:

Liquidus : T_Ae, T_Be
Solidus : T_Aa, T_Bb
Solvus : ac, bd

Eutectic reaction isotherm: $a\ e\ b$

3.2 APPLICATION OF THE PHASE RULE

The phase diagram of Fig. 3.1 shows three single-phase regions, α, β and L. Application of the phase rule indicates that there are two degrees of freedom in a single phase field of the phase diagram:

$$P + F = C + 1, \qquad F = 2 + 1 - 1 = 2$$

In order to characterize one phase field of the binary system, two independent variables, temperature and composition of one of the components in the phase, are essential. In the two-phase region of the phase diagram, $(\alpha + L)$, $(\beta + L)$ or $(\alpha + \beta)$, there is only one degree of freedom.

$$P + F = C + 1, \qquad F = 1$$

Thus, out of the three independent variables, T and one composition value of each phase, say X_B^{α} and X_B^{L} for the $(\alpha + L)$ phase field, only one can be independently selected. Suppose, we select the temperature T_1 as the independent variable, then, compositions of the two phases are determined by drawing a tie-line at T_1. The composition values at T_1 are $X_B^{\alpha_1}$ and $X_B^{L_1}$, Fig. 3.2. The details have been discussed in Chapter 2. The three-phase equilibrium has been shown in the phase diagram as line *aeb*. Application of the phase rule indicates that it is an invariant, i.e., there are zero degrees of freedom.

$$P + F = C + 1, \quad F = 2 + 1 - 3 = 0$$

The temperature T_e and composition of the three phases, X_B^{α} (point a), X_B^{L} (point e), and X_B^{β} (point b), are fixed.

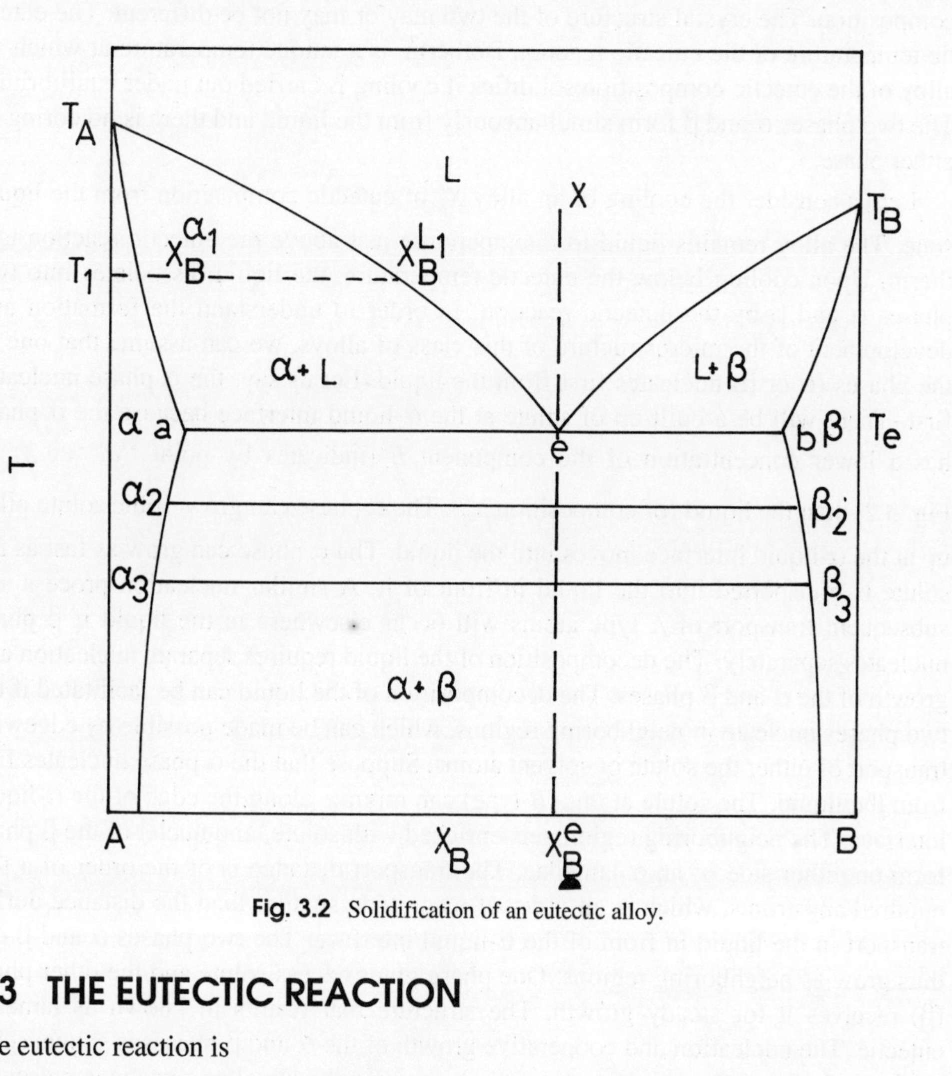

Fig. 3.2 Solidification of an eutectic alloy.

3.3 THE EUTECTIC REACTION

The eutectic reaction is

$$L \underset{\text{heating}}{\overset{\text{cooling}}{\rightleftharpoons}} \alpha + \beta$$

An alloy of the eutectic composition dissociates into two solid phases α and β upon cooling below the eutectic temperature T_e, Fig. 3.2. The two solid phases will differ in composition. The crystal structure of the two may or may not be different. The eutectic temperature or the eutectic reaction isotherm, is a unique temperature at which an alloy of the eutectic composition solidifies if cooling is carried out under equilibrium. The two phases α and β form simultaneously from the liquid and there is no coring of either phase.

Let us consider the cooling of an alloy X_B^e of eutectic composition from the liquid state. The alloy remains liquid to a temperature just above the eutectic reaction isotherm. Upon cooling below the eutectic temperature, the liquid dissociates into two phases α and β by the eutectic reaction. In order to understand the formation and development of the microstructure of this class of alloys, we can assume that one of the phases (α or β) nucleates first from the liquid. Let us say, the α phase nucleates first. There will be a built-up of solute at the α-liquid interface because the α phase has a lower concentration of the component *B* (indicates by point "*a*" or X_B^a in Fig. 3.2) than the liquid (of composition X_B^e). The α phase can grow if the solute piled up at the α-liquid interface moves into the liquid. The α phase can grow as fast as the solute is transported into the liquid in front of it. A similar nucleation process and subsequent transport of *A* type atoms will occur elsewhere in the liquid if β phase nucleates separately. The decomposition of the liquid requires separate nucleation and growth of the α and β phases. The decomposition of the liquid can be facilitated if the two phases nucleate in neighboring regions, which can be made possible by edgewize transport of either the solute or solvent atoms. Suppose that the α phase nucleates first from the liquid. The solute atoms (*B*-type) can migrate along the edge of the α-liquid interface. The neighboring region gets enriched with solute, and nuclei of the β phase form on either side of an α lamellae. The transport distance is of the order of a few hundred angstroms, which is an order of magnitude smaller than the distance during transport in the liquid in front of the α-liquid interface. The two phases α and β can thus grow as neighboring regions. One phase gives excess solute and the other phase (β) receives it for steady growth. The structure that results in known as lamellar eutectic. The nucleation and cooperative growth of the α and β phases is shown schematically in Fig. 3.3a. (A photomicrograph showing the lamellar eutectic is presented in Fig. 3.4a).

The relative amount of the two phases can be calculated by applying the lever rule. From the phase diagram of Fig. 3.2 the following composition values can be obtained at a temperature just below T_e.

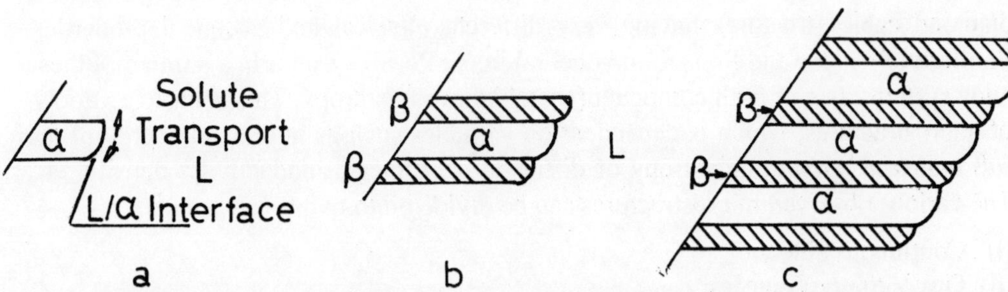

Fig. 3.3 Cooperative growth of eutectics, schematic. The direction of solute transport is shown by arrows in (a).

$$X_{\beta}^{\alpha} = 0.1, \quad X_B^L = X_B^e = 0.6, \quad X_B^{\beta} = 0.9$$

The relative amounts of the α and β phases are

$$\%\,\alpha = \frac{0.9 - 0.6}{0.9 - 0.1} \times 100 = 37.5\%$$

$$\%\,\beta = \frac{0.6 - 0.1}{0.9 - 0.1} \times 100 = 62.5\%$$

With further cooling below the eutectic temperature, compositions of the α and β phases change along the respective solvus lines and there are minor adjustments in the relative amounts of the two phases. This, however, is limited to temperatures lying about 100°C below the eutectic reaction isotherm. At temperature far below the eutectic, the rate of diffusion of the two species becomes very slow and further adjustment, in composition, as well as the relative amounts of the two phases, do not occur. The α and β phases are retained at room temperature as such.

3.4 The Microstructure of Eutectic Alloys

A large number of binary alloy systems show the eutectic reaction. Examples are: Al-Si, Al-Ge, Ag-Si, Ag-Ge, Au-Si, Au-Ge, Pb-Sn, Pb-Sb, Pb-Bi, Cu-Al, Cd-Bi, Mg-Zn, Al-Sn, Cd-Zn, Ag-Cu, Fe-C, etc. The crystal structure of the two component metals vary considerably. For example, Ag and Cu in the Ag-Cu eutectic system are both *fcc*, and Mg-Zn and Cd-Zn systems have both components with *hcp* structures. In contrast, Al is *fcc*, and Si and Ge, of the Al-Si and Al-Ge systems, respectively, are diamond cubic structures having very different physical and chemical properties. Similarly, Pb is *fcc* and Sb is rhombohedral in the Pb-Sb system. In a number of these alloy systems, one or both component metals show anisotropy. This leads to a variety, of microstructures, which is dependent on variables such as interfacial energy of the α/β interface, growth anisotropy of diffusion coefficient, conductivity, density, etc. The various observed microstructures can be divided into two broad groups:

(i) Continuous eutectic
(ii) Discontinuous eutectic

In the continuous group of eutectics, the β phase grows along with the α phase and continuity of individual lamellae or rods has been observed to be maintained to a length of up to 1 cm. In the discontinuous eutectic, the β phase does not grow to significant lengths of the order previously mentioned. Instead, the eutectic forms by repeated nucleation of the β phase from the eutectic liquid. The lamellar, rod shaped and, to a lesser extent, the spiral eutectic microstructures belong to the continuous class. The nodular. Chinese Script and acicular microstructures of the eutectic belong to the discontinuous class.

3.4.1 Continuous Eutectics

3.4.1a Lamellar Eutectic

The most commonly observed microstructure of the eutectic in the binary alloy systems is lamellar in nature. This consists of alternate slabs of the α and β phases (with convex or sometimes concave interface with the liquid while they are growing). The α/β interface, Fig. 3.3, is generally planar and the two phases maintain a rigid habit and orientation relationship with each other. The low index planes and directions of the two phases, match with each other across a common interface with low specific interfacial energy, permitting appreciable growth of the lamellae. The thickness of the lamellae, α or β, is generally very small compared to its length. The lamellar eutectic structure is observed in a large number of alloys. In the Cd-Zn alloy, the basal planes {0001} of Cd and Zn match at the interface. The $\langle 01\bar{1}0 \rangle$ directions of Cd and Zn which are along one of the principal axes are common. This gives a very low energy interface. In the Al-$CuAl_2$ pseudo-binary alloy, {001} plane of Al matches with the {001} plane of $CuAl_2$, and one of the cubic directions, $\langle 100 \rangle$, of the two, matches

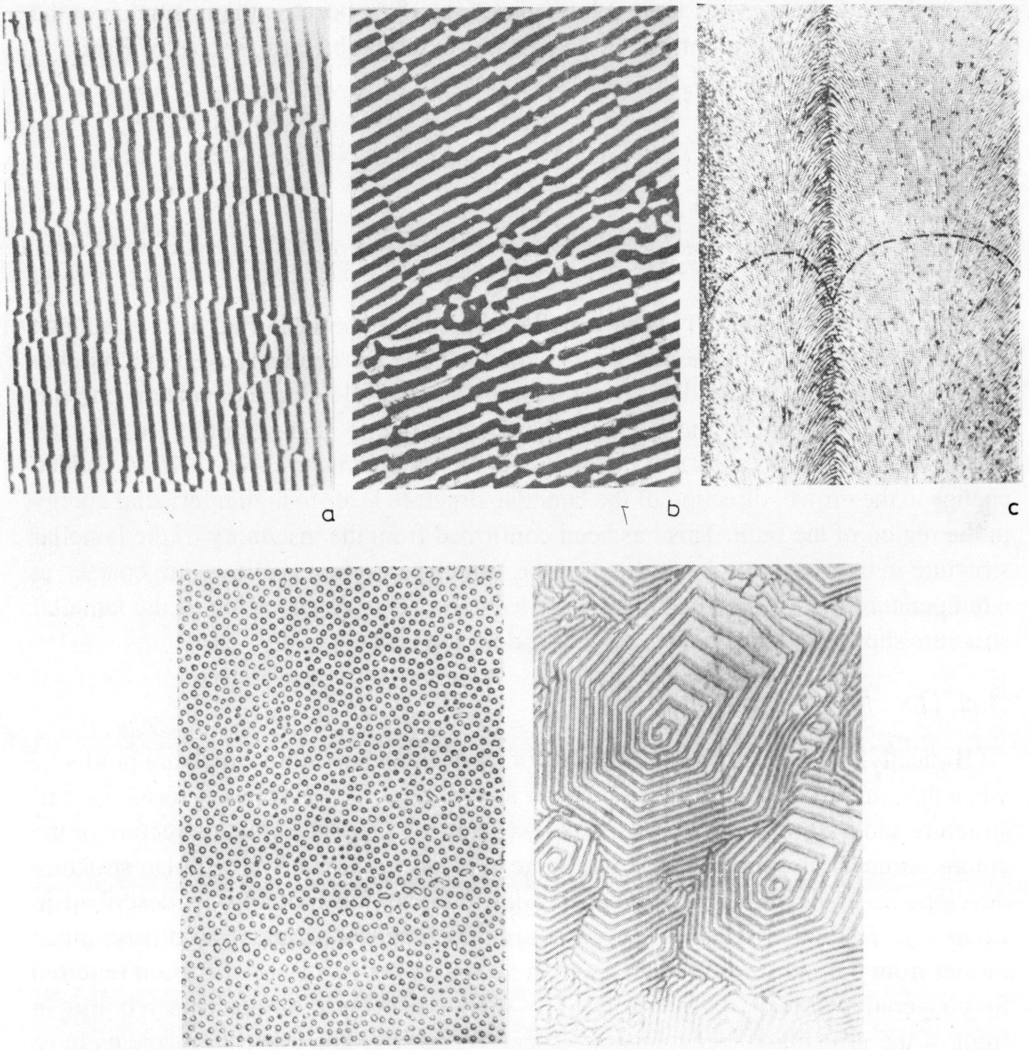

Fig. 3.4 Mircrostructures of continuous eutectic alloys (a) lamellar, Cu-Al alloy (b) lamellar with faults, Cu-Al alloy, (after Kraft, R.W., *Trans. Metall. Soc. AIME*, 224 (1962), 65), (c) cellular structure (after Weart, H.W. & Mack, J.D., Trans. AIME, 212 (1958), 664), (d) rod-type, Ag-Cu alloy (after Chadwick, G.L., ''Eutectic Alloy Solidification'', *Progress in Materials Science*, (ed.) B. Chalmers, Pergamon Press, Oxford (1963), 153), (e) spiral type, Zn-Mg alloy (after Fullman, R.L. & Wood, D.L., *Acta Metall.*, 2 (1954), 188.

with each other thus giving again a low energy interface because the mismatch at the common interface is minimized. In a separate investigation carried out by Kraft (1) the following orientation relationship was observed,

$$\{111\}_{Al} \quad || \quad \{211\}_{CuAl_2}$$

$$[101]_{Al} \quad || \quad [120]_{CuAl_2}$$

An optical photomicrograph of the lamellar structure is shown in Fig. 3.4a. A sudden change in the growth direction of the lamellar eutectic has been observed in a number of alloy systems, which is due to one or more of the following: convection current, impurities, adjustment of the interlamellar spacing due to change in the growth rate, etc. There are growth faults that developed in the microstructure, Fig. 3.4b. A sudden change in the growth direction of the lamellar structure leads to high interfacial energy in the region of the fault. This has been confirmed from the instability of the lamellar structure in the region of the fault when the lamellar structure is allowed to coarsen at a temperature below the eutectic reaction isotherm. The planar region of the lamellar structure shows considerable stability as it does not coarsen easily.

3.4.1b Rod-Type Eutectic

Basically, there are two modifications of the lamellar structure which are produced when the component metals of the eutectic are not pure. These alternate forms are cell structure and rod structure, as described by Chadwick (2). The cellular structure or the colony structure is produced by the same process by which the cellular structure develops in single phase alloys due to constitutional supercooling, as described in Chapter 2. The impurity elements present in the component metals can diffuse much farther from the solid-liquid interface than necessary for the lateral diffusion required for cooperative growth of the eutectic. This gives rise to constitutional supercooling in front of the growing eutectic, leading to cell formation. The impurity elements have very similar distribution coefficients, K (<1), for the two phases, α and β. A photomicrograph showing the cellular structure of the eutectic is presented in Fig. 3.4c from the work of Weart et al. (see in ref. 2).

The rod structure has been described by Chadwick (2) to result from different distribution coefficients of the impurity elements for the two phases of the eutectic. The lamellae of one of the phases, say α, will grow faster than the other phase in the liquid. The other phase β will lag behind and break up into smaller cells. The resulting structure has isolated cylindrical cell morphology of the β phase in a continuous matrix of the α. Although Chadwick (2) has not described the rod-type structure on the basis of interfacial energy, the circular geometry of the rod indicates that the interfacial energy of the α/β interface is independent of orientation in alloy systems where rod-type eutectic structure is observed. This is substantiated from observation of rod-type eutectic in the Ag-Cu system, Fig. 3.4d, in which all planes and directions are observed to be parallel. It is presumed that the presence of impurities modifies the interface to the extent that the interfacial energy is isotropic.

3.4.1c Spiral Eutectic

The spiral eutectic structure has been observed in the Zn-Mg eutectic alloy, Fig. 3.4e. The phase diagram of the alloy system, Fig. 3.5, shows the eutectic composition to be 92.2 at. pct. Zn, and the balance Mg. The eutectic forms between the

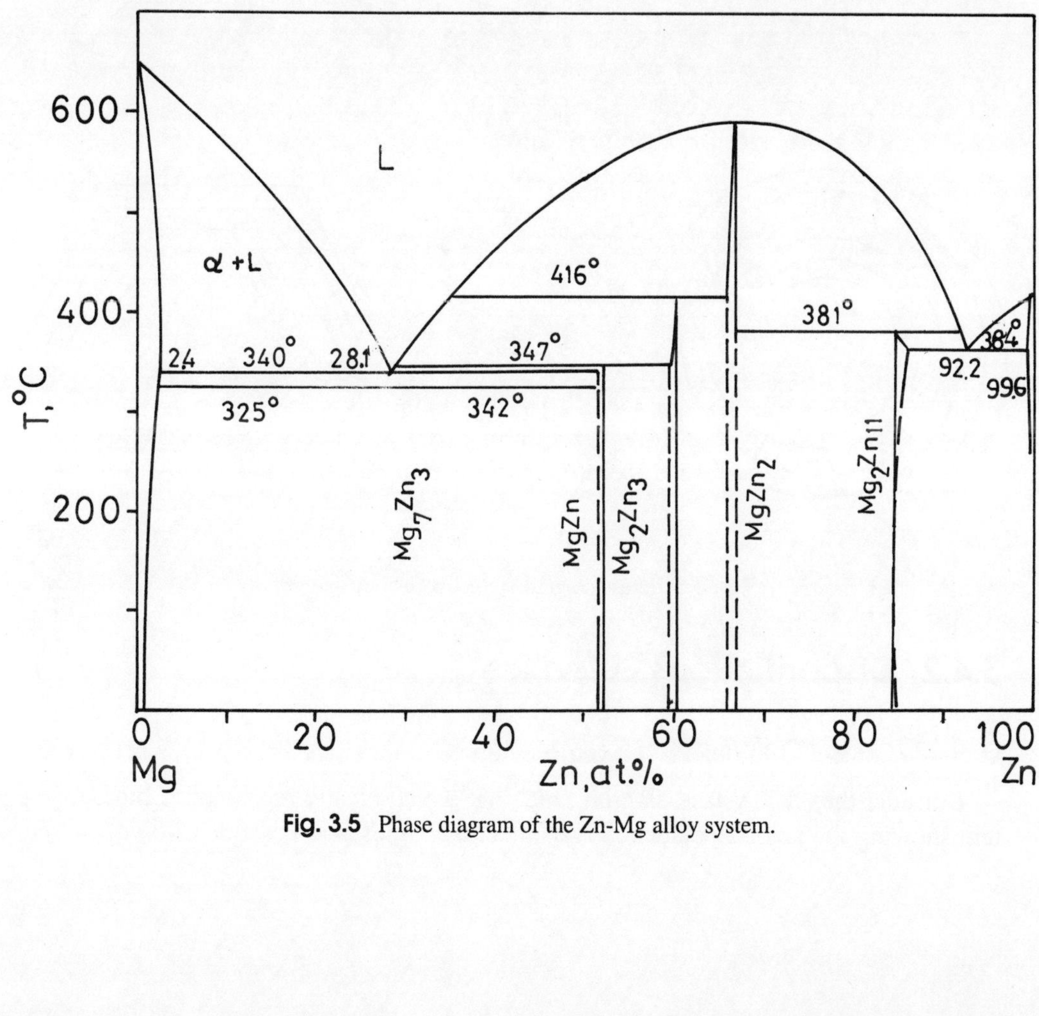

Fig. 3.5 Phase diagram of the Zn-Mg alloy system.

intermediate phase $MgZn_2$ and Zn. In the eutectic microstructure, the β phase forms as a continuous spiral in a hexagonal arrangement. It has been proposed by Fullman and Wood (3) that such a microstructure results from anisotropy of growth of one of the phases. In the Zn-Mg alloy, the zinc-rich phase (α) grows faster than the $MgZn_2$ phase, as shown in Fig. 3.6. This makes the two phases curl up. However, the leading phase (α) does not touch the tail but grows around it in the form of a spiral, as is made obvious from the fact that if the leading and the trailing ends come too close there will be paucity of solute for growth of the β phase. The final microstructure consists of the spiral with double cone.

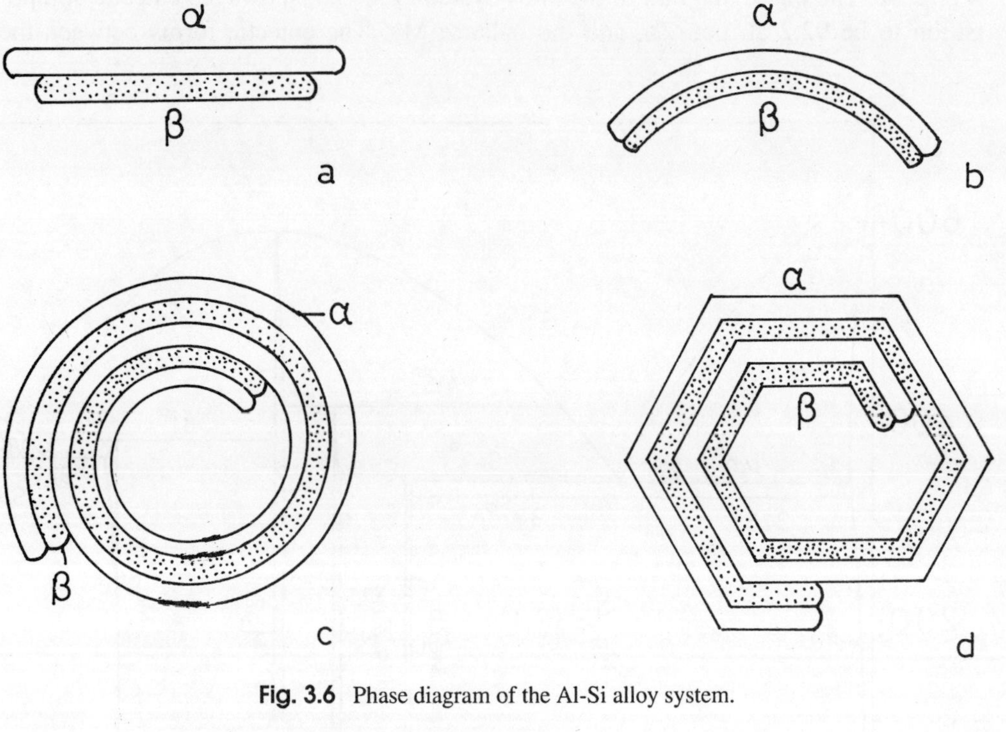

Fig. 3.6 Phase diagram of the Al-Si alloy system.

3.4.2 Discontinuous Eutectics

3.4.2a Acicular Eutectic

Consider the Al-Si phase diagram, Fig. 3.7, which ideally represents a binary system showing the acicular eutectic. The eutectic composition is set at 12.6 wt. pct. Si

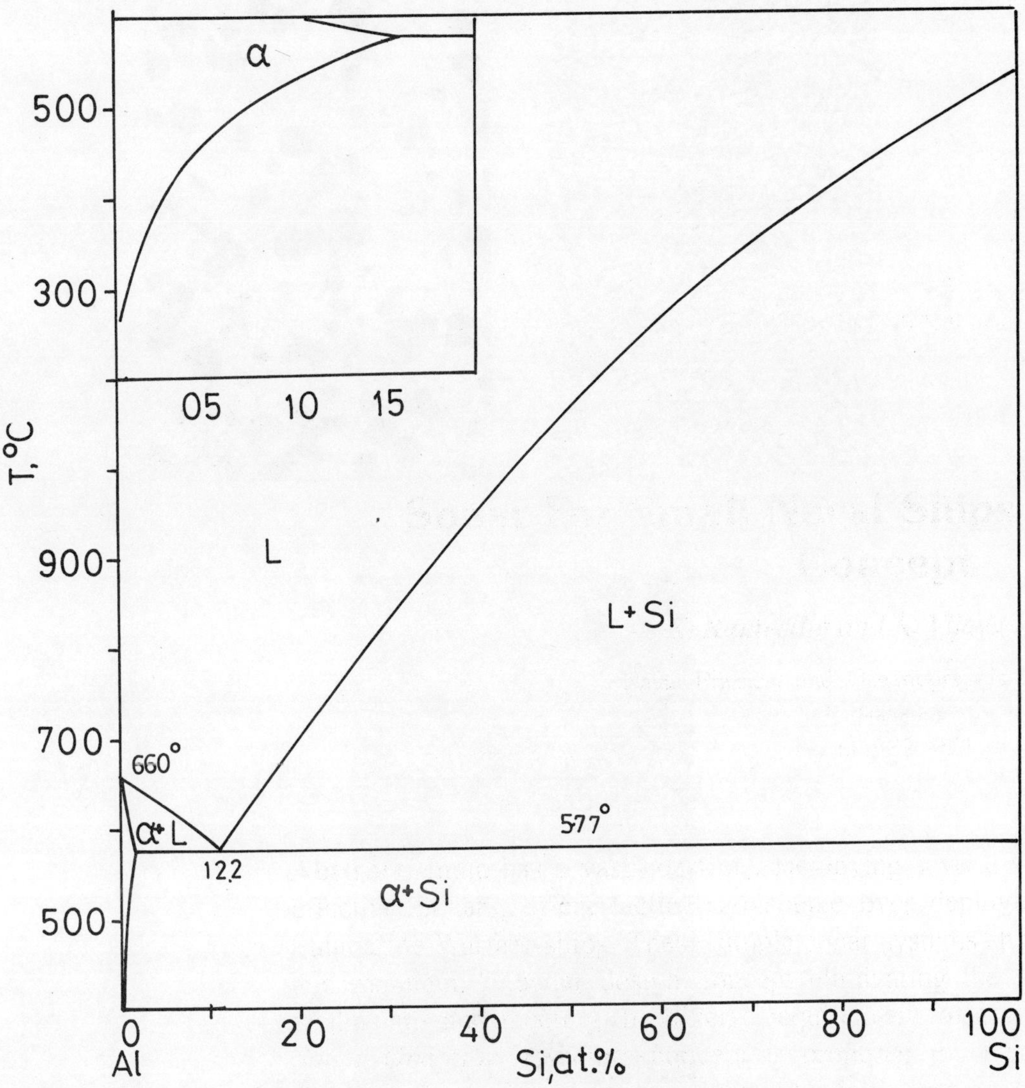

Fig. 3.7 Phase diagram of the Al-Si alloy system.

and the balance Al. The maximum solubility of Al in Si is 0.0016 at. pct. Al and that of Si in Al is 1.5 at. pct. Si, at the equilibrium eutectic temperature of 577°C. The slow cooling of the eutectic liquid produces a structure consisting of plate-shaped particles of Si phase (β) in a continuous matrix of Al-rich solid solution (α), Figs. 3.8a and 3.9.

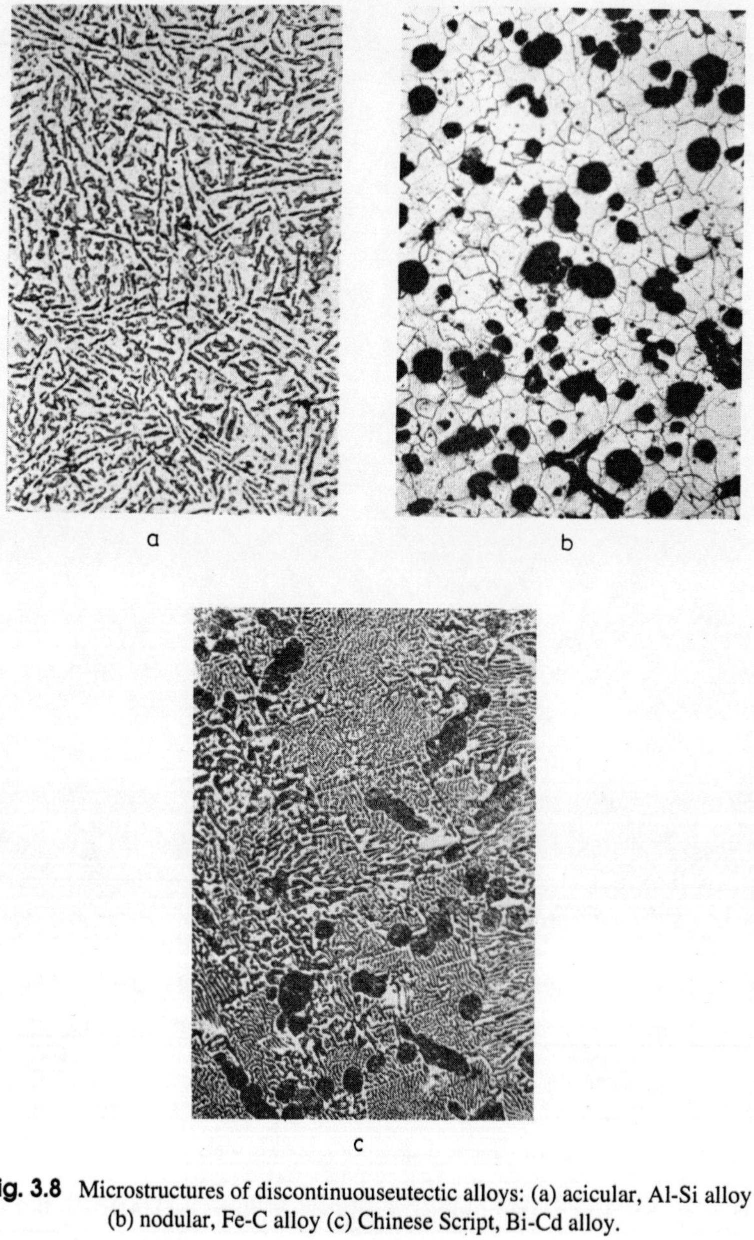

Fig. 3.8 Microstructures of discontinuouseutectic alloys: (a) acicular, Al-Si alloy (b) nodular, Fe-C alloy (c) Chinese Script, Bi-Cd alloy.

The Si plates are bounded by a pair of {111} planes of the Al-rich matrix. The thickness of the plate is very small compared to its length, and most of the plates are isolated and not connected with each other. The plates are distributed randomly in the matrix of the α phase. They remain nearly parallel only in a very small segment of a cell, as the photomicrograph of a slowly cooled Al-Si eutectic alloy illustrates, Fig. 3.8a.

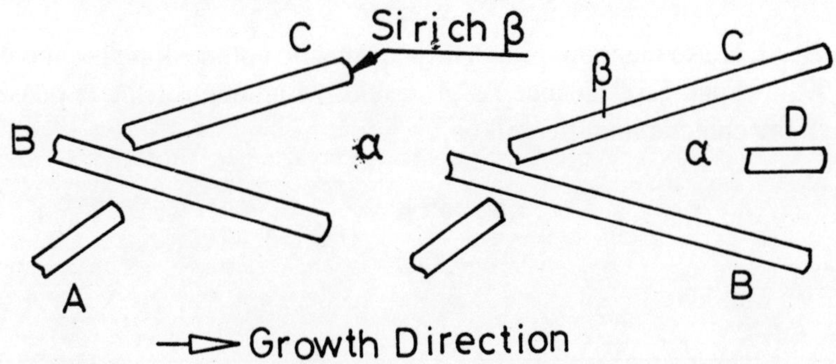

Fig. 3.9 Schematic illustration of the formation of the acicular eutectic.

The acicular eutectic has been proposed by Chalmers (4) to grow due to strong anisotropy in the growth direction. The individual plates grow randomly in the eutectic liquid (shown schematically in Fig. 3.9). The plate marked *A* has grown near the edge of plate *B*, and cannot find the necessary excess solute from the liquid to continue growing. If plates marked *C* and *B* continue growing, the distance between them will become large. After some time, when the excess Si in the liquid due to formation of α (Al-rich solution) is not able to reach the tip of the growing Si plates (because of the large distance between them), the Si concentration in the region reaches a level at which nucleating of a new plate of Si, marked *D*, occurs. The acicular eutectic growth requires repeated nucleation of Si-rich phase (β) but is not difficult to realize it because of the build up of Si concentration in the liquid when the distance between two random plates becomes large.

3.4.2b Nodular Eutectic

The nodular, globular or spheroidal eutectic structure results when the β phase nucleates in the shape of a sphere or near spheroid in a continuous matrix of the α phase. The spherical shape has the least surface area to volume ratio among all possible geometries. The associated interfacial energy per unit volume will be a minimum for the spherical shape. The only difficulty with the nodular shape of the eutectic is that formation of the β phase requires repeated nucleation. This limits the occurrence of nodular eutectics to very few alloy systems and the Fe-C alloys belonging to the cast iron group. An optical photomicrograph illustrating the nodular eutectic is shown in Fig. 3.8b for an Fe-C alloy. In the Al-Sn alloy system, the nodular eutectic occurs in the absence of any impurity; however, in the Fe-C alloys it occurs in the presence of Mg. The normal eutectic structure of the Fe-C alloy in the absence of Mg shows flaky graphite.

In the Al-Sn phase diagram, Fig. 3.10, the eutectic composition is shown at 97.6 at. pct. Sn (99.4 wt.pct. Sn), balance Al. The relative amount of the α phase (Al-solid solution) in the eutectic mixture will be,

$$\% \ \alpha = \frac{99 - 97.6}{99 - 00.0} \times 100 = 1.42\%$$

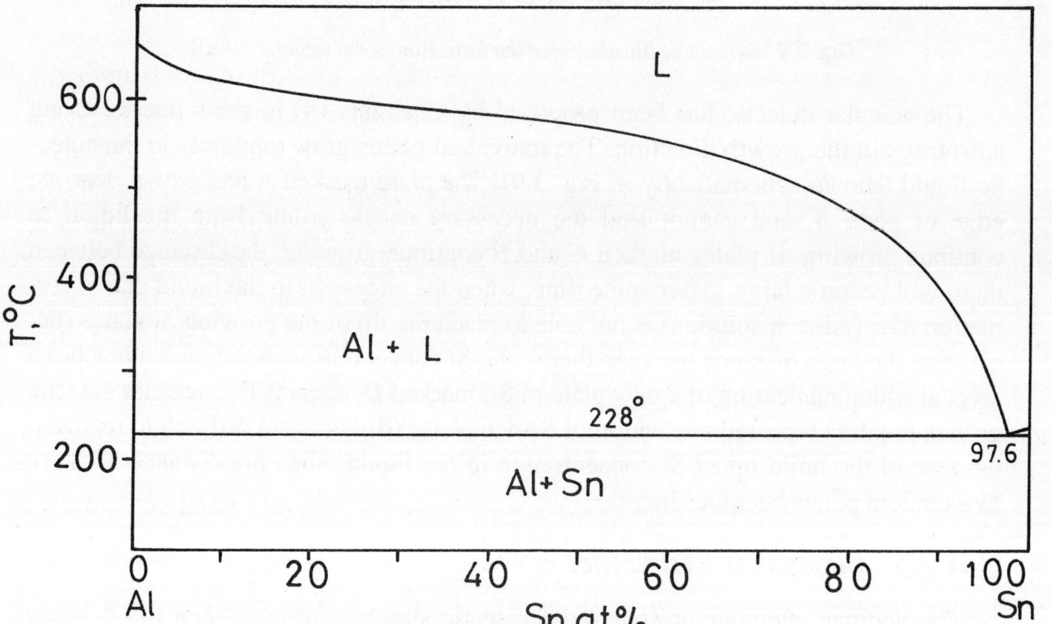

Fig. 3.10 Phase diagram of the Al-Sn alloy system.

$$\% \ \beta = 98.58\% \ ,$$

calculated on the atom percent basis. The volume fraction of the α phase in the two-phase mixture will be higher than the above value. However, the ratio of the phases α and β by volume will be approximately 1:20. The nodular eutectic is proposed to form in those systems where one of the phases in the eutectic mixture is present in a much smaller proportion by volume. This is not a sufficient condition for formation of a discontinuous eutectic. In the Sn-Zn alloys, the two phases are in the ratio 1:12 but the eutectic structure has a lamellar morphology.

3.4.2c Chinese Script Eutectic

The last group of microstructures which should be included in the discontinuous eutectic class are those which show dendritic skeleton in an intricate pattern known as "Chinese Script" structure, Fig. 3.8c. A number of binary and ternary eutectic alloys are observed to solidify with a Chinese Script structure. These include, Pb-56.6 wt.pct.Bi, Bi-43 wt.pct.Sn, Bi-40 wt.pct.Cd, etc. The Bi-Cd and Bi-Sn phase diagrams are shown in Figs. 3.11a and b. In the Bi-Cd phase diagram, the eutectic composition is at 40 wt.pct. Cd. The eutectic reaction occurs at 145°C. There is no solubility of Bi in Cd or Cd in Bi, i.e.; the two phases of the eutectic mixture are almost pure Cd and Bi. In the Bi-Sn alloy system the eutectic reaction occurs when an alloy contain-

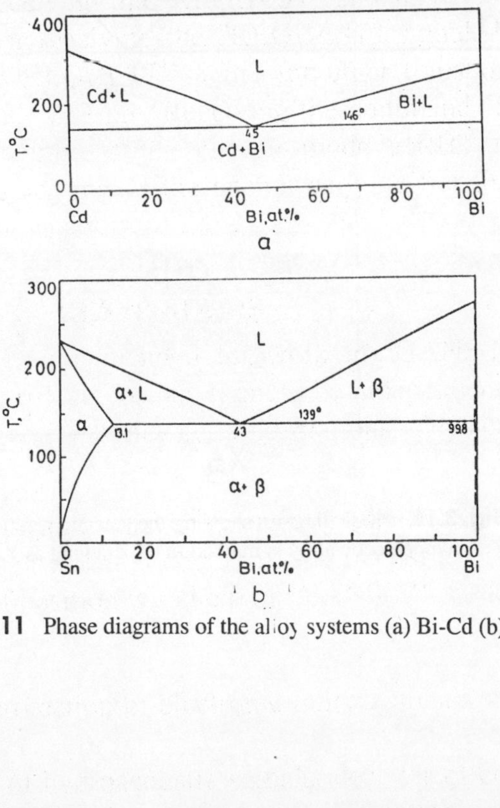

Fig. 3.11 Phase diagrams of the alloy systems (a) Bi-Cd (b) Bi-Sn.

ing Bi-43 wt.pct.Sn is cooled below 139°C. The eutectic microstructure consists of α phase which is almost pure Bi and a tin-rich β phase which has 21 wt.pct. Bi in it. In the Bi-Cd alloy, particles of almost pure Bi solidify as dendrites in a complex three-dimensional pattern in a continuous matrix of Cd.

3.5 HYPOEUTECTIC AND HYPEREUTECTIC ALLOYS—EQUILIBRIUM SOLIDIFICATION

Binary alloys whose solute concentration is less than the eutectic composition but lie to the right of the point "*a*" (of Fig. 3.12) are known as hypoeutectic alloys. The

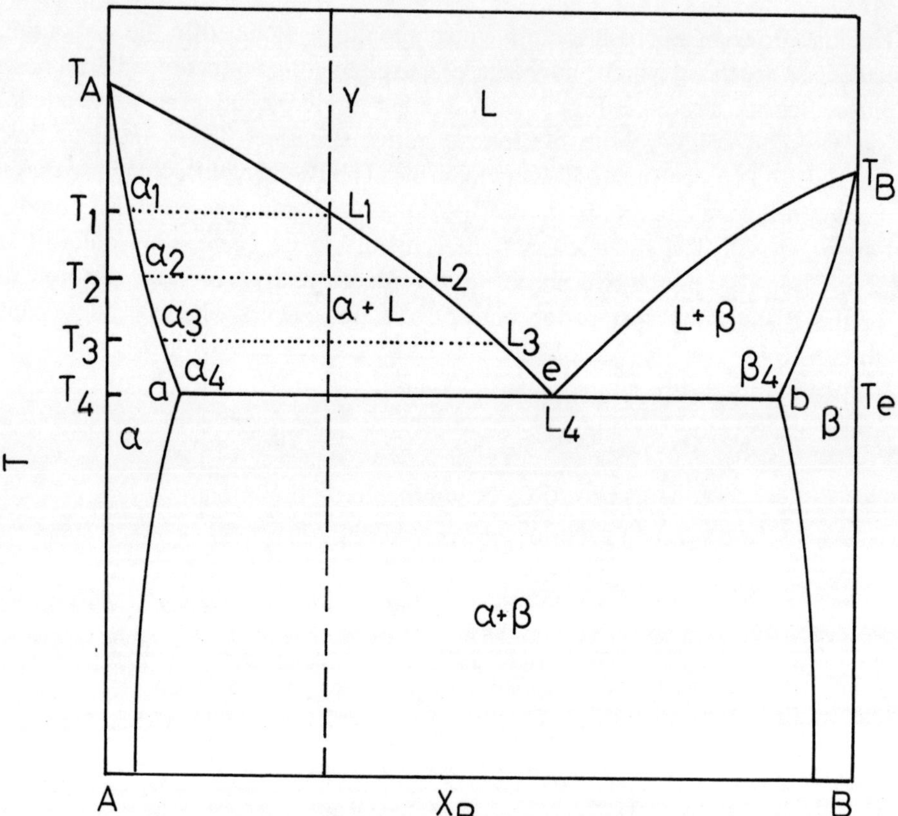

Fig. 3.12 Phase diagram showing the eutectic reaction. A hypoeutectic alloy is marked in the drawing as *Y*.

manner of selection of solute is arbitrary; however, if a more common metal of the two components is termed the solvent, then a hypoeutectic alloy will always show primary α crystals to be identified with the more common metal. The alloy composition *Y* in Fig. 3.12 is a hypoeutectic alloy. Let us consider solidification of a hypoeutectic alloy under equilibrium cooling conditions. The alloy is completely liquid at the temperature T_0. As the cooling proceeds, nuclei of the α phase appear in the melt at the temperature T_1. The α phase is rich in the solvent metal. At the temperature T_1, the α phase of a composition, indicated by the point α_1, is in equilibrium with liquid L_1 of almost the original alloy composition. The composition of the liquid moves along the solvus towards point ''e'' and that of the solid α along the solidus towards the composition point *a* with further cooling. At a temperature just above the eutectic reaction isotherm, the α phase of composition α_4 (point *a*) is in equilibrium with liquid of the eutectic composition. The relative amount of the primary α or proeutectic α phase can be obtained by applying the lever rule at the tie-line $\alpha_4 L_4$.

$$\% \text{ primary } \alpha = \frac{0.6-0.3}{0.6-0.1} \times 100 = 60\ \%$$

$$\% \text{ Liquid } = \frac{0.3-0.1}{0.6-0.1} \times 100 = 40\%.$$

The microstructure at this stage of partial solidification will consist of primary α of composition α_4 in a liquid of the eutectic composition, as shown schematically in Fig. 3.13.

Upon cooling below the eutectic reaction isotherm, the remaining liquid of composition L_4 decomposes into α and β phases of compositions α_4 and β_4, respectively, by the eutectic reaction described earlier. The relative proportions of the α and β phases formed from the eutectic liquid will remain the same as in the alloy of the eutectic composition studied earlier. However, since the eutectic liquid constitutes only 40% of the total alloy of the hypoeutectic composition *Y* the amounts of the eutectic α and β phases are

$$\%\ \alpha = \frac{0.9-0.6}{0.9-0.1} \times 0.4 \times 100 = 15\ \%$$

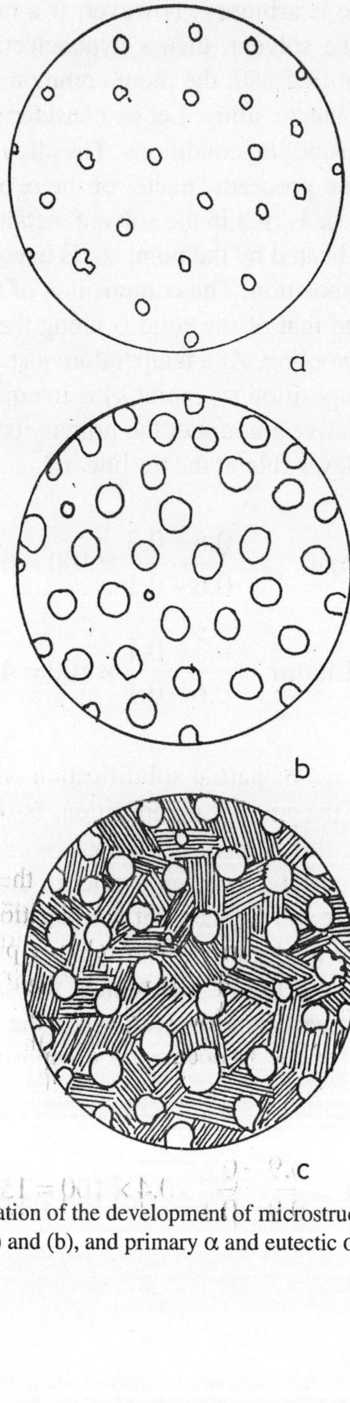

Fig. 3.13 Schematic representation of the development of microstructure in a hypoeutectic alloy. The primary α phase is shown in (a) and (b), and primary α and eutectic α and β phases are shown in (c).

$$\% \ \beta = \frac{0.6-0.1}{0.9-0.1} \times 0.4 \times 100 = 25\%$$

The total amount of α in the hypoeutectic alloy is

$$\% \text{ Total } \alpha = 60 + 15 = 75\%$$

and $$\% \ \beta = 25\%.$$

Fig. 3.14 The microstructure of a hypoeutectic Al-Si alloy; dendrites of primary α (Al-rich solid solution) are seen.

The final microstructure of the alloy is schematically shown in Fig. 3.13 for a lamellar eutectic. This is substantiated with the help of an actual microstructure shown in Fig. 3.14 for a hypoeutectic Al-Si alloy.

Binary alloys whose solute concentration lies to the right of the eutectic composition (point *e* in Fig. 3.15) but is less than the composition represented by point *b* in Fig. 3.15 are known as hypereutectic alloys. The solidification microstructure of hypereutectic alloys follows a similar course as described for the hypoeutectic alloy *Y*. Let us consider an alloy of the hypereutectic composition represented by the composition vertical *Z* in Fig. 3.15. The solidification begins with the formation of primary β crystals in the melt. The composition of the liquid changes along the liquidus and

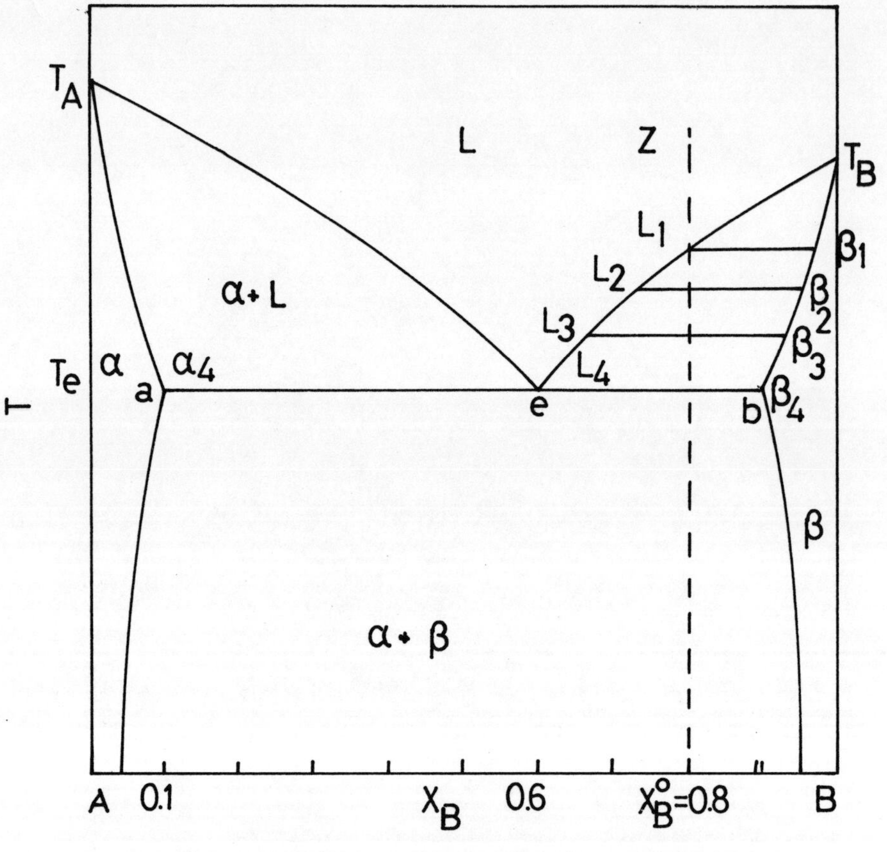

Fig. 3.15 Phase diagram showing the eutectic reaction. A hypereutectic alloy is marked in the drawing by composition vertical *Z*.

that of the β phase along the solidus (as shown by arrows in Fig. 3.15). As the solidification progresses, the amount of the β phase gradually increases at the expense of the liquid. Just above the eutectic reaction isotherm the liquid phase of composition L_4 (point *e*) is in equilibrium with the β phase of composition β_4 (point *b*). The relative amounts of the two phases in equilibrium with each other are,

$$\% \text{ Primary } \beta = \frac{0.8-0.6}{0.9-0.6} \times 100 = 66.66\%$$

$$\% \text{ Liquid} = 33.33\%$$

The liquid has reached the eutectic composition, which upon further cooling will give the eutectic α and β phases by the eutectic reaction. The relative amounts of the α and β phases are:

$$\% \, \alpha = \frac{0.9-0.6}{0.9-0.1} \times 33.33 = 12.5\%$$

$$\% \, \beta = \frac{0.6-0.1}{0.9-0.1} \times 33.33 = 20.83\%$$

The total amount of the β phase in the alloy is 87.50%. The final microstructure will consist of the primary β phase crystals and the eutectic α and β phases, Fig. 3.16. This is substantiated with the help of an actual microstructure derived from an Al-20wt.pct.Si alloy. The structure shows polyhedras of primary Si crystals in a matrix consisting of the eutectic structure. Similar structures are observed in other alloy systems, as shown in Fig. 3.16d for Sn-Bi hypereutectic alloy. The primary β phase which appears as plates is rich in Bi.

3.6 HYPOEUTECTIC ALLOYS—NON-EQUILIBRIUM SOLIDIFICATION

In the preceding sections we have described the solidification of eutectic, hypoeutectic and hypereutectic alloys under conditions in which equilibrium is maintained at

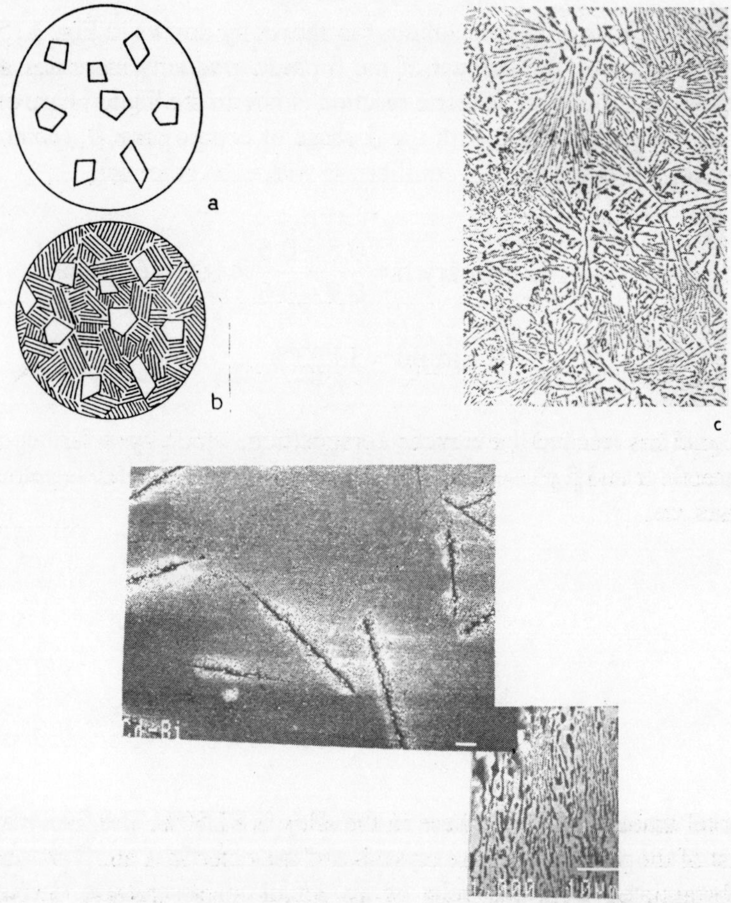

Fig. 3.16 Schematic showing development of microstructure of a hypereutectic alloy. It shows plates of primary β (Si-rich) phase in (a) and primary β and eutectic α and β phases formed below T_e in (b). Actual microstructure of a hypereutectic Al-20wt.pct. Si alloy showing primary β crystals (c) and hypereutectic Cd-Bi alloy showing plates of primary β and the eutectic structure (d).

each decrement of temperature during the solidification process. The solidification under natural or non-equilibrium cooling conditions results in differences in the relative amounts of the phases present and the resulting microstructures.

Consider the solidification of a hypoeutectic alloy indicated by the composition vertical *Y*, Fig. 3.17. At higher temperatures (above T_1) the two components, *A* and *B*, exist as a homogeneous liquid solution because of complete mutual solubility of these components in each other. At the temperature T_1, the α solid solution of composition given by the point α_1 begins to nucleate in the liquid. The α phase will become stable

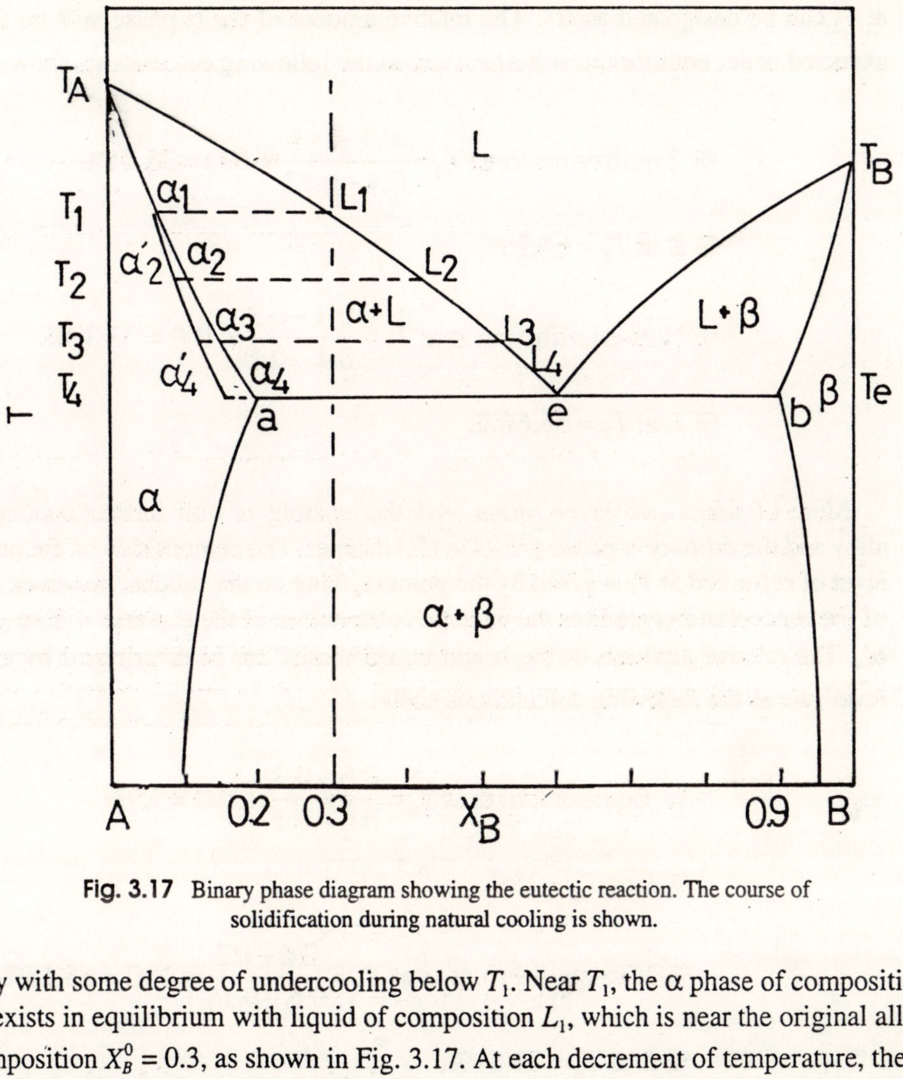

Fig. 3.17 Binary phase diagram showing the eutectic reaction. The course of solidification during natural cooling is shown.

only with some degree of undercooling below T_1. Near T_1, the α phase of composition α_1 exists in equilibrium with liquid of composition L_1, which is near the original alloy composition $X_B^0 = 0.3$, as shown in Fig. 3.17. At each decrement of temperature, the α phase of composition corresponding to the solidus forms over the existing α. In addition, new α regions nucleate and grow in the liquid. At the temperature T_2, the α phase of composition given by the point α_2 forms over α compositions formed above T_2. This is due to insufficient time being available for homogenization of the solid during natural cooling. This results in non-equilibrium α with a solute concentration gradient from the core to the periphery of the α mass. The average composition of the α phase at T_2 can be designated as α'_2. The relative amount of the α phase will be less than expected under equilibrium solidification, as the following calculations show:

$$\% \text{ Equilibrium } \alpha \text{ at } T_2 = \frac{0.4-0.3}{0.4-0.12} \times 100 = 35.71\%$$

$$\% L \text{ at } T_2 = 64.28\%$$

$$\% \text{ Non-equilibrium } \alpha \text{ at } T_2 = \frac{0.4-0.3}{0.4-0.1} \times 100 = 33.33\%$$

$$\% L \text{ at } T_2 = 66.66\%.$$

More of solute-rich layer forms over the existing α with further cooling of the alloy and the primary α phase grows in this manner. The composition of the outermost layer of α formed at T_4 is given by the point α_4 lying on the solidus; however, because of the concentration gradient the average composition of the α phase will be given by α'_4. The relative amounts of the α and liquid phases can be determined by using the lever rule as the following calculations show:

$$\% \text{ Equilibrium } \alpha \text{ at } T_4 = \frac{0.6-0.3}{0.6-0.2} \times 100 = 75\%$$

$$\% L \text{ at } T_4 = 25\%$$

$$\% \text{ Non-equilibrium } \alpha \text{ at } T_4 = \frac{0.6-0.3}{0.6-0.16} \times 100 = 68.18\%$$

$$\% L \text{ at } T_4 = 31.81\%.$$

The relative amount of the liquid under non-equilibrium solidification is higher than that under the equilibrium condition. For solute to be conserved, the average composition of the α phase must be lower. At the temperature T_4 (= T_e) the liquid phase has reached the composition corresponding to the eutectic and will dissociate into α and β phases by the eutectic reaction. The α phase of the eutectic will be continuous with the primary α as the compositions of the outermost layer of non-equilibrium α and β phases formed by the eutectic reaction are given as,

$$\% \text{ eutectic } \alpha = \frac{0.9-0.6}{0.9-0.2} \times 31.81 = 13.63\%$$

$$\% \, \beta = 18.17\%$$

The above calculations show that the relative amounts of the eutectic α and β phases are higher under natural cooling conditions when a comparison is made with results of equilibrium solidification. The primary α phase will show "coring". The development of the microstructure is sketched in Fig. 3.18.

Fig. 3.18 Development of microstructure during natural cooling of a hypoeutectic alloy. α'_2 and α'_4 are average compositions of the primary α at T_2 and T_4, respectively.

The solidification of a hypereutectic alloy will follow a similar course during natural cooling. In this case the primary β phase will show coring and its relative amount will be less than expected under equilibrium solidification of the alloy. In a number of alloy systems, the solubility of the component *A* in the β phase is negligibly small, i.e., the β phase is almost pure *B*. The extent of coring will be negligible if hypereutectic alloys of such alloy systems are allowed to cool naturally. As an example, we can consider the equilibrium phase diagram of the Al-Si binary system (Fig. 3.7). The solubility of Al in Si at the eutectic temperature is 0.0016 at. % Al. No coring of the Si-rich β phase is therefore expected when a hypereutectic alloy, Al-20 at.pct.Si for example, is allowed to cool in air. The structure will consist of faceted crystals of almost pure Si in a fine eutectic mixture consisting of α and β phases.

3.7 TERMINAL SOLID SOLUTIONS

The terminal solid solutions are those alloys which lie outside the composition range of the eutectic reaction, as indicated by composition verticals *M* and *N*, Fig. 3.19. Alloy composition *M* when cooled under equilibrium will form the α solid solution and will not undergo the eutectic reaction because it falls outside the range of the eutectic reaction.

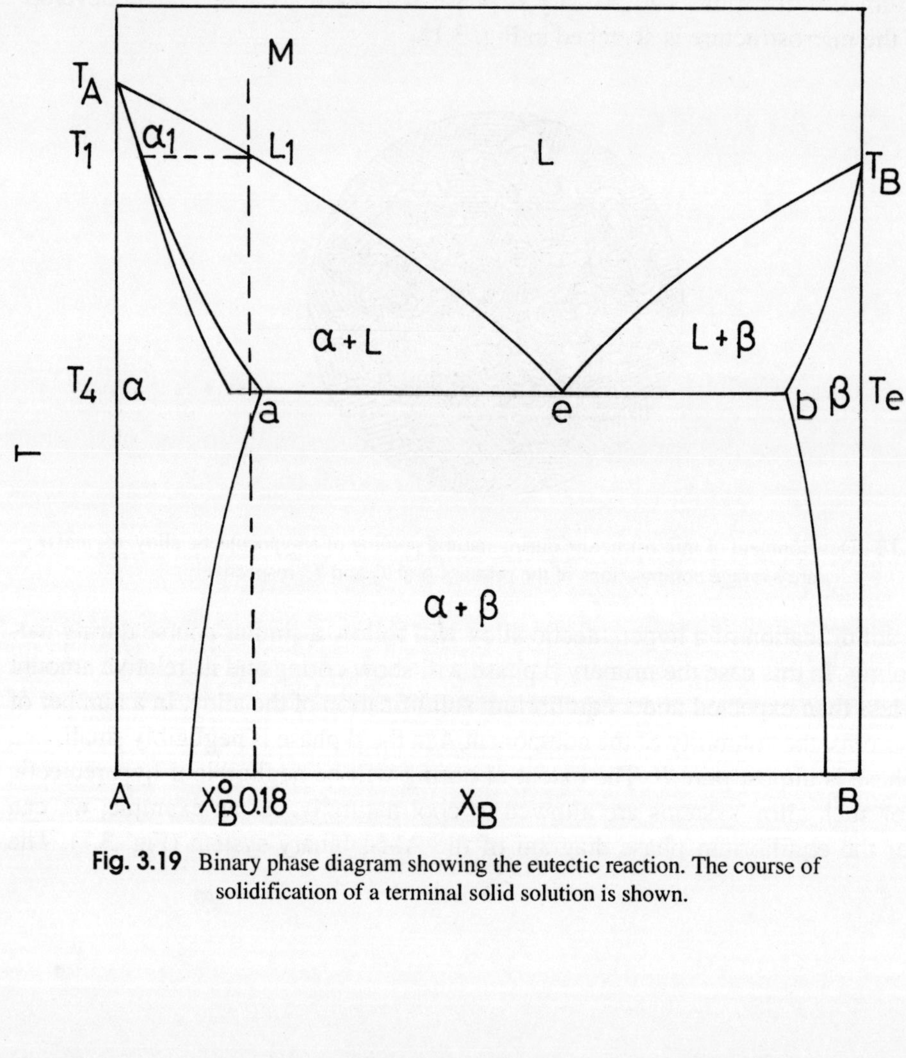

Fig. 3.19 Binary phase diagram showing the eutectic reaction. The course of solidification of a terminal solid solution is shown.

Consider the solidification of an alloy *M* (Fig. 3.19) under natural cooling conditions. The slow diffusion of solute in the solid α and insufficient time available at each decrement of temperature during natural cooling, will give rise to coring of the primary α, as described earlier. The solidification will remain incomplete at the eutectic temperature with the liquid having reached the eutectic composition. The average composition of the α phase is given by the point α′, Fig. 3.19. Upon cooling below the eutectic temperature, the remaining liquid dissociates into α and β phases by the eutectic reaction. The relative amounts of the various constituents are,

$$\% \text{ Primary } \alpha \text{ (Cored) } = \frac{0.6-0.18}{0.6-0.16} \times 100 = 93.33\%$$

$$\% L = 6.66\%,$$

which dissociates into,

$$\% \text{ eutectic } \alpha = \frac{0.9-0.6}{0.9-0.2} \times 6.66 = 2.86\%$$

and $$\% \text{ eutectic } \beta = 3.8\% .$$

The eutectic α phase will grow out of the primary α and will be physically continuous with it. The β phase may not form as a normal eutectic with α. The growth of the eutectic α will leave gap-like regions between the dendritic arms of α, which become rich in solute. These regions will solidify as the β phase. The structure of the eutectic will consist of one layer of β sandwiched between two layers of the α phase. The structure is termed as a ''divorced eutectic'', as illustrated by the optical photomicrograph of Fig. 3.20. The growth of the divorced eutectic does not occur by the cooperative growth mechanism.

The eutectic constituent of the terminal solid solution can be eliminated by annealing the alloy in the single α phase field below the eutectic reaction isotherm. The α phase grows at the expense of the unstable β phase which dissolves. The excess solute released due to dissolution of β will diffuse into the cored α, thus making it uniform in composition. The homogeneous solid solution α, when allowed to cool below the solvus will transform into depleted α and β phases, as illustrated schematically in Fig. 3.21a. The resulting microstructure is shown in Fig. 3.21b for a Cu-4 Ag alloy.

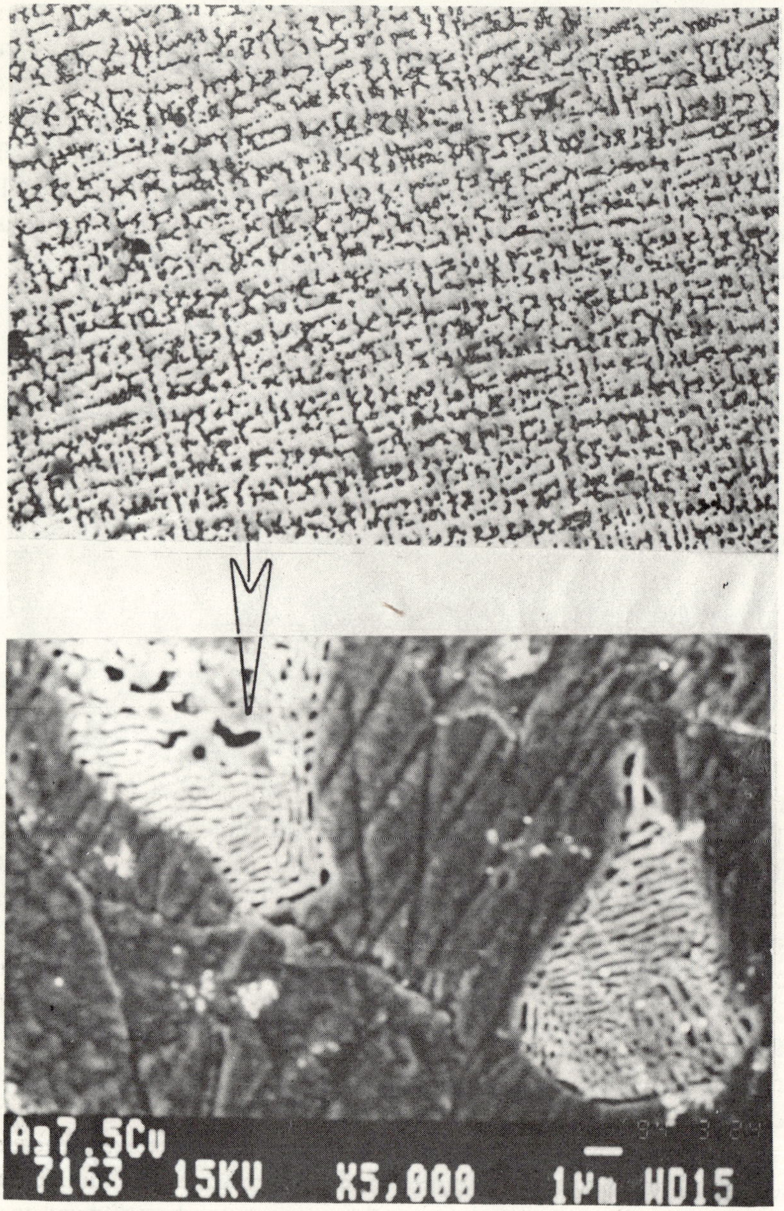

Fig. 3.20 Optical photomicrograph showing eutectic microstructure in a terminal solid solution, Ag-7.5 at.pct.Cu alloy. The Ag-rich solid solution α is shown here as light coloured region and the eutectic structure is dark coloured. It is resolved in the scanning electron microscope image shown here.

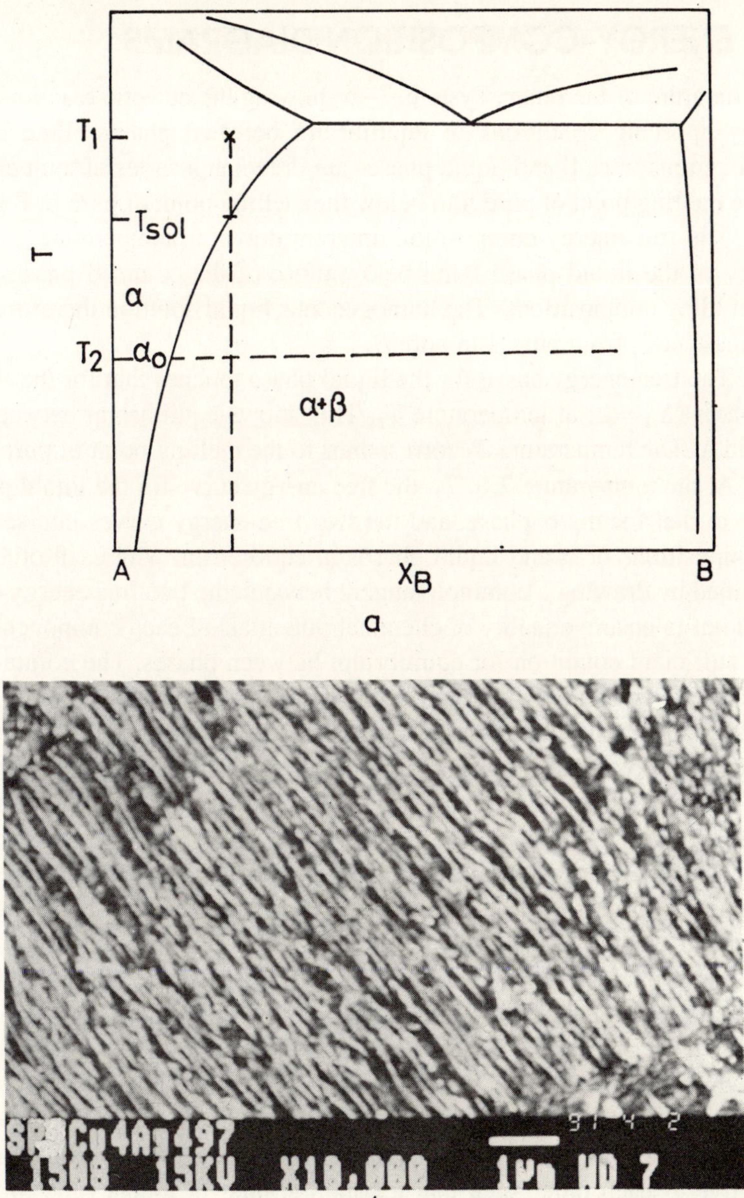

Fig. 3.21 (a) Schematic illustrating the transformation of a supersaturated solid solution α into depleted α and β phases, (b) Actual photomicrograph derived from a Cu-4 at.pct.Ag alloy.

3.8 FREE ENERGY-COMPOSITION DIAGRAMS

The phase diagram of the binary system A–B showing the eutectic reaction can be constructed by applying conditions of equilibrium between phases. Free energy-composition diagrams of α, β and liquid phases are drawn at a series of temperatures, from above the melting point of pure A to below the melting point of pure B, Fig. 3.22.

Fig. 3.22a. The free energy-composition diagram drawn at temperature T_1 shows the free energy of the liquid phase lying below those of the α and β phases in the whole range of alloy compositions. The homogeneous liquid solution therefore exists as the stable phase at T_1 from pure A to pure B.

Fig. 3.22b. The free energy curve for the liquid phase touches that for the α phase at the pure A axis ($X_B = 0$) at temperature T_2. This shows equilibrium between pure liquid and solid A. The temperature T_2 corresponds to the melting point of pure A, T_A.

Fig. 3.22c. At the temperature $T_3 < T_2$, the free energy curve for the liquid phase is raised relative to that for the α phase, and the two free energy curves intersect each other. The compositions of α and liquid phases in equilibrium with each other at T_3 can be determined by drawing a common tangent between the two free energy curves. This is carried out to ensure equality of chemical potentials of each component in the two phases, a sufficient condition for equilibrium between phases. The common tangent line touches the free energy curves for the α and liquid phases at points P_3 and Q_3, respectively, which represent compositions of the two phases in equilibrium with each other at T_3. Moreover, the free energy curve for the β phase touches that for the liquid at $X_B = 1$ indicating that the temperature T_3 corresponds to the melting point of pure B, T_B.

Fig. 3.22d. The free energy-composition diagrams for both α and β phases intersect the free energy curve for the liquid phase at temperature T_4. Points P_4 and Q_4, which are common tangent points on the free energy curves, represent compositions of the α and liquid phases, respectively, in equilibrium with each other. Similarly, composition points N_4 and M_4 represents compositions of the liquid and β phases in equilibrium with each other at T_4. The various phase fields are: α, (α + β), L (L + β) and β, as shown in Fig. 3.22d. It is to be noted that every two-phase region is separated by two single-phase regions involving the same two phases.

Fig. 3.22e. The free energy-composition diagrams of the α, β and liquid phases are displaced relative to each other such that a common tangent touches the three free energy curves at points P_5, Q_5 (= N_5), and M_5 at temperature T_5. The three phases α, β and liquid are in equilibrium with each other at T_5 with points P_5, Q_5 and M_5 representing compositions of the α, liquid and β phases, respectively. The temperature T_5 corresponds to the eutectic reaction isotherm.

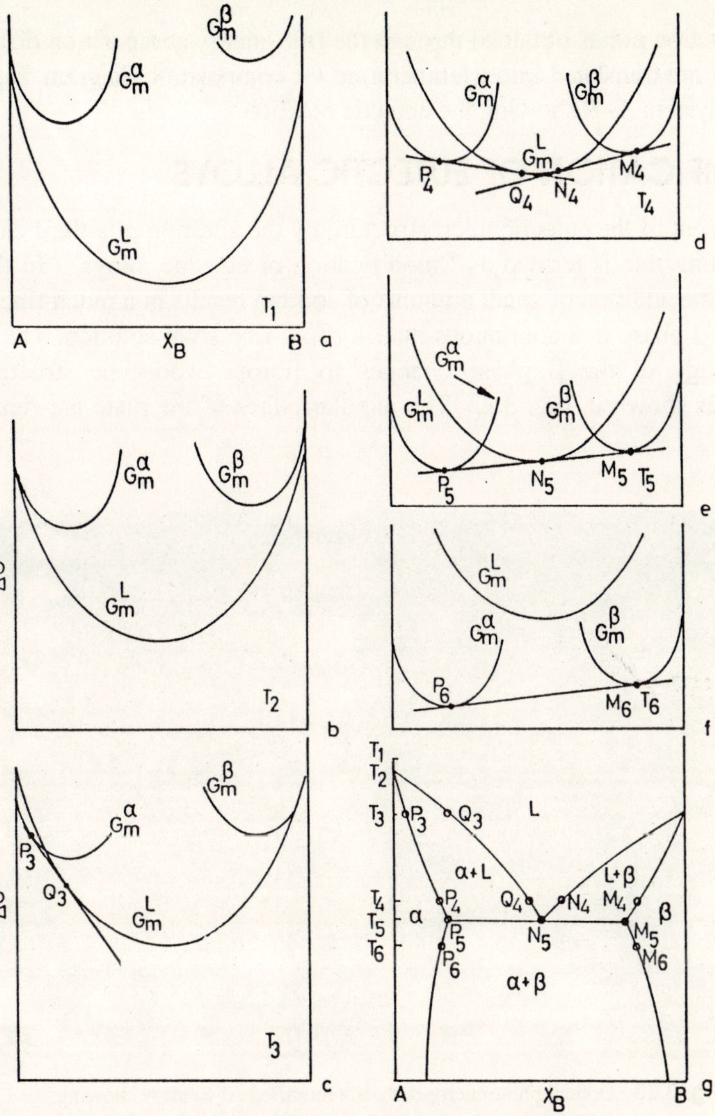

Fig. 3.22 Free energy-composition diagrams of the α, β and liquid phases at a series of temperatures (a to f), and the phase diagram (g).

Fig. 3.22f. The liquid phase becomes unstable at T_6. The free energy-composition diagram of the liquid phase is raised to the extent that the liquid does not maintain equilibrium with either α or β phases. Thus α and β phases will maintain equilibrium with each other. The composition of the α and β phases are given by points P_6 and M_6, respectively, at the temperature T_6.

The composition points obtained through the free energy composition diagrams of Figs. 3.22a to f are translated into a temperature vs. composition diagram, Fig. 3.22g, for the binary system A–B showing the eutectic reaction.

3.9 MODIFICATION OF EUTECTIC ALLOYS

The refinement of the eutectic microstructure by the addition of a third element or change in cooling rate is termed as "modification of eutectic alloys". In the Al-Si eutectic alloy, the addition of small amounts of sodium results in a much finer dispersion of Si-rich β phase in a continuous matrix of Al-rich solid solution. The acicular plate morphology of the β phase changes to fibrous wool-type structure after modification, as shown in Fig. 3.23. The angular edges of the plate are replaced by rounded ones.

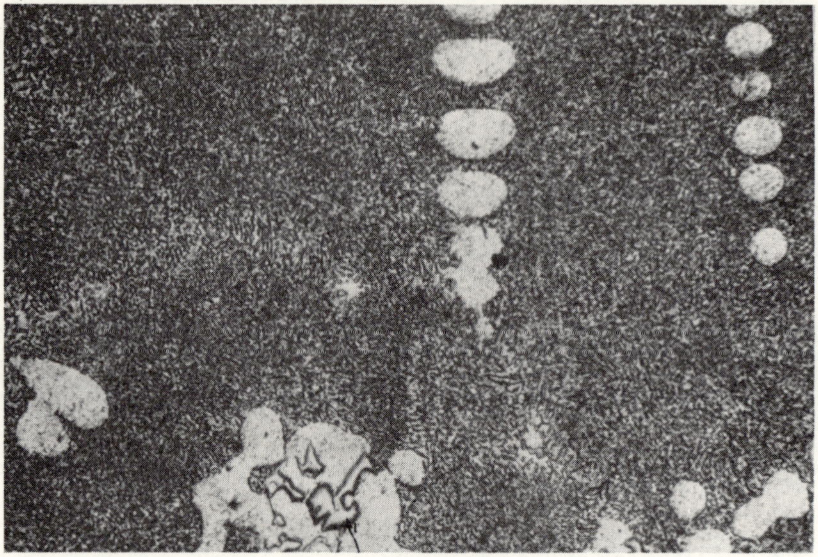

Fig. 3.23 Optical photomicrograph of a modified Al-Si alloy showing fibrous wool-type structure of the eutectic.

The effect of increasing the cooling rate on the phase boundaries and the resulting microstructure can be explained with the help of free energy-composition diagrams, Fig. 3.24, drawn at T_1, T_e and T_2 defined by $T_1 > T_e > T_2$. The free energy-composition diagram drawn at the temperature T_1 illustrates the compositions of α and liquid phases in equilibrium with each other for large particles of the α phase. The particle size decreases upon increasing the rate of cooling. The free energy composition diagram of the α phase will be raised by an amount equal to the additional surface energy associated with the finer structure, due to Gibbs-Thomson effect.

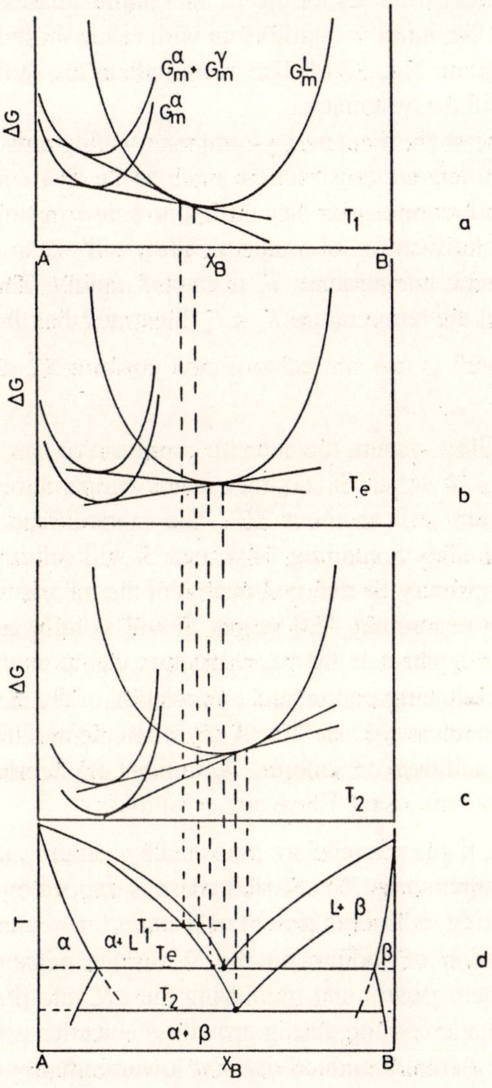

Fig. 3.24 The effect of cooling rate on the free energy-composition diagram and the resulting phase diagram.

The magnitude of the increase in free energy is given by $\gamma V_m/d$, where d is some characteristic linear dimension of the particle such as diameter, or half the interlamellar spacing etc., as shown in Fig. 3.24a. The common tangent drawn between the modified free energy curves of the α and liquid phases illustrates that the solute concentration of the liquid in equilibrium with α has shifted to a lower value as shown in the phase diagram, Fig. 3.24d. The magnitude of the shift will depend upon the rate of cooling but will be systematic.

Fig. 3.24b shows the free energy-composition diagrams at the eutectic temperature T_e. The common tangent construction made at the free energy curves illustrates that the eutectic liquid composition has shifted to a new position due to rapid cooling of the alloy. The solidification of a eutectic alloy will occur at a temperature below the equilibrium eutectic temperature, T_e if cooled rapidly. The free energy-composition diagram drawn at the temperature $T_2 < T_e$ illustrates that the composition of the liquid in equilibrium with α has shifted to a new position $X_B^{e_2}$ due to rapid cooling of the alloy.

In the Al-Si alloy system, the eutectic composition has been reported to shift from 12.6 wt.pct. Si to 14 wt.pct. Si and the eutectic temperature to decrease from 577°C to 555°C, a maximum shift to about 22°C due to modification, as shown in Fig. 3.25. Thus, an original alloy containing 14 wt.pct. Si will solidify with a eutectic structure. It will not show primary Si-rich polyhedras in the microstructure. Similarly, an original eutectic alloy containing 12.6 wt.pct. Si will solidify as a hypoeutectic alloy with dendrites of Al-rich phase in the microstructure due to modification.

A similar shift in temperature and composition of the eutectic has been reported by a number of researchers e.g., Hellawell (5), when the modification of the Al-Si alloy is affected by the addition of sodium. A number of theories for the modification of eutectic have been proposed. These are as follows:

1. The Si-rich, β phase nuclei are poisoned by sodium such that growth of Si occurs at lower temperatures. The Si-rich phase is trapped by the faster growing Al-rich phase resulting in limited growth of β and a finer eutectic microstructure.
2. The adsorption of sodium on the Si surface poisons the Si-rich nuclei, thus retarding their growth and modifying the α/L and β/L interfacial energies. The interfacial undercooling during growth of eutectics is also affected.
3. The higher thermal conductivity and lower enthalpy of fusion of Al provides a conduit for faster growth of the Al-rich phase. The Si-rich phase is trapped.
4. The solubility of sodium in the Al-Si liquid is in some way responsible for the modification of the Al-Si alloy through the Al-Si-Na phase diagram.

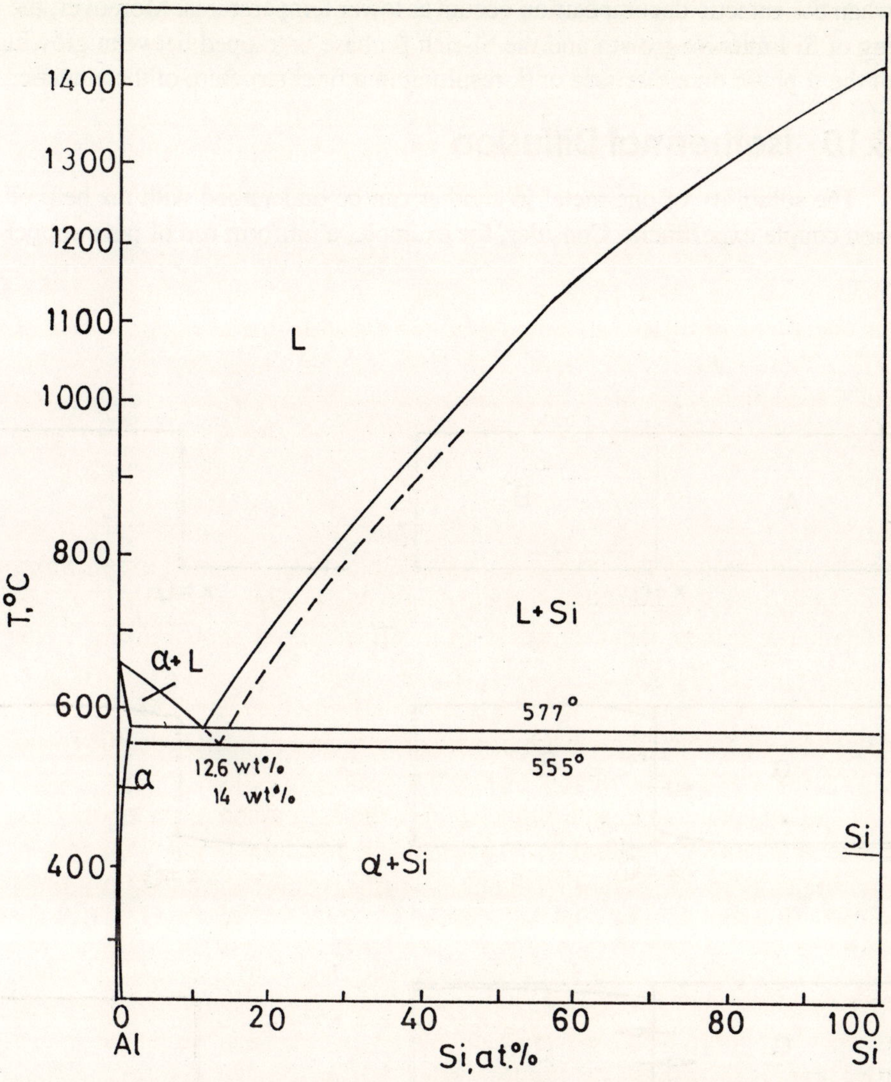

Fig. 3.25 The Al-Si binary phase diagram after modification.

The eutectic structure produced by rapid solidification and that produced by modification with Na can be explained from one or more of the above theories. The kinetic limitations of the growth of Si into an acicular structure retards its rate of growth when the eutectic decomposition occurs at lower temperatures. Moreover, the poisoning of Si limits its growth and the Si-rich β phase is trapped between growing nuclei of the α phase on either side of β, resulting in a finer structure of the eutectic.

3.10 Isothermal Diffusion

The solubility of one metal in another can be understood with the help of a diffusion couple experiment. Consider, for example, a uniform rod of pure copper welded

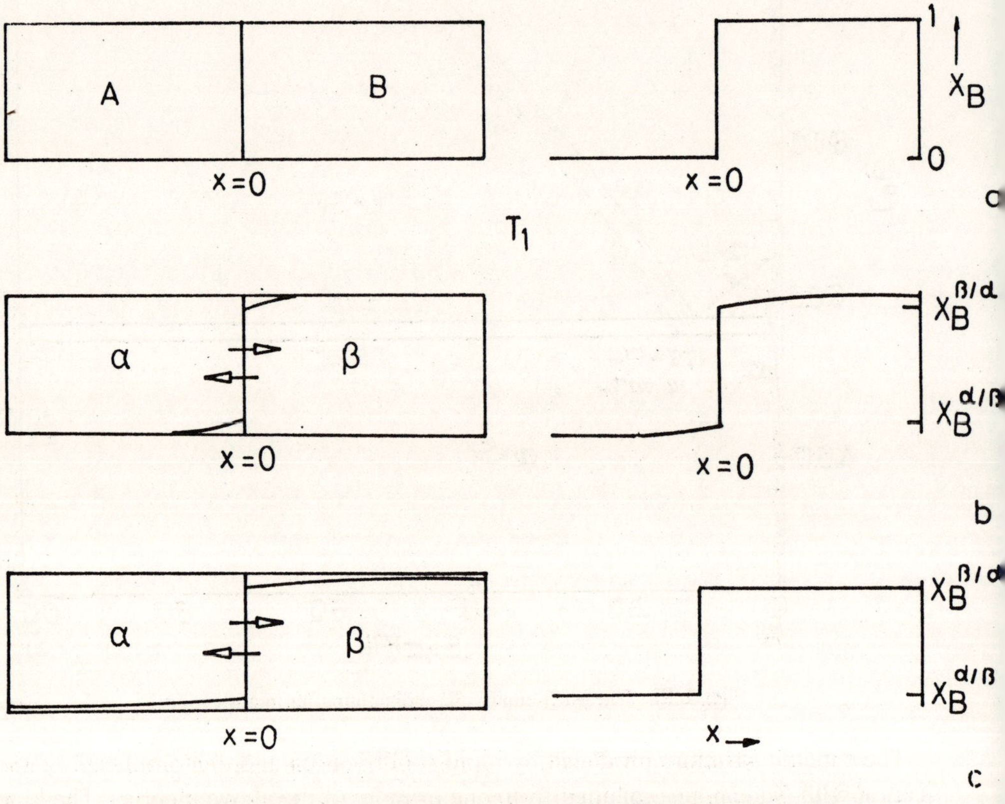

Fig. 3.26 Diffusion couple and the concentration-distance profile (a) initial (b) intermediate and (c) long times of anneal. The interface compositions are shown on the side of each diagram.

to a similar rod of pure silver. The initial concentration-distance profile of silver is shown in Fig. 3.26a. The diffusion couple is allowed to anneal at a temperature $T_1 < T_e$, Fig. 3.27. The phase diagram of the Cu-Ag system indicates that pure copper and silver cannot remain in equilibrium with each other at T_1, say 750°C. The metal Ag will start dissolving in Cu and Cu will dissolve in Ag till saturation is reached. The phase diagram indicates that phases α and β are in equilibrium with each other at T_1. At the beginning of the annealing, process, a two-phase interface consisting of α and β phases will form in the region of the weld. The concentration-distance profile, Fig. 3.26b shows that the solute concentration varies from pure copper to the satura-

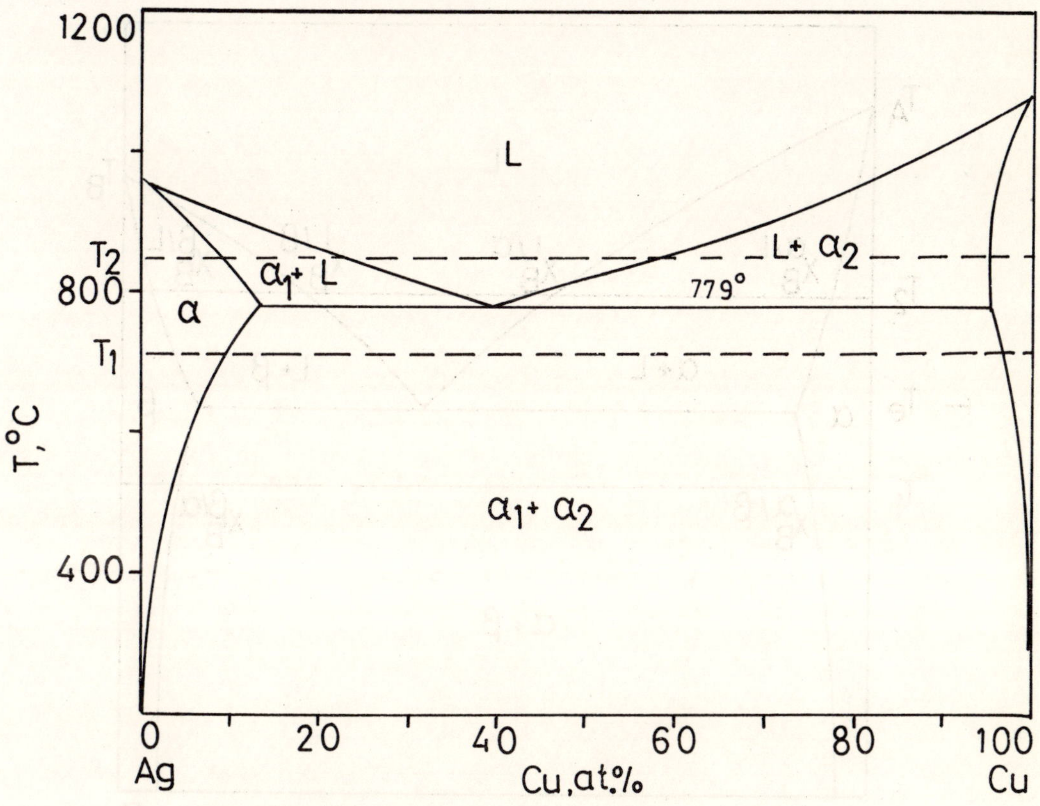

Fig. 3.27a Binary phase diagram illustrating composition of the α, β and liquid phases at the interface.

tion value $X_{Ag}^{\alpha/\beta}$ in the α phase, and from $X_{Ag}^{\beta/\alpha}$ to pure Ag in the β phase. The interface compositions can be obtained from the phase diagram as shown in Fig. 3.27. The two-phase structure corresponding to the (α + β) phase field is not produced. Instead, the two-phase region is represented by the common interface which can migrate in either direction depending upon the relative amounts of the two phases.

The solute will diffuse down the concentration gradient in β towards the α/β interface and then through the concentration gradient in the α phase till equilibrium is established. The concentration-distance profile after a longer annealing time is shown in Fig. 3.26c. It shows uniform compositions of the α and β phases and their relative amounts as required by the lever rule.

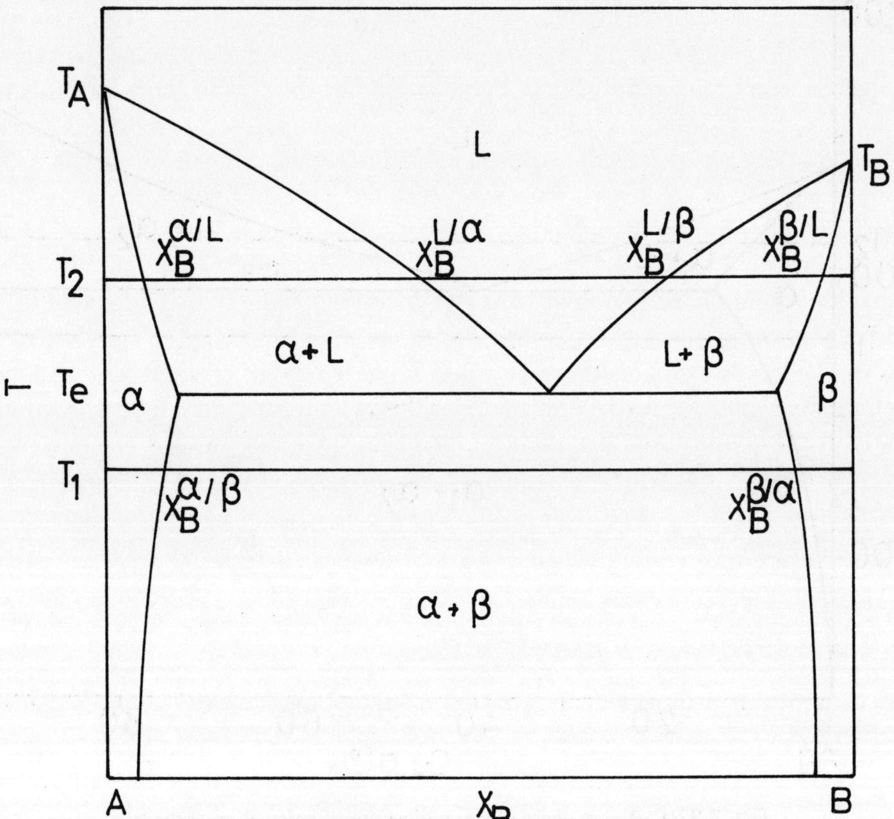

Fig. 3.27b Binary phase diagram illustrating composition of the α, β and liquid phases at the interface.

If the diffusion couple is allowed to anneal at a temperature $T_2 > T_e$, Fig. 3.27b, the concentration-distance profiles at $t > 0$ and $t >> 0$ will consist of a third phase, liquid. This is consistent with the phase diagram which shows that at T_2 three single-phase fields α, β and liquid, are present. If the time of diffusion is small, a thin layer of the liquid will form in the region of the weld, as shown in the concentration-distance profile of Fig. 3.28a. The solute concentration varies in each of the three single-phase fields. In the α phase field, the silver concentration varies from pure Cu to $X_{Ag}^{\alpha/L}$. In the liquid-phase field, the variation in composition is from $X_{Ag}^{L/\alpha}$ to $X_{Ag}^{L/\beta}$ and in the β phase from $X_{Ag}^{\beta/L}$ to $X_{Ag} = 1$, as shown in Fig. 3.28b. The diffusion couple experiment illustrates that if a piece of silver is placed in contact with copper, it will start melting at the Ag/Cu interface below the melting point of either metal.

If the diffusion couple is allowed to anneal for a longer time, the solute will move down the concentration gradients in β, liquid and α phases so as to bring these phases to a uniform composition. In addition, there will be migration of interfaces whose direction will depend upon the relative amounts of the two component metals. Consider the relative sizes of the two rods being such as to make an alloy of composition X, Fig. 3.27b. At $T_2 = 900°C$, the alloy should exist as a liquid solution as the phase diagram indicates. The two interfaces α/L and L/β will move in opposite directions such that the liquid-phase region grows. The direction of migration of the interfaces and the new position of the two interfaces after some time has elapsed is indicated in Fig. 3.28b. If the diffusion continues, the single-phase regions α and β will be eliminated ultimately and the two component metals will form 100% liquid solutions. Similarly, if the composition lies in the (L/β)-phase field, the α/L and L/β interfaces will migrate in such a way that the α-phase field will gradually be eliminated.

The diffusion couple experiment illustrates that all single phase regions present in the phase diagram at the annealing temperature appear in the microstructure. They appear in the same sequence as depicted by the phase diagram.

3.11 The Growth of Eutectics

The theory of growth of eutectics has been studied by a number of investigators. The earlier theory of growth of eutectics by Jackson and Chalmers (6) treats the problem by the simple approach of the growth of the interface in a direction perpendicular to the interface. At the outset it is treated as a problem of diffusion and interfacial energy. When the time available for growth is short, the solute can diffuse to short distances and the interlamellar spacing will be small. A small interlamellar spacing will have large interfacial energy $(2\gamma V_m/s)$ per unit volume of the lamellar structure. Thus, a relatively large fraction of the available driving force will be used in creating

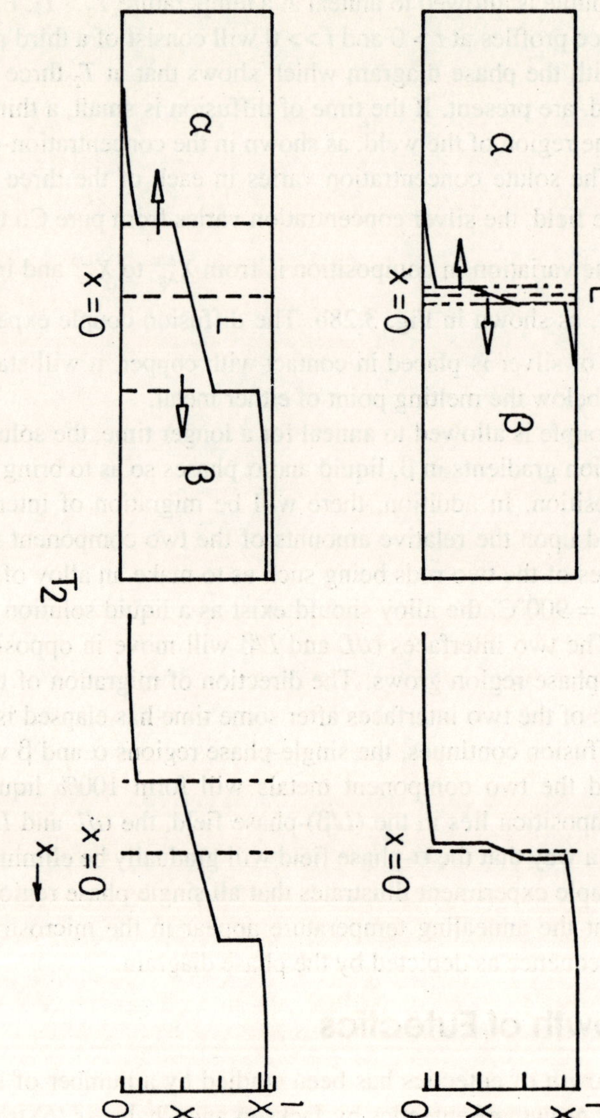

Fig. 3.28 Diffusion couple and the concentration-distance profile (a) $t > 0$ (b) after anneal, $t >> 0$

the interface. The available volume free energy change which drives edge-wise diffusion of solute, favors a small interlamellar spacing. However, the interfacial free energy associated with the α/β interface decreases the magnitude of the available driving force, thus, reducing the rate of growth and subsequently increasing the interlamellar spacing.

Consider an alloy of the eutectic composition (Fig. 3.29) growing into a eutectic structure with a plane front. The individual lamellae are slightly curved, as shown in Fig. 3.30. The growth of α phase (solvent-rich) leads to the rejection of solute which builds up at the α/L interface. Similarly, the growth of β phase leads to the rejection of solvent atoms which pile up at the β/L interface. The build up of solute and solvent

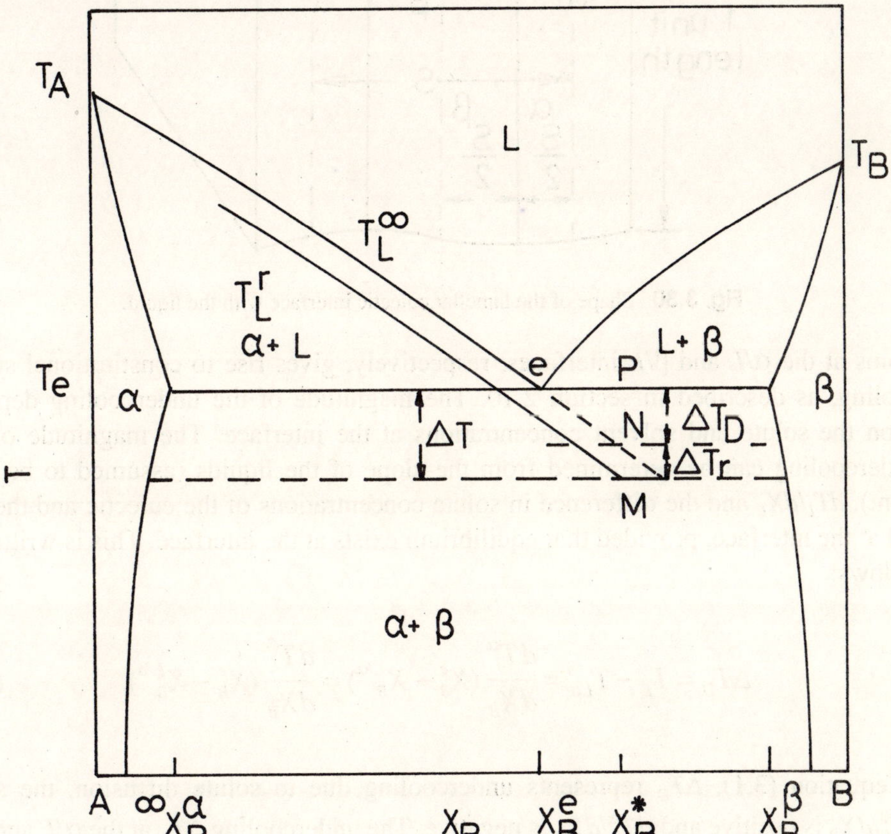

Fig. 3.29 Phase diagram showing undercooling and interface compositions.

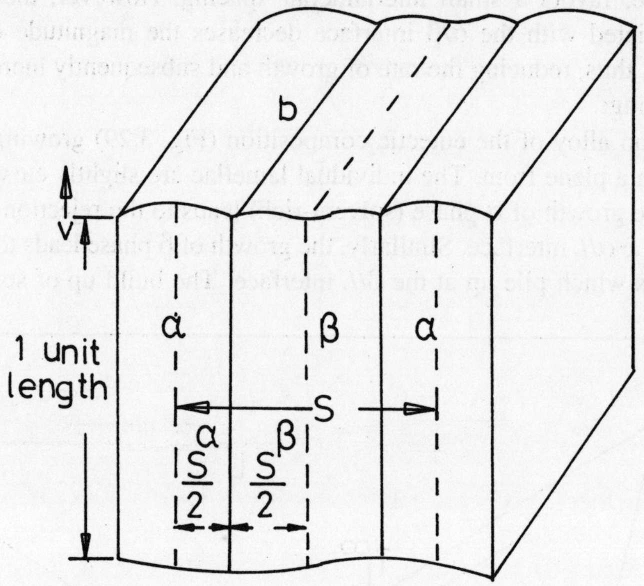

Fig. 3.30 Shape of the lamellar eutectic interface with the liquid.

atoms at the α/L and β/L interfaces, respectively, gives rise to constitutional supercooling, as described in section 2.10. The magnitude of the undercooling depends upon the solute and solvent concentrations at the interface. The magnitude of the undercooling can be determined from the slope of the liquids (assumed to be constant), dT_L/dX_B and the difference in solute concentrations of the eutectic and the liquid at the interface, provided that equilibrium exists at the interface. This is written as follows:

$$\Delta T_D = T_E - T_{L\alpha} = \frac{dT_L^{\alpha}}{dX_B}(X_B^e - X_B^{L/\alpha}) = \frac{dT_L^{\beta}}{dX_B}(X_B^e - X_B^{L/\beta}). \tag{3.1}$$

In equation (3.1), ΔT_D represents undercooling due to solute diffusion, the slope dT_L^{β}/dX_B is positive and dT_L^{α}/dX_B is negative. The undercooling ΔT_D at the α/L and β/L interfaces will be different due to different slopes of the two liquidus curves and differences in solute concentration at the two interfaces. This is shown schematically in Fig. 3.31.

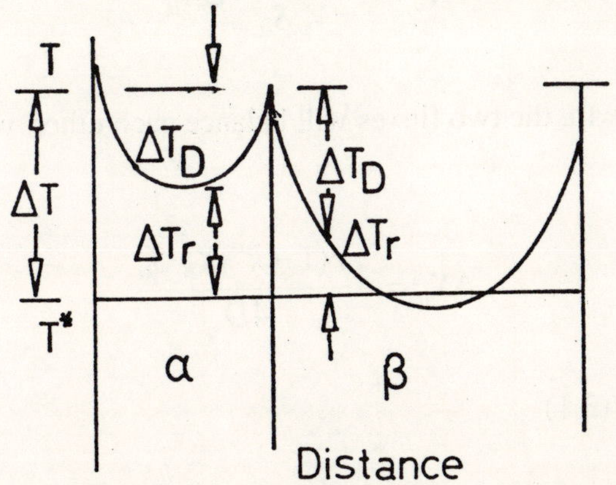

Fig. 3.31 The undercooling as a function of distance along the width the lamellae.

Assuming that the α/L and β/L interfaces move out at a steady state rate v, the flux of solute in the liquid at the α/L interface is given by the following,

$$J_1 = \frac{S_\alpha v b}{2V_m}(X_B^L - X_B^\alpha) = \frac{S_\alpha v b}{2\,V_m}(1 - K^\alpha)\,X_B^L \tag{3.2}$$

where b is the dimension perpendicular to both thc growth direction and width of the lamellae. It is parallel to the α/β interface. The solute rejected at the α/L interface will diffuse laterally along the edge on either side of the α towards the β lamellae. In equation (3.2), S_α is the width of the α lamellae, V_m is the molar volume and K^α is the distribution ratio of solute between α and liquid phases.

The flux of solute from Fick's first law is

$$J_2 = \frac{DA^\alpha}{V_m}\frac{\Delta X_B}{\Delta x}, \tag{3.3}$$

where D is the diffusion coefficient, A^α is the area through which solute diffusion occurs and $\Delta X_B/\Delta x$ is the concentration gradient of solute. Substituting for $A^\alpha = S_\alpha x b$ and $\Delta x = S_\alpha/2$, the effective diffusion distance, in equation (3.3) yields,

$$J_2 = -\frac{2DS_\alpha b}{V_m S_\alpha} \Delta X_B \tag{3.4}$$

For steady state growth, the two fluxes will balance each other, which upon simplication yields,

$$\Delta X_B = -\frac{v(1-k^\alpha)X_B^L S_\alpha}{4D} \tag{3.5}$$

Now, from equation (3.1)

$$\Delta X_B = (X_B^{L/\alpha} - X_B^{L/\beta}) = \Delta T_D \left(\frac{dX_B}{dT_L^\beta} - \frac{dX_B}{dT_L^\alpha} \right)$$

$$= -\frac{v(1-K^\alpha)\, X_B^L}{4D} \cdot S_\alpha$$

$$\Delta T_D = \frac{v(1-K^\alpha)\, X_B^L}{4D\left(\frac{1}{m^\alpha} - \frac{1}{m^\beta}\right)} \cdot S_\alpha \tag{3.6}$$

where m^α and m^β are the slopes of the liquidus curves.
A second undercooling ΔT_r due to the radius of curvature (Gibbs-Thomson Effect) of the lamellae occurs. The eutectic transformation can not occur at the eutectic reaction isotherm T_e, because the change in Gibbs free energy is zero. The driving force must be sufficient to overcome the interfacial energy associated with the α/β interface. The free energy change for the transformation of liquid into α and β phases is written as,

$$\Delta G = \Delta H_f - T\Delta S_f$$

where ΔH_f and ΔS_f are the enthalpy and entropy of fusion, respectively. From $\Delta S_f = \Delta H_f / T_e$, we can write,

$$\Delta G = \frac{\Delta H_f \, \Delta T}{T_e} \tag{3.7}$$

Consider unit length of the slab of the lamellar structure, Fig. 3.30. The area of the α/β interface is $(2 \times 1 \times b)$. The volume of the structure contained within a lamellar spacing S is $(1 \times S \times b)$. The interfacial area of the α/β interface per mole is written as $(2 \times 1 \times b \,/\, 1 \times S \times b \times V_m)$.

The interfacial energy is equal to the specific interfacial energy per unit area of the interface

$$\Delta G^{\gamma} = \gamma \times 2V_m/S = 2\gamma V_m/S \tag{3.8}$$

Equating the free energies from equations (3.7) and (3.8) yields,

$$\Delta H_f \frac{\Delta T}{T_e} = \frac{2\gamma V_m}{S}$$

or

$$\Delta T = \Delta T_r = \frac{2\gamma V_m T_e}{S \cdot \Delta H_f}. \tag{3.9}$$

The undercooling due to the radius of curvature of the lamellae is given by equation (3.9) and is shown in Fig. 3.31.

The total undercooling is the sum of the undercooling due to constitutional supercooling and the radius of curvature. Thus,

$$\Delta T = \Delta T_D + \Delta T_r$$

$$\Delta T = \frac{v(1-K^{\alpha})X_B^L S_{\alpha}}{4D\left(\frac{1}{m^{\alpha}} - \frac{1}{m^{\beta}}\right)} + \frac{2\gamma\, V_m\, T_e}{S \cdot \Delta H_f} \tag{3.10}$$

In order to determine a relationship between the interlamellar spacing and growth rate, the concept of the rate of entropy production is used, which is assumed to be equivalent to minimizing the rate of change of undercooling, ΔT, as a function of interlamellar spacing. Thus differentiating ΔT with respect to S and setting $\partial \Delta T/\partial S = 0$ yields:

$$vS^2 = \frac{8\gamma V_m T_e}{\Delta H_f} \cdot \frac{\left(\frac{1}{m^\alpha} - \frac{1}{m^\beta}\right)}{(1-k^\alpha)\, X_B^L f^\alpha} \tag{3.11}$$

where f^α is the fraction of the α phase determined from the equality, $S_\alpha = f^\alpha$. S in equation (3.10).

As was shown in section 3.9 on the modification of eutectics, the phase boundaries are affected by the change in the rate of cooling. The rate of cooling directly affects the interlamellar spacing and, hence, the liquidus temperature is depressed compared to the equilibrium condition, Fig. 3.29. The undercooling due to diffusion, ΔT_D, length PN corresponds to the liquid composition at the interface, $C_L^*(X_B^*)$ as shown in Fig. 3.29. Similarly, the metastable liquidus T_L^r when extended parallel to the equilibrium liquidus meets the composition vertical C_L^* at the point M. The undercooling due to the radius of curvature ΔT_r equals the length MN. The undercooling due to diffusion and radius of curvature is shown in Fig. 3.31b for the interface shape shown in Fig. 3.30.

In the theory of lamellar eutectic growth by Jackson and Chalmers (6), it has been assumed that the interface is planar and the relative volumes of the two phases are equal. A formal theory of lamellar eutectic growth has been developed by Jackson and Hunt (7), giving a complete description of the shape of the interface, interlamellar spacing, undercooling etc. It is based on the steady state solution of the diffusion equation.

Consider a plane interface of the lamellar eutectic with the liquid with S_α and S_β* being the half widths of the α and β phases, respectively. The origin of the coordinate system is taken at the center of the α lamellae at the α/L interface. The growth of the eutectic occurs along the z direction and x represents the lateral diffusion direction along the interface, Fig. 3.32. The direction y is parallel to the α/β interface. The diffusion problem is essentially two-dimensional. The diffusion equation under steady state is written as

$$\frac{\partial^2 X_B}{\partial x^2} + \frac{\partial^2 X_B}{\partial z^2} + \frac{v}{D_L}\frac{\partial X_B}{\partial z} = 0, \tag{3.12}$$

---

*This follows from the original derivation given by Jackson and Hunt (7).

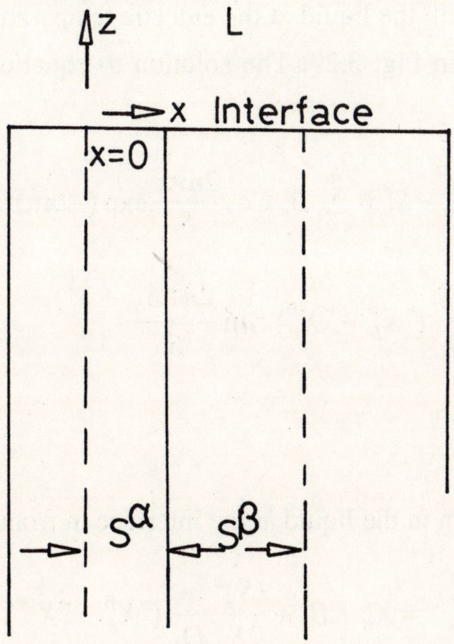

Fig. 3.32 Planar lamellar eutectic interface with the liquid and the coordinate system.

where v is the rate of eutectic growth as given earlier.

The symmetry of the problem is sufficient to determine the solution to the diffusion equation in the region $0 < x < (S_\alpha + S_\beta)$. The initial and boundary conditions are,

$$X_B^L = X_B^e \qquad \text{at} \quad z = \propto$$

and $\partial X_B^L/\partial x = 0$ at $x = 0$ and $\partial X_B/\partial x = 0$ at $x = (S_\alpha + S_\beta)$.

Conservation of matter requires that at the interface,

$$-D_L\,(\partial X_B^L/\partial z)_{z=0} = v\,(X_B^e - {}^{\propto}X_B^{\alpha}), \qquad 0 \le x \le S_\alpha \,. \tag{3.13}$$

and

$$-D_L\,(\partial X_B^L/\partial z)_{z=0} = v\,(X_B^e - {}^{\propto}X_B^{\beta}), \quad S_\alpha \le x \le (S_\alpha + S_\beta). \tag{3.14}$$

In the above equations X_B^α and X_B^β are the compositions of the α and β phases, respectively, in equilibrium with the liquid at the eutectic temperature and X_B^e is the eutectic composition as shown in Fig. 3.29. The solution to equation (3.12) with the above boundary conditions is

$$X_B^L - X_B^e = \sum_{n=1}^{\infty} B_n \operatorname{Cos} \frac{2n\pi x}{S} \exp(-2n\pi z/S) \tag{3.15}$$

where $B_n = \dfrac{1}{(n\pi)^2} \cdot \dfrac{vS}{D_L} ({}^{\infty}X_B^\beta - {}^{\infty}X_B^\alpha) \operatorname{Sin} \dfrac{2n\pi S_\alpha}{S}$

and $S = 2(S_\alpha + S_\beta)$.

The average composition in the liquid at the interface in front of the α is given by

$$X_B^{L/\alpha} = X_B^e + B_0 + \frac{(S)^2}{2S_\alpha} \frac{v}{D_L} ({}^{\infty}X_B^\beta - {}^{\infty}X_B^\alpha) P. \tag{3.16}$$

and in front of the β phase, it is given by

$$X_B^{L/\beta} = X_B^e + B_0 - \frac{S^2}{2S_\beta} \frac{v}{D_L} ({}^{\infty}X_B^\beta - {}^{\infty}X_B^\alpha) P.$$

where $P = \sum_{n=1}^{\infty} \left(\dfrac{1}{n\pi}\right)^3 \operatorname{Sin}^2 \left(\dfrac{2n\pi S_\alpha}{S}\right)$.

The composition of the liquid as a function of distance from the interface is shown schematically in Fig. 3.33, (a) at the interface, z = 0, (b) $z/(S_\alpha + S_\beta) = 0.2$ and (c) $z = S_\alpha + S_\beta$. There is a small composition difference from the eutectic composition along the interface. The composition difference $(X_B^L - X_B^e)$ gradually decreases as the distance from the interface into the liquid increases and disappears completely at a distance $z = S_\alpha + S_\beta$.

In order to determine quantitatively the liquid composition as a function of distance from the interface and along the interface, apart from the diffusional undercooling, ΔT_r, the angle of contact and the interfacial energies at the three-phase junction,

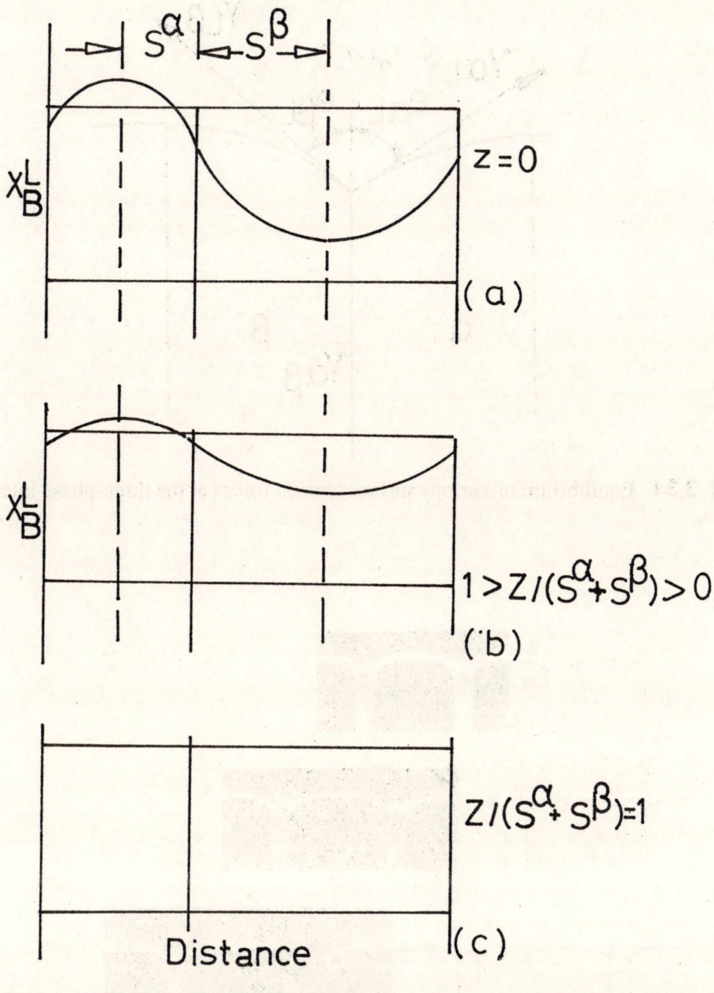

Fig. 3.33 Calculated values of the liquid composition at various positions in the growth direction.

α–β–*L*, are required. Interfacial energies and contact angles at the interface are related by the following relationship (this can be easily done by resolving surface tension force at the three-phase junction, as shown in Fig. 3.34).

$$\gamma_{\alpha L} \cos \theta_{\alpha L} + \gamma_{\beta L} \cos \theta_{\beta L} = \gamma_{\alpha\beta} \tag{3.18}$$

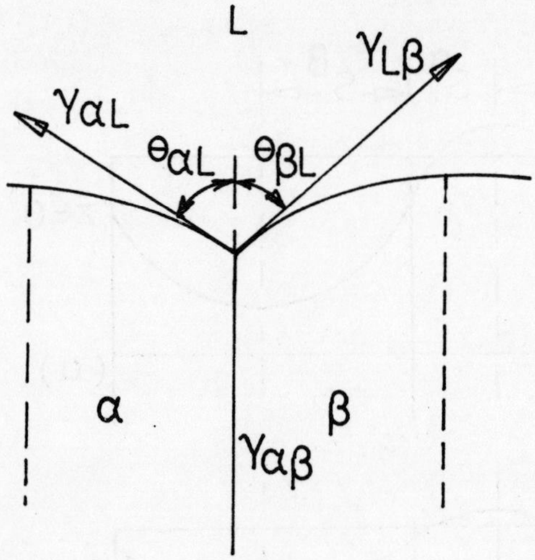

Fig. 3.34 Equilibrium of various surface tension forces at the three-phase interface.

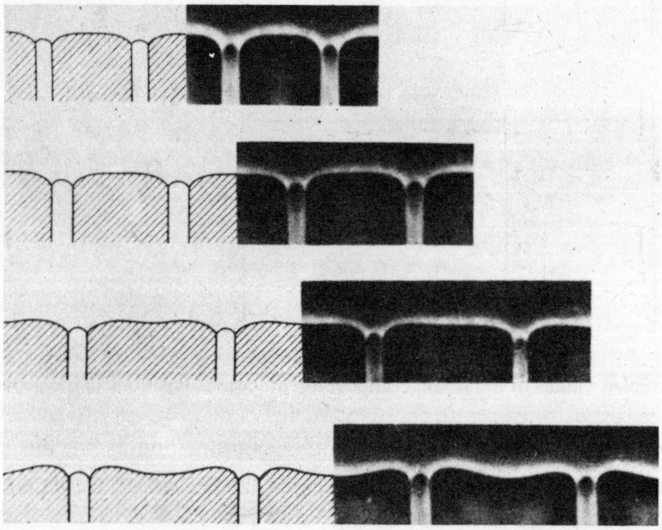

Fig. 3.35 Comparison of calculated and observed shapes of lamellar eutectic for a transparent organic eutectic (after Hunt, J.D. & Jackson, *Trans. AIME*, 236 (1966), 843).

The interface shape has been calculated by Jackson and Hunt (7) and compared with those actually observed for a transparent organic liquid, Fig. 3.35.

A relation between the interlamellar spacing and growth rate, similar to that derived earlier equation (3.11), can be formulated using equations (3.1), (3.9) and (3.15). The equation has the following form:

$$\Delta T = K v S + \frac{L}{S} \tag{3.19}$$

where K and L are constants given by

$$K = -\frac{{}^{\infty}X_B^{\beta} - {}^{\infty}X_B^{\alpha}}{D_L} \sum_{n=1}^{\infty} \frac{1}{(n\pi)^2} \operatorname{Sin}\left(\frac{2n\pi S_\alpha}{S}\right) \operatorname{Cos}\left(\frac{2n\pi x}{S}\right) \exp\left(-2n\pi z/Z\right)$$

$$L = \frac{2\gamma V_m T_e}{\Delta H_t}$$

Following arguments similar to that used in arriving at equation (3.11), we can write,

$$\frac{\partial \Delta T}{\partial S} = 0 = K v - \frac{L}{S^2}$$

or

$$v S^2 = \frac{L}{K} \tag{3.20a}$$

$$(\Delta T)^2 = 4\, v K L \tag{3.20b}$$

Equation (3.20a) predicts that the product of growth rate and the square of the interlamellar spacing is a constant. Experiments carried out (2) on a number of alloy systems confirm this relationship, Fig. 3.36, a to e. Similarly equation (3.20b) predicts that the ΔT vs. $\sqrt{v}$ relationship should follow a straight line. Experimental evidence to support this has come from the work of Hunt and Chilton (8) for a Pb-Sn eutectic alloy, Fig. 3.36f.

The minimum undercooling criterion can be utilized to understand the interlamellar spacing that a system selects under a given growth velocity condition. A plot of ΔT vs. lamellar spacing S in Fig. 3.37 illustrates that the undercooling initially decreases

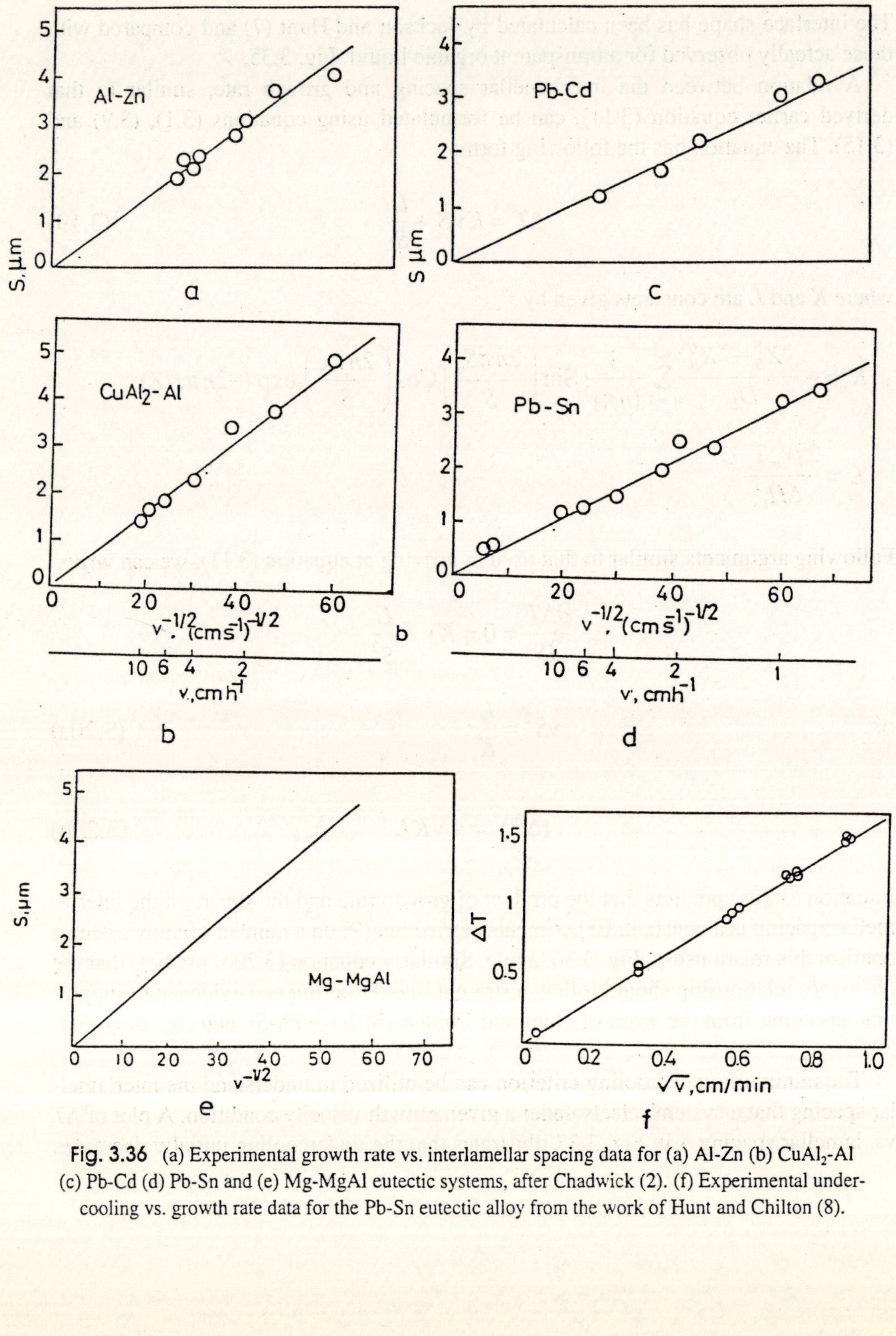

Fig. 3.36 (a) Experimental growth rate vs. interlamellar spacing data for (a) Al-Zn (b) $CuAl_2$-Al (c) Pb-Cd (d) Pb-Sn and (e) Mg-MgAl eutectic systems, after Chadwick (2). (f) Experimental undercooling vs. growth rate data for the Pb-Sn eutectic alloy from the work of Hunt and Chilton (8).

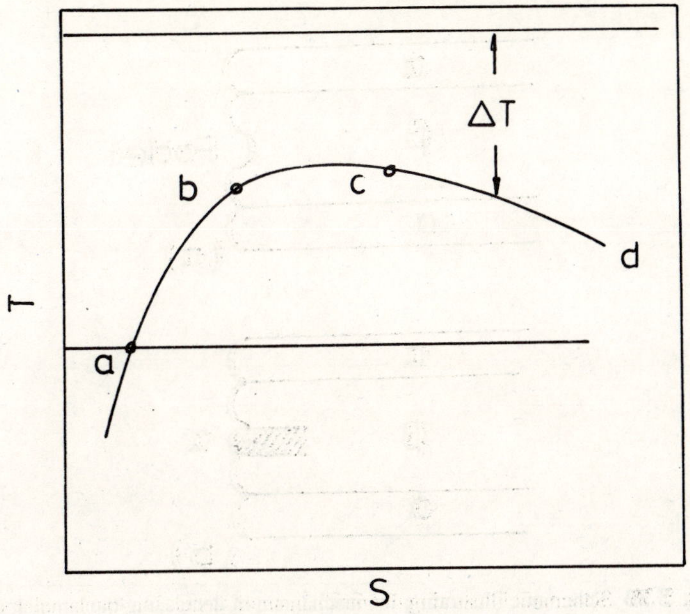

Fig. 3.37 T vs. interlamellar spacing. The magnitude of ΔT is seen to be a function of the interlamellar spacing.

as the interlamellar spacing increases, reaches a minimum value (known as extremum), and then increases again. The curve can be divided into three parts from a to b, b to c and c to d for large spacing. The undercooling in the range a to b leads to increasing growth rates and those lamellae nearer b will dominate the microstructure. Interlamellar spacings in the range b to c are all stable and depending upon the local condition the system will strive towards a particular spacing in this range if the growth rate is constant. At large ΔT in the range c to d, the growth rate slows down and the interlamellar spacing becomes large. The interface curvature cannot maintain a uniform isothermal temperature throughout the interface. There is no definite shape of the interface at large spacings. The interface will either double back or a cylindrical depression will form in the middle of the lamellae. In either case, the system supporting large interlamellar spacings becomes unstable leading to nucleation of the other phase. The interlamellar spacing decreases, thereby reducing the undercooling towards the extremum which in turn brings stability to the interface curvature. The change in lamellar spacing is schematically illustrated in Fig. 3.38. The development of additional lamellae has been described in terms of growth faults by Jackson and Chalmers (6) and by Jackson and Hunt (7).

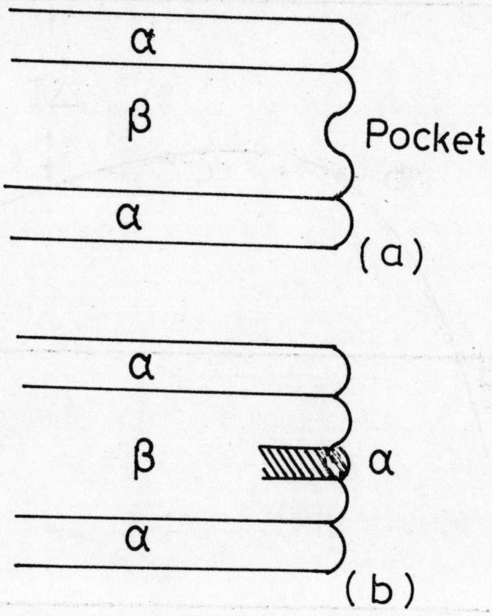

Fig. 3.38 Schematic illustrating the mechanism of decreasing the lamellar spacing so as to adjust to increasing growth rate.

3.12 The Binary Peritectic Systems

If there is a considerable difference in the melting points of thc two component metals, A and B, then upon adding component B to A, the system lowers its melting temperature through a peritectic reaction,

$$L + \alpha \underset{}{\overset{T_p}{\rightleftharpoons}} \beta.$$

Accordingly, solid phase α reacts with liquid to give another solid phase β of a different composition, Fig. 3.39. The crystal structures of the two solids α and β are different in most of the alloy systems. The peritectic reaction occurs at a fixed temperature T_p known as the peritectic reaction isotherm. Compositions of the three phases α, β and liquid in equilibrium with each other at T_p are invariant as shown by

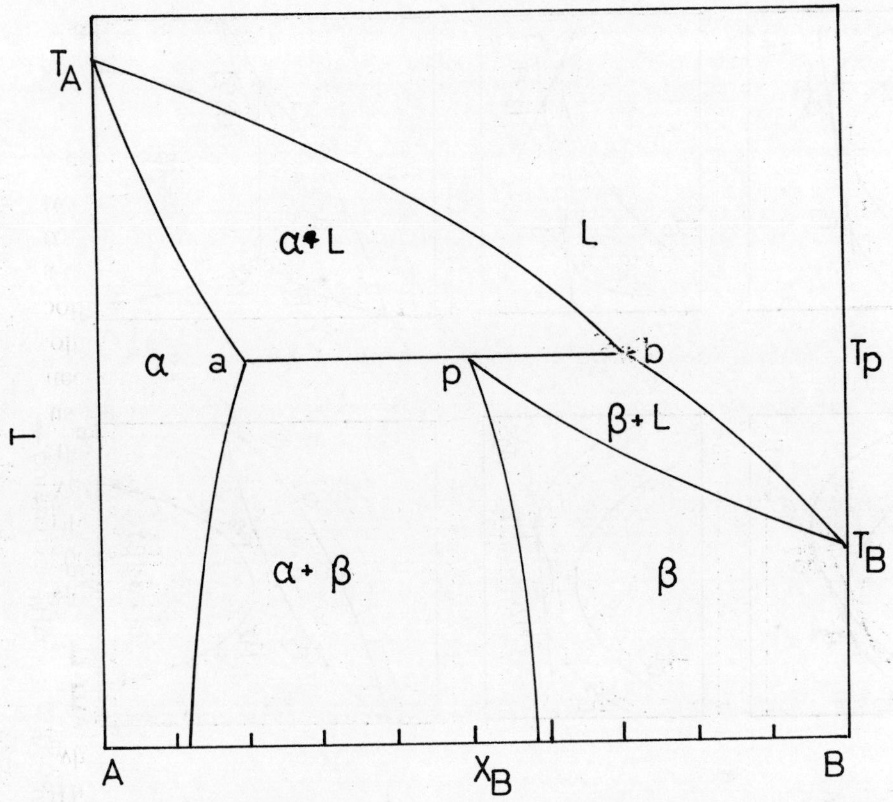

Fig. 3.39 A binary phase diagram between components *A* and *B* showing the peritectic reaction.

points *a*, *p* and *b* respectively, in Fig. 3.39. This can be easily demonstrated by applying the phase rule in a three-phase region of the phase diagram. Accordingly, $F = C - P + 1 = 2 - 3 + 1 = 0$. A simple phase diagram showing only the peritectic reaction has the following boundaries (Fig. 3.39).

Liquidus : T_Ab and bT_B
Solidus : T_Aa and pT_B
Solvus : *ac* and *pq*

Peritectic isotherm: *apb*.

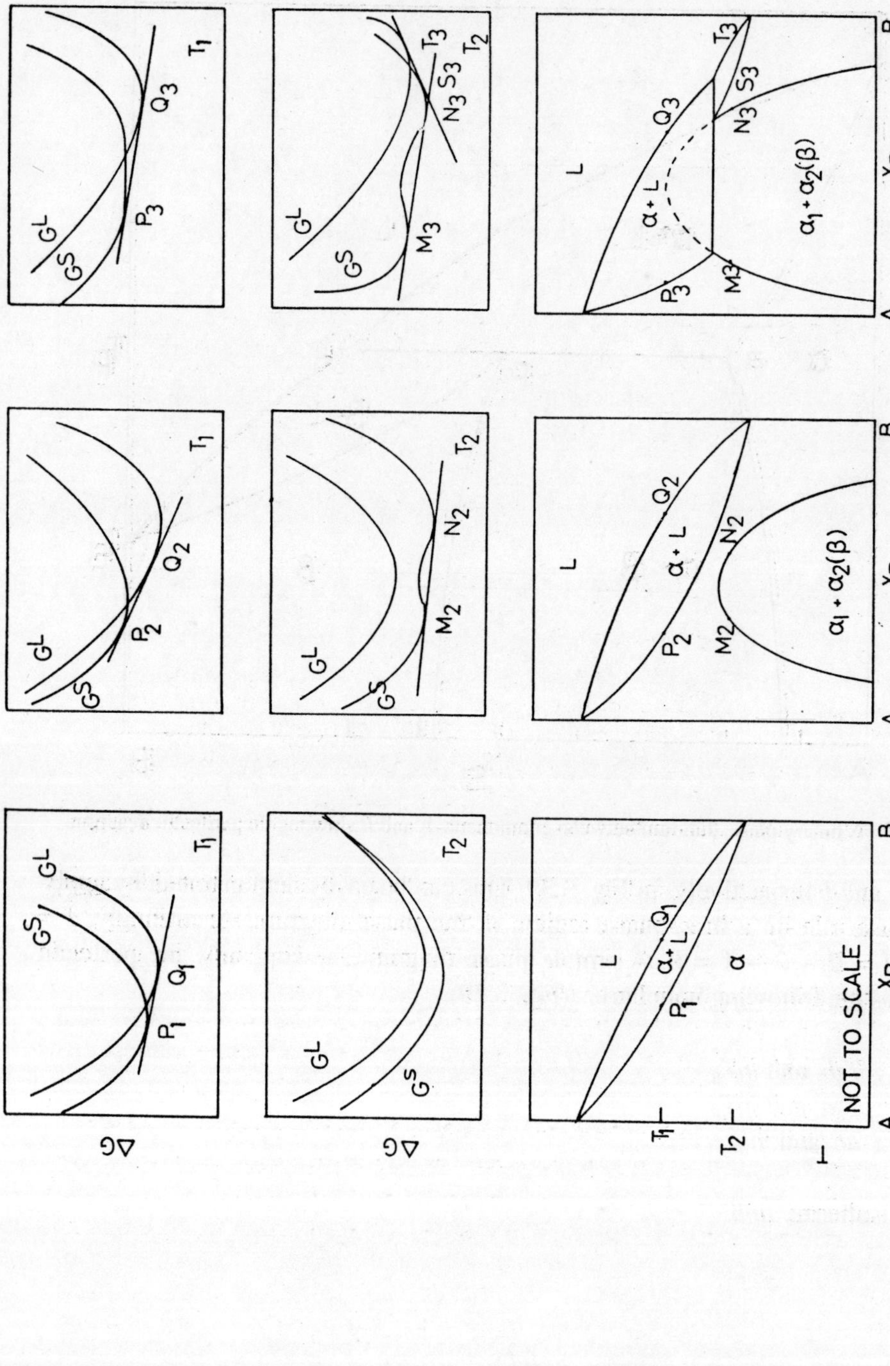

Fig. 3.40 Free energy-composition diagrams with increasing ΔH_m. The resulting phase diagrams are shown at the bottom in each panel.

If there is a positive departure from ideality such that $\Delta H_m^{\alpha} > \Delta H_m^{L} > 0$, then the phase diagram with a solid solution in the whole range of compositions can gradually change to two solid solutions; one α and the other β, maintaining equilibrium with the liquid. This is illustrated with the help of a series of free energy-composition diagrams, when ΔH_m is allowed to increase, Fig. 3.40.

3.13 EQUILIBRIUM SOLIDIFICATION OF A PERITECTIC ALLOY

As with the binary eutectic system, alloy compositions in a binary peritectic system can be designated as peritectic, hypoperitectic and hyperperitectic. An alloy composition lying in the composition range *a* to *p* is termed hypoperitectic whereas the one between *p* and *b* is a hyperperitectic alloy, Fig. 3.41. This convention is again relative to the component *A* being a more common metal.

Let us first consider the equilibrium solidification of a liquid alloy, marked *x*, of the peritectic composition, Fig. 3.41. At temperature T_0, the alloy is in the form of a liquid solution of *A* and *B* and remains so till the temperature T_1 is reached. At small undercoolings near T_1, the solid of composition α_1 forms from the liquid. Upon further cooling, compositions of the liquid move along $L_1L_2L_3L_4$ and those of the solid along $\alpha_1\alpha_2\alpha_3\alpha_4$. The composition of the α phase is uniform at each decrement of temperature between T_1 and T_4 and is dictated by the solidus boundary. Just above the temperature T_4, the α phase of composition α_4 is in equilibrium with liquid of composition L_4. The relative amounts of the two phases are:

$$\%\ \alpha = \frac{pb}{ab} \times 100 = \frac{0.7 - 0.5}{0.7 - 0.2} \times 100 = 40\%$$

$$\%\ L = 60\%.$$

Thus 60% α is in equilibrium with 40% liquid just above T_p. Upon lowering the temperature just below T_p, these two phases will react with each other with the formation of the product phase β. If the cooling is carried out under equilibrium conditions (very slowly) all of the α phase will react with the liquid to yield 100% β phase of composition $X_B^{\beta_4}$.

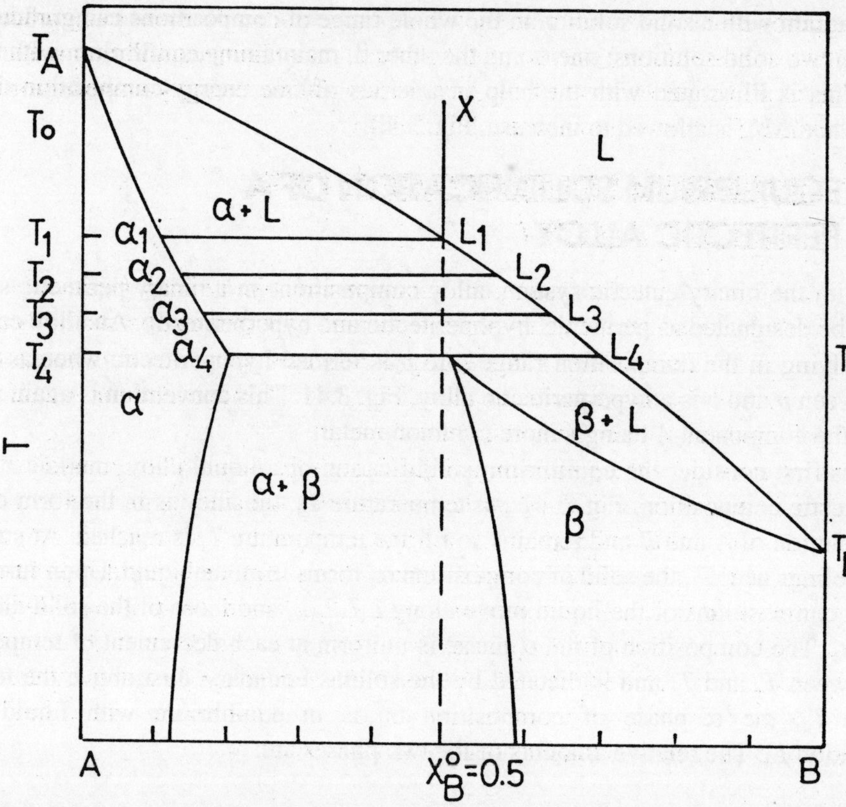

Fig. 3.41 Binary phase diagram showing a peritectic reaction. Compositions of the solid and liquid phases during equilibrium solidification of the peritectic composition are shown.

According to the phase diagram of Fig. 3.41, 3 parts liquid will always react with 2 parts α to yield 100% β phase. Now, consider the resulting microstructure. Just above the peritectic reaction isotherm, an alloy containing 40% *B* and the balance *A* contains 60% liquid and 40% α phase, Fig. 3.42. The peritectic reaction only occurs upon cooling the alloy below T_p. At this stage the α phase will react with the liquid to give the β phase. The reaction in all probability begins at the α/*L* interface. A layer of the β phase forms initially at the interface. Further growth of the β phase occurs by the net diffusion of *B* atoms from the liquid towards the α phase and simultaneous transport of *A* atoms from the α phase towards the liquid. This is evident from the fact that the composition of the β phase lies between the solute-rich liquid and the solvent-rich α

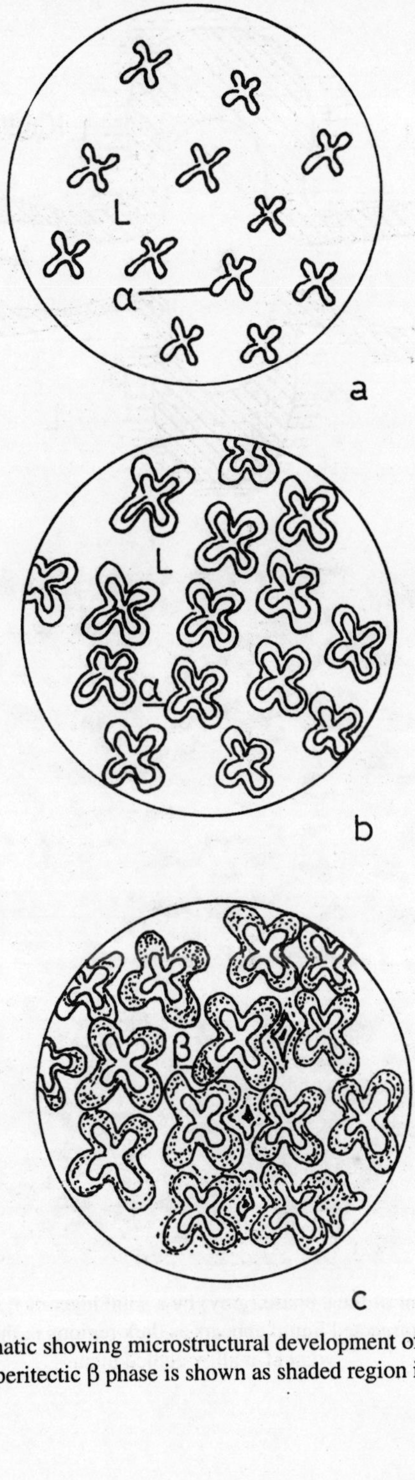

Fig. 3.42 Schematic showing microstructural development of a peritectic alloy. The peritectic β phase is shown as shaded region in (c).

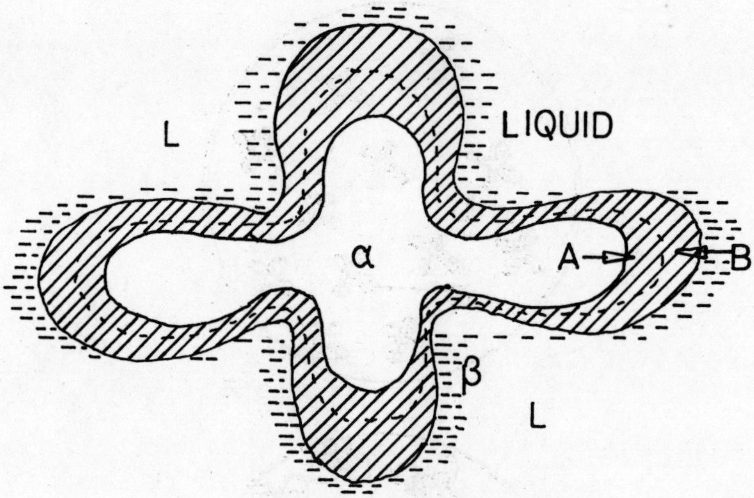

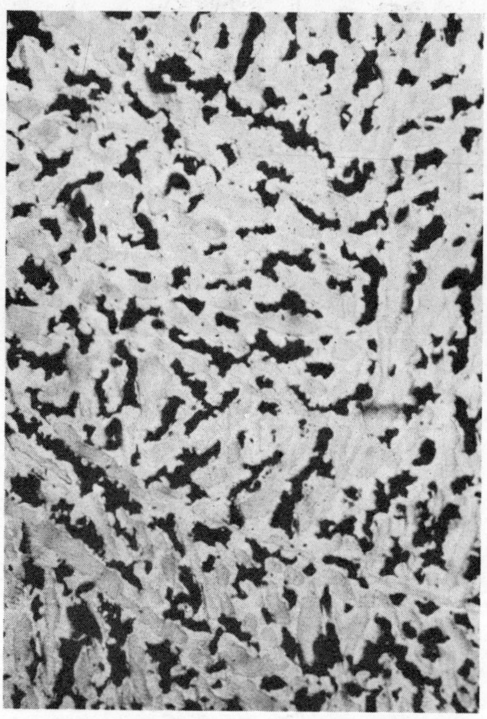

Fig. 3.43 The envelopment of the ε phase (gray) by a solid layer of η (white) which forms from the peritectic reaction. The unreacted liquid appears as dark regions in the photomicrograph, Sn-30 wt.pct.Cu alloy cooled in air.

phase. The diffusion of *A* and *B* type atoms occurs through the solid crust of β enveloping the α phase, Fig. 3.43. As the β phase grows by the migration of β/*L* interface towards the liquid and the α/β interface into the α phase, its thickness increases and the distance that the solute and solvent atoms have to diffuse becomes larger. The lower free energy of the β phase as compared to the free energy of phase mixtures of the α and liquid phase provides the necessary driving force for the transport of atoms. Because of the slow diffusion of the solute in the solid, it generally takes longer for the peritectic reaction to reach completion. The reaction, therefore, remains incomplete until and unless the alloy is cooled very slowly. Under equilibrium cooling, the final microstructure will consist of differently oriented β-phase regions separated by interfaces, as shown in Fig. 3.42.

3.14 EQUILIBRIUM SOLIDIFICATION OF HYPOPERITECTIC AND HYPERPERITECTIC ALLOYS

Next, let us consider the solidification of a hypoperitectic alloy, marked *y* in Fig. 3.44, consisting of 30% component *B*, i.e., $X_B^0 = 0.3$. The solidification of the alloy begins at the temperature T_1 with formation of the primary α phase of composition α_1. As for the alloy of peritectic composition, the equilibrium cooling of the hypoperitectic alloy will result in the composition of the α phase changing along the solidus and that of the liquid phase along the liquidus with the lowering of temperature below T_1. The α and liquid phases will have the following relative amounts just above the peritectic reaction isotherm:

$$\% \,\alpha = \frac{0.7-0.3}{0.7-0.2} \times 100 = 80\%$$

$$\% \,L = 20\%.$$

Upon cooling below the peritectic temperature, the α phase will react with the liquid to give β as the product phase. In this case 20% liquid will react with 13.33% α $(= 20 \times 40 / 60 \times 100)$. The relative amount of the β phase formed as product of the peritectic reaction will be 33.33% (20 + 13.33) provided that the solidification is carried out very slowly such that equilibrium is maintained at each stage. Just below T_p, the alloy will consist of 66.66% primary α and 33.33% β phase. The relative amounts of the α and β phases can also be determined by applying the lever rule just below T_p on the lever *ap* with the fulcrum at $X_B^0 = 0.3$. The values are,

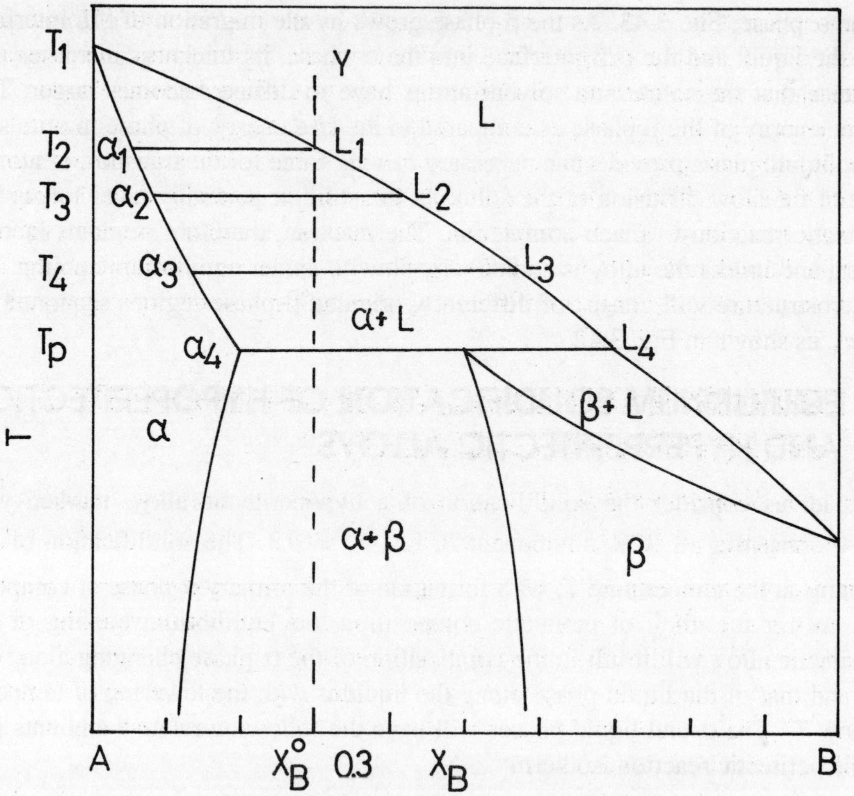

Fig. 3.44 Compositions of the solid and liquid phases during equilibrium solidification of a hypoperitectic alloy.

$$\% \alpha = \frac{0.5-0.3}{0.5-0.2} \times 100 = 66.66\%$$

$$\% \beta = 33.33\%.$$

The α phase formed above the peritectic reaction isotherm is the primary constituent and the β phase, therefore, becomes the secondary constituent, having formed from the peritectic reaction. Further adjustments in the relative amount of the two phases is possible when the alloy cools below the peritectic temperature. This is due to change in solubility of the component B in the α and β phases as characterized by the solvus.

The resulting microstructure for a Sn-Cu alloy would consists of β phase enveloping the α phase. The (α+β) brass structure is shown for a cu-40 wt. pct. Zn alloy, Fig. 3.45.

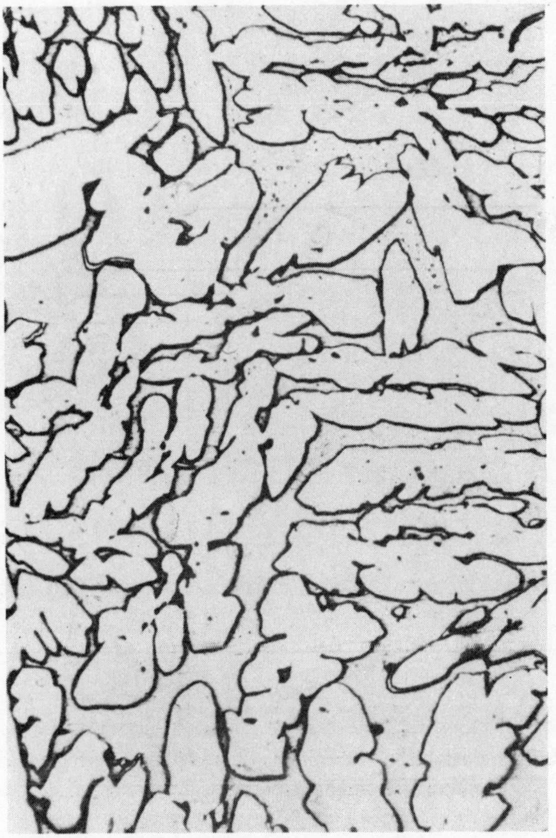

Fig. 3.45 The microstructure of the two-phase β-brass structure in a Cu-40 wt.pct.Zn alloy.

An alloy composition indicated by the composition vertical z ($X_b^0 = 0.6$) is termed as a hyperperitectic alloy, Fig. 3.46. The nuclei of the α phase of composition α_1 will develop in the alloy at temperature T_1 when the alloy is allowed to cool from the liquid solution state at T_0, Fig. 3.46. As the temperature is lowered, more of primary α phase will nucleate and grow at the expense of the liquid. The relative amounts of the α and liquid phases formed in the temperature interval T_1 to T_p can be determined from the lever rule as follows,

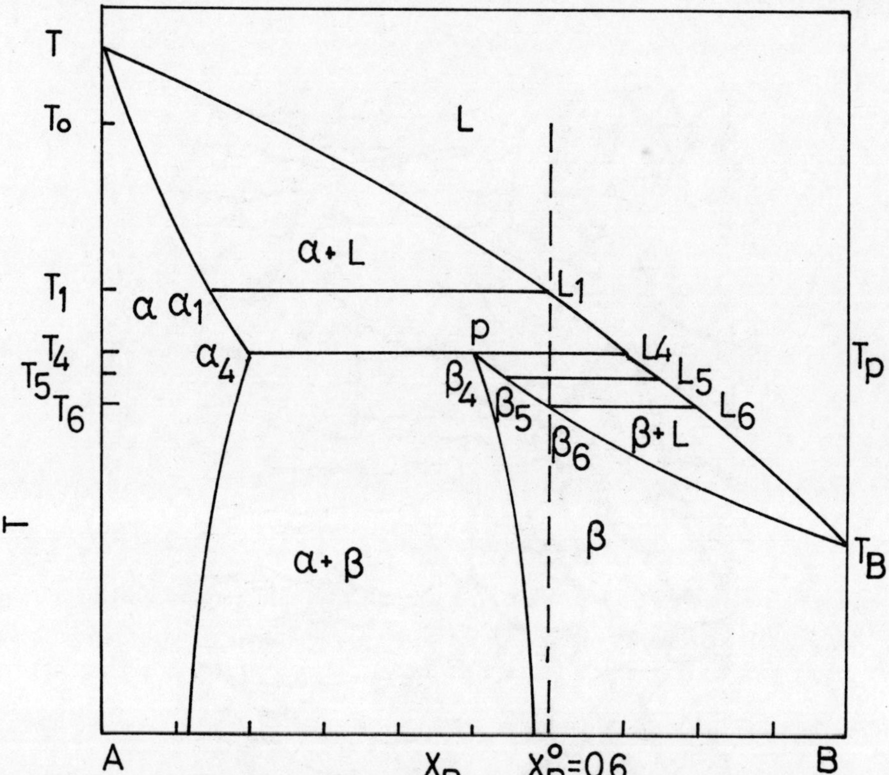

Fig. 3.46 Compositions of the solid and liquid phases during equilibrium solidification of a hyperperitectic alloy.

$$\% \, \alpha = \frac{0.7-0.6}{0.7-0.2} \times 100 = 20\%$$

$$\% \, L = 80\%.$$

Since the relative amount of the liquid is relatively larger than the α phase, all of the primary α will be consumed when it reacts with the liquid to give β as the product phase. Some liquid of composition X_B^L will remain unreacted below T_p. The relative amounts of the α and liquid phases below the peritectic reaction isotherm will be

$$\%\,\beta = \frac{70-60}{70-50} \times 100 = 50\%$$

$$\%\,L = \frac{60-50}{70-50} \times 100 = 50\% \,.$$

Further cooling below the peritectic temperature will result in the deposition of β over the existing peritectic β. This would be easier than nucleation of new β regions from kinetic considerations. The peritectic β phase is also of the appropriate composition for deposition of the solute-rich β over it. Under equilibrium cooling, the composition of the peritectic β will have to change to new values at each decrement of temperature as dictated by the solidus pT_B. The composition of the β phase thus changes along $\beta_4\beta_5\beta_6$ and that of the liquid along $L_4L_5L_6$ till the liquid solidifies completely. The final microstructure will consist of grains of β as an assembly of polyhedra, Fig. 3.47d.

3.15 NATURAL COOLING OF PERITECTIC, HYPOPERITECTIC AND HYPERPERITECTIC ALLOYS

The relative amounts of the phases and the microstructures obtained during equilibrium solidification of peritectic alloys is guided by the equilibrium phase diagram. During natural solidification of such alloys, there is a relatively large departure from equilibrium. This is due to reasons beyond control because of the slower diffusion of solute (or solvent) in the solid layer of the product phase that forms between the reactants. Consider the solidification of an alloy of hypoperitectic composition ($X_B^0 = 0.3$) under natural cooling conditions, Fig. 3.48. Primary crystals of the α phase of composition α_1 form in the liquid solution at the temperature T_1. At every decrement of temperature, primary α of a composition dictated by the solidus will form at existing α. For example, the composition of the layer of α formed at T_2 will be given by the point α_2 on the solidus. Thus, in the temperature interval from T_1 to T_2, layers of α ranging in composition from α_1 to α_2 form as thin layers. Because of rapid solidification, the time available for diffusion is insufficient, causing an inhomogeneity in the composition of the α phase. The concentration of solute in the α will increase from the core to the periphery of α. The average composition of the α phase will show a departure from the equilibrium value α_2 at the temperature T_2. At the temperature T_4, point α_4 on the solidus will represent the composition of the outermost layer of the primary α. The relative amounts of the non-equilibrium α and liquid phases, just above T_4 are,

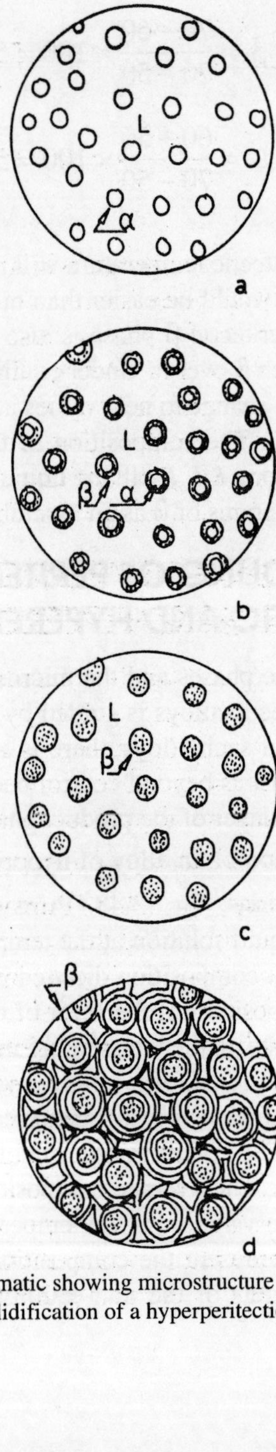

Fig. 3.47 Schematic showing microstructure of the β phase during solidification of a hyperperitectic alloy.

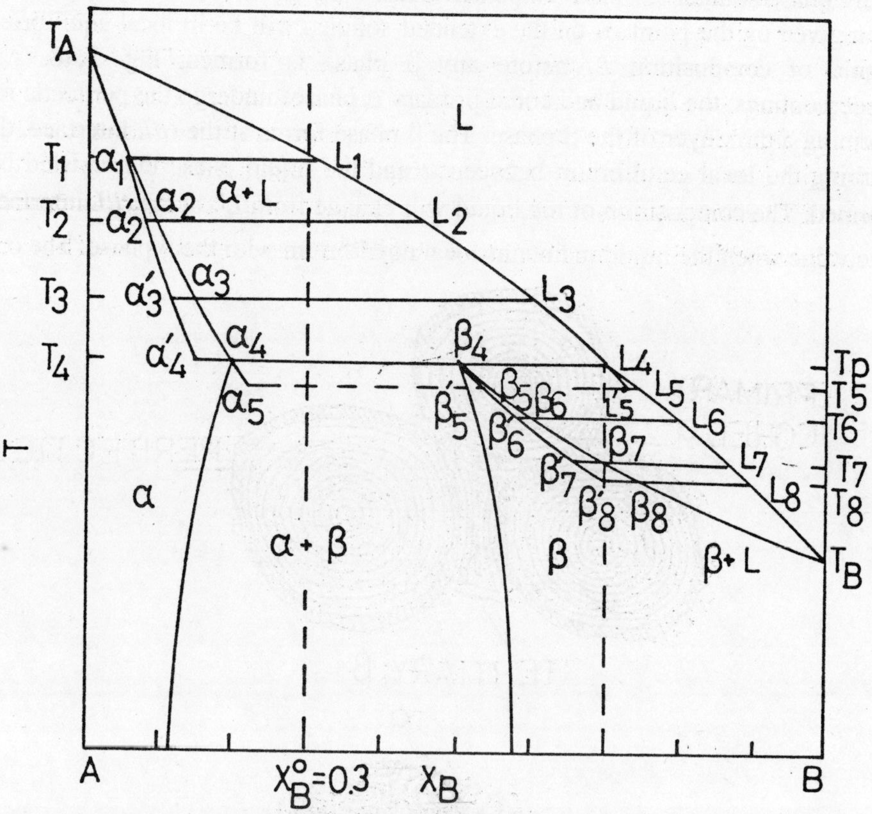

Fig. 3.48 Compositions of the solid and liquid phases during natural cooling of a hypoperitectic alloy.

$$\% \, \alpha = \frac{0.7 - 0.3}{0.7 - 0.15} \times 100 = 72.72\%$$

$$\% \, L = 27.27\%,$$

showing that a relatively larger proportion of the liquid solution remains at T_4. Compare the above result with the 20% liquid obtained under equilibrium solidification.

The primary α phase can continue forming below the peritectic temperature during natural cooling of the alloy. The compositions of the α and liquid phases that will be in local equilibrium with each other can be obtained by extension of the high temperature phase boundaries. At a temperature below T_p, say at T_5, the α phase of composition given by the point α_5 on the extended solidus, will be in local equilibrium with liquid of composition L_5 before any β phase is formed, Fig. 3.48. At small undercoolings, the liquid and cored primary α phases undergo the peritectic reaction, forming a thin layer of the β phase. The β phase forms at the α/L interface, thus disturbing the local equilibrium between α and the liquid phase that existed before β formed. The composition of the liquid will change from L'_5 at the α/L interface to L_5, the value when the liquid maintains local equilibrium with the β phase. The α and the

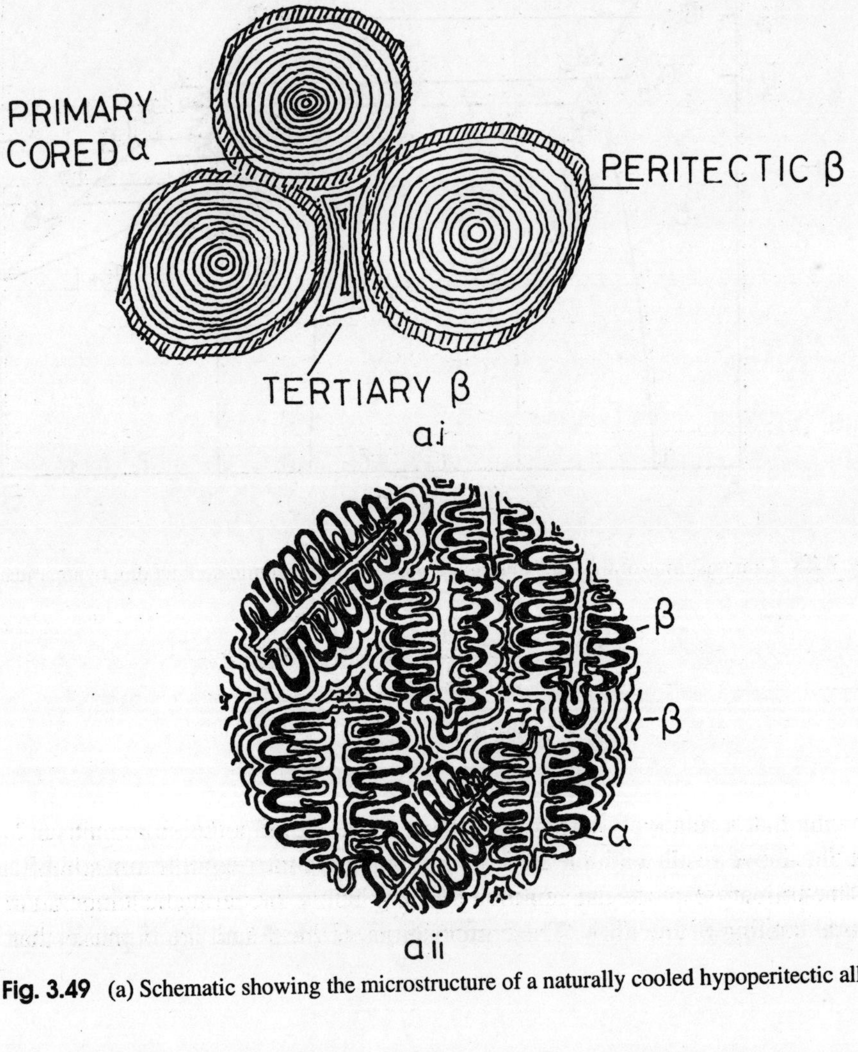

Fig. 3.49 (a) Schematic showing the microstructure of a naturally cooled hypoperitectic alloy.

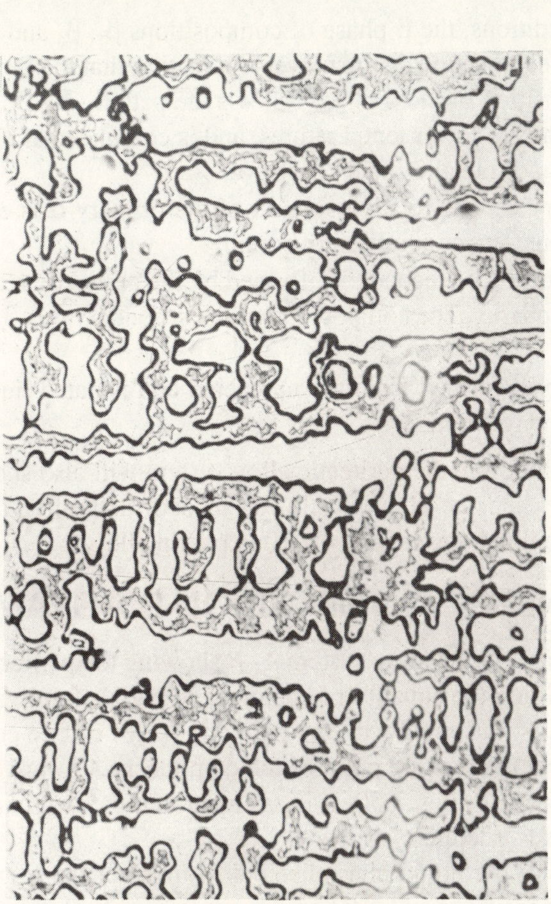

Fig. 3.49 (b) Microstructure of a Cu-10 wt.pct.Sn alloy cooled in air.

liquid phases remain isolated because of the presence of a layer of β between them. In order to form more of the β phase, *A* atoms must diffuse from α towards the α/β interface and *B* atoms must diffuse from the bulk liquid towards the β/*L* interface. The build up of concentration gradient in the β phase makes it grow. As the thickness of the β phase layer increases, the distance that the solute and solvent atoms must diffuse in order to build up the composition necessary for the β phase formation increases. Thus, a thin layer of the β phase forms quickly; however, the rate of migration of α/β and β/*L* interfaces in opposite directions slows down with the thickening of the β layer. The peritectic reaction, therefore, remains incomplete; the liquid remaining unreacted is isolated, and solidifies as a liquid of composition L_5. The solidification of the liquid occurs by the deposition of β over the existing β of composition β_5. Under natural cooling conditions, the β phase of compositions β_5, β_6 and β_7 that form at T_5, T_6 and T_7, respectively, occupy distinct layers indicating that the β phase is also cored. The average composition of the β phase follows the path β_5, β_6, β_7. The solidification of the β phase extends to lower temperatures, and is completed at T_8. The final microstructure, Fig. 3.49a, of the alloy will consist of:

(i) Cored primary α. The relative amount of the primary α is expected to be less than the amount under equilibrium cooling.

(ii) A thin layer of the β (secondary), formed by the peritectic reaction between the α and liquid phases. The composition of the secondary β is β_4 if formed at T_4 or near it.

(iii) Cored tertiary β formed from the unreacted and isolated liquid due to incomplete peritectic reaction.

A terminal solid solution in the peritectic alloy system will also show products of the peritectic reaction when the alloy is allowed to cool naturally. The microstructure shown in Fig. 3.49b illustrates it for a Cu-10wt.pct.Sn alloy.

3.16 FREE ENERGY-COMPOSITION DIAGRAMS

The phase diagram for the alloy system A–B showing the peritectic reaction can be constructed by applying the equality of chemical potentials for a given component in all the phases. This is illustrated with the help of a series of free energy-composition diagrams from above the melting point of the component A to just below the melting point of the component B, Fig. 3.50. It is assumed that the two components A and B have different crystal structures.

The free energy of the liquid phase lies below those of the α and β phases in the whole range of compositions at T_1. A homogeneous liquid solution therefore exists as the stable phase.

The free energy curve of the liquid phase touches that of the α phase at $X_B = 0$, thus establishing equilibrium between the liquid and solid A. The temperature T_2 corresponds to the melting point of pure A.

The solid solution α will become more stable compared to the liquid solution with decreasing temperature. The free energy-composition diagram of the liquid phase will be raised relative to that of the α phase at $T_3 < T_2$. The two free energy curves intersect each other. Compositions of the two phases α and liquid can be determined by drawing a common tangent to the two curves, thus establishing equality of chemical potentials. Compositions of the α and liquid phases are represented by points P_3 and Q_3, respectively, on the common tangent line.

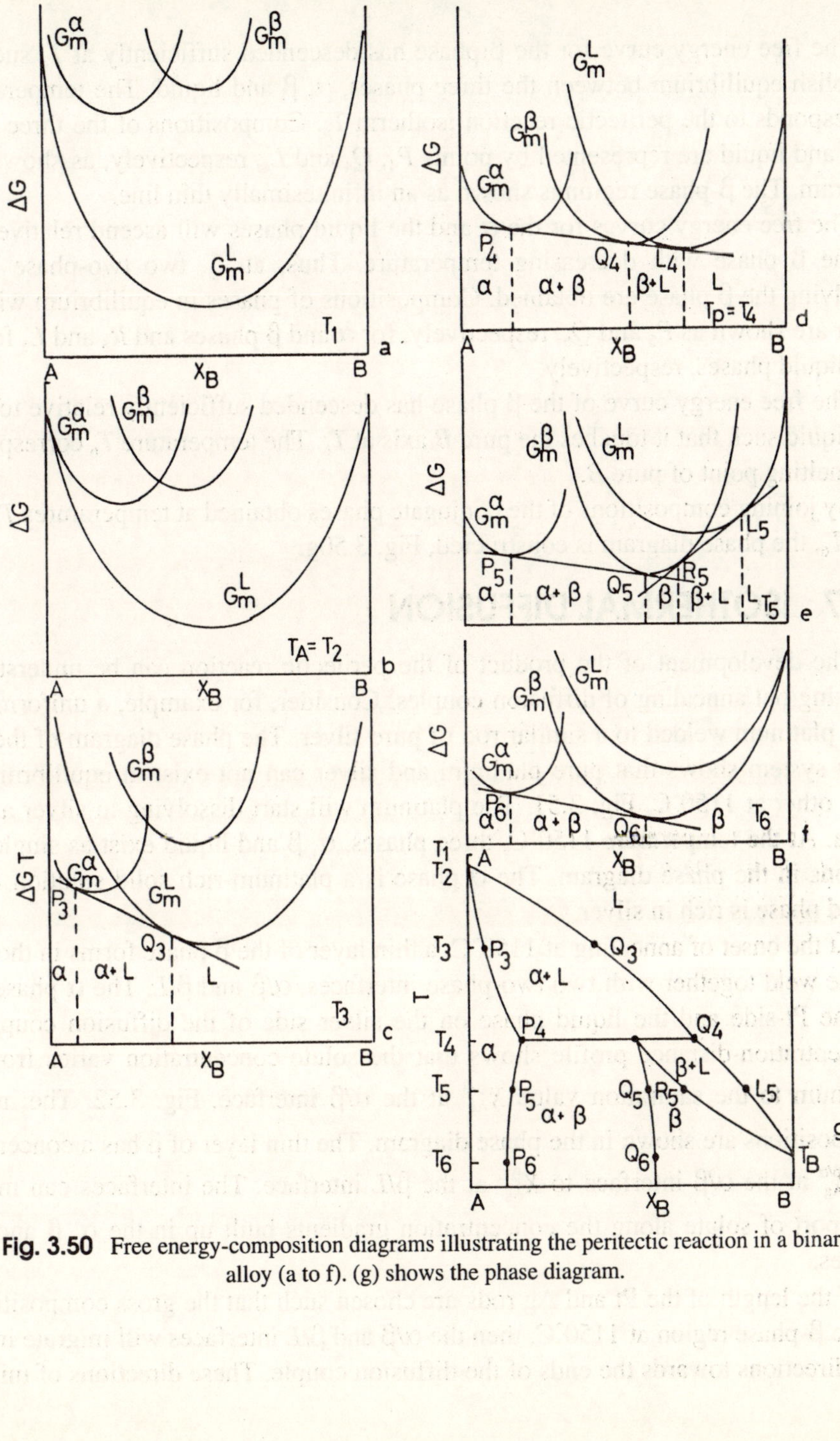

Fig. 3.50 Free energy-composition diagrams illustrating the peritectic reaction in a binary alloy (a to f). (g) shows the phase diagram.

The free energy curve for the β phase has descended sufficiently at T_4 such as to establish equilibrium between the three phases, α, β and liquid. The temperature T_4 corresponds to the peritectic reaction isotherm T_p. Compositions of the three phases, α, β and liquid are represented by points P_4, Q_4 and L_4, respectively, as shown in the diagram. The β-phase region is shown as an infinitesimally thin line.

The free energy curves for the α and the liquid phases will ascend relative to that of the β phase with decreasing temperature. Thus, at T_5, two two-phase regions involving the β phase are obtained. Compositions of phases in equilibrium with each other are shown as P_5 and Q_5, respectively, for α and β phases and R_5 and L_5 for the β and liquid phases, respectively.

The free energy curve of the β phase has descended sufficiently relative to that of the liquid such that it touches the pure B axis at T_6. The temperature T_6 corresponds to the melting point of pure B.

By joining compositions of the conjugate phases obtained at temperatures T_3, T_4, T_5 and T_6, the phase diagram is constructed, Fig. 3.50g.

3.17 ISOTHERMAL DIFFUSION

The development of the product of the peritectic reaction can be understood by carrying out annealing of diffusion couples. Consider, for example, a uniform rod of pure platinum welded to a similar rod of pure silver. The phase diagram of the Pt-Ag alloy system shows that pure platinum and silver can not exist in equilibrium with each other at 1150°C, Fig. 3.51. The platinum will start dissolving in silver and vice versa. At the temperature 1150°C, three phases, α, β and liquid exist as single-phase regions in the phase diagram. The α phase is a platinum-rich solid solution and the liquid phase is rich in silver.

At the onset of annealing at 1150°C, a thin layer of the β phase forms in the region of the weld together with two two-phase interfaces, α/β and β/L. The α phase forms on the Pt-side and the liquid phase on the silver side of the diffusion couple. The concentration-distance profile shows that the solute concentration varies from pure platinum to the saturation value $X_{Ag}^{\alpha/\beta}$ at the α/β interface, Fig. 3.52. The interface compositions are shown in the phase diagram. The thin layer of β has a concentration of $X_{Ag}^{\beta/\alpha}$ at the α/β interface to $X_{Ag}^{\beta/L}$ at the β/L interface. The interfaces can move by transport of solute along the concentration gradients built up in the α, β and liquid phases.

If the length of the Pt and Ag rods are chosen such that the gross composition lies in the β-phase region at 1150°C, then the α/β and β/L interfaces will migrate in opposite directions towards the ends of the diffusion couple. These directions of migration

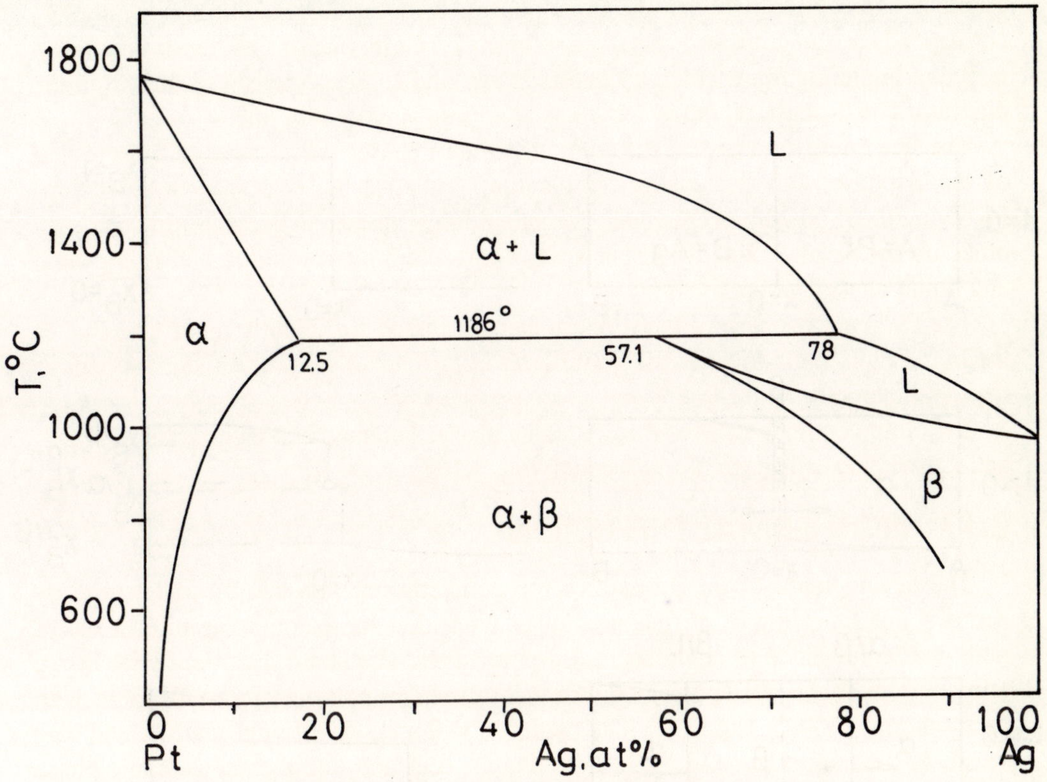

Fig. 3.51 Binary phase diagram of the Pt-Ag system.

of the interfaces are consistent with the growth of the β phase. After a long annealing time, the two interfaces will reach their respective ends and the alloy will be 100% β phase.

The peritectic reaction has been studied by a number of investigators in the past (9–12). It has been observed in most cases that although the peritectic reaction initiates at the α/L interface, it does not grow to any extent because crystallization of the product of the peritectic reaction, β, occurs directly from the undercooled liquid. In order to understand the reaction, let us consider a binary phase diagram between components *A* and *B* showing the peritectic reaction, Fig. 3.53a. At or near the peritectic temperature, the liquid of composition $X_B^{L/\alpha}$ maintains equilibrium with the α phase of composition $X_B^{\alpha/L}$. However, the reaction can not occur at the peritectic

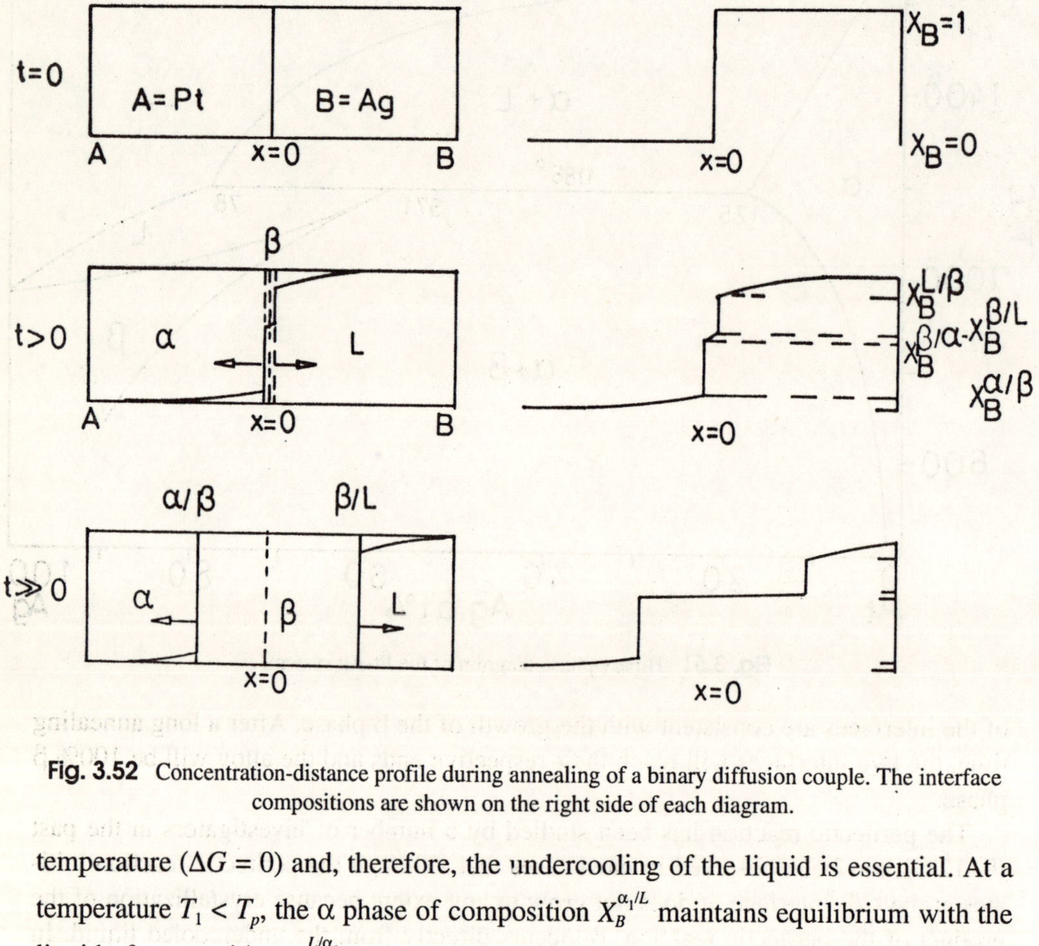

Fig. 3.52 Concentration-distance profile during annealing of a binary diffusion couple. The interface compositions are shown on the right side of each diagram.

temperature ($\Delta G = 0$) and, therefore, the undercooling of the liquid is essential. At a temperature $T_1 < T_p$, the α phase of composition $X_B^{\alpha_1/L}$ maintains equilibrium with the liquid of composition X^{L/α_1} which are obtained by metastable extensions of the upper liquidus and solidus curves to temperatures below T_p. On the other hand, if the β phase grows directly from the supercooled liquid at T_1, it will maintain equilibrium with

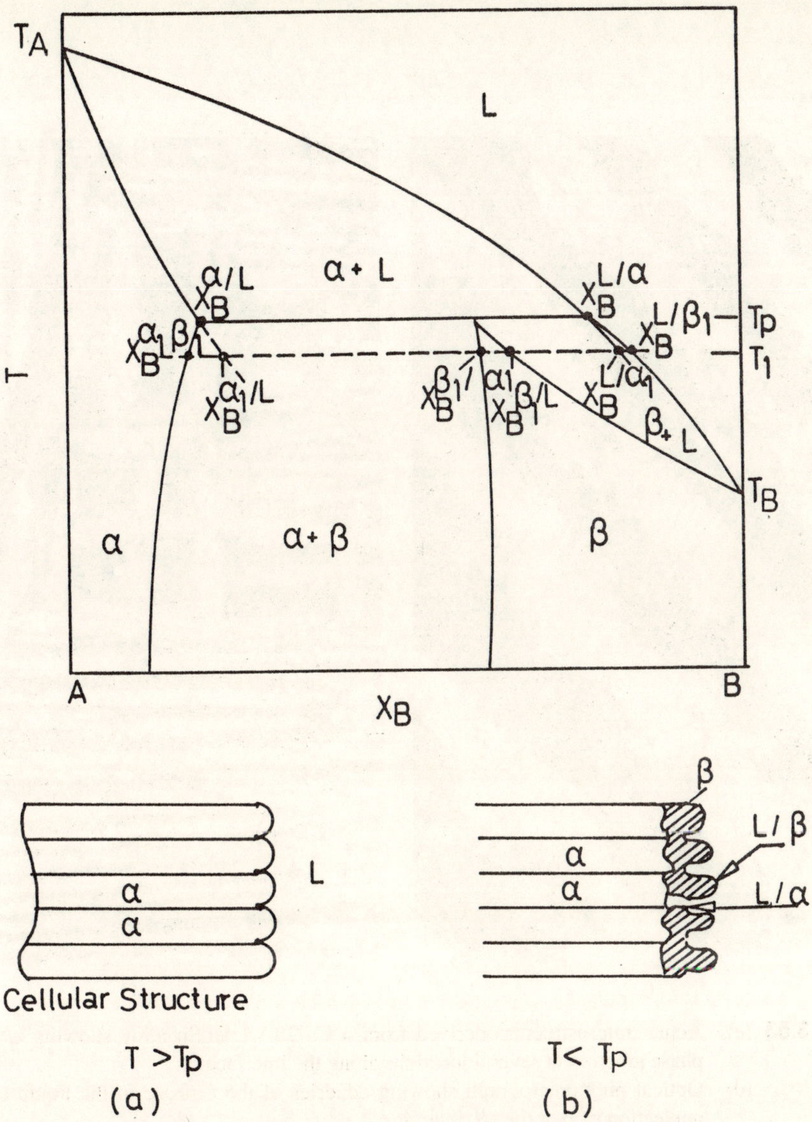

Fig. 3.53 (a) Phase diagram of the binary system *A-B* showing peritectic reaction.
(b) Schematic showing possible growth mechanism of the product of the peritectic reaction.

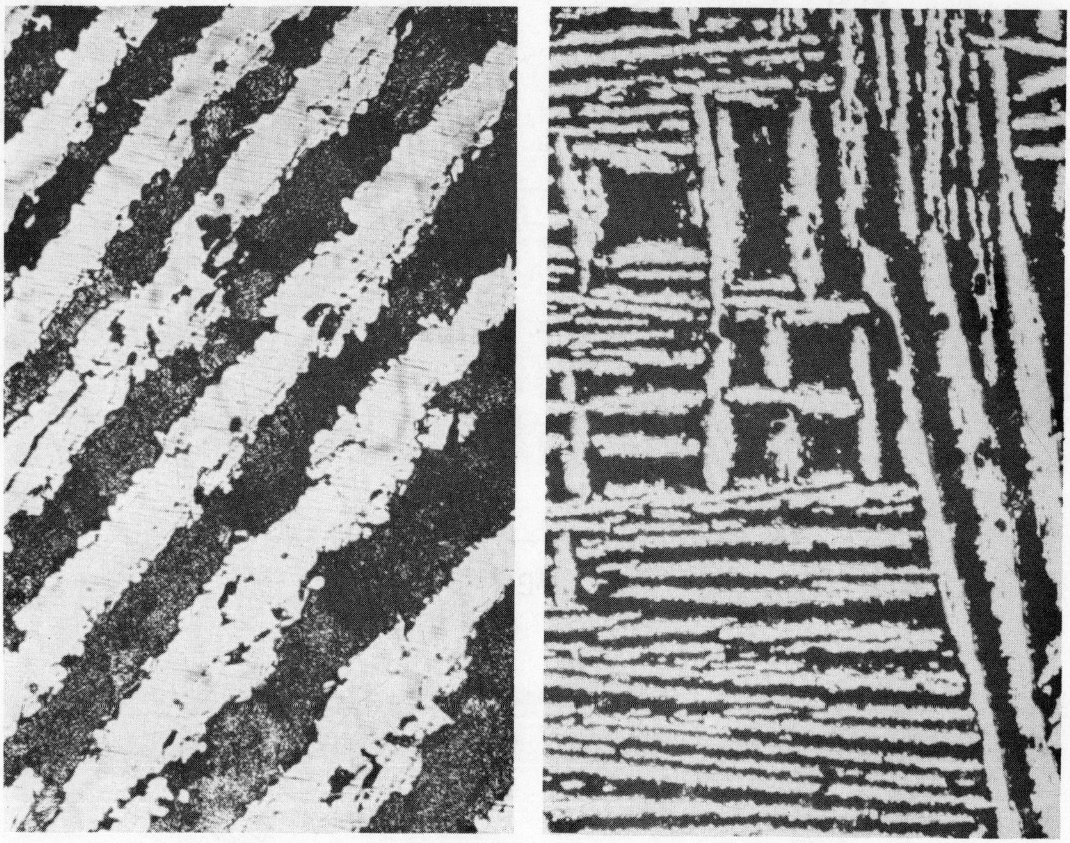

c d

Fig. 3.53 (c) Actual microstructure derived from a Cu-70 wt.pct.Sn alloy showing $\varepsilon/\eta/L$ three-phase junction at several locations along the interface.
(d) Optical photomicrograph showing dendries of the ε phase in the liquid (dark) and nucleation of η at the ε/L interface.

liquid of composition X_B^{L/β_1}. Thus, the α and β phases maintain equilibrium with liquids of different compositions and both phases can not grow together. This will be possible if the metastable extension of the upper liquidus coincides with the β-liquidus or lower liquidus.

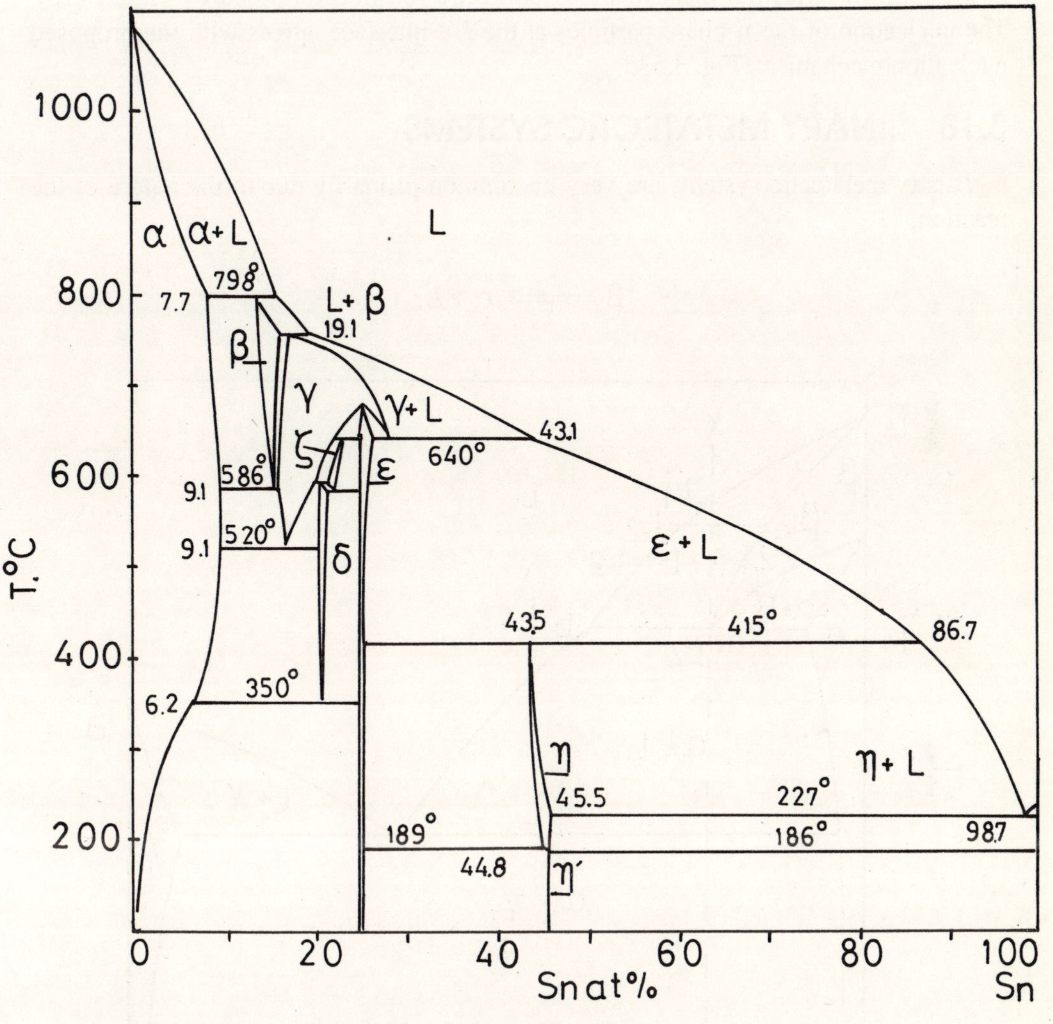

Fig. 3.53 (e) Phase diagram of the Cu-Sn binary system.

In general, the β phase forms at the α/L interface by the peritectic reaction. Further growth of β will require access to the liquid. Thus, in order for the β phase to grow by the peritectic reaction and not by the peritectic transformation, the three-phase junction α/β/*L* must be kept open. According to Hillert (10) this is possible if the secondary or peritectic β phase grows in the manner shown in Fig. 3.53b, whereby an open channel is maintained between α and liquid at the growth front of β. The microstructure of Fig. 3.53c, which is derived from a naturally cooled Cu-70wt.pct.Sn alloy, confirms with the mechanism of peritectic reaction proposed by Hillert (10). The nucleation of the η phase particles at the *L*/ε interface agrees with the proposed nucleation mechanism, Fig. 3.53d.

3.18 BINARY METATECTIC SYSTEMS

Binary metatectic systems are very uncommon primarily due to the nature of the reaction,

$$\beta \rightleftharpoons \alpha + L.$$

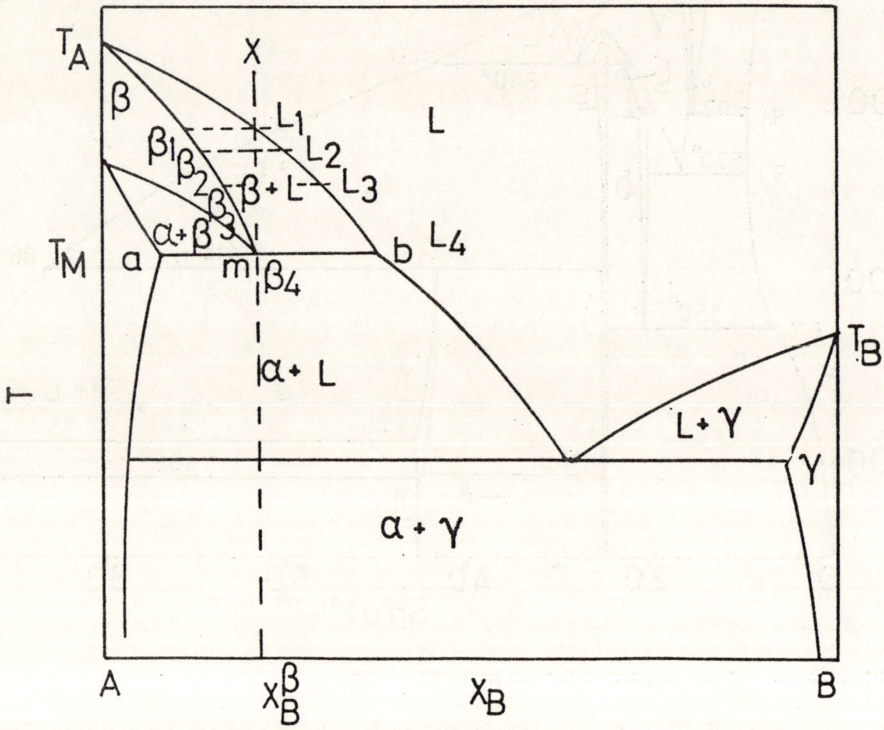

Fig. 3.54 Binary phase diagram showing the metatectic reaction.

Accordingly, a sold phase β dissociates, upon cooling, to a liquid and another solid α having a different composition (and crystal structure). The formation of liquid from solid during cooling of the alloy is a unique feature of the reaction.

A hypothetical binary phase diagram showing the metatectic reaction is presented in Fig. 3.54. The reaction occurs at the metatectic reaction isotherm T_m. Compositions of the α, β and liquid phases are given by the points *a*, *m* and *b*, respectively. Consider the solidification of a metatectic alloy, marked *X* on the diagram, Fig. 3.54. The β phase of composition given by the point β_1 forms at the temperature T_1. Further cooling of the alloy results in the formation of more β whose composition moves along the solidus $\beta_1\beta_2\beta_3\beta_4$. The composition of the liquid changes along the liquidus $L_1L_2L_3L_4$. Under equilibrium cooling, the alloy contains 100% β phase at the temperature T_4 ($= T_m$).

The complete solidification of the alloy is short-lived, as the β phase dissociates into α and liquid phases by the metatectic reaction when the temperature of the system is brought below T_m. The grains of high-temperature phase β are transformed into α with the solute-rich liquid occupying the grain boundary region. The liquid will be held at the grain boundary and grain edges by wetting these regions of the microstructure, Fig. 3.55. The surface tension force play an important role. However, if the relative amount of the liquid is large, the structure will collapse.

A hypometatectic alloy, if cooled from a high temperature, will remain solid for quite some time before melting because the first stage of solidification is completed at a temperature above T_m. The microstructure is a mixture of α and β.

3.19 FREE ENERGY-COMPOSITION DIAGRAMS

The schematic free energy-composition diagrams for the metatectic system are given in Fig. 3.56. At temperature $T_1 = T_{Cr} > T_m$, the free energy curves for both the α and β phases make contact at their minimum point, Fig. 3.56a. The β phase maintains equilibrium with the liquid at T_1. The common tangent construction gives compositions of the β and liquid phases in equilibrium with each other, indicated by points P_1 and Q_1, respectively.

At the temperature $T_2 = T_m$, the three phases, α, β and liquid, are in equilibrium with each other with compositions N_2, P_2 and Q_2, respectively, Fig. 3.56b. The free energy curve for the β phase is raised with respect to that of the liquid when the temperature is lowered to $T_3 < T_m$. The α and liquid phases maintain equilibrium with each other with compositions represented by N_3 and Q_3, respectively, Fig. 3.56c.

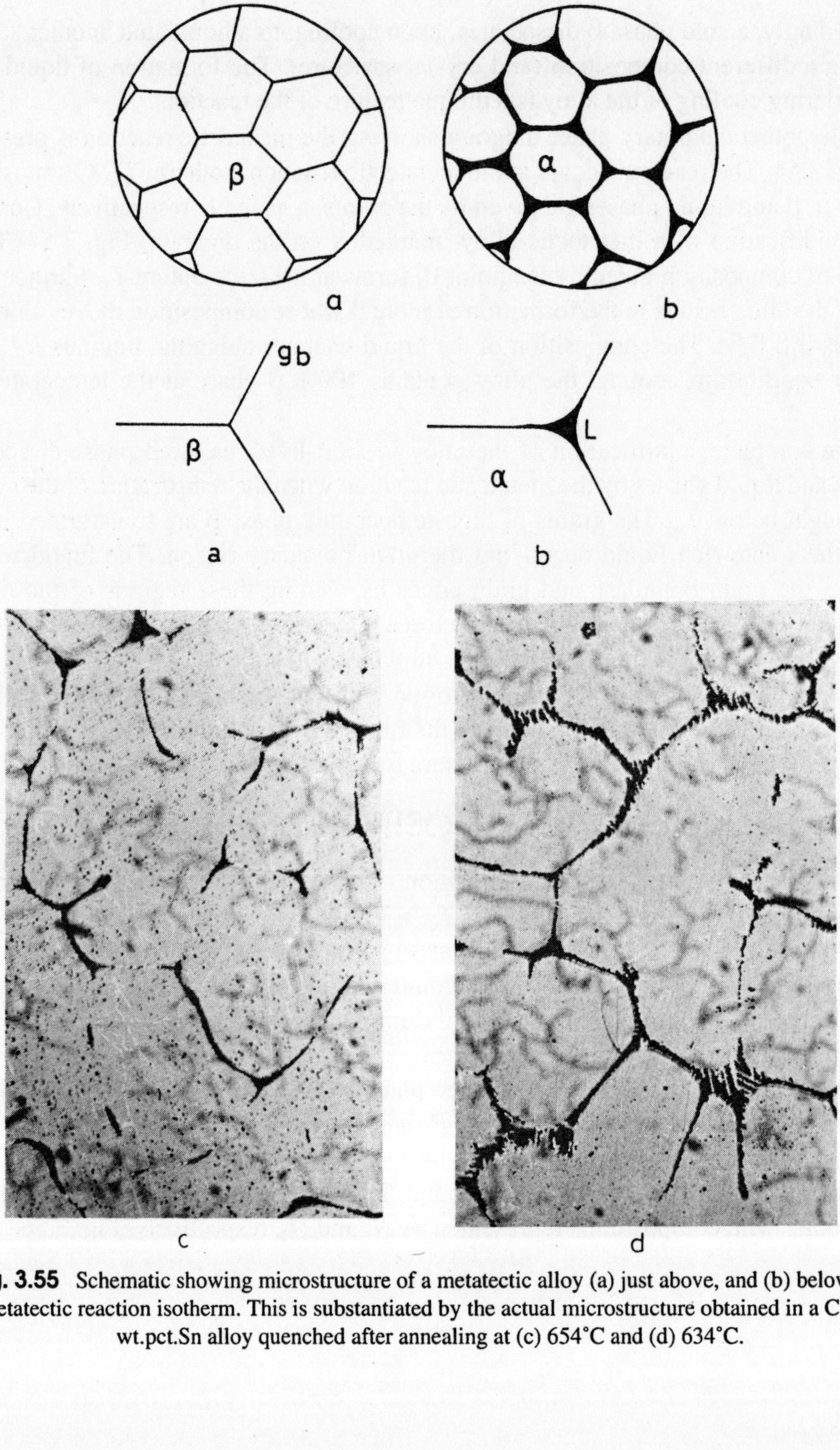

Fig. 3.55 Schematic showing microstructure of a metatectic alloy (a) just above, and (b) below, the metatectic reaction isotherm. This is substantiated by the actual microstructure obtained in a Cu-70 wt.pct.Sn alloy quenched after annealing at (c) 654°C and (d) 634°C.

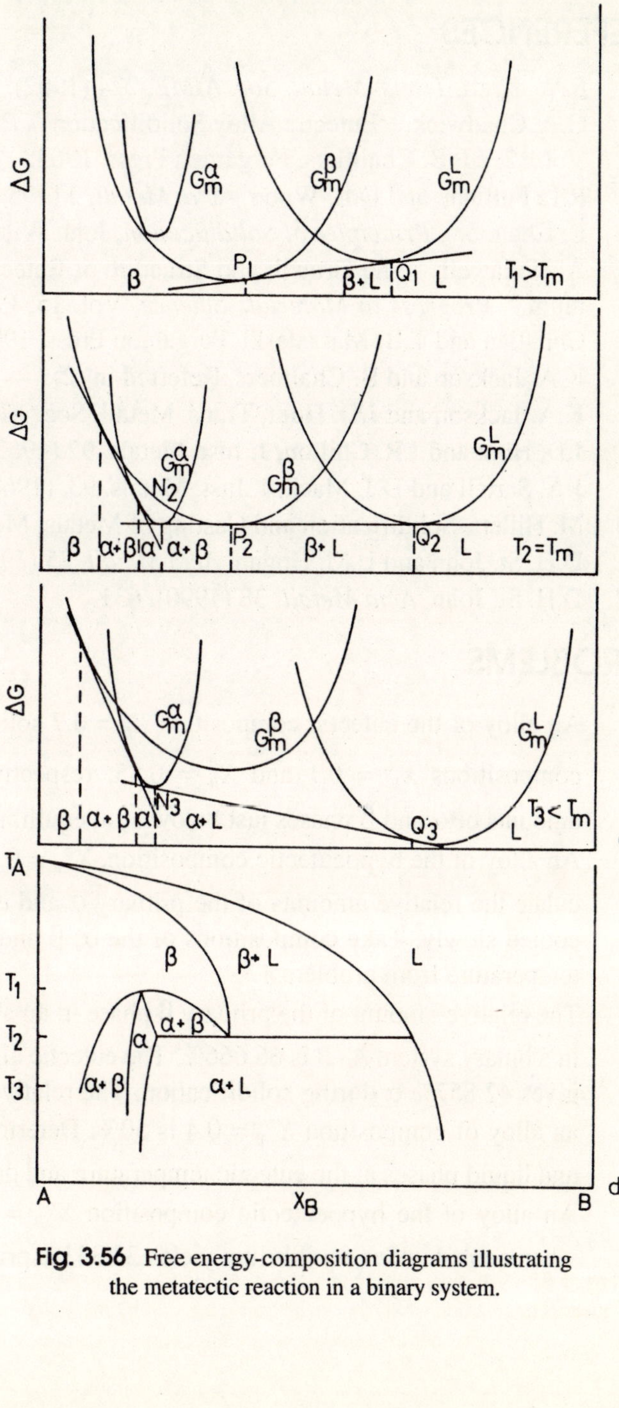

Fig. 3.56 Free energy-composition diagrams illustrating the metatectic reaction in a binary system.

REFERENCES

1. R.W. Kraft, *Trans. Metall. Soc. AIME*, 224 (1962), 65.
2. G.A. Chadwick, "Eutectic Alloy Solidification", *Progress in Materials Science*, Vol. 12, ed. B. Chalmers, Pergamon Press, 1963.
3. R.L. Fullman and D.L. Wood, *Acta. Metall*, 2 (1954), 188.
4. B. Chalmers, *Principles of Solidification*, John Wiley and Sons Inc., 1964.
5. A. Hellawell, "The Growth and Structure of Eutectics with Silicon and Germanium," *Progress in Materials Science*, Vol. 15, Part , (ed.) B. Chalmers, J.W. Christian and T.B. Massalaski, Pergamon Press, 1970.
6. K.A. Jackson and B. Chalmers, Referred in (2).
7. K.A. Jackson and J.D. Hunt, Trans. Metall. Soc. AIME, 236 (1966), 1129.
8. J.D. Hunt and J.R. Chilton, J. Inst. Metals, 92 (1963), 21.
9. J.A. Sartell and D.J. Mack, J. Inst. Metals, 93, (1964-65), 19.
10. M. Hillert, Solidification and Casting of Metals, Metals Soc. London (1979), 81.
11. D.H. St. John and L.M. Hogan, *Acta Metall*, 25 (1977), 77.
12. D.H. St. John, *Acta Metall*, 38 (1990), 631.

PROBLEMS

1. An alloy of the eutectic composition $X_B^e = 0.7$ solidifies into α and β phases of compositions $X_B^\alpha = 0.1$ and $X_B^\beta = 0.85$, respectively. Determine the relative amounts of α and β phases just below T_e at equilibrium.
2. An alloy of the hypoeutectic composition, $X°_B = 0.3$, is allowed to solidify. Calculate the relative amounts of the primary α and eutectic α and β phases when cooled slowly. Take compositions of the α, β and liquid phases at the eutectic temperature from problem 1.
3. The relative amount of the primary β phase in an alloy of composition $X°_B = 0.8$ in a binary system $A–B$ is 66.666%. The eutectic alloy of the same binary system gives 42.857% α during solidification. The relative amount of the primary α in an alloy of composition $X°_\beta = 0.4$ is 50%. Determine compositions of the α, β and liquid phases at the eutectic temperature and draw the phase diagrams.
4. An alloy of the hypoeutectic composition $X°_B = 0.4$ of a binary system $A–B$ when cooled under equilibrium yields 33.333% primary α and 33.333% eutectic

β. The same alloy when cooled under natural cooling conditions yields 30% primary cored α. Another alloy of the same binary system $X°_B = 0.6$ when cooled slowly yields 33.33% primary β. Determine compositions of the α, β and liquid phases at the eutectic temperature and the average composition of the cored α.

5. Draw free energy-composition diagrams of the α, β and liquid phases at a temperature T defined by $T_A > T_B > T > T_e$. Determine compositions of the α and β phase in equilibrium with the liquid. If alloys in the binary system are allowed to cool rapidly, what will be the compositions of the α and β phases in equilibrium with the liquid? The free energy-composition diagram of the bulk liquid phase at the temperature T is independent of the cooling rate.

6. A binary alloy system $A–B$ shows a peritectic reaction, L (80% B) + α (10% B) ⇔ β (50% B). A hypoperitectic alloy of composition $X°_B = 0.4$ is allowed to cool under equilibrium. Determine the relative amount of the primary α just above T_p. What is the relative amount of the peritectic β formed in the alloy?

7. Component A melts at 1000°C and B melts at 750°C. The binary system $A–B$ shows the following reactions:

   α (10% B) + L (50% B) $\xrightarrow[\overline{}]{700^\circ\text{C}}$ β (40% B)

   L (70% B) $\xrightarrow[\overline{}]{600^\circ\text{C}}$ β (45% B) + γ (95% B)

   An alloy containing 40% B is allowed to cool at a rate which is just sufficient to provide 20% completion of the peritectic reaction. The remaining liquid is allowed to cool slowly towards completion of the eutectic reaction to a temperature just below T_e. Draw the phase diagram of the binary system and determine

   (a) (i) relative amount of the unreacted α just below T_p.

   (ii) relative amount of the proeutectic β above T_e.

   (iii) relative amount of the eutectic β and γ phases.

   (b) Draw the free energy-composition diagram at 650°C and indicate composition of all phases.

Chapter 4

BINARY MONOTECTIC AND SYNTECTIC SYSTEMS

4.1 INTRODUCTION

It has been shown in Chapter 1 that immiscibility in the solid occurs when the enthalpy of mixing to form a solid solution is a large positive quantity. The α phase separates into two solid solutions, α_1 and α_2, both with the same crystal structure but differing in composition. There is a tendency towards clustering of *A* and *B* type atoms in distinct regions of the microstructure. The immiscibility also occurs in the liquid when the enthalpy of mixing to form a liquid solution is positive. This is illustrated with the help of a series of phase diagrams with constant positive value of ΔH_m^α but increasing $\Delta H_m^L > 0$, Fig. 4.1. A eutectic type phase diagram results when the magnitude of ΔH_m^L is small. The liquidus curves slope gently towards the eutectic temperature from the melting points of pure components *A* and *B*, Fig. 4.1a. Flattening of the liquidus curve occurs with increasing values of ΔH_m^L Fig. 4.1b. The magnitude

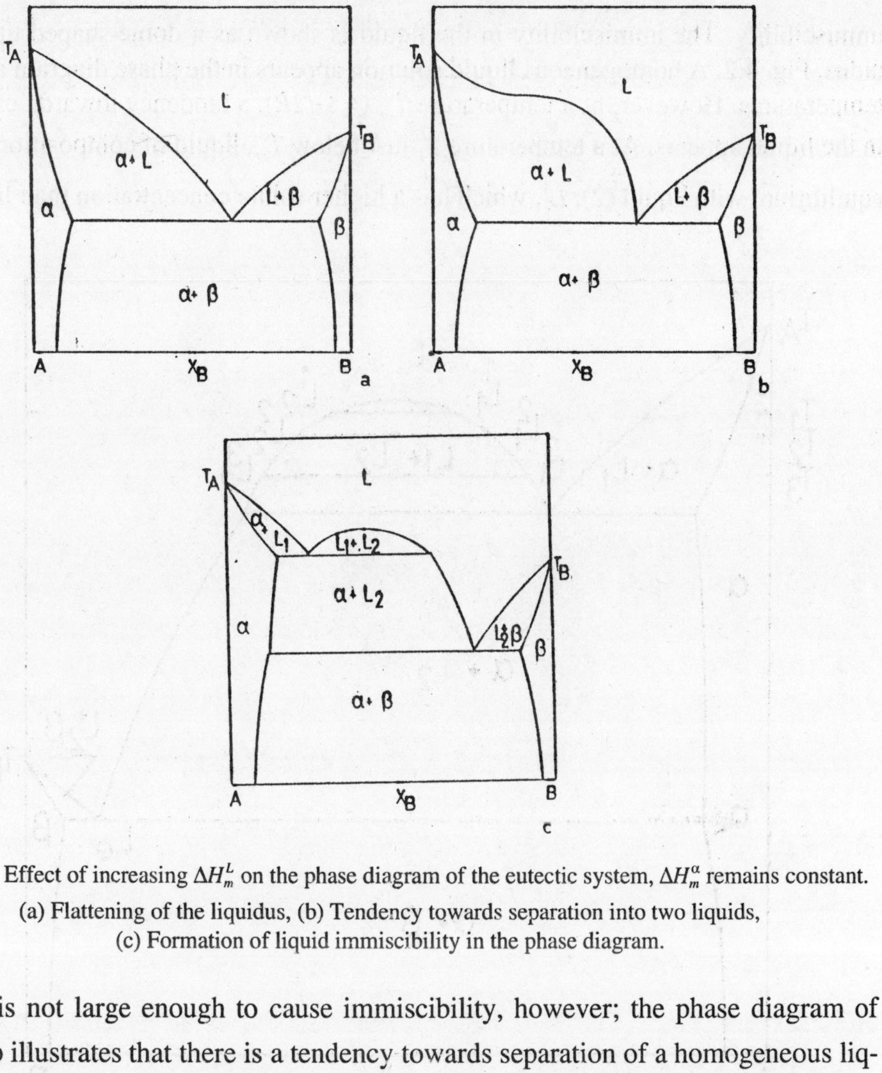

Fig. 4.1 Effect of increasing ΔH_m^L on the phase diagram of the eutectic system, ΔH_m^α remains constant. (a) Flattening of the liquidus, (b) Tendency towards separation into two liquids, (c) Formation of liquid immiscibility in the phase diagram.

of ΔH_m^L is not large enough to cause immiscibility, however; the phase diagram of Fig. 4.1b illustrates that there is a tendency towards separation of a homogeneous liquid into two liquids. With further increase in ΔH_m^L, the homogeneous liquid separates into the two liquids L_1 and L_2, as illustrated in Fig. 4.1c. Generally, there is a tendency of the liquid to accomodate the two types of atoms, *A* and *B*, to form a homogenous solution. However, under large positive ΔH_m^L unlimited solubility of one component in the other is not supported by the system below a critical temperature T_{cr}, hence the immiscibility. The immiscibility in the liquid is shown as a dome-shaped upper liquidus, Fig. 4.2. A homogeneous liquid solution appears in the phase diagram at higher temperatures. However, at a temperature T_{cr} (= $\Omega/2R$), a tendency towards clustering in the liquid appears. At a temperature T_1 just below T_{cr}, liquid of composition L_1^1 is in equilibrium with liquid (2), L_2^1, which has a higher solute concentration than liquid(1).

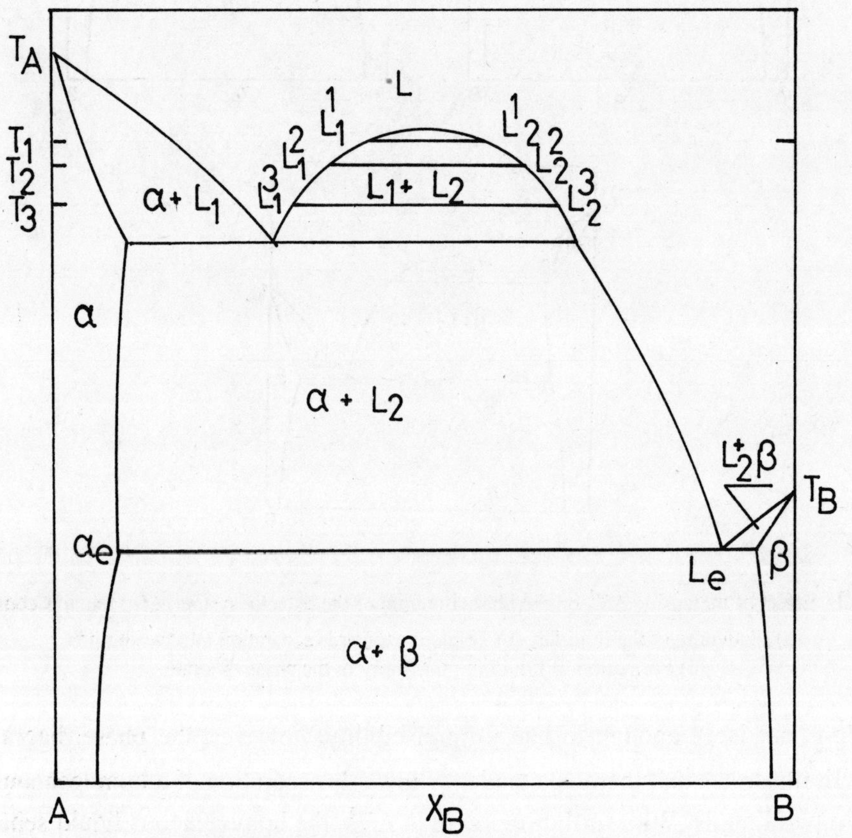

Fig. 4.2 Binary phase diagram showing the monotectic reaction where a homogeneous liquid separates into two liquids L_1 and L_2 below the critical temperature.

There is an increase in the clustering of A and B type atoms in the liquid as the temperature is lowered. This is shown as a departure from the composition of the homogeneous liquid solution. The composition of the liquid (1) moves along the curve L_1^1 L_1^2 L_1^3 and that of liquid (2) along the curve L_2^1 L_2^2 L_2^3.

4.2 THE MONOTECTIC REACTION

The monotectic reaction is written as,

$$L_1 \rightleftharpoons \alpha + L_2,$$

that is, liquid of composition L_1 dissociates upon cooling into a solid α and another liquid L_2 of a composition richer in solute, Fig. 4.3. The α phase is depleted of solute compared to L_1. The two liquids are immiscible in each other over a temperature and composition range just like oil is immiscible in water. This reaction occurs at the monotectic temperature, T_{mono}.

4.3 EQUILIBRIUM SOLIDIFICATION OF MONOTECTIC ALLOYS

The monotectic alloy $X_B^{L_1}$ is composed solely of a single liquid phase L_1 at higher temperatures (Fig. 4.3). Upon cooling the alloy to the monotectic reaction isotherm (or infinitesimally below it), the parent liquid dissociates into the α phase of composition X_B^{α} and a second liquid L_2 of composition $X_B^{L_2}$. The products of the monotectic reaction are termed as monotectic constituents or secondary constituents. The relative amounts of the two phases just below the monotectic reaction isotherm is calculated by using the lever rule as follows:

$$\%\ \alpha = \frac{0.7 - 0.3}{0.7 - 0.1} \times 100 = 66.66\%$$

$$\%\ L_2 = \frac{0.3 - 0.1}{0.7 - 0.1} \times 100 = 33.33\%.$$

The monotectic reaction is analogous to the eutectic reaction, the only difference being that, whereas the products of the eutectic reaction are both solid phases, one of the products of the monotectic reaction is a liquid. The equilibrium between the α and liquid(2) phases is maintained below the monotectic reaction isotherm. If the lower liquidus of the (α + L_2) phase field has a small slope corresponding to a large change in composition per unit drop in temperature and the solubility of the component *B* in *A* in the α phase remains the same or changes very slightly with decreasing temperature, then some more α will form at the expense of L_2 while the alloy cools below the monotectic reaction isotherm. The composition of the liquid moves along the lower liquidus towards L_e and that of the α phase along the solidus towards α_e. The relative amounts of total α and liquid just above the eutectic temperature is

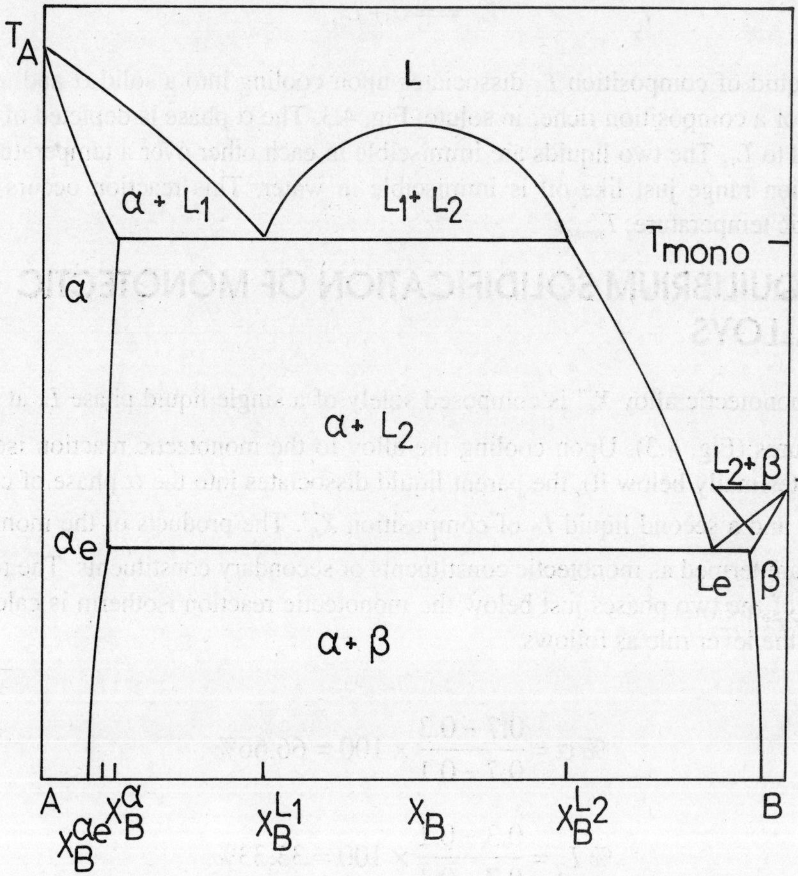

Fig. 4.3 Binary phase diagram showing the monotectic reaction. Compositions of the α and liquid phases are shown during equilibrium solidification of a monotectic alloy.

$$\% \text{ Total } \alpha = \frac{0.9 - 0.3}{0.9 - 0.09} \times 100 = 74.074\%$$

$$\% L_2 = \frac{0.3 - 0.09}{0.9 - 0.09} \times 100 = 25.925\%.$$

Thus, the relative amount of the α formed during cooling between the monotectic and eutectic reaction isotherms is 7.414%. A part of the monotectic α should dissolve when the α phase composition changes from $X_B^{\alpha} = 0.1$ to $X_B^{\alpha_e} = 0.09$ along the lower solidus of the $(\alpha + L_2)$ phase field. However, due to changes in composition of the liquid L_2 along the lower liquidus, a larger proportion of the α is formed, giving the net α formed between T_{mono} and T_e as 7.414%. This can be easily understood from the fact that if we take the liquid (2) of composition L_2 of relative amount 33.33%, then the amount of α formed between T_{mono} and T_e is given as:

$$\%\alpha = \frac{0.9 - 0.7}{0.9 - 0.09} \times 33.33 = 8.23\%.$$

The above figure is higher than the net α calculated earlier (7.414%). This is due to the decreasing solubility of the component B in A in the α phase. The α phase thus formed is termed as ''tertiary α'' and is physically continuous with the monotectic α.

At the eutectic temperature, liquid(2) of composition L_e dissociates into the α and β phases by the eutectic reaction. The eutectic α thus formed is the fourth order α, which is generally continuous with the α formed before it. The β phase gets divorced and forms as nodules or spheroids in the microstructure. The relative amount of the α and β phases in the eutectic mixture is

$$\%\alpha = \frac{0.95 - 0.9}{0.95 - 0.09} \times 25.925 = 1.507\%$$

and

$$\%\beta = \frac{0.9 - 0.09}{0.95 - 0.09} \times 25.925 = 24.41\%,$$

thus giving a total α of 75.59% in the final equilibrium microstructure. The evolution of the microstructure is shown schematically in Fig. 4.4. This is substantiated with an actual photomicrograph obtained during cooling of a monotectic Cu-Pb alloy, Fig. 4.5. In the Cu-Pb alloy system, the monotectic reaction occurs at 1228 K and the monotectic composition is Cu-36wt.pct.Pb.

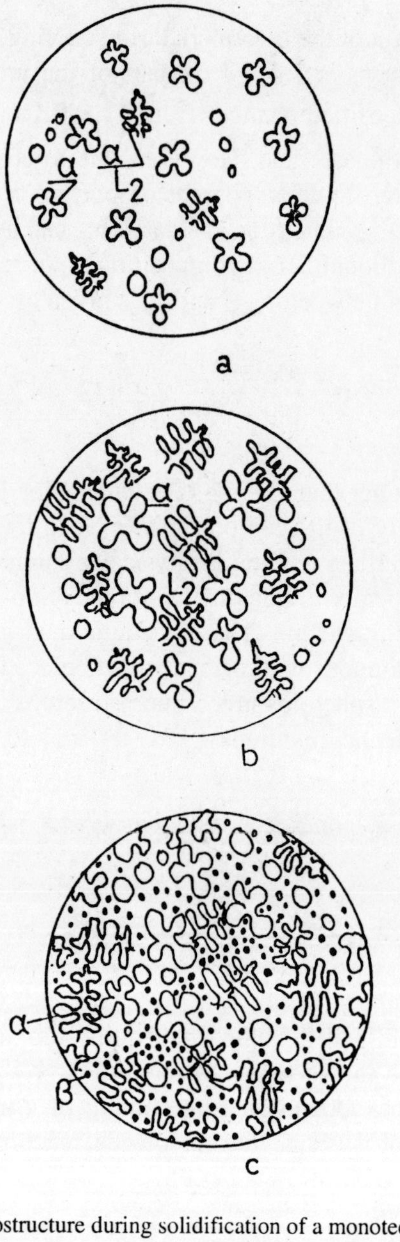

Fig. 4.4 Evolution of microstructure during solidification of a monotectic alloy, (schematic).

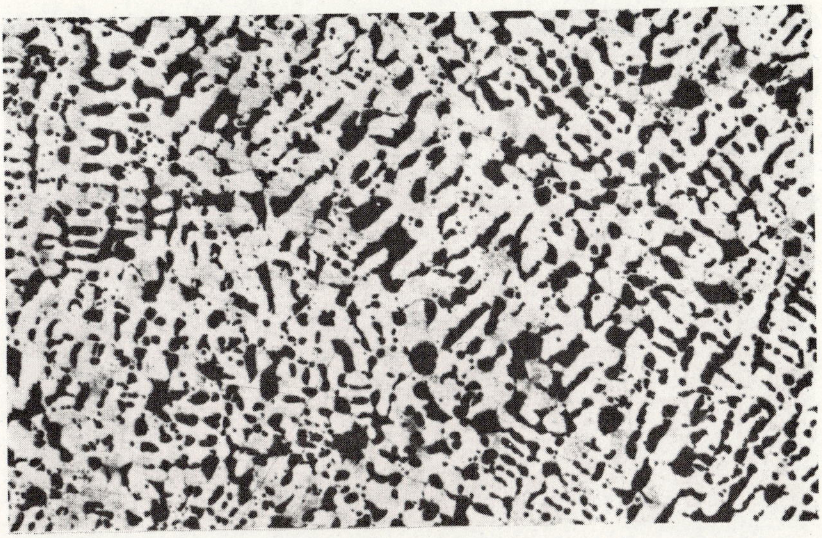

Fig. 4.5 Optical photomicrograph showing products of the monotectic reaction; Pb-rich phase is dark and Cu-rich phase is light.

4.4 EQUILIBRIUM SOLIDIFICATION OF HYPOMONOTECTIC AND HYPERMONOTECTIC ALLOYS

All alloy compositions lying to the left of the monotectic composition point *m* and to the right of the maximum solubility of the component *B* in α, represented by the point *a*, are termed as hypomonotectic alloys, Fig. 4.6. Consider equilibrium solidification of a hypomonotectic alloy Y ($X_B = 0.2$). In this case the primary α phase forms before liquid (1) can undergo the monotectic reaction. The primary α forms in the temperature interval T_1 to T_{mono}, as shown in Fig. 4.6. The relative amount of the primary α can be calculated using the lever rule as follows:

$$\% \text{ Primary } \alpha = \frac{0.3 - 0.2}{0.3 - 0.1} \times 100 = 50\%$$

$$\% \ L_1 = 50\%.$$

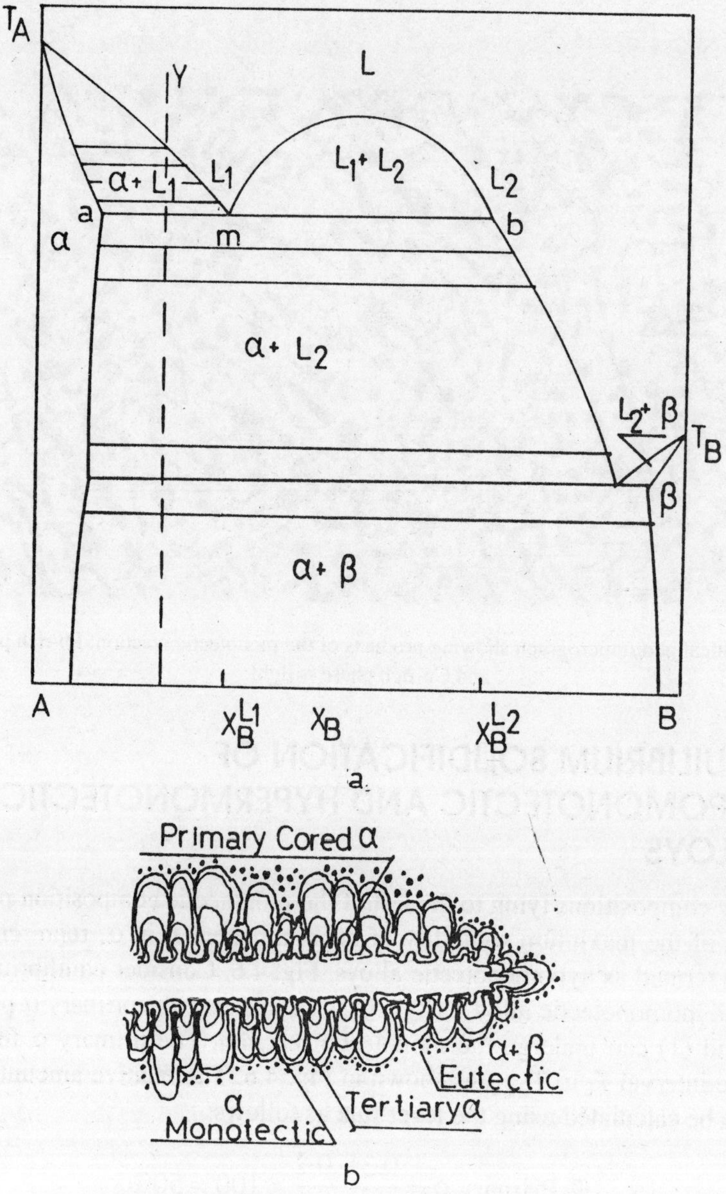

Fig. 4.6 (a) Binary phase diagram showing the monotectic reaction. Hypomonotectic alloy composition is shown by the composition vertical *Y*. (b) Microstructure, (schematic).

The course of solidification of liquid (1) below the monotectic temperature is identical to that described for the monotectic alloy. The only difference is that the relative amounts of the secondary, tertiary and fourth order α and β phases are reduced by approximately 50% w.r.t. the percentages calculated in section 4.3. The final microstructure will consist of:

$$\% \text{ Primary } \alpha = 50\%$$
$$\% \text{ Secondary } \alpha = 33.33\%$$
$$\% \text{ Tertiary } \alpha = 3.09\%$$
$$\% \text{ Fourth order } \alpha = 0.79\%$$
$$\% \ \beta \text{ phase} = 12.8\%$$

Since the relative amount of the α phase in the eutectic mixture is very small, the eutectic liquid does not solidify into a lamellar morphology. Instead, the eutectic or fourth order α is physically continuous with the α phase formed before it and, therefore, is indistinguishable. The β phase is embedded in the matrix of α and the morphology is very similar to that described for the monotectic alloy.

All alloy compositions lying in the composition range represented by points *m* and *b* are termed as hypermonotectic alloys, Fig. 4.7. At higher temperatures, components *A* and *B* form a homogeneous liquid solution, which dissociates into two liquids, L_1 and L_2, when cooled below T_{cr}. Relative to the original alloy composition, the two liquids, L_1 and L_2, are, respectively, richer in components *A* and *B*. The deviation increases with the fall in temperature within the dome. The compositions of the liquids L_1 and L_2 reach $X_B^{L_1}$ and $X_B^{L_2}$, respectively, just above the monotectic reaction isotherm. The relative amounts of the two liquids at a temperature just above T_{mono} in an original alloy of composition $X_B^0 = 0.5$ are,

$$\% \ L_1 = \frac{0.7 - 0.5}{0.7 - 0.3} \times 100 = 50\%,$$

and

$$\% L_2 = \frac{0.50 - 0.30}{0.7 - 0.3} \times 100 = 50\%.$$

The second liquid L_2, forms from the homogeneous liquid solution near the top liquid layer, walls of the container and throughout the bulk of the liquid homogeneously. If there is a substantial difference in the density of the two liquids, they will occupy distinct layers in the container by gravity segregation. For example, in the Cu-50wt.pct.Pb alloy, the liquid (2) being richer in Pb will have a higher density than liquid (1), and thus will settle and occupy the lower part of the container into which it

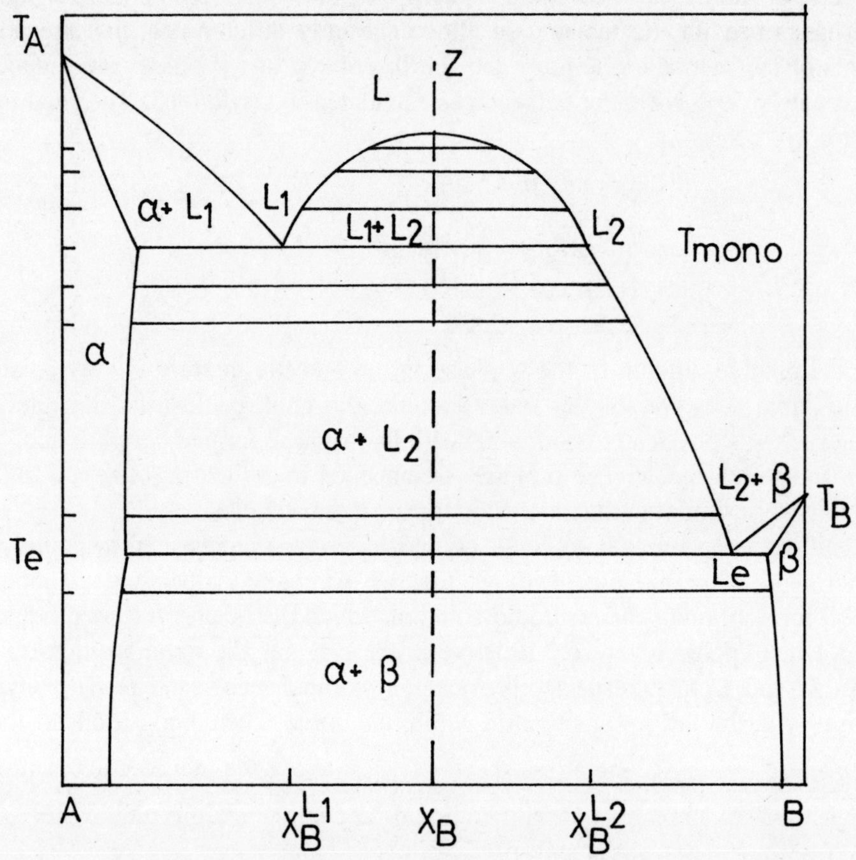

Fig. 4.7 Binary phase diagram showing the monotectic reaction. Hypermonotectic alloy composition is shown by the composition vertical Z.

is poured. This situation is similar to a mixture of oil and water where oil (L_1) floats on top and water (L_2) occupies the lower part of the container.

Upon continued cooling of the alloy, liquid L_1 undergoes the monotectic reaction at T_{mono}. The relative amount of the α and liquid phases formed from the dissociation of L_1 is

$$\%\alpha = \frac{0.7-0.3}{0.7-0.1} \times 50 = 33.33\%$$

$$\%\, L_2 = 16.66\%$$

The total amount of the liquid L_2 in the alloy at this juncture is 66.66%, out of which 50% has formed above T_{mono} and the remaining 16.66% as a product of the monotectic

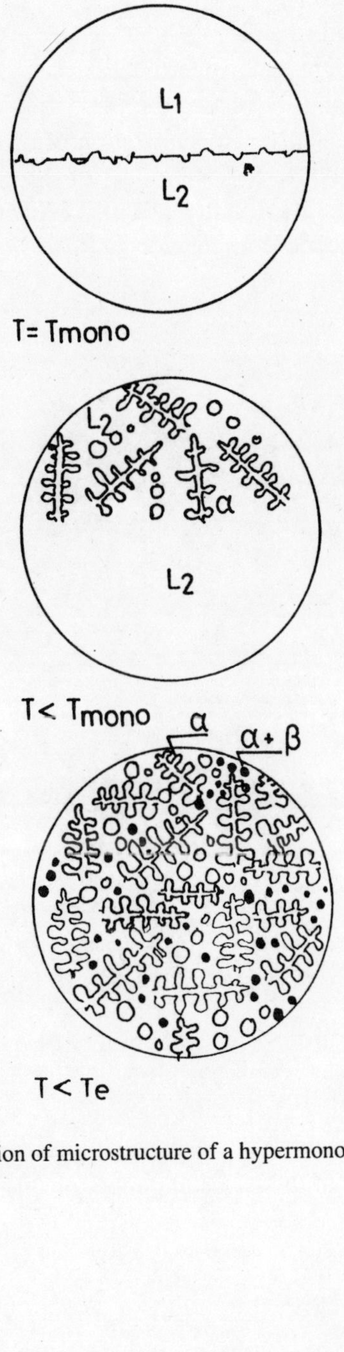

Fig. 4.8 The evolution of microstructure of a hypermonotectic alloy, (schematic).

reaction. A small amount of the tertiary α will form from L_2 while it is cooling through the monotectic and eutectic reaction isotherms. The remaining liquid L_2 dissociates by the eutectic reaction at T_e. The evolution of the microstructure of a hypermonotectic alloy is shown in Fig. 4.8.

The actual microstructure reveals spheroidal dark regions dispersed in a continuous matrix of the (light-etched) α phase, Fig. 4.9. The dark regions were L_2 at the monotectic temperature, which after crystallization of some tertiary α dissociated by the eutectic reaction. The β phase of the product of the eutectic reaction is a Pb-rich solid solution with a maximum solubility of 0.007 wt.pct. Cu. The eutectic reaction occurs at 326°C and the eutectic composition is 99.93% Pb, Fig. 4.10. The eutectic structure remains unresolved.

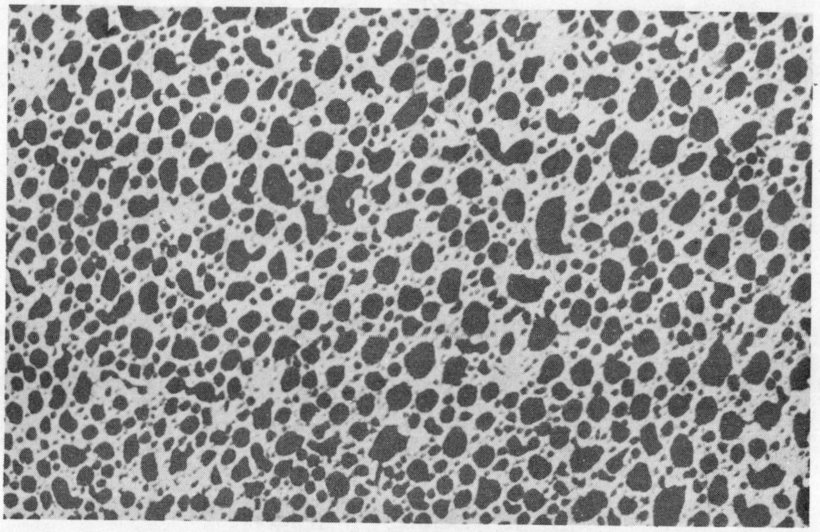

Fig. 4.9 The optical photomicrograph showing microstructure of a hypermonotectic Cu-50wt.pct.Pb alloy. Dark regions are Pb-rich and light regions are Cu-rich.

It is also quite likely that, instead of separation of the two liquids by gravity segregation, one of the liquid phases (say L_1) forms as tiny droplets within a continuous liquid (1) in the form of emulsion. The formation of L_1 and L_2 as separate layers by gravity segregation or as an emulsion will depend upon the following factors:

1. Physical characteristics of the two component metals forming a binary monotectic system.

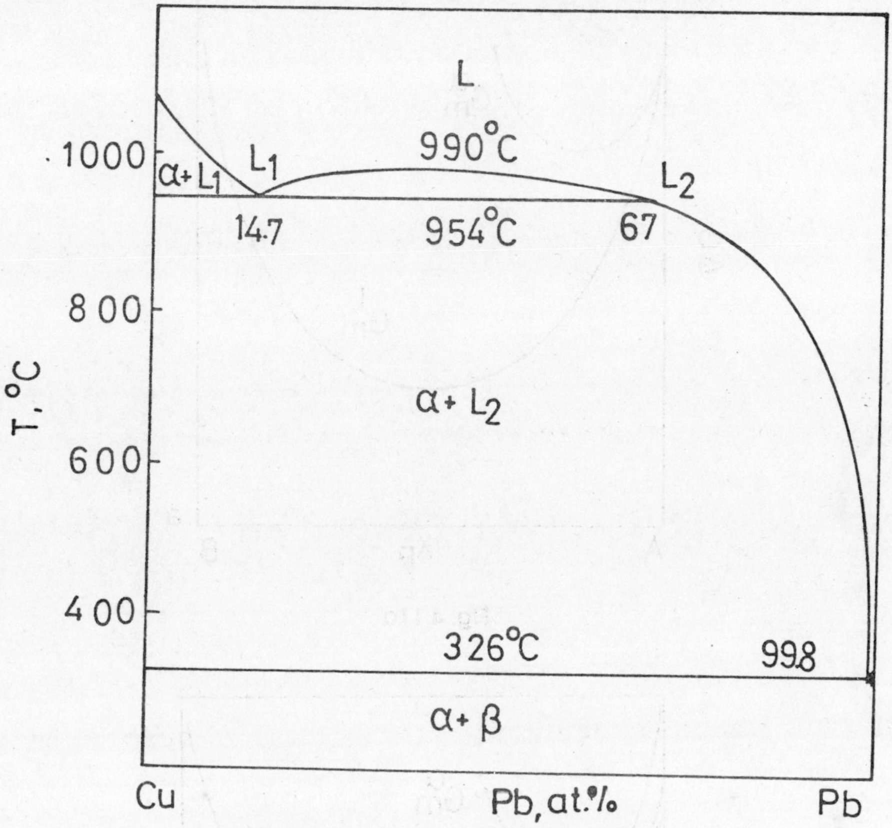

Fig. 4.10 The Cu-Pb binary phase diagram.

2. The condition of formation of the second liquid.
3. The rate of cooling which decides the segregation behavior of the liquid under consideration.
4. The relative density of the two component metals and hence of the two liquids.

4.5 FREE ENERGY–COMPOSITION DIAGRAMS

A binary phase diagram between components *A* and *B* showing the monotectic reaction can be constructed from the free energy-composition diagrams, Fig. 4.11. Fig. 4.11a shows the free energy-composition diagram drawn at the melting point of pure component *A*. The Gibbs free energy of the liquid solution is shown as a parabola, thus illustrating the stability of homogeneous liquid at T_1.

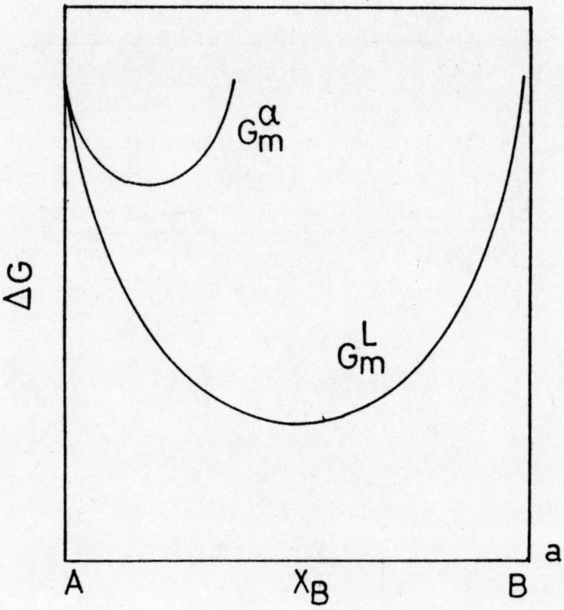

Fig. 4.11a

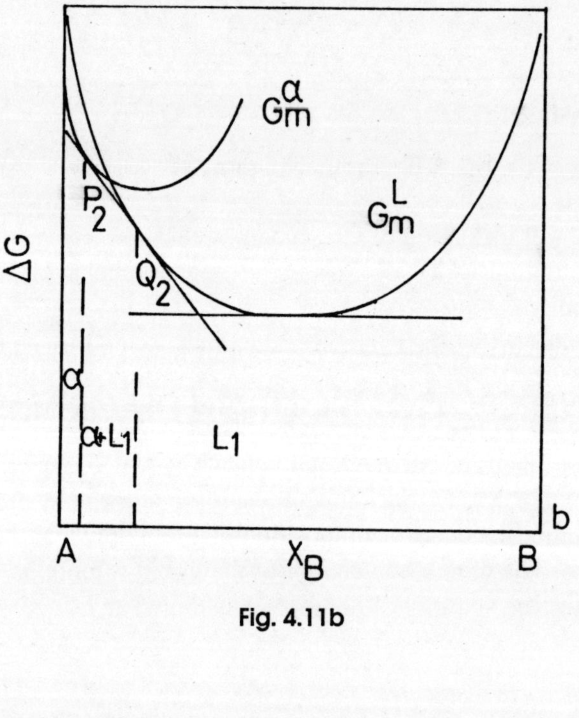

Fig. 4.11b

The free energy curves for the α and liquid phases intersect each other near component *A*. The common tangent line drawn to the two curves meets them at points P_2 and Q_2 which represent compositions of the α and liquid phases, respectively, in equilibrium with each other at T_2. The free energy curve for the liquid shows merger of the minima and inflection points at T_2. The free energy curve is flat and the temperature at which it occurs corresponds to the critical value T_{cr}. The departure from the normal behavior is due to large positive enthalpy of mixing of components *A* and *B* in the liquid state.

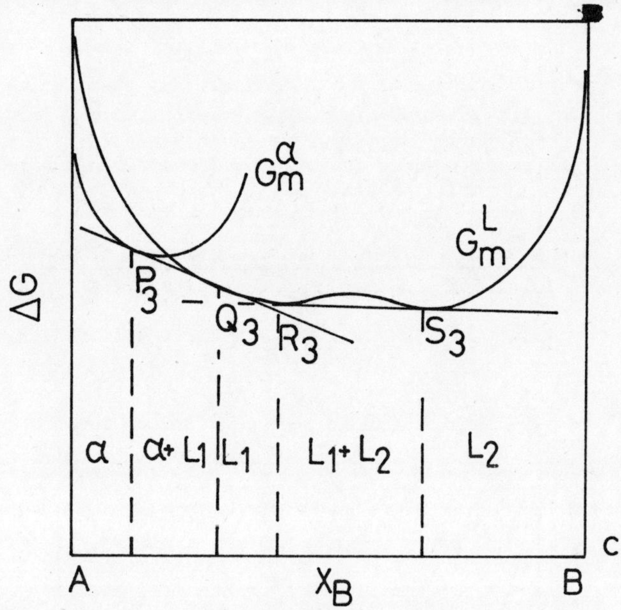

Fig. 4.11c

The free energy curve of the α phase has descended relative to that of the liquid at $T_3 > T_2 = T_{cr}$. The common tangent line indicates that the compositions of α and liquid phases have shifted to new values (enriched with solute) as represented by points P_3 and Q_3, respectively. The Gibbs free energy of the liquid solution shows a maximum flanked on either side by a minimum. The liquid solution splits into two liquids, L_1 and L_2, at T_3 because the free energy of homogeneous liquid solution will be higher than a mixture of two liquids at this temperature. One common tangent line meets the two limbs of the curve at points R_3 and S_3, which represent the compositions of L_1 and L_2, respectively. The transition from one homogeneous liquid solution to a mixture of two liquids is gradual.

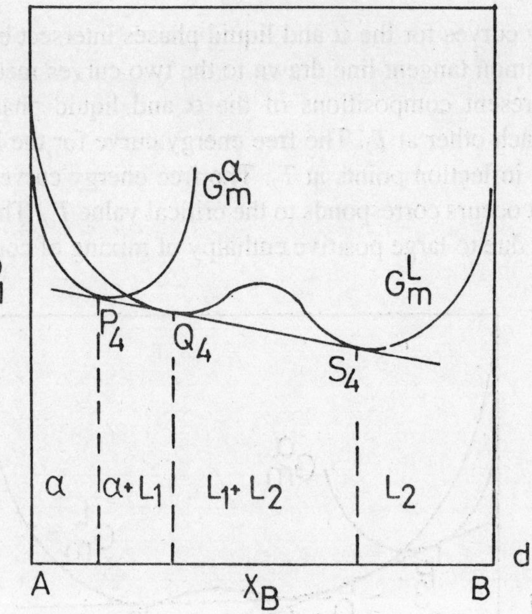

Fig. 4.11d

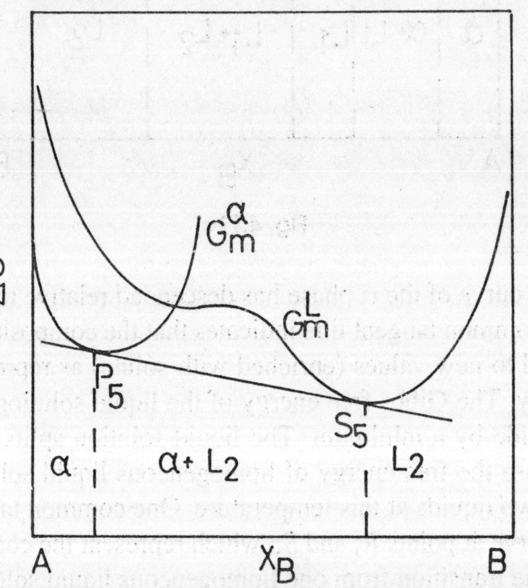

Fig. 4.11e

The tendency towards clustering in the liquid increases with decreasing temperature, and at the temperature T_4 the common tangent line on the free energy curve of the liquid when extended also becomes tangent to the free energy curve of the α phase. The temperature T_4, therefore, corresponds to the monotectic reaction isotherm with α, L_1 and L_2 as coexisting phases.

Due to differences in the relative stability of liquids L_1 and L_2, part of the free energy curve (designated as L_1) ascends more rapidly than L_2 as the temperature is lowered. At the temperature $T_5 < T_{mono}$, the α phase coexists with liquid L_2. Coexistence of α with liquid L_1 will raise the free energy.

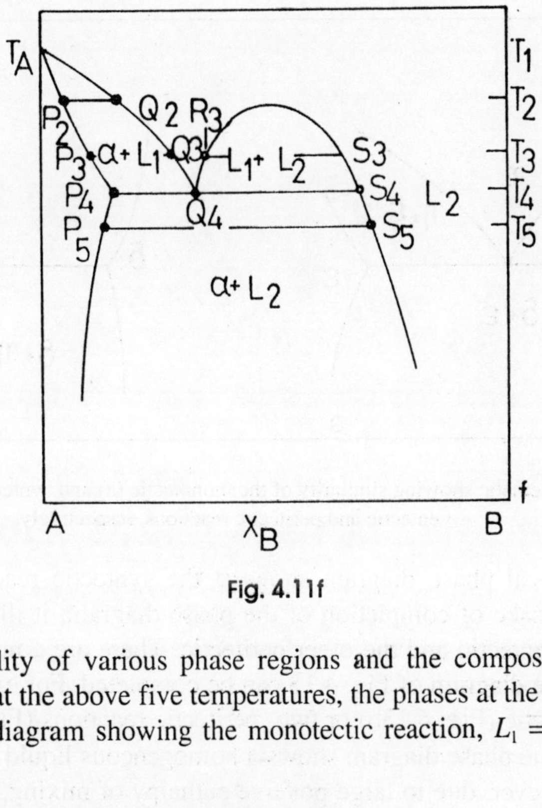

Fig. 4.11f

From the stability of various phase regions and the composition points of the coexisting phases at the above five temperatures, the phases at the above five temperatures, the phase diagram showing the monotectic reaction, $L_1 \rightleftharpoons \alpha + L_2$, is constructed.

4.6 BINARY SYNTECTIC SYSTEM

In the preceding section, a monotectic reaction has been characterized by $L_1 \rightleftharpoons \alpha + L_2$. The reaction belongs to the eutectic group in which there are two two-phase fields above the reaction temperature and one two-phase fields below the reaction temperature, Fig. 4.12a. Accordingly, the η phase dissociates into two phases δ and ε. The syntectic reaction belongs to the peritectic group and is characterized by one two-phase field above the reaction temperature and two two-phase fields below the reaction temperature, Fig. 4.12b. The phases participating in the reaction are two liquids, L_1 and L_2, and one solid β. The syntectic reaction is written as:

$$L_1 + L_2 \rightleftharpoons \beta.$$

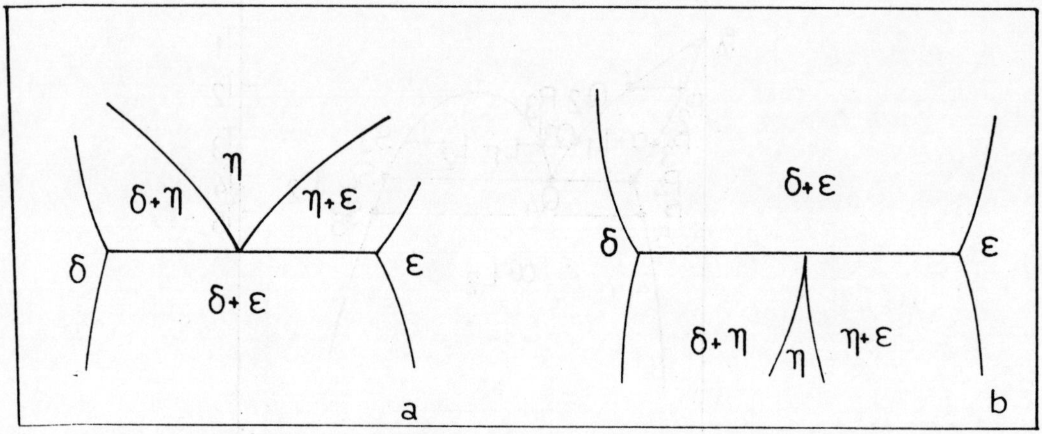

Fig. 4.12 Schematic showing similarity of the monotectic (a) and syntectic (b) reactions with the eutectic and peritectic reactions, respectively.

A hypothetical phase diagram showing the syntectic reaction is shown in Fig. 4.13a. For the sake of completion of the phase diagram, it illustrates two additional reactions; one eutectic and the other peritectic. There are a number of other ways in which the phase diagram of Fig. 4.13 can be completed. For example, one may select either two eutectic (Fig. 4.13b) or two peritectic reactions (Fig. 4.13c) and complete the diagram. The phase diagram shows a homogeneous liquid solution at higher temperatures. However, due to large positive enthalpy of mixing, the homogeneous, liquid solution shows clustering at lower temperature. The splitting of the homogeneous liquid solution into two liquids reflects this behavior. The two separate liquid solutions do not remain stable over a large temperature interval and ultimately react with each other to produce β phase, which is solid.

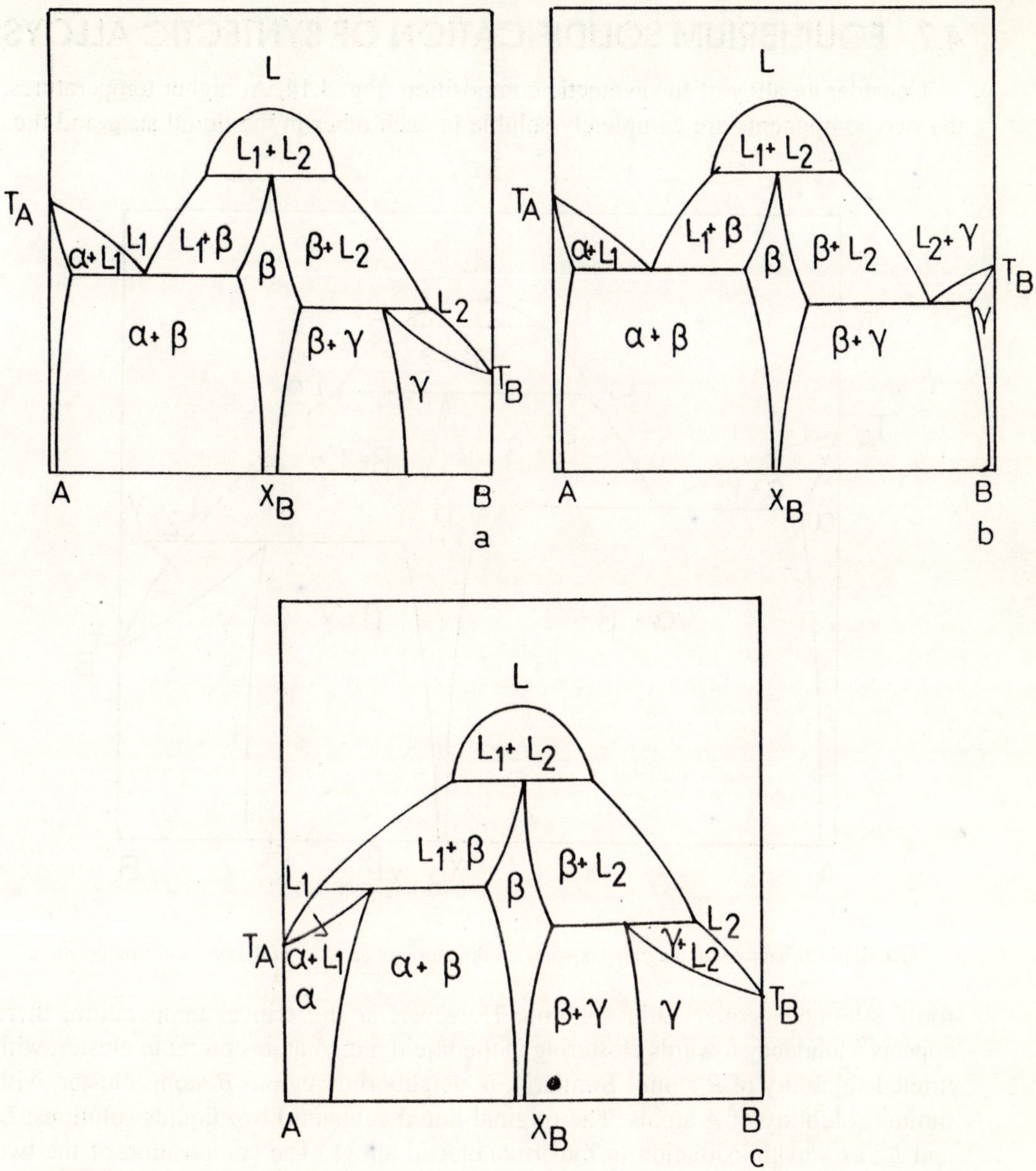

Fig. 4.13 A hypothetical binary phase diagram showing the syntectic reaction. The rest of the reactions are shown for the sake of completion of the diagram: (a) one eutectic and one peritectic, (b) two eutectic, and (c) two peritectic reactions.

4.7 EQUILIBRIUM SOLIDIFICATION OF SYNTECTIC ALLOYS

Consider an alloy of the syntectic composition, Fig. 4.14. At higher temperatures, the two components are completely soluble in each other in the liquid state and thus

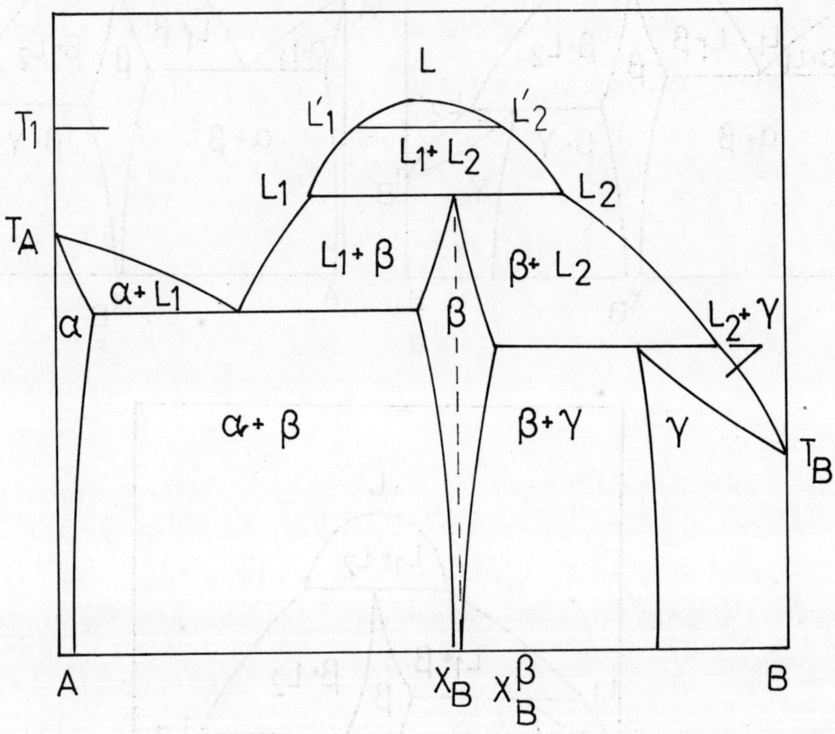

Fig. 4.14 Binary phase diagram showing solidification of an alloy of the syntectic composition.

form a homogeneous liquid solution. However, at the critical temperature, there appears a tendency towards clustering in the liquid, i.e., *A* atoms prefer to cluster, with limited solubility of *B* atoms. Similarly, in neighboring regions *B* atoms cluster, with limited solubility of *A* atoms. The original liquid splits into two liquids solutions, L_1 and L_2, as was the situation in hypermonotectic alloys. The composition of the two liquid solutions can be determined by drawing a tie-line at any temperature within the immiscibility gap. For example, at temperature T_1, liquid L_1 of composition L_1^1 is in equilibrium with L_2 of composition L_2^1. The liquid L_1 gets enriched with component *A* and L_2 gets enriched with component B as the temperature decreases. At the syntectic reaction isotherm, the two liquids react with each other to form β phase of composition X_B^β.

There are a very limited number of alloy systems showing the syntectic reaction. A number of them that do show the syntectic reaction are the alkali metals, Na, K, Ca, etc. alloyed with metals like Zn, Cd, Pb, etc. The commercial value of such alloy systems is yet to be explored fully as very limited work has been done on the properties of such alloys.

The β phase forms at the interface between the two liquids. Direct contact between the two liquids is lost as a consequence and the syntectic reaction stops, just like the peritectic reaction. Further growth of the β phase occurs by the syntectic transformation. This involves net transport of A atoms from L_1 and B atoms from L_2 towards the β phase. As the thickness of the β phase layer increases, the distance that A and B atoms have to diffuse increase and it become difficult for the transformation to proceed as rapidly as it did before. The syntectic transformation can reach completion only when the alloy is kept below the syntectic reaction isotherm for a long time. A single-phase alloy will result, as shown in Fig. 4.15.

4.8 THE EFFECT OF GRAVITY SEGREGATION ON MICROSTRUCTURAL EVOLUTION DURING NATURAL COOLING OF A SYNTECTIC ALLOY

Consider the solidification of a syntectic alloy under natural cooling. As shown before, the homogeneous liquid will separate into two liquid solutions L_1 and L_2 (as the alloy is cooled through the immiscibility gap of the phase diagram, Fig. 4.16), which preferably occupy distinct layers in the mold. This will occur if the component metals have a significant difference in densities. Solidification of the alloy will begin at the syntectic reaction isotherm. The β phase will form at the interface between L_1 and L_2, as illustrated in Fig. 4.17. The growth of the β phase is restricted during natural cooling of the alloy as the two liquids have lost direct contact with each other. Liquids L_1 and L_2 will remain isolated and solidify independently; i.e., liquid L_1 will solidify as a hypereutectic alloy and L_2 as a hypoperitectic alloy, according to the hypothetical phase diagram of Fig. 4.16.

The secondary β phase will form both as a proeutectic constituent from L_1, depositing over the existing syntectic β phase, and as homogeneously formed nuclei into L_1 and grow. At the eutectic temperature, the liquid(1) L_1, now enriched with component

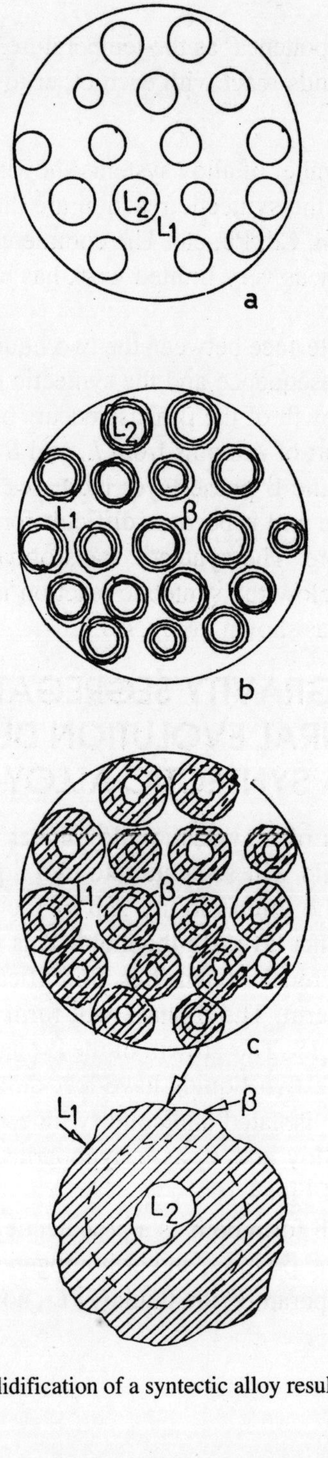

Fig. 4.15 Progress of solidification of a syntectic alloy resulting in single-phase β.

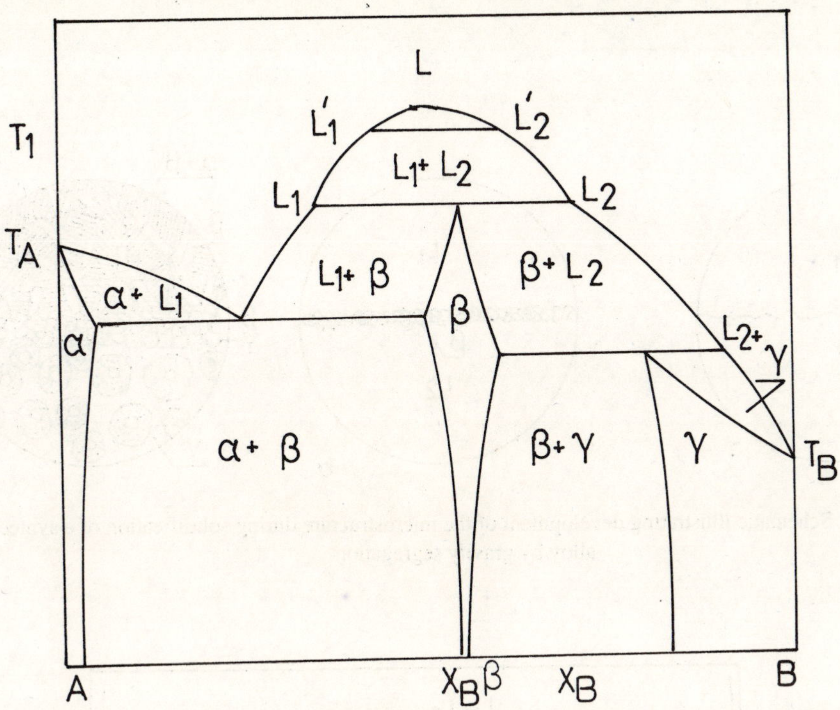

Fig. 4.16 Binary phase diagram showing a syntectic reaction. The separation of the liquid is by gravity segregation.

A, will dissociate into α and β phases by the eutectic reaction. The microstructure in the layer originally occupied by L_1 will consist of secondary β and the eutectic α + β phases, as shown schematically in Fig. 4.17. The solidification of the independent liquid L_2 proceeds in the same manner by deposition of the properitectic β constituent. At the peritectic temperature, the solute enriched liquid reacts with the secondary β to form the γ phase. The solidification of L_2 will proceed with coring of the secondary β and tertiary and fourth order γ phases. The relative amounts of the two liquids will change for hyposyntectic and hypersyntectic alloy compositions. However, no microstructural changes are expected during the course of solidification of these alloys under natural cooling. The K-Zn binary system showing syntectic reaction is presented in Fig. 4.18.

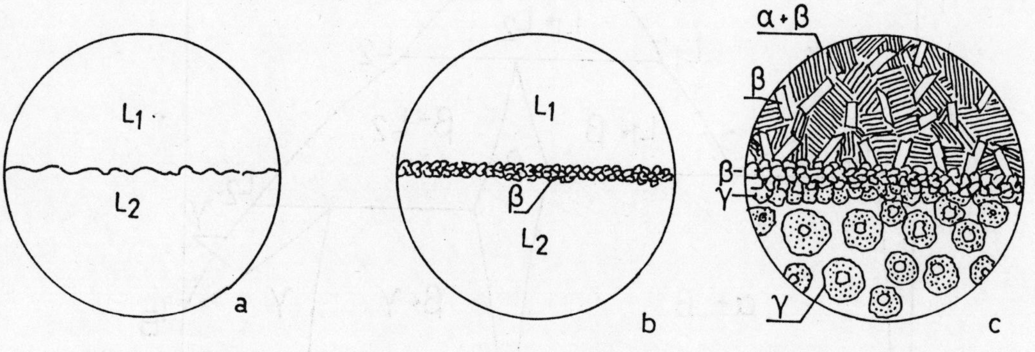

Fig. 4.17 Schematic illustrating development of the microstructure during solidification of a syntectic alloy by gravity segregation.

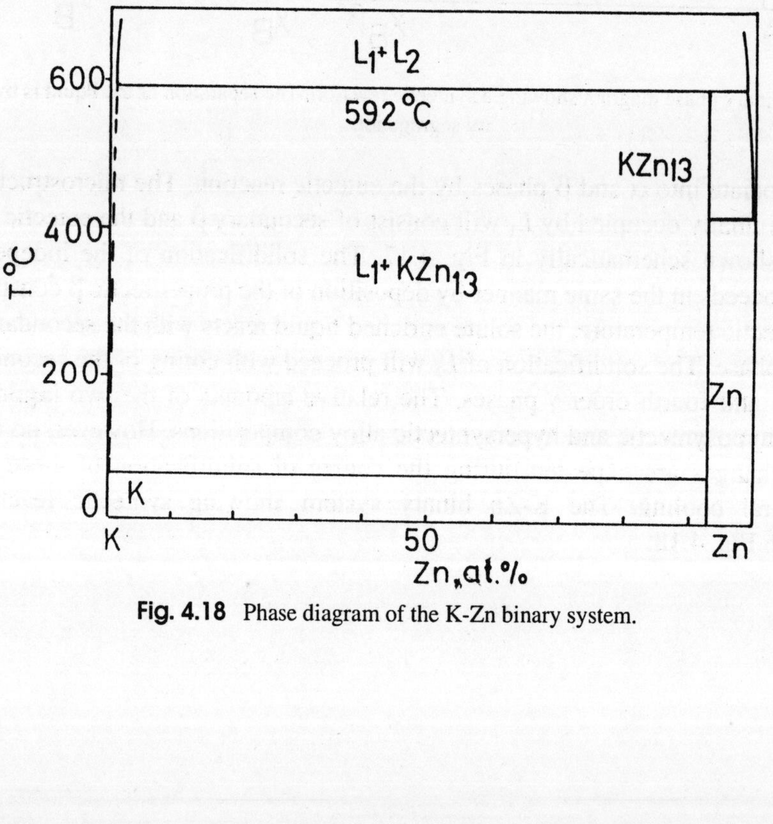

Fig. 4.18 Phase diagram of the K-Zn binary system.

4.9 FREE ENERGY-COMPOSITION DIAGRAMS

As described above, the phase diagram shows immiscibility in the liquid. This is

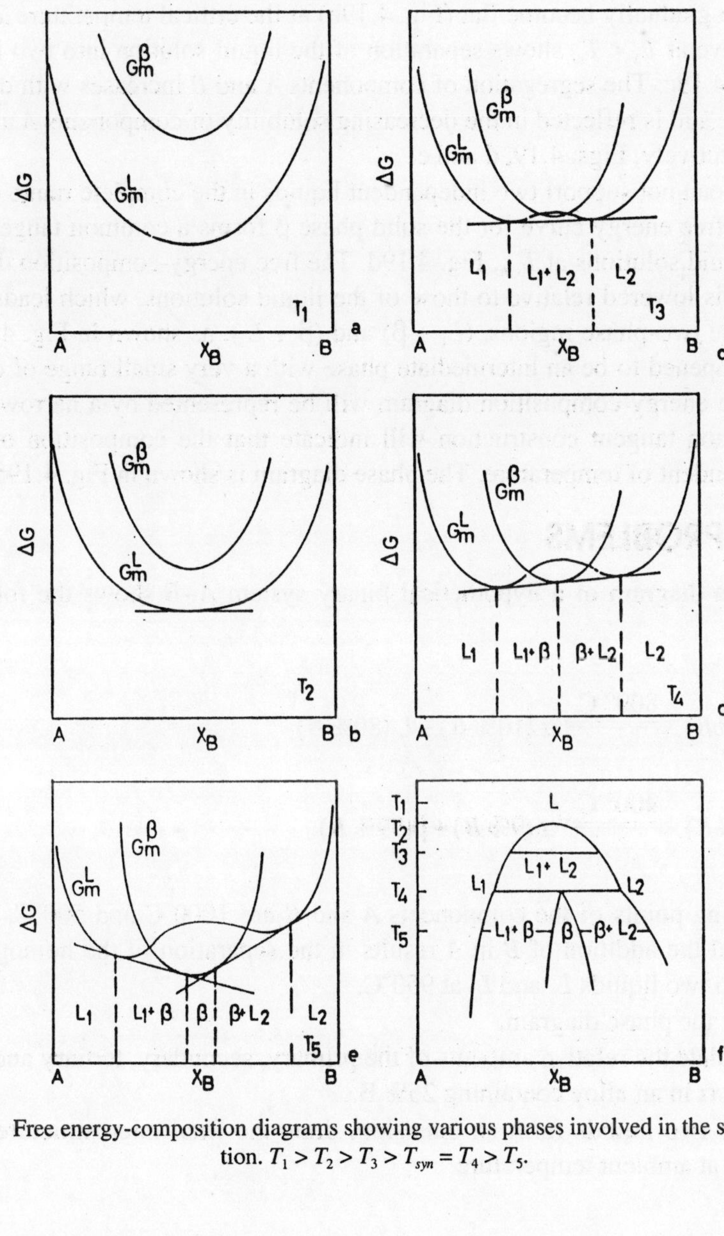

Fig. 4.19 Free energy-composition diagrams showing various phases involved in the syntectic reaction. $T_1 > T_2 > T_3 > T_{syn} = T_4 > T_5$.

possible when the interaction term Ω^L or excess free energy of mixing of the two components in the liquid is large and positive. At higher temperatures, the two components form a homogeneous liquid and the free energy curve is represented by a parabola, Fig. 4.19a. As the temperature is lowered, there is a tendency for the free energy curve to gradually become flat (Fig. 4.19b) at the critical temperature T_{cr}. The free energy curve at $T_3 < T_{cr}$ shows separation of the liquid solution into two liquids, L_1 and L_2, Fig. 4.19c. The segregation of components A and B increases with decreasing temperature and is reflected in the decreasing solubility of components A and B in L_2 and L_1, respectively, Figs. 4.19, d and e.

The system can not support two independent liquids in the complete range of temperatures. The free energy curve for the solid phase β forms a common tangent with those of the liquid solutions at T_{syn}, Fig. 4.19d. The free energy-composition diagram of the β phase is lowered relative to those of the liquid solutions, which leads to the formation of the two-phase regions, (L_1 + β) and (β + L_2), as shown in Fig. 4.19e. If the β phase happened to be an intermediate phase with a very small range of compositions, the free energy-composition diagram will be represented by a narrow parabola. The common tangent construction will indicate that the composition of the β phase is independent of temperature. The phase diagram is shown in Fig. 4.19f.

SELECTED PROBLEMS

1. The phase diagram of a hypothetical binary system A–B shows the following reactions:

$$L_1(40\%B) \xrightleftharpoons{800^\circ\text{ C}} \alpha\,(10\%\,B) + L_2(80\%\,B)$$

$$L_2(95\%B) \xrightleftharpoons{400^\circ\text{ C}} \alpha\,(9\%\,B) + \beta(99\%\,B)$$

The melting points of the components A and B are 1000°C and 500°C, respectively, and the addition of B in A results in the separation of the homogeneous liquid into two liquids L_1 and L_2 at 950°C.

a. Draw the phase diagram.
b. Calculate the relative amounts of the primary, secondary, tertiary and fourth order α in an alloy containing 25% B.
c. If the two liquids form an emulsion, draw the final microstructure of the alloy at ambient temperature.

2. Metal *A* melts at 1000°C and *B* melts at 500°C. The addition of the component *B* in *A* results in the following reactions:

$$L_1(40\%B) \xrightleftharpoons{900°C} \alpha\,(10\%B) + L_2(80\%B),\ T_{cr} = 1050°C$$

$$\alpha\,(9\%B) + L_2(89\%B) \xrightleftharpoons{600°C} \beta\,(79\%B).$$

   a. Draw the phase diagram.
   b. Calculate the relative amounts of the primary, secondary and tertiary α phases in an alloy containing 25% B.
   c. Calculate the relative amount of the β phase just below 600°C after complete equilibrium.
   d. Draw schematic free energy-composition diagrams at (i) 1025°C (ii) 900°C (iii) 700°C (iv) 550°C.
   e. Draw the composition-distance profile for (i) short times and (ii) intermediate times of annealing for a diffusion couple between components *A* and *B* (*A*:*B* = 3:1) at 575°C and 950°C. Show the direction of migration of the interface(s).

3. Component *A* melts at 1000°C and *B* melts at 650°C. The hypothetical binary system shows the following reactions.

$$L_1(30\%B) + L_2(60\%B) \xrightleftharpoons{1000°\,C} \beta(50\%B),\ T_{cr} = 1100°C \text{ at } X_B = 0.5$$

$$L_2(70\%\,B) \xrightleftharpoons{900°C} \beta(55\%\,B) + L_3(80\%B),\ T_{cr} = 970°C \text{ at } X_B = 0.75$$

$$L_1(20\%B) \xrightleftharpoons{800°C} \alpha(5\%B) + \beta(45\%B)$$

$$L_3(95\%B) + \beta(52\%B) \xrightleftharpoons{700°C} \gamma\,(90\%B)$$

   a. Draw the phase diagram of the binary system *A*–*B*.

b. An alloy containing 50% B is cooled from the homogeneous liquid state. The cooling rate is such that only 30% β forms by the syntectic reaction. The remaining liquids L_1 and L_2 are allowed to cool slowly but independently. Liquids L_1 and L_2 undergo the eutectic and monotectic reactions, respectively, and liquid L_3 combines with the β phase to form γ.
   (i) Determine the relative amounts of L_1 and L_2 remaining unreacted just below 1000°C.
   (ii) Determine the relative amounts of the proeutectic and eutectic β phases forming from the remaining liquid L_1. Assume equilibrium.
   (iii) Determine the relative amount of the promonotectic β phase formed just above 900°C and the monotectic β phase and liquid L_3 just below 900°C forming from the remaining liquid L_2. Assume equilibrium.
   (iv) Determine the relative amount of the γ phase formed just below 700°C.

c. Draw the free energy-composition diagram at 950°C, 850°C and 750°C.

4. Component A melts at 500°C and B melts at 700°C. The binary system A–B shows the following reactions:

$$L_1(40\%B)+L_2(60\%B)\xrightleftharpoons{900°C}\alpha(50\%B), T_{cr}=1000°C, X_B=0.5$$

$$L_2(70\%B)\xrightleftharpoons{800°C}\alpha(52\%B)+L_3(80\%B), T_{cr}=900°C, X_B=0.75$$

$$L_1(20\%B)+\alpha(45\%B)\xrightleftharpoons{700°C}\beta(30\%B)$$

$$L_3(90\%B)\xrightleftharpoons{600°C}\alpha(51\%B)+\gamma(95\%B)$$

An alloy containing 45% B is cooled from the homogeneous liquid state at a rate such that only 10% α phase forms by the syntectic reaction. The remaining liquids L_1 and L_2 are allowed to cool slowly so as to give the equilibrium microstructure.

a. Draw the phase diagram and label all phase fields.
b. Determine the relative amounts of liquids L_1 and L_2 remaining unreacted just below 900°C.

c. Determine the relative amounts of the properitectic α forming from L_1 and promonotectic α forming from L_2.
d. Determine the relative amounts of the monotectic α and L_3 phases.
e. Determine the relative amounts of the peritectic β phase.
f. Draw the free energy-composition diagram at 850°C.
g. Draw the microstructure of the alloy (consider gravity segregation).

5. "Equilibrium solidification of monotectic and syntectic alloys leads to an inhomogeneous microstructure". Discuss the above statement with reference to the gravity segregation in these alloys.
6. With the information provided below, draw the phase diagrams of the Cd-K, K-Zn, Na-Zn, Cd-Cs and Cd-Rb alloy systems and then answer the following:

Cd-K System

$$L_1(0.01 \text{ at.\% K}) \underset{}{\overset{321°\text{C}}{\rightleftharpoons}} \alpha(0.005\%) + \text{Cd}_{13}\,\text{K}(7.143\%)$$

$$L_1 \overset{490°\text{C}}{\rightleftharpoons} \text{Cd}_{13}\,\text{K}(7.143\% \text{ K}) \text{ congruently melting}$$

$$L_1(15\% \text{ K}) \overset{468°\text{C}}{\rightleftharpoons} \text{Cd}_{13}\text{K}(7.143\%) + L_2(94\% K)$$

$$L_2(99.99\% \text{ K}) \overset{637°\text{ C}}{\rightleftharpoons} \text{Cd}_{13}\,\text{K}(7.143\%) + \text{K}\ (100\%)$$

melting points: Cd = 321.108°C and K = 63.7°C.

K-Zn System

$$L_1(1 \text{ at.\% Zn}) + L_2(98 \text{ at.\%Zn}) \overset{592°\text{ C}}{\rightleftharpoons} \text{KZn}_{13}(92.86\% \text{ Zn}).$$

$$L_2(99.9\% \text{ Zn}) \overset{419.58°\text{C}}{\rightleftharpoons} \text{KZn}_{13}(92.86\% \text{ Zn}) + \text{Zn}(100\%)$$

$$L_1(0.01\%\ Zn) \xrightleftharpoons{637°C} K + KZn_{13}(92.86\%\ Zn)$$

melting point: Zn = 419.58°C.

Na-Zn System

$$L_1(0.8\%Zn) + L_2(93.5\%Zn) \xrightleftharpoons{557°C} NaZn_{13}$$

$$L_2(99.9\%Zn) \xrightleftharpoons{418.86°C} NaZn_{13} + Zn$$

$$L_1(0.0001\%Zn) \xrightleftharpoons{97.8°C} Na + NaZn_{13}$$

melting point: Na = 97.8°C.

Cd-Rb System

$$L_1(5at.\%Rb) + L_2(99\%Rb) \xrightleftharpoons{500°C} Cd_{13}Rb$$

$$L_1(0.001\%Rb) \xrightleftharpoons{321°C} Cd + Cd_{13}Rb$$

$$L_2(99.99\%Rb) \xrightleftharpoons{39.4°C} Cd_{13}Rb + Rb.$$

melting point : Rb = 39.48°C.

Cd-Cs System

$$L_1(\sim 1\text{at.}\%\text{Cd}) + L_2(\sim 99\%\text{Cd}) \xrightleftharpoons{400^\circ\text{C}} \text{Cd}_{13}\text{Cs}$$

$$L_2(99.99\%\text{Cd}) \xrightleftharpoons{321^\circ\text{C}} \text{Cd}_{13}\text{Cs} + \text{Cd}$$

$$L_1(0.001\%\text{Cd}) \xrightleftharpoons{28.3^\circ\text{C}} \text{Cs} + \text{Cd}_{13}\text{Cs},$$

melting point: Cs = 28.39°C.

a. What is the effect of the atomic diameter on the (i) width of the immiscibility gap, (ii) stability of the intermediate phases, and, therefore, (iii) on the melting or dissociation temperature?

b. Which of the two, syntectic or monotectic, reactions will occur in a system with a low melting or dissociation temperature of the intermediate phase? Explain.

Chapter 5

INTERMEDIATE PHASES

5.1 INTRODUCTION

It was shown in Chapter 1 that when two metals are allowed to mix with each other, they may either form a solid solution in the whole range of compositions or have a limited solid solubility of one element in another. Consider for example, the Cu-Ni and Cu-Ag alloy systems. The metals Cu and Ni are completely soluble in each other in all proportions and form a single solid solution having a crystal structure consistent with either Cu or Ni. In the Cu-Ag alloy system on the other hand, the two metals have very limited solubility in each other. Thus copper can dissolve only up to 5.1 at. pct. Ag and Ag can dissolve up to 15.9 at.pct. Cu. The terminal solid solutions that form have the crystal structure of the solvent-rich component. In the Cu-Ag alloy system, both terminal solid solutions are *fcc*.

A large number of alloy systems show intermediate phases which, as the name suggests, are phases intermediate between the two terminal solid solutions. The crystal structure of an intermediate phase is different from that of the terminal solid solutions on either side of it. Among the large number of binary alloy systems, an intermediate phase commonly forms by the peritectic reaction. Intermediate phases can also form in alloy systems by the syntectic or peritectoid reactions. As an example, the phase diagram of Fig. 5.1 represents the intermediate phase in the alloy system Mo-Hf. The liquid reacts with α to form Mo_2Hf as the following reaction shows:

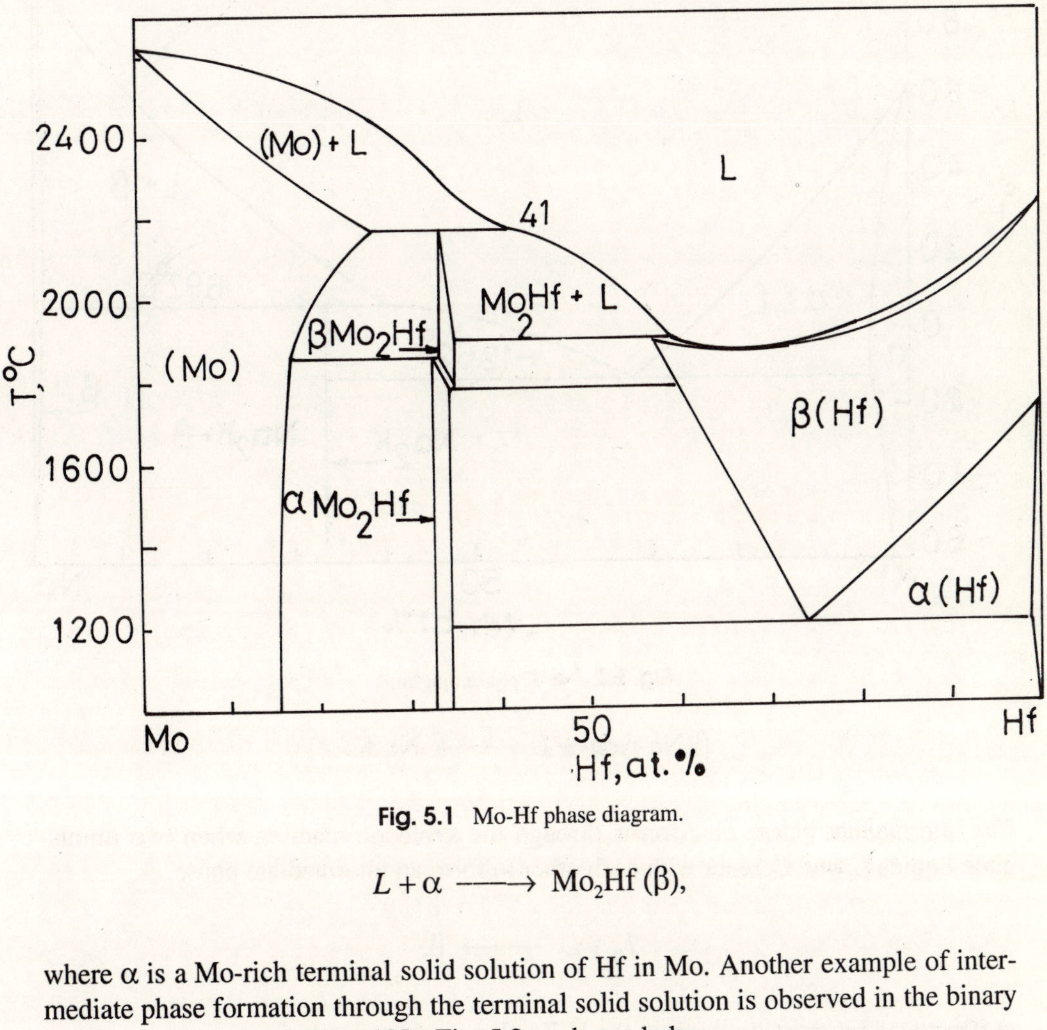

Fig. 5.1 Mo-Hf phase diagram.

$$L + \alpha \longrightarrow Mo_2Hf\ (\beta),$$

where α is a Mo-rich terminal solid solution of Hf in Mo. Another example of intermediate phase formation through the terminal solid solution is observed in the binary system of alkali metals K and Na, Fig. 5.2 as shown below:

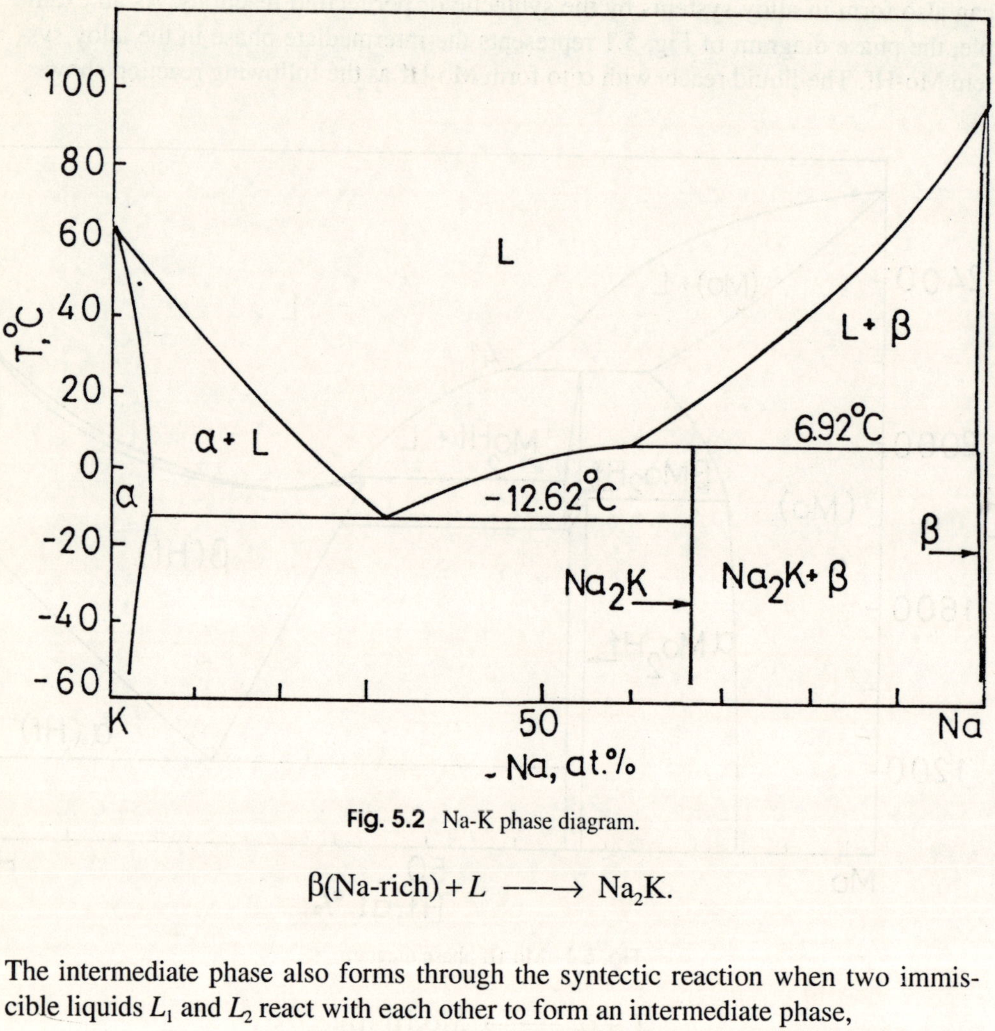

Fig. 5.2 Na-K phase diagram.

$$\beta(\text{Na-rich}) + L \longrightarrow Na_2K.$$

The intermediate phase also forms through the syntectic reaction when two immiscible liquids L_1 and L_2 react with each other to form an intermediate phase,

$$L_1 + L_2 \longrightarrow \beta,$$

as illustrated by an example from the K-Zn alloy system, Fig. 5.3,

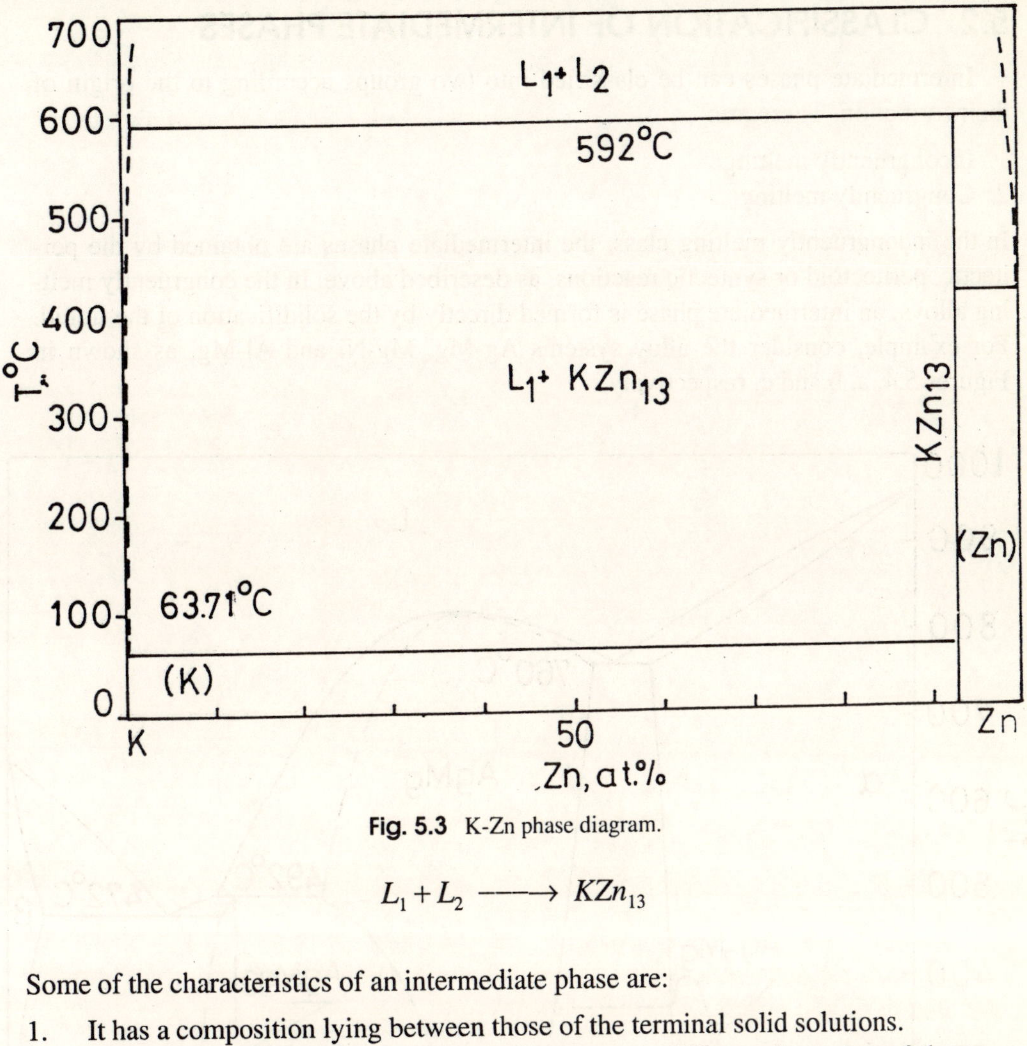

Fig. 5.3 K-Zn phase diagram.

$$L_1 + L_2 \longrightarrow KZn_{13}$$

Some of the characteristics of an intermediate phase are:

1. It has a composition lying between those of the terminal solid solutions.
2. The crystal structure of the intermediate phase is different from that of the terminal solid solutions.
3. Intermediate phases exist over a range of compositions.
4. They do not completely conform to the valency consideration, as the bonding required to form them is of a mixed type and all the valency electrons are not used in bonding them (due to some electrons being free, which maintain the conductivity of these phases).

5.2 CLASSIFICATION OF INTERMEDIATE PHASES

Intermediate phases can be classified into two groups according to the origin of their formation. These are:

1. Incongruently melting
2. Congruently melting

In the incongruently melting class, the intermediate phases are obtained by the peritectic, peritectoid or syntectic reactions, as described above. In the congruently melting alloys, an intermediate phase is formed directly by the solidification of the liquid. For example, consider the alloy systems Ag-Mg, Mg-Ni and Al-Mg, as shown in Figures 5.4, a, b and c, respectively.

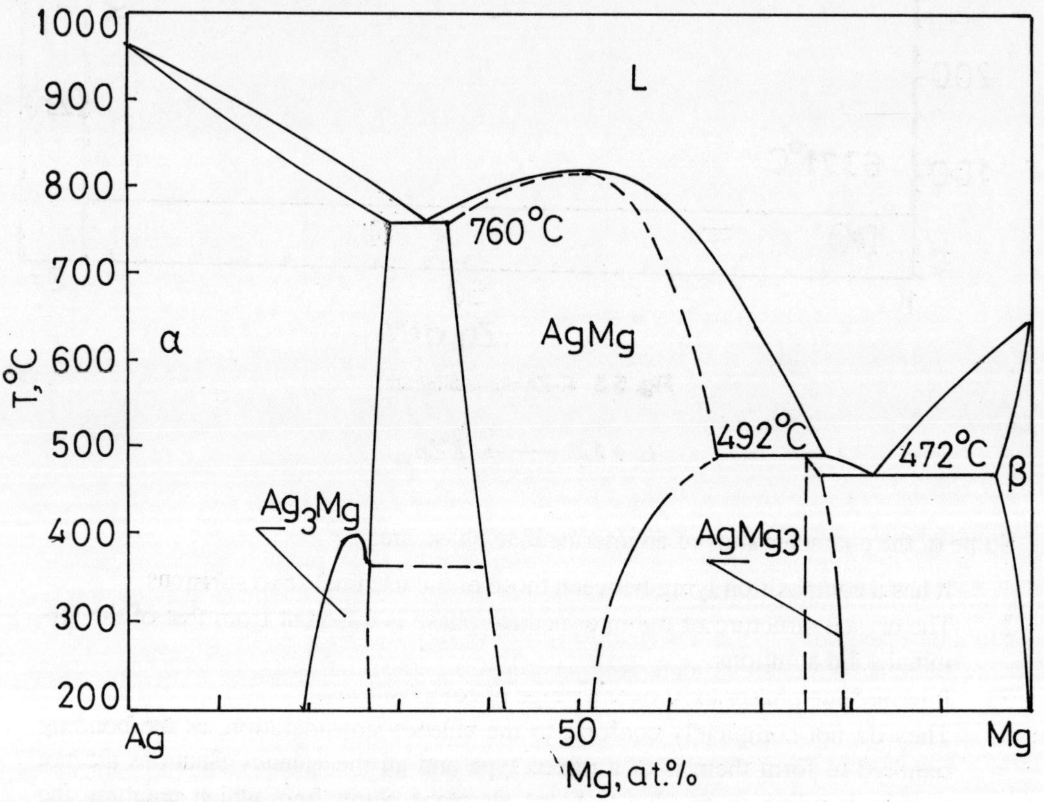

Fig. 5.4a Phase diagram of the alloy systems (a) Ag-Mg

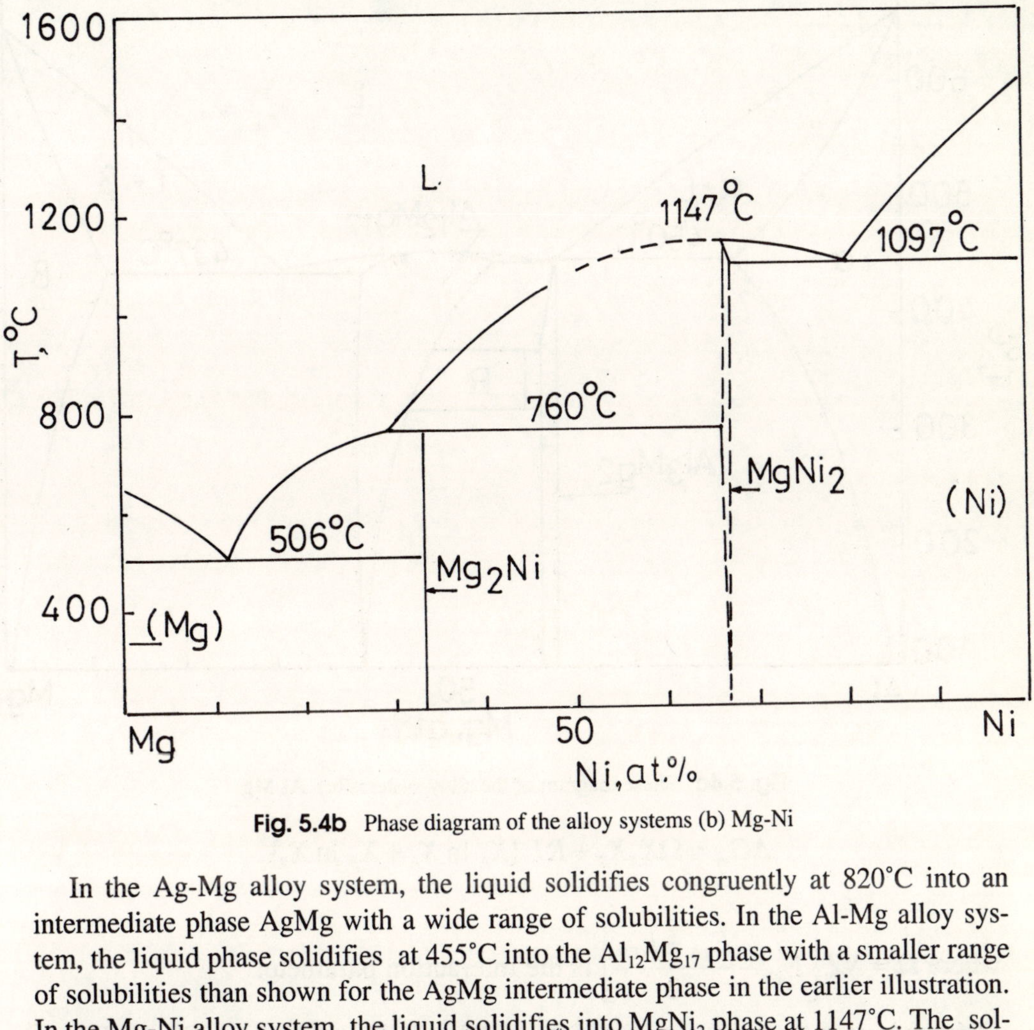

Fig. 5.4b Phase diagram of the alloy systems (b) Mg-Ni

In the Ag-Mg alloy system, the liquid solidifies congruently at 820°C into an intermediate phase AgMg with a wide range of solubilities. In the Al-Mg alloy system, the liquid phase solidifies at 455°C into the $Al_{12}Mg_{17}$ phase with a smaller range of solubilities than shown for the AgMg intermediate phase in the earlier illustration. In the Mg-Ni alloy system, the liquid solidifies into $MgNi_2$ phase at 1147°C. The solubility range is very restricted, varying from 66.2 to 67.3 at. pct. Ni. The intermediate phases in these systems behave as components and can be considered to divide or partition the phase diagram. However, no particular benifit can be derived from making such pseudo-binary diagrams. Constructing the phase diagram with the intermediate phase as a component is advantageous in ternary systems.

As described in Chapter 1, the free energy of mixing of a binary solution is written as,

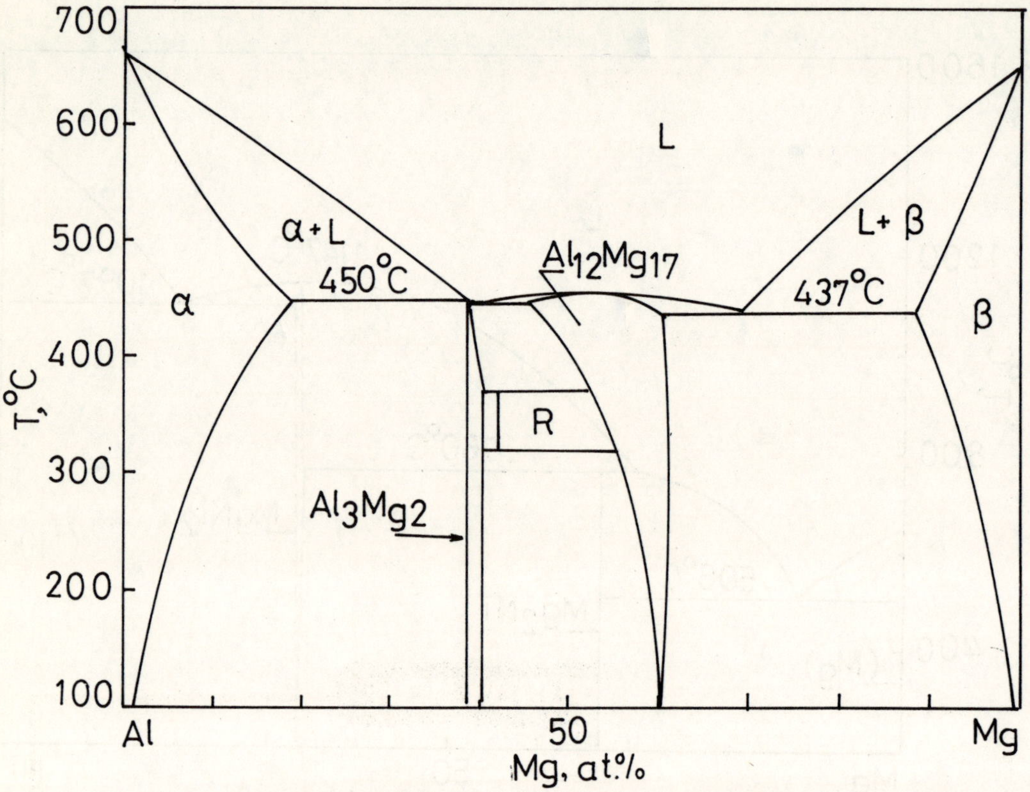

Fig. 5.4c Phase diagram of the alloy systems (c) Al-Mg.

$$\Delta G_m = \Omega X_A X_B + RT\,[X_A \ln X_A + X_B \ln X_B],$$

where $\Omega = NZ\left[E_{AB} - \dfrac{E_{AA} + E_{BB}}{2}\right]$ is the interaction parameter.

Ω depends upon the bond energies of the A–B bonds E_{AB}, and the pure bonds E_{AA} and E_{BB}. If $|E_{AB}| > |E_{AA} + E_{BB}|/2$, there will be a tendency for dissimilar atoms to be neighbors. That is, A atoms will prefer to be neighbors of B atoms and vice versa. With $\Delta H_m^S < \Delta H_m^L < 0$, there will be a strong attractive force between A and B atoms in the solid as compared to that in the liquid. The melting point of the solid solution will be raised due to strong A–B bonds. The phase diagram will show a maximum, as discussed in Chapter 2. At low temperatures, the solid will try to order itself so as to

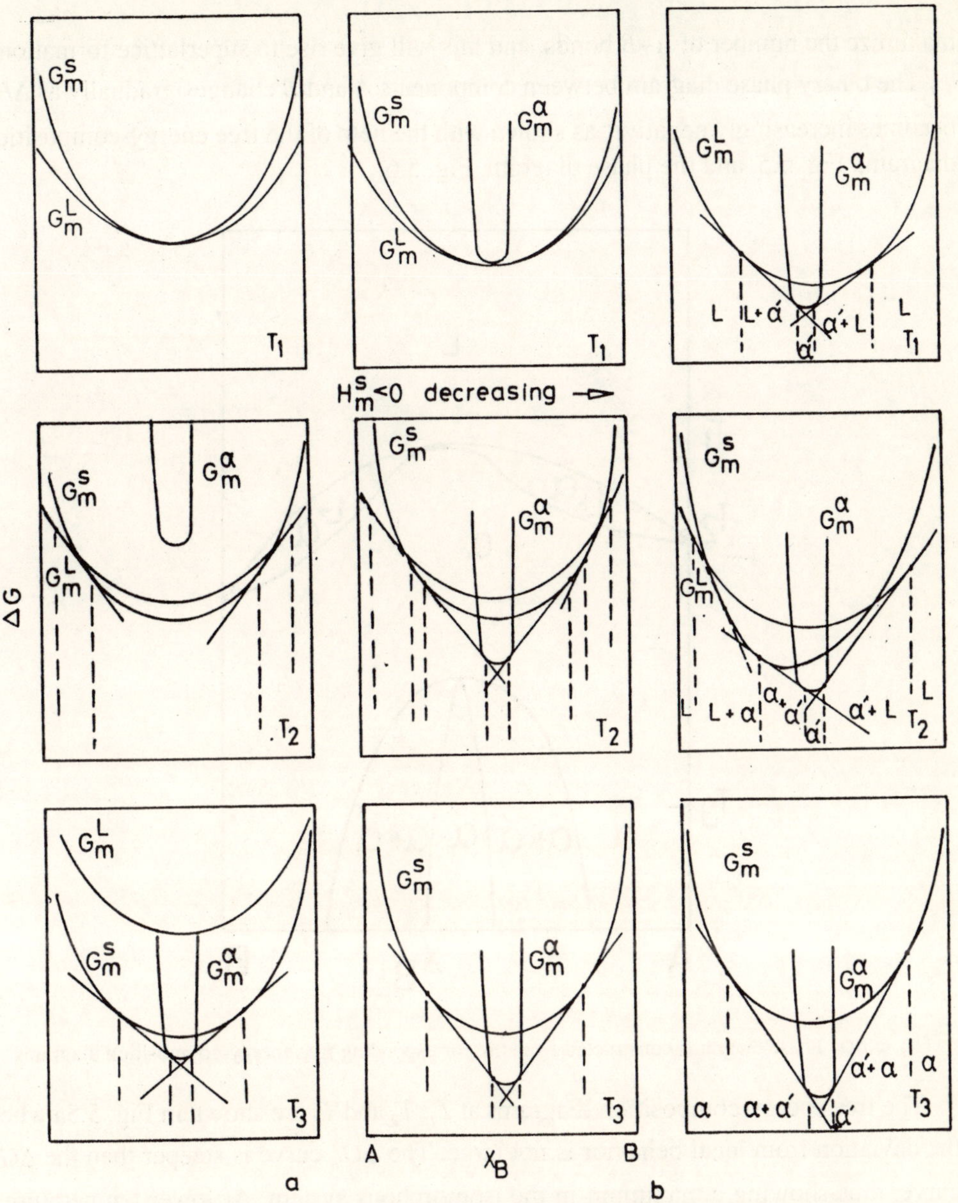

Fig. 5.5 Free energy-composition diagrams for $\Delta H_m^S < \Delta H_m^L < 0$ with ΔH_m^S becoming increasingly negative.

maximize the number of A–B bonds, and this will give rise to superlattice formation.

The binary phase diagram between components A and B changes gradually as ΔH_m^S becomes increasingly negative, as shown with the help of the free energy-composition diagram, Fig. 5.5, and the phase diagram, Fig. 5.6.

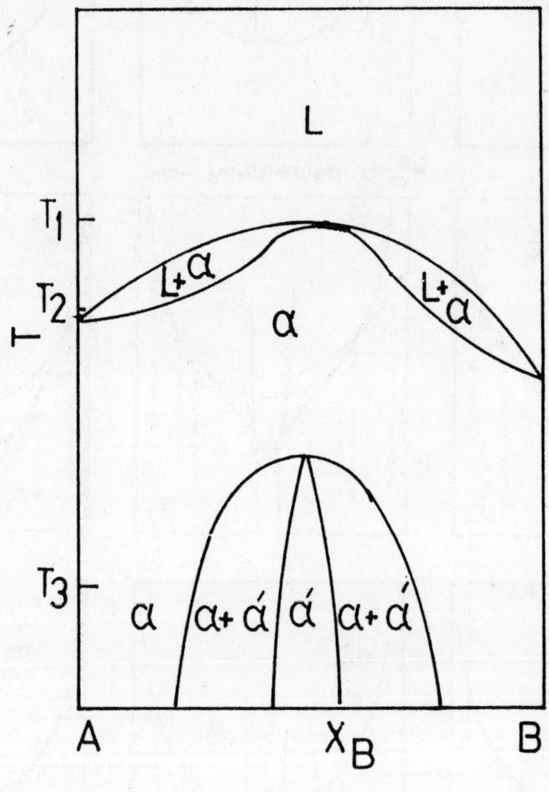

Fig. 5.6a Phase diagrams constructed from the corresponding free energy-composition diagrams.

The free energy-composition diagrams at T_1, T_2 and T_3 are shown in Fig. 5.5a when the deviation from ideal behavior is not large. The ΔG_m^S curve is steeper than the ΔG_m^L curve, thus showing a maximum in the isomorphous system. At lower temperatures, there is a tendency towards ordering of the α phase. The phase diagram is shown in Fig. 5.6a.

With ΔH_m^S becoming increasingly negative, a stage is reached at which T_{max}

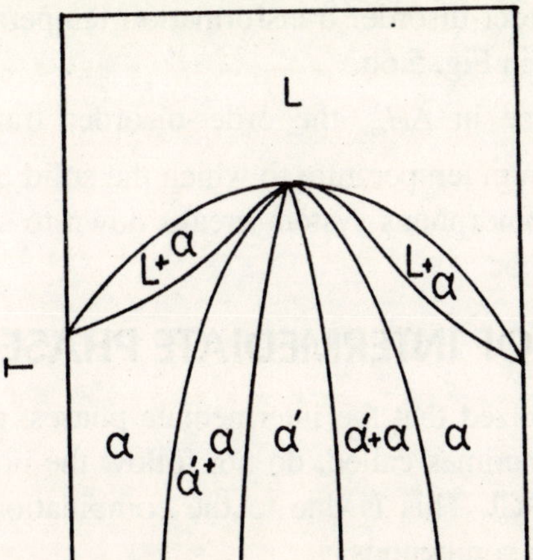

Fig. 5.6b

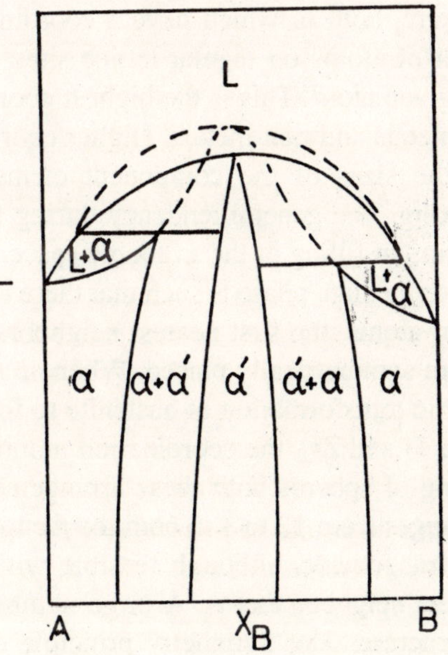

Fig. 5.6c

becomes equal to the order-disorder transformation temperature. The corresponding phase diagram is shown in Fig. 5.6b.

With further decrease in ΔH_m^S, the order-disorder transformation temperature exceeds T_{max}, the maximum temperature to which the solid is stable in the absence of ordering. The binary isomorphous system breaks down to show two peritectic reactions, as shown in Fig. 5.6c.

5.3 STRUCTURE OF INTERMEDIATE PHASES-PRINCIPLES

It is generally recognized that the intermediate phases, or the intermetallic compounds as they are sometimes called, do not follow the normal valency rules as in ionic solids such as NaCl. This is due to the combination of ionic, covalent and metallic bonding in such compounds.

The crystal structure of an intermediate phase depends to an extent on geometrical principles, which are,

a. The Space-filling principle.
b. The Symmetry principle.
c. The Connection principle.

Examination of the periodic table reveals that a large number of elements crystallize in the *fcc* and *hcp* structure, both of which have a coordination number of 12. In a symmetrical arrangement of atoms on regular lattice sites, there are 12 first nearest neighbor atoms for any given atom. This is the highest coordination number geometrically possible in pure metals and non-metals. Higher coordination numbers may be found in alloys when the sizes of the component elements differ suitably, thus allowing for denser packing. The general tendency during formation of intermediate phases is to achieve maximum filling of the available space.

The structure of an intermediate phase is such that there is symmetry. For example, in the *fcc* arrangement of atoms, the first nearest neighbors are at a distance $a\sqrt{2}/2$, Fig. 5.7, and all atoms are symmetrically placed. When an *fcc* lattice changes to *bcc*, (as during the polymorphic transformation of austenite to ferrite), or during an *hcp* to *bcc* transformation (as in Ti and Zr), the coordination number does not change to 11, 10 or 9, although packing of spheres with these arrangements is also possible. The coordination number changes from 12 to 8 in both the *fcc* to *bcc* and *hcp* to *bcc* transformations. The other arrangements although feasible will not yield a symmetrical arrangement of all nearest neighbor atoms. A large number of elements (33 or so) crystallize in the *bcc* structure. The Symmetry principle dictates that the resulting crystal structure of the intermediate phase be highly symmetric when two or more elements are mixed with each other.

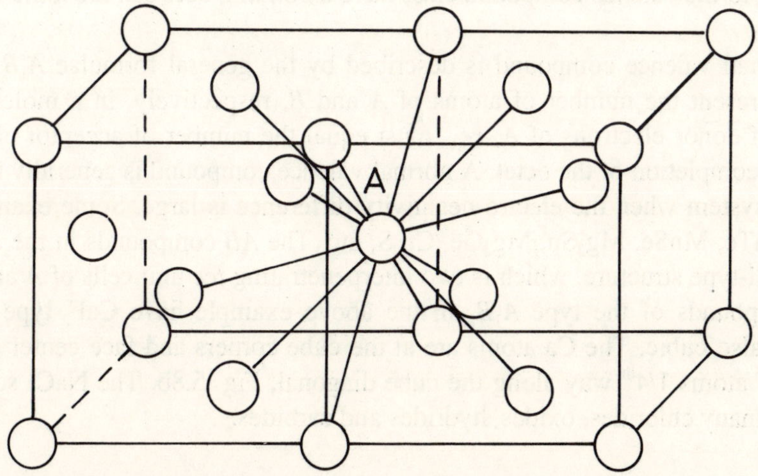

Fig. 5.7 Arrangement of atoms in an *fcc* lattice showing the first nearest neighbor atoms to an atom marked "*A*".

Consider a close packed arrangement of atoms, *fcc*, for example. Connect all atoms to one another through links or bonds. In the three-dimensional array of spheres, there will always be some short and some long links. Now remove all links except for the shortest ones. Those atoms that are still connected to each other are said to form a connection. The connection is said to be homogeneous if all atoms in the link are of the same kind; otherwise, it is known as heterogeneous. The connection could be one, two or three dimensional, and finite or, infinite. The intermediate phases with multi or high connections will be favored and govern the crystal structure.

5.4 CLASSIFICATION OF THE INTERMEDIATE PHASE

The intermediate phase can be broadly classified as either Valence compounds, Size-factor compounds or Electron compounds.

5.4.1 Valence Compounds

In the valence compound formation, the two atoms forming the intermediate phase behave as a donor acceptor pair for the electrons. The cations donate the valence electrons which are accepted by the anions which complete their octet. The valence compound group forms a stable octet configuration $ns^2\ np^6$. These can be completed in a manner akin to that of the ionic compounds, NaCl, LiF, etc., or by the sharing of electrons between atoms, as in covalent bonding in diamond. Intermediate phases belonging to the valence compound class have a bonding between the ionic and covalent bonds.

A normal valence compound is described by the general formulae A_xB_y where x and y represent the number of atoms of A and B, respectively, in a molecule. The number of donor electrons of A, xe_A, must equal the number of acceptor electrons y $(8-e)$ for completion of the octet. A normal valence compound is generally formed in a binary system when the electro-negativity difference is large. Some examples are: MgSe, BaTe, MnSe, Mg_2Sn, Mg_2Ge, Cu_2S, etc. The AB compounds in the above list have NaCl-type structure, which is two interpenetrating *fcc* unit cells of A and B, Fig. 5.8. Compounds of the type A_1B_2 in the above example have CaF_2-type structure which is also cubic. The Ca atoms are at the cube corners and face center positions, and the F atoms 1/4th way along the cube diagonal, Fig. 5.8b. The NaCl structure is taken by many chlorides, oxides, hydrides and carbides.

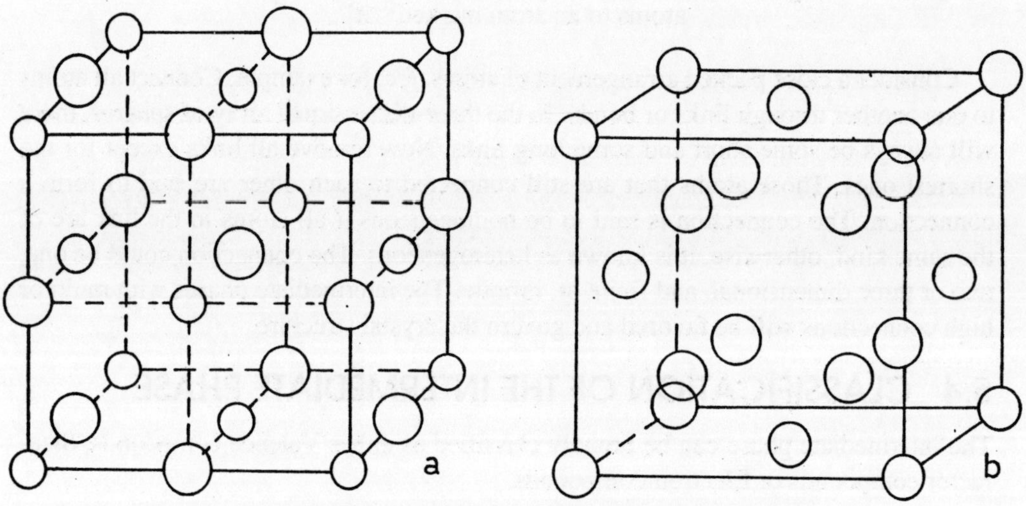

Fig. 5.8 Atom positions in (a) NaCl and (b) CaF_2 structures.

The valence compounds also form with atoms in a tetrahedral arrangement. Since there are four atoms surrounding a central atom in such an arrangement, there have to be four bonds in all between A and B atoms. The compound A_xB_y must satisfy the condition:

$$\frac{x\, e_A + y\, e_B}{x + y} = 4,$$

where e_A and e_B are the number of valence electrons of A and B atoms, respectively. If one of the sites of the tetrahedron is not occupied by atoms, it is a defect valence compound with a tetrahedral structure.

5.4.2 Size-Factor Compounds

An intermediate phase is known as a size-factor compound if the final structure depends upon the relative sizes of the two component metals. The formation of such structures strictly depends upon the relative volume of the two elements under consideration which indirectly influences the solubility of one element in another.

The Laves phases belong to this class of intermediate phases. In general, the structure of Laves phases is based on atoms occupying regular positions on the apex of a tetrahedron. The small atoms occupy such positions. The larger of the two atoms lies in the holes between the tetrahedral. Majority of the Laves phases belong to one of the following three structure types,

$MgCu_2$, $MgZn_2$, or $MgNi_2$.

Most of the original work on these phases has been carried out by Laves and his co-workers. These phases are considered to have their origin in geometrical factors. The following table shows a few intermediate phases having the above structure types.

$MgCu_2$-type	$MgZn_2$-type	$MgNi_2$-type
Cubic	Hexagonal	Hexagonal
$TiBe_2$	$CaMg_2$	HfG_2Cr_2
$AgBe_2$	$TaFe_2$	$NbZn_2$
$BiAu_2$	$NbMn_2$	$SeFe_2$

The structure of the Laves phases can be described in terms of the double layers. For example, in Fig. 5.9, are shown the basic, structures representing atomic positions occupied by the larger A atoms (Mg). The lattice of the A atoms can be considered as a hexagonal network of atoms with A atoms in the upper layer directly above the ones in the lower layer. The distinct arrangements of the double layers are termed X, Y, and Z. The double layer occupies 8 atoms followed by two each in the Y and Z layers. The

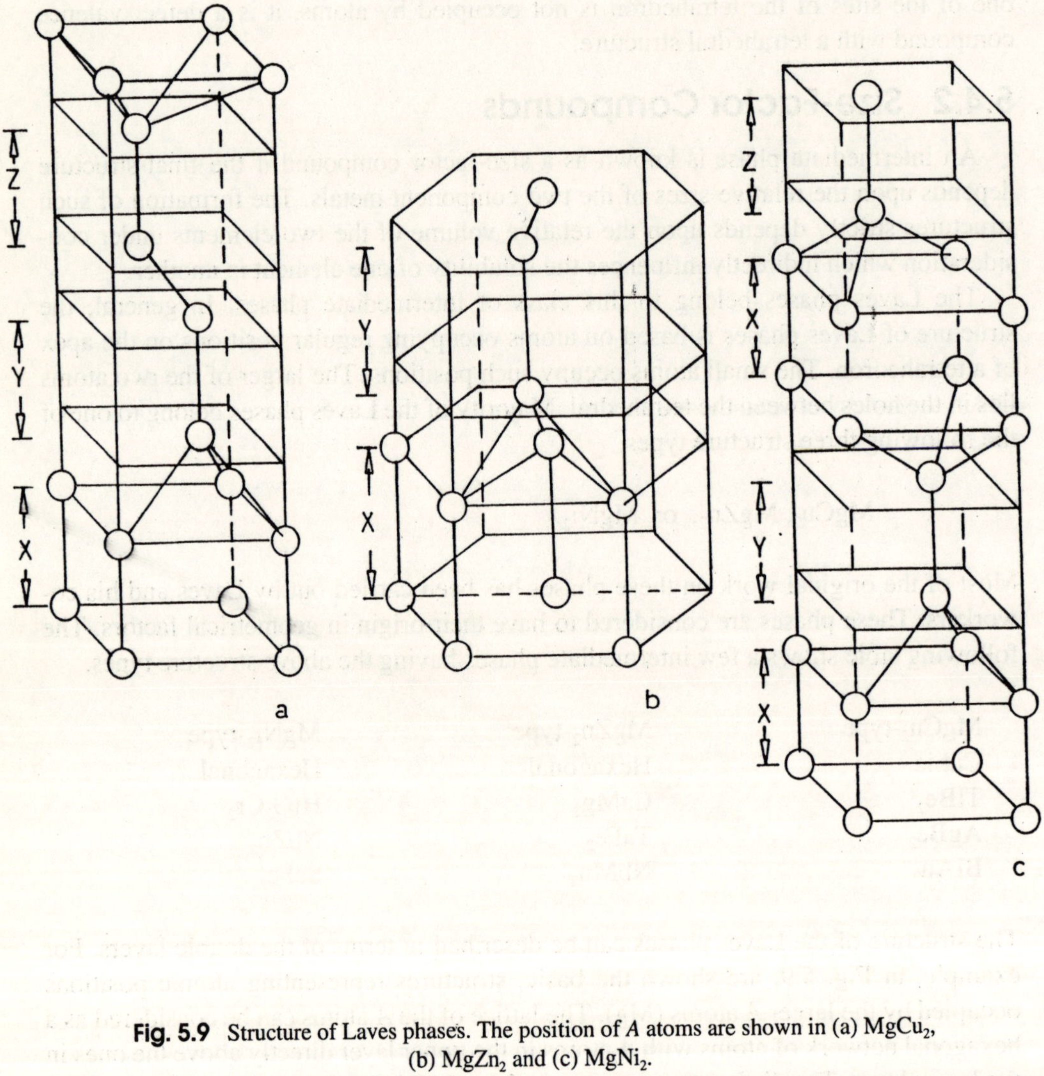

Fig. 5.9 Structure of Laves phases. The position of *A* atoms are shown in (a) $MgCu_2$, (b) $MgZn_2$ and (c) $MgNi_2$.

positions of *A* atoms in the *Y* and *Z* double layer are shifted relative to those in the *X* layer. In the terminology of the double layer arrangement of atoms, the Laves phases can be described as,

$MgCu_2$ – *XYZXYZ*...
$MgZn_2$ – *XYXYXY*...
$MgNi_2$ – *XYXZXYXZ*...

In the $MgCu_2$ structure type, the smaller Cu atoms occupy the apex of the tetrahedron and the larger Mg atoms occupy the hole between the tetrahedra. The Mg atoms form an *fcc* lattice, as shown in Fig. 5.10.

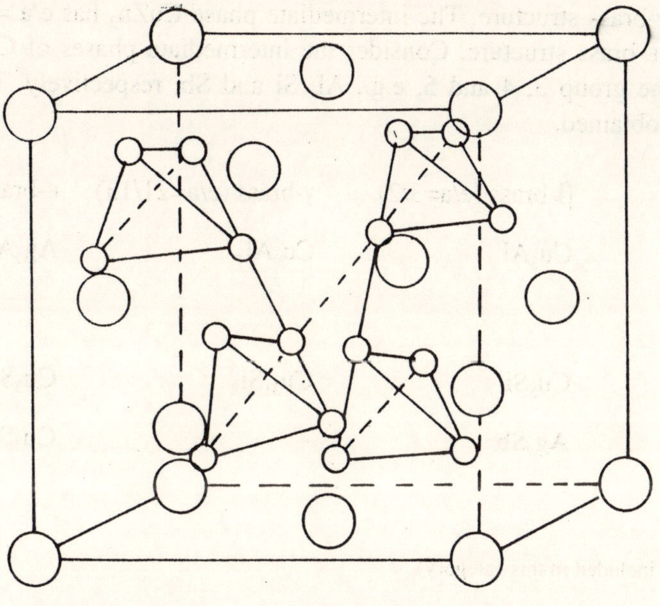

Fig. 5.10 The *fcc* arrangement of the $MgCu_2$ structure.

5.4.3 Electron Compounds

There are a large number of intermediate phases having a fixed electron to atom ratio. These are known as Hume Rothery phases or electron compounds. The electron to atom ratios are 3/2, 7/4 and 21/13. In the determination of the electron to atom ratios, it is usual to consider the valence electrons according to the following scheme:

Elements	No. of Valence Electrons
Cu, Ag, Au	1
Pb, Mg, Zn, Cd, Be	2
Al, Ga, In	3
Sn, Si, Ge	4
Sb, As, P, Bi	5
Pt and transition metals	0

The formation of electron compounds can be explained by taking the example of Cu-Zn alloys, where the intermediate phases CuZn, Cu_5Zn_8 and $CuZn_3$ are observed. According to the above scheme, the CuZn phase has an electron to atom ratio of 3/2. It is *bcc* with β-brass structure. The Cu_5Zn_8 has an electron to atom ratio 21/13 which is cubic with a γ-brass structure. The intermediate phase $CuZn_3$ has e/a = 7/4 which is *hcp* with an ε-brass structure. Consider the intermediate phases of Cu or Ag with elements of the group 3, 4 and 5, e.g., Al, Si and Sb, respectively. The following structures are obtained.

	β-brass (e/a=3/2)	γ-brass (e/a=21/13)	ε-brass (e/a=7/4)
Cu-Al, Cu-In or Ag–Al	Cu_3Al	Cu_9Al_4	Ag_5Al_3
Cu–Si	Cu_5Si	$Cu_{31}Si_8$	Cu_3Si
Cu–Sb or Ag–Sb	Ag_7Sb	–	Cu_3Sb*

* (e/a=8/4 but is included in this category)

5.5 NON-STOICHIOMETRIC COMPOUNDS

The intermediate phases in congruently melting alloys exist over a range of compositions. The maximum or minimum in the temperature corresponds to a stoichiometric composition A_xB_y, where x and y are integers. Intermediate phases in binary systems exist over a range of compositions with excess A and B type atoms. For example, in the Al-Ni alloy system, the AlNi phase melts congruently at 1638°C and exists in the composition range from 43 to 69 at.pct. Ni. This range of composition

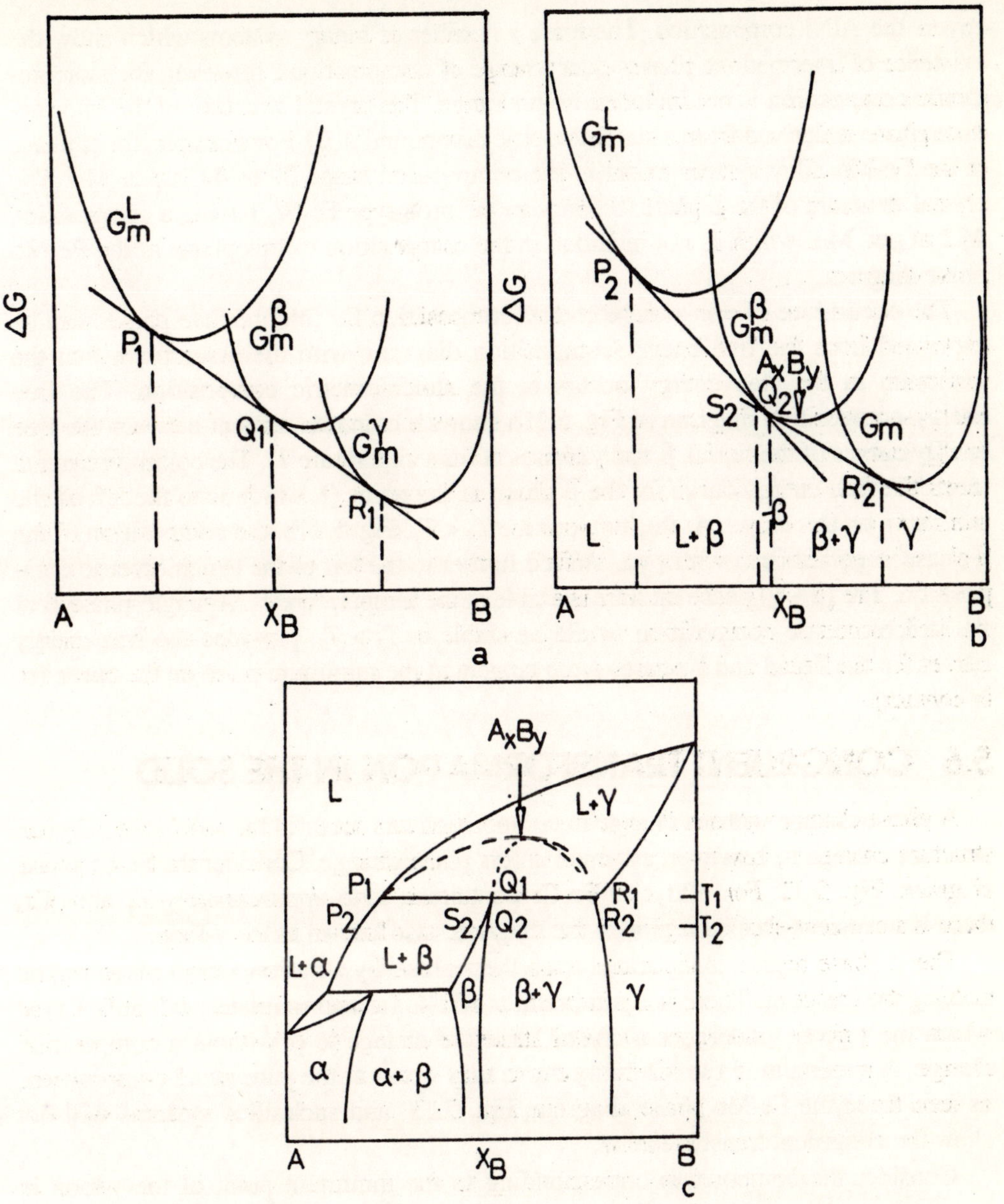

Fig. 5.11 Free energy-composition diagrams showing occurrence of non-stoichiometric compositions for the intermediate phase (a) at the peritectic temperature, T_1 (b) at $T_2 < T_1$; (c) shows the corresponding phase diagram.

covers the AlNi composition. There are a number of binary systems which show the existence of intermediate phases over a range of compositions; however, the stoichiometric composition is not included in this range. The crystal structure of the intermediate phase is derived from a stoichiometric compound A_xB_y. For example, the μ phase in the Fe-Mo alloy system exists in the composition range 39 to 44 at.pct. Mo. The crystal structure of the μ phase belongs to the prototype Fe_7W_6 having a composition 46.2 at.pct. Mo, which is not included in the composition of this phase in the Fe-Mo phase diagram.

The occurrence of non-stoichiometric composition for intermediate phases can be explained from the free energy-composition diagram, with the assumption that the minimum in the free energy occurs at the stoichiometric composition. The free energy-composition diagram of Fig. 5.11a shows a common tangent between the free energy curves of the liquid, β and γ phases at the temperature T_1. The common tangent meets the free energy curve for the β phase at the point Q_1 which is to the left of the minimum on this curve. At the temperature $T_2 < T_1$, Fig. 5.11b, the composition of the β phase in equilibrium with γ has shifted further to the left of the stoichiometric composition. The (β + γ) phase mixture is stable at the temperature T_2. A single-phase β of the stoichiometric composition would be stable at $T_3 > T_1$, provided the free energy curves for the liquid and β phases were tangent at the minimum point on the curve (or in contact).

5.6 CONGRUENT TRANSFORMATION IN THE SOLID

A phase change without change in composition can occur in the solid state. Crystal structure change is, however, assumed in this phase change. Consider the Fe-Cr phase diagram, Fig. 5.12. For alloys of Fe-Cr containing upto approximately 12 at.% Cr, there is a crescent-shaped region in the diagram, also known as the γ-loop.

The α phase region is separated from the γ phase by a narrow (α+γ) phase region making the crescent. There is a minimum at 831°C (at approximately 6.5 at.% Cr) at which the γ phase undergoes a crystal structure change to α without a composition change. A minimum in the solubility curve may occur at the pure metal composition, as seen from the Fe-Mo phase diagram, Fig. 5.13, and such alloy systems will not show the congruent transformation.

Consider the composition corresponding to the minimum point of the γ-loop in Fig. 5.12. An alloy which is originally 100% α at higher temperatures, will gradually transform into γ if cooled slowly. This γ phase, upon further cooling, will transform again to the α phase at 831°C. Other alloy compositions in the range of compositions of the γ-loop will transform in the same manner, except for the congruent transformation. The final structure below the lower solubility curve will consist of α.

A crescent shaped γ-loop with a minimum at the pure metal composition is observed in the Fe-Sn, Fe-P, Fe-W, and Fe-V alloys.

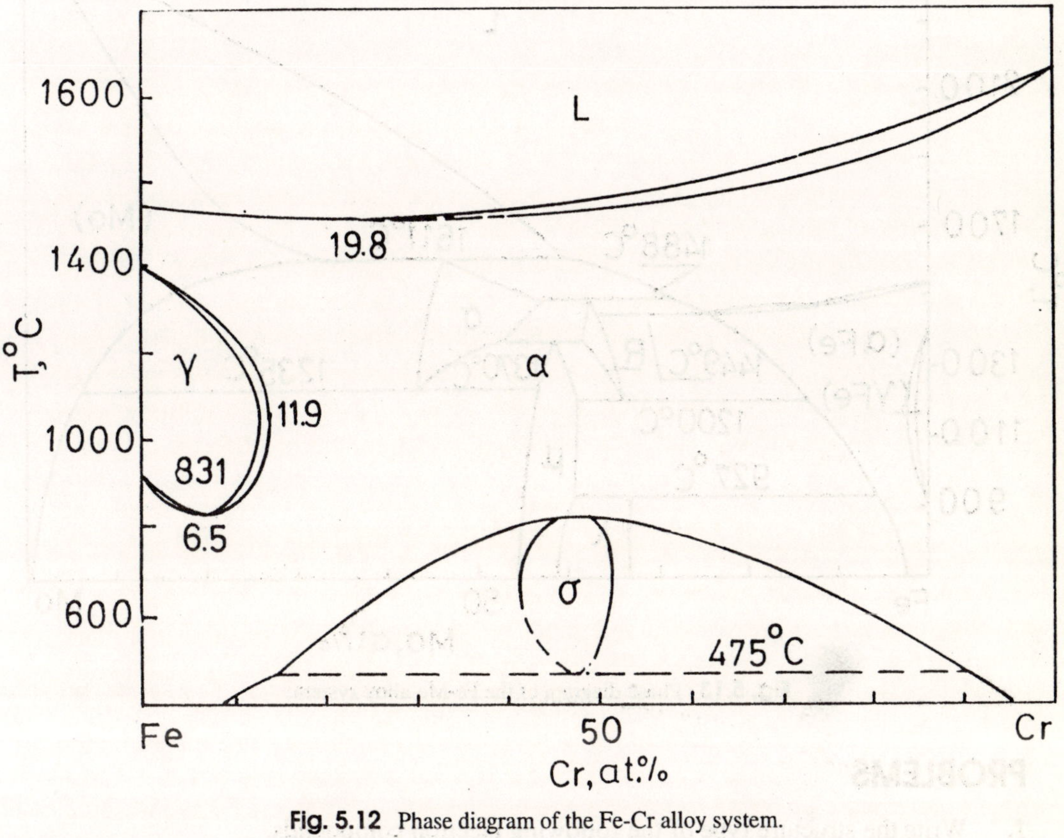

Fig. 5.12 Phase diagram of the Fe-Cr alloy system.

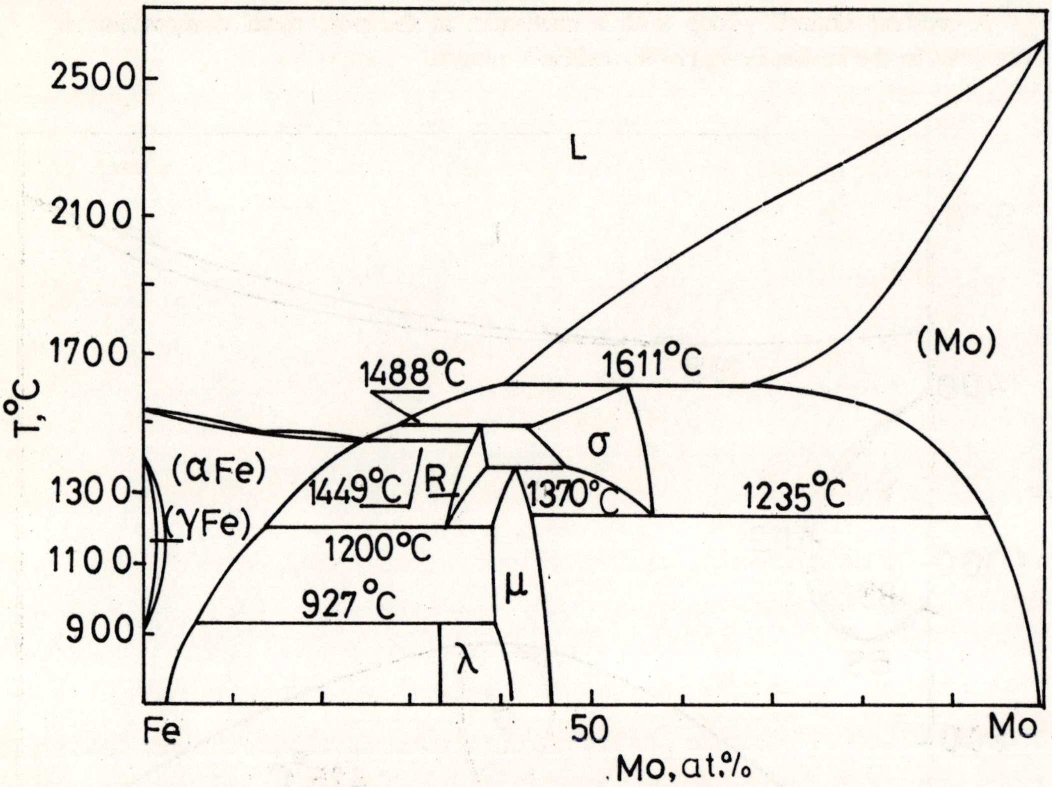

Fig. 5.13 Phase diagram of the Fe-Mo alloy system.

PROBLEMS

1. Write the structure type of the following electron compounds.
   (i) $PtCd_3$
   (ii) NiAl
   (iii) Cu_3Sn
   (iv) $Cu_{13}Sb_3$
2. Write the formulae for the γ-brass structure in the following binary systems.
   (i) Cu–Ga
   (ii) Ni Zn

(iii) Cu–In
(iv) Cu–Sn
(v) Ni–Ga

3. Write the structure type of the following valency compounds.
(i) Mg_2Si
(ii) SnTe

4. Write the formulae for the ε-brass structure in the following binary systems.
(i) Cu–Zn
(ii) Cu–Sn
(iii) Cu–Sb
(iv) Li–Zn

Chapter 6

BINARY PHASE DIAGRAMS EQUILIBRIUM OF PHASES IN THE SOLID STATE

Basically, there are three reactions involving phases in the solid state. These are the eutectoid, peritectoid and monotectoid. They are represented by the following reactions:

Eutectoid reaction: $\gamma \rightleftharpoons \alpha + \beta$

Peritectoid reaction: $\alpha + \gamma \rightleftharpoons \beta$

Monotectoid reaction: $\alpha_1 \rightleftharpoons \alpha_2 + \beta$

6.1 BINARY EUTECTOID SYSTEM

In the binary eutectoid reaction, a solid phase γ dissociates into two solid phases α and β when the γ phase is allowed to cool. The reaction occurs at the eutectoid reaction isotherm T_E. The binary eutectoid system is analogous to the binary eutectic system, the only difference being that the liquid phase of the binary eutectic system is replaced by the solid phase γ of the eutectoid system. This difference will show up in the time taken for completion of the reaction when the γ phase is allowed to cool continuously or transformed isothermally below T_E.

A hypothetical binary system between components A and B showing the eutectoid reaction is presented in Fig. 6.1. Since the high temperature phase is solid (γ), it has to be obtained from the liquid during solidification of the alloy. It can occur in the phase diagram either by an isomorphous behavior, $L \rightleftharpoons \gamma$, or by means of a peritectic

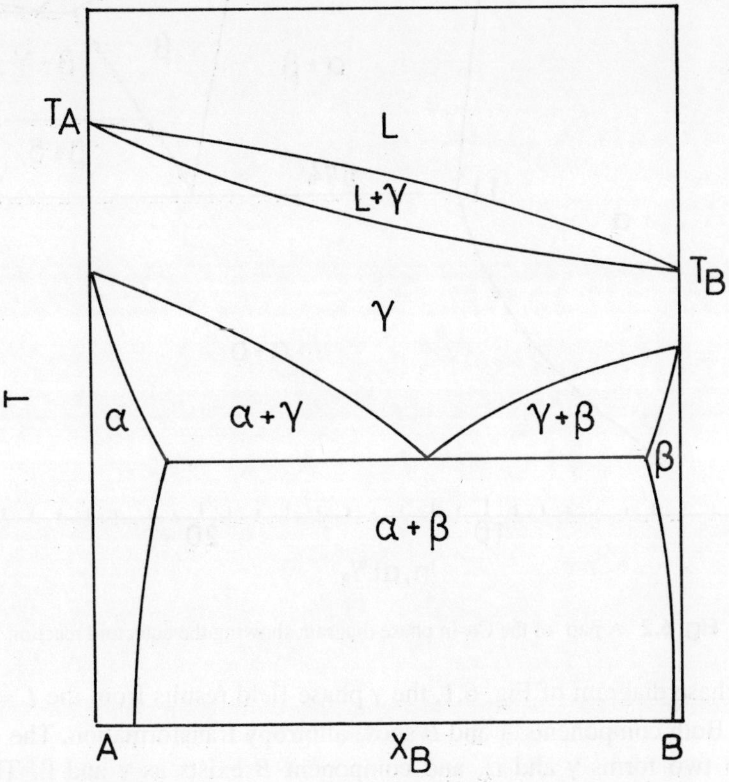

Fig. 6.1 A hypothetical binary phase diagram showing the eutectoid reaction.

reaction, $L + \delta \rightleftharpoons \gamma$. An intermediate phase can also dissociate into two solid phases at lower temperatures by the eutectoid reaction.

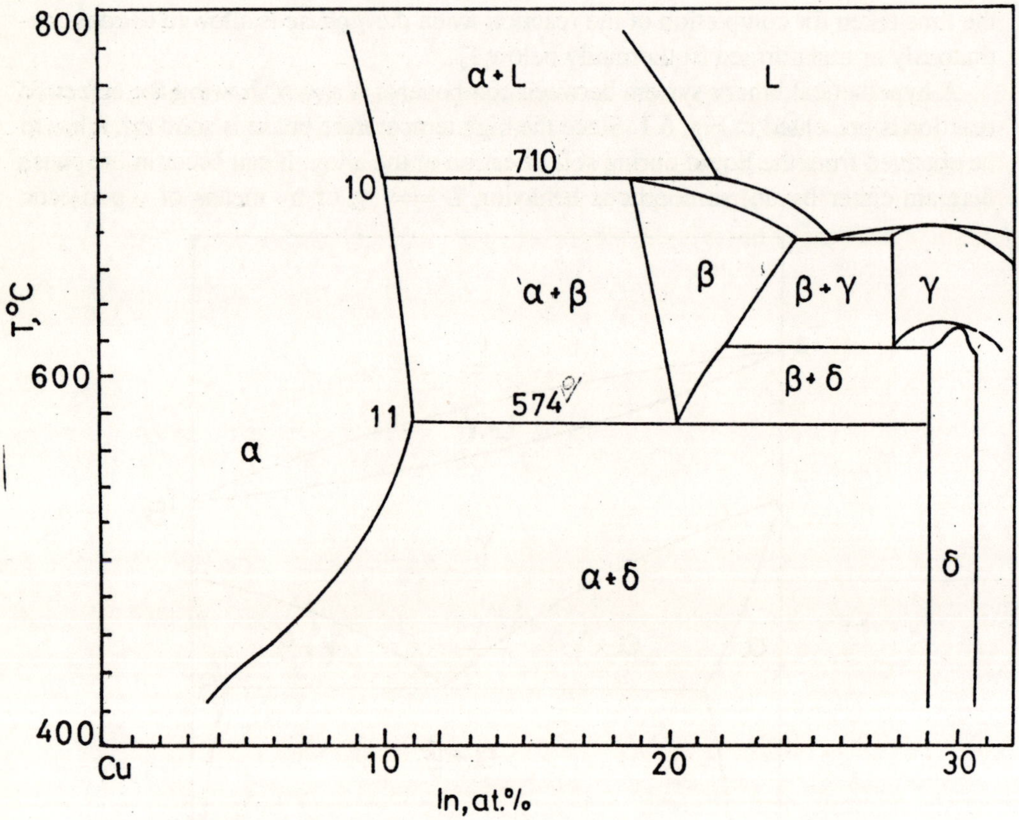

Fig. 6.2 A part of the Cu-In phase diagram showing the eutectoid reaction.

In the phase diagram of Fig. 6.1, the γ phase field results from the $L \rightleftharpoons \gamma$ transformation. Both components A and B show allotropy transformation. The component A exists in two forms γ and α, and component B exists as γ and β. The γ phase transforms into A-rich phase α, and B-rich phase β, of compositions X_B^α and X_B^β, respectively, just below the eutectoid reaction isotherm T_E. A part of the Cu-In phase diagram showing the eutectoid reaction is presented in Fig. 6.2. The high temperature phase β, undergoes the eutectoid reaction at 847 K to give α and δ phases represented by the following reaction:

$$\beta(X_B^{\beta}=0.20) \xrightarrow{T_E = 847\text{ K}} \alpha(X_B^{\alpha}=0.109)+\delta(X_B^{\delta}=0.29)$$

The β phase is *bcc*, the δ phase is a γ-brass related structure and the α phase is an *fcc* solid solution of In in Cu. The δ phase is an electron compound with electron concentration 21:13 and with formula Cu_9In_4. An optical photomicrograph showing the product of the eutectoid reaction is presented in Fig. 6.3. The microstructure shows alternate lamellae of the α and δ phases.

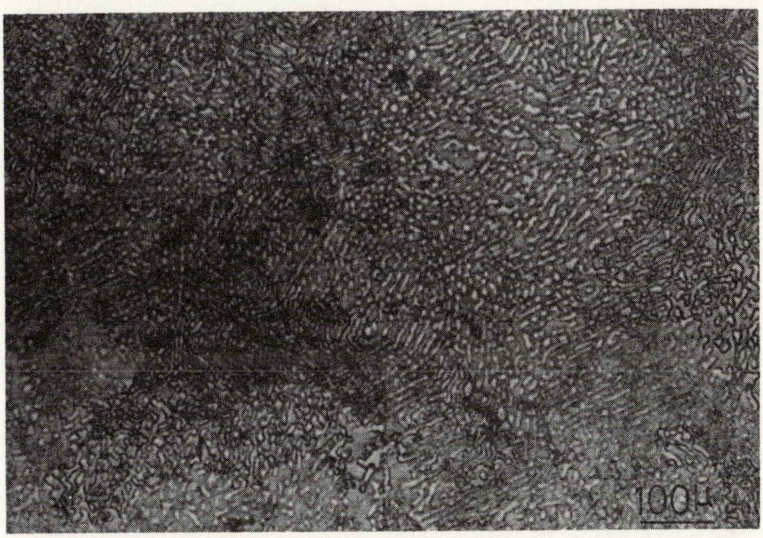

Fig. 6.3 An optical photomicrograph showing the product of the eutectoid reaction, specimen aged for 5 h at 710 K.

6.1.1 Eutectoid Transformation in Fe-C alloys

The Fe-C binary or Fe-C-*X* ternary systems (where *X* is a substitutional solute) have commercial importance in that the Fe-C alloys (plain carbon steels and cast irons) find

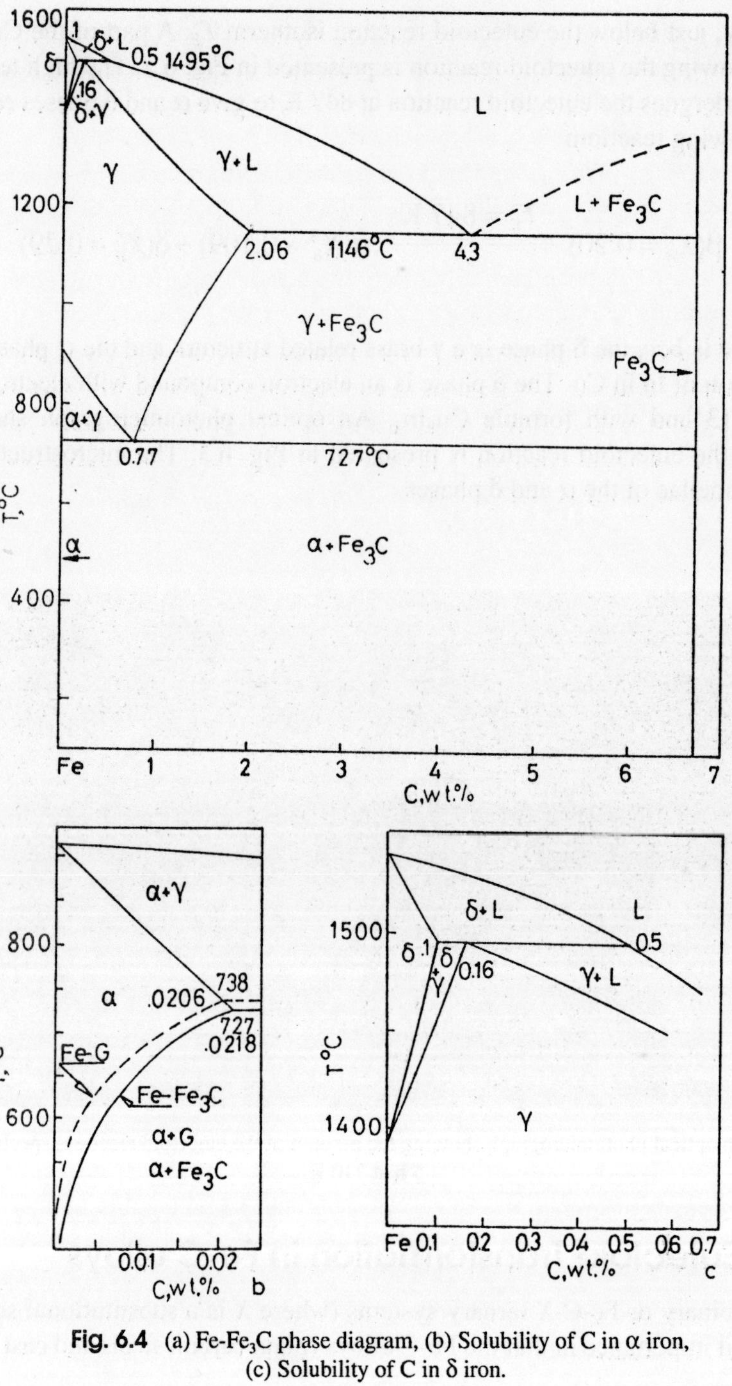

Fig. 6.4 (a) Fe-Fe_3C phase diagram, (b) Solubility of C in α iron, (c) Solubility of C in δ iron.

application in all industries. The phase diagram of the Fe-C systems and microstructure of the product phases, both stable and metastable, will be considered in detail. The Fe-C phase diagram is represented by the Fe-Fe_3C pseudo-binary system, Fig. 6.4. The alloy compositions can be divided into two classes. Fe-C alloys containing 0.02 to 2.0 wt.pct. C belong to the first class and constitute compositions of the plain carbon steels. Fe-C alloys containing 2 to 4.5 wt.pct. C belong to the second class and constitute the family of cast irons. The distinctive feature of the two classes is that, whereas the alloy compositions in the first class undergo only the eutectoid reaction, alloy compositions belonging to the second class undergo both eutectic and eutectoid reactions.

6.1.2 Transformation of Austenite to Pearlite

An alloy of the eutectoid composition (0.77 wt.pct. C) undergoes the eutectoid reaction at 1000 K (727° C) to give the product phases by the following reaction:

$$\gamma \xrightleftharpoons{1000\text{ K}} \alpha + Fe_3C.$$

The austenite phase in an interstitial solid solution of the *fcc* form of iron. The ferrite phase is an interstitial solid solution of C in the *bcc* form of iron. The cementite phase (Fe_3C) is an intermediate phase with orthorhombic structure. These are shown in Fig. 6.5. The product phases of the eutectoid reaction appear in a lamellar morphology. The structure consists of alternate lamellae of the α and Fe_3C phases and is termed as pearlite. The microstructure of pearlite is shown in Fig. 6.6. The pearlite nucleates at the grain boundaries of austenite of the eutectoid composition. Either, phase, α or Fe_3C has been observed to nucleate pearlite by what is termed as the branching mechanism. In the plain carbon steels of hypoeutectoid composition, the pearlite nucleates from proeutectoid ferrite with the ferrite phase of pearlite being physically continuous with the proeutectoid ferrite. Similarly, in hypereutectoid steels, the pearlite nucleates from proeutectoid cementite.

The parent austenite does not transform at the eutectoid temperature because the volume free energy change is zero. Because of the slower rates of diffusion during the solid to solid transformation, the austenite phase can be retained to temperatures well below the eutectoid and the progress of the transformation can thus be studied. The free energy-composition diagrams of Fig. 6.7 illustrate that the volume free energy change becomes negative below the eutectoid temperature. When the magnitude of the chemical free energy change more than compensates for the interfacial energy of the α/Fe_3C interface, the austenite to pearlite transformation will occur. Near the eutectoid temperature, the interlamellar spacing being large, the interfacial energy associated with the α/Fe_3C interface is small. However, at lower transformation temperatures, the interlamellar spacing is small with a large associated interfacial energy. If an Fe-C alloy of the eutectoid composition is allowed to transform isothermally at a number of temperatures below T_E, there is a gradual decrease in the interlamellar spacing, the relative amounts of the α and Fe_3C phases remaining more or less the same.

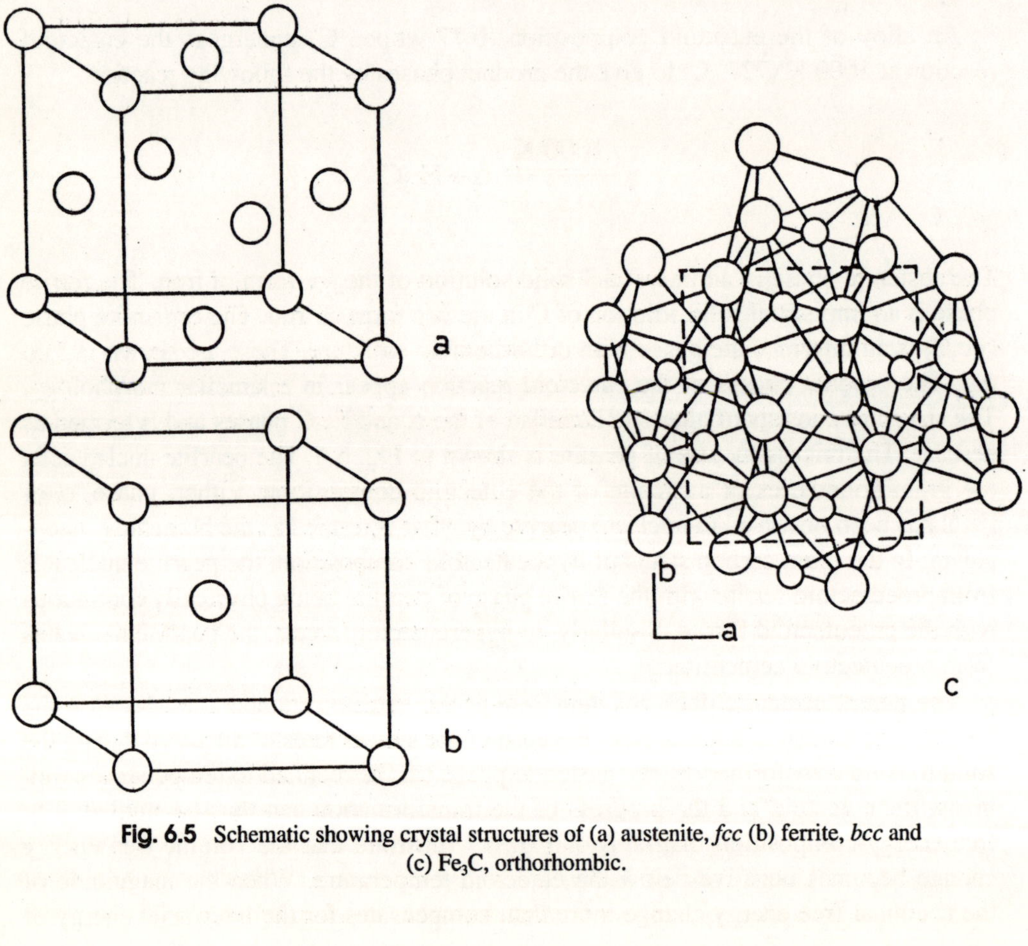

Fig. 6.5 Schematic showing crystal structures of (a) austenite, *fcc* (b) ferrite, *bcc* and (c) Fe_3C, orthorhombic.

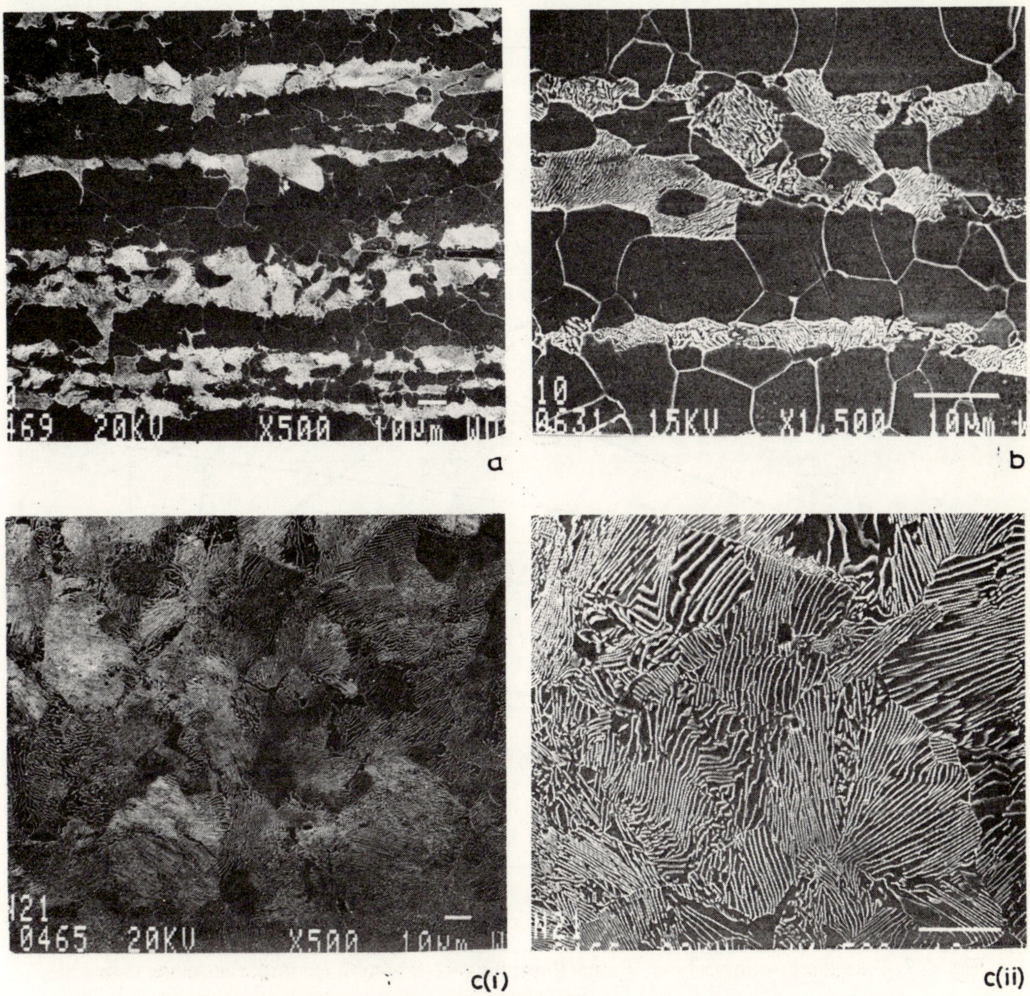

Fig. 6.6 Photomicrographs showing the structure of pearlite: (a) Nodules or cells of pearlite at the austenite grain boundaries, Fe–0.23 wt.pct.C steel. The structure shows banded appearance. (b) Well-resolved lamellae of the α and Fe_3C phases. (c) Fe–0.8 wt.pct.C steel, as annealed, (i) low and (ii) high magnification.

The transformation of austenite to pearlite in the eutectoid steel is thought to occur by the nucleation of one of the phases, say α. The α phase being depleted of C, the austenite in front of α gets enriched with carbon. A concentration gradient, from the interface to the far-away region of austenite, is built up. The ferrite phase can grow only as fast as the diffusion of carbon is allowed to occur. The concentration-distance profile illustrates formation of ferrite from austenite, Fig. 6.8. When the carbon atoms

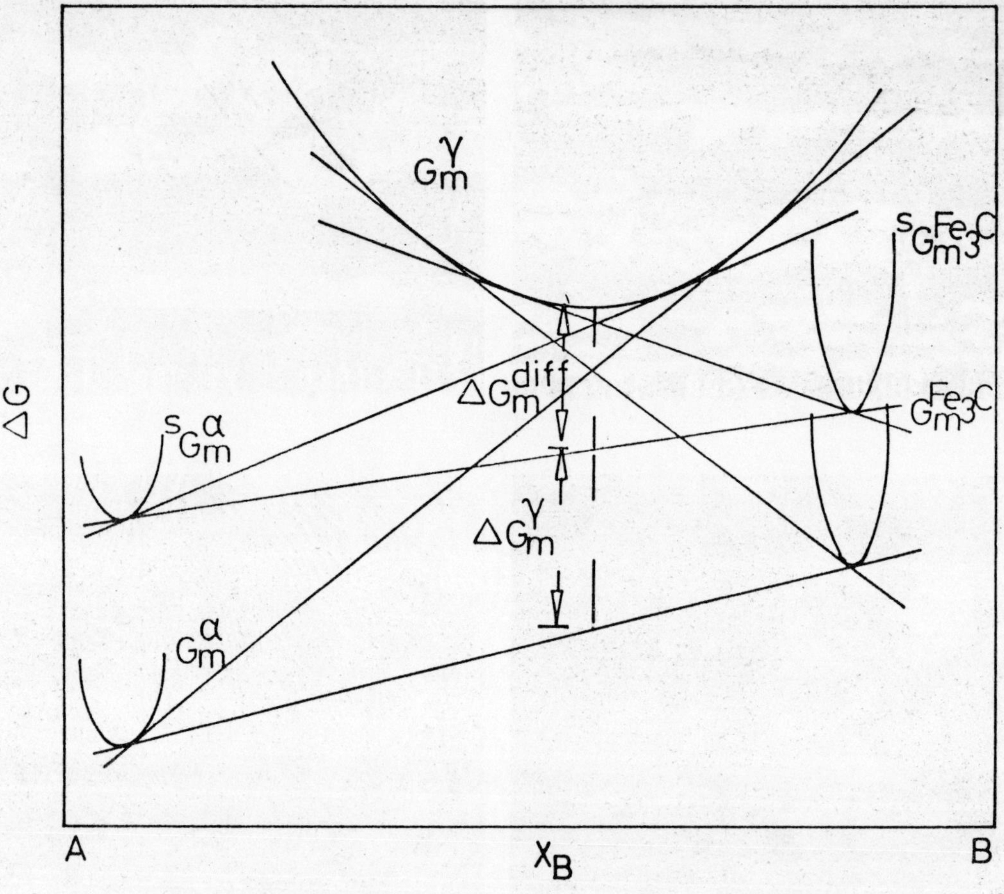

Fig. 6.7 Free energy-composition diagram illustrating the driving force for the austenite to pearlite transformation.

diffuse to the region of austenite, far-away from the interface, it takes a very long time and the progress of the ferrite is restricted. However, if sufficient number of carbon atoms move along the edge of ferrite and achieve the concentration of carbon necessary for the nucleation of cementite, the eutectoid reaction is facilitated. The edgewise transport of carbon achieves two objectives. The first and the foremost is formation of the second phase of the product of the eutectoid reaction, namely Fe_3C; and the second is the relieving of carbon built up at the α/γ interface, so that the ferrite phase can advance into austenite. Fig. 6.8b shows the concentration-distance profile when the

Fe_3C phase forms from austenite. In the nucleation and growth of cementite, neighboring regions of the Fe_3C/γ interface get depleted of carbon, and there must be continued transport of C from far-away regions of austenite for continued growth of cementite. Instead, the time taken for the transport of solute atoms will become shorter if carbon atoms diffuse from the C-enriched neighboring region of the α/γ interface along the edge of the lamella. The two phases, α and Fe_3C, thus, cooperate with each other, one supplying excess carbon and the other receiving it, for the growth of both phases. The mechanism of growth of pearlite is termed the "cooperative growth mechanism".

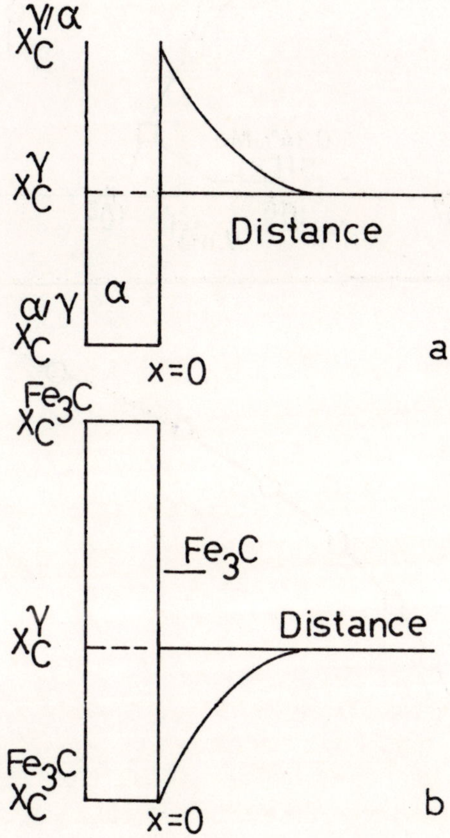

Fig. 6.8 Concentration-distance profile, for (a) ferrite-austenite (b) cementite-austenite.

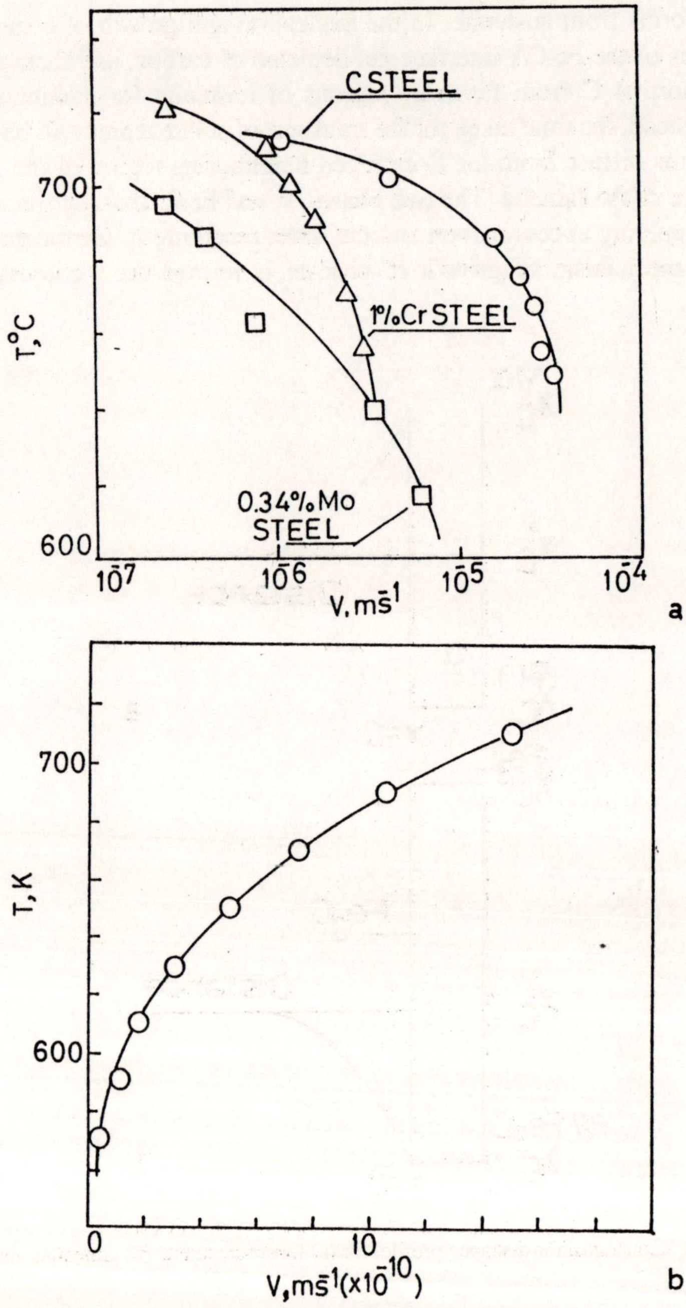

Fig. 6.9 Growth rate vs. transformation temperature of pearlite for (a) a number of steels (after Brown, D. and Ridley, N., *J. Iron Steel Inst.*, 207 (1969), 1232). (b) Cu-20.15at.pct.In alloy.

The interlamellar spacing of pearlite is dependent on the isothermal transformation temperature. As the temperature of transformation decreases, the distance that carbon atoms can diffuse in a given time ($X \cong \sqrt{Dt}$) decreases due to decreasing diffusivity ($D = D_0 \exp^{-Q/RT}$). The pearlite grows with smaller interlamellar spacing, which has a higher interfacial energy associated with the α/Fe_3C interface per unit volume. With a decrease in the reaction temperature, the chemical free energy change associated with the $\gamma \Rightarrow \alpha + Fe_3C$ transformation increases, Fig. 6.7. However, as mentioned earlier, the interfacial energy also increases. The available driving force increases with decreasing transformation temperature, reaches a maximum, and then decreases again. The growth rate of pearlite therefore increases initially, reaches a maximum, and then decreases again as the temperature of transformation is decreased. The growth rate vs. temperature data experimentally observed for a number of Fe-C alloys (1, 2) and a Cu-20.15 at.pct. In alloy (3) are represented in Fig. 6.9. The transformation temperatures were not low enough, for the decreasing growth rate after the maximum, to be recorded. From the principle of maximum entropy production, Puls and Kirkaldy (4) have shown that the interlamellar spacing of pearlite is inversely proportional to the degree of undercooling below T_E, and is given by the following expression:

$$S = \frac{6\gamma V_m T_E}{\Delta H_m \cdot \Delta T} \tag{6.1}$$

In equation (6.1), γ is the interfacial energy of the α/Fe_3C interface, V_m is the molar volume, ΔH_m is the change in enthalpy per mole between the parent and the product phases. The interlamellar spacing is proportional to the reciprocal of the undercooling $(\Delta T)^{-1}$, as shown in Fig. 10a after the work of Hawkes et al. (5) for plain carbon steel, Al-78 wt.pct. Zn (6) and a Cu-20.15 at.pct. In alloy (3).

6.1.3 Transformation of Austenite to Ferrite

In hypoeutectoid steels (composition from 0 to 0.77% C, excluding 0.77% C), the austenite phase does not transform directly to pearlite upon cooling. Instead, the austenite first transforms to ferrite, referred to as proeutectoid ferrite. The Fe-C phase diagram, Fig. 6.4, shows that the austenite containing low and medium carbon concentration goes through the $(\alpha + \gamma)$ phase field when cooled. The temperature of γ

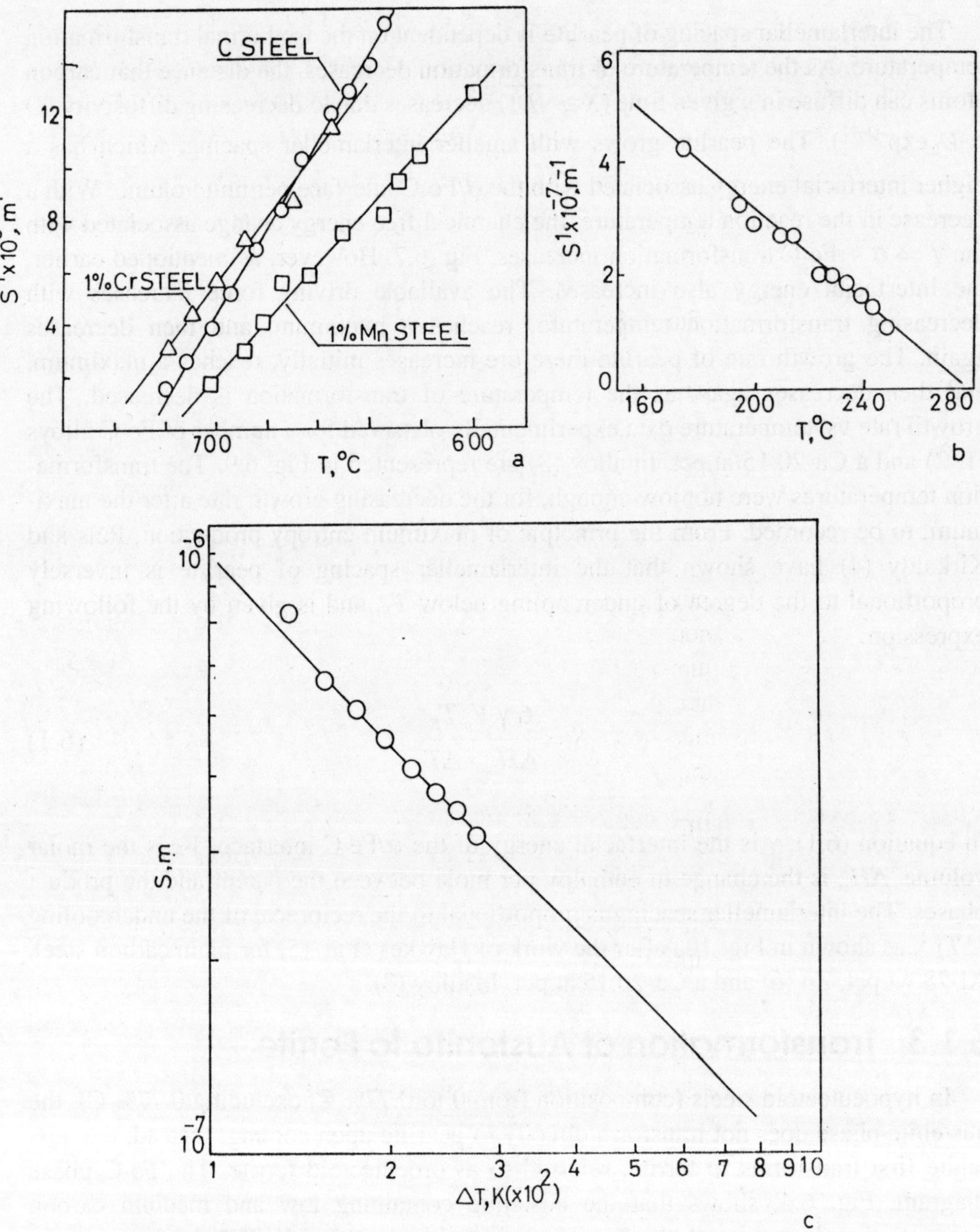

Fig. 6.10 Interlamellar spacing vs. undercooling ΔT in (a) plain C steel (after Brown, D. and Ridley, N., *J. Iron Steel Inst.*, 207 (1969), 1232). (b) Al-78 wt.pct.Zn alloy (after Cheetham, D. and Ridley, N., *J. Inst. Metals*, 99 (1971), 371) and (c) Cu-20.15 at.pct.In alloy.

$\gamma \Rightarrow \alpha$ transformation decreases with increasing carbon content of hypoeutectoid steels. Let us consider a binary Fe-C alloy containing 0.4% C. The relative amount of ferrite will increase as the temperature decreases. Thus, at a temperature just above the eutectoid, the austenite phase containing 0.77% C will be in equilibrium with ferrite (0.02% C) and the relative amount of ferrite, as calculated by using the lever rule will be,

$$\%\,\alpha = \frac{0.77 - 0.4}{0.77 - 0.02} \times 100 = 49.33\%.$$

The remaining austenite will transform to pearlite upon further cooling as described earlier. The microstructure will consist of about 50% ferrite and 50% pearlite, as shown in the photomicrograph of Fig. 6.11.

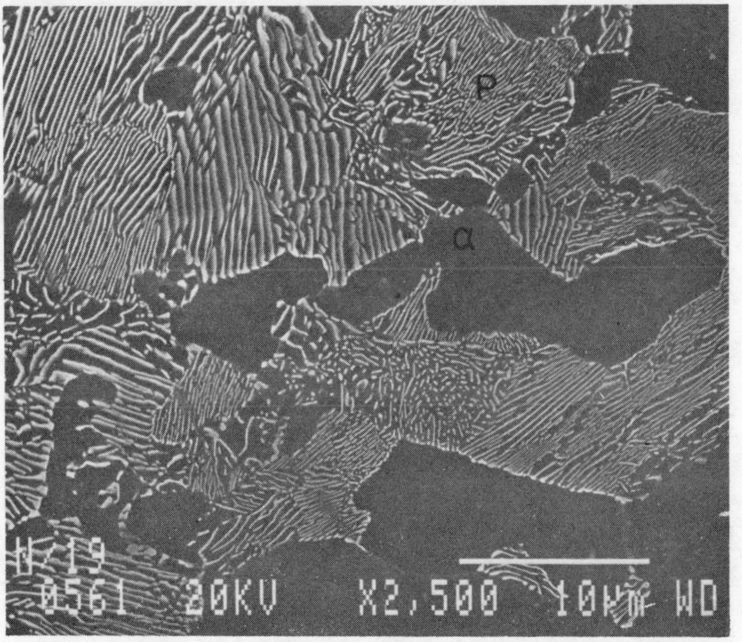

Fig. 6.11 Photomicrograph showing structure of medium carbon steel (hypoeutectoid); proeutectoid α and pearlite are easily distinguishable, Fe-O.4 pct.C steel, annealed.

The ferrite phase has been observed to occur in various shapes. Dube′ (7) was the first to classify these shapes into distinct morphologies. These are:

(i) Grain boundary allotriomorphs, as sketched in Fig. 6.12a, are doubly spherical lens shapes with maximum chord diameter situated in the plane of the boundary. Although the morphology shown in Fig. 6.12a is most common, a number of variants are also observed. In alloy systems in which the product phases forms a coherent interface, the allotriomorph is observed to develop facets. These could be planar sections only on one side of the grain boundary, Fig. 6.12b, or on both sides, Fig. 6.12c. The planar section is generally connected with a curved interface terminating on the grain boundary plane. The allotriomorphs grow preferentially along grain boundaries rather than in a direction normal to it.

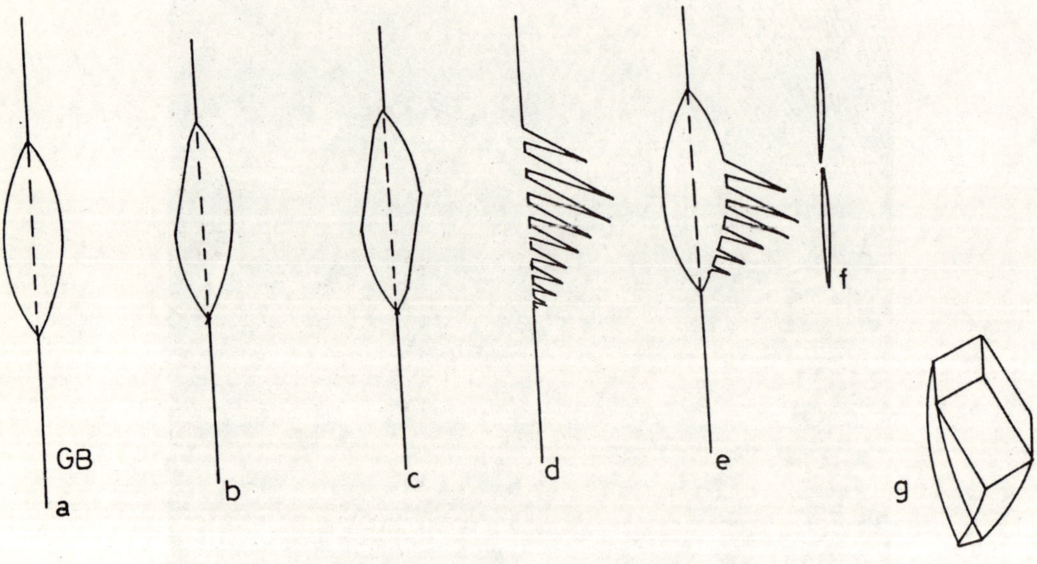

Fig. 6.12 Shapes of grain boundary allotriomorphs.

(ii) Widmanstätten side plates, are plate (or needle) shaped crystals which nucleate in the vicinity of the grain boundary and grow into the matrix from there. The primary side plates grow directly from the grain boundaries, Fig. 6.12d, whereas the secondary side plates nucleate from crystals of a different morphology, for example allotriomorphs, and grow into the matrix, Fig. 6.12e.

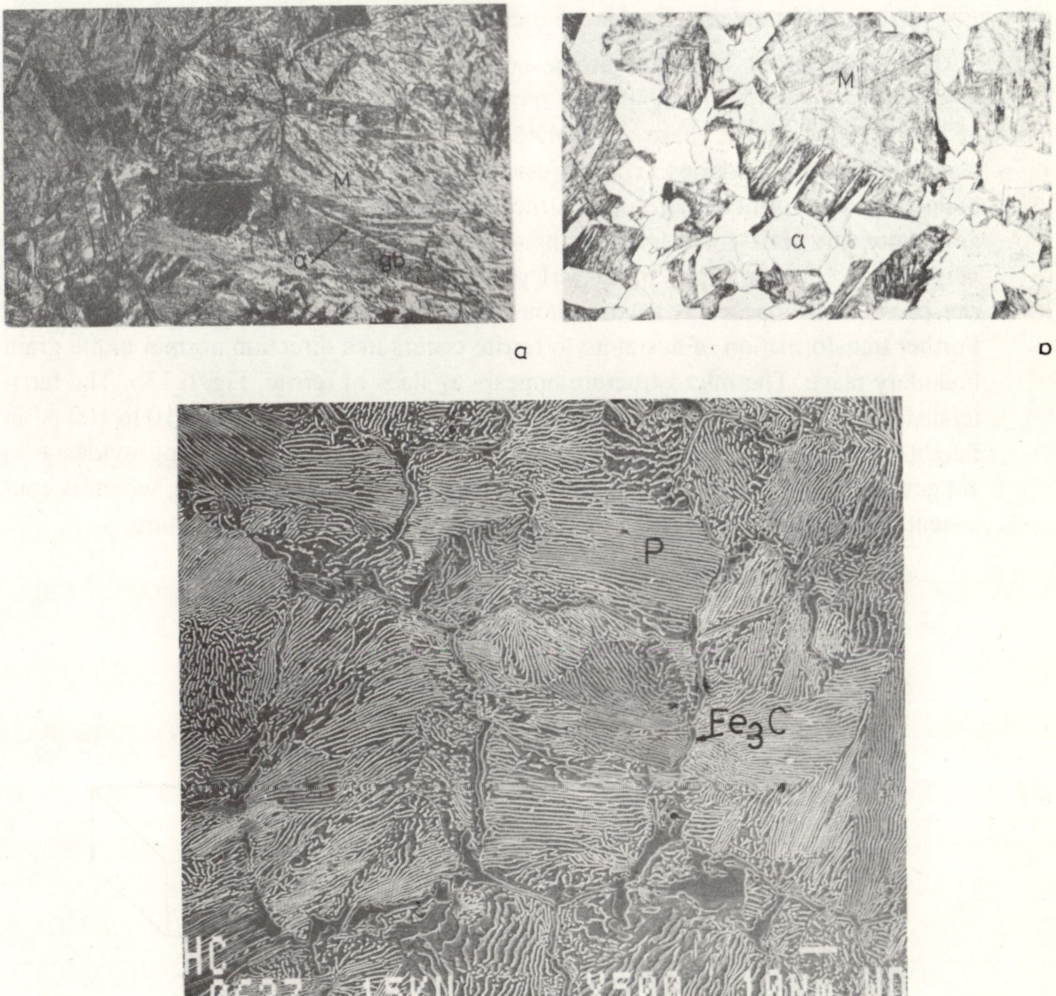

Fig. 6.13 Various stages of the austenite to ferrite transformation in steel (a) early stage (b) advanced stage. The structure of pearlite and cementite in hypereutectoid steel is shown in (c), Fe-1.1 wt.pct.C steel in the annealed condition.

(iii) Intragranular Widmanstätten plates, are plate shaped ferrite which grow from the interior or from within the matrix, Fig. 6.12f. Impurity particles are observed to be nucleation sites for these plates.

(iv) Idiomorphs, are roughly equiaxed crystals of ferrite which develop entirely from within the matrix of austenite, Fig. 6.12g

The ferrite phase nucleates at the austenite grain boundaries. An experimental observation illustrating nucleation of ferrite is shown in the optical photomicrograph of Fig. 6.13a. Initially, these are isolated doubly spherical lens shaped particles all along the grain boundaries. The diffusion of carbon is more rapid along the grain boundaries due to their more open structure. The allotriomorphs lengthen along the grain boundary at first. The lengthening of ferrite stops when the diffusion field of two neighboring allotriomorphs start overlapping each other after some growth. The ferrite phase now appears as a continuous network along austenite grain boundaries. Further transformation of austenite to ferrite occurs in a direction normal to the grain boundary plane. The microstructure appears as slabs of ferrite, Fig. 6.13b. The ferrite/austenite interface has a ledged structure which are disordered steps 10 to 100 A° in height on an otherwise planar interface, Fig. 6.14. There is increasing evidence to suggest that the $\gamma \Rightarrow \alpha$ transformation occurs by the ledge mechanism, which is consistent with the high mobility of the disordered step of the ledged structure.

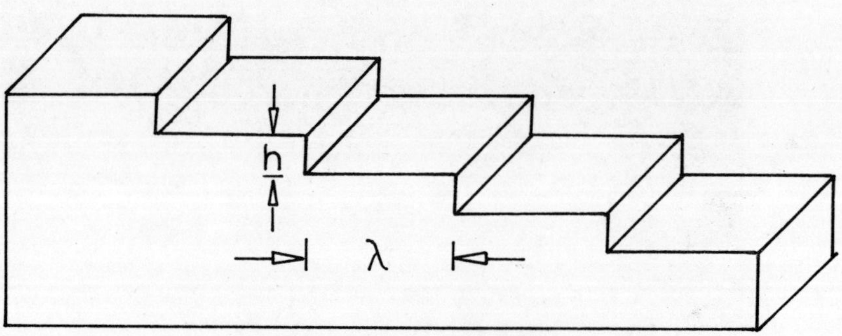

Fig. 6.14 α/γ interface showing the ledged structure.

The other morphology of ferrite which forms in low carbon steels consists of plates whose length to thickness ratio is very high. This morphology is termed as Widmanstätten ferrite. The two phases, austenite and ferrite, bear a definite orientation relationship, termed after Kurdjumov and Sachs (8). The close-packed plane and direction of the *fcc* and *bcc* lattices match each other across a common interface, as illustrated in Fig. 6.15, and represented by the following:

$$\{111\}_{fcc} \;||\; \{110\}_{bcc}$$

$$<110>_{fcc} \;||\; <111>_{bcc}$$

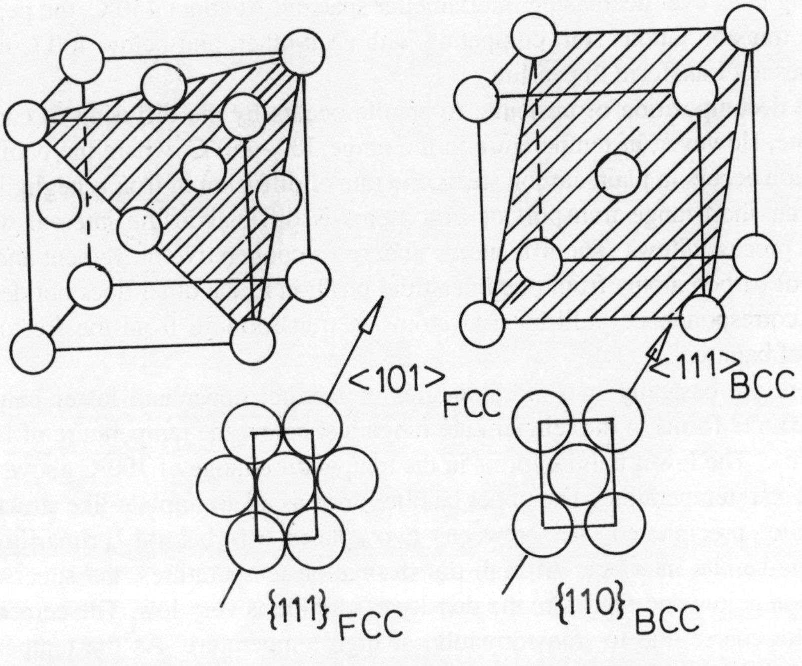

Fig. 6.15 The orientation relationship between the austenite and ferrite lattices.

In hypereutectoid steels containing 0.77 to 1.3 wt.pct. C, the austenite transforms into primary cementite at first. The cementite phase also nucleates on the grain boundaries of austenite. The lengthening of the cementite nuclei occurs along the grain boundary, and in a few minutes the cementite phase appears as a fine network along the grain boundaries, Fig. 6.13c. Further transformation of austenite occurs by growth of cementite in a direction perpendicular to the grain boundary, similar to that observed in the austenite to ferrite transformation in hypoeutectoid steels. However, the relative amount of cementite in hypereutectoid steel with 1.2 wt.pct. C, is so small (1.2–0.77)/(6.67–0.77) × 100 = 7.3%, that, even after all the proeutectoid cementite has formed, it appears as a fine network structure along the grain boundaries.

6.1.4 Transformation of Austenite to Bainite

The bainite phase is steel refers to the aggregate of ferrite and cementite structures forming from metastable austenite at intermediate temperature lying between the temperatures at which pearlite and martensite form. The rate of diffusion of carbon decreases as the temperature of transformation of austenite to pearlite decrease, resulting in an ever decreasing interlamellar spacing. At about 450°C, the pearlite and bainite transformations start competing with each other, and below 400°C the austenite does not transform to pearlite.

The decomposition of austenite to bainite occurs by the diffusion of carbon into austenite. However, at temperature in the range 300–450°C, where the bainite transformation occurs in plain carbon steels, the rate of diffusion of iron is negligibly small and even short-range transport of iron atoms is difficult in the interval which the kinetic process allows. The iron atoms undergo a cooperative movement and the diffusion of carbon atoms from one interstitial position to the other does not destroy the lattice correspondence held by iron atoms in transforming from the *fcc* to the *bcc* lattice of bainite.

There are basically two morphologies of bainite: upper and lower bainite. The upper bainite forms in the temperature range just below the temperature of formation of pearlite. The lower bainite forms in the temperature range of 100°C above the martensitic start temperature. The upper bainite forms as a lath or plate-like structure with cementite precipitated in between two plates of bainite primarily at the austenite-bainite interface. At high transformation temperatures, the supersaturation of carbon is low and therefore the density of carbide is very low. The cementite particles are coarse due to transformation at high temperature. As the temperature of transformation is lowered, the density of carbide increases due to increased supersaturation of carbon as can be seen by extrapolation of the $\alpha/(\alpha + \gamma)$ phase boundary below the eutectoid temperature.

The lower bainite consists of plates similar to the Widmanstätten ferrite with high supersaturation of carbon. Fine cementite particles precipitate within the plates to relieve the supersaturation. The basic difference between the Widmanstätten ferrite and lower bainite is that, whereas lower bainite has cementite precipitated within the plates, the Widmanstätten ferrite does not have cementite. The microstructure of Fig. 6.16. illustrates the structure of bainite.

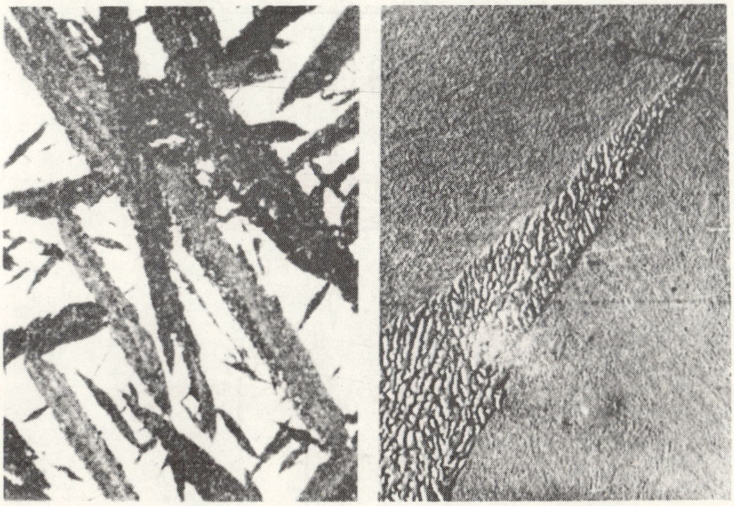

a b

Fig. 6.16 (a) An optical photomicrograph showing the microstructure of bainite, (b) Resolved microstructure of carbides within a bainite plate (after G.R. Speich, *Decomposition of Austenite by Diffusional Processes*, (V.F. Zackay & H.I. Aaronson, Interscience Publishers, New York (1962), 353).

6.1.5 Transformation of Austenite to Martensite

With decreasing transformation temperature, the rate of diffusion of carbon decreases to the extent that austenite does not transform by mechanisms requiring diffusion of carbon. Instead, metastable austenite transforms into martensite by a diffusionless displacive transformation mechanism. The transformation occurs by the cooperative movement of atoms by shearing of the austenite lattice.

The martensitic transformation occurs by two deformations to accomodate the change in shape. The first deformation is the homogeneous plane strain which changes the crystal structure. In the case of iron-carbon alloys, the *fcc* lattice of austenite transforms to a *bcc* lattice of martensite, Fig. 6.17a. This is realized by a compressive strain of approximately 20% along the z axis and a tensile strain of 12% each along the x and y axis of the body-centered tetragonal lattice delineated from the *fcc* lattice. According to the theory of martensitic transformations, after Wechler, et al. (9), and Bowles and Mackenzie(10), there remains an unrotated, undistorted habit plane after the transformation; that is, some plane of the austenite does not undergo

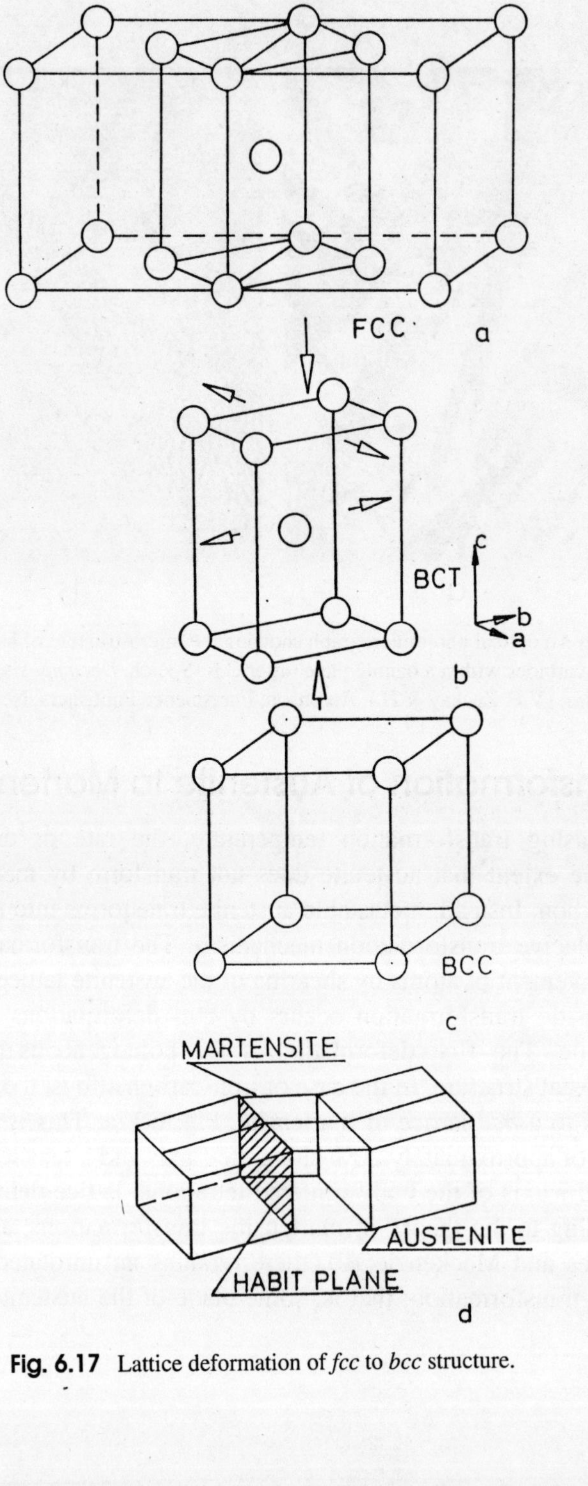

Fig. 6.17 Lattice deformation of *fcc* to *bcc* structure.

distortion and becomes the habit plane of the martensite lattice, as shown in Fig. 6.17b. In order to keep an unrotated and undistorted habit plane, another deformation in the form of slip or twinning is required. The second deformation is termed as a lattice invariant deformation, suggesting that the structure of the lattice does not change in the second deformation. Fig. 6.17a illustrates how the *bcc* lattice of martensite is generated from the fcc lattice of austenite. The orientation relationship observed during martensitic transformations in steel is the Kurdjumov-Sachs (8) type, illustrated by the following:

$$\{111\}_{\text{austenite}} \;||\; \{110\}_{\text{martensite}}$$

$$<110>_{\text{austenite}} \;||\; <111>_{\text{martensite}}$$

The other orientation relationship as determined by Greninger and Troiano (11) is given by

$$\{111\}_{\text{austenite}} \;||\; \{110\}_{\text{martensite}}$$

$$<111>_{\text{austenite}} \;||\; <110>_{\text{martensite}}$$

In very low carbon steels, the martensite lattice that forms from austenite is *bcc*. However, as the carbon concentration of steel is increased, the crystal structure of martensite becomes body-centered tetragonal. The carbon atoms occupy interstitial sites preferentially along the *c* axis. The tetragonality of martensite, i.e., c/a ratio, increases with increasing C content of steel, as given by Winchell et al. (12), $c/a = 1.0 + 0.045 \times$ wt.pct. C and shown in Fig. 6.18.

The martensitic transformation begins at a temperature termed as the martensitic start, M_S, temperature and gets completed at the martensitic finish, M_f, temperature. The transformation is athermal in nature, that is, only a certain volume fraction of the austenite transforms to martensite below M_S. The volume fraction of martensite formed at any temperature between M_s and M_f is independent of time, unlike the diffusion controlled transformation of austenite to pearlite or ferrite. The M_s temperature in plain carbon steels is a function of the carbon content. Increasing the carbon content of steel decreases the M_s temperature, as illustrated in Fig. 6.19 after the work of Marder and Krauss (13).

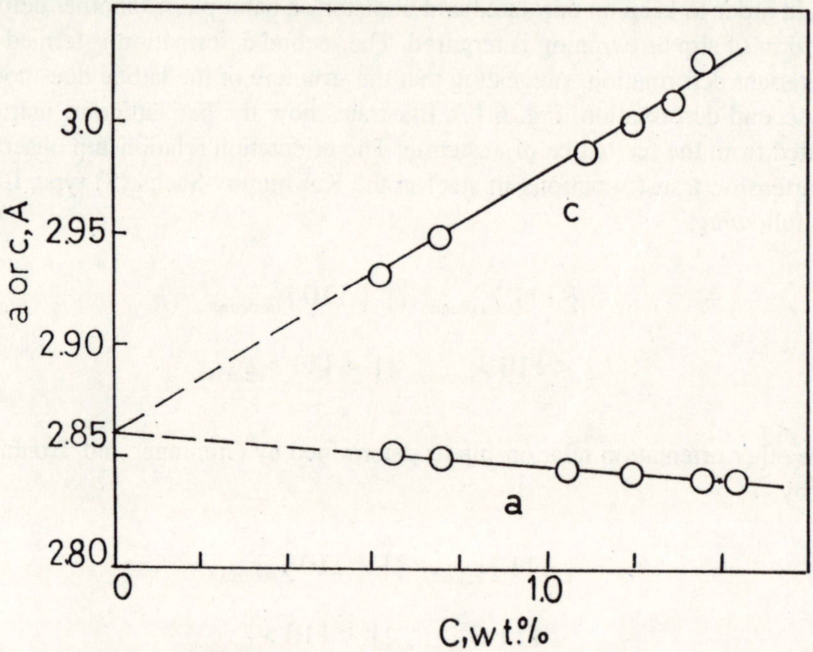

Fig. 6.18 The effect of carbon on the tetragonality of martensite in plain C steel. The c/a ratio will increase with increasing C content (after Bain, E.C. & Paxton, H.W., *Alloying Elements in Steel*, 3rd ed., American Society for Metals, Ohio (1966).

The martensitic transformations in plain carbon steels results in two basic morphologies of martensite, lath and plates. A large number of thin parallel plates form as a board or lath-shaped structure of lath martensite in low to medium carbon steels with a high M_s temperature, Fig. 6.20a. Some retained austenite with tangled dislocations is observed at the interface. These dislocations are generated during the lattice invariant deformation as a part of the crystallographic feature. The plate martensitic structure consists of acicular plates which are quite broad compared to the fine structure of the lath. The plate morphology is generally observed in high carbon steels whose M_s temperature is low. The plates are not parallel but form at an angle to each other. This leaves a higher volume fraction of untransformed austenite, which is retained. The microstructure of the plate martensite is shown in Fig. 6.20b.

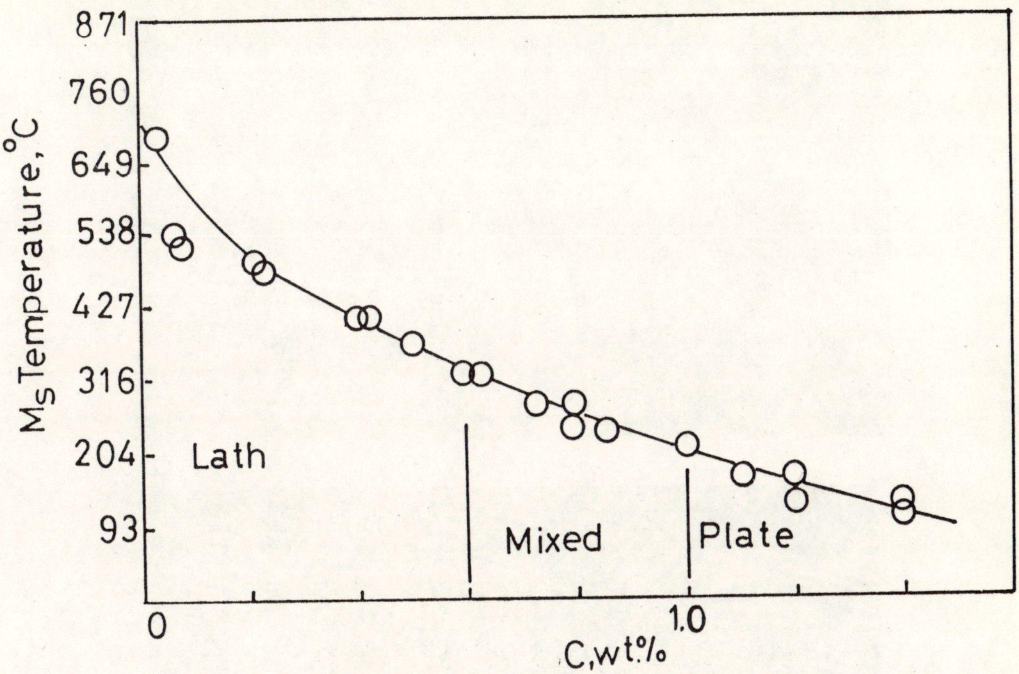

Fig. 6.19 M_s temperature vs. carbon content in steel (after Marder, A.R. & Kraus, G., *Trans. ASM*, 60 (1967), 651).

6.1.6 Tempering of Martensite

The plain carbon steels when quenched from high temperature to produce the martensitic structure have high strength. However, since the ductility of freshly quenched martensite is very low, it has a low toughness and, therefore, becomes useless for many engineering applications. The basic idea of tempering is to improve the ductility and hence the toughness of steel. This is achieved by sacrificing the very high strength of martensite steel. By a proper control of the time and temperature of tempering, optimum properties can be achieved. Basically, the process of tempering involves heating a piece of steel which has been quenched (rapidly cooled) from the austenite region. The martensitic structure characteristic of the steel is allowed to age in the temperature range 0–700°C. The changes in structure during tempering are dependent to a large extent upon the carbon content, alloying elements and temperature of tempering. The process of tempering can be divided into four stages. These are as follows:

Fig. 6.20 (a) An optical photomicrograph showing lath martensite in a 0.1% C steel.
(b) Photomicrograph showing plate martensite, Fe-Ni-Cr alloy.

Stage I

Temperature range from 0 to 100°C. Segregation of carbon occurs at dislocations.

The process of preferential segregation of carbon atoms to dislocations occurs during the brief period that the martensite phase cools to the temperature of the quench bath after transformation from the parent austenite. This process of preferential segregation continues when the temperature of steel is raised. In the first stage of tempering, energy of the strained martensite is reduced, the supersaturation of C is reduced, and a part of the energy is released when C-dislocation complexes are formed.

Stage II Precipitation of ε Carbide

When the plain carbon steel containing the martensitic structure is heated in the temperature range 100° to 250°C, ε carbide is the first precipitate to form. In carbon steels containing 0.15 wt.pct. C, most of the carbon atoms are bound to the dislocations and the precipitation of ε carbide becomes difficult. However, in plain carbon steels containing more than 0.2 wt.pct. C, there are sufficient free carbon atoms to form ε carbide. The structure of ε carbide ($Fe_{2.4}C$) is hexagonal close packed. It forms as thin plates with a coherent broad face maintaining the following orientation relationship with martensite.

$$\{011\}_{\alpha'} \parallel \{0001\}_{\varepsilon}$$

$$<11\bar{1}>_{\alpha'} \parallel <12\bar{1}0>_{\varepsilon}$$

Stage III Transformation of Retained Austenite

The austenite transformation is invariably incomplete, and retained austenite appears in the microstructure along with martensite. The retained austenite is not a desirable structure in steels as the failure occurs primarily along the austenite/martensite interface due to preferential segregation. The retained austenite transforms to bainite during heating in the temperature range 200–350°C. The carbide particles precipitate within the matrix to relieve the supersaturation of carbon in austenite.

Stage IV Precipitation of Cementite

The fourth stage of tempering occurs when the steel is heated in the temperature range 250 to 700°C. The cementite phase forms initially as needle-shaped particles. At higher temperatures, the surface area to volume ratio of cementite decreases and spheroidal cementite results, Fig. 6.21. Further transformation occurs by precipitate coarsening of spheroidal cementite. The crystal structure of cementite is orthorhombic, with the following orientation relationship with the matrix:

$$\{211\}_{\alpha'} \parallel \{001\}_{Fe_3C}$$

$$[01\bar{1}]_{\alpha'} \parallel [100]_{Fe_3C}$$

$$[\bar{1}11]_{\alpha'} \parallel [010]_{Fe_3C}$$

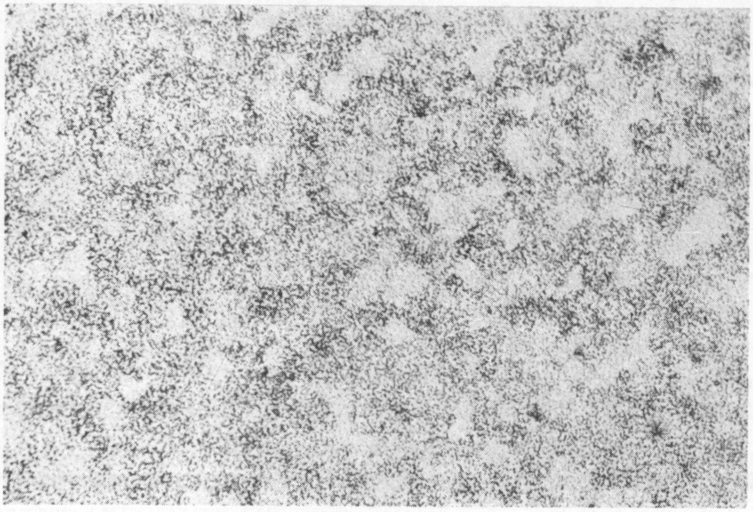

Fig. 6.21 An optical photomicrograph showing spheroidal cementite in a 1.1 wt.pct. C steel.

6.1.7 Transformation at Fixed Subcritical Temperature—The Time-Temperature-Transformation Diagram

The transformation of parent austenite to various microstructures, ferrite, cementite, pearlite, bainite and martensite, has been described in the preceding sections. Relatively slow reactions in the solid state usually makes it possible to cool steel of the eutectoid composition far below the eutectoid temperature without decomposition of the high temperature phase, provided, of course, that the rate of cooling is sufficient. If a piece of plain carbon steel of the eutectoid composition is rapidly cooled to and then held at a temperature somewhat below the eutectoid reaction isotherm, the transformation will proceed at a definite rate characteristic of that temperature. The volume fraction of various phases in the final microstructure is to a large extent dependent upon the time and temperature of the isothermal transformation. This information can be presented in a time-temperature-transformation diagram. The relative proportion of various phases can be determined by volume fraction analysis using quantitative microscopy. A number of specimens of the steel are isothermally transformed for times ranging from a few seconds to approximately one hour and cooled rapidly to preserve the high temperature phase. The specimens are ground, and prepared for metallographic examination using a standard specimen preparation technique. The volume fraction of the various phases present in the specimen is measured using point count technique (see Chapter 8 for details). For plain carbon steel of the eutectoid composition, the volume fractions of pearlite and bainite are measured as a function of time at each isothermal transformation temperature. The experiment is carried out at a number of temperatures in the interval of approximately 20 K. The volume fraction as a function of time is shown in Fig. 6.22 at temperature T_1. Similar graphical representation of the volume fraction data is made at each transformation temperature. The time taken for the transformation of austenite to the product phase pearlite or bainite at an interval of 10 volume percent of the phase is determined at each temperature and plotted as a function of the isothermal transformation temperature, Fig. 6.23. The temperature range over which a particular phase is stable is also indicated in Fig. 6.23.

If it is desired to know the phase or phases which will be present in the final microstructure during continuous cooling, the appropriate cooling curve is superimposed on the *T–T–T* diagram. In the diagram of Fig. 6.23, three different cooling rates *a*, *b* and *c* are superimposed. If the steel is cooled slowly such as shown by curve "*a*", it will transform into coarse pearlite. A mixture of bainite and fine pearlite will be observed in the microstructure during continuous cooling at rate "*b*". The martensite structure will result when the steel is cooled very rapidly, such as shown by curve "*c*". The microstructure containing 100% bainite cannot be obtained by continuous cooling of plain carbon steels. An interrupted cooling curve, such as that shown by "*d*", can primarily give bainite from austenite.

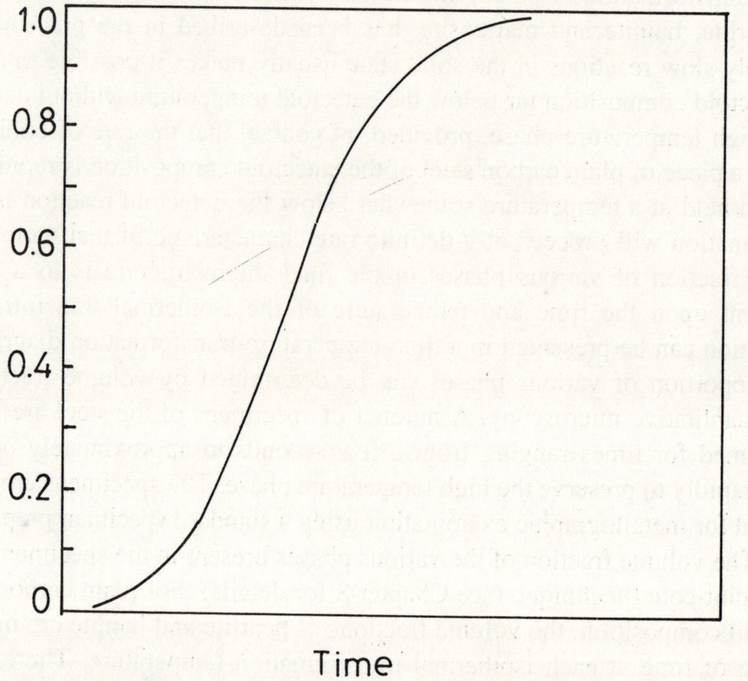

Fig. 6.22 Volume fraction vs. time of transformation.

In the previous paragraphs we discussed the T-T-T diagram and the resulting microstructure of eutectoid steel under different cooling rates. The proeutectoid ferrite will form during continuous cooling of a hypoeutectoid steel. The austenite composition will be displaced towards the eutectoid composition. The final structure will consist of primary ferrite and pearlite, bainte or martensite or a mixture of these morphological features. Accordingly, the T-T-T diagram will show an additional austenite to ferrite transformation curve, Fig. 6.24a. A similar behaviour is expected in steel of hypereutectoid compositions. The proeutectoid cementite phase will form during continuous cooling of these steels as shown in the T-T-T diagram of Fig. 6.24b.

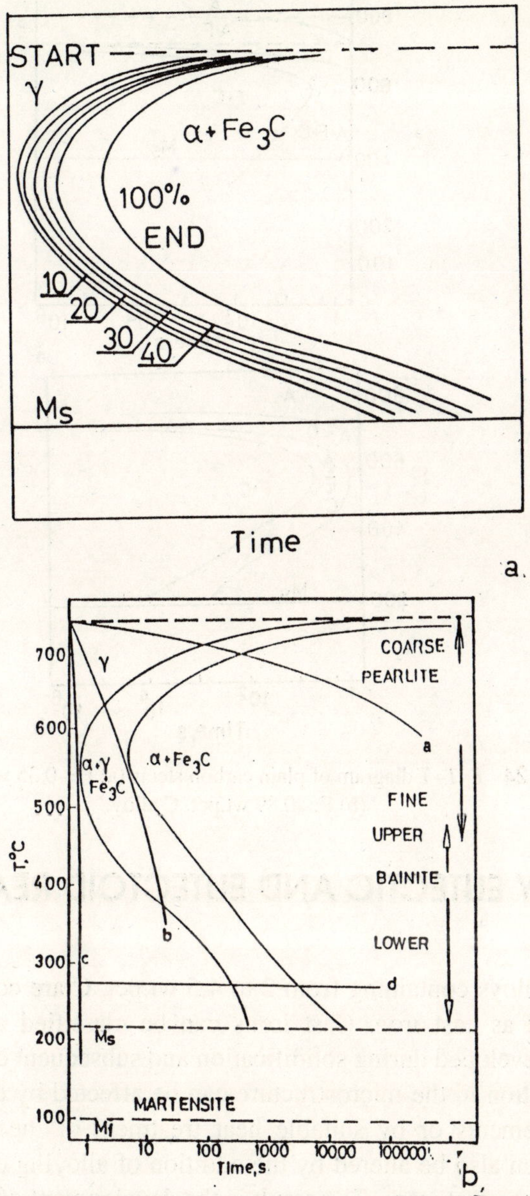

Fig. 6.23 (a) A hypothetical *T–T–T* diagram, (b) *T–T–T* diagram of an eutectoid steel. Three different cooling curves *a*, *b* and *c* are superimposed on the diagram resulting in a different microstructure.

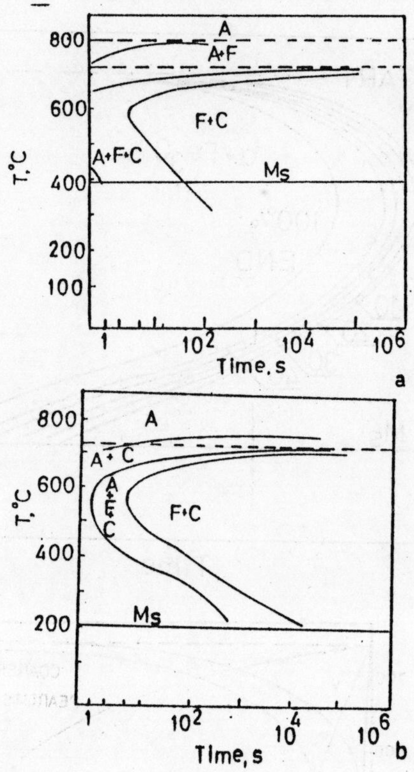

Fig. 6.24 *T–T–T* diagram of plain carbon steels (a) Fe–0.35 wt.pct. C alloy (b) Fe–0.89 wt.pct. C alloy.

6.2 BINARY EUTECTIC AND EUTECTOID REACTIONS-CAST IRON

Iron-carbon alloys containing from 2 to 4.5 wt.pct. C are commercially important materials termed as cast iron. Cast irons can be classified according to the final microstructure developed during solidification and subsequent cooling of these alloys. Further modification in the microstructure can be affected by either inoculation with substitutional elements or by suitable heat treatment of the basic cast irons. The microstructure can also be altered by the addition of alloying elements, as for example, special purpose cast irons. The result is the development of alloys with a range of physical and mechanical properties. The basic cast irons are:

(i) White cast iron
(ii) Gray cast iron
(iii) Ductile cast iron

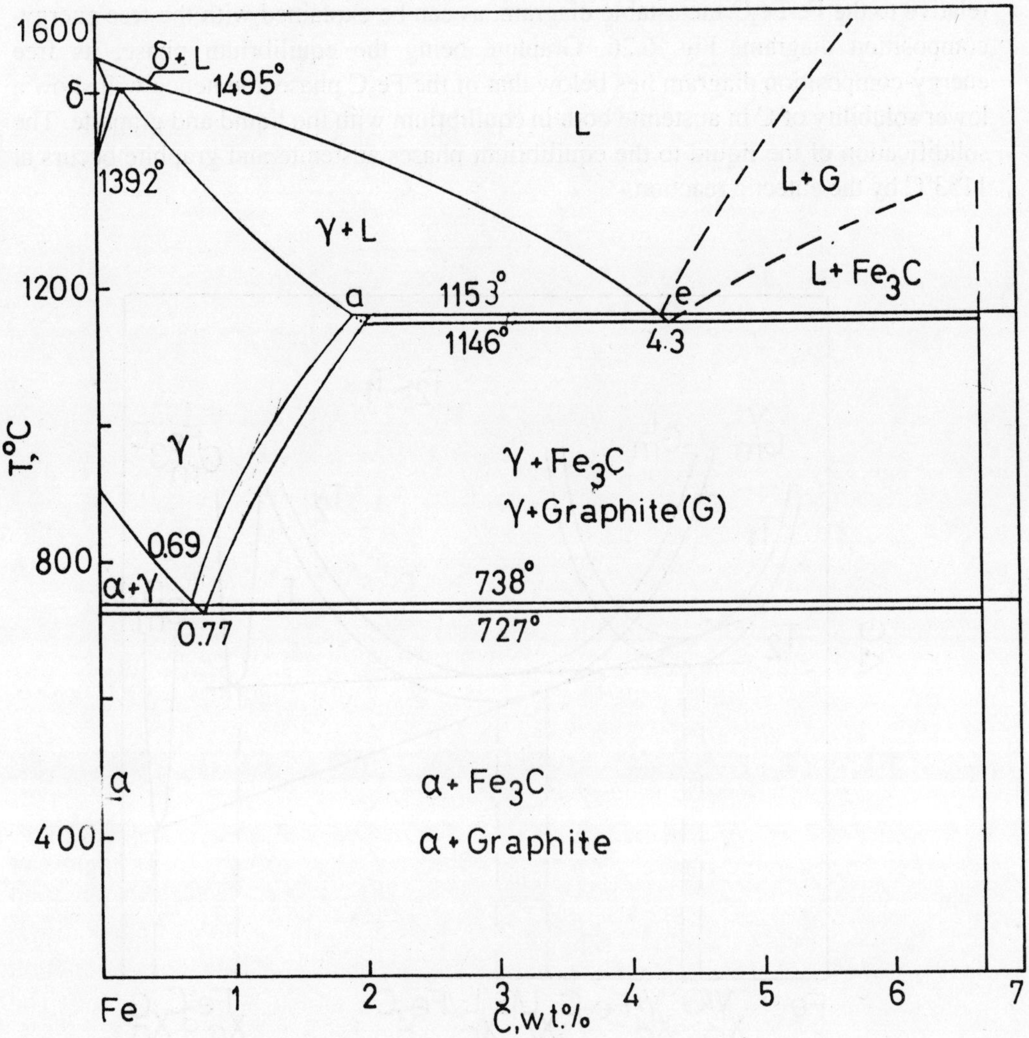

Fig. 6.25 Fe–Fe_3C and Fe-graphite phase diagrams.

The microstructure developed after solidification of the liquid can be best understood with the help of the equilibrium and metastable phase diagrams of the Fe-C alloy system (14), Fig. 6.25. The equilibrium iron-graphite diagram is displaced relative to the Fe-Fe_3C metastable diagram, as can be explained with the free energy-composition diagram, Fig. 6.26. Graphite being the equilibrium phase, its free energy-composition diagram lies below that of the Fe_3C phase and hence will show a lower solubility of C in austenite both in equilibrium with the liquid and graphite. The solidification of the liquid to the equilibrium phases austenite and graphite occurs at 1153°C by the eutectic reaction.

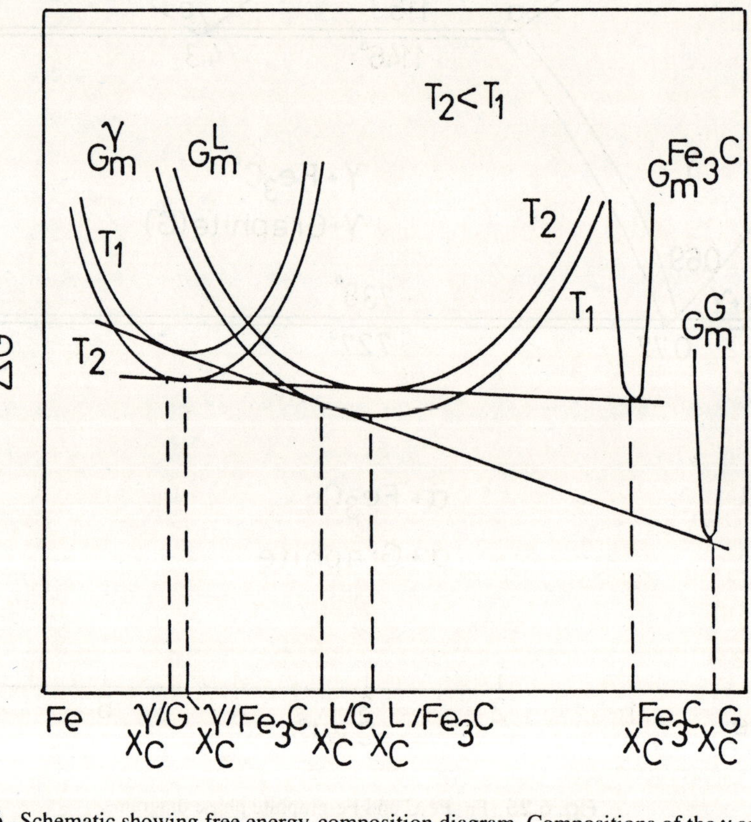

Fig. 6.26 Schematic showing free energy-composition diagram. Compositions of the γ and liquid phase during transformation under equilibrium and metastable equilibrium are shown.

$$L \rightleftharpoons \gamma + \text{Graphite (G)},$$

The solidification of the liquid occurs at 1146°C by the eutectic reaction,

$$L \rightleftharpoons \gamma + Fe_3C$$

when the liquid is cooled rapidly resulting in the lowering of the eutectic temperature, as discussed in Chapter 3. The free energy-composition diagram of Fig. 6.26 illustrates that austenite, liquid and graphite phases are in equilibrium with each other at T_e = 1153°C. When the temperature of solidification is lowered, the free energy-composition diagram of the liquid phase is raised relative to that for the γ and liquid phases to a higher concentration of carbon. A similar shift in carbon concentration occurs during transformation of austenite by the eutectoid reaction. The compositions and temperatures of transformation are shown in Table 6.1.

Table 6.1 **Showing compositions of α, γ, liquid and Fe_3C or graphite phases according to the equilibrium and metastable equilibrium diagrams.**

	Eutectic				Eutectoid		
	T, °C	γ	Liquid	C in Fe_3C/G	T, °C	γ	α
Equilibrium	1153	1.99	4.26	100	738	0.69	–
Metastable Equilibrium	1146	2.06	4.3	6.67	727	0.77	0.02

There is a difference of about 7°C in the equilibrium and metastable equilibrium eutectic reaction isotherms. The solidification of the eutectic liquid will be according to the equilibrium diagram during slow cooling of the alloy from the liquid state. The solidification should be completed before the liquid reaches 1146°C. The final microstructure of cast iron is dependent upon the rate of cooling of the liquid, the isothermal transformation temperature, and to some extent on the presence of alloying elements.

6.2.1 White Cast Iron

When the transformation of the liquid occurs below the metastable eutectic temperature, a highly brittle iron with good wear resistance results. This iron is termed as white cast iron. Let us consider the cooling of an Fe-3 wt.pct.C alloy from the liquid state. The austenite phase nucleates in the liquid when the temperature corresponding to the liquidus is reached. Subsequent cooling through the (γ + liquid) region gives rise to the growth of austenite from the existing nuclei that formed below the liquidus temperature. The composition of the liquid moves towards the eutectic composition (point *e* in Fig. 6.25) and that of the γ phase towards point *a*. If the rate of cooling is relatively fast, the eutectic liquid transforms according to the Fe-Fe_3C diagram by the reaction, $L \rightleftharpoons \gamma + Fe_3C$. The two phases γ and Fe_3C occupy neighboring regions not necessarily in an ideal lamellar morphology. This mixture of $\gamma + Fe_3C$ phases obtained through the eutectic reaction is termed as "ledeburite". Further cooling through the two-phase region ($\gamma + Fe_3C$) results in formation of more cementite at the expense of austenite because of the decreasing solid solubility of C in austenite

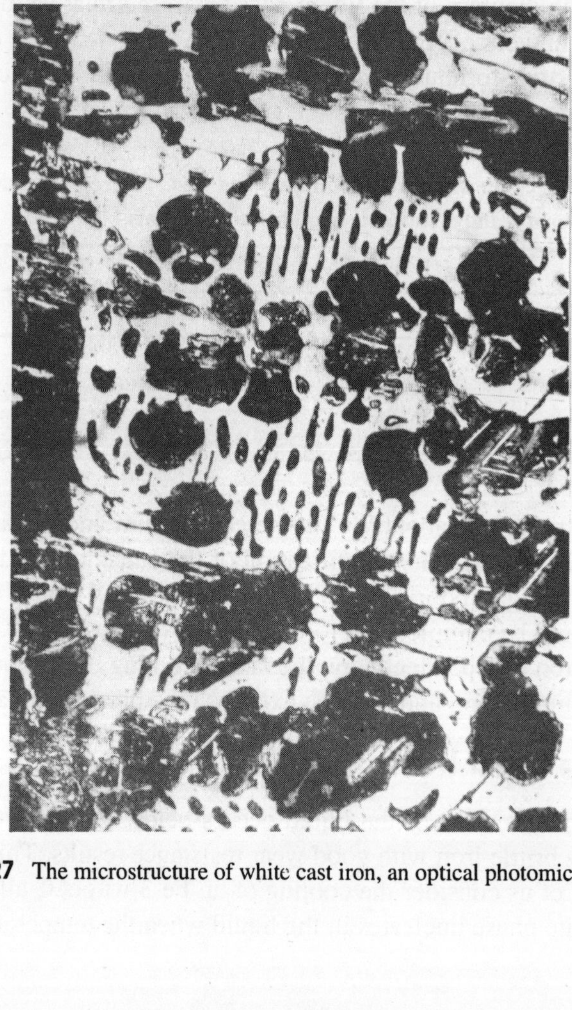

Fig. 6.27 The microstructure of white cast iron, an optical photomicrograph.

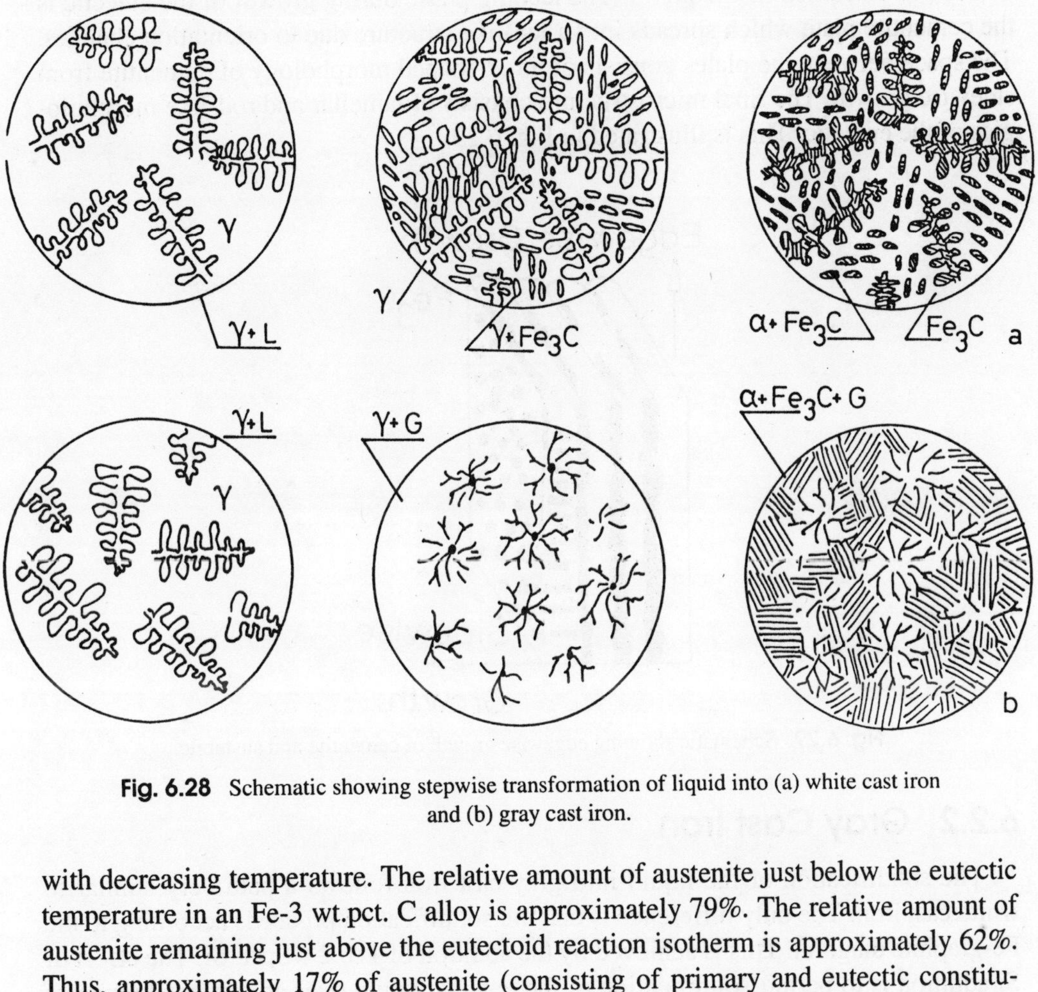

Fig. 6.28 Schematic showing stepwise transformation of liquid into (a) white cast iron and (b) gray cast iron.

with decreasing temperature. The relative amount of austenite just below the eutectic temperature in an Fe-3 wt.pct. C alloy is approximately 79%. The relative amount of austenite remaining just above the eutectoid reaction isotherm is approximately 62%. Thus, approximately 17% of austenite (consisting of primary and eutectic constituents) would have transformed into cementite during cooling between the eutectic and eutectoid temperatures. The austenite transforms into pearlite (α + Fe_3C) below the eutectoid temperature. The final microstructure consists of cementite and lamellar pearlite as shown in the optical photomicrograph of Fig. 6.27. Fig. 6.28a illustrates the stepwise microstructural development of white cast iron.

A number of models have been proposed for the solidification of the eutectic; however, the edgewise growth model proposed by Hillert and Subba Rao (15) tallies with the observed microstructure. The mechanism is similar to the growth of the eutectic as discussed in Chapter 3. The leading phase during growth of the eutectic is the cementite plate which spreads into a fan-like structure due to orientation changes. The space between the plates consists of a rod-shaped morphology of cementite from sidewise growth. The final microstructure consists of lamellar and rod-like morphologies of the eutectic. This is illustrated in Fig. 6.29.

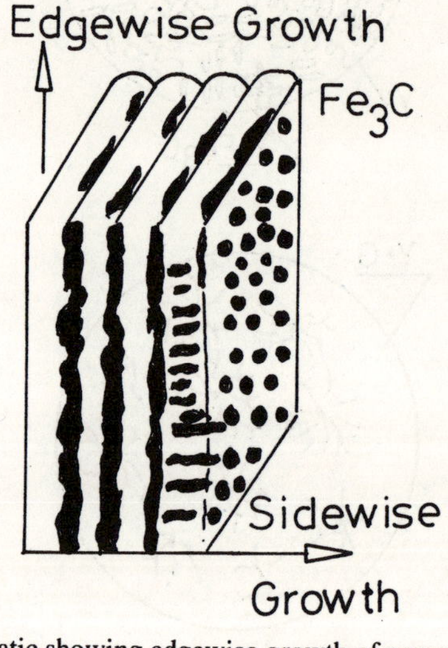

Fig. 6.29 Schematic showing edgewise growth of cementite and austenite.

6.2.2 Gray Cast Iron

The solidification of the liquid into gray cast iron follows a path very similar to white cast iron. The only difference is that the solidification proceeds according to the Fe-graphite diagram. This is achieved by the addition of 1 to 2 wt.pct. Si. The effect of Si addition is to permit solidification of the eutectic liquid over an extended range of temperature from 1153°C to 1122°C. A large thermal gap of approximately 31°C permits nucleation and growth of the graphite in the liquid.

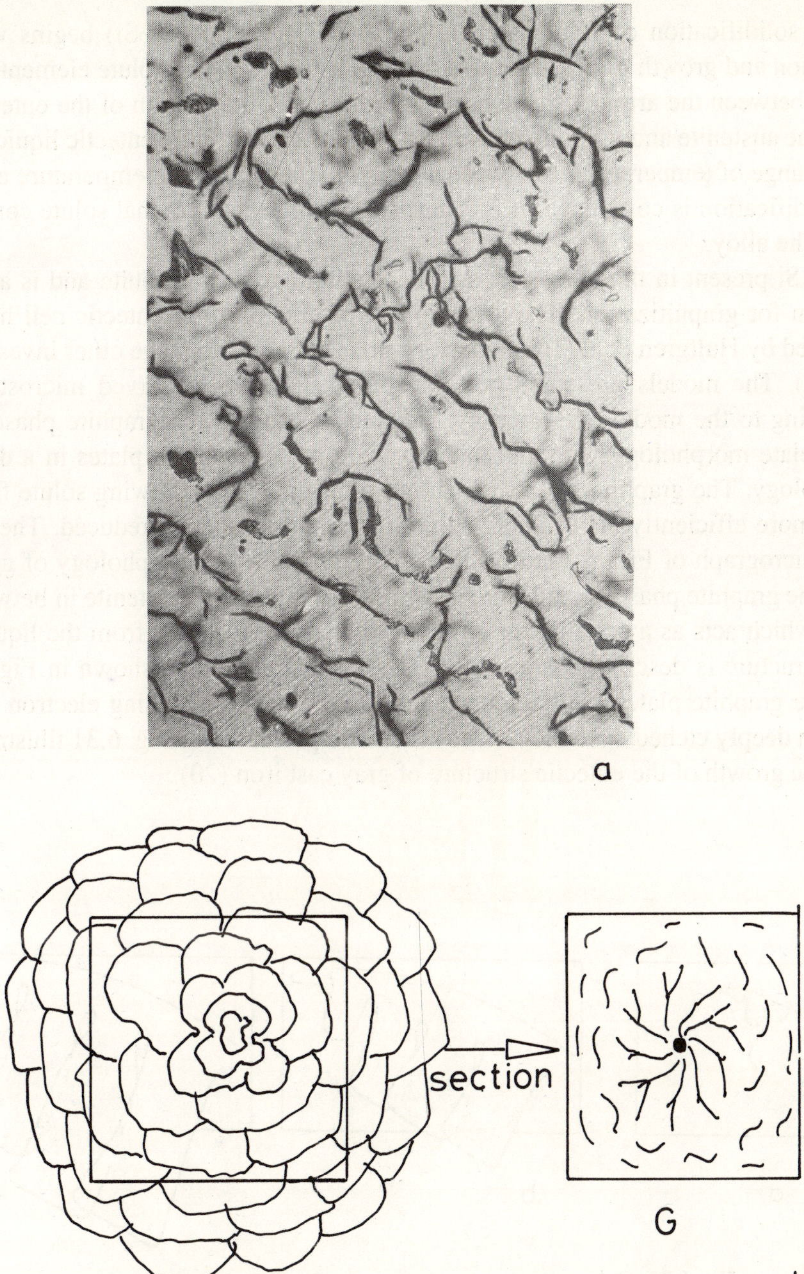

Fig. 6.30 (a) Graphite flake morphology of gray cast iron.
(b) The cabbage leaf structure of graphite, (schematic).

The solidification of a hypothetical alloy (Fe-3%C–1 to 2%Si) begins with the nucleation and growth of austenite to a dendritic structure. The solute elements segregate in between the arms of the dendrite, permitting solidification of the eutectic liquid to the austenite and graphite phases. The solidification of the eutectic liquid occurs over a range of temperatures between T_e and T_f, where T_f is the temperature at which the solidification is completed. It is a function of the substitutional solute concentration in the alloy.

The Si present in the alloy acts as a nucleating agent of graphite and is added in cast iron for graphitization. The arrangement of graphite in a eutectic cell has been described by Hultgren et al (16), and Morrogh et al (17), and some other investigators (18, 19). The models presented here are based upon the observed microstructure. According to the model presented by Morrogh et al (17), the graphite phase grows into a plate morphology with austenite growing in between the plates in a dendritic morphology. The graphite plates branch out frequently, thus drawing solute from the liquid more efficiently, as in doing so the diffusion distance is reduced. The optical photomicrograph of Fig. 6.30a illustrates the graphite flake morphology of gray cast iron. The graphite phase spreads into a fan-like structure with austenite in between the plates which acts as a conduct for eifficient transfer of C atoms from the liquid. The microstructure is described as a cabbage leaf-like structure, as shown in Fig. 6.30b. That the graphite plates are interconnected is revealed by scanning electron microscopy on deeply etched specimens. The schematic presented in Fig. 6.31 illustrates the stepwise growth of the eutectic structure of gray cast iron (20).

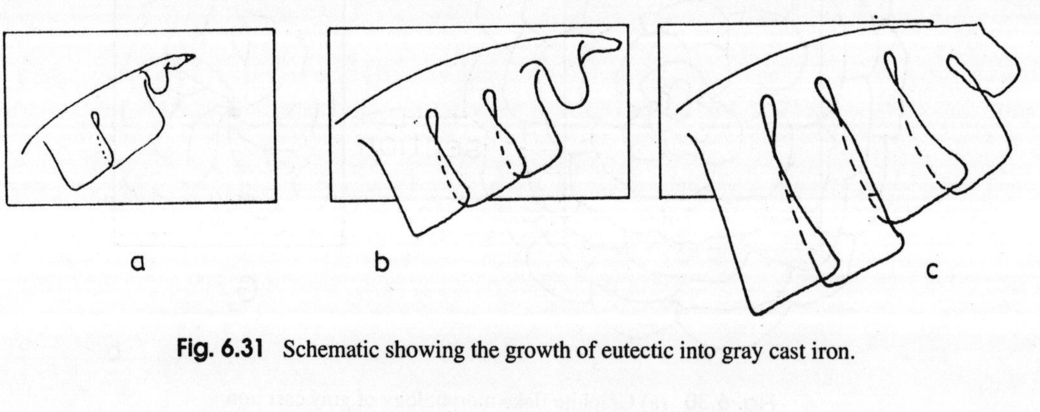

Fig. 6.31 Schematic showing the growth of eutectic into gray cast iron.

The concentration of carbon in austenite decreases during cooling between the eutectic and eutectoid temperatures. The rejected carbon appears in the form of additional graphite. If the alloy is cooled slowly, the austenite decomposes according to the stable Fe-C phase diagram. The final microstructure consists of graphite plates in a matrix of ferrite. On the other hand, the austenite phase transforms to pearlite if the metastable eutectoid reaction the temperature (727°C) is reached before the $\gamma \Rightarrow \alpha +$ graphite transformation can occur. Factors inhibiting the diffusion of carbon in austenite will prevent formation of graphite. There will thus be a tendency for the austenite to be retained with a subsequent transformation into pearlite.

The graphite phase can grow in a number of morphologies. It is classified according to its shape, size and distribution.

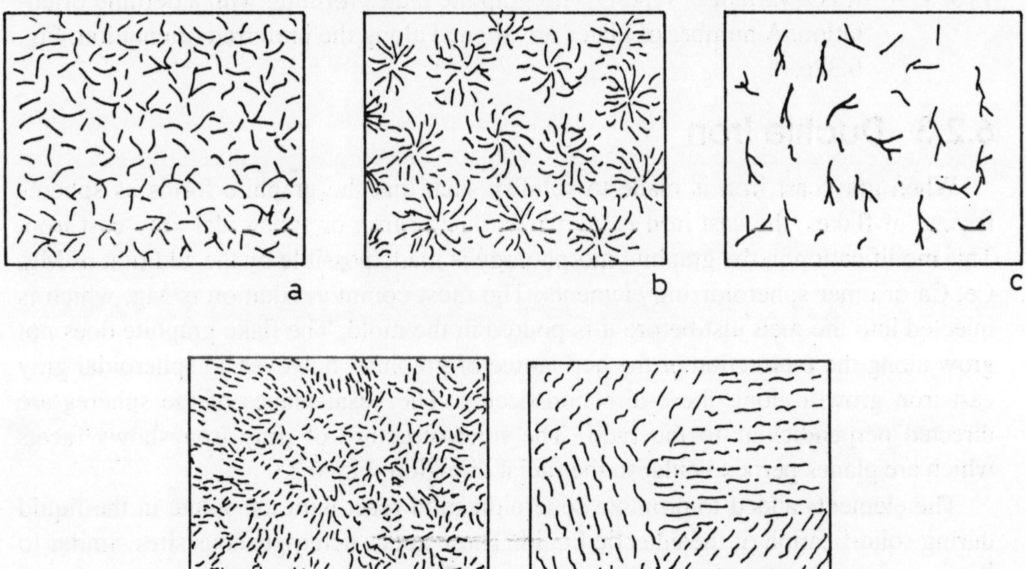

Fig. 6.32 Graphite flake morphologies (a) Type A-uniform and randomly distributed (b) Type B-rossette (c) Type C-random flakes (d) Type D-fine graphite (e) Type E-oriented graphite.

Type A – The flakes of graphite are of uniform size and randomly distributed throughout the matrix, Fig. 6.32a. This occurs when solidification of the eutectic liquid occurs close to the equilibrium temperature.

Type B – The graphite forms in a rosette morphology. This occurs due to solidification of the eutectic liquid at lower temperatures when the flakes are very fine, Fig. 6.32b.

Type C – Graphite forms as random flakes. This is observed in hypereutectic alloys where graphite forms from the liquid before eutectic solidification, Fig. 6.32c.

Type D – When the graphite phase forms in an undercooled melt between the arms of dendrites, it has a very fine structure. It forms in the presence of Ti in a rapidly cooled melt. The cast iron contains sufficient Si to promote graphitizations. Fig. 6.32d illustrates this structure.

Type E – It is a variant of type D with graphite plates forming with a definite orientation. A number of plates are aligned along the preferred orientation, Fig. 6.32e.

6.2.3 Ductile Iron

When gray cast iron is made to solidify such that the graphite forms as spheres instead of flakes, the cast iron is known as ductile iron or spheroidal gray cast iron. This modification in the graphite morphology is made possible by the addition of Mg, Ce, Ca or other spheroidizing elements. The most common addition is Mg, which is injected into the melt just before it is poured in the mold. The flake graphite does not grow along the *c*-direction of the hcp lattice of graphite; however, in spheroidal gray cast iron growth along the *c*-direction occurs. The basal planes of the spheres are directed perpendicular to the radii. The microstructure of gray iron shows facets which are planes perpendicular to the radial direction, Fig. 6.33.

The elements added to promote spheroidization react with the solute in the liquid during solidification of the eutectic liquid. These act as heterogeneous sites similar to those associated with non-metallic inclusions. The graphite phase generally nucleates in the liquid pockets created by the proeutectic austenite. The spheroidal growth of graphite is very similar to that described for spheroidal or nodular eutectic growth in Chapter 3. The interfacial energy of the graphite/liquid interface is modified in such a way that the growth of spheroids is feasible. It is presumed that it will be independent of the orientation, thus making it possible for growth to occur along both "*a*" and

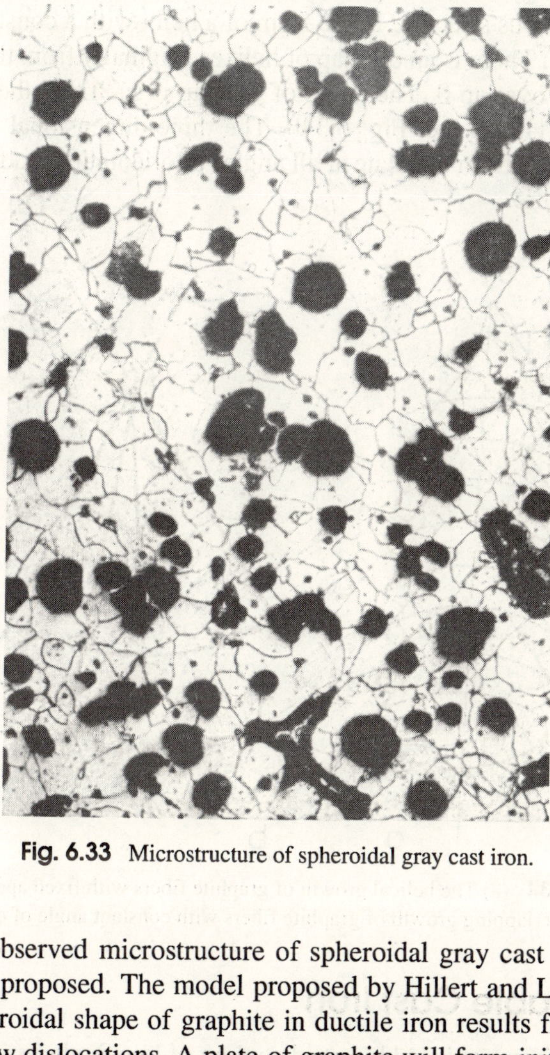

Fig. 6.33 Microstructure of spheroidal gray cast iron.

"*c*" directions.

Based on the observed microstructure of spheroidal gray cast iron, a number of models have been proposed. The model proposed by Hillert and Lindblom (21) suggests that the spheroidal shape of graphite in ductile iron results from the growth of graphite from screw dislocations. A plate of graphite will form initially in the liquid. The alloying elements Ce and Mg will attach themselves at the growing edge of the graphite plate, thus creating screw dislocations. The carbon atoms will attach themselves for the growth of spirals. After some growth, the spirals will not fit together and there will thus be a tendency towards branching. These branches will form new spirals and the final structure will appear spheroidal.

The model proposed by Hunter and Chadwick (22) suggests that graphite, initially, grows as plates. Subsequent branching of the plate, three-dimensionaly, leads to the spheroidal morphology. According to Double and Hellawell (23), the graphite grows in the liquid as a fibrous structure in the form of a helix with a constant apex angle, as shown in Fig. 6.34a. There is an overlap of helixes originally from the same plate with a constant angle of overlap θ. The angle of overlap is such that the two fibers match along a coincident lattice site, Fig. 6.34b. The three-dimensional development of a large number of fibers from the plate at all angles of orientation leads to the spheroidal or spherulitic structure.

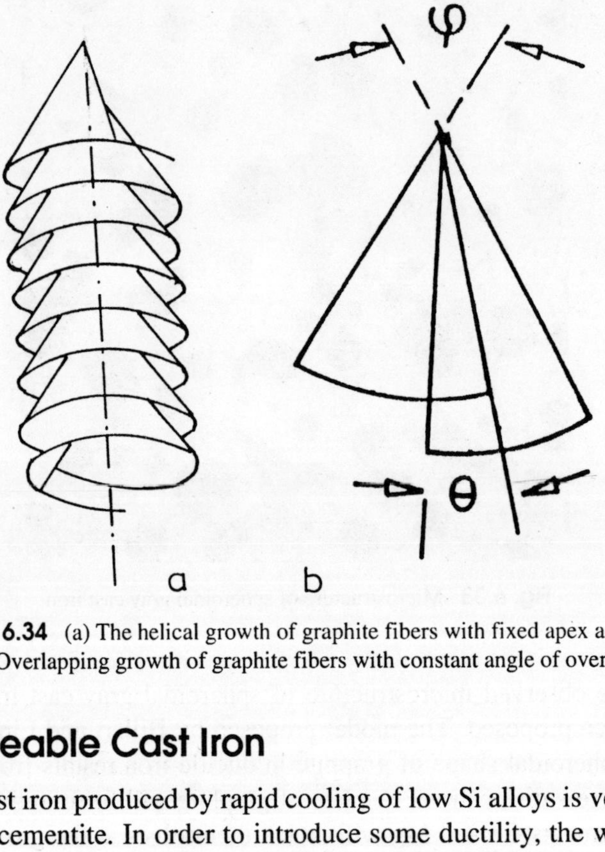

Fig. 6.34 (a) The helical growth of graphite fibers with fixed apex angle. (b) Overlapping growth of graphite fibers with constant angle of overlap.

6.2.4 Malleable Cast Iron

The white cast iron produced by rapid cooling of low Si alloys is very brittle due to the presence of cementite. In order to introduce some ductility, the white cast iron is heat treated (malleablized). The iron produced through such a treatment is known as malleable cast iron. The basic idea is to convert the cementite phase into graphite temper nodules (roughly spherical structures). Depending upon the microstructural requirements, the graphitization heat treatment is carried out in two stages. In the first stage, the white cast iron is heated in the temperature range 940 to 960°C, which is above the eutectoid temperature. In the second stage additional graphitization can be carried out in the temperature range 720 to 730°C, which lies below the eutectoid temperature of the stable Fe-graphite phase diagram.

I-Stage Graphitization

The white cast iron is slowly heated from the ambient temperature to the temperature range 940–960°C and held there for some time. The microstructural changes that occur are:

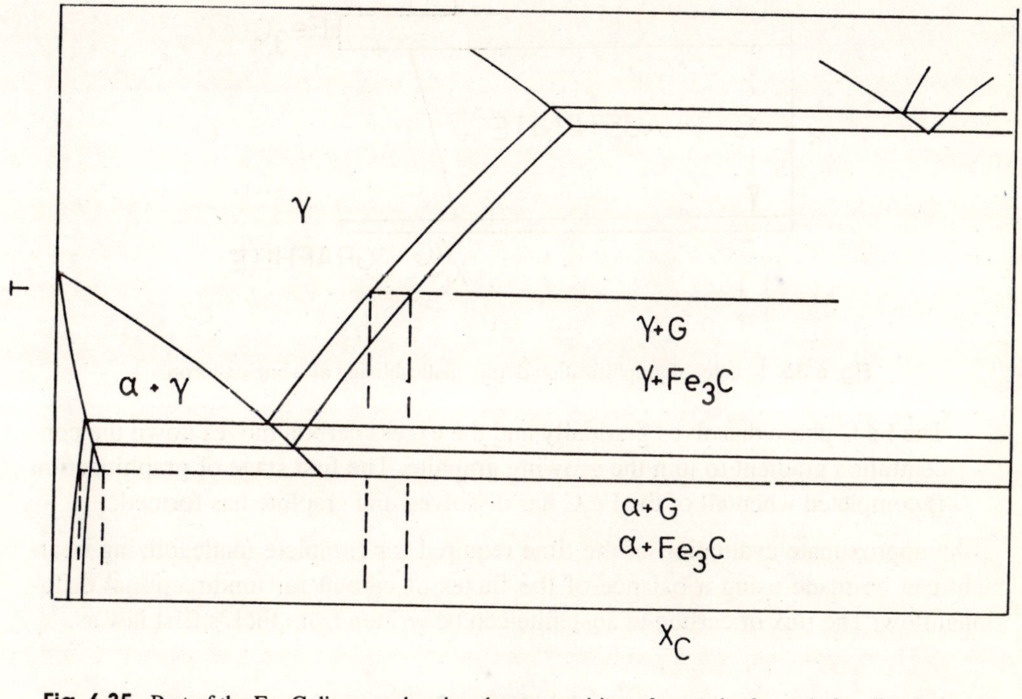

Fig. 6.35 Part of the Fe–C diagram showing the composition of austenite formed after dissolution of cementite.

a. The low temperature structure, i.e., ferrite, pearlite or martensite transform into austenite of a composition corresponding to the γ/Fe_3C boundary of the $(\gamma+Fe_3C)$ two-phase region, Fig. 6.35.

b. The graphite phase nucleates at the saturated γ/Fe_3C interface. The rate of nucleation is promoted by C and Si. The presence of Si in cast iron decreases the solubility of C in austenite, thus increasing the driving force available for the growth of graphite. As shown in Fig. 6.36, the driving force stems from the difference in solubility of C in austenite in equilibrium with cementite and graphite. The concentration gradient of C is increased in the presence of Si.

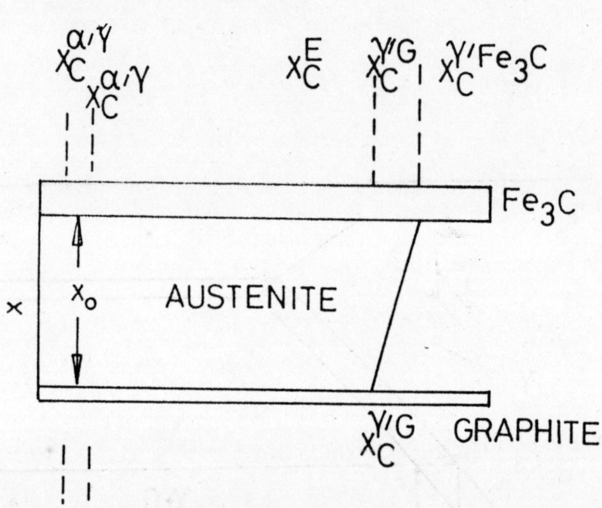

Fig. 6.36 I-stage of graphitization during malleablizing of white cast iron.

c. The Fe_3C phase dissolves gradually and the excess carbon moves down the concentration gradient to join the growing graphite. The first stage of graphitization is completed when all of the Fe_3C has dissolved and graphite has formed.

An approximate evaluation of the time required for complete malleablizing treatment can be made using a balance of the fluxes of carbon for unidirectional diffusional flow. The flux of carbon in austenite can be written from Fick's first law as,

$$J_1 = -\frac{AD_C^{\gamma}}{V_m}\frac{X_C^{\gamma/G} - X_C^{\gamma/Fe_3C}}{\Delta x}, \tag{6.2}$$

where A is the cross-sectional area through which diffusion occurs, D_C^{γ} is the diffusion coefficient of C in austenite, $X_C^{\gamma/G}$ and X_C^{γ/Fe_3C} are the mole fractions of C in austenite in equilibrium with graphite and cementite, respectively, and Δx is the effective diffusion distance taken as x_0, which is the spacing between Fe_3C and graphite. The flux of carbon appears entirely from the dissolution of Fe_3C, whose initial volume fraction is V_f^0. The flux of carbon J_2 is related to the rate of decrease of volume fraction of cementite, written as,

$$J_2 = -\frac{Ax_0}{V_m} X_C^{Fe_3C} \frac{dV_f}{dt}, \tag{6.3}$$

where $X_C^{Fe_3C}$ is the mole fraction of C in the Fe_3C phase. The rate of flow of C through austenite equals the rate at which Fe_3C phase dissolves, giving a steady rate of growth of graphite, and J_1 equals J_2.

$$-Ax_0X_C^{Fe_3C} \frac{dV_f}{dt} = -A\, D_C^{\gamma} \frac{X_C^{\gamma/G} - X_C^{\gamma/Fe_3C}}{x_0}$$

or

$$-X_C^{Fe_3C} \int_{V_f^0}^{V_f} dV_f = -D_C^{\gamma} \int_0^t \frac{X_C^{\gamma/G} - X_C^{\gamma/Fe_3C}}{x_0^2}\, dt$$

or

$$X_C^{Fe_3C} (V_f^0 - V_f) = D_C^{\gamma} \frac{X_C^{\gamma/Fe_3C} - X_C^{\gamma/G}}{x_0^2}\, t \tag{6.4}$$

The volume fraction of Fe_3C will become zero at $t = t_{critical}$, the time required for complete graphitization. Thus, the time required for complete graphitization in the first stage is

$$t_{critical} = \frac{x_0^2 X_C^{Fe_3C} V_f^0}{D_C^{\gamma}\left(X_C^{\gamma/Fe_3C} - X_C^{\gamma/G}\right)} \tag{6.5}$$

The time required for graphitization in the first stage of graphitization depends upon the following factors:

(a) The spacing between cementite and graphite. The smaller the spacing x_0 between cementite and graphite, the shorter will be the time required for complete graphitization. This can be controlled by cooling the liquid rapidly so that the spacing between austenite and cementite in the eutectic structure becomes smaller.

(b) Addition of alloying elements. Such elements should be added in cast iron which promote the rate of nucleation and growth of graphite temper nodules during malleablizing.

(c) Si content in cast iron. The effect of increasing Si content in cast iron is to separate the γ/Fe_3C and γ/G boundaries. The effective driving force which is related to the composition difference $(X_C^{\gamma/Fe_3C} - X_C^{\gamma/G})$ increases. The effect of increasing the composition difference of carbon in austenite in equilibrium with Fe_3C and graphite, on decreasing the time required for malleable heat treatment is apparent from equation (6.5) as well.

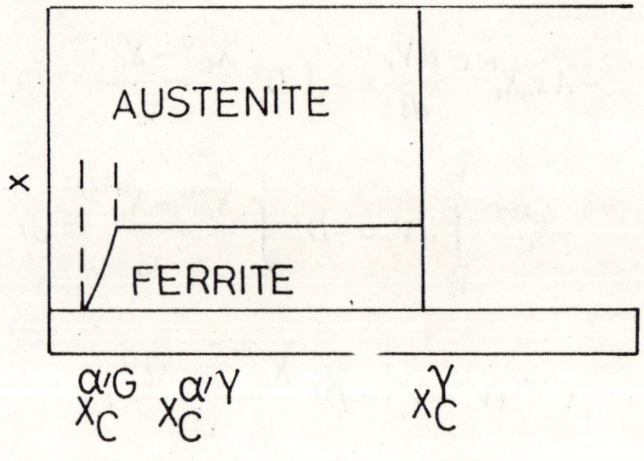

Fig. 6.37 II-stage of graphitization during malleablizing of white cast iron.

II-Stage Graphitization

In the second stage of graphitization, the alloy is allowed to cool very slowly after complete graphitization in the first stage, the aim being to not allow the transformation of austenite into cementite. The excess carbon in the austenite diffuses to graphite temper nodules with the diffusion of C occurring through austenite. This process is also known as a ferritizing anneal. The complete graphitization of cast iron can be

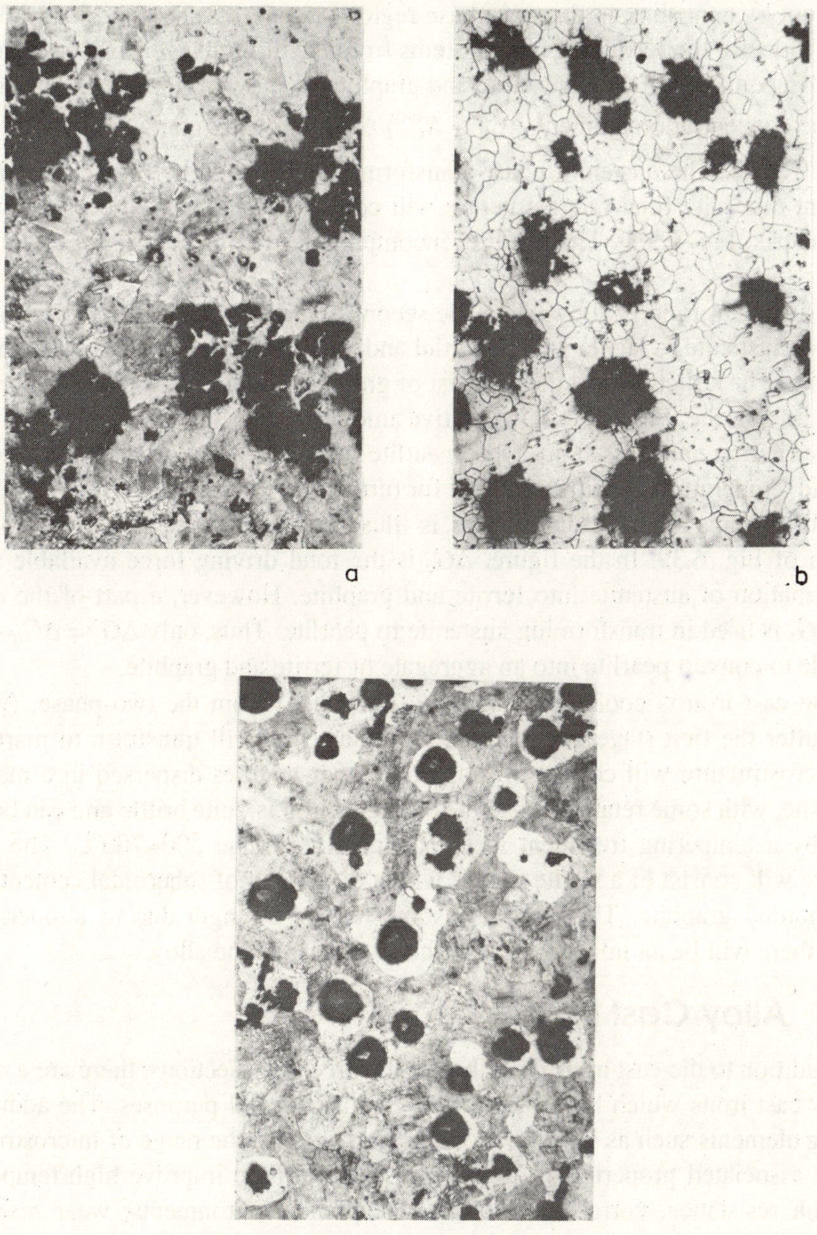

Fig. 6.38 (a) An optical photomicrograph showing microstructure of malleable cast iron: graphite dark, ferrite light and pearlite gray, (b) Fully malleablised cast iron, (c) An optical photomicrograph showing nodular cast iron. Graphite nodules are surrounded by a thin layer of ferrite in pearlite matrix.

carried out by annealing in the two-phase region (α + G), as shown in Fig. 6.37. The driving force for the ferritizing anneal stems from the difference in composition of the α phase in equilibrium with austenite and graphite as shown. The carbon atoms move down the concentration gradient, $(X_C^{\alpha/\gamma} - X_C^{\alpha/G})/\Delta x$, to growing graphite phase through a layer of ferrite. The austenite phase transforms gradually in the process, and given sufficient time, the final microstructure will consist of graphite temper nodules in a ferrite matrix, Fig. 6.38b. The result of incomplete ferritizing anneal is shown in Fig. 6.38a.

If insufficient time is allowed for the second stage of graphitization, the transformation of austenite to ferrite will be partial and the remaining austenite will transform to pearlite. The structure will thus consist of graphite nodules surrounded by ferrite in a matrix of pearlite, Fig. 6.38c. The relative amount of pearlite will be large if the time of the ferritizing anneal is short. Once pearlite has formed out of austenite below the eutectoid temperature, the time required for further ferritizing will be very large due to the small driving force available. This is illustrated in the free energy-composition diagram of Fig. 6.39. In the figure, ΔG_0 is the total driving force available for the transformation of austenite into ferrite and graphite. However, a part of the driving force ΔG_1 is used in transforming austenite to pearlite. Thus, only $\Delta G_2 = \Delta G_0 - \Delta G_1$ is available to convert pearlite into an aggregate of ferrite and graphite.

If the cast iron is cooled very rapidly (quenched) from the two-phase, (γ + G), region after the first stage graphitization, the austenite will transform to martensite. The microstructure will consist of graphite temper nodules dispersed in a matrix of martensite, with some retained austenite. The cast iron is quite brittle and can be made useful by a tempering treatment in the temperature range 500–700°C. The microstructure will consist of a ferrite matrix with a dispersion of spheroidal cementite and large mottled graphite. There will be some loss of strength due to tempering but overall there will be an improvement in the toughness of the alloy.

6.2.5 Alloy Cast Irons

In addition to the cast irons described in the preceding sections, there are a number of alloy cast irons which have been developed for special purposes. The addition of alloying elements such as Cr, Mo, Si, Ni and Al extends the range of microstructures and the associated properties in cast irons. The aim is to improve high temperature oxidation resistance, corrosion resistance in acidic environments, wear resistance, abrasion resistance, etc. Alloy cast irons can be divided into two groups: graphite-free and graphite-bearing. The graphite-free irons are designated as alloy white irons. They may contain Cr or Cr and Ni.

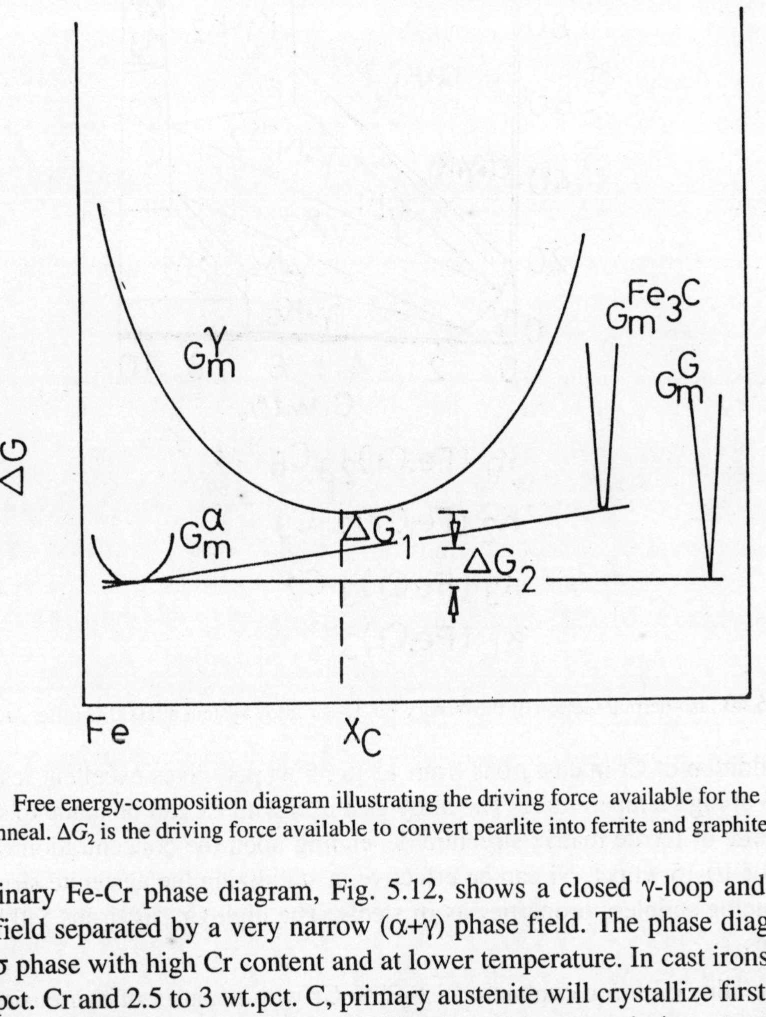

Fig. 6.39 Free energy-composition diagram illustrating the driving force available for the ferritizing anneal. ΔG_2 is the driving force available to convert pearlite into ferrite and graphite.

The binary Fe-Cr phase diagram, Fig. 5.12, shows a closed γ-loop and an open α-phase field separated by a very narrow (α+γ) phase field. The phase diagram also shows a σ phase with high Cr content and at lower temperature. In cast irons containing 2 wt.pct. Cr and 2.5 to 3 wt.pct. C, primary austenite will crystallize first from the liquid. This will be followed by the solidification of the eutectic into γ and carbide phases. The carbide phase is $(Cr, Fe)_3C$, and because of the low Cr content in cast iron all of the Cr goes into the carbide phase. The ternary isothermal section [after Jackson (24)] shows that γ and carbide will be in equilibrium with each other at 1000°C, Fig. 6.40.

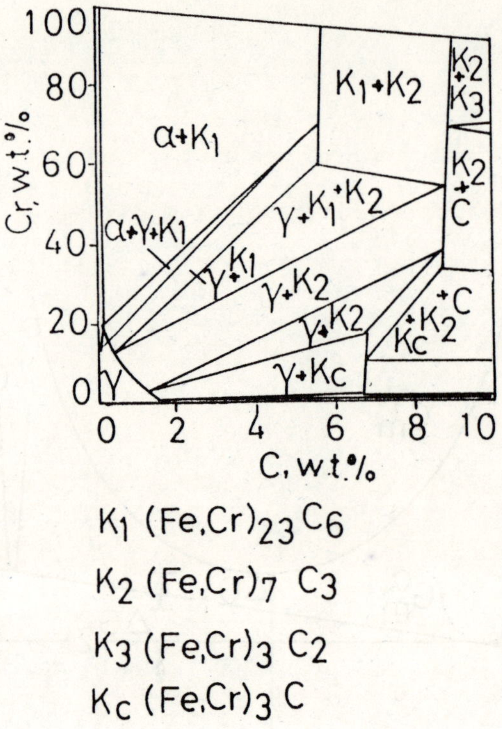

Fig. 6.40 Isothermal section of the ternary Fe–C–Cr alloy system at 1000°C (after Jackson).

The addition of Cr in cast irons from 12 to 35 wt.pct. gives excellent resistance to oxidation at high temperatures. The alloy cast iron with Cr can be made to solidify in the austenite or ferrite matrix structure depending upon the concentration of Cr. The addition of 10-15 wt.pct. Ni can be effective in stabilizing the austenite structure and in introducing stainless properties as in steels. The high Cr cast irons fall into three basic types.

(i) The alloy cast iron containing 12–28% Cr with a matrix of martensite and dispersed carbide.

(ii) The alloy cast iron containing 29-34 wt.pct. Cr with a matrix of ferrite and a dispersion of alloy carbides $(Cr, Fe)_{23}C_6$ and $(Cr, Fe)_7C_3$. The microstructure is shown in Fig. 6.41 in a cast iron containing 29.3% Cr and 2.95% C.

(iii) The alloy cast iron containing 15–30 wt.pct. Cr and 10–15 wt.pct. Ni with a stable austenite structure at low temperatures and carbides, $(Cr, Fe)_{23}C_6$ and $(Cr, Fe)_7C_3$, dispersed in the matrix.

Fig. 6.41 Microstructure of high-Cr iron showing dispersed alloy carbides in a matrix of ferrite.

The Fe-Ni phase diagram, Fig. 6.42, shows that the addition of Ni to cast iron is effective in stabilizing austenite. It also tends to promote graphitization. The beneficial effect of Ni addition is to reduce the C content of the eutectic. The thermal gap between γ–G and γ–Fe_3C eutectics is increased by the addition of Ni, thus promoting graphitization and suppressing the formation of carbide. The effect of Ni is to move the knee of the T–T–T diagram to longer times and to suppress the M_s temperature, thus making it possible to form martensite without severe quenching.

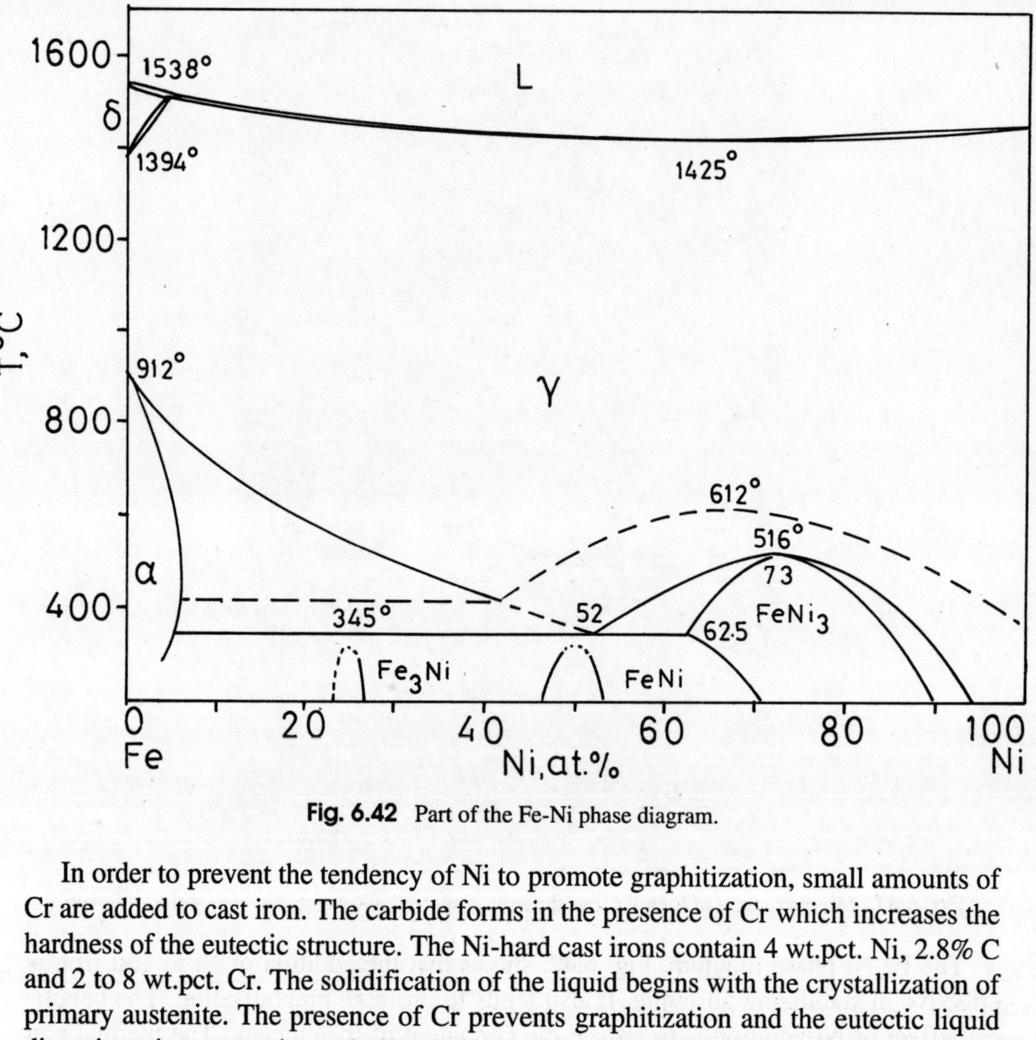

Fig. 6.42 Part of the Fe-Ni phase diagram.

In order to prevent the tendency of Ni to promote graphitization, small amounts of Cr are added to cast iron. The carbide forms in the presence of Cr which increases the hardness of the eutectic structure. The Ni-hard cast irons contain 4 wt.pct. Ni, 2.8% C and 2 to 8 wt.pct. Cr. The solidification of the liquid begins with the crystallization of primary austenite. The presence of Cr prevents graphitization and the eutectic liquid dissociates into austenite and alloy carbide. The austenite transforms into martensite at lower temperatures. The Ni-hard cast iron contains needles of martensite and the austenite-martensite/carbide eutectic structure of ledeburite, Fig. 6.43. This alloy cast iron is used for superior abrasion resistance.

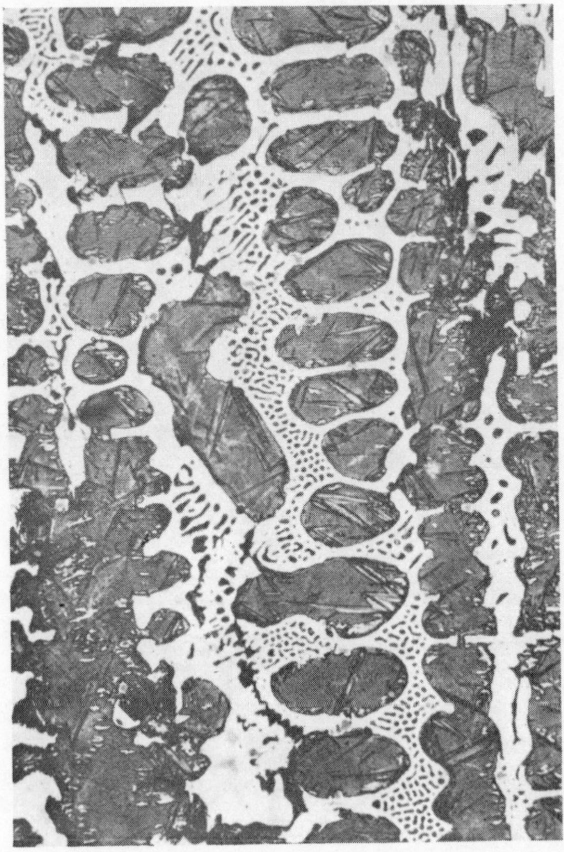

Fig. 6.43 The microstructure of Ni-hard cast iron.

The alloy cast iron containing 15 to 30 wt.pct. Ni and a small amount of Cr is known as Ni-resist iron. The microstructure consists of austenite in the form of dendrites and graphite as plates or flakes. The microstructure may contain inter-dendritic carbides due to the presence of Cr, Fig. 6.44. The carbides can be graphitized in the (γ+G) region of the phase diagram, if strength is not the primary requirement. This alloy cast iron is resistant to oxidation. These alloy cast irons are also used in chemical processing plants, sea water, oil handling operations and in food handling plants.

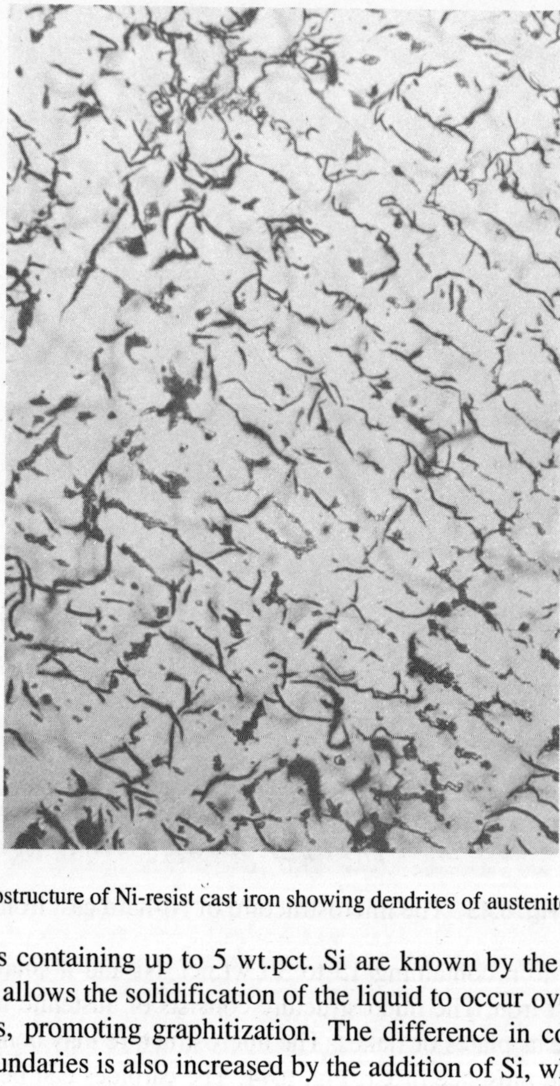

Fig. 6.44 The microstructure of Ni-resist cast iron showing dendrites of austenite and graphite plates.

Alloy cast irons containing up to 5 wt.pct. Si are known by the trade name Silal. The addition of Si allows the solidification of the liquid to occur over a large temperature interval, thus, promoting graphitization. The difference in composition of the γ/G and γ/Fe_3C boundaries is also increased by the addition of Si, which increases the effective driving force thus facilitating the formation of graphite flakes, Fig. 6.45. The addition of 5.0 wt.pct. Si in cast iron forms a surface film of iron silicate, thus making the cast iron resistant to acid corrosion.

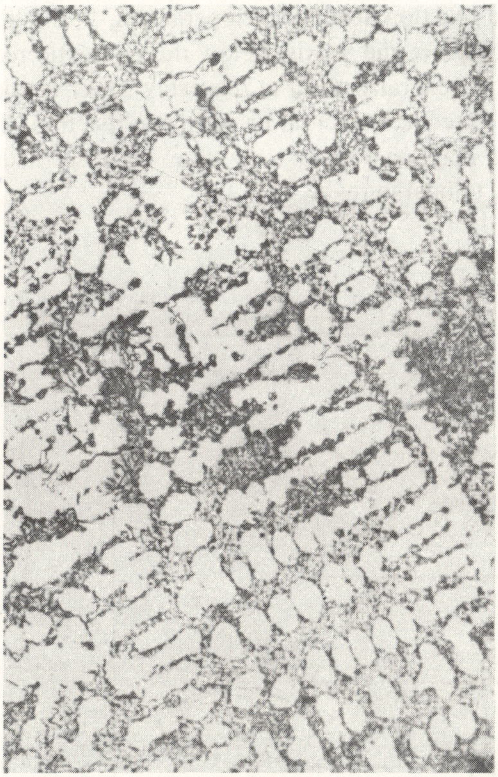

Fig. 6.45 The microstructure of cast iron containing 5% Si showing graphite phase in the microstructure.

6.3 BINARY PERITECTOID SYSTEMS

In a binary peritectoid system, two solid phases react with each other to give a third solid phase with a different composition and crystal structure. This reaction is related to that of the binary peritectic system; the only difference is that the liquid phase of the peritectic is replaced by a solid phase in the peritectoid.

$$\alpha + \gamma \rightleftharpoons \beta$$

A hypothetical phase diagram with the peritectoid reaction is shown in Fig. 6.46. Since the reactants involve two solid phases, the phase diagram may show a peritectic, eutectic or a eutectoid reaction at higher temperatures. In the phase diagram of Fig. 6.49, the two solid phases α and γ exist below the peritectic reaction isotherm. The peritectoid reaction will generally occur at relatively lower temperatures because it is always followed by a eutectic, eutectoid or peritectic reaction. It is expected that the rate of the peritectoid reaction will be very slow because of the very slow rate of solute diffusion at low temperatures.

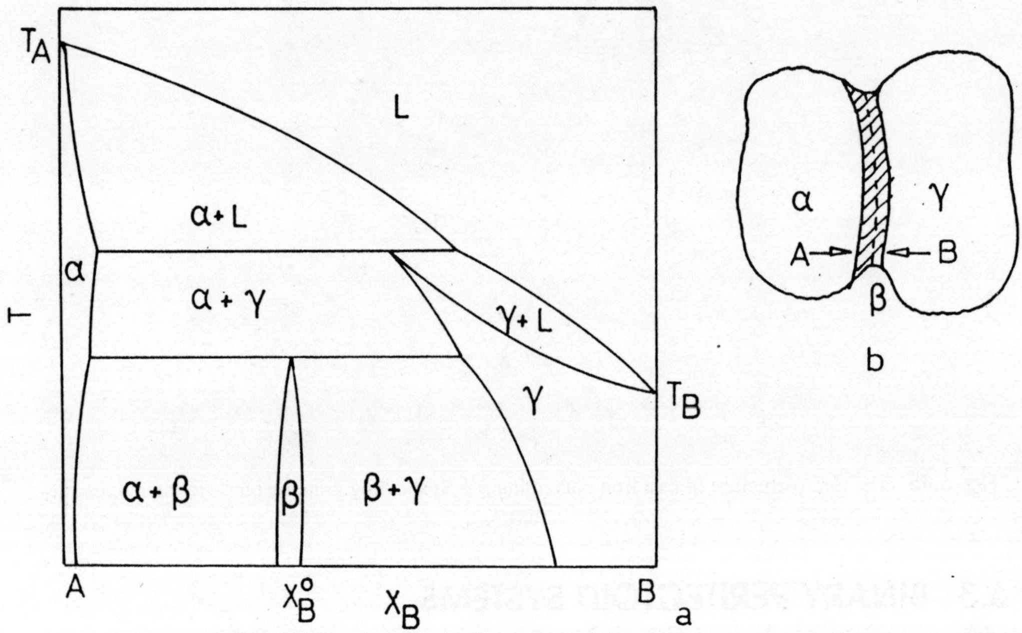

Fig. 6.46 A hypothetical binary phase diagram showing the peritectoid reaction.

Consider an alloy of the peritectoid composition X_B^0 as shown in the diagram. At the peritectoid temperature, α and γ phases of composition, X_B^α and X_B^γ, respectively, will react with each other to give the β phase of composition X_B^β. The reaction will initiate at the α/γ interface. A thin layer of the β phase will form as a product of the reaction. Further growth of β will occur by migration of the α/β and γ/β phase interfaces in opposite directions. The diffusion of *A* atoms will occur from α towards γ and

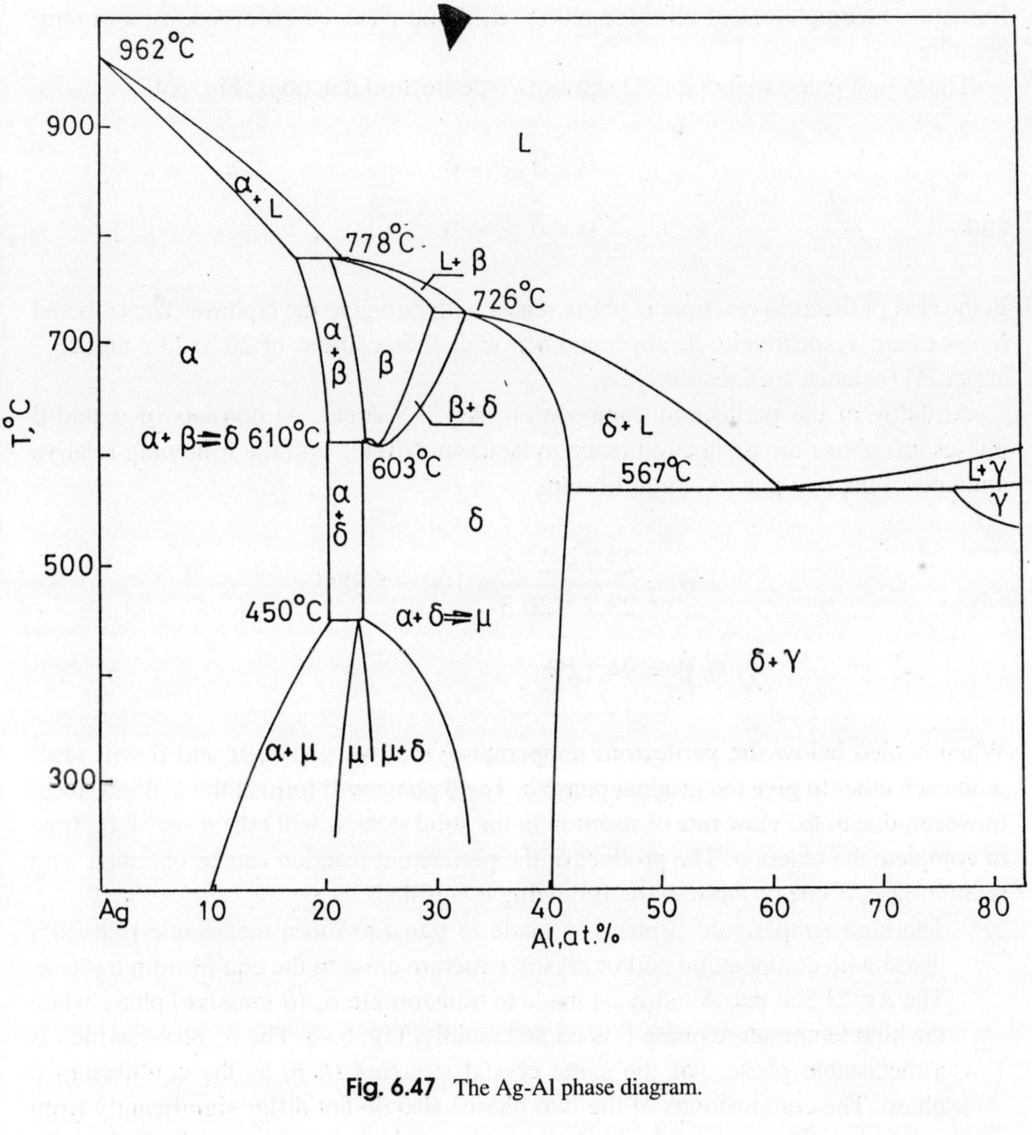

Fig. 6.47 The Ag-Al phase diagram.

that of B atoms from γ towards α. The solute and solvent atoms have to diffuse through an ever increasing thickness of the β phase layer thus decreasing the rate of growth of the product β. The peritectoid reaction is generally very slow and will reach completion only after a long reaction time. It is, therefore, common to find the transformation incomplete, and all three phases α, β and γ can be observed at room temperature.

The Ag-Al phase diagram (25) shows two peritectoid reactions, Fig. 6.47,

$$\alpha+\beta \rightleftharpoons \delta$$

and

$$\alpha+\delta \rightleftharpoons \mu.$$

In the first peritectoid reaction, α phase reacts with β to give the δ phase. The α, β and δ phases are, respectively, *fcc*, *bcc*, and *hcp* with compositions of 20.3, 23.5 and 23.7 at.pct. Al (balance Ag), respectively.

An alloy of the peritectoid composition, Ag-23.5 at.pct. Al consists of α and β phases just above the peritectoid reaction isotherm 610°C, with the following relative amounts of the two phases at equilibrium.

$$\%\,\alpha = \frac{23.7-23.5}{23.7-20.3} \times 100 = 5.88\%$$

$$\%\,\beta = 94.12\%$$

When cooled below the peritectoid temperature, the two phases α and β will react with each other to give the product phase δ. The δ phase will form at the α/β interface; however, due to the slow rate of reaction in the solid state, it will take a very long time to complete the reaction. The product of the peritectoid reaction can be obtained with relative ease, if one or more of the following is fulfilled:

1. The high temperature β phase is made to transform to a metastable transition phase with composition and/or crystal structure close to the equilibrium δ phase. The Ag-23.5 at.pct. Al alloy, is made to transform to δ_m (δ-massive) phase when the high temperature phase β is cooled rapidly, Fig. 6.48. The δ_m phase, which is a metastable phase, has the same crystal structure (*hcp*) as the equilibrium δ phase. The compositions of the two phases also do not differ significantly from each other. The metastable δ_m phase can be made to transform to the δ phase by annealing it below the peritectoid temperature for a short time.

Fig. 6.48 The microstructure of the δ_m phase.

2. The composition of one of the parent phases is close to the product phase. In the Ag-Al alloy considered above, the composition of the δ phase is close to the β phase near the peritectoid reaction isotherm. The change in composition required to transform β to δ is small (0.2 at.pct.). A crystal structure change from *bcc* to *hcp* is primarily required to transform the β to the δ phase. The β phase in the (α + β) phase mixture occupies a volume fraction of approximately 94%.
3. The product phase at times has a certain crystallographic orientation relationship with the parent phase. The common interface is a low index plane of low interfacial energy. From energetic considerations, a low energy interface provides a higher driving force ($\Delta G = \Delta G^c - \Delta G^\gamma$) for diffusion than an interface of average interfacial energy, where ΔG^c and ΔG^γ are, respectively, the chemical free energy available for transformation and the interfacial energy.

6.4 BINARY MONOTECTOID SYSTEMS

The binary monotectoid system is synonymous with the binary monotectic system; the only difference between the two is that, whereas a binary monotectic reaction involves two liquids, L_1 and L_2, and a solid α, the monotectoid reaction involves three solids α_1 and α_2 and β. It is written as

$$\alpha_1 \rightleftharpoons \alpha_2 + \beta.$$

In general, the two component metals form a series of solid solutions in a large composition range at high temperatures, as shown in the hypothetical phase diagram, Fig. 6.49. At lower temperature, the homogeneous solid solution dissociates into two solids having the same crystal structure but different compositions. This occurs through an immiscibility dome consisting of phases α_1 and α_2. The departure from a homogeneous solution increases as the temperature is decreased, as shown by arrows in Fig. 6.49. The phase α_1 gradually gets enriched with the component *A* and α_2 with the component *B*. Finally, at the monotectoid reaction isotherm, the α_1 phase dissociates into α_2 and β phases. The α_2 phase differs from α_1 only with respect to the composition. The β phase, however, has different composition and crystal structure as compared to the α_1 or α_2 phase.

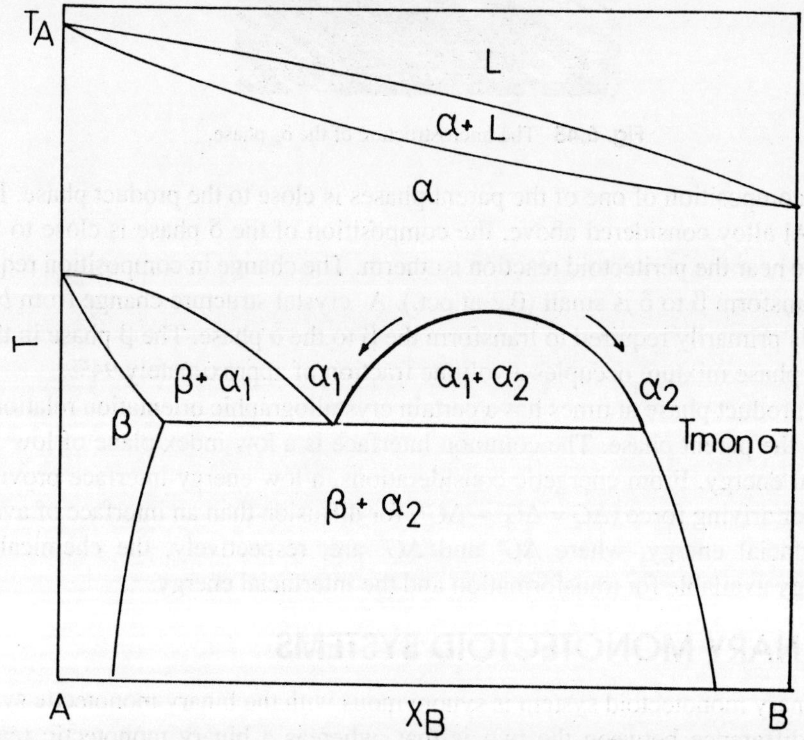

Fig. 6.49 A hypothetical phase diagram with monotectoid reaction.

The monotectoid reaction occurs in binary systems when one of the component shows allotropic transformation, for example, the Nb–Zr system, Fig. 6.50. The refractory metal Zr exists in two allotropy forms: β (*bcc*) and α (*hcp*). The *bcc* form of Zr, β, forms solid solution with Nb (*bcc*) in the whole range of compositions at higher temperatures. An immiscibility gap appears at T_{cr} = 988°C at Zr–60.6 at.pct. Nb when the homogeneous solid solution β begins to split into β_1 and β_2. The β_1 solid solution dissociates into α and β_2 phases at 620°C given by,

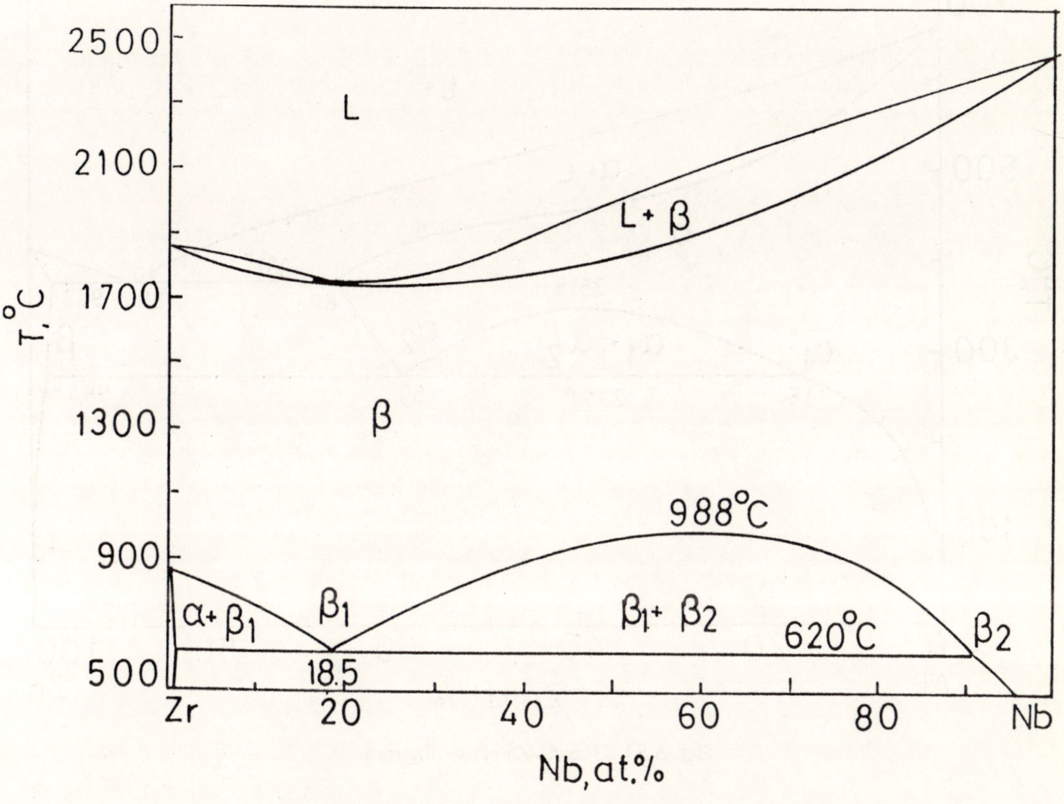

Fig. 6.50 The Nb-Zr phase diagram.

$$\beta_1(18.5 \text{ at.pct. Nb}) \xrightleftharpoons{620°C} \alpha\ (0.6 \text{ at.pct. Nb}) + \beta_2\ (91 \text{ at.pct. Nb}).$$

The monotectoid reaction can also occur in binary systems when neither component shows allotropic transformations; for example, the Al-Zn alloy system, Fig. 6.51. It shows a maximum solubility of 67 at.pct. Zn in Al at the eutectic temperature. The α phase is not stable below 351°C as a homogeneous solid solution in the whole range of compositions. The following reaction is observed at the monotectoid reaction isotherm,

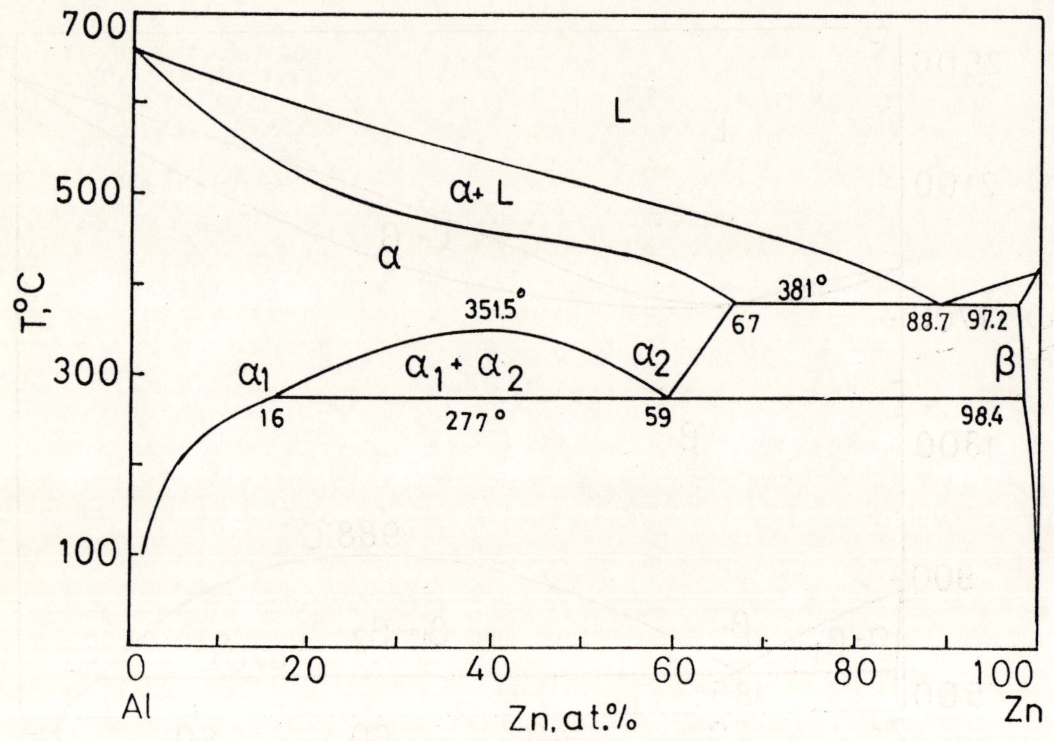

Fig. 6.51 The Al-Zn phase diagram.

$$\alpha_1(59 \text{ at.pct. Zn}) \xrightleftharpoons{277^\circ\text{C}} \beta\ (98.4 \text{ at.pct. Zn}) + \alpha_2\ (16.5 \text{ at.pct. Zn}).$$

The crystal structures of α, α_1 and α_2 conform to the *fcc* structure of pure Al and that of the β phase with the *hcp* structure of pure Zn. The products of the monotectoid reaction generally appear as a duplex structure.

REFERENCES

1. Brown and N. Ridley, *J. Iron and Steel Inst.*, 270 (1969), 1232.
2. Pickalsmier, McElny, Kegley, Stansbury and Frye, *Trans AIME*, 218 (1960), 473.
3. M.K. Bhatia and S.P. Gupta, Z. Metallkde, 85 (1994), 192.
4. M.P. Puls and J.S. Kirkaldy, *Met. Trans.*, 3 (1972), 2772.
5. Johnson Hawkes and R.F. Mehl, *Trans. ASM*, 30 (1942), 1049.
6. D. Cheetham and N. Ridley, *J. Inst. Metals*, 99 (1971), 371.
7. C.A. Dubé, Ph.D. Thesis, Carnegie Institute of Technology (1948). (See 4.1 Aaronson: *Decomposition of Austenite by diffusional processes*, Interscience Publishers, New York (1962)).
8. G.V. Kurdjumov and G. Sachs, *Z. Physik*, 64, (1939), 325.
9. M.S. Weschler, D.S. Lieberman and T.A. Read, Trans. *TMS-AIME*, 197 (1953), 503.
10. J.S. Bowles and J.K. Mackenzie, *Acta Metall.* 2, (1954), 129, 138, 224.
11. A.D. Greninger, and A.R. Troiano, *Trans. TMS-AIME*, 185 (1949), 590.
12. P.G. Winchell and M. Cohen, *Trans. Am. Soc. Met.*, 55 (1962), 347.
13. A.R. Marder and G. Krauss, *Trans. ASM*, 60 (1967), 651.
14. M.G. Benz and J.F. Elliott, *Trans. Metall. Soc. AIME*, 221 (1961), 323.
15. M. Hillert and V.V. Subba Rao, *The Solidification of Metals*, Iron Steel Inst. Publ. 110, London (1968).
16. A. Hultgren, Y. Lindblom and E. Ruclberg, *J. Iron Steel* Inst., London, 176 (1954), 365.
17. H. Morrogh and W. Oldfield, *Iron Steel*, 32 (11) (1959), 431.
18. I. Minkoff and B. Lux, *Cast Metals Res. J.*, 6 (1970), 181.
19. K.P. Bunin, Y. Malinochka and S. Fedorova, *Litenoe Proizvod*, 4 (1953), 21.
20. I. Minkoff, *The Physical Metallurgy of Cast Iron*, Wiley Interscience Publication, 1983.
21. M. Hillert and Y. Lindblom, *J. Iron Steel Inst.*, London, 176 (1954), 388.
22. M.J. Hunter and G.A. Chadwick, *J. Iron Steel Inst.*, London, 210 (1972), 707.
23. D.D. Double and A. Hellawell, *Acta Metall.*, 17 (1969), 1071.
24. R.S. Jackson, *British Foundryman*, 67 (1974), 34.
25. M. Hansen and K. Anderko, *Constitution of Binary Alloys*, 2nd ed., McGraw Hill Book Company, New York, 1958.

PROBLEMS

1. An iron-carbon alloy containing 0.3 wt.pct. C is allowed to cool slowly from the austenite range. Calculate,
   (i) the amount of proeutectoid ferrite.
   (ii) the amount of ferrite and cementite in pearlite.
   The same steel is allowed to cool to 800°C and subsequently quenched rapidly so as to transform the remaining austenite into martensite. Calculate the amount of proeutectoid ferrite.
2. An iron-carbon alloy containing 1.2 wt.pct. C is allowed to cool slowly from the austenite range. Calculate,
   (i) the amount of proeutectoid cementite.
   (ii) the amount of ferrite and cementite in pearlite.
   Look up the *T–T–T* diagram for a C-steel alloy containing 1 wt.pct. C and examine if bainite can form during continuous cooling. Explain.
3. How would you distinguish between martensite and bainite from observations of the microstructure? Write distinguishing features of each.
4. A rod of pure iron is joined to a small rod of pure graphite and the diffusion couple allowed to anneal (i) at 850°C (ii) at 1000°C. Draw the concentration-distance profile during (a) early stage (b) intermediate stage of annealing of the couple. Draw the microstructure of the Fe-C alloy if the alloy is cooled slowly to room temperature.
5. What is the driving force for I-stage graphitization of white cast iron? Explain with the help of free energy-composition diagrams.
6. What is the driving force for II-stage graphitization of white cast iron? Explain using free energy-composition diagrams. Explain why it is so difficult to graphitize pearlitic cast iron near the eutectoid temperature?
7. An Fe-4 wt.pct. C alloy is allowed to cool so as to obtain (i) white cast iron with pearlite matrix (ii) gray cast iron with ferrite matrix. Calculate the relative amounts of proeutectic, eutectic, proeutectoid and eutectoid product phase(s) in the microstructure. Show the development of microstructure in a series of sketches in each case.
8. What modification in the solidification or alloy chemistry can be made to enhance the rate of I-stage graphitization?
9. Draw the heat treatment cycle (superimposed on the Fe-C diagram) necessary to convert
   (i) spheroidal gray cast iron with pearlite matrix to spheroidal gray cast iron with ferrite matrix.

(ii) spheroidal gray cast iron with ferrite matrix to spheroidal gray cast iron with pearlite matrix.

(iii) spheroidal gray cast iron with pearlite matrix to graphite spheres surrounded by a thin layer of ferrite in a pearlite matrix.

(iv) Spheroidal gray cast iron with ferrite matrix into graphite spheres surrounded by a thin layer of pearlite in a ferrite matrix.

(v) Spheroidal gray cast iron with ferrite matrix into graphite spheres surrounded by a thin layer of martensite in a ferrite matrix.

10. Draw the Cu-Al phase diagram. Write all peritectoid reactions occurring in this binary system.
11. The peritectoid reaction does not go to completion. Explain.

Chapter 7

BINARY PHASE DIAGRAM CALCULATIONS

The basic thermodynamics relating the Gibbs free energy to composition, activity, etc. has been described in Chapter 1. It has been understood that a system is under equilibrium at a given temperature and pressure when the free energy has a minimum value. For two phases to be in equilibrium, it has been shown that the chemical potential of each component is the same. This can be expressed in mathematical form as,

$$\mu_A^{\alpha}(X_B^{\alpha}, T, P) = \mu_A^{\beta}\,(X_B^{\beta}, T, P)$$

and (7.1)

$$\mu_B^{\alpha}(X_B^{\alpha}, T, P) = \mu_B^{\beta}(X_B^{\beta}, T, P).$$

The phase diagrams for a number of binary systems will be calculated using the available thermodynamic data. The phase diagrams will include most of the binary invariant reactions involving liquid phases. In some cases hypothetical phase diagrams for the binary system $A–B$ will be calculated at first by using assumed values for different thermodynamic parameters. Thereafter, it will be shown that such systems do exist. In most cases, the free energy-composition diagram will be drawn at a number of temperatures using equations relating the free energy to the composition and temperature. A common tangent construction which satisfies the condition for equality of chemical potentials will be made to determine compositions of different phases in equilibrium with each other at a given temperature, thus leading to the construction of the phase diagram. A linear least square optimization method of calculating phase diagrams will be presented at the end of this chapter. The numerical method optimizes the thermodynamic and composition vs. temperature data to yield relevant free energy values used in the phase diagram calculations.

7.1 BINARY ISOMORPHOUS SYSTEMS

Simple phase diagrams can be calculated if appropriate thermodynamic data exist. To begin with, we will calculate the simple lens-shaped phase diagram of a binary system with components A and B both having the same crystal structure. It is assumed that the two components are completely soluble in each other in all proportions, in the liquid as well as in the solid state, and form ideal solutions. The melting points of the two components A and B are T_A and T_B, respectively, with the condition $T_A > T_B$. In the simple lens-shaped diagram, solidification will occur only below T_A and gets completed above T_B. The standard states for the system are, therefore, taken as pure solid A and pure liquid B. The free energies of the components may be expressed as,

$$G_i^{0(j)} = G_i^0 + RT \ln a_i^j \tag{7.2}$$

where G_i^0 is the standard free energy per mole for the component i and a_i^j is the activities of the component i in the jth phase. For the component A, we can write

$$\ln (a_A^\beta / a_A^\alpha) = -\frac{\Delta G_{fA}^0}{RT} (\beta \Rightarrow \alpha) \tag{7.3}$$

where ΔG^0_{fA} is the free energy of fusion of the component A, and β and α are the liquid and solid A, respectively. Assuming specific heats of the components at constant pressure to remain constant in the two phases, i.e., $C^{\beta}_{PA} = C^{\alpha}_{PA}$, equation (7.3) is written as

$$\ln(a^{\beta}_{A}/a^{\alpha}_{A}) = \frac{\Delta H^0_{fA}}{R}(L \Rightarrow S)\ [1/T - 1/T_A] \tag{7.4}$$

Equation (7.4) is arrived at, by writing,

$$\Delta G^0_{fA}(L \Rightarrow S) = H^{0(S)}_{A} - H^{0(L)}_{A} - T(S^{0(S)}_{A} - S^{0(L)}_{A})$$

$$= \Delta H^0_{fA} - T\,\Delta S^0_{fA}$$

$$\Delta G^0_{fA} = \Delta H^0_{fA} - \frac{T\Delta H^0_{fA}}{T_A}$$

$$= \Delta H^0_{fA}\left(1 - \frac{T}{T_A}\right)$$

For ideal or near ideal solution $a^L_A = X^L_A$ and $a^S_A = X^S_A$. Substituting for the activities in equation (7.4) yields,

$$X^L_A = 1 - X^L_B = X^S_A \exp\left[-\frac{\Delta H^0_{fA}}{R}\left(\frac{1}{T} - \frac{1}{T_A}\right)\right]. \tag{7.5}$$

We can write a similar expression for the component B,

$$X^L_B = X^S_B \exp\left[-\frac{\Delta H^0_{fB}}{R}\left(\frac{1}{T} - \frac{1}{T_B}\right)\right] \tag{7.6}$$

Substituting for X^L_B from equation (7.5) gives the temperature vs. composition relation for the solidus line.

$$1 = X_A^S \exp\left[-\frac{\Delta H_{fA}^0}{R}\left(\frac{1}{T}-\frac{1}{T_A}\right)\right] + X_B^S \exp\left[-\frac{\Delta H_{fB}^0}{R}\left(\frac{1}{T}-\frac{1}{T_B}\right)\right] \qquad (7.7)$$

Similarly, we can write an expression for the liquidus line as,

$$1 = X_A^L \exp\left[\frac{\Delta H_{fA}^0}{R}\left(\frac{1}{T}-\frac{1}{T_A}\right)\right] + X_B^L \exp\left[\frac{\Delta H_{fB}^0}{R}\left(\frac{1}{T}-\frac{1}{T_B}\right)\right] \qquad (7.8)$$

From a knowledge of the heats of fusion and the melting points of the components A and B, compositions of the solid and liquid phases in equilibrium with each other can be determined. The calculation has been carried out for the Ge-Si binary system from the following data (1, 2),

$$\Delta H_{f\text{Si}}^0 = 50.5 \text{ kJ mol}^{-1}$$

$$\Delta H_{f\text{Ge}}^0 = 36.94 \text{ kJ mol}^{-1}$$

$$T_{\text{Si}} = 1685 \text{ K}$$

$$T_{\text{Ge}} = 1210.4 \text{ K}$$

$$C_{p\text{Si}}^L = C_{p\text{Si}}^S \quad \text{and} \quad C_{p\text{Ge}}^L = C_{p\text{Ge}}^S.$$

The calculated binary phase diagram of the Ge-Si alloy system is shown in Fig. 7.1 by full lines, with the published solidus and liquidus curves from the work of Thurmond (3).

In order to determine how the calculated phase diagram compares with the published one, it is important to determine the composition difference between the liquidus and solidus at a given temperature T, defined as $T_A > T > T_B$. The difference in composition is written as $(X_B^L - X_B^S)$. The composition calculated at 1400 K yields,

$$X_B^L = 0.7346$$

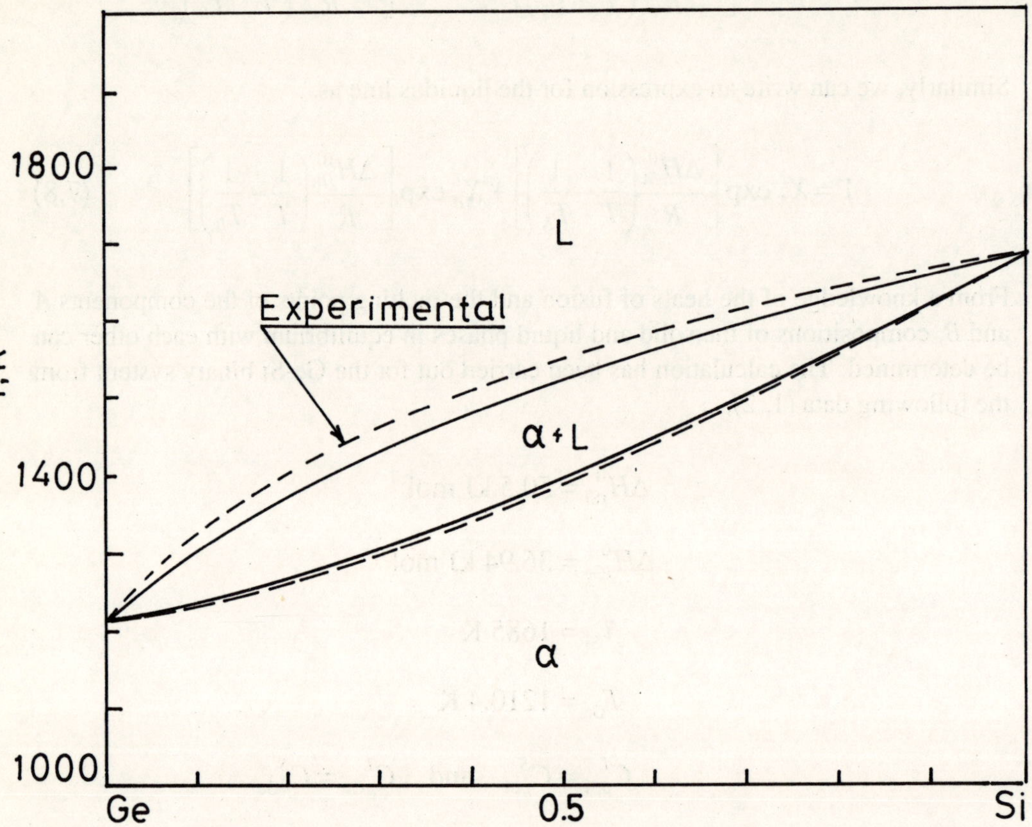

Fig. 7.1 Calculated phase diagram of the Ge-Si alloy system (full line). The broken lines are from the work of Thurmond (3).

$$X_B^S = 0.44688 \qquad (\text{Ge} \equiv \text{component} B)$$

$$\Delta X_B = 0.2877$$

The compositions according to the published phase diagram at 1400 K are,

$$X_B^L = 0.805, \quad X_B^S = 0.467 \quad \text{and} \quad \Delta X_B = 0.338.$$

The difference appears to be small considering that the calculation of these compositions have been made by assuming ideal solutions and equal specific heats for each of the two components in both phases.

The published phase diagram of the Ge-Si system has been evaluated by considering the regular solution model. The interaction parameters (or the enthalpy of mixing coefficients) Ω^S and Ω^L are taken to be 6.5 × 10^3 J mol^{-1} and 3.5 × 10^3 $Jmol^{-1}$, respectively.

In deriving equations (7.5) and (7.6), it was assumed that both solid and liquid solutions are ideal, when the enthalpy of mixing is zero. In the regular solution model, it is assumed that enthalpies of mixing ΔH_m for both solid and liquid solutions are not zero, but the entropy of mixing equals the ideal entropy of mixing, $\Delta S_m = \Delta S_m$ (ideal). The excess entropy ΔS^E is zero for both solid and liquid solution. It is assumed that the standard state for A is pure solid A and that for B is pure liquid B, as before. Following the derivation given in Chapter 2, the free energy of the solid and liquid solutions are written as:

$$\Delta G^S = \Delta H_m^S - X_B^S \Delta H_{fB}^0 \left(1 - \frac{T}{T_B}\right) + RT\,[X_A^S \ln X_A^S + X_B^L \ln X_B^L] \qquad (7.9)$$

and

$$\Delta G^L = \Delta H_m^L + X_A^L \Delta H_{fA}^0 \left(1 - \frac{T}{T_A}\right) + RT\,[X_A^L \ln X_A^L + X_B^L \ln X_B^L] \qquad (7.10)$$

The enthalpies of mixing in equations (7.9) and (7.10) are written as

$$\Delta H_m^S = \Omega^S X_A^S X_B^S = 6.5 \times 10^3 X_A^S X_B^S,$$

and

$$\Delta H_m^L = \Omega^L X_A^L X_B^L = 3.5 \times 10^3 X_A^L X_B^L.$$

Substituting values of T_A, T_B, T, and the enthalpies of fusion and mixing of the two components, the free energy vs. composition curve can be obtained. For the Ge-Si alloy system, this has been carried out at a number of temperatures, as shown in Figs. 7.2, a, b, c and d at 1550, 1450, 1350 and 1300 K, respectively. The composition of the two phases, solid and liquid, at each temperature, can be obtained by drawing a common tangent between the two free energy curves. The phase diagram of the Ge-Si alloy system is shown in Fig. 7.3.

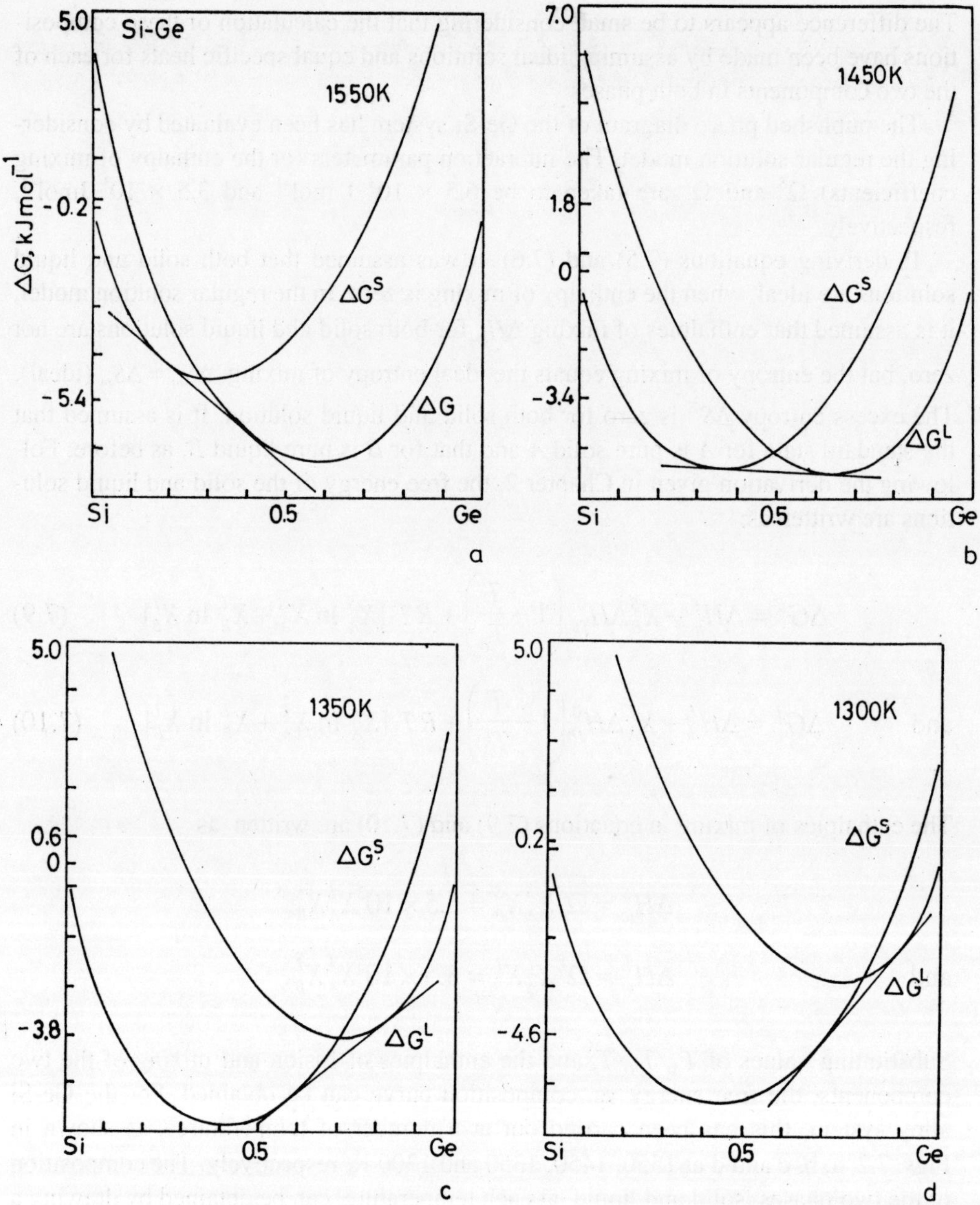

Fig. 7.2 The calculated free energy-composition diagrams using equations (7.9) and (7.10) for the Ge-Si binary alloy system at (a) 1550 K (b) 1450 K (c) 1350 K and (d) 1300 K.

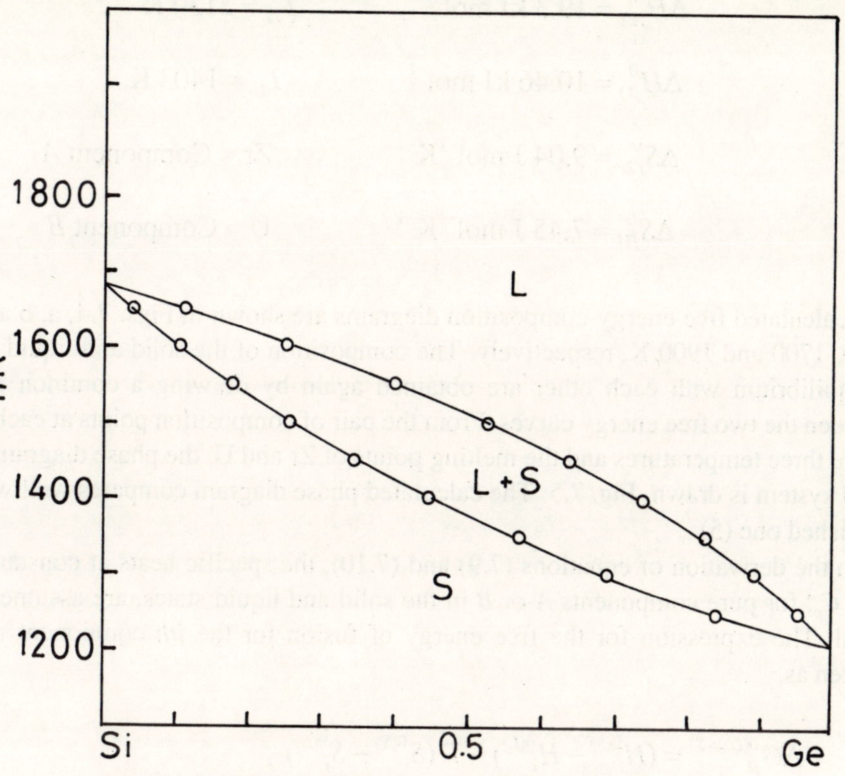

Fig. 7.3 The calculated phase diagram of the Ge-Si binary system.

Rand and Kubaschewski (4) have calculated the Zr–U phase diagram by using the regular solution model for both solid and liquid solutions. The enthalpies of mixing for the solid and liquid solutions are equal but composition dependent as the following data demonstrates:

$X_B =$	0.1	0.2	0.3	0.4	0.5	0.6	0.7	0.8	0.9
$\Delta H_m =$ (J mol^{-1})	1422	2468	3347	3933	4226	4184	3807	3096	1958

The enthalpies and entropies of fusion, and the melting temperature of the two components, U and Zr are taken to be,

$$\Delta H^0_{f\mathrm{Zr}} = 19.3 \text{ kJ mol}^{-1} \qquad T_{\mathrm{Zr}} = 2130 \text{ K}$$

$$\Delta H^0_{f\mathrm{U}} = 10.46 \text{ kJ mol}^{-1} \qquad T_U = 1403 \text{ K}$$

$$\Delta S^0_{f\mathrm{Zr}} = 9.04 \text{ J mol}^{-1}\text{K}^{-1} \qquad \mathrm{Zr} = \text{Component } A$$

$$\Delta S^0_{f\mathrm{U}} = 7.45 \text{ J mol}^{-1}\text{K}^{-1} \qquad \mathrm{U} = \text{Component } B$$

The calculated free energy-composition diagrams are shown in Figs. 7.4, a, b and c at 1500, 1700 and 1900 K, respectively. The composition of the solid and liquid phases in equilibrium with each other are obtained again by drawing a common tangent between the two free energy curves. From the pair of composition points at each of the above three temperatures and the melting points of Zr and U, the phase diagram of the Zr-U system is drawn, Fig. 7.5. The calculated phase diagram compares well with the published one (5).

In the derivation of equations (7.9) and (7.10), the specific heats at constant pressure C_p, for pure components A or B in the solid and liquid states, are assumed to be equal. The expression for the free energy of fusion for the *ith* component may be written as,

$$\Delta G_{fi}^{0(L\Rightarrow S)} = (H_i^{0(S)} - H_i^{0(L)}) - T\,(S_i^{0(S)} - S_i^{0(L)})$$

$$= \left[\Delta H^0_{fi} + \int_{T_i}^{T} \Delta C^0_{pi}\, dT\right] - T\left[\Delta S^0_{fi} + \int_{T_i}^{T} \frac{\Delta C^0_{pi}}{T}\, dT\right], \qquad (7.11)$$

where $\Delta C^0_{pi} = C^{0(S)}_{pi} - C^{0(L)}_{pi}$. The heat capacity of pure substances is generally represented by polynomials of the form,

$$C^0_{pi} = a_i + b_i T + c_i T^{-2},$$

when a_i, b_i and c_i are constants. Substituting for C_p for the component B in equation (7.11) yields,

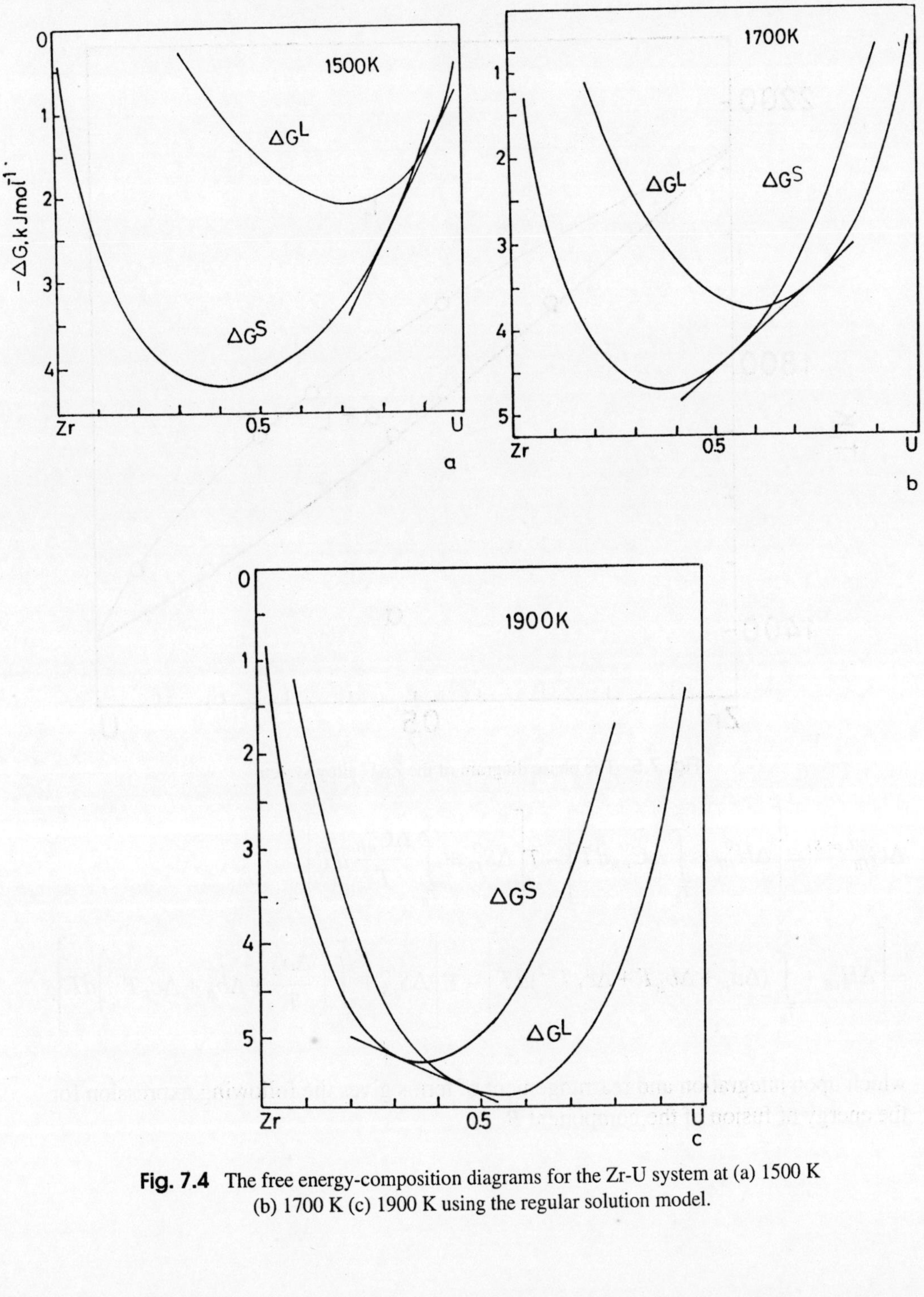

Fig. 7.4 The free energy-composition diagrams for the Zr-U system at (a) 1500 K (b) 1700 K (c) 1900 K using the regular solution model.

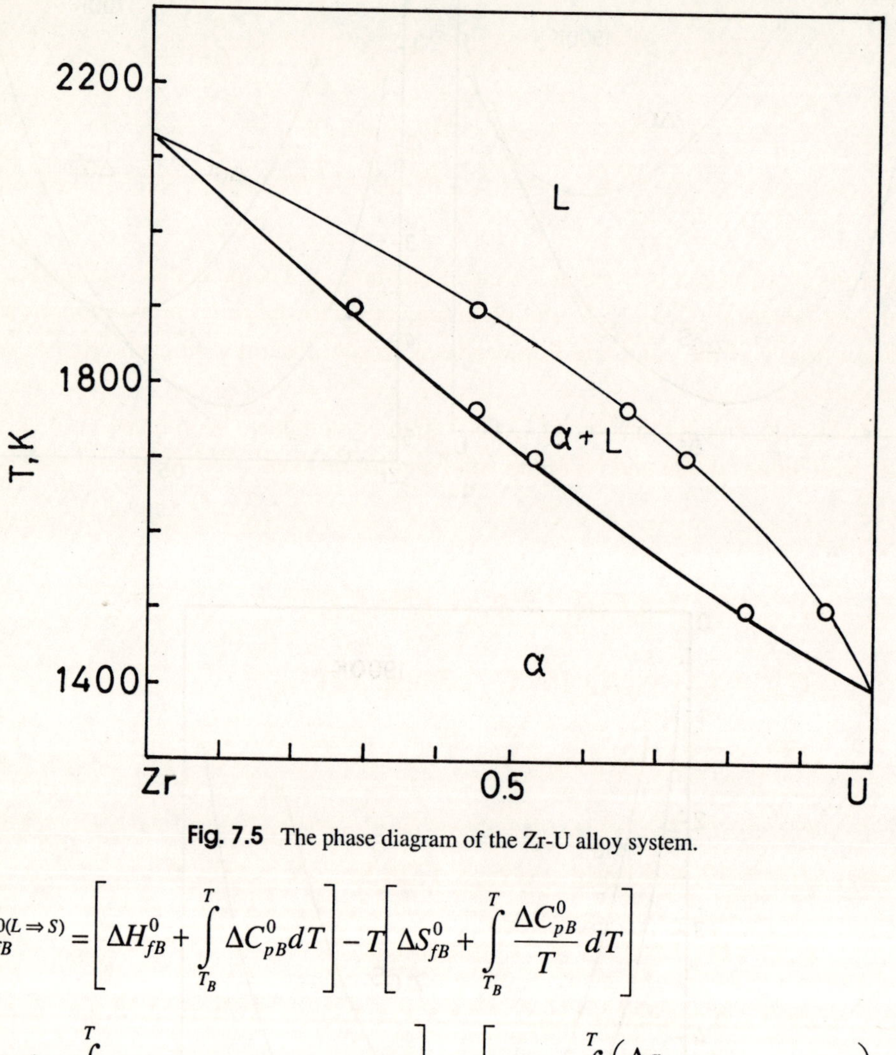

Fig. 7.5 The phase diagram of the Zr-U alloy system.

$$\Delta G_{fB}^{0(L\Rightarrow S)} = \left[\Delta H_{fB}^0 + \int_{T_B}^{T} \Delta C_{pB}^0 dT\right] - T\left[\Delta S_{fB}^0 + \int_{T_B}^{T} \frac{\Delta C_{pB}^0}{T} dT\right]$$

$$= \left[\Delta H_{fB}^0 + \int_{T_B}^{T} (\Delta a_B + \Delta b_B T + \Delta c_B T^{-2}) dT\right] - T\left[\Delta S_{fB}^0 + \int_{T_B}^{T} \left(\frac{\Delta a_B}{T} + \Delta b_B + \Delta c_B T^{-3}\right) dT\right],$$

which upon integration and rearrangement of terms gives the following expression for the energy of fusion of the component B.

$$\frac{\Delta G_{fB}^0}{RT} = \Delta H_{fB}^0\left(\frac{1}{T}-\frac{1}{T_B}\right)+\frac{\Delta a_B}{R}\left(1-\frac{T_B}{T}+\ln\frac{T_B}{T}\right)$$

$$-\frac{\Delta b_B}{2RT}(T-T_B)^2-\frac{\Delta c_B}{2R}\left(\frac{1}{T}-\frac{1}{T_B}\right)^2. \tag{7.12}$$

A similar expression can be written for the component *A*. The procedure outlined earlier through equations (7.3), (7.5) and (7.6) may be followed to write expressions for the compositions of the solid and liquid phases in equilibrium with each other at the temperature *T*.

Phase diagram calculations of the Cu-Ni binary system have been carried out using specific heat values of Cu and Ni in the solid and liquid states. The following data are used (6).

For Cu: $\Delta H_{f\text{Cu}}^0 = 13.04$ kJ mol^{-1}, $T_{\text{Cu}} = 1356.5$ K

$C_{p\text{Cu}}^{0(S)} = 5.41 + 1.4\times10^{-3}\text{T}$ cal/deg. mol

$C_{p\text{Cu}}^{0(L)} = 7.5$ cal/deg. mol

For Ni: $\Delta H_{f\text{Ni}}^0 = 17.47$ kJ mol^{-1}, $T_{\text{Ni}} = 1726$ K

$C_{p\text{Ni}}^{0(S)} = 6 + 1.8\times10^{-3}\text{T}$ cal/deg. mol

$C_{p\text{Ni}}^{0(L)} = 9.2$ cal/deg. mol

The calculated free energy-composition diagrams at 1670 K, 1610 K, 1550 K, 1490 K, 1430 K and 1370 K are shown in Fig. 7.6. The phase diagram of the Cu-Ni alloy system calculated using the above data is shown in Fig. 7.7. The phase diagram compares reasonably well with that published for the Cu-Ni alloy system (7).

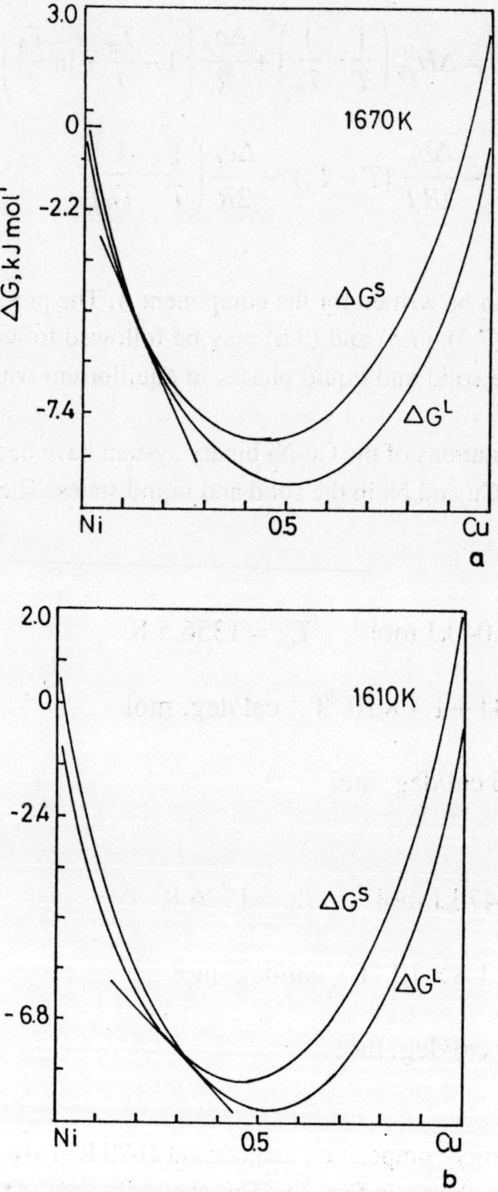

Fig. 7.6 Free energy-composition diagrams for the Cu-Ni binary system using specific heat data for pure copper and nickel at (a) 1670 K (b) 1610 K. (Contd.)

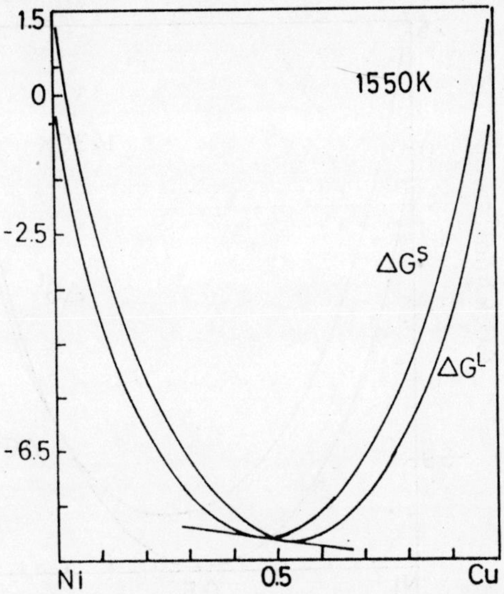

c

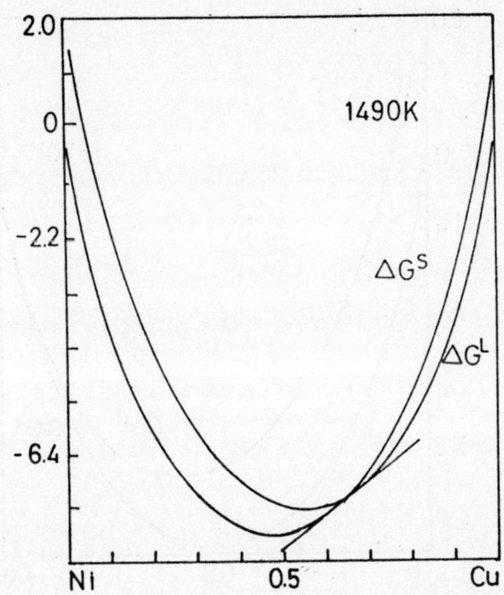

d

Fig. 7.6 Free energy-composition diagrams for the Cu-Ni binary system using specific heat data for pure copper and nickel at (c) 1550 K (d) 1490 K. (Contd.)

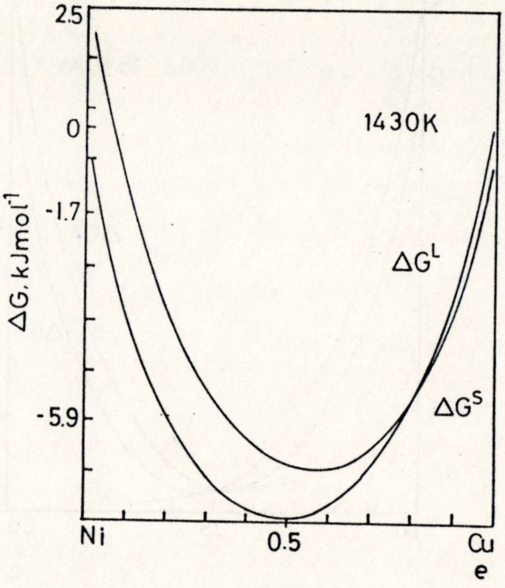

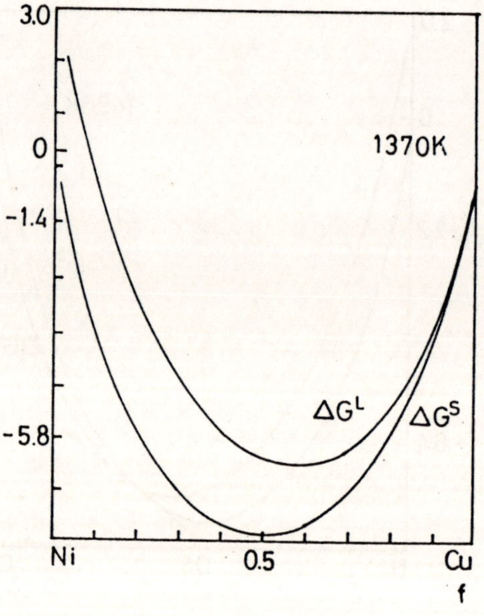

Fig. 7.6 Free energy-composition diagrams for the Cu-Ni binary system using specific heat data for pure copper and nickel at (e) 1430 K (f) 1370 K.

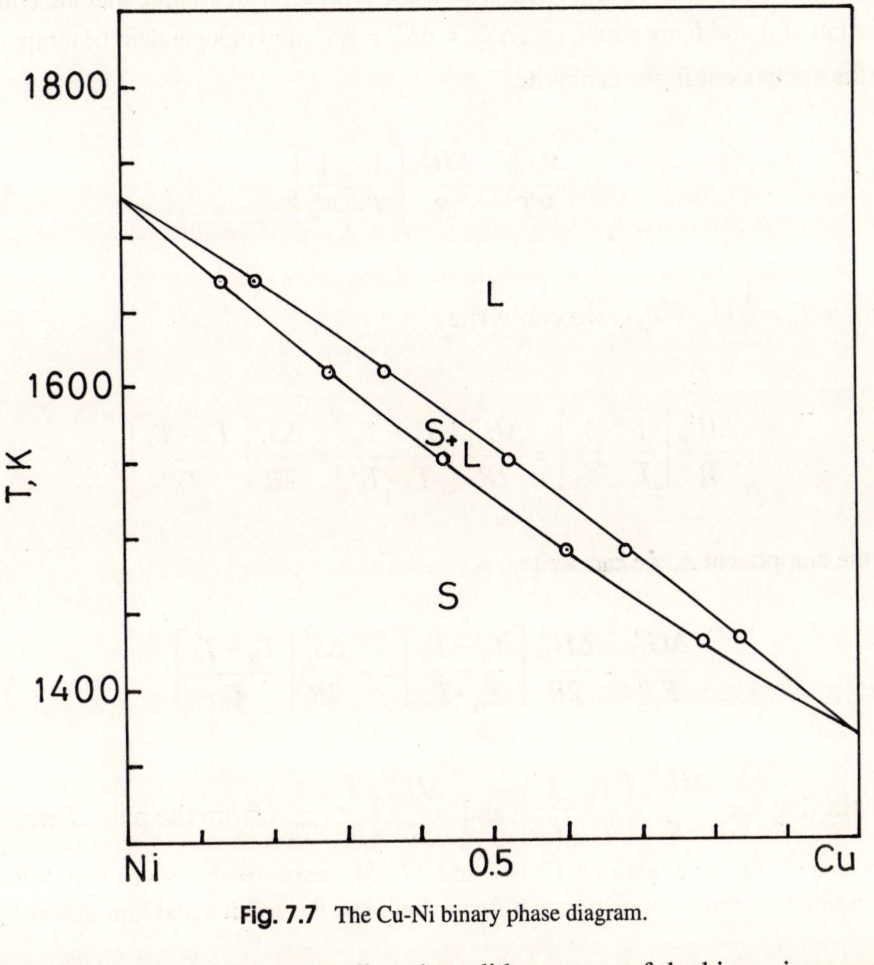

Fig. 7.7 The Cu-Ni binary phase diagram.

The shape of the liquidus as well as the solidus curves of the binary isomorphous system is determined by the enthalpies of fusion of the two components and the free energy of mixing term. The shape can be qualitatively represented in terms of the composition difference between the liquidus and solidus compositions at a given temperature.

This difference is measured in terms of the width $(X_B^L - X_B^\alpha)$ at the temperature T_0 halfway between the melting points of the two component metals, $T_0 = 1/2\ (T_A + T_B)$.

Let us consider, for simplicity, an ideal Raoultian solution for both liquid and solid that forms when the two component metals are mixed. Also, assume that the entropies of fusion of A and B are equal, i.e., $\Delta S^0_{fA} = \Delta S^0_{fB} = \Delta S^0_f$, and independent of temperature. For the component B, we can write,

$$\frac{\Delta G^0_{fB}}{RT} = \frac{\Delta H^0_{fB}}{R}\left[\frac{1}{T} - \frac{1}{T_B}\right], \tag{7.13}$$

For $T = T_0 = \frac{1}{2}(T_A + T_B)$, we can write,

$$\frac{\Delta H^0_{fB}}{R}\left[\frac{1}{T} - \frac{1}{T_B}\right] = \frac{\Delta H^0_{fB}}{2R}\left[\frac{T_B - T_A}{T_B \cdot T_0}\right] = \frac{\Delta S^0_f}{2R}\left[\frac{T_B - T_A}{T_0}\right]. \tag{7.14}$$

For the component A, we can write,

$$\frac{\Delta G^0_{fA}}{RT} = \frac{\Delta H^0_{fA}}{2R}\left[\frac{T_A - T_B}{T_A \cdot T_0}\right] = -\frac{\Delta S^0_f}{2R}\left[\frac{T_B - T_A}{T_0}\right] \tag{7.15}$$

Substituting for $\frac{\Delta H_{0fB}}{R}\left(\frac{1}{T} - \frac{1}{T_B}\right)$ and $\frac{\Delta H^0_{fA}}{R}\left(\frac{1}{T} - \frac{1}{T_A}\right)$ from the pair of equations (7.7) and (7.8), in equations (7.14) and (7.15), respectively, gives the following expressions for the composition difference between the solidus and liquidus at T_0,

$$(X^S_B - X^L_B) = \left[\exp\left\{\frac{\Delta S^0_f}{2R}\left(\frac{T_B - T_A}{T_0}\right)\right\} - 1\right] / \left[\exp\left\{\frac{\Delta S^0_f}{2R}\left(\frac{T_B - T_A}{T_0}\right)\right\} + 1\right]. \tag{7.16}$$

Equation (7.16) can be written in simplified form as

$$(X^L_B - X^S_B) = \frac{\Delta S^0_f}{4R}\left(\frac{T_A - T_B}{T_0}\right) \tag{7.17}$$

The above equation illustrates that the separation between the liquidus and solidus curves is directly proportional to the entropy of fusion and the difference in the melting temperature of the two components *A* and *B*. This is illustrated by utilizing the entropy of fusion data for the Ge-Si and Cu-Ni binary systems.

For the Ge-Si alloy system, the semiconducting metals Si and Ge have entropies of fusion 30 and 30.4 J mol^{-1}K^{-1}, respectively. The composition difference $\Delta X_B = (X_B^L - X_B^S)$, calculated at $\Delta S_f^0 = 30$ J mol^{-1}K^{-1} and $(T_A+T_B)/2 = 1445.7$ K, is 0.296. For the Cu-Ni alloy system, $\Delta S_f^0 = 10$ J mol^{-1}K^{-1} and $\Delta X_B = 0.072$ at $T_0 = 1541$ K. These values are in excellent agreement with the published liquidus and solidus curves of the above two alloy systems.

In order to illustrate how the shape of the phase diagram is affected by the entropy of fusion of the components under consideration, three hypothetical phase diagrams between components A and B are calculated. The following data are used:

	T_A, K	T_B, K	ΔH_{fA}^0, kJ mol^{-1}	ΔH_{fB}^0, kJ mol^{-1}	ΔS_f^0, J mol^{-1} K^{-1}
(i)	1200	800	12	8	10
(ii)	1200	800	36	24	30
(iii)	1200	800	4	3	$\cong$ 3.5*

*value used in the calculation.

Using the ideal solution model, the free energy-composition diagrams were calculated at a number of temperatures between 800 and 1200 K, some of which are shown in Figs. 7.8, a, b, c, d, e, and f. The three phase diagrams drawn in Figs. 7.8, g, h and i illustrate the effect of entropy of fusion on the width ΔX_B. A value of $\Delta S_f^0 = 10$ J mol^{-1}K^{-1} is typical of most metals and in such cases the width of the lens-shaped region is reasonable, Fig. 7.8g. For materials with large entropies of fusion, such as metal oxides, halides etc., the entropy of fusion is large since there are several ions per compound unit. The width of the lens-shaped region is quite large in such cases, Fig. 7.8h. Similar results are expected if vapor-liquid equilibria are considered. This is because of the higher enthalpy of vaporization at the equilibrium boiling point. The enthalpy of transformation, and hence the entropy of transformation, during solid to solid transformation is usually much smaller than the enthalpy and, therefore, the entropy of fusion, of most metals. In such cases, the gap of the lens-shaped region is very narrow, as illustrated in Fig. 7.8i. The phase diagrams of Figs. 7.8, g, h and i are constructed from the corresponding free energy-composition diagrams.

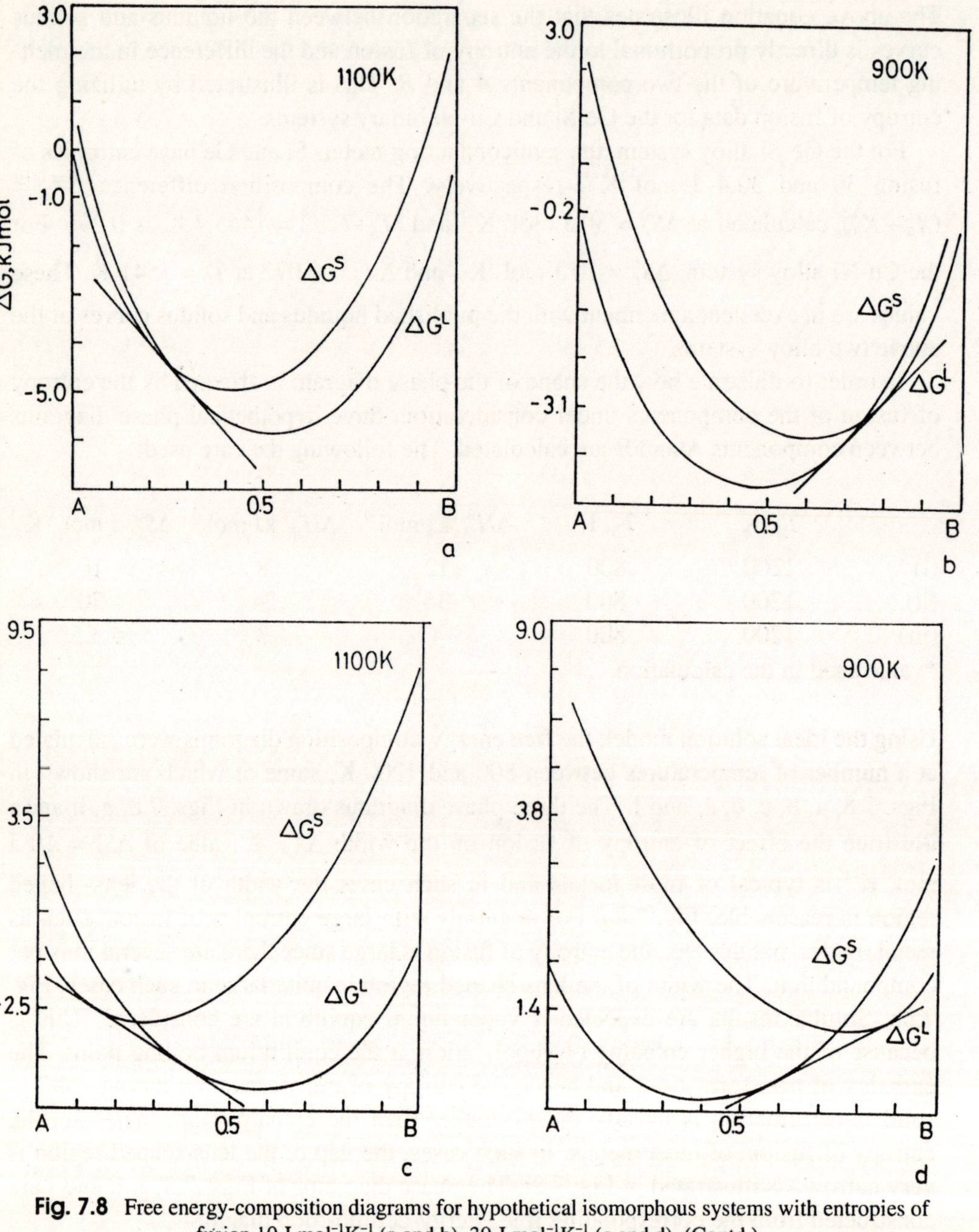

Fig. 7.8 Free energy-composition diagrams for hypothetical isomorphous systems with entropies of fusion 10 J mol^{-1}K^{-1} (a and b), 30 J mol^{-1}K^{-1} (c and d). (Contd.)

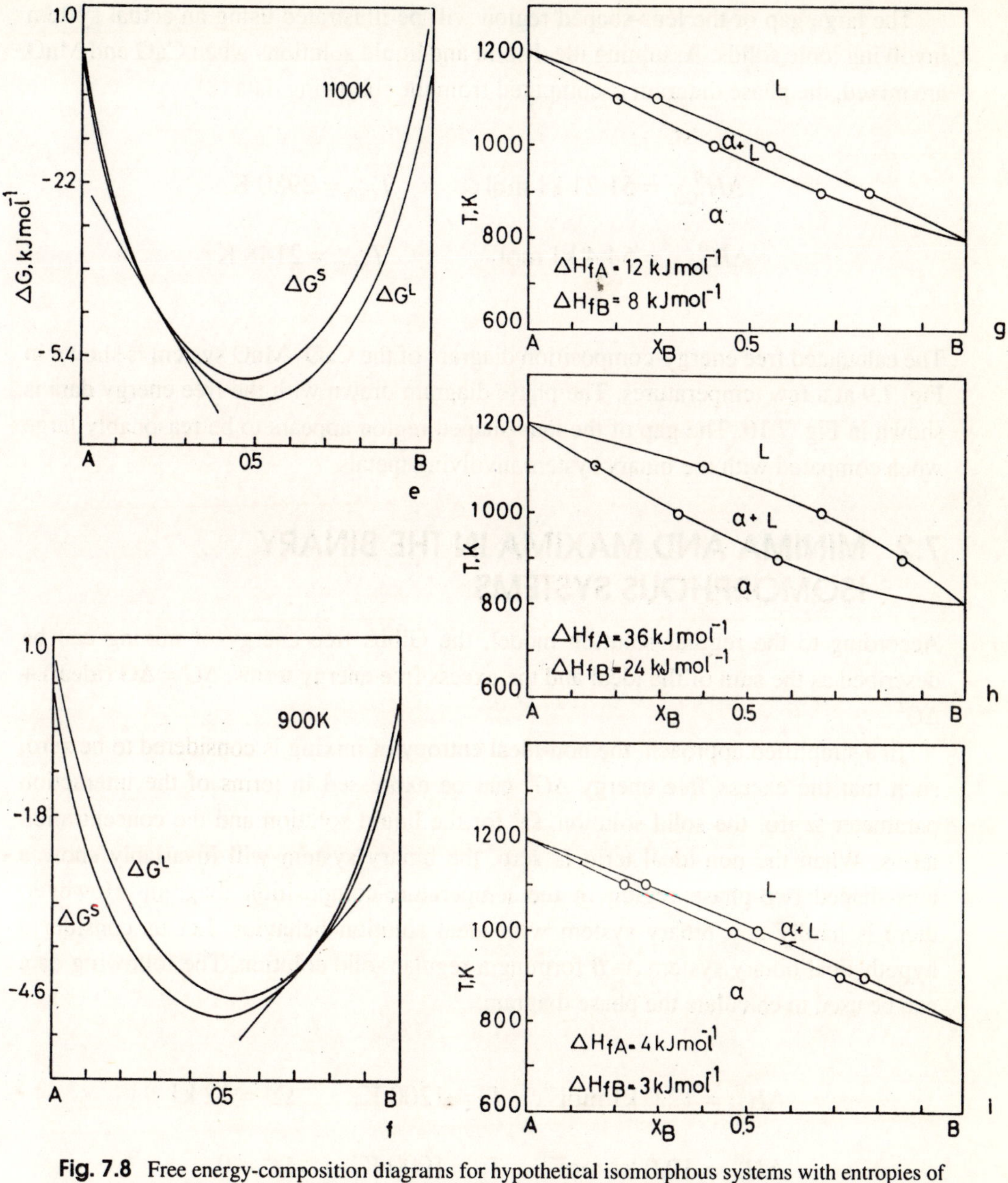

Fig. 7.8 Free energy-composition diagrams for hypothetical isomorphous systems with entropies of fusion 3.5 J mol^{-1}K^{-1} (e and f). The corresponding phase diagrams are shown in g, h and i, respectively.

The large gap of the lens-shaped region will be illustrated using an actual system involving ionic solids. Assuming ideal solid and liquid solutions when CaO and MnO are mixed, the phase diagram is computed from the following data (8),

$$\Delta H^0_{fCaO} = 51.21 \text{ kJ mol}^{-1}, \qquad T_{CaO} = 2980 \text{ K}$$

$$\Delta H^0_{fMnO} = 54.4 \text{ kJ mol}^{-1}, \qquad T_{MnO} = 2148 \text{ K}$$

The calculated free energy-composition diagram of the CaO–MnO system is shown in Fig. 7.9 at a few temperatures. The phase diagram drawn with the free energy data is shown in Fig. 7.10. The gap of the lens-shaped region appears to be reasonably large when compared with the binary system involving metals.

7.2 MINIMA AND MAXIMA IN THE BINARY ISOMORPHOUS SYSTEMS

According to the regular solution model, the Gibbs free energy of mixing can be described as the sum of the ideal and the excess free energy terms, $\Delta G = \Delta G \text{ (ideal)} + \Delta G^E$.

In a simplified approach, the non-ideal entropy of mixing is considered to be zero, such that the excess free energy ΔG^E can be expressed in terms of the interaction parameter Ω^S for the solid solution, Ω^L for the liquid solution and the concentration terms. When the non-ideal term is zero, the binary system will invariably show a lens-shaped two-phase region in the temperature-composition diagram. However, there is hardly any binary system with ideal solution behavior. Let us consider a hypothetical binary system A–B forming a regular solid solution. The following data can be used to calculate the phase diagram:

$$\Delta H^0_{fA} = 12.0 \text{ kJ mol}^{-1}, \quad T_A = 1200 \text{ K}, \qquad \Omega^S = 12 \text{ kJ}$$

$$\Delta H^0_{fB} = 10.0 \text{ kJ mol}^{-1}, \quad T_B = 1000 \text{ K}, \qquad \Omega^L = 0$$

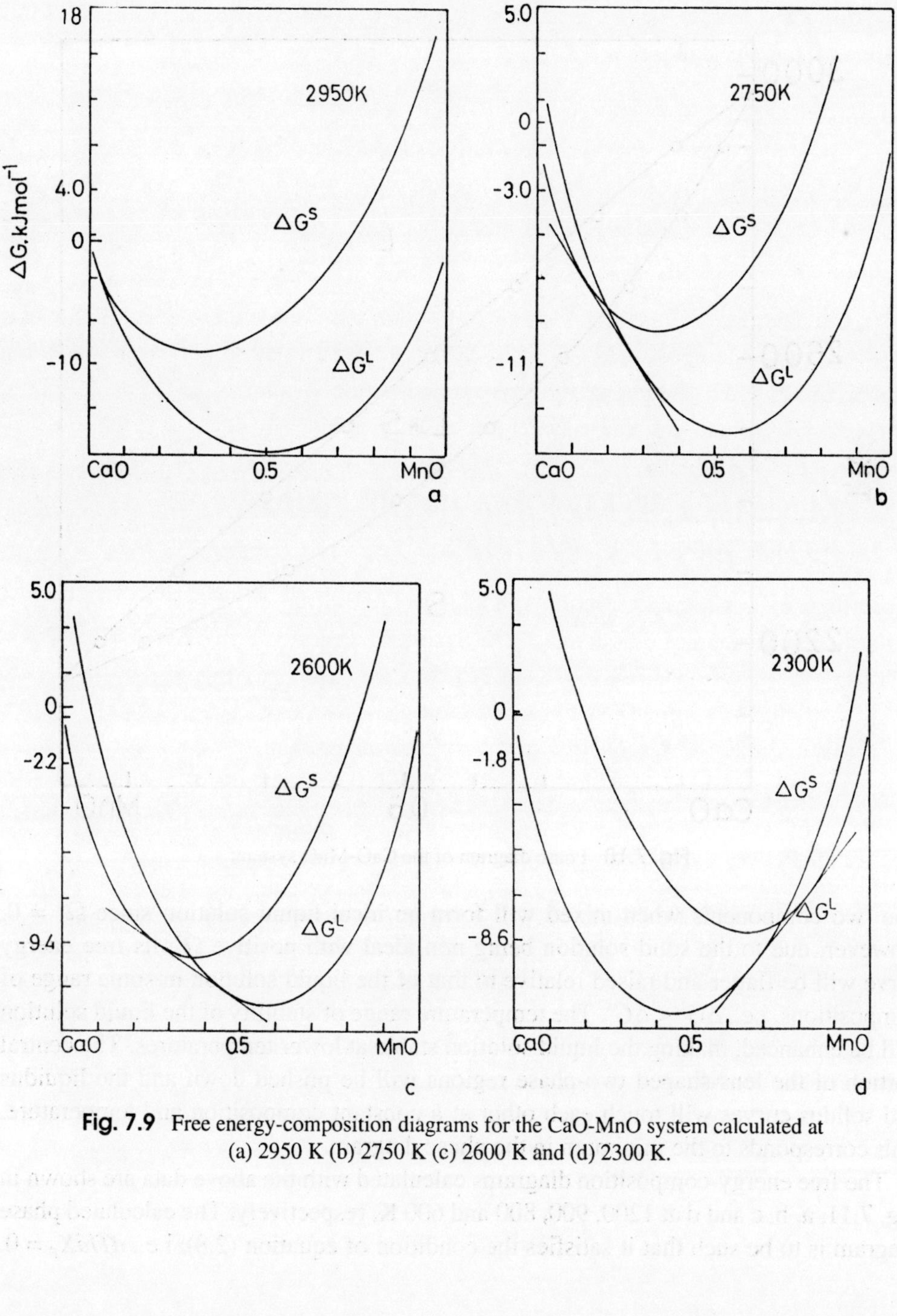

Fig. 7.9 Free energy-composition diagrams for the CaO-MnO system calculated at (a) 2950 K (b) 2750 K (c) 2600 K and (d) 2300 K.

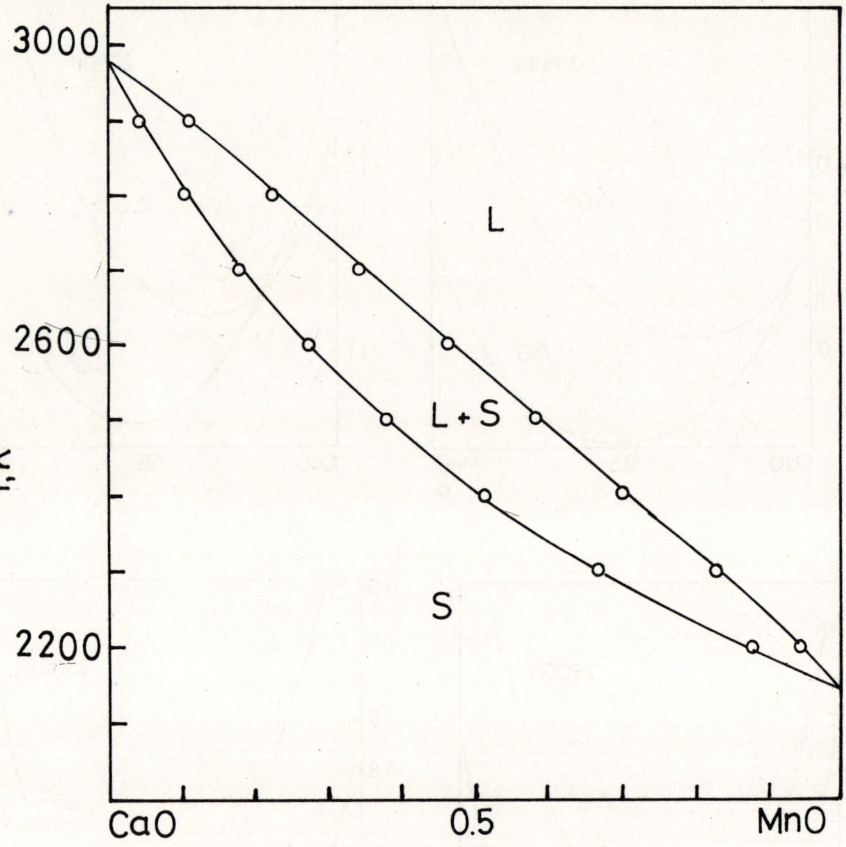

Fig. 7.10 Phase diagram of the CaO-MnO system.

The two components when mixed will form an ideal liquid solution since $\Omega^L = 0$. However, due to the solid solution being non-ideal with positive Ω^S, its free energy curve will be flatter and raised relative to that of the liquid solution in some range of compositions, i.e., $\Delta G^L < \Delta G^S$. The temperature range of stability of the liquid solution will be enhanced, making the liquid solution stable at lower temperatures. The central portion of the lens-shaped two-phase regions will be pushed down and the liquidus and solidus curves will touch each other at a constant composition and temperature. This corresponds to the minimum in the phase diagram.

The free energy-composition diagrams calculated with the above data are shown in Fig. 7.11, a, b, c and d at 1200, 900, 800 and 600 K, respectively. The calculated phase diagram is to be such that it satisfies the condition of equation (2.8), i.e., $dT/dX_B = 0$.

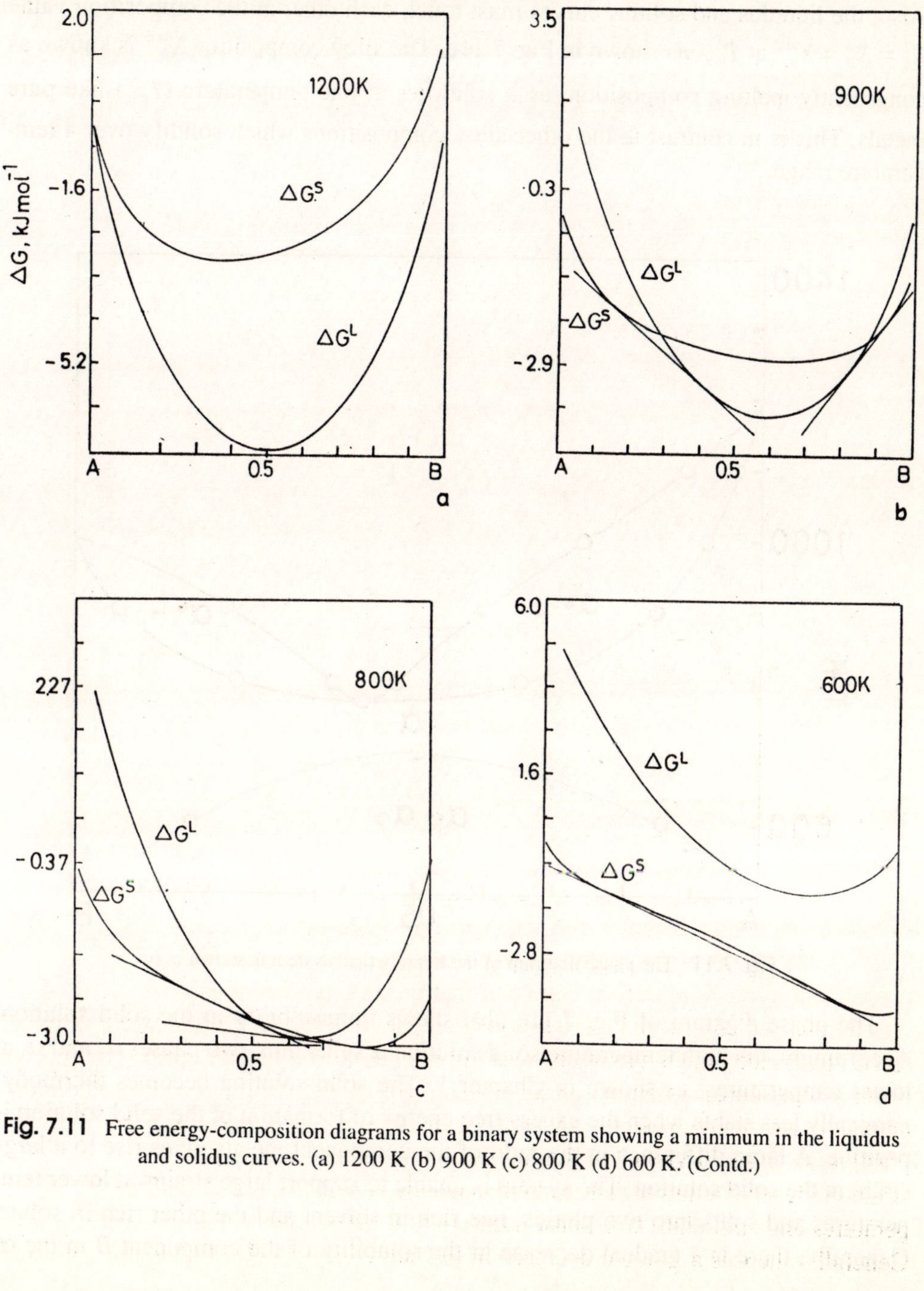

Fig. 7.11 Free energy-composition diagrams for a binary system showing a minimum in the liquidus and solidus curves. (a) 1200 K (b) 900 K (c) 800 K (d) 600 K. (Contd.)

Also, the liquidus and solidus curves must touch each other at the composition value $X_B^L = X_B^S = X_B^{min}$ at T_{min}, as shown in Fig. 7.11e. The alloy composition X_B^{min} is known as congruently melting composition, as it solidifies at one temperature (T_{min}) like pure metals. This is in contrast to the other alloy compositions which solidify over a temperature range.

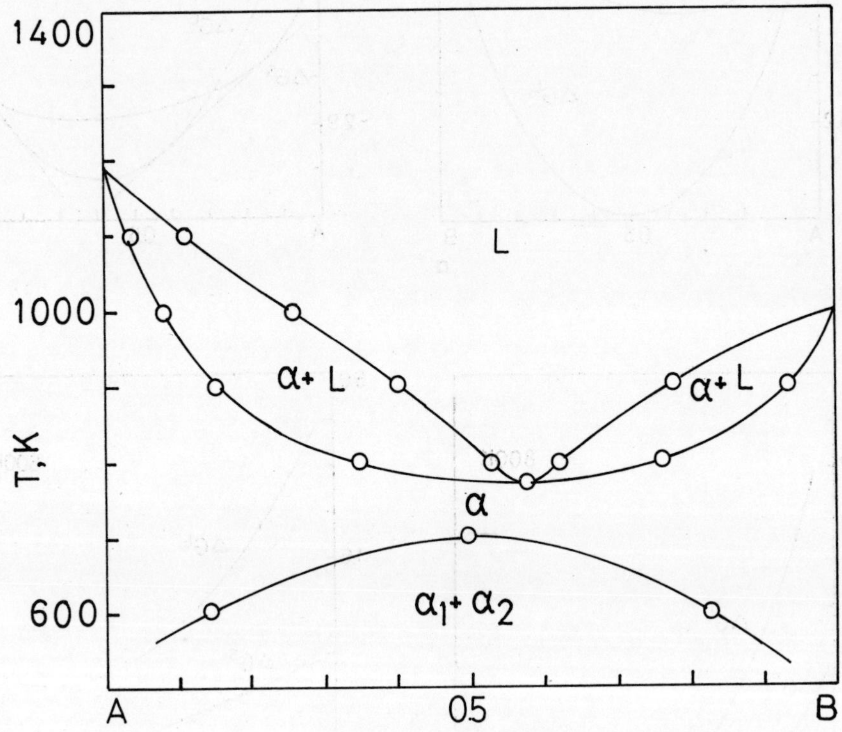

Fig. 7.11 The phase diagram of the hypothetical system is shown in (e).

The phase diagram of Fig. 7.11e also shows immiscibility in the solid solution. Accordingly, the high temperature solid solution α splits into two phases α_1 and α_2 at lower temperatures, as shown in Chapter 1. The solid solution becomes thermodynamically less stable when the excess free energy of formation of the solid solution is positive. A large difference in the radii of the component metals gives rise to a large strain in the solid solution. The system is unable to support large strains at lower temperatures and splits into two phases; one rich in solvent and the other rich in solute. Generally, there is a gradual decrease in the solubility of the component B in the α_1

phase and the component A is the α_2 phase. The structure of the liquid has the flexibility to accommodate strain energy arising from differences in the atomic radii of the two component metals.

This is demonstrated from the calculated phase diagram of the Au-Ni system. The following data are used (9).

$$\Delta H^0_{f\text{Au}} = 12.534 \text{ kJ mol}^{-1}, \quad T_{\text{Au}} = 1336 \text{ K}$$

Crystal structure: Au = *fcc*, Ni = *fcc*

$$\Delta H^0_{f\text{Ni}} = 17.618 \text{ kJ mol}^{-1}, \quad T_{\text{Ni}} = 1726 \text{ K},$$

$$\Delta C^{0(S \Rightarrow L)}_{p\text{Au}} = (5.607 - 5.1894 \times 10^{-3}\text{T}) \text{ J mol}^{-1}\text{K}^{-1}$$

$$\Delta C^{0(S \Rightarrow L)}_{p\text{Ni}} = (13.392 - 7.533 \times 10^{-3}\text{T}) \text{ J mol}^{-1}\text{K}^{-1}$$

$$\Delta G^{E(S)} = X_{\text{Au}}X_{\text{Ni}}(24147X_{\text{Au}} + 38293X_{\text{Ni}} - 14229X_{\text{Au}}X_{\text{Ni}})\left(1 - \frac{T}{2600}\right)$$

$$\Delta G^{E(L)} = X_{\text{Au}}X_{\text{Ni}}(4310.55\, X_{\text{Au}} + 1862\, X_{\text{Ni}})$$

The calculation of the free energy of the solid and liquid solutions has been carried out with both liquid A and liquid B as standard states. The expressions for the free energy of the solid as well as liquid solutions are modified as follows,

$$\Delta G^L = RT\,(X_{\text{Au}} \ln X_{\text{Au}} + X_{\text{Ni}} \ln X_{\text{Ni}}) + \Delta G^{E(L)}$$

$$\Delta G^S = RT\,(X_{\text{Au}} \ln X_{\text{Au}} + X_{\text{Ni}} \ln X_{\text{Ni}}) + X_A \Delta G^0_{fA} + X_B \Delta G^0_{fB} + \Delta G^{E(S)}$$

The free energy of fusion of the component B, ΔG^0_{fB}, can be calculated using equation (7.12) and from a similar expression for the component A. The free energy-composition diagrams at a few temperatures are shown in Fig. 7.12. Observation of the two terms of the free energy of non-ideal solutions indicates that as $X_{\text{Au}} \Rightarrow 1$ and

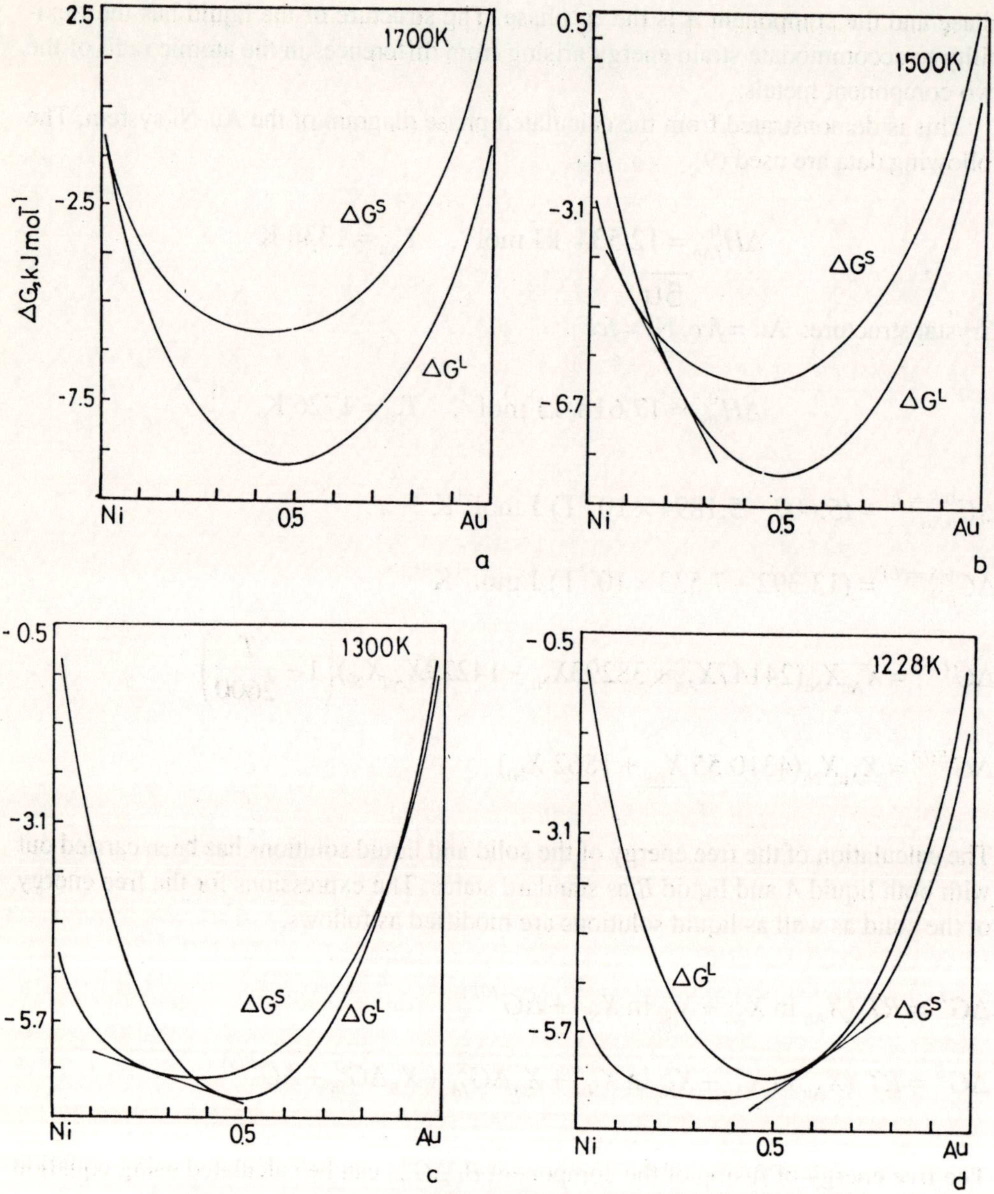

Fig. 7.12 Free energy-composition diagram of the Au-Ni binary system at (a) 1700 K (b) 1500 K (c) 1300 K (d) 1228 K. (Contd.)

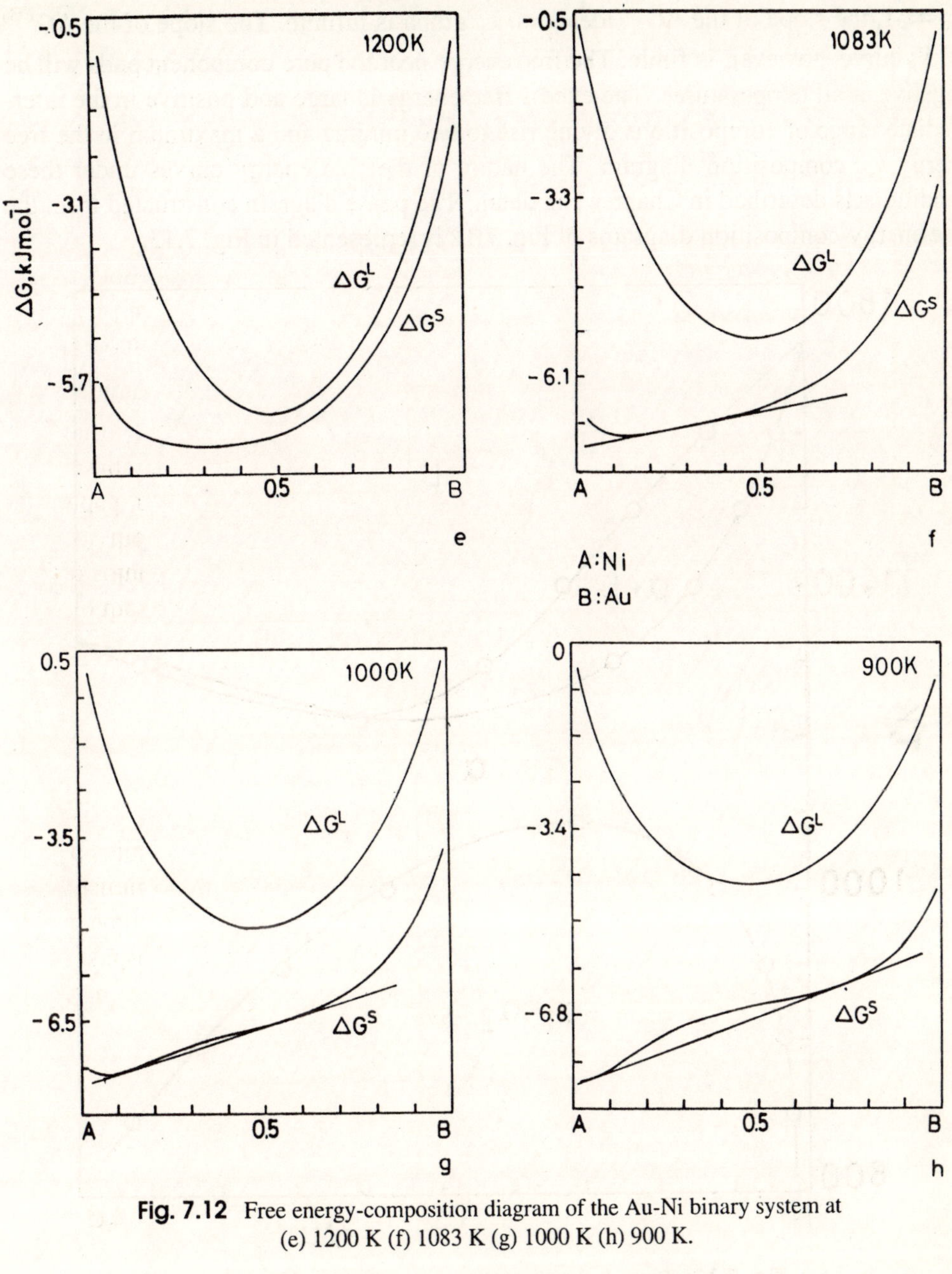

Fig. 7.12 Free energy-composition diagram of the Au-Ni binary system at (e) 1200 K (f) 1083 K (g) 1000 K (h) 900 K.

$X_{Ni} \Rightarrow 1$, the slope of the ΔG_m (ideal) vs. X_B graph is infinite. The slope of the $\Delta G^{E(S)}$ vs. X_B curve, however, is finite. The free energy near the pure component ends will be negative at all temperatures. The excess free energy is large and positive in the intermediate range of compositions giving rise to two minima and a maximum in the free energy vs. composition diagram. The nature of the free energy curves under these conditions is described in Chapter 1 in detail. The phase diagram constructed from the free energy-composition diagrams of Fig. 7.12 is represented in Fig. 7.13.

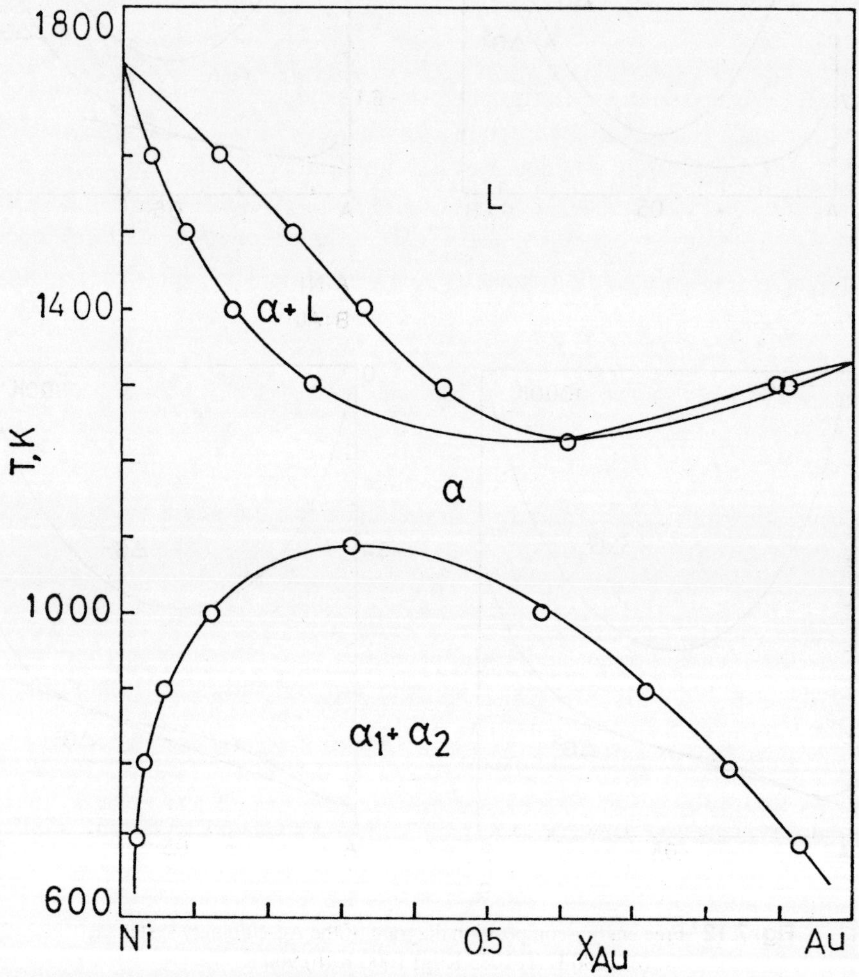

Fig. 7.13 The calculated phase diagram of the Au-Ni system.

It is also possible to have a maximum in the liquidus and solidus curves when the liquid solution is more non-ideal relative to the solid solution. For simplicity, this will be illustrated with the following data for a hypothetical system A–B forming non-ideal liquid solution and ideal solid solution.

$$\Delta H_{fA}^{0} = 12.0 \text{ kJ mol}^{-1}, \quad T_A = 1200 \text{ K}, \quad \Omega^L = 14 \text{ kJ}$$

$$\Delta G_{fB}^{0} = 10.0 \text{ kJ mol}^{-1}, \quad T_B = 1000 \text{ K}, \quad \Omega^S = 0$$

Due to the positive non-ideal enthalpy of mixing of the two components in forming a liquid solution, the free energy of mixing curve for the liquid will be raised relative to that of the solid. The temperature range of stability of the solid solution will be extended, making the solid solution exist at higher temperatures. This manifests itself in the liquidus and solidus lines being raised as compared to the smooth lens-shaped region of the binary isomorphous system. The liquidus and solidus lines meet at a temperature $T_{\max}$ at composition value $X_B^{\max}$, which is the composition of an alloy that melts congruently. The calculated free energy-composition diagrams are shown in Fig. 7.14 at a few temperatures, using the above thermodynamic data. The phase diagram shown in Fig. 7.14 satisfies the condition $dT/dX_B = 0$.

7.3 BINARY EUTECTIC SYSTEMS

It has been shown in the previous section that there is a minimum in the liquidus and solidus curves of the binary isomorphous system when the enthalpy of mixing of the solid solution is sufficiently positive. However, there is a critical temperature T_{cr} below which a homogeneous solid solution dissociates into two phases α_1 and α_2, shown in the phase diagram as the immiscibility gap. Formation of A–A and B–B bonds over A–B bonds is preferred. The solid solution shows clustering of A and B type atoms in neighboring regions. The positive non-ideal enthalpy of mixing due to positive values of Ω^S makes the excess free energy of the solid solution positive as was observed for the Au–Ni alloy system.

If the Ω^S is further increased, a stage will reach when the critical temperature exceeds the temperature minimum in the liquidus and solidus curves, $T_{\min}$. The phase diagram will gradually change from the lens-shaped isomorphous system to a eutectic with increasing Ω^S, as shown in the series of drawings in Fig. 7.15. If it is assumed that one of the components, say A, has negligible solubility for the component B in the solid state, then it is possible to derive an analytical expression for the liquidus curve.

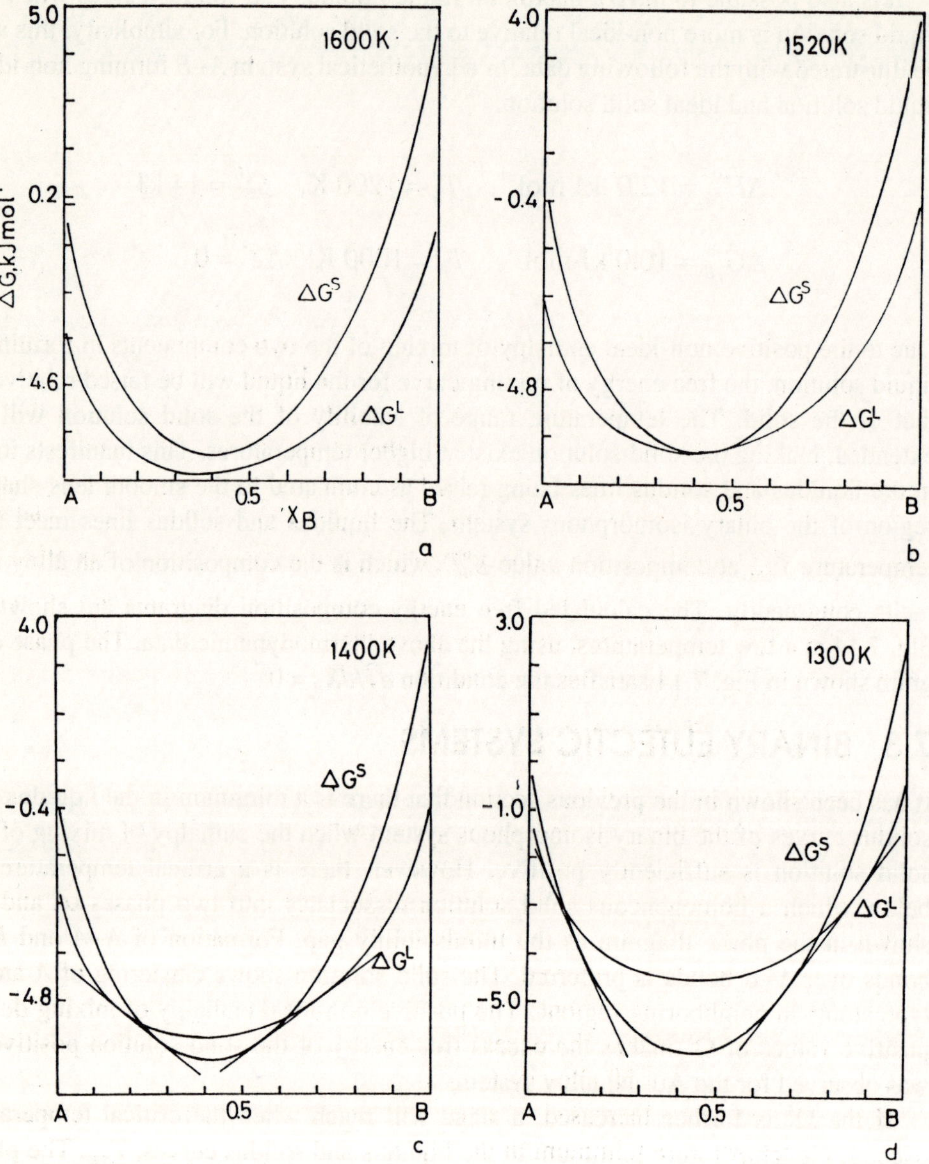

Fig. 7.14 Free energy-composition diagrams of a hypothetical binary system A–B with non-ideal enthalpy of mixing of the liquid solution at (a) 1500 K (b) 1450 K (c) 1400 K (d) 1300 K. (Contd.)

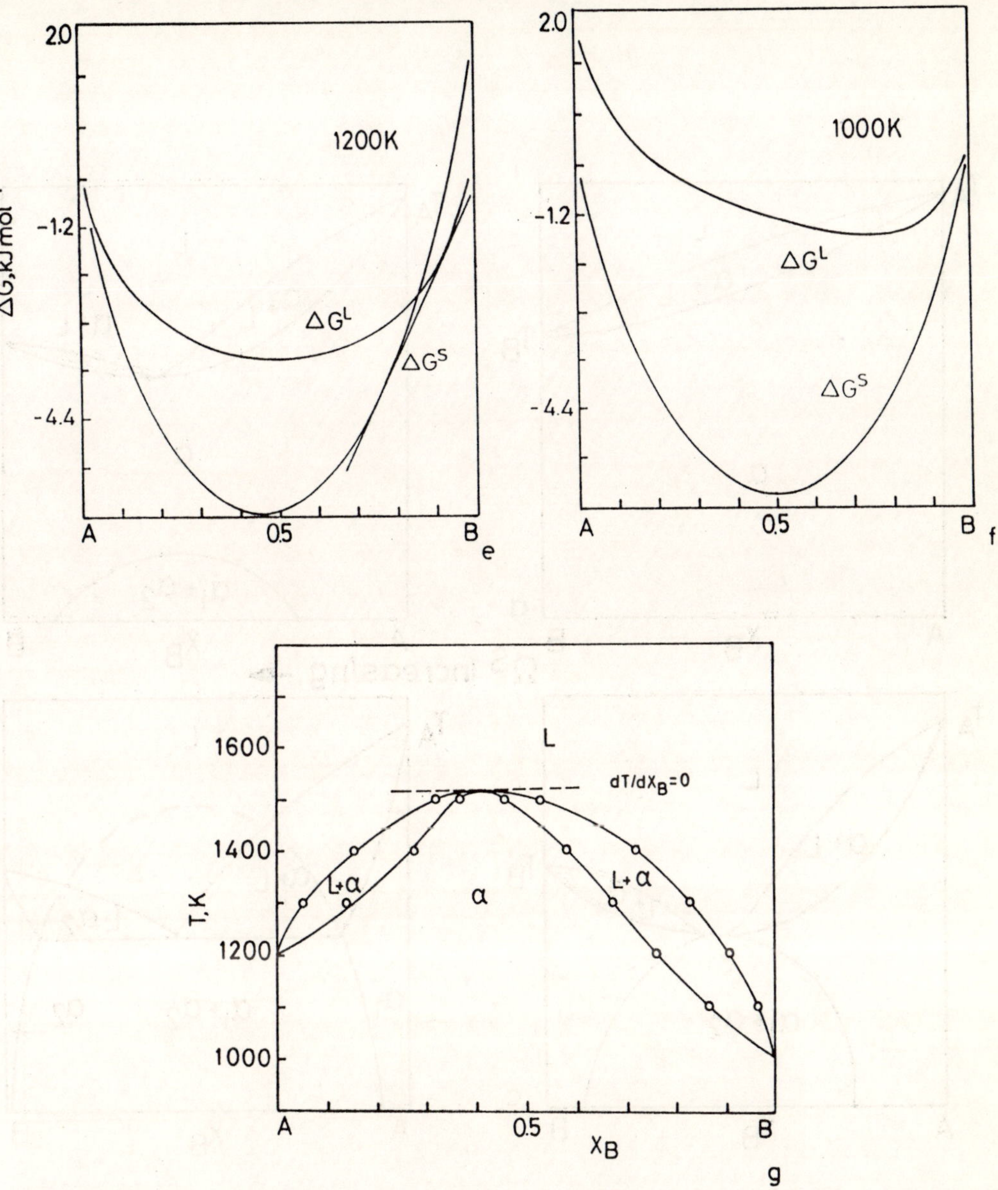

Fig. 7.14 Free energy-composition diagrams of a hypothetical binary system A–B with non-ideal enthalpy of mixing of the liquid solution at (e) 1200 K (f) 100 K. The phase diagram is shown in (g).

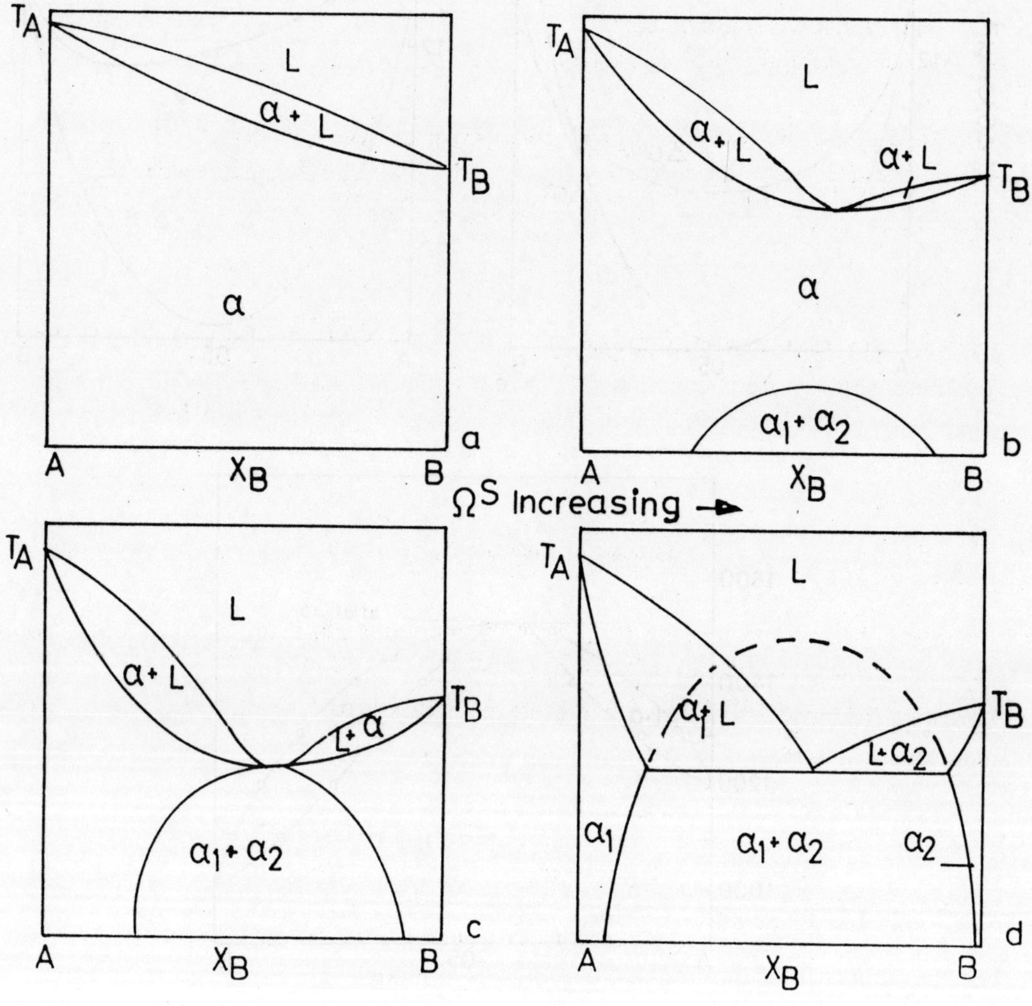

Fig. 7.15 Gradual change in the binary phase diagram A–B from the lens-shaped isomorphous system to a eutectic with increasing Ω^s.

For pure A, $a_A^S = 1$ and $a_A^L = \gamma_A^L \cdot X_A^L$. Substitution of the activities of the component A for the solid and liquid in equation (7.4) yields,

$$\ln \gamma_A^L X_A^L = -\frac{\Delta H_{fA}^0}{R}\left[\frac{1}{T}-\frac{1}{T_A}\right], \quad (7.18)$$

where γ_A^L is the activity coefficient of the component A in the liquid. The activity coefficient is related to the interaction parameter by the following expression,

$$\ln \gamma_A^L = \frac{\Omega^L}{RT}(X_B^L)^2 \quad (7.19)$$

Substituting for γ_A^L from equation (7.19) into equation (7.18) yields the following expression for the composition of the liquid phase,

$$\ln X_A^L + \frac{\Omega^L}{RT}(X_B^L)^2 = -\frac{\Delta H_{fA}^0}{R}\left(\frac{1}{T}-\frac{1}{T_A}\right) \quad (7.20)$$

If the solubility of the component A is negligible in the solid B in the α_2 or β phase, as the case may be an analytical expression for the other branch of the liquidus curve can be written, from which the composition of the liquid in equilibrium with the β or α_2 phase can then be estimated. Thus, we can write,

$$\ln X_B^L + \frac{\Omega^L}{RT}(X_A^L)^2 = -\frac{\Delta H_{fB}^0}{R}\left(\frac{1}{T}-\frac{1}{T_B}\right) \quad (7.21)$$

The two branches of the liquidus curve meet at the eutectic composition X_B^L at the temperature T_e. Equations (7.20) and (7.21) should be simultaneously satisfied at X_B^e and T_e. The following data have been used to illustrate the application of the above analytical expressions in calculating phase diagrams of the eutectic system (10).

$$\Delta H^0_{fA} = 15.0 \text{ kJ mol}^{-1}, \quad T_A = 1500 \text{ K}, \quad \Omega^L = 2100\left(1 - \frac{T}{3000}\right) \text{J}$$

$$\Delta H^0_{fB} = 11 \text{ kJ mol}^{-1}, \quad T_B = 1200 \text{ K}.$$

Solutions to the two equations (7.20) and (7.21) are simultaneously satisfied at the composition $X^e_B = 0.625$ and temperature $T_e = 859.8$ K. The phase diagram is shown in Fig. 7.16.

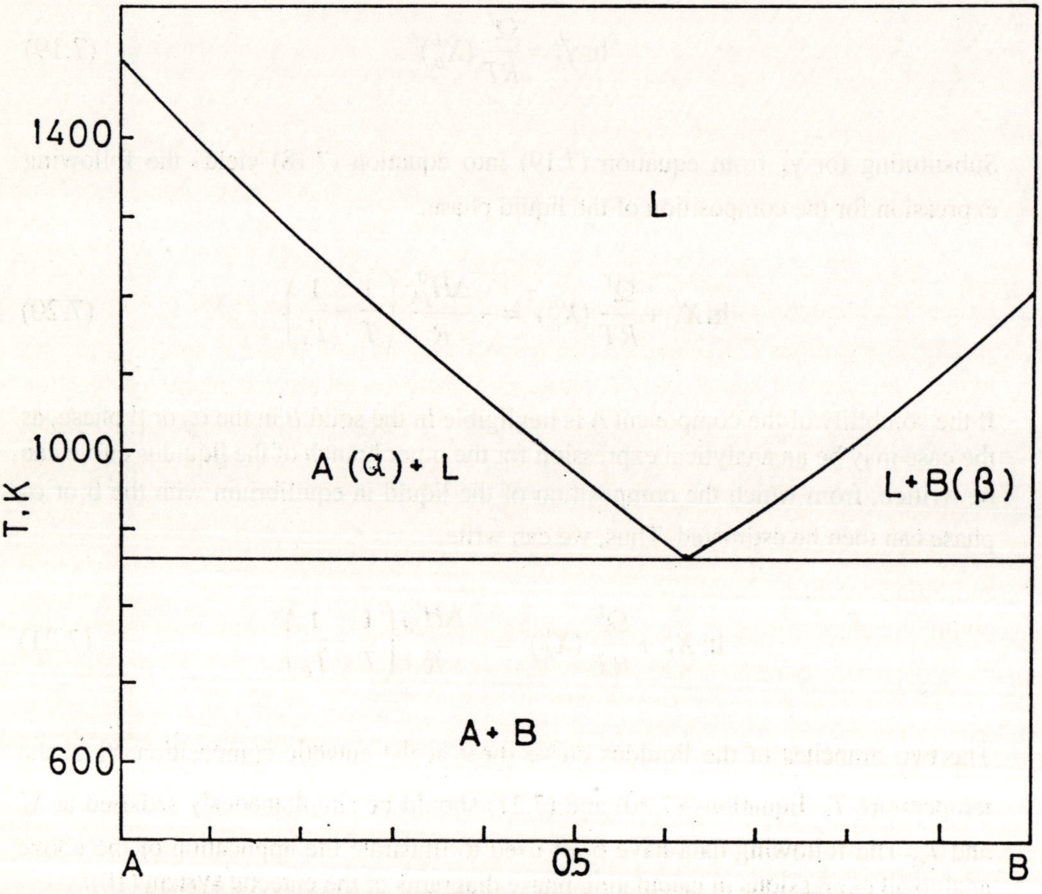

Fig. 7.16 Phase diagram of the binary system A–B calculated using the analytical expressions, equations (7.20) and (7.21).

The binary phase diagram, showing an invariant eutectic reaction, can also be calculated using regular or sub-regular solution models. According to the regular solution model, the Gibbs free energy of solution is written as a sum of an ideal term and a symmetric interaction (Ω) Gibbs free energy term due to non-ideal enthalpy of mixing. The sub-regular solution model has an additional term which skews the composition dependence of *A–B* interaction Gibbs free energy of the solid and liquid solutions. The free energies of the solid and liquid solutions are written as,

$$\Delta G_m^L = (1 - X_B^L)\Delta G_{fA}^0 + RT\,[X_A^L \ln X_A^L + X_B^L \ln X_B^L] + \Omega^L X_B^L(1 - X_B^L) + \\ + \eta^L(1 - 2X_B^L)(1 - X_B^L)X_B^L, \qquad (7.22)$$

and

$$\Delta G_m^S = -X_B^S \Delta G_{fB}^0 + RT\,[X_A^S \ln X_A^S + X_B^S \ln X_B^S] + \Omega^S X_B^S(1 - X_B^S) + \\ + \eta^S(1 - 2X_B^S)(1 - X_B^S)X_B^S, \qquad (7.23)$$

Except for the additional terms containing η^S and η^L, equations (7.22) and (7.23) are similar to equations (2.12) and (2.14), respectively. If both liquid *A* and liquid *B* are treated as standard states, as the phase equilibria involving the invariant reaction eutectic requires, then equation (7.22) will be devoid of the first term on the right-hand side with ΔG_{fA}^0. Instead, an additional term $(1 - X_B^S)\,\Delta G_{fA}^0$ will appear in the expression for the free energy of the solid solution ΔG_m^S, in equation (7.23). This is trivial as far as the results are concerned, because the free energy curves for the solid and liquid solutions are simply displaced in the same direction by the same measure, giving the composition of the solid and liquid phases (in equilibrium with each other) as obtained through the pair of equations (7.22) and (7.23).

The phase diagram showing a eutectic reaction will be calculated for binary systems when the two component metals have the same crystal structure, such as Ag–Cu and Cd–Zn. The following data obtained from optimization of the experimental data are used (11).

$$\Delta G_{f\text{Ag}}^0 = -11945 + 9.67T, \quad \text{J mol}^{-1}, \quad T_{\text{Ag}} = 1233.8\ \text{K}$$

$$\Delta G^0_{f\text{Cu}} = -13054 + 9.62T, \quad \text{J mol}^{-1}, \quad T_{\text{Cu}} = 1356.4 \text{ K}$$

$$\Omega^L = 15171 - 2.537\,T, \quad \Omega^S = 34532 - 9.178\,T$$

$$\eta^L = -2425 + 0.946\,T, \quad \eta^S = -5996 + 1.725T$$

For the Cd–Zn system

$$\Delta G^0_{f\text{Cd}} = -6110 + 10.286T, \text{ J mol}^{-1}, \quad T_{\text{Cd}} = 593.9 \text{ K}$$

$$\Delta G^0_{f\text{Zn}} = -7390 + 10.668T, \text{ J mol}^{-1}, \quad T_{\text{Zn}} = 692.5 \text{ K}$$

$$\Omega^L = 8625 - 1.235T, \quad \Omega^S = 21665 - 8.139T$$

$$\eta^L = -78 - 0.564\,T, \quad \eta^S = -7062 + 7.145T$$

The free energy-composition diagrams for the Ag-Cu alloy system, calculated at a number of temperatures using the above data, are shown in Fig. 7.17. The free energy curves for the solid solutions are flatter in a significant part of the alloy composition. The common tangent drawn between the free energy curves of the solid and liquid solutions gives the composition of the phases in equilibrium with each other. The phase diagram is drawn with the composition values thus obtained, Fig. 7.18. The following observations can be made:

(i) The critical temperature below which a single solid solution does not remain stable is raised to a temperature above the melting points of the pure components, thus suggesting that a liquid will dissociate into two solid phases at a lower temperature.

(ii) The free energy-composition diagram at 1052 K is such that the free energy curves for the liquid solution and two branches of the solid solution make a common tangent. The temperature corresponds to the eutectic reaction isotherm. The composition of the liquid in equilibrium with two solid phases can be determined at the eutectic temperature. These values are: $X_B^{\alpha_1} = 0.14$, $X_B^L = 0.4$, $X_B^{\alpha_2} = 0.95$.

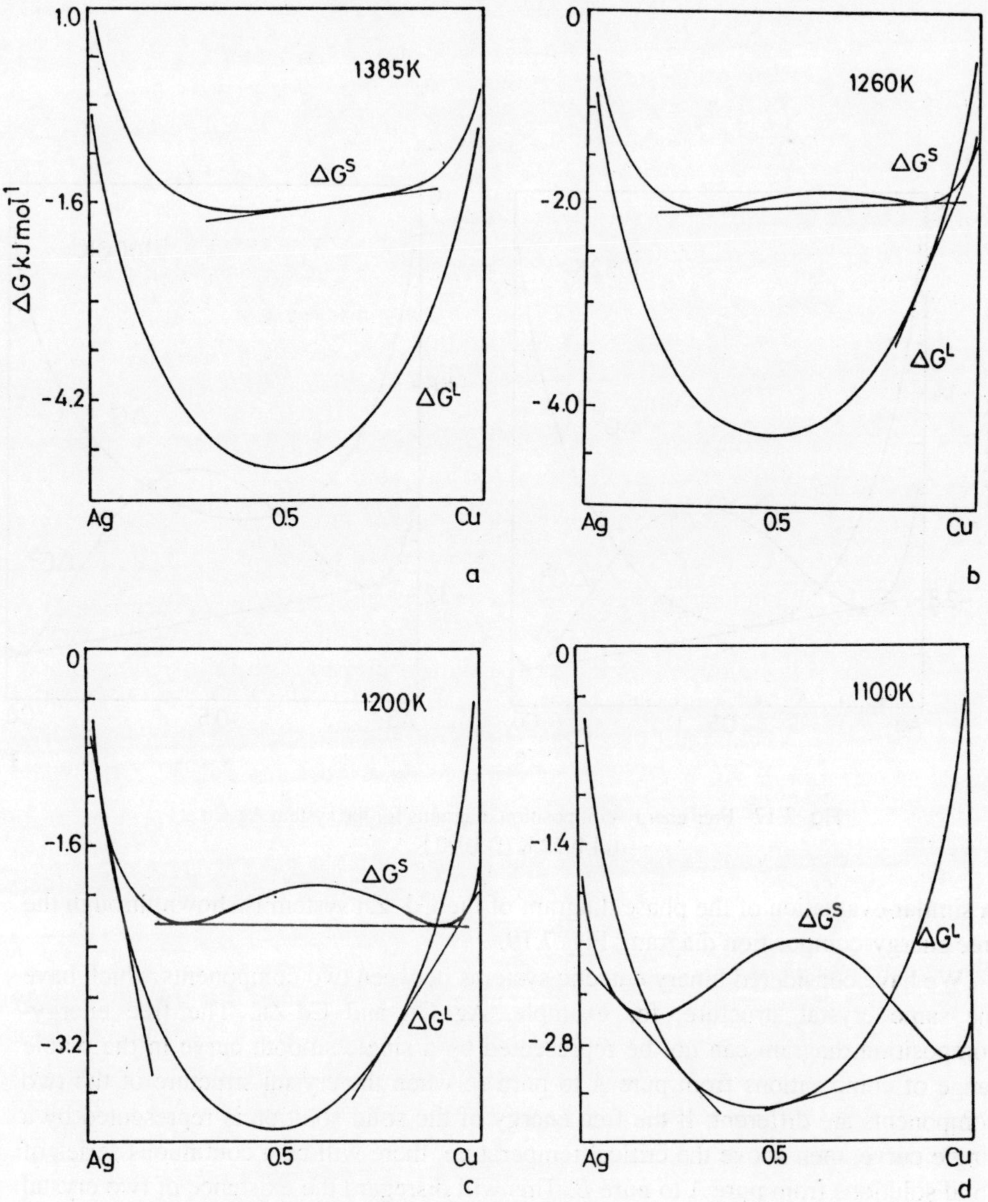

Fig. 7.17 Free energy-composition diagrams for the system Ag-Cu at (a) 1385 K (b) 1260 K (c) 1200 K (d) 1100 K. (Contd.)

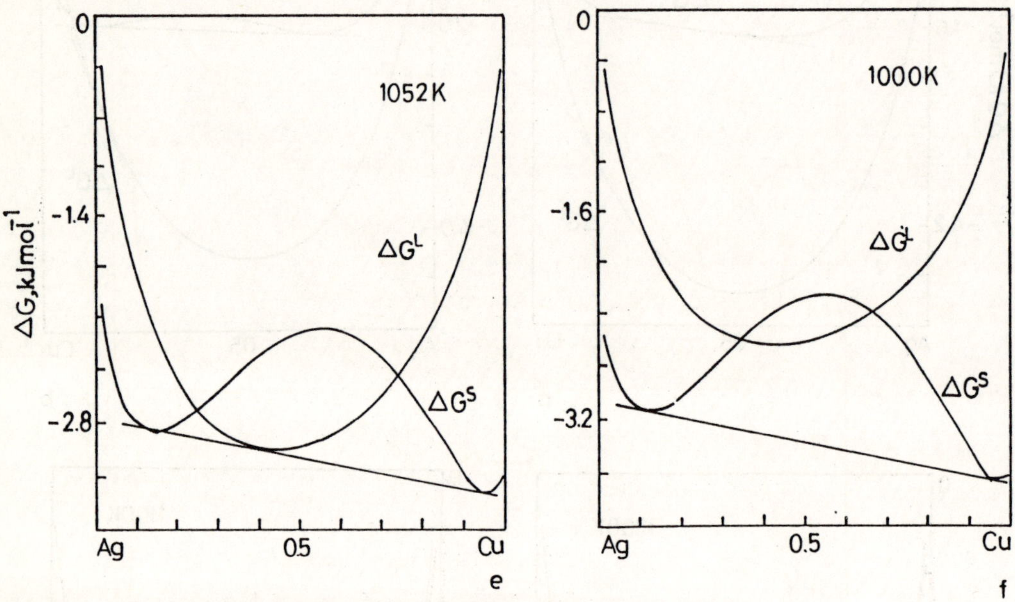

Fig. 7.17 Free energy-composition diagrams for the system Ag-Cu at (e) 1052 K (f) 1000 K.

A similar evaluation of the phase diagram of the Cd–Zn system is shown through the free energy-composition diagram, Fig. 7.19.

We have considered binary eutectic systems between two components which have the same crystal structure, for example, Ag–Cu and Cd-Zn. The free energy-composition diagram can not be represented by a single smooth curve in the whole range of compositions from pure *A* to pure *B*, when the crystal structure of the two components are different. If the free energy of the solid solution is represented by a single curve, then above the critical temperature, there will be a continuous series of solid solutions from pure *A* to pure *B*. This will disregard the existence of two crystal systems. Thus, for binary systems with different crystal structures of the components, each solid phase must be represented by a separate free energy curve. This is illustrated with the phase diagram calculations of the Pb–Sn system, where Pb and Sn crystallize in *fcc* and tetragonal structures, respectively.

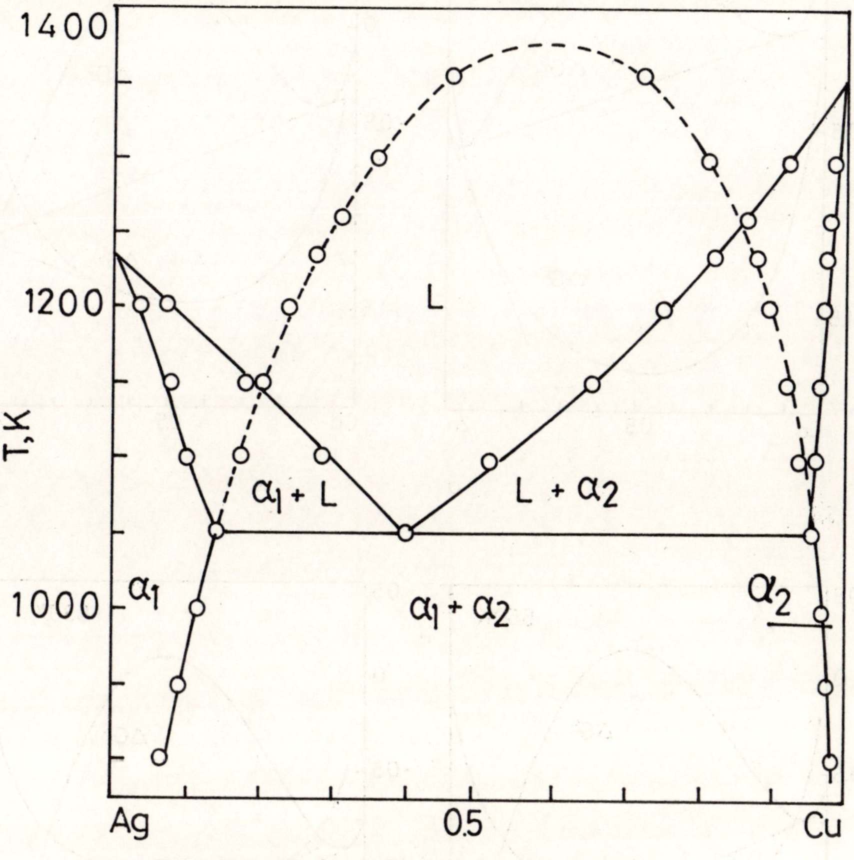

Fig. 7.18 Calculated phase diagram of the Ag-Cu system.

In a Sn-rich solid solution (β), atoms of Pb will exist in the body-centered tetragonal configuration. It requires the hypothetical transformation of *fcc* position of the Pb lattice. The corresponding free energy change (12) is,

$$\text{Sn}(bct) \Leftrightarrow \text{Sn}\,(fcc), \quad \Delta G^0 = 5510 - 9.49\text{T J mol}^{-1}.$$

Considering pure liquid Pb and pure liquid Sn as standard states, we can write the free energy of mixing of the liquid and solid solutions as

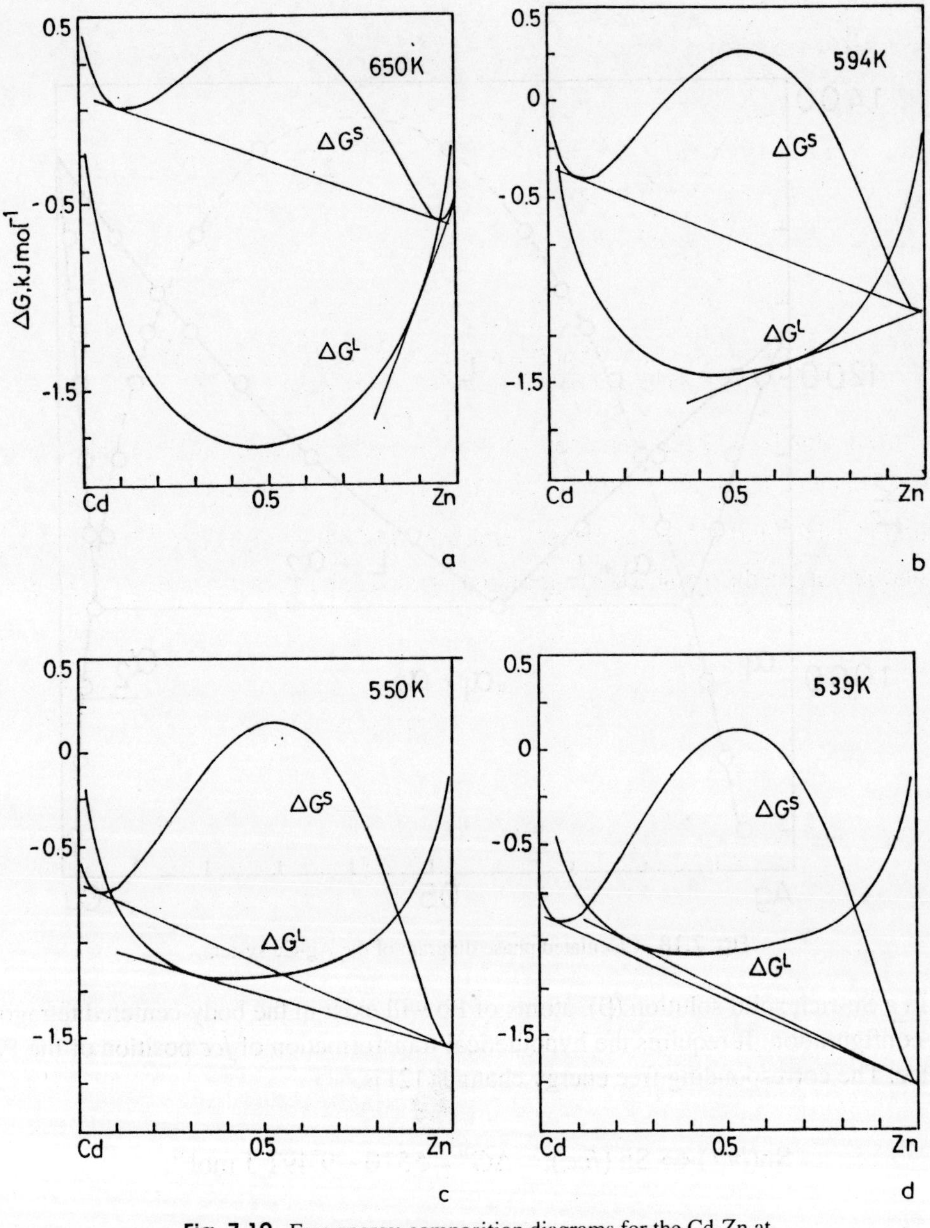

Fig. 7.19 Free energy-composition diagrams for the Cd-Zn at (a) 650 K (b) 594 K (c) 550 K (d) 539 K. (Contd.)

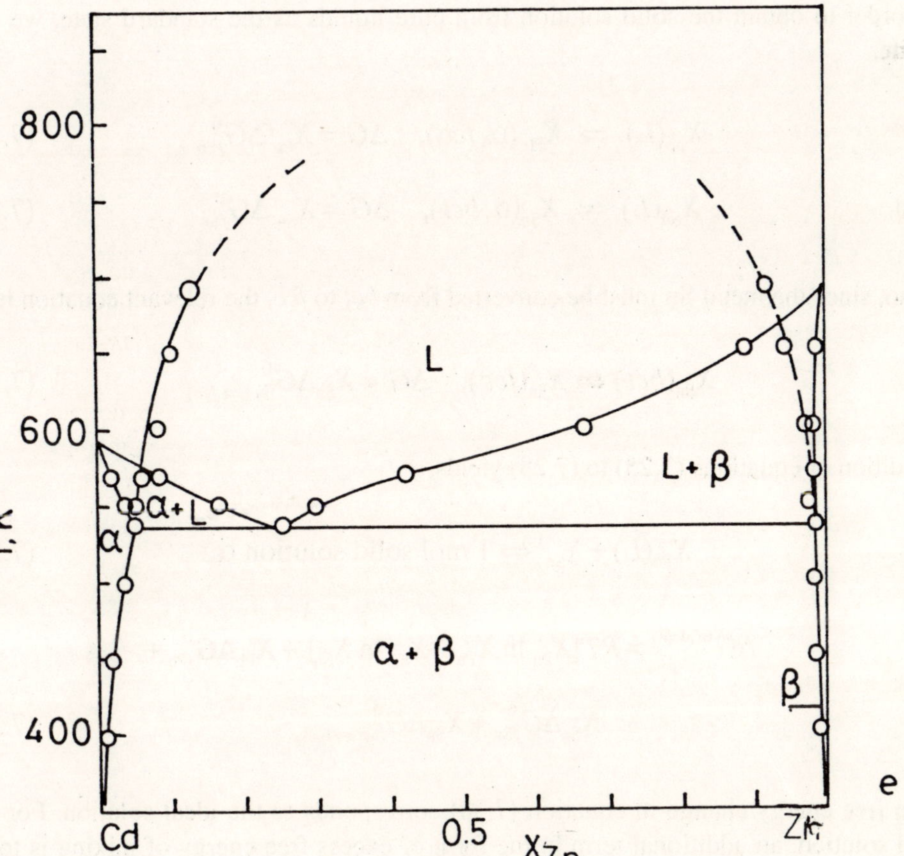

Fig. 7.19 The phase diagram is shown in (e).

$X_{Pb}(L) + X_{Sn}(L) \Leftrightarrow$ 1mol liquid solution,

$$\Delta G^{L(\text{ideal})} = RT\ [X_{Pb} \ln X_{Pb} + X_{Sn} \ln X_{Sn}] \qquad (7.24)$$

$X_{Pb}(\alpha, fcc) + X_{Sn}(\alpha, fcc) \Leftrightarrow$ 1mol solid solution α,

$$\Delta G^{\alpha(\text{ideal})} = RT\ [X_{Pb} \ln X_{Pb} + X_{Sn} \ln X_{Sn}] \qquad (7.25)$$

In order to obtain the solid solution from pure liquids as the standard state, we can write,

$$X_{pb}(L) \Leftrightarrow X_{Pb}(\alpha, fcc), \quad \Delta G = X_{Pb}\, \Delta G^0_{fPb} \qquad (7.26)$$

and

$$X_{Sn}(L) \Leftrightarrow X_{Sn}(\alpha, bct), \quad \Delta G = X_{Sn}\, \Delta G^0_{fSn} \qquad (7.27)$$

Also, since the metal Sn must be converted from *bct* to *fcc*, the relevant equation is,

$$X_{Sn}(bct) \Leftrightarrow X_{Sn}(fcc), \quad \Delta G = X_{Sn} \Delta G^0_{(bct \Rightarrow fcc)} \qquad (7.28)$$

Addition of equations (7.25) to (7.28) yields,

$$X_{Pb}(L) + X_{Sn}^{(L)} \Leftrightarrow 1 \text{ mol solid solution } \alpha. \qquad (7.29)$$

$$\Delta G^{\alpha(\text{ideal})} = RT[X_{Pb} \ln X_{Pb} + X_{Sn} \ln X_{Sn}] + X_{Pb}\Delta G^0_{fPb} + X_{Sn}\Delta G^0_{fSn} + X_{Sn}\Delta G^0_{(\text{bct} \Rightarrow \text{fcc})} \qquad (7.30)$$

The free energy change in equation (7.30) corresponds to the ideal solution. For the real solution, an additional term in the form of excess free energy of mixing is to be added on the right-hand side of equation (7.30). The free energy of the α solid solution is represented by the complete expression of equation (7.31).

$$\Delta G^{0} = RT[X_{Pb}\ln X_{Pb} + X_{Sn}\ln X_{Sn}] + X_{Pb}\Delta G^{0}_{fPb} + X_{Sn}\Delta G^{0}_{fSn} + X_{Sn}\Delta G^{0}_{(fcc \Rightarrow bct)} + \Delta G^{E} \quad (7.31)$$

A similar expression can be written for the β solid solution.

$$\Delta G^{\beta} = RT[X_{Pb}\ln X_{Pb} + X_{Sn}\ln X_{Sn}] + X_{Pb}\Delta G^{0}_{fPb} + X_{Sn}\Delta G^{0}_{fSn} + X_{Pb}\Delta G^{0}_{(fcc \Rightarrow bct)} + \Delta G^{E} \quad (7.32)$$

Using linear least square optimization, Karakaya et al (12) have calculated the free energies of fusion for the components A and B and the excess free energies of the liquid and the two solid phases. These values are,

$$\Delta G^{0}_{fPb} = -4700 + 7.99\,T$$

$$\Delta G^{0}_{fSn} = -11131.8 + 22.874\,T - 0.5975 \times 10^{-2}\,T^{2} - 0.055\,T\ln T + 644170/T$$

$$\Delta G^{E(\alpha)} = 6700\,X_{Pb}\,X_{Sn} + 0.365\,X_{Pb}\,X_{Sn}\,T$$

$$\Delta G^{E(\beta)} = -203068\,X_{Pb}\,X_{Sn},\ \text{J mol}^{-1}$$

$$\Delta G^{E(L)} = (4800 + 200\,X_{Sn})X_{Pb}X_{Sn} + T(2.815 - 1.215\,X_{Sn})\,X_{Pb}\,X_{Sn},\ \text{J mol}^{-1}.$$

The calculated free energy-composition diagrams at a number of temperatures are shown in Fig. 7.20 (a, b, c, d, e and f) and the phase diagram is determined by drawing a common tangent to the free energy curves for the solid and liquid solutions is shown in Fig. 7.20g.

Next, we will consider an eutectic system in which the two components have different crystal structures but the solubility of one of the components in the other is negligibly small. A real system showing the binary invariant reaction satisfying the above conditions is the Cd–Pb alloy system. In the Cd–Pb alloy system, the solubility of Pb in Cd in negligibly small and the solvent Cd (*hcp*) is treated as ideal with $a^{0}_{Cd} = X_{Cd}$ with $\gamma^{0}_{Cd} = 1$. A dilute solution of Cd in Pb may be treated as a Henrian solution with $a^{0}_{Cd} = \gamma^{0}_{Cd} \cdot X_{Cd}$, when the activity coefficient is independent of composition.

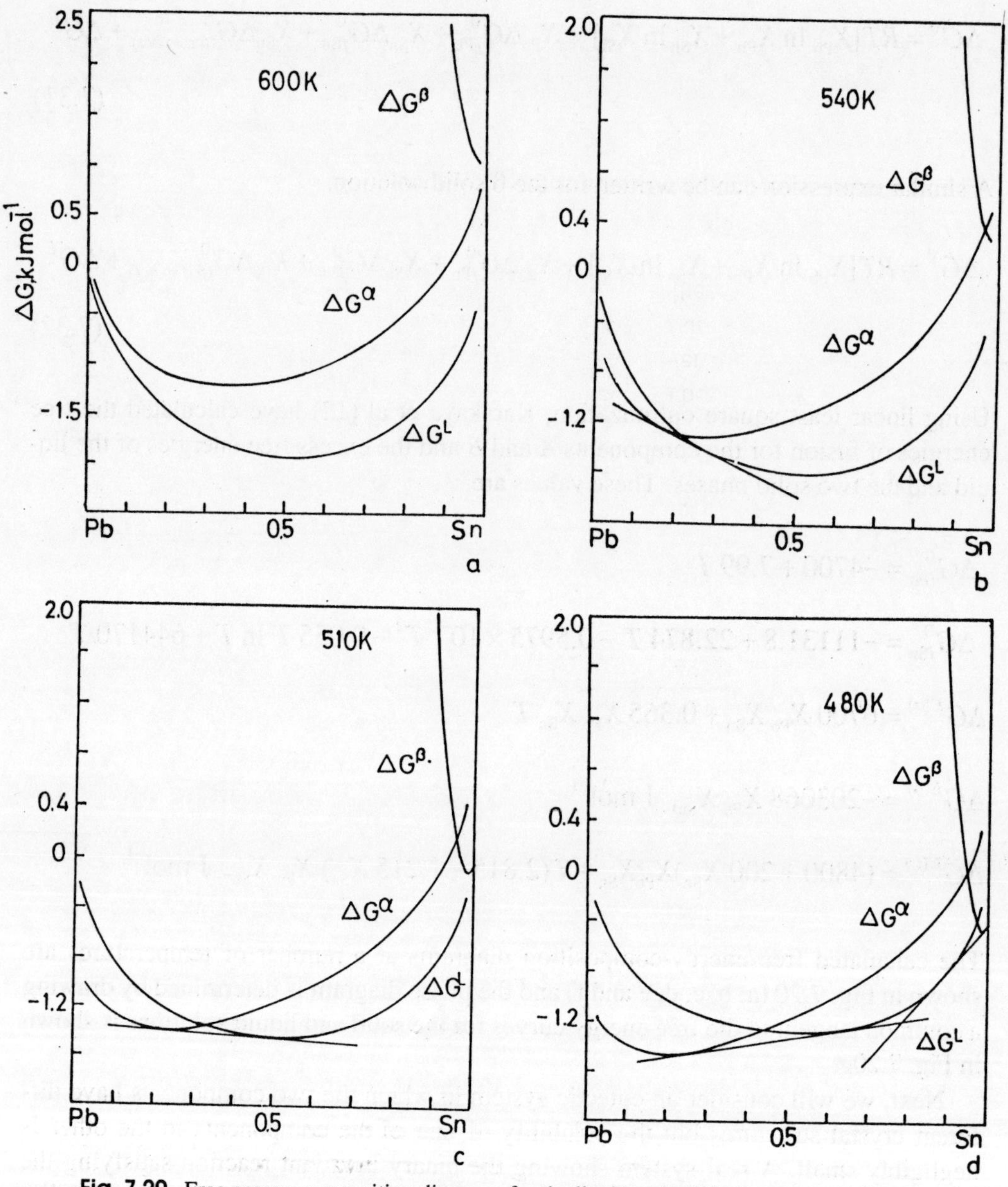

Fig. 7.20 Free energy-composition diagrams for the liquid and solid phases (α and β) at (a) 600 K (b) 540 K (c) 510 K (d) 480 K. (Contd.)

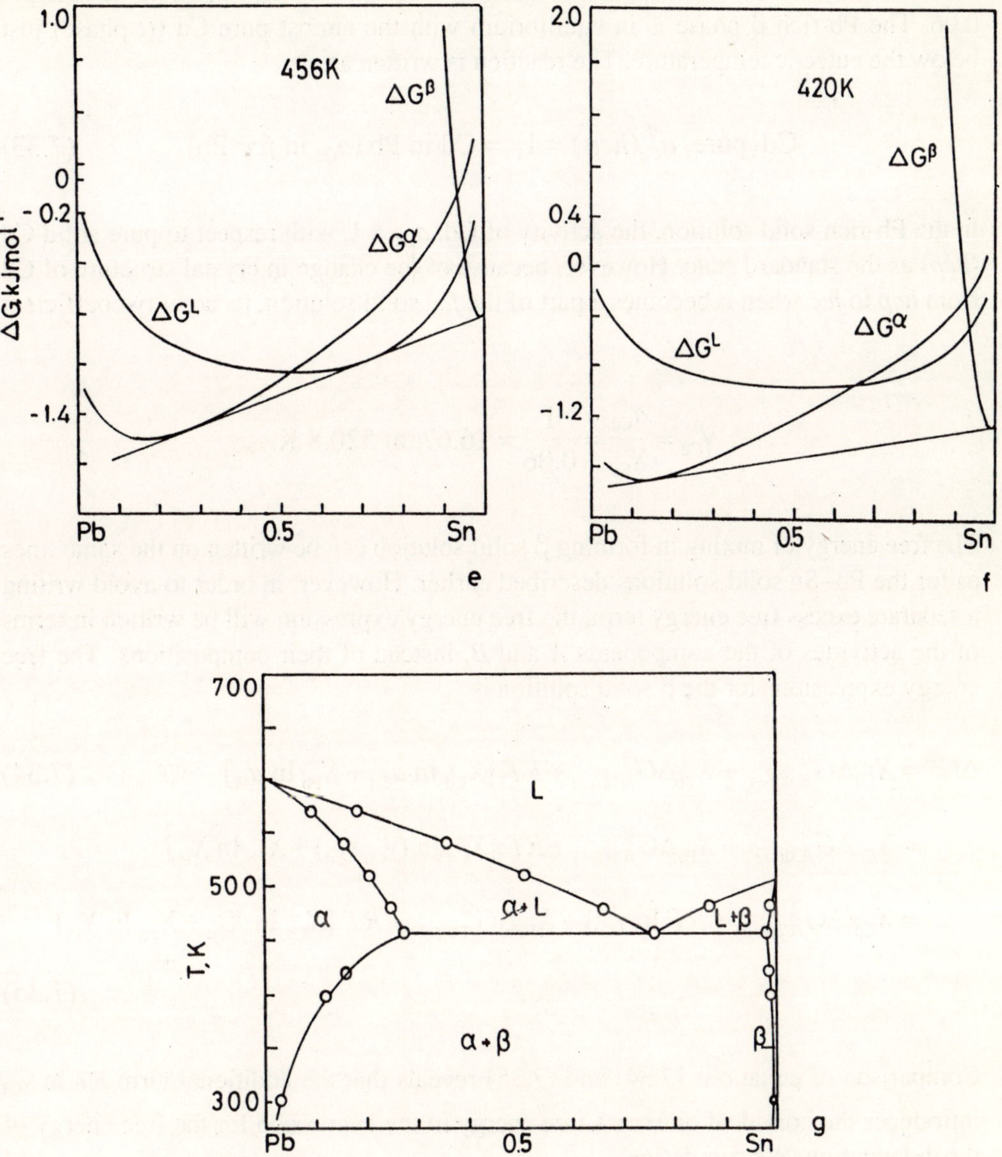

Fig. 7.20 Free energy-composition diagrams for the liquid and solid phases (α and β) at (e) 456 K (f) 420 K. The phase diagram is shown in (g).

The solubility of Cd in Pb (β) at the eutectic reaction isotherm at 520.8 K is X_{Cd} = 0.06. The Pb-rich β phase is in equilibrium with the almost pure Cd (α phase) just below the eutectic temperature. The reaction is written as,

$$\text{Cd}\{\text{pure}, a^0_{\text{Cd}}(hcp) = 1\} = \text{Cd in Pb } (a_{\text{Cd}} \text{ in } fcc \text{ Pb}) \tag{7.33}$$

In the Pb-rich solid solution, the activity of Cd, $a_{Cd} = 1$, with respect to pure solid Cd (*hcp*) as the standard state. However, because of the change in crystal structure of Cd from *hcp* to *fcc* when it becomes a part of the *fcc* solid solution, its activity coefficient is

$$\gamma^0_{\text{Cd}} = \frac{a_{\text{Cd}}}{X_{\text{Cd}}} = \frac{1}{0.06} = 16.67, \text{ at } 520.8 \text{ K.}$$

The free energy of mixing in forming β solid solution can be written on the same lines as for the Pb–Sn solid solutions described earlier. However, in order to avoid writing a separate excess free energy term, the free energy expression will be written in terms of the activities of the components *A* and *B*, instead of their compositions. The free energy expressions for the β solid solution is

$$\Delta G^{\beta} = X_{\text{Cd}}\Delta G^0_{f\text{Cd}(hcp)} + X_{\text{Pb}}\Delta G^0_{f\text{Pb}(fcc)} + RT\,[X_{\text{Cd}} \ln a_{\text{Cd}} + X_{\text{Pb}} \ln a_{\text{Pb}}] \tag{7.34}$$

$$= X_{\text{Cd}}\Delta G^0_{f\text{Cd}(hcp)} + X_{\text{Pb}}\Delta G^0_{f\text{Pb}(fcc)} + RT\,[X_{\text{Cd}} \ln (\gamma^0_{\text{Cd}} X_{\text{Cd}}) + X_{\text{Pb}} \ln X_{\text{Pb}}]$$

$$= X_{\text{Cd}}(\Delta G^0_{f\text{Cd}(hcp)} + RT \ln \gamma^0_{\text{Cd}}) + X_{\text{Pb}}\Delta G^0_{f\text{Pb}(fcc)} + RT\,[X_{\text{Cd}} \ln X_{\text{Cd}} + X_{\text{Pb}} \ln X_{\text{Pb}}] \tag{7.35}$$

Comparison of equations (7.34) and (7.35) reveals that the additional term $RT \ln \gamma^0_{Cd}$ introduces the non-ideal or excess free energy in the expression for the free energy of β solid solution. We can define,

$$\Delta G^0_{f\text{Cd}(fcc)} = [\Delta G^0_{f\text{Cd}(hcp)} + RT \ln \gamma^0_{\text{Cd}}] \tag{7.36}$$

and write equation (7.35) as,

$$\Delta G^{\beta} = X_{Cd}\Delta G^{0}_{fCd(fcc)} + X_{Pb}\Delta G^{0}_{fPb(fcc)} + RT\ [X_{Cd} \ln X_{Cd} + X_{Pb} \ln X_{Pb}] \tag{7.37}$$

Defining the free energy of fusion for pure Cd (*fcc*) in this manner, makes the β solid solution ideal. The phase diagram can be calculated from the activity coefficient data as a function of temperature and the excess free energy of the liquid. The activity coefficient is obtained from the solubility of Cd in Pb as a function of temperature. This is shown in Table 7.1. The excess free energy for the liquid solution has been obtained using the solid/liquid equilibria and the linear least square optimization to fit the experimental data (β), expressed in the form of the following polynomial:

$$\Delta G^{E(L)} = (15609 - 6.45T)X_{Pb} + (-38034 + 22.887\ T)X^{2}_{Pb} + (602034 - 40.26\ T)X^{3}_{Pb}$$
$$+(-70925 + 37.607\ T)\ X^{4}_{Pb}.$$

Table 7.1 **The activity coefficient and excess free energy of the β solid solution as a function of temperature.**

T, K	γ^{0}_{Cd}	RT ln γ^{0}_{Cd}	T, K	γ^{0}_{Cd}	RT ln γ^{0}_{Cd}
590	90.9	22.1			
580	50	18.8	521	17.85	12.6
570	35.7	16.9	500	17.54	12.4
560	27.8	15.5	480	24.39	13.3
540	23.8	14.5	460	34.48	14.1
530	20.4	13.5	440	47.61	14.8
525	18.5	12.8	420	71.42	16.1

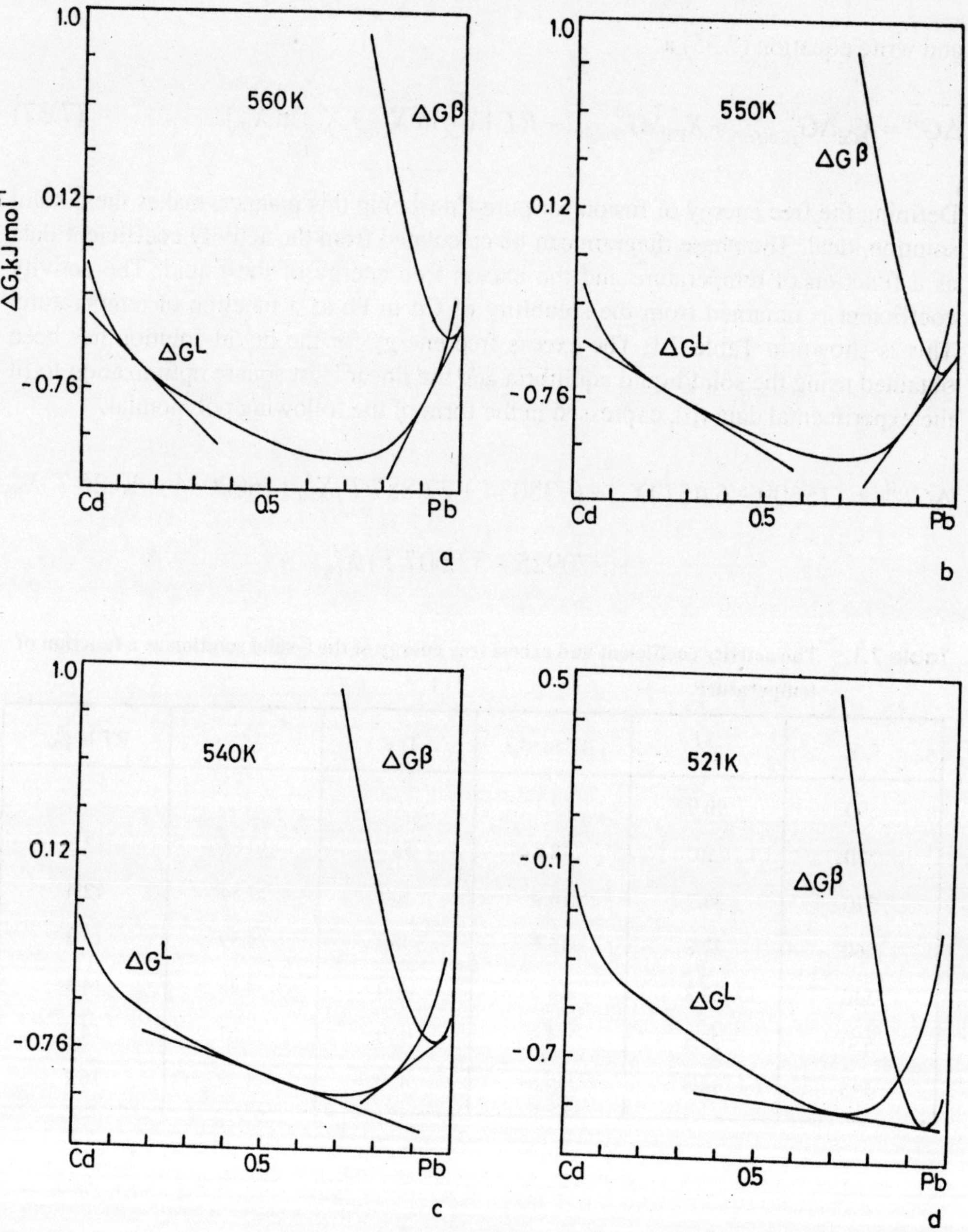

Fig. 7.21 Free energy-composition diagrams for the Cd-Pb system calculated at (a) 560 K (b) 550 K (c) 540 K and (d) 521 K. The phase diagram is shown in (e). (Contd.)

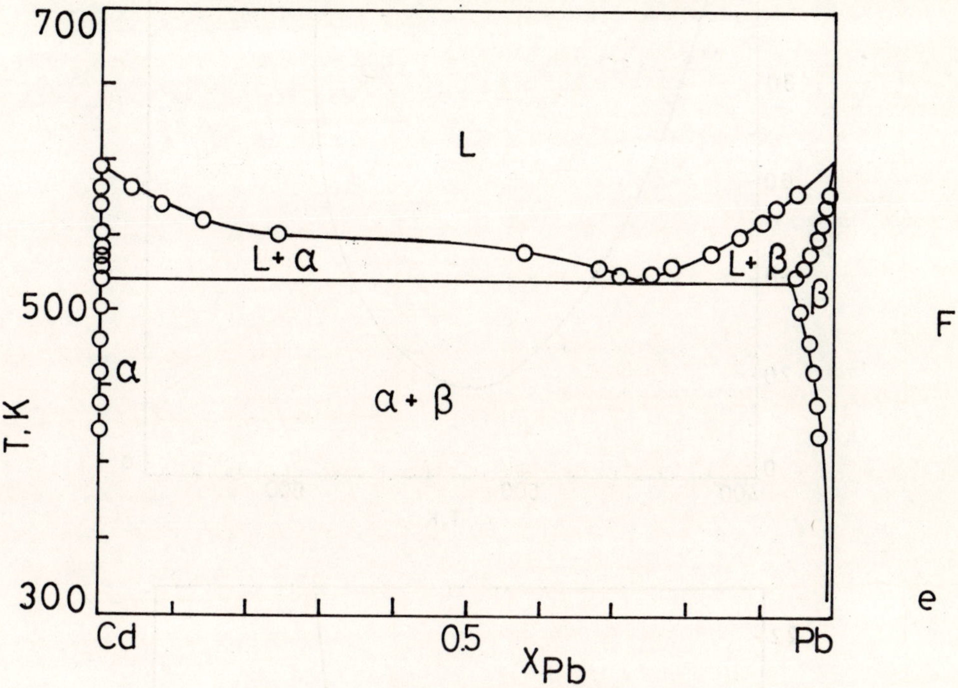

Fig. 7.21 The phase diagram is shown in (e).

The free energies of fusion for pure Cd (*hcp*) and Pb are given as

$$\Delta G^0_{f\text{Cd}(hcp)} = -6410\left(\frac{T_{\text{Cd}} - T}{T_{\text{Cd}}}\right), \text{J mol}^{-1}, \quad T_{\text{Cd}} = 594.1 \text{ K}$$

$$\Delta G^0_{f\text{Pb}} = 4810\left(\frac{T_{\text{Pb}} - T}{T_{\text{Pb}}}\right), \text{J mol}^{-1}, \quad T_{\text{Pb}} = 600.5 \text{ K}$$

The free energy curves for the liquid and β solid solution are shown in Fig. 7.21. The free energy for the α solid solution is taken on the pure Cd axis as a point calculated from the expression for the free energy of fusion for pure Cd (*hcp*). The phase equilibria between solid α and liquid, and α and β phases, are established using this value on the pure Cd axis. The phase diagram is presented in Fig. 7.21e.

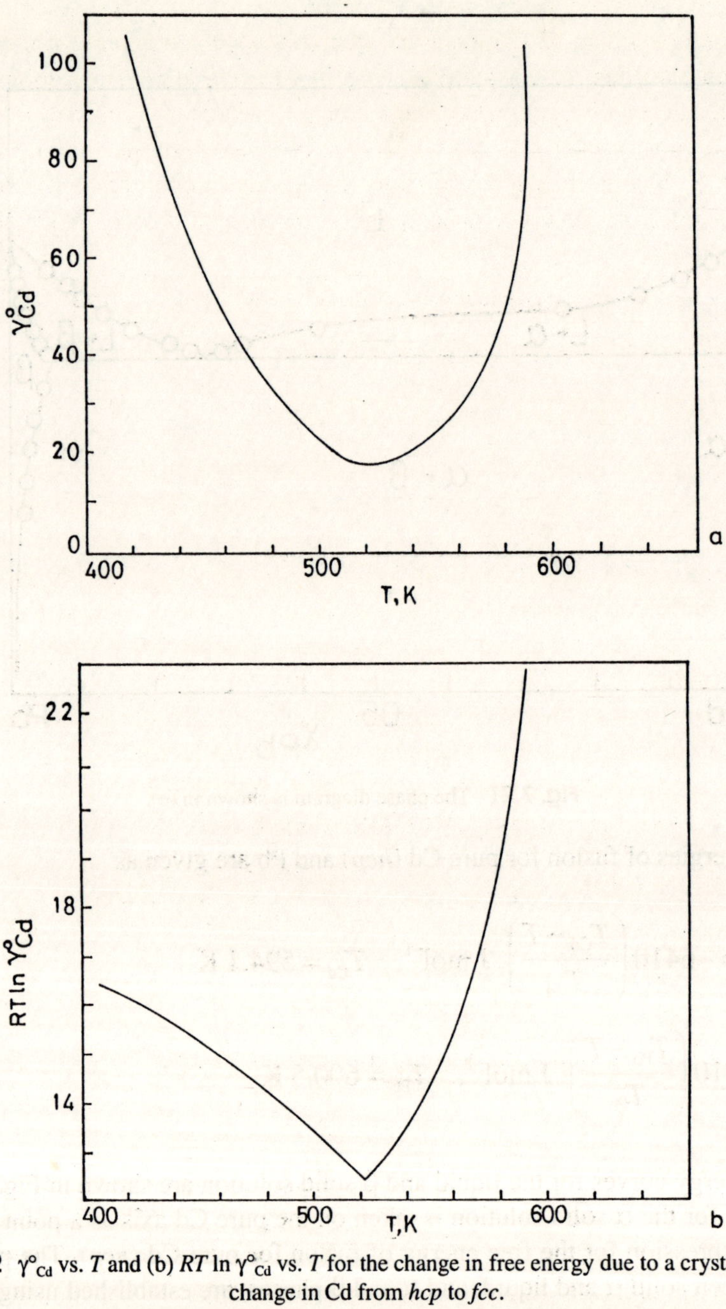

Fig. 7.22 γ°_{Cd} vs. T and (b) $RT \ln \gamma^\circ_{Cd}$ vs. T for the change in free energy due to a crystal structure change in Cd from *hcp* to *fcc*.

In order to calculate the free energy change due to a hypothetical change in the crystal structure of Cd from *hcp* to *fcc*, we can write equation (7.36) in the following form,

$$\Delta G^0_{f\text{Cd}(fcc)} - \Delta G^0_{f\text{Cd}(hcp)} = RT \ln \gamma^0_{\text{Cd}}$$

The calculated values, as shown in Table 7.1, are temperature dependent and non-linear, Fig. 7.22. In general, the change in the free energy due to a crystal structure change is dependent upon the binary system under consideration.

7.4 BINARY PERITECTIC SYSTEMS

A peritectic reaction in the binary system *A–B* occurs when the liquid reacts with the solid at a higher temperature to give another solid phase. The crystal structure of the second solid (stable at lower temperatures) may or may not be the same as that of the solid phase at higher temperatures. In a number of alloy systems, the product of the peritectic reaction is an intermediate phase. As in the case of a eutectic, the enthalpy of mixing of both the solid and liquid solutions influence the peritectic temperature and composition.

In order to illustrate the phase diagram calculations for the binary peritectic system, we will, at first, take the simple approach of considering both solid and liquid solutions as regular with the following data for a hypothetical system *A–B*.

$$\Delta G^0_{fA} = 12.0 \text{ kJ mol}^{-1}, \quad T_A = 1200 \text{ K}, \quad \Delta G^0_{fA} = \Delta H^0_{fA}\left(1 - \frac{T}{T_A}\right)$$

$$\Delta H^0_{fB} = 8.0 \text{ kJ mol}^{-1}, \quad T_B = 800 \text{ K}, \quad \Delta G^0_{fB} = \Delta H^0_{fB}\left(1 - \frac{T}{T_B}\right)$$

$$\Omega^L = \Omega^S = 16.0 \text{ kJ}$$

The following equation are used to calculate the free energy curves,

$$\Delta G^L = RT\,[X_A \ln X_A + X_B \ln X_B] + \Omega^L X_A X_B$$

$$\Delta G^S = X_A \Delta G^0_{fA} + X_B \Delta G^0_{fB} + RT\,[X_A \ln X_A + X_B \ln X_B] + \Omega^S X_A X_B$$

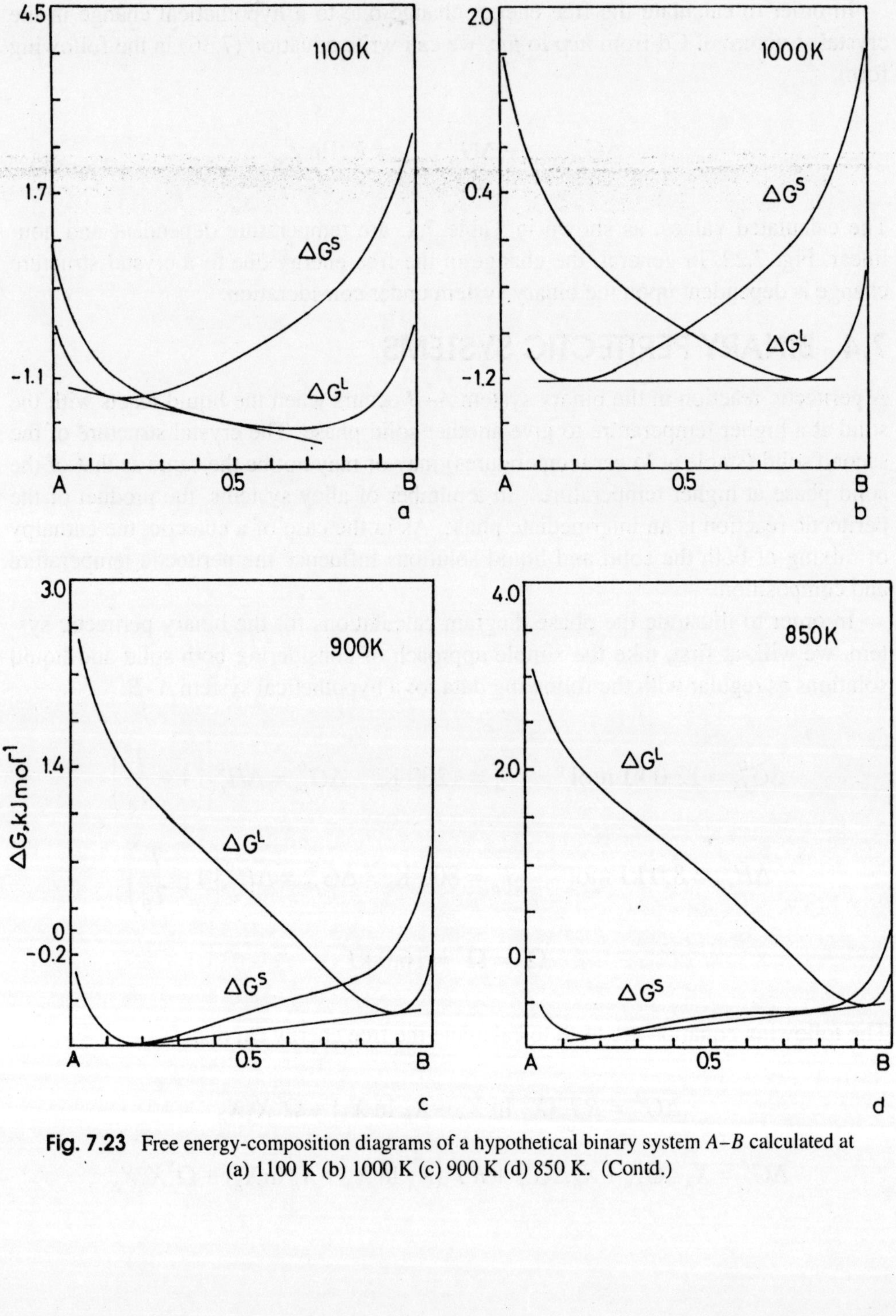

Fig. 7.23 Free energy-composition diagrams of a hypothetical binary system A–B calculated at (a) 1100 K (b) 1000 K (c) 900 K (d) 850 K. (Contd.)

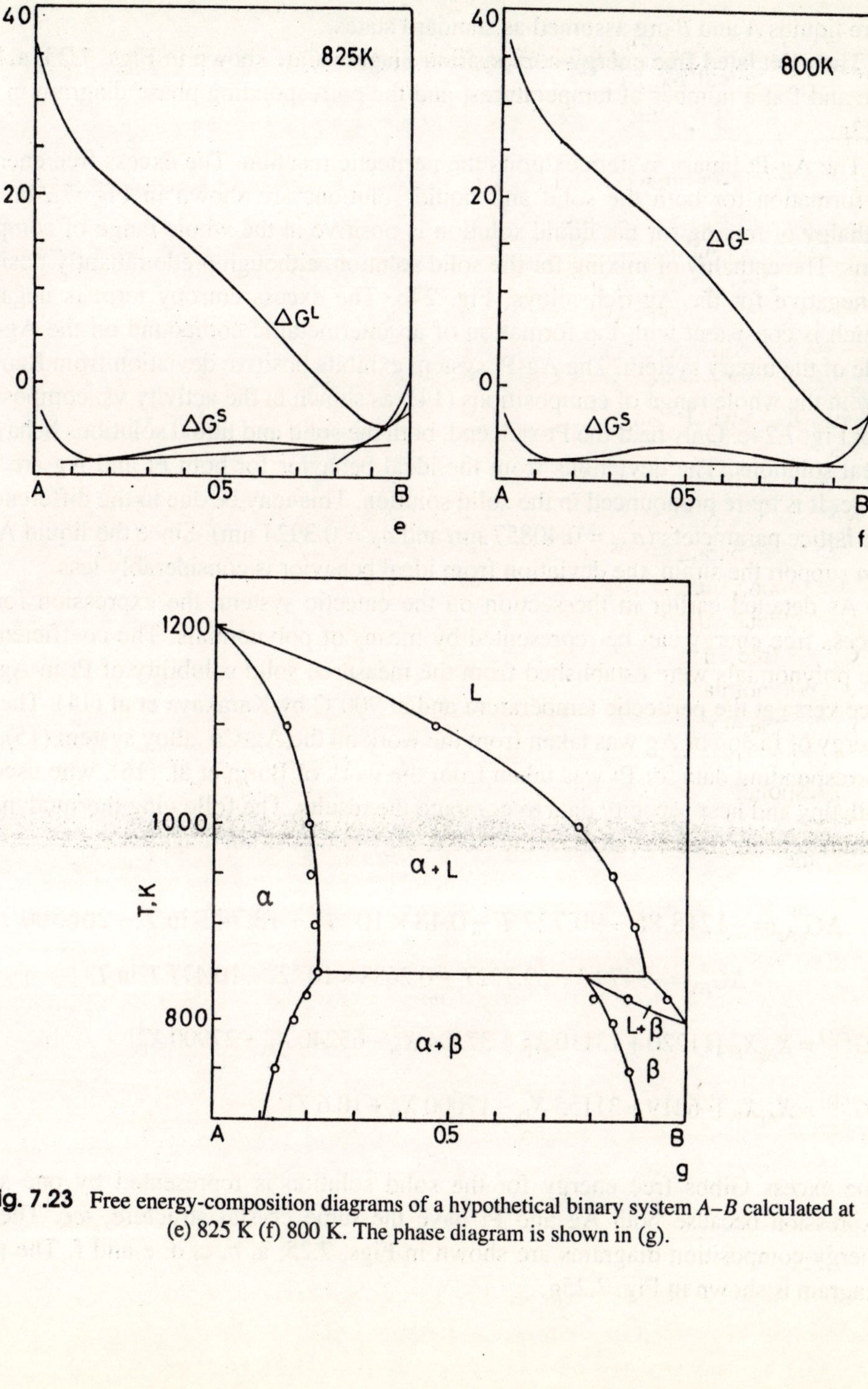

Fig. 7.23 Free energy-composition diagrams of a hypothetical binary system *A–B* calculated at (e) 825 K (f) 800 K. The phase diagram is shown in (g).

Pure liquids *A* and *B* are assumed as standard states.

The calculated free energy-composition diagrams are shown in Figs. 7.23, a, b, c, d, e and f at a number of temperatures, and the corresponding phase diagram in Fig. 7.23g.

The Ag-Pt binary system exhibits the peritectic reaction. The excess free energies of formation for both the solid and liquid solutions are shown in Fig. 7.24a. The enthalpy of mixing for the liquid solution is positive in the whole range of compositions. The enthalpy of mixing for the solid solution, although predominantly positive, is negative for the Ag-rich alloys, Fig. 24b. The excess entropy term is negative, which is consistent with the formation of an intermetallic compound on the Ag-rich side of the binary system. The Ag-Pt system exhibits positive deviation from Raoult's law in the whole range of compositions (14), as shown in the activity vs. composition plot Fig. 7.24c. Only near the Pt-rich end, both the solid and liquid solutions behave as ideal solutions. The deviations from the ideal behavior for both Pt and Ag are very large. It is more pronounced in the solid solution. This may be due to the difference in the lattice parameters (a_{Ag} = 0.40857 nm and a_{Pt} = 0.3924 nm). Since the liquid Ag-Pt can support the strain, the deviation from ideal behavior is considerably less.

As detailed earlier in the section on the eutectic system, the expression for the excess free energy can be represented by means of polynomials. The coefficients in the polynomials were established from the measured solid solubility of Pt in Ag and vice versa at the peritectic temperature and at 900°C by Karakaya et al (14). The free energy of fusion of Ag was taken from the work on the Ag-Co alloy system (15). The corresponding data for Pt was taken from the work of Barin et al. (16), who used the enthalpy and heat capacity data to compute the results. The following thermodynamic parameters are used to calculate the free energy-composition diagrams:

$$\Delta G^0_{f\text{Ag}} = -1218.86 - 90.727\,T - 0.48 \times 10^{-2}T^2 + 13.74T \ln T - 266500/T$$

$$\Delta G^0_{f\text{Pt}} = -9479.3 - 69.722T - 0.2688 \times 10^{-2}T^2 + 10.477\,T \ln T$$

$$\Delta G^{E(L)} = X_{\text{Ag}}X_{\text{Pt}}\,[11220 + 13110\,X_{\text{Pt}} + 37304\,X^2_{\text{Pt}} - 65240\,X^3_{\text{Pt}} + 27900\,X^4_{\text{Pt}}]$$

$$\Delta G^{E(S)} = X_{\text{Ag}}X_{\text{Pt}}\,[-6219 + 31155\,X_{\text{Pt}} - 17000\,X^2_{\text{Pt}} + 10.6\,T]$$

The excess Gibbs free energy for the solid solution is represented by one single expression because both Ag and Pt have the same crystal structure, *fcc*. The free energy-composition diagrams are shown in Figs. 7.25, a, b, c, d, e and f. The phase diagram is shown in Fig. 7.25g.

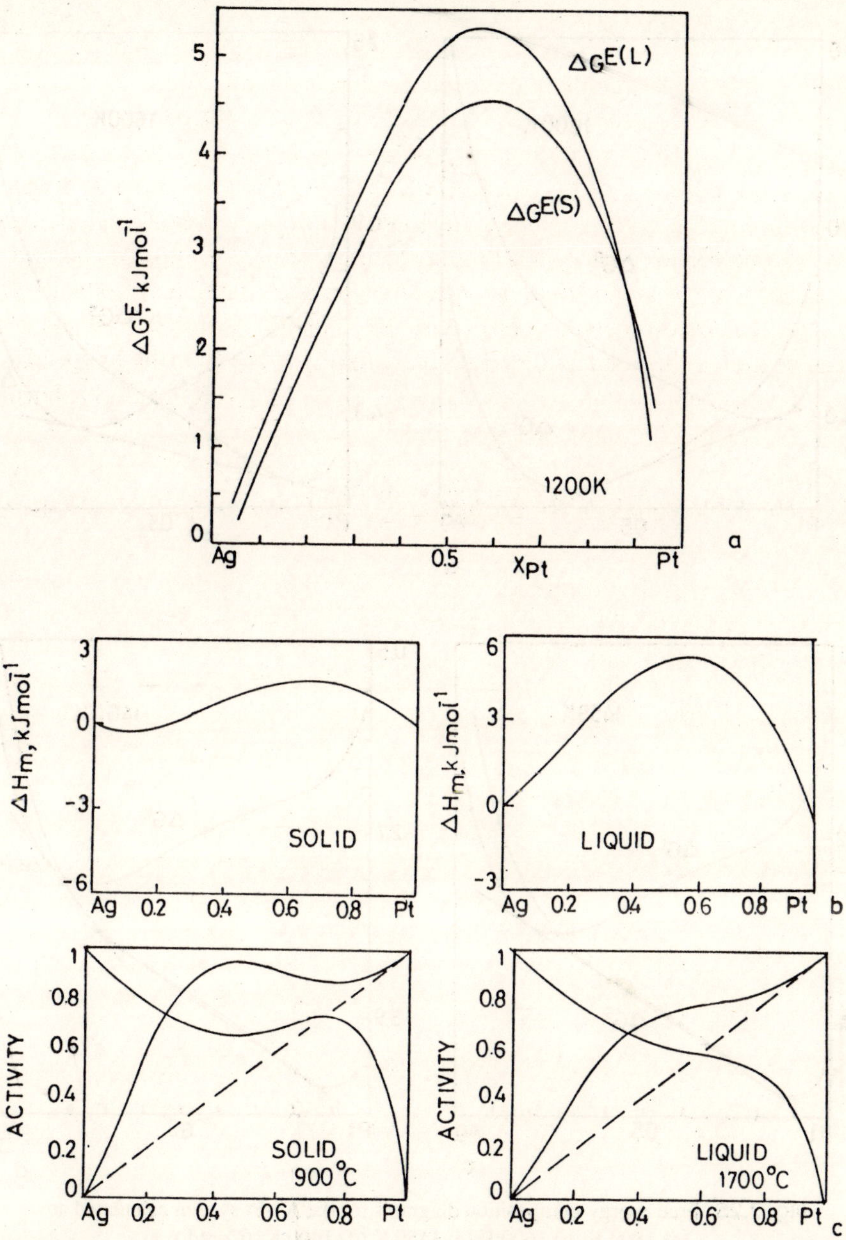

Fig. 7.24 (a) Excess free energy vs. composition graph for the solid and liquid solutions of the Ag-Pt system. (b) The enthalpy of mixing of solid and liquid solutions. (c) The activity vs. composition data for both solid and liquid solutions.

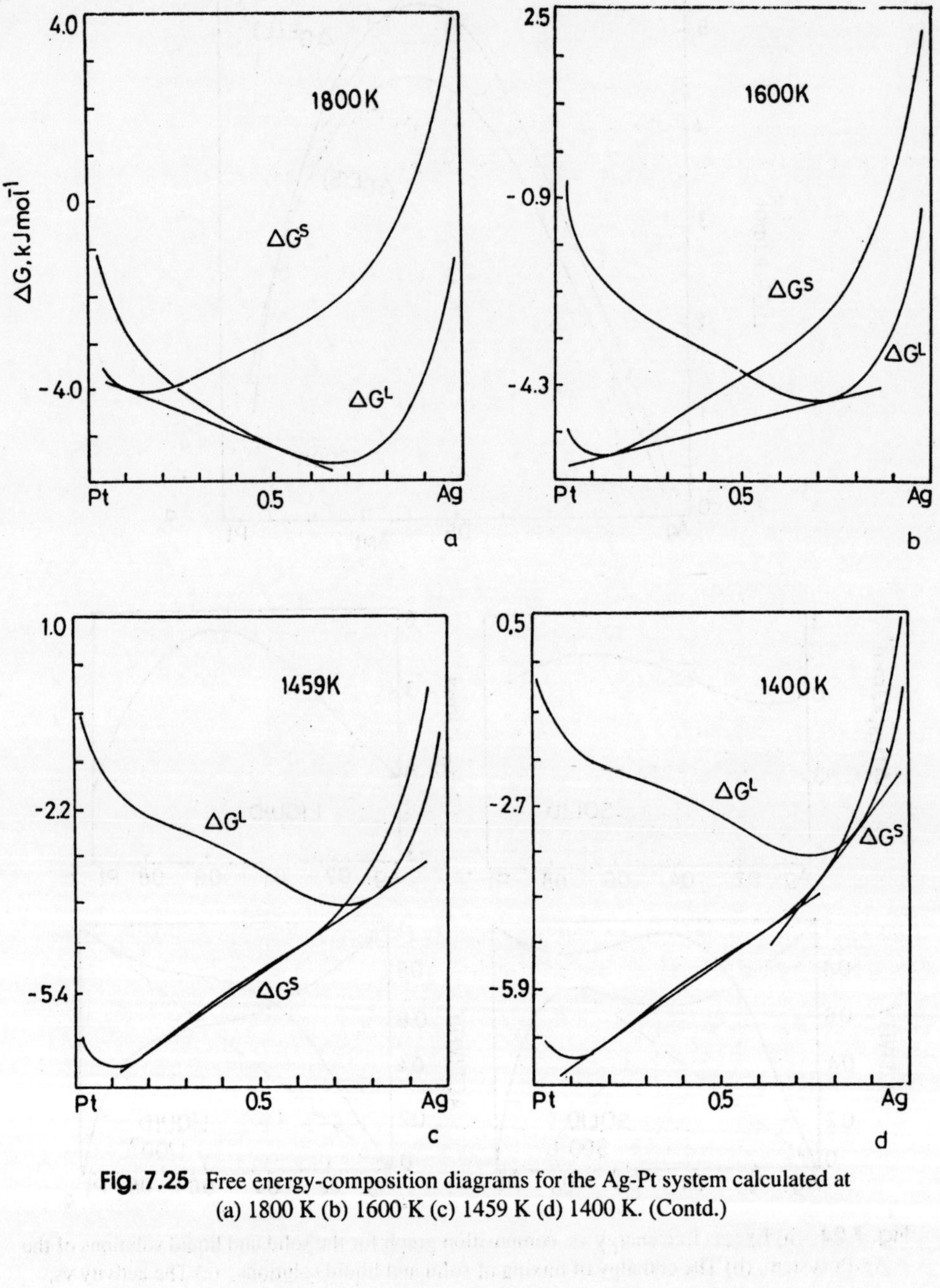

Fig. 7.25 Free energy-composition diagrams for the Ag-Pt system calculated at (a) 1800 K (b) 1600 K (c) 1459 K (d) 1400 K. (Contd.)

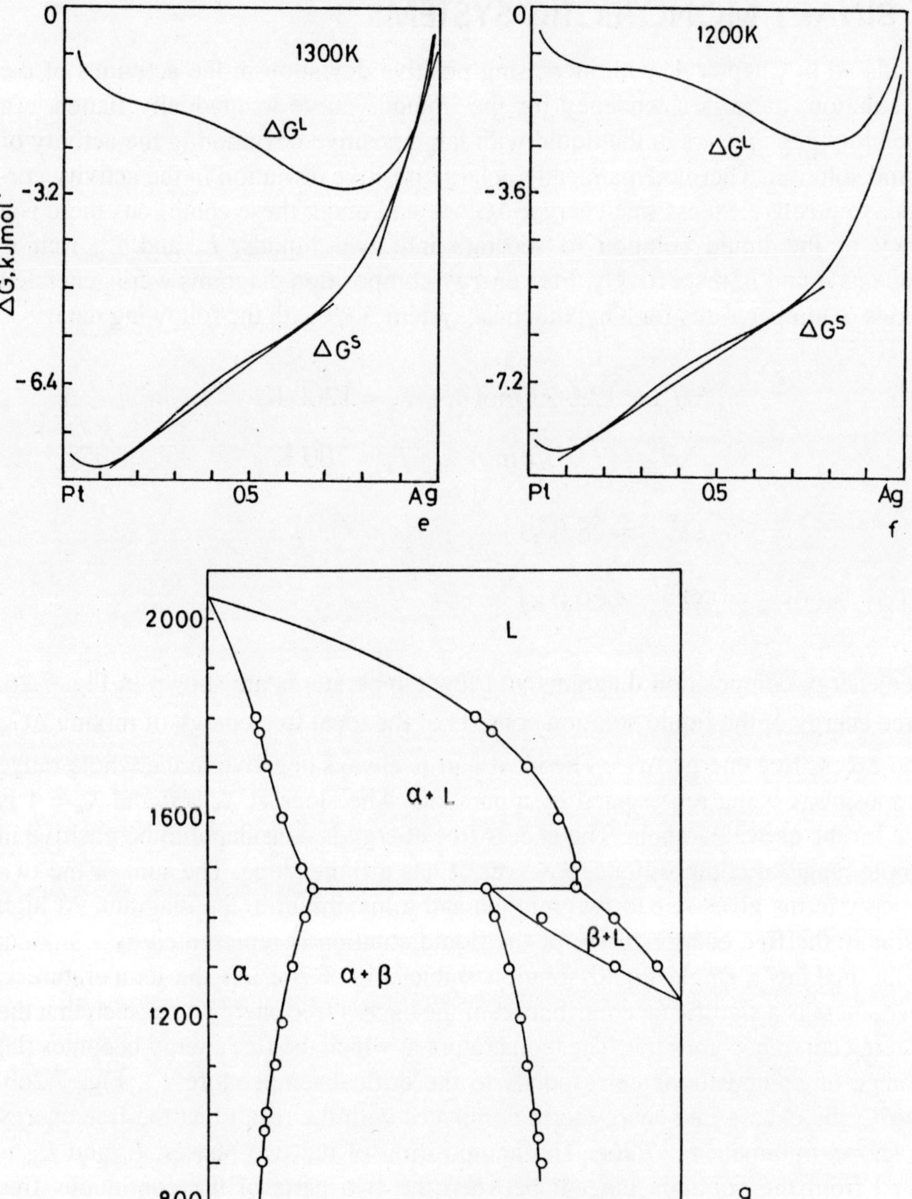

Fig. 7.25 Free energy-composition diagrams for the Ag-Pt system calculated at (e) 1300 K (f) 1200 K. The phase diagram is shown in (g).

7.5 BINARY MONOTECTIC SYSTEMS

As discussed in Chapter 4, with increasing positive deviation in the activities of the liquid solution, there is a tendency for the liquidus curve to gradually flatten. An immiscibility gap appears in the liquid with large positive deviation in the activity of the liquid solution. Thermodynamically, a large positive deviation in the activity corresponds to positive excess free energy, $\Delta G^E>0$, and under these conditions there is a tendency of the liquid solution to separate into two liquids, L_1 and L_2, rich is components A and B, respectively. Free energy-composition diagrams were generated at a series of temperatures for a hypothetical system $A-B$ with the following data:

$$\Delta H^0_{fA} = 12.0 \text{ kJ mol}^{-1}, \quad T_A = 1200 \text{ K}$$

$$\Delta H^0_{fB} = 7.0 \text{ kJ mol}^{-1}, \quad T_B = 700 \text{ K}$$

$$\Omega^S = 28.0 \text{ kJ}$$

$$\Omega^L = 20.0 \text{ kJ}$$

Free energy-composition diagrams at a few temperatures are shown in Fig. 7.26. The free energy of the liquid solution consists of the ideal free energy of mixing ΔG_m and the excess free energy ΔG^E. The ideal part is always negative in the whole range of compositions being represented by a parabola. The slope at $X_B = 0$ and $X_B = 1$ is infinite for the above parabola. The excess free energy is considered to be positive in the whole range of compositions; however, it has a finite slope. The sum of the two free energy terms gives rise to two minima and a maximum in the diagram. At high temperature the free energy curve for the liquid solution is represented by a smooth parabola, making a single liquid solution stable, Fig. 7.26a. As the temperature is lowered, there is a significant contribution of the excess free energy term such that the free energy curve becomes flat. The temperature at which the free energy becomes flat in a range of compositions corresponds to the critical temperature T_{cr}, Fig. 7.26b. Below T_{cr}, the excess free energy term dominates with the result that the free energy curve shows minima, Fig. 7.26c. The composition of the two phases, L_1 and L_2, is obtained from the common tangent between the two parts of the continuous free energy curve. This trend continues with the solubility of B in A (forming L_1) and A in B (forming L_2) decreasing with decreasing temperature.

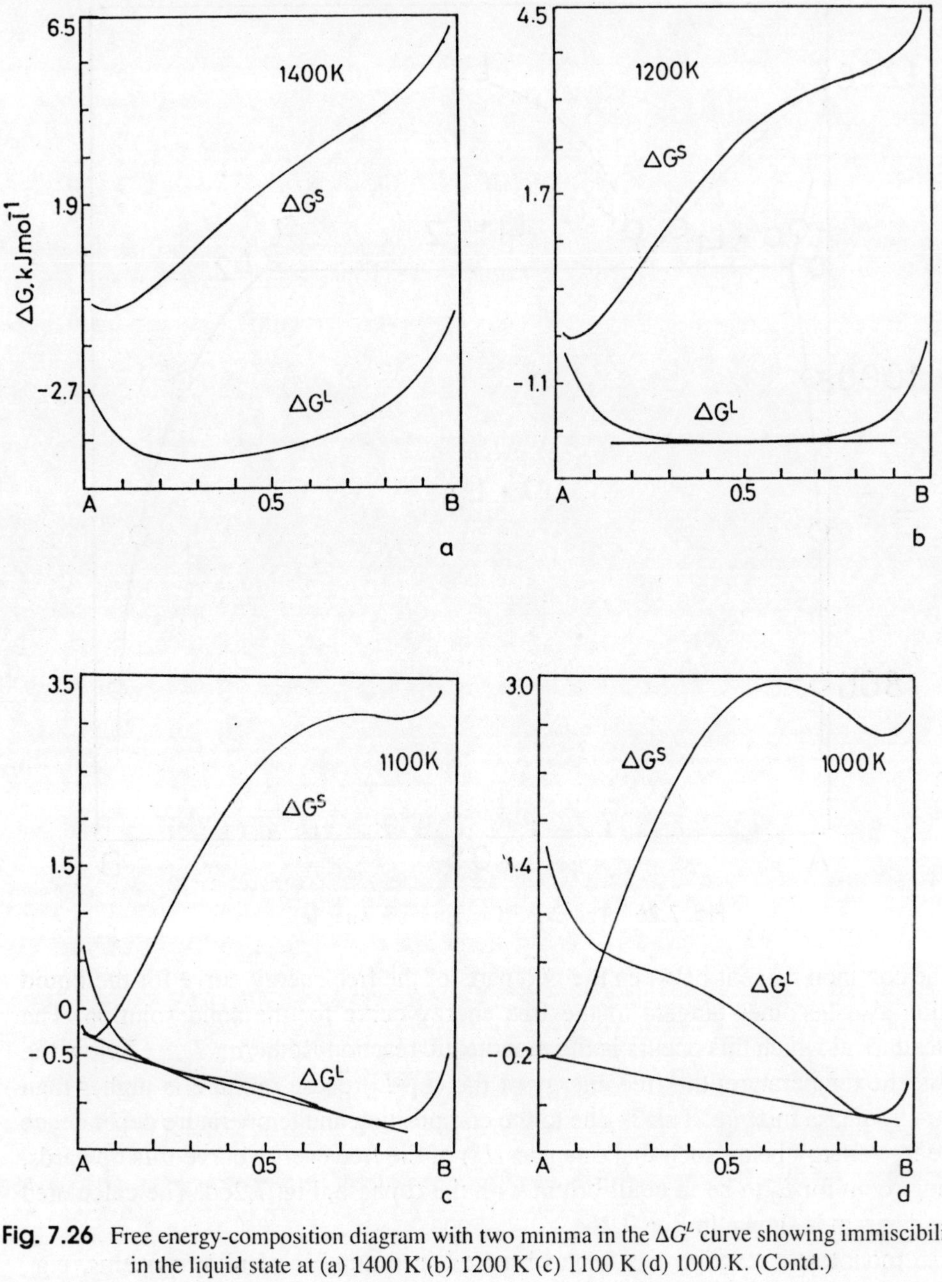

Fig. 7.26 Free energy-composition diagram with two minima in the ΔG^L curve showing immiscibility in the liquid state at (a) 1400 K (b) 1200 K (c) 1100 K (d) 1000 K. (Contd.)

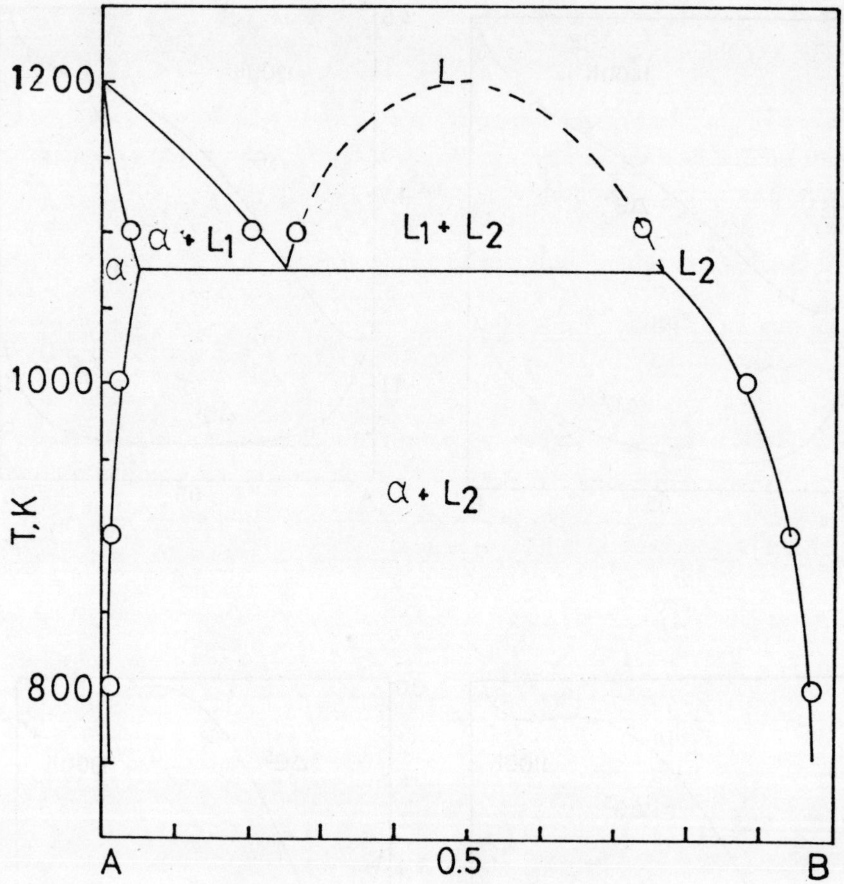

Fig. 7.26 The phase diagram is shown in (e).

The common tangent between the two parts of the free energy curve for the liquid solution also becomes tangent to the free energy curve for the solid solution. The temperature at which this occurs is the monotectic reaction isotherm, T_{mono}. Below the monotectic temperature, the free energy of the (L_1+L_2) phase mixture is higher than the $(\alpha+L_2)$ phase mixture. This is due to the composition and temperature dependence of the free energy being such that one part (L_1) of the free energy curve tilts upwards, making room for L_2 to be in equilibrium with the α phase, Fig. 7.26d. The calculated phase diagram is shown in Fig. 7.26e.

The monotectic reaction has been observed in a number of alloy systems, e.g., Cu-Pb, Al-In, Ag-Rh, Ag-Co, etc. The two components, Cu and Pb and Ag and Rh, have the same crystal structure, *fcc*, in the Cu-Pb and Ag-Rh alloy systems, respectively. The crystal structures of Ag and Co in the Ag-Co alloy system are different below 1394 K.

Thermodynamic data of condensed phases are not available in the published literature. The thermodynamic modelling of the Ag-Rh alloy system has been carried out by Karakaya et al (17) from known compositions of the solid and liquid phases in equilibrium with each other and the solid solubility values, such that the compositions obtained from the free energy-composition diagrams are self-consistent.

The Gibbs free energy of fusion of pure silver has been taken from the thermodynamic modelling of the Ag-Pd system (18). The free energy of fusion of the Rh has been obtained from the work of Barin et al (16), who used specific heat values of the solid and liquid Rh phases. The immiscibility gap in the Ag-Rh alloy system has been reported to have a large difference in the compositions of the two liquid phases, L_1 and L_2 (19, 20), thus implying that the enthalpy of mixing of the liquid solution is the major contributing factor to the excess free energy of the liquid solution. The excess entropy term is treated as insignificant. The enthalpy of mixing of the liquid has been obtained by modelling it to be a sub-regular solution; this is represented by the following expression,

$$\Delta H^L = X_{Ag} X_{Rh} [a + b X_{Rh}] \tag{7.38}$$

Similarly, for the solid solution on the Rh-rich side of the phase diagram, the following expressions are used to represent the enthalpy of mixing and excess entropy:

$$\left.\begin{aligned} \Delta H^S &= X_{Ag}(c + d X_{Rh}) \\ \text{and} \qquad \Delta S^E &= f X_{Ag} X_{Rh} \end{aligned}\right\}$$

In all there are five constants, a, b, c, d and f, the evaluation of which will give the expression for the excess free energy of liquid and solid solutions. These constants have been evaluated by Karakaya et al (17) from the measured temperature and composition data associated with the eutectic and monotectic reactions of the Ag-Rh alloy system. The excess terms are represented by the following expressions:

$$\Delta H^L = X_{Ag}\, X_{Rh}(46000 - 700\, X_{Rh}), \quad \text{J mol}^{-1}$$

$$\Delta G^{E(L)} = 0$$

$$\Delta H^S = X_{Ag}(1600 + 3750\, X_{Rh}), \quad \text{J mol}^{-1} \quad \text{(applicable on the Rh-rich side of the phase diagram)}$$

$$\Delta S^{E(S)} = -16.8\, X_{Ag}\, X_{Rh}, \text{ J mol}^{-1}\text{ K}^{-1}$$

$$\Delta G^0_{f\,Ag} = -1218.86 - 90.7247\, T - 0.4799\; 10^{-2}T^2 + 0.378 \times 10^{-6}T^3 + \\ +13.74\, T \ln T - 266500/T, \text{ J mol}^{-1}$$

$$\Delta G^0_{f\,Rh} = 383.168 - 149.209\, T - 0.67235 \times 10^{-2}T^{-2} + 0.378 \times 10^{-6}T \\ +21.029\, T \ln T - 16950/T, \text{ J mol}^{-1}$$

The free energy-composition diagrams at a few temperatures near the invariant equilibria, monotectic and eutectic, are shown in Fig. 7.27, from which the phase diagram is calculated, Fig. 7.27h.

The phase diagram of the Ag-Co system shows immiscibility in the liquid with the solubility of Ag given by the expression (21),

$$\log X_{Ag} = -5500/T + 0.69.$$

The solubility of Co in Ag has been reported to fall in the range 0.02 to 0.9 at. pct. Co in the temperature range 600–940°C. It is expressed in the following form (22),

$$\ln X_{Co} = -11500/T + 4.5$$

The recently assessed phase diagram of the Ag-Co system does not show any solid solubility of Ag in the high temperature form of Co (*fcc*). The free energy of fusion for pure Ag was taken again from the work on Ag-Pd (18) and that of Co from Barin et al (16). These values are given below:

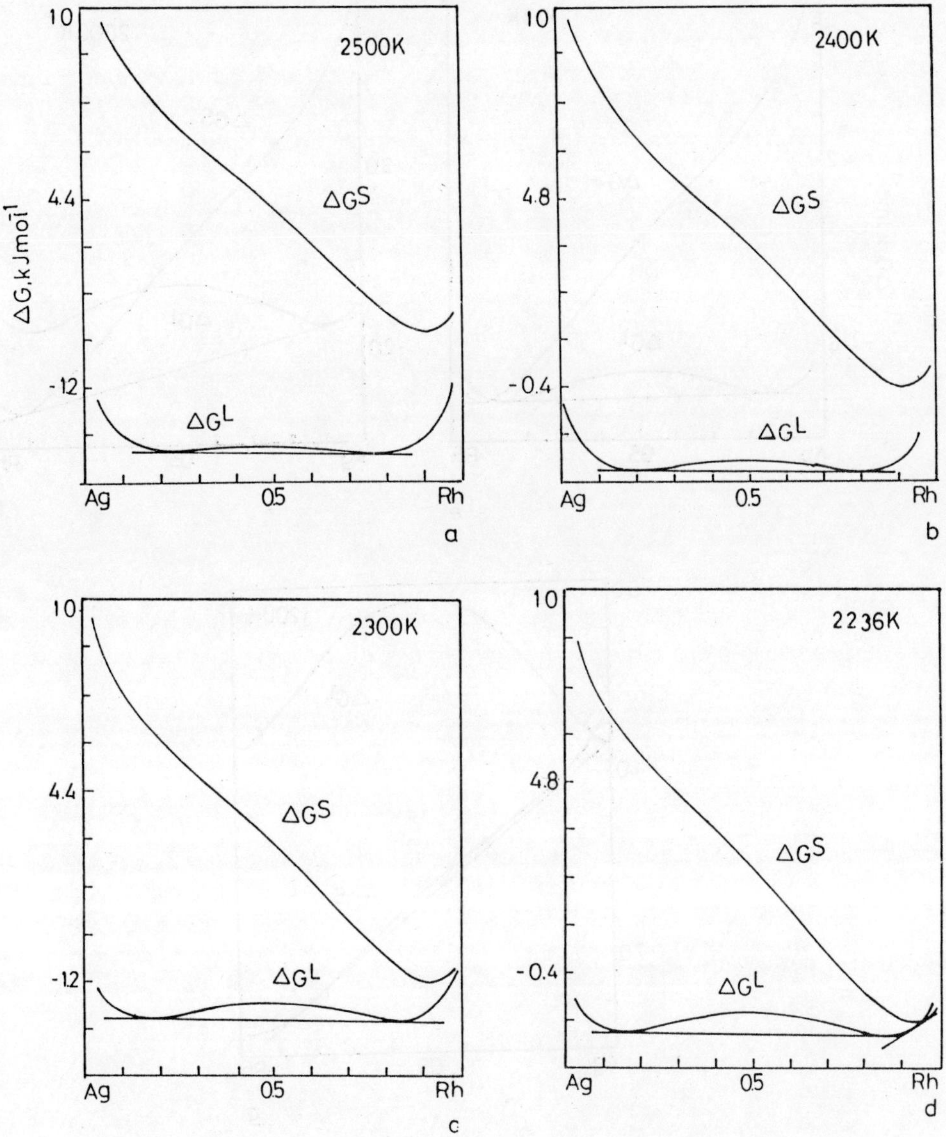

Fig. 7.27 Free energy-composition diagrams of the Ag-Rh system at (a) 2500 K (b) 2400 K (c) 2300 K (d) 2236 K. (Contd.)

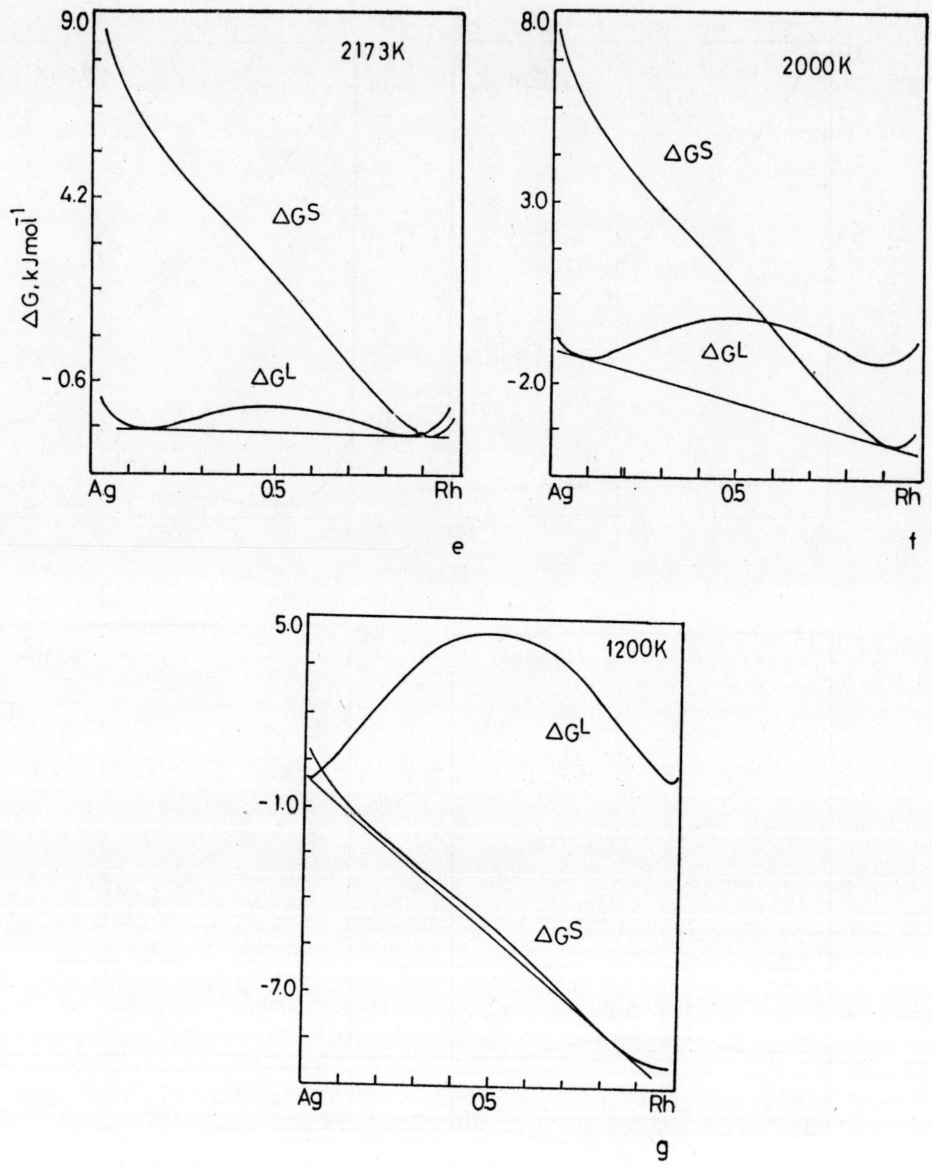

Fig. 7.27 Free energy-composition diagrams of the Ag-Rh system at (e) 2173 K (f) 2000 K (g) 1200 K. (Contd.)

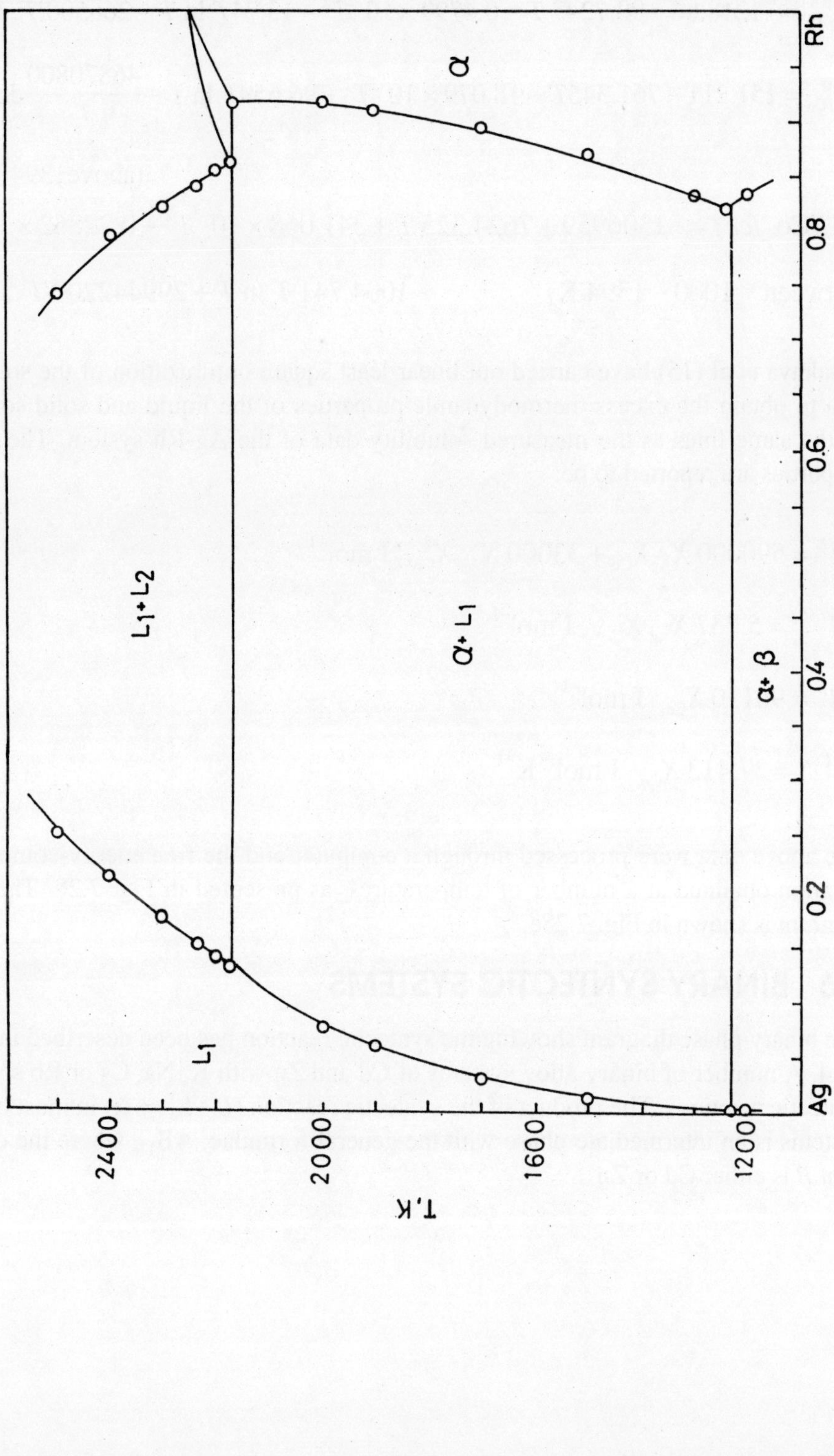

Fig. 7.27 The phase diagram is shown in (h).

$$\Delta G^0_{f\text{Ag}} = -1218.86 - 90.7247\,T - 0.4799 \times 10^{-2}T^2 - 13.74T\ln T - 266500/T,\ \text{J mol}^{-1}$$

$$\Delta G^0_{f\text{Co}} = 151.211 - 761.345T - 18.079 \times 10^{-3}T^2 + 96.659T\ln T - \frac{46870800}{T}\ \text{J mol}^{-1}$$

(above1394 K)

$$\Delta G^0(\text{Co}, fcc) = -1306959 + 7624.325\,T + 341.068 \times 10^{-3}T^2 - 0.22862 \times 10^{-4}T^3$$

(between 1000 – 1394 K) $\qquad -1004.741\,T\ln T + 299442200/T\ \text{J mol}^{-1}$

Karakaya et al (15) have carried out linear least square optimization of the solubility data to obtain the excess thermodynamic properties of the liquid and solid solutions on the same lines as the measured solubility data of the Ag-Rh system. The excess properties are reported to be:

$$\Delta H^L = 590000\,X_{\text{Ag}}X_{\text{Co}} + 33000\,X_{\text{Ag}}\,X^2_{\text{Co}},\ \text{J mol}^{-1}$$

$$\Delta G^{E(L)} = 5.737\,X_{\text{Ag}}\,X_{\text{Co}},\ \text{J mol}^{-1}$$

$$\Delta H^S = 96110\,X_{\text{Co},}\ \text{J mol}^{-1}$$

$$\Delta S^{E(S)} = 37.413\,X_{\text{Co},}\ \text{J mol}^{-1}\text{K}^{-1}$$

The above data were processed through a computer and the free energy-composition diagram obtained at a number of temperatures, as presented in Fig. 7.28. The phase diagram is shown in Fig. 7.28e.

7.6 BINARY SYNTECTIC SYSTEMS

The binary phase diagram showing the syntectic reaction has been described in Chapter 4. A number of binary alloy systems of Cd and Zn with K, Na, Cs or Rb show the syntectic reactions. The product of the syntectic reaction (L_1+$L_2 \Rightarrow \alpha$) in most of these systems is an intermediate phase with the general formulae, AB_{13}, where the component B is either Cd or Zn.

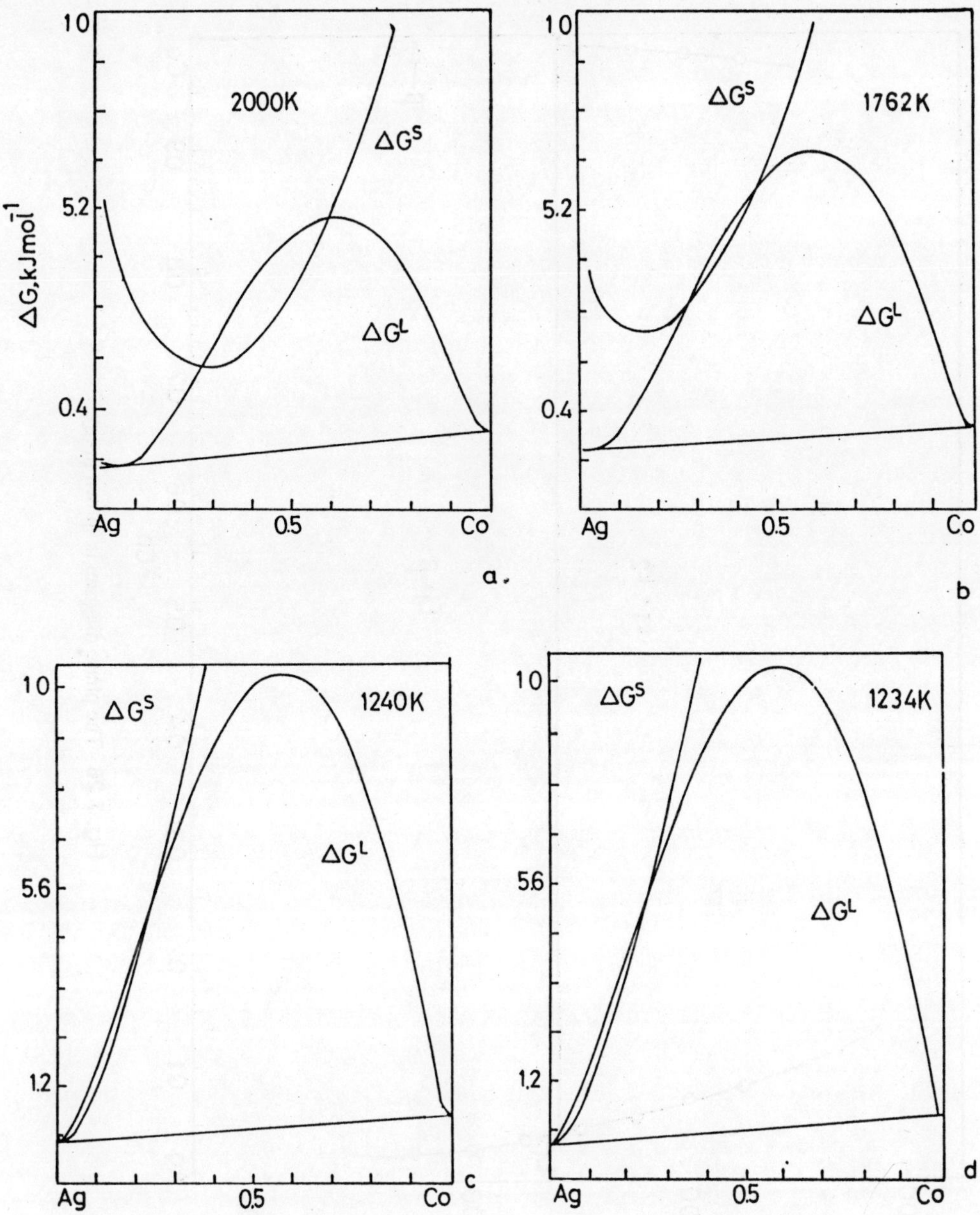

Fig. 7.28 Free energy-composition diagrams for the Ag-Co binary system. The diagrams are drawn at temperatures (a) 2000 K (b) 1762 K (c) 1240 K (d) 1234 K. (Contd.)

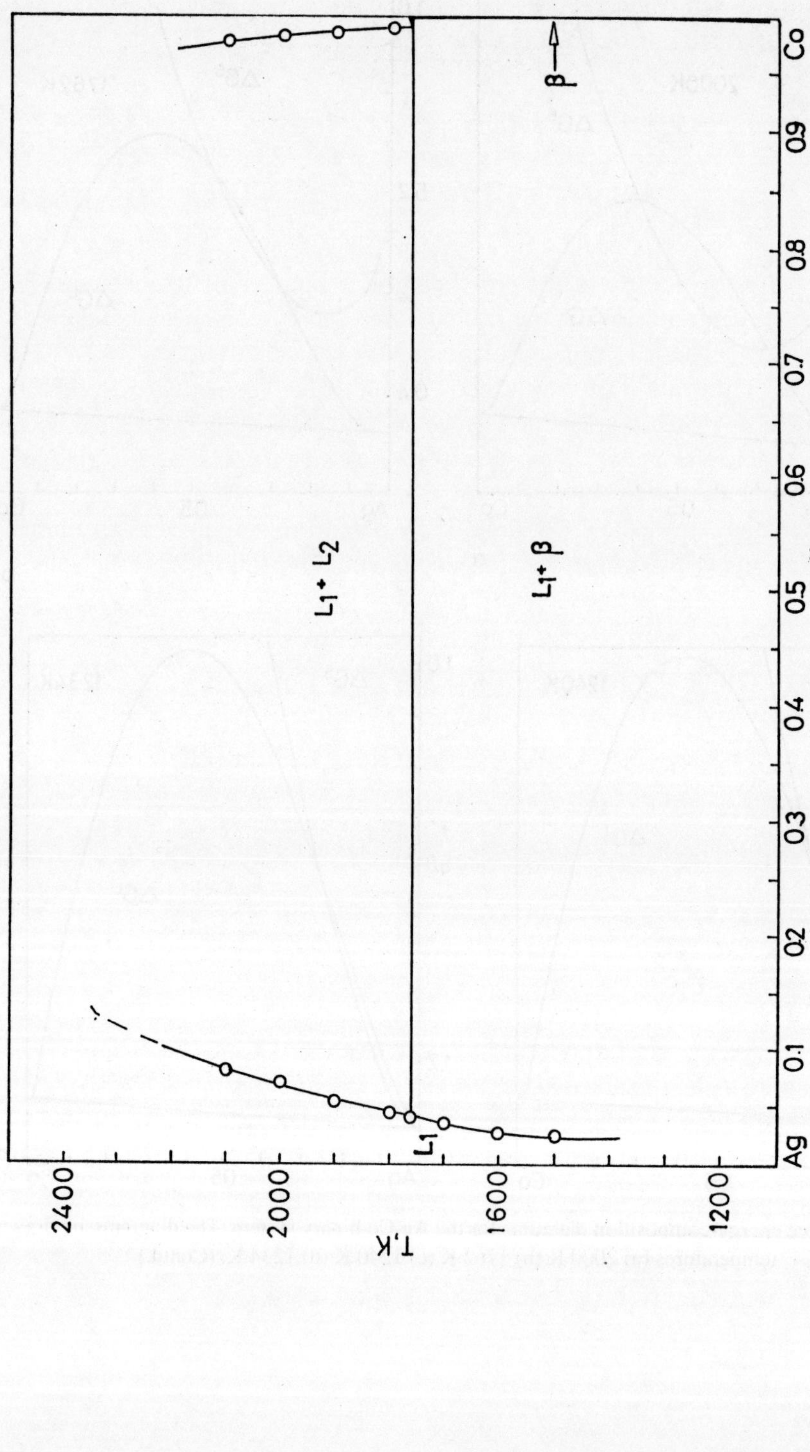

Fig. 7.28 The phase diagram is shown in (e).

To begin with, we will calculate the free energy-composition diagram of a hypothetical binary system using the following data:

$$\Delta H^0_{fA} = 12 \text{ kJ mol}^{-1} \quad T_A = 1200 \text{ K}$$

$$\Delta H^0_{fB} = 7 \text{ kJ mol}^{-1}, \quad T_B = 700 \text{ K}, \quad \Omega^S = 14 \text{ kJ}, \quad \Omega^L = 28 \text{ kJ}.$$

The free energy-composition diagrams are shown at a number of temperatures in Fig. 7.29. The phase diagram constructed from the free energy-composition diagrams is shown in Fig. 7.29e. The Na-Zn phase diagram has been calculated by Pelton (23) using least square optimization of the thermodynamic data. The activities of Na in liquid Na-Zn alloys over the composition range 93.1 to 99.4 at. pct. Zn have been determined by Morachewskii et al (24) in a temperature range from below the liquidus to 600°C using e.m.f. measurements. The partial molar enthalpies and excess entropies of Na were obtained from the e.m.f. data. These data were optimized to obtain the enthalpy of mixing and excess entropy of forming the liquid solution (23). The values are:

$$\Delta H(L) = X_{\text{Zn}} X_{\text{Na}}(-27838 + 266805\, X_{\text{Na}} - 638240\, X^2_{\text{Na}}), \text{ J mol}^{-1}$$

$$\Delta S^E(L) = X_{\text{Zn}} X_{\text{na}}(-53.936 + 281.45\, X_{\text{Na}} - 720.0254\, X^2_{\text{Na}}), \text{ J mol}^{-1}\text{K}^{-1}$$

The free energy of formation of the compound $NaZn_{13}$ from liquid Na and Zn has been given by the expression (23),

$$\Delta G^0(\text{NaZn}_{13}) = -9526 + 10.859\, T, \quad \text{J mol}^{-1}$$

The phase diagram of the Na-Zn system has been evaluated from the free energy-composition diagram using the above data, Fig. 7.30. The liquidus on the Zn-rich side of the phase diagram is in complete agreement with reported values (23). However, the liquidus on the Na-rich side of the phase diagram shows unreasonably high solubility for Zn in Na. This may be due to the ambiguous result of the partial excess free energy of Na in liquid solution remaining constant with composition, as discussed by Pelton (23).

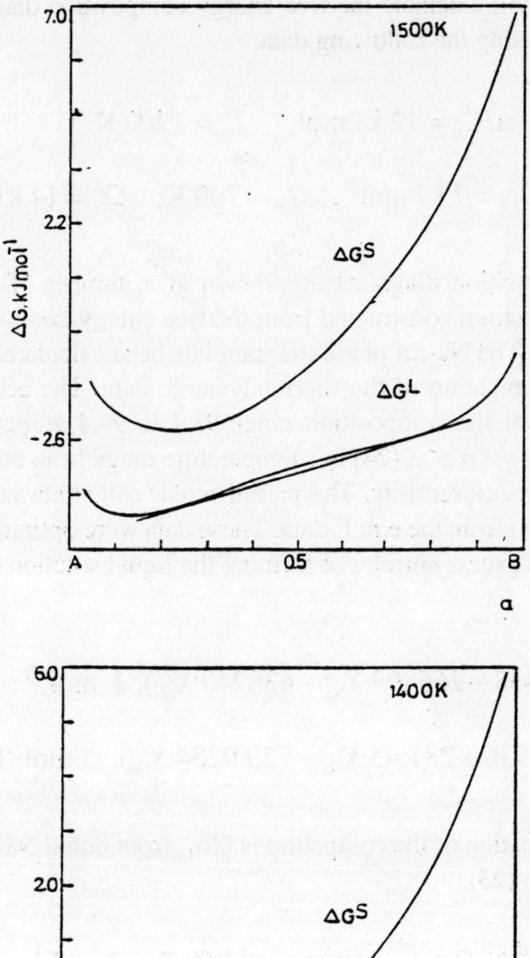

Fig. 7.29 Free energy-composition diagram with two minima in the ΔG^L curves showing immiscibility in the liquid. The free energy curves were calculated at (a) 1500 K (b) 1400 K. (Contd.)

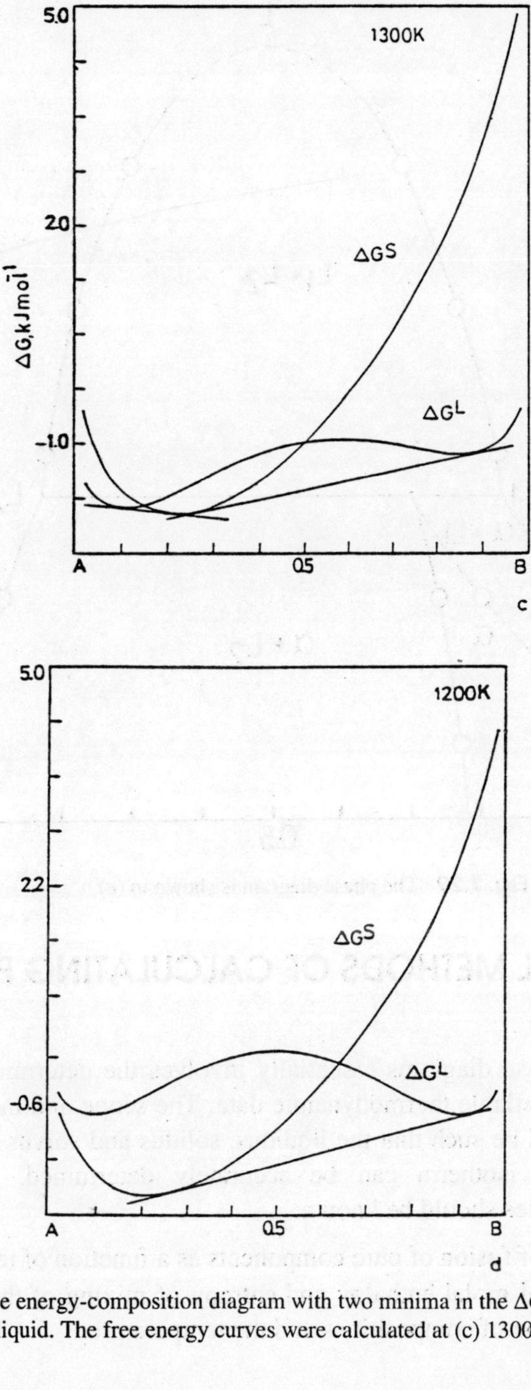

Fig. 7.29 Free energy-composition diagram with two minima in the ΔG^L curves showing immiscibility in the liquid. The free energy curves were calculated at (c) 1300 K (d) 1200 K. (Contd.)

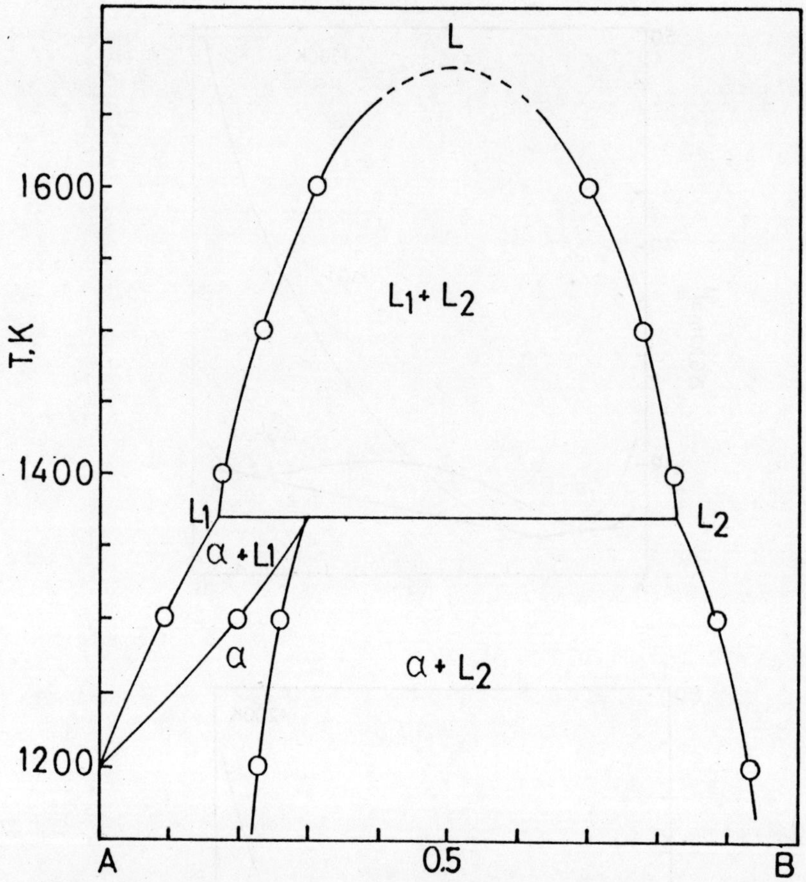

Fig. 7.29 The phase diagram is shown in (e).

7.7 NUMERICAL METHODS OF CALCULATING PHASE DIAGRAMS

The calculations of phase diagrams essentially involves the determination of phase boundaries from the available thermodynamic data. The scope and merit of the thermodynamic data should be such that the liquidus, solidus and solvus boundaries and the invariant reaction isotherm can be accurately determined. The following thermodynamic properties should be known:

(i) The free energy of fusion of pure components as a function of temperature.

(ii) The excess partial molal enthalpy and entropy of mixing of the component *A* and *B* as a function of compositions and the temperature.

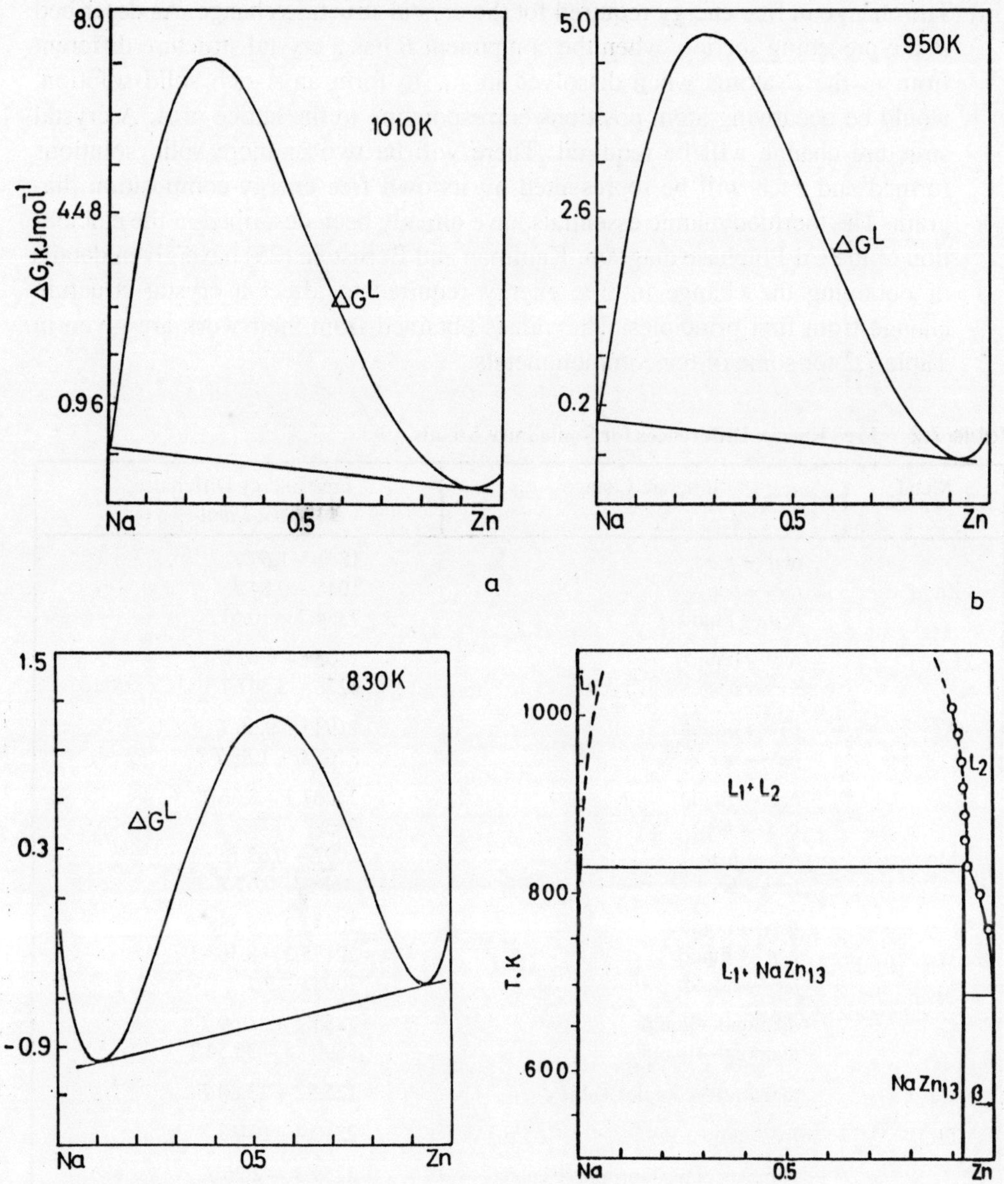

Fig. 7.30 Free energy-composition diagrams for the Na-Zn system at (a) 1010 K (b) 950 K (c) 830 K. The phase diagram is shown in (d).

(iii) The change in free energy required for the crystal structure change. As described in the preceding section, when the component *B* has a crystal structure different from *A*, the *B* atoms when dissolved in *A*, to form an *A*-rich solid solution, would be occupying atom positions corresponding to the lattice of *A*. A crystal structure change will be required. There will be two or more solid solutions formed and each will be represented by its own free energy-composition diagram. The thermodynamic essentials have already been described in the calculation of the Cd-Pb phase diagram. Kaufman and Bernstein (25) have given details of obtaining the change in free energy required to affect a crystal structure change from first principles. The values obtained from their work are given in Table 7.2 for some of the common metals.

Table 7.2 Free Energy Differences for Some Pure Metals

Metal	Structure Change	Free Energy Difference, ΔG, J mol^{-1}
Zn	*hcp* → *fcc*	1841 – 1.67 *T*
	fcc → *bcc*	1046 – 0.84 *T*
	hcp → liquid	7384.7 – 10.67*T*
Cu	*fcc* → liquid	13054 – 9.62 *T*
	fcc → *bcc*	6276 – 3.347 *T*
Ag	*fcc* → liquid	11945 – 9.66 *T*
	fcc → *bcc*	3765.6 – 1.88 *T*
Mo	*bcc* → liquid	24267.2 – 8.36 *T*
	bcc → *hcp*	8368
	fcc → *hcp*	– 2092 – 0.62 *T*
	fcc → *bcc*	– 10460 – 0.62 *T*
W	*bcc* → liquid	30543.2 – 8.368 *T*
	hcp → liquid	22175.2 – 8.368 *T*
	fcc → liquid	20083 – 9 *T*
C	diamond→liquid	1255.2 – 4.769 *T*
	diamond→liquid	36909.4 – 30.54 T
Ge	diamond→complex cubic	125.52 + 13.80 *T*
Pb	*fcc*→*hcp*	2510.4 – 0.418 *T*
Mn	complex cubic→primitive cubic	2259.3 – 2.26 *T*
	primitive cubic→*fcc*	2217.5 – 1.63 *T*
	fcc→*bcc*	1757.3 – 1.25 *T*

(iv) The free energy of formation of an intermediate phase as a function of temperature.

The free energy of fusion of components A and B can be obtained for a large number of elements, from published literature, at the equilibrium melting temperature. The free energy of fusion as a function of temperature can be determined from the latent heat of fusion and specific heats at constant pressure for the pure components in the liquid and solid states. The procedure of calculating the free energy of fusion has been described in section (7.1), equation (7.12), and illustrated for the Cu-Ni and Au-Ni alloy systems.

The excess thermodynamic properties can be evaluated from the activities and activity coefficients data for a particular component in the liquid and solid solutions in a range of compositions and temperatures. The Gibbs-Duhem integration may be used to calculate the activities and activity coefficients of the other component when those of a component of a binary is known. For dilute solutions, assuming that the solute follows the Henry's law, the activity of the solvent may be determined. From the condition of equality of activity of a given component in two phases at equilibrium, the activity of the component in one of the phases can be determined if its activity in the other phase is known. The activities of the components as functions of temperature and composition are a source of available thermodynamic information. Even an equation relating the solubility of a component in solid or liquid solution as a function of composition and temperature, becomes a source of thermodynamic information, as the assumed values may be assessed for their accuracy, and, hence, provide useful information in phase diagram calculations.

If sufficient thermodynamic data are available for a given binary system as a function of temperature and composition, it may be possible to perform simultaneous critical evaluation of the data and thereby calculate the phase diagram. The technique is referred to as the linear least square optimization, as described by Lukas et al (26) and Bale et al (27). The technique yields optimized equations for the Gibbs free energy of each phase representing all the information.

The calculation of the phase diagram can be carried out with the thermodynamic equations relating free energies of liquid and solid phases with composition and temperature. Considering both pure liquid A and liquid B as standard states, the free energy of formation of a liquid solution is given for a binary system A–B as

$$\Delta G_m^L = RT\,[X_A \ln X_A + X_B \ln X_B] + \Delta G^{E(L)}$$

where ΔG^E, as defined earlier, is the excess free energy represented by the equation,

$$\Delta G^{E(L)} = \Delta H^L - T\,\Delta S^{E(L)}$$

For a large number of binary substitutional solutions, the enthalpy of mixing and excess entropy or non-ideal entropy can be represented by polynomials, equations (7.40) and (7.41),

$$\Delta H^L = X_A X_B\,[A_0 + A_1 X_B + A_2 X_B^2 + A_3 X_B^3 + \ldots + A_n X_B^n] \qquad (7.40)$$

and $$\Delta S^{E(L)} = X_A X_B [B_0 + B_1 X_B + B_2 X_B^2 + B_3 X_B^3 + \ldots + B_b X_B^n] \qquad (7.41)$$

For a regular solution, A_1, A_2 etc. = 0 and B_0, B_1, B_2 etc. = 0, and the excess free energy term reduces to,

$$\Delta G^{E,(L)} = A_0 X_A X_B \quad (\text{where } A_0 = \Omega^L \text{ as used earlier}),$$

and the polynomial representation of the thermodynamics of the solution becomes an extension of the regular solution theory. The partial enthalpies and excess entropies of the components A and B can be obtained from the relation derived in Chapter 1. We will write L or S without a superscript as the expressions are the same for both solutions.

$$\Delta H_A = \Delta H - X_B \frac{\partial \Delta H}{\partial X_B}, \quad \Delta H_B = \Delta H + X_A \frac{\partial \Delta H}{\partial X_B}$$

$$\Delta S_A^E = \Delta S - X_B \frac{\partial \Delta S^E}{\partial X_B} \quad \text{and} \quad \Delta S_B^E = \Delta S + X_A \frac{\partial \Delta S^E}{\partial X_B}.$$

The partial molal enthalpy of the component A is written as

$$\Delta H_A = X_A X_B\,[A_0 + A_1 X_B + A_2 X_B^2 + \ldots + A_n X^n] + (1 - 2X_B)\,[A_0 + A_1 X_B + A_2 X_B^2 + \ldots$$

$$+ A_n X_B^n] + X_A X_B\,[A_1 + 2A_2 X_B + 3A_3 X_B^2 + \ldots + nA_n X_B^{n-1}]$$

$$= X_B^2[A_0 + A_1(X_B - X_A) + A_2 X_B(X_B - 2X_A) + A_3 X_B^2(X_B - 3X_A) + A_n X_B^{n-1}(X_B - nX_A)]$$

or

$$\Delta H_A = \sum_{i=0}^{n} A_i\,[X_B - i\,X_A]\,X_B^{i+1} \tag{7.42}$$

Similarly, we can write the enthalpy for the component *B* and partial excess entropies of *A* and *B*, as,

$$\Delta H_B = \sum_{i=0}^{n} A_i\,(i+1)\,X_A^2\,X_B^i \tag{7.43}$$

$$\Delta S_A^E = \sum_{i=0}^{n} B_i\,[X_B - iX_A]\,X_B^{i+1} \tag{7.44}$$

$$\Delta S_B^E = \sum_{i=0}^{n} B_i\,(i+1)\,X_A^2\,X_B^i \tag{7.45}$$

The partial excess free energies of the components *A* and *B* can be written using equations (7.42) to (7.45). These expressions are given in equation (7.46) and (7.47).

$$\Delta G_A^E = \sum_{i=0}^{n} (A_i - TB_i)\,(X_B - iX_A)\,X_B^{i+1} \tag{7.46}$$

and

$$\Delta G_b^E = \sum_{i=0}^{n} (A_i - TB_i)(i+1)\,X_A^2 X_B^i \tag{4.47}$$

The integral excess free energy of formation of the solutions is

$$\Delta G^E = X_A \Delta G_A^E + X_B \Delta G_B^E$$

$$= X_A \sum_{i=0}^{n} (A_i - TB_i)(X_B - iX_A) X_B^{i+1} + X_B \sum_{i=0}^{n} (A_i - TB_i)(i+1) X_A^2 X_B^i$$

$$= \sum_{i=0}^{n} (A_i - TB_i) X_A X_B^{i+1} \tag{7.48}$$

$$= \sum_{i=0}^{n} \phi_i X_A X_B^{i+1}, \quad \phi_i = (A_i - TB_i)$$

$$= X_A X_B \sum_{i=0}^{n} \phi_i X_B^i, \tag{7.49}$$

which in the expanded form can be written as

$$\Delta G^E = X_A X_B \, [\phi_0 + \phi_1 X_B + \phi_2 X_B^2 + \phi_3 X_B^3 + \ldots\ldots] \tag{7.50}$$

The least square regression analysis is used as a method of calculating an expression for some quantity which fits the experimental data as closely as possible. At present, the thermodynamic quantities of interest are: ΔG^E, ΔG_A^E, ΔG_B^E, ΔH, ΔH_A, ΔH_B, ΔS^E, ΔS_A^E and ΔS_B^E. Any of these thermodynamic parameters can be dependent upon the composition of the alloy under consideration. If we assign a value X_B to the composition, then ΔG_B^E, for example, has some value. The partial excess free energy of the component B becomes a dependent variable, say y, the composition being the independent variable, say x. For n pair of experimental points, (x_1, y_1), (x_2, y_2), (x_3, y_3), ... (x_n, y_n), the data can be fitted by least square regression analysis to a polynomial of the form, for example,

$$y = a + bx + cx^2 + d\,x \ln x \tag{7.51}$$

If the data are scattered, the vertical distance in the y direction of the experimental coordinate, (x_i, y_i), from the curve of equation (7.51) is

$$y_i - (a + bx_i + cx_i^2 + d\,x_i \ln x_i) \tag{7.52}$$

The sum of the square of these distances, p, from the curve is

$$p = \sum_{i=1}^{n} \{y_i - (a + bx_i + cx_i^2 + d\, x_i \ln x_i)\}^2 \tag{7.53}$$

In the method of least square regression analysis, the coefficients a, b, c and d are selected such that the value of p is a minimum. The condition necessary for p to be a minimum is that the differentials of p w.r.t. a, b, c and d individually be zero, i.e.,

$$\frac{\partial p}{\partial a} = 0,\ \frac{\partial p}{\partial b} = 0,\ \frac{\partial p}{\partial c} = 0 \ \text{ and } \ \frac{\partial p}{\partial d} = 0. \tag{7.54}$$

The operation can be carried out to yield,

$$\frac{\partial p}{\partial a} = -2 \sum_{i=1}^{n} \{y_i - (a + bx_i + cx_i^2 + d\, x_i \ln x_i)\} = 0$$

$$\frac{\partial p}{\partial b} = -2 \sum_{i=1}^{n} x_i \{y_i - (a + bx_i + cx_i^2 + d\, x_i \ln x_i)\} = 0 \tag{7.55}$$

$$\frac{\partial p}{\partial c} = -2 \sum_{i=1}^{n} x_i^2 (y_i - (a + bx_i + cx_i + cx_i^2 + d\, x_i \ln x_i)\} = 0$$

and $$\frac{\partial p}{\partial d} = -2 \sum_{i=1}^{n} x \ln x_i \{y_i(a + bx_i + cx_i^2 + d\, x_i \ln x_i)\} = 0$$

For $i = 1$ to 4, we can write these equations as,

$$na + b \sum x_i + c \sum x_i^2 + d \sum x_i \ln x_i = \sum y_i = u$$

$$a \sum x_i + b \sum x_i^2 + c \sum x_i^3 + d \sum x_i^2 \ln x_i = \sum x_i y_i = v \tag{7.56}$$

$$a \sum x_i^2 + b \sum x_i^3 + d \sum x_i^4 + d \sum x_i^3 \ln x_i = \sum x_i^2 \ln x_i = w,$$

and $$a \sum x_i \ln x_i + b \sum x_i^2 \ln x_i + c \sum x_i^3 \ln x_i + d \sum x_i^2 \ln x_i^2 = z.$$

The solution to the above equation in matrix notation is,

$$\begin{vmatrix} a \\ b \\ c \\ d \end{vmatrix} = A^{-1} \begin{vmatrix} u \\ v \\ w \\ z \end{vmatrix} \tag{7.57}$$

where A^{-1} is the inverse of the matrix A, represented by

$$A = \begin{vmatrix} M_{11} & M_{12} & M_{13} & M_{14} \\ M_{21} & M_{22} & M_{23} & M_{24} \\ M_{31} & M_{32} & M_{33} & M_{34} \\ M_{41} & M_{42} & M_{43} & M_{44} \end{vmatrix} \tag{7.58}$$

The elements of the matrix M_{ij} have the following values,

$$M_{11} = n, M_{12} = \sum x_i, M_{13} = \sum x_i^2, M_{14} = \sum x_i \ln x_i$$

$$M_{21} = \sum x_i, M_{22} = \sum x_i^2, M_{23} = \sum x_i^3, M_{24} = \sum x_i^2 \ln x_i$$

$$M_{31} = \sum x_i^2, M_{32} = \sum x_i^3, M_{33} = \sum x_i^4, M_{34} = \sum x_i^3 \ln x_i$$

$$M_{41} = \sum x_i \ln x_i, M_{42} = \sum x_i^2 \ln x_i, M_{43}, \sum x_i^3 \ln x_i, M_{44} = \sum x_i^2 \ln x_i^2$$

which can be calculated if the pair of experimentally measured coordinates (x_i, y_i), i = 1 to 4, are known. The unknowns a, b, c and d can be calculated using Cramer's Rule by replacing the *jth* column of the matrix with the column matrix on the right-hand side of equation (7.57). The values of a, b, c and d are given by the following determinant ratios:

$$a = \frac{\det M_1}{\det A} = \frac{\begin{vmatrix} u & M_{12} & M_{13} & M_{14} \\ v & M_{22} & M_{23} & M_{24} \\ w & M_{32} & M_{33} & M_{34} \\ z & M_{42} & M_{43} & M_{44} \end{vmatrix}}{\begin{vmatrix} M_{11} & M_{12} & M_{13} & M_{14} \\ M_{21} & M_{22} & M_{23} & M_{24} \\ M_{31} & M_{32} & M_{33} & M_{34} \\ M_{41} & M_{42} & M_{43} & M_{44} \end{vmatrix}}$$

Similar expressions can be written for the evaluation of b, c and d, i.e.,

$$b = \frac{\det M_2}{\det A}, \quad c = \frac{\det M_3}{\det A} \quad \text{and} \quad d = \frac{\det M_4}{\det A} \cdot \tag{7.60}$$

The application of the least square optimization method of calculating phase boundaries will now be demonstrated for liquid-solid and solid-solid equilibria.

The compositions of liquid and solid phases in equilibria with each other in the two-phase region of the binary phase diagram have been reported for a large number of binary systems. The data are quite accurate in most cases and can be used in the evaluation of coefficients A_i and B_i which will give the partial excess free energy values, from which the integral excess free energy of formation of a solution can be determined.

The activity of a given component, when the solid and liquid phases are in equilibrium with each other, of a binary system is given by

$$RT \ln a_A^L - RT \ln a_A^S = -\Delta G_{fA}^0 \tag{7.61}$$

A similar expression can be written for the component B. Equation (7.61) can be rewritten in the following forms:

$$RT \ln \gamma_A^L X_A^L - RT \ln \gamma_A^S X_A^S = -\Delta G_{fA}^0$$

or

$$RT \ln \gamma_A^L + RT \ln X_A^L - RT \ln \gamma_A^S X_A^S = -\Delta G_{fA}^0$$

or

$$RT \ln X_A^L + \Delta G_A^{E(L)} - RT \ln \gamma_A^S X_A^S = -\Delta G_{fA}^0 \quad (7.62)$$

Let us assume that the component B has negligible solid solubility in the component A. The component B can be assumed to follow the Raoult's law, and we can write

$$a_B^S = X_B^S \quad \text{and} \quad a_A^S \cong 1$$

Substituting for the activity values in equation (7.62) yields,

$$RT \ln X_A^L + \Delta G_A^{E(L)} = -\Delta G_{fA}^0$$

and

$$RT \ln X_B^L + \Delta G_B^{E(L)} = -\Delta G_{fB}^0 + RT \ln X_B^S,$$

when $\Delta G_A^{E(L)}$ and $\Delta G_B^{E(L)}$ are given by equations (7.46) and (7.47), respectively. Each tie-line in the (liquid + solid) region results in two equations, one for each component. From the free energies of fusion of components A and B, we can form simultaneous equations,

$$\ln X_A^L + \frac{1}{RT} \Delta G_{fA}^0 = -\frac{1}{RT} \Delta G_A^{E(L)} = \sum_{i=0}^{n} (A_i - TB_i)(X_B - iX_A) X_B^{i+1} \quad (7.63)$$

and

$$\ln(X_B^L / X_B^S) + \frac{1}{RT} \Delta G_{fB}^0 = -\frac{1}{RT} \Delta G_B^{E(L)} = \sum_{i=0}^{n} (A_i - TB_i)(i+1) X_A^2 X_B^i \quad (7.64)$$

At each tie-line corresponding to some T in the $(L{+}S)$ region, compositions X_A^L, X_B^L and X_B^S are known. Substituting for the free energies of fusion and composition values, a series of simultaneous equations can be written. Using the method of least square optimization, coefficients A_i and B_i can be evaluated using the procedure outlined. From the computed values of the coefficients, the partial excess free energies can be written as a polynomial from which the expression for integral excess free energy can be derived.

In the Cd-Pb alloy system, Pb has negligible solubility in solid Cd. The above set of equations can be directly applicable to this alloy system. By using the least square optimization method, Ashtakala et al (28) have determined the enthalpy of mixing of the liquid

$$\Delta H^L = X_{Cd}X_{Pb}[15564 - 21184\,X_{Pb} + 35731\,X_{Pb}^2 - 31752\,X_{Pb}^3 + 11042\,X_{Pb}^4], \text{J mol}^{-1}$$

From the enthalpies of mixing data, the partial molar enthalpies of components A and B can be determined using the equation,

$$\Delta H_A^L = \Delta H - X_B \frac{\partial \Delta H^L}{\partial H_B} \quad \text{and} \quad \Delta H_B^L = \Delta H + X_A \frac{\partial \Delta H^L}{\partial X_B}$$

Having calculated $\Delta G_A^{E(L)}$ and $\Delta G_B^{E(L)}$ from equations (7.63) and (7.64), the partial excess entropies ΔS_A^E and ΔS_B^E can be calculated. A process of smoothening the data is carried out by least square regression analysis. The phase diagram can be calculated using the optimized values.

The compositions of α_1 and α_2 phases across the immiscibility gap of a phase diagram can be used as an important set of data in phase diagram evaluations. The activity of each component is the same in the two phases, α_1 and α_2, in equilibrium with each other. This is written as,

$$a_A^{\alpha_1} = a_A^{\alpha_2}$$

or $$RT \ln a_A^{\alpha_1} = RT \ln a_A^{\alpha_2}$$

or $$RT \ln X_A^{\alpha_1} + RT \ln \gamma_A^{\alpha_1} = RT \ln X_A^{\alpha_2} + RT \ln \gamma_A^{\alpha_2}$$

or $$RT \ln X_A^{\alpha_1} + \Delta G_A^{E(\alpha_1)} = RT \ln X_A^{\alpha_2} + \Delta G_A^{E(\alpha_2)} \tag{7.65}$$

where $\Delta G_A^{E(\alpha_1)}\left(= RT \ln \gamma_A^{\alpha_1}\right)$ and $\Delta G_A^{E(\alpha_2)}$ are the excess free energy of the component A in the α_1 and α_2 phases, respectively. The partial excess free energies $\Delta G_A^{E(\alpha_1)}$ and $\Delta G_A^{E(\alpha_2)}$ can be represented as polynomials with compositions $X_B^{\alpha_1}$ and $X_B^{\alpha_2}$, equation (7.46), which yields,

$$RT \ln\left(X_A^{\alpha_1}/X_A^{\alpha_2}\right) = \sum_{i=0}^{n} (A_i - TB_i) \left\{\left(X_B^{\alpha_2} - iX_B^{\alpha_2}\right)X_B^{\alpha_2\, i+1} - \left(X_B^{\alpha_1} - iX_A^{\alpha_1}\right)X_B^{\alpha_1\, i+1}\right\}$$

A similar expression can be written for the component B. Each tie-line in the immiscibility gap of the phase diagram yields two data points, one for each component. The optimization can now be carried out from the compositions of the immiscibility gap boundaries measured experimentally at a number of temperatures. The procedure will yield coefficients A_i and B_i, from which expressions for the enthalpy of mixing in the solid and excess entropy can be written. The optimization has been carried out for the Au-Ni system by Bale and Pelton (2) with the resulting values as follows,

$$\Delta H^S = X_{Au}X_{Ni}(21.506 + 18.887X_{Ni} + 8.858\, X_{Ni}^2 - 22.121\, X_{Ni}^3), \quad \text{J mol}^{-1}$$

$$\Delta S^{E(S)} = X_{Au}X_{Ni}(19.104 - 20.928\, X_{Ni} + 42.986X_{Ni}^2 - 35.095\, X_{Ni}^3), \quad \text{J mol}^{-1}.$$

7.8 CALCULATION OF SLOPES OF PHASE BOUNDARIES

The solid solubility of a component in a binary solid solution can be obtained from the experimentally measured limiting slope dT/dX_B. At first, we will derive a general relationship for the slopes of the phase boundaries, from the condition that the chemical potential of each component is the same in all the phases at equilibrium under constant temperature and pressure. Accordingly,

$$\mu_A^{\alpha}\,(X_B^{\alpha}, T, P) = \mu_A^{\beta}\,(X_B^{\beta}, T, P) \tag{7.66}$$

$$\mu_B^{\alpha}\,(X_B^{\alpha}, T, P) = \mu_B^{\beta}\,(X_B^{\beta}, T, P)$$

The chemical potential of a given component is related to the activity of that component in the phase by the relation,

$$\mu_i^\alpha = \mu_i^{0\alpha} + RT \ln a_i^\alpha \tag{7.67}$$

where $\mu_i^{0\alpha}$ is the chemical potential of the *ith* component in the standard state in the α phase. Substituting the value of μ_i^α and μ_i^β in the pair of equations (7.66) yields,

$$\mu_A^{0\alpha} + RT \ln a_A^\alpha = \mu_A^{0\beta} + RT \ln a_A^\beta$$

$$\mu_B^{0\alpha} + RT \ln a_B^\alpha = \mu_B^{0\beta} + RT \ln a_B^\beta. \tag{7.68}$$

Rearrangement of terms in equation (7.68) gives the following pair of equations

$$\ln a_A^\beta - \ln a_A^\alpha = -\frac{\Delta\mu_A^{0(\alpha \Rightarrow \beta)}}{RT}$$

$$\ln a_B^\beta - \ln a_B^\alpha = -\frac{\Delta\mu_B^{0(\alpha \Rightarrow \beta)}}{RT}$$

Substituting for the activity of the component *i* in terms of the activity coefficient from the equation, $a_i^j = \gamma_i^j \times X_i^j$, yields,

$$\ln X_A^\beta - \ln X_A^\alpha + \ln \gamma_A^\beta - \ln \gamma_A^\alpha + \frac{\Delta\mu_A^{0(\alpha \Rightarrow \beta)}}{RT} = 0 \tag{7.69a}$$

$$\ln X_B^\beta - \ln X_B^\alpha + \ln \gamma_B^\beta - \ln \gamma_B^\alpha + \frac{\Delta\mu_B^{0(\alpha \Rightarrow \beta)}}{RT} = 0 \tag{7.69b}$$

If ψ is a function of the left-hand side of equations (7.69), it can be represented as

$$\psi = f(T, X_A, X_B) \quad \text{and}$$

$$\left(\frac{\partial\psi}{\partial T}\right) = \left(\frac{\partial\psi}{\partial T}\right)_{X_i} + \left(\frac{\partial\psi}{\partial X_B^\alpha}\right)_{T,X_B^\beta}\left(\frac{dX_B^\alpha}{dT}\right) + \left(\frac{\partial\psi}{\partial X_B^\beta}\right)_{T,X_B^\alpha}\left(\frac{dX_B^\beta}{dT}\right) = 0 \qquad (7.70)$$

Differentiation of the pair of equations (7.69) yields,

$$\frac{d\psi}{dT} = 0 + 0 + \frac{\partial}{\partial T}(\ln\gamma_A^\beta) - \frac{\partial}{\partial T}(\ln\gamma_A^\alpha) = \frac{\Delta H_A^0}{RT^2}$$

$$\left(\frac{\partial\psi}{\partial X_B^\alpha}\right)_{T,X_B^\beta} = \frac{1}{X_A^\alpha} + \frac{\partial}{\partial X_B^\alpha}(\ln\gamma_A^\beta) - \frac{\partial}{\partial X_B^\alpha}(\ln\gamma_A^\alpha) = \frac{1}{X_A^\alpha} + \frac{\partial\ln\gamma_A^\alpha}{\partial X_B^\alpha}$$

$$= \frac{1 + X_A^\alpha\left(\dfrac{\partial\ln\gamma_A^\alpha}{[\partial x_B^\alpha]}\right)}{X_A^\alpha} = \frac{\phi^\alpha}{X_A^\alpha}$$

$$\left(\frac{d\psi}{\partial X_B^\beta}\right)_{T,X_B^\alpha} = -\ \frac{1 + X_B^\beta\dfrac{\partial\ln\gamma_A^\beta}{\partial x_A^\alpha}}{X_A^\beta} = -\ \frac{\phi^\beta}{X_A^\beta}, \quad \text{also}$$

$$\left(\frac{d\psi}{dT}\right) = \frac{\partial}{\partial T}(\ln\gamma_B^\beta) - \frac{\partial}{\partial T}(\ln\gamma_B^\alpha) - \frac{\Delta H_B^0}{RT^2}$$

$$\left(\frac{\partial\psi}{\partial X_B^\alpha}\right)_{T,X_B^\beta} = -\frac{1}{X_B^\alpha} - \frac{\partial}{\partial X_B^\alpha}(\ln\gamma_B^\alpha) = -\frac{\phi^\alpha}{X_B^\alpha}$$

$$\left(\frac{\partial\psi}{\partial X_B^\beta}\right)_{T,X_B^\alpha} = \frac{\phi^\beta}{X_B^\beta} \quad \text{from equation (7.69b).}$$

Substitution of each set separately in equation (7.70) yields,

$$\frac{\partial}{\partial T}(\ln \gamma_A^\beta) - \frac{\partial}{\partial T}(\ln \gamma_A^\alpha) - \frac{\Delta H_A^0}{RT^2} + \frac{\phi^\alpha}{X_A^\alpha}\left(\frac{dX_B^\alpha}{dT}\right) - \frac{\phi^\beta}{X_A^\beta}\left(\frac{dX_B^\beta}{dT}\right) = 0$$

and
$$\frac{\partial}{\partial T}(\ln \gamma_B^\beta) - \frac{\partial}{\partial T}(\ln \gamma_B^\alpha) - \frac{\Delta H_B^0}{RT^2} + \frac{\phi^\alpha}{X_B^\alpha}\left(\frac{dX_B^\alpha}{dT}\right) + \frac{\phi^\beta}{X_B^\beta}\left(\frac{dX_B^\beta}{dT}\right) = 0$$

Solving for $\left(\frac{dX_B^\alpha}{dT}\right)$ and $\left(\frac{dX_B^\beta}{dT}\right)$ yields,

$$\left(\frac{dX_B^\alpha}{dT}\right) = \frac{X_A^\alpha X_B^\alpha}{(X_B^\beta - X_B^\alpha)\,\phi^\alpha}\left[X_B^\beta\left\{\frac{\partial}{\partial T}(\ln X_B^\beta - \ln \gamma_B^\alpha) - \frac{\Delta H_B^0}{RT^2}\right\} + X_A^\beta\left\{\frac{\partial}{\partial T}(\ln \gamma_A^\beta - \ln \gamma_A^\alpha) - \frac{\Delta H_A^0}{RT^2}\right\}\right]$$

$$\left(\frac{dX_B^\beta}{dT}\right) = \frac{X_A^\beta X_B^\beta}{(X_B^\beta - X_B^\alpha)\,\phi^\beta}\left[X_A^\alpha\left\{\frac{\partial}{\partial T}(\ln \gamma_A^\beta - \ln \gamma_A^\alpha) - \frac{\Delta H_A^0}{RT^2}\right\} + X_B^\alpha\left\{\frac{\partial}{\partial T}(\ln \gamma_B^\beta - \ln \gamma_B^\alpha) - \frac{\Delta H_B^0}{RT^2}\right\}\right] \tag{7.71}$$

Thus, slopes of the phase boundaries (dT/dX_B) for both the $\alpha/(\alpha+\beta)$ and $\beta/(\alpha+\beta)$ phase boundaries can be determined if experimental values of the temperature dependence of the activity coefficients, compositions and the enthalpies of the two components are known.

The limiting slopes of the phase boundaries can be calculated from the same consideration of equality of chemical potential of a given component in both the phases, equation (7.66). The condition implicit in the equality of chemical potential is described by equations (7.69),

$$\ln X_A^{\beta} - \ln X_A^{\alpha} + \ln \gamma_A^{\beta} - \ln \gamma_A^{\alpha} + \frac{\Delta\mu_A^{0(\alpha \Rightarrow \beta)}}{RT} = 0 \tag{7.69a}$$

$$\ln X_B^{\beta} - \ln X_B^{\alpha} + \ln \gamma_B^{\beta} - \ln \gamma_B^{\alpha} + \frac{\Delta\mu_B^{0(\alpha \Rightarrow \beta)}}{RT} = 0 \tag{7.69b}$$

The phase boundaries converge at the pure component axes, $X_B = 0$ and $X_B = 1$. For the equilibrium liquid (β) ⇒ solid (α) as $X_A \Rightarrow 1$, the liquidus and solidus curves converge at the melting point of the component A. The relevant equation can be written by replacing β in the superscript with L for the liquid. For dilute solutions, an ideal solution behavior can be assumed for both solid and liquid phases. Thus $a_A^L = X_A^L$ and $a_A^{\alpha} = X_A^L$, etc. Considering the free energy of fusion, $\Delta\mu_A^0 (= \Delta G_{fA}^0)$ to be given by $\Delta H_{fA}^0\,(1 - T/T_A)$, and

$$\lim_{X_A \to 1} \ln X_A = \lim_{X_A \to 1} \ln (1 - X_B) = -X_B\,,$$

We can substitute for these values in equation (7.69), and obtain,

$$-X_B^L + X_B^{\alpha} = -\frac{\Delta H_{fA}^0}{R} \cdot \left(\frac{1}{T} - \frac{1}{T_A}\right). \tag{7.72}$$

Differentiating equation (7.72) with respect to T yields,

$$-\frac{dX_B^L}{dT} + \frac{dX_B^{\alpha}}{dT} = \frac{\Delta H_{fA}^0}{RT^2}$$

or
$$-\frac{dX_B^L}{dT} + \frac{dX_B^{\alpha}}{dT} = \frac{\Delta H_{fA}^0}{RT_A^2} \quad \text{at} \quad T = T_A.$$

If the solute has negligible solubility in the α phase, the solidus curve will be very steep and $dT/dX_B^{\alpha} = \infty$, or $dX_B^{\alpha}/dT = 0$.

$$-\frac{dX_B^L}{dT}=\frac{\Delta H_{fA}^0}{RT_A^2}. \tag{7.73}$$

For non-ideal solutions,

$$-\frac{dX_B^L}{dT}+\frac{dX_B^\alpha}{dT}+\frac{d}{dT}(\ln\gamma_A^L)-\frac{d}{dT}(\ln\gamma_A^\alpha)=\frac{\Delta H_{fA}^0}{RT_A^2} \quad \text{at} \quad T=T_A$$

or

$$-\frac{dX_B^L}{dT}+\frac{dX_B^\alpha}{dT}+\frac{d}{dT}\{\ln\gamma_A^L-\ln\gamma_A^\alpha\}=\frac{\Delta H_{fA}^0}{RT_A^2}$$

Thus, if the temperature dependence of the activity coefficients of the components in the liquid and solid solutions are known, the slope of the phase boundaries of binary solutions can be calculated.

REFERENCES

1. L.V. Shchipanova and P.V. Geld, *Chem. Abstract*, 59 (1963), 3371.
2. O Kubaschewski, F.L. Evans and C.B. Alcock, *Metallurgical Electrochemistry*, Pergamon Press, 1967 (pp. 347, 384, 398, 405).
3. C.D. Thurmond, *J. Electrochem Soc.*, 57 (1953), 827.
4. M.H. Rand and O. Kubaschewski, *The Thermomechanical Properties of U Compounds*, Oliver and Boyd, Edinwigh (1963), 89.
5. R.P. Larsen, R.S. Shor, H.M. Fedder and D.S. Flikkema, U.S. Atomic Energy Commission Publ. ANL (1954), 3135.
   Also see: O. Kubaschewski, Z. Electrochem., 54 (1950), 275.
   O. Kubaschewski, Z. Electrochem., 41 (1950), 445.
6. K.K. Kelly, *Bull U.S. Bur. Mines*, 476 (1949).
7. M. Hansen and K. Anderko, *Constitution of Binary Alloys*, 2nd ed., McGraw Hill Book Co., (1958), 681.
8. I. Barin and O. Knacks, *Thermomechanical Properties of Inorganic Substances*, Springer Verlag (1973).
9. R. Hultgren, P.D. Desai, D.T. Hawkins, M. Gleiser and K.K. Kelly, ''Selected Values of the Thermodynamic Properties of Elements of Binary Alloys, *ASM*, Metals Park, Ohio, (1973).

10. C.H.P. Lupis, *Chemical Thermodynamics of Materials*, North Holland, Elsevier Science Publishing Co. Inc., (1983).
11. J.L. Murray, *Met. Trans.*, 15A, USA (1984), 261.
12. I. Karakaya and W.T. Thomson, *Bull. Alloy Phase Diag.*, 9 (1984), 144.
13. J. Dutkiewictz, Z. Mosser and W. Zakulski, Bull. Alloy Phase Diag., 9 (1988), 694.
14. I. Karakaya and W.T. Thomson, *Bull. Alloy Phase Diag.*, 8 (1987), 334.
15. I. Karakaya and W.T. Thomson, *Bull. Alloy Phase Diag.*, 7 (1986), 259.
16. I Barin, O. Knack and O. Kubaschewski, ''Thermochemical Properties of Inorganic substances,'' *Springer Verlag* (1973).
17. I. Karakaya and W.T. Thomson, *Bull. Alloy Phase Diag.*, 7 (1986), 362.
18. I. Karakaya and W.T. Thomson, *Bull. Alloy Phase Diag.*, 9 (3) (1988), 237.
19. H. Rossler, *Chem. Ztg.*, 2 (1900), 733.
20. R.W. Drier and H.L. Walker, *Phil Mag.*, 16 (1983), 294.
21. B.P. Burylev and V.D. Ivanova, Russian Journal of Phys. Chem., 50 (1976), 1286.
22. J. Barnardini, A. Combe-Brun and J. Cabane, *Scripta Metall.*, 4 (1970), 985.
23. A.D. Pelton, *Bull. Alloy Phase Diagrams*, 8 (1987), 550.
24. A.G. Morachewskii, E.A. Meiorova and O.I. Vorobeva, *Elektro Khim.*, 18(1) (1982), 148.
25. L. Kaufmann and H. Bernstein, *Computer Calculations of Phase Diagrams*, Academic Press, New York (1970).
26. H.L. Lukas, E-Th. Henig and B. Zimmermann, *Calphad Journal*,1 (1977), 225.
27. C.W. Bale and A.D. Pelton, *Trans. Metall.*, 14B (1983), 77.
28. S. Ashtakala, A.D. Pelton and C.W. Bale, *Bull. Alloy Phase Diagrams*, 2 (1) (1981), 83.

PROBLEMS

1. Calculate and plot the phase diagram of the MgO-NiO system with the following data.

$$\Delta H_{f\mathrm{MgO}} = 77 \text{ kJ mol}^{-1},\ \Delta H_f^{\mathrm{NiO}} = 52.32 \text{ kJ mol}^{-1},\ T_{\mathrm{MgO}} = 3073 \text{ K}\ T_{\mathrm{NiO}} = 2233 \text{ K}$$

2. The Ag-Ge binary system shows a eutectic reaction. The thermodynamic properties have been assessed to give the following values:

$$\Delta H^L_{\mathrm{Ni}} = (1 - X_{\mathrm{Ag}})X_{\mathrm{Ag}}(18.6 - 38X_{\mathrm{Ag}} + 91.5X^2_{\mathrm{Ag}} - 137X^3_{\mathrm{Ag}} + 48X^4_{\mathrm{Ag}}) \text{ kJ mol}^{-1}$$

$$\Delta S^E = (1 - X_{Ag})X_{Ag}(13.5 - 32.7X_{Ag} + 90.8X_{Ag}^2 - 128X_{Ag}^3 + 515X_{Ag}^4), \text{ J mol}^{-1}$$

$$\Delta G_{fAg}^0 = 32940 + 23.45T - 7.76T \ln T + 3.67 \times 10^{-3}T^2, \text{J mol}^{-1}$$

$$\Delta G_{fGe}^0 = 1221 + 90.709T - 13.738T \ln T + 4.8 \times 10^{-3}T^2 + 2.66 \times 10^5 T^{-1}, \text{J mol}^{-1}$$

$RT \ln \gamma_{Ge}^0 = 8.8 + \Delta G_{fGe}^0 = 8.8 + \Delta G_{fGe}^0$ for the solid solution.

Compute the phase diagram.

3. The free energy of mixing of a binary system is given by
$\Delta G_m = 10000\, X_A X_B + RT(X_A \ln X_A + X_B \ln X_B)$
Determine the critical composition and temperature for the immiscibility gap and the spinodal phase boundaries at 500, 400 and 300 K.

4. What is the effect of the entropy of fusion on the separation between the liquidus and solidus curves?

5. Calculate the separation between the liquidus and solidus curves for the system at $T = (T_{fNb} + T_{fTa}) / 2$ and $(T_{fCaO} + T_{fMnO})/2$.
(a) Nb–Ta (T_{fNb} = 2469°C, T_{fTa} = 3020°C, $\overline{\Delta S}°_f$ = 9 J mol^{-1} K^{-1})
(b) CaO–MnO (T_{fCaO} = 2980 K, T_{fMnO} = 2148 K, $\overline{\Delta S}°_f$ = 21 J mol^{-1}K^{-1})

6. Components *A* and *B* have negligible mutual solubility in each other in the solid state. The phase diagram shows a eutectic reaction. The excess free energy of mixing in the liquid is represented by the relation,

$$\Delta G_m^E = 2000\, X_A X_B \left(1 - \frac{T}{3000}\right)$$

The melting points and the heats of fusion of components *A* and *B* are 1200 K and 1000 K and 12 kJ mol^{-1} and 9 kJ mol^{-1} respectively. The specific heats of the two components C_p $(S \rightarrow L)$ are assumed to the negligible. Calculate the phase diagram of the system *A*–*B*.

7. In Chapter 2, expressions for the free energy of mixing for the solid and liquid solutions were derived using pure solid *A* as the standard state for *A* and pure liquid *B* as the standard state for the component *B*. There are a number of other possible standard states for components *A* and *B*, that is (i) *A*-solid, *B*-solid (ii) *A*-liquid, *B*-liquid (iii) *A-liquid, B*-solid.
Determine expressions for the free energy of mixing of the solid and liquid

solutions for each of the above combinations of standard states. Also, show that the change in reference state does not change the relative position of phase boundaries.

8. The regular solution is represented by an expression of the form:

$$\Delta G_m = X_A X_B(aX_A + bX_B) + RT(X_A \ln X_A + X_B \ln X_B)$$

Calculate the critical composition and temperature for the immiscibility gap for $a = 5$ kJ mol^{-1} and $b = 6$ kJ mol^{-1}

9. The following data are reported in the literature for the Na–K binary system:

$\Delta G°_{fK} = -2.53 + 0.163\lambda\, T + 4.55 \times 10^{-5}\, T^2 - 2.05 \times 10^{-9}\, T^3 - 2.93 \times 10^{-2} T \ln T$, kJ mol^{-1}

$\Delta G°_{fNa} = -1.63 + 0.127\, \mathrm{T} + 3.17 \times 10^{-5}\, T^2 - 1.77 \times 10^{-9}\, T^3 - 2.27 \times 10^{-2}\, T \ln T$, kJ mol^{-1}

$$G^{E(S)}_{\mathrm{Na}} = 0$$

$$\Delta H^L_m = X_{\mathrm{K}} X_{\mathrm{Na}}(2.25 + 1.40X_{\mathrm{Na}}), \text{kJ mol}^{-1}$$

$$S^{E(L)} = X_{\mathrm{K}} X_{\mathrm{Na}}\,(-6.31 + 1.3X_{\mathrm{Na}} + 5.1\, X^2_{\mathrm{Na}} - 5.85\, X^3_{\mathrm{Na}}), \text{J mol}^{-1}\text{K}^{-1}$$

For the terminal solid solution,

$$\left.\begin{aligned} RT\gamma°_{\mathrm{Na}} &= 5.535 \text{ kJ mol}^{-1} \\ RT\gamma°_{\mathrm{K}} &= 9.996 \text{ kJ mol} - 1 \end{aligned}\right\} \text{ standard state, pure liquid}$$

$$\Delta G°_{f(\mathrm{Na_2K})} = 11.295 - 40.23\, T \text{ kJ mol}^{-1} \text{ \{free energy of fusion of Na}_2\text{K)}$$

Calculate the phase diagram and plot it.

Chapter 8

QUANTITATIVE MICROSCOPY

8.1 INTRODUCTION

The physical and mechanical properties of materials are largely dependent on the microstructure. As an example, it is well-known that the stress required to initiate yielding in a metal or an alloy depends to some extent on the grain-size. As the surface area of the grain boundaries per unit volume increases, the grain size decreases and hence the yield stress of the material increases. This is represented by the well-known Hall-Petch (1) equation:

$$\sigma_y = \sigma_i + K_y d^{-1/2} \,. \tag{8.1}$$

In equation (8.1), σ_i is the lattice friction stress, K_y is a material constant, and d is the grain diameter. Similarly, the precipitation hardening due to the second phase particles embedded in the depleted matrix is dependent on a number of parameters, such as volume fraction of the particles, interparticle spacing, mean free path, particle size, etc. In order to characterize the properties of a material, it is, therefore, essential to relate these with the stereological parameters such as volume fraction of the second phase particles, surface area per unit volume, fraction of the second phase particles, surface area per unit volume, number of particles in a volume, particle size and particle size distribution, etc. In the study of the kinetics of phase transformation, parameters such as growth rate, interlamellar spacing, true average particle diameter, mean curvature, etc. are frequently required. The true shape and size of the three dimensional microstructural features is not apparent when studied on a plane of polish which is two-dimensional. Quantitative microscopy is developed primarily to relate the three-dimensional structure to the structural parameters in the plane of observation of opaque materials. Since the structural features are randomly dispersed in the three dimensions, the mathematical probability that the structure will be intercepted by a plane or line plays a key role. This is pertinent because each structural element has a finite dimension. We will discuss briefly the theory of probability as applicable to the theory of quantitative microscopy. We will begin with the definition of a few simple terms used in the theory of probability.

8.2 THEORY OF PROBABILITY

8.2.1 Sample Space and Elementary Events

The set of all possible outcomes of a random experiment is termed the sample space. Consider the tossing of a coin. There are two possible outcomes: a head or a tail. The sample space can be written as the set $\{H, T\}$. Similarly, if we throw a die, the possible outcomes will be the numbers from 1 to 6. The sample space in the experiment is $\{1, 2, 3, 4, 5, 6\}$.

Suppose we toss the coin twice. The possible outcomes of the experiment are, two heads (H, H), head on the first toss and tail on the second (H, T), tail on the first toss and head on the second (T, H), and both tails (T, T).

The sample space of the experiment can be represented by $\{(H, H), (H, T), (T, H), (T, T)\}$. Similarly, roll a pair of dice. The possible outcomes are:

$$\begin{array}{cccccc}
1,1 & 1,2 & 1,3 & 1,4 & 1,5 & 1,6 \\
2,1 & 2,2 & 2,3 & 2,4 & 2,5 & 2,6 \\
3,1 & 3,2 & 3,3 & 3,4 & 3,5 & 3,6 \\
4,1 & 4,2 & 4,3 & 4,4 & 4,5 & 4,6 \\
5,1 & 5,2 & 5,3 & 5,4 & 5,5 & 5,6 \\
6,1 & 6,2 & 6,3 & 6,4 & 6,5 & 6,6
\end{array}$$

The sample space consists of 36 elements, and each element has an equal chance of occurring.

In general, consider a random experiment with p outcomes ($a_1, a_2, a_3, \ldots, a_p$) and another with q outcomes ($b_1, b_2, b_3, \ldots, b_q$), then the sample space of the two experiments carried out together consists of $p \times q$ outcomes and can be represented by the set:

$$
\begin{array}{ccccc}
(a_1, b_1) & (a_1, b_2) & (a_1, b_3) & \ldots & (a_1, b_q) \\
(a_2, b_1) & (a_2, b_2) & (a_2, b_3) & \ldots & (a_2, b_q) \\
\cdot & \cdot & \cdot & \cdot & \cdot \\
\cdot & \cdot & \cdot & \cdot & \cdot \\
\cdot & \cdot & \cdot & \cdot & \cdot \\
(a_p, b_1) & (a_p, b_2) & (a_p, b_3) & \ldots & (a_p, b_q)
\end{array}
$$

This represented by the set in shortened notation:

$$\{(a_1, b_j)\} \qquad \begin{array}{l} i = 1, 2, \ldots, p \\ j = 1, 2, \ldots, q. \end{array}$$

The elements of a sample space on random sampling are termed elementary events. Thus, the throw of a die may result in any of the six elementary events denoted by 1, 2, 3, 4, 5, and 6. Similarly, throwing two dice results in any of the 36 elementary events as indicated earlier. The tossing of a coin results in either a head or a tail so there are two elementary events in this experiment.

Consider some events of a random experiment: Event A "The rolling of a die results in an odd number". This is represented by the subset {1, 3, 5}. Event B "The number on the dice is less than 3", will be represented by the subset {1, 2}.

8.2.2 Probability of an Event

Let us consider a box containing some white balls and some red balls of the same size. If the balls are randomly placed in the box, the chance that a red ball is drawn is related to the proportion of red balls in the container. Suppose there are 30 white balls and 70 red balls in the container. The chance that a red ball is drawn is more. However, if the number of white balls is 70 and red balls is 30, then the chance of drawing a white ball is more.

Thus, if we have two events, A and B, associated with a random experiment, we can talk about the event A being more or less likely to happen than event B. The event which is more likely to happen has a higher probability of occurrence. In the example of the container filled with 70 red balls and 30 white balls, the probability of drawing a red ball is $P(A) = 70/100$, and white ball is $P(B) = 30/100$. The probability of an event A is defined as the ratio of the number of elementary events favorable to A divided by the total number of elementary events which are equally likely to occur.

$$\text{Thus}\, P(A) = \frac{\text{number of elementary events favorable to A}}{\text{total no. of elementary events equally likely to occur}}$$

If two events A and B are mutually exclusive, i.e., independent of each other, the probability that either A or B will occur equals the sum of the probabilities of the two events $P(A)$ and $P(B)$,

$$P(A \text{ or } B) = P(A) + P(B) \tag{8.2}$$

In the example of the container having red and white balls, the probability that the ball drawn is either red or white is 1.

$P(\text{red or white}) = 0.7 + 0.3 = 1.$

Consider all equally likely events of a random experiment. There may be some mutually exclusive events. In such a case, the probability that event A or B will occur is equal to

$$P(A \text{ or } B) = P(A) + P(B) - P(A \text{ and } B) \tag{8.3}$$

Let us assume a pack of cards. The probability that the card drawn is either red or an ace is

$$P(\text{red}) = 1/2$$

$$P(\text{ace}) = 1/13$$

$$P(\text{red and ace}) = 1/26$$

$$P(\text{red or an ace}) = 1/2 + 1/13 - 1/26 = 7/13$$

If the probability of an event depends upon the events preceding it, the chance of occurrence of such an event is known as conditional probability. Consider a ternary alloy with mole fractions $X_A = 0.3$, $X_B = 0.2$ and $X_C = 0.5$ for the components *A*, *B* and *C*, respectively. The probability of the event "a particular lattice site is occupied by *A*-type atom" is equal to 0.3/1 = 0.3. If we place a subsequent condition that the lattice site is not occupied by *C*-type atom, then it is occupied either by an *A* or a *B*-type atom. Hence the probability that the lattice site is occupied by an *A* atom is 0.3/(0.2+0.3) = 0.6. The subsequent conditions imposed on the event modify the probability, and this is known as conditional probability. This is expressed as

$$P(A) = \frac{\text{mol. fraction of } A \text{ atoms}}{\text{mol. fraction } A + \text{mol. fraction } B} = \frac{0.3}{(0.2+0.3)} = 0.6$$

In general, we can discuss the occurrence of a conditional event *A*, having known that event B has occurred. The conditional probability is written as

$$P(A/B) = \frac{P(A \text{ and } B)}{P(B)} \tag{8.4}$$

when *P* (*A* and *B*) is the number of elementary events favorable to both *A* and *B* and *P* (*B*) is the number of events favorable to *B*. The following example illustrates the above formula.

During the coarsening of a precipitate, particle coalescence also occurs. Let us assume coalescence of two particles, the size range of particles being 1 to 6 mm. It is known that no more than one pair each combination of equal size particles and no more than two pairs of unequal size particles are considered in the experiment. A pair of particles in picked up and the sum of the particle sizes of a pair is 6. What is the conditional probability that the particle size 4 has appeared at least once?

If *A* is the event "particle size 4 has appeared at least once", then *P* (*A*) = 11/36. The event *B* "the sum of the particle sizes of the coalesced particles is 6" gives the probability equal to *P* (*B*) = (5/36). The probability that both events *A* and *B* have occurred is (2/36). Thus,

$$P\ (A/B) = \frac{2/36}{5/36} = \frac{2}{5} = 0.4$$

Consider a ternary alloy with $X_A = 0.4$, $X_B = 0.2$, and $X_C = 0.4$ as the mole fractions of components *A*, *B*, and *C*, respectively. What are the probabilities of two neighboring sites being occupied by *A–A*, *B–B*, *C–C*, *A–B*, *A–C*, and *B–C* pairs?

The probability that one of the sites is occupied by *A*, *B*, or *C*–type atoms is $P(A) = 0.4$, $P(B) = 0.2$, $P(C) = 0.4$. The probability of two neighboring sites being occupied by *A* atoms is $P(A\text{–}A) = 0.4 \times 0.4 = 0.16$. Similar probability values can be written for different combination of *A*, *B*, and *C* as given below:

$$P(A-A) = 0.4 \times 0.4 = 0.16$$

$$P(B-B) = 0.2 \times 0.2 = 0.04$$

$$P(C-C) = 0.4 \times 0.4 = 0.16$$

$$P(A-B) = 0.4 \times 0.2 + 0.2 \times 0.4 = 0.16$$

$$P(A-C) = 0.4 \times 0.4 + 0.4 \times 0.4 = 0.32$$

$$P(B-C) = 0.2 \times 0.4 + 0.4 \times 0.2 = 0.16$$

$$\text{Total} = 0.16 + 0.04 + 0.16 + 0.16 + 0.32 + 0.16 = 1$$

The above example illustrates that, in the case of independent events, for every pair of events *A* and *B* where *A* and *B* are associated with one of the experiments, the probability of simultaneous occurrence of *A* and *B* is the product of $P(A)$ and $P(B)$. Thus,

$$P(A \text{ and } B) = P(A) \times P(B) \tag{8.5}$$

8.2.3 Probability Distribution

Let us consider the distribution of precipitate particles of the β phase in a matrix of the α phase. The particles belong to classes 1 to 10 mm. The number of particles of each class in given in Table 8.1.

Table 8.1

Particle class, x, size in mm	No. of particles
1	1
2	3
3	5
4	8
5	10
6	8
7	6
8	4
9	3
10	2

If all particle classes are equally likely to be selected, the probability that a particle of class 1 is selected is equal to 1/50 = 0.02. The probability of selecting particles of each class is written as

$$P(1) = 0.02, \quad P(2) = 0.06$$

$$P(3) = 0.1, \quad P(4) = 0.16$$

$$P(5) = 0.2, \quad P(6) = 0.16$$

$$P(7) = 0.12, \quad P(8) = 0.08$$

$$P(9) = 0.06, \quad P(10) = 0.04$$

The result illustrates the probability distribution of particles belonging to each class, as shown in Fig. 8.1.

Let us consider an experiment to be carried out in such a manner that all outcomes are equally likely. Let us say that, if the experiment results in a success (S) its probability is denoted by s, and if it results in failure (F), it is f. Let the experiment be carried out two times, both independent of each other and let us count both the experiments as one. If X represents success, then we can write the probabilities as follows:

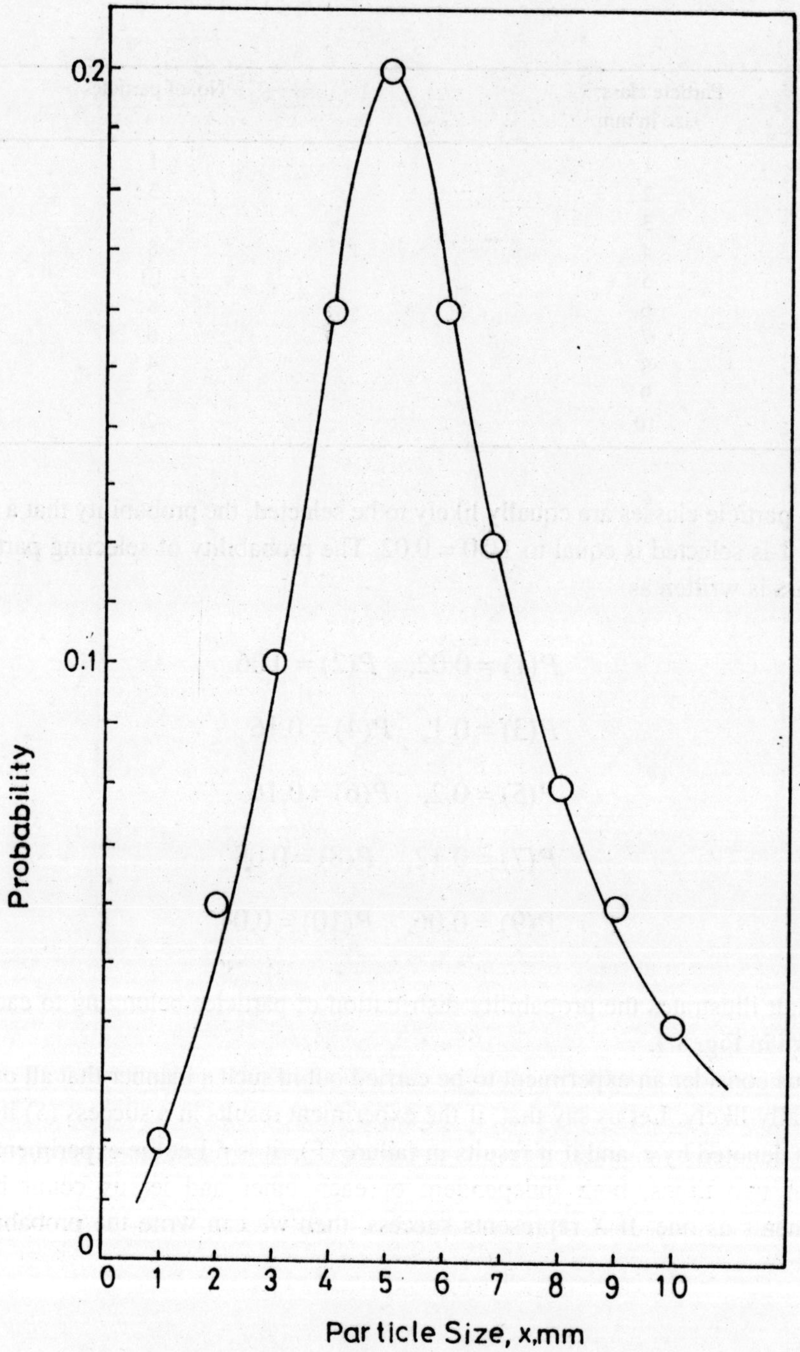

Fig. 8.1 The probability distribution of particles.

$$P(X=0)=P(FF)=f^2$$

$$P(X=1)=P(SF \text{ or } FS)=sf+fs=2sf$$

$$P(X=2)=P(SS)=s^2$$

or

$$s^2+2sf+f^2=1 \tag{8.6}$$

If the same experiment is carried out three times and the combined experiment treated as a single experiment, we can write,

$$P(X=0)=P(FFF)=f^3$$

$$P(X=1)=P(SFF), P(FSF), P(FFS)=3sf^2$$

$$P(X=2)=P(SSF), P(SFS), P(FSS)=3s^2f$$

$$P(X=3)=P(SSS)=s^3$$

The sum of the probabilities is $s^3 + 3s^2f + 3sf^2 + f^3 = 1$ (8.7)

If the experiment is carried out n times and the number of successes is r, then we can write,

$$P(X=r)=C(n,r)\, s^r f^{n-r} \tag{8.8}$$

The probability distribution of the random variable is expressed as:

$$P(X=0)=C(n,0)\, s^0 f^{n-0}$$

$$P(X=1)=C(n,1)\, s^1 f^{n-1}$$

$$P(X=2)=C(n,2)\, s^2 f^{n-2}$$

$$P(X=3) = C(n,3)\, s^3 f^{n-3}$$

$$P(X=r) = C(n,r)\, s^r f^{n-r}$$

$$P(X=n) = C(n,n)\, s^n f^{n-n}$$

The value of $C(n, r) = n!/r!\,(n-r)\,!$. The probability distribution with values of random variable $X = 0, 1, 2, \ldots, r, \ldots n$, thus, shows a binominal distribution. This is illustrated with the help of the following example.

A coin is tossed 10 times. If getting a head is a success, what are the probabilities of getting $X = 0$ (complete failure), $X = 4$ (four successes and six failures), and $X = 8$ (8 successes and 2 failures)?

$$P(X=0) = C(10,0)\,(1/2)^0\,(1/2)^{10} = 0.00097656.$$

$$P(X=4) = C(10,4)\,(1/2)^4\,(1/2)^6 = 0.205.$$

$$P(X=8) = C(10,8)\,(1/2)^8\,(1/2)^2 = 0.0439.$$

8.2.4 Frequency and Cumulative Frequency

In a statistical experiment, it is usual to record the data in the order that they occur. For example, the result of repeated tosses of a coin can be recorded as *HTTHHT* . . . . In this section, we learn how to represent data in a tabular form, and determine the frequency and cumulative frequency of occurrence of a particular event.

The grain size of a polycrystalline sample of copper has been measured and the data recorded in the sequence they occurred. From the data, we can group all the grain size values that belong to the same size class, as represented in Table 8.2.

The table illustrates how often a particular grain size x, occurs in the sample, i.e., the absolute frequency for a particular value of x in the statistical experiment on measurement of grain size. Since the total number of measurements is $n = 100$, the relative frequency $f(x)$ of each grain size can be written. For example, for $x = 200$ μm, the absolute frequency is 15 and the relative frequency $f(x = 200) = 0.15$.

Table 8.2 Frequency Table of the Grain Size

Grain size, μm (x)	Absolute frequency	Relative frequency	Cumulative frequency	Cumulative Relative frequency
140	2	0.02	2	0.02
150	3	0.03	5	0.05
160	4	0.04	9	0.09
170	6	0.06	15	0.15
180	10	0.1	25	0.25
190	13	0.13	38	0.38
200	15	0.15	53	0.53
210	14	0.14	67	0.67
220	12	0.12	79	0.79
230	10	0.1	89	0.89
240	6	0.06	95	0.95
250	3	0.03	98	0.98
260	2	0.02	100	1.0

If we sum the relative frequency values up to a certain value of $x \le a$, we get the cumulative relative frequency $F(a)$ corresponding to that value of a. Suppose we sum all absolute frequency values smaller than or equal to $x = 200$ μm, then the cumulative frequency is 53 and the cumulative relative frequency is $F(x \le 200) = 0.53$.

The above idea can be represented in a generalized form. Consider a statistical sample containing n measurements and belonging to p classes,

$$x_1, x_2, x_3, ..., x_p$$

with relative frequencies,

$$f_1, f_2, f_3, ..., f_p$$

The frequency function can be written as

$$f(x) = \begin{cases} f_i, & x = x_i \quad (i = 1, 2, ..., p) \\ 0 & x \ne x_i \end{cases} \tag{8.9}$$

The sum of the relative frequencies in the sample equals 1, as shown in Table 2. This is represented as

$$F(x) = \sum_{i=1}^{p} f(x_i) = f(x_1) + f(x_2) + f(x_3) + \ldots + f(x_p) \tag{8.10}$$

$$= f_1 + f_2 + f_3 + \ldots + f_p$$

$$= 1.$$

The cumulative relative frequency function $F(x)$, can also be measured for the value of $i = m$, when $m \le p$. Thus

$$F(x) = \sum_{i=1}^{m} f(x_i)$$

The frequency function $f(x)$ can be shown in a diagram as individual points of each class, known as a dot frequency diagram, Fig. 8.2a, or a histogram drawn with x as the mid-point of each class, Fig. 8.2b.

If the data consist of a large number of numerically different values, the frequency function can be represented by grouping. This is carried out by choosing an interval covering x from the smallest to the largest value of the sample. This is illustrated with the help of percent elongation of a large number of steel specimens hardened by heat treatment.

7.6, 7.9, 3.1, 3.6, 3.4, 4.3, 3.4, 4.7, 4.1, 4.6, 7.1,
7.8, 6.5, 6.5, 4.2, 5.1, 6.3, 5.2, 5.3, 3.2, 6.5, 6.4,
3.8, 5.6, 5.7, 6.2, 6.1, 8.0, 7.5, 8.2, 8.3, 7.2, 7.5,
7.6, 6.1, 2.6, 2.7, 5.7, 5.6, 5.7, 6.1, 6.3, 7.2, 6.6,
8.1, 7.0, 3.8, 4.1, 6.1, 6.0, 5.0, 3.9, 4.0, 3.8, 5.8,
2.7, 6.1, 6.2, 5.8, 7.0, 6.3, 6.4, 5.9, 5.7, 8.0, 6.3,
6.4, 5.5, 5.4, 5.3, 6.0, 5.0, 5.1, 7.1, 8.0, 3.3, 2.0,
4.9, 6.1, 5.8, 5.7, 6.0, 8.1, 2.3, 4.0 4.1, 4.3, 4.5,
5.6, 6.0 5.3, 5.5, 5.4, 6.7, 6.8.

The above data can be grouped into class intervals from 2 to 3 including 3, 3 to 4, 4 to 5, 5 to 6, 6 to 7, 7 to 8 and 8 to 9 as given in Table 8.3.

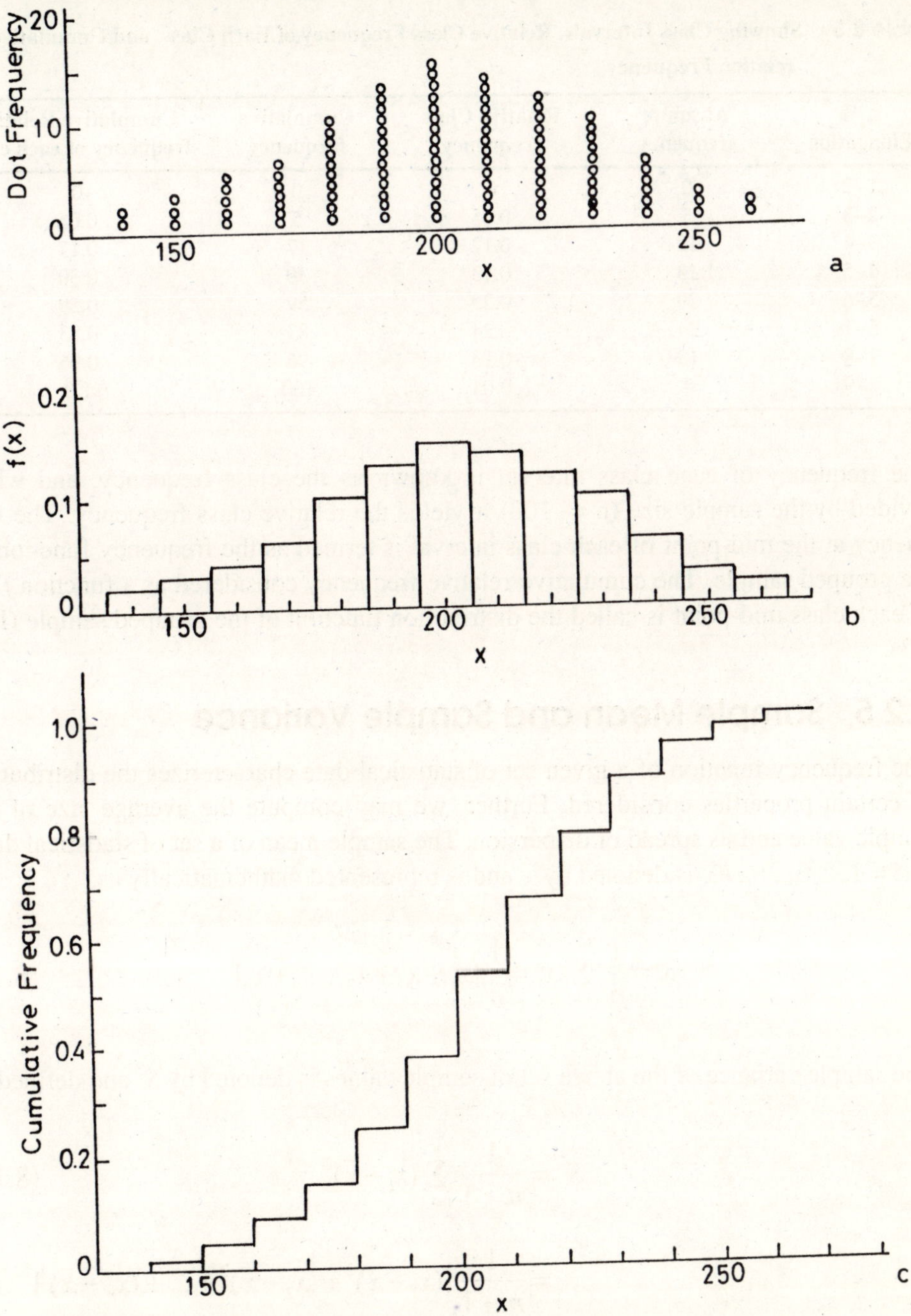

Fig. 8.2 (a) Dot frequency diagrams showing frequency function (b) Histogram showing frequency function (c) Cumulative frequency vs. x.

Table 8.3 Showing Class Intervals, Relative Class Frequency of Each Class and Cumulative relation Frequency

x, % Elongation	Absolute frequency	Relative Class frequency	Cumulative frequency	Cumulative Relative frequency of each class
1–2	0	0	0	0
2–3	5	0.05	5	0.05
3–4	12	0.12	17	0.17
4–5	13	0.13	30	0.30
5–6	29	0.29	59	0.59
6–7	24	0.24	83	0.83
7–8	13	0.13	96	0.96
8–9	4	0.04	100	1.0

The frequency of each class interval is known as the class frequency, and when divided by the sample size (n = 100) it yields the relative class frequency. The frequency at the mid-point of each class interval is termed as the frequency function of the grouped sample. The cumulative relative frequency considered as a function $f(x)$ of each class mid-point is called the distribution function of the grouped sample (Fig. 8.3).

8.2.5 Sample Mean and Sample Variance

The frequency function of a given set of statistical data characterizes the distribution of certain properties considered. Further, we may compute the average size of the sample value and its spread or dispersion. The sample mean of a set of statistical data, x_i ($i = 1, 2, 3, \ldots, n$), is denoted by $\overline{x}$ and is represented mathematically as,

$$\overline{x} = \frac{1}{n}\sum_{i=1}^{n} x_i = \frac{1}{n}[x_1 + x_2 + x_3 + \ldots + x_n] \tag{8.11}$$

The sample variance of the above set of sample values is denoted by S^2 and defined as

$$S^2 = \frac{1}{n-1}\sum_{i=1}^{n}(x_i - \overline{x})^2 \tag{8.12}$$

$$= \frac{1}{n-1}[(x_1 - \overline{x})^2 + (x_2 - \overline{x})^2 + \ldots + (x_n - \overline{x})^2]$$

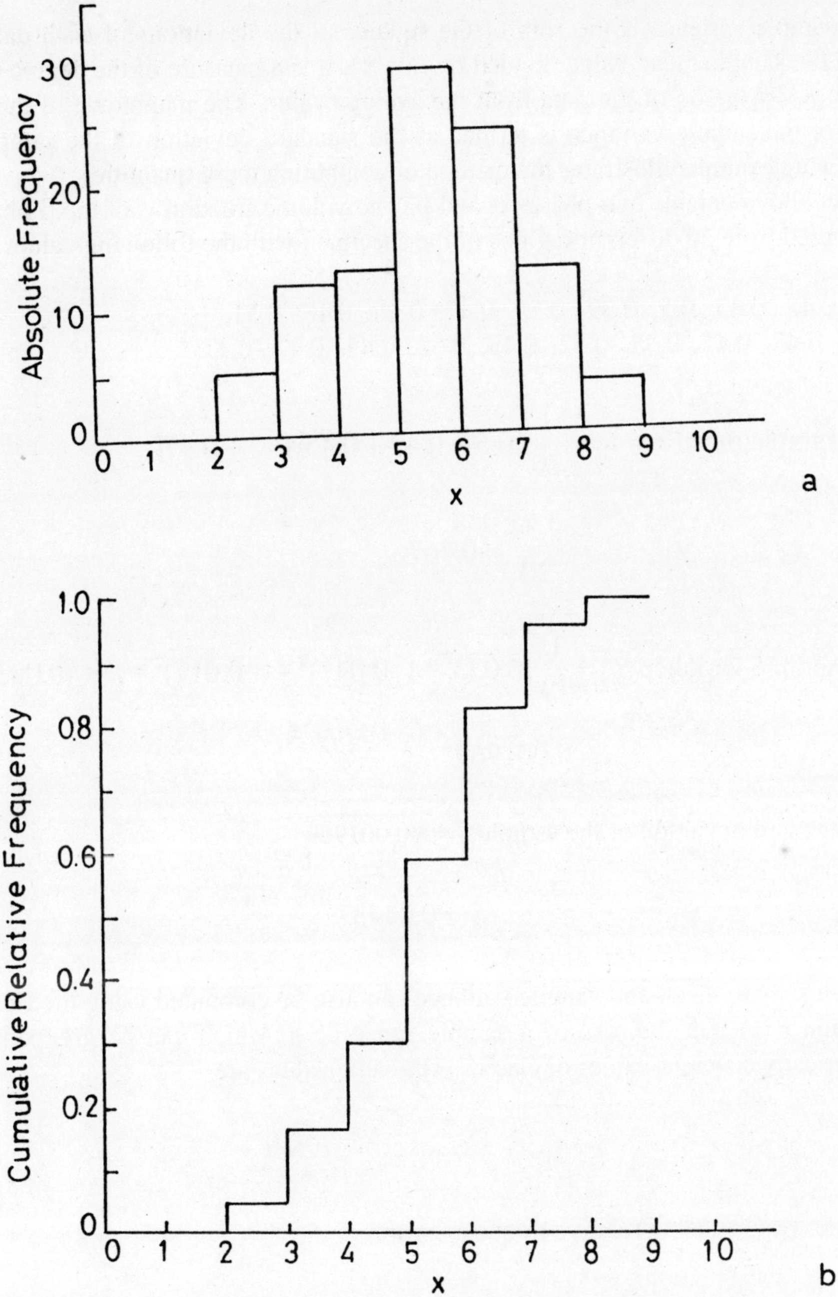

Fig. 8.3 (a) The absolute frequency vs. x (b) The cumulative relative frequency or distribution function, $f(x)$.

The sample variance is the sum of the squares of the deviations of each data value from the sample mean value divided by (n – 1). It is a measure of the degree of deviation or dispersion of the data from the average value. The magnitude of the square root of the sample variance is termed as the standard deviation of the sample. The following example illustrates the method of computing these quantities.

An alloy contains two phases α and β. The volume fraction v_f of the β phase was measured from 20 different regions of the specimen with the following values.

0.5, 0.42, 0.45, 0.5, 0.39, 0.55, 0.47, 0.46, 0.48, 0.51,
0.44, 0.48, 0.42, 0.38, 0.52, 0.49, 0.52, 0.45, 0.44, 0.47.

The sample mean $\bar{x} = \bar{v}_f = \frac{1}{20}[0.5 + 0.42 + 0.45 + ... + 0.47]$

$$= \frac{9.34}{20} = 0.467$$

The sample variance $S^2 = \frac{1}{19}[0.033^2 + (-0.047)^2 + (-0.017)^2 + ... + (0.003)^2)$

$$= 0.001969$$

and standard deviation of the sample $S = \sqrt{0.001969}$

$$S = 0.04437.$$

The sample mean and sample variance can also be computed using the frequency function $f(x)$. Let the size of a sample space be n, which can be grouped into p numerically different values or classes. The same values are

$$x_1, x_2, x_3, ..., x_p \qquad p \leq n.$$

and the corresponding relative frequencies are,

$$f(x_1), f(x_2), f(x_3), ..., f(x_p).$$

The number of times each group or class appears, equals the relative frequency times the number of values of the sample space, n. The corresponding frequency values required for the computation of the sample mean are, $nf(x_1)$, $nf(x_2)$, $nf(x_3)$, . . . and $nf(x_p)$. The value x_i appears $nf(x_i)$ times in the sample space. The sample mean $\bar{x}$ is

$$\bar{x} = \frac{1}{n}\sum_{i=1}^{p} x_i\, nf(x_i) \tag{8.13}$$

$$= [x_1 f(x_1) + x_2 f(x_2) + x_3 f(x_3) + \ldots + x_p f(x_p)]$$

The sample variance is,

$$S^2 = \frac{1}{n-1}\sum_{i=1}^{p} (x_i - \bar{x})^2\, nf(x_i). \tag{8.14}$$

The following example illustrates the method of computation. The chord lengths which are intercepts of disc-shaped particles with the plane of polish are measured.

Table 8.4 Computation of Sample Mean and Sample Variance

Chord Length x in μm	Absolute Frequency n = 20	Relative Frequency $f(x_i)$	$nf(x_i)$	$x_i nf(x_i)$	$(x_i-\bar{x})^2$	$(x_i-\bar{x})^2\, nf(x_i)$
180	2	0.1	2	360	552.25	1104.5
190	3	0.15	3	570	182.25	546.75
200	6	0.3	6	1200	12.25	73.5
210	5	0.25	5	1050	42.25	211.25
220	3	0.15	3	660	272.25	816.75
230	1	0.05	1	230	702.25	702.25

$$\sum x_i nf(x_i) = 4070, \quad \sum(x_i - \bar{x})^2 nf(x_i) = 3455$$

$$\bar{x} = 1/n \sum x_i nf(x_i) = \frac{4070}{20} = 203.5\ \mu\text{m}.$$

$$S^2 = 1/19 \sum(x_i - \bar{x})^2\, nf(x_i) = 1/19 \times 3455 = 181.84.$$

$$S = 13.48\ \mu\text{m}.$$

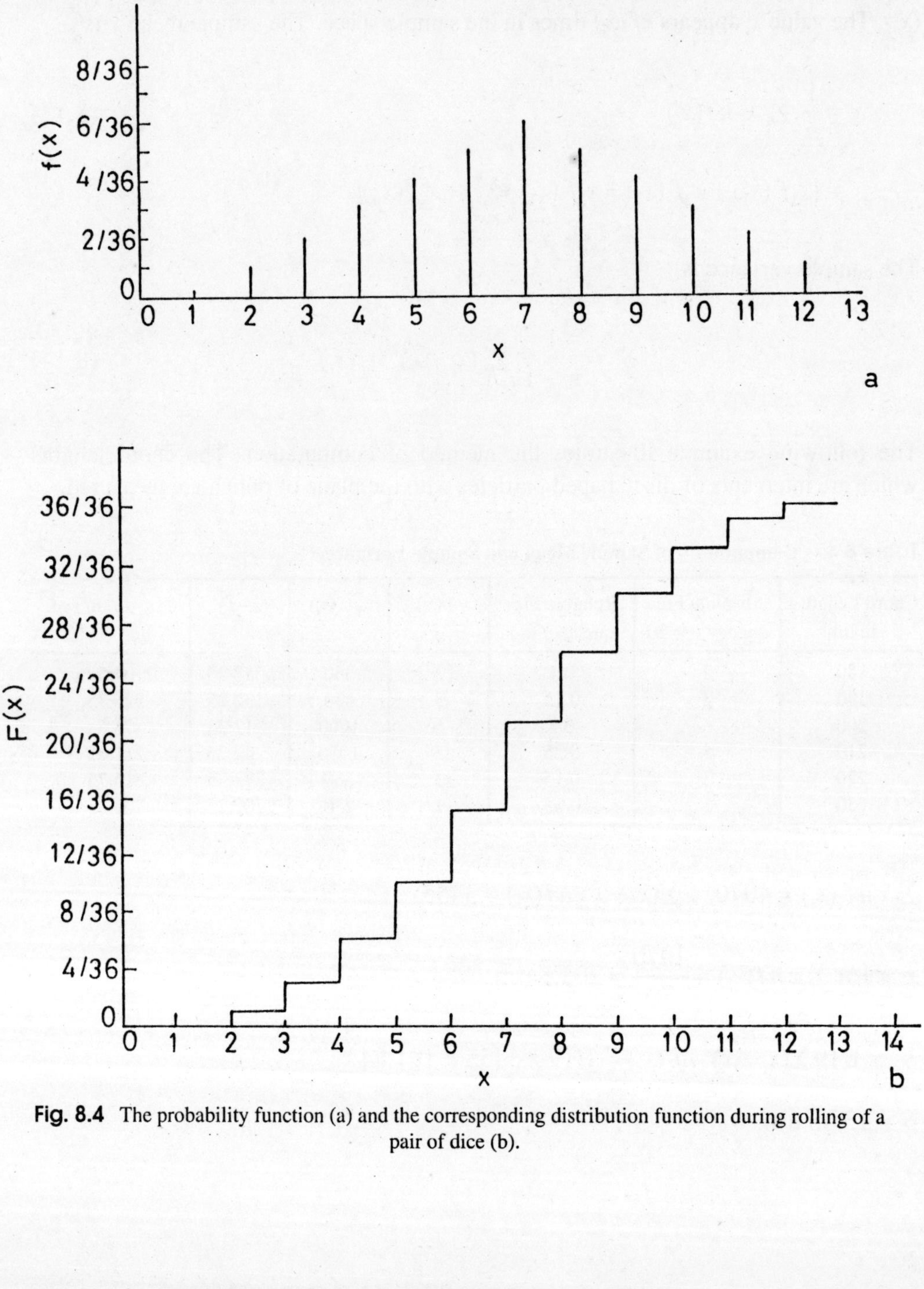

Fig. 8.4 The probability function (a) and the corresponding distribution function during rolling of a pair of dice (b).

8.2.6 Random Variable and Mean and Variance of a Distribution

Consider an experiment in which a die is rolled. The outcome of the experiment is any number from 1 to 6. It is not possible to predict which number will exactly appear on the die. The outcome of a rolled die is, therefore, a random process. If the number 3 appears on the die it is mere chance that this number has appeared. The chance that number 3 has appeared is represented by a random variable X.

The above example can be extended to the rolling of a pair of dice. The sum of the numbers appearing on the two dice can be any integer from 2 to 12, which the random variable X, can take. The random variable X is a function whose value is a real number. In a given interval I, the random variable can take any of the values, $X = a, b, c, d$ where a, b, c etc. lie within that interval and have a certain probability of occurrence. If X takes the value b, when b is contained in the interval I, then the probability is denoted by $P\,(X = b)$.

If X lies between a and b, $a < X < b$, then the probability is

$$P(a < X < b)$$

$X \leq a$, when X assumes any value smaller than or equal to a, means that its probability is $P\,(X \leq a)$.

$X > a$ means that X assumes values greater than "a" with a probability $P\,(X > a)$.

The random variable $X \leq a$ and $X > a$ covers the whole range of real numbers in the interval I and is represented by $-\infty < X < +\infty$ with $P\,(-\infty < X < +\infty) = 1$.

Thus $$P(X > a) + P(X \leq a) = 1.$$

or $$P(X \leq a) = 1 - P(X > a).$$

When a pair of dice is rolled, the sum of the numbers appearing on the two dice, X, can have values from 2 to 12 with the following probability.

$P\,(X = 2) = 1/36$, $P\,(X = 3) = 2/36$, $P\,(X = 4) = 3/36$, $P\,(X = 5) = 4/36$,
$P\,(X = 6) = 5/36$, $P\,(X = 7) = 6/36$, $P\,(X = 8) = 5/36$, $P\,(X = 9) = 4/36$,
$P\,(X = 10) = 3/36$, $P\,(X = 11) = 2/36$, $P\,(X = 12) = 1/36$,

In the experiment on rolling a pair of dice

$$P(X = 6.5) = 0,$$

$$P(2.5 < X \le 6) = 14/36,$$

and

$$P(X > 6) = 21/36.$$

The random variable X can be discrete or continuous. In the above example, X can take only certain finite integral values, 2, 3, . . ., 12 and, thus, represents a discrete random variable, as the probability value $P\,(X = 6.5) = 0$ suggests. The concept of a discrete random variable can be represented in functional form.

Let $x_1, x_2, x_3, \ldots, x_m$ be the values of X selected such that there exist the corresponding probabilities

$$P(x_1), P(x_2), P(x_3), \ldots, P(x_m).$$

The probability function of X is

$$f(x_i) = \begin{cases} P_i & \text{when } x = x_i \quad (i = 1, 2, 3, \ldots, m) \\ 0 & \text{when } x = x_i \quad (1 < i > m) \end{cases} \tag{8.15}$$

and $\sum_{i=1}^{m} f(x_i) = 1$ when the sample covers m discrete values.

When a pair of dice are rolled, the random variable and probability functions can be written as

$x = 2,\; 3,\; 4,\; 5,\; 6,\; 7,\; 8,\; 9,\; 10,\; 11,\; 12,$

$f(x) = 1/36, 2/36, 3/36, 4/36, 5/36, 6/36, 5/36, 4/36, 4/36, 3/36, 2/36, 2/36, 1/36,$

and $\sum f(x_i) = F(x) =$

1/36, 3/36, 6/36, 10/36, 15/36, 21/36, 26/36, 26/36, 30/36, 33/36, 35/36, 1.

The probability function $f(x)$ is a measure of the probability distribution in a statistical experiment. This is also known as the distribution function, $F(x)$. For $X \leq x$, the probability is $P(X \leq x)$, and the distribution function is $F(x) = \sum_{x_i \leq x} f(x_i)$. (8.16)

The probability function and the distribution function are represented in Figs. 8.4, a and b, respectively, for the random variable X which takes integral values from 2 to 12.

Now, let us define a random variable which is continuous. Consider a bar of metal A being deposited with metal B at one end. A similar bar of metal A is joined at the deposited end and the diffusion couple is allowed to anneal. The metal B will disperse into A on either side with a concentration-distance profile as shown in Fig. 8.5. The solute concentration exists all along the bar for all values of x, i.e., $-\infty < X < +\infty$. The probability of finding solute at any position along the bar exists. Thus $X = x$ (positional coordinate) becomes a random variable which is continuous. For every $X = x$, there exists a probability $P(X = x)$ of the occurrence of solute.

The probability function depends upon the continuous random variable X. This is represented in terms of the distribution function $F(x) = P(X \leq x)$ in integral form:

$$F(x) = \int_{-\infty}^{x} f(y)\,dy \tag{8.17}$$

where $f(y)$ is continuous. The distribution function is also continuous for every value of x. The probability function $f(x)$ (written as $f(y)$ under the integral to avoid the upper limit x) is the probability density or the density of the distribution. The distribution function can be determined by computing the area under the curve within the interval of interest. For example $F(x) = P(a < X < b)$ is the area under the curve between the continuous variables x = a and $x = b$ in Fig. 8.5. Moreover, since the solute is contained within the bar,

$$F(x) = \int_{-\infty}^{+\infty} f(y)dy = 1 = P(-\infty < X < +\infty) \tag{8.18}$$

The method of computing sample mean and sample variance was introduced in section 8.2.5. We can also compute the mean of a distribution μ, and variance of distribution σ^2. These are expressed as

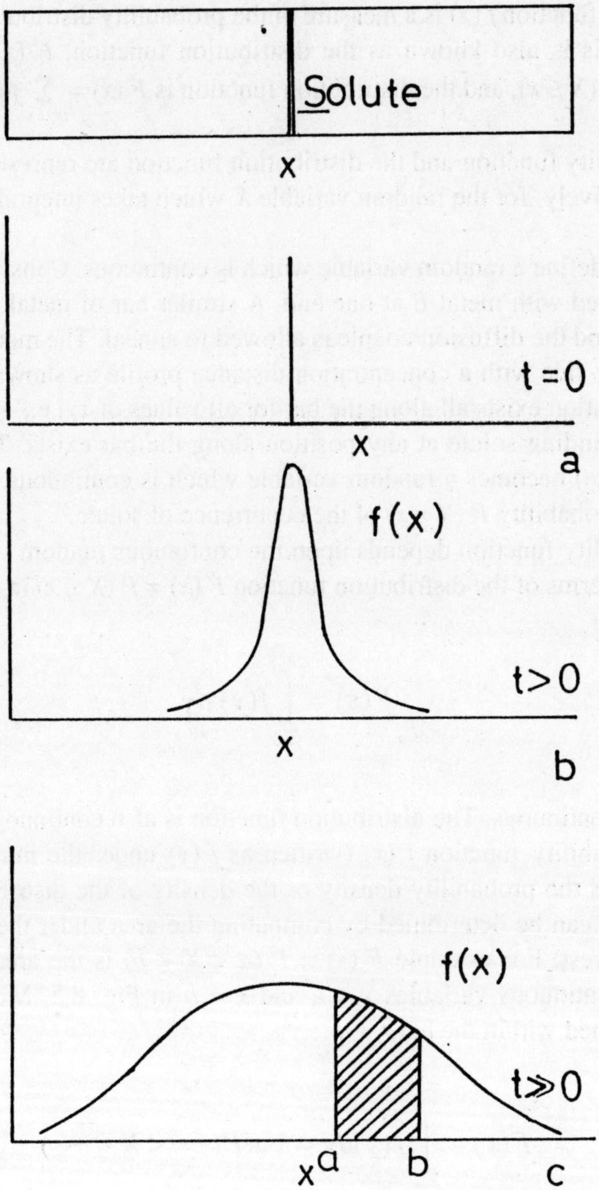

Fig. 8.5 Concentration-distance profile showing the distribution of solute for a normal distribution: (a) $t = 0$, (b) short time $t > 0$ (c) $t >> 0$.

$$\mu = \sum_i X_i f(x_i) \quad \text{for discrete variables} \tag{8.19}$$

and
$$\mu = \int_{-\infty}^{+\infty} x f(x)\, dx \quad \text{for continuous variables} \tag{8.20}$$

where $f(x)$ is the probability function for discrete variables and density distribution for continuous variables.

The variance of a distribution is similarly denoted by

$$\sigma^2 = \sum_i (x_i - \mu)^2 f(x_i), \quad \text{for discrete distributions} \tag{8.21}$$

and
$$\sigma^2 = \int_{-\infty}^{+\infty} (x_i - \mu)^2 f(x) dx \quad \text{for continuous distributions} \tag{8.22}$$

The magnitude of the square root of σ^2 is known as the standard deviation of the distribution.

If x is any random variable in a statistical experiment and $g(x)$ is any continuous function which is defined for all real x, then the expected (or sometimes known as the average) value of the function $g(x)$ is

$$E(g(x)) = \sum_i g(x_i) f(x_i), \quad \text{discrete function} \tag{8.23}$$

and
$$E(g(x)) = \int_{-\infty}^{+\infty} g(x) f(x)\, dx, \quad \text{continuous function} \tag{8.24}$$

For continuous functions,

$$g(x) = \frac{1}{a}, \quad E(g(x)) = \int_{-\infty}^{+\infty} \frac{1}{a} f(x)\, dx$$

$$g(x) = 1, \quad E(1) = \int_{-\infty}^{+\infty} f(x)\, dx = 1$$

$$g(x) = x^k, E(x^k) = \int_{-\infty}^{+\infty} x^k f(x)\, dx$$

$$g(x) = x, E(x) = \int_{-\infty}^{+\infty} x f(x)\, dx = \mu$$

$$g(x) = x - \mu, E(x - \mu) = \int_{-\infty}^{+\infty} (x - \mu)\, f(x) dx$$

$$= \int_{-\infty}^{+\infty} x f(x) dx - \mu \int_{-\infty}^{+\infty} f(x)\, dx = \mu - \mu = 0$$

In a statistical experiment, some times it is necessary to measure two parameters associated with the experiment. These parameters or quantities will be associated with two random variables, x and y. For example, the random variable x may be the yield strength and y the concentration of solute in a binary alloy. If we carry out the experiment, we will get a pair of number $x = x_1$ and $y = y_1$ or (x_1, y_1) in the xy–plane. If a given event is bounded by $C_1 < x < d_1$ and $C_2 < y < d_2$, then the outcome of the event will lie in a rectangle bounded by C_1d_1 on the x-axis and C_2d_2 on the y-axis, as shown in Fig. 8.6. The definition of the probability function, distribution function, and the expected value are identical except for the addition of one or more variables, as shown in Table 8.5.

The expected value of a function $g\,(x, y)$ for continuous random variables x and y is given as

$$E(g(x, y)) = \int_{-\infty}^{+\infty}\int_{-\infty}^{+\infty} g(x, y)\, f(x, y)\, dx\, dy \tag{8.25}$$

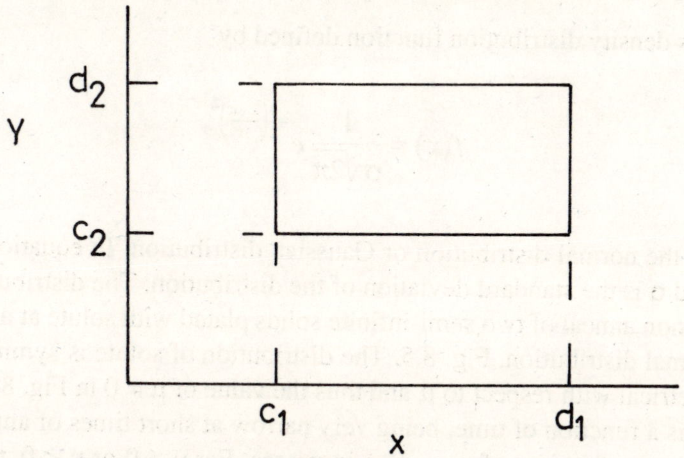

Fig. 8.6 The diagram shown the method of determining probability for an event which depends upon two random variables *x* and *y*.

Table 8.5 Probability function, distribution function and expected values for the single random variable and two random variables.

	Single random variable		Two random variables	
	Discrete	Continuous	Discrete	Continuous
Probability	$p_i, x = x_i$	$p_i, x = x_i$	$p_{ij}, x = x_i, y = y_j$	$p_j, x = x_i, y = y_j$
Probability Function	$f(x)$	$f(x)$	$f(x, y)$	$f(x, y)$
Distribution Function	$F(x) = \sum_{x_i \le x} f(x_i)$	$F(x) = \int_{-\infty}^{x} f(y)dy$	$F(x, y) = \sum_{x \le x_i} \sum_{y \le y_j} f(x_i y_j)$	$F(x, y) \int_{-\infty}^{x} \int_{-\infty}^{y} f(u, v)du\, dv.$
Expected or Average value	$E(g(x)) = \sum_i g(x_i) f(x_i)$	$E(\dot{g}(x)) = \int_{-\infty}^{+\infty} g(x) f(x)\, dx$	$E(g(x, y)) = \sum_x \sum_y g(x, y)\, dxdy$	$E(g(x, y)) = \int_{-\infty}^{+\infty} \int_{-\infty}^{+\infty} g(x, y) f(x, y)\, dxdy$
	$F(x) = \sum_i f(x_i) = 1$	$F(x) = \int_{-\infty}^{+\infty} f(y)\, dy = 1$	$F(x, y) = \sum_i \sum_j f(x_i y_j) = 1$	$F(x, y) = \int_{-\infty}^{+\infty} \int_{-\infty}^{+\infty} f(x, y)\, dxdy = 1$

8.2.7 Normal Distribution

A continuous density distribution function defined by

$$f(x) = \frac{1}{\sigma\sqrt{2\pi}} e^{-\frac{1}{2}\left(\frac{x-\mu}{\sigma}\right)^2} \tag{8.26}$$

is known as the normal distribution or Gaussian distribution. In equation (8.26), μ is the mean and σ is the standard deviation of the distribution. The distribution of solute during diffusion anneal of two semi-infinite solids plated with solute at a common end shows a normal distribution, Fig. 8.5. The distribution of solute is symmetrical, i.e., $f(x)$ is symmetrical with respect to μ and thus the value of $\mu = 0$ in Fig. 8.5. The solute distribution is a function of time, being very narrow at short times of anneal but gradually spreading as the time of annealing increases. For $\mu > 0$ or $\mu < 0$, the solute distribution function will shift to the right or left, respectively, by μ units.

The standard deviation of the distribution is small at short times but gradually increases with the time of anneal. The distribution function for the normal distribution is represented by

$$F(x) = \frac{1}{\sigma\sqrt{\pi - 2}} \int_{-\infty}^{y} \exp\left\{-\frac{1}{2}\left(\frac{y-\mu}{\sigma}\right)^2\right\} dy \tag{8.27}$$

When x, the random variable, lies between a and b, $(a < x \leq b)$, the distribution function is,

$$P(a < x \leq b) = F(b) - F(a) = \int_{a}^{b} \exp\left\{-\frac{1}{2}\left(\frac{y-\mu}{\sigma}\right)^2\right\} dy \tag{8.28}$$

The above integral cannot be evaluated by regular integration. The following procedure for evaluation is adopted.

Let $p = \dfrac{y-\mu}{\sigma}$, $dp = \dfrac{1}{\sigma} dy$, substituting for these in equation (8.27), we get

$$\phi(y) = \frac{1}{\sqrt{2\pi}} \int_{-\infty}^{y} e^{-1/2\,p^2}\, dp \tag{8.29}$$

The value of $\phi(y)$ as a function of y can be obtained from Fig. 8.7.

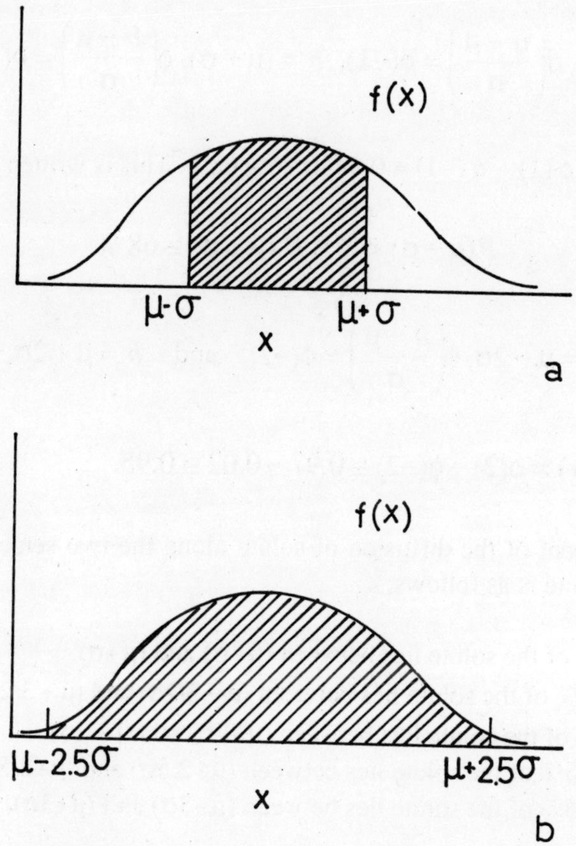

Fig. 8.7 The distribution of solute in a pair of semi-infinite solids after diffusion: (a) $a = \mu - \sigma$, $b = \mu + \sigma$ (b) $a = \mu - 2.5\sigma$, $b = \mu + 2.5\sigma$.

If we set $y = \dfrac{x-\mu}{\sigma}$, then $F(x) = \dfrac{1}{\sqrt{2\pi}} \displaystyle\int_{-\infty}^{\frac{x-\mu}{\sigma}} e^{-\frac{1}{2}y^2}\, dy = \phi\left(\dfrac{x-\mu}{\sigma}\right)$

Then, $F(b) - F(a) = \phi\left(\dfrac{b-\mu}{\sigma}\right) - \phi\left(\dfrac{a-\mu}{\sigma}\right)$

For $a = (\mu - \sigma),\ \sigma\left(\dfrac{a-\mu}{\sigma}\right) = \phi(-1),\ b = (\mu + \sigma),\ \phi\left(\dfrac{b-\mu}{\sigma}\right) = \phi(1)$

$F(b) - F(a) = \phi(1) - \phi(-1) = 0.84 - 0.16 = 68\%$. This is written as

$$P(\mu - \sigma) < X \le P(\mu + \sigma) \cong 68\ \%$$

Similarly, for $a = \mu - 2\sigma,\ \phi\left(\dfrac{a-\mu}{\sigma}\right) = \phi(-2)$ and $b = \mu + 2\sigma,\ \phi\left(\dfrac{b-\mu}{\sigma}\right) = \phi(2)$

and $F(b) - F(a) = \phi(2) - \phi(-2) \cong 0.97 - 0.02 \cong 0.95.$

In the experiment of the diffusion of solute along the two semi-infinite bars, the distribution of solute is as follows:

(i) About 68% of the solute lies between $(\mu - \sigma)$ and $(\mu + \sigma)$.
(ii) About 87.5% of the solute lies between $(\mu - 3/2\sigma)$ and $(\mu + 3/2\sigma)$.
(iii) About 95% of the solute lies between $(\mu - 2\sigma)$ and $(\mu + 2\sigma)$.
(iv) About 98.75% of the solute lies between $(\mu - 2.5\sigma)$ and $(\mu + 2.5\sigma)$.
(v) About 99.75% of the solute lies between $(\mu - 3\sigma)$ and $(\mu + 3\sigma)$.

Some of these are shown in Figs. 8.7, a and b, as shaded areas under the normal distribution curve.

8.3 GEOMETRICAL PROBABILITY OF INTERSECTION OF MICROSTRUCTURES WITH TEST LINES AND PLANES

The metallurgical microstructure consists of grain boundaries, second phase particles, dislocations, etc. The aim of quantitative microscopy is to make measurements in two dimensions (in the plane of polish) of objects (structures) which are three-dimensional. This is particularly applicable to most metals, alloys, ceramics, etc., which are opaque, implying that measurements on these materials cannot be made in three dimensions.

Grain boundaries are planar or curved surfaces. The determination of the grain boundary surface area will require measurements in the plane of polish where these boundaries appear as lines. Similarly, the grain boundary edges which are lines in three dimensions will appear as points in the plane section. The spherical-shaped particles of the second phase will appear as circles when intersected by the plane of polish. The diameter of the circle will be the chord diameter of the sphere intersected by the plane. The shape of randomly shaped particles will depend on the geometry of the particle in three dimensions and the position at which the intersection is made. Dislocation lines which are one-dimensional objects will appear as points in the plane section.

Quantitative microscopy aims at determining the true average value of a given parameter, like surface area of the grain boundary, length of a dislocation line, particle size, number of particles, interlamellar spacing, etc. The important condition is that the structure under consideration should be uniformly distributed so as to keep the deviation from the average to as low a value as possible, because measurements of the above structural parameters are based on geometric probability.

The above ideas will be applied to determine the geometric probability in a few cases. Consider a particle defined by its orientation (θ, ψ) contained within a cube of edge length "*a*", Fig. 8.8. Place a large number of planes parallel to the top face of the cube in such a way that the planes are randomly distributed within the cube. Each of the planes is described by its distance from the origin within the limit *O* to *a*. This constitutes a statistical experiment which will define the probability. The probability that a given plane intersects the particle is related to the distance $D(\theta, \psi)$ between the planes that are parallel to the test planes and tangential to the particle.

$$P \text{ (Probability)} = \frac{D(\theta, \psi)}{a} \tag{8.30}$$

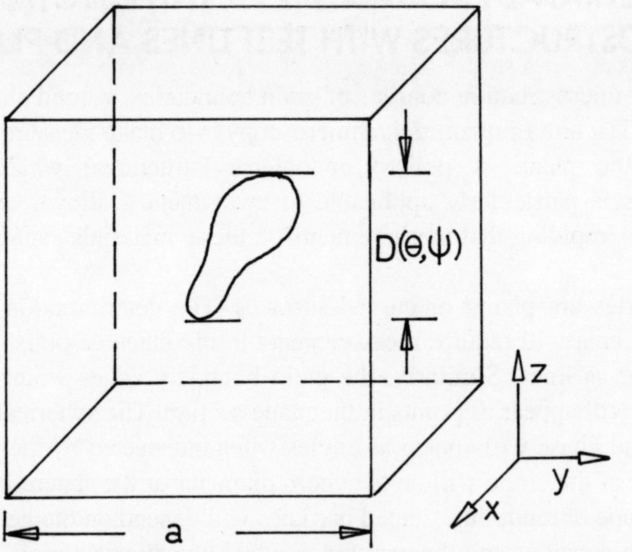

Fig. 8.8 The determination of the geometrical probability of intersection of a test plane with the particle.

In order to determine the distance between tangent planes, it is necessary to define the orientation of the particle in terms of θ, ψ.

A similar geometric probability can be written for linear features. Consider a differential element of length dl of a dislocation line in three dimensions, Fig. 8.9. Place a number of planes parallel to the X–Z plane. The probability that the test planes intersect the element dl is related to the projection of the line element on a line perpendicular to the test planes. These lines wiii be parallel to the y-axis. The projected length on the y-axis is dy (θ, ψ), and the probability of its intersection with a plane is

$$P\text{ (test plane intersects the element } dl) = \frac{dy(\theta, \psi)}{a} \tag{8.31}$$

In considering two-dimensional structural features in three dimensions, e.g. grain boundary surfaces, the probability of intersection can be determined by drawing a large number of test lines parallel to one of the axes. Consider a differential area element of area dA contained within a cube of edge length "a", Fig. 8.10. If a number of test lines are drawn parallel to the y-axis, then the position of each line can be defined in terms of the coordinates (x_i, z_i) for the ith test line. The probability that a given test line is contained within the differential element dA is related to the projection of dA on a plane perpendicular to the test line. The projected area dS is a function of (θ, ψ), i.e., orientation of the surface in three dimensions. The probability is written as

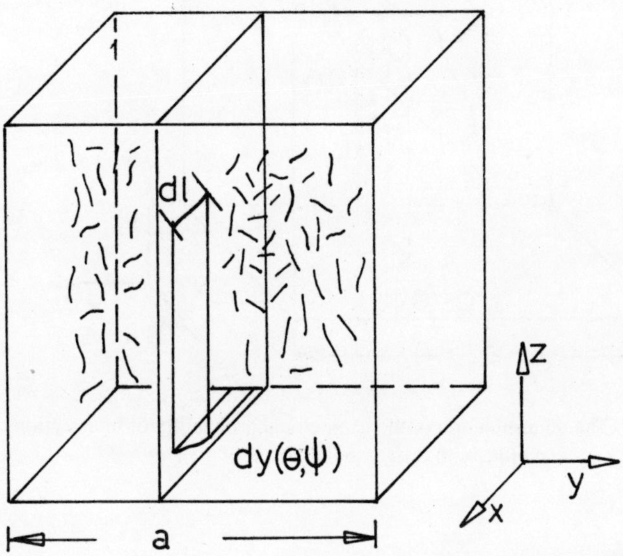

Fig. 8.9 The determination of the geometrical probability of intersection of a test plane with differential element dl.

$$P \text{ (test line meets the element of area } dA) = \frac{dS(\theta, \psi)}{a^2} \tag{8.32}$$

In a number of instances, the microstructure may appear anisotropic, for example, the elongated grain structure of a heavily cold deformed metal after annealing. It is necessary to average each geometric probability over the range of orientations to get a realistic value for the quantity under consideration, grain diameter in this case.

Let X (θ) be some property of a two-dimensional structure dependent upon its orientation θ. The fraction of the orientation lying within the angular range $d\theta$ (θ + $d\theta$)) gives the probability of finding an orientation for the circle of orientation, Fig. 8.11. This is written as

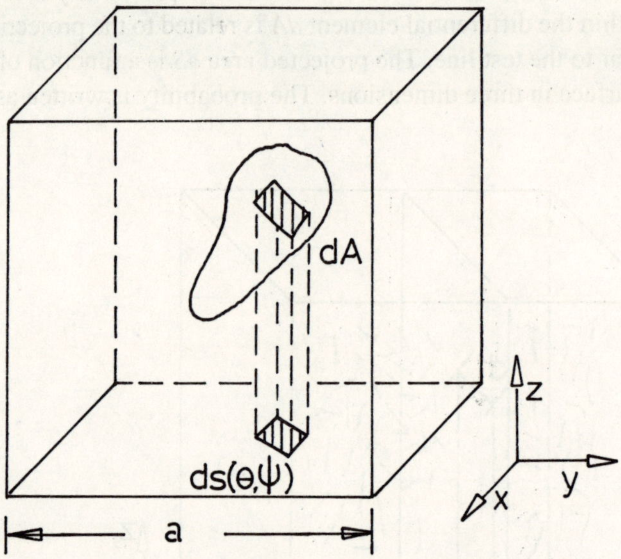

Fig. 8.10 The determination of the geometrical probability of intersection of a test line with differential element of area dA.

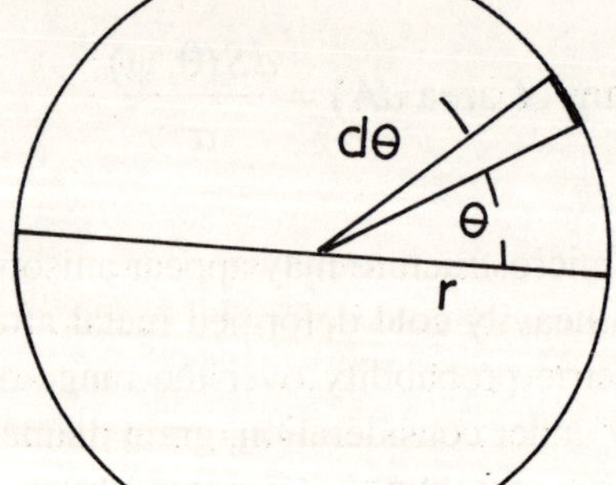

Fig. 8.11 Averaging over a circle of orientation in two-dimension.

$$\text{Probability } P \text{ (orientation lying within } \theta \text{ and } (\theta + d\theta) \text{ is} = \frac{r\,d\theta}{2\pi r} \tag{8.33}$$

The probability function, $f(\theta) = 1/2\pi$. The expected value of x from equation (8.24) is,

$$E(g(x)) = \bar{x} = \int_0^{2\pi} x(\theta)\, f(\theta)\, d\theta$$

$$= \int_0^{2\pi} x(\theta) \frac{d\theta}{2\pi}. \tag{8.34}$$

A similar derivation for the expected value of the random variable x (θ, ψ) can be carried out for a three-dimensional structure which is dependent on θ and ψ. Let us consider a differential element of area dA lying on the surface of a sphere of radius r, Fig. 8.12. The differential element of the surface covers an orientation θ to (θ + $d\theta$) and ψ to (ψ + $d\psi$). The area dA on the sphere is formed from two circles of latitude differing by $d\psi$ and two circles of longitude differing by $d\theta$, as shown in Fig. 8.12. The area *ABCD* is formed from areas *AB*, *BC*, *CD*, and *DA*.

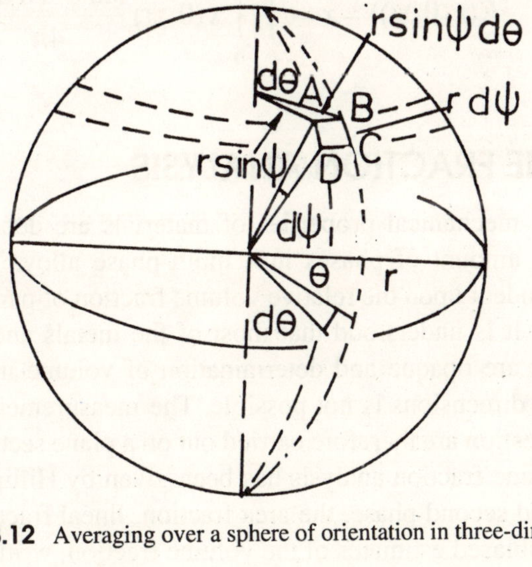

Fig. 8.12 Averaging over a sphere of orientation in three-dimension.

The arc $AB = CD = r \sin \psi d\theta$ and the arc $BC = DA = r\, d\psi$.

$$\text{Area } dA = r^2 \sin \psi \, d\theta \, d\psi \tag{8.35}$$

The combined probability of finding a given orientation within the range of orientation $d\theta$ and $d\psi$ is given by

$$f(\theta, \psi)\, d\theta \, d\psi = \frac{dA}{\text{area of the sphere}} = \frac{r^2 \sin \psi \, d\theta \, d\psi}{4\pi r^2},$$

and $$f(\theta, \psi)\, d\theta \, d\psi = \frac{\sin \psi \, d\theta \, d\psi}{4\pi},$$

where the probability function, $f(\theta, \psi) = \dfrac{\sin \psi}{4\pi}$.

The expected value x for two random variables θ and ψ is

$$E(x(\theta, \psi)) = \bar{x} = \int_0^{\pi} \int_0^{2\pi} x(\theta, \psi) \frac{\sin \psi \, d\theta \, d\psi}{4\pi} \tag{8.37}$$

8.4 VOLUME FRACTION ANALYSIS

The physical and mechanical properties of materials are dependent to some extent upon the relative amount of phases in a multi-phase alloy. The economics of ore extraction is dependent upon the relative volume fraction of particular compounds in a complex mineral. It is understood that most of the metals and alloys, minerals, and ceramic materials are opaque and determination of volume in a volume from measurement in three dimensions is not possible. The measurements of area, length, etc. of the phase in question are therefore carried out on a plane section. A good account of the theory of volume fraction analysis has been given by Hilliard (2). For a homogeneously distributed second phase, the area fraction, lineal fraction, and point fraction are statistically unbiased estimates of the volume fraction, written as

$$x = V_f = A_f = L_f = p_f \tag{8.38}$$

where V_f = volume fraction (m^3/m^3)
A_f = area fraction (m^2/m^2)
L_f = lineal fraction (m/m)
p_f = point fraction (number/number)

8.4.1 Area Fraction

The volume occupied by the second phase particles cannot be measured directly in opaque objects. Measurement of the intercepted area in a convenient way to represent the volume fraction. The aim at this point, therefore, is to show that the volume fraction of the second phase particles is equal to the area fraction when measurements are made in the plane of polish. We will follow the simple procedure outlined by Hilliard (2). Let us consider a homogeneous distribution of the second phase particles within a cube of edge length "a", Fig. 8.13. It is convenient to select a plane (the test plane) at a distance y from the origin and perpendicular to the y-axis. The fraction of the area of the test plane occupied by the second phase particles is

$$A_f(y) = \frac{A(y)}{a^2} = \frac{\sum_{i=1}^{n} A_i(y)}{a^2} \tag{8.39}$$

where $A(y)$ is the total area of intersection of the β phase with the test plane and $A_i(y)$ is the area of the ith particle on a plane situated at a distance y from the origin. The expected or average area over the domain of y from equation (8.24) is,

$$\overline{A}_f = \int_0^a A_f(y)\, f(y)\, dy, \tag{8.40}$$

where $f(y)\,dy$ is the probability of finding a test plane at a position between y and $(y + dy)$. The variable y is treated as a continuous random variable. Since we can easily assume a uniform distribution of the test planes, and these can take any position between 0 and a, the probability of finding a test plane in the interval dy is

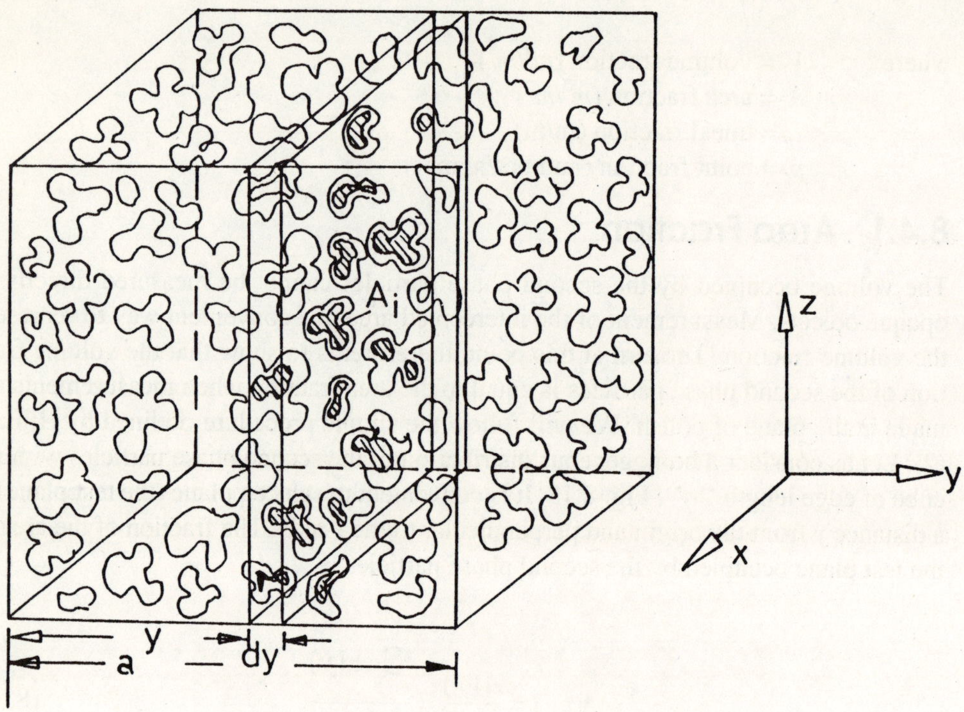

Fig. 8.13 Intersection of particles with a test plane, $A(y) = A_1 + A_2 + A_3 + \ldots + A_n$.

$$f(y)\,dy = \frac{dy}{a} \tag{8.41}$$

Substituting for $f(y)\,dy$ from equation (8.41) and $A_f(y)$ from equation (8.39) in equation (8.40) yields

$$\overline{A}_f = \int_0^a \frac{A(y)}{a^2}\frac{dy}{a} \tag{8.42}$$

The quantity $A\,(y)\,dy$ is the area of the base times the height; the integral $\int_0^a A\,(y)\,dy$ is the volume occupied by the second phase particles within the cube. Thus,

$$\overline{A}_f = \frac{\text{Volume of the second phase}}{a^3} = V_f \tag{8.43}$$

8.4.2 Lineal Fraction

A lineal fraction analysis can be carried out in an identical manner by considering a line of length "a" parallel to the y-axis. The line lies within a cube of edge length "a" and is defined by positional coordinates x and z from the origin, Fig. 8.14. If the second phase particles are uniformly distributed within the volume, a number of such particles will be intersected by the line for each possible position of the line. The lineal fraction L_f can be computed from the sum of all line segments intersected by the particles. Thus

$$L_f\,(x,z) = \frac{l\,(x,z)}{a} = \sum_{i=1}^{n} l_i(x,z) \tag{8.44}$$

where $l\,(x, z)$ is the total length of the line segments occupied by the second phase and $l_i\,(x, z)$ is the length of the line segment intersected by the ith particle in the plane of polish. The expected or average value of $L_f\,(x, z)$ over the domain of the continuous random variables x and z is

$$\overline{L}_f = \int_0^a \int_0^a L_f(x,z)\, f(x,z)\, dx\, dz \tag{8.45}$$

Here x and z are continuous variables because they can take any value in their respective domains. In equation (8.45), $f\,(x, z)\,dx\,dz$ is the combined probability of finding a test line in the interval x to $(x + dx)$ and z to $(z + dz)$. For a uniform distribution of test lines, the probability of finding a test line within an area $dx\,dz$ is

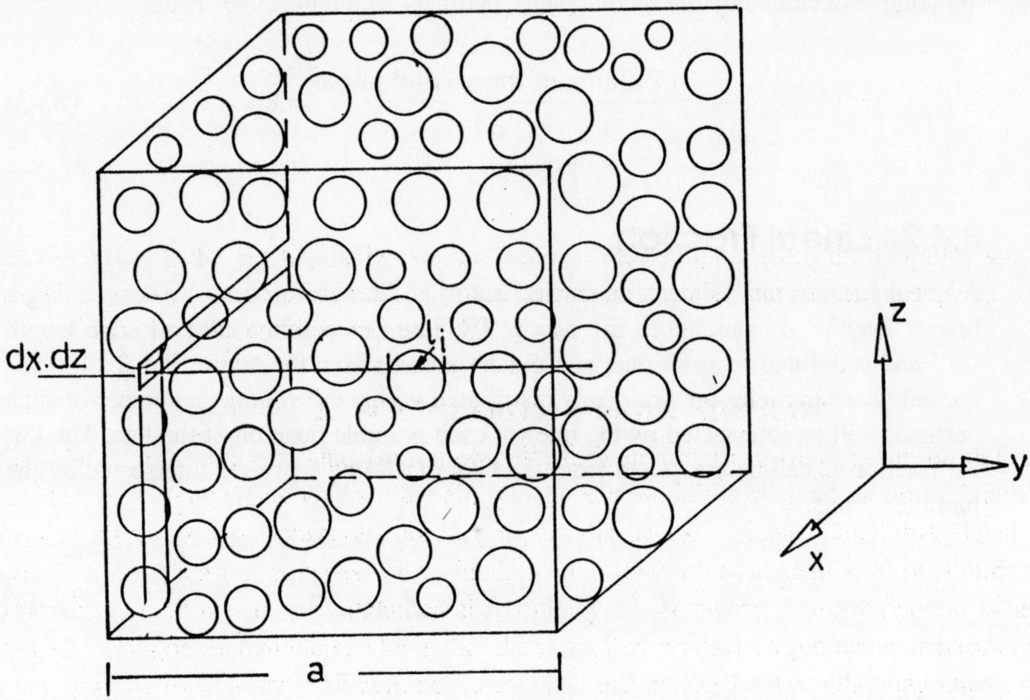

Fig. 8.14 Intersection of particles with a test line, $l(x, z) = (l_1 + l_2 + l_3 + \ldots + l_n) = \sum_{l=1}^{n} l_i(x, z)$

$$f(x,z)\,dx\,dz = \frac{dx\,dz}{a^2} \tag{8.46}$$

where $f(x, z)$ is the probability function (= $1/axa$) and a^2 is the area within which all test lines are distributed. Substituting for $L_f(x, z)$ and $f(x, z)\,dx\,dy$ in equation (8.45), the following result is obtained:

$$\overline{L}_f = \int_0^a \int_0^a \frac{l(x,z)}{a} \cdot \frac{1}{a^2}\,dx\,dz \tag{8.47}$$

or

$$\overline{L}_f = V_f \tag{8.48}$$

In equation (8.47), $l\,(x, z)\,dx\,dz$ is the volume of the second phase, contained within a bar of material whose area is $dx\,dz$ and whose height is $l\,(x, z)$.

8.4.3 Point Fraction

If a point is placed at any random position $P\,(x, y, z)$ within a volume, then the probability that it will be contained within the second phase particles is proportional to the volume fraction of these particles, i.e.,

$$\overline{P}_f = V_f \tag{8.49}$$

8.4.4 To show that $\overline{\mathbf{A}}_f = \overline{\mathbf{L}}_f$

In order to prove that the area fraction of the second phase particles equals the lineal fraction (L_f), consider a square of edge length ''a''. The projection of the three-dimensional particles on the above plane (plane of polish) is shown in Fig. 8.15. If we draw a line within the square, it will intersect a number of particles in the plane of projection (Fig. 8.15) and a number of particles will be intersected by each position of the line for a homogeneous distribution. The lineal fraction L_f can be calculated from the sum of all line segments intersected by the particles. This gives

$$L_f(x) = \frac{l_f}{a} = \frac{l_1 + l_2 + l_3 + l_4 + \ldots + l_n}{a} = \frac{\sum\limits_{i=1}^{n} l_i(x)}{a} \tag{8.50}$$

where $l_i(x)$ is the length of the line segment intersected by the ith particle in the plane of polish. The expected value of L_f over the domain of x is

$$E = \overline{L}_f = \int_0^a \frac{l_f(x)\, f(x)\, dx}{a} \tag{8.51}$$

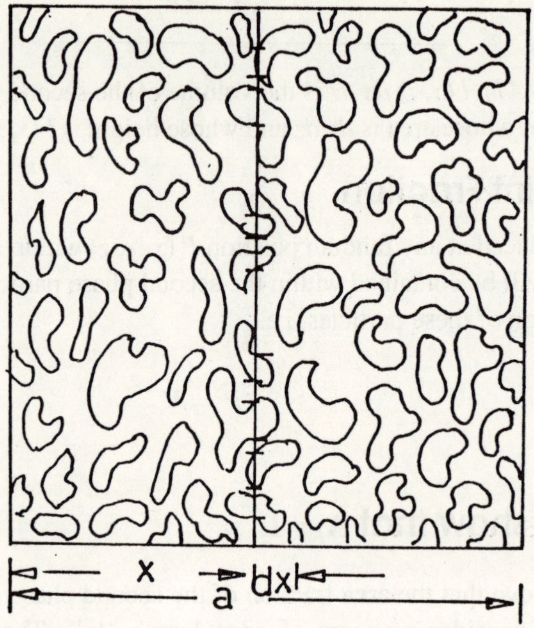

Fig. 8.15 Projection of a three-dimensional structure on a plane. The test line drawn parallel to the y-axis intersects the projected particles with intercepts $l_1, l_2, \ldots l_n$.

$$l(x) = l_1 + l_2 + l_3 + \ldots + l_n = \sum_{1=1}^{n} l_i.$$

In equation (8.51), $f(x)$ is the probability function of finding the test line in the interval between x and $(x + dx)$. For a uniform distribution of test lines, the probability of finding a test line in the interval x and $(x + dx)$ is dx/a. Substitution of the probability function, $f(x)\, dx = dx/a$, in equation (8.51) yields,

$$\overline{L}_f = \int_0^a \frac{l_f(x)}{a}\frac{dx}{a} = \overline{A}_f, \tag{8.52}$$

where $L_f(x)\, dx$ is the area of the particles in the interval 0 to a.

The volume fraction of the second phase particles can be measured experimentally by counting either the area fraction, lineal fraction or point fraction of all particles contained within a given microstructure. The area fraction is determined by a graphical method. This requires superimposition of a transparent graph sheet on the microstructure. The number of squares contained within the second phase particles is counted. By summing up all the areas occupied by the second phase particles, and dividing it by the total area occupied by the structure, gives the area fraction of the second phase. In a slightly different approach, the microstructure to be evaluated for the volume fraction measurement is first recorded on photographic paper. The area occupied by the second phase particles is cut out and weighed. The ratio of the weight of the second phase to the total weight also yields the area fraction. The procedure for determining the volume fraction from the area fraction analysis is quite accurate; however, because of the difficulty encountered in the measurement, it is not commonly used.

In the measurement of the volume fraction from the lineal fraction, a number of lines at specified intervals are drawn on the microstructure. The sum of the lengths of line segments contained within the second phase, when divided by the total length of the line, yields the desired result. The procedure is simple and straightforward; however, some difficulty is experienced when the second phase forms with a preferred orientation. In order to minimize the error of measurement in such cases, it is usual to make measurements on lines covering all possible orientations.

The point count technique is the most frequently used method of determining the volume fraction of the given phase in multi-phase materials. The measurement is made with the help of a reticule etched on a plane glass and fitted in the eyepiece lens of a metallurgical microscope. Basically, there are three types of reticules available based on the total number of points on the grid. These are $10 \times 10 = 100$ points, Fig. 8.16a, $20 \times 20 = 400$ points, Fig. 8.16b, and $30 \times 30 = 900$ points.

The procedure of measuring volume fraction from the point count technique is illustrated in Fig. 8.17. The microstructure consists of pearlite and ferrite in plain carbon steel. The measurement requires counting the number of corner points of the square lying on the designated structures. The analysis is carried out by traversing one line at a time and recording the number of points that lie on the structure to be evaluated. The measurement is easier when the number of points on a line is 10 (for the 10×10 grid). The strain in measurement increases with increase in the number of points along a line. However, the accuracy of the result improves with an increase in the number of points on the grid as illustrated by the following equation,

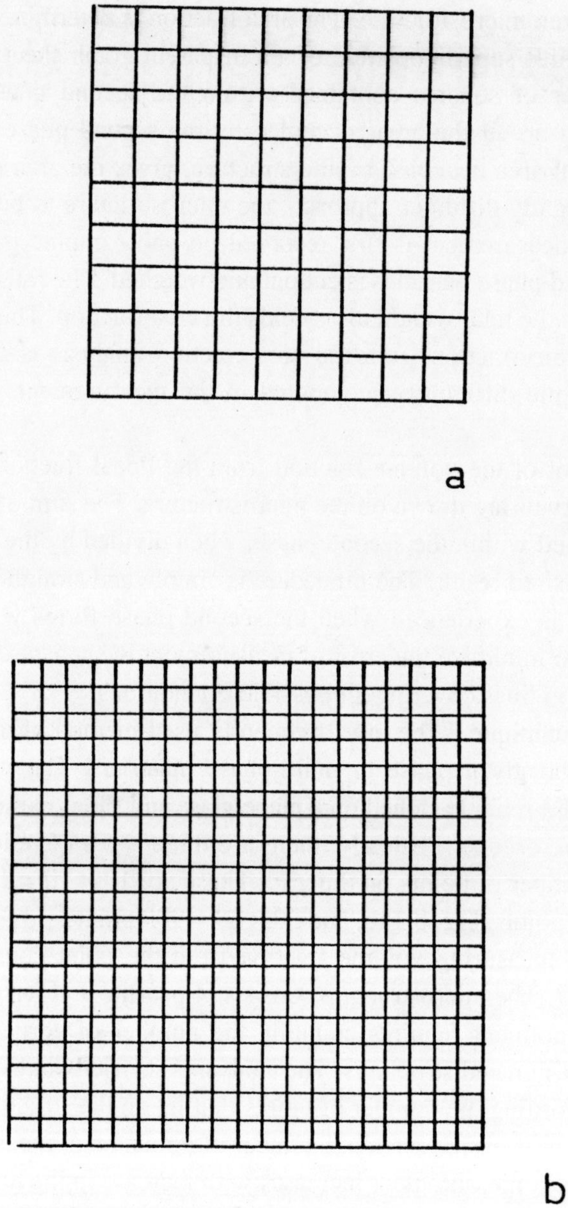

Fig. 8.16 Reticule with (a) 10×10 = 100 points (b) 20×20 = 400 points.

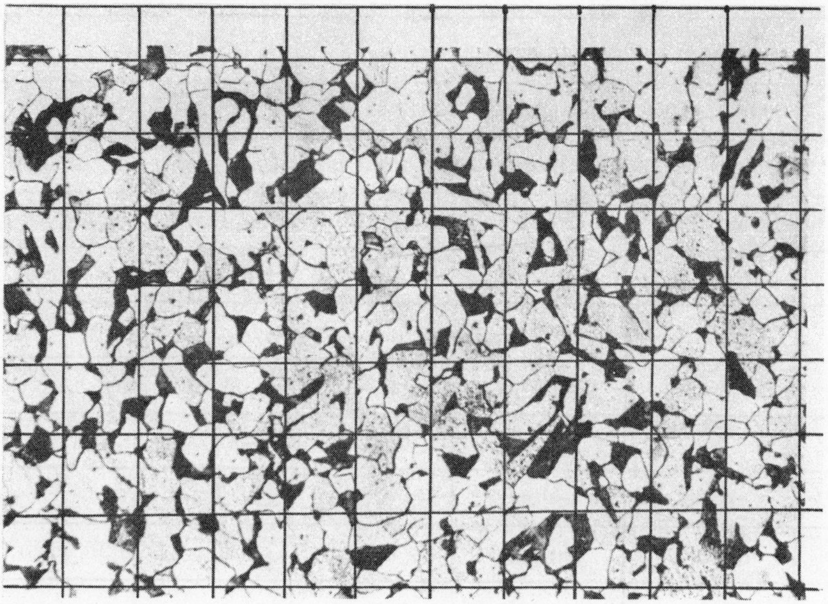

Fig. 8.17 The microstructure consisting of ferrite-pearlite in a plain carbon steel is superimposed on a square grid for evaluating the volume fraction of pearlite.

$$\pm \Delta V_f = \frac{2\sqrt{p_f(1-p_f)}}{p} \tag{8.54}$$

where p is the total number of points on the test grid. The use of a 20×20 grid provides a compromise of yielding reasonably good results with acceptable strain on the eye. The volume fraction obtained in the pearlite-ferrite aggregate of plain carbon steel is

$$V_f = \frac{22}{88} = 0.25$$

The relative class frequency and the distribution functions are shown in Fig. 8.18. The methods of calculating mean and variance of the volume fraction are shown in Table 8.6.

Table 8.6 **Mean ($x = \overline{V}_f$) and variance (s) of the volume fraction of pearlite in a mild steel.**

S.No.	V_f	$V_f - \overline{V}_f$	$(V_f - \overline{V}_f)^2$	S^2	S
1	0.2154	−0.0258	6.656×10^{-4}		
2	0.2675	+0.0263	6.917×10^{-4}		
3	0.2403	−0.0009	8.1×10^{-7}		
4	0.2675	+0.0263	6.917×10^{-4}	0.00066	0.0256
5	0.2879	+0.0467	2.18×10^{-3}		
6	0.2426	0.0014	1.96×10^{-6}		
7	0.1972	−0.044	1.936×10^{-3}		
8	0.2244	−0.168	1.936×10^{-4}		
9	0.2403	−0.0009	8.1×10^{-7}		
10	0.229	−0.0122	1.488×10^{-4}		
Mean, x = $\overline{V}_f = 0.2412$					

The volume fraction of the second phase is the parameter which controls the mechanical properties of the two-phase alloys. It is frequently used in quality control of materials. The relative volume of phases in the multi-phase field of an equilibrium phase diagram is closely related to the composition of phases through the lever rule. The volume fraction measurement, therefore, serves as a guide to check the accuracy of the equilibrium phase diagram if accurate data is available. This has been carried out in a few instances and excellent results obtained, such as, in the Cu-Al system.

The volume fraction analysis is extensively used to establish the time-temperature-transformation diagram of a multi-phase alloy. Such diagrams give information about the stable range of temperatures of the existence of each phase, the relative amount of each phase and the volume fraction of the parent phase remaining untransformed after a certain time of holding at a given isothermal transformation temperature. The influence of the rate of cooling on the resulting microstructure in commercial steels is useful in quality control and has been extensively used in the area of materials research. A typical T–T–T diagram for a commercial steel is shown in

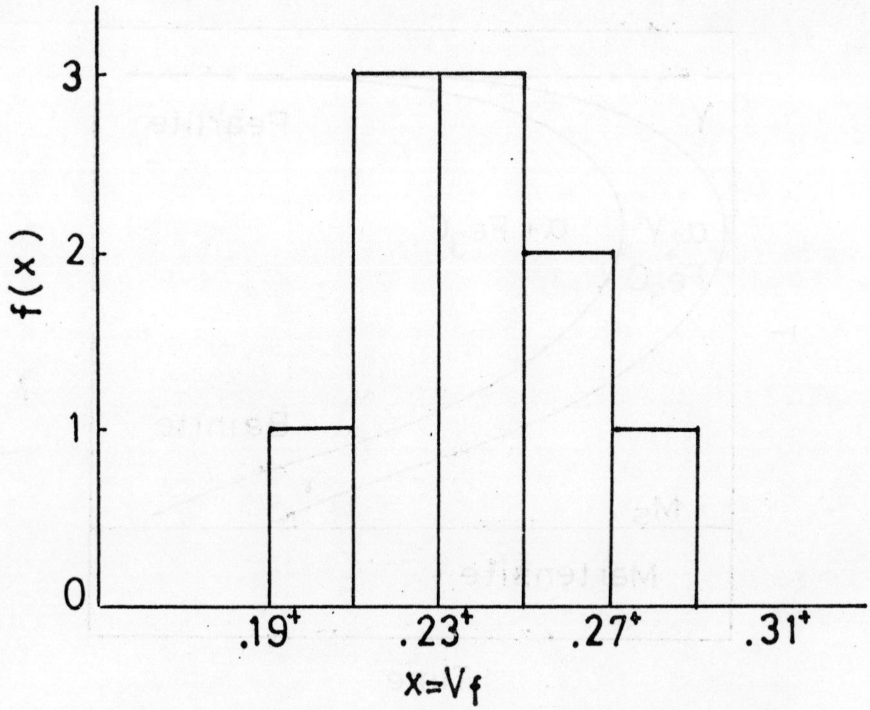

Fig. 8.18 The relative class frequency and the distribution function.

Fig. 8.19. The diagram illustrates the temperature range of stability of ferrite, bainite and martensite phases. The desired microstructure in this steel can be obtained by a suitable rate of cooling or isothermal transformation can be carried out by measurements of volume fraction of the transformed region. The increase in the volume fraction of the transformed region as a function of the time of aging is shown in Fig. 8.20 for a Cu-In alloy. The curve has three distinct regions. The increasing rate of change of the volume fraction initially pertains to the nucleation stage. This is followed by the steady state growth of cells represented the linear part of the curve. Finally, the decreasing rate of growth of cells is due to the impingement of cells originating from different grain boundaries. By plotting the data as log ln $(1 - v_f]^{-1}$ vs. log t, the process or processes controlling the transformation can be understood. A very interesting aspect of the volume fraction analysis is the possibility of determining the local composition of the depleted matrix. The composition is related to the volume fraction by the following equation

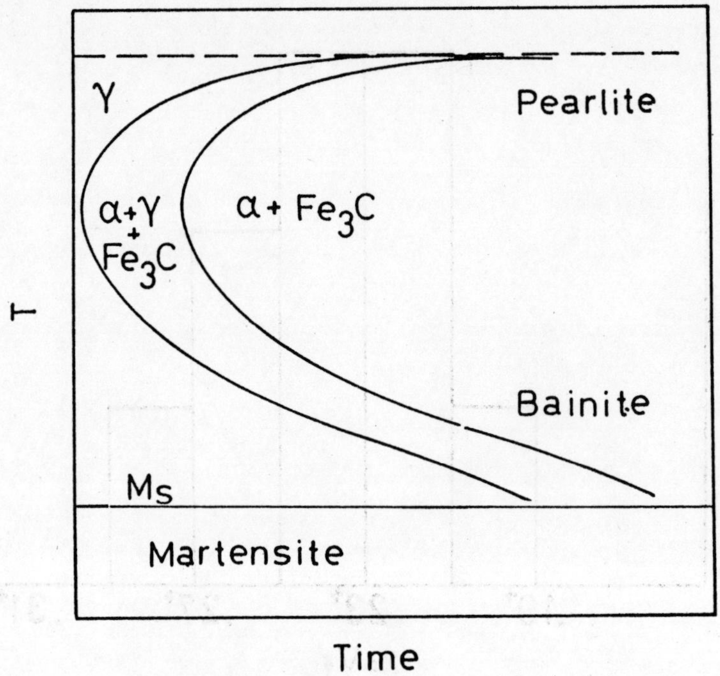

Fig. 8.19 *T–T–T* diagram for a commercial steel.

$$X_B^{\alpha} = X_B^0 - (X_B^{\beta} - X_B^0)\frac{V_m^{alloy}}{V_m^{\beta}} \cdot \frac{V_f}{(1 - V_f)} \tag{8.55}$$

where X_B^0 is the original alloy composition

X_B^{α} is the composition of the α phase

V_m^{alloy} is the molar volume of the alloy

V_m^{β} is the molar volume of the β phase.

X_B^{β} is the composition of the β phase.

The average local composition of the depleted matrix in local equilibrium with the β phase of the (α+β) phase field, as determined by the lineal fraction analysis of the lamellar structure, is shown in Fig. 8.21 for an Fe-Zn alloy. The diffusivity values

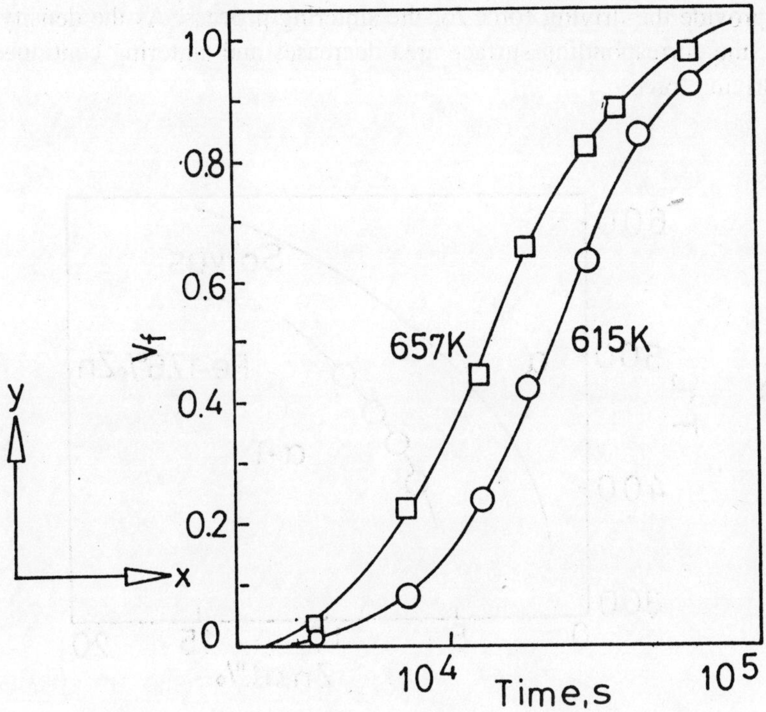

Fig. 8.20 Volume fraction vs. time of aging of a Fe-Zn alloy.

calculated by using the composition, growth rate and interlamellar spacing data of Fig. 8.21, predicts that the kinetics of the cellular phase transformation in Fe-Zn alloys is controlled by the diffusion of Zn along the grain boundaries.

8.5 SPECIFIC SURFACE AREA AND SPECIFIC LENGTH

The specific surface area or surface area per unit volume S_v of the microstructure plays an important role in controlling the mechanical properties. For example, the well known fact that a fine-grained material has superior strength relates to the grain boundary area per unit volume of the metal or an alloy. A precipitate phase with a fine dispersion has a higher surfaces area and thus a higher total interfacial free energy. This is useful in the study of the kinetics of precipitate coarsening because the driving force for the coarsening process is capillarity. In transformation nucleated on surfaces, the rate of nucleation is directly related to the surface area per unit volume. The rate of nucleation increases if the specific surface area is higher. The pores of a solid-interface provide the driving force for the sintering process. As the density of pores decreases, the corresponding surface area decreases and sintering continues under a reduced driving force.

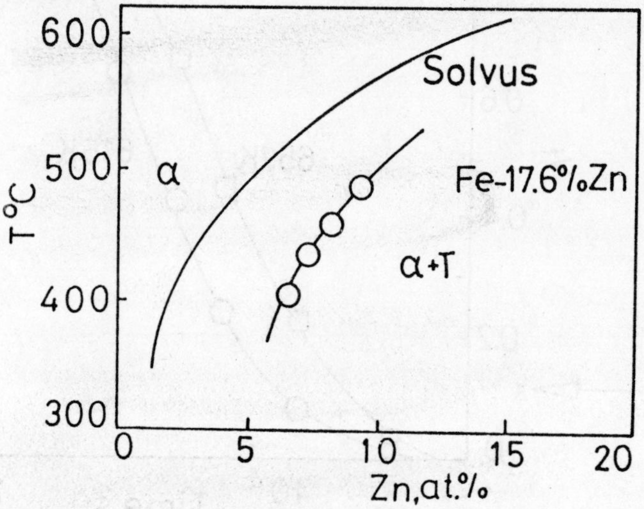

Fig. 8.21 The average local composition of the depleted matrix due to aging of an Fe-Zn alloy.

The specific surface area of a microstructural feature can be best described quantitatively by the following equation

$$S_v = 2\,\overline{N}_L \tag{8.56}$$

where $\overline{N}_L$ is the number of intercepts that the test line makes with the intersection of the two-dimensional microstructural feature on the plane of polish, per unit length of the test line. Equation (8.56) has been derived by Saltykov (3) and Underwood (4) as summarized below.

Let us consider a system of surfaces contained within a cube of edge length "*a*". The basic derivation is based on the principle that the probability of a test line intersecting an element of the surface dA (θ, ψ) in space is proportional to the projected area on a plane perpendicular to the test line, as shown in Fig. 8.22. Thus,

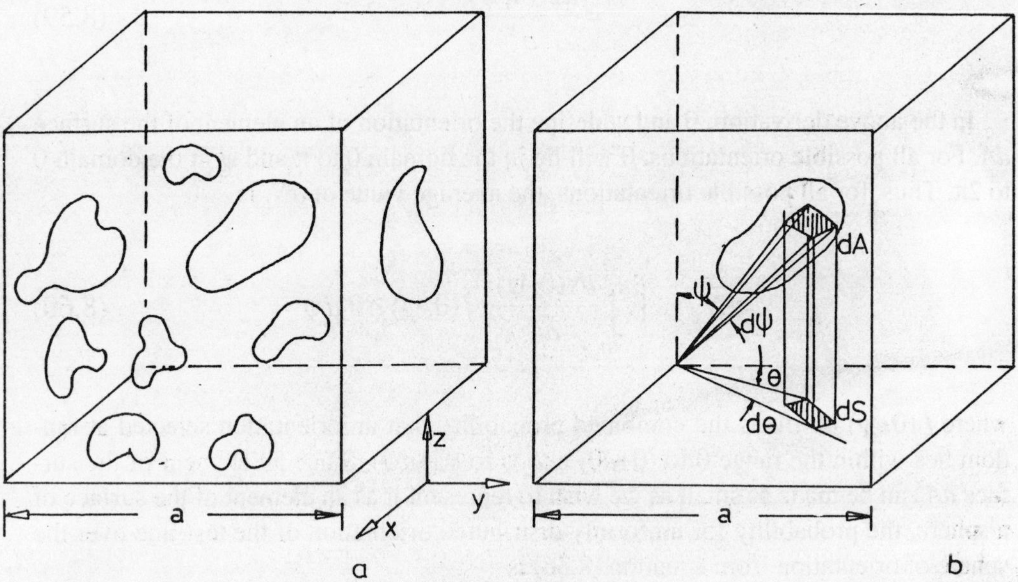

Fig. 8.22 Projection of an element of area dA on the x–y plane and its intersection with a test line. $ds(\theta, \psi) = dA\,|\cos\psi|$.

$$\text{Probability} = \frac{ds\,(\theta, \psi)}{a^2} \tag{8.57}$$

where $ds\,(\theta, \psi)$ is the projected area dA on the x–y plane and a^2 is the total area of the base of the cube. If a large number of parallel test lines are considered, then the geometric probability is simply multiplied by the number and we can write,

$$p = \frac{N \cdot ds(\theta, \psi)}{a^2} \tag{8.58}$$

Now, since the total length of all test lines in *N.a*, the number of intersections per unit length of the test line is

$$dN_L = \frac{Nds\ (\theta, \psi)}{a^2} \cdot \frac{1}{Na}$$

$$= \frac{ds\ (\theta, \psi)}{a^3} \tag{8.59}$$

In the above derivation, θ and ψ define the orientation of an element of the surface *dA*. For all possible orientations, θ will lie in the domain 0 to π and ψ in the domain 0 to 2π. Thus, for all possible orientations, the average value of dN_L is

$$d\overline{N}_L = \int_0^{\pi}\int_0^{2\pi} \frac{ds(\theta, \psi)}{a^3} \cdot f(\theta, \psi)\, d\theta\, d\psi \tag{8.60}$$

where $f(\theta, \psi)\, d\theta\, d\psi$ is the combined probability that an orientation selected at random lies within the range θ to (θ+*d*θ) and ψ to (ψ+*d*ψ). Since an element of the surface *dA* can be made as small as we wish to represent it as an element of the surface of a sphere, the probability for uniformly distributed orientation of the test line over the sphere of orientation from equation (8.36) is

$$f(\theta, \psi)\, d\theta\, d\psi = \frac{\sin \psi\, d\theta\, d\psi}{4\pi}$$

where $$f(\theta, \psi) = \frac{\sin \psi}{4\pi}.$$

Substituting for $f(\theta, \psi)$ from equation (8.36) into equation (8.60) yields,

$$d\overline{N}_L = \int_0^{\pi}\int_0^{2\pi} \frac{ds\ (\theta, \psi)}{4\pi a^3} \sin \psi\, d\theta\, d\psi, \tag{8.61}$$

where the factor 4π arises from the range of orientations covered by a sphere. Substitution for $ds\,(\theta, \psi) = dA|\cos\psi|$ in equation (8.60) yields,

$$d\overline{N}_L = \int_0^{\pi}\int_0^{2\pi} \frac{dA\,|\cos\psi|}{4\pi a^3} \sin\psi \, d\theta \, d\psi$$

$$d\overline{N}_L = \frac{dA}{2a^3}$$

Since the result is applied to each element of the surface confined within the volume, the number of intersections formed with all surfaces in the domain of the surface A is

$$\overline{N}_L = \int_s \frac{dA}{2a^3} = \frac{A}{2a^3} = \frac{S_v}{2}$$

or

$$S_v = 2\overline{N}_L \tag{8.61}$$

When a poly-dispersed assembly of the second phase particles is intersected by a plane of polish, a number of closed loop shapes appear. Similarly, for a polycrystalline material consisting of a system of tetrakidecahedra, a network of lines representing grain boundaries appear on the plane of polish. The length of such lines per unit area of the surface can be determined by proceeding in a similar manner as that for determining surface area per unit volume. The detailed derivation is presented by Underwood (4). The derivation is based on the principle that the probability that a test line will meet an element of the loop (perimeter) of length dl is proportional to the projected length of the element on a line perpendicular to the test line. Proceeding as before, we get the result

$$L_A = \frac{\pi}{2}\overline{N}_L \tag{8.62}$$

where L_A is the length per unit area and $\overline{N}_L$ is the average number of intercepts made by a test line with lineal features per unit length of the test line.

In the glossary of metallurgical microstructures, there are instances when one of the dimensions of the phase predominates. The structure of such phases are lenticular in shape, for example, Widmanstätten ferrite, dendritic arms, needle-shaped precipitates, stringers of MnS in steel, etc. The structure of the dislocation line also belongs to this class of microstructures. Specific length L_V of such one-dimensional features can be determined by counting the number of points per unit area in the plane of polish. The detailed quantitative treatment has been carried out by Underwood (4) and is given by the following equation,

$$L_v = 2\,\overline{p}_A \tag{8.63}$$

where $\overline{p}_A$ is the number of points per unit area.

Consider a line element *dl* (an element of the grain edge) in a three-dimensional structure, Fig. 8.23. Our aim at this point is to determine the length of grain edges per unit volume of the polycrystalline structure. A test plane drawn parallel to the *z*-axis meets the line element *dl* at a point. Thus, the grain edges will appear as a distribution of points in the plane of polish. The geometrical probability of intersection of a test plane with the infinitesimal element *dl* of the three-dimensional feature is given by

$$\text{Probability that the test plane intersects the line element,} \quad p = \frac{dy(\theta, \psi)}{a}$$

where $dy\,(\theta, \psi)$ is the projected length of the line upon a line which is perpendicular to the test plane selected. If a large number of test planes (*N*) parallel to each other and uniformally distributed within the cube are selected, the probability simply gets multiplied by *N*. The number of intersections per unit area is

$$dP_A(\theta, \psi) = \frac{1}{Na^3}\,[N\,dy\,(\theta, \psi)] = \frac{dy(\theta, \psi)}{a^3} \tag{8.64}$$

Equation (8.64) indicates that the number of intersections is a function of the orientation θ & ψ of the line element with respect to the test plane and is related to the projection of *dl*. Thus

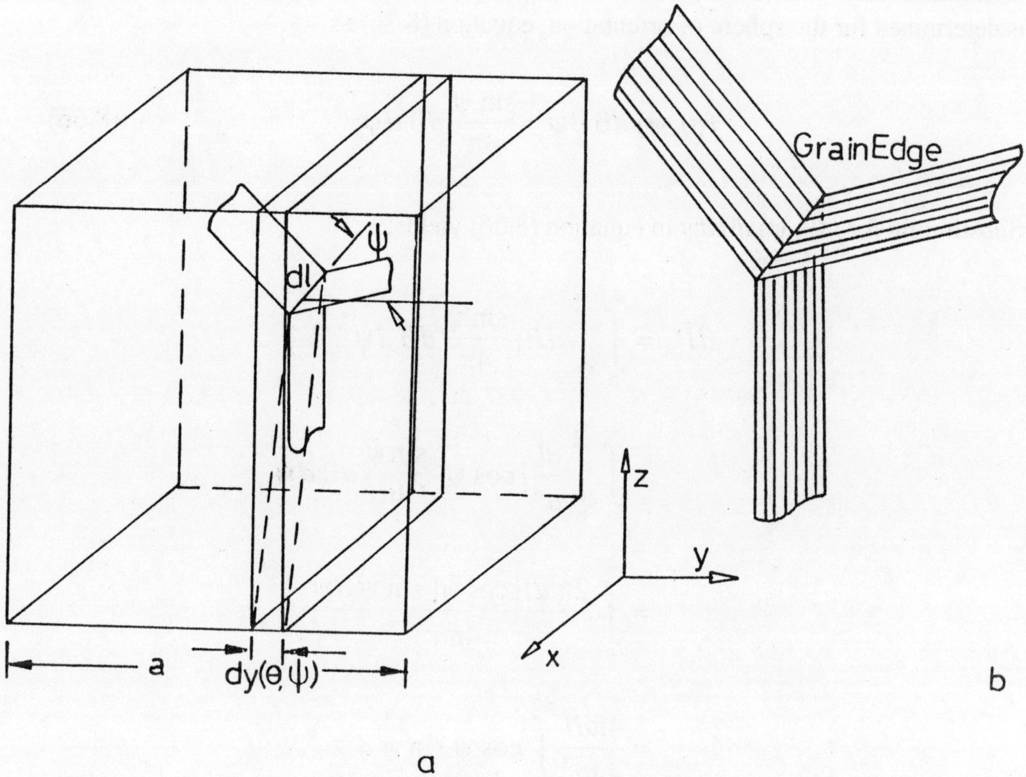

Fig. 8.23 Intersection of a lineal feature, grain edge, with the x–z plane; $dy\ (\theta, \psi)$ is the projected length of a differential element dl (a). The grain edge is shown separately (b).

$$dy\ (\theta, \psi) = |\ \text{Cos}\ \psi\ |\ dl \tag{8.65}$$

For uniformally distributed test planes, the average number of intersections formed with the line element per unit area of the test plane is determined by averaging over the sphere of orientation. Thus,

$$d\overline{P}_A = \int_0^{\pi} \int_0^{2\pi} dP_A f\ (\theta, \psi)\ d\theta\ d\psi \tag{8.66}$$

when $f(\theta, \psi)\, d\theta\, d\psi$ is the combined probability of determining a test plane in the orientation range θ to $(\theta+d\theta)$ and ψ to $(\psi+d\psi)$. The value of the probability function is determined for the sphere of orientation, equation (8.36) as

$$f(\theta,\psi)\, d\theta\, d\psi = \frac{\sin\psi}{4\pi}\, d\theta\, d\psi. \tag{8.66}$$

Substituting for $f(\theta, \psi)\, d\theta\, d\psi$ in equation (8.66) yields:

$$\begin{aligned} d\overline{P}_A &= \int_0^{\pi}\int_0^{2\pi} dP_A \frac{\sin\psi}{4\pi}\, d\theta\, d\psi \\ &= \int_0^{\pi}\int_0^{2\pi} \frac{dl}{a^3} |\cos\psi| \frac{\sin\psi}{4\pi}\, d\theta\, d\psi \\ &= \int_0^{\pi} \frac{2\pi\, dl |\cos\psi| \sin\psi\, d\psi}{4\pi a^3} \\ &= \frac{4\pi dl}{4\pi a^3}\int_0^{\pi/2} \cos\psi \sin\psi\, d\psi \\ &= \frac{dl}{a^3}[x dx]_0^1 \\ &= \frac{dl}{2a^3}. \end{aligned} \tag{8.67}$$

The above derivation has been made for an infinitesimal element of length dl, but is valid for all such elements. Summation over the whole length of the lineal feature yields the number of intersections per unit area of the test plane of all lineal features in a three-dimensional structure. Thus,

$$\overline{P}_A = \int_l \frac{dl}{2a^3} = \frac{1}{2}\frac{l}{a^3} = \frac{1}{2}L_v.$$

$$L_v = 2\overline{P}_A \tag{8.63}$$

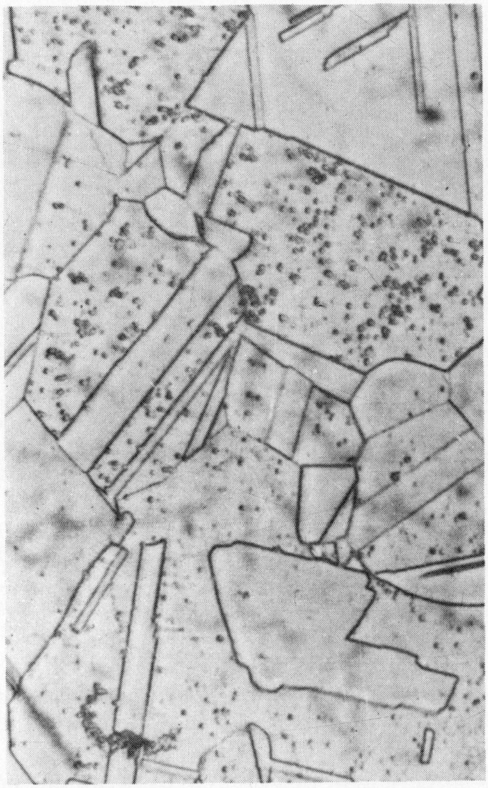

Fig. 8.24 The intersection of dislocation with the plane of polish appear as points (etch pits), Cu–15 wt.pct.In alloy.

Equation (8.63) can be used to determine the specific length of the grain edges where three grain boundaries meet. This is carried out by counting the number of triple-points in a unit area on the test plane. An illustrative example of the density of the dislocation lines is shown in Fig. 8.24 for a Cu-In alloy, alternately processed through single and two-phase regions of the equilibrium phase diagrams. From the quantitative evaluation of the etch pits, it has become clear that the density of dislocations in thermally cycled alloys is an order of magnitude higher than in the well annealed alloy. This is expected, as the interfacial dislocations at the α/β interface formed during cellular phase transformation could not be recovered in the short time that the alloy was kept at the solution treatment temperature. The mechanical strength and ductility of the alloy was substantially improved due to contributions from both the grain size and the dislocation density effects.

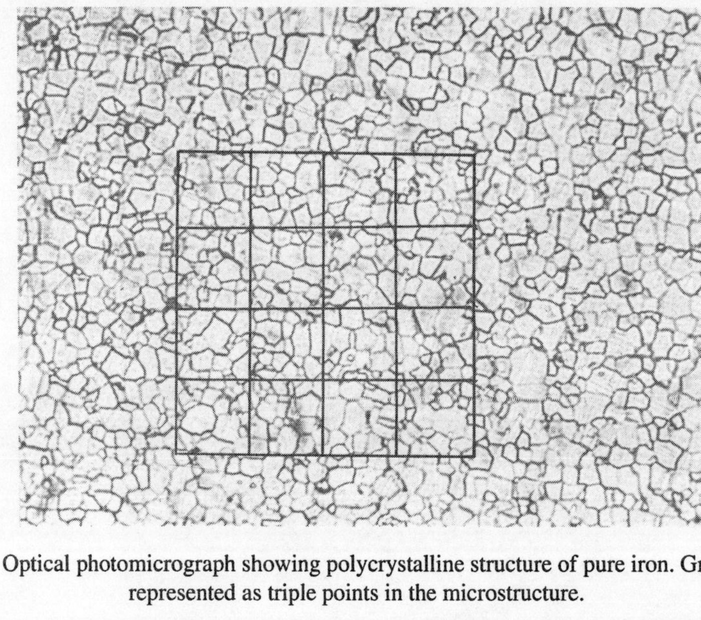

Fig. 8.25 Optical photomicrograph showing polycrystalline structure of pure iron. Grain edges are represented as triple points in the microstructure.

In order to determine the length of grain edges, a similar procedure is followed. The polycrystalline structure of pure iron derived at a magnification of 100x is presented in Fig. 8.25. The procedure is to select an area on the photomicrograph (say 4 × 4 cm^2 in this case) and count the number of triple points contained within this area. Let the number thus counted be n = 496. If the measurements were made at 1x the number of points contained within the same area would have been 100 × 100 times the number obtained above. Thus, in order to take into account the photographic magnification, the number counted is multiplied by the square of the actual magnification.

The actual number of points $= n \times 10^4 = 496 \times 10^4$

The number of points per unit area = $\dfrac{n \times 10^4}{a \times a} = \dfrac{496 \times 10^4}{4 \times 4 \times 10^{-4} \text{m}^2}$

The average length of the grain edges = $2 \times \dfrac{469 \times 10^8}{4 \times 4} = 0.62 \times 10^{10} \text{m}^{-2}$.

The grain boundary area per unit volume is indicative of the grain size. The higher the grain boundary area per unit volume, the smaller the grain size. In fact, the reciprocal of S_v defines the grain diameter. In order to determine the surface area per unit volume and hence the average grain diameter, the polycrystalline structure of a metal or an alloy is selected, Fig. 8.26. A number of lines of known length are projected on the microstructure at an interval of, say, 10 mm. The number of intercepts with the grain boundaries are measured for each line superimposed on the structure. Taking into account the magnification (100x) of the photomicrograph, the number of intercepts per unit length of the test line is recorded and the data averaged.

Number of intercepts, n = 10+8+11+8+8+6+13 (7 lines of length 10 cm)
7+8+7+5+5+4+4+7+9+7+9 (11 lines of length 7 cm each)

$N_L = (1 + .8 + 1.1 + .8 + .8 + .6 + 1.3) + (1 + 1.14 + 1 + .7 + .7 + .57 + .57 + 1 + 1.28 + 1 + 1.28)$

Actual average number of intercepts per unit length, $\overline{N}_L = 0.92 \times 10^4\ m^{-1}$

$$S_v = 2\overline{N}_L = 1.84 \times 10^4 \text{ m}^2/\text{m}^3$$

The grain boundary area per unit volume plays an important role in determining the degree of segregation in metals and alloys. Preferential segregation of undesirable impurity elements occurs if they have strong attraction to the grain boundaries. The mole fraction of the impurity element segregated at the grain boundary will be small in a very dilute alloy with small grain size. This is due to large grain boundary area per unit volume. During application at relatively high temperatures, there is a tendency for grain growth to occur. The rate of grain growth is dependent upon a number of parameters, e.g., the number of particles, interparticle spacing, etc. Coarsening of the

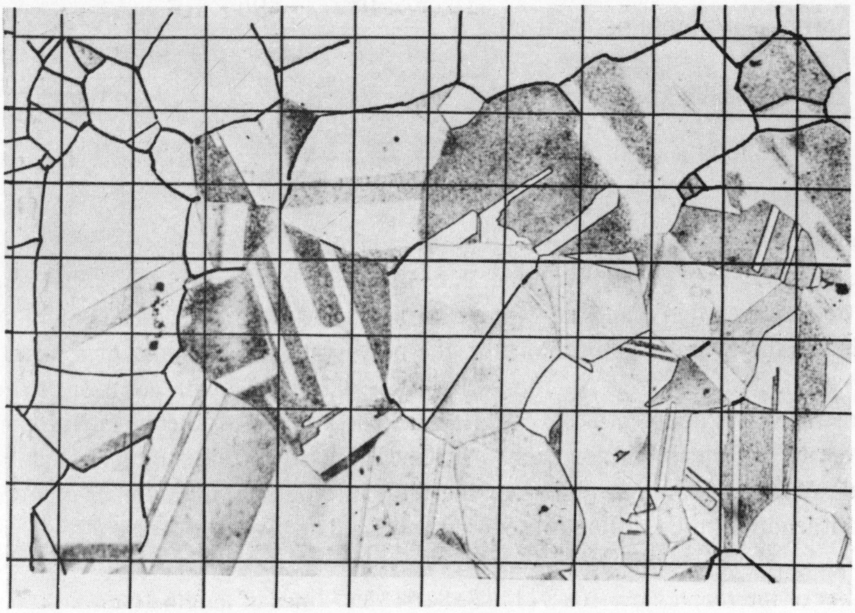

Fig. 8.26 Polycrystalline structure of Cu–In alloy.

particles occurs at elevated temperature application. The number of particles per unit volume decreases and the interparticle spacing increases during coarsening, thus increasing the rate of migration of the grain boundaries. The same mole fraction of impurity elements now distributes on a small area of the grain boundary per unit volume, thus increasing the fraction of monolayer of the impurity element segregated. The monolayer of the solute segregated may be critical and the material may fail by intercrystalline fracture. An evaluation of the surface area of the grain per unit volume helps provide knowledge of the level of segregation of a given solute.

The work hardening characteristics of an alloy having a dispersion of second phase particles depends upon the density of particles and the interparticle spacing. If the density of the particles is low, the surface area of the particles per unit volume will also be low. The interfacial dislocations, whose density is dependent upon the surface area, offer resistance to the motion of dislocation during deformation. An evaluation of the surface area per unit volume of the dispersed particles is useful in understanding the deformation characteristics of the material. The surface area per unit volume of the second phase particles is determined on the same lines as the procedure followed for the grain boundary area.

A photomicrograph representing dispersed assembly of particles is selected, Fig. 8.27. A number of lines of known length are drawn at a regular interval. The following procedure is followed in recording the data:

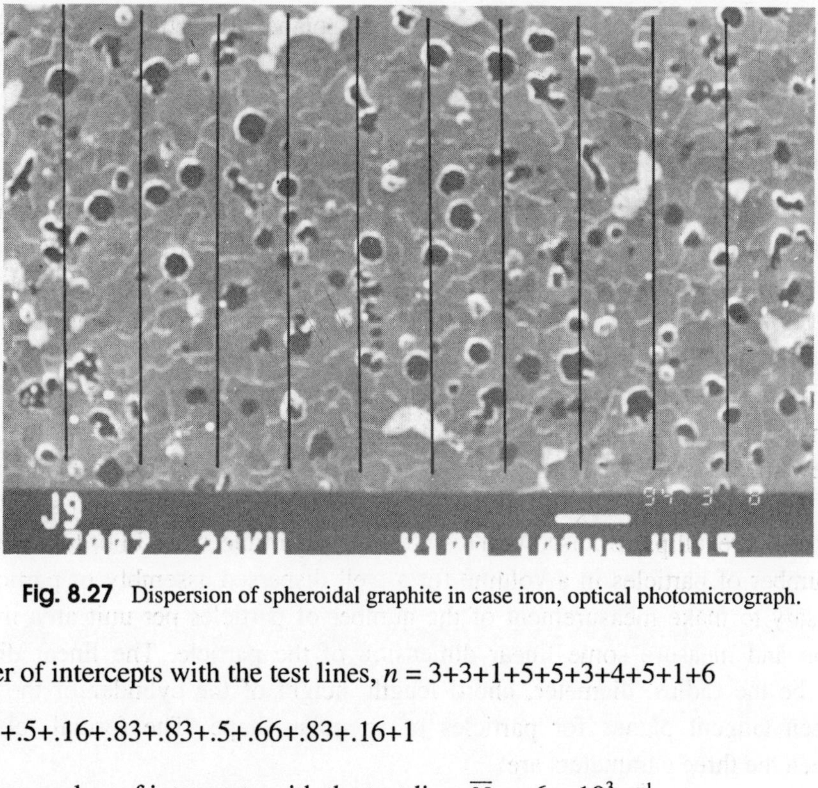

Fig. 8.27 Dispersion of spheroidal graphite in case iron, optical photomicrograph.

Number of intercepts with the test lines, n = 3+3+1+5+5+3+4+5+1+6

N_L = .5+.5+.16+.83+.83+.5+.66+.83+.16+1

Average number of intercepts with the test line, $\overline{N}_L = 6 \times 10^3 \text{m}^{-1}$

Surface area per unit volume, $S_v = 1.2 \times 10^4 \text{m}^2/\text{m}^3$

8.6 NUMBER OF PARTICLES AND AVERAGE SIZE OF PARTICLES

8.6.1 Introduction

In the study of coarsening of precipitate particles, it has been observed that the number of particles per unit volume decreases and the average particle size increases with increase in the time of aging. In a given material system, the particles generally have the same shape but show a distribution of size. Since the kinetics of coarsening is based on the premise that the larger particles grow and smaller ones dissolve, the distribution is generally quite large.

Since the geometric probability that a test plane selected randomly within the sample depends upon the tangent diameter, as defined in section 8.3, the probability of intersection will be different for different particle sizes. If the measurement is to be made on a plane section, then it is likely that a large-size particle may give a small linear dimension. This creates problems as it is difficult to ascertain the true size of the particle from its intersection on a plane. This can be illustrated very conveniently for spherical particles. The intersection of spheres with a plane are circles whose diameters are the chord diameters. A small-size sphere intersected by the plane near its diameter will appear as a circle of large diameter as compared to a large-size sphere intersected near the periphery of the sphere.

With the problems associated in the measurement of true particle sizes in three dimensions, it has become possible to apply quantitative microscopy principles only to a few specific cases. These include (i) structures in which all particles belong to the same shape and size class (ii) structures in which all particles have a simple shape, such as sphere, ellipse or disc, with distribution of particle sizes. In order to determine the number of particles in a volume for a well dispersed assembly of particles, it is necessary to make measurement of the number of particles per unit area in a plane section and measure some linear dimension of the particle. The linear dimension could be the radius, diameter, chord length, height of the cylinder or the distance between tangent planes for particles of irregular shape. The formal relationship between the three parameters are:

$$\overline{N_A} = N_v \overline{D} \tag{8.68}$$

where $\overline{N}_A$, N_v and $\overline{D}$ are, respectively, the average number of particles per unit area, number per unit volume and the distance between tangent planes in three dimensions, Fig. 8.28. For particles of all shapes we can write $\overline{D}$ to be dependent upon the angles θ, ψ as $D(\theta, \psi)$. For spheres, $\overline{D}$ is independent of the orientation and its value equals $2r$, where r is the radius of the particle. The basic quantitative relationship can be established by noting that the probability that a test plane will intersect the particle is related to the tangent diameter as described by equation (8.30),

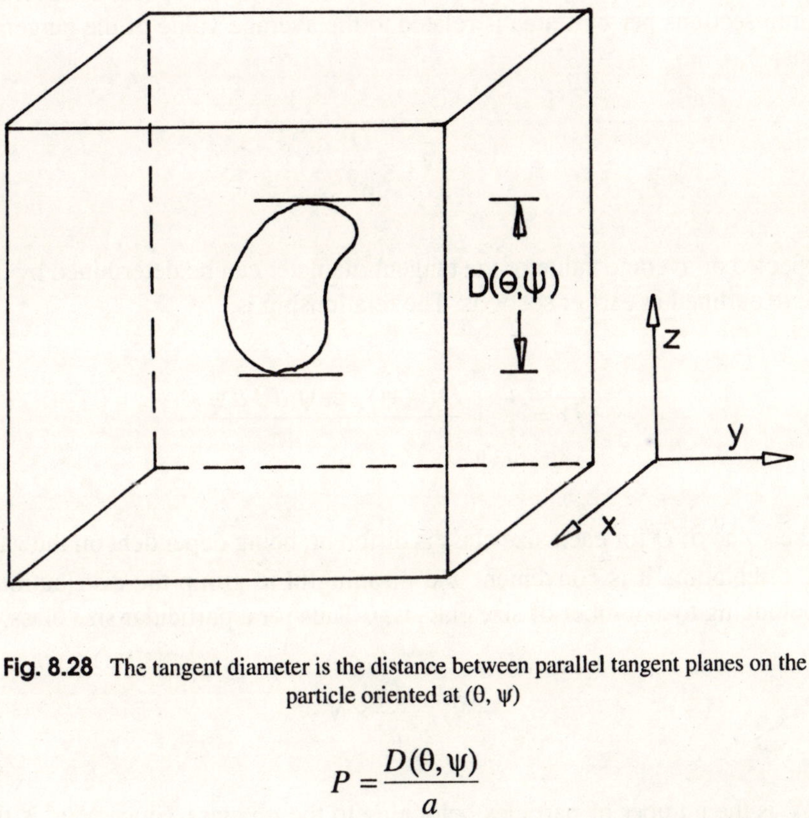

Fig. 8.28 The tangent diameter is the distance between parallel tangent planes on the particle oriented at (θ, ψ)

$$P = \frac{D(\theta, \psi)}{a} \tag{8.30}$$

For a large number of planes N intersecting the particle, the probability can be written as

$$P = \frac{N\,D\,(\theta,\psi)}{a}$$

and the number of intersections per unit area is

$$N_A = \frac{N\,D\,(\theta,\psi)}{a} \times \frac{1}{Na^2} = \frac{D\,(\theta,\psi)}{a^3}$$

For all orientations (of the particle) uniformly distributed in space, the average number of intersections per unit area is related to the average value of the tangent diameter. Thus,

$$\overline{N}_A = \frac{\overline{D}}{a^3} \tag{8.69}$$

The expected or average value of the tangent diameter can be determined by using the procedure outlined in earlier sections. The relationship is,

$$\overline{D} = \int_0^{\pi}\int_0^{2\pi} \frac{D(\theta,\psi)}{a}\,\frac{\sin\psi\,d\theta\,d\psi}{4\pi}$$

Since the value of $\overline{D}$ for each size class is different, being dependent on the value of D and the orientation, it is convenient and meaningful to group the distribution of particles belonging to a number of size classes, j. Thus for a particular size class, j,

$$\overline{N}_{Aj} = \frac{\overline{D}_j}{a^3} \times N_j \tag{8.70}$$

where N_j is the number of particles belonging to the jth class. Since N_j/a^3 is the number of particles per unit volume N_{vj} belonging to the jth class, equation (8.70) can be written as

$$\overline{N}_{Aj} = \overline{D}_j\, N_{vj} \tag{8.71}$$

The test plane intersects particles belonging to all classes. The average number of intersections per unit area for particles belonging to all classes can be determined by summing over the domain of j,

$$\overline{N}_A = \sum_{j=1}^{n} \overline{N}_{Aj} = \sum_{j=1}^{n} \overline{D}_j N_{vj} = \frac{\sum_{j=1}^{n} N_{vj} \sum_{j=1}^{n} \overline{D}_j N_{vj}}{\sum_{j=1}^{n} \overline{D}_j N_{vj}}$$

$$= \frac{N_v \sum_{j=1}^{n} \overline{D}_j N_{vj}}{\sum_{j=1}^{n} N_{vj}}, \text{ since } \; N_v = \sum_{j=1}^{n} N_{vj},$$

when N_v is the number of particles per unit volume of the material of all classes considered together. The value of $\sum_{j=1}^{n} \overline{D}_j N_{vj} / \sum_{j=1}^{n} N_{vj} = \overline{D}$. It can be determined by measuring the distance between parallel tangent planes for all particles in the microstructure and averaging the value. We thus obtain the result

$$\overline{N}_A = N_v \overline{D} \tag{8.68}$$

Equation (8.68) is applicable to particle of all shapes because no assumption of the shape was made in its derivation.

8.6.2 Evaluation of the Number of Particles Per Unit Volume-Constant Shape and Arbinary Size Distribution

Consider a system consisting of particles dispersed in the matrix. The particles are all of the same shape with an arbitrary size distribution. When the three-dimensional structure is intersected by a plane section, the particle intercept on the plane can be characterized in terms of some linear dimension, say l. As an illustration, if the particles are in the shape of spheres, the diameter of the circles can be taken to be the linear dimension. Since the distribution of linear dimension l is not directly related to some linear dimension of the three-dimensional structure, *l cannot represent the size class.* Let us assume that there is a quantity z (1) which is a function of l and z has a form which makes the measurement of average particle size and number of particles per unit volume possible. Then we can write the average value of z as $\bar{z}$ in the following form,

$$\bar{z} = \frac{\sum N_{Aj}\bar{z}_j}{\sum N_{Aj}}, \tag{8.72}$$

when N_{Aj} is the number of particles per unit area and $\bar{z}_j$ is the average value of z for particles belonging to the jth class. $\bar{z}_j$ covers all possible orientations of the particles (θ, ψ) and their positions. From equation (8.71) we can substitute for N_{Aj} in equation (8.72) and write $\bar{z}$ as,

$$\bar{z} = \frac{\sum N_{Vj}\,\bar{D}_j\,\bar{z}_j}{\sum N_{Aj}} \tag{8.73}$$

$\bar{D}_j$ is the average distance between parallel tangent planes and $\bar{z}_j$ is a function of l. If the function $z\,(l)$ is such that $(\bar{D}_j\,\bar{z}_j)$ is a constant (η) and independent of the size class, then it becomes possible to evaluate N_v. Let $\bar{D}_j\bar{z}_j = \eta$, which upon substitution in equation (8.73) yields

$$\bar{z} = \frac{\eta \sum_{v=1}^{n} N_{vj}}{\sum_{v=1}^{n} N_{Aj}} = \frac{\eta\, N_v}{N_A}$$

or

$$N_v = \frac{\bar{z} \cdot N_A}{\eta} \tag{8.74}$$

For the product $\bar{D}_j\,\bar{z}_j$ to be constant, $\bar{z}_j$ must be the reciprocal of some linear dimension of the particle intercept in the plane section, if $\bar{D}_j$ is some linear dimension of the particle in three dimensions. Thus $z = 1/l$. In order that $\bar{z}$ can be evaluated, it is necessary to measure some characteristic linear dimension of the particle in the plane section for all particles belonging to the jth class. Take the reciprocal of l and then average the result for all possible positions and orientations (θ, ψ). If the average exists, it will be found to be inversely proportional to the linear dimension L, of the particle in three dimensions. Thus $\bar{z}_j = \eta_1 \; 1/L_j$. The proportionality constant η_1 is dimensionless and depends upon the shape of the particle. $\overline{D}_j$ can also be written in terms of some linear dimension L_j with a proportionality constant, i.e., $\overline{D}_j = \eta_2 L_j$. Substituting values of $\overline{D}_j$ and $\bar{z}_j$ in the relation $\overline{D}_j \, \bar{z}_j = \eta$, yields,

$$\eta_2 \times 1/L_j \times \eta_2 \, L_j = \eta$$

or

$$\eta_1 \times \eta_2 = \eta \tag{8.75}$$

Thus η is a constant and independent of the size class as assumed earlier because it is dependent upon two constants η_1 and η_2 which are shape dependent. Substituting for η in equation (8.74) yields

$$N_v = \frac{\bar{z}\, N_A}{\eta_1 \, \eta_2} \tag{8.76}$$

The quantities, $\bar{z}$ and N_A and shape factors η_1 and η_2 can be determined experimentally. In the following, we evaluate N_v for spherical shaped particles.

For spheres, the distance between parallel tangent planes is the diameter which can be represented in terms of the radius as $\overline{D}_j = 2R_j$, giving the value of $\eta_2 = 2$. In order to evaluate $\bar{z}_j$, we can take it to be the reciprocal value for all positions and orientations. Let us assume that the selected particle has a diameter D_j for particle belonging to the jth class. Furthermore, the plane intersects the sphere at a position h from the center, Fig. 8.29. If R_j is the radius of the sphere, then,

$$d_j = 2\sqrt{R_j^2 - h^2}$$

In order to evaluate $\bar{z}_j$, it is necessary to take the reciprocal of d_j and average it for all possible positions of the plane section. Let us assume that the planes are distributed between the center and the periphery of the spherical particles (domain R_j). Then the

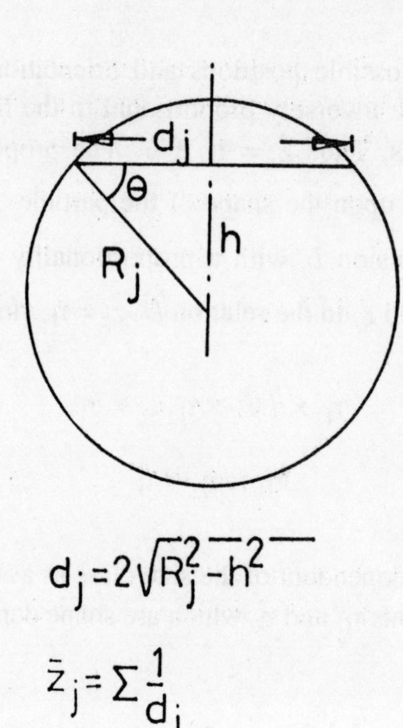

Fig. 8.29 Intersection of particle by the plane at a position h from the center.

probabilities that the plane lies in the interval h and $(h + dh)$ is dh/R_j. The average or the expected value of z_j is

$$\bar{z}_j = \int_0^{R_j} \frac{1}{2\sqrt{R_j^2 - h^2}} \frac{dh}{R_j}$$

The integral can be evaluated by making the substitution $h = R_j$ Sin θ. Thus

$$\bar{z}_j = \int_0^{\pi/2} \frac{d\theta}{2R_j} = \frac{\pi}{4R_j} \tag{8.77}$$

The shape factor $\eta_1 = \pi/4$. For spherical particles equation (8.76) can be represented in the following form

$$N_v = \frac{\bar{z} \cdot N_A}{2 \times \pi/4} = \frac{2\,\bar{z}\,N_A}{\pi} \tag{8.78}$$

and $\overline{R} = \pi/4\bar{z}$ from equation (8.77)

Example: The chord diameter of dispersed spheres is measured at a magnification of 100*x* in the plane section within an area 8 cm × 8 cm. The diameters (in mm) are:

2.1, 3.5, 4.0, 4.2, 3.8, 4.3, 2.0, 3.2, 3.7, 4.3, 3.6, 2.0,
2.6, 3.1, 4.1, 2.5, 2.0, 3.5, 2.7, 3.8, 2.9, 3.3, 4.0, 2.8, 2.9.

Determine $\overline{R}$ and N_v.

From the given data, $N_A = \dfrac{25 \text{ (No. of particles)}}{64 \times 10^{-4}} \times 10^4 \text{ (No. m}^{-2})$

$$\bar{z} = \Sigma \frac{1}{d} = 0.3283371 \times 10^3 \times 10^2 = 3.283371 \times 10^4 \text{ m}^{-1}$$

at a magnification of 1x.

$$\overline{R} = \pi/4\bar{z} = 2.39 \times 10^{-5} \text{ m}$$

and

$$N_v = \frac{2\,\bar{z}\,N_A}{\pi} = 8.169 \times 10^{11}/\text{m}^3$$

8.6.3 Evaluation of N_v and $\overline{R}$ for disc-shaped particles

Consider the distribution of thin discs of different diameters in three dimensions. If the thickness of the disc is negligibly small compared to the diameter, then the intercept with a plane will appear as line segments in the microstructure. The line segments are the chord lengths at the position of intercept with the disc. The tangent diameter can be determined by orienting the disc at ψ which is the angle between the normals to the plane of the disc and the test plane, Fig. 8.30.

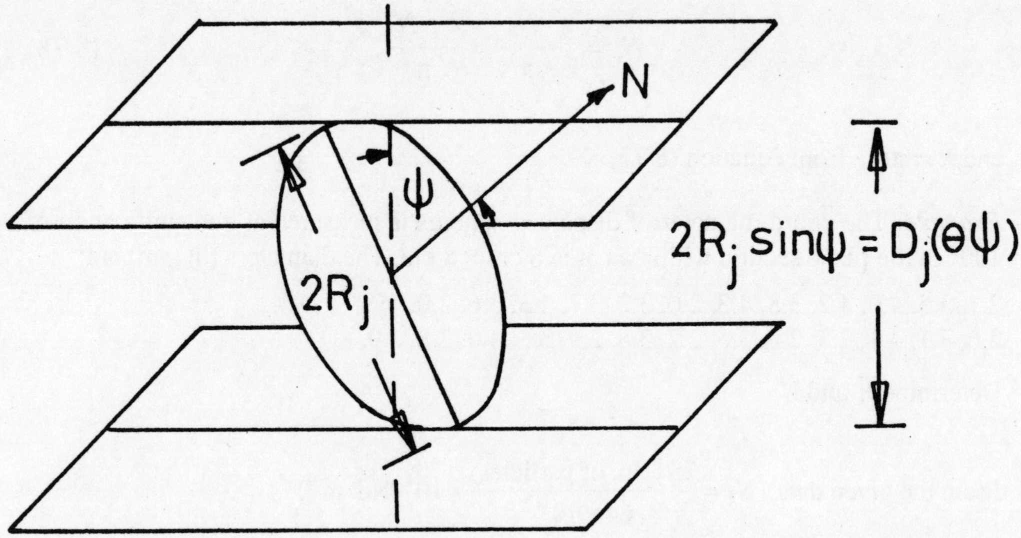

Fig. 8.30 The tangent diameter $\overline{D}$ is a function of particle orientation ψ, which is the angle between the normals to the plane of the disc and the test plane.

$$D_j = 2R_j \,|\sin\psi| \tag{8.79}$$

The expected or average value of D_j for all discs belonging to the jth class is

$$\overline{D}_j = \int_0^{\pi}\int_0^{2\pi} 2R_j \,|\sin\psi|\, \frac{\sin\psi}{4\pi}\, d\theta\, d\psi$$

$$= R_j \int_0^{\pi} \sin^2\psi\, d\psi$$

$$= 2R_j \int_0^{\pi/2} \sin^2\psi\, d\psi \quad \text{with the substitution } \sin^2\psi = \frac{1-\cos 2\psi}{2}$$

$$\overline{D}_j = 2R_j\left[\frac{1}{2}\psi\right]^{\pi/2} - \left[\frac{\sin 2\psi}{4}\right]_0^{\pi}$$

$$\overline{D}_j = \frac{\pi R_j}{2}.$$

The shape factor constant η_1 for a disc equals $\pi/2$. Since particles have circular geometry, the function z can be taken as the reciprocal of line segments which are chord lengths, instead of chord diameters as in the case of spheres, Thus, $\overline{z}$ will have the same relation in the case of disc-shaped particles as it had with the spheres, giving the second constant $\eta_2 = \pi/4$. Substituting values of η_1 and η_2 in equation (8.76) yields,

$$N_v = \frac{N_A\,\overline{z}}{\frac{\pi}{2}\times\frac{\pi}{4}} = \frac{8}{\pi^2}N_A\,\overline{z} \tag{8.80}$$

Example: The length of line segments of dispersed disc-shaped particles is measured at a magnification of 100*x* in a plane section within an area 10 cm × 10 cm. Determine $\overline{R}$ and N_v.

Length of line segments in mm:

1.5, 2.3, 5.1, 6.0, 2.3, 4.1, 5.0, 4.6, 1.7, 2.1,
2.3, 4.2, 4.0, 2.7, 3.2, 3.5, 2.1, 2.6, 2.8, 3.9.

$$N_A = \frac{20}{10\times 10\times 10^{-4}}\times 10^4 \text{ (No. m}^{-2}\text{)}$$

$$\overline{z} = \Sigma\,\frac{1}{d} = 0.3495\times 10^5\text{m};$$ d is the length of line segments.

$$N_v = 5.67\times 10^{11}\text{ m}^{-3} \quad\text{and}\quad \overline{R} = 2.246\times 10^{-5}\text{ m}$$

8.6.4 Evaluation of N_v and $\overline{R}$ for constant size particles

For particles of the second phase having the same shape and size, the number of particles per unit volume N_v can be determined very easily by writing the tangent diameter, surface area and the volume of the particle in terms of some characteristic dimension of the particle and dimensionless shape factors. These can be written by the following set of equations:

$$\text{The tangent diameter, } \overline{D} = \eta_1 Y$$

$$\text{Surface area, } S = \eta_3 Y^2$$

and
$$\text{Volume, } V = \eta_4 Y^3 \tag{8.81}$$

where Y is some linear dimension of the particle, i.e., length, radius, diameter, etc. and η_1, η_3 and η_4 are the shape factors. For a sphere,

$$\eta_1 = 2$$

$$\eta_3 = 4\pi$$

and
$$\eta_4 = 4\pi/3$$

The volume fraction of the second phase is written as

$$V_f = N_v \cdot V$$

$$= N_v \,.\, \eta_4 Y^3 = p_f \tag{8.82}$$

Similarly, the surface area of the particles is

$$S_V = N_V \cdot S$$

$$= N_V \cdot \eta_3 Y^2 = 2\overline{N}_L \tag{8.83}$$

and the relation,

$$N_A = N_V \cdot \overline{D} = N_V \cdot \eta_1 Y \tag{8.84}$$

The parameter N_V can be determined by eliminating Y from any pair of equations (8.82) to (8.86) taken at a time. Thus, we get,

$$N_V = \sqrt{\frac{N_A^3}{P_f} \frac{\eta_4}{\eta_1^3}}$$

$$N_V = \frac{8\,\overline{N}_L}{p_f^2} \cdot \frac{\eta_4}{\eta_3} \tag{8.85}$$

and

$$N_V = \frac{N_A^2}{2N_L} \cdot \frac{\eta_3}{\eta_1^2}$$

The value of Y is $\dfrac{2\overline{N}_L}{N_A} \cdot \dfrac{\eta_1}{\eta_3}$ (8.86)

For a sphere of radius $r\ (= y)$,

$$r = \frac{\overline{N}_L}{\pi N_A} \tag{8.87}$$

The particle size of spherical particles can be determined by counting the number of intercepts per unit length $\overline{N}_L$ and the number of particles per unit area in the plane of polish. The procedure of evaluating $\overline{N}_L$ and N_A has been outlined earlier.

Rod-shaped or Cylindrical Particles

While considering the second phase particles to assume the morphology of a cylinder with flat ends, the first step is to write the tangent diameter, surface area and volume of the cylinder in terms of some linear dimension Y and shape factors η_1, η_3 and η_4 as written in the set of equation (8.81). The tangent diameter is determined by writing $\overline{D}$ in terms of $D(\psi)$ with the help of Fig. 8.31. Thus

$$D(\psi) = (h \text{ Cos } \psi + 2r \sin \psi), \tag{8.88}$$

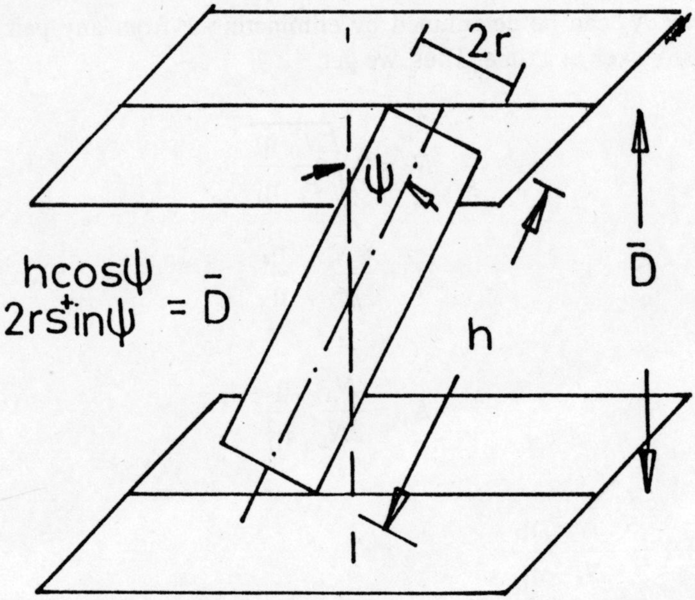

Fig. 8.31 The tangent diameter *D* for a cylindrical particle.

where ψ is the angle of inclination of the cylinder axis with the plane normal. The expected value of *D* is

$$\overline{D} = \int_0^{\pi}\int_0^{2\pi} (h \cos \psi + 2r \sin \psi) \frac{\sin \psi}{4\pi} \, d\theta \, d\psi$$

where *h* is the height of the cylinder and *r* the radius.

$$\overline{D} = \left(\frac{h}{2} + \frac{\pi r}{2}\right).$$

We can write

$$\overline{D} = \left(\frac{h}{2r} + \frac{\pi}{2}\right) r$$

$$S = 2\pi r h + 2\pi r^2 = 2\pi\left(\frac{h}{r}+1\right)r^2$$

and
$$V = \pi r^2 h = \frac{\pi h}{r} r^3 \tag{8.89}$$

Considering the radius of the cylinder to be the characteristic linear dimension Y, we can write the shape factors as

$$\eta_1 = \frac{1}{2}\left(\frac{h}{r}+\pi\right)$$

$$\eta_3 = 2\pi\left(\frac{h}{r}+1\right) \tag{8.90}$$

and
$$\eta_4 = \frac{\pi h}{r}.$$

The value of N_v can be determined from one of the equations (8.85) as,

$$N_v = \frac{4\pi N_A^2}{N_L} \frac{\left(\frac{h}{r}+1\right)}{\left(\pi+\frac{h}{r}\right)^2} \tag{8.91}$$

and the radius of the cylinder as,

$$r = \frac{1}{2\pi} \frac{\overline{N}_L}{N_A}\left[\frac{\pi+\frac{h}{r}}{1+\frac{h}{r}}\right] \tag{8.92}$$

Since all the shape factors are contained in the term h/r, the ratio of the height to the radius of the cylinder can be determined by experimentally measuring $\overline{p}_f$, N_A and $\overline{N}_L$ and substituting in the relation

$$\frac{\eta_1 \eta_4}{\eta_3^2} = \frac{\overline{P}_f N_A}{4\overline{N}_L^2} \tag{8.93}$$

Equation (8.93) can be obtained from the set of equations (8.85).

8.6.5 Separation Between Particles of a Dispersed Phase

The separation between particle-matrix interfaces in a dispersed assembly of particles is central to determining the ease (or for that matter, the difficulty) with which a dislocation glides in its slip plane when it interacts with the particles of the second phase. The dislocation passes relatively easily if the distance between two particles is large. The strength of the alloy and its work hardening rate is directly related to the mean free path, defined as the average separation of particle-matrix interfaces measured linearly through the matrix in all directions. We can also adopt a definition of the mean free path of the dispersed particles, if, measurement of separation between particles is made on a random plane passing through the matrix. The value thus obtained would be different from the mean free path measured linearly because some neighboring particles may not get intersected and others may give a smaller chord projection in the plane.

The mean free path measured linearly in all directions in an assembly of dispersed particles is given by the relation

$$\overline{\lambda}_L = \frac{1 - L_f}{0.5\, N_L} \tag{8.94}$$

where L_f is the lineal fraction of the particles and N_L is the number of intersections per unit length of the test line with the α/β interface. From equations (8.48) and (8.56), we can write,

$$\overline{L}_f = V_f$$

and

$$N_L = \frac{S_V}{2}$$

$$= \frac{N_V \cdot S}{2}$$

$$\overline{N}_L = \frac{V_f \cdot S}{2V}$$

where S is the surface area of the particle and V is its volume. Substituting for $\overline{N}_L$ and $\overline{L}_f$ in equation (8.94) yields,

$$\overline{\lambda}_L = 4\left(\frac{1 - V_f}{V_f}\right) \cdot \frac{V}{S} \tag{8.95}$$

Equation (8.95) is valid, regardless of the particle distribution, size and shape, and

for spherical particles : $\overline{\lambda}_L = \frac{4}{3}\left(\frac{1 - V_f}{V_f}\right) r$

for cylinders or discs : $\overline{\lambda}_L = 2\left(\frac{1 - V_f}{V_f}\right)\left[\frac{1}{1 + \left(\frac{r}{h}\right)}\right] r$ (8.96)

for cube-shaped particles : $\overline{\lambda}_L = \frac{2}{3}\left(\frac{1 - V_f}{V_f}\right) a,$

where r is the radius of particles with circular geometry and a is the edge length of the cube.

The average center to center distance between particles in a random distribution of particles is given by Chandrashekhar (5) for point particles as:

$$\overline{\lambda}_V = \frac{0.554}{(N_V)^{1/3}} \tag{8.97}$$

For a sphere,

$$\overline{\lambda}_V = \frac{0.89\, r}{(V_f)^{1/3}} \tag{8.98}$$

Similar derivations can be made for other particle shapes. The average center to center distance between particles on a plane passing through a random array is

$$\overline{\lambda}_S = \frac{0.5}{(N_A)^{1/2}} \tag{8.99}$$

$$= \frac{0.5}{(N_V \cdot \overline{D})^{1/2}}$$

$$= \frac{0.5}{\sqrt{V_f}} \sqrt{\left(\frac{V}{\eta_1 Y}\right)}$$

For spherical particles, $$\overline{\lambda}_S = \frac{0.723}{\sqrt{V_f}}\, r \tag{8.100}$$

Thus, from a knowledge of the volume fraction of the particles and the radius or any other convenient one-dimensional parameter of the particles, the average separations, $\overline{\lambda}_L$, $\overline{\lambda}_V$ and $\overline{\lambda}_S$ can be calculated.

Example: The volume fraction of spheres of the second phase dispersed in the matrix is 0.1 and the radius of the sphere is 0.4 cm measured at 100x. Determine $\overline{\lambda}_L$, $\overline{\lambda}_S$ and $\overline{\lambda}_V$. If the volume fraction of the particles is doubled, how would it affect the mean free path?

Actual radius of the sphere $= 0.4 \times 10^{-2} \times 10^{-2}$m

$$\overline{\lambda}_L = \frac{4}{3}\left(\frac{1-0.1}{0.1}\right) \times 0.4 \times 10^{-4} = 4.8 \times 10^{-4} \text{ m}$$

$$\bar{\lambda}_S = \frac{0.723}{\sqrt{0.1}} \times 0.4 \times 10^{-4} = 9.14 \times 10^{-5}\text{m}$$

$$\bar{\lambda}_V = \frac{0.89 \times 0.4 \times 10^{-4}}{(0.1)^{1/3}} = 7.669 \times 10^{-5}\text{ m}$$

By increasing the volume fraction to 0.2, the mean free paths are $\bar{\lambda}_L = 2.13 \times 10^{-4}$m, $\bar{\lambda}_S = 6.46 \times 10^{-5}$m and $\bar{\lambda}_V = 6.08 \times 10^{-5}$m.

8.7 GRAIN SIZE MEASUREMENTS

The polycrystalline structure of materials consists of grains interconnected with each other, and can be best described as a tetrakaidecahedron, Fig. 8.32. In order to determine the true grain size, the measurement must be made in three dimensions, which is not possible in most metals and alloys and ceramic materials. Methods have to be devised to measure the grain size. The number thus obtained would represent the corresponding three-dimensional structure. Whatever method of measuring the grain size is devised, it must be consistent with respect to grain size distribution and small and large grain sizes must be measured without any ambiguity. The grain size measured must relate to physical properties of materials.

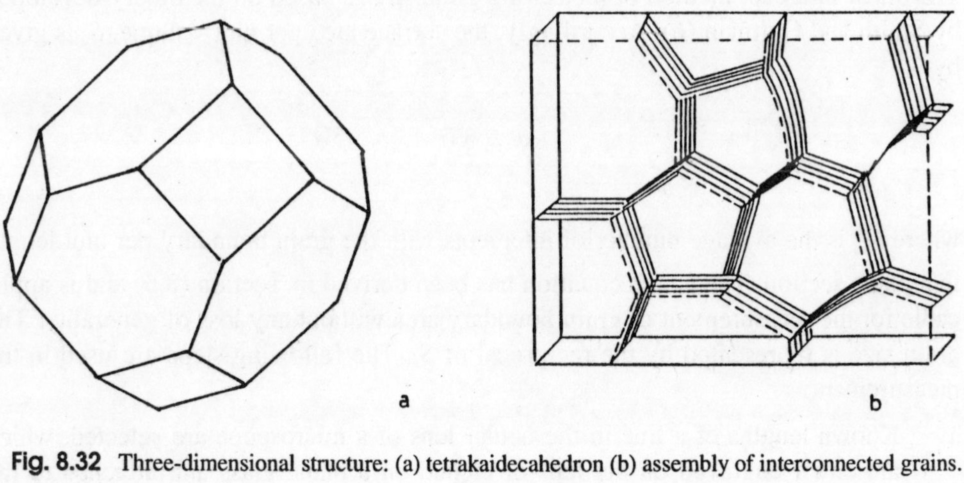

a b

Fig. 8.32 Three-dimensional structure: (a) tetrakaidecahedron (b) assembly of interconnected grains.

The grain size can be represented in three dimensions in terms of the average volume of the grain. The grain diameter in such a system of measure will represent the diameter of a sphere having the same volume as the volume of a grain. The grain size can also be measured in two dimensions in terms of the grain boundary area in a plane section. The surface area of the grain provides a method of representing the grain size. The grain size can also be measured in one dimension as the line intercept across a grain.

The one-dimensional line intercept does not truly represent the grain diameter because the intercept length on a plane section (test plane) depends upon the position of the plane within the tetrakaidecahedron. In order for the grain diameter thus obtained to have any significance and to correlate to the physical properties, a very large number of measurements have to be made. The average value of the line intercept which would lie between zero and the maximum grain diameter in three dimensions, must relate to the diameter of the sphere of equivalent volume as the tetrakaidecahedron. There is now a simple relationship which correlates these two quantities. The line intercept method of defining the grain size is not very useful.

The method of measuring grain boundary area is more appropriate as the numbers obtained show consistency and relate to the physical properties. The following methods are generally used to measure the grain size:

8.7.1 Linear Intercept Method

The linear intercept method of measuring grain size is based on the theory developed by Smith and Guttman (6). Accordingly, the surface area per unit volume, S_v is given by

$$S_v = 2\overline{N}_L ,$$

where $\overline{N}_L$ is the average number of intercepts with the grain boundary per unit length in a plane section. The above equation has been derived in section (8.5) and is applicable for the measurement of grain boundary area without any loss of generality. The grain size is represented by the reciprocal of S_v. The following steps are used in the measurement:

1. Known lengths of a line in the ocular lens of a microscope are selected, which are either engraved on the lens or etched on a plane glass and attached to the lens.

2. The number of intercepts the line makes with the grain boundary trace in the plane section, as observed through the microscope, are counted.
3. The ocular lens is rotated and the number of intercepts measured at 10° interval.
4. Similar counting of the number of intercepts from different regions of the specimen is carried out and the results averaged.
5. The grain size is $1/S_v = 1/2\overline{N}_L$.

If there is no preferential orientation of the grain and the grain structure is equiaxed, the grain size can be measured by the linear intercept method by drawing lines at, say, 10 mm intervals in two perpendicular directions. The method of measurement is shown in Fig. 8.33,

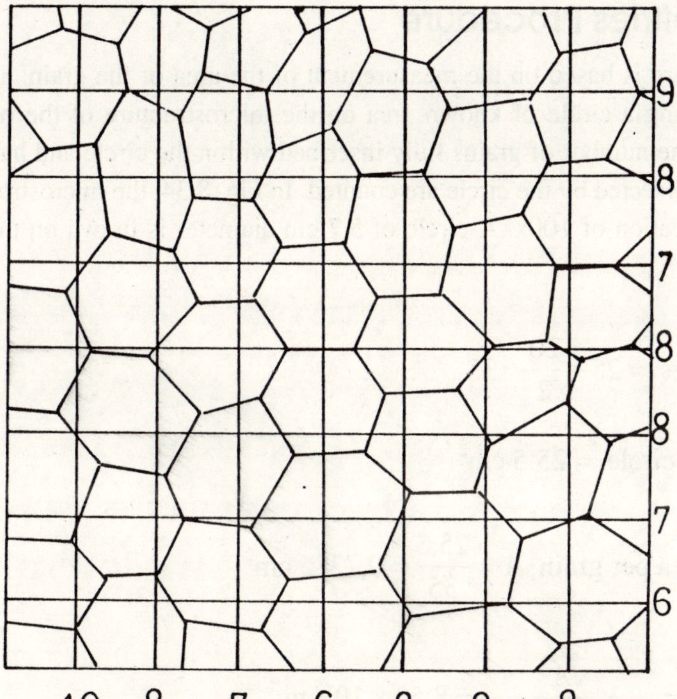

Fig. 8.33 Grain size determination by the linear intercept method.

$$\overline{N}_L = \frac{108}{14} \times \frac{1}{8 \times 10^{-2}} = 0.9642 \times 10^2 \text{ m}^{-1}$$

$$S_v = 2\overline{N}_L$$

$$\text{and Grain size } = \frac{1}{2N_L} = \frac{1}{2 \times 0.9642 \times 10^2} \times \frac{1}{M},$$

where M is the magnification of the figure.
The grain size is 5.185×10^{-5}m.

8.7.2 Jeffries Procedure

This procedure is based on the measurement of the area of the grain. This is carried out by drawing a circle of known area on the microstructure of the polycrystalline specimen. The number of grains fully inscribed within the circle and half the number of grains intersected by the circle are counted. In Fig. 8.34, the microstructure is taken at a magnification of 100x. A circle of 5.7 cm diameter is drawn on the microstructure.

$$\text{No. of grains } = 25 + \frac{20}{2} = 35$$

$$\text{Area of the circle } = 25.5 \text{ cm}^2$$

$$\text{Average area per grain, } \overline{A} = \frac{25.5}{35} = 0.7285 \text{ cm}^2$$

$$\text{Grain size } = \frac{\sqrt{A}}{\text{Magnification}} = 8.53 \times 10^{-5} \text{ m}$$

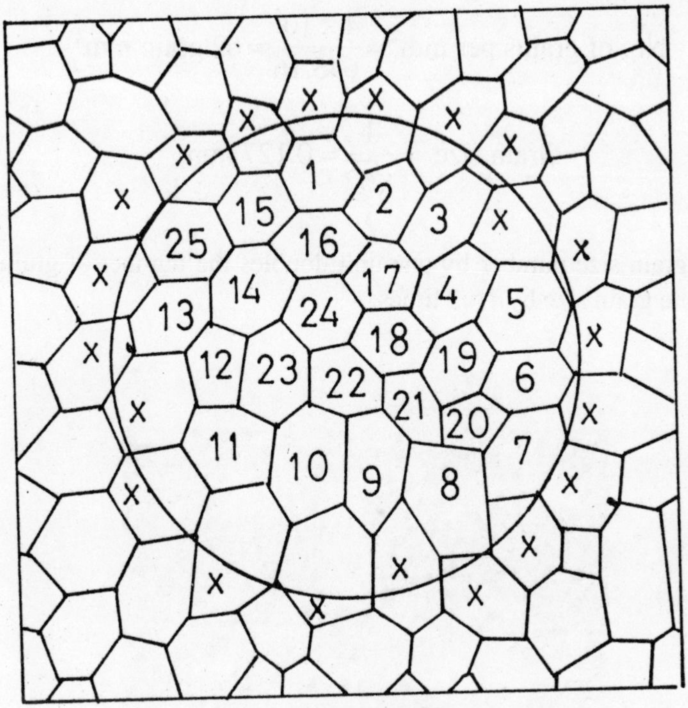

x=1/2

Fig. 8.34 Grain size determination by Jeffries method.

8.7.3 The ASTM Grain Size Number

The ASTM grain size measurement system is based on the number of grains per unit area and is represented by the following relation,

$$\ln N_A = (n - 1) \ln 2,$$

where N_A is the number of grains per square inch at a magnification of 100x and n is the ASTM grain size number. Let $n = 3$, then the number of grains per square inch are $2^{n-1} = 2^{3-1} = 4$. The number of grains in an area of 25.4 × 25.4 mm^2 are 4×10^4 at a magnification of 1x.

$$\text{No. of grains per mm}^2 = \frac{4\times10^4}{645.16} = 62 \text{ grain mm}^2$$

$$\text{Grain size } = \frac{1}{\sqrt{62}} = 0.127 \text{ mm.}$$

Increasing the grain size number by one unit doubles the number of grains per mm^2 and decreases the grain size by $1/\sqrt{2}$ times.

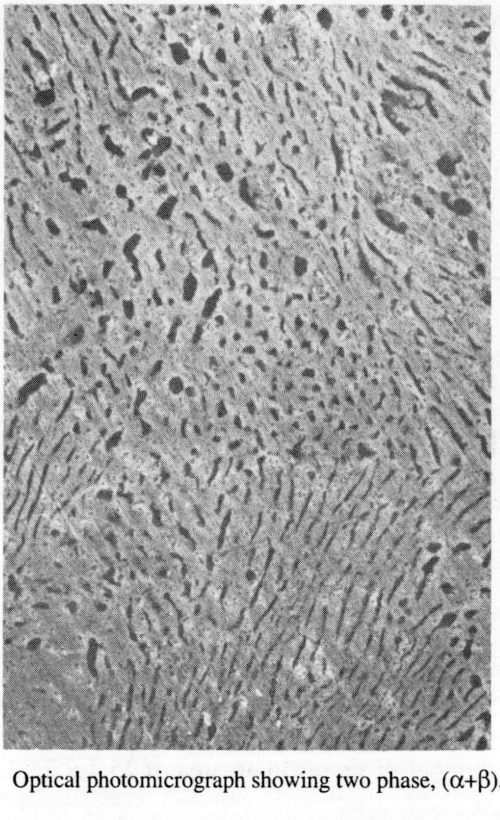

Fig. 8.35 Optical photomicrograph showing two phase, ($\alpha+\beta$), structure.

For each increment in number, there will be a three-fold increase in the number of grains per unit volume. The number of grain boundaries intersected per unit length n_L, and the number of grains per unit area n_A, are related to the number per unit volume by the following.

$$n_v = 0.422\, n_L^3 = 0.667\, n_A^{3/2}\,.$$

REFERENCES

1. R.T. DeHoff & F.N. Rhines, *Quantitative Microscopy*, McGraw Hill Book Company, New York (1968).
2. J.E. Hilliard "*Measurement of Volume in Volume*," in reference 1, McGraw Hill Book Company, New York (1968).
3. S.A. Saltykov, *Stereometric Metallography*, 2nd ed., Metallurgizdat, Moscow (1958).
4. E.E. Underwood, "*Surface Area and Length in Volume*," in reference 1, McGraw Hill Book Company, New York (1968).
5. S. Chandrashekhar, *Rev. Mod. Phys.*, (1943), 15.
6. C.S. Smith & L. Guttman, Trans. Metall. Soc. AIME, 197 (1953), 81.

SELECTED PROBLEMS

1. From the grain size and absolute frequency data provided in Table 8.2, determine the sample mean and sample variance.
2. The chord diameters of dispersed spheres were measured at a magnification of 200x in the test plane of area 10 × 10 cm. The diameters (in mm) are

   4.5, 3.1, 2.7, 4.1, 4.6, 5.2, 6.7, 5.3, 4.9, 4.8, 5.3, 6.5, 2.8, 3.1, 3.5, 6.1, 6.5, 4.6, 3.3, 4.9, 5.0, 6.2, 6.7, 4.5, 2.9.

   Determine the average radius of the sphere and the number of spheres per unit volume.
3. The number of intercepts with the grain boundaries on a line of length 10 cm was measured on a photomicrograph of a polycrystalline structure derived at a magnification of 200x. Determine the surface area of the grain boundaries per unit volume and the average grain size. The number of intercepts are:

   6, 7, 8, 6, 9, 7, 8, 9, 8, 7, 9, 6, 7, 9, 8, 10, 5, 6, 7, 9.

4. Show that the grain size decreases by 1/2 for every increase of 2 in the ASTM grain size number.
5. The volume fraction of the second phase was measured by point count technique. The following data were obtained:

   0.37, 0.4, 0.46, 0.43, 0.5, 0.55, 0.39, 0.41, 0.48, 0.46, 0.48, 0.4, 0.44, 0.47, 0.52, 0.53, 0.5, 0.49, 0.42, 0.44 0.46, 0.53, 0.46, 0.48 0.5.

   Determine the mean and variance. What is the accuracy of the results?
6. Determine the length of the dislocation lines per unit volume from the etch pits shown in Fig. 8.24.
7. Determine the volume fraction of the β phase from the two phase structure (shown in Fig. 8.35) from (i) point fraction and (ii) line fraction analysis.
8. Equal sized spheres of SiO_2 are dispersed in a matrix of pure copper. There were 20 particles in an area measuring 10×10 cm^2 at a magnification of 100x. The volume fraction of SiO_2 in Cu is 0.1. Determine N_v and r.

Chapter 9

TERNARY SYSTEM–GENERAL

9.1 INTRODUCTION–APPLICATION OF THE PHASE RULE

A ternary system consists of three components. We can consider these components to be A, B and C. In order to describe the composition of a ternary alloy, two independent composition variables are required. This is unlike the binary system which required only one independent composition variable. Let us assume that an alloy of Cu-Ni-Al consists of 40 at.pct. Cu, 30 at.pct. Ni. and 30 at.pct. Al. The mole fractions or atom fractions are $X_{Cu} = 0.4$, $X_{Ni} = 0.3$ and $X_{Al} = 0.3$, respectively, for Cu, Ni and Al. If two composition variables are independently selected, for example X_{Cu} and X_{Ni}, then the composition of the third is known from,

$$X_A + X_B + X_C = 1,$$

or in this case, $X_{Cu} + X_{Ni} + X_{Al} = 1$.

A ternary system can be described by using two composition variables and the temperature. A three-dimensional diagram, or space model as it is known, is therefore necessary to represent the ternary system. The diagram may have one, two, three and four phase fields. It is possible to have more than one of each of the above phase fields in the three-dimensional diagram. The phase regions may be one or more of the following:

One phase region : α, L.
Two phase region : $\alpha + L\,\alpha + \beta$, $L_1 + L_2$,
Three phase region : $\alpha + \beta + L$, $\alpha + L_1 + L_2$, $\alpha + \beta + \gamma$, $L_1 + L_2 + L_3$
Four phase region : $\alpha+\beta+\gamma+\delta$, $\alpha+\beta+\gamma+L$, $\alpha+\beta+L_1+L_2$, $\alpha+L_1+L_2+L_3$.

Application of the phase rule in a single phase region (solid or liquid) illustrates that there are three degrees of freedom

$$P + F = C + 1$$

$$F = 3 + 1 - 1 = 3$$

For the α phase we can have the following variables,

$$X_A^{\alpha}, X_B^{\alpha}, X_C^{\alpha} \quad \text{and} \quad T$$

A single-phase region can be described by two compositions and the temperature variables. The phase region is trivariant.

A two-phase region of the ternary phase diagram (for example, $\alpha + L$) can be described by two independent variables and therefore is bivariant. Once the two independent variables are defined, the remaining composition and temperature variables are automatically fixed. The following variables are at our disposal in two phase regions of a ternary alloy:

$$X_A^{\alpha}, X_B^{\alpha}, X_C^{\alpha}, X_A^{L}, X_B^{L}, X_C^{L} \quad \text{and} \quad T.$$

In order to describe the two-phase region completely, we can select any one of the following combinations:

(i) Two composition variables of one of the phases, for example, X_A^α and X_B^α (X_C^α is fixed). The composition of the α phase is fixed and according to the phase rule the α phase of a definite composition can only be in equilibrium with the liquid phase at a definite temperature. The temperature and composition of the liquid phase in equilibrium with a definite composition of the α phase is dictated by the equality of chemical potential of the two phases under consideration.

(ii) The temperature variable and composition of one of the components in one of the above phases, for example X_A^α. The temperature fixes all possible combinations of the α and liquid phase compositions which can be in equilibrium with each other. Selecting the composition of one component in one of the phases fixes the location of that phase. If composition of the component *A* in the α phase is selected, then the location of the ternary composition of the α is known on the solidus surface, which can only be in equilibrium with the liquid phase of a definite composition.

(iii) Composition of one of the components in one phase and composition of one of the components in the other phase. For example, we can select composition X_B^α and X_C^L. This combination of compositions can only exist for a definite composition of the α and liquid phases at a definite temperature in the two-phase region of the phase diagram. The equilibrium is established through the ternary tie-lines.

A three-phase region of a ternary alloy system shows only one degree of freedom ($F = 3 + 1 - 3 = 1$) and, therefore, is monovariant. If we select α, β and liquid (*L*) phases to constitute the three-phase region, we have the following variables at our disposal out of which only one variable is independent.

$$X_A^\alpha, X_B^\alpha, X_C^\alpha, X_A^\beta, X_B^\beta, X_C^\beta, X_A^L, X_B^L, X_C^L, \quad \text{and} \quad T.$$

By exercising temperature as one degree of freedom, all composition variables become fixed. That is, the compositions of the α, β and liquid phases that exist in equilibrium with each other at the temperature *T* are fixed. Similarly, by selecting composition of one component in one of the phases, say X_B^β, the temperatures and the remaining composition variables are fixed. This is again due to the equality of chemical potentials, of each component in all the phases.

The four-phase region of a ternary system is invariant ($F = 3 + 1 - 4 = 0$). That is, all available composition and temperature variables are fixed. Since the temperature is also fixed, the four-phase reaction in a ternary system occurs on an isothermal plane, be it a ternary eutectic or peritectic-type reaction.

9.2 REPRESENTATION OF THE TERNARY SYSTEM

As described in the previous section, a maximum of two composition variables and temperature are required to represent the ternary system, and thus can be represented only in a three-dimensional diagram or the space model. The composition is represented on a horizontal plane and the temperature on an axis perpendicular to this plane. Any two composition variables are sufficient to describe the composition of a ternary alloy. The composition can be represented in terms of the atom or weight percent or as atom or mole fraction. The change from atom percent to weight percent or vice versa is similar to that used for the binary system.

When all the three components, *A*, *B* and *C*, of the alloy have equal importance, it is usual to plot the composition of the alloy in an equilateral triangle, also known as the Gibbs triangle after the author who devised this method of representation of ternary alloys, Fig. 9.1. The pure components, *A*, *B* and *C*, are represented along the corners of the equilateral triangle. The sides, *AB*, *BC* and *AC* represent the compositions of the respected binary alloys. The ternary alloy compositions are represented within the triangle as points if all three components are present in a given phase.

The selection of an equilateral triangle to represent composition of the ternary alloy stems from the unique property of the triangle that the sum of the perpendiculars drawn from any point within the triangle to the sides of the triangle is constant and equals the height of the triangle. In Fig. 9.2, the sum of the perpendiculars drawn from the point *P* on the sides *AC*, *AB* and *BC* is ($PQ + PR + PS$), which is equal to the height of the triangle, *BO*. The point *P* may lie anywhere within the triangle. The perpendicular distance is thus selected as a convenient and uniform method of representing the alloy composition. The method is uniform because the sum of the three perpendiculars is a constant equal to the height of the triangle. In Figure 9.2, the perpendiculars are divided into twenty equal parts at an interval of 5 percent. Any point lying on the line *AC* represents a binary alloy composition between components *A* and *C* and therefore will show zero percent *B*. The composition point lying at the point *B* represents pure component *B*. Thus, the perpendicular distance from *B* to the opposite side *AC*, shown by *BO* in Fig. 9.2, represents 100 percent. The farther is the composition point from the corner *B* on the perpendicular *BO*, the smaller is the amount of the component *B* in the alloy..

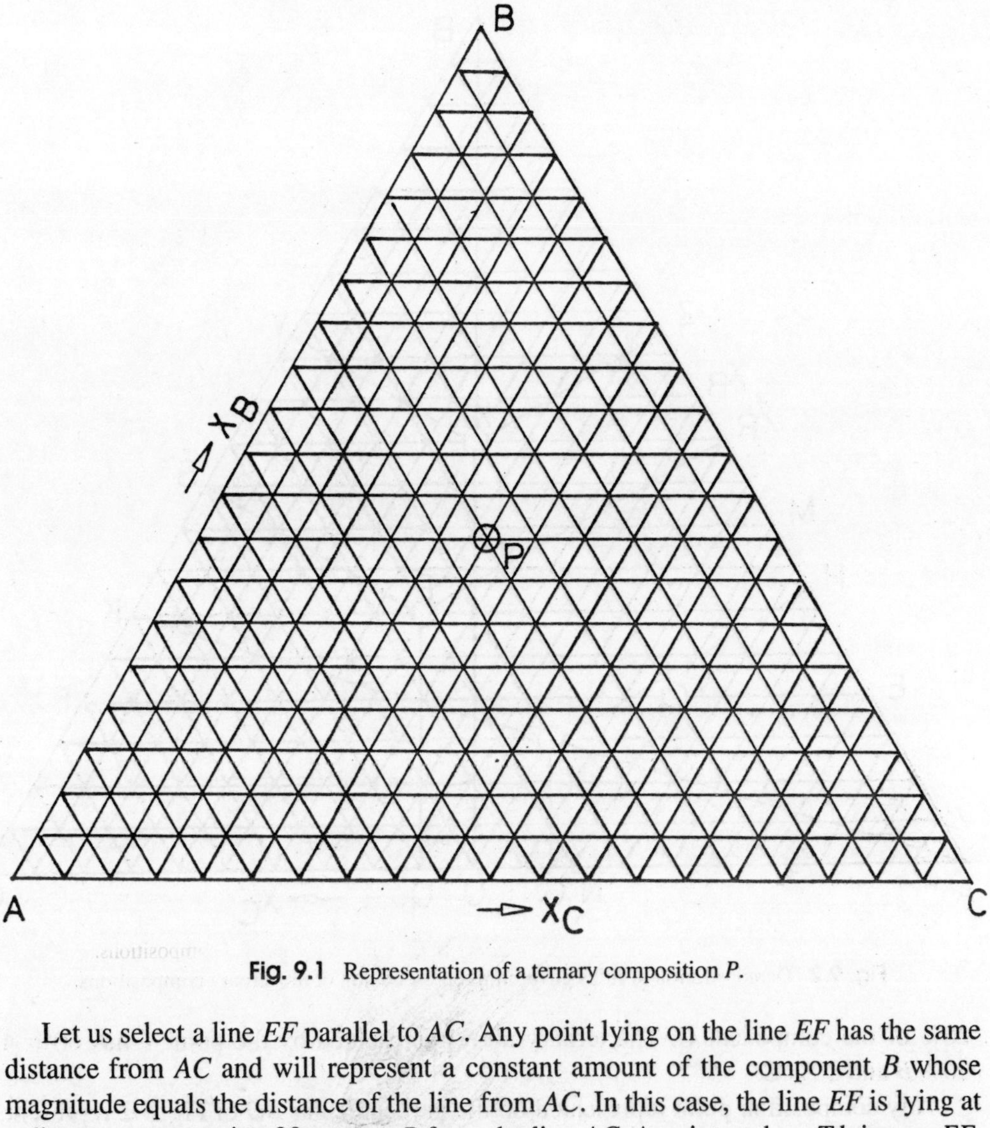

Fig. 9.1 Representation of a ternary composition *P*.

Let us select a line *EF* parallel to *AC*. Any point lying on the line *EF* has the same distance from *AC* and will represent a constant amount of the component *B* whose magnitude equals the distance of the line from *AC*. In this case, the line *EF* is lying at a distance representing 20 percent *B* from the line *AC*. A point such as *T* lying on *EF*, therefore, represents 20% *B* in the alloy. The line *MN* passing through point *T* is drawn parallel to the side *BC*. The distance of the point *T* from the line *BC* will represent the composition of the component *A* (the component opposite the side) in the alloy. Thus, point *T* represents 60% of the component *A*. Similarly, point *T* represents

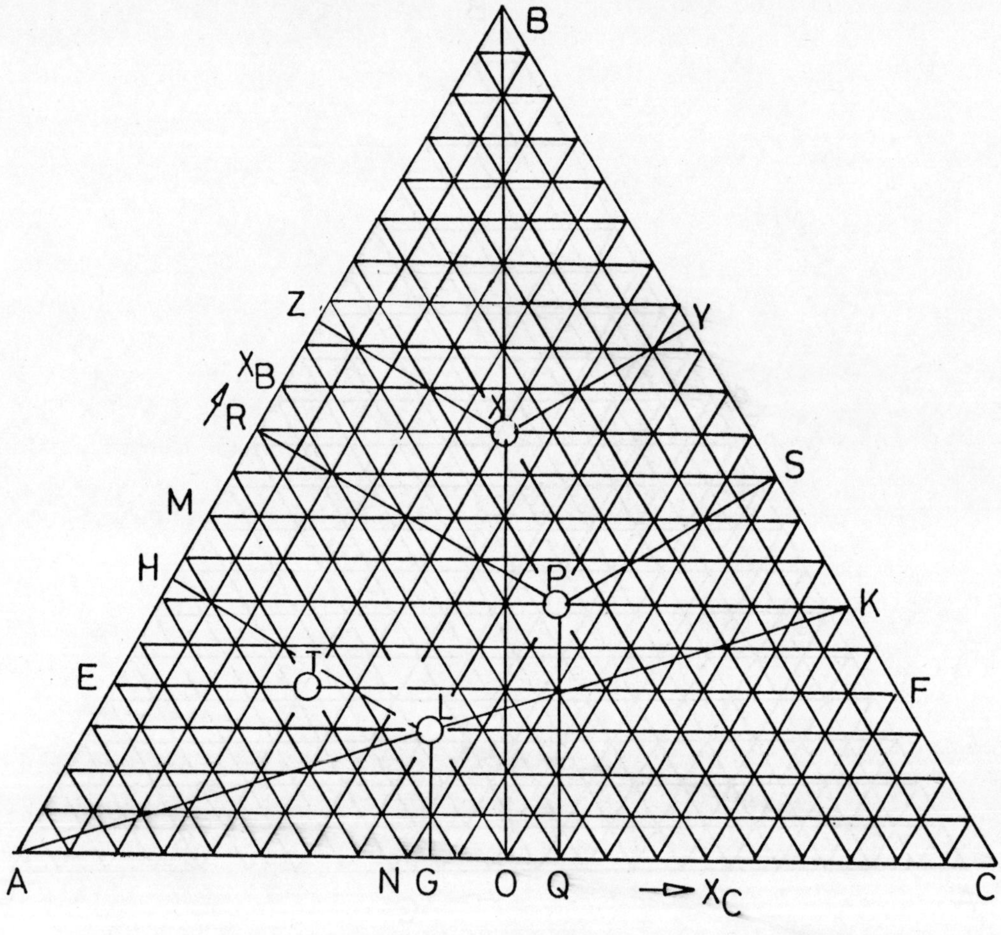

Fig. 9.2 Demonstration of rules governing representation of the ternary compositions.

20% of the component *C*. The ternary alloy represented by the point *T* has 60% *A*, 20% *B* and 20% *C*.

Any composition point represented on the perpendicular *BO* of Fig. 9.2 represents equal amounts of the components *A* and *C* because the perpendicular distances on the sides *BC* and *AB* will be equal. The composition point *X* lying on the line *BO* has 25% *A* and 25% *C* and the balance is 50% *B*. Any line drawn from the corner of the triangle to the opposite side (not necessarily perpendicular) will show a constant proportion of the other two components. If a line *AK* is drawn from the corner *A* to the side *BC*, it will show the same proportion of the components B and C in the alloy no matter where the composition point lies on the line AK. The ternary alloy represented by the point L which lies on the line AK has the ratio B:C::LG:LH or B:C::15:35. The same ratio between the components B and C is maintained no matter where the point L lies on AK as can be proved by using simple geometrical arguments.

9.3 APPLICATION OF THE LEVER RULE–TIE-LINES AND TIE-TRIANGLES

Application of the lever rule can be extended to two and three-phase regions of the ternary system in determining relative amounts of phases in equilibrium with each other. Consider a ternary alloy composition X^0 dissociating into two phases α and β in a two-phase field of the ternary system, Fig. 9.3. The composition of the α and β phases is represented by X^α and X^β where the X's represent the gross composition which can be shown by appropriate subscript when considering the composition of each component in the α and β phases and the original alloys.

From the lever rule, the relative amount of the α phase is given by

$$\%\,\alpha = \frac{P\beta}{\alpha\beta} \times 100$$

In order to determine the composition, the lengths $P\beta$ and $\alpha\beta$ can be measured and the relative amount of the α phase determined. Sincc the Gibbs triangle contains divisions of composition parallel to the sides of the triangle, it is not necessary to measure lengths $P\beta$ and $\alpha\beta$.

This can be carried out by first drawing lines parallel to one of the sides, say AB, from points α, P and β which meet the side AC at G, H and K, respectively. Draw a line from the point α parallel to AC which meets PH and βK at points M and N, respectively. Now, from triangles $\alpha\beta N$ and αPM.

$$\frac{P\beta}{\alpha\beta} = \frac{MN}{\alpha N} = \frac{HK}{GK} = \frac{X_C^\beta - X_C^0}{X_C^\beta - X_C^\alpha}$$

$$\therefore \qquad \%\,\alpha = \frac{P\beta}{\alpha\beta} \times 100 = \frac{X_C^\beta - X_C^0}{X_C^\beta - X_C^\alpha} 100 = \frac{X_B^\beta - X_B^0}{X_B^\beta - X_B^\alpha} \times 100.$$

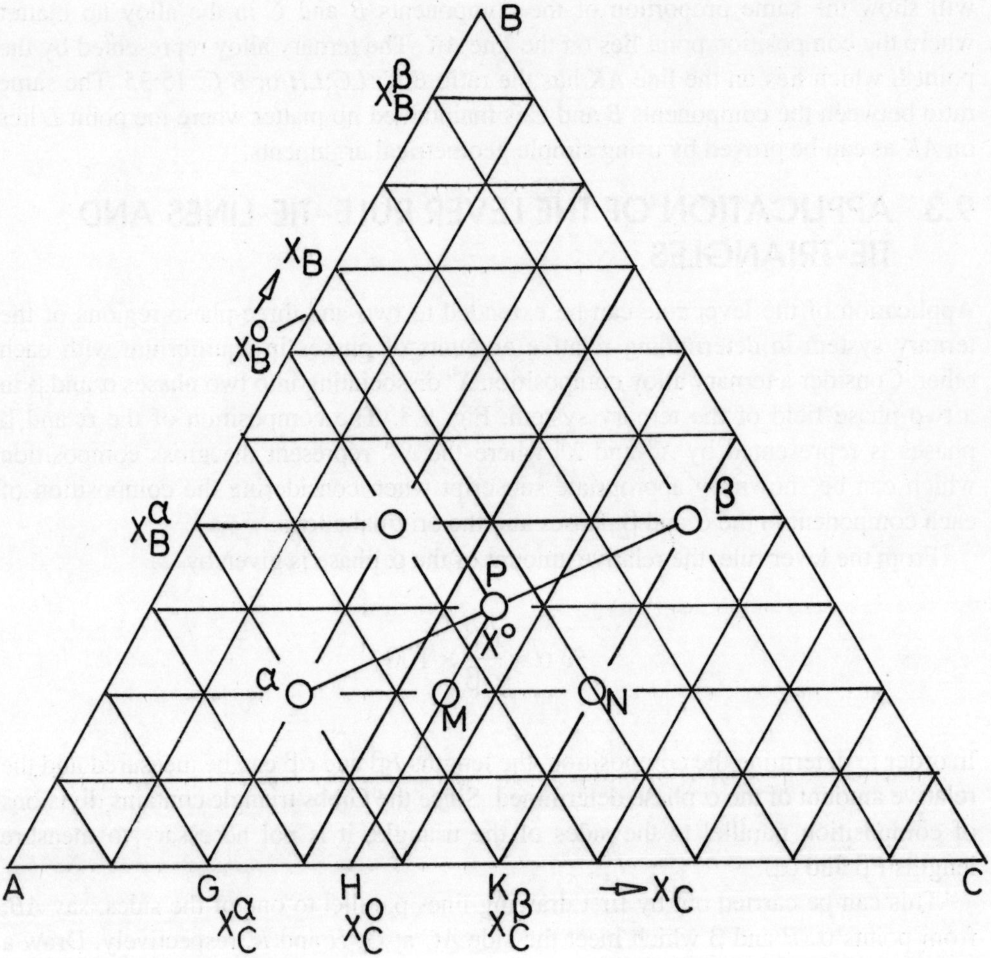

Fig. 9.3 Application of the lever rule in calculating relative amounts of the two phases in equilibrium with each other in a ternary system.

By reading composition values on the binaries, the relative amounts of the phases can be determined. The same rule can be applied to any ternary alloy which separates into two phases. The line αβ is known as the tie-line.

Three phases in equilibrium with each other are represented by a tie-triangle in a ternary system with each line of the triangle representing equilibrium between two phases. Let us consider α, β and γ phases in equilibrium with each other at the temperature *T*. The composition of the three phases are,

$$\alpha: \quad X_A^\alpha = 0.6, \quad X_B^\alpha = 0.2, \quad X_C^\alpha = 0.2$$

$$\beta: \quad X_A^\beta = 0.2, \quad X_B^\beta = 0.5, \quad X_C^\beta = 0.3$$

$$\gamma: \quad X_A^\gamma = 0.3, \quad X_B^\gamma = 0.1, \quad X_C^\gamma = 0.6$$

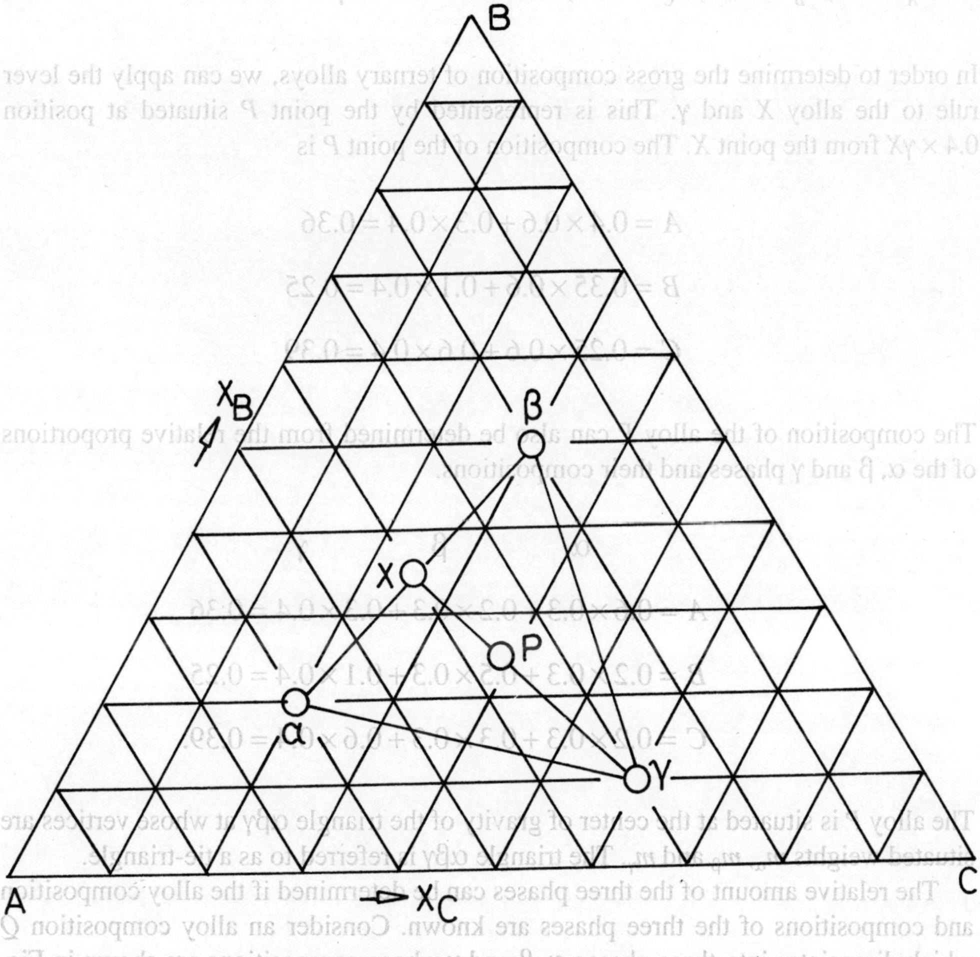

Fig. 9.4 Extension of the lever rule in calculating relative amounts of three phases in equilibrium with each other in a ternary system.

and the relative proportions are, $\alpha:\beta:\gamma = 0.3:0.3:0.4$. The composition of the ternary alloy which dissociates into three phases α, β and γ at the temperature T can be determined from the following.

Since the relative amount of the α and β phases are the same in the alloy, these two phases are formed from an alloy X halfway along αβ, as shown in Fig. 9.4. The composition of the alloy X would be,

$$X:\ X_A = 0.4, X_B = 0.35, X_C = 0.25, \text{ and the ratio } X:\gamma = 0.6:0.4.$$

In order to determine the gross composition of ternary alloys, we can apply the lever rule to the alloy X and γ. This is represented by the point P situated at position $0.4 \times \gamma X$ from the point X. The composition of the point P is

$$A = 0.4 \times 0.6 + 0.3 \times 0.4 = 0.36$$

$$B = 0.35 \times 0.6 + 0.1 \times 0.4 = 0.25$$

$$C = 0.25 \times 0.6 + 0.6 \times 0.4 = 0.39$$

The composition of the alloy P can also be determined from the relative proportions of the α, β and γ phases and their compositions.

$$\qquad\quad \alpha \qquad\qquad \beta \qquad\qquad \gamma$$

$$A = 0.6 \times 0.3 + 0.2 \times 0.3 + 0.3 \times 0.4 = 0.36$$

$$B = 0.2 \times 0.3 + 0.5 \times 0.3 + 0.1 \times 0.4 = 0.25$$

$$C = 0.2 \times 0.3 + 0.3 \times 0.3 + 0.6 \times 0.4 = 0.39.$$

The alloy P is situated at the center of gravity of the triangle αβγ at whose vertices are situated weights m_α, m_β and m_γ. The triangle αβγ is referred to as a tie-triangle.

The relative amount of the three phases can be determined if the alloy composition and compositions of the three phases are known. Consider an alloy composition Q which dissociates into three phases α, β and γ whose compositions are shown in Fig. 9.5. Join αQ and extend it to meet the line βγ at P. The relative amount of the α phase in the alloy is obtained by applying the lever rule between the α phase and the alloy P.

$$\% \, \alpha = \frac{PQ}{\alpha P} \times 100 = \frac{0.47 - 0.4}{0.47 - 0.2} \times 100 = 25.92\%$$

$$\% \, P = \frac{Q\alpha}{\alpha P} \times 100 = \frac{0.4 - 0.2}{0.47 - 0.2} \times 100 = 74.08\%$$

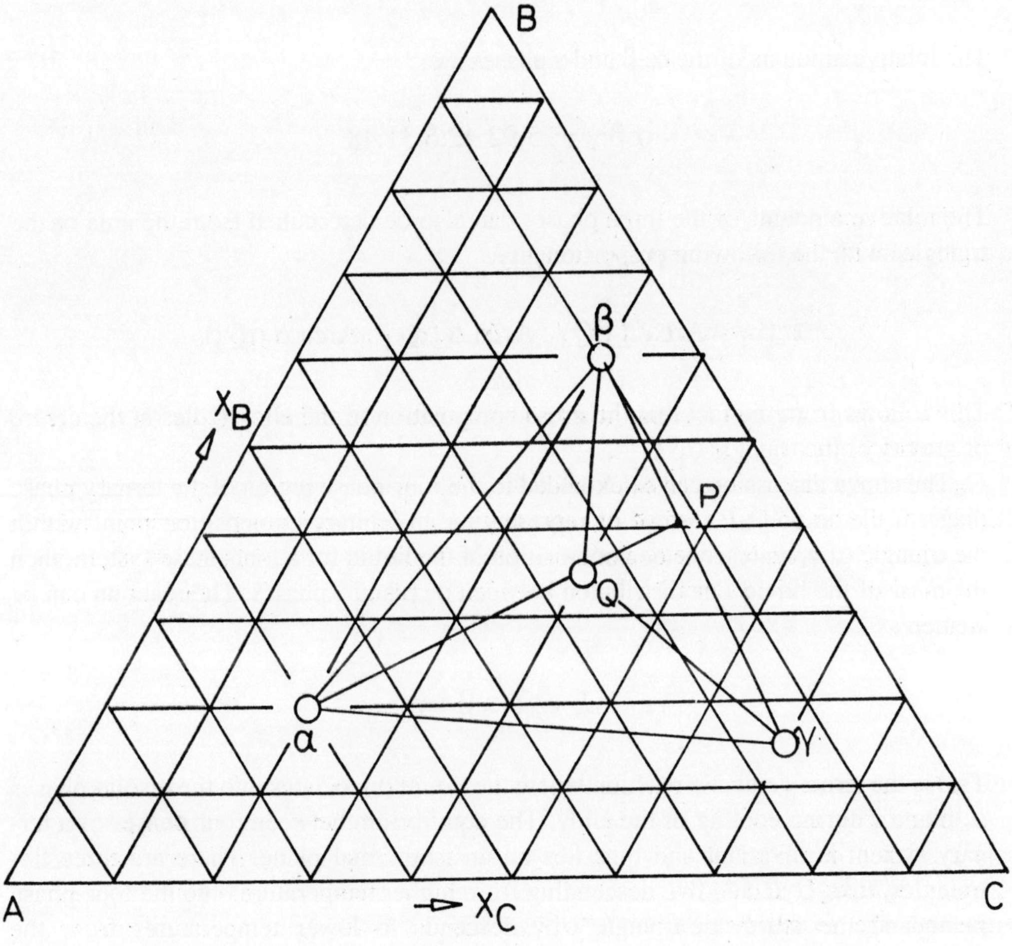

Fig. 9.5 Dissociation of an alloy composition Q into three phases α, β and γ.

Alloy of composition P is now distributed between β and γ phases.

$$\therefore \qquad \% \beta = \frac{P\gamma}{\beta\gamma} \times \% P = \frac{P\gamma}{\beta\gamma} \times \frac{Q\alpha}{\alpha P} \times 100 = \frac{0.7-0.47}{0.7-0.3} \times 74.08 = 42.6\%$$

$$\% \gamma = \frac{\beta P}{\beta\gamma} \times \% P = \frac{\beta P}{\beta\gamma} \times \frac{Q\alpha}{\alpha P} \times 100 = \frac{0.47-0.3}{0.7-0.3} \times 74.08 = 31.48\%$$

The relative amounts of the α, β and γ phases are,

$$\alpha{:}\beta{:}\gamma = 25.92{:}42.6{:}31.48$$

The relative amounts of the three phases can also be determined from the area of the triangles with the following proportionality.

$$\alpha{:}\beta{:}\gamma = \text{Area}\ \Delta\ \beta Q\gamma : \text{Area}\ \Delta\ \alpha Q\gamma : \text{Area}\ \Delta\ \alpha Q\beta.$$

This follows from the fact that the gross composition of the alloy Q lies at the centre of gravity of the triangle αβγ.

The above discussion can be extended to the four-phase region of the ternary phase diagram. If the point P instead of representing an arbitary composition point within the triangle αβγ, represents the composition of the liquid for a four-phase system, then the mass of the liquid L is distributed between α, β and γ phases. The reaction can be written as

$$L \rightleftharpoons \alpha + \beta + \gamma.$$

This is the ternary eutectic reaction where the liquid dissociates into three solid phases α, β and γ during cooling of the alloy. The equilibrium between four phases of a ternary system is invariant and thus lies on an isothermal plane. There are three tie-triangles, $\alpha\beta L$, $\alpha\gamma L$, and $\beta\gamma L$ descending from higher temperature onto the four-phase plane and the fourth tie-triangle αβγ descends to lower temperatures from the four-phase plane, as shown in Fig. 9.6.

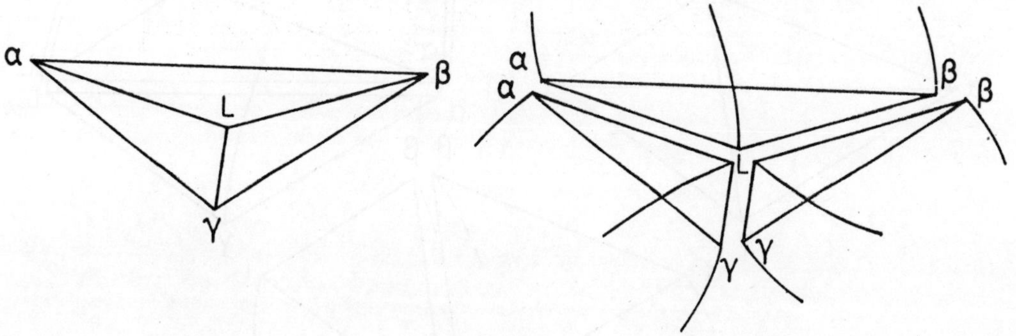

Fig. 9.6 The shape of the invariant plane for the reaction $L \Leftrightarrow \alpha + \beta + \gamma$.

The liquid composition may also lie either opposite one of the vertices α, β or γ, Fig. 9.7a, or opposite one of the sides, αβ, αγ, or βγ, Fig. 9.7b. In Fig. 9.7a, the composition of the liquid is drawn opposite the corner α. It forms a four-sided figure. The following invariant reaction takes place:

$$L + \alpha == \beta + \gamma.$$

There are 4 three-phase regions in this quasi-peritectic reaction of the ternary. Two of the three-phase regions, L+α+β and L+α+γ, descend from higher temperatures on to the four-phase plane. The remaining two three-phase regions, L+β+γ and α+β+γ, descend from the four-phase plane to ambient temperatures. The gross composition of the alloy is represented by the point P. Just above the four-phase plane $\alpha\beta\gamma L$, and along the line αL, the alloy contains α and liquid phases in equilibrium with each other. The relative amounts of the two phases, α and liquid, can be determined by applying the lever rule on the line αL with fulcrum at P, Fig. 9.8.

$$\% \, \alpha = \frac{PL}{\alpha L} \times 100 \quad \text{and} \quad \% \, L = \frac{\alpha P}{\alpha L} \times 100.$$

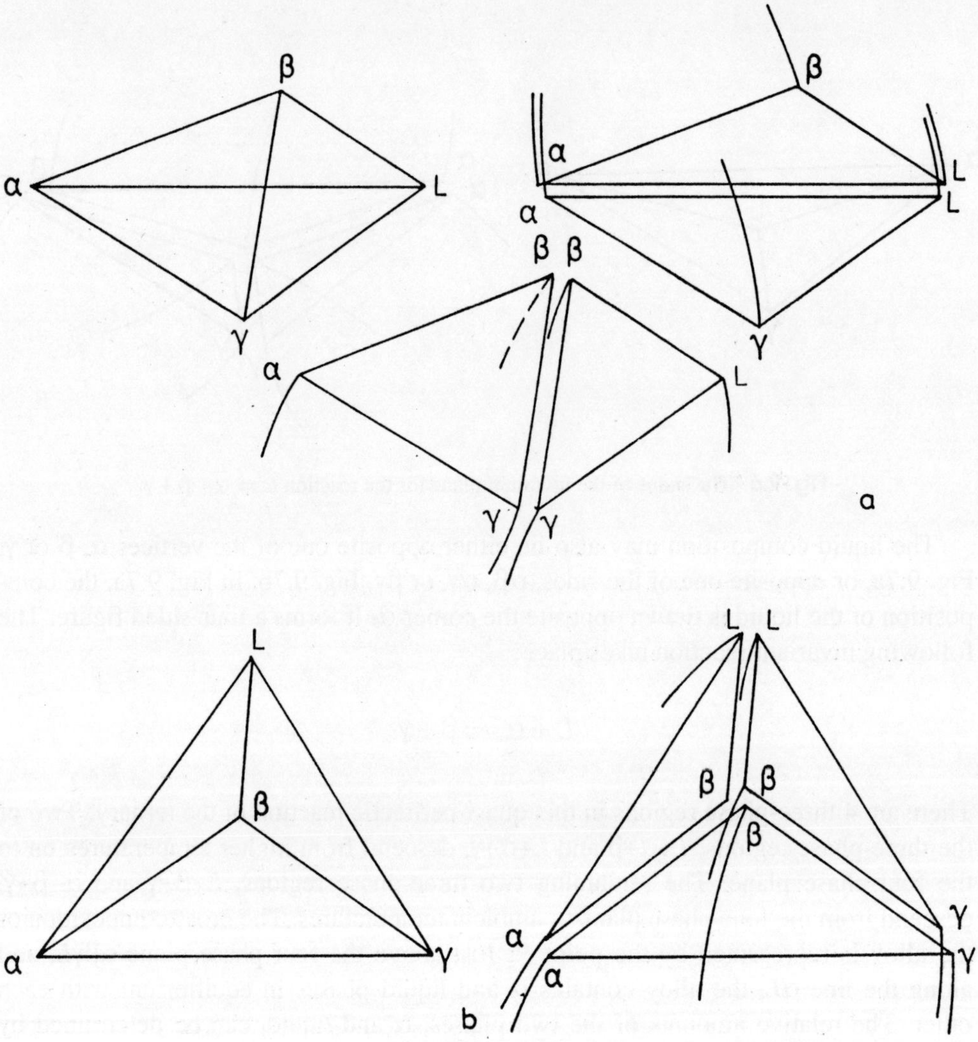

Fig. 9.7 The position of three-phase regions relative to the four phase plane in the reactions: (a) $L + \alpha \Leftrightarrow \beta + \gamma$ and (b) $L + \alpha + \gamma \Leftrightarrow \beta$.

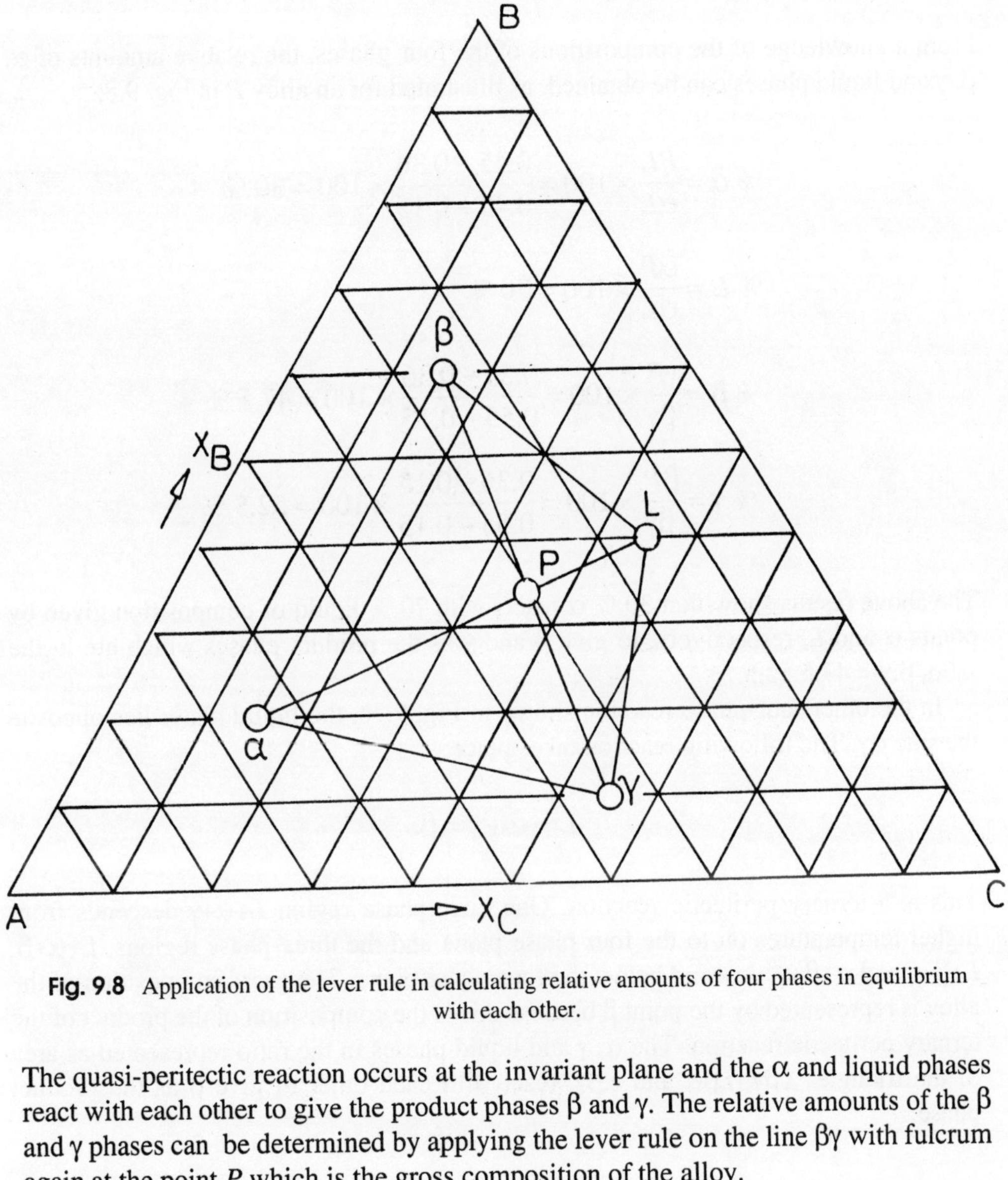

Fig. 9.8 Application of the lever rule in calculating relative amounts of four phases in equilibrium with each other.

The quasi-peritectic reaction occurs at the invariant plane and the α and liquid phases react with each other to give the product phases β and γ. The relative amounts of the β and γ phases can be determined by applying the lever rule on the line βγ with fulcrum again at the point *P* which is the gross composition of the alloy.

$$\% \beta = \frac{\gamma P}{\beta\gamma} \times 100 \quad \text{and} \quad \% \gamma = \frac{\beta P}{\beta\gamma} \times 100.$$

From a knowledge of the compositions of the four phases, the relative amounts of α, β, γ and liquid phases can be obtained, as illustrated for an alloy *P* in Fig. 9.8.

$$\% \alpha = \frac{PL}{\alpha L} \times 100 = \frac{0.45 - 0.36}{0.45 - 0.15} \times 100 = 30\ \%$$

$$\% L = \frac{\alpha P}{\alpha L} \times 100 = 70\ \%$$

$$\% \beta = \frac{\gamma P}{\beta\gamma} \times 100 = \frac{0.55 - 0.36}{0.55 - 0.15} \times 100 = 47.5\ \%$$

$$\% \gamma = \frac{\beta P}{\beta\gamma} \times 100 = \frac{0.36 - 0.15}{0.55 - 0.15} \times 100 = 52.5\ \%$$

The above results show that 30 % α reacts with 70 % liquid of composition given by points α and *L*, respectively, to give β and γ as the product phases which are in the ratio, β:γ = 47.5:52.5.

In the other four-phase reaction shown in Fig. 9.7b, the liquid phase lies opposite the side αγ. The following reaction takes place:

$$L + \alpha + \gamma = \beta.$$

This is a ternary peritectic reaction. One three-phase region *L*+α+γ descends from higher temperatures on to the four-phase plane and the three-phase regions, *L*+α+β, *L*+β+γ and α+β+γ, descend below the four-phase plane. The gross composition of the alloy is represented by the point β because this is the composition of the product of the ternary peritectic reaction. The α, γ and liquid phases in the ratio represented as area of the triangles *L*βγ, *L*βα and αβγ, react with each other to give β as the product phase.

PROBLEM

1. Plot the following ternary compositions in the Gibbs triangle
   a. 20 at.pct. *A*, 50 at.pct. *B*, 30 at.pct. *C*.
   b. 60 at.pct. *A*, 10 at.pct. *B*, 20 at.pct. *C*.
2. Three phases α, β and γ are in equilibrium with each other (in a three-phase region) at a given temperature in a ternary system *A–B–C*. The compositions of the three phases (in atom fraction of the components) are as follows:

	A	*B*	*C*
α	0.6	0.2	0.2
β	0.1	0.7	0.2
γ	0.15	0.3	0.55

   (a) Plot the composition of all three phases in the concentration triangle. Calculate the relative amount of each phase for a ternary alloy composition 0.25*A*, 0.4*B* and 0.35*C*.
   (b) What will be the composition of the alloy if it contains equal amounts of α and β phases only?
   (c) What will be the composition of the alloy if it contains equal amounts of α, β and γ phases?
3. Write all composition variables in a three-phase region of a ternary system and explain how selecting any one of these variables fixes the remaining composition variables and temperature.
4. A ternary system of components *A*, *B* and *C* shows an invariant reaction between
   (a) two solids (α and β) and two liquids (L_1 and L_2).
   (b) one liquid (*L*) and three solids (α, β and γ).
   (c) three liquids (L_1, L_2 and L_3) and one solid (α).
   Write all possible reactions between the four phases. Identify some of them in terms of the nomenclature used in the binary system.
5. Three phases α, β and γ are in the ratio α:β:γ :: 3:3:4 in a ternary system *A–B–C*. Determine the composition of the alloy if the three phases have the following compositions:

	A	*B*	*C*
α:	0.6	0.3	0.1
β:	0.2	0.6	0.2

γ: 0.2 0.3 0.5

6. Show that any point drawn on a line from a corner to the opposite edge represents a constant ratio of the components along the edge.
7. Compositions of the α, β, γ and liquid phase are given as follows. What are the relative amounts of the α and liquid phases above the invariant plane and β and γ phases below the same plane for an alloy composition at the intersection of lines α*L* and βγ?

	A	*B*	*C*
α:	70%	15%	15%
β:	20%	70%	10%
γ:	20%	5%	75%
L:	5%	45%	50%

Chapter 10

TERNARY ALLOY SYSTEM–TWO-PHASE EQUILIBRIA

10.1 THE SPACE MODEL

Two-phase equilibrium in the ternary system can occur between liquid and solid solutions, (α+L), two liquid phases, (L_1+L_2), or two solid phases(α_1+α_2 or α+β). Consider the ternary isomorphous system to be constructed from the three binary isomorphous systems, A–B, B–C and A–C, Fig. 10.1. The space model of the ternary isomorphous system is shown in Fig. 10.2a. The three liquidus curves of the binaries generate a liquidus surface $T_AL_1T_BL_2T_CL_3T_A$. Similarly, the three solidus lines of the binaries make up the solidus surface, $T_AS_1T_BS_2T_CS_3T_A$, of the ternary.

The liquid phase is stable above the liquidus surface and solid, α, is stable below the solidus surface. The two surfaces envelope the two-phase region, (α+L), Fig. 10.2b. In contrast to the binary system where one tie-line appears at each isothermal section, a large number of tie-lines exist at each isothermal plane in the ternary system. The bundle of tie-lines which have varying direction at each isothermal plane connect the conjugate solid and liquid phases.

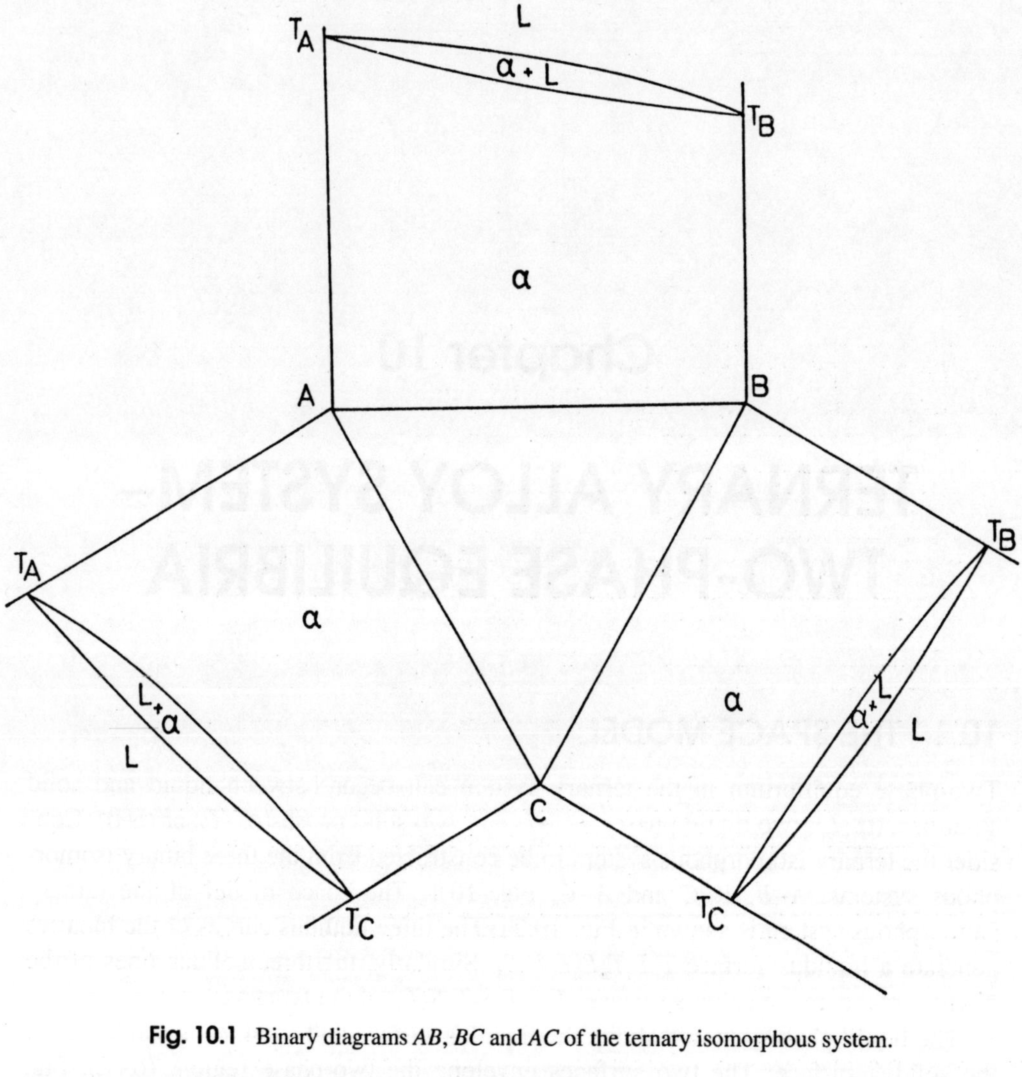

Fig. 10.1 Binary diagrams *AB*, *BC* and *AC* of the ternary isomorphous system.

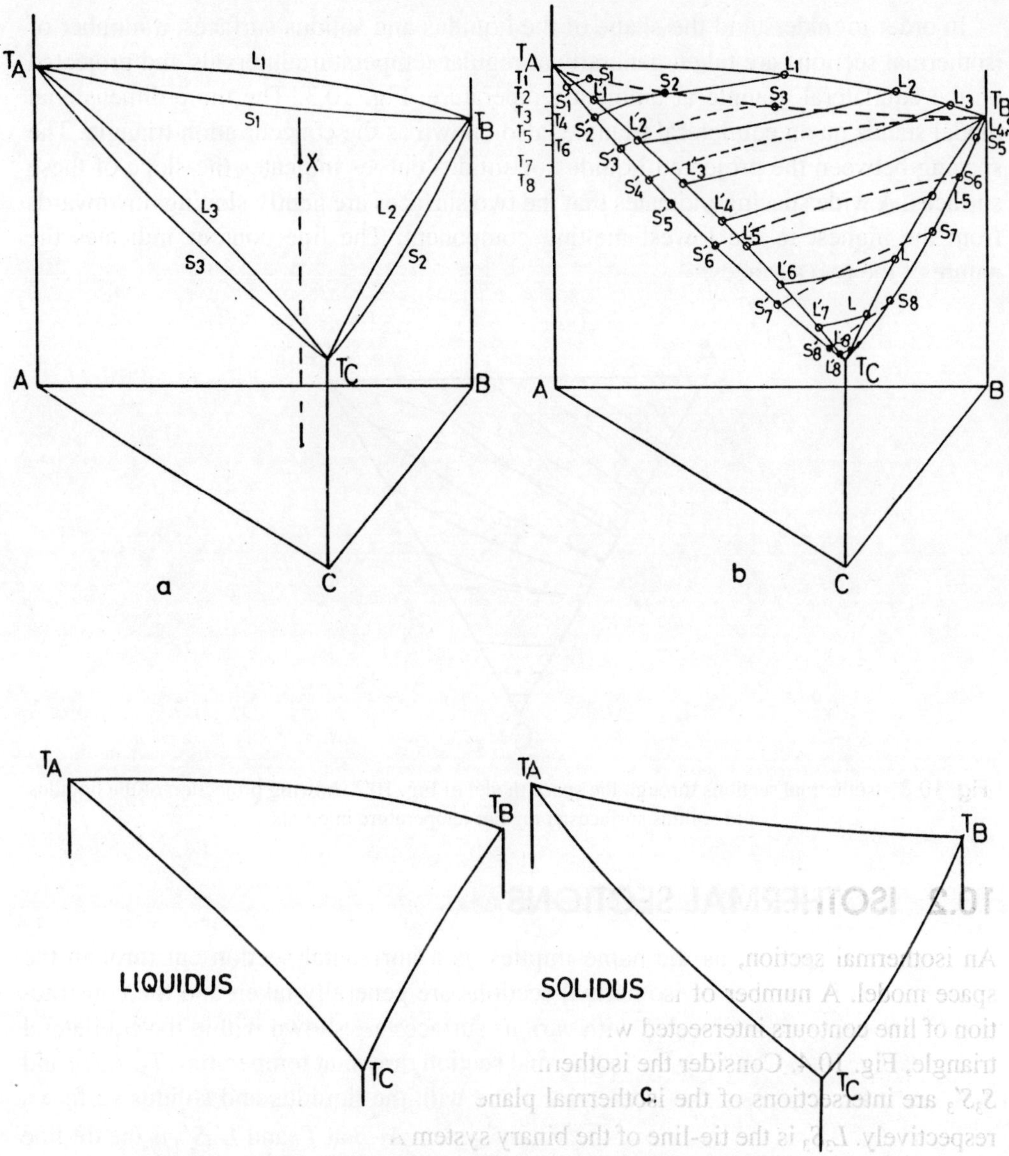

Fig. 10.2 (a) Space model of the ternary isomorphous system (b) The shape of the liquidus and solidus surfaces shown through a number of isothermal sections (c) Shape of the liquidus and solidus surfaces.

In order to understand the shape of the liquidus and solidus surfaces, a number of isothermal sections are taken generally at regular temperature intervals and projected on the equilateral triangle at ambient temperature, Fig. 10.3. The three-dimensional model stands on an equilateral triangle, also known as the concentration triangle. The spacing between the projected liquidus or solidus curves indicates the slope of these surfaces. A wide spacing indicates that the two surfaces are gently sloping downwards from the highest to the lowest melting component. The line contour indicates the nature of the two surfaces.

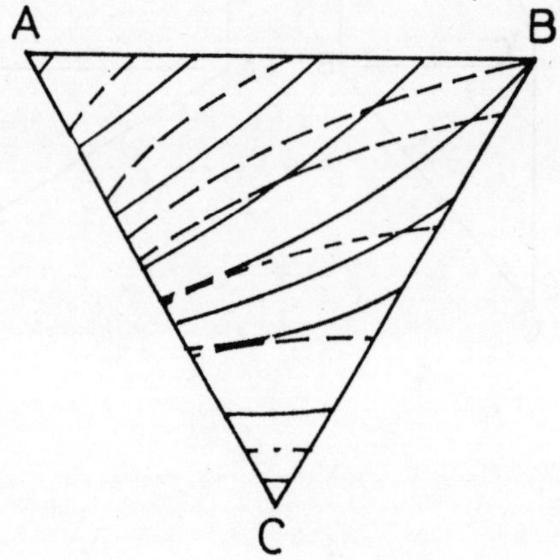

Fig. 10.3 Isothermal sections through the space model of Fig. 10.2 showing projection of the liquidus and solidus surfaces at regular temperature intervals.

10.2 ISOTHERMAL SECTIONS

An isothermal section, as the name implies, is a horizontal section cut through the space model. A number of isothermal sections are generally taken and the construction of line contours intersected with various surfaces are shown within the equilateral triangle, Fig. 10.4. Consider the isothermal section drawn at temperature T_3. $L_3L'_3$ and $S_3S'_3$ are intersections of the isothermal plane with the liquidus and solidus surfaces, respectively. L_3S_3 is the tie-line of the binary system A–B at T_3 and $L'_3S'_3$ is the tie-line of the binary system A–C at the same temperature. These two tie-lines along with the curves $S_3S'_3$ and $L_3L'_3$ form the boundaries of the two-phase, $(\alpha+L)$, region. Each ternary tie-line is similar to the binary tie-line and gives the composition of the conjugate solid and liquid phases at a given temperature. The solid phase α exists between the

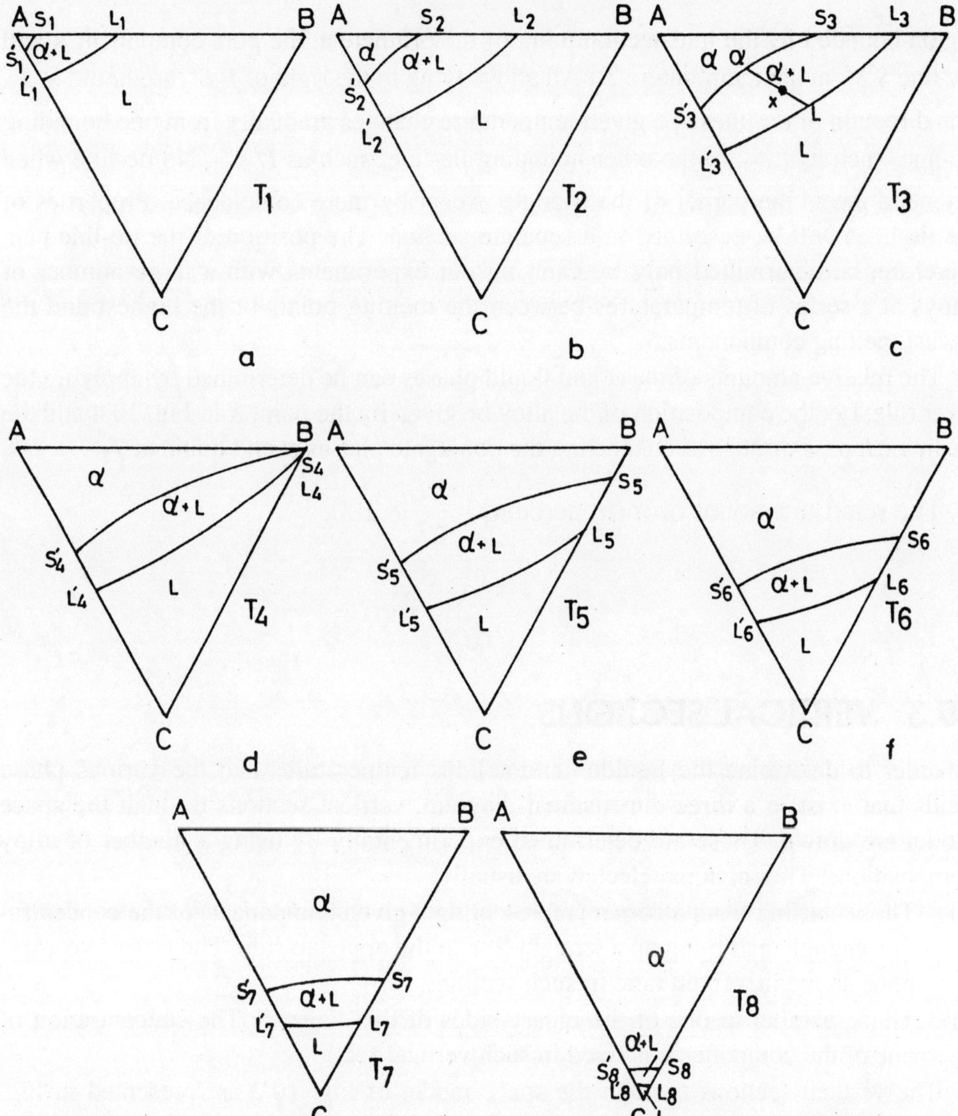

Fig. 10.4 Isothermal sections through the space model of Fig. 10.2.

region bounded by the intersection point of the ordinate at the pure component A and the line $S_3S'_3$ at the temperature T_3. All alloys lying to the right of $L_3L'_3$ are liquid at T_3. The direction of tie-lines at a given temperature changes gradually from one bounding tie-line, such as L_3S_3, to the other bounding tie-line, such as $L'_3S'_3$. No tie-line when extended meets the corner of the triangle except by mere coincidence. Properties of the tie-lines will be described in a separate section. The position of the tie-line can, therefore, be determined only by carrying out experiments with a large number of alloys at a series of temperatures between the melting points of the highest and the lowest melting components.

The relative amounts of the α and liquid phases can be determined by applying the lever rule. Let the composition of the alloy be given by the point X in Fig. 10.4 and the tie-line αL pass through X connecting the conjugate phases α and liquid at T_3.

$$\text{The relative amount of } \alpha \text{ (in percent)} = \frac{XL}{\alpha L} \times 100,$$

and

$$\% \, L = \frac{\alpha X}{\alpha L} \times 100.$$

10.3 VERTICAL SECTIONS

In order to determine the liquidus and solidus temperatures and the various phase fields that exist in a three-dimensional diagram, vertical sections through the space model are drawn. These are determined experimentally by using a number of alloy compositions. The sections selected are usually:

(i) Those starting from a corner (representing a given component) of the concentration triangle and lying on a straight line to the opposite side. The other two components are in a fixed ratio in such sections.

(ii) Those parallel to one of the binary sides of the diagram. The concentration of one of the components is fixed in such vertical sections.

The vertical sections through the space model of Fig. 10.2 are presented in Fig. 10.5. The vertical section shown in Fig. 10.5a is lying on the straight line AM joining the concentration triangle at the corner A to the point M on the side BC. The other section PQ is drawn on a line parallel to A–B, Fig. 5.10b. In order to construct the vertical section through the space model, lines are drawn parallel to the temperature axis from the end points of the straight line AM or PQ. The lines drawn from P and Q meet the liquidus and solidus, respectively, at L'_1 and S_1 and L'_2 and S_2. The vertical

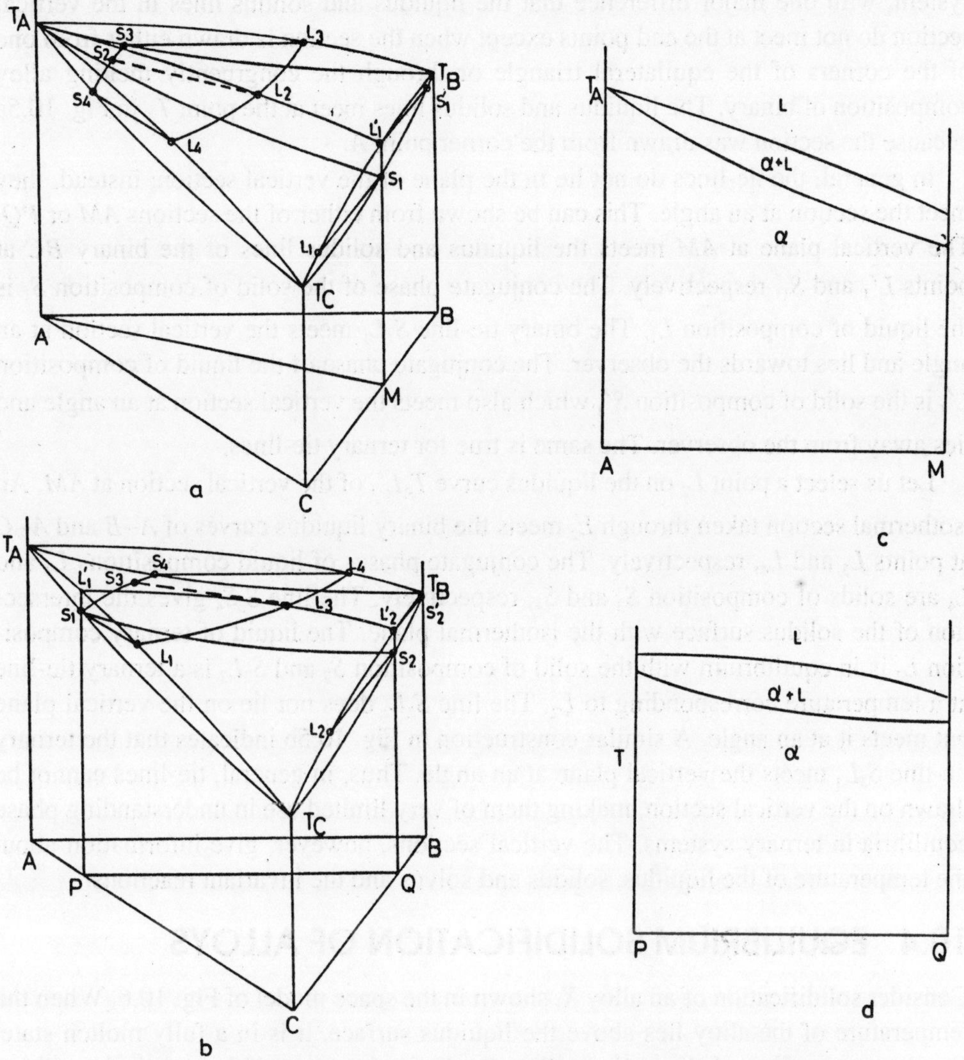

Fig. 10.5 Vertical sections through the space model of Fig. 10.2. The three-dimensional representation is shown in (a) and (b) and the corresponding two-dimensional representation in (c) and (d), respectively.

section meets the liquidus and solidus surfaces along lines $L'_1L'_2$ and S_1S_2, respectively. The vertical sections are shown separately in Figs. 10.5, a and b. The liquidus and solidus lines are very similar to those observed for the binary isomorphous system, with one major difference that the liquidus and solidus lines in the vertical section do not meet at the end points except when the section is drawn either from one of the corners of the equilateral triangle or through the congruently melting alloy composition of binary. The liquidus and solidus lines meet at the point T_A in Fig. 10.5a because the section was drawn from the corner point A.

In general, the tie-lines do not lie in the plane of the vertical section; instead, they meet the section at an angle. This can be shown from either of the sections AM or PQ. The vertical plane at AM meets the liquidus and solidus lines of the binary BC at points L'_1 and S_1, respectively. The conjugate phase of the solid of composition S_1 is the liquid of composition L_1. The binary tie-line S_1L_1 meets the vertical section at an angle and lies towards the observer. The conjugate phase of the liquid of composition L'_1 is the solid of composition S'_1 which also meets the vertical section at an angle and lies away from the observer. The same is true for ternary tie-lines.

Let us select a point L_2 on the liquidus curve $T_AL'_1$ of the vertical section at AM. An isothermal section taken through L_2 meets the binary liquidus curves of $A–B$ and $A–C$ at points L_3 and L_4, respectively. The conjugate phases of liquid compositions L_3 and L_4 are solids of composition S_3 and S_4, respectively. The line S_3S_4 gives the intersection of the solidus surface with the isothermal plane. The liquid of ternary composition L_2 is in equilibrium with the solid of composition S_2 and S_2L_2 is a ternary tie-line at a temperature corresponding to L_2. The line S_2L_2 does not lie on the vertical plane but meets it at an angle. A similar construction in Fig. 10.5b indicates that the ternary tie-line S_3L_3 meets the vertical plane at an angle. Thus, in general, tie-lines cannot be drawn on the vertical section, making them of very limited use in understanding phase equilibria in ternary systems. The vertical sections, however, give information about the temperature of the liquidus, solidus and solvus and the invariant reactions.

10.4 EQUILIBRIUM SOLIDIFICATION OF ALLOYS

Consider solidification of an alloy X, shown in the space model of Fig. 10.6. When the temperature of the alloy lies above the liquidus surface, it is in a fully molten state. Continuous cooling of the molten alloy results in the composition vertical touching the liquidus surface at the temperature T_2. The solidification of the liquid begins with the formation of nuclei of the α phase (Fig. 10.6). The solid of composition S_2 is in equilibrium with the liquid of almost original alloy composition. The equilibrium between the solid and liquid phases is shown in the isothermal section by the tie-line S_2L_2 (X) at the temperature T_2, Fig. 10.7 b. The relative amount of the solid is negligibly small. If the liquid is cooled slowly, such that equilibrium is maintained at each small decrement in temperature, then the solid of composition S_3 will be in

equilibrium with liquid of composition L_3 at $T_3 < T_2$.
The relative amount of the solid as well as liquid phases can be determined by applying the lever rule, Fig. 10.7c. Accordingly,

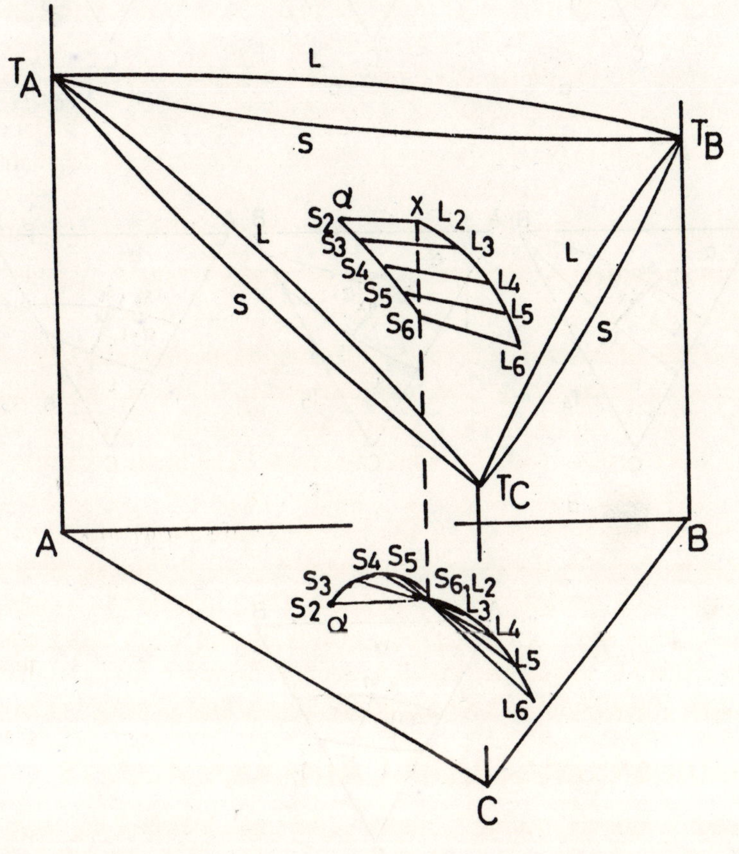

Fig. 10.6 Solidification of an alloy *X* shown in the space model of Fig. 10.2a.

$$\% \alpha_3 = \frac{L_3X}{S_3L_3} \times 100 = 27 \%$$

$$\% \text{ Liquid} = \frac{XS_3}{S_3L_3} \times 100 = 73 \%$$

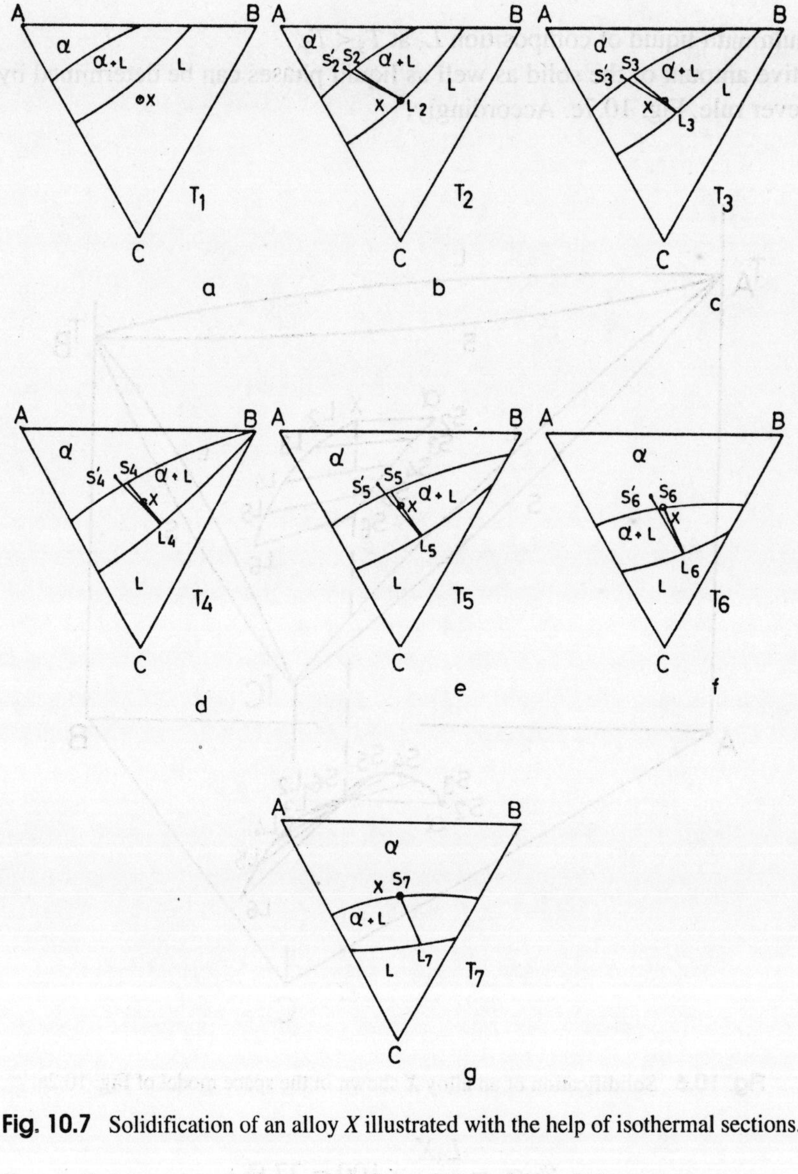

Fig. 10.7 Solidification of an alloy *X* illustrated with the help of isothermal sections.

The tie-line L_3S_3 has rotated clockwise from its position S_2L_2 at temperature T_2. The rotation is around the composition vertical. Since the solid phase formed is richer in the component *A*, the liquid will get impoverished with respect to *A* and its composition will move away from *A* towards the lowest melting component *C*. The composition of the liquid changes along points on the liquidus surface $L_2L_3L_4 \ldots L_6$ and the conjugate solid along points on the solidus surface $S_2S_3S_4 \ldots S_6$. Tie-lines S_2L_2 through S_6L_6 lie at different isotherms and have rotated clock-wise around the vertical line at X.

The relative amount of the α increases with every small decrement in temperature. The relative amounts of the solid at T_4 and T_5 are,

$$\% \, \alpha \text{ at } T_4 = \frac{L_4X}{S_4L_4} \times 100 = 52\ \%, \ \% \, L = 48\ \%$$

$$\% \, \alpha \text{ at } T_5 = \frac{L_5X}{S_5L_5} \times 100 = 79\ \%, \ \% \, L = 21\ \%$$

The original alloy composition touches the solidus surface at the temperature T_6. The last trace of liquid solidifies, with the compositions of the conjugate phases solid and liquid being represented by S_6 (X) and L_6, respectively. The microstructure of the ternary alloy X appears very similar to the structure of the solid formed during solidification in binary alloys.

Projections of compositions of the conjugate solid and liquid phases are shown on the concentration triangle, Fig. 10.6. The composition of the solid changes along the curve S_2S_6 and that of the liquid along L_2L_6 with a cusp at X (L_2, S_6). Since the solid has just started forming at the temperature T_2, the tie-line S_2L_2 will be tangent on the liquidus projection with the point of tangency at L_2. Similarly, since solidification is completed at T_6, the line L_6S_6 will be tangent to the solidus projection at the point S_6.

We can now consider natural cooling of an alloy X when the diffusion rates of the components A, B and C along with convection allows good mixing of components in the liquid. The composition of the liquid at all temperatures can be represented by the bulk liquid composition and follows the liquids surface. However, the relatively slow rates of diffusion of components of the ternary in the solid, results in an inhomogeneous α solid solution with a cored structure.

The first solid α crystals to form in the liquid are of a composition represented by point S_2 at the temperature T_2, Fig. 10.7. Subsequent cooling through the two-phase field forms solids of compositions represented by point S_3 at T_3, S_4 at T_4, etc. The subsequent solid layers that form over α of the composition S_2 have a higher concentration of the other two components B and C and do not homogenize during natural cooling. The average composition of the solid formed after each decrement in temperature will deviate from the equilibrium composition at that temperature. At the temperature T_3, the equilibrium composition is represented by the point S_3 lying on the solidus but the average composition of the cored α is represented by point S'_3, having more of the component A. The tie-line will not turn as much as during equilibrium solidification. The average composition of the solid will lie to the left of the equilibrium composition, as shown in Fig. 10.7. The relative amount of the liquid remaining to be solidified will be more at each temperature when compared with the liquid to be solidified under equilibrium conditions. At the temperature T_6, some liquid will remain to be solidified because the average composition of the solid does not coincide with the original alloy composition (Fig. 10.7). The solidification will extend to lower temperatures and will be completed at T_7. The tie-lines S'_3L_3, S'_4L_4, etc. do not pass through the original alloy composition because these are not true tie-lines of the ternary. These have been constructed for the purpose of illustration by averaging compositions of all solid layers formed at and above a given temperature under consideration. The microstructure of the cored solid solution will be very similar to that observed in binary alloys.

10.5 RULES GOVERNING CONSTRUCTION OF TERNARY TIE-LINES

Two-phase equilibrium in ternary systems is governed by some simple rules for the construction of tie-lines:

(i) If the two-phase region extends from one binary to the other through the ternary system at a given temperature, the tie-lines gradually change their orientation from one binary tie-line to the other. This is illustrated in Fig. 10.8 where the two-phase region extends from the binary A–B to binary A–C. The tie-lines gradually change orientation from *ab* to *ac*, as shown in Fig. 10.8.

(ii) The ternary tie-lines do not intersect each other. Application of the phase rule reveals that there are two degrees of freedom in a two-phase region of the ternary system. An additional degree of freedom (over the binary system) will be in the form of at least an additional composition variable of one of the components in one of the two phases. An isothermal section of the ternary system consists of a very large number of tie-lines representing composition of conjugate phases, liquid and α.

Consider tie-lines L_1S_1 and L_2S_2 in the two-phase region of the ternary system at temperature T, Fig. 10.9. Let the tie-lines intersect at point L_1 such that L_1 and L_2 coincide and lie on the liquidus surface. For an original alloy composition X, coincident with the compositions (L_1 or L_2), the liquid will be in equili-

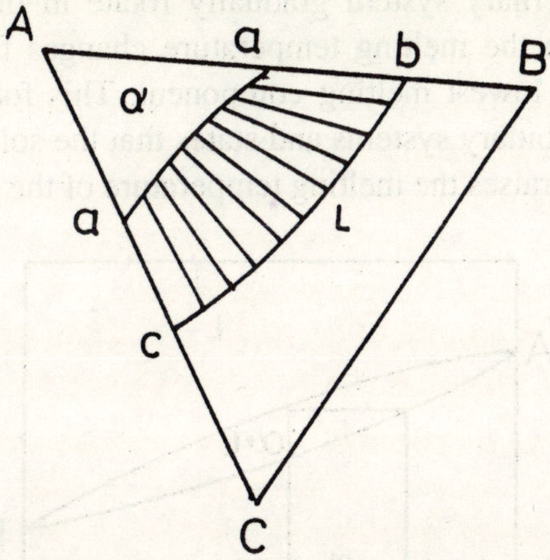

Fig. 10.8 Properties of tie-lines illustrating rules governing their construction.

brium with two solid phases α_1 and α_2 whose compositions are represented by points S_1 and S_2 lying on the solidus. This violates the phase rule because we have three phases $(L + \alpha_1 + \alpha_2)$ at temperature T, and can be represented only by monovariant equilibrium. Thus, liquid of composition L_1 (or L_2) cannot be in equilibrium with both α_1 and α_2 simultaneously. This is possible only when the tie-lines do not intersect each other.

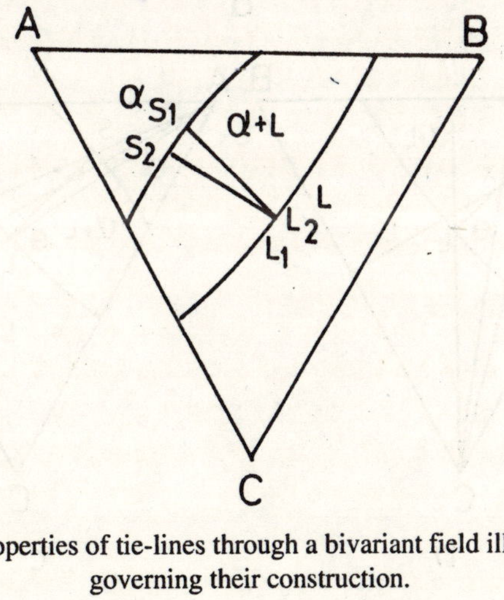

Fig. 10.9 Properties of tie-lines through a bivariant field illustrating rules governing their construction.

(iii) Tie-lines in the ternary system gradually rotate in the same direction as the direction in which the melting temperature changes from the highest melting component to the lowest melting component. This follows from Konovalov's rule applicable to binary systems and states that the solid is always richer in the component which raises the melting temperature of the alloy.

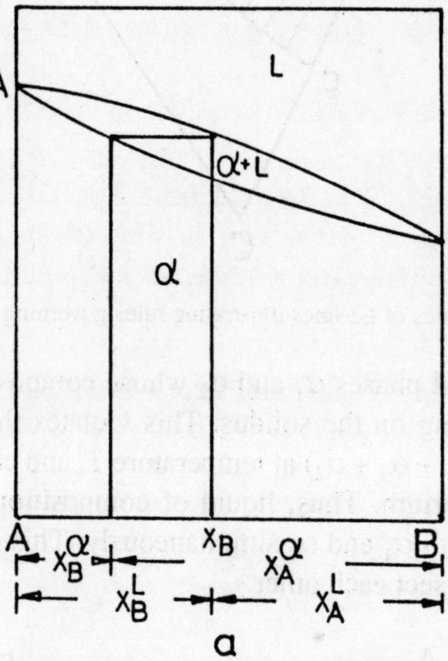

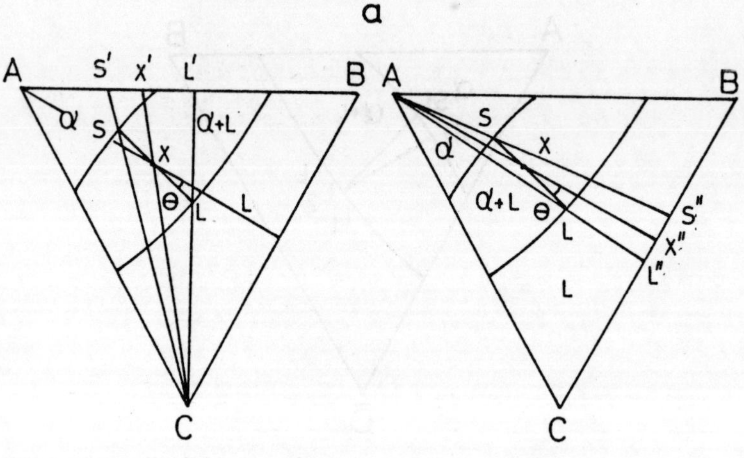

Fig. 10.10 Konovalov's rule of rotation of tie-lines: (a) binary isomorphous system; (b) and (c) isothermal sections through the space model at *T*.

Let us consider the binary isomorphous system with component *A* having a higher melting point than component *B*, Fig. 10.10a. The α phase is richer in the component *A* than the liquid, at all temperatures. We can write,

$$X_A^\alpha > X_A^L.$$

From $\quad X_A^\alpha + X_B^\alpha = 1 \quad$ and $\quad X_A^L + X_B^L = 1, \quad$ we have,

$$\frac{X_A^\alpha}{X_A^\alpha + X_B^\alpha} > \frac{X_A^L}{X_A^L + X_B^L}$$

or
$$\frac{X_A^\alpha}{X_A^\alpha + X_B^\alpha - X_A^\alpha} \gg \frac{X_A^L}{X_A^L + X_B^L - X_A^L}$$

or
$$\frac{X_A^\alpha}{X_B^\alpha} > \frac{X_A^L}{X_B^L} \quad \text{for a binary system.}$$

This rule can be extended to the ternary system with $T_A > T_B > T_C$ by considering an isothermal section at the temperature *T*, Fig. 10.10b. Let the composition of the conjugate solid and liquid phases be represented by *S* and *L*, respectively, for an original alloy composition *X*. Straight lines joining points *S*, *X* and *L* with the corner *C* meet the side *A–B* at points *S′*, *X′* and *L′*, respectively. The tie-line *SL* is inclined (in a clockwise direction) by an angle θ to the line connecting the corner *A* to the original alloy composition point *X*. Since the component *A* has a higher melting point than *B*, the following inequality holds for the Kanovalov's rule to be applicable:

$$\frac{X_A^\alpha}{X_B^\alpha} > \frac{X_A^L}{X_B^L}$$

Now, $\quad X_A^\alpha = BS', \; X_B^\alpha = AS', \; \dfrac{X_A^\alpha}{X_B^\alpha} = \dfrac{BS'}{AS'}$

$$X_A^L = BL', \; X_B^L = AL', \; \frac{X_A^L}{X_B^L} = \frac{BL'}{AL'} \,.$$

and since
$$\frac{BS'}{AS'} > \frac{BL'}{AL'}$$

$$\frac{X_A^{\alpha}}{X_B^{\alpha}} > \frac{X_A^L}{X_B^L} \,.$$

The argument can be extended to cover the inequality in ratios of compositions of components A and C and B and C. For Konovalov's rule to be applicable,

$$\frac{X_B^{\alpha}}{X_C^{\alpha}} > \frac{X_B^L}{X_C^L} \quad \text{and} \quad \frac{X_A^{\alpha}}{X_C^{\alpha}} > \frac{X_A^L}{X_C^L}$$

The first inequality can be proved by considering the isothermal section again at the temperature T, Fig. 10.10c. Join points S, X and L to the corner A and extend them to meet the side BC at points S'', X'' and L'', respectively.

$$X_B^{\alpha} = CS'', X_C^{\alpha} = BS'', \; \frac{X_B^{\alpha}}{X_C^{\alpha}} = \frac{CS''}{BS''} \,,$$

and
$$X_B^L = CL'', \; X_C^L = BL'', \; \frac{X_B^L}{X_C^L} = \frac{CL''}{BL''} \,.$$

Since,
$$\frac{CS''}{BS''} > \frac{CL''}{BL''} \,, \; \frac{X_B^{\alpha}}{X_C^{\alpha}} > \frac{X_B^L}{X_C^L} \,.$$

Similarly, it can be shown that $X_A^{\alpha}/X_C^{\alpha} > X_A^L/X_C^L$ and Konovalov's rule is satisfied in the two-phase field of the ternary system. The tie-line SL drawn in the diagram of

Fig. 10.10b has the correct orientation, i.e., has rotated clockwise from the straight line connecting *A* to *X*. This direction of rotation coincides with the direction in which the melting points are decreasing from the highest to the lowest melting component.

(iv) Tie-lines when extended do not meet the corner of the equilateral triangle except when the composition of a phase in a two-phase region lies close to a corner of the triangle, i.e., the phase under consideration has a very low solubility for the other two components. This can be shown by negating the Konovalov's rule. Consider an isothermal section at temperature *T*, Fig. 10.11. The tie-line *SL* when produced meets the corner *A* and the point *Y* on the side *BC*. We can write,

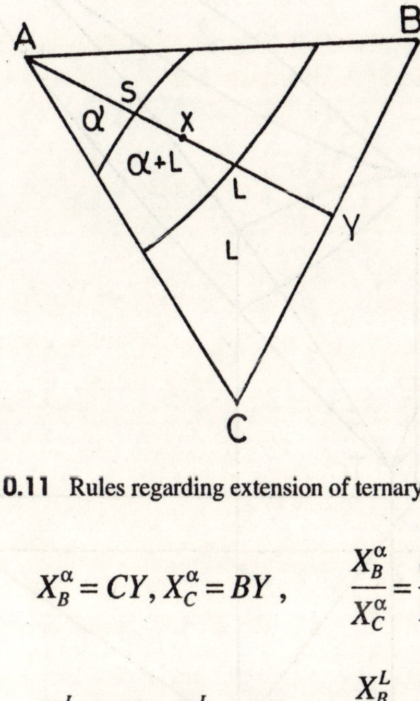

Fig. 10.11 Rules regarding extension of ternary tie-lines.

$$X_B^{\alpha} = CY, X_C^{\alpha} = BY, \qquad \frac{X_B^{\alpha}}{X_C^{\alpha}} = \frac{CY}{BY},$$

$$X_B^{L} = CY, \; X_C^{L} = BY, \qquad \frac{X_B^{L}}{X_C^{L}} = \frac{CY}{BY},$$

and $X_B^{\alpha}/X_C^{\alpha} = X_B^{L}/X_C^{L}$, which violates Konovalov's rule. Thus, ternary tie-lines when extended do not meet the corner of the equilateral triangle.

10.6 VARIANTS OF THE TERNARY ISOMORPHOUS SYSTEM

In a variant of the ternary isomorphous system, one of the binary systems may be congruently melting with a minimum in temperature at which the composition of the solid and liquid phases are the same. The other two binary systems are regular with

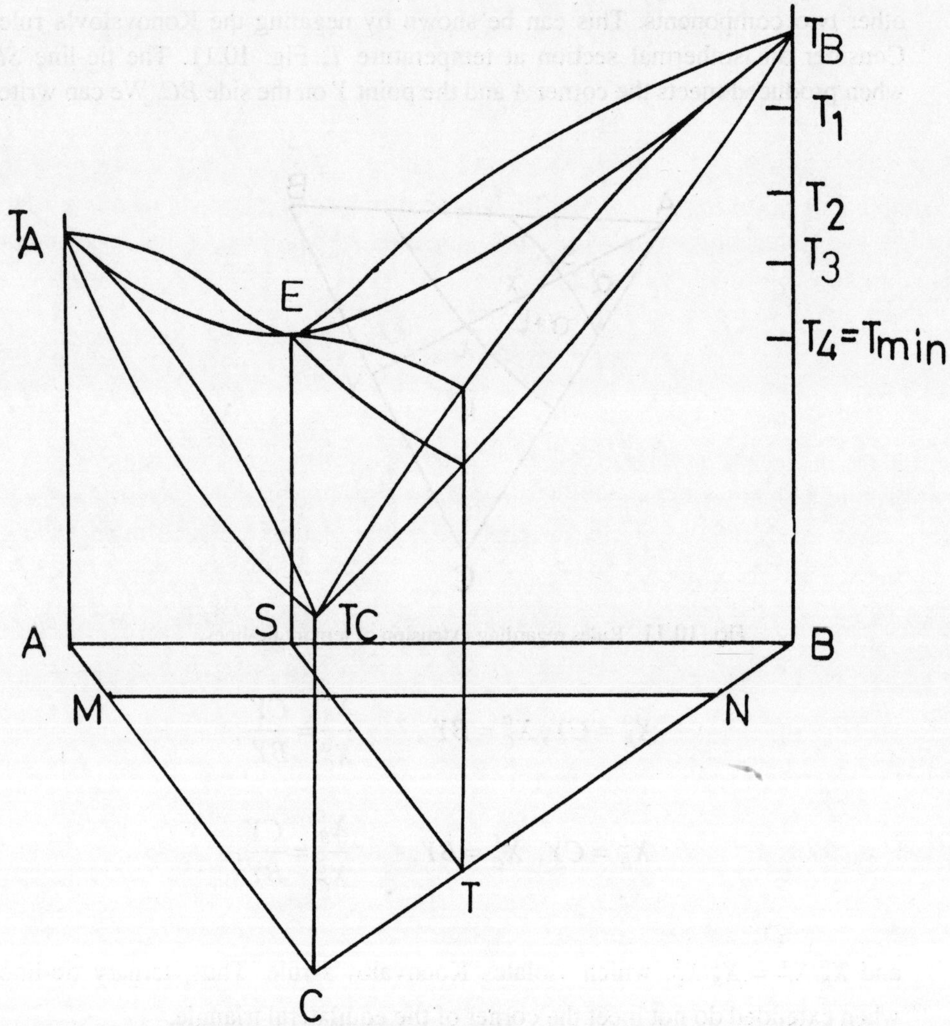

Fig. 10.12 Variant of the ternary isomorphous system-space model. Binary system *AB* shows a minimum.

lens-shaped two-phase regions, as shown in the space model of Fig. 10.12. The congruently melting composition of the binary behaves as a pure component (point E in the diagram). The liquidus and solidus surfaces will meet at the point E in addition to meeting at T_A, T_B and T_C. Elsewhere, the two-phase region (α+L) separates the liquidus and solidus surfaces. The liquidus surface slopes down from the melting temperature T_A and T_B towards the melting temperature of component C with a trough in the region ET_C. The slope of the trough will depend upon the temperatures T_C and T_{min}. Details of the space model are illustrated in a series of isothermal and vertical sections. The isothermal sections at T_1 and T_2 (defined by $T_B>T_1>T_2T_A>T_3>T_4 = T_{min}>T_C$) do not show any special feature and, therefore, need no explanation, Fig. 10.13. The isothermal section at $T_3<T_A$ shows two two-phase regions (α+L) with the liquid lying in the region of the trough corresponding to the depression in the solidification temperature near the minimum in one binary, Fig. 10.13c. At $T_4 = T_{min}$, the liquidus and solidus surfaces meet at the point E and separate as two-phase regions, Fig. 10.13d.

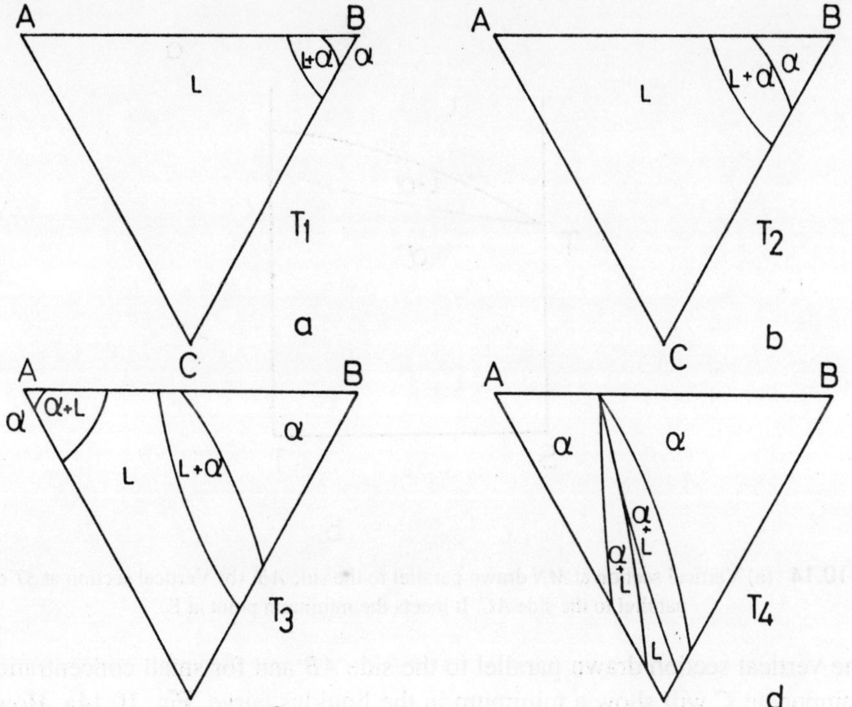

Fig. 10.13 Isothermal sections through the space model of Fig. 10.12.

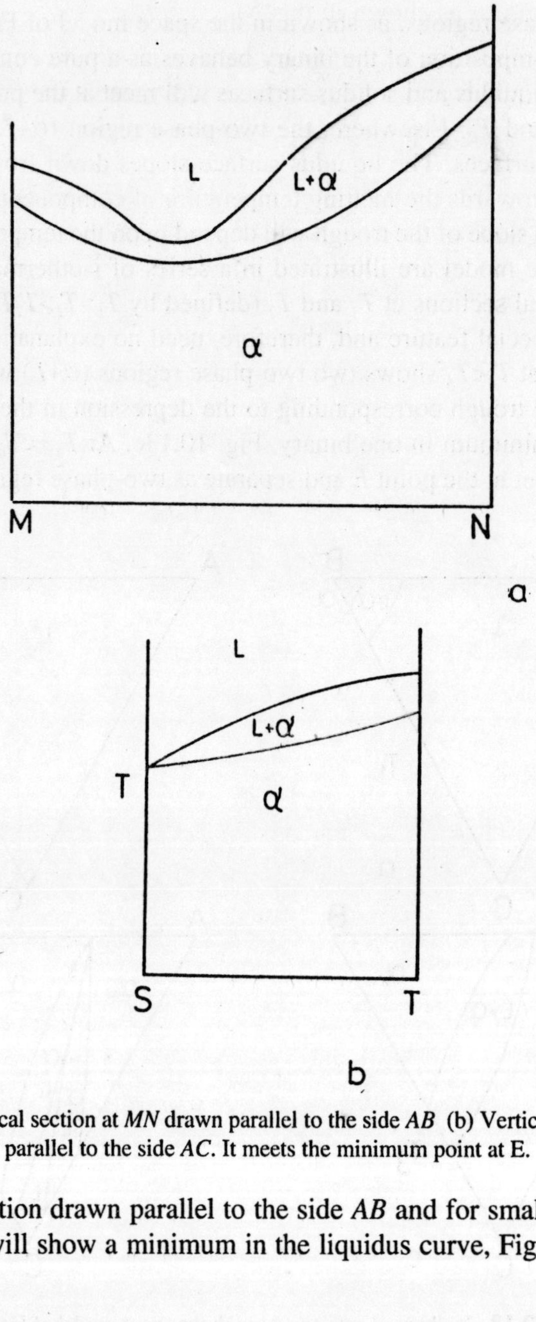

Fig. 10.14 (a) Vertical section at *MN* drawn parallel to the side *AB* (b) Vertical section at *ST* drawn parallel to the side *AC*. It meets the minimum point at E.

The vertical section drawn parallel to the side *AB* and for small concentrations of the component *C* will show a minimum in the liquidus curve, Fig. 10.14a. However, the solidus will not touch the liquidus curve at any point in this section. Of special interest is the vertical section *ST* which is drawn parallel to the side *AC* touching the point *E*, Fig. 10.14b. Since the liquidus and solidus surfaces meet at the point *E*, the two curves will meet at point *E* in the vertical section, as shown.

10.7 TWO-PHASE EQUILIBRIA INVOLVING IMMISCIBILITY GAP

In a large number of binary systems, a homogeneous solid solution separates into two solids at lower temperatures. The transformation occurs at a critical temperature T_c.

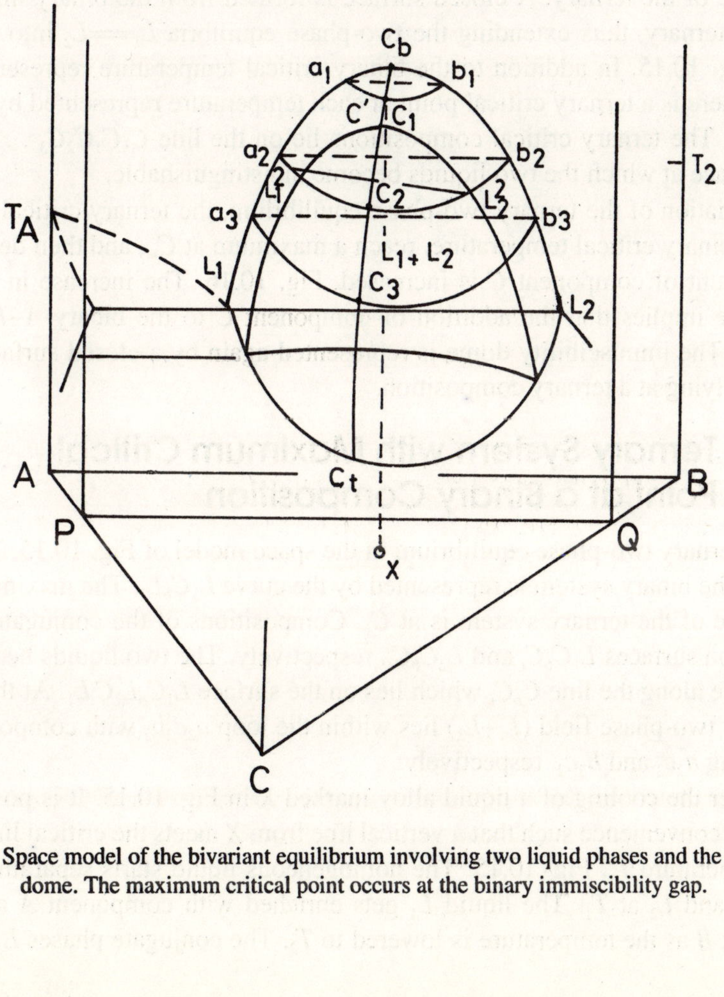

Fig. 10.15 Space model of the bivariant equilibrium involving two liquid phases and the immiscibility dome. The maximum critical point occurs at the binary immiscibility gap.

The thermodynamics of solutions has been presented in Chapter 1. Similar separation of a homogeneous liquid solution also occurs. Liquids L_1 and L_2 are rich in components A and B, respectively.

Let us consider the behavior of solutions both solid and liquid as affected by the presence of a third component. Consider a binary system A–B which shows a homogeneous liquid solution L at higher temperatures but begins to separate into liquids L_1 and L_2 at the critical temperature. The immiscibility in the liquid, as shown by the dome-shaped region of the phase diagram, cannot remain limited to the binary system when a third component C is added. The immiscibility is extended to the ternary. There are two possible modes by which the third component C interacts with liquids L_1 and L_2. In the first, the addition of the third component does not raise the critical temperature of the ternary. A closed surface is formed from the binary immiscibility gap in the ternary, thus extending the two-phase equilibria $L_1 \rightleftharpoons L_2$ into the ternary system, Fig. 10.15. In addition to the binary critical temperature represented by the point C_b, there is a ternary critical point at each temperature represented by points C_1, C_2, C_3, etc. The ternary critical compositions lie on the line $C_bC_1C_2C_3 \ldots C_t$ on the closed surface at which the two liquids become indistinguishable.

In a variation of the ternary two-phase equilibrium, the ternary critical points rise above the binary critical temperature, reach a maximum at C_m, and then descend to C_t as the amount of component C is increased, Fig. 10.16. The increase in the critical temperature implies that the addition of component C to the binary A–B promotes clustering. The immiscibility dome is represented again by a closed surface with the apex at C_m lying at a ternary composition.

10.7.1 Ternary System with Maximum Critical Point at a Binary Composition

Consider ternary two-phase equilibrium in the space model of Fig. 10.15. The immiscibility in the binary system is represented by the curve $L_1C_bL_2$. The maximum critical temperature of the ternary system is at C_b. Compositions of the conjugate phases L_1 and L_2 lie on surfaces $L_1C_bC_t$ and $L_2C_bC_t$, respectively. The two liquids become indistinguishable along the line C_bC_t which lies on the surface $L_1C_bL_2C_tL_1$. At the temperature T_2, the two-phase field (L_1+L_2) lies within the loop $a_2c_2b_2$ with composition of L_1 and L_2 along a_2c_2 and b_2c_2, respectively.

Consider the cooling of a liquid alloy marked X in Fig. 10.15. It is positioned for the sake of convenience such that a vertical line from X meets the critical line C_bc_t at c_1 at the temperature T_1, Fig. 10.15. The homogeneous liquid starts separating into two liquids L_1 and L_2 at T_1. The liquid L_1 gets enriched with component A and L_2 with component B as the temperature is lowered to T_2. The conjugate phases L_1 and L_2 are

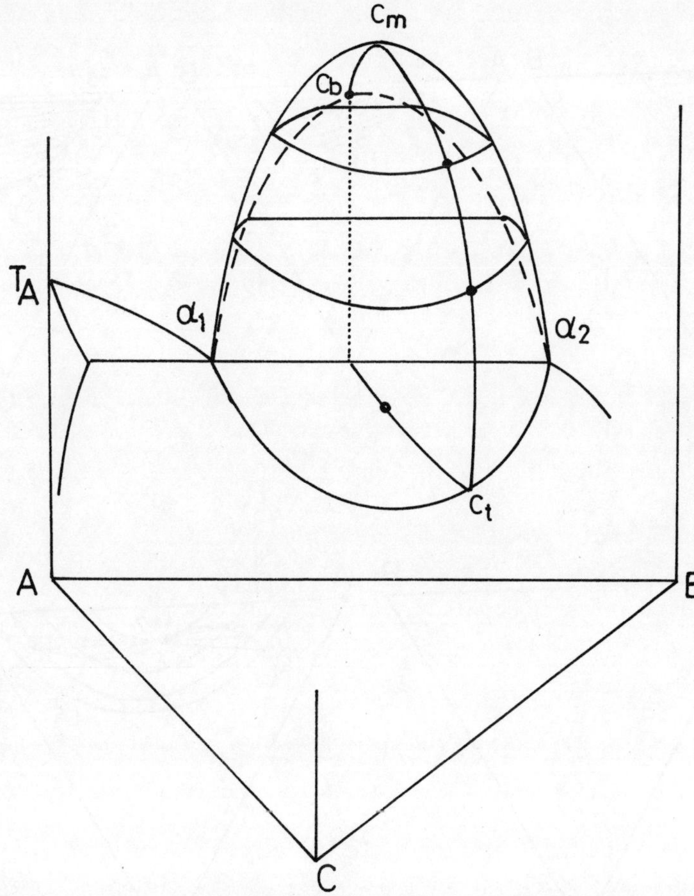

Fig. 10.16 Space model of the bivariant equilibrium involving two solid phases and the immiscibility dome. The maximum critical point occurs at a ternary composition.

in equilibrium with each other and are of compositions L_1^2 and L_2^2 lying on the loop $a_2c_2b_2$. Further cooling to T_3 results in liquids L_1 and L_2 of composition L_1^3 and L_2^3, respectively, in equilibrium with each other. The two composition points lie on the loop $a_3c_3b_3$.

The details are shown in the isothermal sections, Fig. 10.17a, b and c. The critical points do not lie on the maximum positions of the loop, m_1, m_2, m_3, etc. but are displaced to one side. This is due to unequal partitioning of the component C in the two liquids. The difference in the partitioning coefficients is responsible for the above displacement of critical compositions.

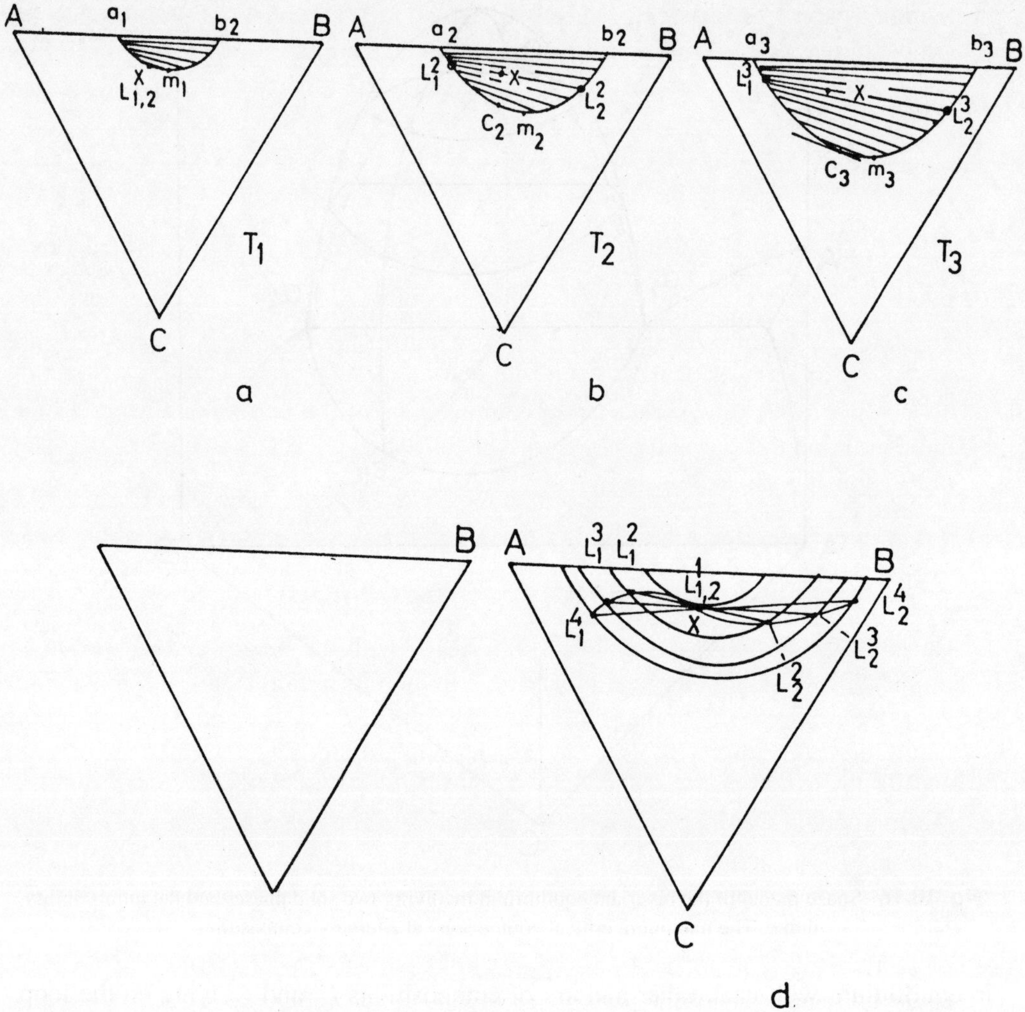

Fig. 10.17 (a), (b) and (c) isothermal section through the space model of Fig. 10.15 (d) the projection of the tie-lines through the space model of Fig. 10.15.

Ternary alloys having a very small amount of the component C will have the composition point very near the line A–B on the concentration triangle. The tie-line representing equilibrium between conjugate phases L_1 and L_2 will be nearly parallel to the side A–B. The tie-line near the critical point at any temperature will be nearly parallel to the tangent to the curve *acb* at the critical point *c* (as shown in Fig. 10.17c at the point c_3) because at the critical point the two liquids become indistinguishable and the loop *acb* cannot be intersected. The loop *acb* on the isothermal section expands as the temperature decreases. The critical point gradually moves away from the original alloy composition. This amounts to saying that the ternary tie-lines will gradually change their orientation towards the binary tie-line, as the temperature is lowered.

The projection of the tie-lines is shown in Fig. 10.17d at temperatures T_2, T_3 and T_4. Points L_1^1, L_1^2, L_1^3 . . . lie on a skew surface whose projection generates the curve $L_1^1 L_1^2 L_1^3 L_1^4$ which is tangent to the loop $a_1c_1b_1$, at the point c_1. Similarly, composition points of the second liquid L_2, represented by points $L_2^1 L_2^2 L_2^3$ . . . lie on a skew surface generated by tie-lines in space as a direct result of the rotation of the tie-lines about the composition vertical at *X*. The tie-lines are rotating in a clockwise direction in this case. The greater the asymmetry in compositions of the two liquids from the maximum point on the curve, the larger will be the skewing. This is due to the large angle of rotation at each decrement in temperature.

10.7.2 Ternary System with Maximum Critical Point at a Ternary Composition

Consider the ternary system *ABC* (Fig. 10.16) with the binary system *AB* showing immiscibility, with the critical point at C_b. In the illustration that will follow, we will consider immiscibility in the solid instead of in the liquid. The addition of the component *C* to the binary *AB* raises the critical temperature. The maximum occurs at c_m. This is due to an enhanced tendency of clustering of *A* and *B* atoms due to addition of the component *C*. The component *C may not partition equally again between the two separated solid solutions,* α_1 and α_2, from a homogeneous solid solution α. The interaction parameter Ω which is related to the difference in the bond energies of the like and unlike pair of atoms will be a large positive quantity. Moreover, since in the case of a ternary system, we have an additional like pair *C–C* with energy E_{CC}, the average of the bond energies of the pure bonds, $(E_{AA} + E_{CC})/2$ and $(E_{BB} + E_{CC})/2$ will dominate over $(E_{AA} + E_{BB})/2$ and E_{AB}, E_{AC} and E_{BC}.

A ternary critical point c_m at the top of the dome will form a critical line $c_bc_mc_t$ with c_t lying on the solid solubility surface at the ambient temperature. The projection of the curve c_bc_m lies within the concentration triangle with c_b lying on the binary *AB*. The critical curve $c_bc_mc_t$ separates the immiscibility dome in two parts. Any point lying on the solubility surface to the right of the curve $c_b c_m c_t$ will represent the composition of the α_2 phase. Similarly, any point lying on the solubility surface to the left of the critical curve will represent the composition of the α_1 phase. The two surfaces are,

$$\alpha_1 c_b c_m c_t \alpha_1 \quad \text{and} \quad \alpha_2 c_b c_m c_t \alpha_2.$$

A vertical section through the space model of Fig. 10.15 at PQ is shown in Fig. 10.18.

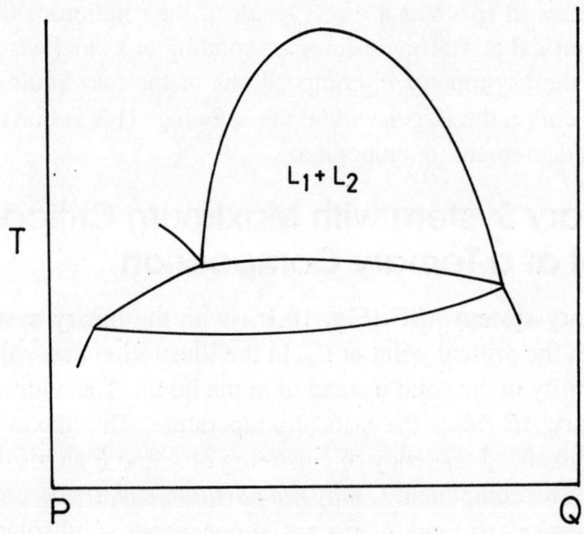

Fig. 10.18 Vertical section through the space model of Fig. 10.15.

A number of isothermal sections through the space model are shown in Fig. 10.19. The isothermal section at a temperature T_1 between the binary and ternary critical points, c_b and c_m, respectively, shows a closed loop with critical points c_1 and c_1', Fig. 10.19a. Any tie-line near the binary AB will be nearly parallel to the line AB and will also be nearly parallel to the tangent drawn at the point c_1'. Similarly, any tie-line drawn near the critical point c_1' will be nearly parallel to the tangent drawn on the loop at the point c_1. The tie-lines in the α_1+α_2 phase field will gently rotate from being parallel to the side AB to being nearly parallel to the tangent on the loop at c_1' as the amount of the component C increases in the alloy.

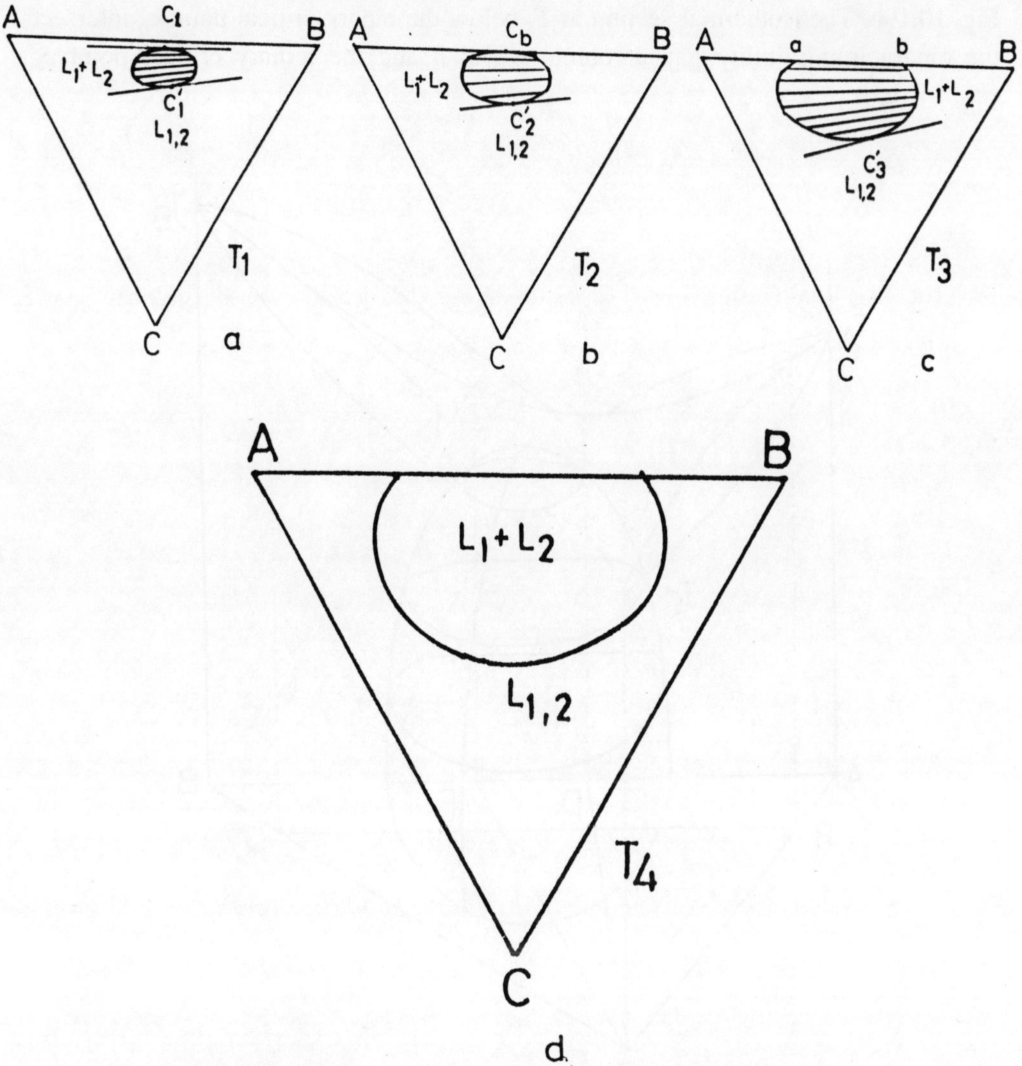

Fig. 10.19 Isothermal section through the space model of Fig. 10.16.

The isothermal section taken at the binary critical point c_b shows that the loop is closed on the binary AB and the line AB is tangent on the loop at the point c_b. Tie-lines will gently rotate to finally become nearly parallel to the tangent on the loop at c_2',

Fig. 10.19b. The isothermal section at T_3 below the binary critical point c_b intersects the binary immiscibility gap at points a and b and the ternary critical point c_3', Fig. 10.19c.

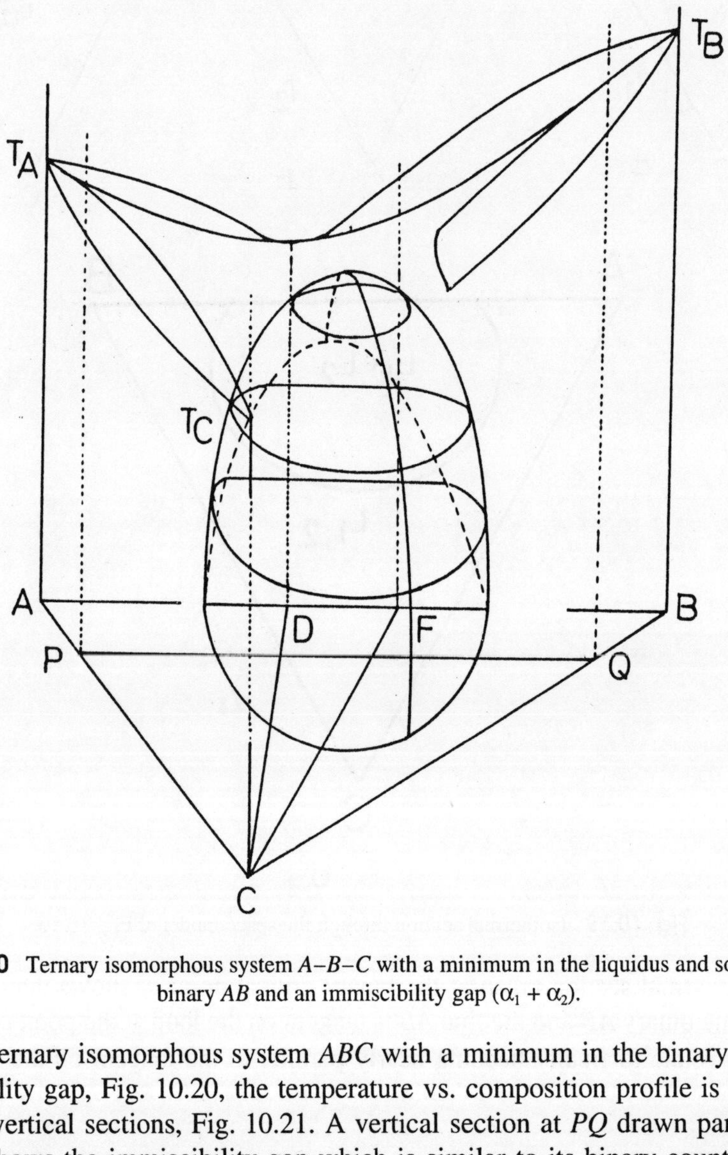

Fig. 10.20 Ternary isomorphous system A–B–C with a minimum in the liquidus and solidus of the binary AB and an immiscibility gap $(\alpha_1 + \alpha_2)$.

For a ternary isomorphous system ABC with a minimum in the binary AB and an immiscibility gap, Fig. 10.20, the temperature vs. composition profile is shown in a series of vertical sections, Fig. 10.21. A vertical section at PQ drawn parallel to the side AB shows the immiscibility gap which is similar to its binary counterpart, Fig.

10.21a. The liquidus and solidus curves do not close at the ordinates at *P* and *Q*. A vertical section drawn at *CD* where the ordinate at *D* touches the minimum in the liquidus and solidus temperatures of the binary *AB* shows that the liquidus and solidus are closed at T_c and T_{min}, Fig. 10.21b. The immiscibility gap reaches a maximum and terminates on the ordinate at *D*. Another vertical section at *CF* shows the nature of the liquidus and solidus surfaces of the ternary system, Fig. 10.21c.

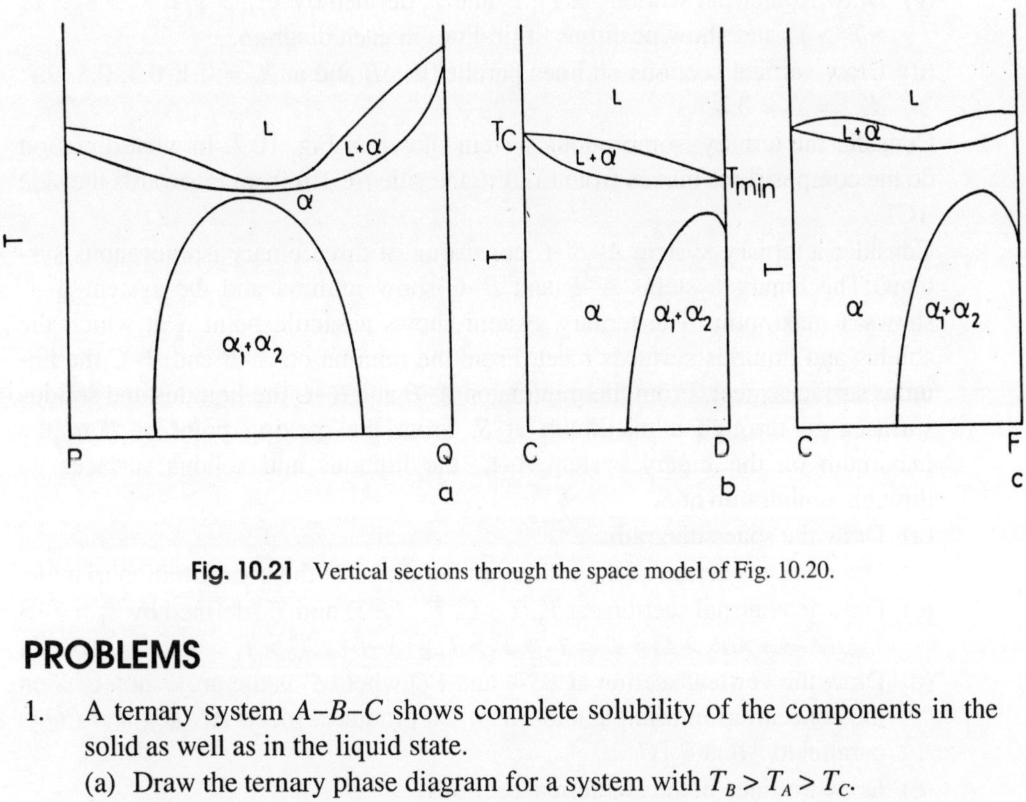

Fig. 10.21 Vertical sections through the space model of Fig. 10.20.

PROBLEMS

1. A ternary system *A–B–C* shows complete solubility of the components in the solid as well as in the liquid state.
   (a) Draw the ternary phase diagram for a system with $T_B > T_A > T_C$.
   (b) Draw the liquidus and solidus projections on the base of the concentration triangle.
   (c) Draw isothermal sections at T_1 and T_2 defined by $T_B > T_1 > T_A > T_2$.
   (d) Draw a number of tie-lines in both isothermal sections. In which direction should the tie-lines turn in going from T_1 to T_2? Explain.

(e) Select an alloy composition and determine the relative amounts of the α and liquid phases in equilibrium with each other at T_1 and T_2 for the alloy composition lying within the two-phase field. The amount of which component(s) will be increasing with decreasing temperature.

(f) Draw a vertical section at *PQ* parallel to *AB*.

2. The liquidus and solidus surfaces of a ternary system exhibit a maximum which lies at a ternary composition.
   (a) Draw the space model of the ternary system with $T_B > T_A > T_C$.
   (b) Draw projections of the liquidus and solidus surfaces on the concentration triangle.
   (c) Draw isothermal sections at T_1, T_2 and T_3 defined by $T_{max} > T_1 > T_B > T_2 > T_A > T_3 > T_C$ and show positions of tie-lines in each diagram.
   (d) Draw vertical sections on lines parallel to *AB* and at $X_C = 0.1, 0.3, 0.5, 0.7$. $X_{max} = X_C = 0.4$.
3. Consider the ternary isomorphous system shown in Fig. 10.2. In what direction do the compositions moves from (a) *A* to the side *BC* (b) from *B* towards the side *AC*?
4. Consider a ternary system *A–B–C* consisting of three binary isomorphous systems. The binary systems *A–B* and *B–C* show minima and the system *A–C* shows a maximum. The ternary system shows a saddle point *S* at which the solidus and liquidus surfaces meet. From the minima on *A–B* and *B–C* the liquidus surfaces meet. From the minima on *A–B* and *B–C* the liquidus and solidus surfaces go through a maximum at *S*. From the melting point of *B* to the maximum on the binary system *A–C*, the liquidus and solidus surfaces go through a minimum at *S*.
   (a) Draw the space diagram.
   (b) Draw the projection of the solidus and liquidus on the concentration triangle.
   (c) Draw isothermal sections at T_1, T_2, T_3, T_4, T_5, T_6 and T_7, defined by $T_B > T_1 > T_{max}\,(A–C) > T_2 > T_3 > T_S = T_4 > T_5 > T_{min}\,(A–B) > T_6 > T_C > T_7 > T_{min}\,(B–C)$.
   (d) Draw the vertical section at *BS′X* and *PQ* where *S′* is the projection of *S* on the concentration triangle and *BS′* when produced meets *AC* at *x* and *PQ* is parallel to *AB* at 0.1*C*.
   (e) Draw tie-lines in the isothermal sections.
   (f) Describe the cooling of an alloy passing through a point on the curve through the saddle point. Would you get coring in the alloy composition *S*?
   (g) If an alloy composition on the curve T_BS is naturally cooled, describe the cooling and draw projection of the skew surface generated by tie-lines on the base of Gibbs' triangle.

5. For the space model of Fig. 10.20, draw a series of isothermal sections below the top of the dome. Show the position of tie-lines in each section.
6. The liquidus and solidus surfaces of a ternary system A–B–C exhibit a maximum at a binary composition.
   (a) Draw the ternary phase diagram with $T_B > T_A > T_C$.
   (b) Draw the projection of the liquidus and solidus surfaces on the Gibbs' triangle.
   (c) Draw isothermal sections at $T_{max} > T_1 > T_B > T_2 > T_A > T_3 > T_C$.
   (d) Draw vertical sections on lines parallel to AB at $X_C = 0.1, 0.3, 0.5, 0.7$ and 0.9.

Chapter 11

TERNARY ALLOY SYSTEMS–THREE-PHASE EQUILIBRIA

As described in Chapter 9, the application of the phase rule in a three-phase region of the ternary system gives one degree of freedom. Thus, out of the six independent composition variables and a temperature variable only one can be selected independently. Let us exercise temperature as the one degree of freedom. The composition variables are fixed in the process. The three-phase equilibria is represented by tie-triangles. The composition of the three phases lie at the corners of the tie-triangle at each isotherm. The following three-phase equilibria can be considered.

$$L \Leftrightarrow \alpha + \beta, \quad L_1 \Leftrightarrow \alpha + L_2, \quad \gamma \Leftrightarrow \alpha + \beta$$

$$L + \alpha \Leftrightarrow \beta, \quad L_1 + L_2 \Leftrightarrow \alpha, \quad \gamma + \alpha \Leftrightarrow \beta$$

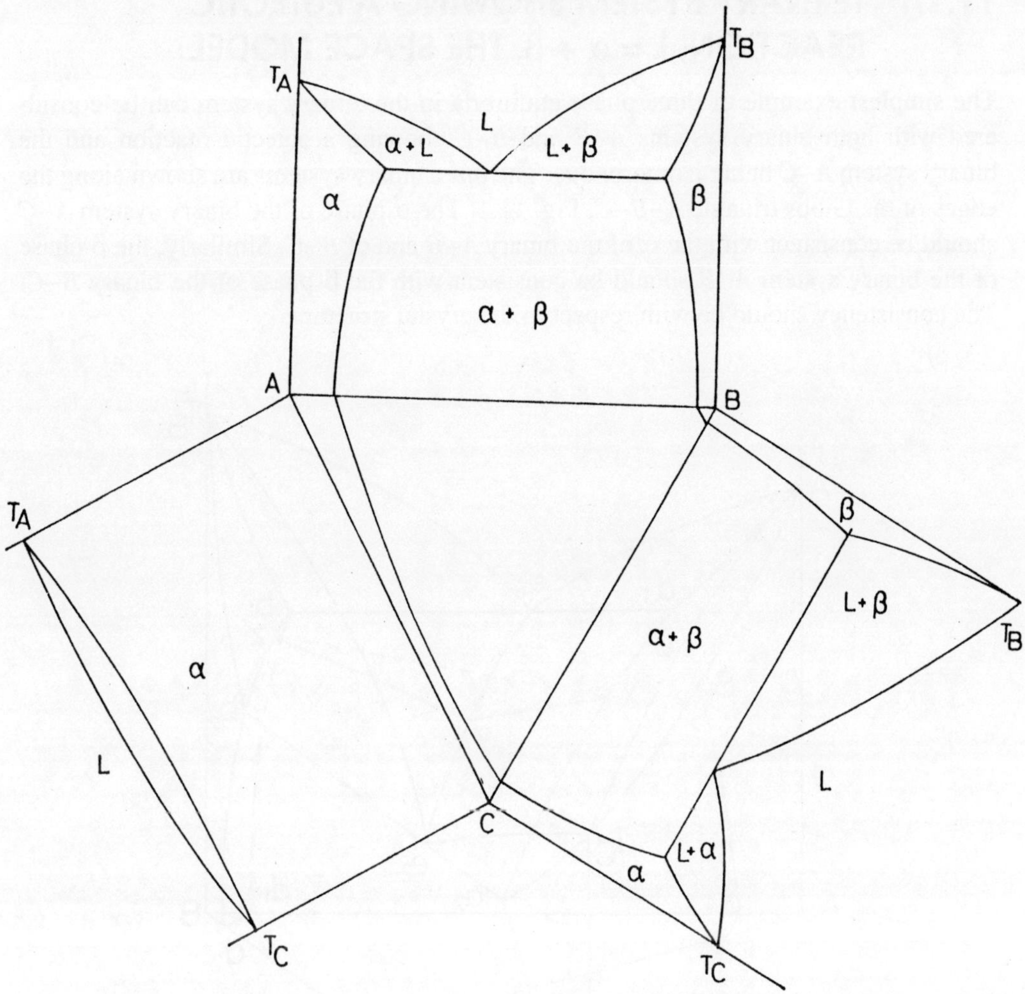

Fig. 11.1 Binary systems A–B and B–C are eutectics and the system A–C is isomorphous as shown on the edges of the Gibbs triangle.

11.1.1 TERNARY SYSTEM SHOWING A EUTECTIC REACTION, L = α + β, THE SPACE MODEL

The simplest example of three-phase equilibria in the ternary system can be considered with both binary systems *A–B* and *B–C* showing a eutectic reaction and the binary system *A–C* being isomorphous. The three binary systems are shown along the edges of the Gibbs triangle *A–B–C*, Fig. 11.1. The α phase of the binary system *A–C* should be consistent with the α of the binary *A–B* and of *B–C*. Similarly, the β phase of the binary system *A–B* should be consistent with the β phase of the binary *B–C*. The consistency should be with respect to the crystal structure.

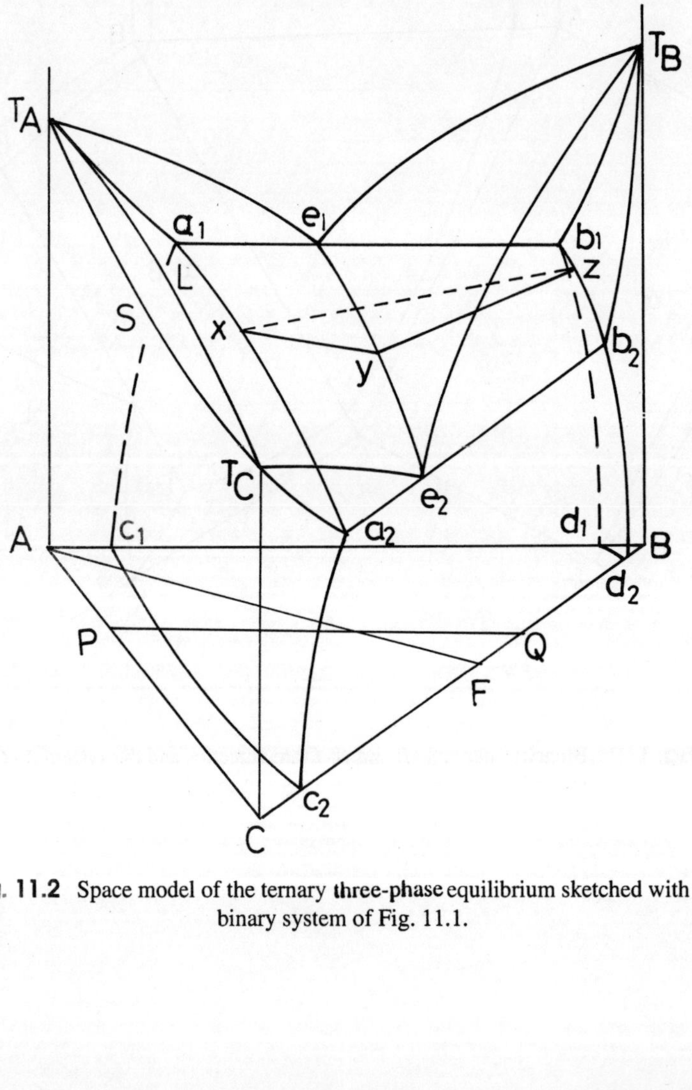

Fig. 11.2 Space model of the ternary three-phase equilibrium sketched with the binary system of Fig. 11.1.

The space model of the ternary system is shown in Fig. 11.2. The space diagram consists of a three-phase region, (L+α+β), three two-phase regions, (α+β), (L+α) and (L+β) and three single-phase regions, L, α and β. These phase regions are shown separately in the exploded model, Fig. 11.3.

As shown in Table 11.1., the phase diagram shows the following:

Table 11.1

Liquidus Surface	$L/(L+\beta)\ T_Be_1e_2T_B$
	$L/(L+\alpha)\ T_Ae_1e_2T_CLT_A$
Solidus Surface	$\beta/(L+\beta) T_Bb_1b_2T_B$
	$\alpha/(L+\alpha)\ T_Aa_1a_2T_CST_A$
Solvus Surface	$\alpha/(\alpha+\beta)\ a_1a_2c_2c_1a_1$
	$\beta/(\alpha+\beta)\ b_1b_2d_2d_1b_1$
Three-Phase Region bounded by	α–L ruled surface $a_1e_1e_2a_2a_1$
	α–β ruled surface $a_1b_1b_2a_2a_1$
Two-Phase Regions bounded by	(α+L) $T_Ae_1e_2T_CLT_A$ and $T_Aa_1a_2T_CST_A$
	(β+L) $T_Be_1e_2T_B$ and $T_Bb_1b_2T_B$
	(α+β) $a_1a_2c_2c_1a_1$, $b_1b_2d_2d_1$ and $a_1b_1b_2a_2a_1$
Single-Phase Regions bounded by	α $T_Aa_1a_2T_CST_A$, $T_Ca_2c_2CT_C$, $T_Aa_1c_1AT_A$
	β $T_Bb_1d_1d_2b_2T_B$, $T_Bb_2d_2BT_B$ and $T_Bb_1d_1BT_B$
Line of critical temperature at which two phases become indistinguishable	Nil

Binary liquidus lines: $T_Ae_1,\ T_Be_1\ (A-B)$

$$T_Be_2,\ T_ce_2\ (B-C)$$

$$T_ALT_c\ (A-C)$$

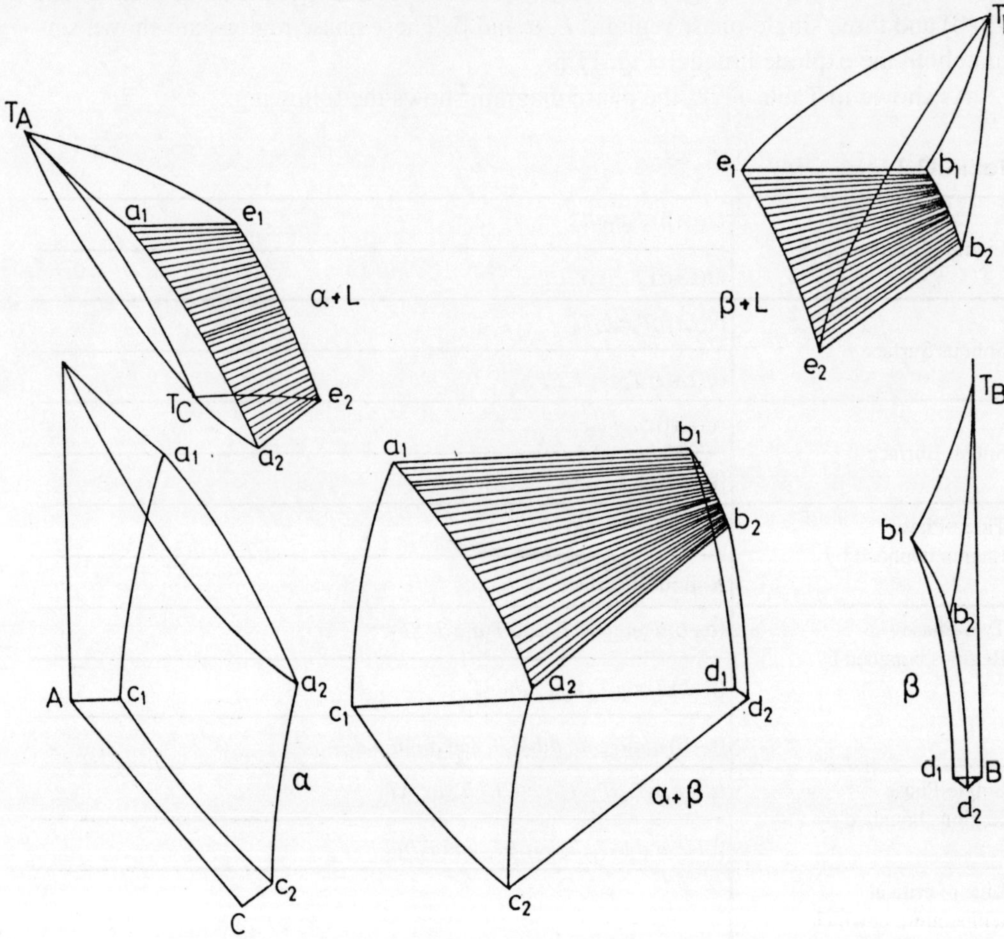

Fig. 11.3 Exploded model of the phase diagram showing various phase fields.

Binary solidus lines: $T_A a_1,\ T_B b_1\ (A - B)$

$T_B b_2,\ T_c a_2\ (B - C)$

$T_A S T_c\ (A - C)$

e_1e_1: Line along which the two liquid surfaces meet. Any alloy with composition on this line will dissociate by the reaction $L = \alpha+\beta$.

Liquidus surfaces of the ternary: $T_Ae_1e_2T_cLT_A$, $T_Be_1e_2T_B$
Solidus surface: $T_Aa_1a_2T_cST_A$, $T_Bb_1b_2T_B$
Solvus surfaces: $a_1a_2c_2c_1a_1$, $b_1b_2d_2d_1b_1$

Now let us describe the various phase fields of the ternary phase diagram as shown in the exploded model, Fig. 11.3. The (α+L) phase region is bounded by the liquidus surface $T_Ae_1e_2T_CLT_A$ from above and the solidus surface $T_Aa_1a_2T_CST_A$ from below. It terminates on top of the three-phase region (α+β+L), $a_1b_1b_2a_2a_1$ forming a ruled surface. The term "ruled surface" here implies that it consists of bundle of tie-lines coplanar with the surface. The (β+L) phase region is bounded by the liquidus $T_Be_1e_2T_B$ from above and the solidus $T_Bb_1b_2T_B$ from below. It also terminates on top of the three-phase region forming a ruled surface. The (L+α) and (L+β) phase fields are very similar to those described in Chapter 10 for the ternary isomorphous system with the tie-lines connecting the conjugate phases at each isotherm. The (α+β) phase region is bounded by the ruled surface $a_1b_1b_2a_2a_1$, which is the bottom of the (α+β+L) phase field, the solvus surfaces $a_1a_2c_2c_1a_1$ and $b_1b_2d_2d_1b_1$ on the sides of the phase diagram. The three-phase region is bounded by ruled surfaces $a_1e_1e_2a_2a_1$, $b_1e_1e_2b_2b_1$ and $a_1b_1b_2a_2a_1$. At an isotherm, the conjugate tie-lines on the three surfaces meet to form a tie-triangle representing equilibrium between α, β and liquid.

The three-phase region (L+α+β) is closed along lines a_1a_2 and b_1b_2 and along the binary reaction isotherms ($a_1e_1b_1$ and $a_2e_2b_2$). Lines a_1a_2, e_1e_2 and b_1b_2 do not lie on the same plane. Just as the two phase region is composed of a bundle of tie-lines, the three-phase region is composed of a stack of tie-triangles. These tie-triangles close on the binary reaction isotherms $a_1e_1b_1$ and $a_2e_2b_2$ forming degenerate tie-lines (tie-triangles become tie-lines).

The liquid-phase region lies above the liquidus surface. The α and β-phase regions are bounded by the solidus and solvus surfaces and the prism planes on the base of the triangle, as clearly seen in the exploded model drawn separately in Fig. 11.3. The single-phase regions, liquid, α and β join the three-phase field along lines e_1e_2, a_1a_2 and b_1b_2, respectively. The intersection of the isothermal plane with the three-plane region is represented by the triangle. The corners of the triangle represent compositions of these phases, for example, in the triangle xyz of Fig. 11.2, which lies on an isothermal plane, points x, y and z represent compositions of the α, liquid, and β

phases, respectively. The three bounding surfaces of the tie-triangle are not planar and it is due to the change in orientation of the tie-lines as the temperature decreases from Te_1 to Te_2.

11.1.2 ISOTHERMAL SECTIONS

The details of the ternary phase diagram and the various phase fields are best illustrated with the help of the isothermal sections, Fig. 11.4. The isothermal sections are drawn at temperature $T_1, T_2, \ldots T_6$ defined as follows:

$$T_B > T_1 > T_A > T_2 > T_C > T_{e_1} > T_3 > T_4 > T_5 > T_{e_2} > T_6$$

Temperature T_1 lies below T_B but above the melting point of pure A, T_A. The isothermal plane will intersect the liquidus and solidus surfaces near corner B of the phase diagram. The (β+L) phase region will appear in the isothermal section at T_1 which will separate the liquid and β phase fields, Fig. 11.4a. Temperature T_2 lies below the melting point of pure A and above T_C and the isothermal plane intersects the liquidus and solidus surfaces near both corners A and B. An additional two-phase field (α+L) will appear in the isothermal section at T_2, Fig. 11.4b. Since the two liquidus surfaces meet along e_1e_2, the liquidus curves at Te_1 will meet at the point e_1 on the binary side AB.

Decreasing the temperature below Te_1 results in the intersection of the isothermal plane with the three-phase region (L+α+β) which appears as a tie-triangle, Fig. 11.4c. This is a new feature in the isothermal section at T_3. The tie-triangle is made up of tie-lines representing conjugate phases $\alpha\beta$, $L\alpha$ and $L\beta$. Since the three two-phase regions terminate on the three-phase field, the isothermal section must also intersect the α+L, β+L and α+β phase regions, as shown in Fig. 11.4c at T_3. Moreover, since the single-phase fields lie near the monovariant lines of the space model, they would appear near the corners of the tie-triangles in the isothermal section (Fig. 11.4c). The tie-triangles gently move with decreasing temperature from being near the side AB at T_3 to being near the side BC at T_5. The composition of the liquid gradually changes from e_1 to e_2 along e_1e_2 with decreasing temperature. The position of the tie-triangle at T_4 and T_5 are shown in Figs. 11.4, d and e, respectively. At a temperature below T_5 (at T_{e_2}), the tie-triangle terminates in a tie-line $a_2e_2b_2$ and the three-phase region will not appear below T_{e_2}. The isothermal section at $T_6 < T_{e_2}$ intersects the α, (α+β) and β phase fields, as shown in Fig. 11.4f. There will be minor adjustments in the relative amounts and compositions of the α and β phases along α/(α+β) and β/(α+β) solvus surfaces.

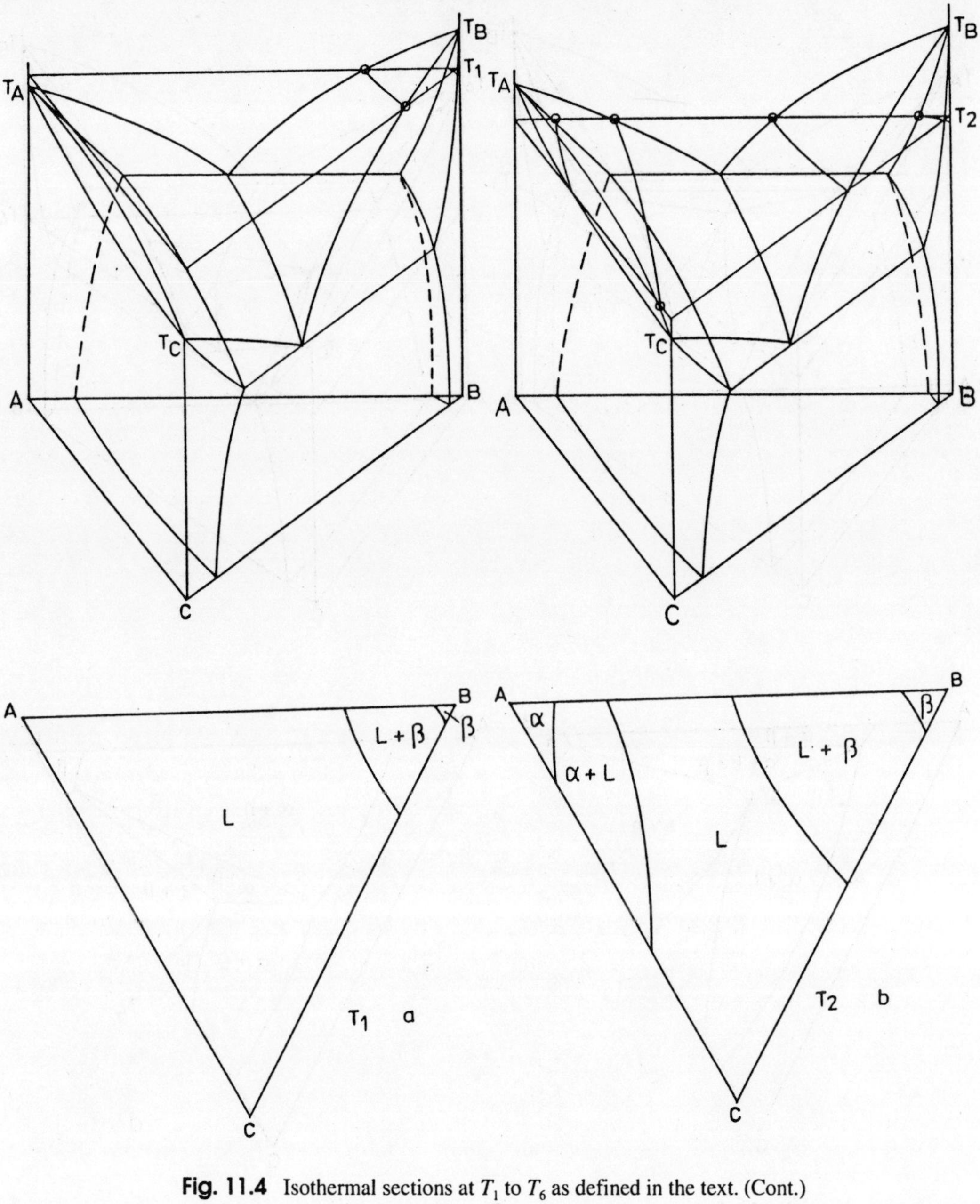

Fig. 11.4 Isothermal sections at T_1 to T_6 as defined in the text. (Cont.)

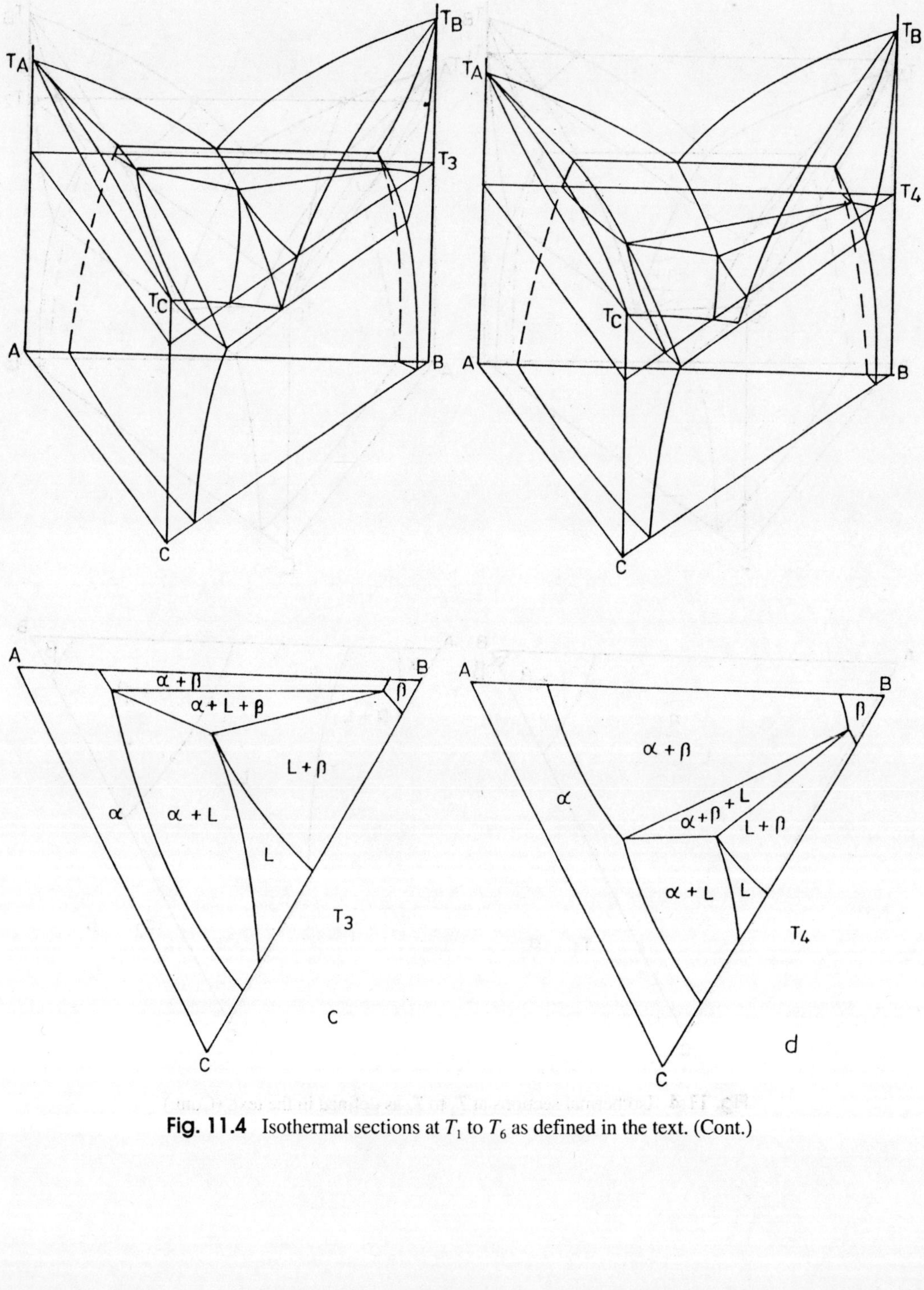

Fig. 11.4 Isothermal sections at T_1 to T_6 as defined in the text. (Cont.)

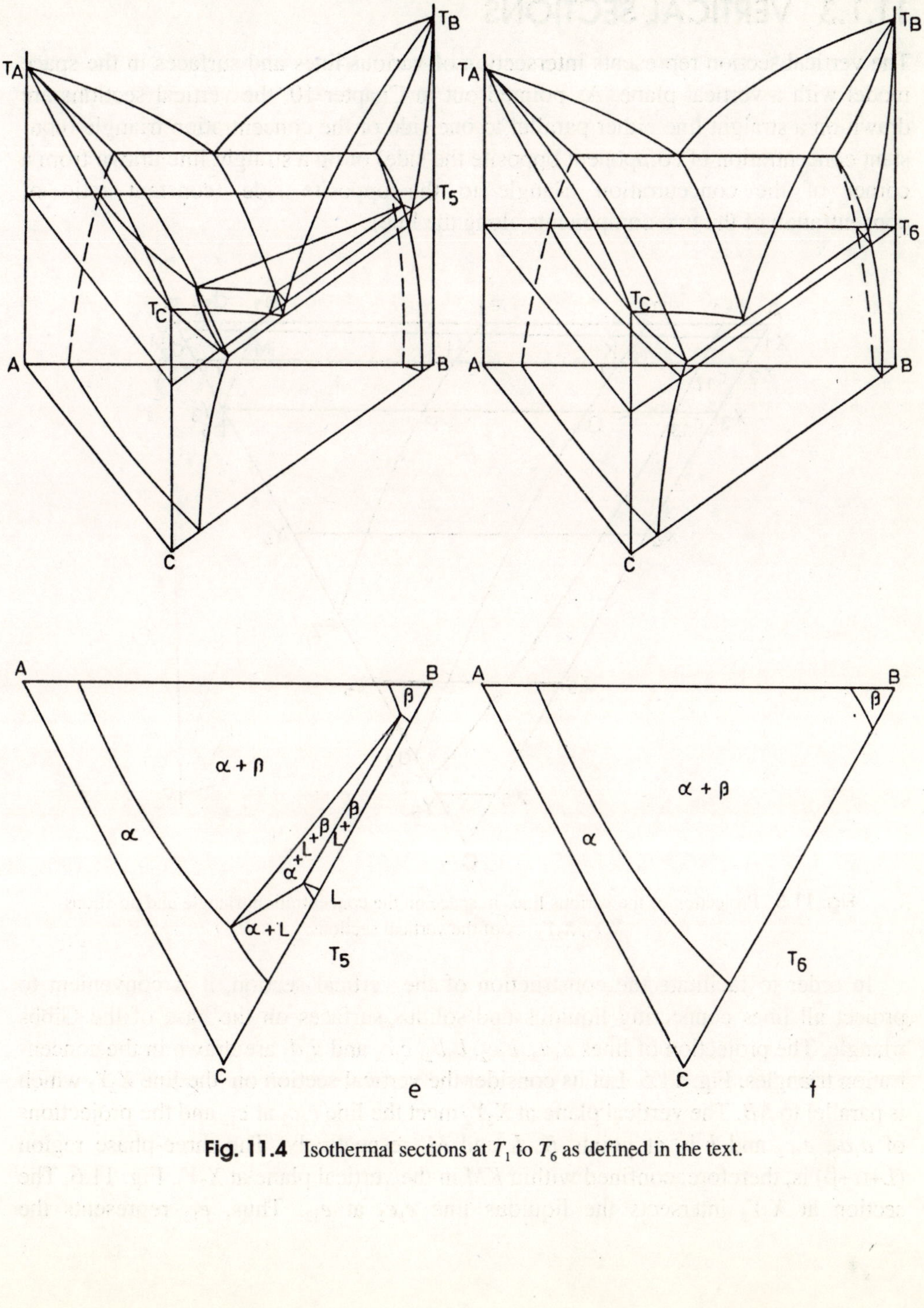

Fig. 11.4 Isothermal sections at T_1 to T_6 as defined in the text.

11.1.3 VERTICAL SECTIONS

The vertical section represents intersection of various lines and surfaces in the space model with a vertical plane. As pointed out in Chapter 10, the vertical sections are drawn on a straight line either parallel to one side of the concentration triangle (constant concentration of component opposite the side) or on a straight line drawn from a corner of the concentration triangle to the opposite side (constant ratio of concentration of the two components along the line).

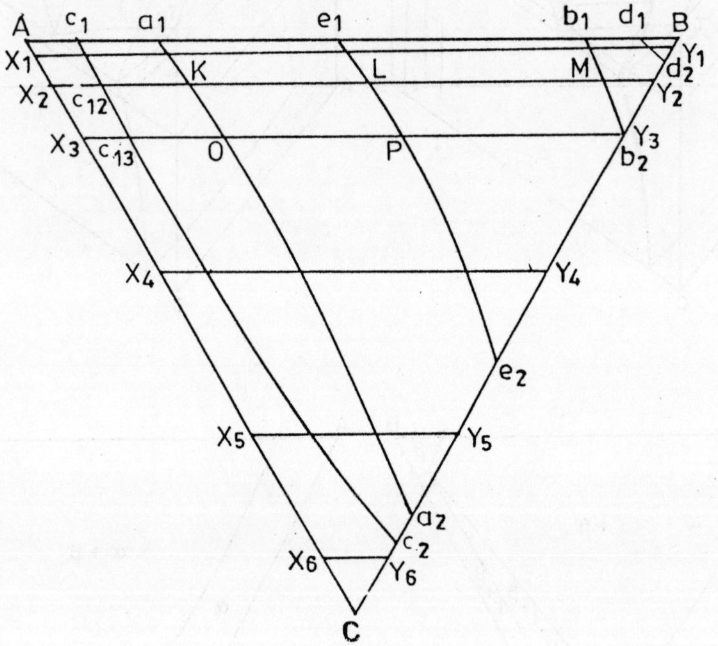

Fig. 11.5 Projection of the various lines in space on the concentration triangle and positions X_1Y_1, X_2Y_2 . . . of the vertical sections.

In order to facilitate the construction of the vertical section, it is convenient to project all lines connecting liquidus and solidus surfaces on the base of the Gibbs triangle. The projection of lines a_1a_2, e_1e_2, b_1b_2, c_1c_2 and d_1d_2 are drawn in the concentration triangles, Fig. 11.5. Let us consider the vertical section on the line X_2Y_2 which is parallel to AB. The vertical plane at X_2Y_2 meet the line c_1c_2 at c_{12} and the projections of a_1a_2, e_1e_2 and b_1b_2 at points K, L and M, respectively. The three-phase region (L+α+β) is, therefore, confined within KM in the vertical plane at X_2Y_2, Fig. 11.6. The section at X_2Y_2 intersects the liquidus line e_1e_2 at e_{12}. Thus, e_{12} represents the

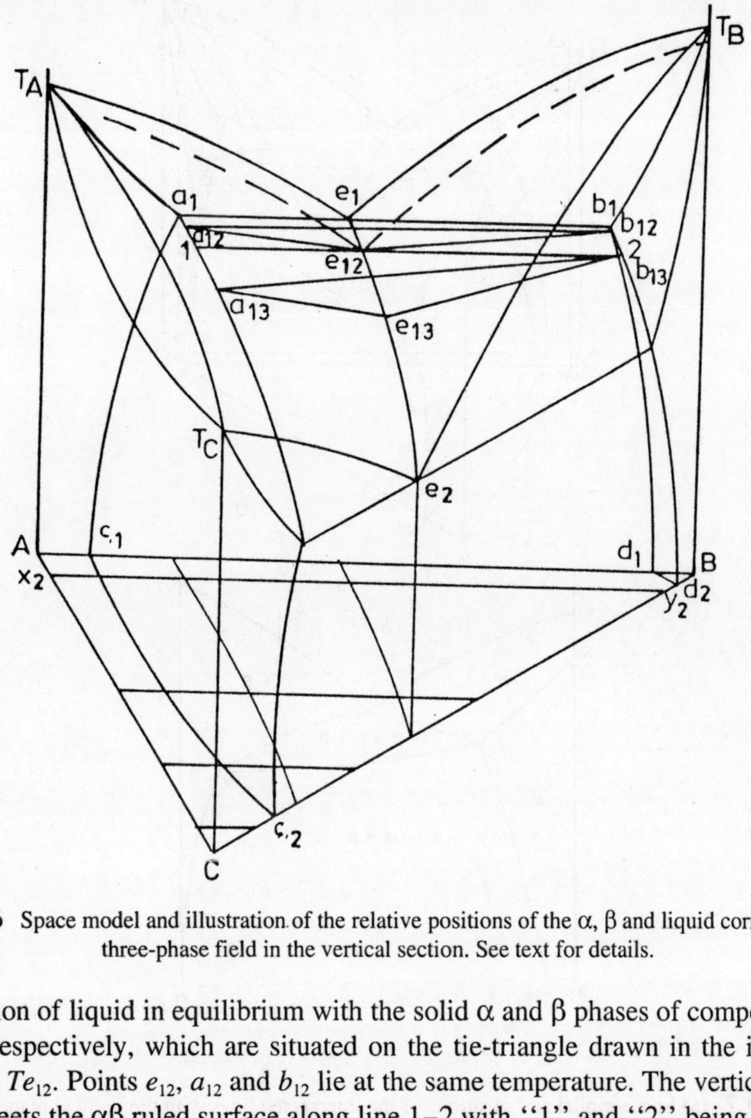

Fig. 11.6 Space model and illustration of the relative positions of the α, β and liquid corners of the three-phase field in the vertical section. See text for details.

composition of liquid in equilibrium with the solid α and β phases of composition a_{12} and b_{12}, respectively, which are situated on the tie-triangle drawn in the isothermal section at Te_{12}. Points e_{12}, a_{12} and b_{12} lie at the same temperature. The vertical section at X_2Y_2 meets the αβ ruled surface along line 1–2 with "1" and "2" being the points of intersection with lines a_1a_2 and b_1b_2, respectively. Since the binary eutectic isotherm a_1b_1 is at a higher temperature than a_2b_2, there is a gentle slope from a_1b_1 to a_2b_2. The point a_{12}, therefore, lies at a higher temperature than point "1" and since e_{12} lies at the same temperature as a_{12}, the intersection point of the vertical plane with e_1e_2 also lies above point "1". Since point "1" represents the composition of the α phase

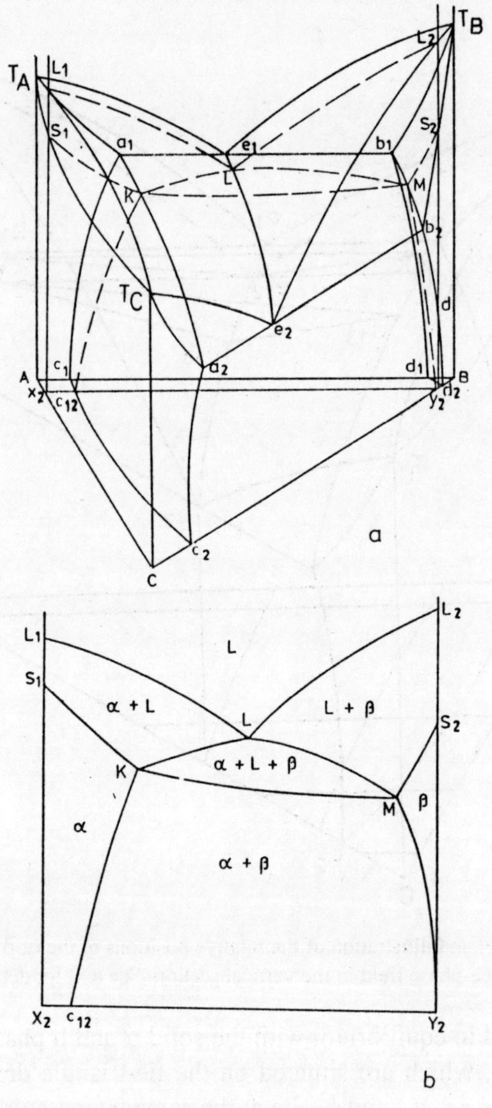

Fig. 11.7 (a) Space model and positions of the intersected lines with the vertical plane at X_2Y_2 (b) The vertical section at X_2Y_2.

along the three-phase region, it lies at a lower temperature than point e_{12}. The point marked "2" is a point of intersection of the vertical plane with line b_1b_2. The isothermal section at point "2" meets lines e_1e_2 and a_1a_2 at e_{13} and a_{13}, respectively, as shown in Fig. 11.6. The point marked "2" (b_{13}) lies at the same temperature as a_{13} and since this lies at a lower temperature than point "1", point b_{13} also lies at a lower temperature than point "1" and a_{12}. Thus, the composition of the β phase of the monovariant equilibrium will lie at a lower temperature than those of the α and liquid phases. The three-phase region will be bounded by a triangular field *KLM* in the vertical section. This is shown in the space model of Fig. 11.7a and the vertical section in Fig. 11.7b.

The ordinate at point X_2 meets the liquidus and solidus curves of the binary *AC* at L_1 and S_1, respectively. The vertical section will meet the liquidus and solidus surfaces of the (α+*L*) phase region along L_1L and S_1K, respectively, as shown in Fig. 11.7a and b. Similarly, the ordinate at Y_2 meets the liquidus and solidus curves of the binary *BC* at L_2 and S_2, respectively. The vertical section at X_2Y_2 will, therefore, meet the liquidus and solidus surface of the (*L*+β) region along L_2L and S_2M, respectively. The vertical section meets the α/(α+β) solvus along Kc_{12} and the β/(α+β) solvus along *Md* as shown. The α phase field lies to the left of Kc_{12} and the β phase field to the right of *Md*. These single-phase regions are separated by the (α+β) phase region.

The vertical section at X_1Y_1 is shown in Fig. 11.8a. The diagram is very similar to that shown in Fig. 11.7b except for the β phase field which continues all the way to the ambient temperature. The intersection of the vertical plane at X_1Y_1 with the αβ, α*L* and β*L* ruled surfaces will show a smaller tilt as compared to those shown in Fig. 11.7b for section at X_2Y_2.

The vertical section at X_3Y_3 meets the α–α, *L*–*L* and β–β lines at position *O*, *P* and Y_3, respectively, in the projection. The three-phase region (*L*+α+β) will be confined within OPY_3' in space, as shown in Fig. 11.9a. Since the β–β line terminates at the point b_2 and the ordinate at Y_3 coincides with b_2, the three-phase field will terminate at b_2. The β-phase region will not appear in the section at X_3Y_3, as shown in Fig. 11.8c. The line of intersection of the vertical plane with the αβ, *L*α and *L*β ruled surfaces will be tilted more, relative to that shown at X_2Y_2. The temperatures at which the various lines in space intersect decrease as the section moves away from the binary line *AB*, because the liquidus slopes down from e_1 to e_2 and *C* is the lowest melting component in this ternary system. The section at X_4Y_4, shown in Fig. 11.8d, is very similar to that drawn at X_3Y_3.

The vertical section at X_5Y_5 does not meet the projection of the line e_1e_2. However, this vertical section does meet the three-phase field which will appear as a closed loop instead of a triangular region, Fig. 11.8e. The liquidus line will be continuous across the section with a gentle change in curvature. The same section is shown in the space model of Fig. 11.9c.

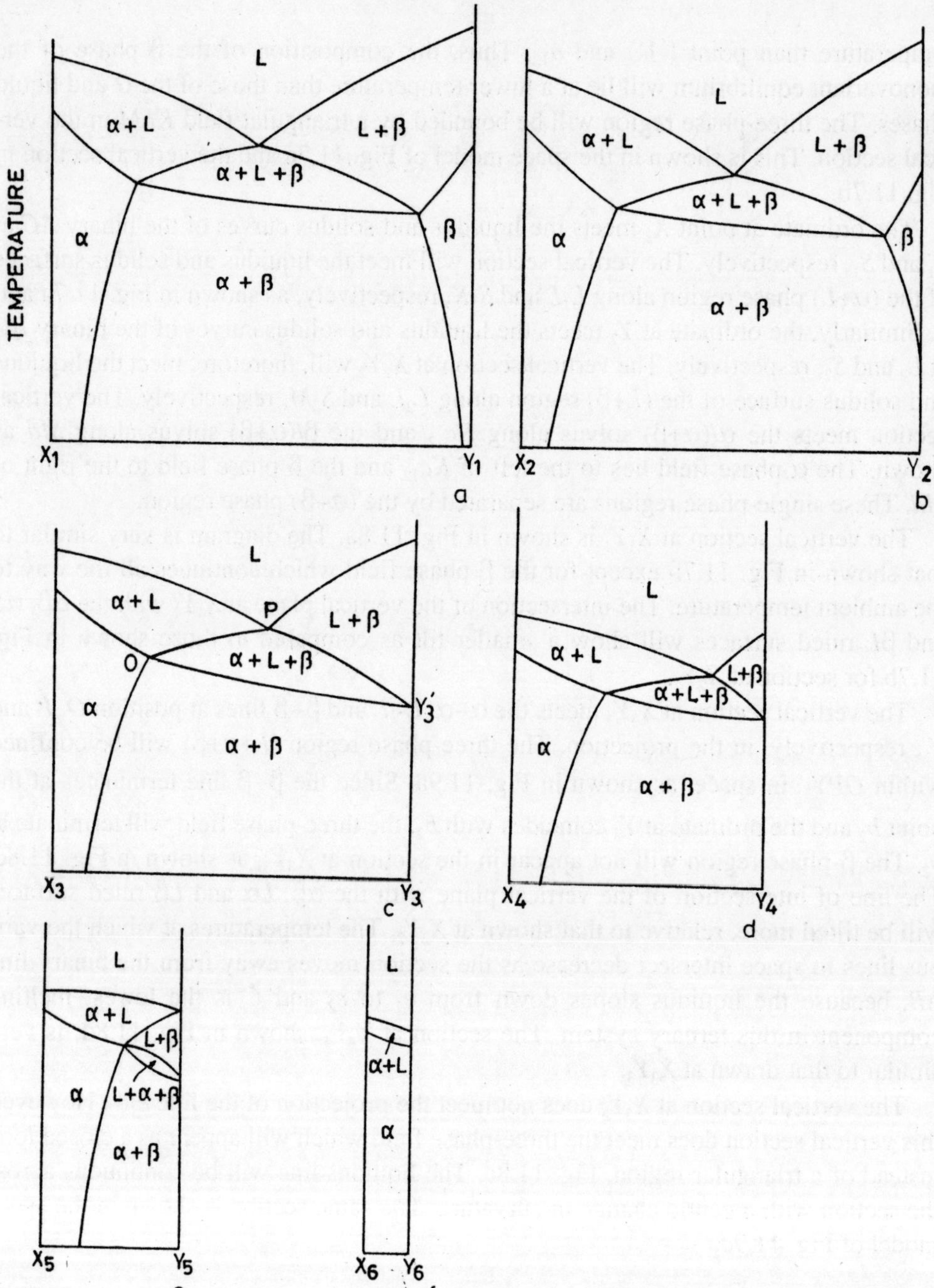

Fig. 11.8 Vertical sections at (a) X_1Y_1 (b) X_2Y_2 (c) X_3Y_3 (d) X_4Y_4 (e) X_5Y_5 and (f) X_6Y_6.

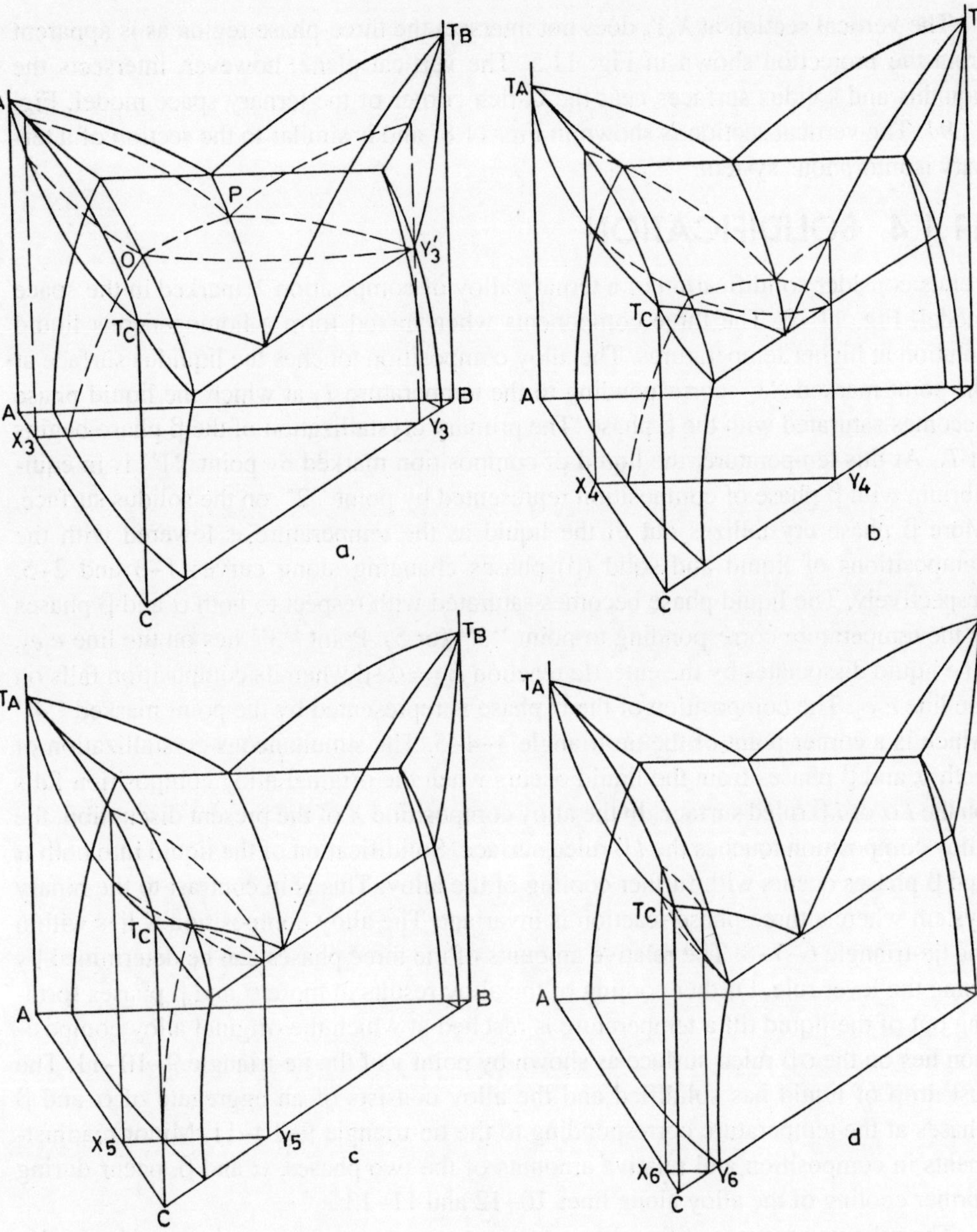

Fig. 11.9 Space models and positions of the lines of intersection with the liquidus, solidus and solvus surfaces and the vertical planes at (a) X_3Y_3 (b) X_4Y_4 (c) X_5Y_5 (d) X_6Y_6.

The vertical section at X_6Y_6 does not intersect the three-phase region as is apparent from the projection shown in Fig. 11.5. The vertical plane, however, intersects the liquidus and solidus surfaces near the C-rich corner of the ternary space model, Fig. 11.9d. The vertical section is shown in Fig. 11.8f and is similar to the section of a ternary isomorphous system.

11.1.4 SOLIDIFICATION

Let us consider solidification of a ternary alloy of composition X marked in the space model, Fig. 11.10. The three components when mixed form a homogeneous liquid solution at higher temperatures. The alloy composition touches the liquidus surface at the point marked "1" corresponding to the temperature T_1 at which the liquid phase becomes saturated with the β phase. The primary crystallization of the β phase begins at T_1. At this temperature, the liquid of composition marked by point "1" is in equilibrium with β phase of composition represented by point "2" on the solidus surface. More β phase crystallizes out of the liquid as the temperature is lowered with the compositions of liquid and solid (β) phases changing along curves 1–3 and 2–5, respectively. The liquid phase becomes saturated with respect to both α and β phases at the temperature corresponding to point "3" (or 5). Point "3" lies on the line e_1e_2. The liquid dissociates by the eutectic reaction $L = \alpha+\beta$ when its composition falls on the line e_1e_2. The composition of the α phase is represented by the point marked "4" which is a corner point of the tie-triangle 3–4–5. The simultaneous crystallization of both α and β phases from the liquid occurs when the original alloy composition falls on the $L\alpha$ or $L\beta$ ruled surface. In the alloy composition X of the present discussion, the alloy composition touches the $L\beta$ ruled surface. Solidification of the liquid into both α and β phases occurs with further cooling of the alloy. This is in contrast to the binary system where a three-phase reaction is invariant. The alloy composition X lies within the tie-triangle 6–7–8. The relative amounts of the three phases can be determined by using the lever rule. Further cooling of the alloy results in more α and β phases forming out of the liquid till a temperature is reached at which the original alloy composition lies on the αβ ruled surface as shown by point y of the tie-triangle 9–10–11. The last drop of liquid has solidified and the alloy consists of an aggregate of α and β phases at the temperature corresponding to the tie-triangle 9–10–11. Minor readjustments in composition and relative amounts of the two phases, α and β, occur during further cooling of the alloy along lines 10–12 and 11–13.

The relative amounts of the phases at any temperature can be calculated by applying the lever rule in the appropriate two or three-phase fields of the isothermal section in Fig. 11.11. The composition vertical at X lies on the liquidus surface at the

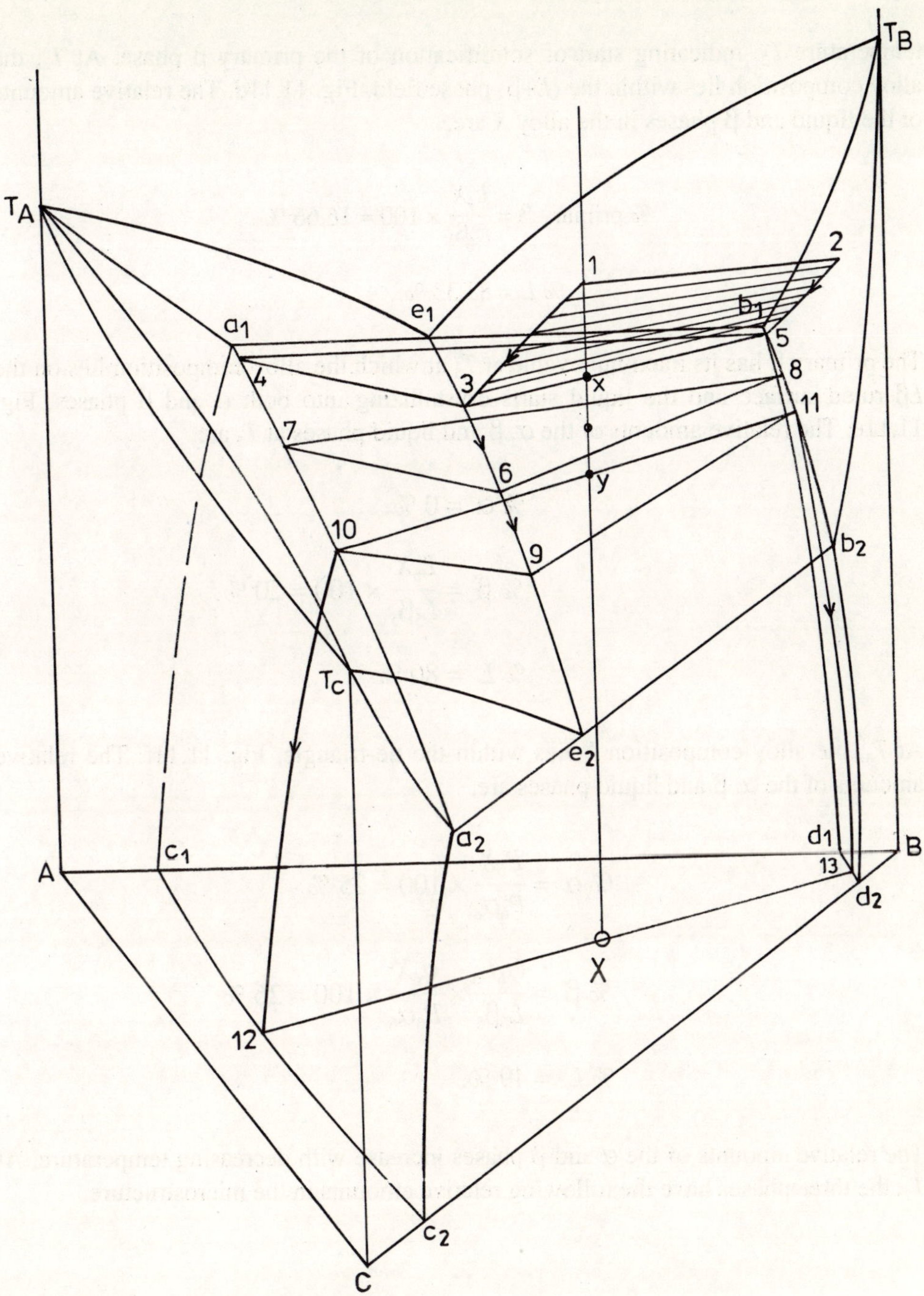

Fig. 11.10 Space model illustrating solidification of an alloy X.

temperature T_3, indicating start of solidification of the primary β phase. At T_4, the alloy composition lies within the $(L+\beta)$ phase field, Fig. 11.11d. The relative amounts of the liquid and β phases in the alloy X are,

$$\% \text{ primary } \beta = \frac{L_4X}{L_4\beta_4} \times 100 = 16.66 \%$$

$$\% L = 83.33 \%.$$

The primary β has its maximum value at T_5 at which the alloy composition lies on the $L\beta$ ruled surface and the liquid starts crystallizing into both α and β phases, Fig. 11.11e. The relative amounts of the α, β and liquid phases at T_5 are,

$$\% \alpha = 0 \%$$

$$\% \beta = \frac{L_5X}{L_5\beta_5} \times 100 = 20 \%$$

$$\% L = 80 \%.$$

At T_6, the alloy composition X lies within the tie-triangle, Fig. 11.11f. The relative amounts of the α, β and liquid phases are,

$$\% \alpha = \frac{P_6X}{P_6\alpha_6} \times 100 = 25 \%$$

$$\% \beta = \frac{O_6L_6}{L_6\beta_6} \times \frac{\alpha_6X}{P_6\alpha_6} \times 100 = 26 \%$$

$$\% L = 49 \%.$$

The relative amounts of the α and β phases increase with decreasing temperature. At T_7, the three phases have the following relative amounts in the microstructure,

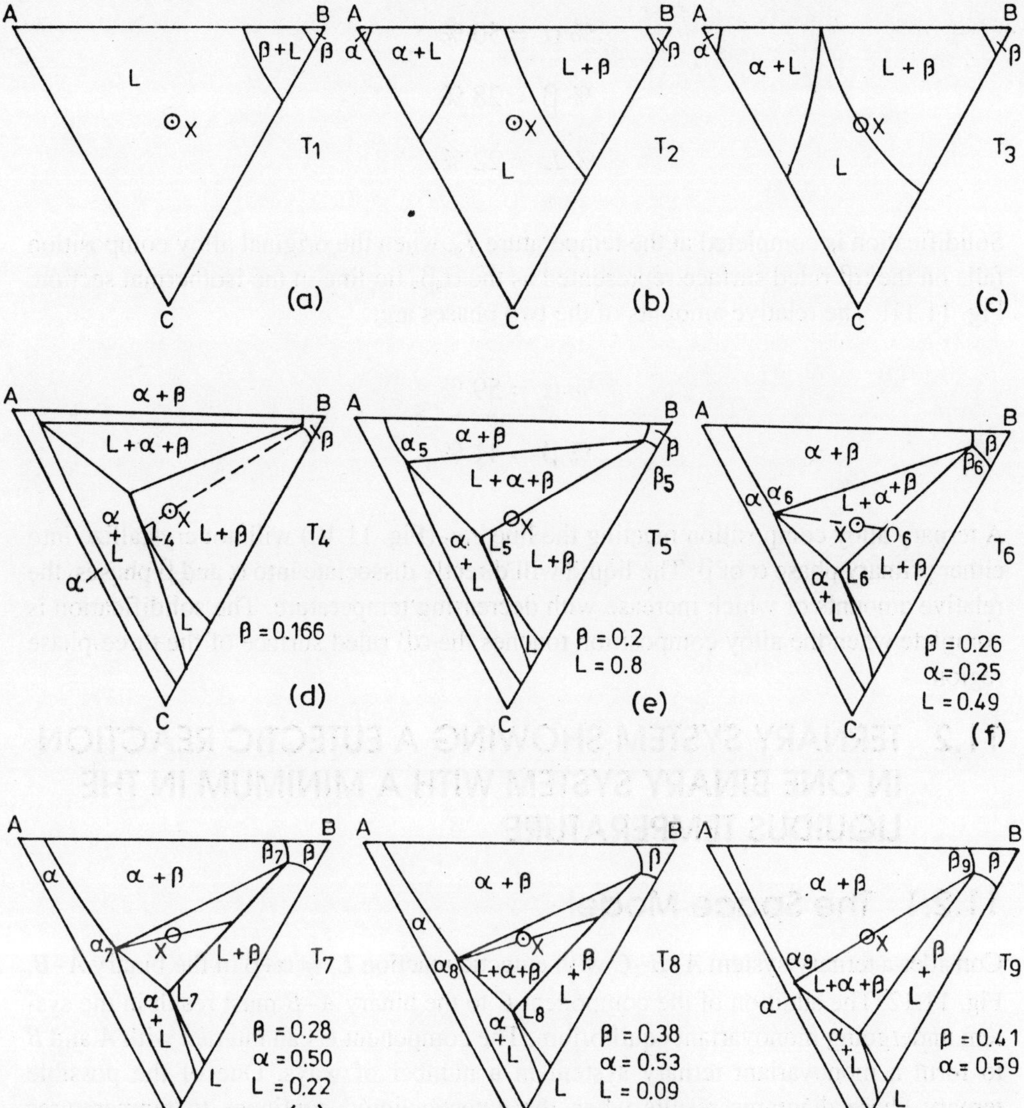

Fig. 11.11 Isothermal section through the space model of Fig. 11.2 governing relative amounts of the α, β and liquid phases in an alloy composition *X*.

$$\% \alpha = 50 \%$$

$$\% \beta = 28 \%$$

$$\% L = 22 \%.$$

Solidification is completed at the temperature T_9, when the original alloy composition falls on the $\alpha\beta$ ruled surface represented as the $\alpha_9\beta_9$ tie-line in the isothermal section, Fig. 11.11i. The relative amounts of the two phases are,

$$\% \alpha = 59 \%$$

$$\% \beta = 41 \%$$

A ternary alloy composition meeting the line e_1e_2 (Fig. 11.10) will not crystallize into either primary phase α or β. The liquid will directly dissociate into α and β phases, the relative amounts of which increase with decreasing temperature. The solidification is complete when the alloy composition touches the $\alpha\beta$ ruled surface of the three-phase region.

11.2 TERNARY SYSTEM SHOWING A EUTECTIC REACTION IN ONE BINARY SYSTEM WITH A MINIMUM IN THE LIQUIDUS TEMPERATURE

11.2.1 The Space Model

Consider a ternary system A–B–C with eutectic reaction $L \rightleftharpoons \alpha+\beta$ in the binary A–B, Fig. 11.12. The addition of the component C to the binary A–B must result in the system undergoing monovariant equilibrium. The component C can interact with A and B to form a monovariant ternary system in a number of ways. One of the possible ternary phase diagrams results when the eutectic liquid continues to temperatures below the binary eutectic isotherm and terminates at a minimum point e_1. The α and β phases are distinct just below T_e, however, the compositions of the two phases approach each other as the temperature is lowered. The α and β phases become indistinguishable at the temperature Te_1. Point c_1 on the curve ac_1b represents the critical composition at which the two phases are indistinguishable. The line e_1c_1 is a degenerate tie-triangle. The three-phase region is formed by the ruled surfaces abc_1 ($\alpha\beta$), $aee_1\,c_1$ (αL) and $bee_1\,c_1$ (βL). Further details of the other phase regions are given in Table 11.2. The tie-lines S_1L_1 and S_2L_2 (L_2 is not shown) on the binary isomorphous systems *A–C* and *B–C*, respectively, are at the same temperature as e_1c_1. Below Tc_1, there is a critical composition at each temperature at which the α and β phases become indistinguishable. The critical composition lies on the line c_1c_2. The α and β phases have a distinct identity within the plane *bacd* and surfaces acc_2c_1 and bdc_2c_1. Elsewhere, they exist as a continuous series of solid solutions or as a single-phase α (β).

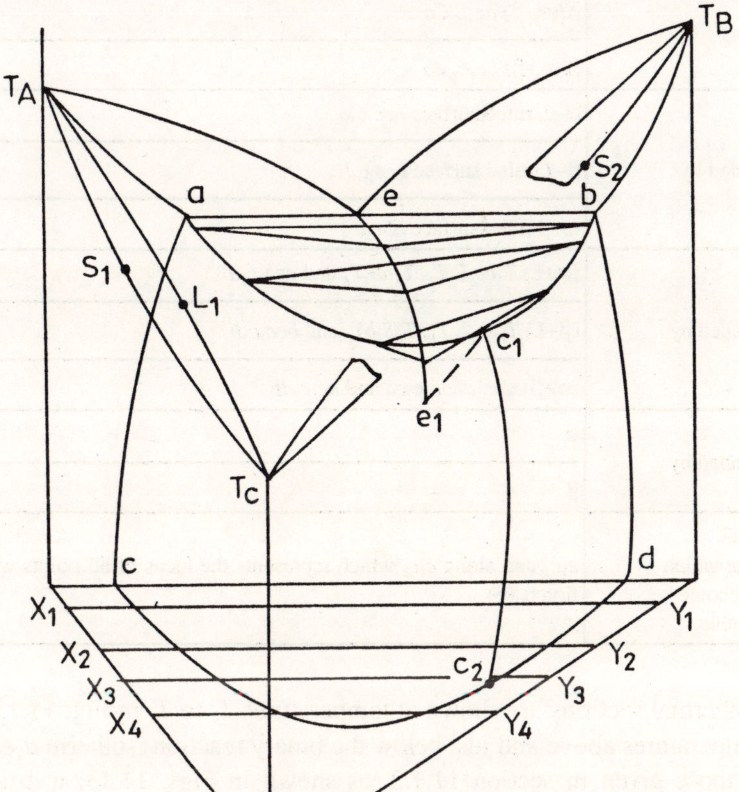

Fig. 11.12 Ternary space model showing a eutectic reaction on the side *A–B* and a minimum critical point on the monovariant liquid curve.

Table 11.2

Liquidus Surface	$L/(L+\beta)$ $T_Bee_1L_2T_B$
	$L/(L+\alpha)$ T_Aee_1 L_1T_A and $L_1L_2T_C$
Solidus Surface	$\beta/(L+\beta)$ $T_BbS_2T_B$
	$\alpha/(L+\alpha)$ $T_AaS_1T_A$ and $S_1T_CS_2S_1$
Solvus Surface	$\alpha/(\alpha+\beta)$ ac_1c_2Ca
	$\beta/(\alpha+\beta)$ bc_1c_2 db
Three-Phase Region bounded by	α–L ruled surface aee_1c_1a
	β–L ruled surface bee_1c_1b
	α–β ruled surface abc_1a
Two-Phase Regions bounded by	$(\alpha+L)$ $T_Aee_1L_1T_A$, $T_AaS_1T_A$ and aee_1c_1a
	$(\beta+L)$ $T_Bee_1L_2T_B$, $T_BS_2bT_B$ and bee_1c_1b
	$(\alpha+\beta)$ abc_1a, ac_1c_2ca and bc_1c_2db
Single-Phase Regions bounded by	α –
	β –
Line of critical temperature at which two phases become indistinguishable	e_1c_1 and along c_1c_2 which represents the locus of all points with composition α (β)

The isothermal sections are shown at temperatures T_1 to T_7 in Fig. 11.13. The sections at temperatures above and just below the binary reaction isotherm a_1eb_1 are very similar to those given in section 11.1.2, as shown in Figs. 11.13, a, b and c. The three-phase region appears just below T_e, Fig. 11.13c. Since the compositions of the α and β phases approach each other as the temperature decreases, there is a tendency the three-phase region ($\alpha+\beta+L$) to shrink gradually, Fig. 11.13d. At the temperature Te_1, the $\alpha\beta$ tie-line shrinks to a point (c_1). The indistinguishable α (β) is in equilibrium with the liquid of composition e_1 as shown in the isothermal section at the temperature T_5, Fig. 11.13e. At temperatures below T_5, the α and β phases are distinct only in a restricted composition range.

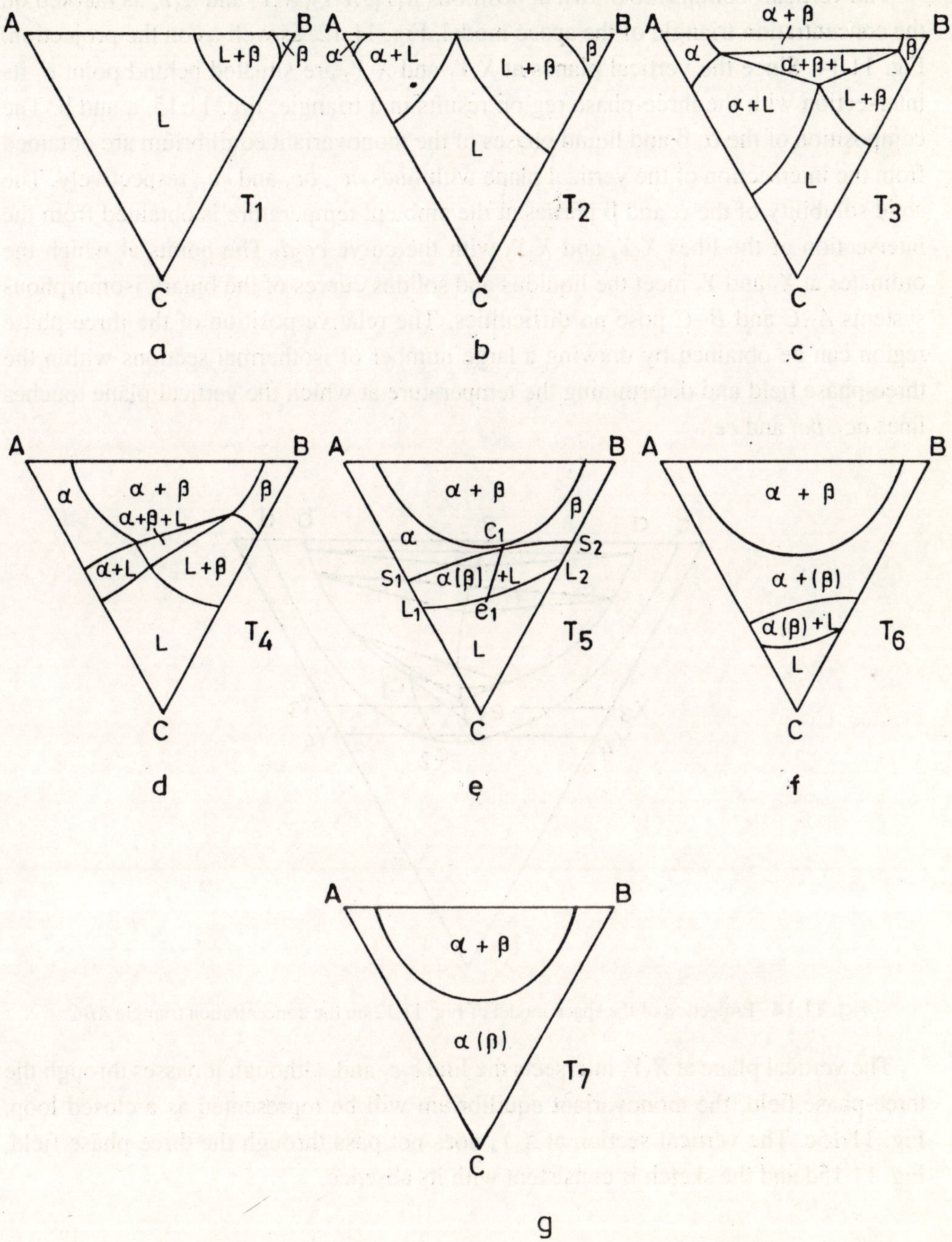

Fig. 11.13 Isothermal sections through the space model of Fig. 11.12.

The vertical sections are drawn at positions X_1Y_1, X_2Y_2, X_3Y_3 and X_4Y_4 as marked on the concentration triangle of the space model, Fig. 11.12, as well as on the projection, Fig. 11.14. Since the vertical planes at X_1Y_1 and X_2Y_2 are situated behind point c_1 its intersection with the three-phase region results in a triangle, Fig. 11.15, a and b. The composition of the α, β and liquid phases of the monovariant equilibrium are obtained from the intersection of the vertical plane with lines ac_1, bc_1 and ee_1, respectively. The solid solubility of the α and β phases at the ambient temperature is obtained from the intersection of the lines X_1Y_1 and X_2Y_2 with the curve cc_2d. The points at which the ordinates at X_1 and Y_1 meet the liquidus and solidus curves of the binary isomorphous systems A–C and B–C pose no difficulties. The relative position of the three-phase region can be obtained by drawing a large number of isothermal sections within the three-phase field and determining the temperature at which the vertical plane touches lines ac_1, bc_1 and ee_1.

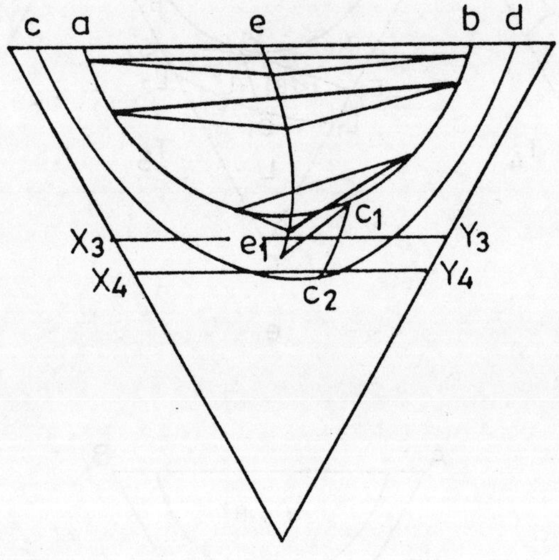

Fig. 11.14 Projection of the space model of Fig. 11.12 on the concentration triangle ABC.

The vertical plane at X_3Y_3 intersects the line e_1c_1 and, although it passes through the three-phase field, the monovariant equilibrium will be represented as a closed loop, Fig. 11.15c. The vertical section at X_4Y_4 does not pass through the three-phase field, Fig. 11.15d and the sketch is consistent with its absence.

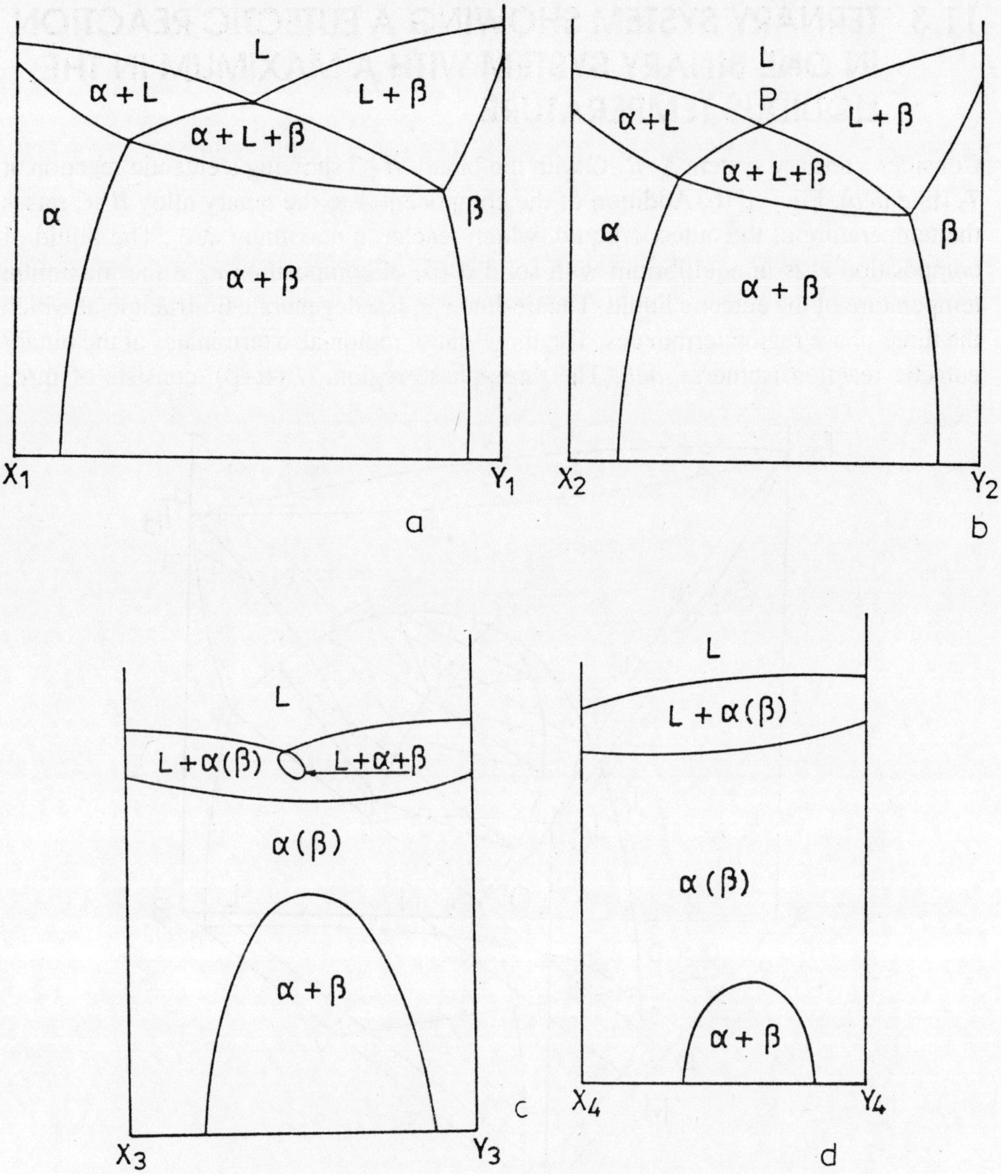

Fig. 11.15 Vertical sections through the space model of Fig. 11.12. The locations of the vertical section are shown in Fig. 11.12.

11.3 TERNARY SYSTEM SHOWING A EUTECTIC REACTION IN ONE BINARY SYSTEM WITH A MAXIMUM IN THE LIQUIDUS TEMPERATURE

Consider a ternary system *A–B–C* with the binary *B–C* showing a eutectic reaction at T_e (line *aeb*), Fig. 11.16. Addition of the component *A* to the binary alloy *B–C* raises the temperature of the eutectic liquid, which reaches a maximum at e_1. The liquid of composition e_1 is in equilibrium with solid α (β) of composition c_1 at the maximum temperature of the eutectic liquid. The tie-line e_1c_1 is a degenerate tie-triangle at which the three-phase region terminates. The three-phase region also terminates at the binary eutectic reaction isotherm, *aeb*. The three-phase region, (*L*+α+β), consists of three

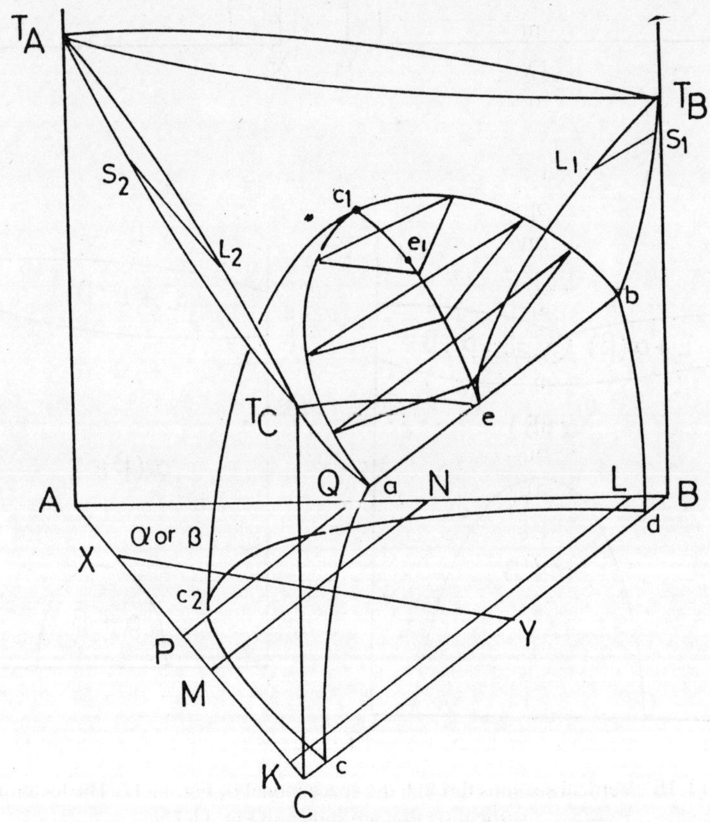

Fig. 11.16 Ternary space model *A–B–C* showing a eutectic reaction on the binary *B–C* and a maximum critical point on the monovariant liquid curve.

ruled surfaces ac_1b ($\alpha\beta$), $aee_1\ c_1a$ (αL) and $bee_1\ c_1\ b$ (βL) and it is closed along ac_1, bc_1, and ee_1. Other details of the phase diagram are given in Table 11.3. The shape of the three-phase region is evident from a number of tie-triangles drawn within the space diagram of this field.

Table 11.3

Liquidus Surface	$L/(L+\beta)$ $L_1ee_1L_2$
	$L/(L+\alpha)$ $L_2T_Cee_1L_2$
Solidus Surface	$L/(L+\alpha(\beta))$ $T_AT_BL_1e_1L_2T_A$
	$\beta/(L/\beta)$ $S_1bC_1S_1$
	$\alpha/(L+\alpha)$ $S_2T_CaC_1S_2$ α $(\beta)/(L+\alpha\ (\beta))$ $T_AS_2C_1S_1T_BT_A$
Solvus Surface	$\alpha/(\alpha+\beta)$ $C_1acC_2C_1$
	$\beta/(\alpha+\beta)$ $C_1bdC_2C_1$
Three-Phase Region bounded by	α–L ruled surface $C_1e_1eaC_1$
	β–L ruled surface $C_1e_1ebC_1$
	α–β ruled surface aC_1b
Two-Phase Regions bounded by	$(\alpha+L)$ $L_2T_Cee_1L_2$, $S_2T_CaC_1S_2$
	$(\beta+L)$ $L_1ee_1L_2$, $S_2bC_1S_1$
	$(\alpha+\beta)$ $C_1acC_2C_1$, $C_1bdC_2C_1$ and aC_1b
Single-Phase Regions bounded by	α –
	β –
Line of critical temperature at which two phases become indistinguishable	e_1C_1 and along C_1C_2 which represents the locus of all points with composition α (β)

The isothermal plane at e_1c_1 will intersect the lens-shaped figure on the side AC along L_2S_2 and BC along L_1S_1. Point c_1 represents the composition of the alloy at which the α and β phases become indistinguishable. The αβ tie-line of the monovariant equilibrium gradually shortens as the temperature is increased from the binary eutectic reaction isotherm, *aeb*. At the temperature corresponding to c_1e_1, the αβ tie-line vanishes and the tie-triangle becomes a tie-line. The composition of the α and β phases approach each other as the temperatures rises above T_e. The locus of the critical compositions generates the curve c_1c_2 where c_2 lies at the ambient temperature.

The isothermal sections through the space model are shown in Fig. 11.17. The section at $T_2 = Te_1$ shows the degenerate tie-triangle as a tie-line c_1e_1 connecting S_1L_1 and S_2L_2 on the sides *BC* and *AC*, respectively, Fig. 11.17b. The three-phase field (*L*+α+β) begins just below Te_1. The αβ tie-line of the monovariant regicn at T_3 is relatively short but will gain in length as the temperature is lowered, Fig. 11.17, c, d, e and f. The α (β) phase field expands as the temperature is lowered and ultimately becomes continuous from the binary *A–B* to *A–C*.

The vertical sections at *KL*, *MN*, *PQ* and *XY* are shown in Figs. 11.18, a, b, c and d, respectively. The tie-line c_1e_1 lies on the vertical plane at *XY*. It thus appears as a horizontal line on the section and clarifies the shape of the liquidus surface on either side of c_1e_1.

11.4 TERNARY SYSTEM WITH A MAXIMUM OR MINIMUM IN LIQUIDUS TEMPERATURE AND EUTECTIC REACTION IN TWO OF THE BINARIES

Consider a ternary system *A–B–C* with binary systems *A–B* and *B–C* each showing the eutectic reaction. The ternary three-phase field passes through a maximum along *gh*, Fig. 11.19. The ternary monovariant curve e_1e_2 rises above e_1, reaches a maximum at *m* on the line *gh*, and descends below to e_2. The line e_1e_2 separates the α*L* and β*L* ruled surfaces $a_1e_1e_2a_2$ and $b_1e_1e_2b_2$, respectively. Points *g* and *h* lie on lines a_1a_2 and b_1b_2, respectively. The αβ ruled surface $a_1b_1b_2a_2$ also rises above a_1b_1, touches the line *gh* and descends below to a_2b_2. The three-phase field is closed along lines a_1ga_2, b_1hb_2, $a_1e_1b_1$, $a_2e_2b_2$ and *gmh*. Since the monovariant region is also closed along *gmh*, it is divided into two parts along the line *gh*. One part of the three-phase region ascends from the binary eutectic reaction isotherm $a_1e_1b_1$ and terminates along *gh*. The other part ascends from $a_2e_2b_2$ and terminates at the same line *gh*. The bounding surfaces of the three-phase region are:

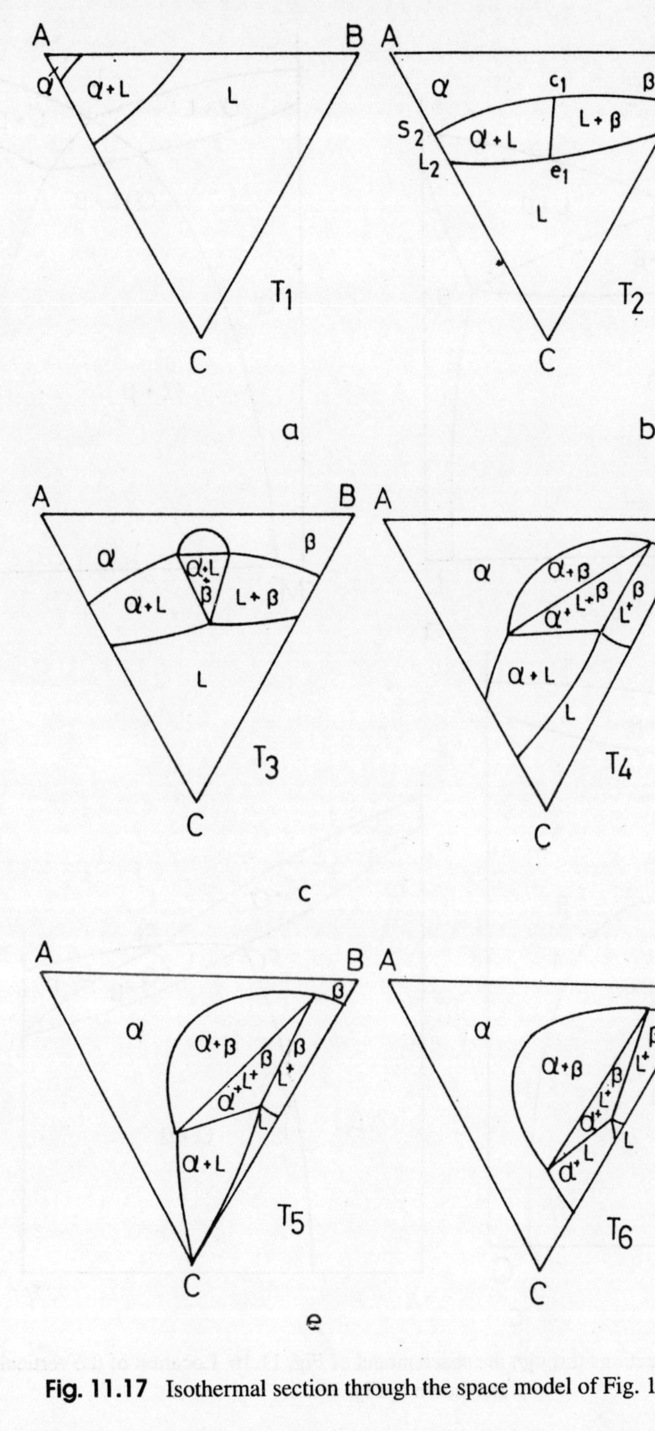

Fig. 11.17 Isothermal section through the space model of Fig. 11.16.

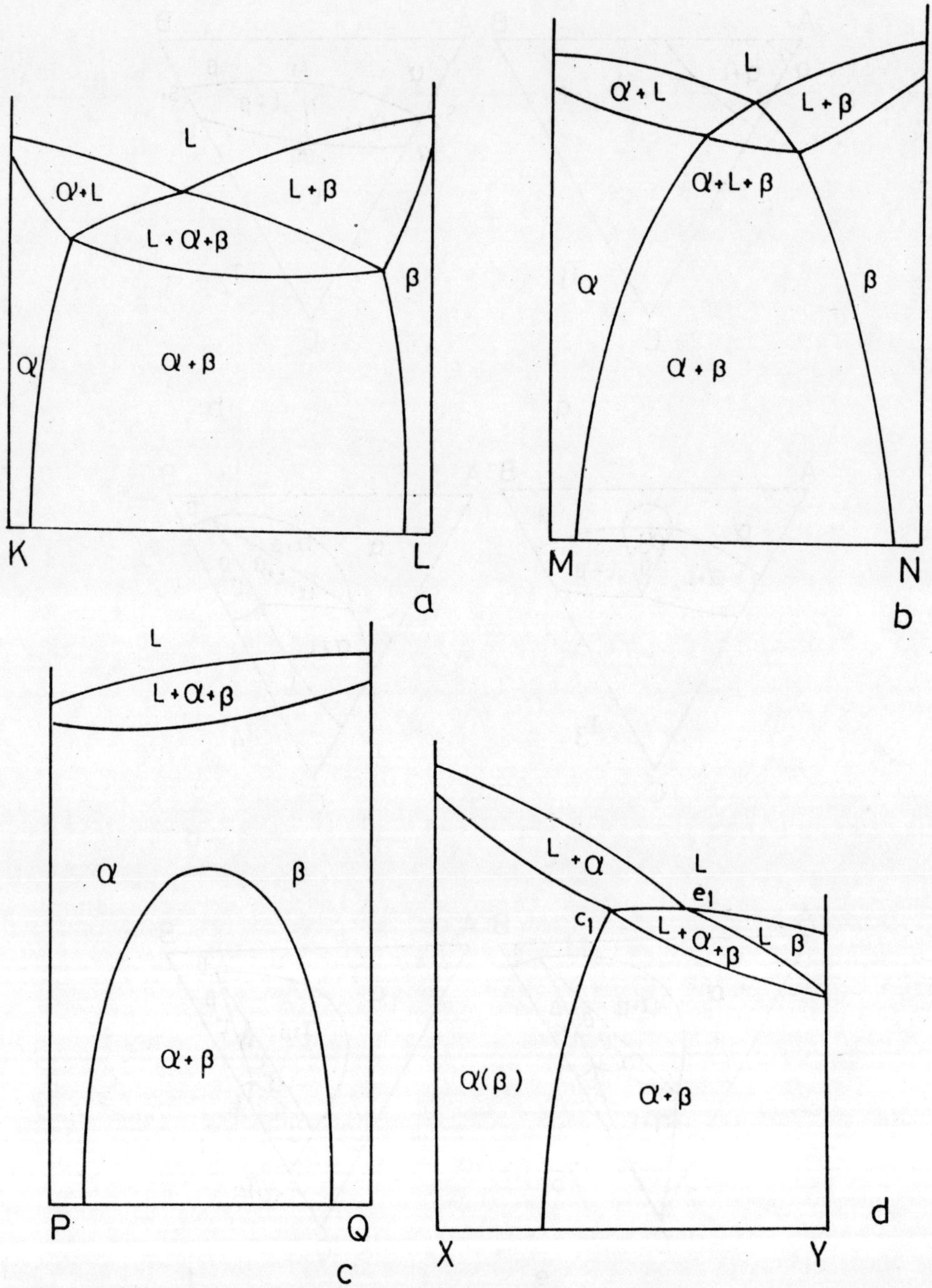

Fig. 11.18 Vertical sections through the space model of Fig. 11.16. Location of the vertical sections are shown in Fig. 11.16.

$$a_1e_1mga_1(\alpha L),\ b_1e_1mhb_1(\beta L) \text{ and } a_1b_1hga_1(\alpha\beta)$$

$$a_2e_2mga_2(\alpha L),\ b_2e_2mhb_2(\beta L) \text{ and } a_2b_2hga_2(\alpha\beta)$$

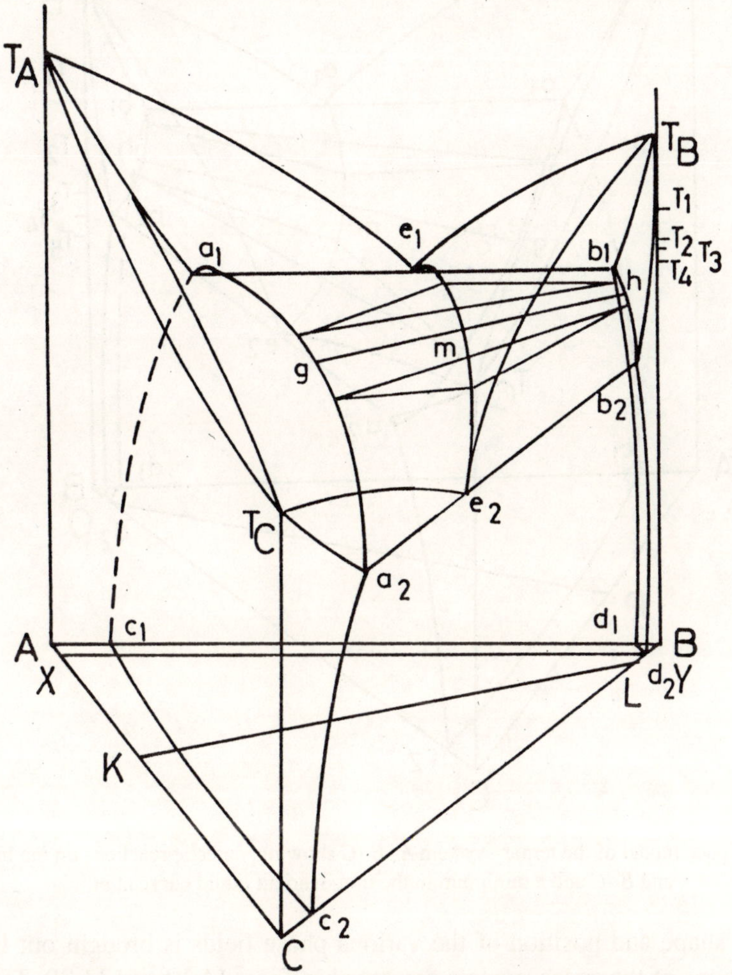

Fig. 11.19 Space model of the ternary system *A–B–C*, showing eutectic reaction on the binaries *A–B* and *B–C* and a maximum in the monovariant liquid curve at *m*.

In the ternary system with a minimum temperature, the monovariant curve e_1e_2 goes through a minimum temperature at *m*, Fig. 11.20. The αβ ruled surface also goes through a minimum along the line *gh* with point *m* lying on *gh*. The three-phase region is also divided into two parts in this variation of the ternary monovariant system.

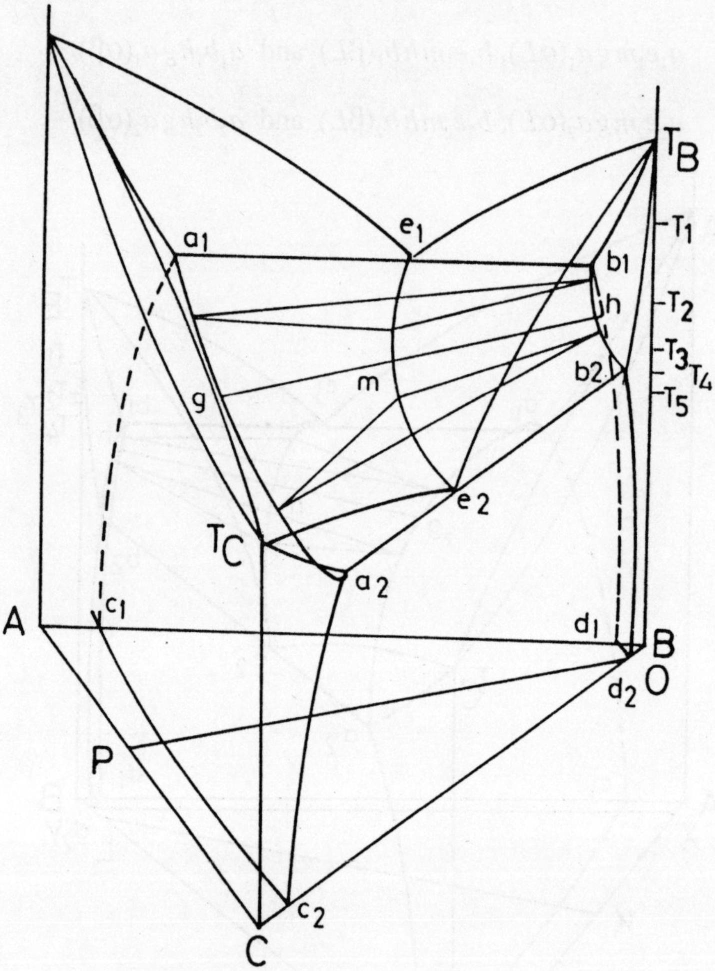

Fig. 11.20 Space model of the ternary system A–B–C showing, eutectic reactions on the binaries A–B and B–C and a minimum in the monovariant liquid curve at m.

The true shape and position of the various phase fields is brought out in the isothermal sections of the space models presented in Figs. 11.19 and 11.20. The isothermal section at the maximum temperature T_m shows that the liquid surface is divided into two parts along e_1e_2 and in contact at the point m, Fig. 11.21. The liquid-phase region L occurs on both sides AB and BC of the point m, Fig. 11.21b. The three-phase region exists on both sides of the common (α+β) phase field at a temperature T_3 just below the maximum temperature, Fig. 11.21c. At a temperature $T_4 < T_3$, the (α+β) phase field expands and the liquid phase field shrinks, as shown in the isothermal

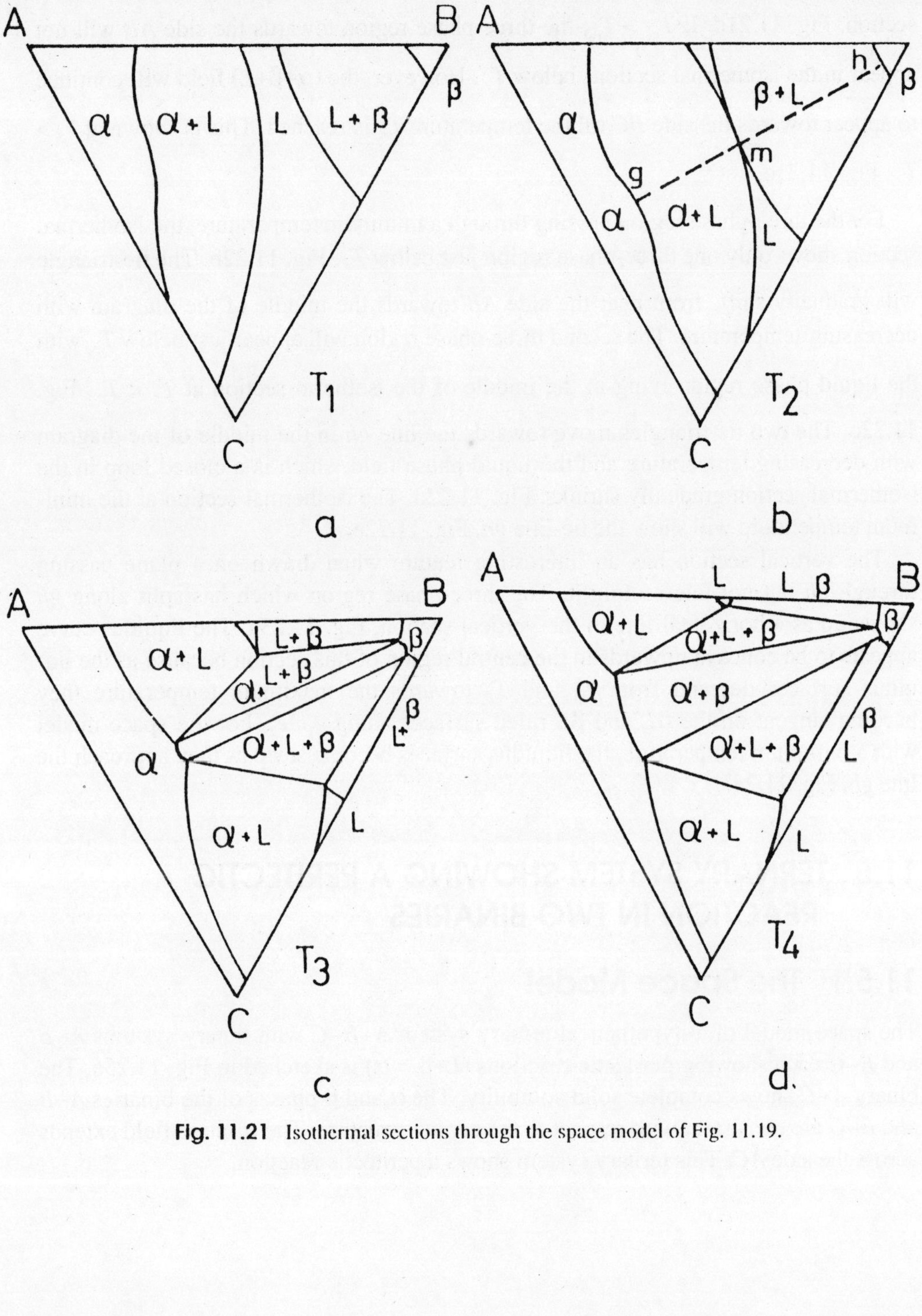

Fig. 11.21 Isothermal sections through the space model of Fig. 11.19.

section, Fig. 11.21d. If $T_{e_1} > T_{e_2}$, the three-phase region towards the side AB will not appear in the isothermal sections below T_{e_1}. However, the (α+β+L) field will continue to appear towards the side BC till the temperature T_{e_2} is reached. This is shown at $T_5 > T_{e_2}$, Fig. 11.21e.

For the three-phase region passing through a minimum temperature, the isothermal section shows only one three-phase region just below T_{e_1}, Fig. 11.22b. The tie-triangle will gradually shift from near the side AB towards the middle of the diagram with decreasing-temperature. The second three-phase region will appear just below T_{e_2} with the liquid phase region lying in the middle of the isotherm section at $T_3 < T_{e_2}$, Fig. 11.22c. The two tie-triangles move towards the line gh in the middle of the diagram with decreasing temperature and the liquid phase field which is a closed loop in the isothermal section gradually shrinks, Fig. 11.22d. The isothermal section at the minimum temperature will show the tie-line gh, Fig. 11.22e.

The vertical section has an interesting feature when drawn on a plane passing through gh but not intersecting it. The three-phase region which has split along gh shows up as a horizontal line in the vertical section, Fig. 11.23a. The liquidus curve appears to be concave upwards in the central region of this section because as the liquidus surfaces descend from T_A and T_B towards the maximum temperature they become tangent on the αL and βL ruled surfaces along e_1me_2. For the space model with a minimum temperature, the liquidus surfaces become steep as they approach the line gh, Fig. 11.24.

11.5 TERNARY SYSTEM SHOWING A PERITECTIC REACTION IN TWO BINARIES

11.5.1 The Space Model

The space model of a hypothetical ternary system A–B–C with binary systems A–B and B–C each showing peritectic reactions (L+β = α) is sketched in Fig. 11.25a. The binary A–C shows complete solid solubility. The α and β phases of the binaries A–B and B–C are consistent with respect to the crystal structure. The α phase field extends across the side AC. This ternary system shows a peritectic reaction.

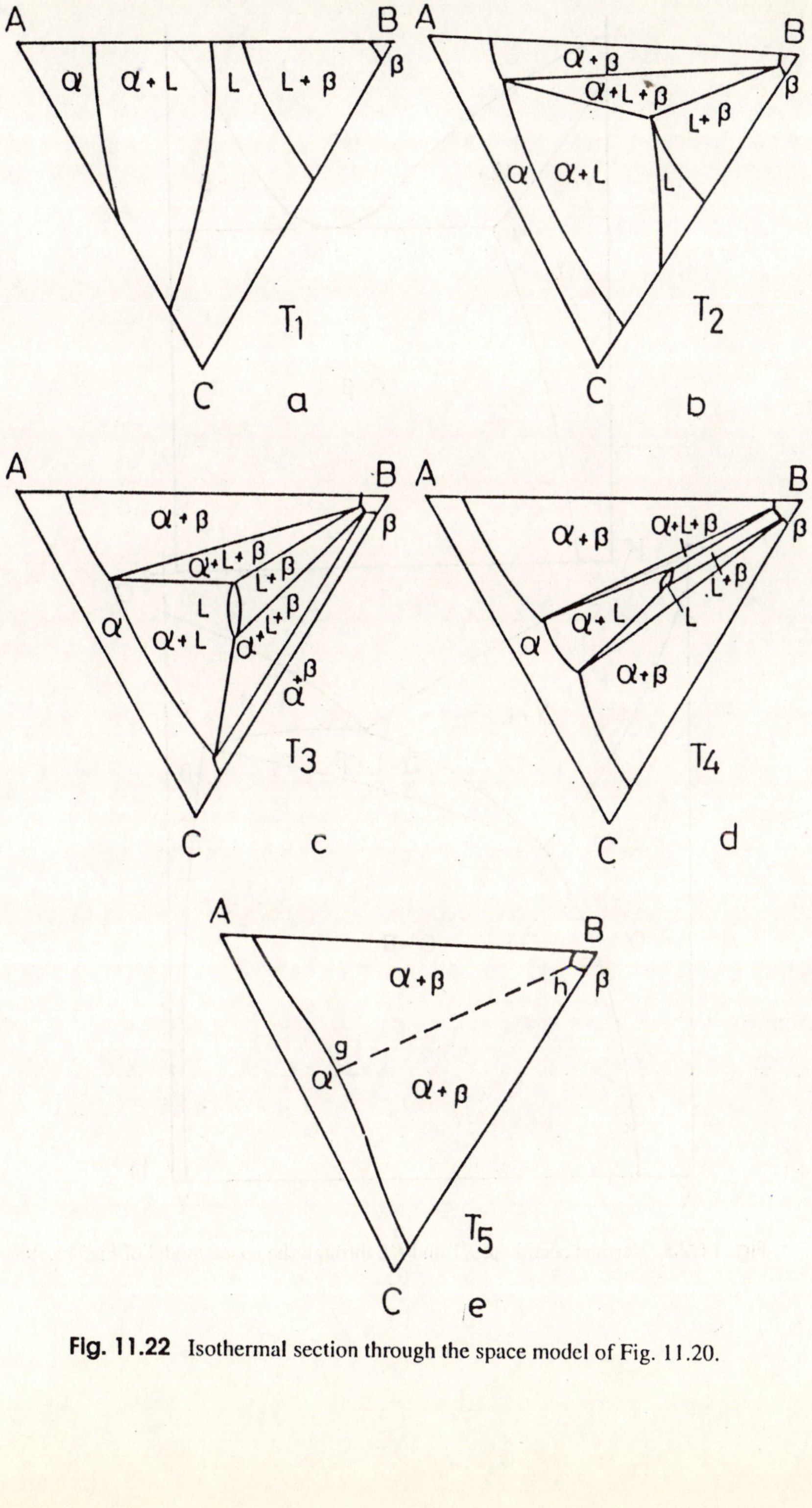

Fig. 11.22 Isothermal section through the space model of Fig. 11.20.

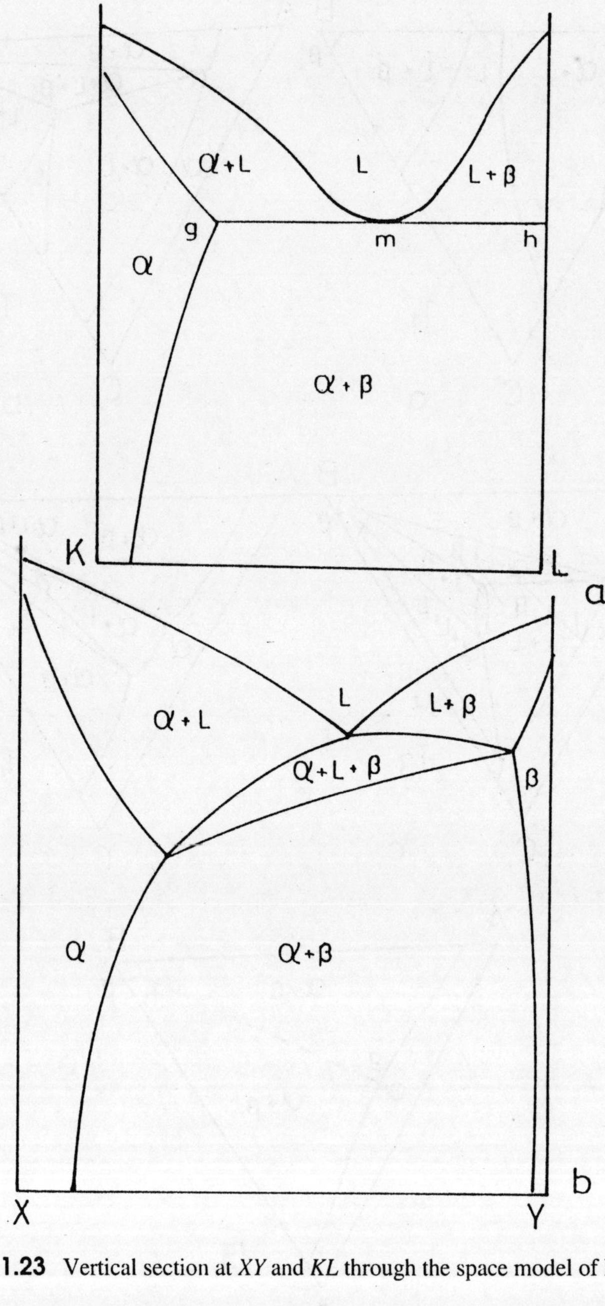

Fig. 11.23 Vertical section at *XY* and *KL* through the space model of Fig. 11.19.

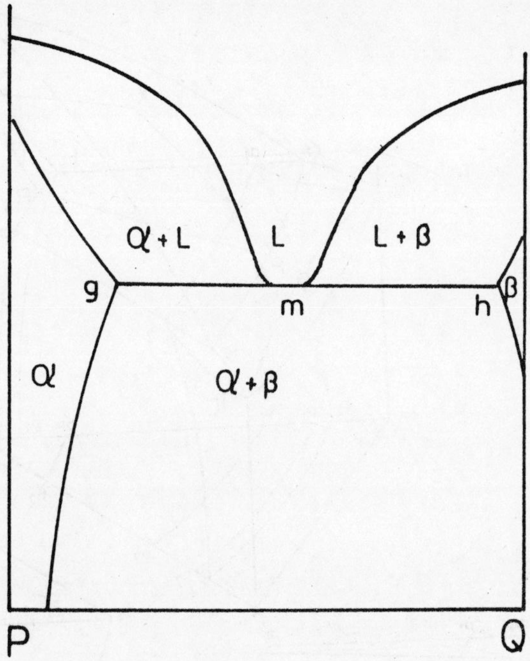

Fig. 11.24 Vertical section at *PQ* through the space model of Fig. 11.20.

The various surfaces and phase fields confining these surfaces are given in Table 11.4. The liquidus consists of two parts. For $T_B > T_{p_1} > T_A > T_{p_2} > T_c$, the liquidus surface $T_Bp_1p_2T_B$ slopes downwards from T_B and terminates on the line p_1p_2. Any ternary composition point lying within $T_Bp_1p_2$ will crystallize into primary β. The second part of the liquidus, $T_Ap_1p_2T_cT_A$, which slopes down from p_1T_A towards p_2T_c will initiate solidification of primary α phase from the liquid.

The three-phase region, (L+α+β) consists of ruled surfaces $p_1b_1b_2p_2p_1$ (Lβ), $p_1a_1a_2p_2p_1$ (αL) and $a_1b_1b_2a_2a_1$ (αβ). The Lβ ruled surface forms as an upper surface of the three-phase region which is closed along p_1p_2, b_1b_2, $p_1a_1b_1$, $p_2a_2b_2$ and a_1a_2, as shown in the exploded model of the three-phase region separately, Fig. 11.25b. The (L+β) phase region exists between the Lβ ruled surface and the liquidus $p_1T_Bp_2$. The (L+α) phase region exists to the left of the αL ruled surface $p_1a_1a_2p_2p_1$. The single-phase regions are very similar in appearance to those shown for the eutectic system in section 11.1.

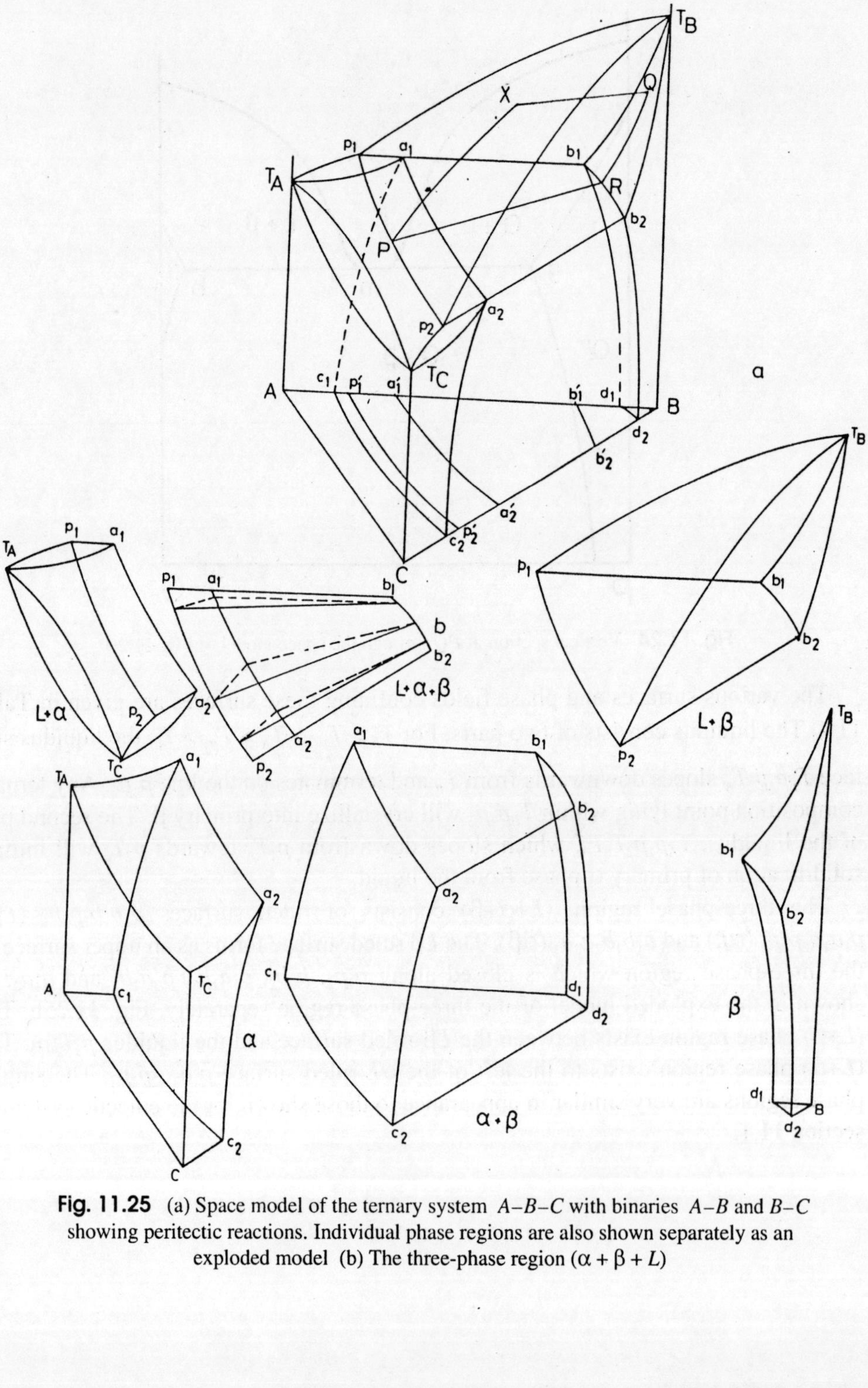

Fig. 11.25 (a) Space model of the ternary system A–B–C with binaries A–B and B–C showing peritectic reactions. Individual phase regions are also shown separately as an exploded model (b) The three-phase region ($\alpha + \beta + L$)

Table 11.4

Liquidus Surface	$L/(L+\beta)$ $T_Bp_1p_2T_B$
	$L/(L+\alpha)$ $T_Ap_1p_2T_CT_A$
Solidus Surface	$\beta/(L+\beta)$ $T_Bb_1b_2T_B$
	$\alpha/(L+\alpha)$ $T_Aa_1a_2T_CT_A$
Solvus Surface	$\alpha/(\alpha+\beta)$ $a_1a_2c_2c_1a_1$
	$\beta/(\alpha+\beta)$ $b_1b_2d_2d_1b_1$
Three-Phase Region bounded by	$\alpha-L$ ruled surface $p_1a_1a_2p_2p_1$
	$\beta-L$ ruled surface $p_1b_1b_2p_2b_1$
	$\alpha-\beta$ ruled surface $a_1b_1b_2a_2a_1$
Two-Phase Regions bounded by	$(\alpha+L)$ $T_Ap_1p_2T_CT_A$ and $T_Aa_1a_2T_CT_A$
	$(\beta+L)$ $T_Bp_1p_2T_B$ and $T_Bb_1b_2T_B$
	$(\alpha+\beta)$ $a_1b_1b_2a_2a_1$, $a_1a_2c_2c_1a_1$ and $b_1b_2d_2d_1b_1$
Single-Phase Regions bounded by	α $T_Aa_1a_2T_CT_A$, (upper surface) $a_1a_2c_2c_1a_1$, $T_CCc_2a_2T_C$ and $T_AAc_1a_1T_A$
	β $T_Bb_1b_2T_B$ (upper surface), $b_1b_2d_2d_1b_1$, $T_Bb_2d_2BT_B$ and $T_Bb_1d_1BT_B$
Line of critical temperature at which two phases become indistinguishable	Nil

11.5.2 The Isothermal Section

In order to indicate the shape of various phase fields, isothermal sections are shown at a number of temperatures, Fig. 11.26. The major difference between the ternary eutectic and ternary peritectic three-phase systems is that whereas the tie-triangles point away from the binary side AB in the eutectic reaction, they point towards the side AB in the case of a peritectic reaction. The reason is obvious from the fact that in the case of a peritectic reaction, the liquid reacts with β to give the product phase α.

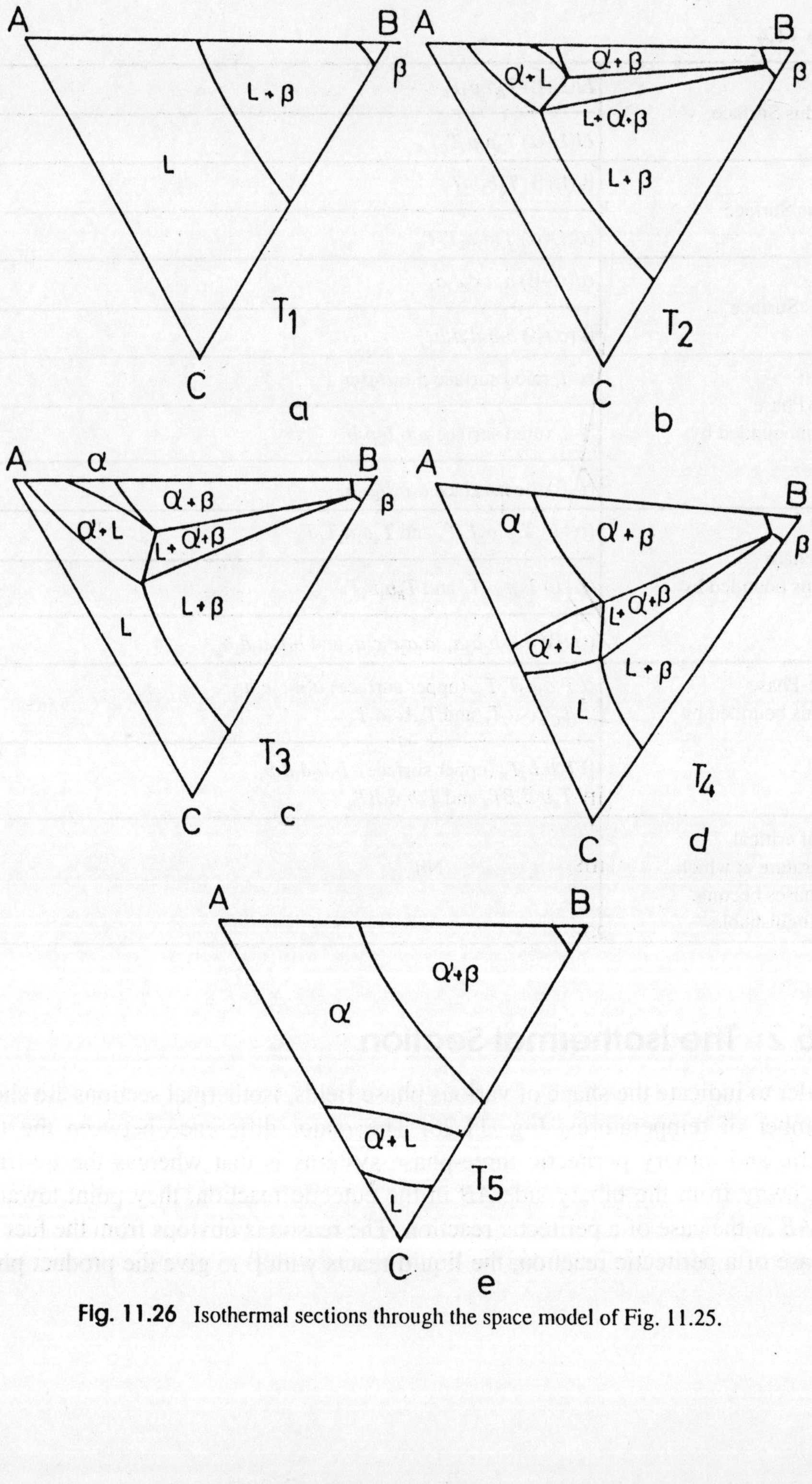

Fig. 11.26 Isothermal sections through the space model of Fig. 11.25.

Any alloy composition selected for study must, therefore, come closer to the α phase composition as the temperature is lowered. In the ternary eutectic case, the alloy composition comes closer to both the α and β phases as the temperature is lowered.

11.5.3 Vertical Sections

The vertical sections are shown at a number of positions X_1Y_1, X_2Y_2, X_3Y_3 and X_4Y_4 all parallel to the side *AB* and at *CD*. The position of the various phase fields are obtained from projection of the lines p_1p_2, a_1a_2 and b_1b_2 on the concentration triangle, as shown in the space model of Fig. 11.25a.

The vertical section at X_1Y_1 passes through the α, (α+β) and β phase fields at the ambient temperature. The α phase field extends from X_1 to *O*, the (α+β) from *O* to 5 and β from 5 to Y_1, Fig. 11.27. The (α+β) phase field is bounded by the ruled surface αβ from above and in the section at X_1Y_1, it meets the ruled surface along *qr*. The three-phase field is confined within *pqr*, Fig. 11.27a. The three points *p*, *q* and *r*, lie at different temperatures. In this case, $T_p > T_q > T_r$ which can be shown by drawing a series of tie-triangles within the (α+β+*L*) phase region and then obtaining the temperature at which the vertical plane meets each corner of the tie-triangle. The ordinate at X_1 meets the solidus and liquidus lines of the binary *A–C* at points *t* and *u*, respectively. Similarly, the ordinate at Y_1 meets the solidus and liquidus curves at points *v* and *w*, respectively. These points are shown in Fig. 11.27a. A similar procedure is used in the construction of the vertical sections at X_2Y_2, X_3Y_3, X_4Y_4 and *CD*, Figs. 11.27, b, c, d and e, respectively.

11.5.4 Solidification of Alloys

The solidification of an alloy in the ternary peritectic system showing a three-phase reaction can be followed from the space model of Fig. 11.25 and the isothermal sections, Fig. 11.28. The composition vertical meets the liquidus surface at T_1 and the primary β phase starts to form in the liquid. The compositions of the conjugate phases are given by the tie-line L_1S_1, Fig. 11.28a. The liquid composition moves along the curve *XP* on the liquidus surface and that of the solid along *QR* on the solidus surface. The liquid is saturated with the β phase at the temperature T_4 at which these two phases react with each other to give the product phase α. The relative amount of the primary β has increased from zero at T_1 to 20 % at T_4. The product phase α begins to form just below T_4 with composition of the *L*, α and β phases changing along curves p_1p_2, a_1a_2 and b_1b_2, respectively. The α phase forms at the expense of both liquid and β. Its relative amount in the alloy increases as the temperature is lowered. The relative amounts of the α, β and liquid phases at the temperature T_5 are,

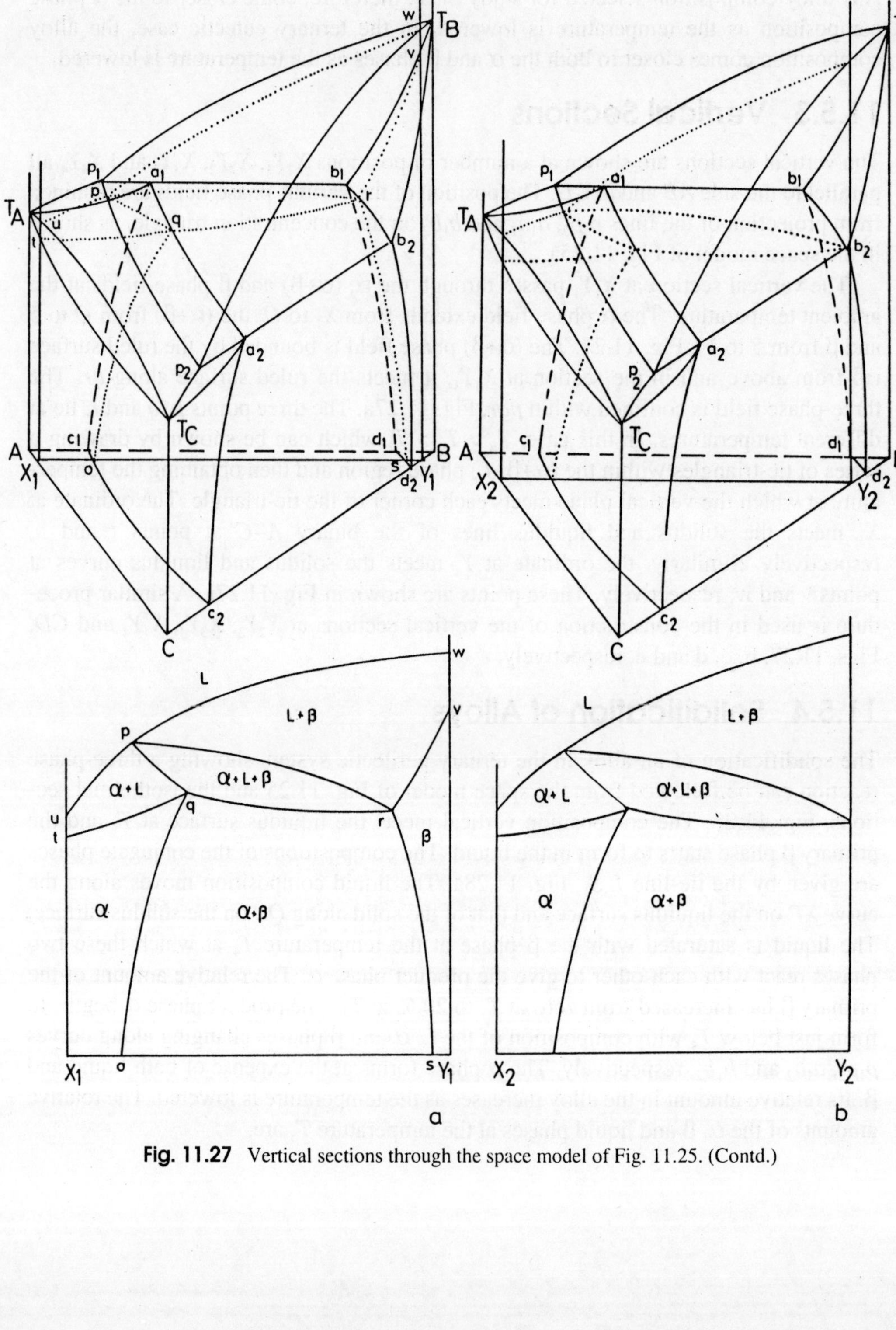

Fig. 11.27 Vertical sections through the space model of Fig. 11.25. (Contd.)

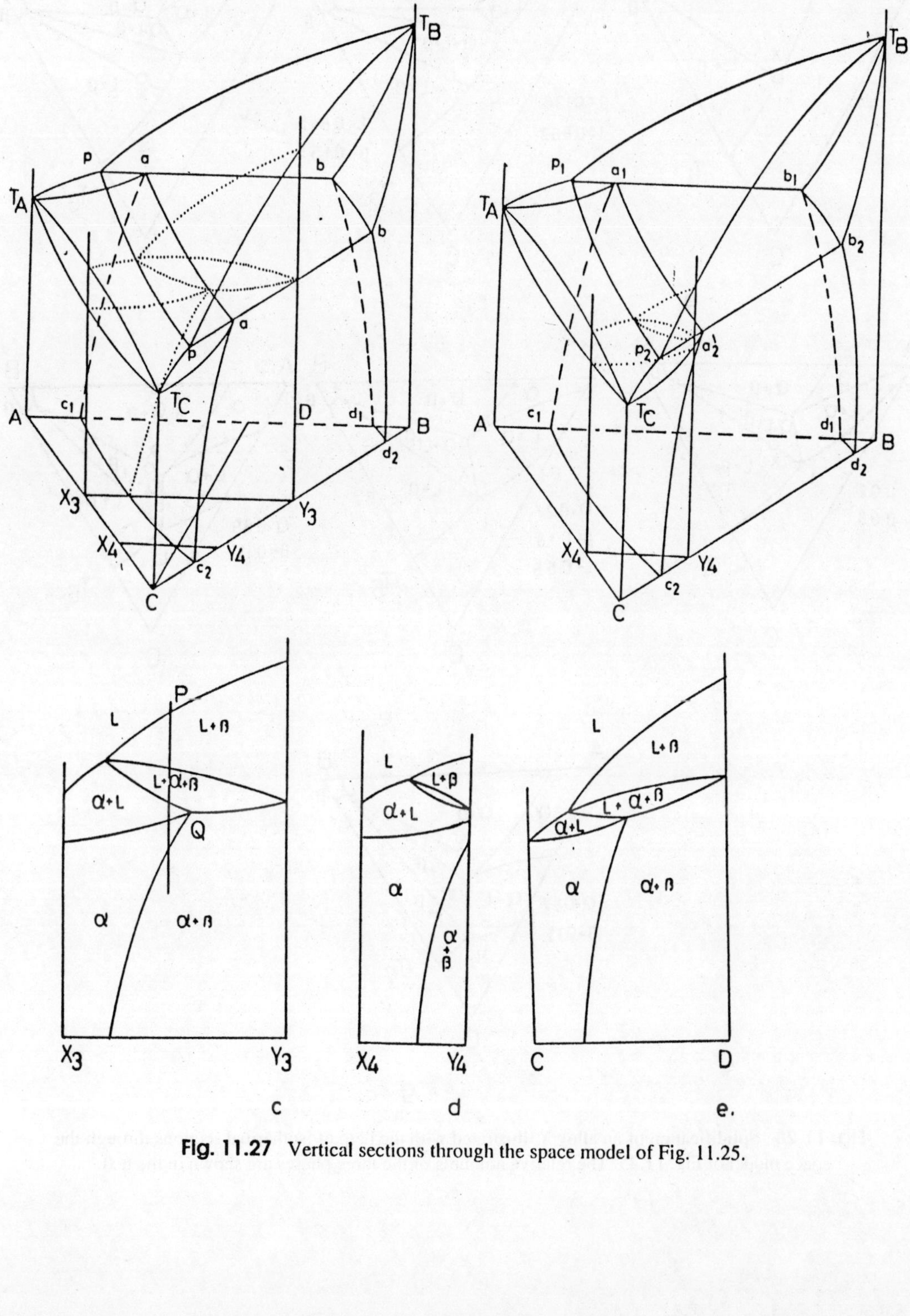

Fig. 11.27 Vertical sections through the space model of Fig. 11.25.

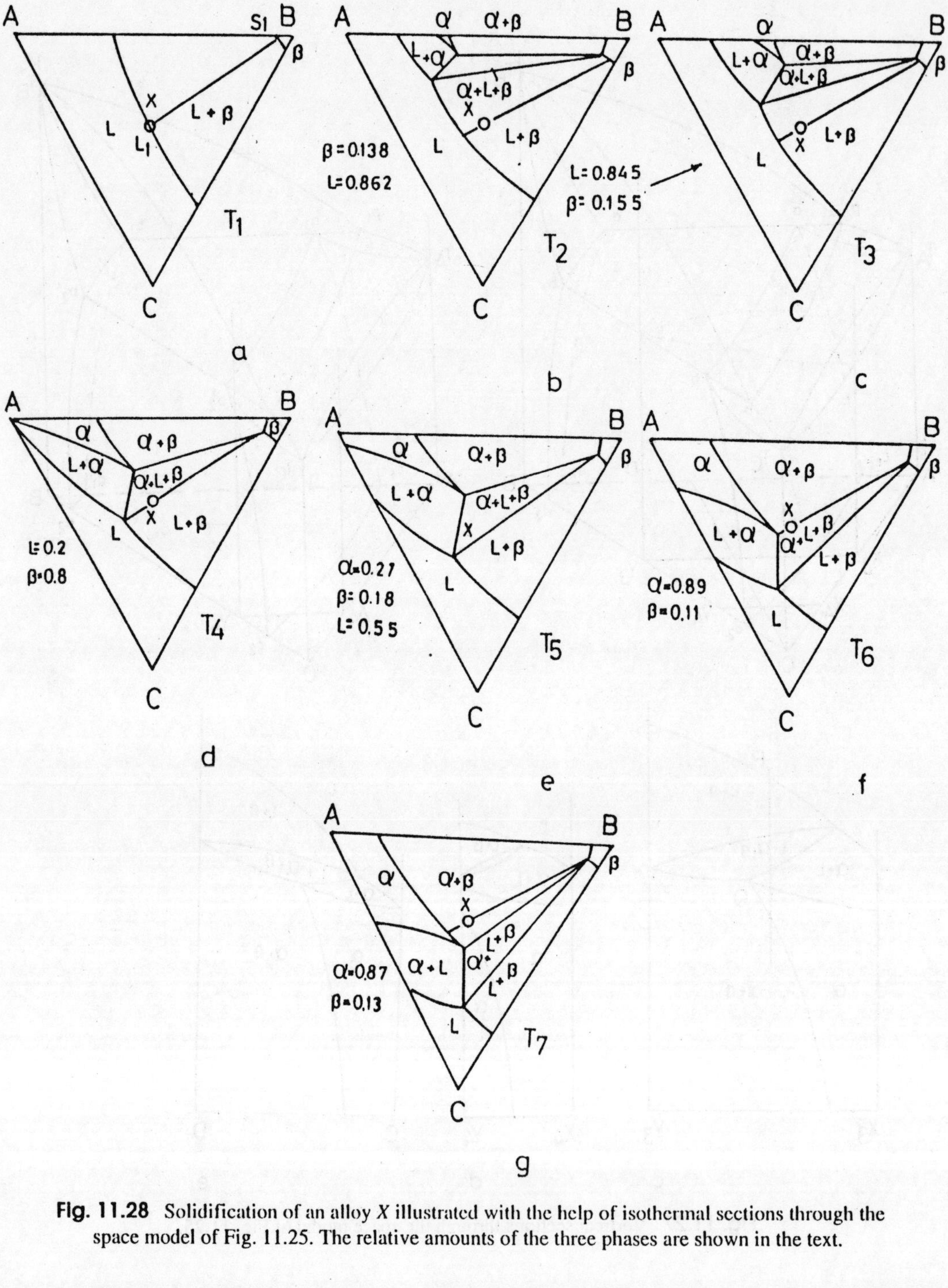

Fig. 11.28 Solidification of an alloy *X* illustrated with the help of isothermal sections through the space model of Fig. 11.25. The relative amounts of the three phases are shown in the text.

$$\alpha = 27\ \%$$

$$\beta = 18\ \%$$

$$L = 55\ \%$$

The composition vertical touches the $\alpha\beta$ ruled surface at the temperature T_6, which is the temperature at which the liquid solidifies completely. The relative amounts of the α and β phases at T_6 are,

$$\alpha = 89\ \%$$

$$\beta = 11\ \%$$

Minor adjustments in composition and relative amounts of the two solid phases occur below T_6.

11.6 TERNARY PERITECTIC SYSTEM WITH ONE BINARY SYSTEM SHOWING THE PERITECTIC REACTION AND A MINIMUM IN THE LIQUIDUS TEMPERATURE

The space model of the ternary system A–B–C with the binary A–B showing a peritectic reaction and a minimum in the liquidus curve, is shown in Fig. 11.29. The three-phase region, (L+α+β), originates at the binary peritectic reaction isotherm *pab*. Composition of the monovariant liquid (associated with the three-phase equilibrium) changes along pp_1, with p_1 being the minimum point on the liquidus. The liquid phase exists in equilibrium with the indistinguishable α (β) phase at T_{p_1}. The composition of the solid at the minimum temperature is represented by c_1. The tie-line p_1c_1 is a degenerate tie-triangle. The temperature T_{p_1} represents the lowest temperature of existence of the monovariant field. The α and β phases become indistinguishable at all temperatures below T_{p_1} at points the locus of which generates the curve c_1c_2, where c_2 lies at ambient temperature. The three bounding surfaces of the three-phase region are,

ac_1b (αβ ruled surface, lower surface)

app_1c_1a (αL ruled surface, lower surface)

bpp_1c_1b (βL ruled surface, upper surface)

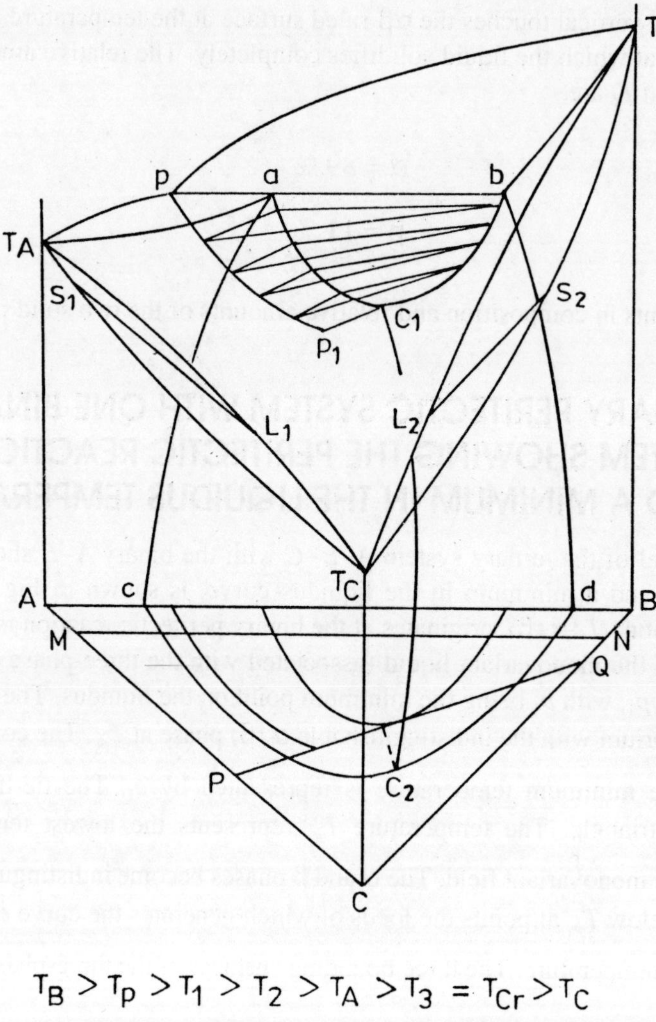

$T_B > T_p > T_1 > T_2 > T_A > T_3 = T_{Cr} > T_C$

Fig. 11.29 Space model of the ternary system A–B–C with the binary A–B showing a peritectic reaction and a minimum critical point on the monovariant liquid curve.

The $\alpha\beta$ tie-line of the $(\alpha+\beta+L)$ phase region gradually becomes shorter as the temperature decreases from T_p to T_{p_1}. At T_{p_1} it has, zero length and the tie-triangle terminates in a tie-line p_1c_1. The other phase boundaries of the ternary phase diagram are given in Table 11.5.

Table 11.5

Liquidus Surface	$L/(L+\beta)$ $T_BL_2p_1pT_B$
	$L/(L+\alpha)$ $pp_1L_1T_A$, $T_CL_1p_1L_2T_C$
Solidus Surface	$\beta/(L+\beta)$ $T_BS_2C_1bT_B$
	$\alpha/(L+\alpha)$ $T_AS_1S_2C_1aT_A$ and $T_CS_1S_2T_C$
Solvus Surface	$\alpha/(\alpha+\beta)$ aC_1C_2ca
	$\beta/(\alpha+\beta)$ bC_1C_2db
Three-Phase Region bounded by	α–L ruled surface paC_1p_1p
	β–L ruled surface bC_1p_1pb
	α–β ruled surface aC_1b
Two-Phase Regions bounded by	$(\alpha+L)$ $pp_1L_1T_A$ and $T_AS_1S_2C_1aT_A$
	$(\beta+L)$ $T_BL_2p_1pT_B$ and $T_BS_2C_1bT_B$
	$(\alpha+\beta)$ aC_1C_2ca and bC_1C_2db
Single-Phase Regions bounded by	α –
	β –
Line of critical temperature at which two phases become indistinguishable	p_1C_1 and along C_1C_2.

The isothermal section just below the binary peritectic reaction isotherm has a very similar appearance to that observed for the ternary system with two binary peritectic reactions, Fig. 11.30a. Isothermal sections are also shown at T_2 and T_3 defined by $T_1 > T_2 > T_3 = T_{p_1}$, Fig. 11.30, b and c. The interpretation of these should pose no difficulty.

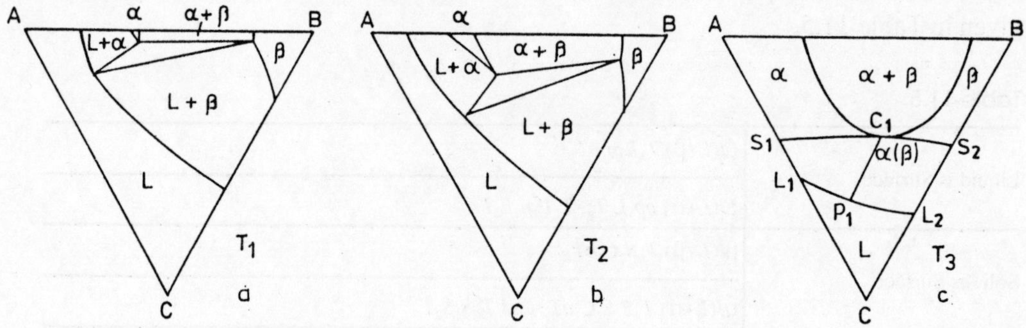

Fig. 11.30 Isothermal sections through the space model of Fig. 11.29.

The vertical section parallel to the side which has a low concentration of the component C is again similar to that observed for the ternary system with two binary peritectic reactions, Fig. 11.31a. The vertical plane at PQ which meets the critical line p_1c_1, such that p_1c_1 lies on it, is shown in Fig. 11.31b. The (α+β) phase field closes at c_1 and the three-phase region is shown along the horizontal line p_1c_1. Alloy compositions lying on the line p_1c_1 undergo the peritectic reaction $L+\beta \Rightarrow \alpha$. This is apparent from the vertical section at PQ, Fig. 11.31b. The solidification begins with the formation of primary β in the liquid. At the temperature corresponding to the minimum in the liquidus, the liquid will react with β to give α as the product phase. Any excess liquid will solidify into secondary α. The alloy compositions lying to the right of the point c_1 will not undergo a peritectic reaction. The liquid will solidify into primary β over a temperature range.

11.7 TERNARY PERITECTIC SYSTEM WITH ONE BINARY SHOWING A PERITECTIC REACTION AND A MAXIMUM IN THE LIQUIDUS TEMPERATURE

The space model of the ternary system $A–B–C$ with the binary $B–C$ showing a peritectic reaction and a maximum in the liquidus temperature is shown in Fig. 11.32a. The projection is shown in Fig. 11.32b. The monovariant liquid curve ascends from p to a maximum point p_1. The three-phase field exists to a maximum temperature of Tp_1.

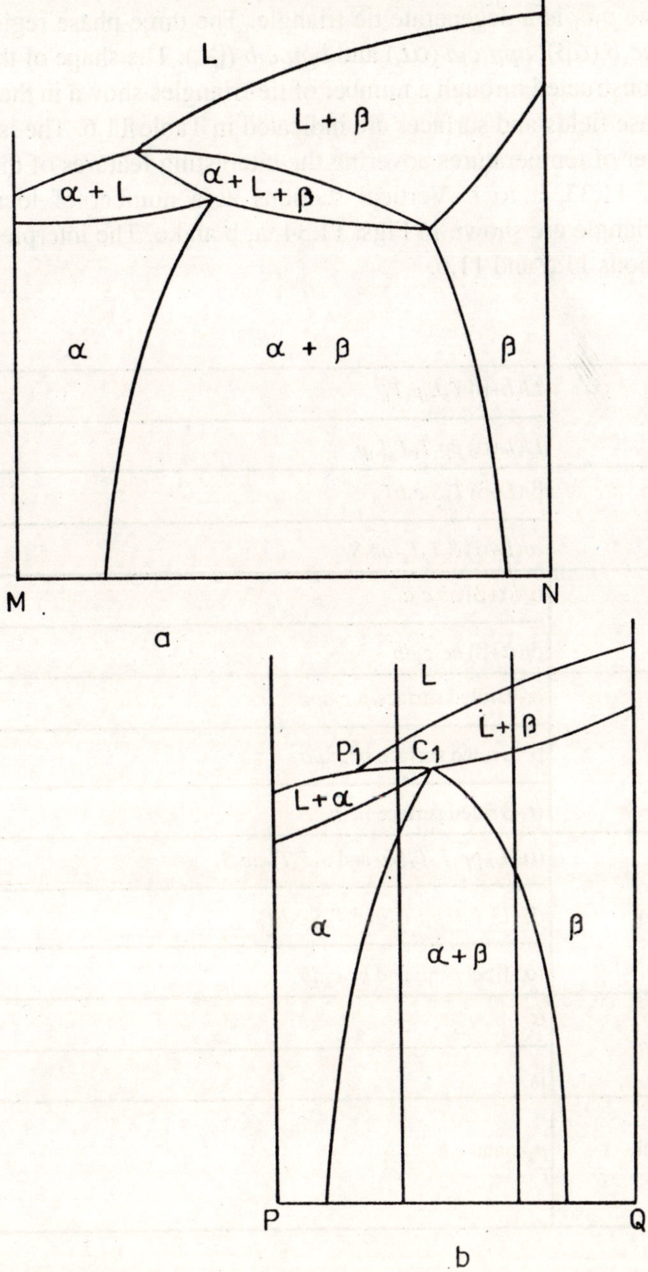

Fig. 11.31 Vertical sections at *PQ* and *MN* of Fig. 11.29.

There is a critical composition c_1 at which the α and β phases become indistinguishable. The tie-line p_1c_1 is a degenerate tie-triangle. The three-phase region consists of ruled surfaces ac_1b (αβ), app_1c_1a (αL) and bpp_1c_1b (βL). The shape of the three-phase region can be constructed through a number of tie-triangles shown in the space model. The various phase fields and surfaces are indicated in Table 11.6. The isothermal sections at a number of temperatures covering the interesting features of the diagram are shown in Figs. 11.33, a to f. Vertical sections at a number of locations on the concentration triangle are shown in Figs. 11.34, a, b and c. The interpretations are on the lines of sections 11.5 and 11.6.

Table 11.6

Liquidus Surface	$L/(L+\beta)$ $T_BL_1p_1T_B$
	$L/(L+\alpha)$ $pp_1T_CT_AL_1p$
Solidus Surface	$\beta/(L+\beta)$ $T_BS_1c_1bT_B$
	$\alpha/(L+\alpha)$ $S_1T_AT_C\,ac_1S_1$
Solvus Surface	$\alpha/(\alpha+\beta)$ ac_2c_1a
	$\beta/(\alpha+\beta)$ bc_1c_2db
Three-Phase Region bounded by	$\alpha-L$ ruled surface $p_1c_1app_1$
	$\beta-L$ ruled surface bc_1p_1pb
	$\alpha-\beta$ ruled surface ac_1b
Two-Phase Regions bounded by	$(\alpha+L)$ $pp_1T_CT_AL_1p$ and $S_1T_AT_C\,ac_1S_1$
	$(\beta+L)$ $T_BL_1p_1pT_B$ and $T_BS_1c_1bT_B$
	$(\alpha+\beta)$ acc_2c_1a and bc_1c_2db
Single-Phase regions bounded by	α –
	β –
Line of critical temperature at which two phases become indistinguishable	p_1c_1 and c_1c_2

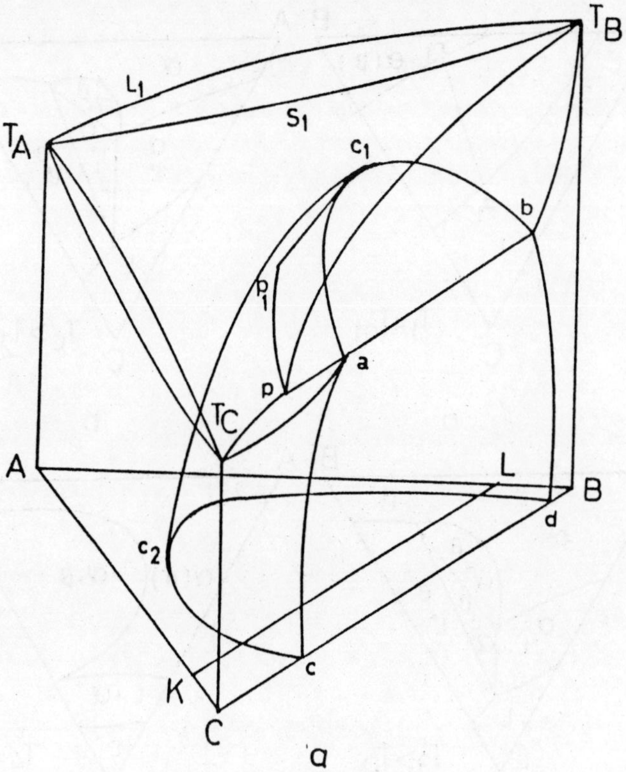

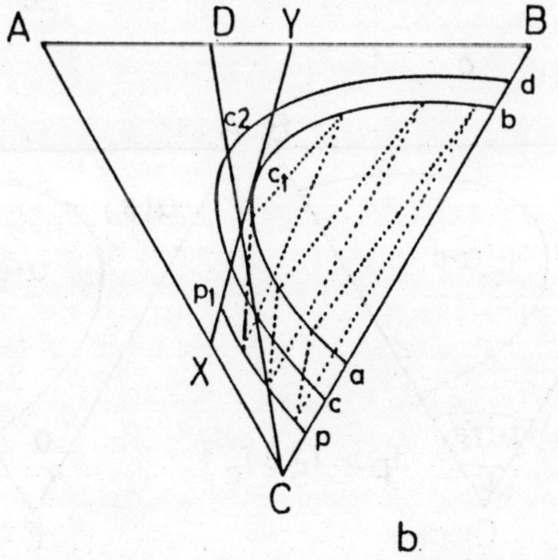

Fig. 11.32 (a) Space model of the ternary system $A–B–C$ with the binary $B–C$ showing a peritectic reaction and a maximum in critical point on the monovariant liquid curve.
(b) Projection on the concentration triangle.

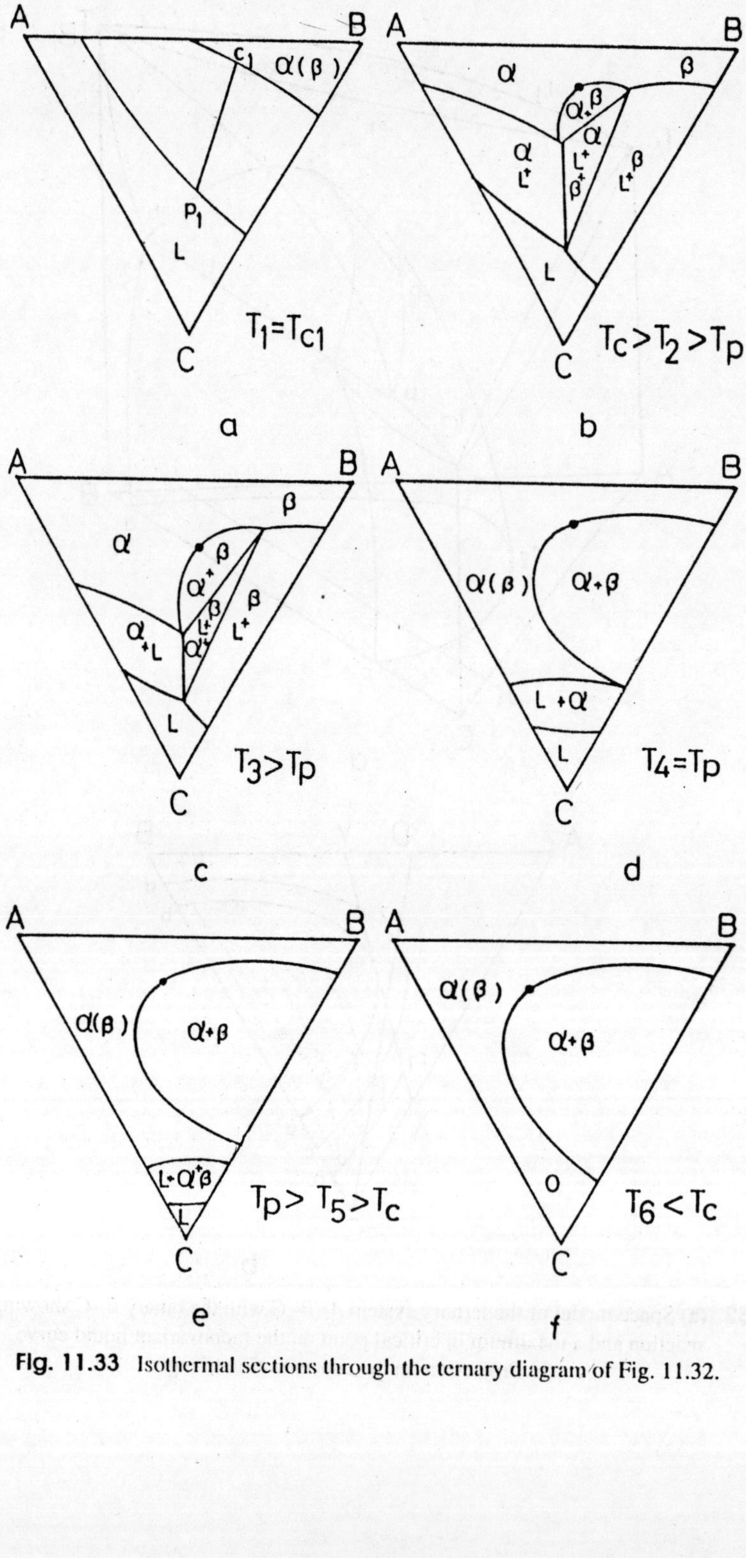

Fig. 11.33 Isothermal sections through the ternary diagram of Fig. 11.32.

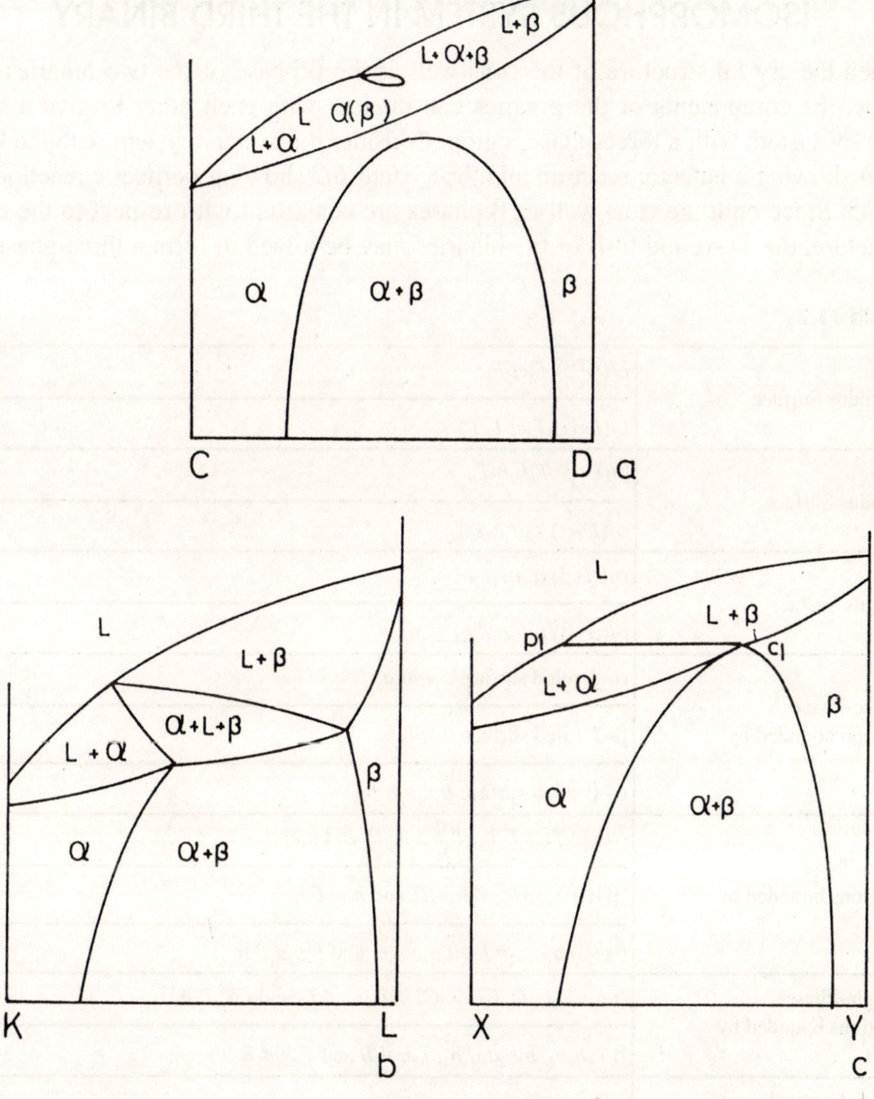

Fig. 11.34 Vertical sections at *CD*, *KL* and *XY* through the ternary diagram of Fig. 11.32.

11.8 TERNARY SYSTEM WITH PERITECTIC AND EUTECTIC REACTIONS IN THE TWO BINARIES AND AN ISOMORPHOUS SYSTEM IN THE THIRD BINARY

When the crystal structure of the α as well as the β phase of the two binaries is the same, the components of the binaries can interact with each other to give a simple ternary system with a three-phase region. Consider the ternary system with the binary A–B showing a eutectic reaction and the system BC showing peritectic reaction, Fig. 11.35. Since both the α as well as β phases are consistent with respect to the crystal structure, the α–α and β–β of the binaries may be joined to form a three-phase field

Table 11.7

Liquidus Surface	$L/(L+\beta)$ $T_B ep T_B$
	$L/(L+\alpha)$ $T_A ep T_C T_A$
Solidus Surface	$\beta/(L+\beta)$ $T_B b_1 b_2 T_B$
	$\alpha/(L+\alpha)$ $T_A a_1 a_2 T_c T_A$
Solvus Surface	$\alpha/(\alpha+\beta)$ $a_1 a_2 c_2 c_1 a_1$
	$\beta/(\alpha+\beta)$ $b_1 b_2 d_2 d_1 b_1$
Three-Phase Region bounded by	α–L ruled surface $a_1 ep a_2 a_1$
	β–L ruled surface $b_1 ep b_2 b_1$
	α–β ruled surface $b_1 a_1 a_2 b_2 b_1$
Two-Phase Regions bounded by	$(\alpha+L)$ $T_A ep T_C T_A$, $T_A a_1 a_2 T_C T_A$ and $a_1 ep a_2 a_1$
	$(\beta+L)$ $T_B ep T_B$, $T_B b_1 b_2 T_B$ and $b_1 ep b_2 b_1$
	$(\alpha+\beta)$ $b_1 a_1 a_2 b_2 b_1$, $a_1 a_2 c_2 c_1 a_1$ and $b_1 b_2 d_2 d_1 b_1$
Single-Phase Regions bounded by	α $a_1 a_2 c_2 c_1 a_1$, $T_C\ a_2 c_2 C T_C$, $T_A a_1 c_1 A T_A$ and $C T_C T_A A$
	β $T_B b_1 b_2$, $b_1 b_2 d_2 d_1 b_1$, $T_B b_2 d_2 B$ and $T_B b_1 d_1 B$
Line of critical temperature at which two phases become indistinguishable	–

running across the two binaries. The various surfaces and phase fields are shown in Table 11.7. A new feature of this diagram is the crossing over of the monovariant liquid and α lines *ep* and a_1a_2, respectively, somewhere within the space. The two lines *ep* and a_1a_2 lie at different temperatures. The $L\beta$ and $\alpha\beta$ ruled surfaces which are designated by epb_2b_1 and $a_1b_1b_2a_2$, respectively, are very similar in shape to those presented in earlier sections on three-phase equilibria. The αL ruled surface epa_2a_1 is twisted due to the crossing over of the lines *ep* and a_1a_2, as shown in Fig. 11.35. The tie-triangles will change direction in going from temperature T_e to T_p. This is shown in the three-phase region of the space model, Fig. 11.35. The tie-lines on the αL ruled surface are also shown separately to indicate the twisted shape of the surface.

The interesting feature of the ternary phase diagram is that whereas alloys deprived of the component *C* will solidify according to the eutectic reaction, alloys rich in the component *C* will solidify by the peritectic reaction. Alloys in the intermediate range of composition will follow a compromise mode of freezing. Thus, there exist all possible reactions, $L+\alpha = \beta$, $L = \alpha+\beta$ or $L+\beta = \alpha$. An alloy compositions will undergo one of the above reactions during solidification.

The isothermal sections of Fig. 11.36 clearly reveal the characteristic reversal in the orientation of the tie-triangles. The change in the direction is gradual as seen in a separate drawing, Fig. 11.36d.

A number of vertical sections parallel to the side *AB* are shown in Fig. 11.37. The vertical section at *PQ* shows all the characteristics of a ternary eutectic monovariant equilibrium. Alloy compositions lying within the plane of the vertical section at *PQ* and within the three-phase triangle will follow a similar course of solidification as the ternary eutectic system, Fig. 11.37a. The solidification will begin with the formation of crystals of either primary α or β phases depending upon the position of the alloy under consideration. At a temperature corresponding to saturation of either of the phases, the remaining liquid will dissociate by the eutectic reaction. Some of the alloy compositions lying on the vertical plane at *ST*, Fig. 11.37c, will undergo the eutectic reaction at first. There will be a reversal at lower temperatures and the β phase will react with the liquid to give the α phase. One such alloy composition *Y* is shown in the plane of the drawing, Fig. 11.37c. The solidification of the alloy begins at the temperature corresponding to the composition vertical touching the liquidus surface, as shown by point "1" in the figure. The product of solidification is the primary β phase. The liquid dissociates into α and β phases by the eutectic reaction in the temperature interval 2–3. The β phase reacts with the remaining liquid to give the α phase by the peritectic reaction below the temperature indicated by point "3" in the diagram.

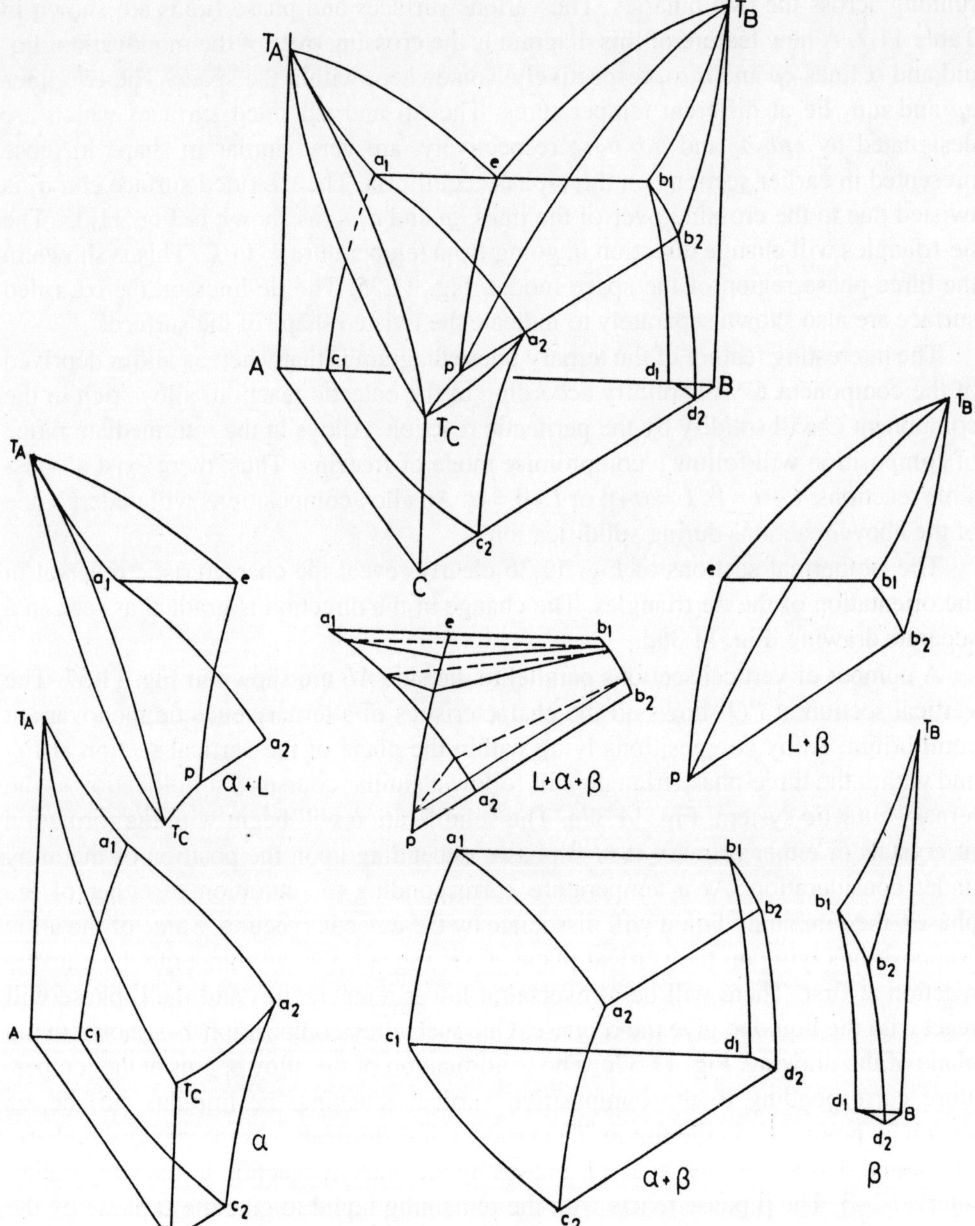

Fig. 11.35 Space model of the ternary system *A–B–C* with the binary *A–B* showing a eutectic and *BC* showing a peritectic reaction.

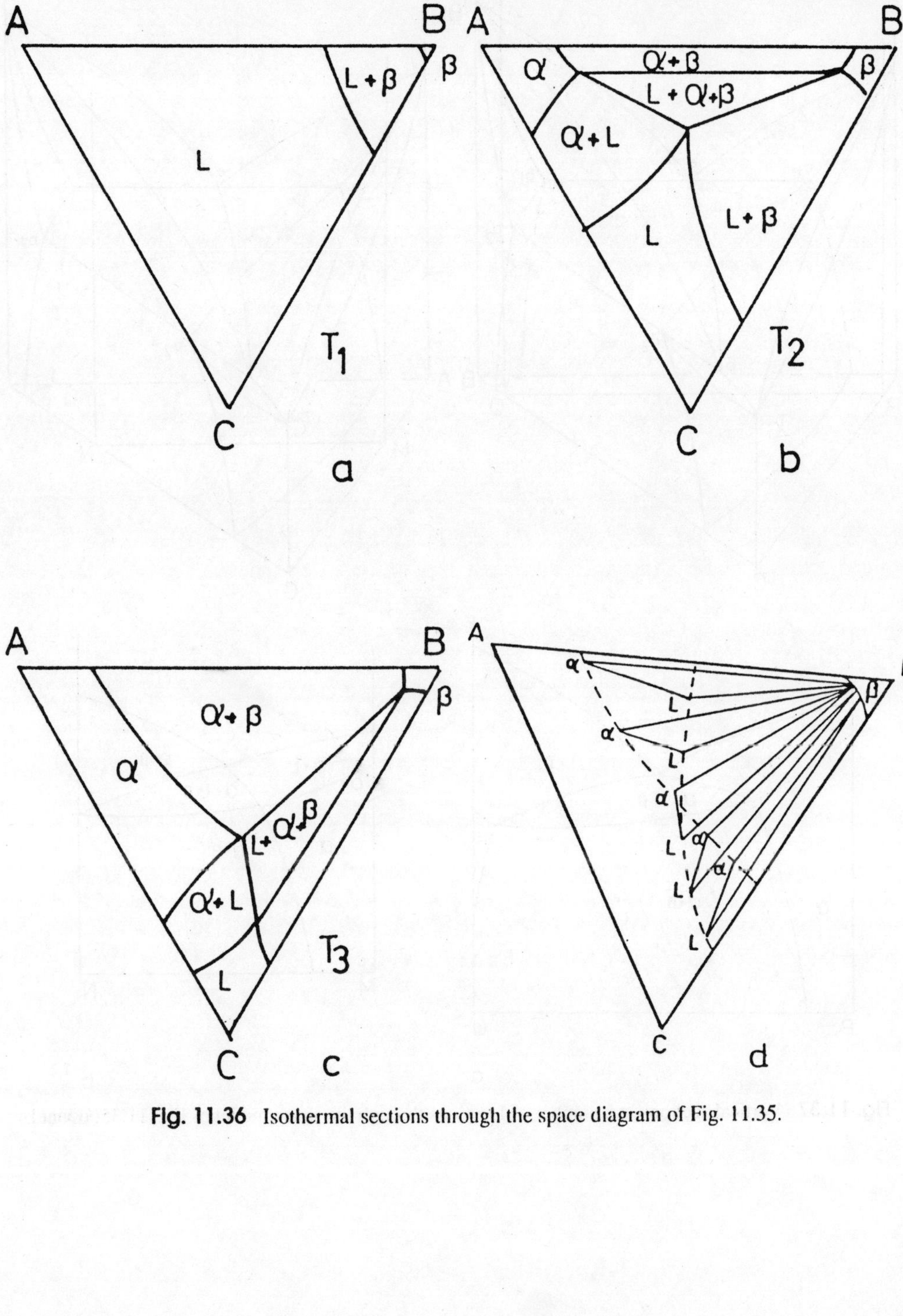

Fig. 11.36 Isothermal sections through the space diagram of Fig. 11.35.

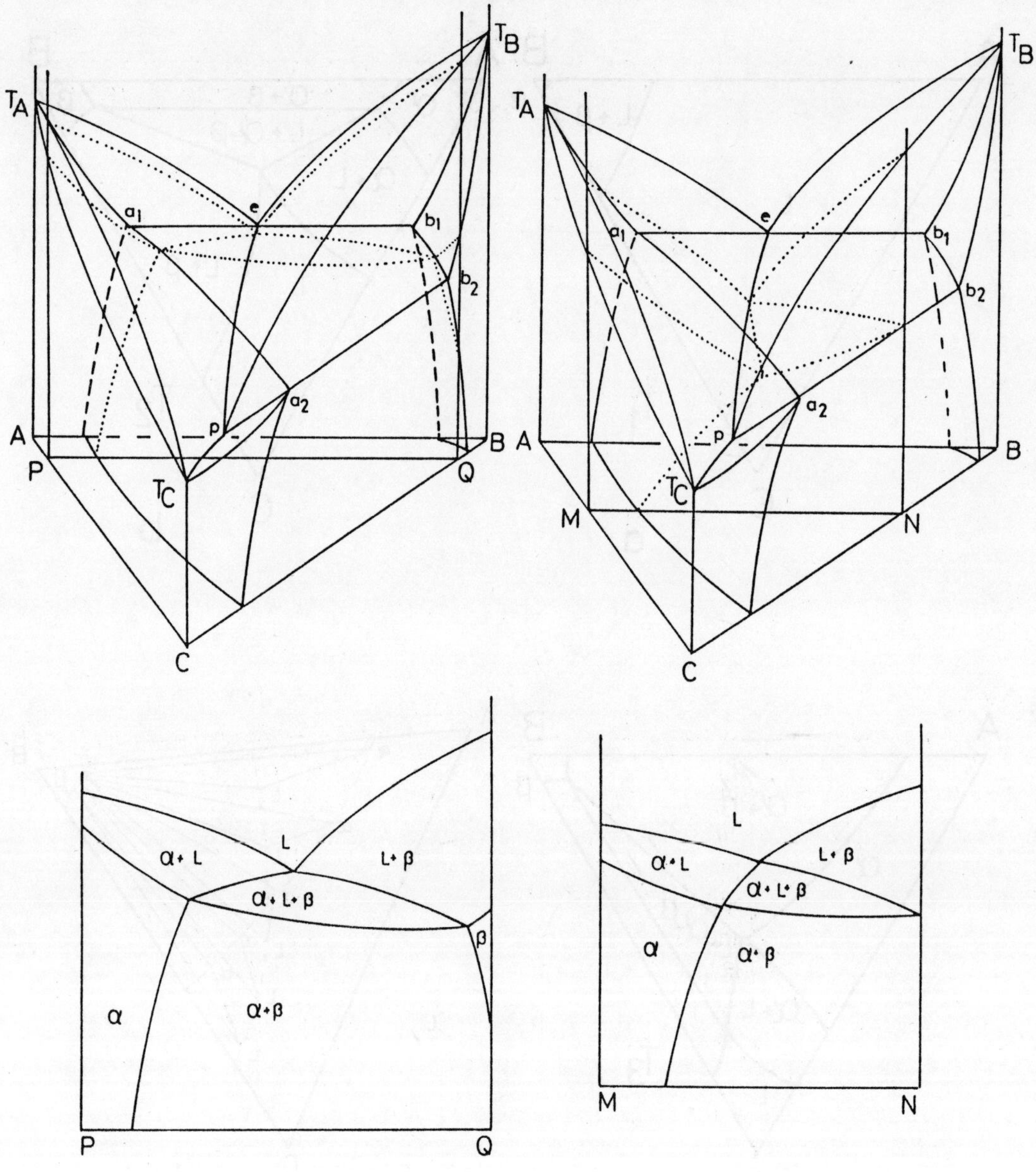

a b

Fig. 11.37 Vertical sections at a number of locations through the space model of Fig. 11.35. (Contd.)

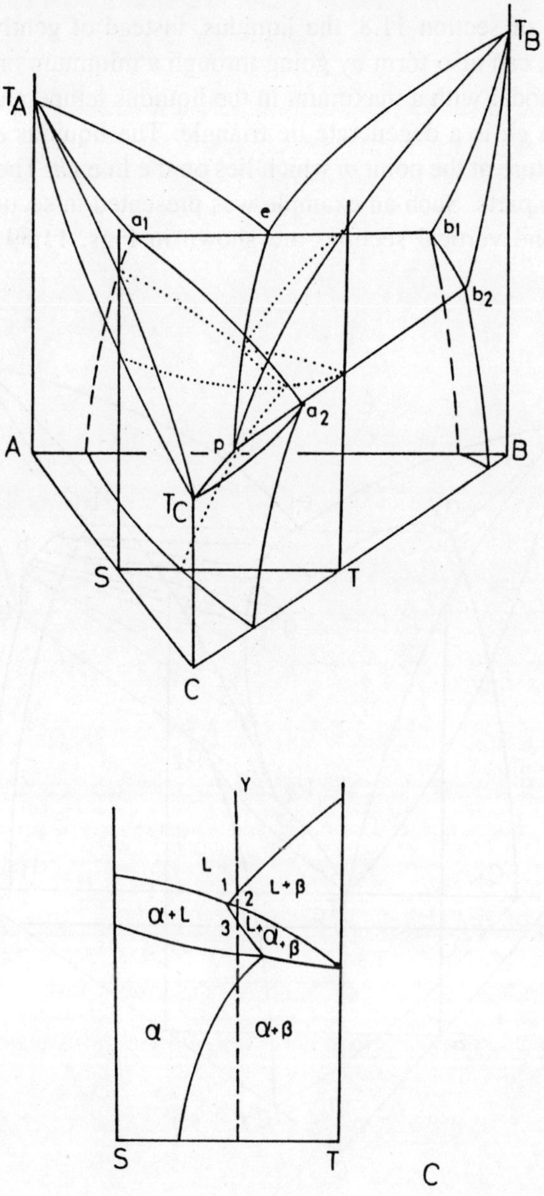

Fig. 11.37 Vertical sections at a number of locations through the space model of Fig. 11.35.

In the example of section 11.8, the liquidus, instead of gently sloping from one binary to the other, can also form by going through a minimum or maximum temperature. The space model with a maximum in the liquidus temperature is shown in Fig. 11.38. The tie-line gh is a degenerate tie-triangle. The liquidus e_1p_2 goes through a maximum temperature at the point m which lies on the line gh. The three-phase region is divided into two parts. Such an example was presented in section 11.4. A few isothermal sections and vertical sections are shown in Figs. 11.39 and 11.40, respectively.

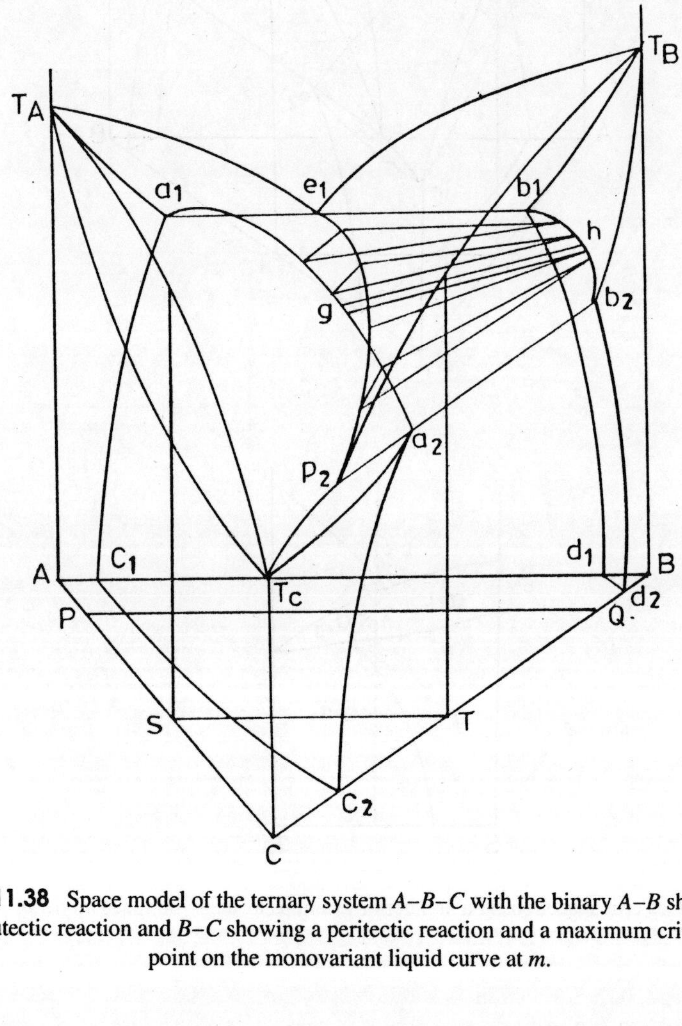

Fig. 11.38 Space model of the ternary system A–B–C with the binary A–B showing a eutectic reaction and B–C showing a peritectic reaction and a maximum critical point on the monovariant liquid curve at m.

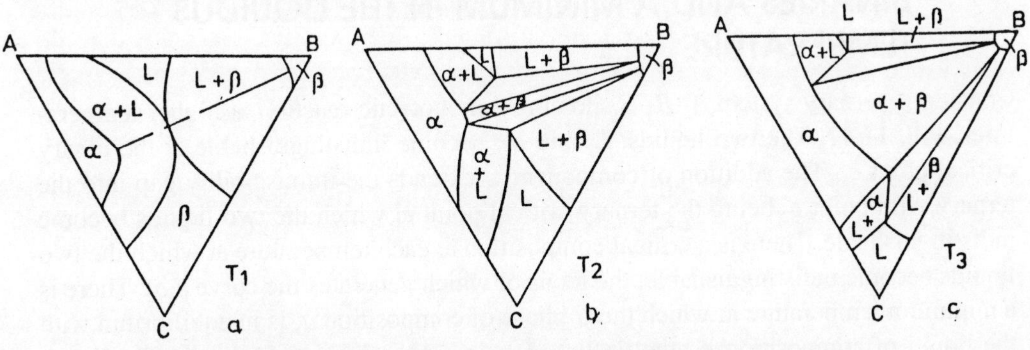

Fig. 11.39 Isothermal sections through the space model of Fig. 11.38.

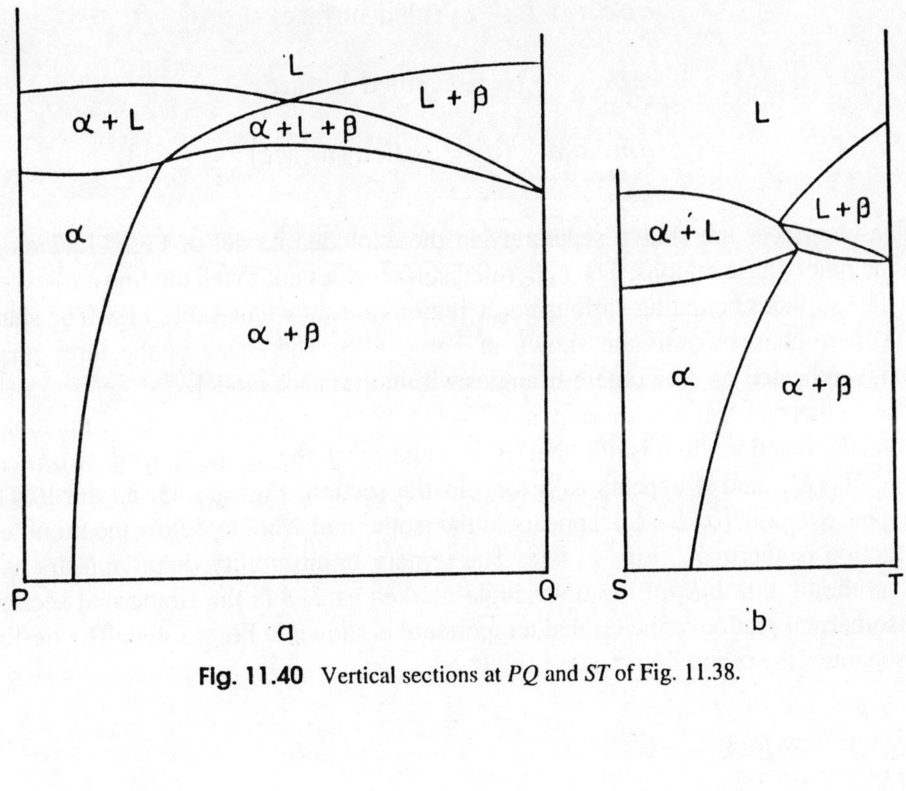

Fig. 11.40 Vertical sections at *PQ* and *ST* of Fig. 11.38.

11.9 TERNARY SYSTEM SHOWING A MONOTECTIC REACTION $L_1 = \alpha + L_2$ IN ONE OF THE BINARIES AND A MINIMUM IN THE LIQUIDUS TEMPERATURE

Consider a ternary system *A–B–C* showing a monotectic reaction at higher temperatures, Fig. 11.41. The two liquids, L_1 and L_2, become indistinguishable at the binary critical point c_1. The addition of component *C* extends the immiscibility gap into the ternary with point c_2 being the ternary critical point at which the two liquids become indistinguishable. There is a critical composition at each temperature at which the two liquids become indistinguishable, the locus of which generates the curve c_1c_2. There is a minimum temperature at which the α phase of composition a_1 is in equilibrium with the liquid of composition c_2. the tie-line a_1c_2 is a degenerate tie-triangle. The three-phase region lies between a_1c_2 and *amb*, Fig. 11.41. The three ruled surfaces are,

$$abc_2a_1a \quad (\alpha + L_2 \text{ ruled surface})$$

$$mbc_2 \quad (L_1 + L_2 \text{ ruled surface})$$

and

$$amc_2a_1a \quad (\alpha + L_1 \text{ ruled surface})$$

These surfaces are shown separately in the exploded model of Fig. 11.42 along with the other phase regions. The L_1L_2 ruled surface does not touch the line c_1c_2 except at c_2. The surfaces bounding various phase regions are shown in Table 11.8. The shape of the three-phase regions are shown in Table 11.8. The shape of the three-phase region is indicated by drawing tie-triangles within the space model.

The isothermal sections are shown in Fig. 11.43. At temperatures above the binary monotectic reaction, the isothermal plane intersects the dome-shaped two-phase region, (L_1+L_2), and it appears as a loop in the section, Figs. 11.43, a, and b. The three-phase region, (α+L_1+L_2), appears in the isothermal sections below the monotectic reaction isotherm T_m, Fig. 11.43c. The ternary immiscibility dome appears as a loop on the tie-line L_1L_2 of the tie-triangle marked as 2–3 in the isothermal section. The isothermal section at the critical temperature is shown in Fig. 11.43d. The tie-line a_1c_2 separates the α and liquid phase fields.

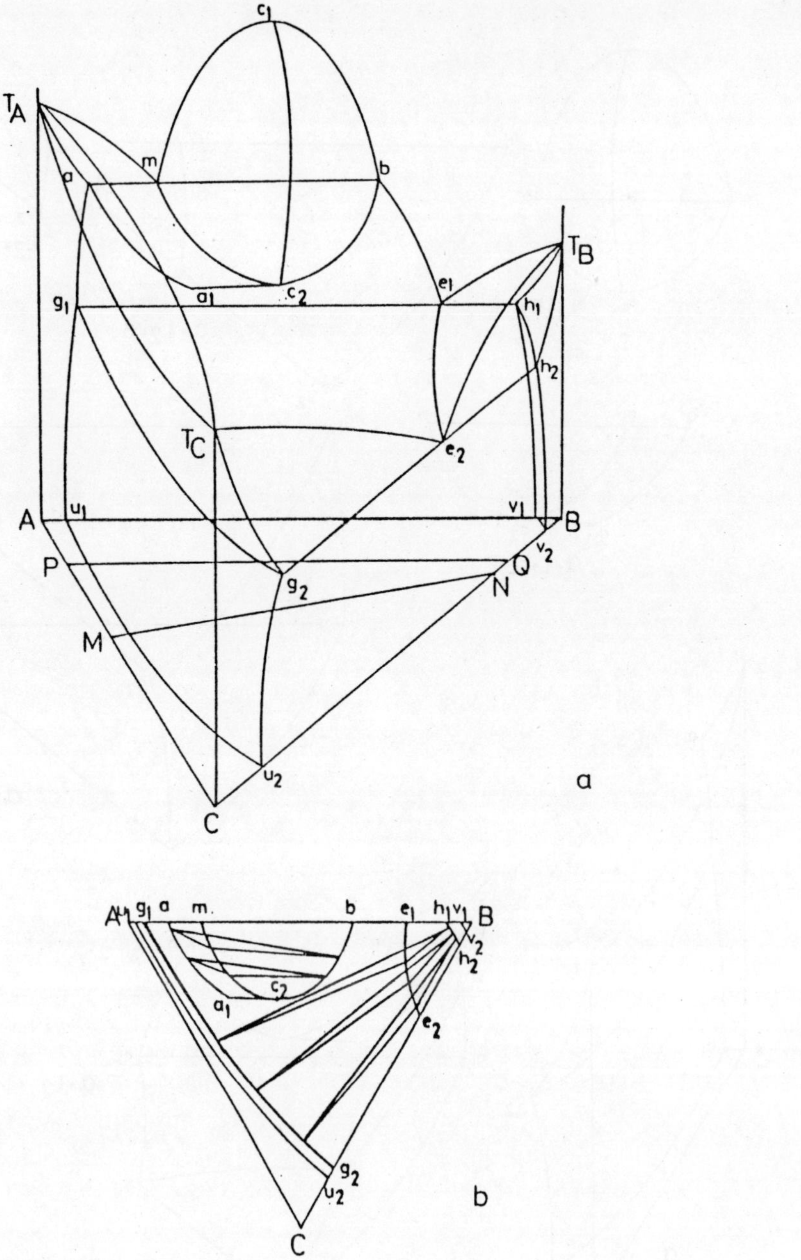

Fig. 11.41 (a) Space model of a ternary system A–B–C with the binary A–B showing a monotectic reaction. The binary reactions at lower temperatures are drawn for the sake of completion. (b) Projection of the three-phase fields $(L_1 + L_2 + \alpha)$ and $(L_2 + \alpha + \beta)$ on the concentration triangle ABC.

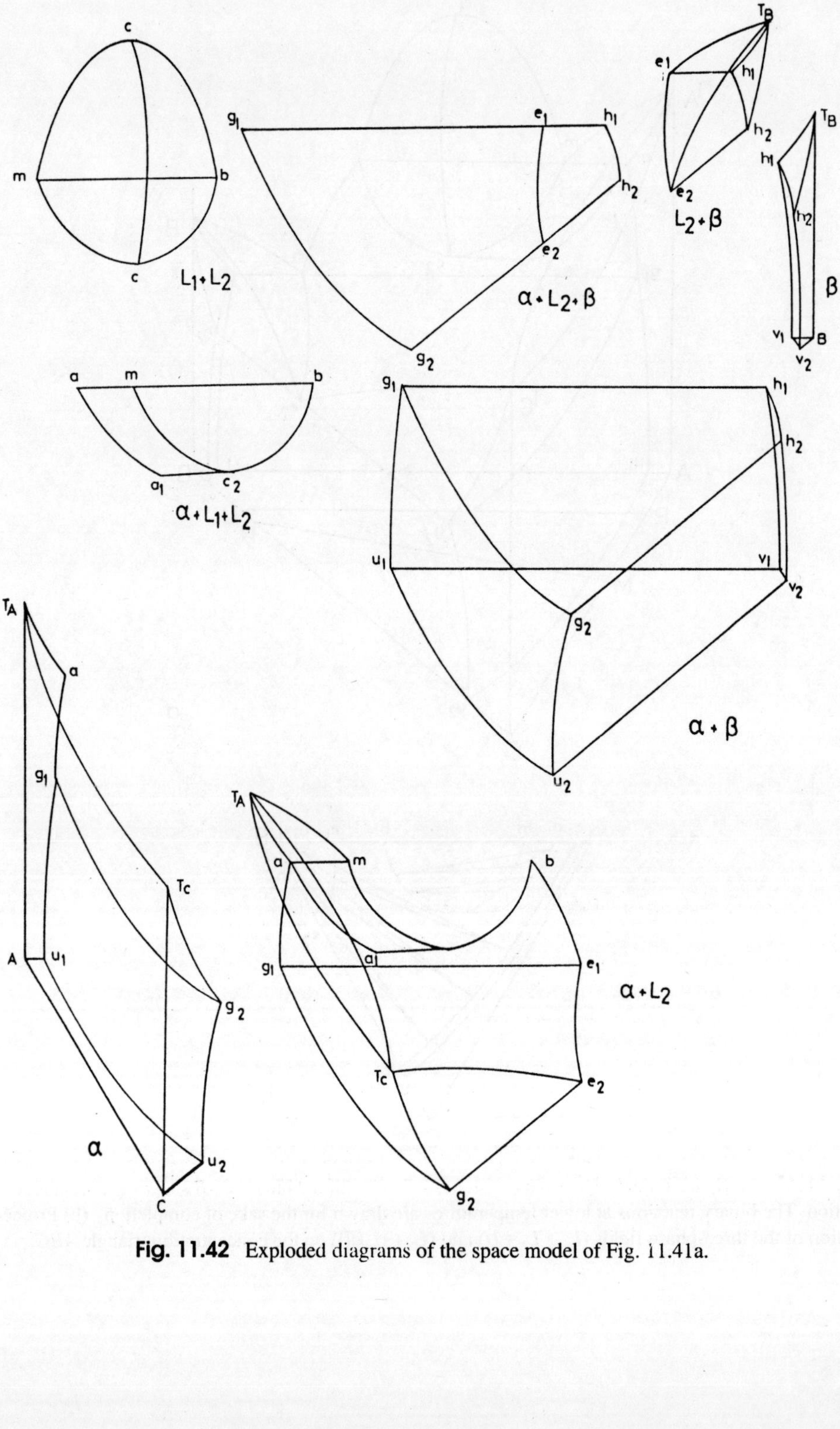

Fig. 11.42 Exploded diagrams of the space model of Fig. 11.41a.

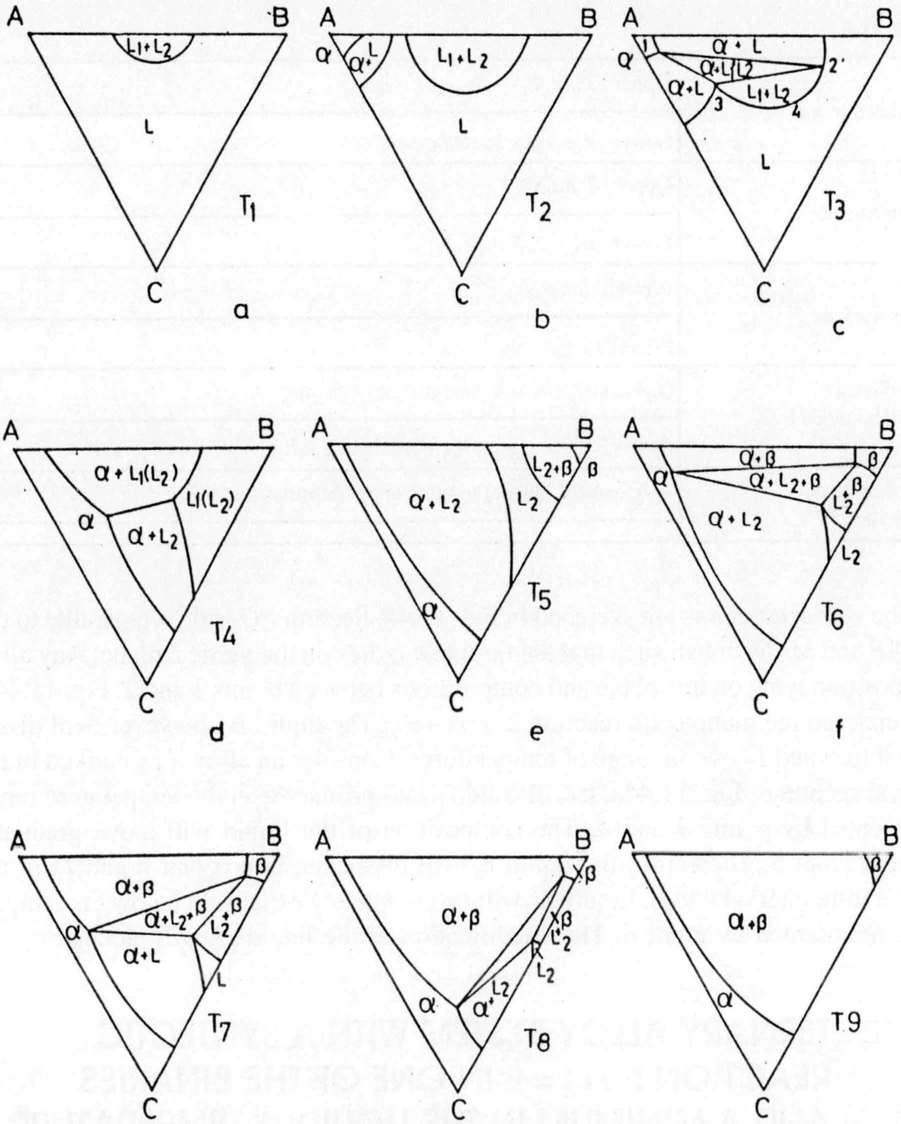

Fig. 11.43 Isothermal sections through the space model of Fig. 11.41a.

Table 11.8

Liquidus Surface	Upper $T_Amc_2L_1T_A$, mc_2c_1m, c_1bc_2
	Lower $T_Be_1e_2T_B$, $T_Ce_2e_1bc_2L_1T_C$
Solidus Surface	Upper $T_Aaa_1S_1T_A$
	Lower $ag_1g_2T_CS_1a_1$, $T_Bh_1h_2T_B$
Solvus Surface	$\alpha/(\alpha+\beta)$ $h_1h_2v_2v_1h_1$
	$\beta/(\alpha+\beta)$ $g_1g_2u_2u_1g_1$
Three-Phase Region bounded by	$(L_1+L_2+\alpha)$, abc_2a_1a, amc_2a_1a and mbc_2m
	$(\alpha+\beta+L_2)$, $g_1e_1e_2g_2g_1$, $h_1e_1e_2h_2h_1$ and $g_1h_1h_2g_1$
Line of critical temperature	a_1c_2, and S_1L_1 lie at the same temperature as a_1c_2

The vertical sections are sketched in Fig. 11.44. Section *PQ* is drawn parallel to the line *AB* and *MN* is drawn such that the tie-line a_1c_2 lies on the vertical plane. Any alloy composition lying on this plane and compositions between points 1 and 2, Fig. 11.44a, will undergo the monotectic reaction $L_1 = \alpha + L_2$. The liquid L_1, however, will dissociate into α and L_2 over a range of temperatures. Consider an alloy *X* as marked in the vertical section of Fig. 11.44a. It will solidify into primary α in the temperature range represented by points 3 and 4. The composition of the liquid will move gradually towards point 5. Thereafter, the liquid L_1 will dissociate into α and liquid L_2 in the temperature interval 4 to 6. Liquid L_1 will be completely exhausted below the temperature represented by point 6. The solidification of the liquid L_2 will proceed by the ternary eutectic reaction $L_2 = \alpha + \beta$, as discussed in section 11.1

11.10 TERNARY ALLOY SYSTEM WITH A SYNTECTIC REACTION $L_1+L_2 = \beta$ IN ONE OF THE BINARIES AND A MINIMUM IN THE LIQUIDUS TEMPERATURE

The space model of the ternary system *A–B–C* with the binary system A–B showing the syntectic reaction is shown in Fig. 11.45. The three-phase field and the region of liquid immiscibility can be described on the same lines as that for the ternary system with a monotectic reaction in one of the binaries, section 11.9. c_1c_2 is the critical curve

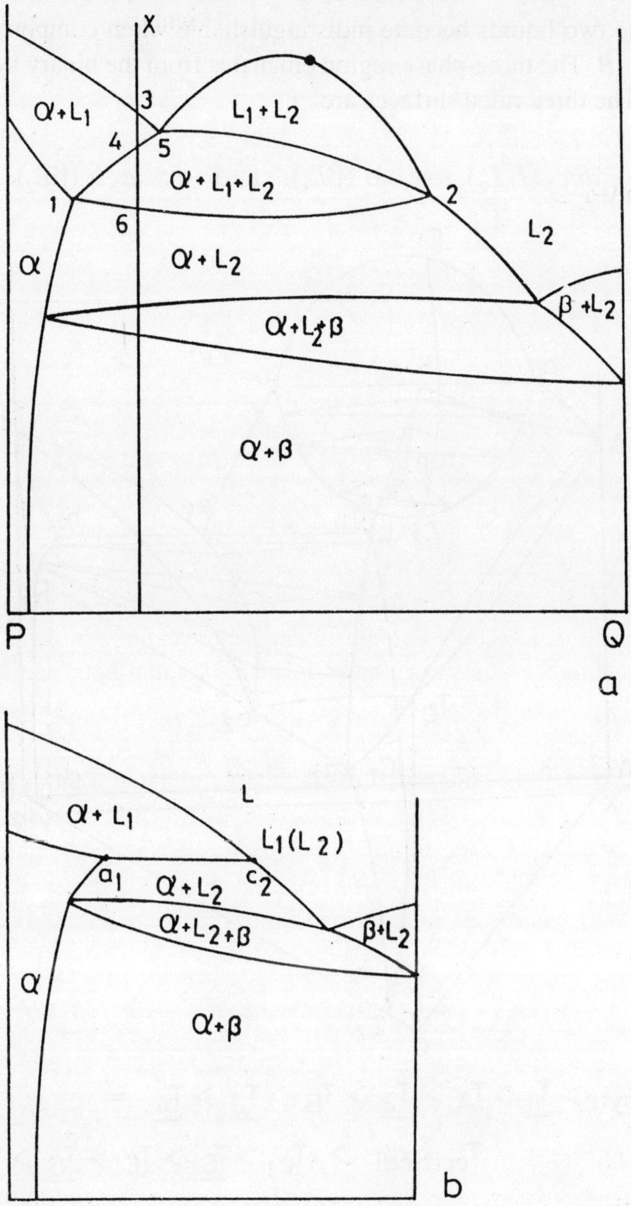

Fig. 11.44 Vertical sections through the space models of Fig. 11.41a.

along which the two liquids become indistinguishable when component C is a added to the binary A–B. The three-phase region emanates from the binary syntectic reaction isotherm asb. The three ruled surfaces are

$$abc_2\ (L_1L_2),\ ass_1c_2a\ (\beta L_1)\quad \text{and}\quad bss_1c_2\,b\ (\beta L_2)$$

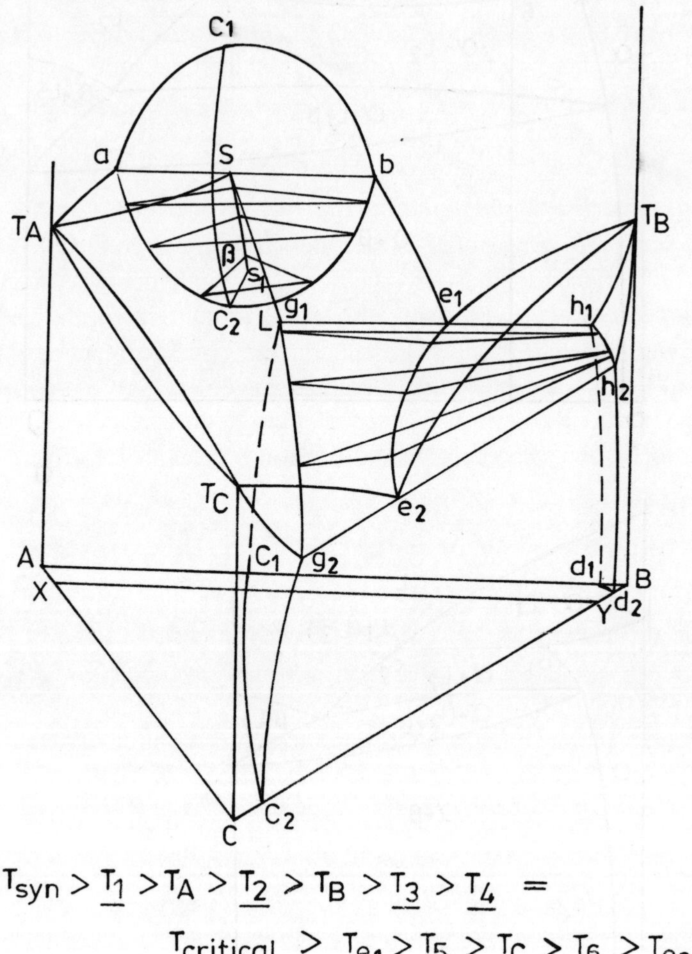

Fig. 11.45 Space model of a ternary system A–B–C showing a syntectic reaction in the binary A–B and a minimum critical point. The ternary three-phase reaction involving eutectics is drawn for completion only.

The tie-line c_2S_1 is a degenerate tie-triangle which crosses the three-phase field, $L_1 + L_2 + \beta$.

The isothermal sections are shown in Fig. 11.46. The two-phase region, L_1+L_2, appears in the form of a loop at all temperatures between T_{c_1} and T_{c_2}. The ($\beta+L_1+L_2$) phase field appears in all isothermal sections below T_s and above T_{s_1}. Since the monovariant syntectic reaction has similarity with the monovariant peritectic reaction, the β corner of the tie-triangle will face the side AB on which the syntectic reaction occurs. At the critical temperature, $T_{c_2} = T_{s_1} = T_4$, the tie-triangle terminates in a tie-line c_2s_1 with ($L_2+\beta$) and ($L_1+\beta$) phase fields lying on either side of it, Fig. 11.46d. Below T_{s_1}, the two liquids exist as a single liquid L_1 (L_2).

A vertical section at KL parallel to the side AB is shown in Fig. 11.47. The orientation of the three-phase region $L_1+L_2+\beta$ is consistent with that observed in the ternary system with a peritectic reaction. Any alloy composition lying in the vertical plane at XY and lying within points 1 and 2 will undergo the syntectic reaction $L_1+L_2 = \beta$. The product phase β will form over a temperature range. An alloy composition passing through point 3 will form 100 % β when the two liquids react with each other. For other alloy compositions, secondary solidification of β will occur from either liquids L_1 or L_2.

11.11 TERNARY ALLOY SYSTEM WITH A SYNTECTIC REACTION IN ONE BINARY AND A MONOTECTIC REACTION IN A SECOND BINARY

The space model of a ternary alloy system $A–B–C$ with a syntectic reaction $L_1+L_2 \Leftrightarrow \alpha$ in the binary $A–B$ and a monotectic reaction $L_1 = \alpha + L_2$ in the binary $B–C$ is shown in Fig. 11.48a. The third binary is an isomorphous system. The critical temperatures of the immiscibility gap of the two binary systems $A–B$ and $B–C$ are shown by points c_1 and c_2, respectively, with $T_{c_1} > T_{c_2}$. A simple ternary monovariant equilibrium may occur in the system with a gentle slope from point c_1 to c_2 along c_1c_2. The three-phase region emanates from the binary syntectic reaction isotherm T_{s_1}, and terminates on the monotectic reaction isotherm T_{m_2}. It is assumed that $T_{s_1} > T_{m_2}$. The three-phase region consists of the following ruled surfaces:

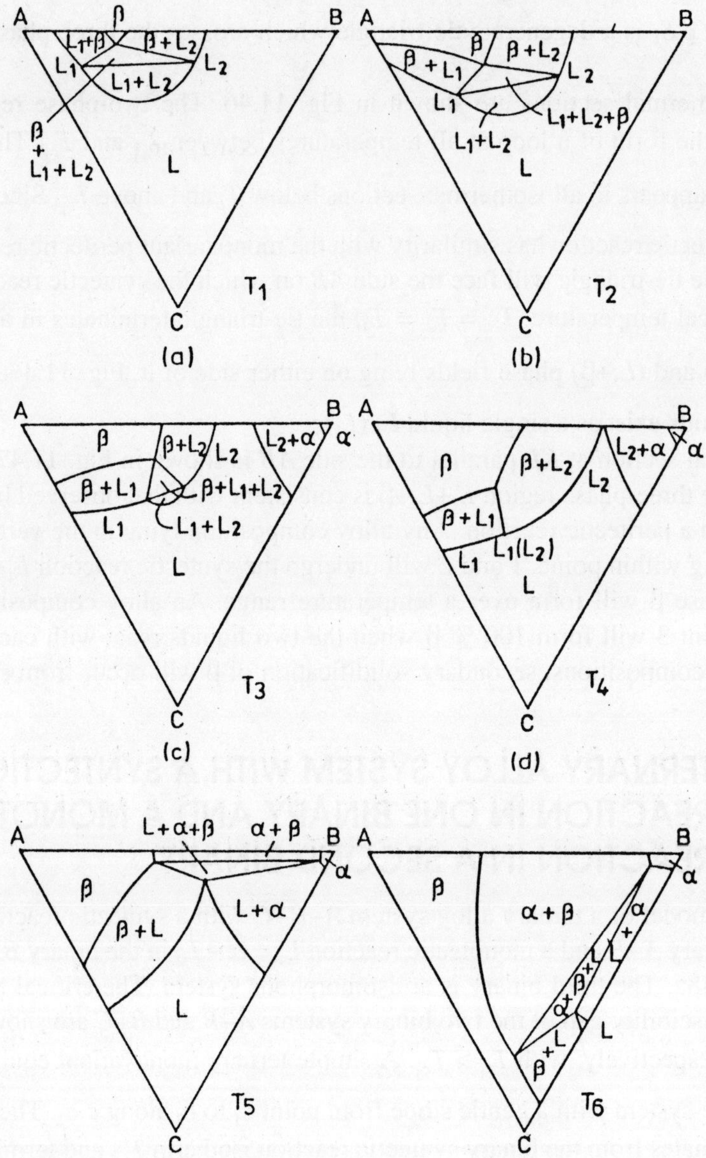

Fig. 11.46 Isothermal sections through the space model of Fig. 11.45.

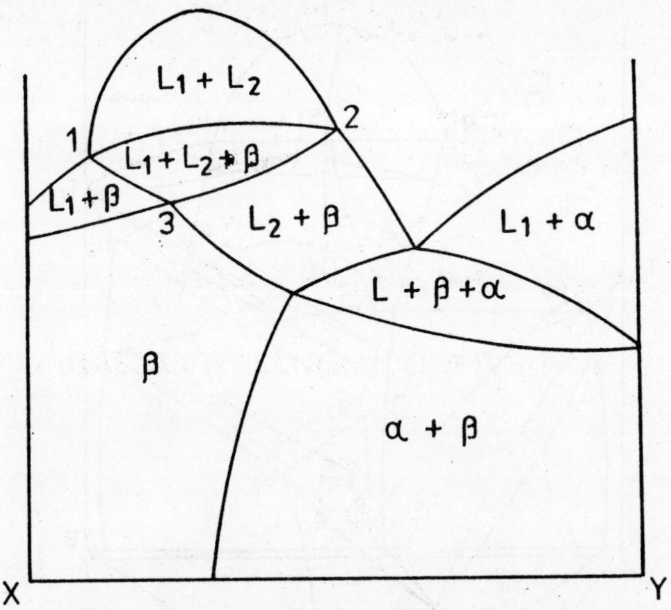

Fig. 11.47 Vertical section *XY* of the diagram in Fig. 11.45.

$s_1h_1m_2h_2s_1$ (αL_2 ruled surface)

$g_1s_1h_2g_2g_1$ (αL_1 ruled surface)

$g_1h_1m_2g_2g_1$ (L_1L_2 ruled surface)

The L_1L_2 ruled surface occupies the upper surface of the three-phase region but lies below the $L_1 + L_2$ phase region. Compositions of the conjugate phases L_1 and L_2 lie on surfaces $g_1c_1c_2g_2g_1$ and $h_1c_1c_2m_2h_1$, respectively. The two liquids become indistinguishable along c_1c_2. The three-phase field is constructed on the same lines as in the ternary system with the peritectic reaction on one of the binaries and the eutectic reaction on a second binary. The αL_2 phase region is twisted due to crossing over of lines s_1h_2 and m_2h_1. This will show up in the shape of the tie-triangle which will have a profound reversal in orientation, as shown in the space model, Fig. 11.48a. At lower temperatures there is an interaction between the binary eutectic ($a_1e_1b_1$) on the side *AB* and peritectic $p_2a_2b_2$ on the side *BC*. The three-phase region (α+β+L_1) is shown separately, Fig. 11.48b.

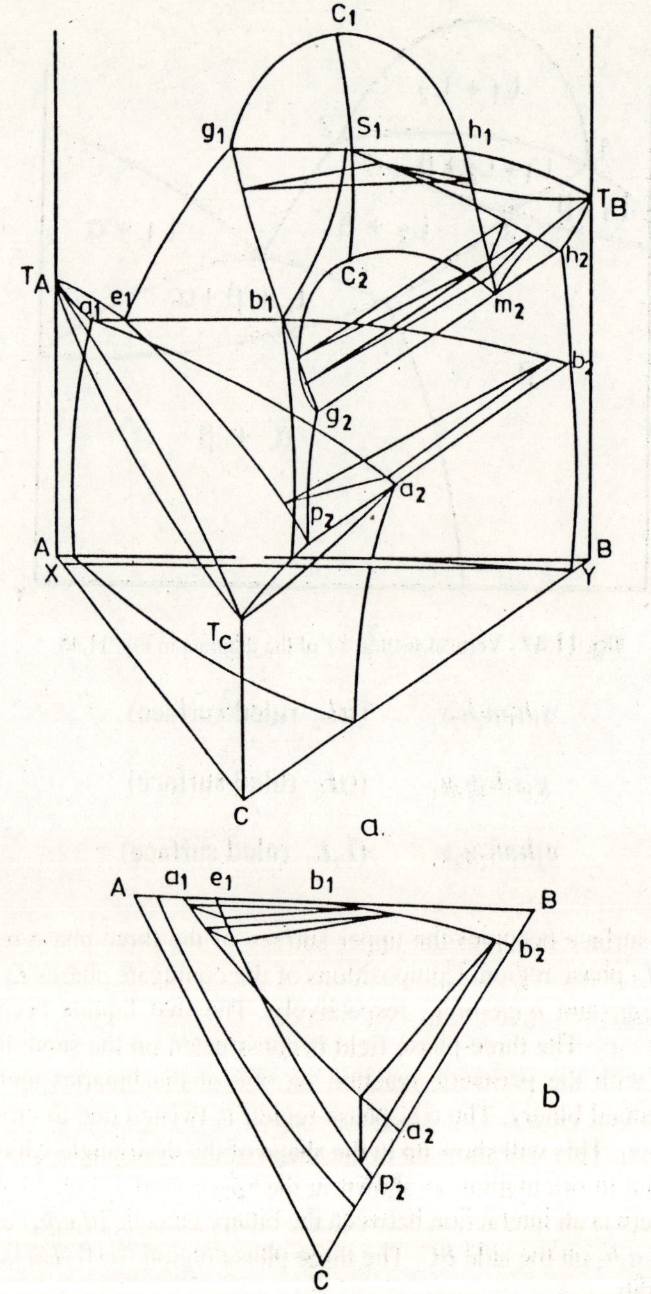

Fig. 11.48 (a) Space model of the ternary system *A–B–C* showing a syntectic reaction in binary *A–B* and a monotectic reaction in the binary *B–C*. (b) Projection of the various lines on the concentration triangle.

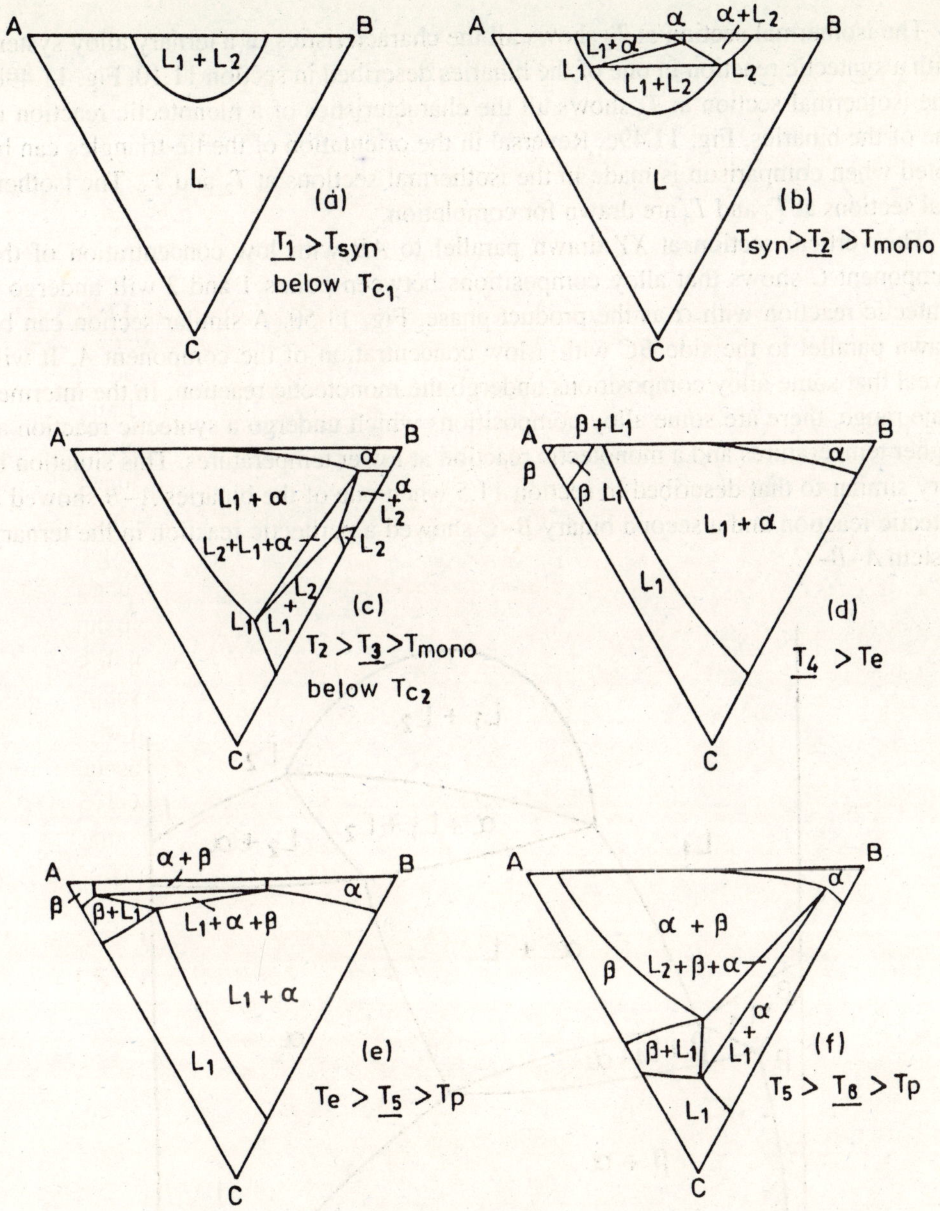

Fig. 11.49 Isothermal sections through the space model of Fig. 11.48.

The isothermal section at T_2 shows all the characteristics of a ternary alloy system with a syntectic reaction in one of the binaries described in section 11.10, Fig. 11.49b. The isothermal section at T_3 shows all the characteristics of a monotectic reaction in one of the binaries, Fig. 11.49c. Reversal in the orientation of the tie-triangles can be noted when comparison is made in the isothermal sections at T_2 and T_3. The isothermal sections at T_4 and T_6 are drawn for completion.

The vertical section at *XY* drawn parallel to *AB* with low concentration of the component *C* shows that alloy compositions between points 1 and 2 will undergo a syntectic reaction with α as the product phase, Fig. 11.50. A similar section can be drawn parallel to the side *BC* with a low concentration of the component *A*. It will reveal that some alloy compositions undergo the monotectic reaction. In the intermediate range, there are some alloy compositions which undergo a syntectic reaction at higher temperatures and a monotectic reaction at lower temperatures. This situation is very similar to that described in section 11.5 when one of the binaries *A–B* showed a eutectic reaction and a second binary *B–C* showed a peritectic reaction in the ternary system *A–B–C*.

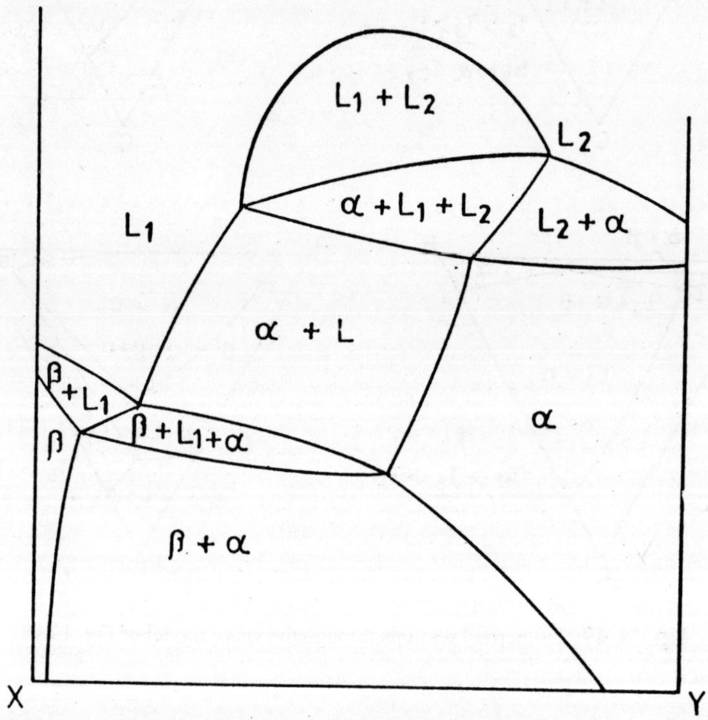

Fig. 11.50 Vertical section at *XY* of Fig. 11.48.

11.12 GENERAL RULES GOVERNING THE CONSTRUCTION OF THREE-PHASE REGIONS

1. Two single-phase regions are separated by a two-phase region involving the same phases.
2. Every three-phase region is surrounded by three two-phase and three single-phase regions.
3. The three two-phase regions surrounding the three-phase region are along the edges of the tie-triangle in isothermal sections.
4. Single-phase regions surrounding the three-phase region are along the corners of the tie-triangle in isothermal sections.
5. Each vertex of the tie-triangle is surrounded by four lines (no less and no more) only. This rule is very strictly followed in the construction of isothermal sections.
6. Each node of the three-phase region is connected to four lines too (only in the vertical section). There may be exceptions in a few cases.
7. The phase boundaries joining the corner of a tie-triangle when extended either lie both within the triangle or completely out of it.

PROBLEMS

1. With reference to Fig. 11.2, state which phase regions are separated by the following surfaces:
   (a) (i) $T_Be_1e_2T_B$ (ii) $a_1e_1e_2a_2$ (iii) $b_1d_1d_2b_2$ (iv) $a_1b_1b_2a_1$.
   (b) Draw the α and (α+β+*L*) phase fields separately and show tie-triangles in the three-phase field.
   (c) Draw vertical sections at (i) *AF* and (ii) *PQ*.
   (d) The vertical plane at *AF* meets the liquidus line e_1e_2 at *G*. Describe the cooling of the alloy passing through the point *G*.
2. An alloy *X* goes through the ternary three-phase reaction, $L \Leftrightarrow \alpha + \beta$. If compositions of the α, β and liquid phases are given, calculate relative amounts of the α, β and liquid phases at temperatures T_1 and T_2.

at T_1	*A*	*B*	*C*	at T_2	*A*	*B*	*C*
α(%)	85	10	5		70	15	15
β(%)	10	85	5		7	86	7
L(%)	40	40	20		25	45	30
X(%)	40	45	15				

3. With reference to Fig. 11.12, state which phase regions are separated by the following surfaces:
   (a) (i) aee_1c_1 (ii) $T_Aee_1L_1T_A$
   (b) Describe the cooling of an alloy composition passing through the point *P* in Fig. 11.15b.
   (c) Draw the vertical section at (i) the plane on *AF* which intersects the line e_1c_1 (ii) the plane on *GH* such that the line e_1c_1 lies on it, (see Fig. 11.14).
   (d) Draw the (α+*L*) and (α+β) phase regions separately and show the tie-lines.
4. (a) Draw the (α+β+*L*) phase region separately for the ternary system shown in Fig. 11.19. Show the shape of the region with the help of a number of tie-triangles.
   (b) Describe the cooling of an alloy composition passing through the point *m* in Fig. 11.19. What special characteristic is associated with the alloy?
5. With reference to the space mode of Fig. 11.25, which phase regions are separated by the following surfaces:
   (i) $p_1a_1a_2p_2p_1$ (ii) $b_1b_2d_2d_1$ (iii) $T_Ap_1p_2T_C$.
6. An alloy composition *X* (40% *A*, 50% *B*, 10% *C*) undergoes a peritectic reaction $L + \beta \Leftrightarrow \alpha$. The composition of the α, β and liquid phases are given at T_1 and T_2. Calculate the relative amount of the three phases at the two temperatures. What do you conclude?

at T_1	*A*	*B*	*C*	at T_2	*A*	*B*	*C*
α(%)	60	35	5		56	35	9
β(%)	8	90	2		6	90	4
L(%)	70	10	20		60	12	48

7. Describe the cooling of alloy compositions passing through the point *P* and *Q* in the vertical section shown in Fig. 11.27c. What difference in the microstructure do you expect? Draw the microstructure of the two alloy compositions.
8. Draw separately all the phase fields of the ternary diagram shown in Fig. 11.32a as an exploded model and outline surfaces bounding various phase fields.
9. (a) State with reference to Fig. 11.35 which phase regions are separated by the following surfaces:
   (i) $a_1e\,pa_2$ (ii) eb_1b_2p
   (b) Draw separately the (α+β+*L*) phase field of the ternary diagram shown in Fig. 11.35. Draw tie-triangles to show the shape of the three-phase field.
   (c) Describe the cooling of alloy compositions lying on the line *ep*: (i) closer to the point *e* (ii) closer to the point *p*.

10. (a) With reference to the ternary phase diagram of Fig. 11.41, state which phase regions are separated by the following surfaces:
    (i) $T_A T_C g_2 g_1 a$ (ii) $mc_1\ c_2$ (iii) $abc_2\ a_1\ a$
    (b) Describe the cooling of an alloy composition passing through point "5" in the vertical section shown in Fig. 11.44a and any point on the line a_1c_2 in Fig. 11.44b.
11. Binary systems *A–B* and *B–C* of the ternary *A–B–C* show the syntectic reaction $L_1+L_2 \Leftrightarrow \beta$. Liquids L_1 and L_2 undergo the following reactions at lower temperatures:

$$A-B\ \ L_1 \overset{T_{e_1}}{\Longleftrightarrow} \alpha+\beta \quad \text{and} \quad L_2+\beta \overset{T_{p_1}}{\Longleftrightarrow} \gamma$$

$$B-C\ \ L_1 \overset{T_{e_2}}{\Longleftrightarrow} \alpha+\beta \quad \text{and} \quad L_2 \overset{T_{e_3}}{\Longleftrightarrow} \beta+\gamma$$

The six binary invariant temperatures are in the order $T_{S_1} > T_{S_2} > T_{e_1} > T_{p_1} > T_{e_2} > T_{e_3}$ and the binary *A–C* is isomorphous. The ternary phase diagram shows the following three-phase fields: $(L_1+L_2+\beta)$, $(L_1+\alpha+\beta)$ and $(L_2+\beta+\gamma)$

    (a) Draw the space model and its projection on the concentration triangle.
    (b) Draw sufficient number of isothermal sections to reveal all phase fields.
    (c) Draw vertical sections parallel to *AB* at a number of positions to bring out the shape of various phase fields.
    (d) Describe cooling of typical alloys going through $(L_1+L_2+\beta)$ and $(L_1+\alpha+\beta)$ phase fields.

12. A ternary alloy composition (25% *A*, 45% *B* and 30% *C*) undergoes three-phase reactions involving α, β and liquid phases. The compositions of the α, β and liquid phases at temperatures T_1 and T_2 are given below:

at T_1	*A*	*B*	*C*	at T_2	*A*	*B*	*C*
α(%)	40	27	33		32	30	38
β(%)	5	90	5		4	90	6
L(%)	30	28	42		25	25	50

Show these compositions in the concentration triangle and calculate the relative amounts of the three phases at T_1 and T_2. What do you conclude in terms of the nature of the three-phase reaction occurring at T_1 and T_2 in this illustration?

Chapter 12

TERNARY ALLOY SYSTEM—FOUR-PHASE EQUILIBRIA

According to the phase rule, in a ternary system, an invariant reaction occurs when four phases are in equilibrium with each other. There are zero degrees of freedom and compositions of all phases and the temperature are fixed. That is, the reaction occurs on an isothermal plane with compositions of all four phases lying on the plane at fixed positions. We will discuss four-phase equilibrium involving a liquid and three solid phases, α, β and γ. The four-phase reaction in a ternary system can be classified into:

	$L = \alpha + \beta + \gamma$,	Class I, Ternary eutectic reaction,
	$L + \alpha = \beta + \gamma$,	Class II, Ternary quasi-peritectic reaction,
and	$L + \alpha + \beta = \gamma$,	Class III, Ternary peritectic reaction.

The quasi-peritectic reaction is intermediate between eutectic and peritectic reactions. Some compositions of the ternary alloy will solidify by the eutectic reaction and others through a peritectic one. The discussion of the four-phase equilibrium in the ternary system can be extended by substituting one of the solid phases by a second liquid L_2, thus involving a monotectic or a quasi-syntectic reaction. Further, the liquid phase can be substituted by a fourth solid phase δ giving rise to eutectoid, quasi-eutectoid or peritectoid reactions. The above three classes of four-phase equilibrium can be studied to illustrate their distinguishing features. The variants of the Class I, II and III reactions will also be discussed.

12.1 CLASS I: THE TERNARY EUTECTIC REACTION

12.1.1 The Space Model

The simplest example of the four-phase Class I reaction can be, considered with binary eutectic reactions,

$$L = \alpha + \beta, L = \beta + \gamma \quad \text{and} \quad L = \alpha + \gamma.$$

It is understood that the crystal structures of the α, β and gamma phases in the above reactions are consistent. That is, the α phase, in the first and third reaction has the same crystal structure. The space model is shown in Fig. 12.1. The three binary reactions are indicated by the horizontal lines $a_1e_1b_1$, $a_2e_2b_2$ and $a_3e_3b_3$. The ternary eutectic reaction, L = α + β + γ, occurs on an isothermal or invariant plane αβγ, as shown in Fig. 12.1. The invariant reaction plane T_E occurs at a temperature below the melting points of the three components A, B and C and the binary reaction isotherms T_{e_1}, T_{e_2} and T_{e_3}. The ternary system shows the following phase regions:

Single-phase fields,	α, β, γ, liquid
Two-phase fields,	L+α, L+β, L+γ, α+β, α+γ, β+γ
Three-phase fields,	L+α+β, L+α+γ, L+β+γ, α+β+γ
Four-phase region,	L+α+β+γ

As a general rule of construction of the complete space model, the liquid compositions of the binaries are joined with the ternary liquid composition on the invariant plane. In the case of the ternary eutectic system, points e_1, e_2 and e_3 are joined to the

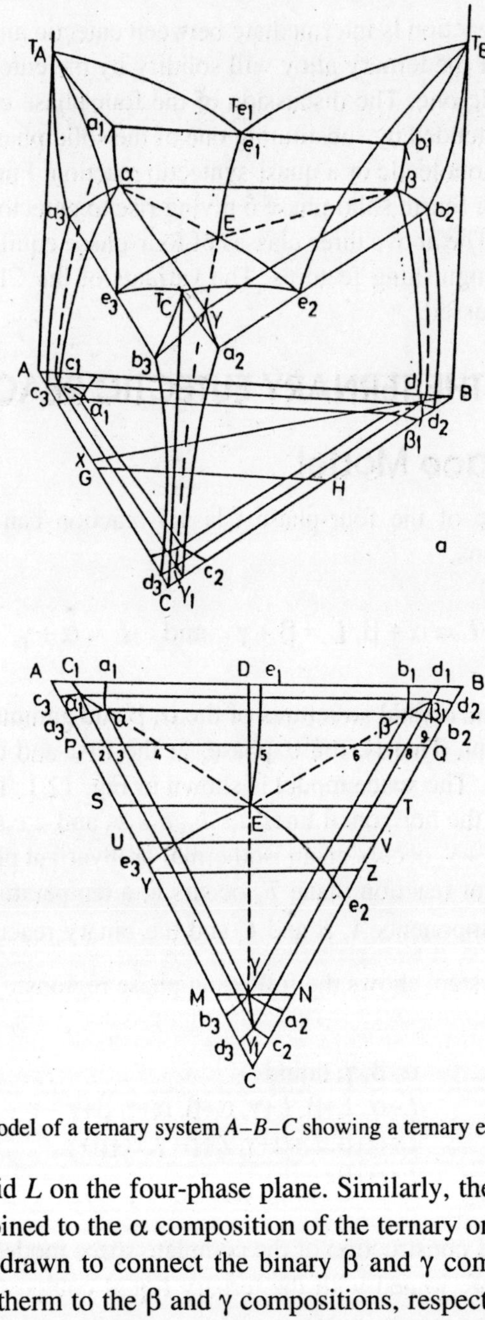

Fig. 12.1 The space model of a ternary system A–B–C showing a ternary eutectic reaction, $L = \alpha+\beta+\gamma$

ternary eutectic liquid L on the four-phase plane. Similarly, the α phase composition of the binaries are joined to the α composition of the ternary on the four-phase plane. Similarly, lines are drawn to connect the binary β and γ composition points at the eutectic reaction isotherm to the β and γ compositions, respectively, on the invariant plane. The solubility of the α, β and γ in each other changes as the temperature decreases below the four-phase plane and lines $\alpha\alpha_1$, $\beta\beta_1$ and $\gamma\gamma_1$ terminate on the triangle $\alpha_1\beta_1\gamma_1$ lying at the ambient temperature.

Following the rules of construction of the three-phase region on an isothermal section, described in Chapter 11, the three two-phase regions must lie along the sides and the single-phase regions on the corners of the tie-triangle $\alpha\beta\gamma$. The three two-phase regions (α+β), (α+γ), and (β+γ) ascent from the base of the space model and terminate on the corresponding ruled surfaces of the three-phase region. For example, the (α+β) phase region terminates on the $\alpha\beta$ ruled surface of the (L+α+β) phase field from below. Similarly, the (β+γ) and (α+γ) phase regions terminate on the $\beta\gamma$ and $\alpha\gamma$ ruled surfaces, respectively, of the (L+β+γ) and (L+α+γ) regions from below.

The three-phase regions involving a liquid and two solids emanate from the binaries and terminate on the four-phase plane. For example, the (L+α+β) phase region lies below the region of primary crystallization of the α and β phases (from the liquid) and involves αL and βL ruled surfaces on either side of the line e_1E which forms a trough from e_1 to E. It emanates from the binary eutectic reaction isotherm $a_1e_1b_1$ and terminates on the triangle $\alpha\beta L$ on the four-phase plane. Similarly, the (L+β+γ) phase region is bounded by the βL and γL ruled surfaces from above and the $\beta\gamma$ ruled surface from below. It emanates from the binary $a_2e_2b_2$ and terminates on the triangle $\beta\gamma L$ on the four-phase plane. The (L+α+γ) phase region emanates from the binary reaction isotherm $a_3e_3b_3$ forming ruled surfaces αL and γL from above and $\alpha\gamma$ from below and terminates on the triangle $L\alpha\gamma$ on the four-phase plane.

The (α+L) phase region which involves primary crystallization of the α phase from the liquid above the αL ruled surfaces of the (L+α+β) and (L+α+γ) phase fields and is bounded by liquidus and solidus surfaces. Details of various ruled surfaces and phase regions are given in Table 12.1.

The single, two and three-phase regions of the space model are drawn separately in Fig. 12.2. The single-phase fields lie between the solidus and the solvus.

12.1.2 Isothermal Sections

The isothermal sections at a number of temperatures are shown below.

Fig. 12.3a For the ternary eutectic system with $T_B > T_A > T_c > T_{e_1} > T_{e_2} > T_{e_3} > T_E$, the isothermal section at T_1 defined by $T_B > T_1 > T_A$ will intersect the (L + β) phase field. The section shows the (L+β) phase region and β and liquid phase fields on either side of it.

Table 12.1 Various Phase Fields in the Ternary Eutectic System (Class I)

Liquidus Surface	(β+L): $T_B e_1 E e_2 T_B$, ($\alpha + L$): $T_A e_1 E e_3 T_A$, (γ+L): $T_C e_3 E e_2 T_C$
Solidus Surface	(β+L): $T_B b_1 \beta b_2 T_B$, (α+L): $T_A a_1 \alpha a_3 T_A$, (γ+L): $T_C b_3 \gamma a_2 T_C$
Three-Phase regions and the corresponding ruled surfaces	(α+β+L):$a_1 e_1 E \alpha(\alpha L)$, $b_1 e_1 E \beta(\beta L)$, $a_1 b_1 \beta \alpha(\alpha\beta)$ (α+γ+L): $a_3 \alpha E e_3(\alpha L)$, $b_3 e_3 E \gamma(\gamma L)$, $a_3 b_3 \gamma \alpha(\alpha\gamma)$ (β+γ+L): $b_2 \beta E a_2(\beta L)$, $a_2 e_2 E \gamma(\gamma L)$, $a_2 b_2 \beta \gamma(\beta\gamma)$ (α+β+γ): $\alpha\alpha_1\beta_1\beta(\alpha\beta)$, $\beta\beta_1\gamma_1\gamma(\beta\gamma)$, $\alpha\alpha_1\gamma_1\gamma(\alpha\gamma)$
Four-phase plane	$\alpha\beta\gamma$
Two-Phase Regions bounded by	(α+L): $T_A e_1 E e_3 T_A$, $T_A a_1 \alpha a_3 T_A$, $a_1 e_1 E \alpha a_1$ and $a_3 e_3 E \alpha a_1$ (β+L): $T_B e_1 E e_2 T_B$, $T_B b_1 \beta b_2 T_B$, $b_1 e_1 E \beta b_1$ and $b_2 e_2 E \beta b_2$ (γ+L): $T_C e_2 E e_3 T_C$, $T_C b_3 \gamma a_2 T_C$, $a_2 e_2 E \gamma a_2$ and $b_3 e_3 E \gamma b_3$ (α+β): $a_1 \alpha \alpha_1 c_1$, $b_1 \beta \beta_1 d_1$ and $\alpha\beta\beta_1\alpha_1$ (α+γ): $a_3 \alpha \alpha_1 c_3$, $b_3 \gamma \gamma_1 d_3$ and $\alpha\gamma\gamma_1\alpha_1$ (β+γ): $b_2 \beta \beta_1 d_2$, $a_2 \gamma \gamma_1 c_2$ and $\gamma\beta\beta_1\gamma_1$
Single-Phase regions bounded by	α: $T_A a_1 c_1 A T_A$, $T_A a_3 c_3 A T_A$, $T_A a_1 \alpha a_3$, $a_3 \alpha \alpha_1 c_3$ and $a_1 \alpha \alpha_1 c_1$. β: $T_B b_1 d_1 B T_B$, $T_B b_2 d_2 B T_B$, $T_B b_1 \beta b_2 T_B$ and $b_1 \beta \beta_1 d_1$ and $b_2 \beta \beta_1 d_2$. γ: $T_C a_2 c_2 C T_C$, $T_C b_3 d_3 C T_C$, $T_C a_2 \gamma b_3$, $b_3 \gamma \gamma_1 d_3$ and $a_2 \gamma \gamma_1 c_2$.

Fig. 12.3b The section at T_2 defined by $T_1 > T_A > T_2 > T_c$ will show the α and $(L + \alpha)$ phase regions in addition to the β and (L + β) phase fields.

Fig. 12.3c The section at $T_3 = T_{e_1}$ shows that the liquidus on the binary A–B meets at e_1. The γ and (γ + L) phase fields are also intersected at T_3 as shown in the figure.

Fig. 12.3d The temperature T_4 lies just below T_{e_1} giving way to the appearance of the (L+α+β) phase region in the isothermal section.

Fig. 12.3e The tie-triangle (α+β+L) moves away from the binary side AB as the temperature gradually decreases below T_{e_1} because the $\alpha\beta$ ruled surface starting from the binary side AB is to move away and terminate on the $\alpha\beta$ line on the four-phase plane. The γ phase field expands as the temperature is lowered.

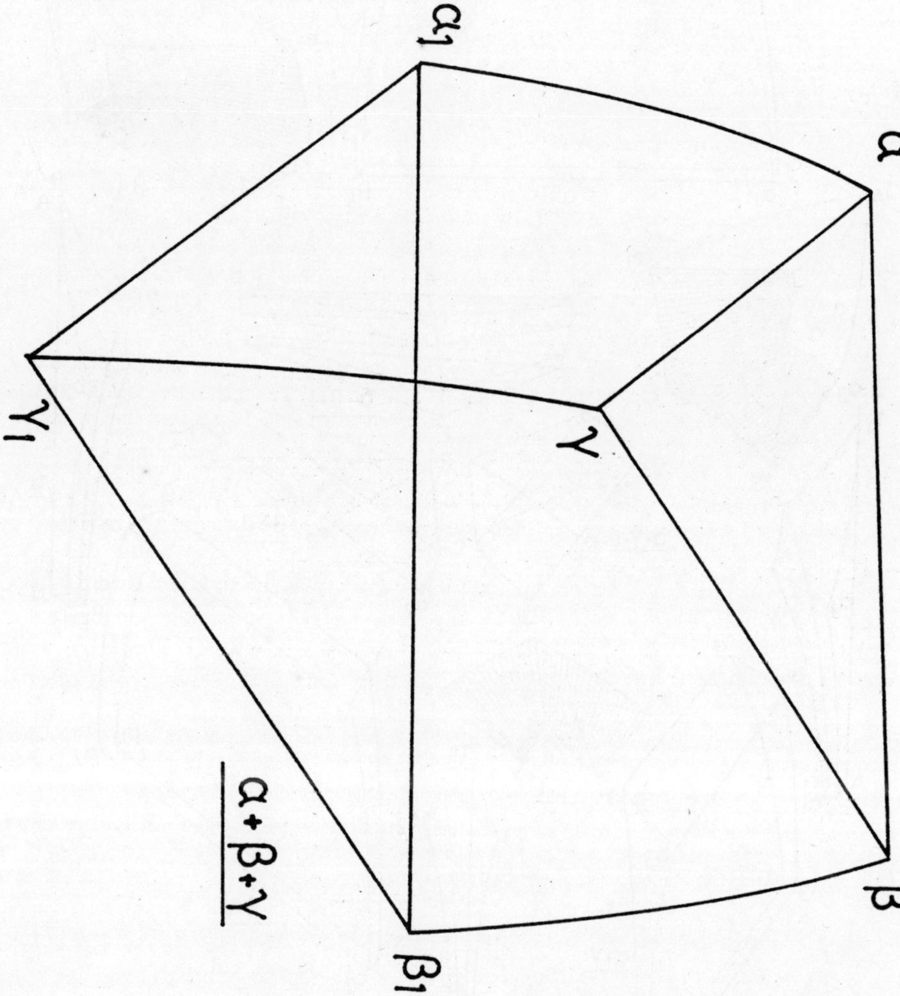

Fig. 12.2 Exploded model of the ternary eutectic system showing separate phase fields (Cont.)

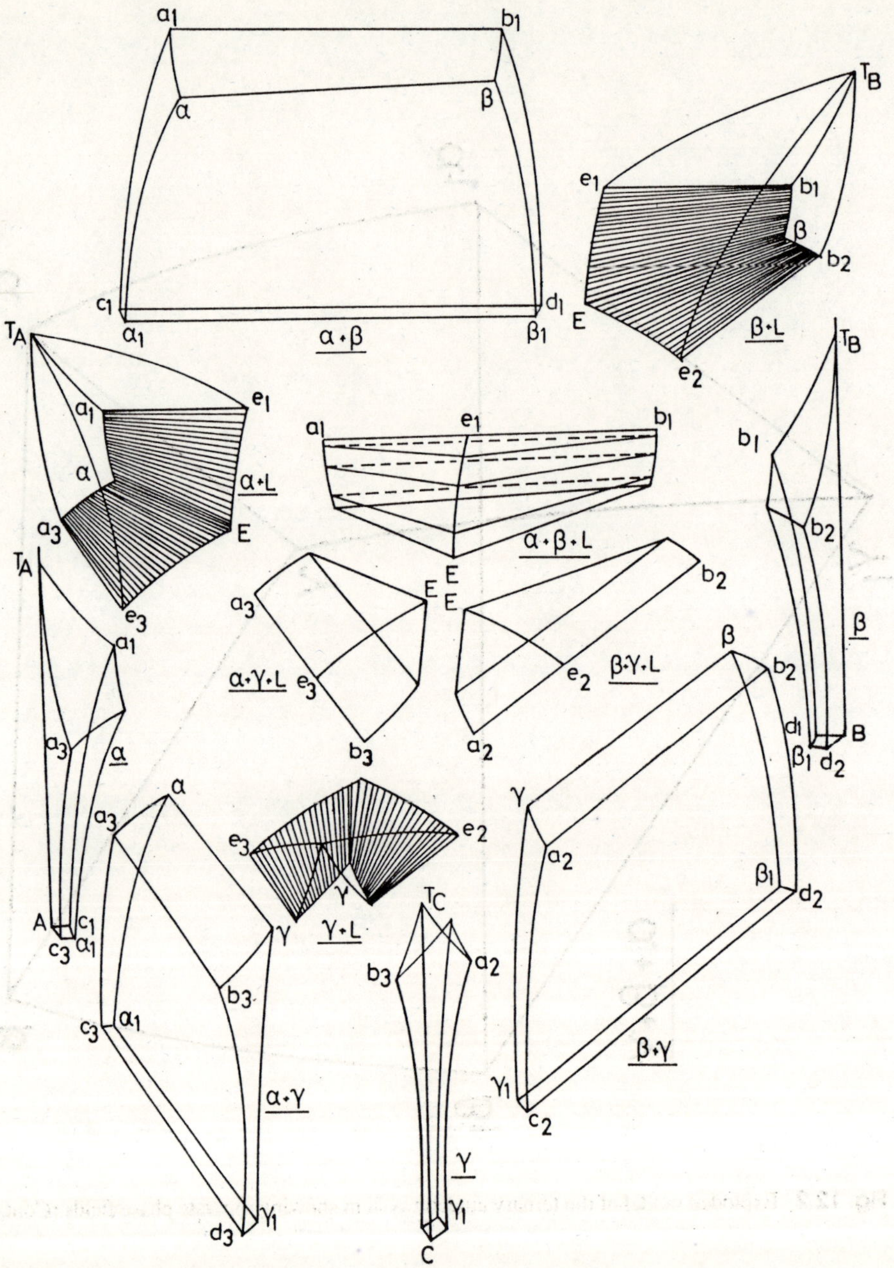

Fig. 12.2 Exploded model of the ternary eutectic system showing separate phase fields.

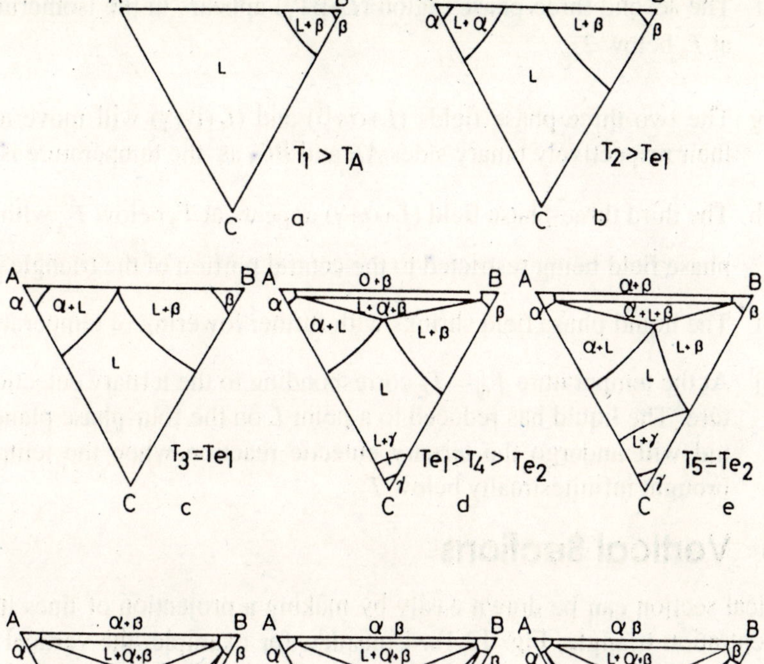

Fig. 12.3 Isothermal sections through the space model of Fig. 12.1

Fig. 12.3f The second three-phase region (L+β+γ) appears in the isothermal section at T_6 below T_{e_2}.

Fig. 12.3g The two three-phase fields (L+α+β) and (L+β+γ) will move away from their respectively binary sides AB and BC, as the temperature is lowered.

Fig. 12.3h The third three-phase field (L+α+γ) appears at T_8 below T_{e_3} with the liquid phase field being restricted to the central portion of the triangle ABC.

Fig. 12.3i The liquid phase field shrinks with further lowering of temperature to T_9.

Fig. 12.3j At the temperature $T_{10} = T_E$ corresponding to the ternary eutectic temperature. The liquid has reduced to a point L on the four-phase plane. The liquid will undergo the ternary eutectic reaction when the temperature is brought infinitesimally below T_E.

12.1.3 Vertical Sections

The vertical section can be drawn easily by making a projection of lines in space on the concentration triangle, Fig. 12.1b. Consider, for example, the vertical section at PQ drawn parallel to the side AB of the triangle ABC. The section at PQ intersects various lines in space at points 1 to 9. The following phase regions must appear in the vertical section between the pair of points.

1 – 2 (α+γ) phase field at the ambient temperature.

2 – 3 Increasing solid solubility of the component B with point "3" lying on the four-phase plane (drawn as a horizontal line parallel to PQ).

3 – 4 The three-phase field (α+γ+L) terminates on the four-phase plane between these points. The αL and αγ ruled surfaces appear as lines. They meet the ordinate at P.

4 – 6 The three-phase field (α+β+L) terminates on the four-phase plane between these points. The monovariant liquid curve is intersected at point "5". Points 4–5–6 form a triangular three-phase region with point "5" being at a higher temperature. Lines 4 – 5 and 5 – 6 are intersections of ruled surfaces αL and βL with the vertical plane.

6 – 7 The three-phase region (β+γ+L) terminates on the four-phase plane between these points. The intersection of the vertical plane with the βL and βγ ruled surfaces appear as lines which terminate on the ordinate at Q.

7 – 8 Increasing solid solubility of the component B in the (β+γ) phase field. The line is an intersection of the solvus surface, (β+γ)/(α+β+γ), with the vertical plane.

8 – 9 (β+γ) phase field at the ambient temperature.

5 – 9 The intersection of the liquidus surface with the vertical plane forming the (β+L) phase field below it.

1 – 5 The intersection of the liquidus surface with the vertical plane forming the (α+L) phase field.

With the above unscrambling, the vertical section at *PQ* can be sketched, Fig. 12.4a. Following a similar procedure, the vertical sections are drawn at *ST*, *UV*, *YZ*, *MN* and *CD*, Fig. 12.4.

12.1.4 Solidification of Alloys

The course of solidification of an alloy in the ternary four-phase (Class I) system depends upon the original alloy composition. We will consider solidification of alloys lying at different positions in the concentration triangle, Fig. 12.5.

(i) Alloy composition E – The alloy does not undergo primary or secondary crystallization of any of the three phases. The liquid dissociates into α, β and γ phases at the invariant temperature.

(ii) Alloy compositions lying on lines αE, βE or γE – The solidification of these alloys will begin by crystallization of primary α, β or γ phases. The remaining liquid will dissociate by the ternary eutectic reaction. For example, the solidification of an alloy lying on the line αE will begin by deposition of the primary α phase. The composition of the α and liquid phases will gradually move towards points α and E, respectively. The remaining liquid will dissociate into α+β+γ phases at the ternary eutectic temperature.

(iii) Alloy compositions lying in regions like $b_1e_1E\beta b_1$ – The liquid upon cooling touches the liquidus surface of the (β+L) phase field, thereby initiating crystallization of the primary β phase. This is shown by the tie-line β_1L_1 in the space diagram of Fig. 12.5. More primary β phase forms from the liquid as the temperature is lowered with compositions of the solid and liquid changing along the solidus and liquidus surfaces as discussed in Chapter 10. The composition of the liquid moves towards the line e_1E and it meets the line e_1E at point L_3 at the temperature T_3. The liquid becomes saturated with solute such that crystallization of both α and β phases occurs below T_3. The composition of the

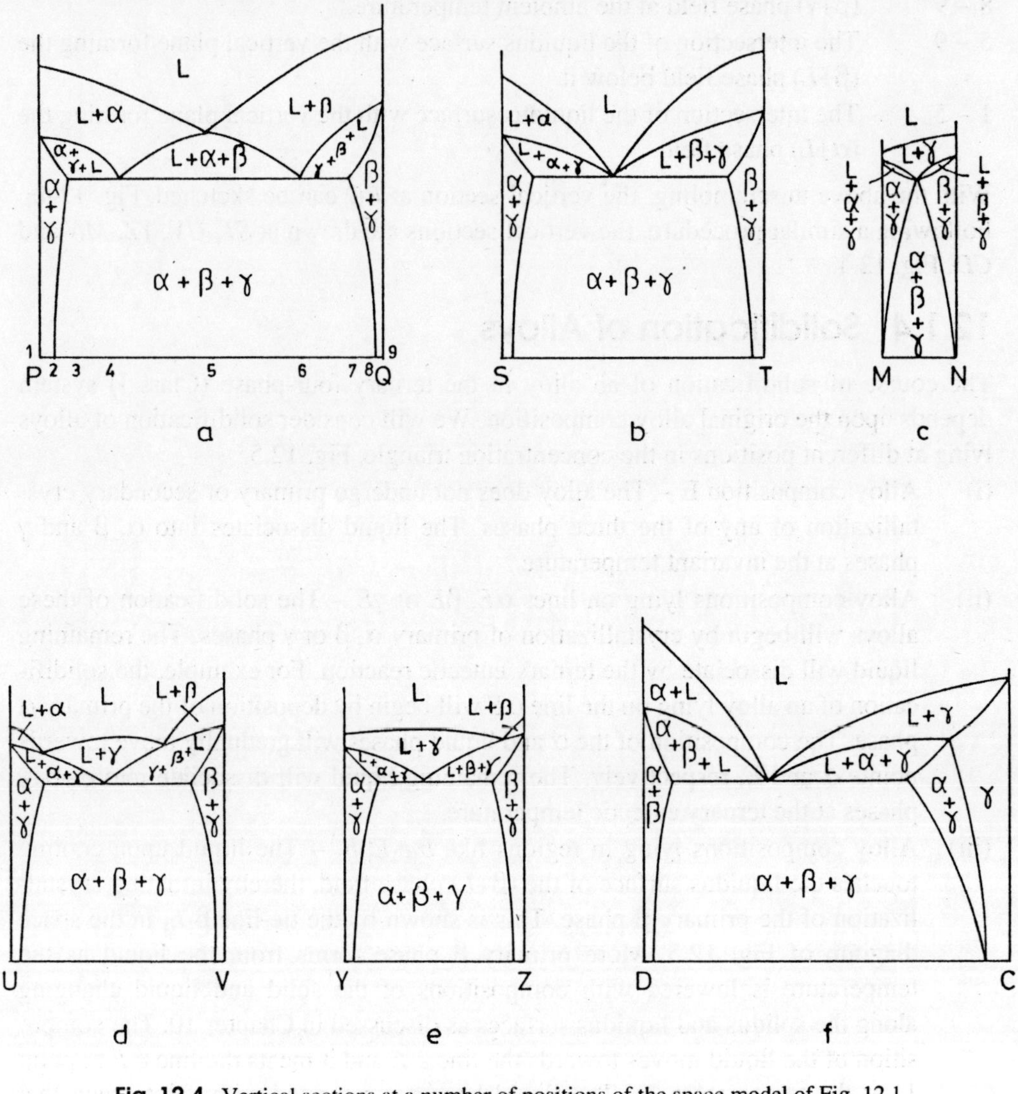

Fig. 12.4 Vertical sections at a number of positions of the space model of Fig. 12.1. The positions *PQ*, *ST*, *UT*, *YZ*, *MN* and *CD* are shown in Fig. 12.1.

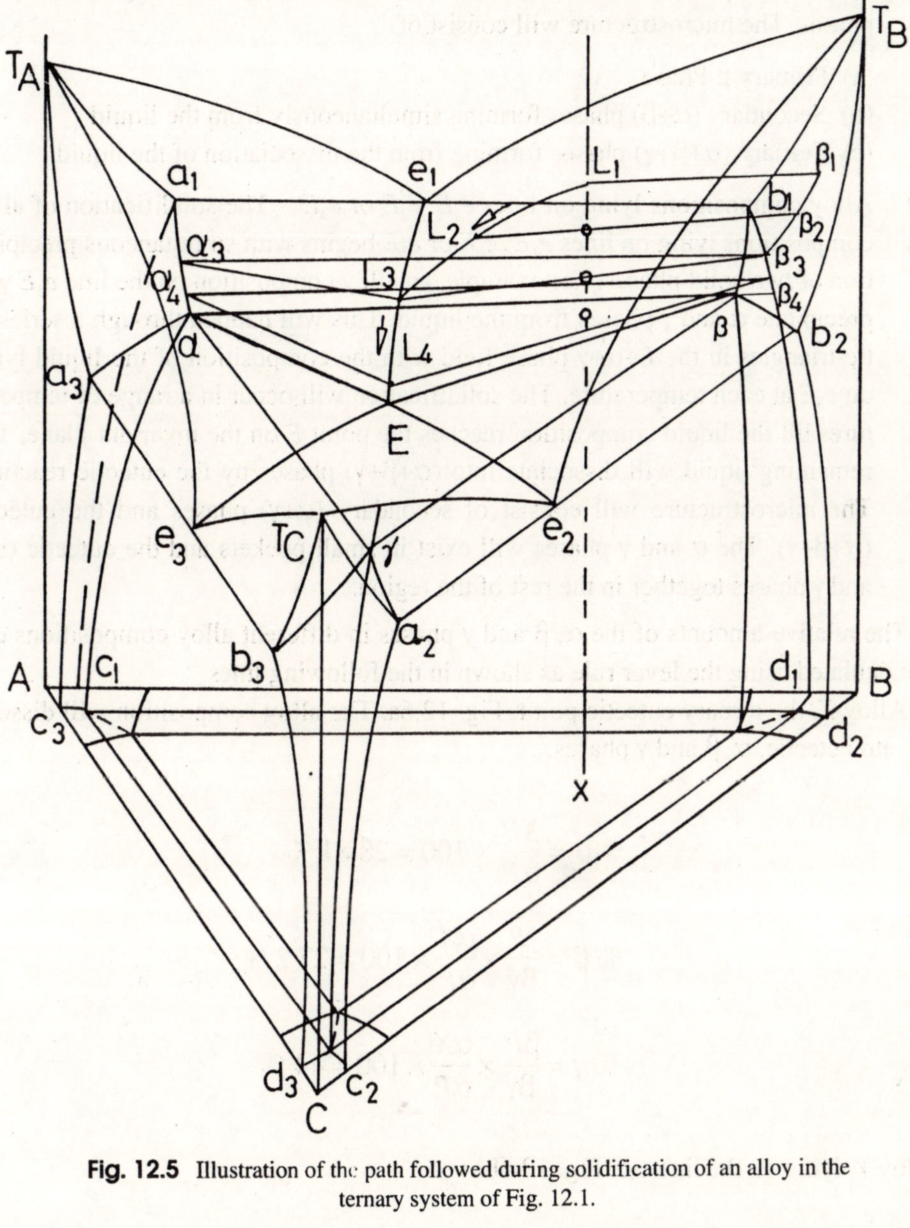

Fig. 12.5 Illustration of the path followed during solidification of an alloy in the ternary system of Fig. 12.1.

liquid gradually moves towards the ternary eutectic E. The remaining liquid dissociates by the eutectic reaction at the invariant temperature T_E into $(\alpha+\beta+\gamma)$ phases. The microstructure will consist of

(a) Primary β Phase
(b) Secondary $(\alpha+\beta)$ phases forming simultaneously from the liquid
(c) Tertiary $(\alpha+\beta+\gamma)$ phases forming from the dissociation of the liquid.

(iv) Alloy compositions lying on lines e_1E, e_2E or e_3E – The solidification of alloy compositions lying on lines e_1E, e_2E or e_3E begins with simultaneous precipitation of two solid phases. For example, an alloy composition on the line e_3E will precipitate α and γ phases from the liquid. This will happen through a series of tie-triangles in the $L+\alpha+\gamma$ phase field with the composition of the liquid lying on e_3E at each temperature. The solidification will occur in a range of temperatures till the liquid composition reaches the point E on the invariant plane. The remaining liquid will dissociate into $(\alpha+\beta+\gamma)$ phases by the eutectic reaction. The microstructure will consist of secondary $(\alpha+\gamma)$ phases and the eutectic $(\alpha+\beta+\gamma)$. The α and γ phases will exist in small pockets and the eutectic α, β and γ phases together in the rest of the region.

The relative amounts of the α, β and γ phases in different alloy compositions can be calculated using the lever rule as shown in the following lines.

Alloy X, the ternary eutectic point, Fig. 12.6a. The alloy composition will dissociate into eutectic, α, β and γ phases.

$$\%\,\alpha = \frac{XP}{\alpha P} \times 100 = 28.81\ \%$$

$$\%\,\beta = \frac{\gamma P}{\beta\gamma} \times \frac{\alpha X}{\alpha P} \times 100 = 27.2\ \%$$

$$\%\,\gamma = \frac{\beta P}{\beta\gamma} \times \frac{\alpha X}{\alpha P} \times 100 = 44\ \%$$

Alloy Y, lying on the line αL, Fig. 12.6b.

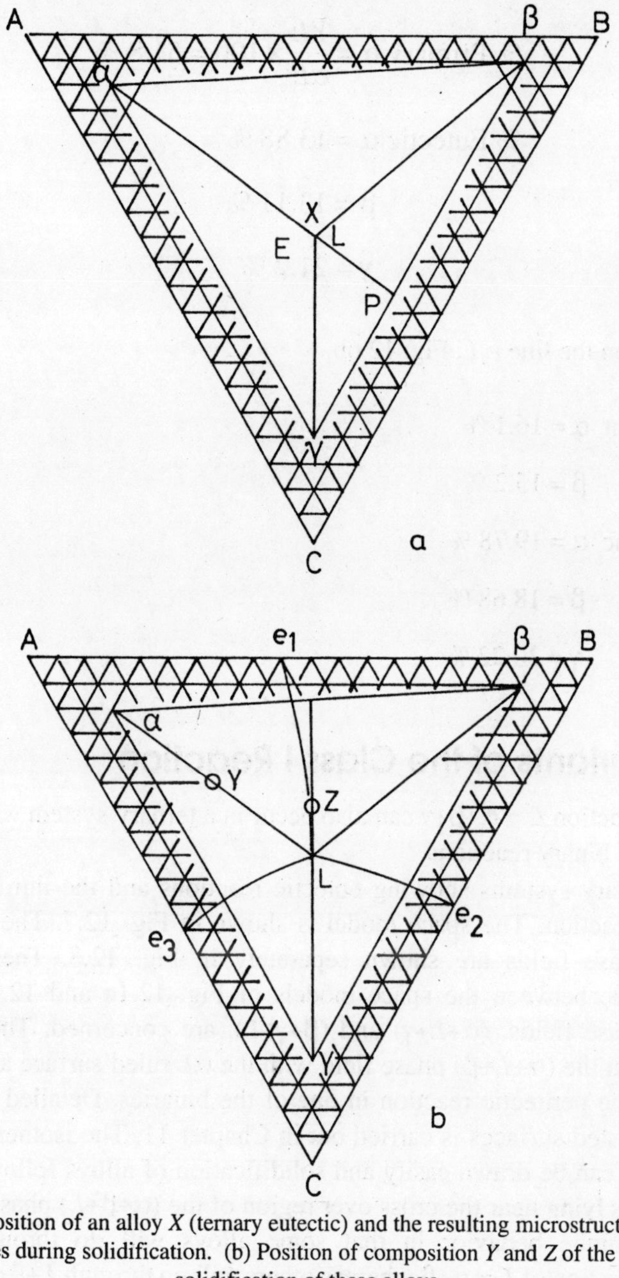

Fig. 12.6 (a) Position of an alloy *X* (ternary eutectic) and the resulting microstructural development of phases during solidification. (b) Position of composition *Y* and *Z* of the text and solidification of these alloys.

$$\% \text{ Primary } \alpha = \frac{YL}{\alpha L} \times 100 = 51.8\ \%$$

$$\% \text{ Eutectic } \alpha = 13.88\ \%$$

$$\beta = 13.11\ \%$$

$$\gamma = 21.2\ \%$$

Alloy Z, lying on the line e_1L, Fig. 12.6b.

The monovariant $\alpha = 16.1\ \%$

$\beta = 15.2\ \%$

Eutectic $\alpha = 19.78\ \%$

$\beta = 18.68\ \%$

$\gamma = 30.22\ \%$

12.1.5 Variants of the Class I Reaction

The eutectic reaction $L = \alpha+\beta+\gamma$ can also occur in a ternary system with the following combination of binary reactions.

(i) Two binary systems showing eutectic reactions and the third showing a peritectic reaction. The space model is shown in Fig. 12.7. The single, two and three-phase fields are shown separately in Fig. 12.8. There is very little difference between the space models of Fig. 12.1a and 12.7a as far as the three-phase fields, ($\alpha+L+\gamma$) and ($\beta+\gamma+L$), are concerned. The difference lies mainly in the ($\alpha+L+\beta$) phase field with the αL ruled surface appearing twisted due to the peritectic reaction in one of the binaries. Detailed interpretation of such twisted surfaces is carried out in Chapter 11. The isothermal and vertical sections can be drawn easily and solidification of alloys followed. Alloy compositions lying near the cross over region of the ($\alpha+\beta+L$) phase field will show some unique behavior in that some alloys will go through a secondary crystallization of $L = \alpha+\beta$ whereas others will go through $L+\beta = \alpha$ reaction. The liquid will always dissociate by the eutectic reaction at the invariant temperature.

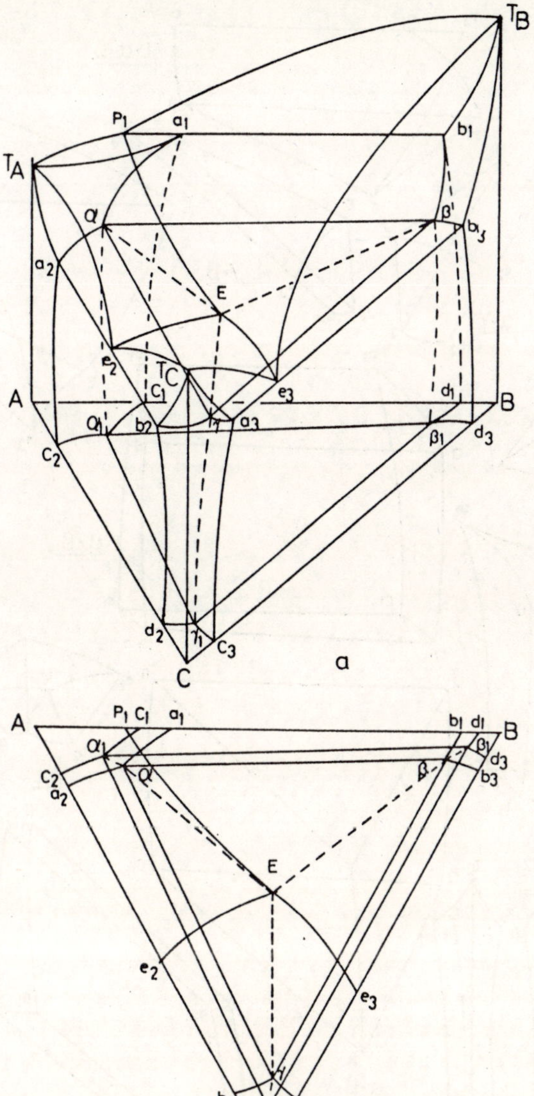

Fig. 12.7 (a) Space model showing a variant of ternary eutectic reaction. (b) Projection of lines in space on the base of the concentration triangle.

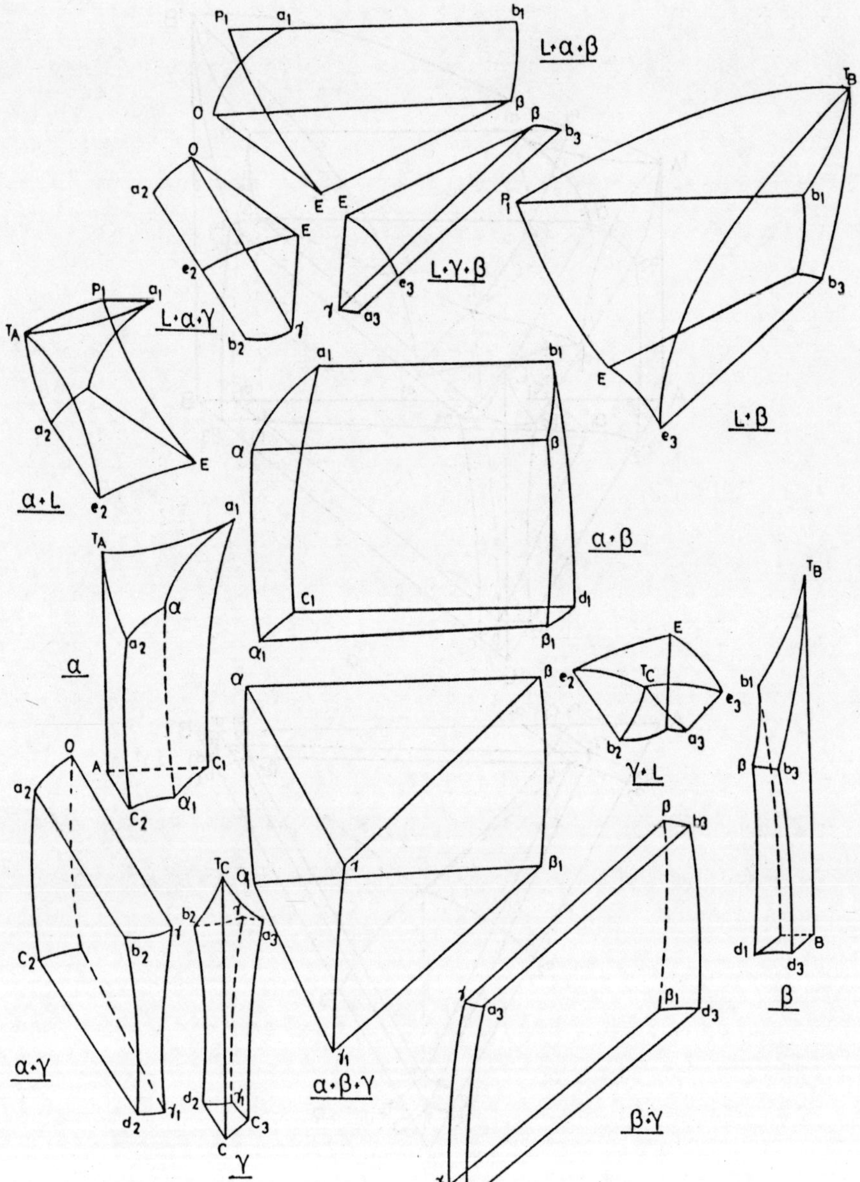

Fig. 12.8 Various phase regions of the space model of Fig. 12.7 shown separately.

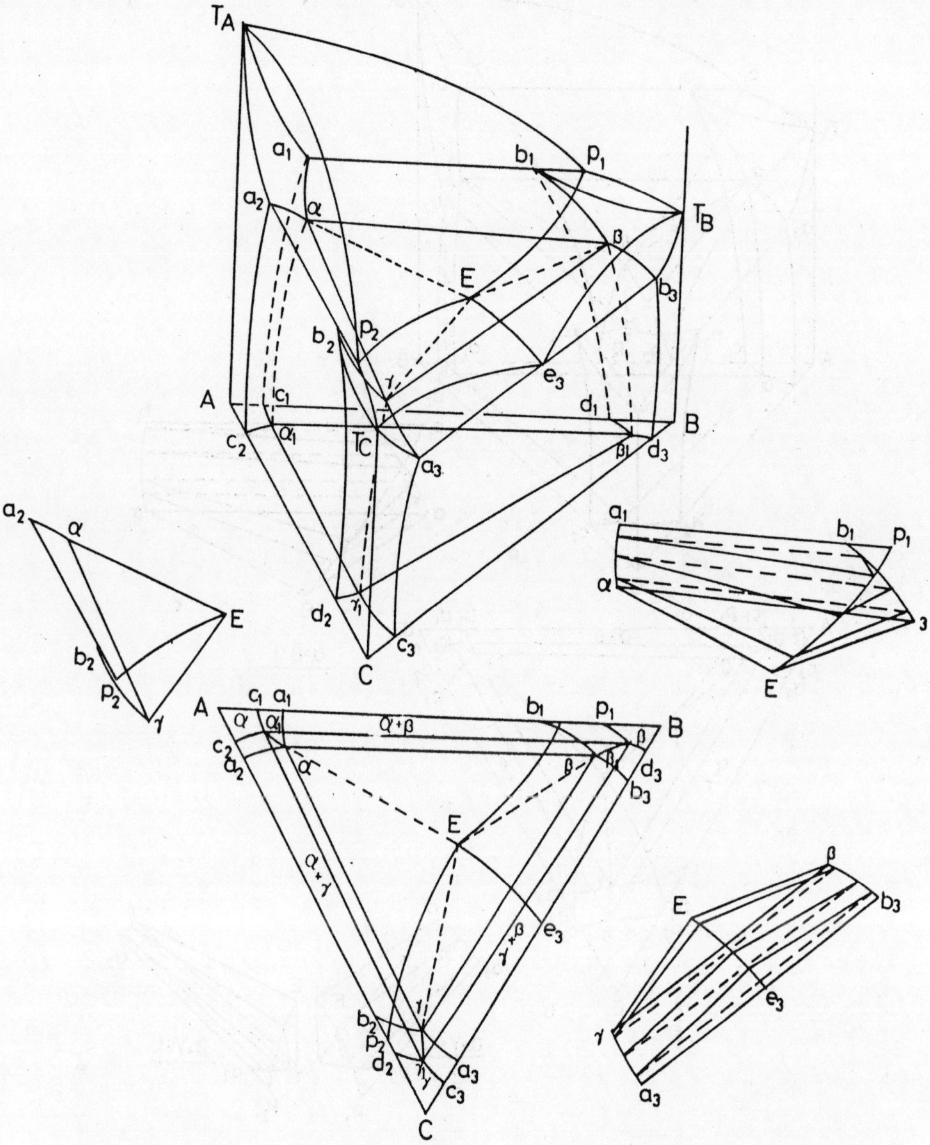

Fig. 12.9 Space model and its projection on the concentration triangle of a ternary system *A–B–C* with one binary system showing a eutectic reaction and the other two binaries showing peritectic reactions.

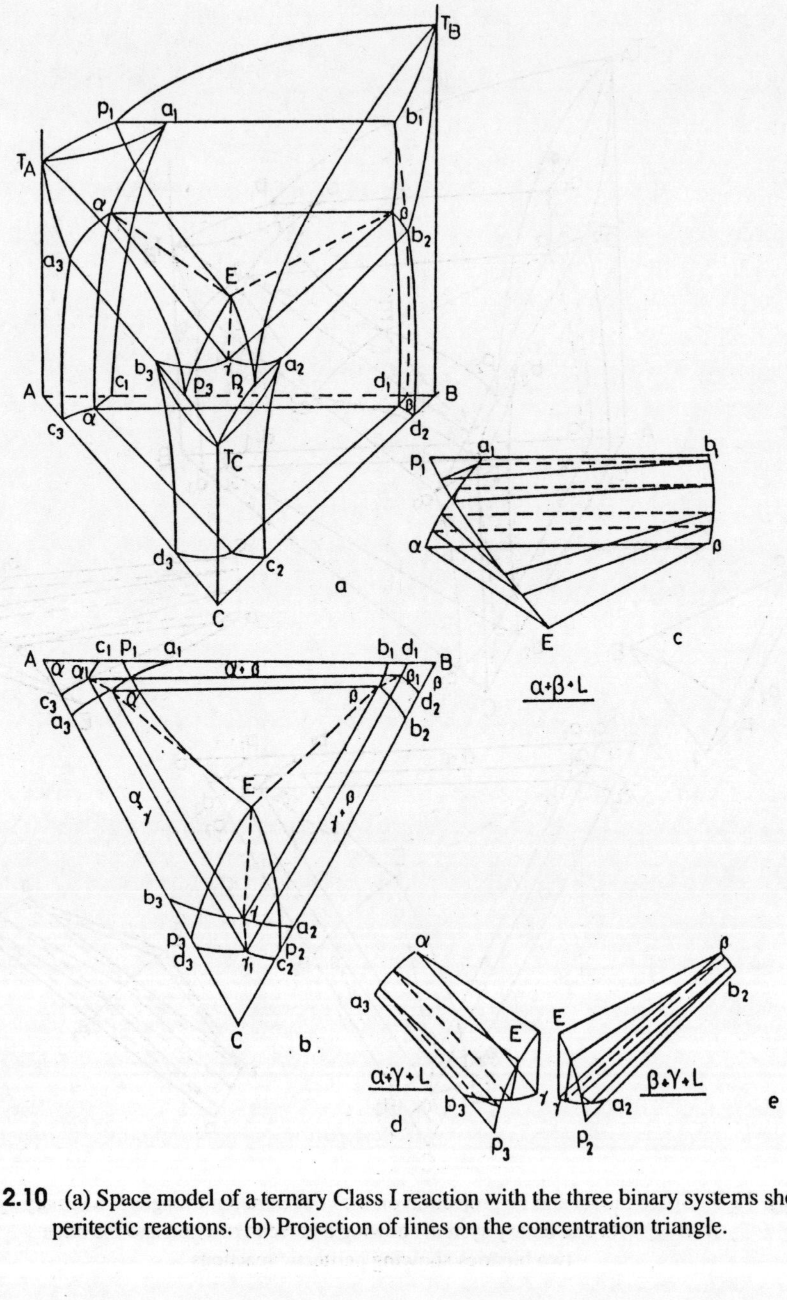

Fig. 12.10 (a) Space model of a ternary Class I reaction with the three binary systems showing peritectic reactions. (b) Projection of lines on the concentration triangle.

(ii) One binary system showing a eutectic reaction and the other two binaries showing peritectic reactions. The space model and projection of lines on the concentration triangle are shown in Fig. 12.9. With the introduction of two binary peritectic reactions, the solidification behavior of alloys will become more complex although the phase diagram as such is easy to understand.

(iii) A ternary Class I reaction is also possible when the three binary systems show peritectic reactions. The space model and its projection on the concentration triangle is shown in Fig. 12.10. In each three-phase region, (α+β+L) (α+γ+L) and (β+γ+L), there are alloy compositions which will undergo a secondary peritectic reaction. Alloy composition on lines αE, βE and γE on the four-phase plane will always dissociate by the eutectic reaction.

(iv) Ternary eutectic reaction $L = \alpha+\beta+\gamma$ can occur in alloy systems when two of the binary systems show eutectic reactions and the third is isomorphous. The binary A–B shows the reaction $L = \alpha+\beta$ and the binary B–C, $L = \beta+\gamma$. The space model is shown in Fig. 12.11a. The (α+β+L) and (β+γ+L) phase fields are similar to those observed for the ternary eutectic with three binary eutectic reactions. The monovariant liquid curve ascends from E on the four-phase plane and terminates at point e_3 in space. The liquid of composition e_3 is in equilibrium with the indistinguishable α (γ) phase at the critical point c_1. The tie-line c_1e_3 is a degenerate tie-triangle and is situated at the maximum temperature to which the (α+γ+L) phase region exists. The projection of the space diagram on the concentration triangle is shown in Fig. 12.11a. The shape of the (β_1+β_2+L) phase region and the three bounding surfaces are shown separately in Fig. 12.11b. The (α+β_1+L) phase region shown separately in Fig. 12.11d is similar to that shown in Fig. 12.2.

12.2 CLASS II: THE TERNARY QUASI-PERITECTIC REACTION

The ternary quasi-peritectic reaction $L+\beta = \alpha+\gamma$ occurs in a number of alloy systems. The reaction occurs on an isothermal plane having the shape of a trapezium, Fig. 12.12. There are two three-phase regions, (L+α+β) and (L+β+γ), which descend from the binary isothermal reaction temperatures on to the four-phase plane and just above the invariant temperature T_I have the shape shown in Fig. 12.12a. The other two three-phase regions (α+γ+L) and (α+β+γ), (Fig. 12.12b) descend from the four phase plane; one terminating at a binary reaction isotherm and the other at the ambient temperature.

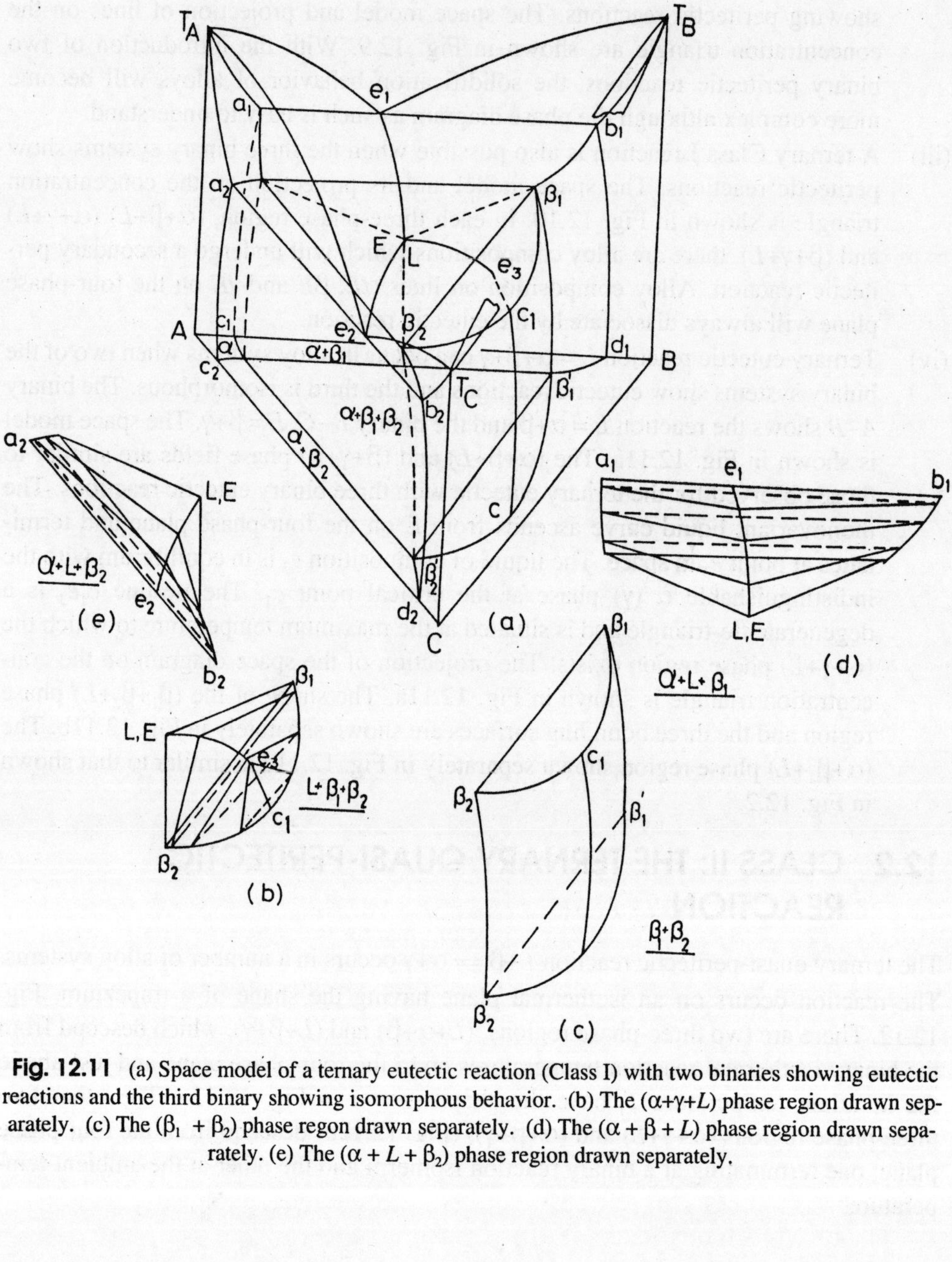

Fig. 12.11 (a) Space model of a ternary eutectic reaction (Class I) with two binaries showing eutectic reactions and the third binary showing isomorphous behavior. (b) The (α+γ+L) phase region drawn separately. (c) The (β_1 + β_2) phase regon drawn separately. (d) The (α + β + L) phase region drawn separately. (e) The (α + L + β_2) phase region drawn separately.

12.2.1 The Space Model

The space model of the ternary quasi-peritectic (Class II) system is shown in Fig. 12.13a with the projection in Fig. 12.13b. The space model is constructed with the binary system *A–B* showing a peritectic reaction and the other two binary systems, *A–C* and *B–C*, showing eutectic reactions. The various phase fields are drawn separately in Fig. 12.14 and also given in Table 12.2. The ternary four-phase reaction in this illustration is $L+\beta = \alpha+\gamma$.

Table 12.2 Various phase fields in the Ternary Quasi-Peritectic system (Class II)

Liquidus Surface	$(\alpha+L)$: $T_BpLe_2T_B$ $(\alpha+L)$: $T_ApLe_3T_A$ $(\gamma+L)$: $T_Ce_3Le_2T_C$
Solidus Surface	$(\beta+L)$: $T_Bb_1\beta b_2T_B$, $(\alpha+L)$:$T_Aa_1\alpha a_3T_A$, $(\gamma+L)$:$T_Ca_2\gamma b_3T_C$
Three-Phase regions and the corresponding ruled surfaces	$(\alpha+\beta+L)$: $a_1\alpha\beta b_1a_1(\alpha\beta)$, $pb_1\beta Lp(\beta L)$, $pa_1\alpha Lp(\alpha L)$ $(\beta+\gamma+L)$: $a_2b_2\beta\gamma a_2(\beta\gamma)$, $e_2\beta Le_2b_2(\beta L)$, $a_2e_2L\gamma a_2(\gamma L)$ $(\alpha+\gamma+L)$: $a_3e_3L\alpha a_3(\alpha L)$, $b_3e_3L\gamma e_3(\gamma L)$, $a_3\alpha\gamma b_3a_3(\alpha\gamma)$ $(\alpha+\beta+\gamma)$: $\alpha\beta\beta_1\alpha_1\alpha(\alpha\beta)$, $\alpha\alpha_1\gamma_1\gamma\alpha(\alpha\gamma)$, $\beta\beta_1\gamma_1\gamma\beta(\beta\gamma)$
Four-phase plane	$\alpha\beta\gamma$
Two-Phase Regions bounded by	$(\alpha+L)$: $T_ApLe_3T_A$, $T_Aa_1\alpha a_3T_A$, $pa_1\alpha Lp$ and $a_3e_3L\alpha a_3$ $(\beta+L)$: $T_BpLe_2T_B$, $T_Bb_1\beta b_2T_B$, $pb_1\beta Lp$ and $e_2\beta Le_2b_2$ $(\gamma+L)$: $T_Ce_3Le_2T_C$, $T_Ca_2\gamma b_3T_C$, $a_2e_2L\gamma a_2$ and $b_3e_3L\gamma e_3$ $(\alpha+\beta)$: $a_1b_1\beta\alpha a_1$, $a_1c_1\alpha_1\alpha a_1$, $b_1\beta\beta_1d_1b_1$ and $\alpha\beta\beta_1\alpha_1$ $(\beta+\gamma)$: $a_2\gamma\beta b_2$, $a_2\gamma\gamma_1c_2a_2$, $b_2\beta\beta_1d_2b_2$ and $\beta\gamma\gamma_1\beta$ $(\alpha+\gamma)$: $a_3\alpha\gamma b_3a_3$, $\alpha\gamma\gamma_1\alpha_1$, $b_3\gamma\gamma_1d_3b_3$ and $a_3\alpha\alpha_1c_3a_3$
Single-Phase regions bounded by	α: $T_Aa_1c_1AT_A$, $T_Aa_1\alpha\alpha_1c_3T_A$, $T_Aa_3c_3AT_A$, $a_1\alpha\alpha_1c_1a_1$ and $a_3\alpha\alpha_1c_3a_3$. β: $T_Bb_1\beta b_2T_B$, $b_1\beta\beta_1d_1b_1$, $b_2\beta\beta_1d_2b_2$, $T_Bb_2d_2BT_B$ and $T_Bb_1d_1BT_B$. γ: $T_Ca_2c_2CT_C$, $T_Cb_3d_3CT_C$, $T_Cb_3d_3\gamma_1\gamma T_C$, $T_Cb_3\gamma a_2T_C$ and $a_2\gamma\gamma_1c_2a_2$.

The two three-phase fields, $(L+\alpha+\beta)$ and $(L+\beta+\gamma)$, start from the binary invariant isotherms of *AB* and *BC*, and terminate on the triangles $\alpha\beta L$ and $L\beta\gamma$, respectively-on the four-phase plane. The $(L+\alpha+\beta)$ phase region is bounded by $L\alpha$, $L\beta$ and $\alpha\beta$ ruled surfaces marked by $Pa_1\alpha Lp$, $pb_1\beta Lp$ and $a_1b_1\beta\alpha$, respectively. Similarly, ruled surfaces $L\beta$, $L\gamma$ and $\beta\gamma$ enclose the $(L+\beta+\gamma)$ phase region. The $(\alpha+\beta+\gamma)$ phase region

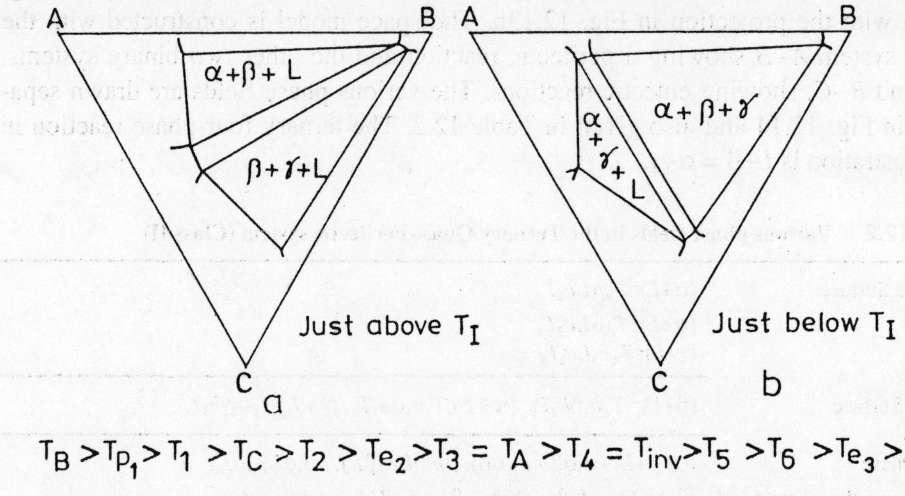

Fig. 12.12 (a) A ternary quasi-peritectic (Class II) system drawn with components A, *B* and *C*. (b) The (γ+α+β) and (*L*+α+γ) phase region drawn separately.

descends below the triangle αβγ on the four-phase plane and terminates on $\alpha_1\beta_1\gamma_1$ at the ambient temperature. The other three-phase region (*L*+α+γ) has the uppermost tie-triangle αβγ on the four-phase plane terminating on the binary invariant line $a_3e_3b_3$ which becomes the degenerate tie-triangle.

12.2.2 Isothermal Sections

The isothermal sections at a number of temperatures are shown in Fig. 12.15. For the ternary quasi-peritectic system with $T_B > T_{p_1} > T_1 > T_c > T_2 > T_{e_2} > T_3 = T_A > T_4 = T_p > T_5 > T_6 > T_{e_3} > T_7$, the section at temperatures T_3, T_4 and T_5 show the relevant features of the Class II reaction. At $T_3 > T_p$ the isothermal section shows (α+β+*L*) and (*L*+β+γ) phase regions separated by (β+*L*) field, which will gradually shrink to a line β*L* on the four-phase plane at T_p. The other two three-phase fields (*L*+α+γ) and (α+β+γ) appear at a temperature T_5 just below the quasi-peritectic reaction isotherm. These three-phase regions are separated by the (α+γ) field.

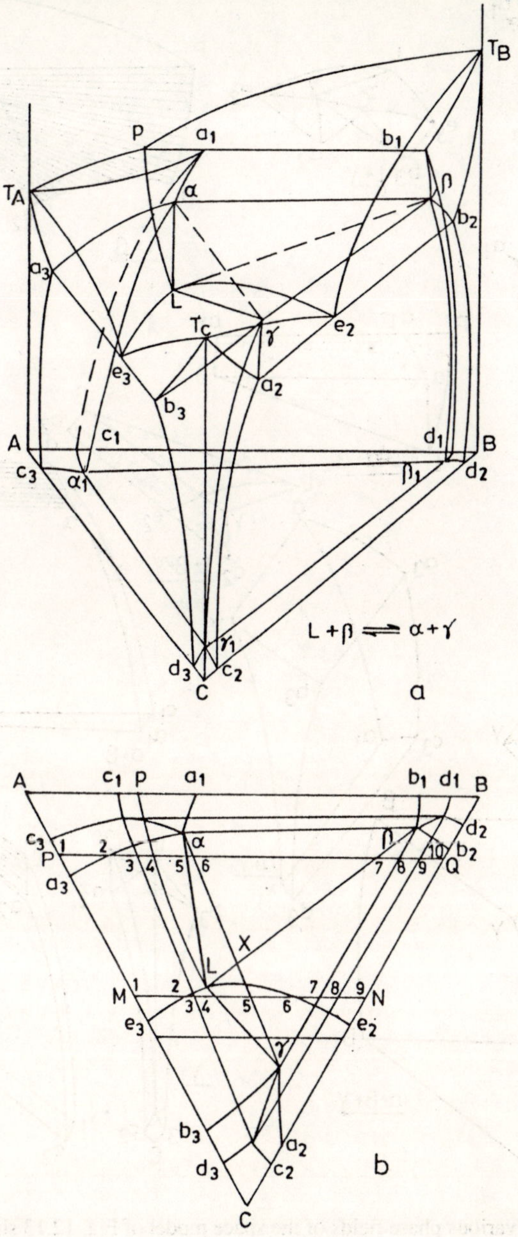

Fig. 12.13 (a) Space model of a ternary system *A–B–C* showing the quasi-peritectic reaction $L+\beta = \alpha+\gamma$. (b) Projection of (a) on the concentration triangle *ABC*.

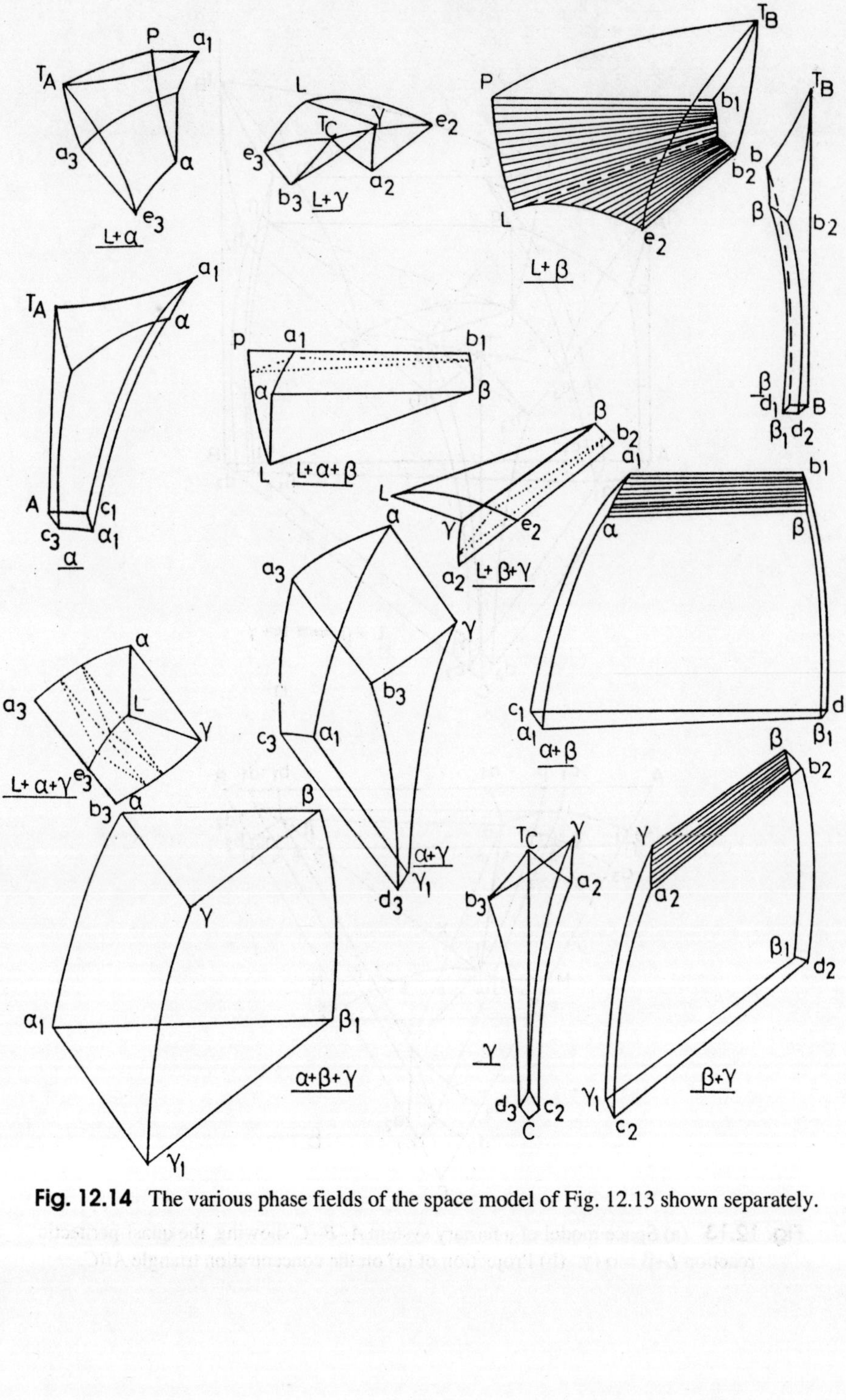

Fig. 12.14 The various phase fields of the space model of Fig. 12.13 shown separately.

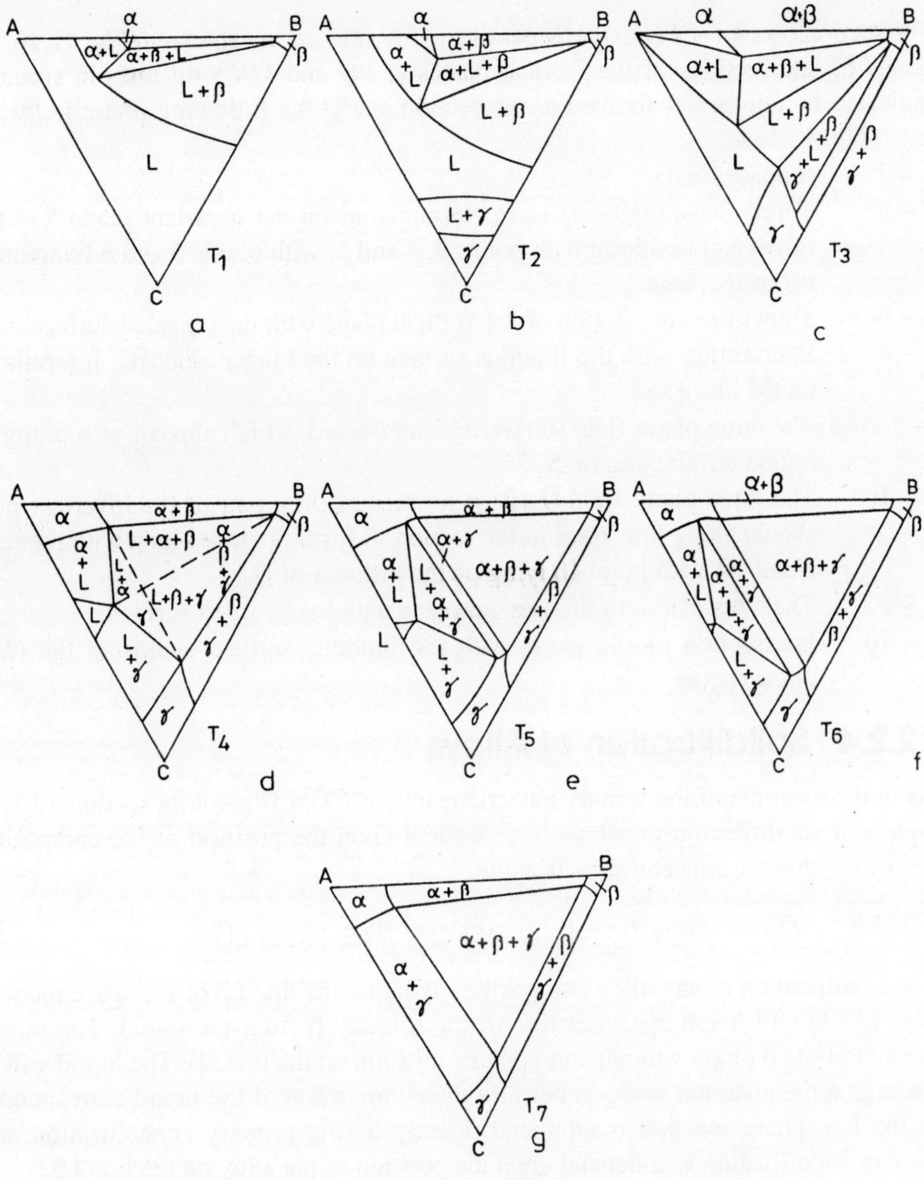

Fig. 12.15 Isothermal sections through the space model of Fig. 12.13.

12.2.3 Vertical Sections

The sections drawn at PQ and MN parallel to the side AB are shown in Fig. 12.16. The points of intersections of the vertical planes at PQ and MN with lines in space are indicated by numbers 1 to 10. For the section at PQ the following phase fields will exist, Fig. 12.16a.

1 – 2	α phase field
2 – 6	Three-phase region (L+α+γ) terminating on the invariant plane 5 – 8. It forms a closed loop with points 2, 5 and 6, with points 5 and 6 lying on the invariant plane.
3 – 6	Shows the intersection of the vertical plane with the αγ ruled surface.
1 – 4	Intersection with the liquidus surface on the binary side AC. It terminates on the line 4 – 5.
4–5–6–7	The three-phase field (α+β+L) is intersected, which appears as a triangular region terminating on 5–7.
7 – 10	The three-phase field (L+β+γ) terminates on a part of the invariant plane shown along line 7 – 8 in the section. It forms a closed loop with points, 7, 8 and 10, with point 10 lying on the ordinate at Q.
8 – 9	The intersection of the vertical plane with the βγ ruled surface.
4 – 10	Intersection of the plane with the liquidus surface enclosing the (L+β) phase region.

12.2.4 Solidification of Alloys

As in the example of the ternary eutectic reaction (Class I) given in section 12.1, the course of solidification of alloys is dependent upon the position of the composition vertical within the concentration triangle.

(i) Alloy Compositions Lying on the Line Lβ

The solidification of any alloy composition lying on the line Lβ of the space model of Fig. 12.13a will begin by deposition of the primary β from the liquid. The relative amount of the β phase will depend upon its position on the line Lβ. The liquid will not undergo a monovariant reaction because the composition of the liquid corresponding to the four-phase reaction is attainend directly during primary crystallization of β. Further solidification will depend upon the position of the alloy on the line Lβ.

(a) On the line βX. Alloy compositions lying on the line βX will undergo the quasi-peritectic reaction L+β = α+γ. The liquid will be completely consumed during the reaction leaving some unreacted primary β and products of the

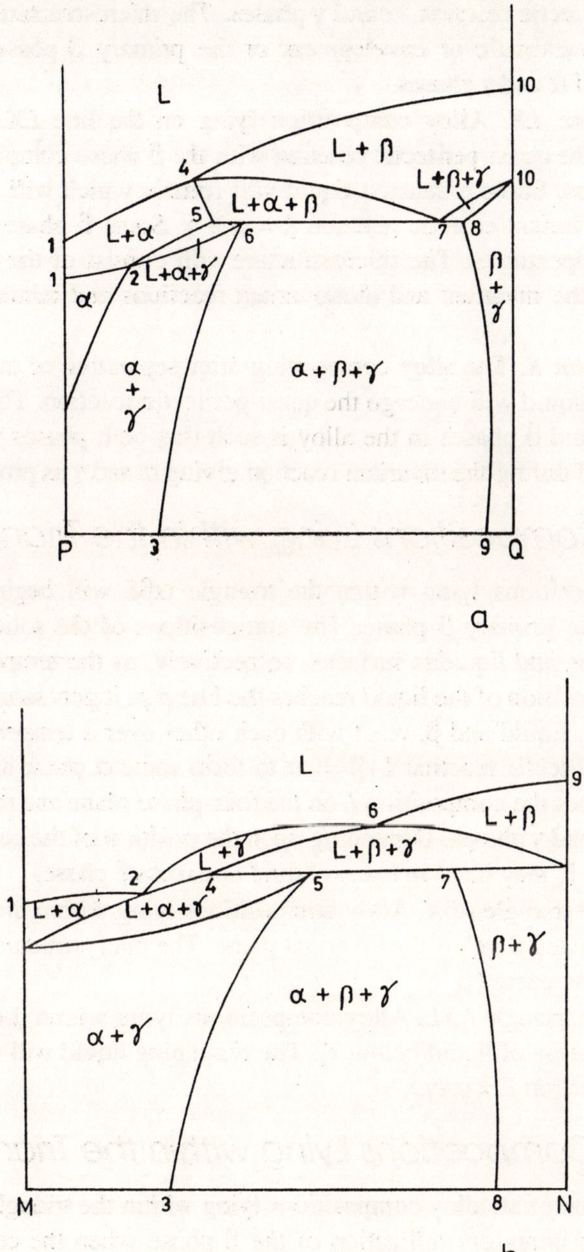

Fig. 12.16 Vertical section at *PQ* as well as *MN* both parallel to the line *AB*.

quasi-peritectic reaction, α and γ phases. The microstructure should show features characteristic of envelopment or the primary β phase surrounded by a mixture of α and γ phases.

(b) On the line *LX*. Alloy composition lying on the line *LX*, Fig. 12.13a, will undergo the quasi-peritectic reaction with the β phase completely consumed in the process. Some unreacted liquid will remain which will solidify further by the monovariant eutectic reaction $L = \alpha + \gamma$. Some β phase may precipitate at lower temperatures. The microstructure will consist of the (α+γ) phases as a result of the invariant and monovariant reactions and minor quantity of the β phase.

(c) At the point *X*. The alloy composition after separation of the primary β phase from the liquid will undergo the quasi-peritectic reaction. The relative amounts of the *L* and β phases in the alloy is such that both phases will be completely consumed during the invariant reaction giving α and γ as product phases.

(ii) Alloy Compositions Lying within the Triangle αβL

All alloy compositions lying within the triangle αβ*L* will begin solidification by deposition of the primary β phase. The compositions of the solid and liquid move along the solidus and liquidus surfaces, respectively, as the temperature is lowered. When the composition of the liquid reaches the line p_1p, it gets saturated with β phase. The two phases, liquid and β, react with each other over a temperature range by the monovariant peritectic reaction $L+\beta \Rightarrow \alpha$ to form some α phase at the *L*/β interface. The liquid reaches the composition *L* on the four-phase plane and reacts with β to give a mixture of α and γ phases. Depending upon the position of the composition vertical, the alloy below T_p may have an excess liquid or excess β phase.

(a) Within the triangle αβ*X*. Alloy compositions lying within the triangle αβ*X* will have unreacted β below the invariant plane. The microstructure will consist of α, α+β, and unreacted β.

(b) Within the triangle α*XL*. Alloy compositions lying within the triangle α*XL* will have an excess of liquid below T_p. The remaining liquid will undergo the monovariant reaction $L = \alpha+\gamma$.

(iii) Alloy Compositions Lying within the Triangle βγL

The solidification of all alloy compositions lying within the triangle βγ*L*, Fig. 12.13a, will begin by primary crystallization of the β phase when the composition vertical touches the liquidus surface. As the composition vertical touches the β*L* ruled surface of the (*L*+β+γ) region, the liquid dissociates into β and γ phases by the monovariant eutectic reaction. This occurs over a range of temperatures. The composition of the liquid will move towards L along the line e_2L as the temperature is lowered. It will reach the composition L at the quasi-peritectic reaction isotherm. The liquid will react with β to give α and γ as product phases. The product phases below T_p depend upon whether there is excess liquid or excess β phase and thus on the alloy composition selected.

(a) Within the triangle βγX. Alloy compositions lying within the triangle $\beta\gamma X$ will undergo the quasi-peritectic reaction such that all liquid is consumed. The microstructure will consist of α+β+γ phases.

(b) Within the triangle γLX. Alloy compositions lying within the triangle γLX will have unreacted liquid below T_p, which will dissociate by the monovariant eutectic reaction into α and γ phases.

(iv) Alloy Composition L

The alloy composition L, Fig. 12.13a, will not undergo the quasi-peritectic reaction as it does not go through the crystallization of primary β phase. The alloy will solidify through the monovariant dissociation reaction $L = \alpha+\gamma$. The relative amounts of phases for alloy compositions lying within a given tie-triangle can be calculated by applying the lever rule. These calculations are shown for the following compositions.

(a) Composition Y lying within the triangle $\alpha L\beta$ in the area $\alpha X\beta$, Fig. 12.17a. The relative amounts of the α, β and liquid phases just above the four-phase plane are,

$$\%\ \alpha = \frac{YZ}{\alpha Z} \times 100 = 20\%$$

$$\%\ \beta = \frac{LZ}{L\beta} \times \frac{\alpha Y}{\alpha Z} \times 100 = 29.33\ \%$$

$$\%\ L = 50.66\ \%$$

The liquid reacts with β to give α and γ phases just below the four-phase plane. Liquid is completey consumed in the process,

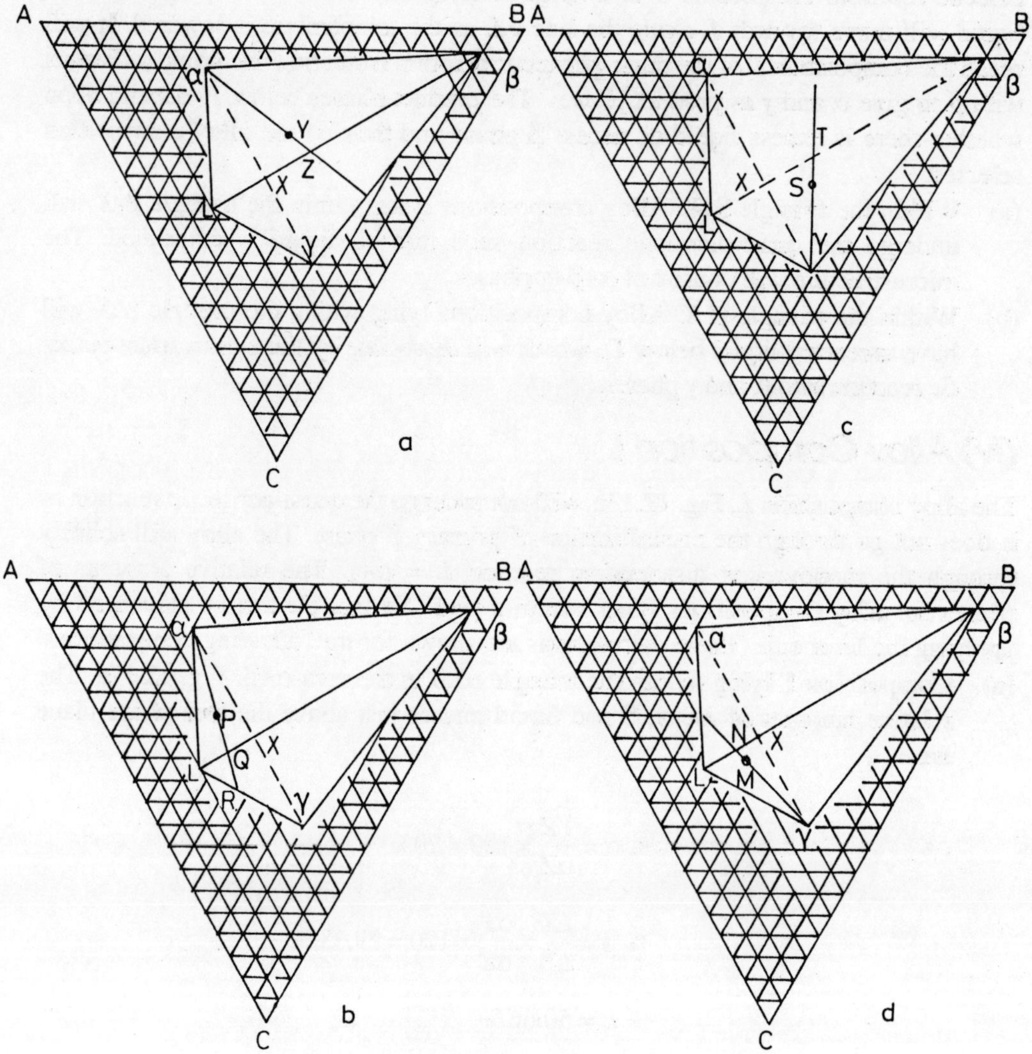

Fig. 12.17 (a) Position of the alloy Y lying within the triangle $\alpha L\beta$.
(b) Alloy composition P lying within the triangle $\alpha L\beta$.
(c) Alloy composition S lying within triangle $L\beta\gamma$.
(d) Alloy M lying within $L\beta\gamma$.

$$\% \, \alpha = \frac{WY}{\alpha W} \times 100 = 47.37 \, \%$$

$$\% \, \beta = \frac{W\gamma}{\beta\gamma} \times \frac{\alpha Y}{\alpha W} \times 100 = 16.66 \, \%$$

$$\% \, \gamma = \frac{W\beta}{\beta\gamma} \times \frac{\alpha Y}{\alpha W} \times 100 = 35.96 \, \%$$

There is a substantial reduction in the amount of the β phase below T_p as it is consumed during the quasi-peritectic reaction.

(b) Alloy composition *P* lying within the triangle α*L*β and area α*XL*, Fig. 12.17b. Relative amounts of the α, liquid and β phase just above the invariant plane are,

$$\% \, \alpha = \frac{PQ}{\alpha Q} \times 100 = 33.33 \, \%$$

$$\% \, \beta = \frac{LQ}{\beta L} \times \frac{\alpha P}{\alpha Q} \times 100 = 6.66 \, \%$$

$$\% \, L = \frac{Q\beta}{\beta L} \times \frac{\alpha P}{\alpha R} \times 100 = 60 \, \%$$

It is apparent from the above that 6.66% β reacts with 26.667% liquid to give α and γ phases in the ratio 4:5 which would be 14.81% α and 18.51% γ phases. This ratio can be calculated by taking the composition *X* on the intersection of the line αγ and β*L*.

(c) Alloy composition *S* lying within the triangle *L*βγ and area γβ*X*, Fig. 12.17c. Relative amounts of the β, γ and liquid phases just above T_p are,

$$\% \, \gamma = \frac{ST}{\gamma T} \times 100 = 25.58 \, \%$$

$$\% \beta = \frac{LT}{L\beta} \times \frac{S\gamma}{\gamma T} \times 100 = 28.06\ \%$$

$$\% L = \frac{T\beta}{L\beta} \times \frac{S\gamma}{\gamma T} \times 100 = 46.36\ \%$$

The liquid and β phases will react with each other at T_p to give α and γ phases. The alloy composition will show unreacted β phase. The relative amounts of phases below T_p are,

$$\% \gamma = \frac{SU}{\gamma U} \times 100 = 57.77\ \%$$

$$\% \beta = \frac{LU}{\alpha\beta} \times \frac{S\gamma}{\gamma U} \times 100 = 16.47\ \%$$

$$\% \alpha = \frac{\beta U}{\alpha\beta} \times \frac{S\gamma}{\gamma U} \times 100 = 25.75\ \%$$

The above result can also be obtained by reacting 46.36% liquid with 46.36 × 1/4 = 11.59% β to yield 25.75% α and 32.43% γ phases. The addition of secondary γ above the four-phase plane to the γ obtained by the quasi-peritectic reaction gives a value of approximately 56% which is close to the relative amount of γ = 57.77%.

(d) Alloy composition M lying within the triangle $L\beta\gamma$ and area $LX\gamma$, Fig. 12.17d. Relative amounts of the β, γ and liquid phases just above T_p are,

$$\% \gamma = 12.7\ \%$$

$$\% \beta = 9.94\ \%$$

$$\% L = 77.4\ \%$$

Relative amounts of the α, γ and liquid phases just below T_p are,

$$\%\ \gamma = 40.27\ \%$$

$$\%\ \alpha = 22.08\ \%$$

$$\%\ L = 37.64\ \%,$$

which is consistent with the quasi-peritectic reaction of the liquid and β phases.

12.2.5 Variants of the Class II (Ternary Quasi-Peritectic) Reaction

The quasi-peritectic reaction can also occur in a ternary system with the following combination of binary reactions:

(i) Two of the binary systems show peritectic reactions and the third shows a eutectic reaction.

As presented in the space model of Fig. 12.18a and its projection in Fig. 12.18b, the binary systems $A–B$ and $A–C$ show peritectic reactions with reaction isotherms $a_1b_1p_1$ and $a_2b_2p_2$, respectively. The third binary alloy system between components B and C shows a eutectic reaction along $a_3e_3b_3$. The quasi-peritectic reaction occurs at T_p shown by the isothermal plane in the shape of a trapezium $\alpha\beta\gamma L$. The three-phase region ($\beta+\gamma+L$) descends below the invariant plane and terminates on the eutectic reaction isotherm $a_3e_3b_3$.

Isothermal sections at temperatures T_1 and T_2, defined by $T_{p_1} > T_{p_2} > T_1 > T_2 > T_p > T_3$, show (Figs. 12.19, a and b) two three-phase regions, ($\alpha+\beta+L$) and ($\alpha+\gamma+L$), with the tie-triangles oriented as in the three-phase equilibrium involving two binary peritectic reactions, discussed in detail in Chapter 11. The isothermal section at $T_3 < T_p$ shows the other two three-phase regions ($\alpha+\beta+\gamma$) and ($\beta+\gamma+L$) with a complete change in the orientation of the tie-triangles, as shown in Fig. 12.12b.

Vertical sections are drawn at positions M_1N_1 and P_1Q_1 parallel to the side AB, Figs. 12.20, a and b. Numbers 1 to 9 marked in the vertical sections at M_1N_1 show the relative position of various boundaries in the space model. The corresponding numbers are marked along the line M_1N_1 in Fig. 12.18b. The vertical sections at M_1N_1 and P_1Q_1 are easy to follow.

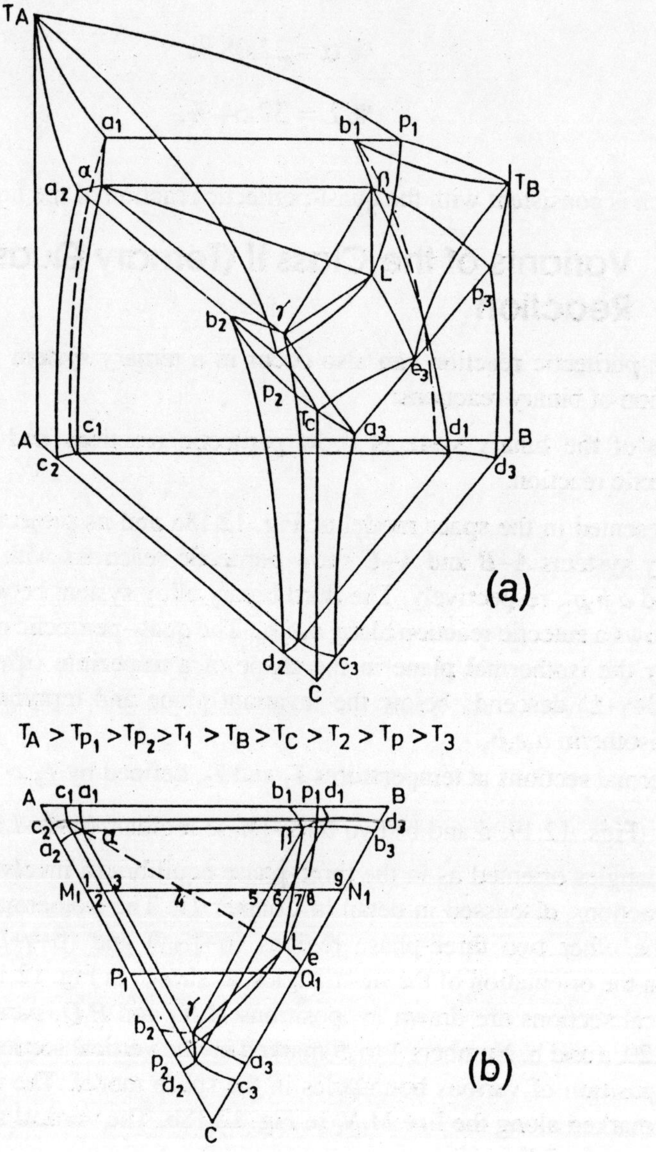

Fig. 12.18 (a) Space model of a variant of the ternary quasi-peritectic system A–B–C with two binary systems showing a peritectic reaction and the third a eutectic one. (b) The projection of (a) on the concentration triangle ABC.

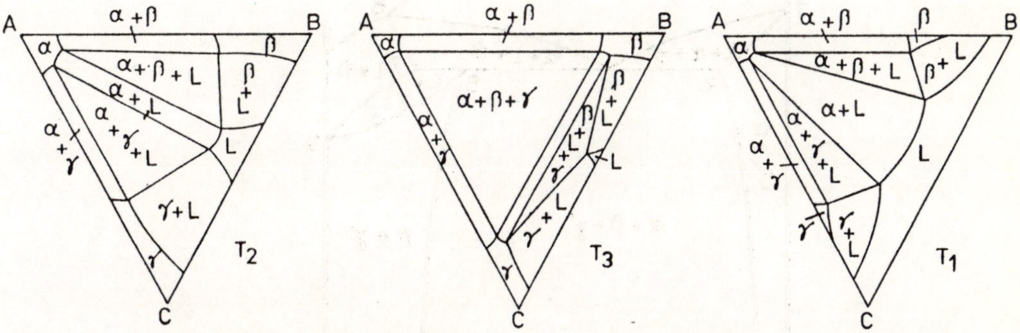

Fig. 12.19 Isothermal sections through the space model of Fig. 12.18.

(ii) All the three binary systems show eutectic reactions.

The phase diagram of the ternary quasi-peritectic system with all the three binaries A–B, B–C and A–C showing eutectic reactions is presented in the space model of Fig. 12.21a. The projection is shown in Fig. 12.21b. The (β+γ+L) phase region descends below the invariant plane and terminates on the binary reaction isotherm $a_3e_3b_3$.

The isothermal sections at T_1 and T_2 above the invariant plane ($T_1 > T_2 > T_p$) show two three-phase regions, (α+β+L) and (α+γ+L), Figs. 12.22, a and b. The orientation of the tie-triangles corresponds to the monovariant eutectic reaction discussed in Chapter 11. This is in contrast to the previous example where the tie-triangles were oriented so as to project a monovariant peritectic reaction. The other features of the isothermal sections at T_1 and T_2 and the one drawn at $T_3 < T_p$ are similar to the previous example.

The vertical sections at M_2N_2 and P_2Q_2 are shown in Figs. 12.23, a and b, respectively, and can be interpreted easily.

(iii) Two of the binary systems show invariant reaction, either two eutectics or one eutectic and one peritectic. The third binary system shows an isomorphous behavior. The space diagram of the ternary system is shown in Fig. 12.24a and its projection in Fig. 12.24b. In this illustration, the binary system A–B shows a eutectic reaction at $a_1e_1b_1$ and A–C shows a peritectic reaction at $a_2b_2p_2$. The (α+β+L) and (α+γ+L) phase regions descend from the binary isotherms $a_1e_1b_1$ and $a_2b_2p_2$, respectively, and terminate on the invariant plane. The monovariant

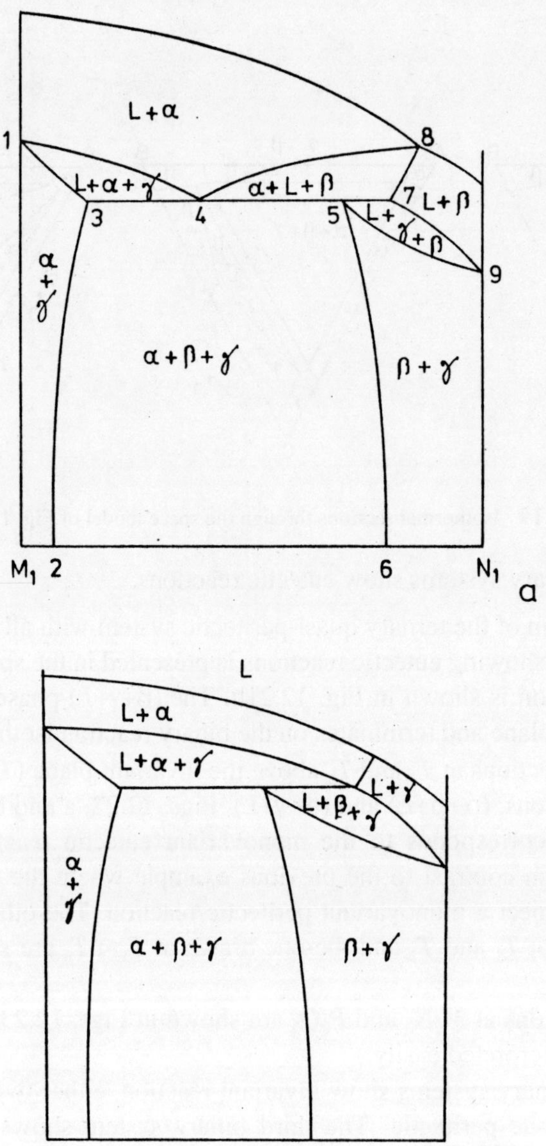

Fig. 12.20 (a), (b) Vertical sections drawn at M_1N_1 and P_1Q_1 parallel to the side AB.

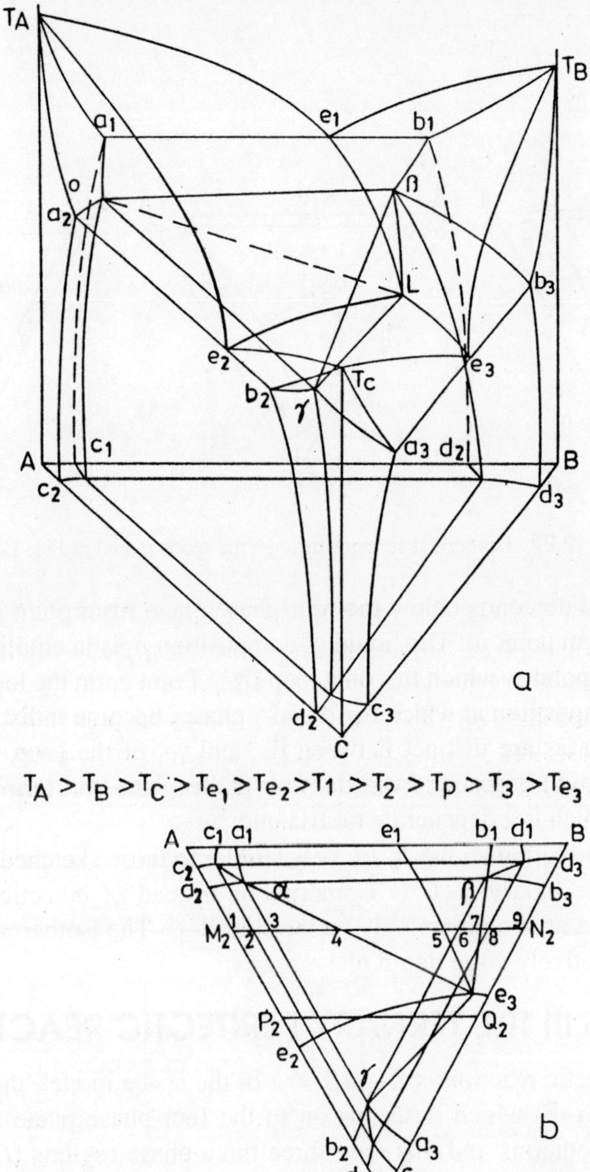

Fig. 12.21 (a) Space model of a variant of the ternary system A–B–C showing a quasi-peritectic reaction with three binary systems showing eutectic reactions. (b) Projection of (a) on the concentration triangle ABC.

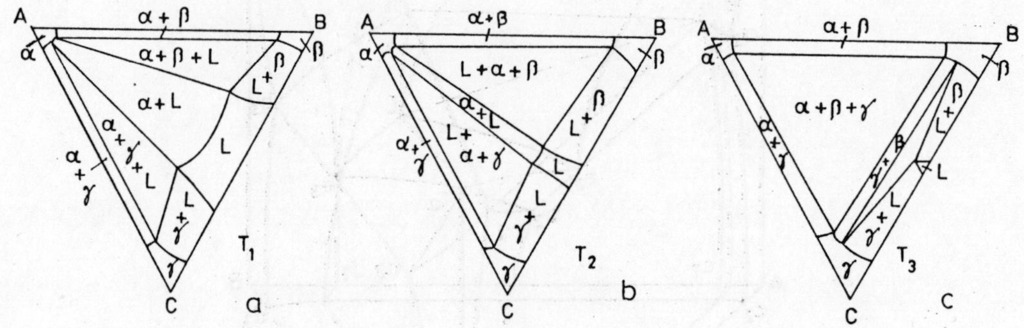

Fig. 12.22 Isothermal sections through the space model of Fig. 12.21.

liquid curve descends below the four-phase plane from point L and terminates at a minimum point p_3. The liquid of composition p_3 is in equilibrium with solid β (γ) at the point c_1 which lies on a loop $\beta\gamma c_1$. Point c_1 on the loop represents the critical composition at which the β and γ phases become indistinguishable. The β and γ phases are distinct between βc_1 and γc_1 of the loop. The three-phase region (β+γ+L) descends from the four-phase plane and terminates at the tie-line p_3c_1 which is a degenerate tie-triangle.

The isothermal section above T_p are very similar to those sketched for the previous variants. Since the binary B–C is isomorphous instead of eutectic, the isothermal plane will intersect at two points only on the side B–C. The isothermal section below T_p will show a relatively large liquid phase region.

12.3 CLASS III THE TERNARY PERITECTIC REACTION

The ternary peritectic reaction is L+α+β = γ. In the space model, there is one three-phase region (L+α+β) which descends on to the four-phase plane from one of the binary reaction isotherms and there are three three-phase regions (L+α+γ), (L+β+γ) and (α+β+γ) which appear below the invariant plane, Figs. 12.25, a and b.

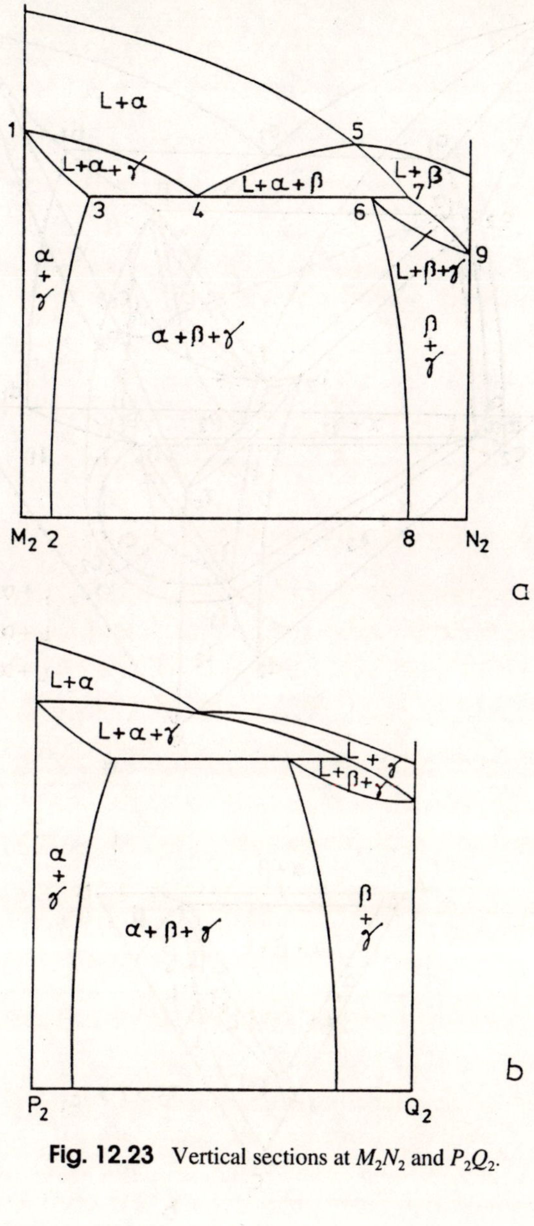

Fig. 12.23 Vertical sections at M_2N_2 and P_2Q_2.

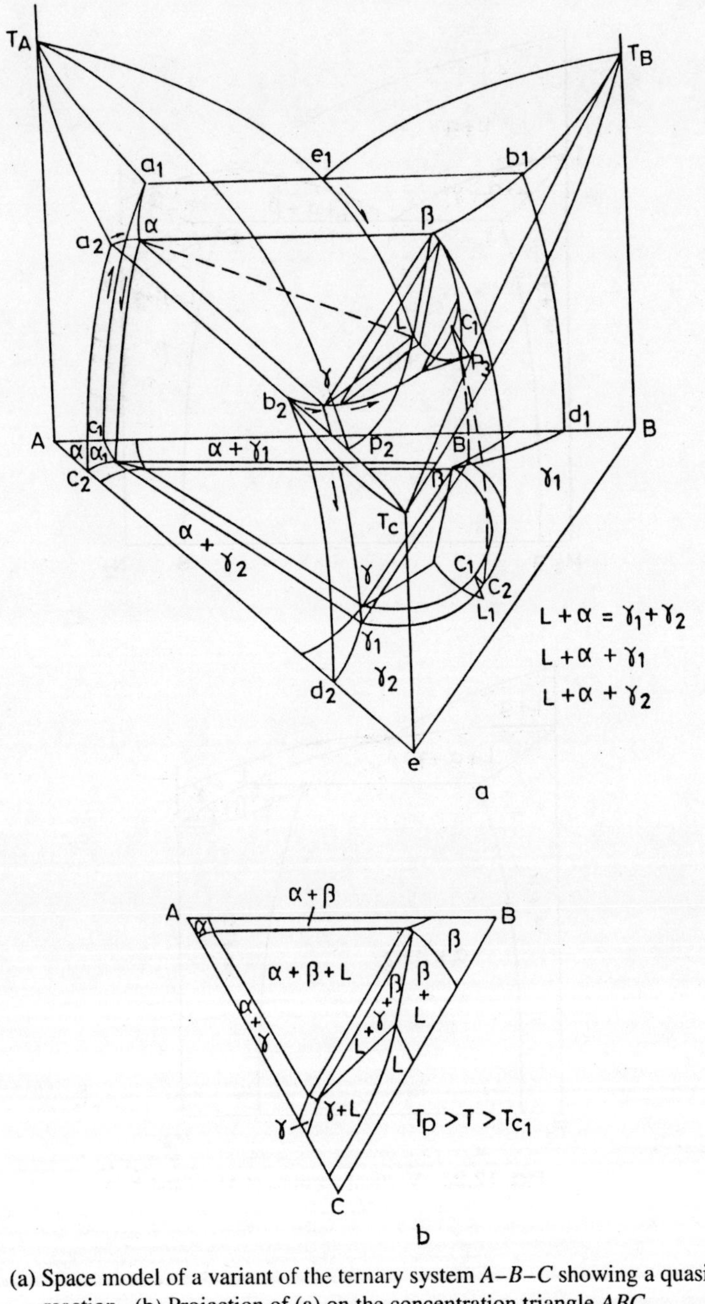

Fig. 12.24 (a) Space model of a variant of the ternary system A–B–C showing a quasi-peritectic reaction. (b) Projection of (a) on the concentration triangle ABC.

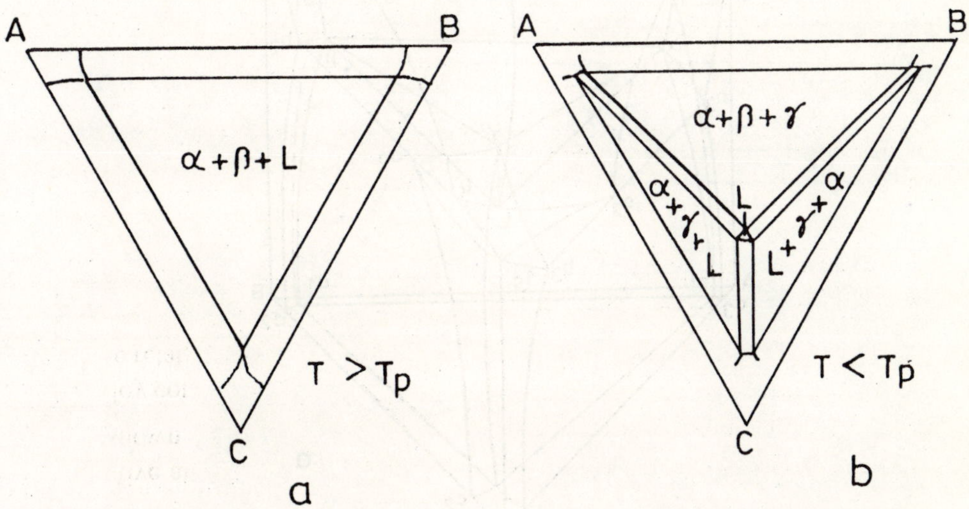

Fig. 12.25 Position of various three-phase regions of the ternary peritectic (Class III) reaction.

12.3.1 The Space Model

An example of the Class III reaction is shown in the space model of Fig. 12.26a with its projection on the concentration triangle in Fig. 12.26b. The ternary system shows eutectic reactions on the binaries *A–B* and *A–C*. The three-phase region ($\alpha+\beta+L$) emanates from the binary reaction isotherm $a_1e_1b_1$ and terminates on the larger triangle $\alpha\beta L$ of the invariant plane. It is bounded by ruled surfaces $a_1b_1\beta\alpha a_1$ ($\alpha\beta$), $a_1e_1L\alpha a_1$ ($L\alpha$) and $b_1e_1L\beta b_1$ ($L\beta$). The ($\alpha+\gamma+L$) and ($\beta+\gamma+L$) phase regions descend from the four-phase plane and terminate on the reaction isotherm $a_3e_3b_3$ and $p_2a_2b_2$, respectively. The ($\alpha+\beta+\gamma$) phase field descends from the triangle $\alpha\beta\gamma$ of the four-phase plane and terminates at $\alpha_1\beta_1\gamma_1$ at the ambient temperature. The various phase fields are drawn separately in Fig. 12.27.

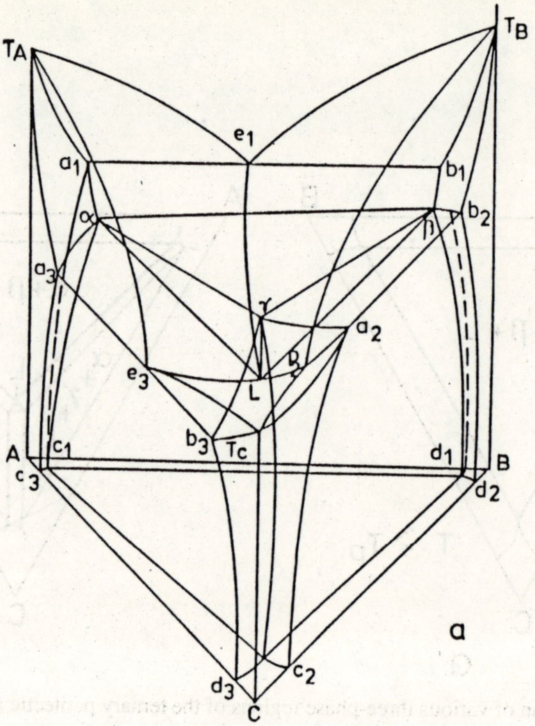

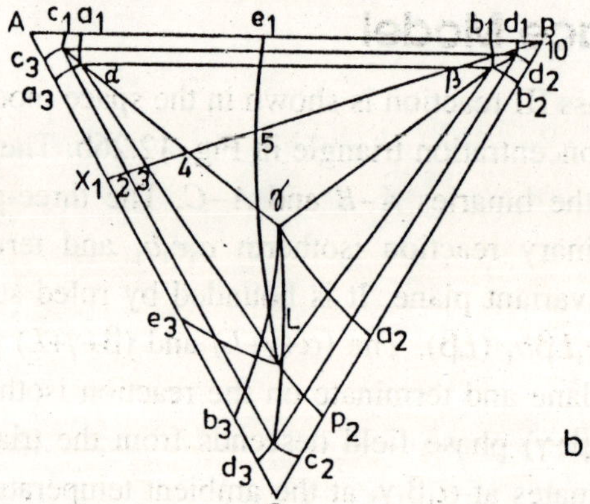

Fig. 12.26 (a) The space model of a ternary system $A-B-C$ showing a ternary peritectic reaction $L+\alpha+\beta = \gamma$. The system shows two binary eutectic reactions and a binary peritectic reaction. (b) Projection of (a) on the base triangle ABC.

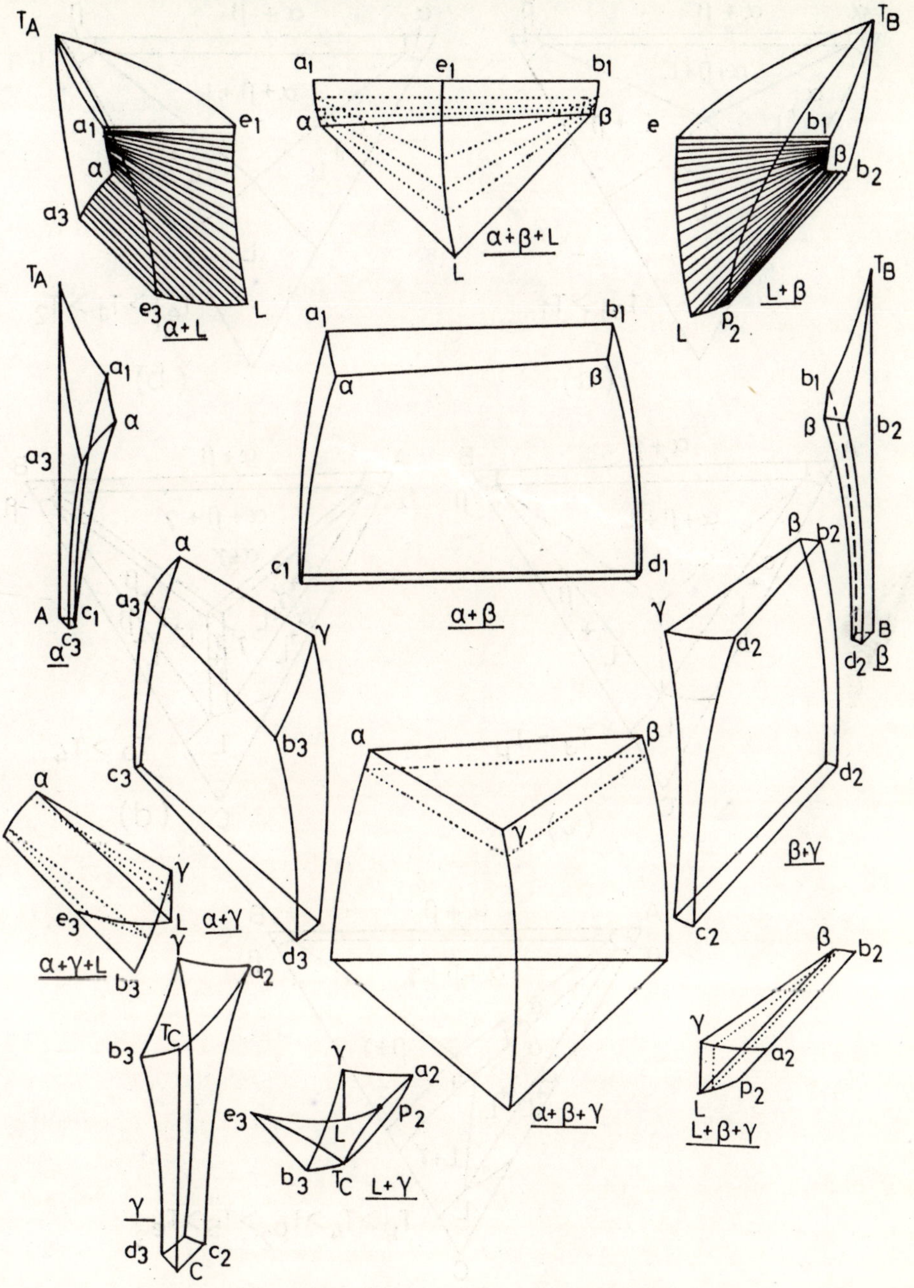

Fig. 12.27 Separate drawing of the phase fields of Fig. 12.26a.

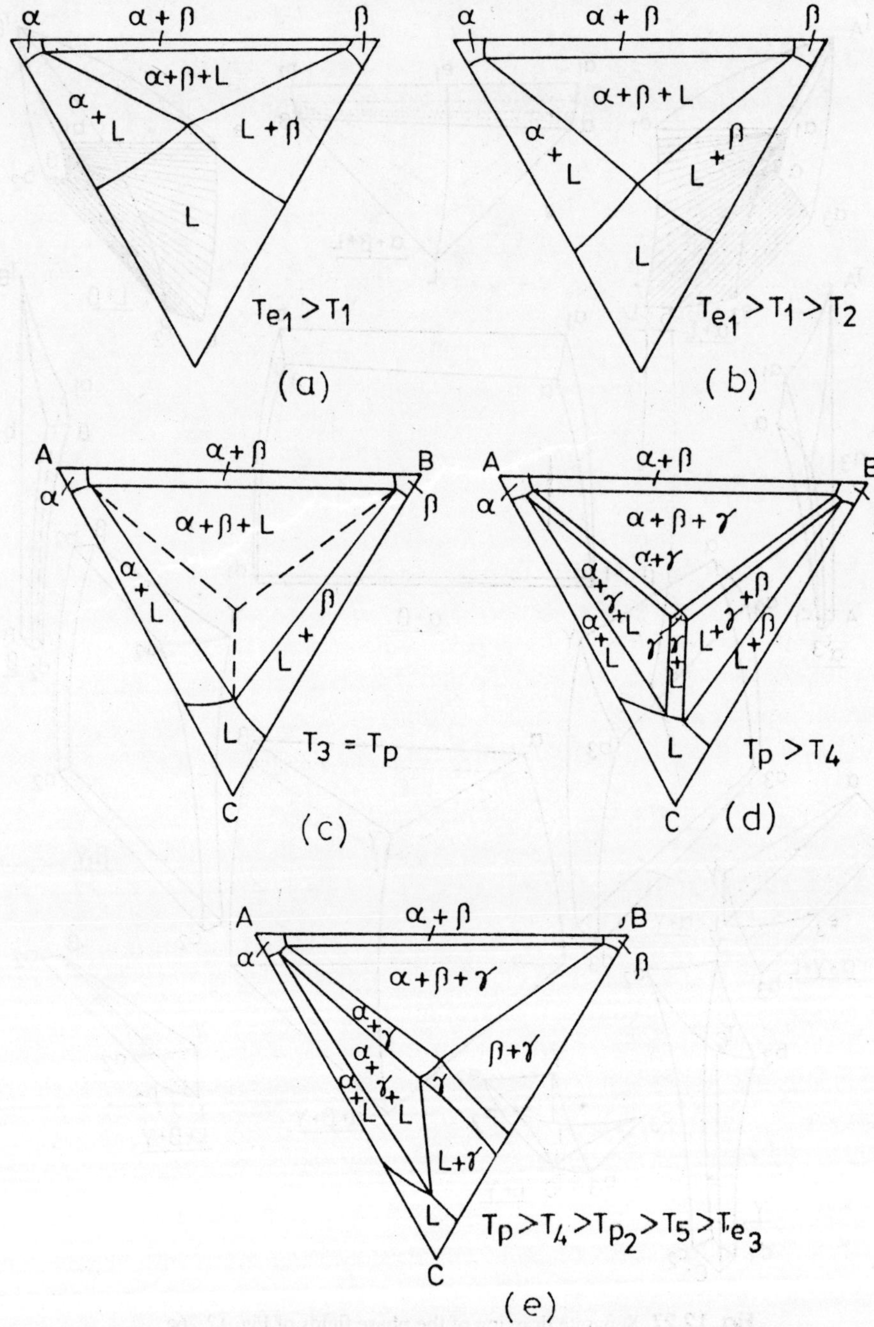

Fig. 12.28 Isothermal sections through the space diagram of Fig. 12.26a.

12.3.2 Isothermal Sections

The isothermal sections drawn at temperatures T_1 to T_5 defined by $T_B > T_A > T_{e_1} > T_1 > T_2 > T_p = T_3 > T_4 > T_{p_2} > T_5 > T_{e_3}$, reveal the true nature of the peritectic reaction, Fig. 12.28. The isothermal section just above the ternary peritectic reaction isotherm shows the (α+β+*L*) and phase field with (α+β), (α+*L*) and (β+*L*) phases along the edges and α, β and liquid phases along the corners of the tie-triangle, Fig. 12.28b. The liquid reacts with α and β phases to give γ as the product phase. The composition point γ lies within the triangle αβ*L*, Fig. 12.28c. The three three-phase regions (α+γ+*L*), (β+γ+*L*) and (α+β+γ) appear in the isothermal sections at T_4 just below T_p, Fig. 12.28d.

12.3.3 Vertical Sections

A vertical section at *BX* from the corner *B* to the point *X* on the side *AC* is shown in Fig. 12.29. The intersection of the vertical plane with various boundaries is labelled with numbers from 1 to 10. The vertical plane at *BX* does not intersect the (β+γ+*L*) phase field and, therefore, it does not appear in the section. The (α+β+*L*) phase field lies above the invariant plane between points 3 and 6 (on the plane). It intersects the monovariant liquid curve e_1L at point 5. The (α+γ+*L*) phase region lies below the invariant plane and terminates on the ordinates at *X*. The vertical section also shows (α+β) and α phase fields between points 6–7 and 7–10, respectively, as shown in Fig. 12.29. The other vertical sections can also be constructed easily.

12.3.4 Solidification of Alloys

Depending on the alloy composition selected, solidification of a liquid alloy in this system begins with crystallization of either primary α or β phases or co-deposition of both α and β. Alloy compositions lying within the area a_1e_1L will solidify into primary α first. The liquid composition will move gradually on the liquidus as the temperature is lowered. The α and β phases start forming simultaneously from the liquid when the liquid composition falls on the line e_1L. The solidification of the liquid occurs by the monovariant reaction $L = \alpha + \beta$ over a range of temperatures. The composition of the liquid at T_p reacts with the α and β phases to give γ as the product phase. If the alloy composition lies within the triangle αβγ, the liquid will be consumed during the peritectic reaction. The final microstructure will consist of the α+β+γ phases. This is shown below for an alloy composition lying within various fields.

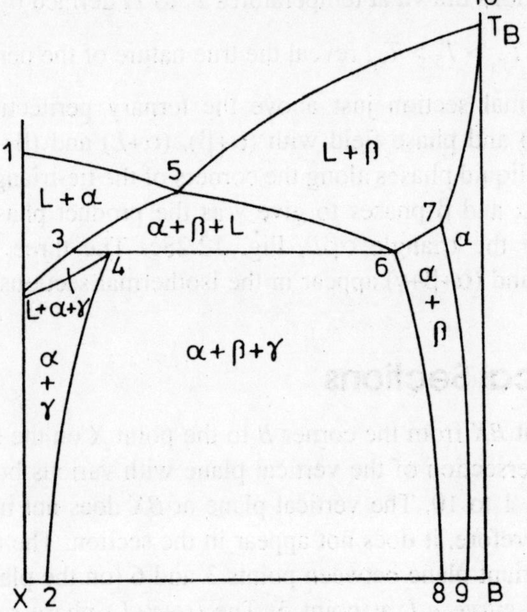

Fig. 12.29 Vertical section at *BX* through the space model of Fig. 12.26a.

a_1e_1L	primary α (α+β) by monovariant reaction, $L = \alpha+\beta$, when the liquid composition touches the monovariant curve e_1L.
Δαβγ	The liquid will react with α and β phases to give γ as the product phase. The final product will be (α+β+γ).
$\Delta\alpha\gamma L$	The liquid will react with α and β phases to give γ as the product phase. The β phase will be consumed. Further solidification of the liquid will occur by the monovariant reaction.
b_1e_1L	Primary β Monovariant (α+β) from the liquid when its composition touches the line e_1L.
Δαβγ	The liquid undergoes the peritectic reaction, $L+\alpha+\beta = \gamma$, to give γ as the product phase. Final microstructure will be (α+β+γ).
$\Delta\beta\gamma L$	The α phase is completely consumed by the peritectic reaction. Further solidification of the liquid will occur by the monovariant reaction.

$\alpha\gamma$ Both liquid and β phases will be consumed by the peritectic reaction. The final microstructure will consist of the α and γ phases with some β percipitated at lower temperatures.

$\beta\gamma$ Both liquid and α phases will be consumed by the peritectic reaction. The final microstructure will consist of the β and γ phases with some α precipitating at lower temperatures.

γL Both α and β phases are consumed by the peritectic reaction. Further solidification occurs by the bivariant reaction. Some α and β phases may form at lower temperatures.

The relative amounts of the various phases can be calculated using the lever rule as will be shown for a number of alloy compositions.

(i) Alloy composition *X*, Fig. 12.30a.
The relative amounts of the α, β and liquid phases just above T_p are,

$$\%\,\beta = \frac{XY}{\beta Y} \times 100 = 46\ \%$$

$$\%\,\alpha = \frac{LY}{\alpha L} \times \frac{X\beta}{\beta Y} \times 100 = 36.15\ \%$$

$$\%\,L = \frac{\alpha Y}{\alpha L} \times \frac{X\beta}{\beta Y} \times 100 = 17.84\ \%$$

The relative amounts of the α, β and γ phases just below T_p are,

$$\%\,\gamma = \frac{XZ}{\gamma Z} \times 100 = 33.33\ \%$$

$$\%\,\alpha = \frac{\beta Z}{\alpha\beta} \times \frac{X\gamma}{XZ} \times 100 = 30.76\ \%$$

$$\%\,\beta = 35.9\ \%$$

The result shows that both α and β phases are consumed during the peritectic reaction with the liquid.

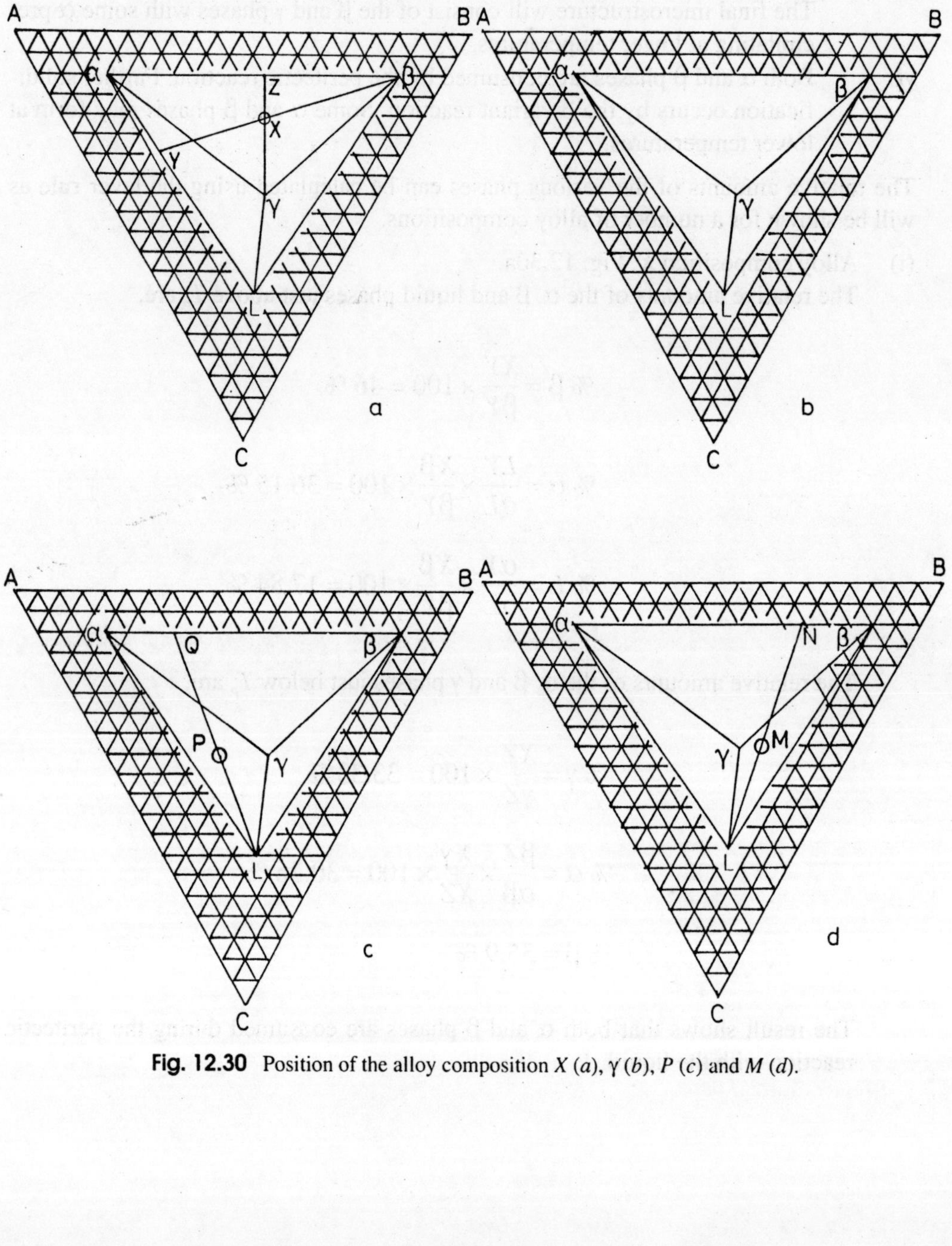

Fig. 12.30 Position of the alloy composition *X* (*a*), γ (*b*), *P* (*c*) and *M* (*d*).

(ii) Alloy composition γ, Fig. 12.30b.
The relative amounts of the α, β and liquid phases just above T_p are,

$$\% L = 57.14\ \%$$

$$\% \alpha = 17.62\ \%$$

$$\% \beta = 25.23\ \%$$

(iii) Alloy composition *P*, Fig. 12.30c.

$$\% L = \frac{PQ}{LQ} \times 100 = 55.55\ \%$$

$$\% \alpha = \frac{\beta Q}{\alpha\beta} \times \frac{LP}{LQ} \times 100 = 34.18\ \%$$

$$\% \beta = \frac{\alpha Q}{\alpha\beta} \times \frac{LP}{LQ} \times 100 = 10.25\ \%$$

Just below T_p, we will get,

$$\% \gamma = \frac{PR}{RQ} = 42.85\ \%$$

$$\% L = \frac{\alpha R}{\alpha L} \times \frac{\gamma P}{\gamma R} \times 100 = 30.95\ \%$$

$$\% \alpha = \frac{LR}{\alpha L} \times \frac{\gamma P}{\gamma R} \times 100 = 26.18\ \%$$

The β phase is completely consumed during the peritectic reaction. Some α is consumed.

(iv) Alloy Composition *M*, Fig. 12.30d.
The relative amounts of the α, β and liquid phases just above the peritectic reaction isotherm T_p are,

$$\% L = \frac{MN}{NL} \times 100 = 55.2\ \%$$

$$\% \alpha = \frac{\beta N}{\alpha\beta} \times \frac{LM}{NL} \times 100 = 10.68\ \%$$

$$\% \beta = \frac{\alpha N}{\alpha\beta} \times \frac{LM}{NL} \times 100 = 34.11\ \%$$

After the peritectic reaction,

$$\% \gamma = 60\ \%$$

$$\% \beta = 18.38\ \%$$

$$\% L = 21.62\ \%$$

The α phase is completely consumed and β phase is partly consumed by the peritectic reaction for this alloy composition.

12.3.5 Variants of the Ternary Peritectic Reaction

The peritectic reaction $L+\alpha+\beta = \gamma$ can also occur in a ternary system with the following combination of binary reactions.

(i) One binary system shows a eutectic reaction and the other two binaries show peritectic reactions.

The space model and the projection of various lines in space on the concentration triangle *ABC* are shown in Fig. 12.31. The three-phase region ($\alpha+\beta+L$) descends to lower temperatures and terminates on the triangle $\alpha\beta L$ of the invariant plane. It is bounded by $a_1b_1\beta\alpha a_1$ ($\alpha\beta$), $a_1e_1L\alpha a_1$ ($L\alpha$) and ($b_1e_1L\beta b_1$ ($L\beta$) ruled surfaces. The three three-phase regions ($\alpha+\beta+\gamma$), ($\alpha+\gamma+L$) and ($\beta+\gamma+L$), descend from the four-phase plane. The triangles $\alpha\beta\gamma$, $\alpha\gamma L$ and $\beta\gamma L$ on the invariant plane are the uppermost triangles of the respective regions. The three-phase region ($\alpha+\gamma+L$) terminates on the peritectic reaction isotherm of the binary *A–C* on line $a_3b_3p_3$ with ruled surfaces $b_3a_3\alpha\gamma b_3$ ($\alpha\gamma$), $b_3\gamma Lp_3b_3$ (γL) and $a_3\alpha Lp_3a_3$ (αL). Similarly, the ($\beta+\gamma+L$) phase region terminates on the peritectic reaction line $a_2b_2p_2$ of the binary *B–C* with ruled surfaces, $b_2a_2\gamma\beta b_2$ ($\beta\gamma$), $a_2\gamma Lp_2a_2$ (γL) and $b_2\beta Lp_2b_2$ (βL). The ($\alpha+\beta+\gamma$) phase region descends from the invariant plane on to the concentration triangle *ABC* with expanded field $\alpha_1\beta_1\gamma_1$. Details of various phase fields are shown in Table 12.3.

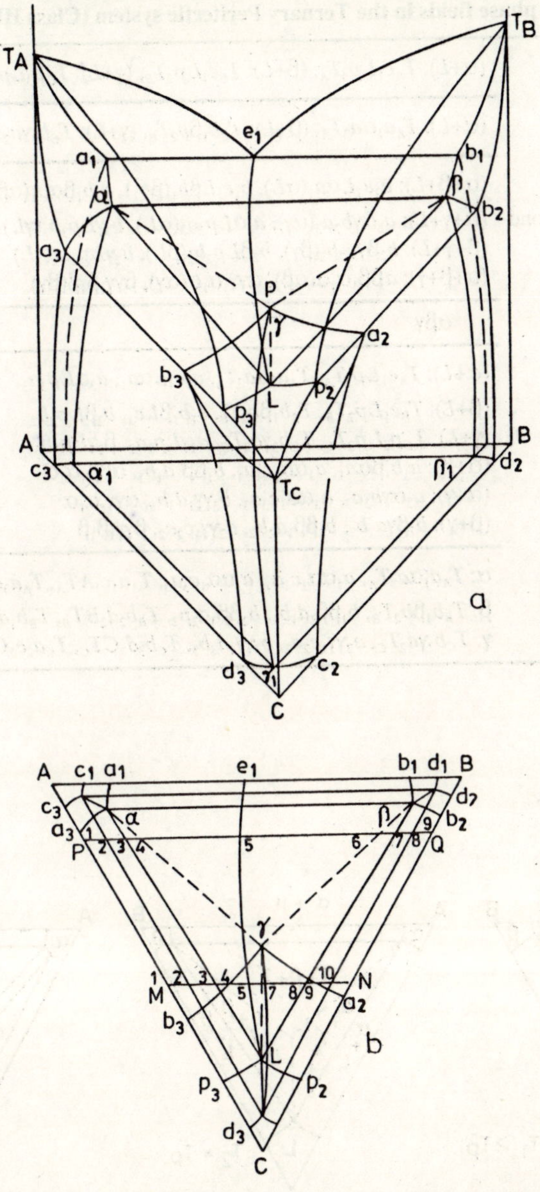

Fig. 12.31 Space model of a variant of the ternary system *A–B–C* showing peritectic reaction with one binary showing a eutectic reaction and the other two binaries showing peritectic reactions.

Table 12.3 Various phase fields in the Ternary Peritectic system (Class III)

Liquidus Surface	(α+L): $T_Ae_1Lp_3T_A$, (β+L): $T_Be_1Lp_2T_B$, (γ+L): $T_Cp_3Lp_2T_C$
Solidus Surface	(α+L): $T_Aa_1\alpha a_3T_A$, (β+L): $T_Bb_1\beta b_2T_B$, (γ+L): $T_Cb_3\gamma a_2T_C$
Three-Phase regions and the corresponding ruled surfaces	(α+β+L): $a_1e_1L\alpha a_1(\alpha L)$, $b_1e_1L\beta b_1(\beta b_1)$, $a_1b_1\beta\alpha a_1(\alpha\beta)$ (α+γ+L): $a_3\alpha\gamma b_3a_3(\alpha\gamma)$, $a_3\alpha Lp_3a_3(\alpha L)$, $b_3\gamma Lp_3b_3(\gamma L)$ (β+γ+L): $b_2\beta\gamma a_2b_2(\beta\gamma)$, $b_2\beta Lp_2b_2(\beta L)$, $a_2\gamma Lp_2a_2(\gamma L)$ (α+β+γ): $a\beta\beta_1\alpha_1\alpha(\alpha\beta)$, $\alpha\gamma\gamma_1\alpha_1\alpha(\alpha\gamma)$, $\beta\gamma\gamma_1\beta_1\beta(\beta\gamma)$
Four-phase plane	$\alpha\beta\gamma$
Two-Phase Regions bounded by	(α+L): $T_Ae_1Lp_3T_A$, $T_Aa_1\alpha a_3T_A$, $a_1e_1L\alpha a_1$, $a_3\alpha Lp_3a_3$ (β+L): $T_Be_1Lp_2T_B$, $T_Bb_1\beta b_2T_B$, $e_1b_1\beta Le_1$, $b_2\beta Lp_2b_2$ (γ+L): $T_Cp_3Lp_2T_C$, $T_Cb_3\gamma a_2T_C$, $a_2\gamma Lp_2a_2$, $\beta_2\gamma Lp_3b_3$ (α+β): $a_1b_1\beta\alpha a_1$, $a_1\alpha\alpha_1c_1a_1$, $b_1\beta\beta_1d_1b_1$, $\alpha\beta\beta_1\alpha_1\alpha$ (α+γ): $a_3\alpha\gamma b_3a_3$, $a_3\alpha\alpha_1c_3a_3$, $b_3\gamma\gamma_1d_3b_3$, $\alpha\gamma\gamma_1\alpha_1\alpha$ (β+γ): $b_2\beta\gamma a_2b_2$, $b_2\beta\beta_1d_2b_2$, $a_2\gamma\gamma_1c_2a_2$, $\beta\gamma\gamma_1\beta_1\beta$
Single-Phase regions bounded by	α: $T_Aa_1\alpha a_3T_A$, $a_1\alpha\alpha_1c_1a_1$, $a_3\alpha\alpha_1c_3a_3$, $T_Aa_1c_1AT_A$, $T_Aa_3c_3AT_A$ β: $T_Bb_1\beta b_2T_B$, $b_1\beta\beta_1d_1b_1$, $b_2\beta\beta_1d_2p_2$, $T_Bb_2d_2BT_B$, $T_Bb_1d_1BT_B$. γ: $T_Cb_3\gamma a_2T_C$, $a_2\gamma\gamma_1c_2a_2$, $b_3\gamma\gamma_1d_3b_3$, $T_Cb_3d_3CT_C$, $T_Ca_2c_2CT_C$.

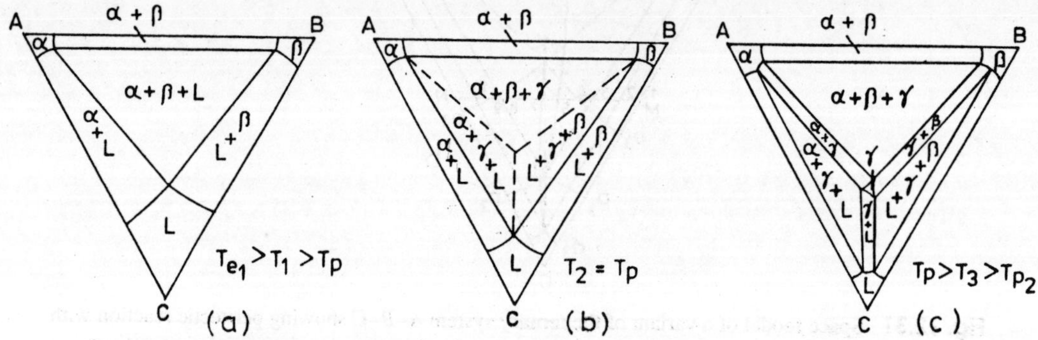

Fig. 12.32 Isothermal sections through the space model of Fig. 12.31.

Isothermal sections at T_1, T_2 and T_3, defined by $T_1 > T_2 = T_p > T_3$, are drawn in Figs. 12.32, a, b and c, respectively. At temperature T_1 just above the peritectic reaction isotherm, the isothermal section shows the (α+β+L) phase region along with single and two-phase regions involving the same three phases, Fig. 12.32a. The isothermal section at T_p shows the same field but now in association with the other three three-phase regions, Fig. 12.32b. At $T_3 < T_p$, the three three-phase regions are separated by (α+γ), (β+γ) and (γ+L) phase fields. The γ phase field appears in the center of the triangle ABC. The vertical sections at PQ and MN are shown in Figs. 12.33, a and b, respectively.

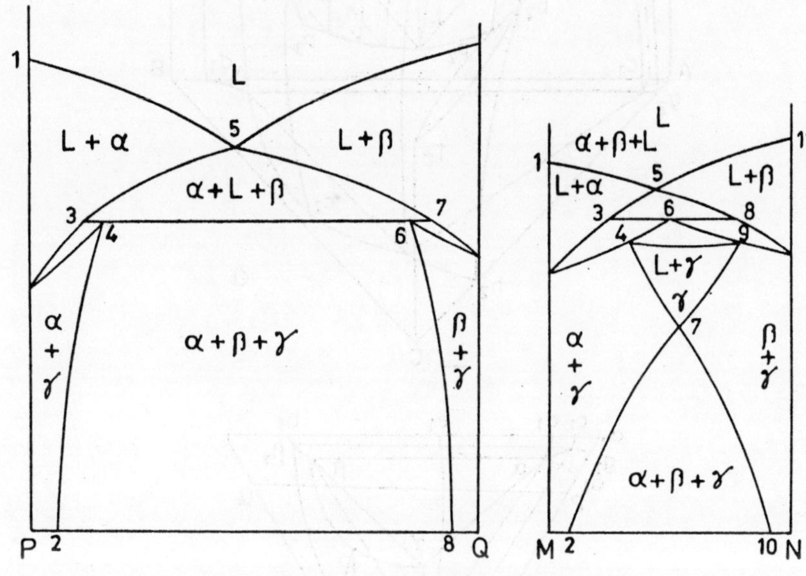

Fig. 12.33 Vertical sections at *PQ* and *MN*.

(ii) The peritectic reaction L+α+β = γ can occur in the ternary system when all the three binaries show peritectic reactions. The space model can be built with relative ease and is being left to the reader as an exercise.

(iii) The peritectic reaction can also occur in the ternary system where only two of the binaries show eutectic or peritectic reactions and the third binary system is an isomorphous. The space model and its projection on the concentration triangle are shown in Figs. 12.34, a and b, respectively. The three-phase

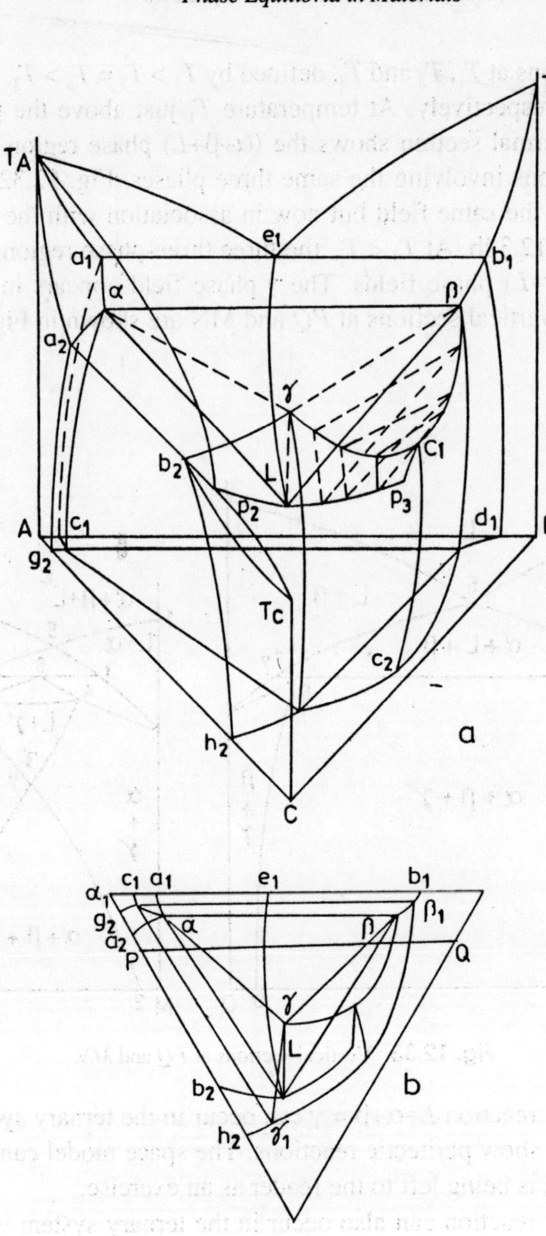

Fig. 12.34 (a) The space model of a variant of the ternary system showing peritectic reaction. (b) Projection of (a) on the concentration triangle.

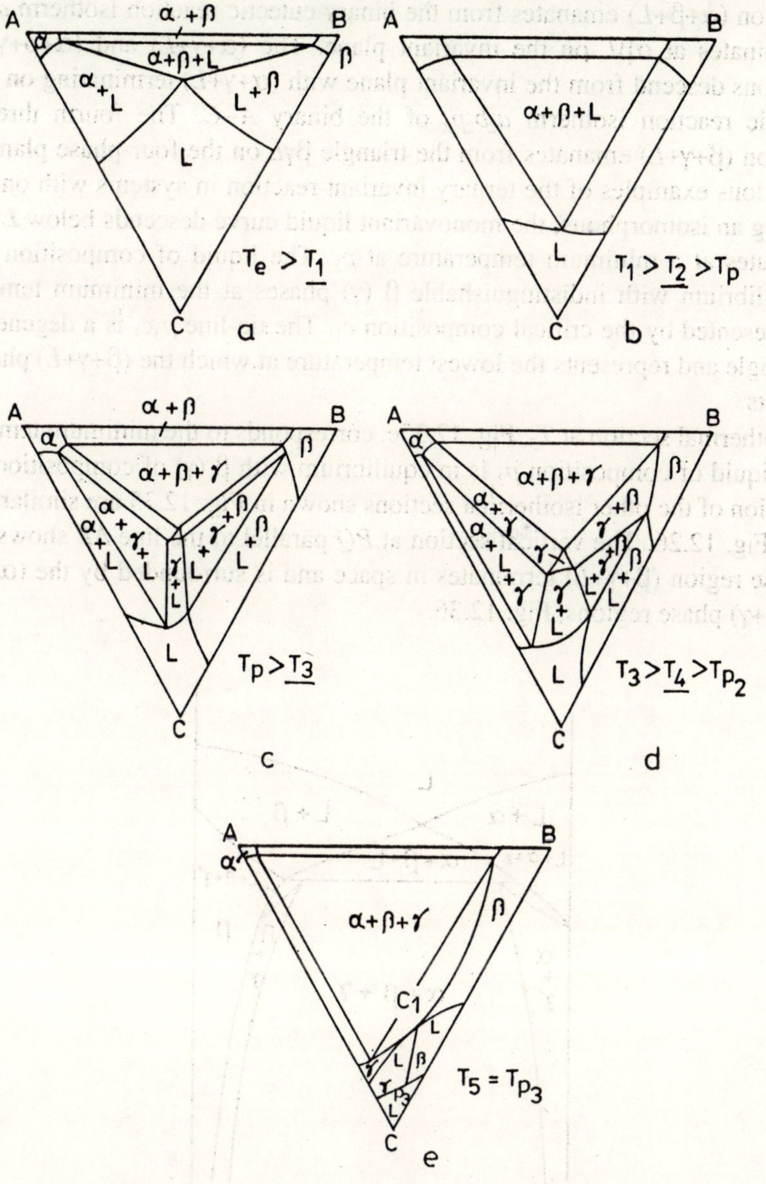

Fig. 12.35 Isothermal sections through the space model of Fig. 12.34.

region (α+β+L) emanates from the binary eutectic reaction isotherm $a_1e_1b_1$. It terminates at αβL on the invariant plane. The (α+γ+L) and (α+β+γ) phase regions descend from the invariant plane with (α+γ+L) terminating on the peritectic reaction isotherm $a_2b_2p_2$ of the binary A–C. The fourth three-phase region (β+γ+L) emanates from the triangle βγL on the four-phase plane. As in previous examples of the ternary invariant reaction in systems with one binary being an isomorphous, the monovariant liquid curve descends below L and terminates at a minimum temperature at p_3. The liquid of composition p_3 is in equilibrium with indistinguishable β (γ) phases at the minimum temperature represented by the critical composition c_1. The tie-line p_3c_1 is a degenerate tie-triangle and represents the lowest temperature at which the (β+γ+L) phase field exists.

The isothermal section at T_5, Fig. 12.35e, corresponds to the minimum temperature at which liquid of composition p_3 is in equilibrium with β (γ) of composition c_1. The interpretation of the other isothermal sections shown in Fig. 12.35 are similar to those shown in Fig. 12.26. The vertical section at PQ parallel to the line AB shows that the three-phase region (β+γ+L) terminates in space and is surrounded by the (α+β+γ), γ (β) and (β+γ) phase regions, Fig. 12.36.

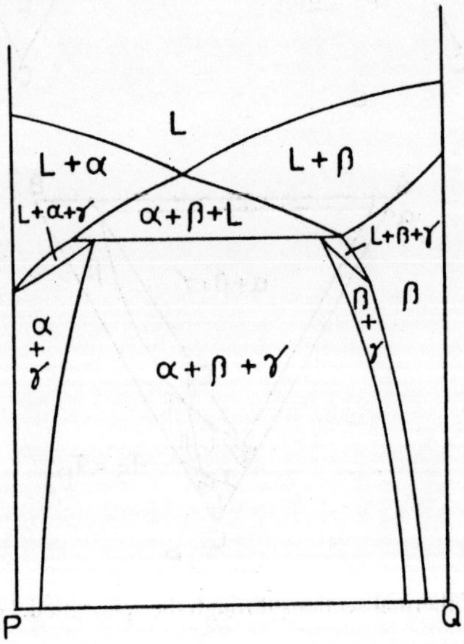

Fig. 12.36 Vertical section at PQ parallel to the side AB.

PROBLEMS

1. (a) With reference to Fig. 12.1, state which phase regions are separated by the following surfaces (i) $a_1b_1\beta\alpha$ (ii) $a_1e_1E\alpha$ (iii) $T_cb_3\gamma a_2$ (iv) $e_3E\gamma b_3$.
   (b) Describe the cooling of an alloy composition passing through a point on the line αE and e_2E (Fig. 12.1).
   (c) Draw vertical sections at (i) BX (ii) GH.
2. Select an alloy composition on the line e_1E of the phase diagram of Fig. 12.1 and compositions of the α, β, γ and liquid phases on the four-phase plane. Calculate the relative amounts of the primary α and β and eutectic, α, β and γ phases in the alloy just below T_E.
3. (a) With reference to the space diagram of Figs. 12.7, 12.9, 12.10 and 12.11, draw sufficient numbers of isothermal sections to reveal the internal structure of the diagram.
   (b) Draw few vertical sections on lines parallel to the side AB in each case.
4. A ternary system A–B–C shows Class I reaction $L \to \alpha + \beta_1 + \beta_2$ and two binaries are associated with a eutectic and peritectic reaction each. The third binary is an isomorphous system.
   (a) Draw the space diagram and show the critical composition at which β_1 and β_2 become indistinguishable.
   (b) Separately draw β, (α+L), (β_2+L) and (α+β_1+L) phase regions.
   (c) Draw sufficient number of isothermal sections to cover all one, two and three-phase regions of the diagram.
   (d) Draw vertical sections on line positions parallel to AB at $X_C = 0.1, 0.2, 0.4, 0.6$ and 0.8.
5. (a) With reference to Fig. 12.13, state which phase regions are separated by the following surfaces (i) $a_3\alpha Le_3$ (ii) $e_2L\beta b_2$
   (b) Draw the vertical section at BM where M is a point on the line AC.
   (c) Describe the cooling of the following alloy compositions (i) at the intersection of lines $\alpha\gamma$ and βL (point X) (ii) on the line βX within the triangle $\alpha\beta L$ (iii) on the line αX within the triangle $\alpha\beta\gamma$. By selecting suitable alloy compositions for the α, β, γ and liquid phases, calculate the relative amount of these phases as applicable.
6. A ternary system A–B–C is associated with three binary peritectic reactions and shows the invariant reaction α+L ⇔ β+γ.
   (a) Draw the space diagram.
   (b) Draw the following phase regions separately (i) (β+α) (ii) (β+γ+L) (iii) (γ+α) and (iv) (α+γ+L).

(c) Draw sufficient numbers of isothermal sections from just below the highest melting component to just below the lowest melting component.

(d) Draw projections of all surfaces on the concentration triangle.

(e) Describe the cooling of an alloy and subsequent development of the microstructure of (i) an alloy passing through the liquid composition on the four-phase plane (ii) a point on the line αL on the invariant plane.

7. A ternary system A–B–C shows Class II reaction and is associated with two binary peritectic reactions and an isomorphous.

(a) Draw the phase diagram.

(b) Draw the (α+L), (α+β_1+L), (β_1+β_2+L) and (β+L) phase regions separately.

(c) Draw a number of isothermal sections through the phase diagram.

(d) Draw a vertical section on a line from A to a point on the side BC.

(e) Indicate the degenerate tie-triangle ec of the type shown in Fig. 12.11. Describe the cooling of an alloy composition passing through point n on the line ec.

8. (a) With reference to Fig. 12.31, state which phase fields are separated by the following surfaces:

(i) $a_1e_1L\alpha$ (ii) $a_3\alpha\gamma b_3$ (iii) $T_CP_3\gamma P_2$.

(b) Draw the following phase fields separately.

(i) α (ii) (γ+L) (iii) (α+β+L) (iv) (β+γ).

(c) Describe the cooling of an alloy composition passing through the point γ in Fig. 12.31.

(d) Calculate the relative amounts of the α, β, γ and liquid phases (whatever is applicable) just below and above the invariant plane for an alloy composition on the line e_1L and within the triangle $\alpha\beta\gamma$.

9. A ternary system A–B–C shows Class III reaction, $L + \alpha + \beta$ <=> γ and is associated with two binary eutectic reactions and a binary peritectic reaction.

(a) Draw the space diagram.

(b) Draw the following phase fields separately.

(i) β (ii) (β+γ) (iii) (α+β+L) (iv) (γ+L).

(c) Draw a number of isothermal sections from just below the highest melting component to a temperature at which the liquid is exhausted during solidification.

(d) Draw vertical sections on lines parallel to the side AB at X_C= 0.1, 0.4 and 0.7.

(e) Describe the solidification of an alloy composition passing through the point γ on the invariant plane.

Chapter 13

TERNARY FOUR-PHASE EQUILIBRIUM WITH CONGRUENTLY MELTING INTERMEDIATE PHASES

13.1 INTRODUCTION

A simple ternary system with a congruently melting intermediate phase in one of the binaries occurs in a number of alloy systems, for example Al-Mg-Si and Al-Sb-Zn. Considering an intermediate phase δ in one of the binary systems as well, there are in all five phases (four solid and one liquid): α, β, γ, δ and liquid. If the δ phase forms in the binary A–B, it can combine with the component C to make a quasi-binary system. There are four possible dissociation reactions of the liquid,

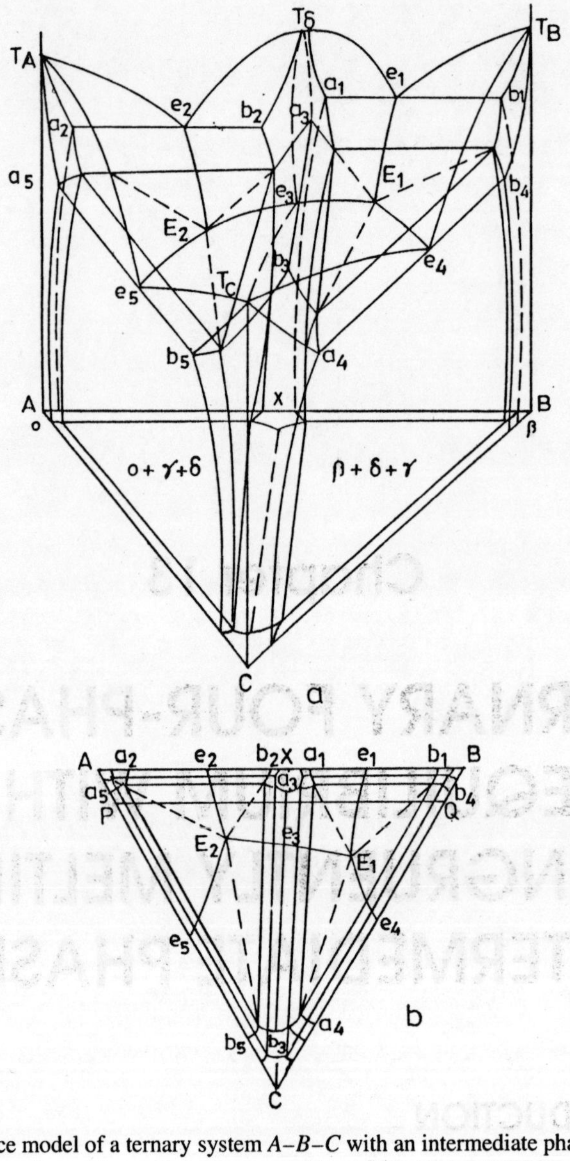

Fig. 13.1 (a) Space model of a ternary system *A–B–C* with an intermediate phase δ on the binary *A–B* showing eutectic reactions. The component *C* and δ phase together form a quasi-binary system. (b) Projection of lines in space on the concentration triangle.

$$L \Rightarrow \alpha + \beta + \gamma \qquad (1)$$

$$L \Rightarrow \alpha + \beta + \delta \qquad (2)$$

$$L \Rightarrow \alpha + \gamma + \delta \qquad (3)$$

$$L \Rightarrow \beta + \gamma + \delta \qquad (4)$$

The ternary phase diagram can be constructed with dissociation reactions (3) and (4) when the intermediate phase forms a quasi-binary system with the component *C*. The formation of a quasi-binary system is not necessary when the liquid dissociates according to the second and fourth reactions.

13.1.1 The Space Model

The space model for the ternary system with the binary system *A–B* showing an intermediate phase δ, and the other two binary systems *A–C* and *B–C* showing eutectic reactions, is presented in Fig. 13.1a, along with its projection on the concentration triangle *ABC*, Fig. 13.1b. The ternary system shows a quasi-binary reaction between the intermediate phase δ and the component *C*. This is given as,

$$L \rightleftharpoons \gamma + \delta.$$

The ternary phase diagram is partitioned into two regions along the eutectic reaction line $a_3e_3b_3$. Obviously, the phase diagram can be constructed with two ternary eutectic (Class I) reactions,

$$L \rightleftharpoons \alpha + \gamma + \delta$$

and

$$L \rightleftharpoons \beta + \gamma + \delta.$$

The eutectic composition e_3 is a saddle point lying at the maximum on the curve $E_2e_3E_1$ and a minimum on the quasi-binary liquidus curve $T_\delta e_3T_C$. This partition of the phase diagram is very similar to that occurring in binary systems with an intermediate phase. The ternary eutectic reactions occur at T_{E_1} and T_{E_2} at liquid composition points E_1 and E_2 on invariant planes. The following three-phase regions will appear in the phase diagram

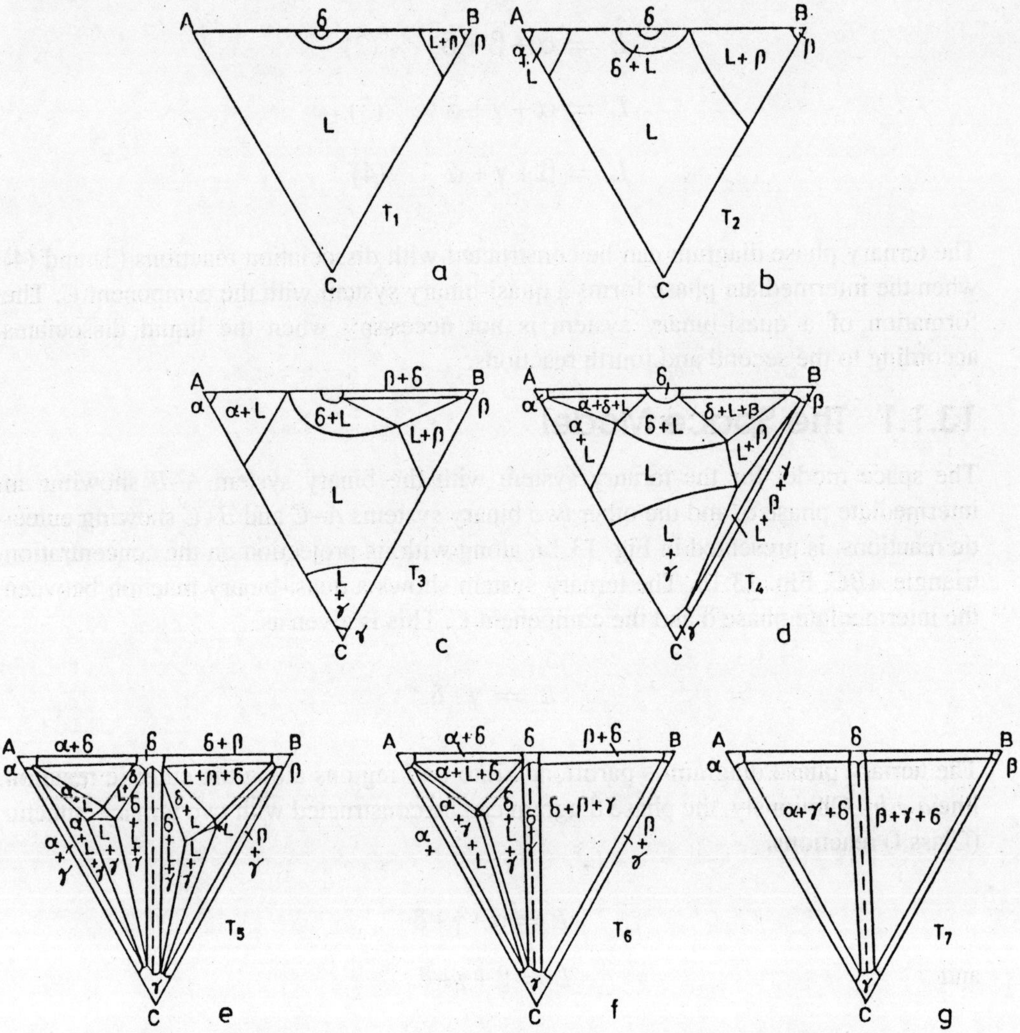

Fig. 13.2 Isothermal sections through the space model of Fig. 13.1.

$$\left.\begin{array}{ccc} \alpha & \delta & L \\ \alpha & \gamma & L \\ \gamma & \delta & L \\ \alpha & \gamma & \delta \end{array}\right\} \quad \text{and} \quad \left.\begin{array}{ccc} \delta & \beta & L \\ \delta & \gamma & L \\ \beta & \gamma & L \\ \beta & \gamma & \delta \end{array}\right\}$$

The ($\gamma + \delta + L$) phase region emanates from the quasi-binary eutectic reaction isotherm at $a_3e_3b_3$ and it descends on both sides of the line *CX* terminating on four-phase planes.

13.1.2 Isothermal Sections

The isothermal sections through the space model are drawn at a number of temperatures covering the temperature range of interest, Fig. 13.2. The result of the interaction of the intermediate phase with the component *C* is shown at T_1, Fig. 13.2a. The first three-phase region, ($\delta + L + \beta$), appears below T_{e_1}, Fig. 13.2c. The partition of the ternary phase diagram along CX is evident in the isothermal section at T_5, Fig. 13.2e. The isothermal sections show two three-phase regions, ($\alpha + \gamma + \delta$) and ($\beta + \gamma + \delta$), separated along the line *CX* at lower temperature, Fig. 13.2g.

13.1.3 Vertical Sections

The vertical section at *CX* shows the quasi-binary eutectic reaction between component *C* and the δ phase, Fig. 13.3a. The horizontal lines in this section are true tie-lines as opposed to the other section where tie-lines meet the vertical plane at an angle.

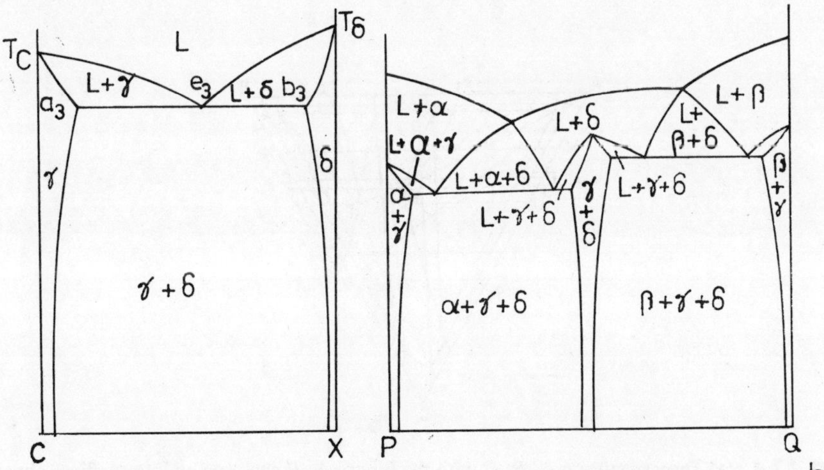

Fig. 13.3 The vertical section at *CX* of Fig. 13.1b.

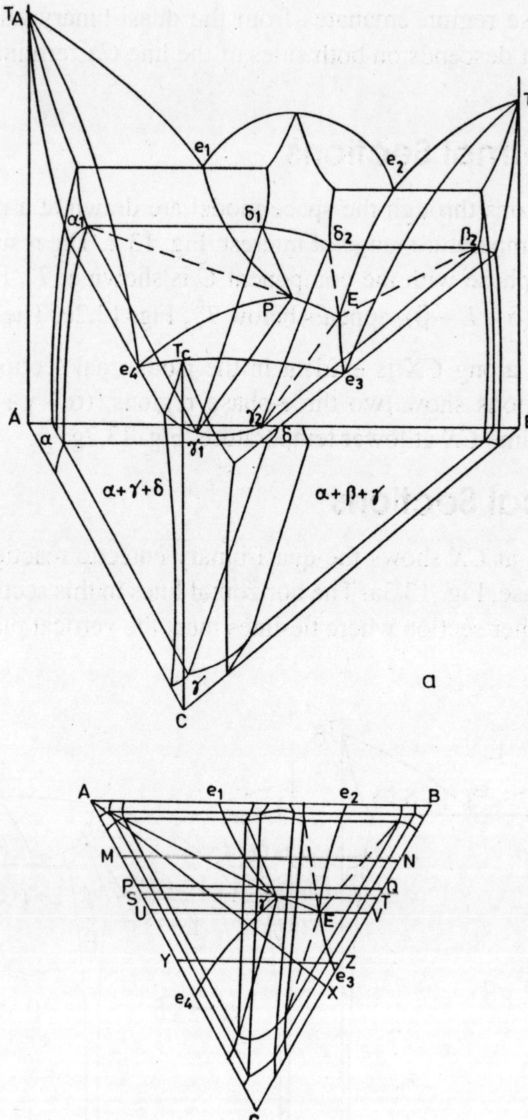

Fig. 13.4 (a) Ternary system A–B–C with the binary A–B showing an intermediate phase δ. There is no quasi-binary between the component C and the δ phase. (b) Projection of (a) on the concentration triangle ABC.

13.2 TERNARY SYSTEM WITH AN INTERMEDIATE PHASE IN ONE OF THE BINARY SYSTEMS WITHOUT A QUASI-BINARY REACTION

Another example of the ternary system with an intermediate phase in one of the binaries is presented in Fig. 13.4. The system does not form a quasi-binary eutectic with component C and the δ phase. The following reactions may occur in the system.

$$L + \alpha \rightleftharpoons \gamma + \delta \quad \text{at} \quad T_p,$$

and

$$L \rightleftharpoons \beta + \gamma + \delta \quad \text{at} \quad T_E.$$

Since the phase diagram does not show any quasi-binary reaction between component C and the δ phase, the $(\mathrm{L} + \gamma + \delta)$ phase region lying in the middle of the diagram is continuous between the two invariant planes. It descends from the plane at T_p and terminates on the ternary eutectic reaction isotherm at T_E. It has the shape of a triangular prism with ruled surfaces $\delta_1\delta_2EP$ (δL), $\delta_1\gamma_1\gamma_2\delta_2$ ($\gamma\delta$) and $PE\gamma_2\gamma_1$ ($L\gamma$). The projection of the space diagram on the concentration triangle is shown in Fig. 13.4b.

Isothermal sections covering the entire temperature range of interest are shown in Fig. 13.5. The three-phase region $(L + \gamma + \delta)$ appears at T_p as shown by the dotted lines, Fig. 13.5a. Vertical sections at a number of positions parallel to the line AB are shown in Fig. 13.5b. The continuity of the $(\mathrm{L} + \gamma + \delta)$ phase field between the invariant planes at T_p and T_E are apparent in all the sections.

13.3 TERNARY SYSTEM WITH AN INTERMEDIATE PHASE IN ONE OF THE BINARIES WITHOUT A QUASI-BINARY REACTION

The ternary system with a quasi-binary reaction between component C and the δ phase was discussed in section 13.1. Reactions (3) and (4) were considered. Now we will consider reactions (1) and (2) for the ternary system,

$$L \rightleftharpoons \alpha + \beta + \gamma$$

$$L \rightleftharpoons \alpha + \beta + \delta.$$

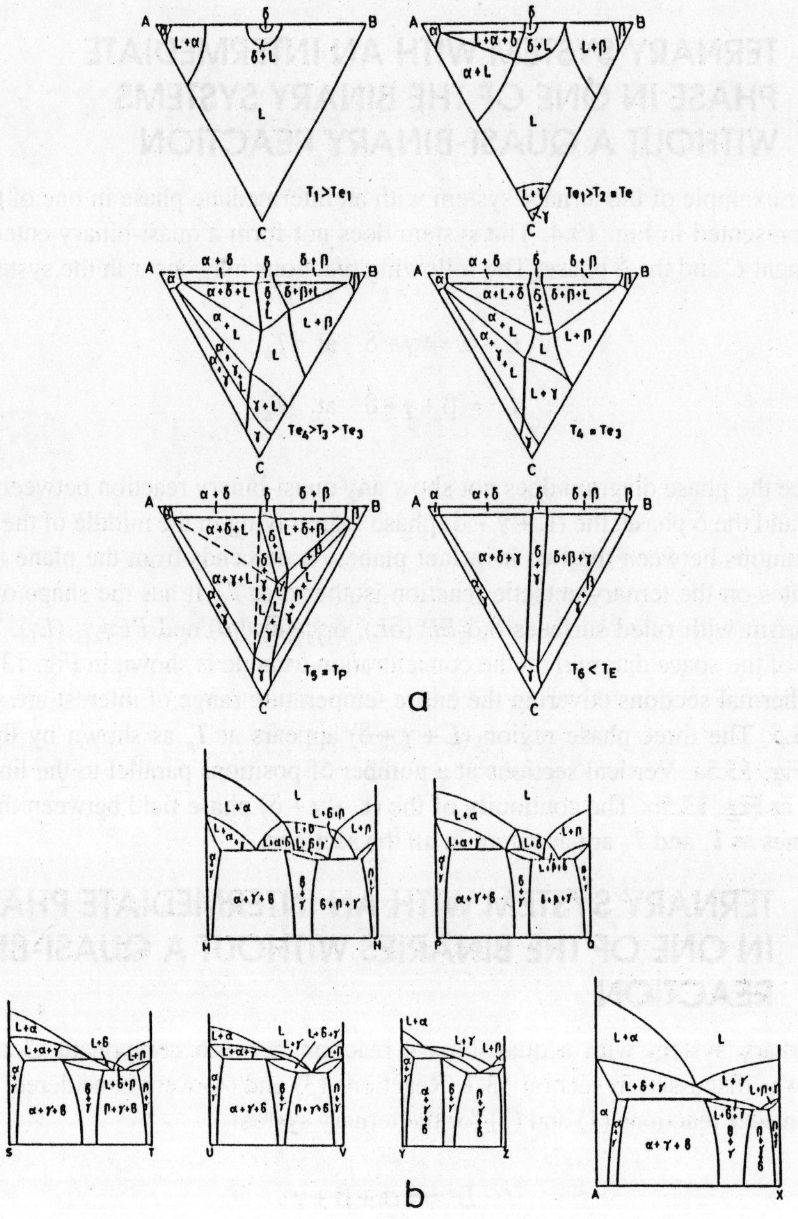

Fig. 13.5 (a) Isothermal sections through the space diagram of Fig. 13.4. (b) Vertical sections at various locations of the space diagram of Fig. 13.4.

The space model shows a saddle point at e_5 which lies at the maximum on the curve $E_1e_5E_2$ and at the minimum on the eutectic at e_5 (not shown), Fig. 13.6a. The projection on the concentration triangle ABC is shown in Fig. 13.6b. Some of the ruled surfaces of the ternary system are shown in Fig. 13.7. Since the $(\alpha + \beta)$ phase region lies across the eutectic reaction isotherm $a_5e_5b_5$ on both sides, the α/β ruled surfaces descend from the line $a_5e_5b_5$ and terminate on invariant planes at E_1 and E_2. Isothermal sections at a number of temperatures through the space model are shown in Fig. 13.8.

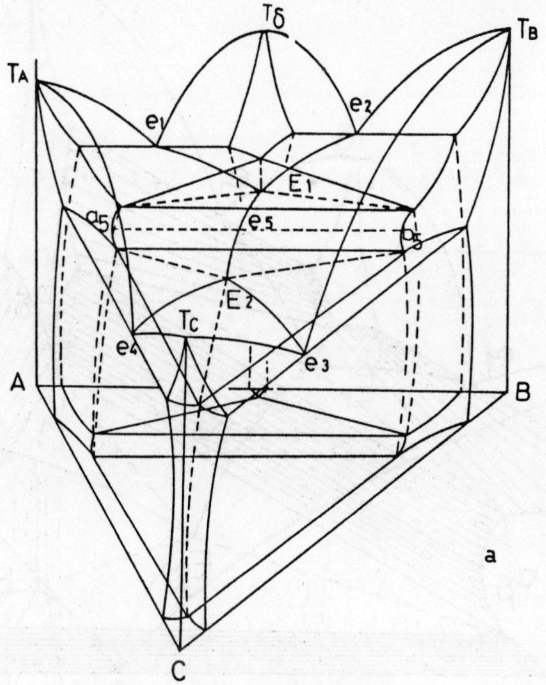

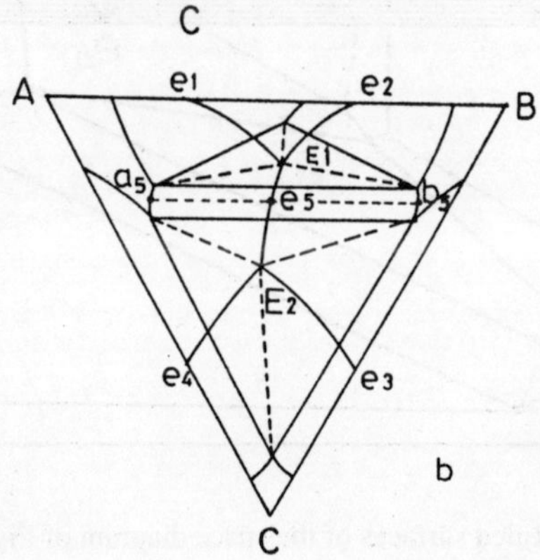

Fig. 13.6 (a) Space model of a ternary system A–B–C with the binary A–B showing an intermediate phase δ but no quasi-binary. (b) The projection of (a) on the concentration triangle ABC.

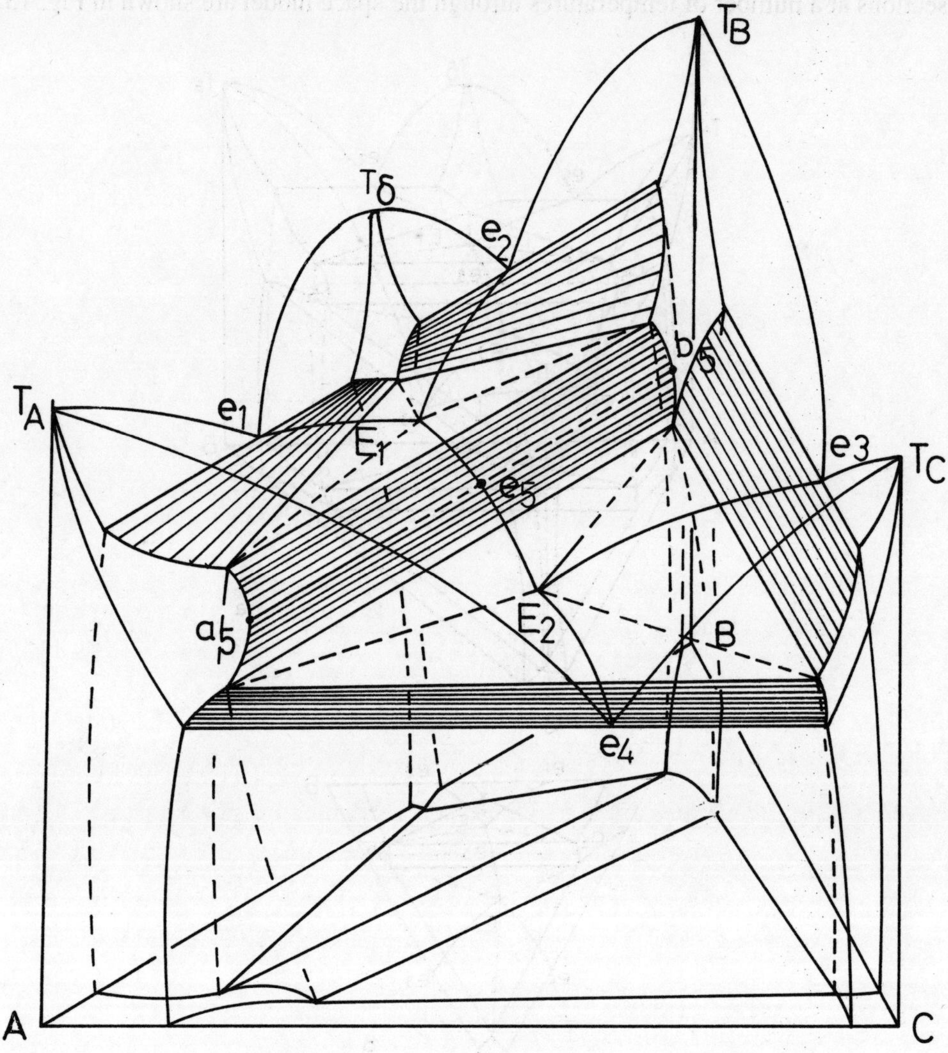

Fig. 13.7 Ruled surfaces of the space diagram of Fig. 13.6.

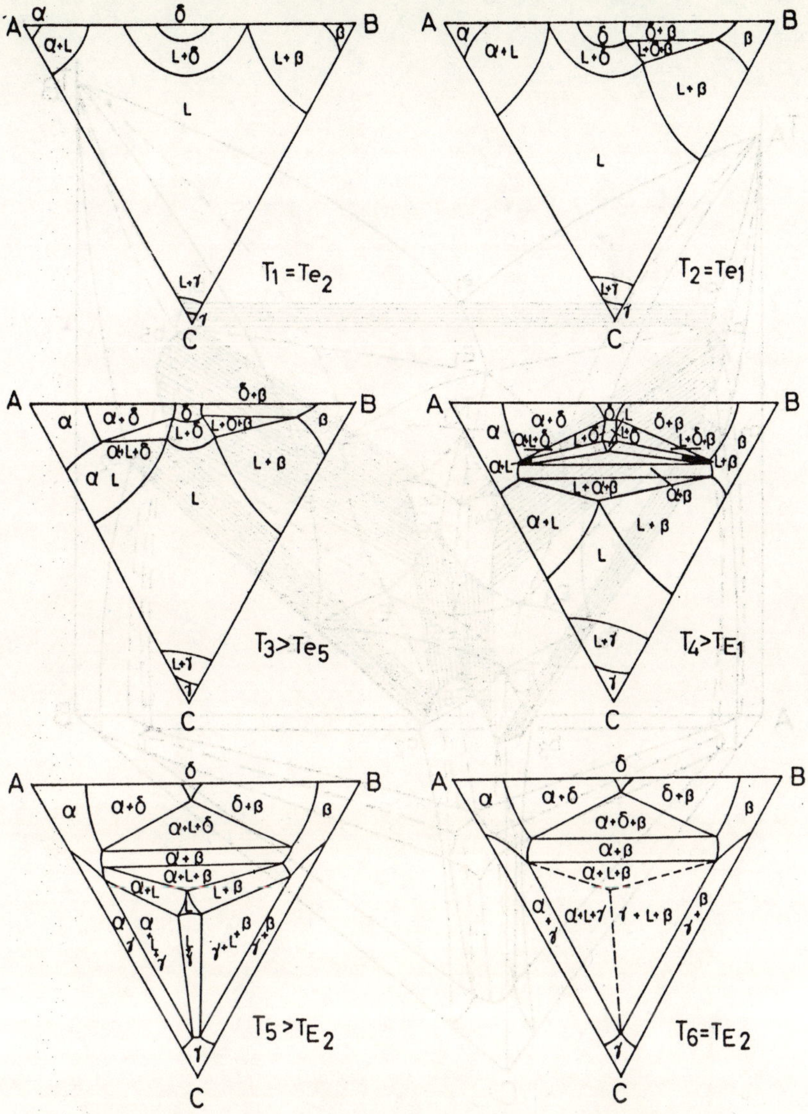

Fig. 13.8 Isothermal sections through the space model of Fig. 13.6.

13.4 PHASE DIAGRAM SHOWING A TERNARY INTERMEDIATE PHASE

Quasi-binary systems can also form in ternary systems with a congruently melting ternary intermediate phase. The space model of the system shows a ternary interme-

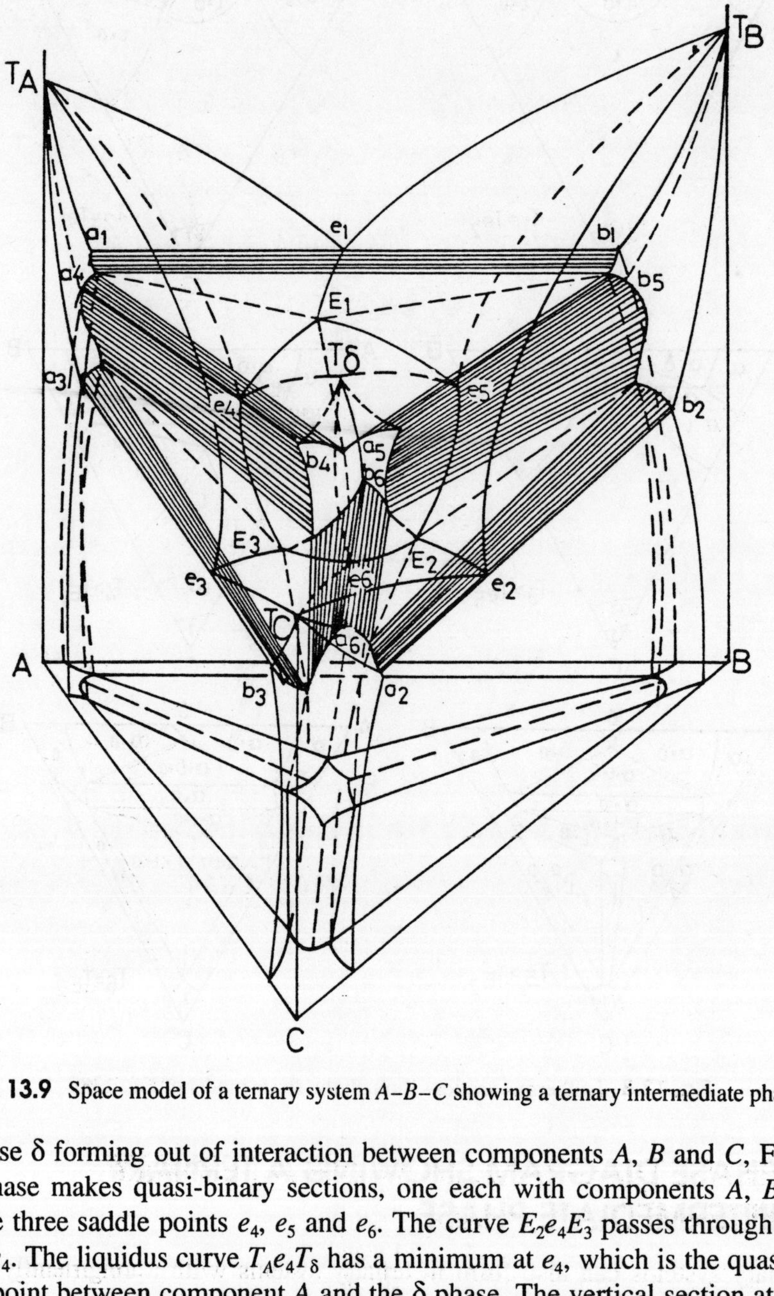

Fig. 13.9 Space model of a ternary system *A–B–C* showing a ternary intermediate phase.

diate phase δ forming out of interaction between components *A*, *B* and *C*, Fig. 13.9. The δ phase makes quasi-binary sections, one each with components *A*, *B* and C. There are three saddle points e_4, e_5 and e_6. The curve $E_2e_4E_3$ passes through a maximum at e_4. The liquidus curve $T_Ae_4T_\delta$ has a minimum at e_4, which is the quasi-binary eutectic point between component *A* and the δ phase. The vertical section at *AX* will show true ternary tie-lines. Similarly, there are two more quasi-binary systems between component B and δ and between C and δ. There are two additional saddle points at e_5 and e_6. The ternary space model is divided into three parts (just like the binary phase diagram is divided into distinct parts by an intermediate phase). The three ternary eutectic reactions are,

$$L \xrightleftharpoons{E_1} \alpha+\beta+\delta$$

$$L \xrightleftharpoons{E_2} \delta+\beta+\gamma$$

$$L \xrightleftharpoons{E_3} \alpha+\delta+\gamma$$

Some of the ruled surfaces involving solid phases are shown in the drawing for clarity. The three quasi-binary sections are shown separately in Fig. 13.10.

The ternary δ phase and its associated phase regions are shown in the isothermal sections, Fig. 13.11. The development of the three-phase regions is brought out clearly in the isothermal sections. Vertical sections can be easily constructed from the guidelines provided in Chapter 12.

13.5 TERNARY SYSTEM WITH CONGRUENTLY MELTING INTERMEDIATE PHASES ASSOCIATED WITH EACH BINARY

The space model for a ternary system with an intermediate phase in each of the binary systems is presented in Fig. 13.12. The binary system A–B is divided into two quasi-binary systems by the intermediate phase δ. Similarly, the binary systems A–C and B–C are divided into two quasi-binary systems each by the presence of intermediate phases η and ε, respectively. The space model in Fig. 13.12 results from the ternary system showing quasi-binaries δ–ε, δ–η and η–ε, with intermediate phases. The ternary phase diagram is divided into four parts with ternary eutectic reactions among the components, A–δ–ε, δ–ε–η, δ–η–B, and ε–η–C. The four invariant reactions and the associated three-phase regions are:

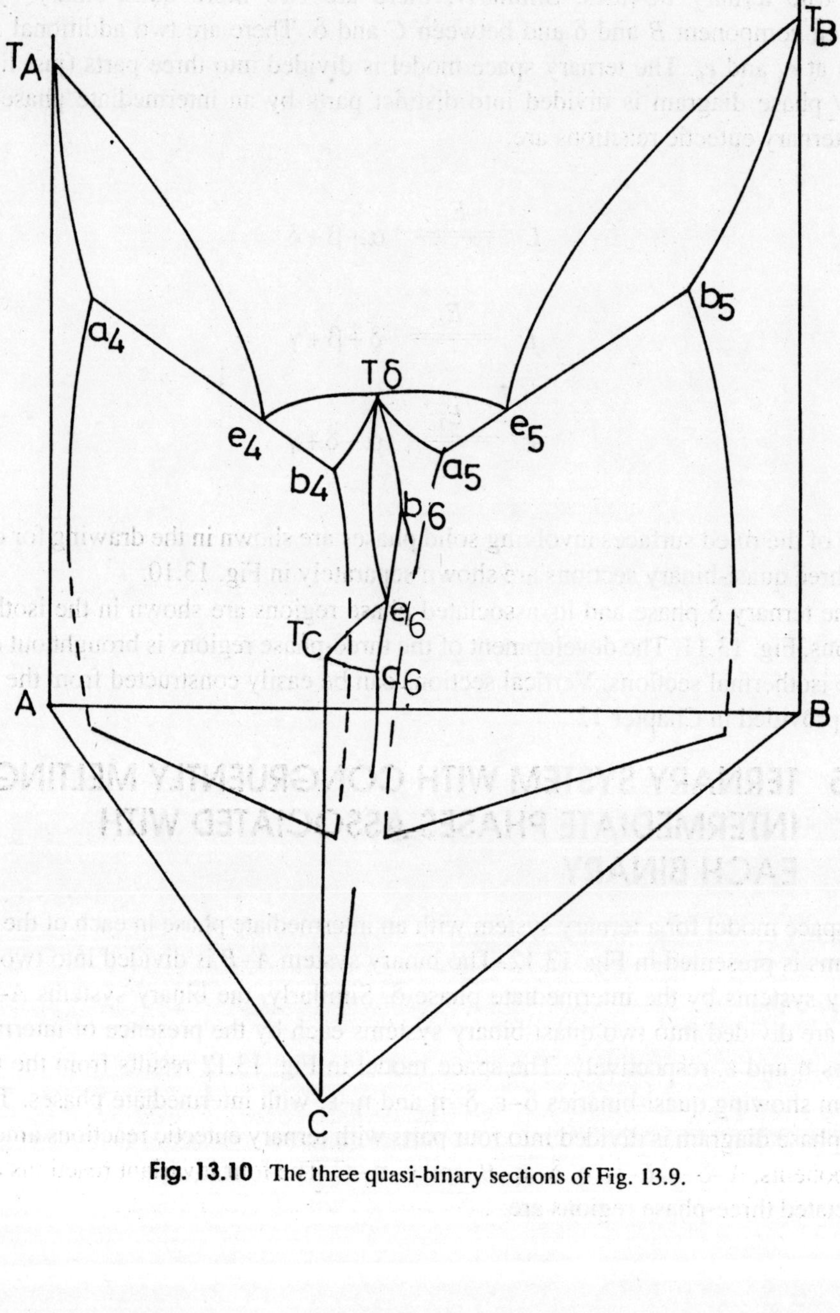

Fig. 13.10 The three quasi-binary sections of Fig. 13.9.

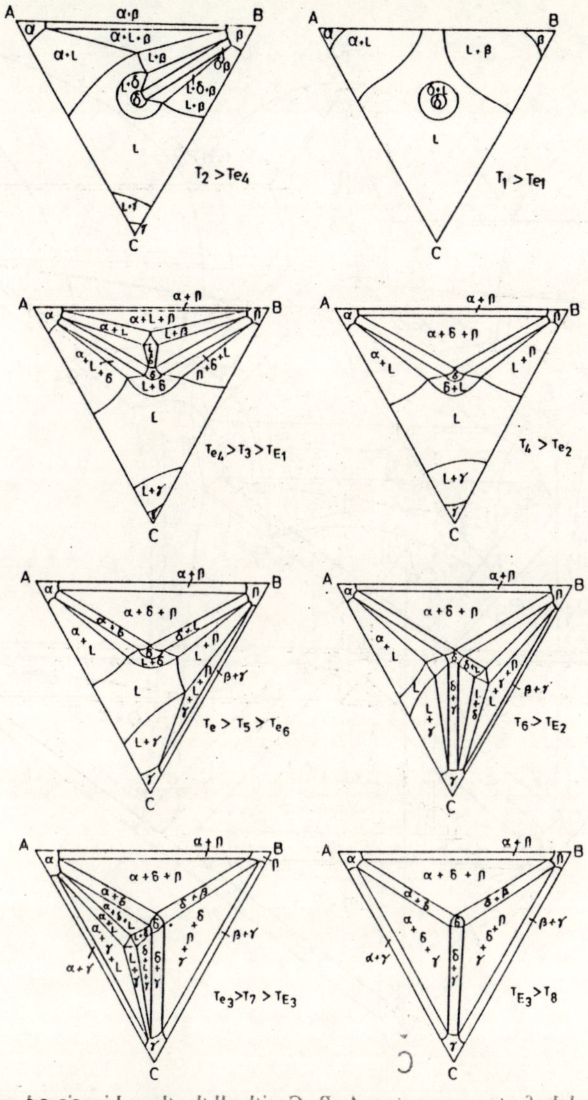

Fig. 13.11 Isothermal sections through the space model of Fig. 13.9.

$L = \alpha + \delta + \varepsilon,$ $L+\alpha+\delta,$ $L+\alpha+\varepsilon,$ $L+\delta+\varepsilon,$ $\alpha+\delta+\varepsilon$

$L=\delta+\beta+\eta,$ $L+\delta+\beta,$ $L+\delta+\eta,$ $L+\beta+\eta,$ $\delta+\beta+\eta$

$L=\delta+\varepsilon+\eta,$ $L+\delta+\varepsilon,$ $L+\delta+\eta,$ $L+\varepsilon+\eta,$ $\delta+\varepsilon+\eta$

$L=\varepsilon+\gamma+\eta,$ $L+\varepsilon+\gamma,$ $L+\varepsilon+\eta,$ $L+\gamma+\eta,$ $\varepsilon+\gamma+\eta$

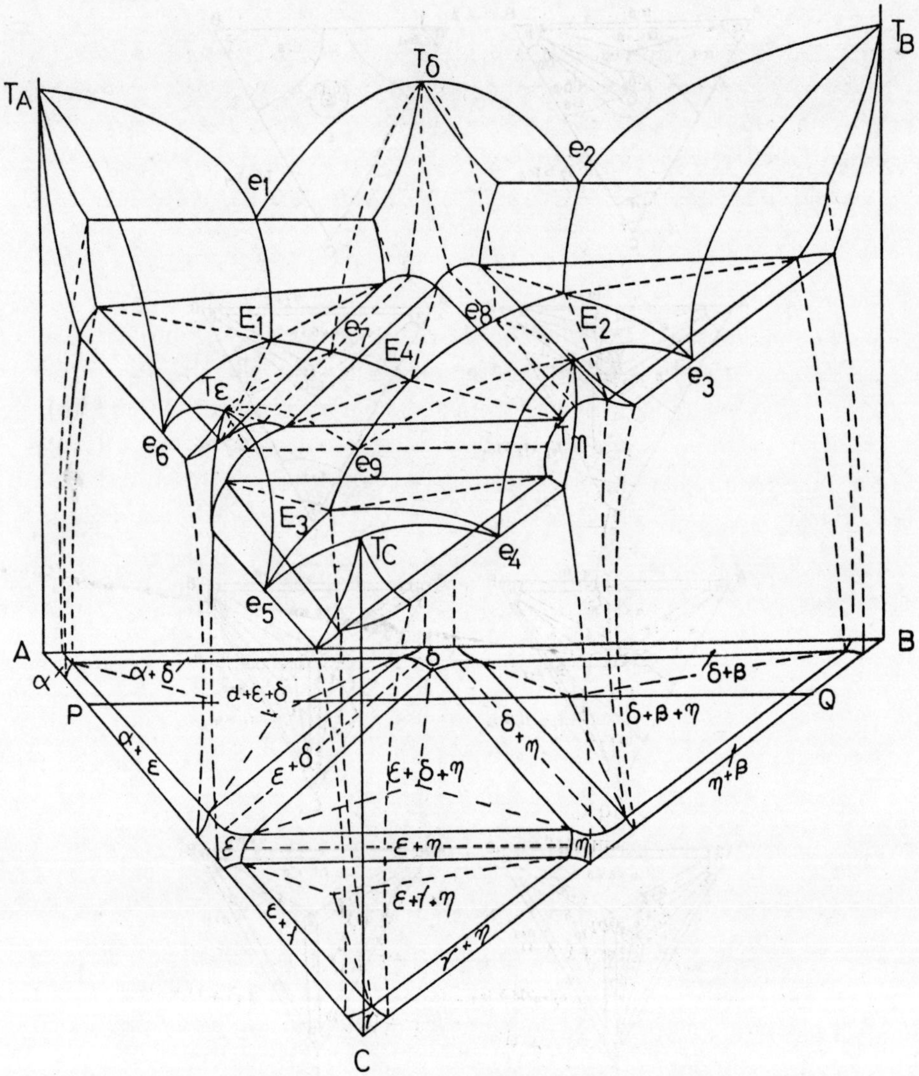

Fig. 13.12 Space model of a ternary system *A–B–C* with all the three binaries showing one intermediate phase. There are a number of such quasi-binary systems.

The common three-phase fields will cut across the quasi-binary sections (outlined above). For example, the L+δ+ε phase field cuts across the quasi-binary section δ–ε. The phase diagram has three saddle points, e_7, e_8 and e_9. The liquidus of the quasi-binary section is formed at a temperature between the melting temperatures of the intermediate phases. The saddle point e_7 is the maximum point on the curve $E_1e_7E_4$

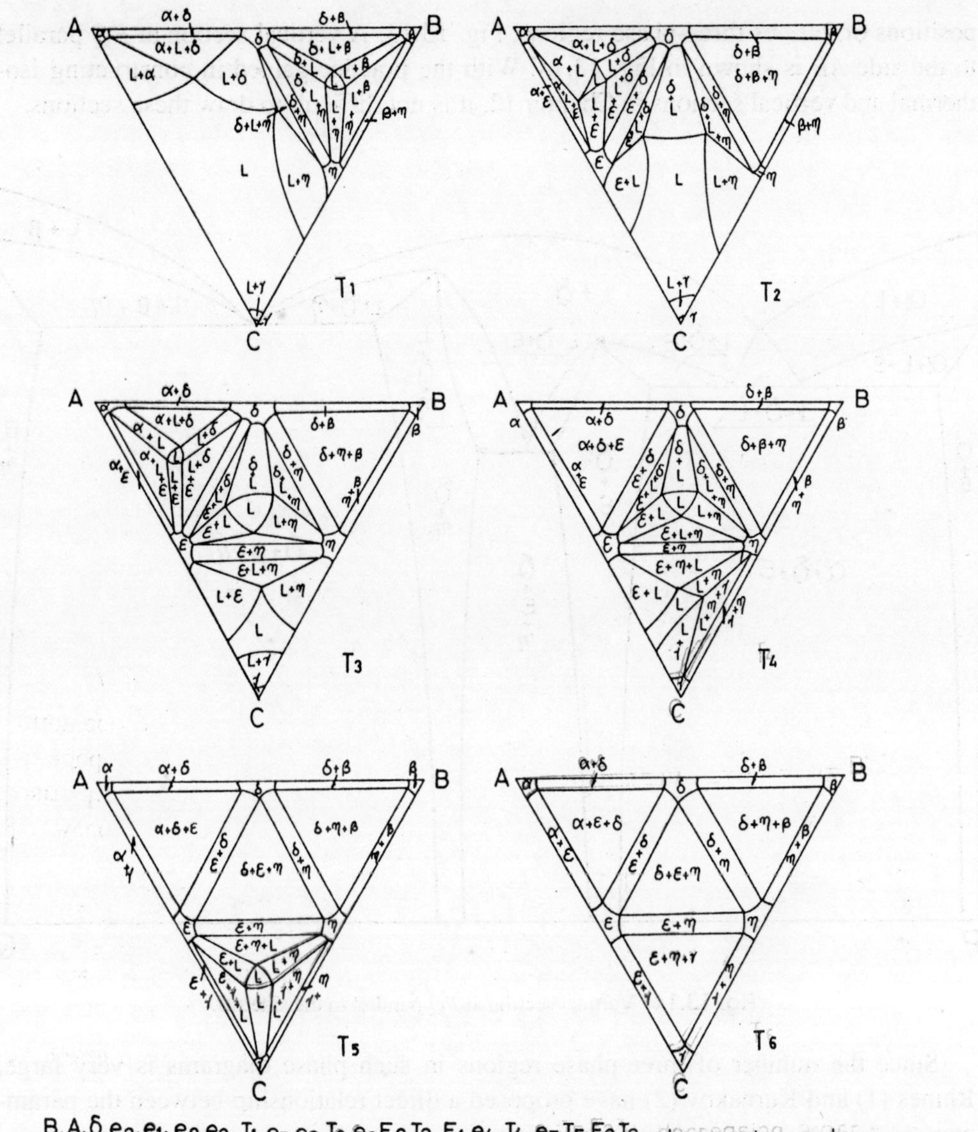

Fig. 13.13 Isothermal sections through the space model of Fig. 13.12.

and the minimum point on the liquidus $T_\delta e_7 T_\varepsilon$. Similar positions are occupied by saddle points e_8 and e_9 in the space model.

Isothermal sections at temperatures T_1 to T_6, defined in each sketch, show the positions of various three-phase regions, Fig. 13.13. A vertical section at *PQ* parallel to the side *AB* is shown in Fig. 13.14. With the practice gained in constructing isothermal and vertical sections in Chapter 12, it is not difficult to draw these sections.

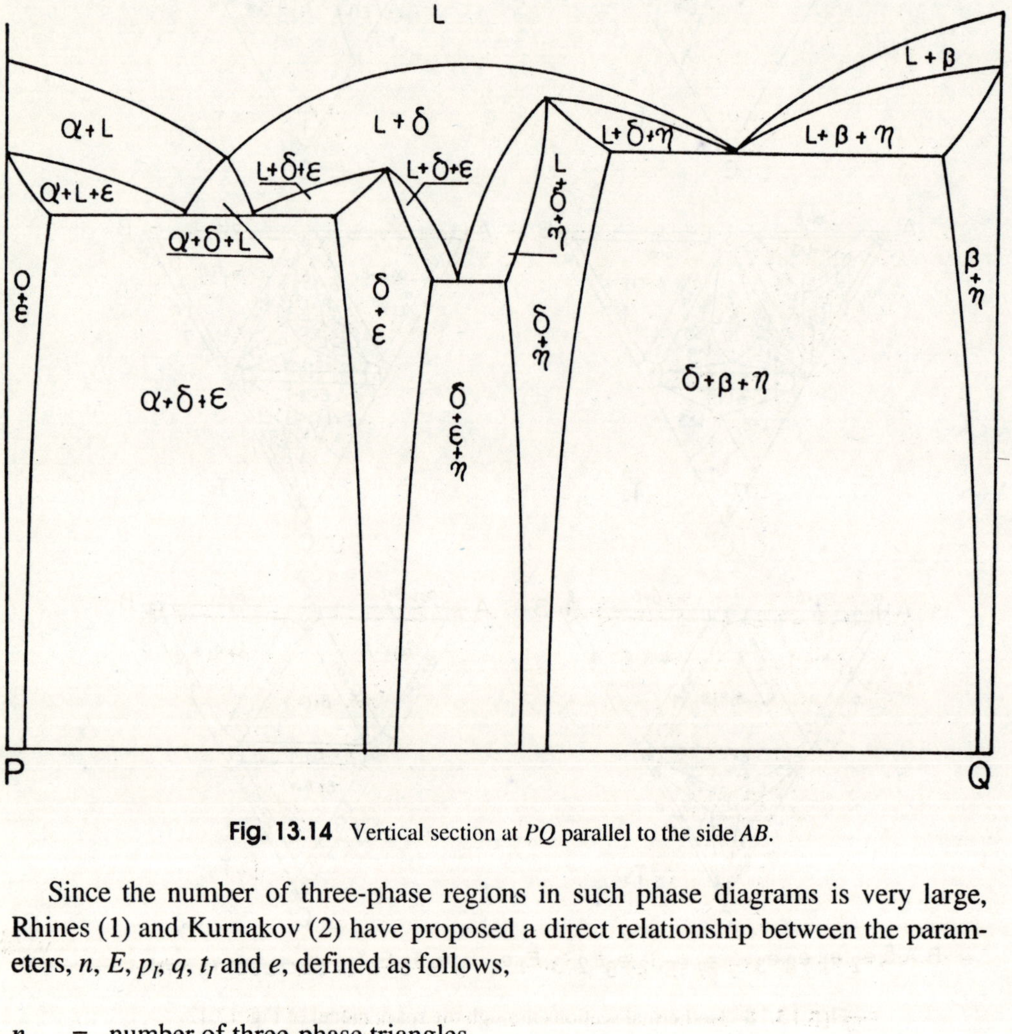

Fig. 13.14 Vertical section at *PQ* parallel to the side *AB*.

Since the number of three-phase regions in such phase diagrams is very large, Rhines (1) and Kurnakov (2) have proposed a direct relationship between the parameters, n, E, p_I, q, t_I and e, defined as follows,

n = number of three-phase triangles
E = ternary eutectic points
p_I = binary congruently melting intermediate phases

q = number of quasi-binary sections
e = number of saddle points
t_l = number of ternary intermediate phases

Accordingly, a single quasi-binary section divides the ternary diagram into two parts, Fig. 13.15a. If quasi-binary sections exist on two binaries, the phase diagram is divided into three parts, Fig. 13.15b. Thus, the number of divisions of the ternary diagram equals the number of binary intermediate phases plus one. This is expressed as

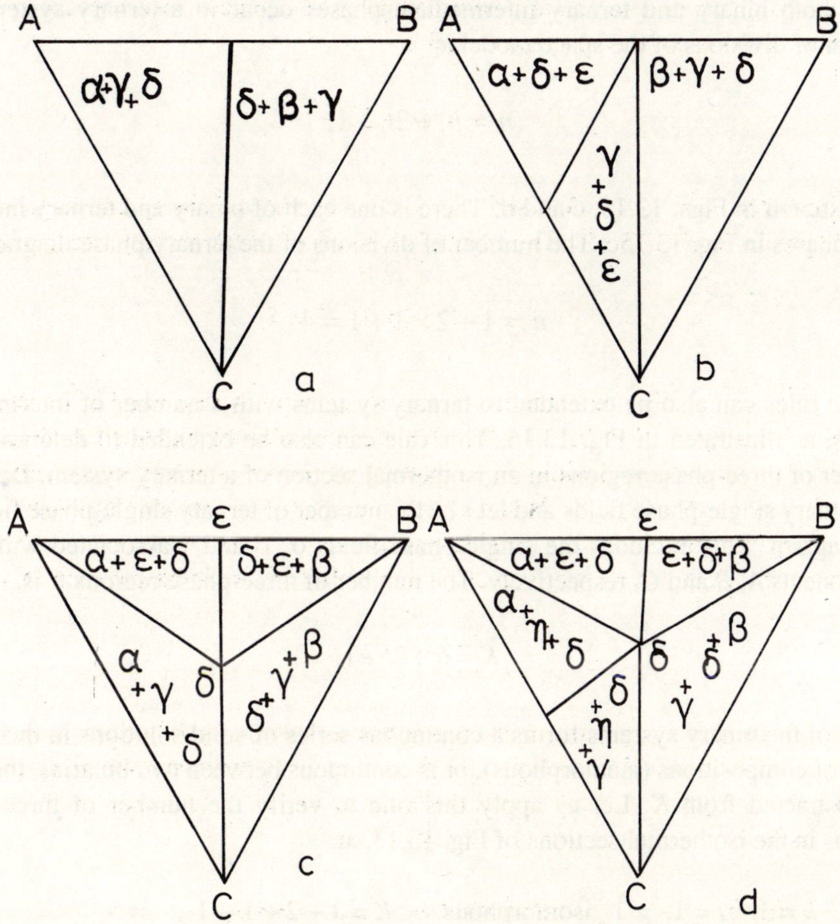

Fig. 13.15 Division of a ternary phase diagram and illustration of the rules governing the number of divisions and the number of tie-triangles.

$$n = b_I + 1.$$

In the space model of Fig. 13.9, it was observed that a single ternary intermediate phase divided the phase diagram into three parts. This can expressed as

$$n = 2\,t_I + 1.$$

When both binary and ternary intermediate phases occur in a ternary system, the number of divisions of the space model is

$$n = b_I + 2t_I + 1,$$

as illustrated in Figs. 13.15, c and d. There is one each of binary and ternary intermediate phases in Fig. 13.15c. The number of divisions of the ternary phase diagram is

$$n = 1 + 2 \times 1 + 1 = 4.$$

The rules can also be extended to ternary systems with a number of intermediate phases, as illustrated in Fig. 13.16. This rule can also be extended to determine the number of three-phase regions in an isothermal section of a ternary system. Let there be b binary single-phase fields and let t be the number of ternary single-phase fields in the diagram. This excludes the single-phase fields α, β and γ associated with pure components A, B and C, respectively. The number of three-phase regions K is,

$$K = b + 2t + 1.$$

If one of the binary systems forms a continuous series of solid solutions in the whole range of compositions (isomorphous), or is continuous between two binaries, then one is substracted from K. Let us apply this rule to verify the number of three-phase regions in the isothermal sections of Fig. 13.13, at,

T_1,	$b = 3$,	$t = 1$,	1 isomorphous,	$K = 3 + 2 + 1 - 1$	$= 5$
T_2,	$b = 4$,	$t = 1$		$K = 4 + 2 + 1$	$= 7$
T_3,	$b = 4$,	$t = 2$,	1 isomorphous,	$K = 4 + 2 \times 2 + 1 - 1$	$= 8$
T_4,	$b = 4$,	$t = 1$,		$K = 4 + 2 \times 1 + 1$	$= 7$

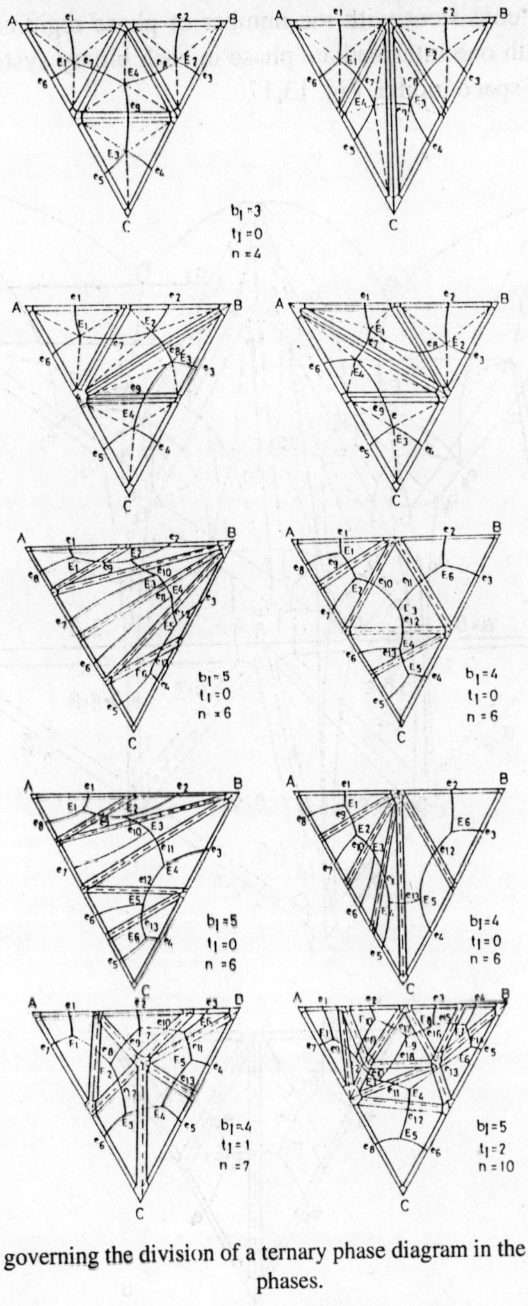

Fig. 13.16 Rules governing the division of a ternary phase diagram in the presence of intermediate phases.

T_5,	$b = 3$,	$t = 1$,	$K = 3 + 2 + 1$	$= 6$
T_6,	$b = 3$,	$t = 0$,	$K = 3 + 1$	$= 4$

These results are consistent with the number of phase regions actually observed. A phase diagram with one intermediate phase in each binary system can be constructed using an alternate space model, Fig. 13.17.

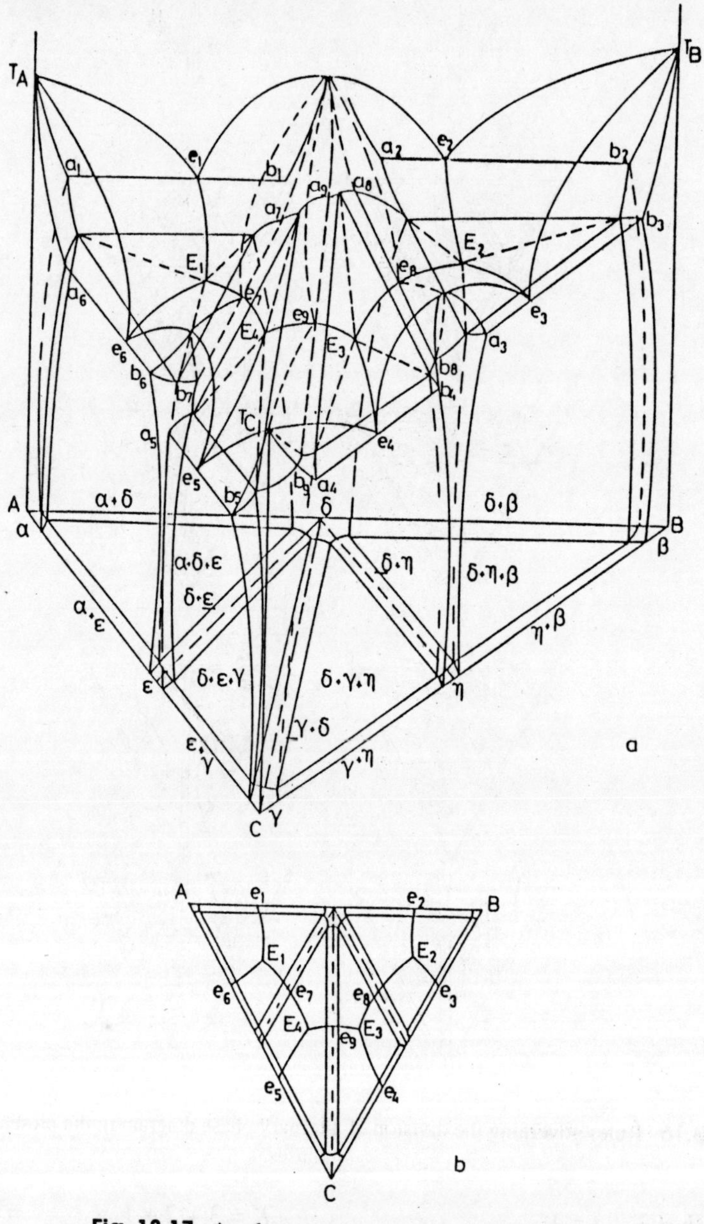

Fig. 13.17 An alternate space model of Fig. 13.12.

REFERENCES

1. F.N. Rhines, *Phase Diagrams in Metallurgy*, McGraw Hill Book Co., New York (1956), 199.
2. N.S. Kurnakov, *Collected Works, Vol. 1*, Acad. Sci., S.S.S.R., Moscow (1961).

PROBLEMS

1. What reaction do you associate with the line a_3b_3 in Fig. 13.1. Describe the cooling of an alloy composition e_3.
2. Given a liquid and four solid phases, α, β, γ and δ, write all possible Class I, Class II and Class III reactions.
3. (a) Draw a ternary phase diagram with intermediate phase δ on the binary *A–B*, which also shows, one each, eutectic and peritectic reactions. The other two binary systems *A–C* and *B–C* show a eutectic and peritectic reactions, respectively. The ternary system shows the following invariant reactions:

   $L \Leftrightarrow \alpha + \gamma + \delta$ and $L + \beta + \gamma \Leftrightarrow \delta$

   (b) Draw the projection of various surfaces on the concentration triangle.
   (c) Draw isothermal sections sufficient in number to illustrate interior details.
   (d) Draw a number of vertical sections on lines parallel to the side *A–B*.
   (e) Write all three-phase regions and indicate which are lying below and which are above the respective invariant planes. Indicate by arrows.
4. A ternary system *A–B–C* shows the following invariant reactions, $\alpha + L \Leftrightarrow \gamma + \delta$ and $L + \beta + \gamma \Leftrightarrow \delta$. The associated binary reactions are:

   $A - B$: $L \Leftrightarrow \alpha + \delta$ and $L \Leftrightarrow \delta + \beta$
   $A - C$: $L \Leftrightarrow \alpha + \gamma$
   $B - C$: $L + \beta \Leftrightarrow \gamma$

   (a) Draw the phase diagram.
   (b) Draw all the three-phase fields separately and their respective positions with respect to the invariant plane.
   (c) Draw a number of isothermal sections.

Chapter 14

TERNARY FOUR-PHASE EQUILIBRIUM-LIQUID IMMISCIBILITY

It was shown in Chapter 11 how liquid immiscibility in a binary system could lead to a three-phase region involving one solid and two liquids. Four-phase equilibrium can also arise in ternary systems when one or more of the binaries show monotectic and/or syntectic reactions. The invariant reaction can occur with the following combination of binary systems:

(i) Two binary systems show monotectic reactions and the third shows a eutectic reaction.

(ii) One binary system shows a monotectic reaction and the other two show eutectic reactions.

(iii) One binary system shows a monotectic reaction, the second reaction eutectic reaction and the third binary is an isomorphous.

(iv) Two binary systems show syntectic reactions.

14.1 LIQUID IMMISCIBILITY IN THE TERNARY PHASE DIAGRAM WITH TWO BINARY SYSTEMS SHOWING MONOTECTIC REACTIONS AND THE THIRD SHOWING A EUTECTIC

Since the binary monotectic or syntectic reactions involve two liquid phases, the ternary invariant reactions will involve the same two liquids. We can consider the following monotectic and eutectic reactions,

binary $A - B$, $L_1 = \alpha + L_2$; also $L_2 = \alpha + \beta$ at lower temperature
binary $B - C$, $L_1 = \gamma + L_2$; also $L_2 = \beta + \gamma$ at lower temperature
binary $A - C$, $L_1 = \alpha + \gamma$

These binary systems are sketched in Fig. 14.1 laid out on sides AB, BC and AC. The space model of the ternary system is shown in Fig. 14.2a and its projection on the concentration triangle ABC in Fig. 14.2b. The ternary system shows an invariant, Class I reaction,

$$L_1 = \alpha + \gamma + L_2$$

and can be termed as quasi-monotectic. The space model has additional complexity due to a ternary eutectic reaction $L_2 = \alpha + \beta + \gamma$ at lower temperatures. The reactions in the phase diagram can be presented in a tabular form, Table 14.1.

Table 14.1

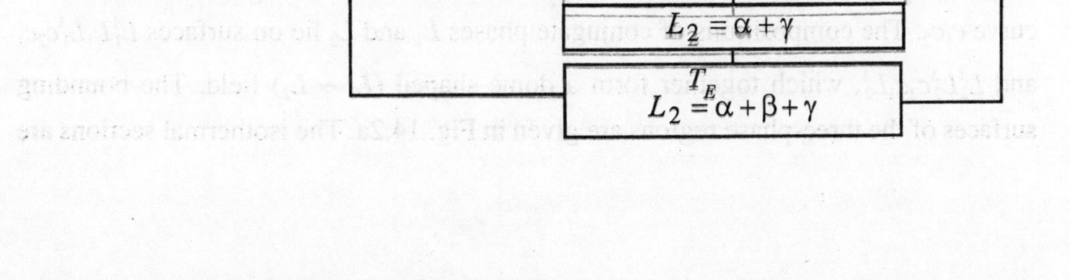

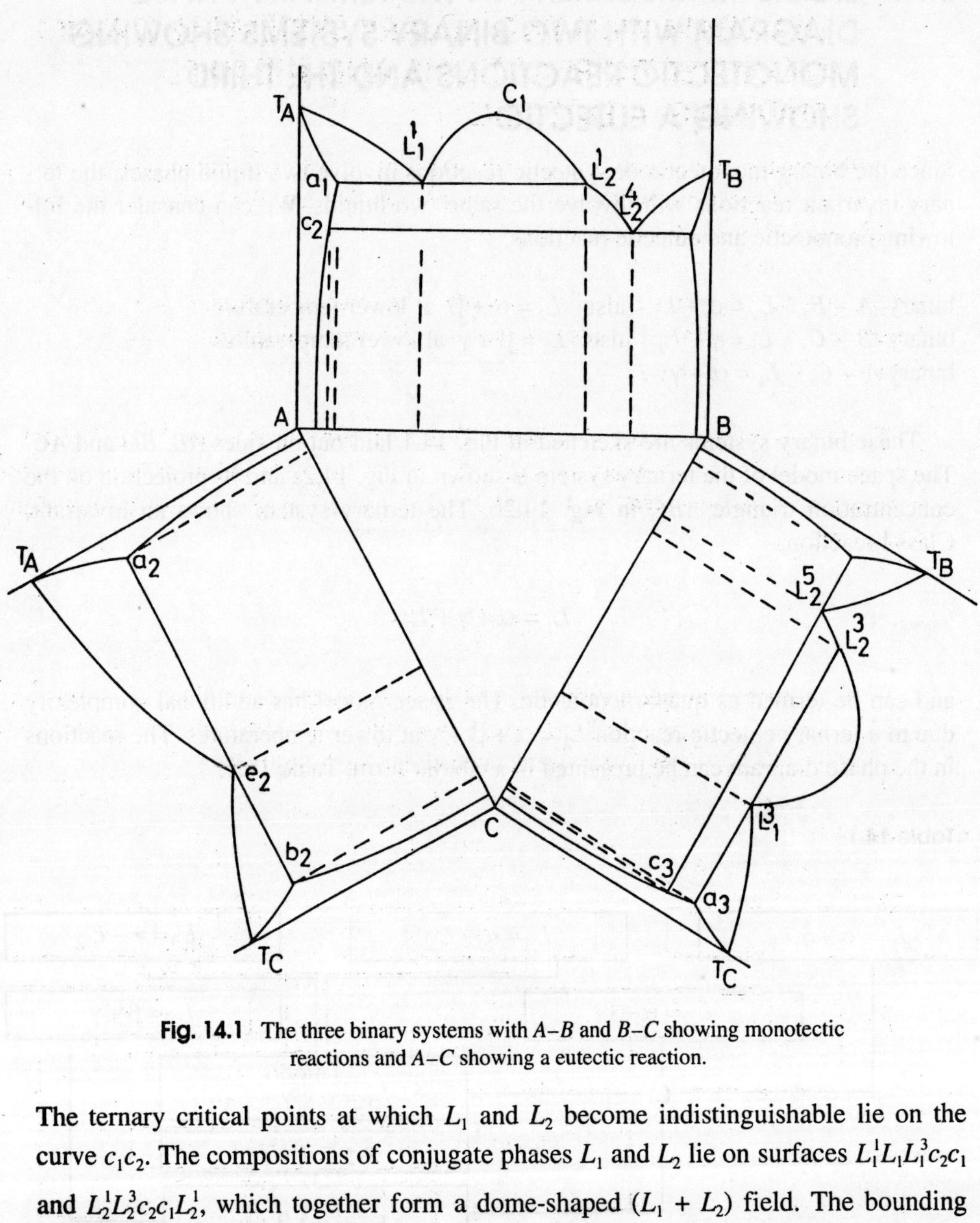

Fig. 14.1 The three binary systems with $A-B$ and $B-C$ showing monotectic reactions and $A-C$ showing a eutectic reaction.

The ternary critical points at which L_1 and L_2 become indistinguishable lie on the curve c_1c_2. The compositions of conjugate phases L_1 and L_2 lie on surfaces $L_1^1L_1L_1^3c_2c_1$ and $L_2^1L_2^3c_2c_1L_2^1$, which together form a dome-shaped ($L_1 + L_2$) field. The bounding surfaces of the three-phase regions are given in Fig. 14.2a. The isothermal sections are

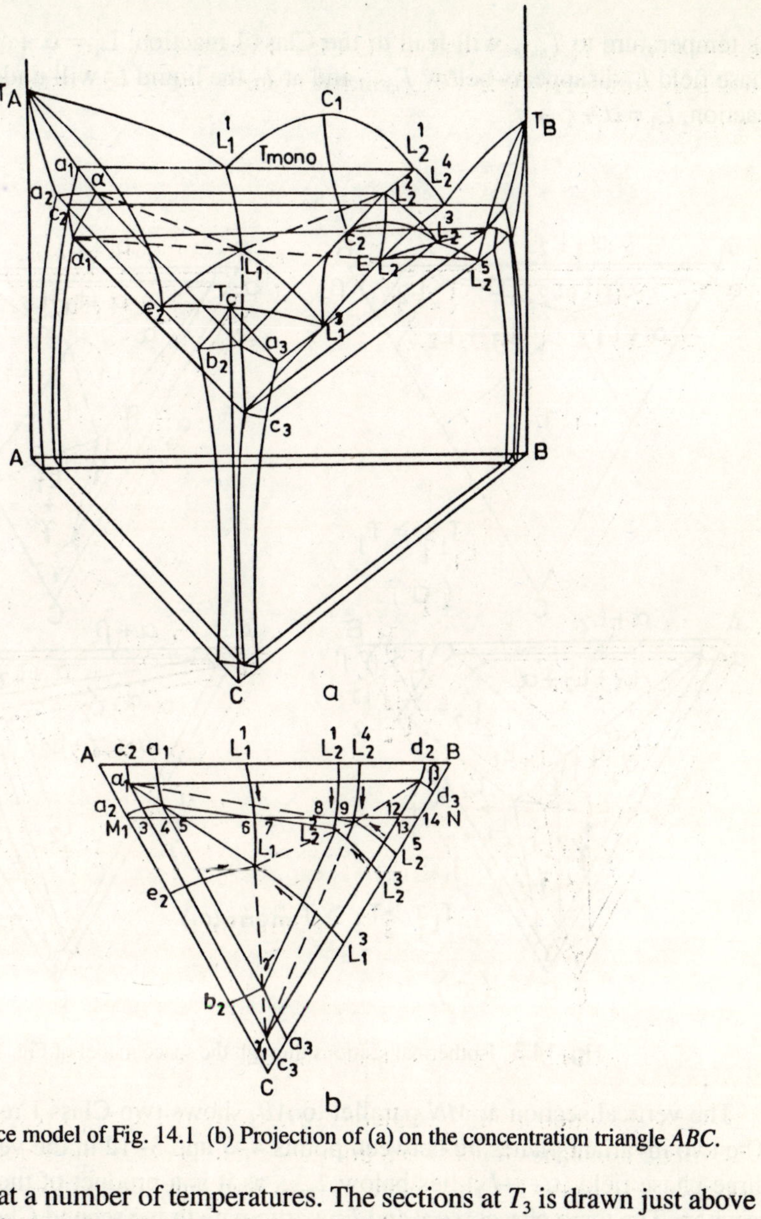

Fig. 14.2 (a) Space model of Fig. 14.1 (b) Projection of (a) on the concentration triangle *ABC*.

shown in Fig. 14.3 at a number of temperatures. The sections at T_3 is drawn just above the quasi-monotectic reaction isotherm, T_{mono}. It shows liquid L_1 in the middle and surrounded by three two-phase and three three-phase regions, Fig. 14.3c. Lowering the temperature to T_{mono} will lead to the Class I reaction, $L_1 = \alpha + \gamma + L_2$. The liquid phase field L_1 disappears below T_{mono} and at T_E the liquid L_2 will undergo the invariant reaction, $L_2 = \alpha + \beta + \gamma$.

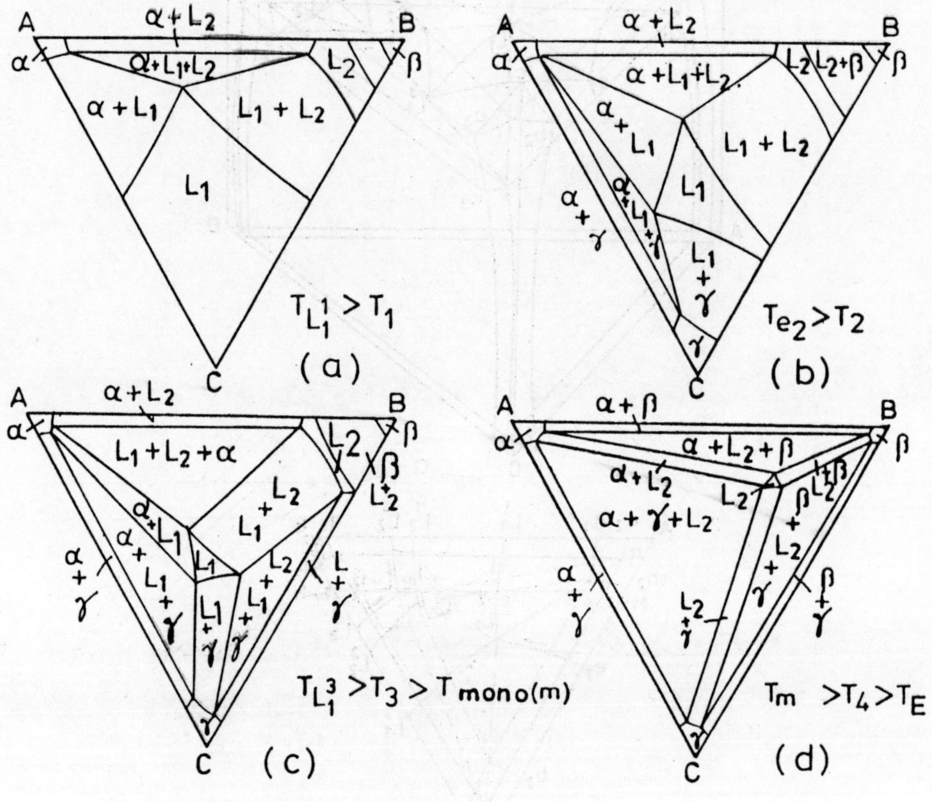

Fig. 14.3 Isothermal sections through the space model of Fig. 14.2.

The vertical section at *MN* parallel to *AB*, shows two Class I reactions, Fig. 14.4. The two invariant planes lie between points 4–7 and 3–12 in the vertical section. The three-phase field ($\alpha+\gamma+L_2$) lies below T_{mono} as it is a product of the quasi-monotectic reaction. The three phases, α, γ and L_2, participate in the second Class I reaction at T_E. The ($\alpha + \gamma + L_2$) phase field is continuous between T_{mono} and T_E as shown. The dome is confined between points 6–9–7, with the critical point lying between points 6 and 9.

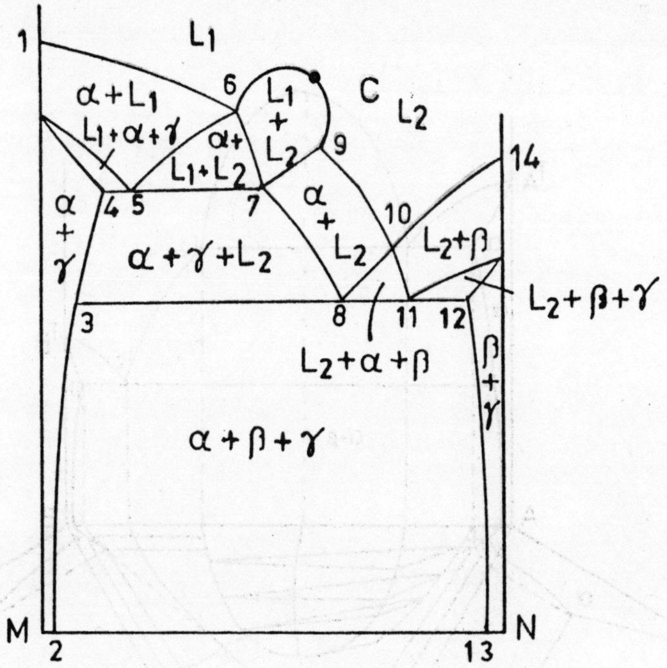

Fig. 14.4 The vertical section at *MN* parallel to *AB*.

The solidification of all alloy compositions can be followed from details provided in section 12.14 for various alloy compositions. The β phase in the ternary eutectic Class I reaction can be replaced by a second liquid L_2 to give the quasi-monotectic reaction. Further, if both L_1 and L_2 appear simultaneously during solidification, the course of solidification will become non-equilibrium due to gravity segregation, especially, when the two liquids have a substantial difference in densities due to a large difference in densities of the components *A*, *B* and *C*.

14.2 LIQUID IMMISCIBILITY IN THE TERNARY PHASE DIAGRAM WITH ONE BINARY SYSTEM SHOWING A MONOTECTIC REACTION AT HIGHER TEMPERATURES AND A EUTECTIC AT LOWER TEMPERATURES. THE OTHER TWO BINARIES SHOW EUTECTIC REACTIONS

The phase diagram for the above system is shown in the spread out format in Fig. 14.5 and the space model in Fig. 14.6. Component *A* and *B* which interact with *C* extend

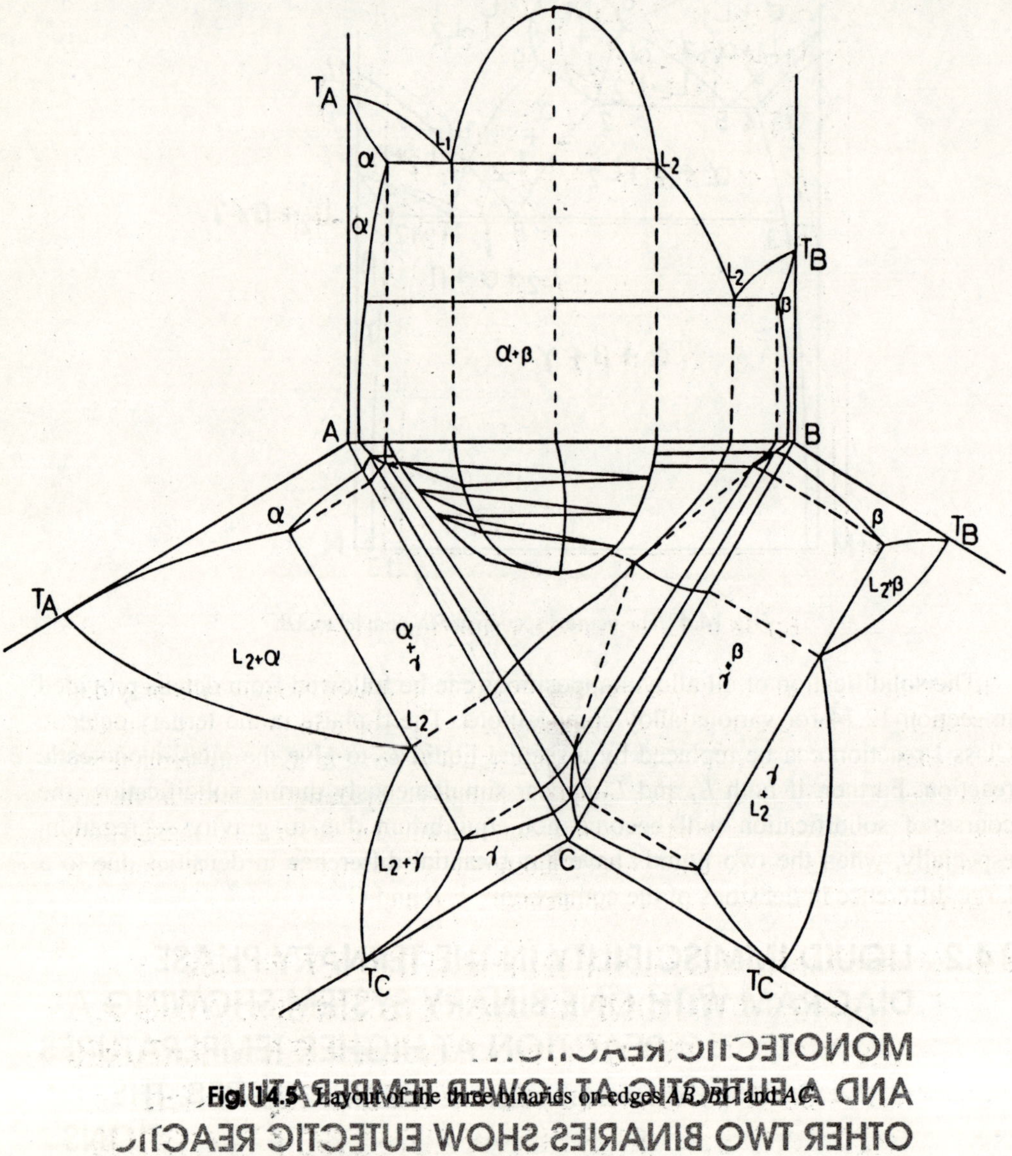

Fig. 14.5 Layout of the three binaries on edges *AB*, *BC* and *AC*.

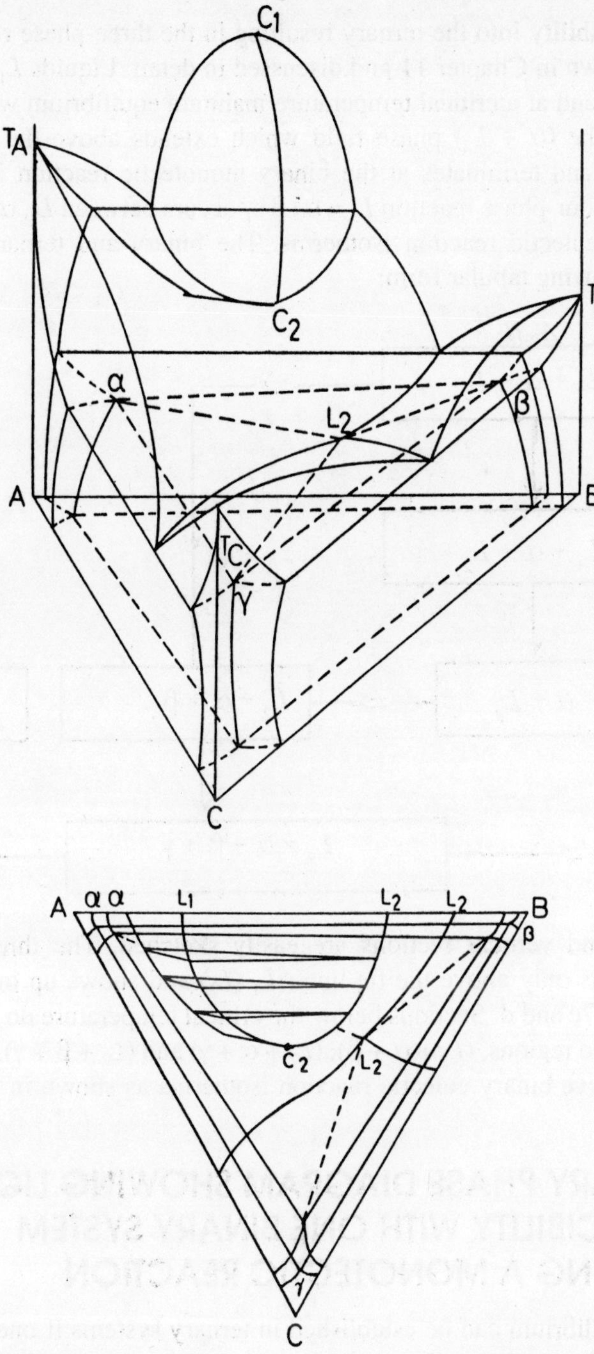

Fig. 14.6 Space model of Fig. 14.5 showing liquid immiscibility.

the liquid immiscibility into the ternary resulting in the three-phase region ($\alpha + L_1 + L_2$). This was shown in Chapter 11 and discussed in detail. Liquids L_1 and L_2 become indistinguishable and at a critical temperature maintain equilibrium with the α phase. This constitutes the ($\alpha + L_2$) phase field which extends above the binary eutectic reaction on *A–B* and terminates at the binary monotectic reaction isotherm on the binary *A–B*. The four-phase reaction $L_2 = \alpha+\beta+\gamma$ occurs between L_2, α, β and γ phases below the three eutectic reaction isotherms. The binary and ternary reactions are shown in the following tabular form:

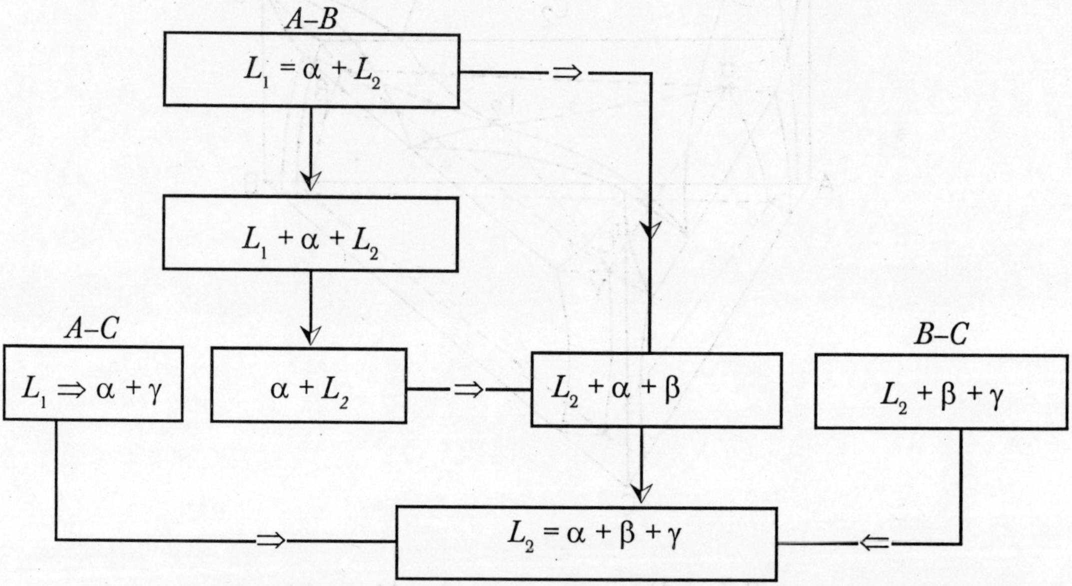

The isothermal and vertical sections are easily sketched. The three-phase region ($\alpha + L_1 + L_2$) exists only above the tie-line αL_1 (L_2) and shows up in the isothermal sections, Figs. 14.7c and d. Sections below the critical temperature do not show liquid L_1. The three-phase regions, ($L_2 + \alpha + \beta$), ($L_2 + \alpha + \gamma$) and ($L_2 + \beta + \gamma$), start appearing below the respective binary eutectic reaction isotherms as shown in Figs. 14.7, g, h and i.

14.3 TERNARY PHASE DIAGRAM SHOWING LIQUID IMMISCIBILITY WITH ONE BINARY SYSTEM SHOWING A MONOTECTIC REACTION

A four-phase equilibrium can be established in ternary systems if one of the binaries shows a monotectic reaction and the other two show eutectic or peritectic reaction.

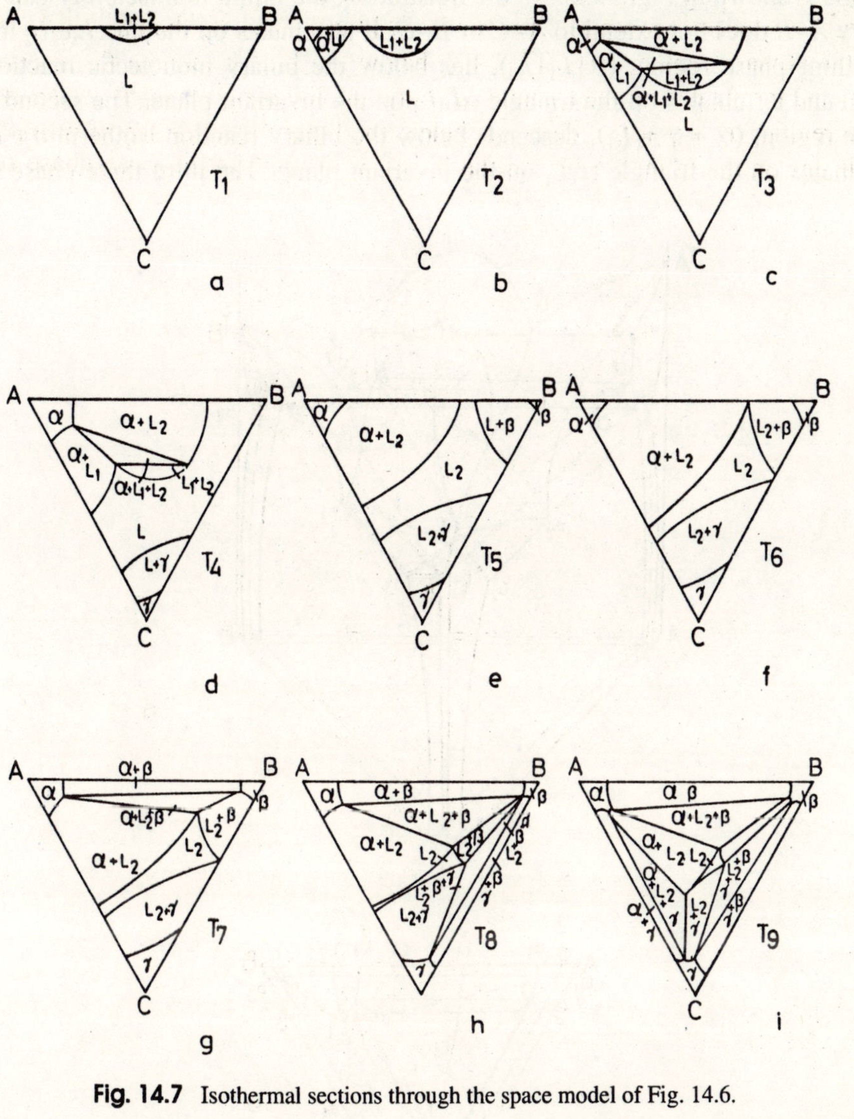

Fig. 14.7 Isothermal sections through the space model of Fig. 14.6.

The ternary four-phase reaction $L_1 = \alpha + \gamma + L_2$ is illustrated in Fig. 14.8a for a system with the binary *A–B* showing a monotectic reaction and binaries *A–C* and *B–C* showing eutectic reactions. However, out of the two binary eutectic reactions, only one participates in the invariant reaction. The projection on the concentration triangle is shown in Fig. 14.8b. In the illustration, the liquid immiscibility gap on the binary A–B does not extend to A–C or B–C. It terminates on the line $L_1c_2L_2$ instead. The three-phase region, $(\alpha+L_1+L_2)$, lies below the binary monotectic reaction isotherm and terminates on the triangle αL_1L_2 on the invariant plane. The second three-phase region, $(\alpha + \gamma + L_1)$, descends below the binary reaction isotherm $a_2e_2b_2$ and terminates on the triangle $\alpha\gamma L_1$ on the invariant plane. The third three-phase region

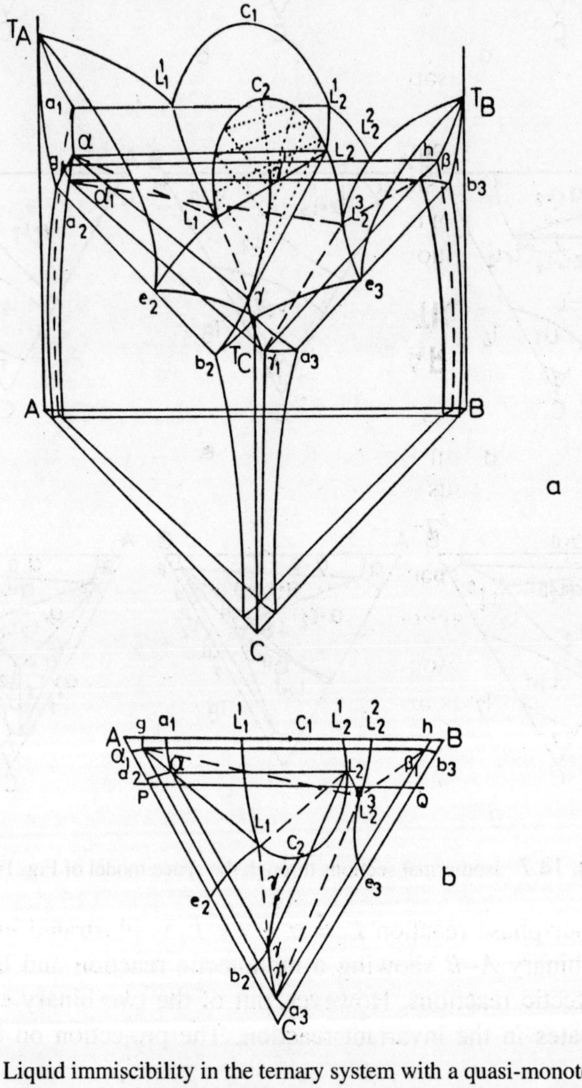

Fig. 14.8 (a) Liquid immiscibility in the ternary system with a quasi-monotectic reaction $L_1 = \alpha + \gamma + L_2$. (b) Projection of (a) on the concentration triangle ABC.

which completes the trio of the three-phase regions rises above L_1L_2 as a liquidus surface and terminates at a critical temperature at c_2. The indistinguishable liquid L_1 (L_2) of composition c_2 is in equilibrium with the γ phase of composition γ' as shown in Fig. 14.8a. The other two ruled surfaces, γL_1 and γL_2, complete the set of three ruled surfaces of the (γ+L_1+L_2) region. The tie-line $\gamma' c_2$ is a degenerate tie-triangle of the three-phase region (L_1+L_2+γ), which terminates on the triangle $\gamma L_1 L_2$ on the four-phase

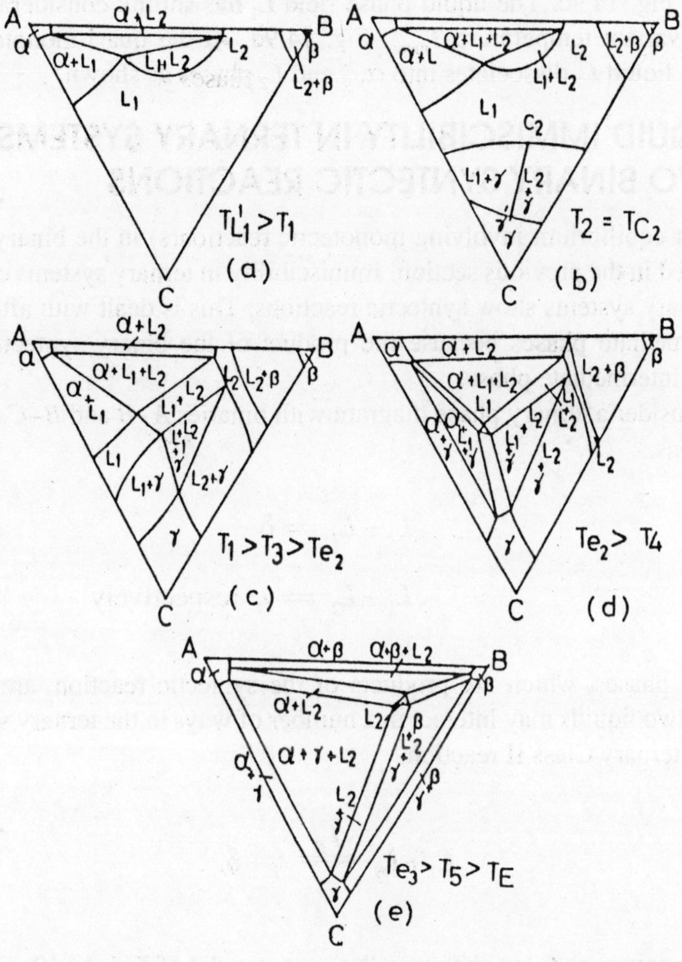

Fig. 14.9 Isothermal sections through the space model of Fig. 14.8.

plane. It exists up to a maximum temperature T_{c_2}. A number of tie-triangles are drawn in the space model to indicate the shape of this phase region. The phase diagram also shows a ternary eutectic reaction, $L_2 \rightleftharpoons \alpha + \beta + \gamma$, at a lower temperature.

Isothermal sections at a number of temperatures are shown in Fig. 14.9. The section drawn at the upper critical temperature, $T_2 = T_{c_2}$ shows the degenerate tie-triangle $c_2\gamma'$, Fig. 14.9b. The rest of the phase fields are similar to that sketched at T_1 just below the binary monotectic reaction isotherm T'_{L_1}. Below the critical temperature at T_3, the isothermal section shows the three-phase region $(L_1+L_2+\gamma)$ in addition to the other phase fields, Fig. 14.9c. The liquid phase field L_1 has shrunk considerably at T_4 just above the invariant temperature T_{mono}, Fig. 14.9d. At the quasi-monotectic reaction isotherm, the liquid L_1 dissociates into α, γ and L_2 phases as shown.

14.4 LIQUID IMMISCIBILITY IN TERNARY SYSTEMS WITH TWO BINARY SYNTECTIC REACTIONS

The invariant equilibrium involving monotectic reaction(s) in the binary systems has been discussed in the previous section. Immiscibility in ternary systems can also occur when the binary systems show syntectic reactions. This is dealt with after the section on the intermediate phases because the product of the binary syntectic reaction is generally an intermediate phase.

Let us consider a ternary phase diagram with binaries A–B and B–C showing syntectic reactions,

$$L_1 + L_2 \rightleftharpoons \delta$$

and

$$L_1 + L_2 \rightleftharpoons \gamma, \text{ respectively.}$$

The γ and δ phases, which are products of the syntectic reaction, are intermediate phases. The two liquids may interact in a number of ways in the ternary system. Let us consider the ternary Class II reaction,

$$L_1 + L_2 \xrightleftharpoons{T_p} \gamma + \delta.$$

The reaction occurs at T_p, as shown in the space model of Fig. 14.10. The two-phase field, γ + δ, is continuous at lower temperatures. The phase diagram shows two ternary eutectic Class I reactions at lower temperatures. These are,

$$L_1 \rightleftharpoons \alpha + \delta + \gamma$$

$$L_2 \rightleftharpoons \beta + \gamma + \delta.$$

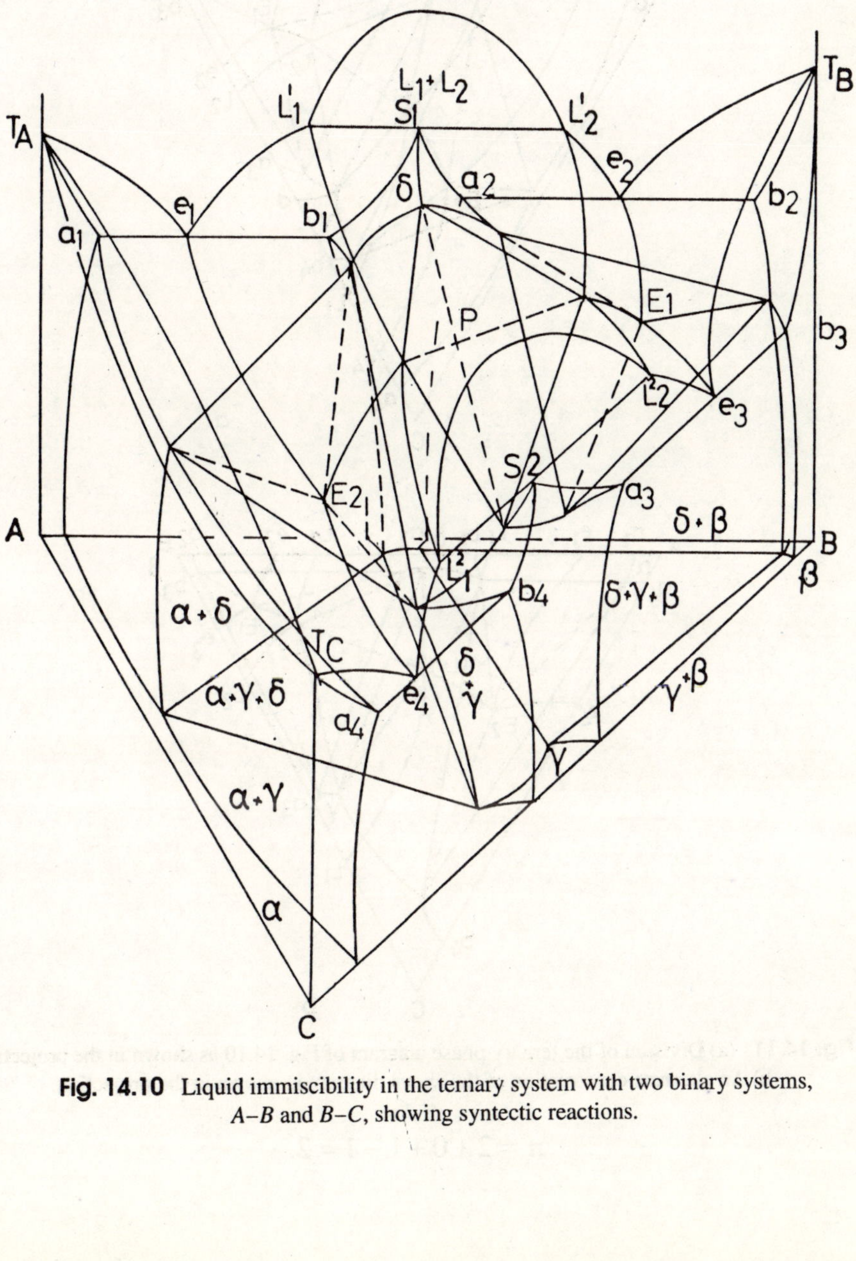

Fig. 14.10 Liquid immiscibility in the ternary system with two binary systems, *A–B* and *B–C*, showing syntectic reactions.

The alloy system has two binary intermediate phases and an isomorphous system. The ternary phase diagram is divided into two parts:

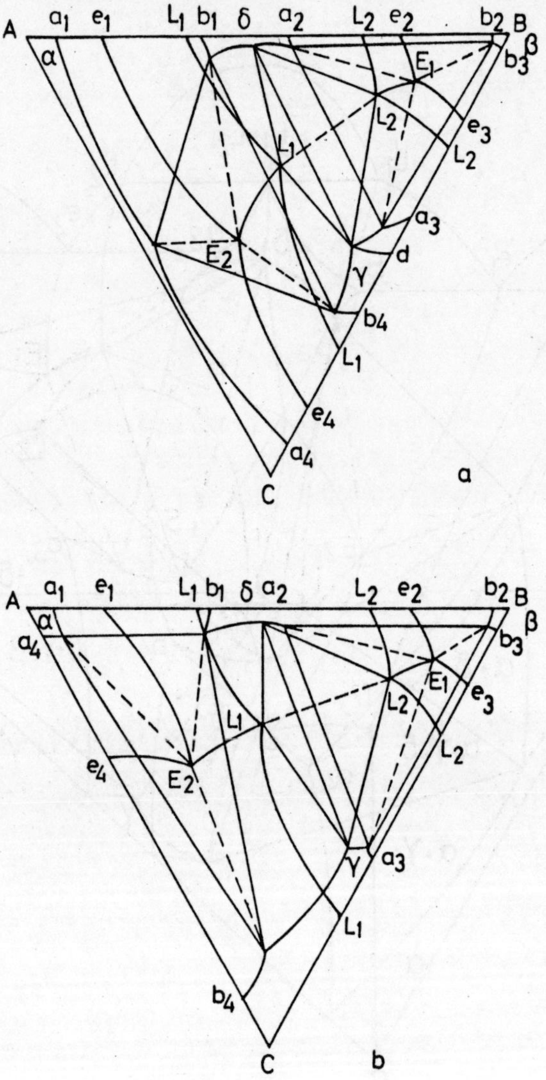

Fig. 14.11 (a) Division of the ternary phase diagram of Fig. 14.10 as shown in the projection. (b) An alternate construction of the above diagram as shown in the projection.

$$n = 2 + 0 + 1 - 1 = 2.$$

This is shown in the projection, Fig. 14.11a. If the γ phase, instead of being an intermediate phase, is contiguous to component *C*, an alternate diagram appears, as shown in the projection, Fig. 14.11b.

PROBLEMS

1. (a) Draw isothermal sections through the space diagram of Fig. 14.10. Label all phase fields.
   (b) Draw a number of vertical sections all parallel to the side *AB* of the space model of Fig. 14.10.
2. A ternary system *A–B–C* shows the reaction $L_1 + \alpha \Leftrightarrow L_2 + \beta$ and is associated with a monotectic reaction on the binary *B–C*, a syntectic reaction on *A–B*, and a eutectic reaction on the binary *A–C*.
   (a) Draw the space diagram.
   (b) Draw $(L_1 + L_2 + \alpha)$ and $(L_1 + L_2 + \beta)$ phase regions separately.
   (c) Draw a number of isothermal sections from the highest critical temperature to a temperature just below the binary monotectic reaction isotherm.
   (d) Draw a vertical section on the line *BX* (*X* lies on the side *AC*).
   (e) Describe the cooling of an alloy composition passing through the point of intersection of αL_1 and βL_2 on the invariant plane. Calculate the relative amounts of the above phases in the alloy.

Chapter 15

SELECTED EXAMPLES OF TERNARY SYSTEMS

15.1 TERNARY ISOMORPHOUS SYSTEM (Ag-Au-Pd)

The Ag-Au-Pd ternary alloy system forms a series of liquid and solid solutions in the whole range of compositions. The ternary space model as constructed from the binary phase diagrams of Ag-Au, Ag-Pd and Au-Pd is shown in Fig. 15.1. The projection of the liquidus on the concentration triangle is shown in Fig. 15.2. The liquidus has been studied by Nemilov et al (1) by thermal analysis of 47 ternary alloys. Miane et al (2) used DTA technique to determine the liquidus and solidus temperatures for a number of ternary alloys positioned on sections Au-50Ag-50Pd, Ag-50Au-50Pd and Pd-50Ag-50Au. A vertical section from the Au-corner to the opposite side with 50% Pd and 50% Ag shows two phase fields, $L + \alpha$ (Au-Ag-Pd), Fig. 15.3. The ordered phases Au_3Pd and $AuPd_3$ are disregarded in the present consideration.

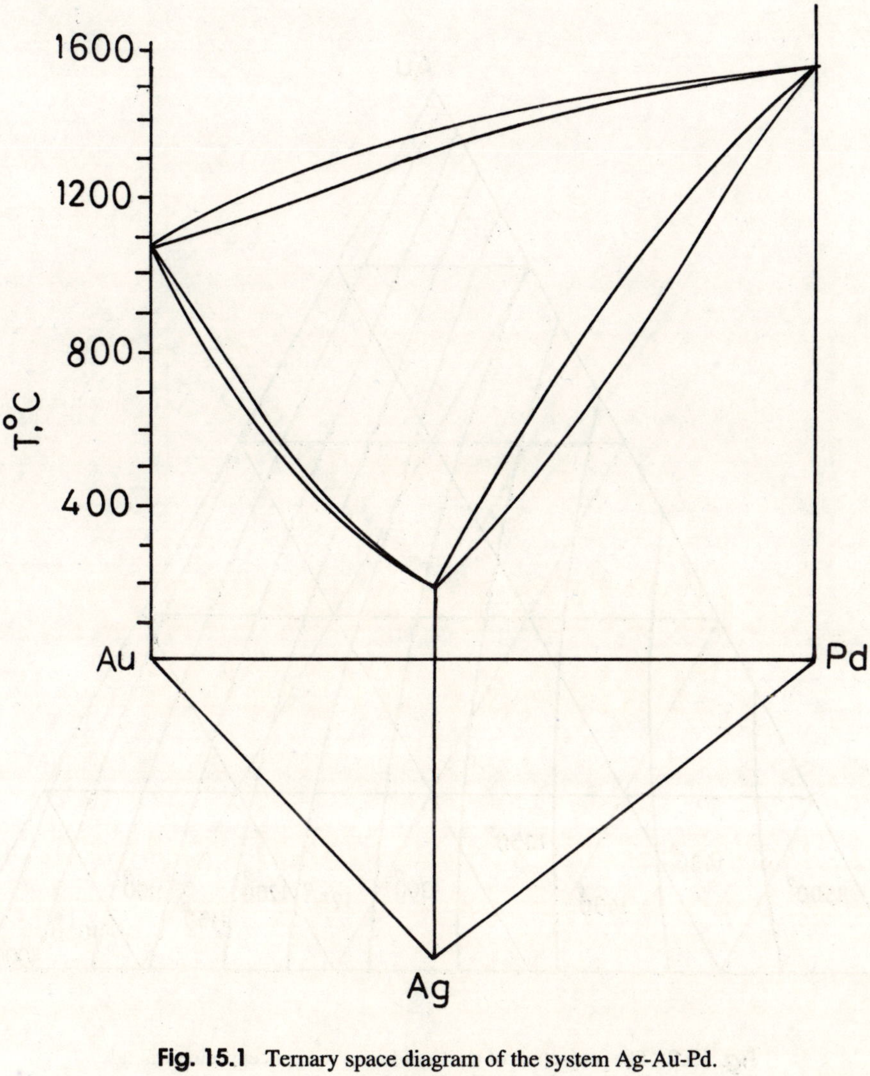

Fig. 15.1 Ternary space diagram of the system Ag-Au-Pd.

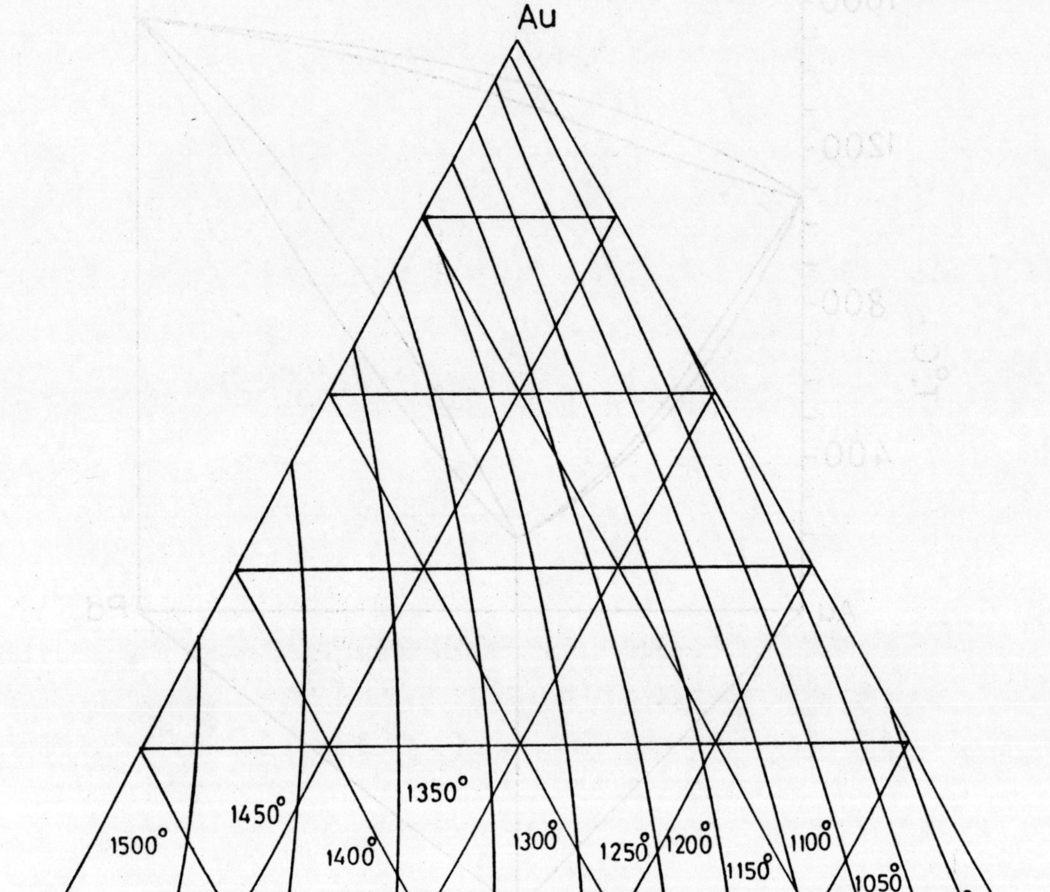

Fig. 15.2 The projection of the liquidus on the concentration triangle, Ag-Au-Pd system.

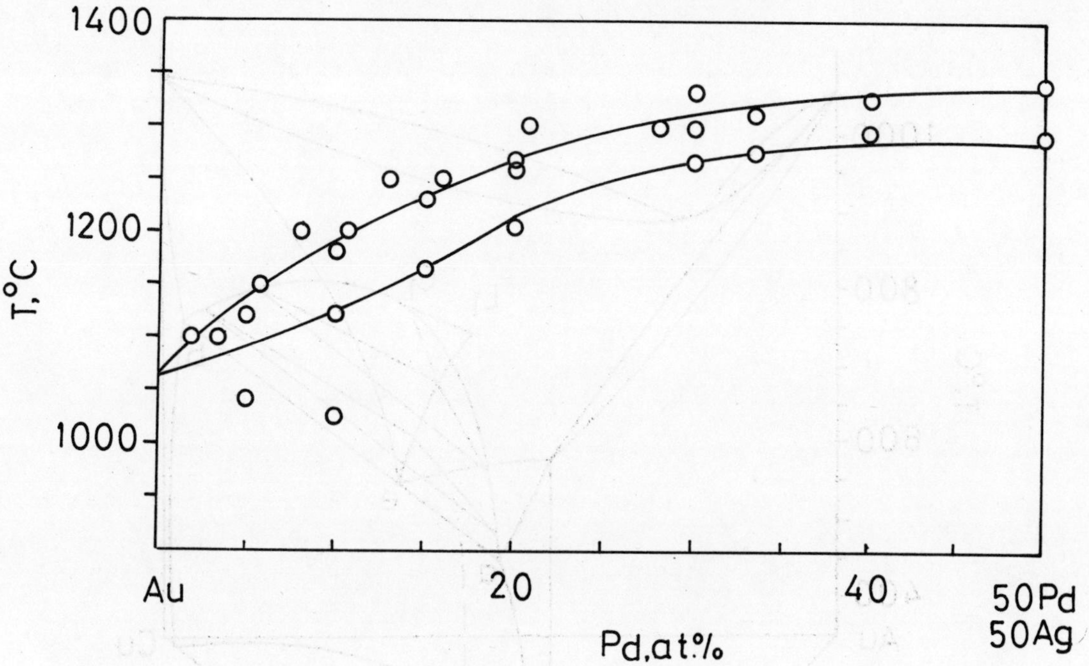

Fig. 15.3 A vertical section through the phase diagram of Fig. 15.1 drawn on a line from the Au corner to the side Ag-Pd.

15.2 TERNARY THREE-PHASE EQUILIBRIUM, $L = \alpha_1 + \alpha_2$ (Ag-Au-Cu)

In the ternary system Ag-Au-Cu, the Ag-Cu binary system shows a eutectic reaction at 779°C with the liquid composition at 39.9 at.pct. Cu. The metal silver has approximately 5 at.pct. solubility in Cu at the eutectic temperature. Copper, on the other hand, has a higher solubility (14.2 at. pct.) in Ag. The Ag-Au binary shows isomorphous behavior. The Au-Cu binary system is an isomorphous with a minimum at 80.1 at. pct. Au at 889°C. The space diagram of the ternary system is shown in Fig. 15.4.

The ternary phase diagram shows a monovariant reaction, $L = \alpha_1 + \alpha_2$. The monovariant liquid curve originates at the critical liquid composition, Cu-33.2Ag-23.4Au at 800°C and descends to a minimum at 767°C with a composition of approximately 14 at.pct. Au (3 to 6). The liquidus surface ascends thereafter towards the Ag-Cu binary and terminates at the eutectic reaction isotherm, 779°C. The liquidus and the two solidus surfaces α_1 and α_2 of the $(L+\alpha_1+\alpha_2)$ phase region touch each other

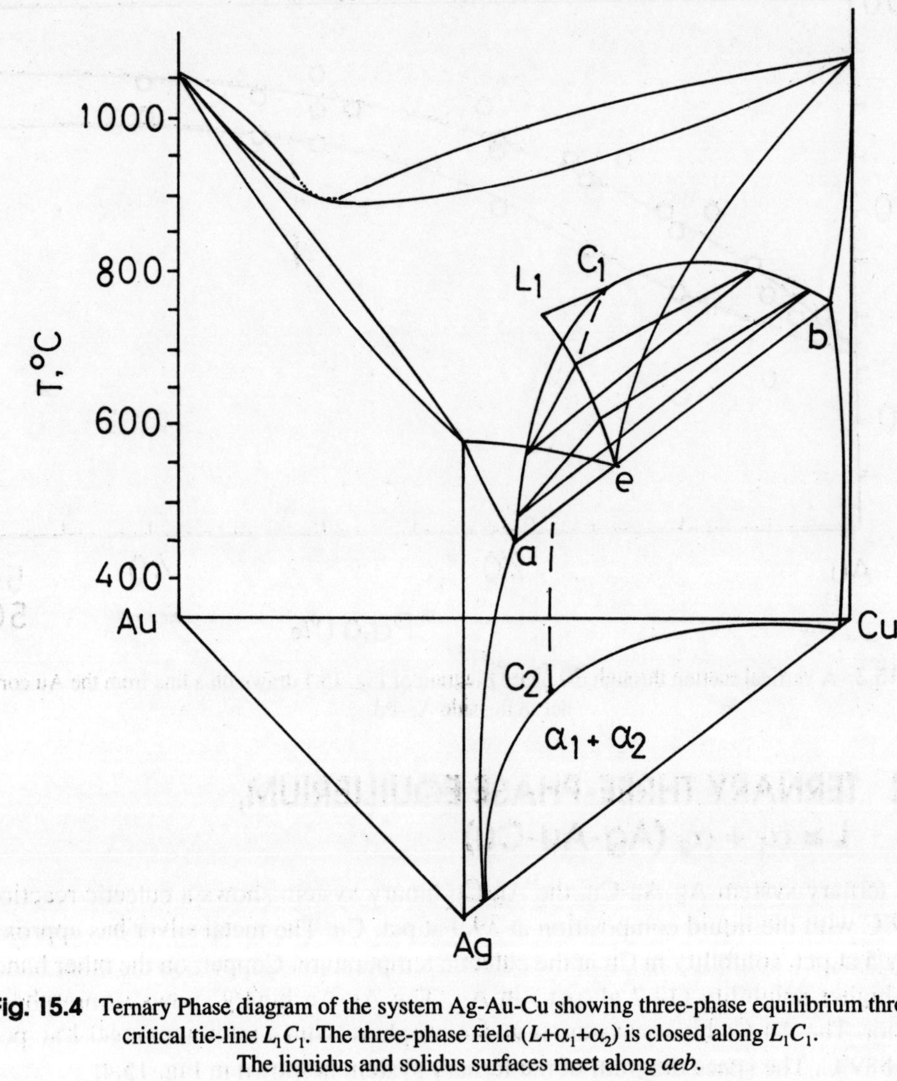

Fig. 15.4 Ternary Phase diagram of the system Ag-Au-Cu showing three-phase equilibrium through a critical tie-line L_1C_1. The three-phase field ($L+\alpha_1+\alpha_2$) is closed along L_1C_1. The liquidus and solidus surfaces meet along *aeb*.

at the Ag-Cu binary reaction isotherm and at the ternary minimum. The projection of the liquidus surface is shown in Fig. 15.5. The critical liquid composition L_1 maintains equilibrium with α_1 (α_2) through the tie line L_1C_1. C_1C_2 represents the critical curve along which the α_1 and α_2 phases become indistinguishable. Projections of the immiscibility gap, $(\alpha_1+\alpha_2)$, are shown at a number of temperatures from the work of (6 to 10) in the isothermal sections of Fig. 15.6. The ternary system has been reviewed by Prince (11).

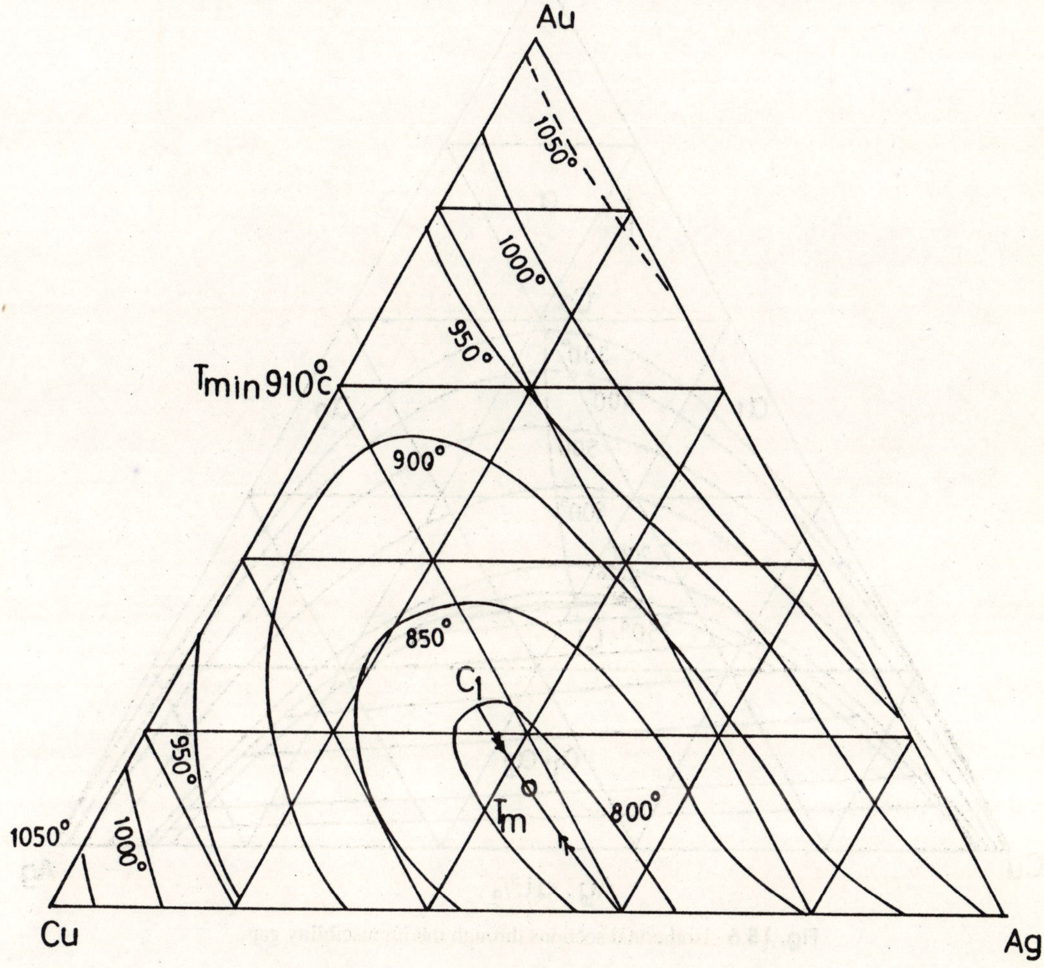

Fig. 15.5 Liquidus projection of the system Ag-Au-Cu.

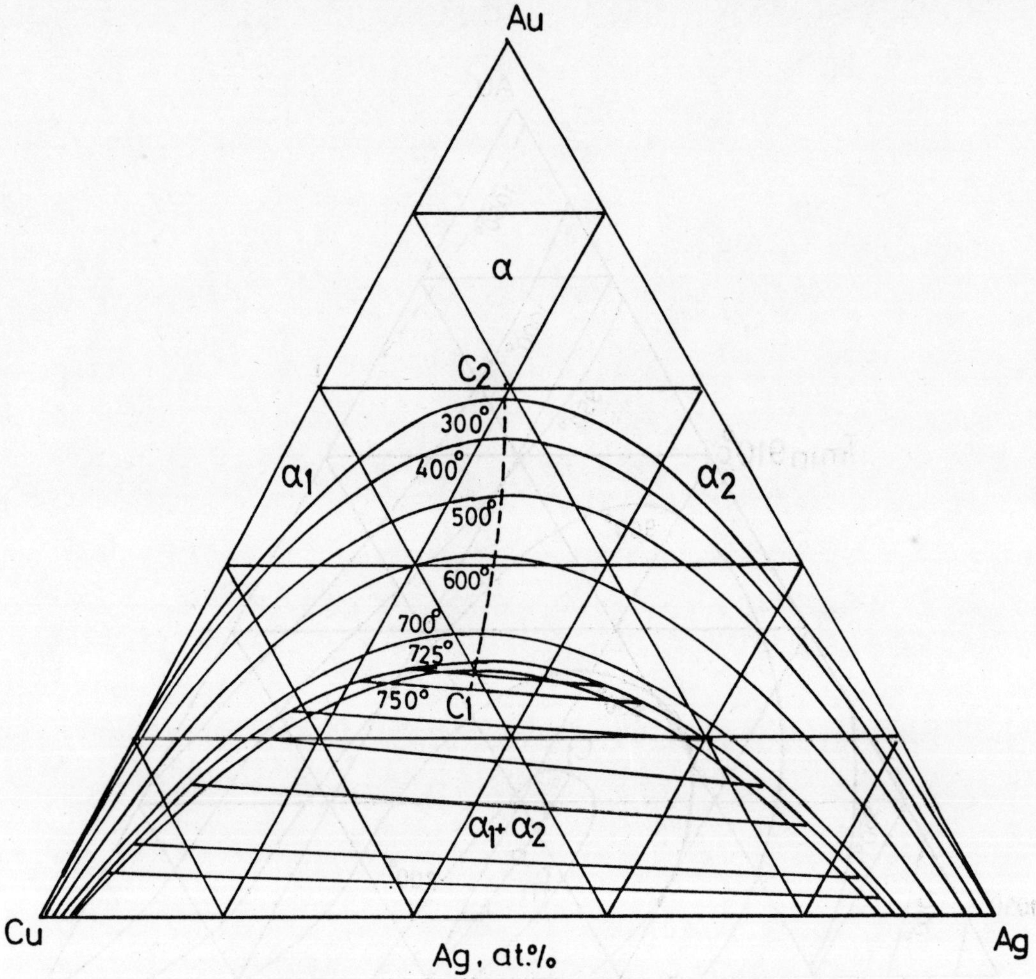

Fig. 15.6 Isothermal sections through the immiscibility gap.

15.3 TERNARY THREE-PHASE EQUILIBRIUM, L ⇌ α + β (Ag-Au-Ge SYSTEM)

The Au-Ge and Ag-Ge binary alloy systems show eutectic reactions. The Au-Ge system shows a eutectic reaction at 361°C. The eutectic liquid has a composition 28 at.pct. Ge. The solubility of Ge in Au at the eutectic temperature is 3 at.pct. However, Au has negligible solubility in pure Ge. The Ag-Ge binary system shows a eutectic reaction at 651°C with the eutectic liquid placed at 75 at.pct. Ag. The solubility of Ge in Ag is 10 at.pct. at the eutectic temperature. Silver has negligible solubility in germanium. The Ag-Au binary system shows complete solubility of Ag in Au in the solid as well as in the liquid state (isomorphous system).

The ternary phase diagram as constructed from the binaries is shown in Fig. 15.7. The liquidus was determined by Zwingmann (12) and runs almost parallel to the Ag-Au edge of the concentration triangle. The liquidus projection has been constructed from the three vertical sections from the work of Hassam-Dalichaouch (13) as reviewed by Prince (14).

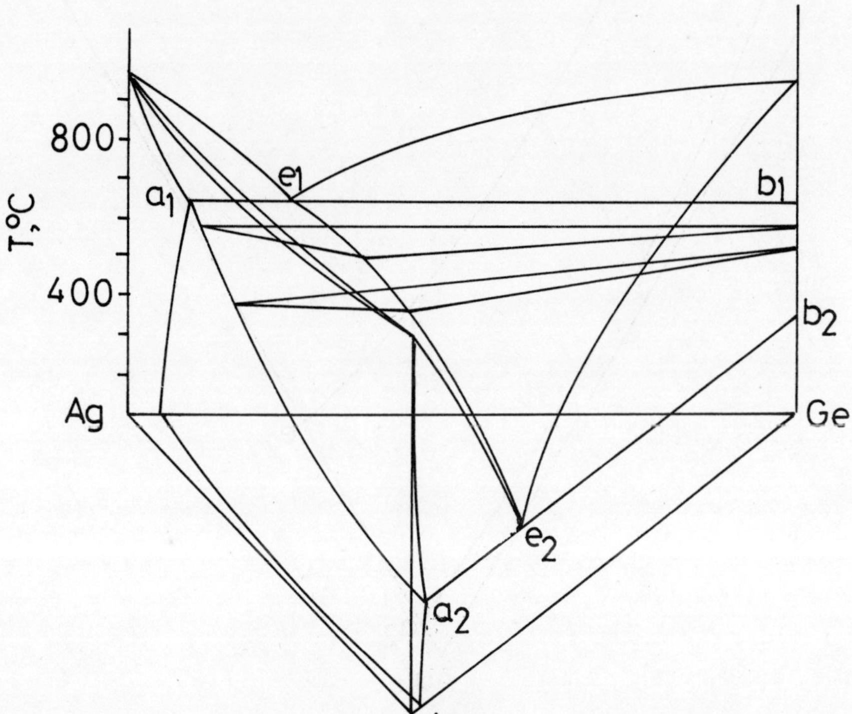

Fig. 15.7 The phase diagram of the ternary system Ag-Au-Ge showing monovariant equilibrium. A few tie-triangles show the extent of the three-phase region.

The monovariant liquid curve which is continuous from Ag-Ge to the Au-Ge eutectic lies close to the composition points 3.65Ag–67.09Au–29.26Ge and 7.13Ag–63.22Au–29.65Ge, Fig. 15.8.

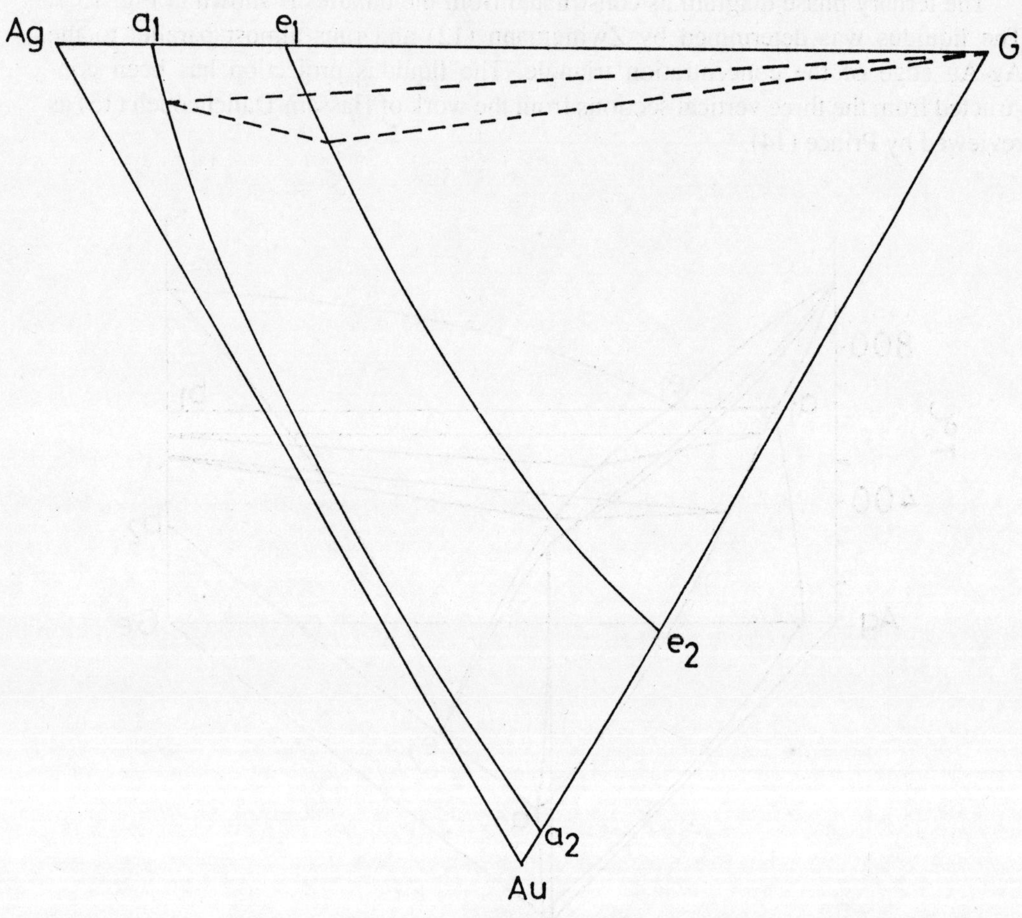

Fig. 15.8 The monovariant liquid and $\alpha_1\alpha_2$ lines bounding the $(L+\alpha_1+\alpha_2)$ phase field. The $\alpha_2(\beta)$ phase is almost pure Ge.

A vertical section on a line from the Ge corner to the opposite side with 50 Ag–50 Au is shown in Fig. 15.9 from the work of Hassam-Dalichaouch (13). The three-phase field $L + \alpha$ (Ag–Au) + β (Ge) shows that the solubility of Ge in liquid and α phases is 20 and 3 at.pct., respectively. The β phase is almost pure Ge. The solubility of Ge in liquid and α phases remains close to the above value in vertical sections drawn on lines from the Ge corner to 75 Ag–25 Au and 75 Au–25 Ag (13). A composite set of isothermal sections shows positions of the triangle ($L + \alpha + \beta$) as they descend from the binary side Ag–Ge to the side Au–Ge, Fig. 15.10.

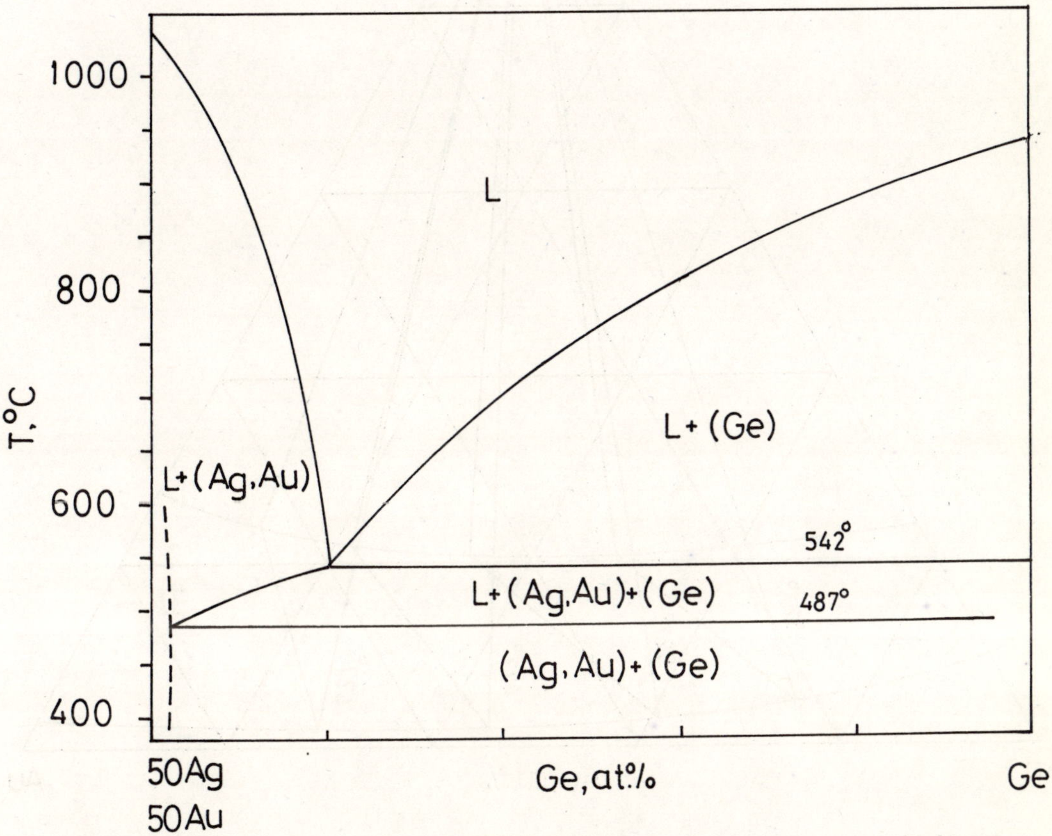

Fig. 15.9 The vertical section drawn on a line from the Ge corner to the opposite side with composition 50Ag-50Au. The (*L*+Ge)/*L*+(Au, Ag) + Ge and *L* + (Au, Ag) + Ge/ (Au, Ag) + Ge lines run almost parallel but must meet at the Ge corner.

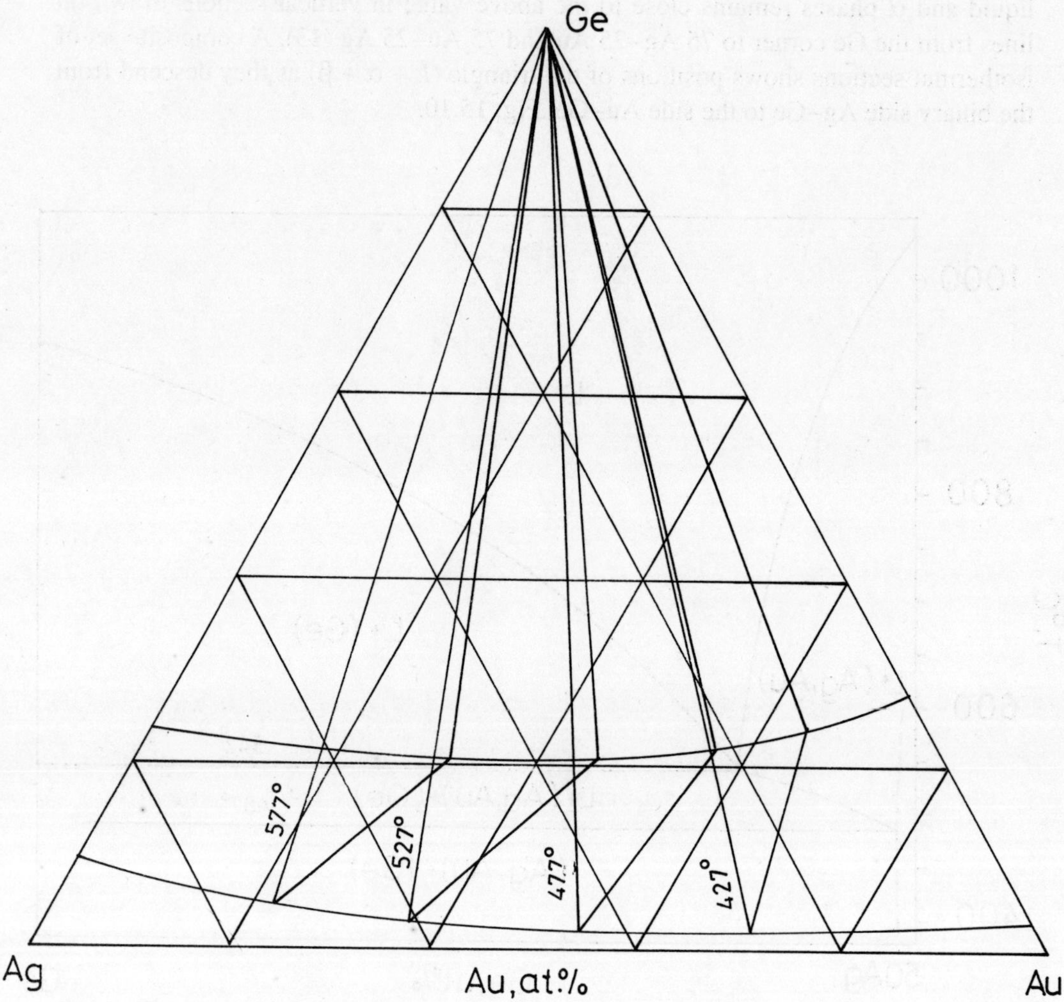

Fig. 15.10 Isothermal sections through the space model of Fig. 15.7 showing the three-phase field, L+α (Au, Ag) + β (Ge) at 427°C, 477°C, 527°C and 577°C.

15.4 TERNARY THREE-PHASE EQUILIBRIUM, $L + \alpha_1 = \alpha_2$ (Ag-Au-Pt SYSTEM)

The Ag-Pt binary system shows a peritectic reaction $L + \alpha_1 = \alpha_2$ at 1186°C. Composition of the three phases at the peritectic reaction isotherm are L: 78 at.pct. Ag,

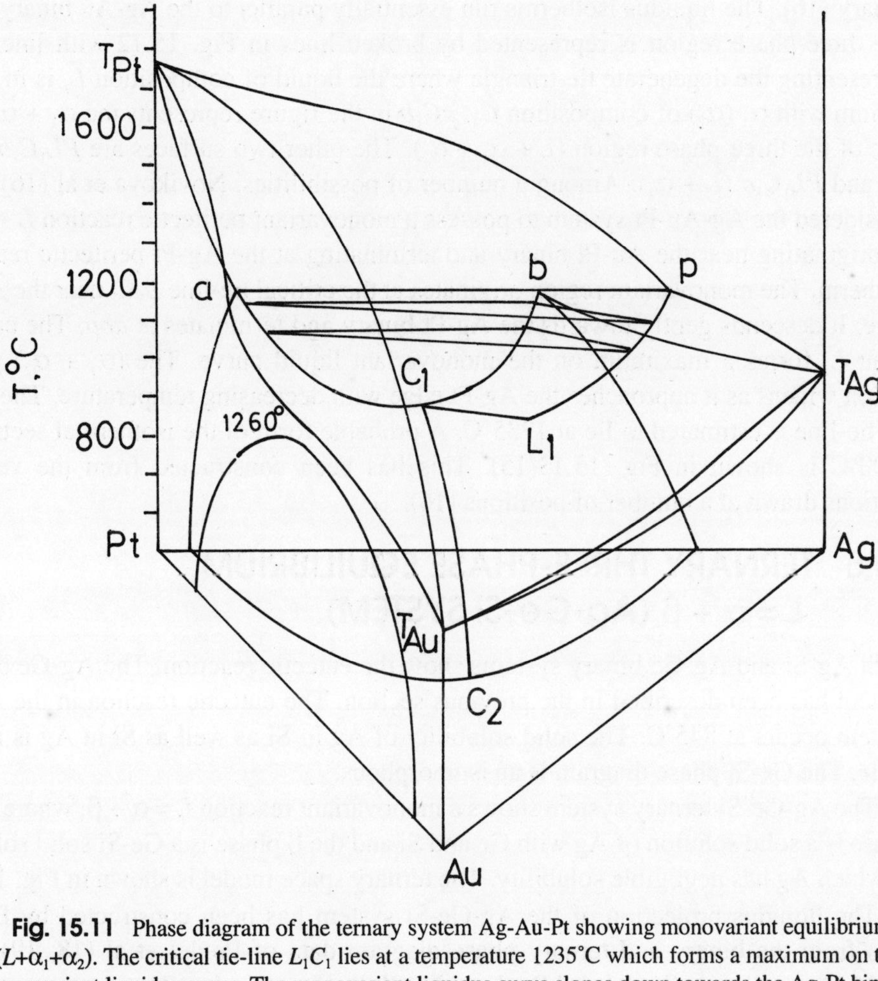

Fig. 15.11 Phase diagram of the ternary system Ag-Au-Pt showing monovariant equilibrium (L+α_1+α_2). The critical tie-line L_1C_1 lies at a temperature 1235°C which forms a maximum on the monovariant liquidus curve. The monovariant liquidus curve slopes down towards the Ag-Pt binary.

α_2: 57.1 at.pct. Ag and α_1:12.5 at.pct. Ag. The Au-Pt binary shows isomorphous behavior with a large separation between the liquidus and solidus curves, i.e., a large difference$\Delta X = X^L_{Au} - X^S_{Au}$. The α phase in the Au-Ag system shows an immiscibility gap at a composition of 61 at.pct. Pt and at the critical temperature 1260°C. The ternary phase diagram as constructed from the three binaries is shown in Fig. 15.11.

The ternary phase diagram of the Ag-Au-Pt system has been assessed by Prince (15). The work is based on the equilibrium phase diagram data of the binaries and the ternary (16). The liquidus isotherms run essentially parallel to the Ag-Au binary side. The three-phase region is represented by broken lines in Fig. 15.12 with line L_1C_1 representing the degenerate tie-triangle where the liquid of composition L_1 is in equilibrium with α_1 (α_2) of composition C_1. aC_1b in the figure represents the $\alpha_1 + \alpha_2$ surface of the three-phase region ($L + \alpha_1 + \alpha_2$). The other two surfaces are PL_1C_1b ($L + \alpha_2$) and PL_1C_1a ($L + \alpha_1$). Among a number of possibilities, Novikova et al (16) have considered the Ag-Au-Pt system to possess a monovariant peritectic reaction $L + \alpha_1 = \alpha_2$ originating near the Au-Pt binary and terminating at the Ag-Pt peritectic reaction isotherm. The monovariant region originates at the critical tie-line L_1C_1 near the Ag-Pt edge. It descends gently towards the Ag-Pt binary and terminates at *abp*. The critical point L_1 forms a maximum on the monovariant liquid curve. The ($\alpha_1 + \alpha_2$) phase region widens as it approaches the Ag-Pt edge with decreasing temperature. The critical tie-line is estimated to lie at 1235°C. A probable form of the isothermal section at 1200°C is shown in Fig. 15.13(15). This has been constructed from the vertical sections drawn at a number of positions (16).

15.5 TERNARY THREE-PHASE EQUILIBRIUM, L = α + β (Ag-Ge-Si SYSTEM)

Both Ag-Si and Ag-Ge binary systems show the eutectic reaction. The Ag-Ge binary system has been described in the previous section. The eutectic reaction in the Ag-Si system occurs at 845°C. The solid solubility of Ag in Si as well as Si in Ag is negligible. The Ge-Si phase diagram is an isomorphous.

The Ag-Ge-Si ternary system shows a monovariant reaction $L = \alpha + \beta$, where the α phase is a solid solution of Ag with Ge and Si and the β phase is a Ge-Si solid solution in which Ag has negligible solubility. The ternary space model is shown in Fig. 15.14.

The liquidus projection of the Ag-Ge-Si system has been constructed by Prince (17) from the binary and ternary phase diagram data of Predel et al (18, 19), Fig. 15.15. According to Predel and Bankstahl (18), the monovariant liquid curve e_1e_2 has an unusual *S*-shape. By taking the Ag-Si eutectic at 11.5 at.pct. Si and drawing the Ag-20Ge-80Si section so that the intersection between the two liquidus curves occurs

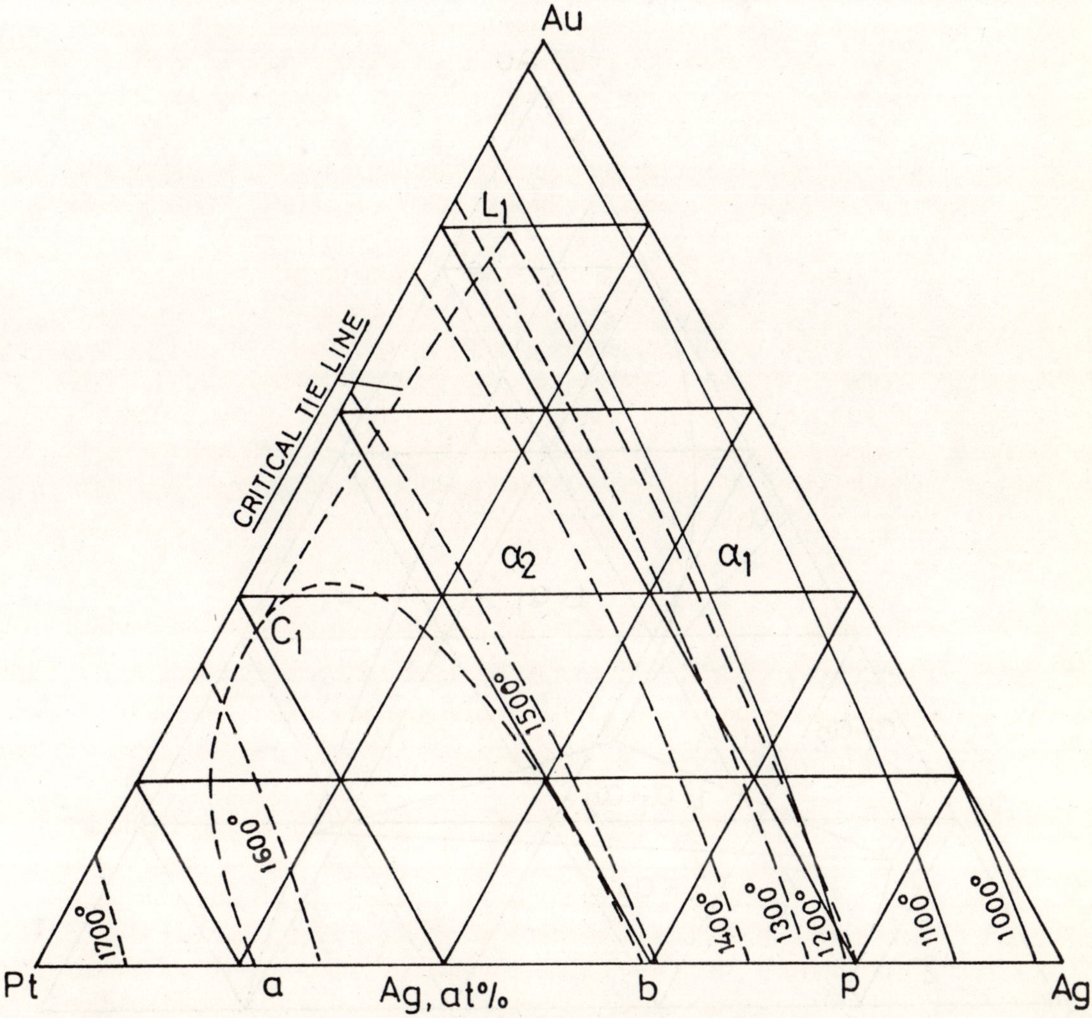

Fig. 15.12 The projection of the liquidus on the concentration triangle. The three-phase region is shown by broken lines.

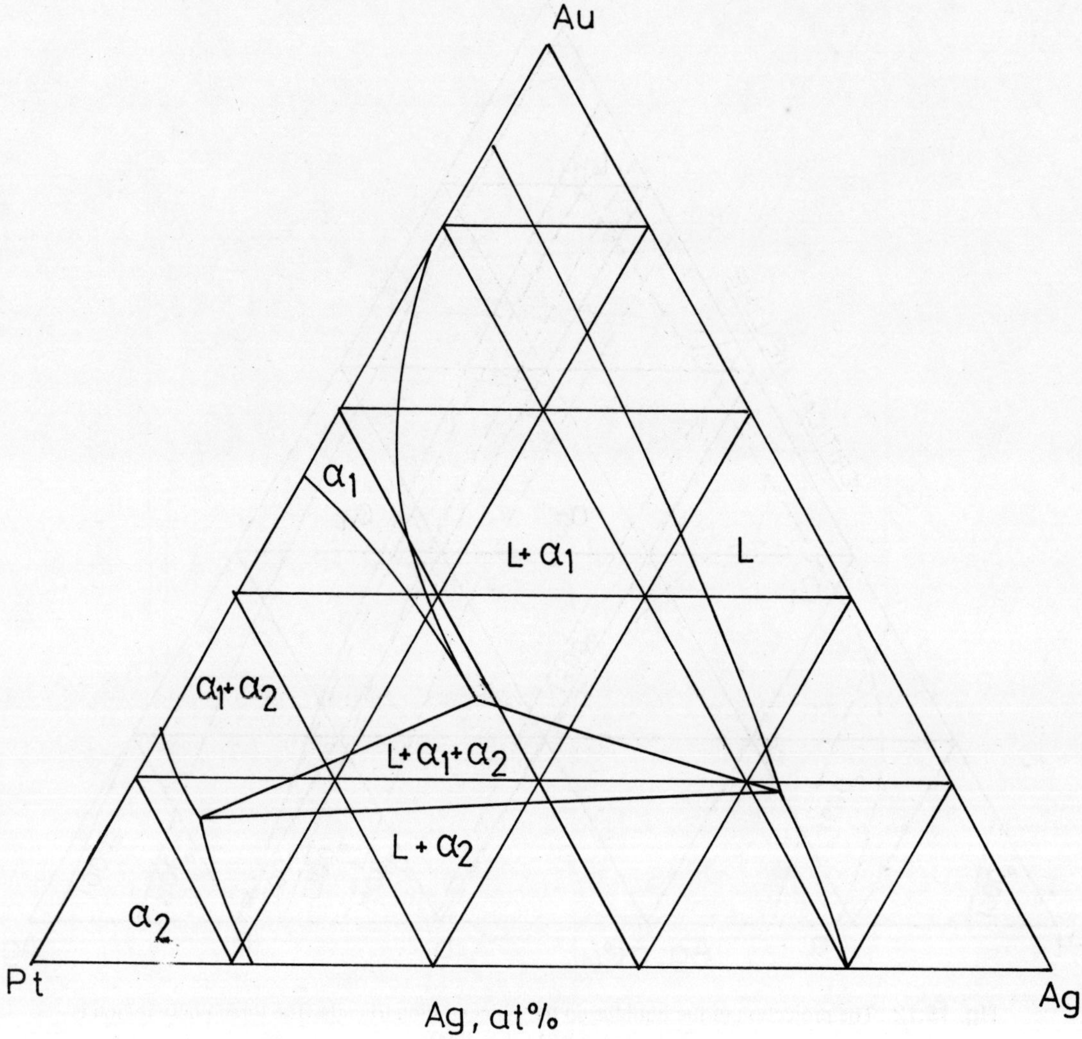

Fig. 15.13 Isothermal section at 1200°C as constructed.

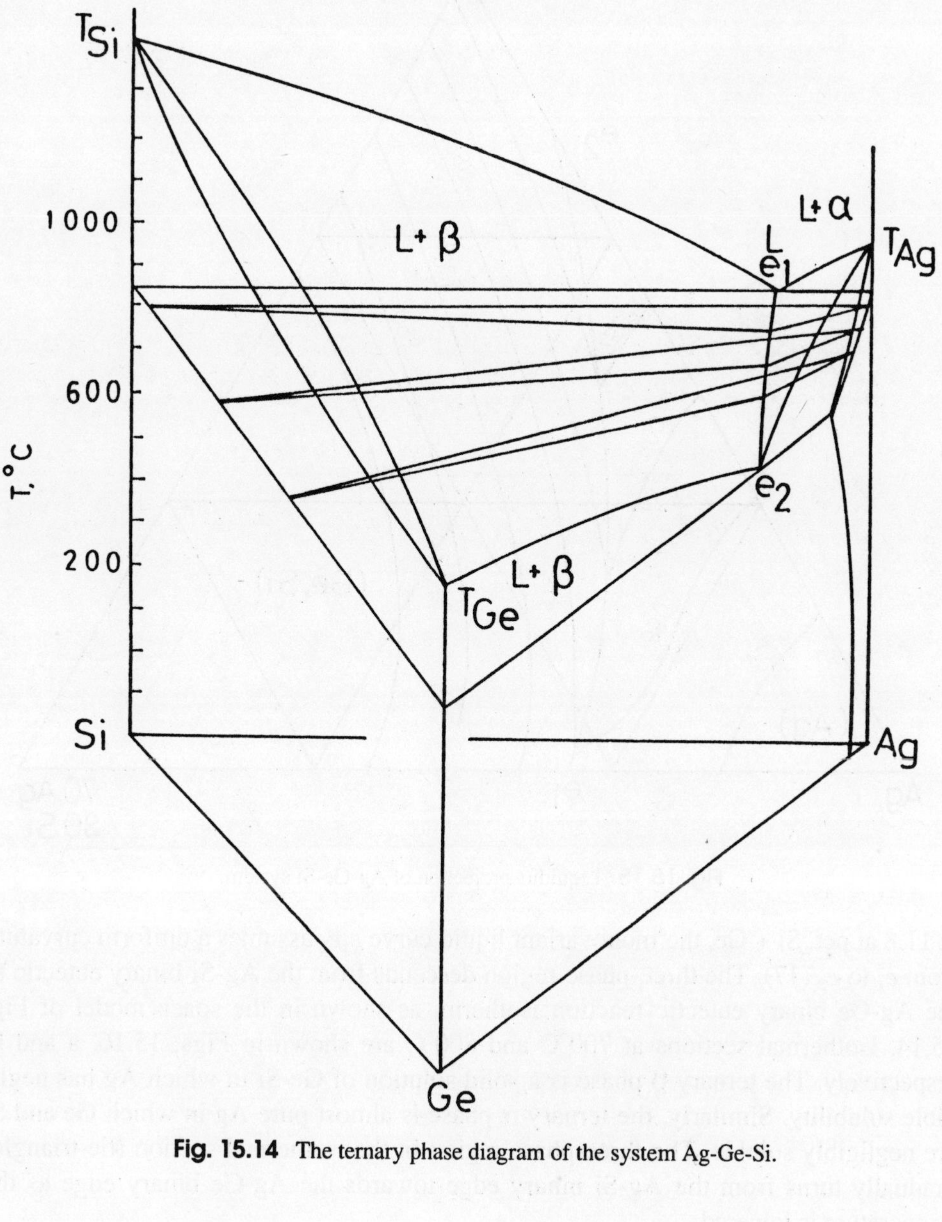

Fig. 15.14 The ternary phase diagram of the system Ag-Ge-Si.

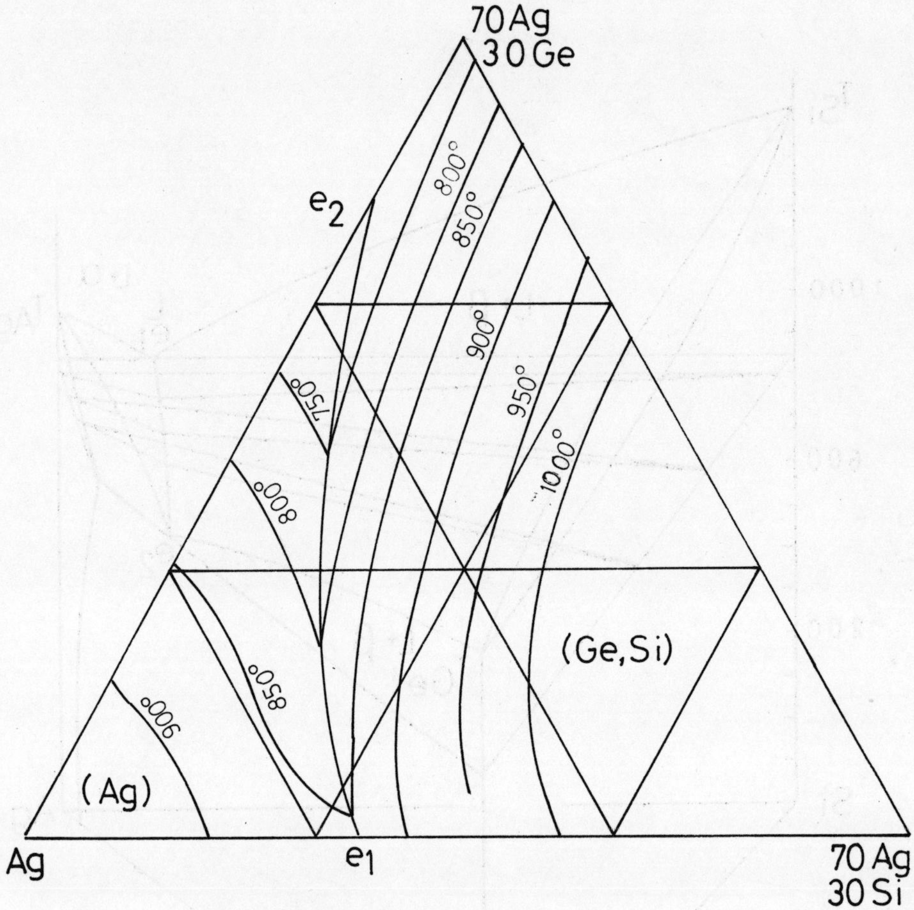

Fig. 15.15 Liquidus projection of Ag-Ge-Si system.

at 11.8 at.pct. Si + Ge, the monovariant liquid curve e_1e_2 assumes a uniform curvature from e_1 to e_2 (17). The three-phase region descends from the Ag-Si binary eutectic to the Ag-Ge binary eutectic reaction isotherm, as shown in the space model of Fig. 15.14. Isothermal sections at 700°C and 800°C are shown in Figs. 15.16, a and b, respectively. The ternary β phase is a solid solution of Ge-Si in which Ag has negligible solubility. Similarly, the ternary α phase is almost pure Ag in which Ge and Si are negligibly soluble. The three-phase region in the isothermal section (tie-triangle) gradually turns from the Ag-Si binary edge towards the Ag-Ge binary edge as the temperature is lowered.

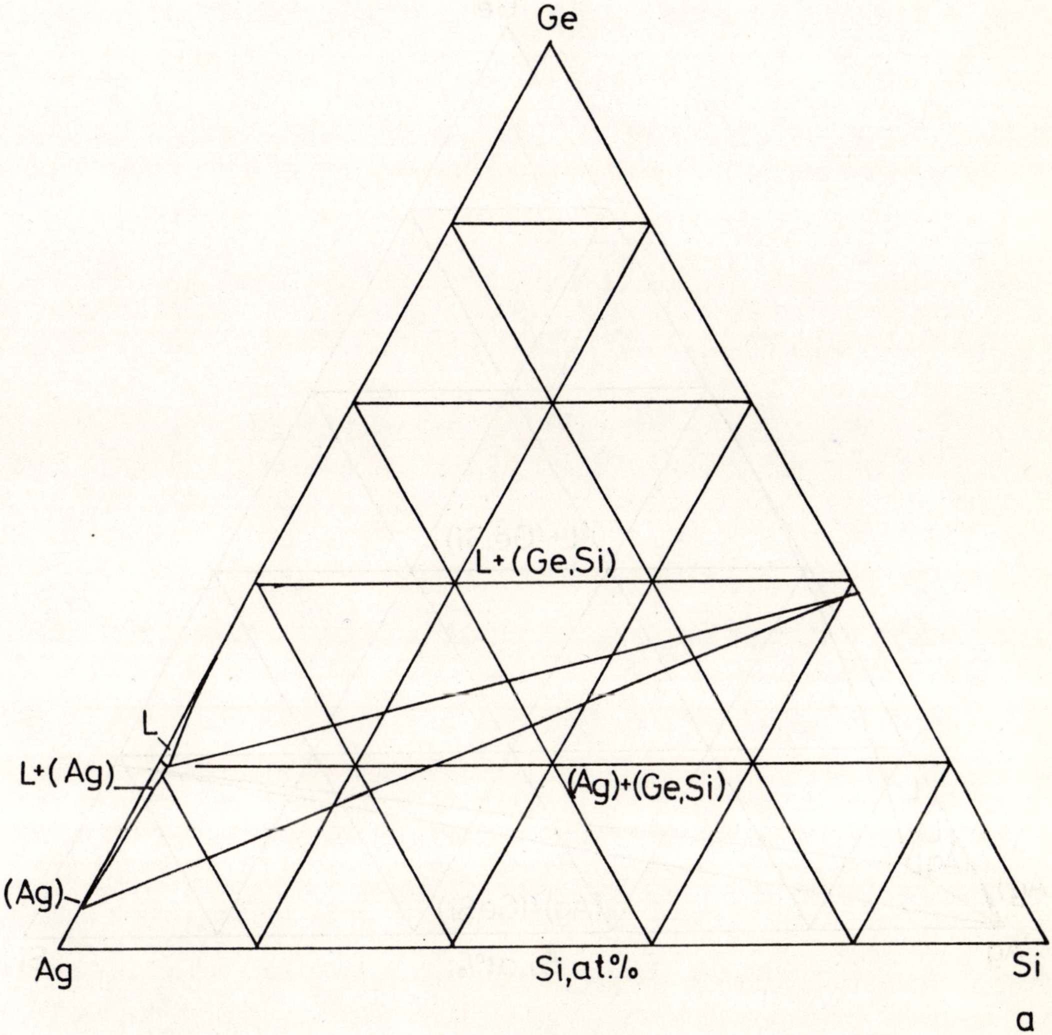

Fig. 15.16 Isothermal sections through the space model of Fig. 15.14 at (a) 700°C.

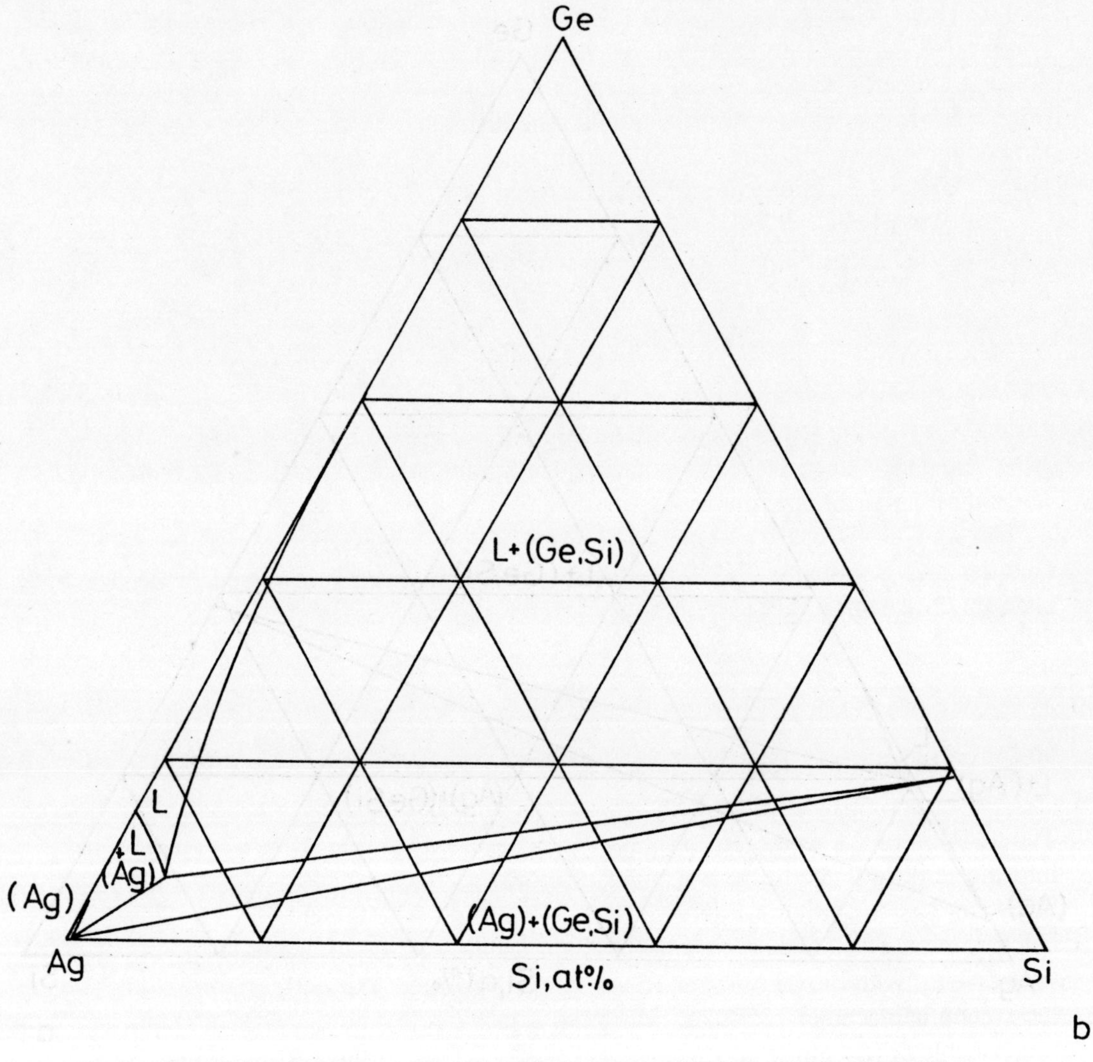

Fig. 15.16 Isothermal sections through the space model of Fig. 15.14 at (b) 800°C.

15.6 TERNARY MONOVARIANT REACTION INVOLVING IMMISCIBILITY IN THE LIQUID (Ag-Cu-Ni SYSTEM)

The Ag-Cu binary system was described in Chapter 7. It shows a eutectic reaction at 779°C. The eutectic liquid shows a composition of 39.9 at.pct. Cu. The solubility of Cu in solid Ag is 14.2 at.pct and that of Ag in Cu is approximately 5 at.pct at the eutectic temperature. The Cu-Ni system is isomorphous, with liquid and solid solutions behaving as almost ideal solutions. The difference in the solidus and liquidus temperatures is small. The Ag-Ni system shows immiscibility in the liquid. The Ni-rich liquid (L_1) undergoes a monotectic reaction at 1435°C, represented as

$$L_1(97\text{at.pct Ni}) \xrightarrow{1435°\text{C}} \alpha(\cong 98.5 \text{ at.pct. Ni}) + L_2(\sim 4 \text{ at.pct. Ni}).$$

The Ag-Ni binary system also shows a eutectic reaction at 961.9°C which is very close to the melting temperature of pure Ag. The solid solubility of Ni in Ag is negligible below the eutectic reaction isotherm. The solubility of Ag in Ni is approximately 1% at the eutectic temperature.

The Ag-Cu-Ni ternary system has been studied by De Cesaris (20) and updated by Guertler and Bergmann (21). This system has been recently reviewed by Kubaschewski (22). The ternary system shows two monovariant reactions.

$$L_1 \rightleftharpoons \alpha + L_2$$

and

$$L_2 \rightleftharpoons \alpha + \beta$$

The addition of Cu to the Ag-Ni binary alloys extends the liquid immiscibility gap into the ternary with the monovariant reaction $L_1 = \alpha + L_2$ extending below the binary monotectic reaction isotherm of 1435°C. The ($\alpha + L_2$) phase region descends below the binary monotectic reaction isotherm and forms a closed three-phase region ($\alpha + L_1 + L_2$) with the ($\alpha + L_1$)and ($L_1 + L_2$) ruled surfaces. The critical temperature in the system is placed at 1250°C at which the α phase is in equilibrium with the indistinguishable L_1 (L_2) along the degenerate tie-line L_1 (L_2) C_1. This is shown in the space diagram of Fig. 15.17.

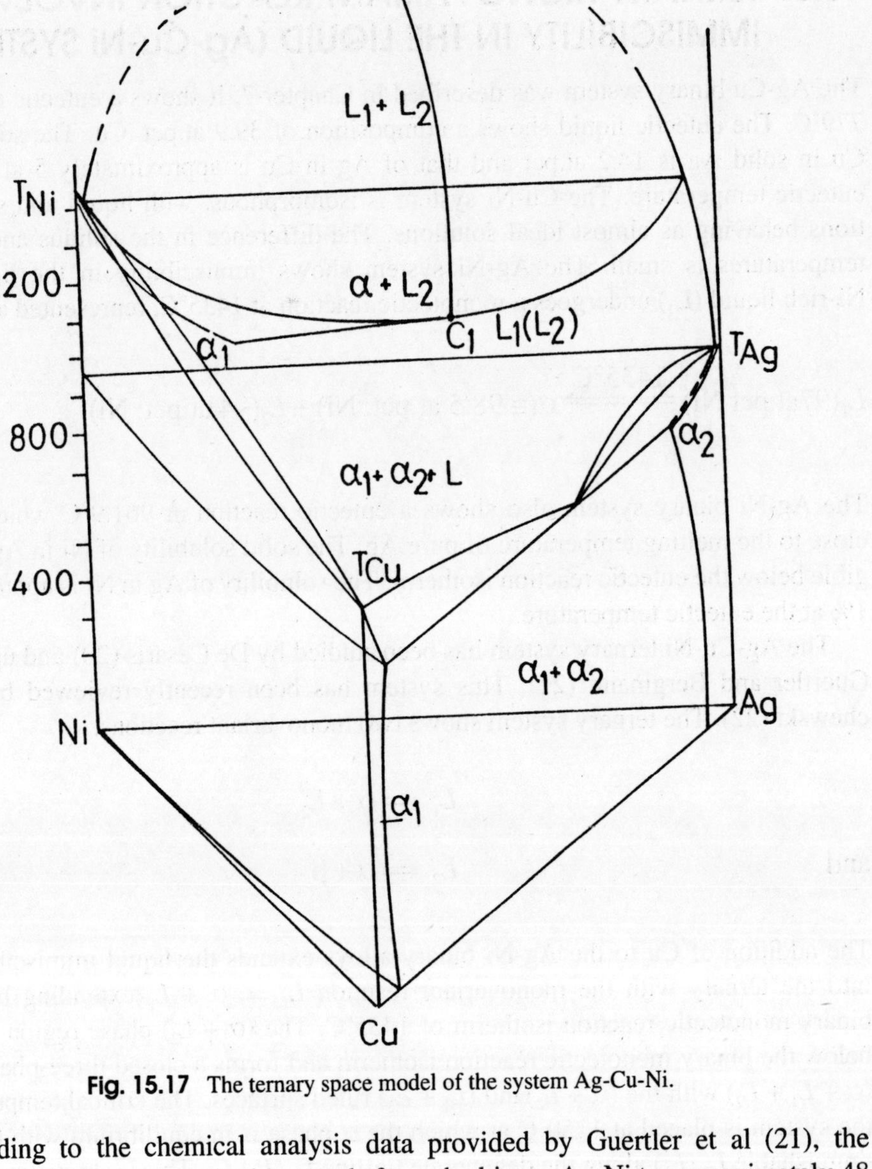

Fig. 15.17 The ternary space model of the system Ag-Cu-Ni.

According to the chemical analysis data provided by Guertler et al (21), the immiscibility in the ternary liquid extends from the binary Ag-Ni to approximately 48 at.pct. Cu at 1250°C. Monovariant equilibrium is clearly revealed in the isothermal sections at 1440°C, and 1300°C, Fig. 15.18. Clearly, the isothermal section at 1440°C does not show the three-phase region. The intersection with the ternary two-phase

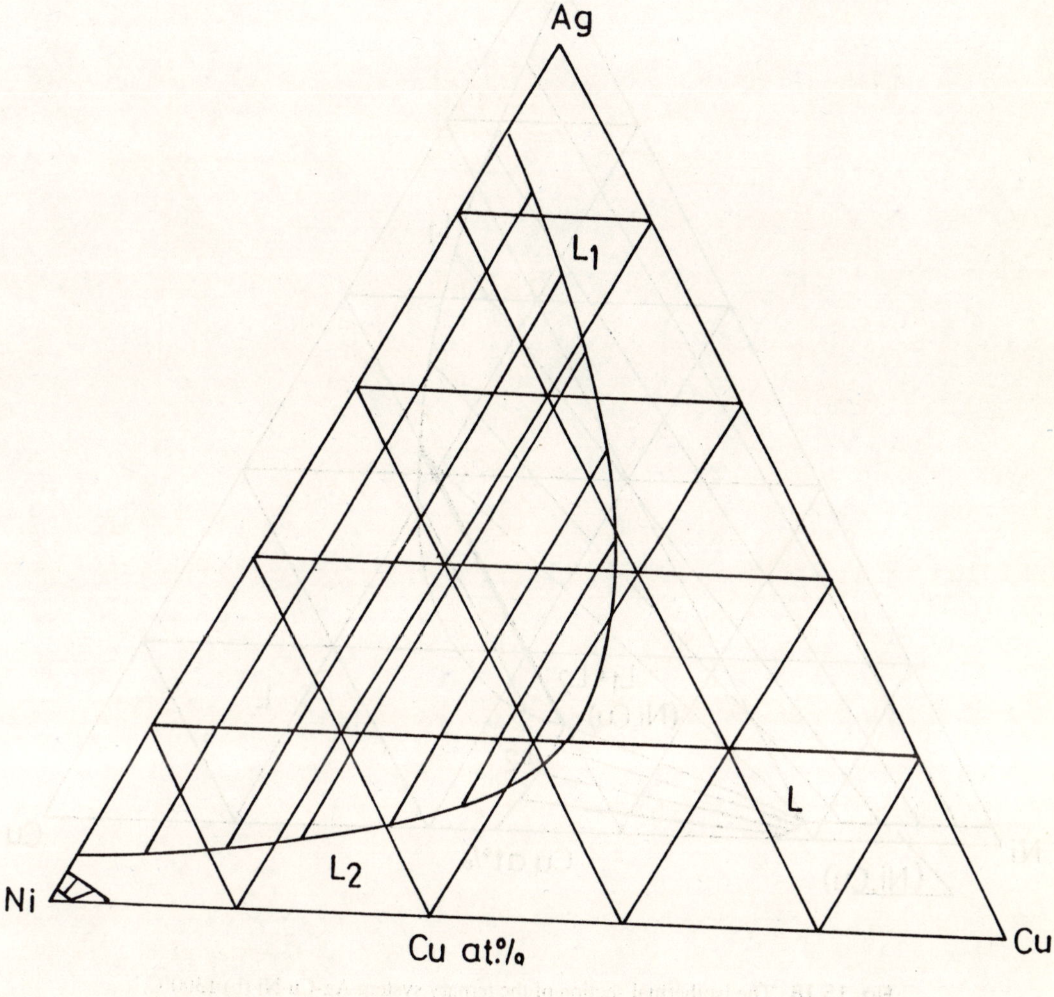

Fig. 15.18 The isothermal section of the ternary system Ag-Cu-Ni (a) 1440°C.

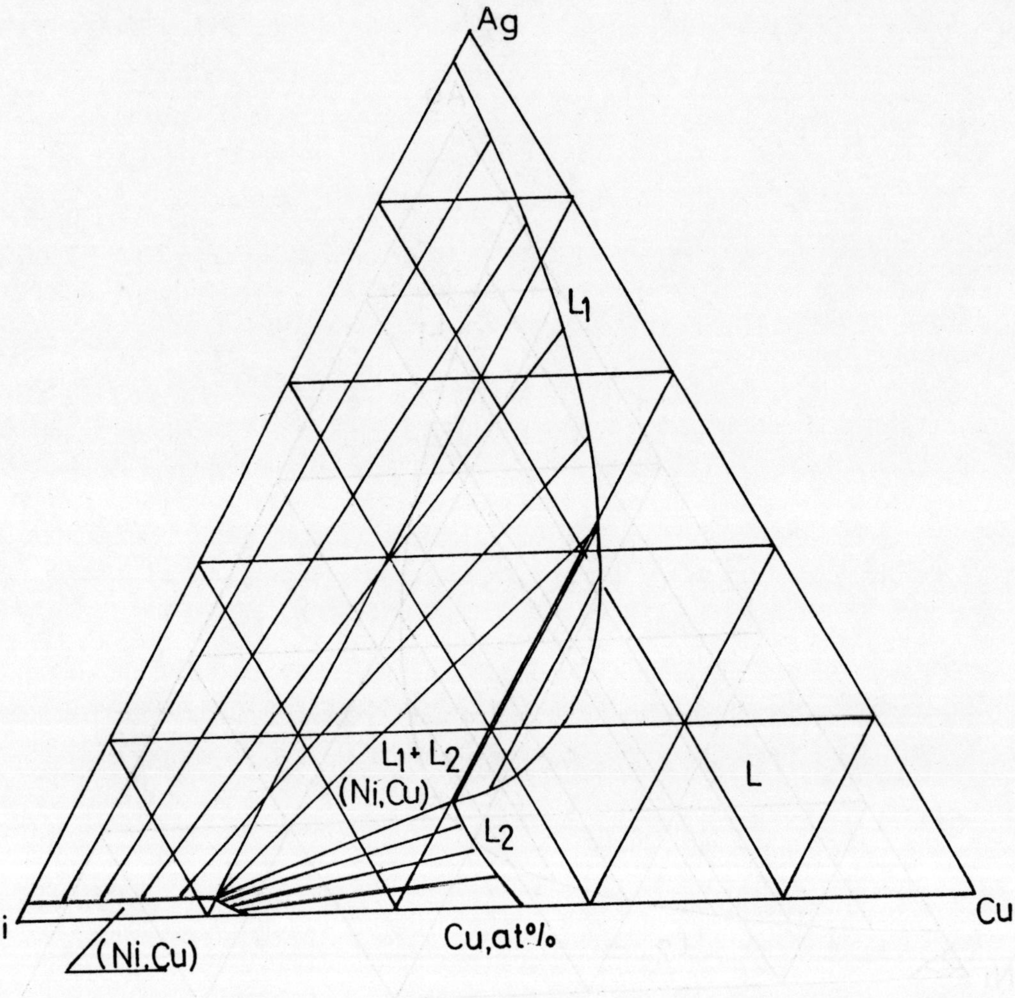

Fig. 15.18 The isothermal section of the ternary system Ag-Cu-Ni (b) 1300°C.

region (L_1 + L_2) appears in the section. The isothermal section at 1300°C shows the three-phase region (L_1+L_2+α) and the associated single and two-phase regions. The three-phase region terminates at 1250°C.

The ternary system also shows a monovariant reaction $L_2 \rightleftharpoons \alpha + \beta$ below 961.9°C. However, since solubilities of both Ag in Ni and Ni in Ag are very small, the monovariant liquid curve runs parallel to and very close to the Ag-Cu binary, as shown in the space model of Fig. 15.17.

15.7 TERNARY EUTECTIC REACTION (INVARIANT) $L \rightleftharpoons \alpha + \beta + \gamma$ (Ag-Cu-Pb system)

The Ag-Cu binary system has been discussed in section 15.6. The Ag-Pb binary phase diagram shows a eutectic reaction at 280°C. The eutectic liquid has a composition 95 at.pct. Pb. The solubility of Pb in Ag at the eutectic temperature is approximately 1 at pct. while Ag has negligible solubility in Pb.

The Cu-Pb binary system shows a monotectic reaction $L_1 \rightleftharpoons \alpha + L_2$at 952°C. The critical temperature is placed at approximately 1006°C (23). The α phase is almost pure Cu. The liquid L_1 of composition 22 at.pct. Pb is in equilibrium with liquid L_2 containing 63 at.pct. Pb at the monotectic temperature. The binary alloy system also shows a eutectic reaction at a fraction of a degree below the melting temperature of pure lead. The product phases α and β are almost pure Cu and Pb, respectively.

The Ag-Cu-Pb ternary system has been investigated by Friedrich et al (24) and reviewed later by Chang et al (25). The ternary system has been assessed by Hayes (26). According to the result published by Chang et al. (25), the binary immiscibility gap in the Cu-Pb system extends to the ternary by the addition of Ag at approximately 36 at.pct. Ag. The critical temperature at which the two liquids become indistinguishable can be placed at approximately 775 ± 10°C. The ternary space diagram is shown in Fig. 15.19.

The projection of the liquidus surface is shown in Fig. 15.20 after the work of Chang et al (25). The ternary immiscibility dome is seen to extend to approximately 36 at.pct. Ag. The calculated liquidus surface from the work of Hayes (26), however, extends the ternary immiscibility gap to approximately 5 at.pct. Ag. The three binary eutectic liquids e_1, e_2 and e_3 interact with each other in the ternary, forming the invariant equilibrium,

$$L \rightleftharpoons \alpha(\text{Cu}) + \beta(\text{Pb}) + (\text{Ag}),$$

at 302°C. The ternary eutectic liquid has a composition 3.73 at.pct. Ag, 1.58 at.pct. Cu and the balance Pb, as shown in Fig. 15.20, after the work of Chang et al (25). Hayes (26) has calculated isothermal sections at a number of temperatures. At 727°C and 527°C, these sections show the three-phase region $L + \alpha$ (Cu) $+ \gamma$ (Ag).

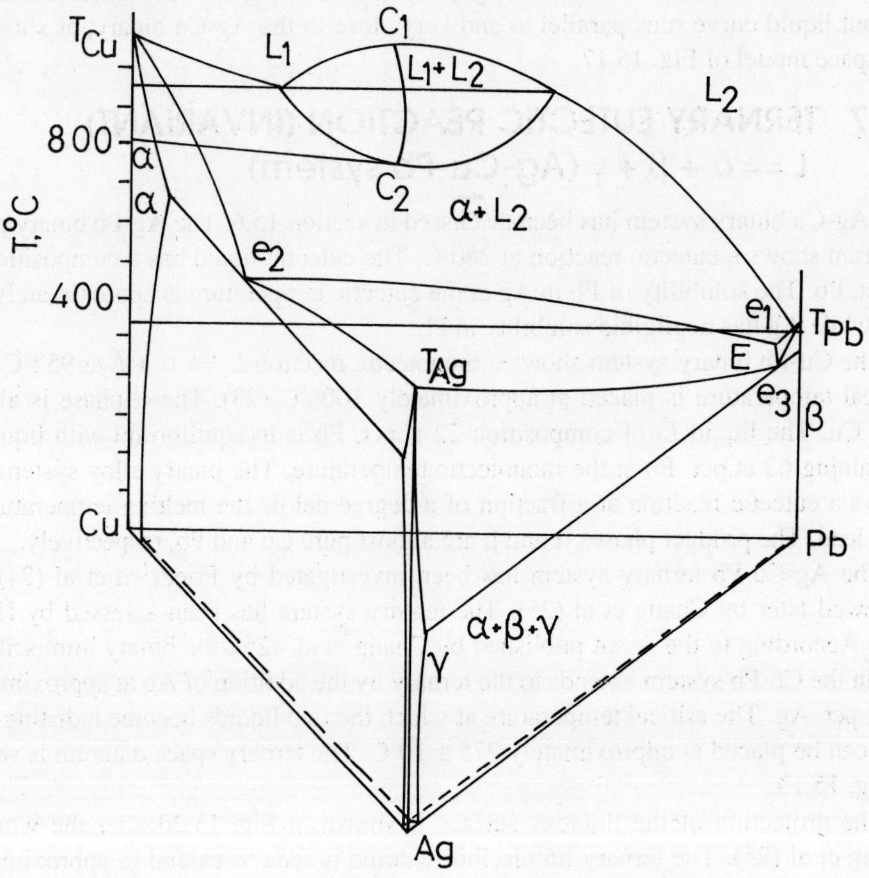

Fig. 15.19 The ternary phase diagram of the system Ag-Cu-Pb.

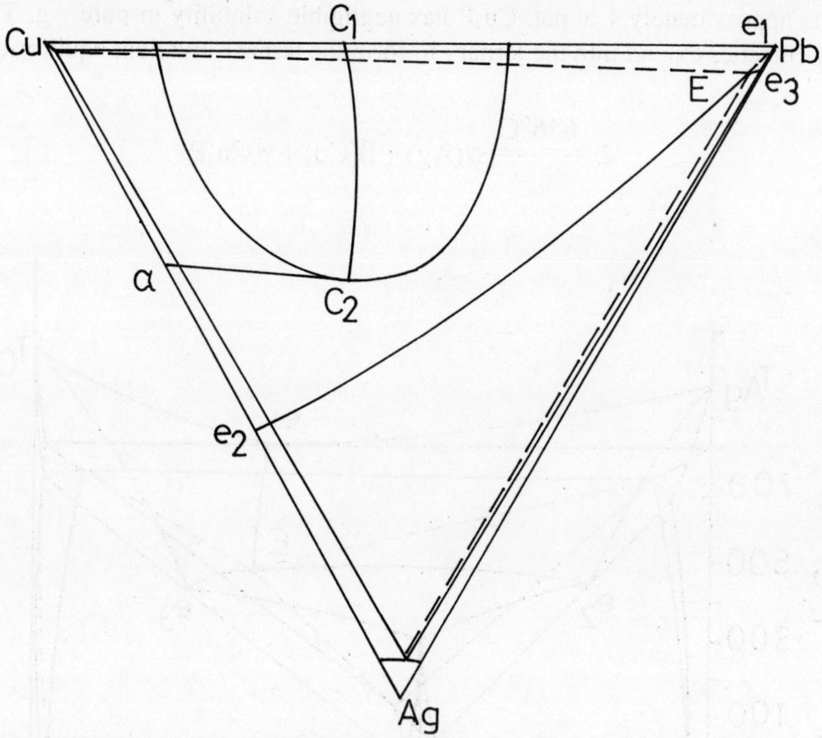

Fig. 15.20 Liquidus projection of the system Ag-Cu-Pb.

15.8 TERNARY EUTECTIC REACTION, L ⇌ α+β+γ (Ag-Cu-Cu_3P SYSTEM)

The Ag-Cu-Cu_3P ternary system shows an invariant reaction $L \rightleftharpoons \alpha+\beta+\gamma$. The Ag-Cu binary system has been described in previous sections. It shows a eutectic reaction at 779°C. The Cu-P binary phase diagram shows a eutectic reaction at 714°C with the eutectic liquid composition at 15.7 at.pct. P. The maximum solubility of P in Cu (β) is 3.5 at.pct. P at the eutectic temperature. The Ag-Cu_3P is a quasi-binary phase diagram with a eutectic reaction at 796°C. The eutectic composition is placed at approximately

33 at.pct. Ag from the work of Moser et al (27). The maximum solubility of Ag in Cu_3P is approximately 1 at.pct. Cu_3P has negligible solubility in pure Ag. The three binary eutectics extend into the ternary to form the ternary invariant equilibrium:

$$L \xrightleftharpoons{646°C} \alpha(Ag) + \beta(Cu) + \gamma(Cu_3P)$$

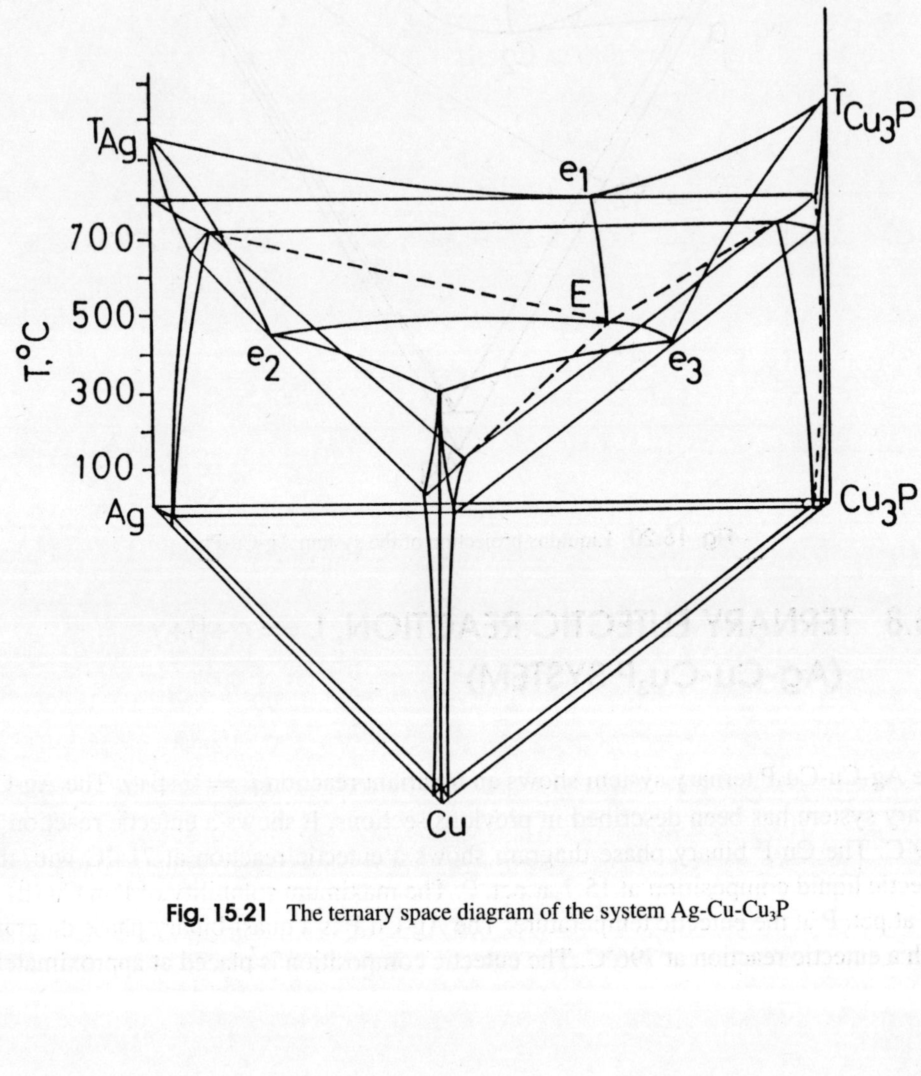

Fig. 15.21 The ternary space diagram of the system Ag-Cu-Cu_3P

The ternary space diagram is shown in Fig. 15.21. The ternary eutectic liquid has a composition of 10.6 at.pct. Ag, 74.8 at.pct. Cu and 14.6 at.pct. P established by Chang et al (25). This composition in terms of the Ag-Cu-Cu_3P ternary system becomes 10.6 Ag, 31 Cu and 58.4 Cu_3P.

15.9 TERNARY EUTECTIC REACTION Al-Si-Sb SYSTEM

The ternary system Al-Si-Sb shows two ternary eutectic reactions. The Al-Si binary system shows a eutectic reaction at 577°C. The Al-Sb phase diagram shows two eutectic reactions: one between pure Al and AlSb at 657°C. The third binary system Si-Sb shows a eutectic reaction at 629°C. The following data (Table 15.1.) of the binary systems are used to construct the ternary space model, Fig. 15.22.

Table 15.1

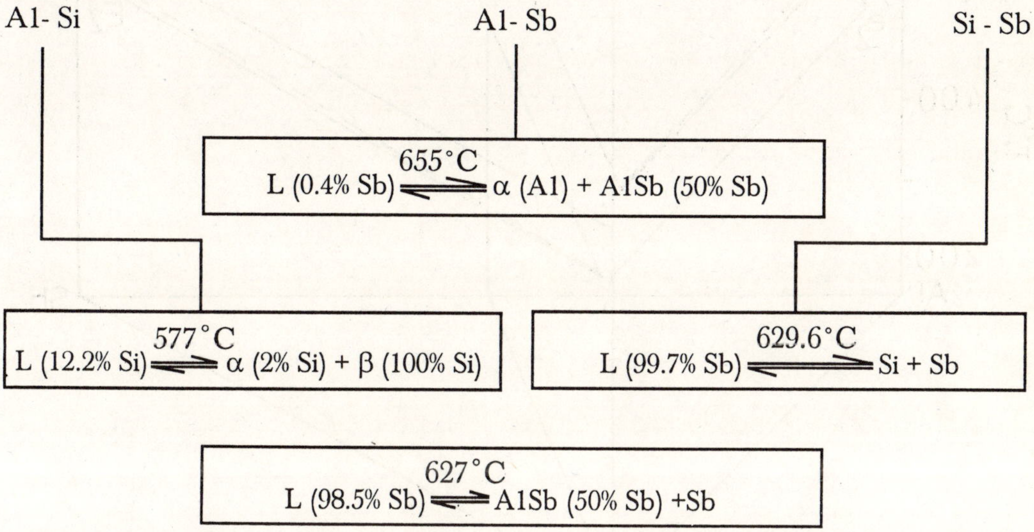

Si forms a quasi-binary system with AlSb. The phase diagram shows a eutectic reaction at 1014°C determined by Glazov et al (28). The solubility of AlSb is less than 1% in Si and that of Si in AlSb is negligible. The ternary phase diagram of the Al-Sb system has been assessed by Hausmann (29) from the data of Hanemann et al (30) and Spengler (31). The two ternary invariant reactions are:

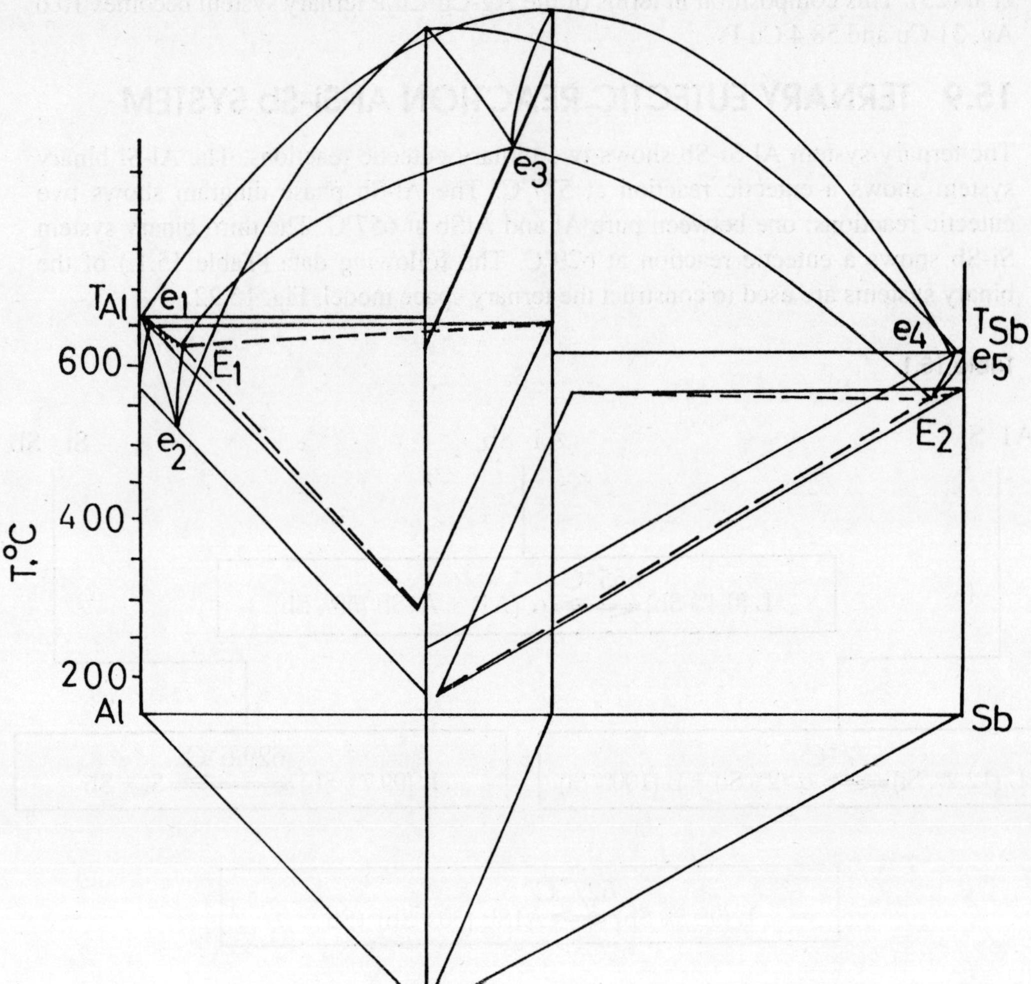

Fig. 15.22 The ternary space diagram of the system Al-Si-Sb.

$$L \xrightleftharpoons{626°C} \beta(\text{Si}) + \gamma(\text{AlSb}) + \delta(\text{Sb})$$

and

$$L \xrightleftharpoons{573°C} \alpha(\text{Al}) + \beta(\text{Si}) + \gamma(\text{AlSb}).$$

The first reaction occurs at 626˚C with the eutectic liquid of composition 1.5 at.pct. Al, 98.2 at.pct. Sb and 0.3 at.pct. Si dissociating into almost pure Si, Sb and the AlSb inter-metallic. The second reaction occurs at 573˚C with the eutectic liquid of composition (89.82% Al, 1% Sb and 9.81% Si) dissociating into α (98.5% Al and 1.5% Si), β (99.98% Si and 0.016% Sb) and γ (AlSb). The ternary invariant equilibria can be represented by the following reaction scheme, Table 15.2.

Table 15.2

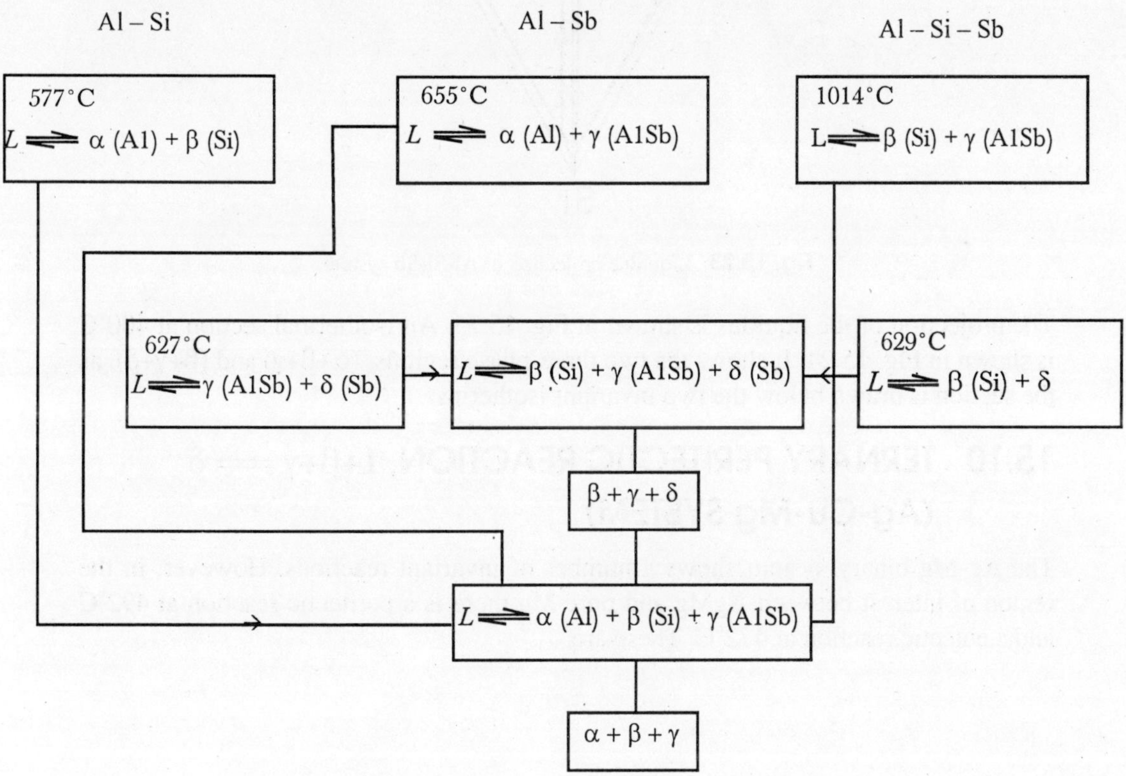

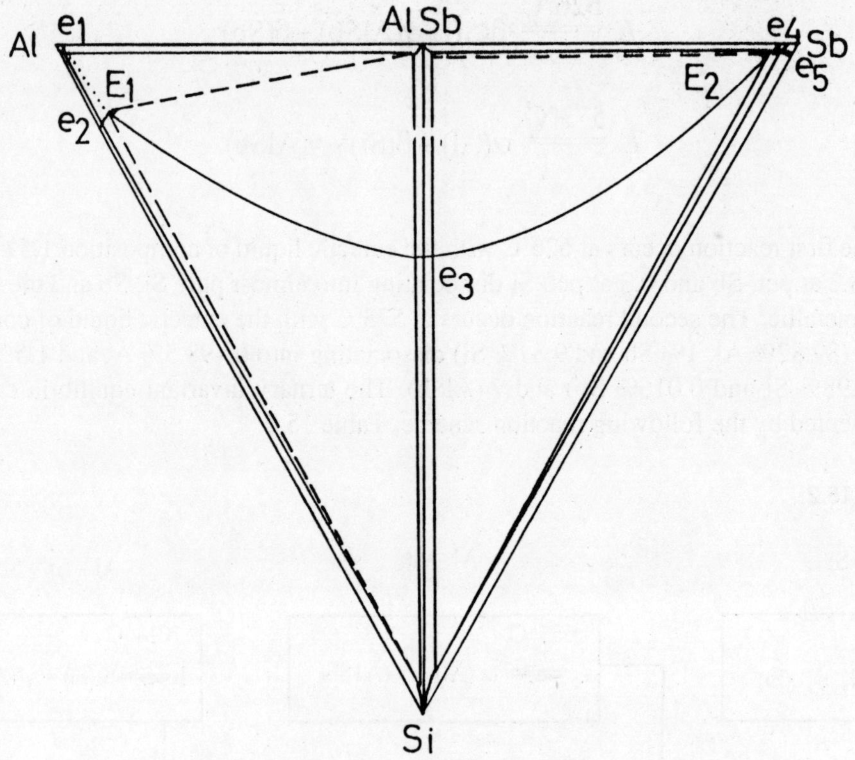

Fig. 15.23 Liquidus projection of Al-Si-Sb system.

The projection of the liquidus is shown in Fig. 15.23. An isothermal section at 400°C is shown in Fig. 15.24. It shows the two three-phase regions, ($\alpha+\beta+\gamma$) and ($\beta+\gamma+\delta$), as the section is drawn below the two invariant isotherms.

15.10 TERNARY PERITECTIC REACTION, $L+\beta+\gamma \rightleftharpoons \delta$ (Ag-Cu-Mg SYSTEM)

The Ag-Mg binary system shows a number of invariant reactions. However, in the region of interest between AgMg and pure Mg there is a peritectic reaction at 492°C and a eutectic reaction at 472°C. These are:

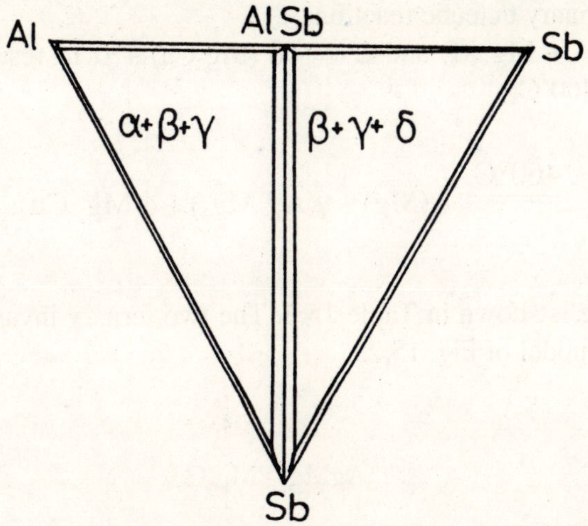

Fig. 15.24 Isothermal section of the system Al-Si-Sb at 400°C.

$$L\ (77.43\%\ \text{Mg}) + \text{AgMg} \xrightleftharpoons{492°\text{C}} \text{Ag}\ \text{Mg}_3$$

and $$L(82.42\%\text{Mg}) \xrightleftharpoons{472°\text{C}} \text{AgMg}_3 + \text{Mg (S.S. } 96.17\%\text{Mg)}.$$

Among a number of binary invariant reactions in the Cu-Mg system, one of the product intermediate phases Mg_2Cu and Ag Mg of the Ag-Mg system show a eutectic reaction:

$$L(12.4\%\text{Ag}) \xrightleftharpoons{530°\text{C}} \text{Mg}_2\text{Cu}\ (4.1\%\text{Ag}) + \text{AgMg}\ (37.4\%\ \text{Ag}).$$

The quasi-binary side between Mg_2Cu and AgMg becomes one of the sides of the ternary system giving rise to the four-phase reaction:

$$L + \beta(\text{AgMg}) + \delta(\text{Mg}_2\text{Cu}) \xrightleftharpoons{505°\text{C}} \gamma\ (\text{AgMg}_3)\ \ (\text{at } T_p)$$

The $(L+\gamma+\delta)$ three-phase region which descends below the four-phase plane at T_p combines with the binary eutectic reactions,

$L \rightleftharpoons \gamma\ (AgMg_3) + Mg\ (\alpha)$ and $L \rightleftharpoons \delta\ (Mg_2Cu) + \alpha$ to result in an invariant eutectic reaction at 460°C:

$$L \xrightleftharpoons{460°C} \alpha(Mg) + \gamma(Ag\,Mg_3) + \delta(Mg_2\,Cu).$$

The reaction scheme is shown in Table 15.3. The two ternary invariant reactions are shown in the space model of Fig. 15.25.

Table 15.3

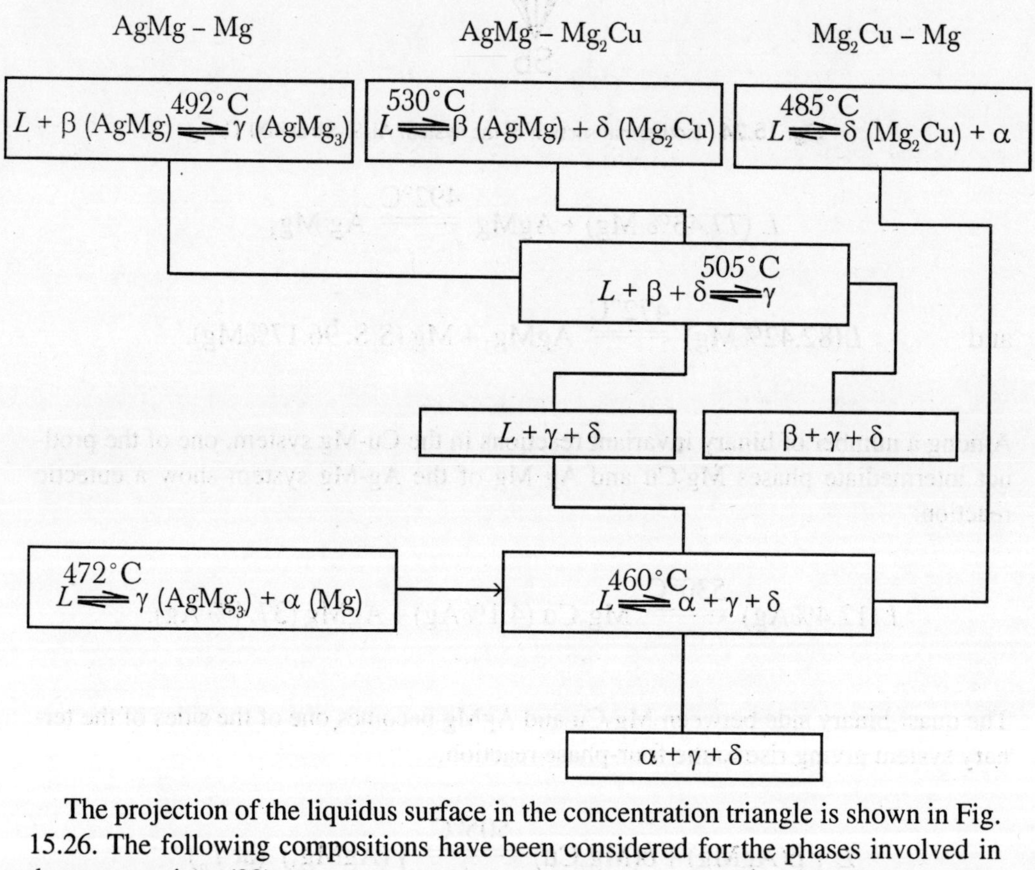

The projection of the liquidus surface in the concentration triangle is shown in Fig. 15.26. The following compositions have been considered for the phases involved in the two reactions (32):

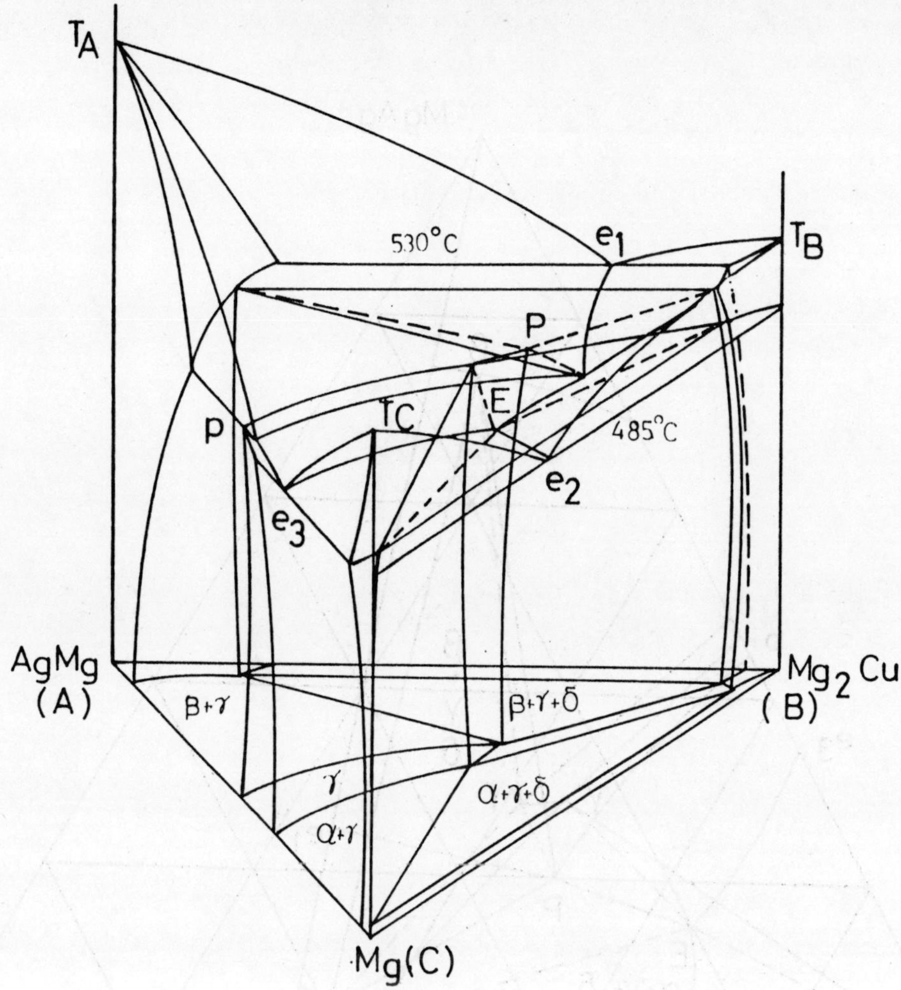

Fig. 15.25 The ternary space diagram of the system AgMg-Mg-Mg_2Cu.

	Ag	Cu	Mg		Ag	Cu	Mg
L	9.8	15.5	74.7	L	7.5	10.1	82.4
γ ($AgMg_3$)	2.5	30.0	67.5	α	0.4	0.1	99.5
δ (Mg_2Cu)	14.0	15.2	70.8	γ	1.4	29.8	68.8
β (AgMg)	36.5	6.8	56.7	δ	14.1	13.0	72.9

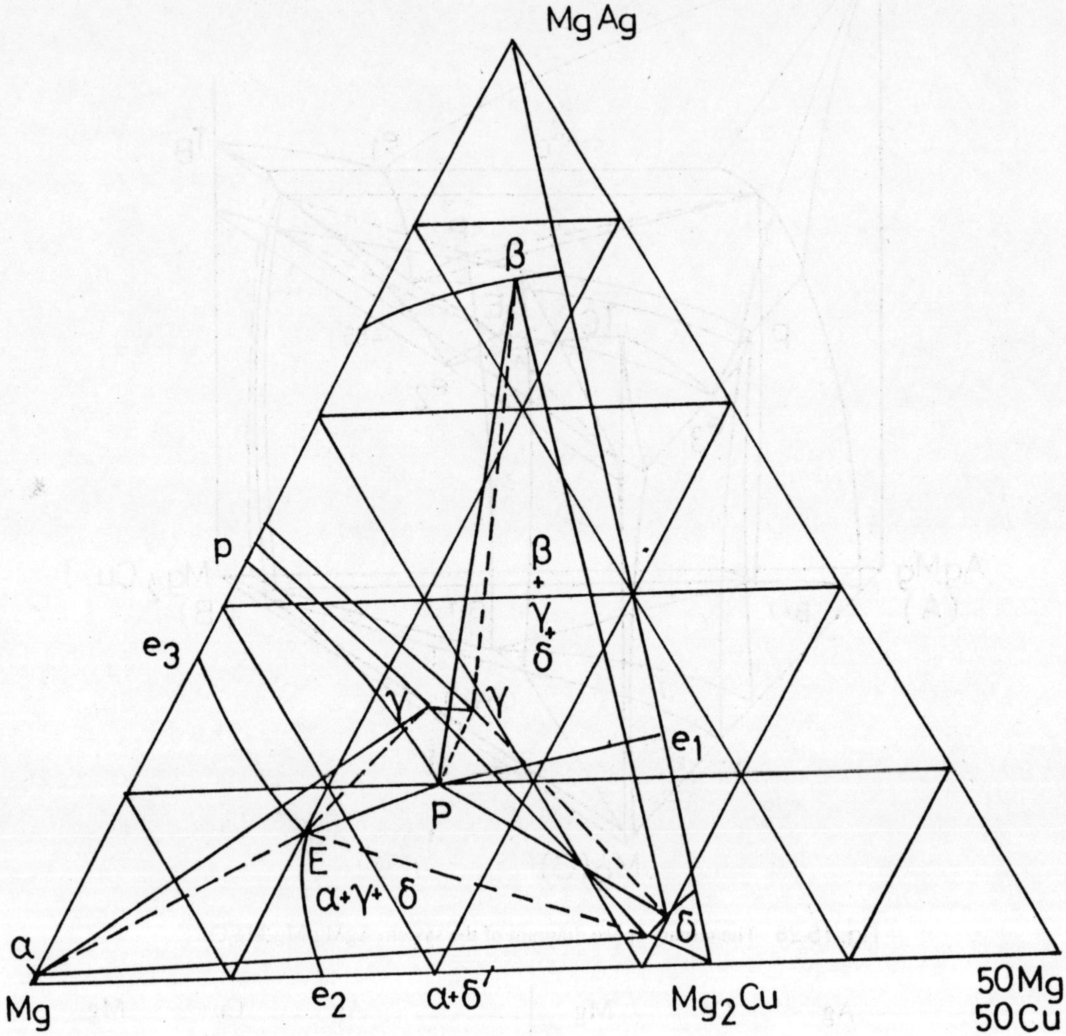

Fig. 15.26 Liquidus projection of the ternary system AgMg-Mg-Mg_2Cu.

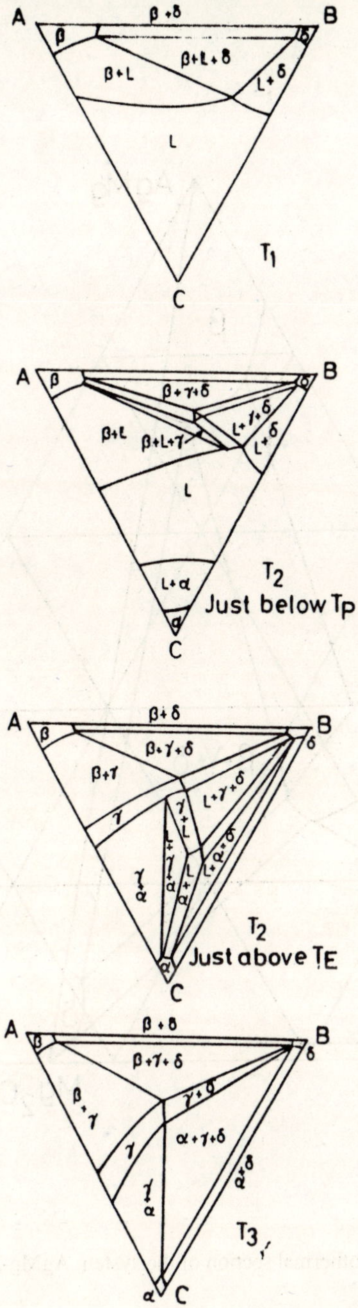

Fig. 15.27 Isothermal sections at $T_1 > T_p > T_2 T_E > T_3$.

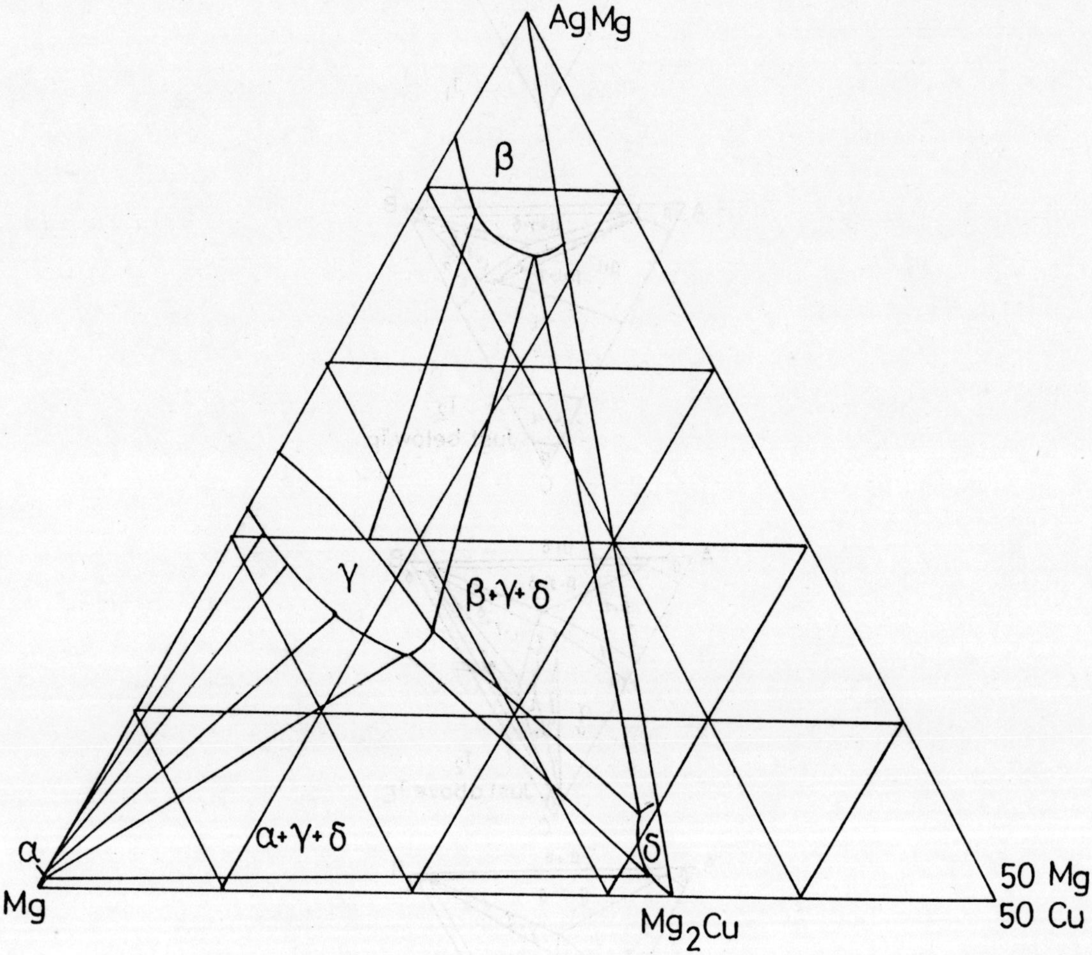

Fig. 15.28 The isothermal section of the system AgMg-Mg-Mg_2Cu at 400°C.

A number of isothermal sections are drawn in Fig. 15.27 which show details of the two invariant reactions. An isothermal section from the work of Shevakin (33) is shown in Fig. 15.28. It shows the two three-phase regions (β+γ+δ) and (α+γ+δ).

15.11 TERNARY PHASE DIAGRAM (Fe-Cr-Ni SYSTEM)

The commercial importance of the Fe-Cr-Ni alloy system has resulted in a very thorough investigation of the constitution of this alloy system. The Cr-Fe binary system forms a series of solid solutions in the whole range of compositions, with a minimum in the liquidus and solidus at 1516°C and at 19.8 at.pct. Cr. The γ-phase appears as a loop at lower temperatures as discussed in Chapter 5. The α (or δ) phase which forms a continuous phase field (both being *bcc*) in the Cr-Fe system transforms to the σ phase at 820°C. The Fe-Ni binary phase diagram shows a peritectic reaction at 1517°C ($L + \delta \Longleftrightarrow \gamma$) with all the three phases being very rich in iron. The Cr-Ni binary phase diagram shows a eutectic reaction at 1345°C with the liquid dissociating into the α and γ phases.

The ternary alloy system Fe-Cr-Ni has been investigated extensively. Among a large body of work on the system, the work of Schurmann et al (34), Wever and Jellinghaus (35), and Jenkins et al (36) are extensively referred to. A review of the Fe-Cr-Ni system has been carried out by Rivlin and Raynor (37). The space model as constructed from the binary systems is shown in Fig. 15.29.

The ternary system shows a monovariant reaction $L \Longleftrightarrow \alpha\ (\delta) + \gamma$. The monovariant liquid curve descends below the peritectic reaction isotherm of the binary side Fe-Ni and terminates at the Cr-Ni eutectic reaction isotherm. Thus, there is a change-over from the peritectic to the eutectic reaction as the monovariant liquid curve passes between the temperature range 1517°C to 1345°C. The liquidus surface gradually slopes on one side downward towards the melting temperature of pure Ni with the monovariant liquid curve petering out at e_1, Fig. 15.29. The liquidus surface has been generated by Rivlin et al (37) after combining the data from references (34–36). It s proposed that the monovariant liquid curve has a minimum located at a temperature just below 1300°C at 49%Cr-8%Fe and 43%Ni. The minimum in the liquidus has been postulated to be associated with an invariant eutectic reaction. This would require a critical tie-line at the minimum, as discussed in Chapter 12. The liquidus and solidus isotherms are shown in Fig. 15.30 using data from Rivlin et al (37).

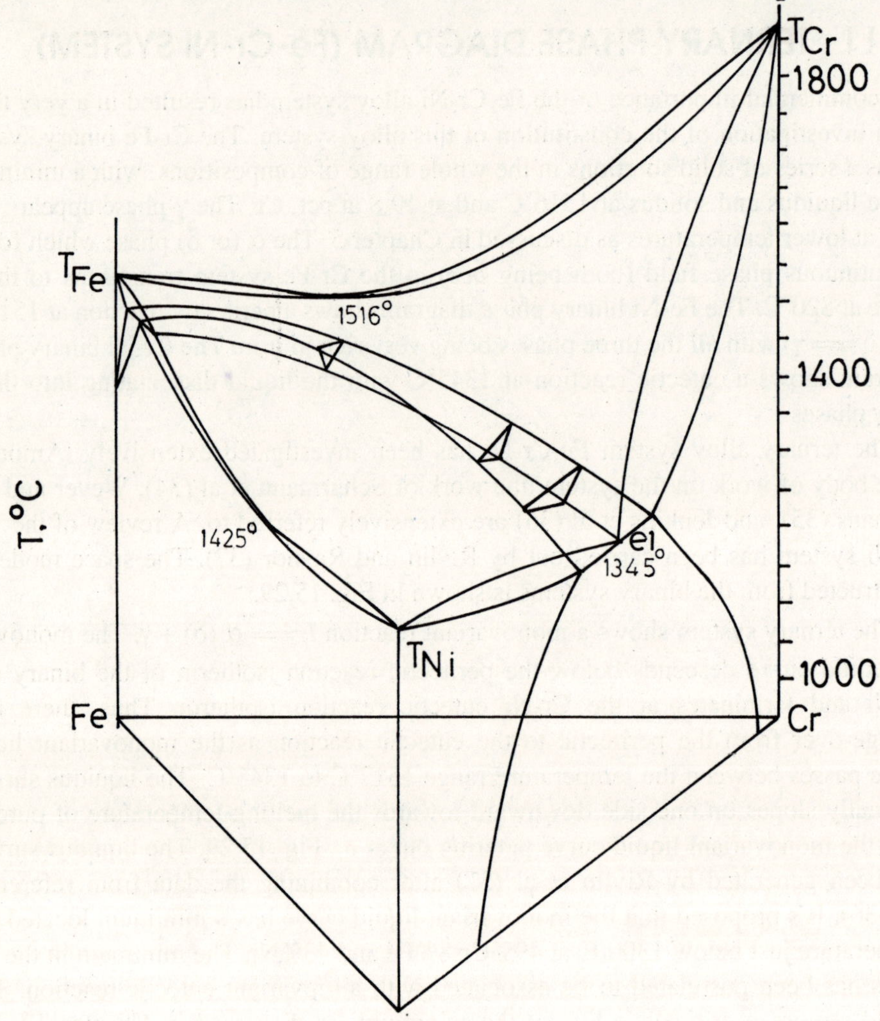

Fig. 15.29 Space Model of the ternary system Fe-Cr-Ni.

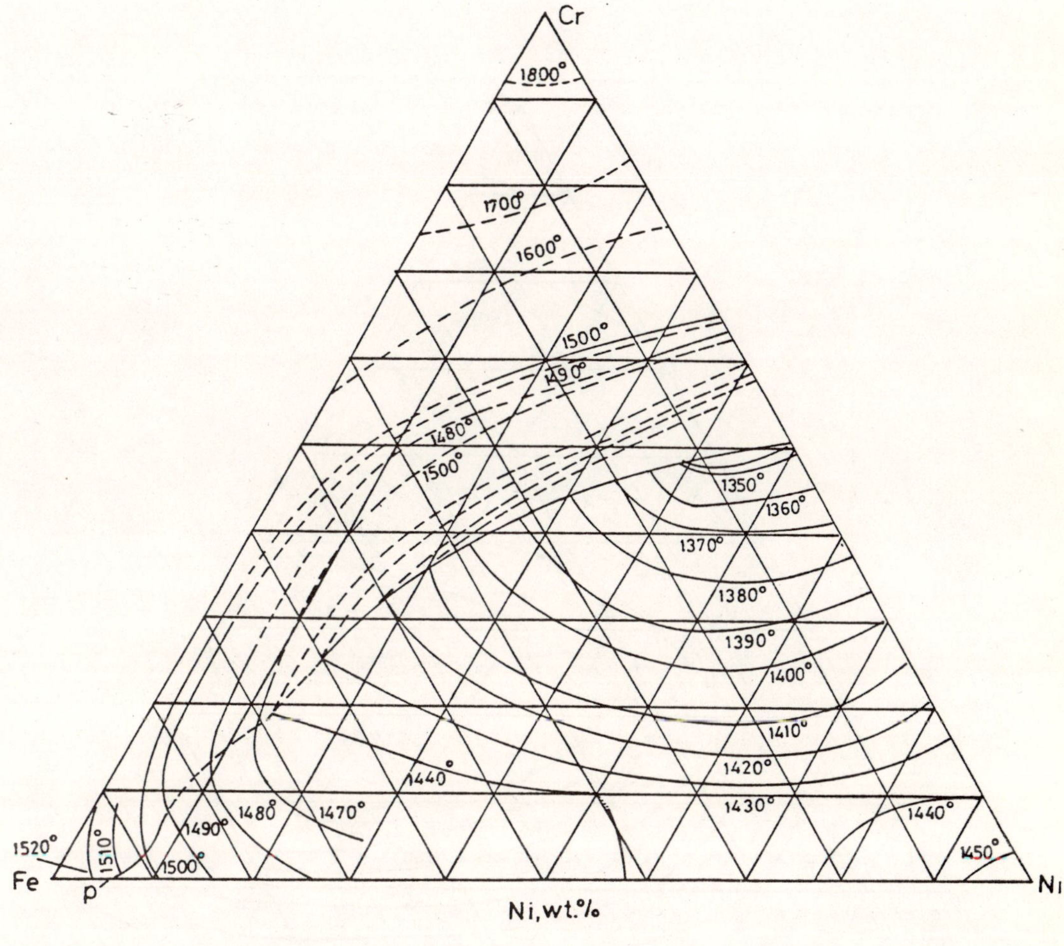

Fig. 15.30 (a) Liquidus projection of Fe-Cr-Ni system.

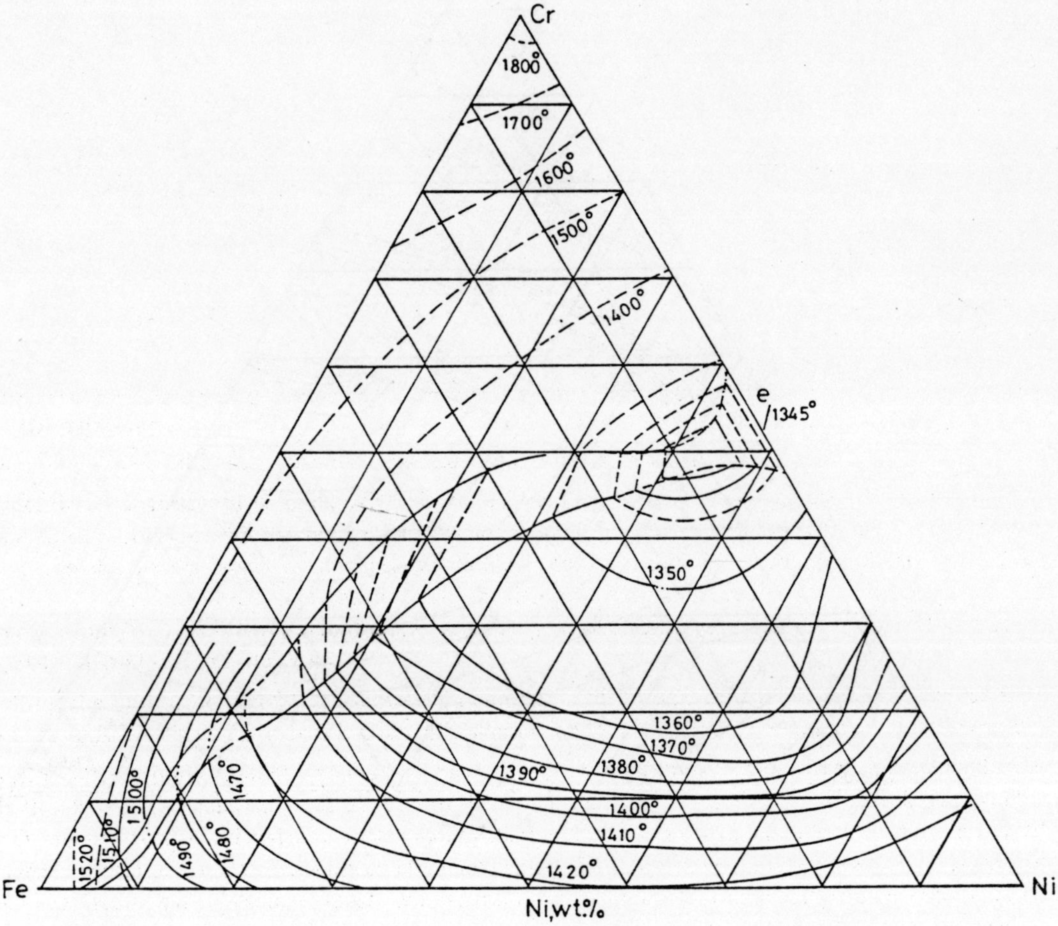

Fig. 15.30 (b) Solidus projection of Fe-Cr-Ni system.

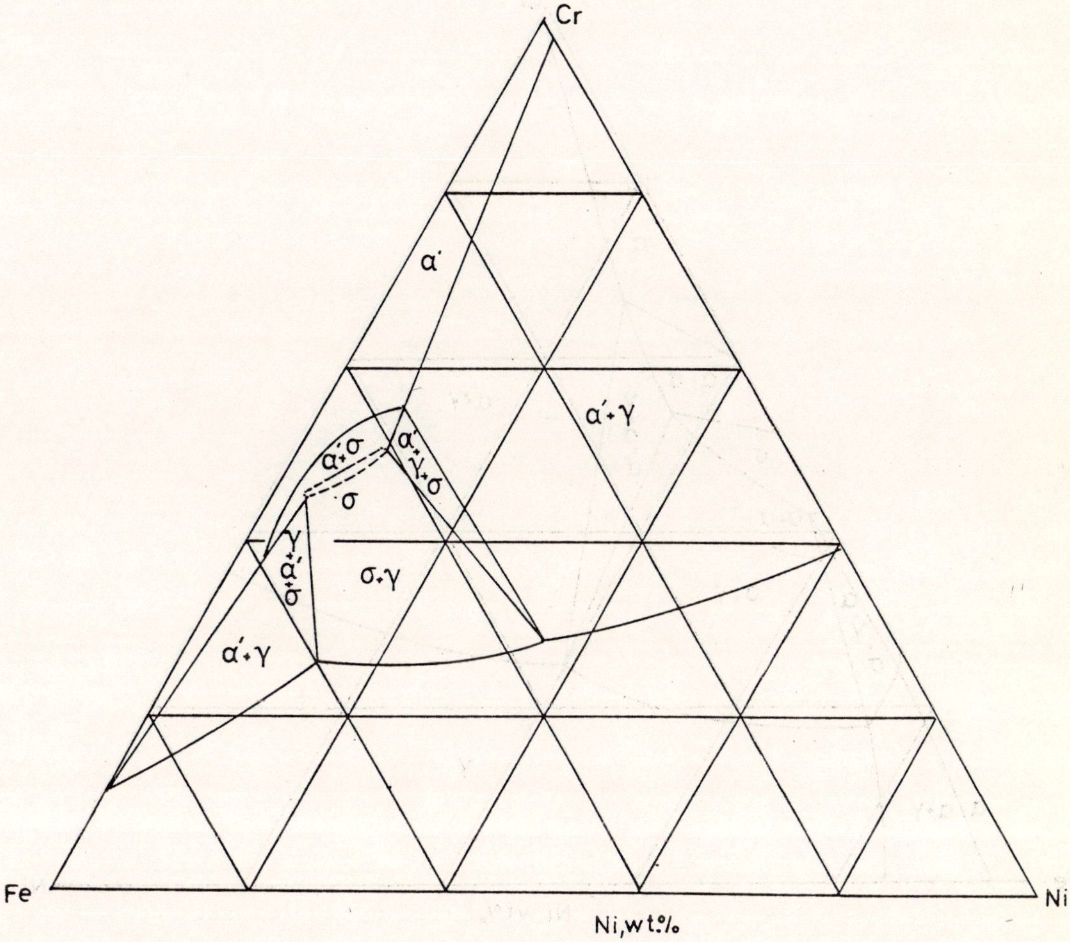

Fig. 15.31 Isothermal section at 900°C.

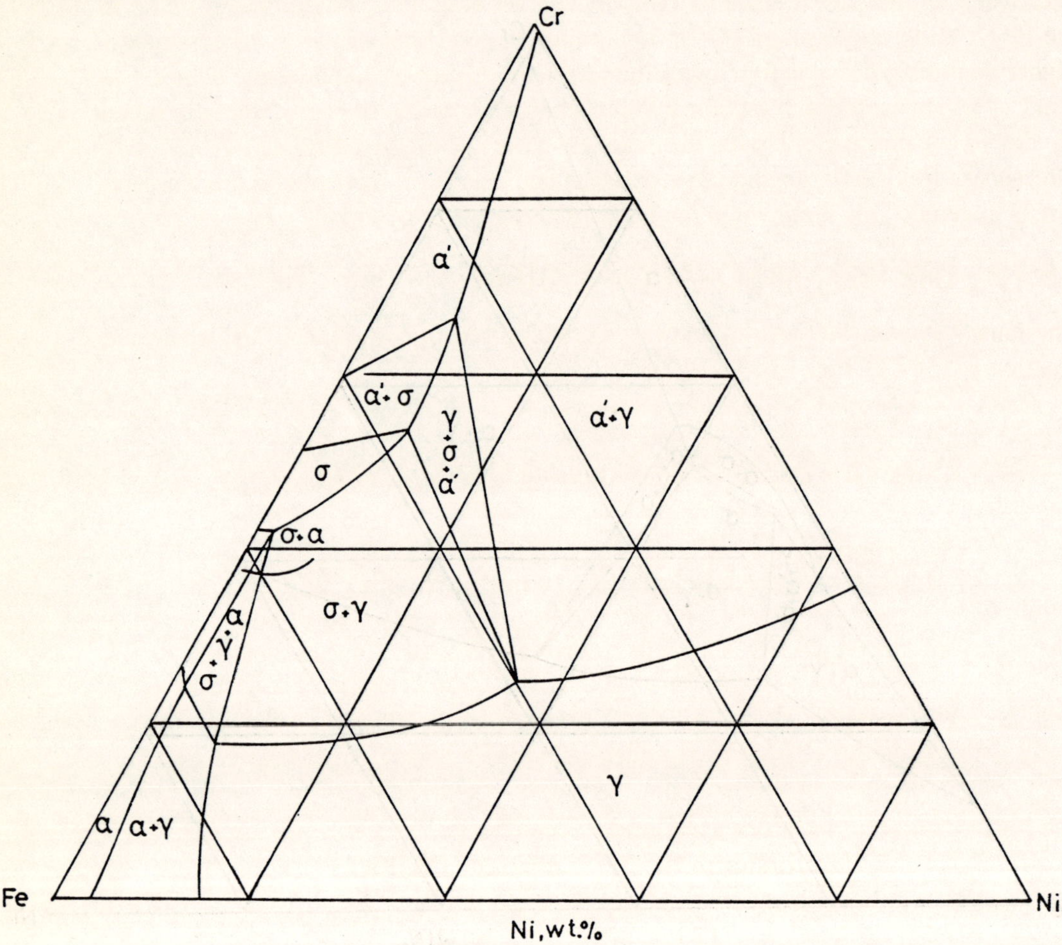

Fig. 15.32 Isothermal section at 650°C.

The ternary system shows a two-phase field below the Cr-Ni binary eutectic. The $(\alpha+\gamma)$ phase region is separated by the α and γ phases as shown in the isothermal section at 1300°C (from the work of Price et al (38)). The $(\alpha+\gamma)$ phase field enlarges with decreasing temperature till the two phases interact with the σ phase. The σ phase in the Fe-Cr-Ni ternary system has an upper temperature limit of 950 ± 10°C which is higher than the corresponding upper limiting temperature of 820°C of the binary system Cr-Fe. The isothermal section at 900°C shows two $(\alpha+\gamma+\sigma)$ phase fields separated by the $(\sigma+\gamma)$ phase field with the reaction $\alpha + \gamma \rightleftharpoons \sigma+\gamma$, Fig. 15.31. The two three-phase fields enlarge and the separation between them increases as the temperature is lowered. This is shown in the isothermal section at 650°C (37), Fig. 15.32.

15.12 THE SiO_2-MgO-Al_2O_3 SYSTEM

The binary system SiO_2-Al_2O_3 shows a peritectic reaction at 1828°C and a eutectic reaction at 1587°C, Fig. 15.33 (39).

$$L + Al_2O_3 \xrightleftharpoons{1828^\circ\ C} \text{mullite } (3Al_2O_3.2\ SiO_2)$$

$$L \xrightleftharpoons{1587^\circ C} \text{cristabolite } (SiO_2) + \text{mullite } (3Al_2O_3.2SiO_2)$$

The binary system MgO-SiO_2 shows the following reactions (Fig. 15.34 (40)):

$$L \xrightleftharpoons{1850^\circ C} MgO + \text{forsterite } (2MgO + SiO_2 = Mg_2SiO_4)$$

$$L + \text{forsterite} \xrightleftharpoons{1557^\circ C} \text{enstatite } (MgSiO_3)$$

$$L \xrightleftharpoons{1543^\circ C} MgSiO_3 + SiO_2.$$

This system also shows an immiscibility gap in the liquid. The MgO-Al_2O_3 binary system shows two invariant reactions, Fig. 15.35 (41).

$$L \xrightleftharpoons{2000°C} \text{periclase (MgO) + spinel } (MgO \cdot Al_2O_3)$$

$$L \xrightleftharpoons{1925°C} \text{spinel } (MgO \cdot Al_2O_3) + \text{corundum } (Al_2O_3).$$

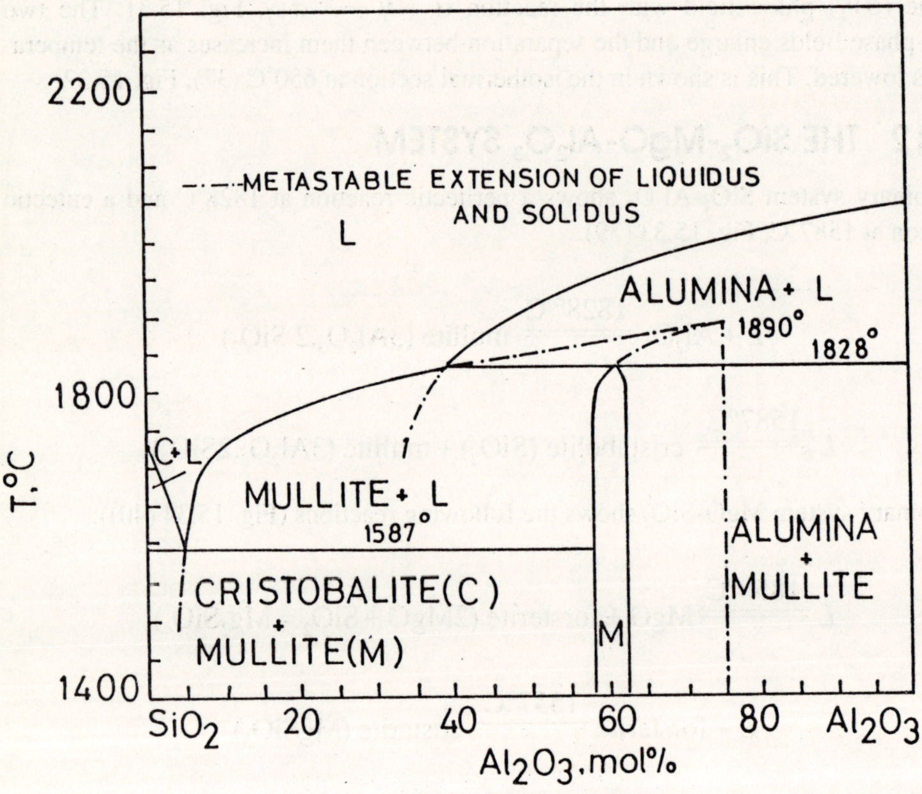

Fig. 15.33 SiO_2-Al_2O_3 phase diagram.

The remaining liquid transforms congruently to spinel.

The SiO_2-MgO-Al_2O_3 ternary system shows a large number of invariant reactions (42). These are written in decreasing order of temperature.

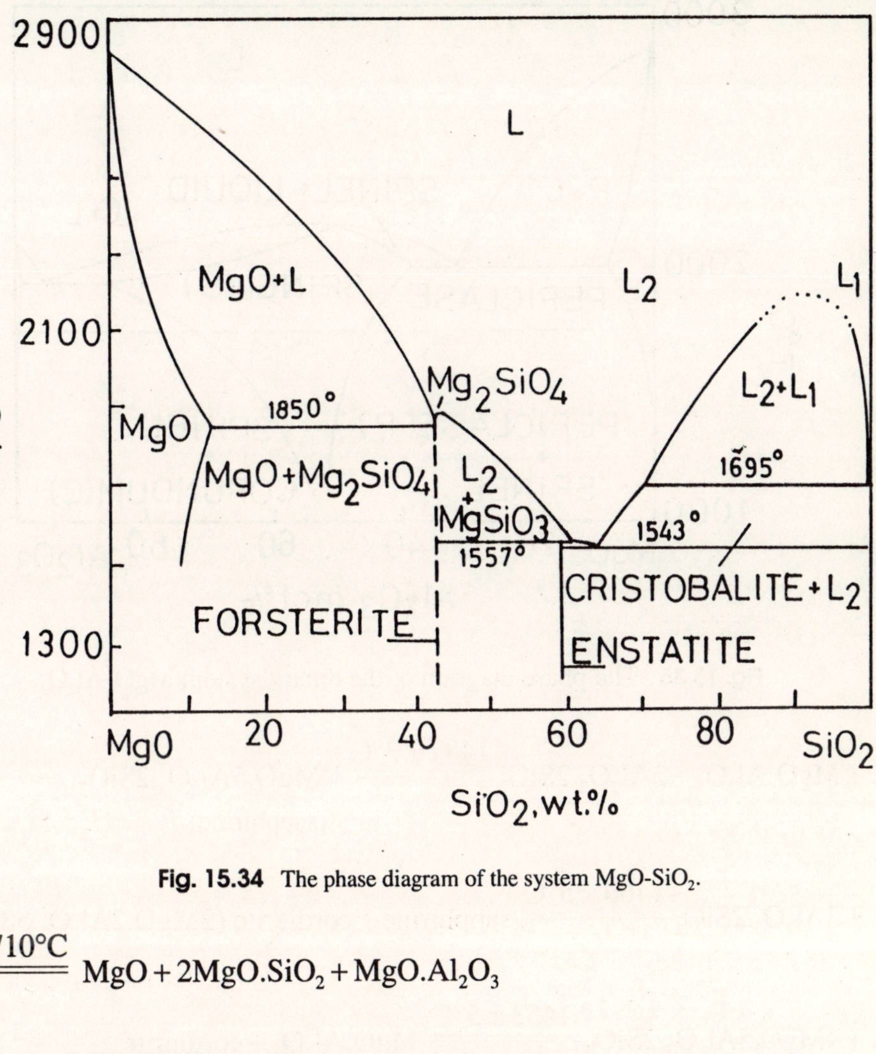

Fig. 15.34 The phase diagram of the system MgO-SiO_2.

$$L \xrightarrow{1710°C} MgO + 2MgO.SiO_2 + MgO.Al_2O_3$$

$$L + Al_2O_3 \xrightarrow{1575 \pm 5°C} MgO.Al_2O_3 + 3Al_2O_3.2SiO_2$$

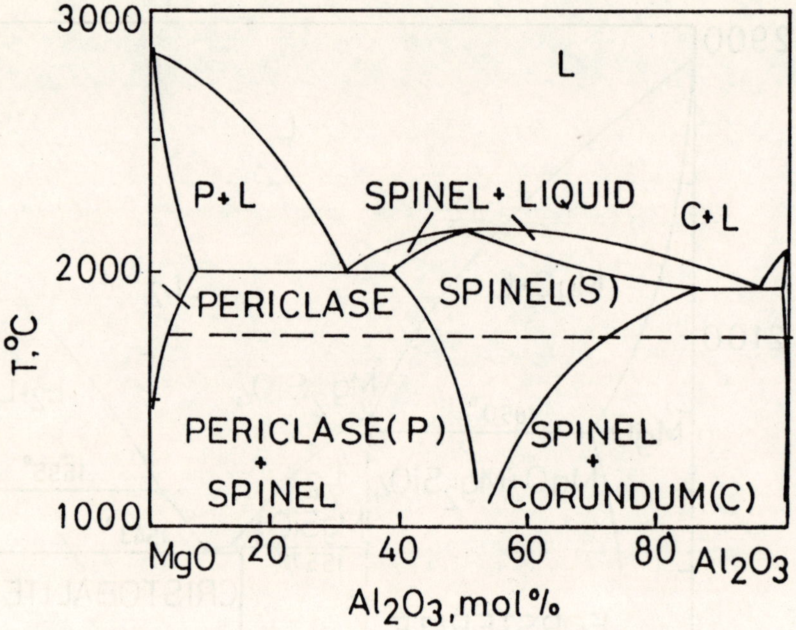

Fig. 15.35 The phase diagram of the binary system MgO-Al_2O_3.

$$L + MgO.Al_2O_3 + 3Al_2O_3.2SiO_2 \xrightleftharpoons{1482 \pm 3°C} 4MgO.5Al_2O_3.2SiO_2 \text{ (sapphirine)}$$

$$L + 3Al_2O_3.2SiO_2 \xrightleftharpoons{1460 \pm 5°C} \text{sapphirine} + \text{cordierite } (2MgO.2Al_2O_3.5SiO_2)$$

$$L + 4MgO.5Al_2O_3.2SiO_2 \xrightleftharpoons{1453 \pm 5°C} MgO.Al_2O_3 + \text{cordierite}$$

$$L + 3Al_2O_3.2SiO_2 \xrightleftharpoons{1443 \pm 5° C} \text{cordierite} + \text{tridymite } (SiO_2)$$

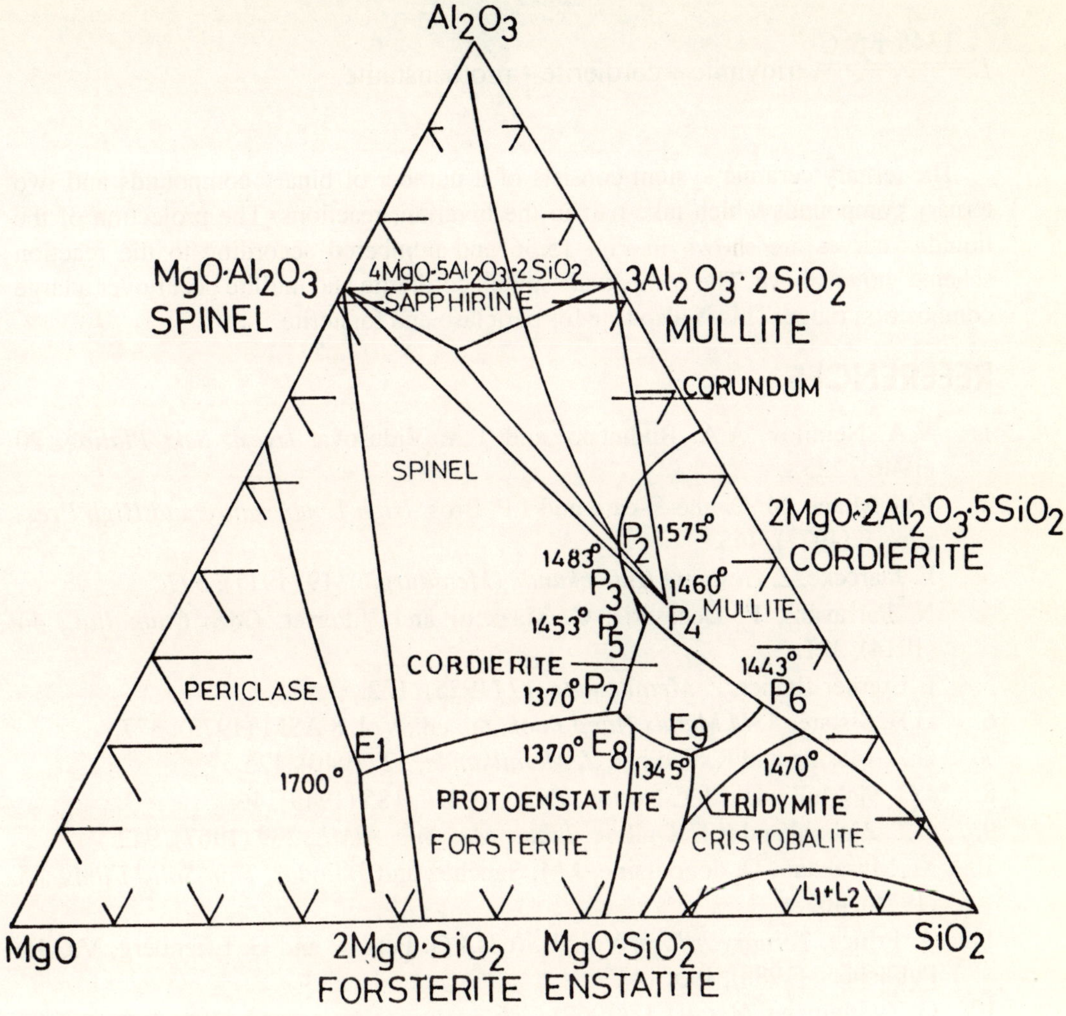

Fig. 15.36 Liquidus projection of the ternary system $MgO\text{-}SiO_2\text{-}Al_2O_3$.

$$L + \text{spinel} \xrightleftharpoons{1370 \pm 5°\text{C}} \text{forsterite} + \text{cordierite}$$

$$L \xrightleftharpoons{1360 \pm 5°\text{C}} \text{forsterite} + \text{protenstatite} + \text{cordierite}$$

$$L \xrightleftharpoons{1345 \pm 5°C} \text{tridymite} + \text{cordierite} + \text{protoenstatite}.$$

The ternary ceramic system consists of a number of binary compounds and two ternary compounds which take part in the invariant reactions. The projection of the liquidus curves are shown in Fig. 15.36 and numbered according to the reaction scheme shown above. The compounds spinel, cordierite and mullite occur over a large composition range. This is also true for periclase and forsterite.

REFERENCES

1. V.A. Nemilov, A.A. Rudnitsky and T.A. Vidusova, *Izvest. Sekt Plating*, 20 (1946), 225.
2. J.M. Miane, M. Gaune-Escard and J.P. Bros, *High Temperature and High Pressure*, 9 (1977), 465.
3. E. Jäarecke, *Z. Gesamte Hûttenkunde* (*Metallurgie*), 19 (1911), 597.
4. N. Parravans, P. Decesaris, C. Mazzetti and V.Perret, *Gazz Chim Ital.*, 44 (1914), 321.
5. L. Sterner-Rainer, *Z. Metallkunde*, 17 (1925), 162.
6. G.H. Sistare, *ASM Metals Hand-book*, 8th ed., Vol. 8 ASM (1973), 377.
7. G.A. Masing and K. Kloiber, *Z. Metallkunde*, 32 (1940), 125.
8. J.G. McMullin and J.T. Norton, *Trans. AIME*, 185 (1949), 46.
9. O.T. Ziebold and R.E. Ogilvie, *Trans. Met. Soc. AIME*, 239 (1967), 942.
10 M. Murakami, D. deFontaine, J.M. Sanchez and J. Fodor, *Thin Solid Films*, 25 (1975), 465.
11. A. Prince, *Ternary Alloys*, Vol. 1., (eds.) G. Petzow and G. Effenberg, V.C.H. Publishers, (1988), 195.
12. G. Zwingmann, *Metall.*, 18(1969), 726.
13. S. Hassam-Dalichaouch, Ph.D. Thesis, Universte'de Piovence Centre de Saint Jerome, (1985).
14. A. Prince (Ref. 11), 178.
15. A. Prince (Ref. 11), 203.
16. O.A. Novikova and A.A. Rudnitsky, *Zhur Neorg Khim*, 3 (1978), 729.
17. A. Prince (Ref. 11), Vol. 2, (1988), 211.
18. B. Predel and H. Bankstahl, *J. Less Common Met.*, 43 (1975), 191.
19. B. Predel, H. Bankstahl and T. Godecke, *J. Less Common Met.*, 44 (1976), 39.
20. P. De Cesaris, *Gazz Chim Ital.*, 43 (1913), 368.

21. W. Guertler and A. Bergmann, *Z. Metallkunde*, 25 (1933), 53.
22. O. Kubaschewski (Ref. 11), 596.
23. J. Niemela, G. Effenberg, K. Hack and P.J.Spencer, Calpad, 10 (1986), 77.
24. K. Friedrich and A. Leroux, *Z. Gesamte. Hûttenkunde*, 10 (1907), 293.
25. Y.A. Chang, D. Goldberg and J.P. Neuman, *J. Phys. Chem. Ref. Data*, 6 (1977), 621.
26. F.H. Hayes, (Ref. 11), Vol. 2, (1988), 1.
27. H. Moser, K.W. Frohlich and E. Raub, *Z. Anorg. Chemie*, 208 (1932), 225.
28. V.M. Glazov and C.Y. Liu., *Izv. Akd. Nauk. SSSR. Met.*, 4 (1960), 150.
29. K. Haussmann, (Ref. 11), Vol. 8, (1993), 209.
30 H. Hanemann and A. Shrader, "Ternary Alloys of Al," *Atlas Metallographics*, Vol. 3, Pt. 2, Verlag. Stahleisen Dusseldorf (1952), 149.
31. H. Spengler, Metall., 14 (1960), 201.
32. E. Henig, (Ref.11), Vol. 1, (1988), 585.
33. Y.F. Shevakin, V.E. Koleswichenko, V.V. Koronik, M.L. Tksypin and A.V. Meshkov, *Izv. Akad, Nauk SSSR. Met.*, 5 (1979), 223.
34. E. Schurmann, J. Brauckmann, Arch. Eisenhûttenwes, 48 (1) (1977), 3.
35. E. Wever and W. Jellinghaus, *Mitt. Kaiser-Wilhelm Inst. Eisenforsh.*,13 (1931), 98.
36. C.H.M. Jenkins, E.H. Bucknall, C.R. Austin and G.A. Mellor, *J. Iron, Steel, Inst.*, 136 (1937), 187.
37. V.G. Rivlin and G.V. Raynor, *International Metals Review*, 1 (1980), 21.
38. P.E. Price and N.J. Grant, *Trans. AIME*, 215 (1959), 635.
39. Aksay and Pask, *Science*, 183 (1974), 69.
40 W.D.Kingery, H.K. Bowen and D.R. Uhlmann, *Introduction to Ceramics*, 2nd ed., John Wiley and Sons (1991).
41. E.F. Osborn and A. Muan, *Phase Equilibrium Diagrams of Oxide Systems*, The American Ceramic Soc. (1960).
42. M.L. Keith and J.F. Schairer, J. Geology, 60 (1952), 182.

Subject Index

A

Allotropy 90
Alloy cast iron 342
Area fraction 487

B

Binary phase diagrams calculations 360
- Activity coefficient 393
- Ag-Co 426
- Ag-Cu 395
- Ag-Pt 414
- Ag-Rh 421
- Au-Ni 385, 386
- Cao-Mno 381
- Cd-Pb 403
- Cd-Zn 396
- Cu-Ni 371, 375
- Effect of entropy of fusion 377
- Enthalpy of mixing 389, 411, 421
- Eutectic system 389
- Excess free energy 407
- Free energy of fusion 361
- Ge-Si 363
- Heat capacity of pure substances 368
- Heat of fusion 362
- Isomorphous system 361
- Minima and maxima 380
- Monotectic 418
- Peritectic system 411
- Pb-Sn 399
- Regular solution 365
- Specific at constant pressure 362
- Specific heats of solids and liquids 368
- Standard states 361
- Syntectic 426
- Zn-Na 429
- Zr-U 367

Binary systems
- Eutectic 155,159
- Eutectoid 294,295
- Mgo-Al_2O_3 808
- Mgo-SiO_2 807
- Metatectic 155,234

- Monotectic 240
- Monotectoid 353
- Peritectic 155,210
- Peritectoid 349
- SiO_2 - Al_2O_3 806
- Syntactic 240,257

C

Cast iron 324
Compressibility 21
Concentration-distance profile 138
Congruent transformation in solids 290
Constitutional supercooling 146
Conversion of heat into work 7

D

Ductile iron 334

E

Efficiency of an engine 7
- Adiabatic process 9
Enthalpy 15
Entropy and disorder 30
- Energy level 31
- Microstates 31
Entropy of the system, surrounding and the universe 15
Eqilibrium constant 42
- Effect of pressure 42
- Effect of precipitate 42
Eqilibrium solidification
- Hypereutectic alloys 172
- Hypermonatectic alloys 247
- Hyperperitectic alloys 219
- Hypereutectic alloys 172
- Hypermoniatectic alloys 247
- Hypopetitectic alloys 217
- Mototectic alloys 243
- Syntectic alloys 260

F

First Law of Thermodynamics 2
- Heat 3
- Heat capacity 4
- Work 4
Four - phase equilibria in ternary system 664
- Eutectic reaction, Class I 665
- Isothermal section 667, 671, 686, 689, 700, 708, 719, 730, 733, 750, 755, 757, 772, 776, 779, 780, 783, 784, 793, 797, 798, 803, 804
- Peritectic reaction, Class III 702
- Phase fields 665, 668, 685, 688, 705, 706, 716, 737, 741, 742, 743, 760
- Projection 681, 764, 767, 775, 778
- Quasi-Peritectic, Class II 683

- Solidification 673, 675, 709, 740
- Space model 660, 669, 670, 679, 680, 682, 685, 698, 705, 715, 718, 725, 728, 731, 732, 734, 738, 744, 749, 753, 756, 759, 763, 766, 769, 770, 773, 775, 777, 782, 786, 788, 790, 800
- Variants, Class I 678
- Variants, Class II 697, 704
- Variants, Class III 714

Free energy - composition diagram 122
- Eutectic 186
- Peritectic 226
- Solid and liquid solutions 122

Free energy change 50

Free energy of solutions 65, 67

Free energy 15
- Gibbs 17
- Helmholtz 15

Frequency 462
- Cumulative 462

G

Grain size 529
- Linear intercept method 530
- ASTM 533
- Jeffries procedure 532

Graphitization 337
- I stage 337
- II stage 339

Gravity segregation 261

Gray cast iron 330

Growth rate
- Pearlite 305

I

Intermediate phases in ternary system 723
- Congruently melting 735
- Quasi - binary reaction 729,736
- Rules of construction 740
- Ternary intermediate phase 733

Intermediate phases 272
- Classification 276
- Crystal structure 282
- Electron compounds 287
- Non - stoichiometric compounds 288
- Principles 282
- Size factor compounds 285
- Valence compounds 283

Isomorphous system 104, 112
- Complete convection in the liquid 135
- Concentration-distance profile 138
- No convection in the liquid 136
- Solute distribution 132

L

Lever Rule 110, 560

Linear fraction 489

Liquid immiscibility in ternary system 746, 754, 756
- Two binary syntectic reactions 758
- Two monotectic and one
- eutectic reactions 747

M

Malleable cast iron 336

Maxwell's relations 19

Melting temperature 94

N

Non equilibrium solidification
- Hypoeutectic alloy 177
- Isomorphous 115, 135, 136
- Peritectic alloys 221
- Syntectic alloys 261
- Termenial solid solutions 182

Normal distribution 478
Number of particles per unit volume 512
- Cylinder 523
- Disc 519
- Particle size 512
- Sphere 515

Numerical methods 432

O

Orientation relationship
- Cementite 320
- Ferrite transformation 311
- Martensite transformation 315

P

P-T-X diagram 105
Partial molar properties 44
Partition function 35
Phase rule
- Application 107, 158
- Condition for equilibrium 59

Point fraction 491
Pressure - Temperature diagrams 82
- Liquid - vapour equilibrium 86
- Shape of the diagram 83
- Single component system 82
- Solid - vapour equlibrium 86

Probability 454
- Distribution 458, 471
- Geometrical 481
- Of an event 455
- Sample mean 466

Q

Quasi - chemical model of solutions 67
- Bond energy 67
- Clustering in solutions 79
- Enthalpy of mixing 70
- Entropy of mixing 72
- Ideal solution 73
- Non ideal solution 70

S

Second law of thermodynamics 6
Separation between particles 526
Solidification and microstructure
- Cells 146
- Complete convection in the liquid 135
- Constitutional supercooling 146
- Coring 115
- Dendrites 146, 150
- Effect of curvature 94
- Effect of particle size 98
- Equilibrium 112, 120, 133
- Isomorphous system 104, 112
- Lever Rule 110, 560
- Melting temperature 94
- No convection 136
- Non - equilibrium 115
- Solute distribution 132

Specific heat 5
- Constant pressure 5
- Constant volume 5
- Relation between C_p and C_v 6

Specific length 499, 503, 504
Specific surface area 499

T

T-T-T diagram 321
Tempering of martensite 317
- Cementite 319

Retained austenite 319

Ternary phase diagrams
- Ag – Au – Cu 765
- Ag – Au – Ge 773
- Ag – Au – Pd 762
- Ag – Au – Pt 773
- Ag – Cu – Mg 792
- Ag – Ge – Si 774
- Ag – Cu – Ni 781
- Ag – Cu – P 787
- Ag – Cu – Pb 785
- Al – Si – Sb 789
- Fe – Cr – Ni 799
- SiO_2 – MgO – Al_2O_3 805

Ternary system
- Gibbs triangle 540
- Representation 537
- Ternary eutectic 548
- Ternary quasi – peritectic 549
- Ternary peritectic 552
- Tie lines 543, 566
- Tie triangle 543

Three phase equilibrium in ternary systems 586
- Application of the lever rule 604
- Eutectic reaction 588
- Isothermal section 593,, 621, 625, 626, 638, 643, 651, 659
- Maximum in the liquidus 612, 634
- Minimum in the liquidus 614, 631
- Monotectic reaction 648
- Peritectic and eutectic 640
- Peritectic reaction 620
- Phase fields 589, 608, 613, 617, 625, 633, 636, 640, 652

Projection of the space model 592, 610

Solidification 602, 627
- Space model 588, 606, 620, 624, 632, 637, 642, 646, 649, 650, 658
- Syntectic and monotectic 655
- Vertical section 596, 622, 627, 628, 629, 635, 644, 645, 647, 660

Transformation of austenite
- Bainite 312
- Cast iron 324
- Cu – Zn 296
- Fe - C alloys 297
- Ferrite 305
- Martensite 313
- Pearlite 299

Two - phase equilibria in ternary system 555
- Application of the lever rule 560
- Immiscibility 575
- Isothermal section 558, 573, 578
- Konovalov's rule 568
- Maximum critical point 576, 579
- Solidification of alloys 562
- The space model 555, 572, 575, 577
- Variants 572
- Vertical section 560, 574, 580

V

Variance 466, 471

Volume expansion coefficient 21

Volume fraction 486

W

White cast iron 327

Z

Zone Refining 143